Strategic Management

An Integrated Approach

Theory & Cases

14e

Charles W. L. Hill

University of Washington — Foster School of Business

Melissa A. Schilling

New York University — Stern School of Business

 Cengage

Australia • Brazil • Canada • Mexico • Singapore • United Kingdom • United States

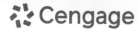

***Strategic Management: Theory & Cases: An
Integrated Approach,*** **14th Edition**
Charles W. L. Hill, Melissa A. Schilling

SVP, Product: Cheryl Costantini

VP, Product: Thais Alencar

Portfolio Product Director: Joe Sabatino

Senior Portfolio Product Manager: Mike Worls

Product Assistant: Vanessa Leahr

Senior Learning Designer: Courtney Wolstoncroft

Senior Content Manager: Meaghan Tomaso

Digital Project Manager: Beth Ross

VP, Product Marketing: Jason Sakos

Associate Director, Product Marketing:
Mary Reynolds

Executive Product Marketing Manager: John Carey

Content Acquisition Analyst: Erin McCullough

Production Service: MPS Limited

Designer: Sara Greenwood

Cover Image Source: Pavel Nesvadba/
Shutterstock.com

Interior image Sources: aragami12345s/
Shutterstock.com
chatchai.b/Shutterstock.com
Michal Sanca/Shutterstock.com
StevanZZ/Shutterstock.com
Pavel Nesvad/Shutterstock.com
IM_photo/Shutterstock.com
Anna Om/Shutterstock.com
Pierre-Yves Babelon/Shutterstock.com
imagIN.gr photography/Shutterstock.com
synto/Shutterstock.com
Dmitry_Tsvetkovba/Shutterstock.com

For product information and technology assistance, contact us at
Cengage Customer & Sales Support, 1-800-354-9706
or support.cengage.com.

For permission to use material from this text or product, submit all
requests online at **www.copyright.com**.

Library of Congress Control Number: 2023903586

Student Edition:
ISBN: 978-0-3577-1662-5

Loose-Leaf Edition:
ISBN: 978-0-3577-1663-2

Cengage
200 Pier 4 Boulevard
Boston, MA 02210
USA

Cengage is a leading provider of customized learning solutions. Our
employees reside in nearly 40 different countries and serve digital learners
in 165 countries around the world. Find your local representative at
www.cengage.com.

To learn more about Cengage platforms and services, register or access
your online learning solution, or purchase materials for your course, visit
www.cengage.com.

Notice to the Reader

Publisher does not warrant or guarantee any of the products described herein or perform any independent analysis in connection with
any of the product information contained herein. Publisher does not assume, and expressly disclaims, any obligation to obtain and
include information other than that provided to it by the manufacturer. The reader is expressly warned to consider and adopt all safety
precautions that might be indicated by the activities described herein and to avoid all potential hazards. By following the instructions
contained herein, the reader willingly assumes all risks in connection with such instructions. The publisher makes no representations
or warranties of any kind, including but not limited to, the warranties of fitness for particular purpose or merchantability, nor are any
such representations implied with respect to the material set forth herein, and the publisher takes no responsibility with respect to such
material. The publisher shall not be liable for any special, consequential, or exemplary damages resulting, in whole or part, from the
readers' use of, or reliance upon, this material.

Printed in the United States of America
Print Number: 01   Print Year: 2023

About the Authors

Charles W. L. Hill

Charles W. L. Hill is an Emeritus Professor of Strategy and International Business at the Foster School of Business, University of Washington, Seattle. He continues to teach strategic management at the Forster School on a part-time basis, one quarter a year. He received his PhD from the University of Manchester's Institute of Science and Technology (UMIST) in Britain. Before joining the University of Washington in 1988, he served on the faculties of UMIST, Texas A&M University, and Michigan State University. Professor Hill has published extensively in top-tier peer-reviewed academic journals. His work is widely cited. Professor Hill has taught courses on strategic management, microeconomics, and international business. He has received numerous awards for teaching excellence. In addition to his academic work, he has worked on a private basis with many organizations including Alaska Airlines, Boeing, Microsoft, Swedish Health Services, Thompson Financial Services, and Wizards of the Coast. His work with Microsoft in particular, spanned more than 20 years. Professor Hill continues to work on strategy development with private organizations.

Melissa A. Schilling

Melissa A. Schilling is the John Herzog Chair Professor of Management at New York University Stern School of Business. She received her PhD in strategic management from the University of Washington. Her research focuses on innovation and strategy in high-technology industries such as smartphones, videogames, pharmaceuticals, biotechnology, electric vehicles, and renewable energies. Her research has earned her awards such as the 2022 "Sumantra Ghoshal Award for Rigour and Relevance in the Study of Management," National Science Foundation's CAREER Award and the Best Paper in *Management Science* and *Organization Science* for 2007 Award. Professor Schilling teaches courses in technology and innovation management, strategic management, corporate strategy, and strategy for social-mission-based organizations. She has also taught workshops or consulted with organizations such as The Motley Fool, Zeta Energy, Bloomberg Corporation, IBM, Siemens, Standard & Poor's, Warner Chilcott, White & Case, PayPal, Facebook, Skullcandy, Behr Paints, The Kauffman Foundation, National Academy of Sciences, the American Antitrust Institute, and others. She has been quoted in or interviewed for articles in *Wall Street Journal, Fortune, Forbes, Inc., Financial Times, Thomson Reuters, CNBC, CNN Money, Bloomberg Business Week, NPR's Marketplace, NPR's Tech Nation, Machine Design, The Brian Lehrer Show, The Huffington Post, Scientific American*, and more.

StevanZZ/Shutterstock.com

Brief Contents

Contents

Contents

Contents

Contents

Contents

Contents

Contents

Contents

Contents

Contents

Pierre-Yves Babelon/Shutterstock.com

Preface

Consistent with our mission to provide students with the most current and up-to-date account of the changes taking place in the world of strategy and management, we continue to update *Strategic Management: An Integrated Approach* with new conceptual content, chapter examples, and cases.

Continuing the trend of the last three editions, there have been significant revisions to the text in this edition. We have changed the organization and flow of the text, placing the chapter on business-level strategy *before* the chapter on functional-level strategy. We have also reworked the chapter on functional-level strategy to stress that business-level strategy is implemented through strategic investments at the functional level (and through the organization—which is covered in Chapter 12). We believe that this represents a better flow of chapters.

We have also added significant new content to update the text and incorporate recent research and trends. For example, Chapter 10 now includes an section on "De-Diversification: Sell-Offs, Spinoffs, Carve-Outs, and Split-Offs." This important topic is often overlooked in strategy texts and is a crucial counterbalance to the heavy focus strategy tends to place on increasing diversification. Chapter 11 now also includes a section discussing the rise of Environmental Social, and Governance (ESG) investing.

Many of the examples and cases contained in each chapter have been revised. Every chapter has a new Opening Case and a new Closing Case. There are also many new Strategy in Action features. In addition, we have significantly updated the examples used in the text to make them both more modern and more globally representative. In making these changes, our goal has been to make the book relevant for students reading it in the third decade of the twenty-first century.

We also have a substantially revised selection of cases for this edition. All cases are either new to this edition or are updates of cases that adopters have indicated they like to see in the book. As with the last edition, we made the decision to use only our own cases. Over the years, it has become increasingly difficult to find high-quality, third-party cases, while we have received consistently positive feedback about the quality of cases that we have written; so, we are sticking with our strategy of only using our own cases. We have also received feedback that many professors like to use shorter cases, instead of, or in addition to, the longer cases normally included in our book.

Consequently, in this edition of the book, we have included 33 cases, 20 of which are the traditional long-form cases, and 13 of which are shorter cases. All of the cases are current. We have made an effort to include cases that have high name recognition with students, and that they will enjoy reading and working on. These include long-form cases on Google, Toyota, IKEA, Boeing, Space X, Tesla, Microsoft, Charles Schwab, and Walmart. Short-form cases include lululemon, Starbucks, McDonald's, and Louis Vuitton.

Practicing Strategic Management: An Interactive Approach

We have received a lot of positive feedback about the usefulness of the end-of-chapter exercises and assignments in the "Practicing Strategic Management" sections of our book. They offer a wide range of hands-on and digital learning experiences for students. We are thrilled to announce that we have moved some of these elements into the MindTap digital learning solution to provide a seamless learning experience for students and instructors. We have enhanced these features to give students engaging, multimedia learning experiences that teach them the case analysis framework and provide them multiple opportunities to step into the shoes of a manager and solve real-world strategic challenges. For instructors, MindTap offers a fully customizable, all-in-one learning suite including a digital gradebook, real-time data analytics, and full integration into your LMS. Select from assignments, including:

- **Cornerstone to Capstone Diagnostic** assesses students' functional area knowledge in the key discipline areas of accounting, finance, economics, marketing and lower-level management, and provides feedback and remediation so that students are up to speed and prepared for the strategic management course material.
- **Learn It Activities:** take concepts from the text and distill them down into consumable summaries. Learn It activities are designed to reinforce the content in the text and simultaneously offer low-stakes assessment and feedback.
- **MindTap eBook:** brings the value, concepts, and applications of the printed text to life. Using the eBook, students can easily search for content and take highlights and notes that enable engaged learning and studying practices.
- **Apply It Chapter Assignments** assess students' comprehension of the reading material and go further in asking learners to apply and analyze the content within varying contexts.
- **Apply It Case Activities** pair a case from the text with assessment questions that are designed to guide them through basic case analysis. These activities, aligned with short chapter-based cases, help prepare learners for more advanced case analysis work later in the course.
- **Study It: Flashcards:** digital flashcards serve to help learners become familiar with course terminology.
- **Study It: StudyPods:** new to this version of MindTap, StudyPods are audio-based summaries of learning objectives that aim to help learners fit studying into their busy lives. These audio features restate the core material using accessible, everyday language to help learners take in essential content in new and different ways.
- **Study It: Practice Tests:** offer learners an opportunity to assess themselves on their knowledge of course content before engaging in higher-stakes, graded assessments like midterms and final exams.
- **"You Make the Decision" Activities:** are scenario-based activities that are included at the part level in MindTap and present challenging business problems that cannot be solved with one specific, correct answer. Students are presented with a series of decisions to be made based upon information they are given about a company, and are scored according to the quality of their decisions.

- **Case Analysis Projects:** are aligned with the cases written by authors Charles Hill and Melissa Schilling and found within the appendix of the core text. These activities challenge students to think and act like tomorrow's strategic leaders. Use our default case analysis activity, written by seasoned strategic management instructors, or customize the project to suit your class. These activities may be completed by a pair or group of students or independently as instructors see fit.

It is not our intention to suggest that *all* exercises should be used for *every* chapter. Strategic management is taught at both undergraduate and graduate levels, and therefore we offer a variety of pedagogically designed activities with numerous challenge levels so that instructors can customize MindTap to best suit their teaching style and the objectives of the course. That said, we have been highly intentional in designing a MindTap learning path that scaffolds learners through the content and offers a multimodal experience to serve learners of varying preferences and levels.

We have found that our interactive approach to teaching strategic management appeals to students. It also greatly improves the quality of their learning experience. Our approach is more fully discussed in the *Instructor's Resource Manual*.

Strategic Management Cases

The 32 cases that we have selected for this edition will appeal, we are certain, to students and professors alike, both because these cases are intrinsically interesting and because of the number of strategic management issues they illuminate. The organizations discussed in the cases range from large, well-known companies, for which students can do research to update the information, to small, entrepreneurial businesses that illustrate the uncertainty and challenge of the strategic management process. In addition, the selections include many international cases, and most of the other cases contain some element of global strategy. Refer to the Table of Contents for a complete listing of the cases.

To help students learn how to effectively analyze and write a case study, we continue to include a special section on this subject. It has a checklist and an explanation of areas to consider, suggested research tools, and tips on financial analysis. Additionally, the MindTap learning activities include Directed Cases that ask students to complete the steps and offer in-depth explanations to guide them through the process, as well as case-based Branching Activities that place students in the shoes of a manager and require them to move through strategic decisions; students are assessed on the quality of their analysis in making their choices, and the activity concludes with a discussion question for you to implement in class.

We feel that our entire selection of cases is unrivaled in breadth and depth.

Teaching and Learning Aids

Taken together, the teaching and learning features of *Strategic Management* provide a package that is unsurpassed in its coverage and that supports the integrated approach that we have taken throughout the book.

- **MindTap.** MindTap is the digital learning solution that helps instructors engage students and help them become tomorrow's strategic leaders. All activities are designed to teach students to problem solve and think like management leaders. Through these activities and real-time course analytics, and an accessible reader, MindTap helps you turn cookie cutter into cutting edge, apathy into engagement, and memorizers into higher-level thinkers.

Customized to the specific needs of this course, activities are built to facilitate mastery of chapter content. We have addressed case analysis from cornerstone to capstone with a functional area diagnostic of prior knowledge, guided cases, branching activities, multimedia presentations of real-world companies facing strategic decisions, and a collaborative environment in which students can complete group case analysis projects together synchronously.

- **Instructor Website.** Access important teaching resources on this companion website. For your convenience, you can download electronic versions of the instructor supplements from the password-protected section of the site, including Instructor's Resource Manual, Comprehensive Case Notes, Cognero Testing, and PowerPoint® slides. To access these additional course materials and companion resources, please visit www.cengage.com.

- **The Instructor's Resource Manual.** For each chapter, we provide a clearly focused synopsis, a list of teaching objectives, a comprehensive lecture outline, teaching notes for the Ethical Dilemma feature, suggested answers to discussion questions, and comments on the end-of-chapter activities. Each Opening Case, Strategy in Action boxed feature, and Closing Case has a synopsis and a corresponding teaching note to help guide class discussion.

- **Case Teaching Notes.** These include a complete list of case discussion questions, as well as comprehensive teaching notes for each case, which give a complete analysis of case issues.

- **Cognero Test Bank.** A completely online test bank allows the instructor the ability to create comprehensive, true/false, multiple-choice, and essay questions for each chapter in the book. The mix of questions has been adjusted to provide fewer fact-based or simple memorization items and to provide more items that rely on synthesis or application.

- **PowerPoint Presentation Slides.** Each chapter comes complete with a robust PowerPoint presentation to aid with class lectures. These slides can be downloaded from the text website.

aragami12345s/Shutterstock.com

Acknowledgments

This book is the product of far more than three authors. We are grateful to our Senior Portfolio Product Manager, Mike Worls; our Senior Learning Designer, Courtney Wolstoncroft; our Senior Content Manager, Meaghan Tomaso; and our Executive Product Marketing Manager, John Carey, for their help in developing and promoting the book and for providing us with timely feedback and information from professors and reviewers, which allowed us to shape the book to meet the needs of its intended market. We also want to thank the departments of management at the University of Washington and New York University for providing the setting and atmosphere in which the book could be written, and the students of these universities who react to and provide input for many of our ideas. In addition, the following reviewers of this and earlier editions gave us valuable suggestions for improving the manuscript from its original version to its current form:

Andac Arikan, *Florida Atlantic University*

Ken Armstrong, *Anderson University*

Richard Babcock, *University of San Francisco*

Kunal Banerji, *West Virginia University*

Kevin Banning, *Auburn University–Montgomery*

Glenn Bassett, *University of Bridgeport*

Thomas H. Berliner, *The University of Texas at Dallas*

Bonnie Bollinger, *Ivy Technical Community College*

Richard G. Brandenburg, *University of Vermont*

Steven Braund, *University of Hull*

Philip Bromiley, *University of Minnesota*

Geoffrey Brooks, *Western Oregon State College*

Jill Brown, *Lehigh University*

Amanda Budde, *University of Hawaii*

Lowell Busenitz, *University of Houston*

Sam Cappel, *Southeastern Louisiana University*

Charles J. Capps III, *Sam Houston State University*

Acknowledgments

Don Caruth, *Texas A&M Commerce*
Gene R. Conaster, *Golden State University*
Steven W. Congden, *University of Hartford*
Catherine M. Daily, *Ohio State University*
Robert DeFillippi, *Suffolk University Sawyer School of Management*
Helen Deresky, *SUNY—Plattsburgh*
Fred J. Dorn, *University of Mississippi*
Gerald E. Evans, *The University of Montana*
John Fahy, *Trinity College, Dublin*
Patricia Feltes, *Southwest Missouri State University*
Bruce Fern, *New York University*
Mark Fiegener, *Oregon State University*
Chuck Foley, *Columbus State Community College*
Isaac Fox, *Washington State University*
Craig Galbraith, *University of North Carolina at Wilmington*
Scott R. Gallagher, *Rutgers University*
Eliezer Geisler, *Northeastern Illinois University*
Gretchen Gemeinhardt, *University of Houston*
Lynn Godkin, *Lamar University*
Sanjay Goel, *University of Minnesota—Duluth*
Robert L. Goldberg, *Northeastern University*
James Grinnell, *Merrimack College*
Russ Hagberg, *Northern Illinois University*
Allen Harmon, *University of Minnesota—Duluth*
Ramon Henson, *Rutgers University*
David Hoopes, *California State University—Dominguez Hills*
Todd Hostager, *University of Wisconsin—Eau Claire*
David Hover, *San Jose State University*
Graham L. Hubbard, *University of Minnesota*
Miriam Huddleston, *Harford Community College*
Tammy G. Hunt, *University of North Carolina at Wilmington*
James Gaius Ibe, *Morris College*
W. Grahm Irwin, *Miami University*
Homer Johnson, *Loyola University—Chicago*
Jonathan L. Johnson, *University of Arkansas Walton College of Business Administration*
Marios Katsioloudes, *St. Joseph's University*
Robert Keating, *University of North Carolina at Wilmington*
Geoffrey King, *California State University—Fullerton*
Rico Lam, *University of Oregon*
Robert J. Litschert, *Virginia Polytechnic Institute and State University*
Franz T. Lohrke, *Louisiana State University*
Paul Mallette, *Colorado State University*
Daniel Marrone, *SUNY Farmingdale*
Lance A. Masters, *California State University—San Bernardino*

Acknowledgments

Robert N. McGrath, *Embry-Riddle Aeronautical University*

Charles Mercer, *Drury College*

Van Miller, *University of Dayton*

Debi Mishra, *Binghamton University*

Tom Morris, *University of San Diego*

Joanna Mulholland, *West Chester University of Pennsylvania*

James Muraski, *Marquette University*

John Nebeck, *Viterbo University*

Jeryl L. Nelson, *Wayne State College*

Louise Nemanich, *Arizona State University*

Francine Newth, *Providence College*

Don Okhomina, *Fayetteville State University*

Phaedon P. Papadopoulos, *Houston Baptist University*

John Pappalardo, *Keen State College*

Paul R. Reed, *Sam Houston State University*

Rhonda K. Reger, *Arizona State University*

Malika Richards, *Indiana University*

Simon Rodan, *San Jose State*

Stuart Rosenberg, *Dowling College*

Douglas Ross, *Towson University*

Ronald Sanchez, *University of Illinois*

Joseph A. Schenk, *University of Dayton*

Brian Shaffer, *University of Kentucky*

Leonard Sholtis, *Eastern Michigan University*

Pradip K. Shukla, *Chapman University*

Mel Sillmon, *University of Michigan—Dearborn*

Dennis L. Smart, *University of Nebraska at Omaha*

Barbara Spencer, *Clemson University*

Lawrence Steenberg, *University of Evansville*

Kim A. Stewart, *University of Denver*

Ted Takamura, *Warner Pacific College*

Scott Taylor, *Florida Metropolitan University*

Thuhang Tran, *Middle Tennessee University*

Bobby Vaught, *Southwest Missouri State*

Robert P. Vichas, *Florida Atlantic University*

John Vitton, *University of North Dakota*

Edward Ward, *St. Cloud State University*

Kenneth Wendeln, *Indiana University*

Daniel L. White, *Drexel University*

Edgar L. Williams, Jr., *Norfolk State University*

Donald Wilson, *Rochester Institute of Technology*

Jun Zhao, *Governors State University*

Charles W. L. Hill

Melissa A. Schilling

Dedication

To my daughters Elizabeth, Charlotte, and Michelle

— Charles W. L. Hill

For my children, Julia and Conor

— Melissa A. Schilling

imagIN.gr photography/Shutterstock.com

Part

1

Introduction to Strategic Management

Chapter 1

Strategic Leadership:
Managing the Strategy-
Making Process for
Competitive Advantage

Chapter

1

Strategic Leadership: Managing the Strategy-Making Process for Competitive Advantage

Opening Case

Peloton

Peloton bills itself as the largest interactive fitness platform in the world, serving a community of more than 6.6 million members. Peloton's mission is to use *technology and design to connect the world through fitness, empowering people to be the best version of themselves anywhere, anytime.* Consistent with this mission, Peloton sells bikes and treadmills that are connected via the internet to instructor-led fitness classes that are offered both live and on-demand.

Peloton was founded in 2012 by John Foley, who at the time was the president of e-commerce at bookseller Barnes & Noble. A fitness aficionado, Foley's time-consuming job and family commitments constrained his ability to attend spin classes at the gym. Foley had to revert to using his home bike, which he described as a "totally unsatisfying experience." Foley realized that he was not alone, and that his problem constituted a business opportunity. He sketched out a vision for an indoor bike with an attached monitor that would stream cycling classes over the internet, raised money from venture capitalists and a kick-starter campaign, and Peloton was born. The vision was to bring into the home the community and excitement of boutique fitness classes offered by companies like SoulCycle and Freewheel.

Peloton had a clear strategy for executing its vision: Build beautifully designed high-end stationary bikes that come equipped with a touch-screen monitor. Target busy upper-middle-class fitness enthusiasts who lacked the flexibility and time to attend gym sessions. Offer a compelling mix of live and prerecorded classes led by personable instructors. Complement those classes with great music, leaderboards that allow riders to compete, compare, and high-five each other, an ability to follow other riders, and access to detailed performance statistics. The business model was to make money on both the sale of the equipment (in 2019 the bikes were $2,245 each) and from a $39 monthly fee that gave subscribers access to streamed exercise sessions.

Shortly before the company went public in mid-2019, Peloton was gaining market traction. The company was going after a share of the more than 180 million users worldwide who paid a monthly fee to go to the gym. Its focus was on the United States, Canada, the United Kingdom, and Germany, four countries with the largest fitness markets in the world. In June 2019, Peloton had over 500,000 active subscribers and annual revenues of $915 million. Its customers included high-profile trendsetters such as former soccer player David Beckham and former President Barack Obama. The high quality and attractive design of its products, coupled with the relative affluence of its target market, allowed Peloton to operate with gross margins on hardware of 43%, higher than even those of Apple. While hardware sales accounted for the bulk of revenues, in 2019 about 20% of revenues came from subscriptions, and that share was growing. Moreover, with an annualized churn rate of around 10%,

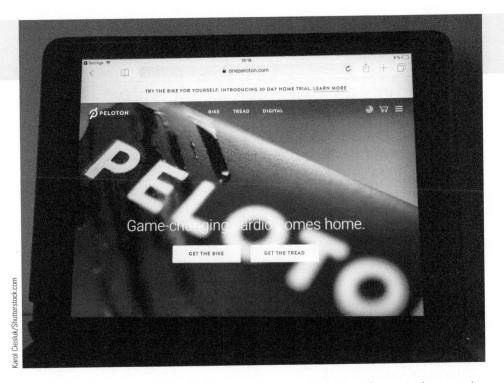

Karol Cieśluk/Shutterstock.com

Sources: Staff reporter, "Peloton Covets Recurring Revenue," *The Economist*, September 5, 2019; N. Trentmann, "How Peloton Plans to Keep Growing after the Pandemic Ends," *Wall Street Journal*, October 23, 2020; S. Terlep, "Inside a Year at Peloton: From Pandemic Winner to HBO Punchline," *Wall Street Journal*, December 31, 2021; Staff reporter, "The Peloton Business Model—How Does Peloton Work?" *Productmint*, February 8, 2022; S. Terlep, "A Peloton Bike and Subscription for One Monthly Fee?" *Wall Street Journal*, March 10, 2022.

significantly below the 22% average for software-as-a-service companies, Peloton was demonstrating strong customer loyalty. True, the company was not making any profits; it lost $196 million in fiscal 2019, but that too was part of the strategy. Peloton was sacrificing current profitability to finance market share gains with the goal of making greater profits down the road.

In early 2020, the COVID-19 pandemic hit. For Peloton, this was a game changer. Gyms were shut down for months on end. Demand for Peloton bikes surged. It was a mixed blessing. The increase in demand quickly outstripped Peloton's ability to supply bikes. Peloton lacked enough manufacturing capacity. Pandemic-related supply chain problems meant that Peloton struggled to get key parts. Bikes were put on back order for months. It took Peloton until late 2020 to work through its supply chain issues. The reward for this effort was that Peloton ended 2020 with over 3 million members and its first quarterly profit. To forestall future manufacturing and supply chain constraints, in December 2020 Peloton announced that it would acquire Precor for $420 million in cash. Precor is one of the largest makers of fitness equipment in the world, with a significant U.S. manufacturing presence.

In 2021, Peloton booked more than $4 billion in revenues, a fourfold increase from 2019, but it still lost $190 million. Moreover, late 2021 and early 2022 brought some new strategic challenges. As the COVID-19 pandemic seemed to wind down, gyms opened and demand for Peloton's bikes and treadmills came in below optimistic projections made during the pandemic. To complicate matters, Bowflex and NordicTrack entered the market with similar bikes that were priced more competitively. Peloton responded by cutting the price of its bikes, offering less expensive models for $1,495, but investors in Peloton were unhappy with the company's slow progress toward profitability. In February 2022, John Foley stepped down as CEO. He was replaced by Barry McCarthy, the former CFO of Netflix and Spotify. McCarthy's strategic formula for fixing the company was as follows: (1) reduce capital spending on hardware; (2) make simpler, lower-cost bikes and treadmills; (3) reduce the corporate head count by 20%; (4) spend more on improving the digital interface and content options; and (5) experiment with different pricing options, including an option in which customers pay a single monthly fee that covers both the bike and the online content (if a customer cancels Peloton, they will take back the bike at no charge). Will this strategy work to recharge Peloton's growth and turn the company profitable? Only time will tell.

1-1 Strategy and Strategic Leadership

Why do some companies succeed, whereas others fail? In the U.S. airline industry, how has Southwest Airlines managed to keep increasing its revenues and profits through both good times and bad, whereas rivals such as United Airlines and American Airlines have struggled to maintain profitability and, on occasion, have had to seek bankruptcy protection? What explains the persistent growth and profitability of Nucor Steel, now the largest steelmaker in the United States, during a period when many of its once-larger rivals disappeared into bankruptcy? How has Microsoft managed to remain a dominant enterprise in an industry characterized by rapid technological change, while some of its rivals have faded? And with reference to the Opening Case, why has Peloton been able to grow so fast, and will it be able to do so going forward, given shifting demand and the entry of new competitors into the home exercise market?

strategy

A set of related actions that managers take to increase their company's performance.

In this book, we explain how the strategies that a company's managers pursue have a major impact on the company's performance relative to that of its competitors. A **strategy** is a set of related actions that managers take to attain a goal or goals. For most, if not all, companies, achieving superior financial performance relative to rivals is the primary goal. If a company's strategies result in superior performance, it is said to have a competitive advantage.

For Peloton, the search for competitive advantage is still a work in progress. Following a clear strategy, Peloton has been able to grow its subscriber base and revenues, but it is still unprofitable, and demand growth has slowed down considerably as restrictions associated with the COVID-19 pandemic have been lifted. To complicate matters, rivals are now appearing. Bowflex and NordicTrack have entered the market with similar bikes that are priced more competitively. In response, Peloton has adjusted its strategy, lowered its own price, and is experimenting with different pricing options. Will Peloton succeed in the long run? That depends to a large degree on the strategies that it pursues, and how well it implements those strategies.

strategic leadership

Creating competitive advantage through effective management of the strategy-making process.

strategy formulation

Selecting strategies based on analysis of an organization's external and internal environment.

strategy implementation

Putting strategies into action.

This book identifies and describes the strategies that managers can pursue to achieve superior performance and provide their companies with a competitive advantage. One of its central aims is to give you a thorough understanding of the analytical techniques and skills necessary to formulate and implement strategies successfully. The first step toward achieving this objective is to describe in more detail what superior performance and competitive advantage mean, and to explain the pivotal role that managers play in leading the strategy-making process.

Strategic leadership is about how to most effectively manage a company's strategy-making process to create competitive advantage. Strategy-making is the process by which managers select and then implement a set of strategies that aim to achieve a competitive advantage. **Strategy formulation** is the task of selecting strategies. **Strategy implementation** is the task of putting strategies into action, which includes designing, delivering, and supporting products; improving the efficiency and effectiveness of operations; and designing a company's organizational structure, control systems, and culture. Peloton's initial strategy was successful under founder John Foley's leadership, not just because he and his team formulated a viable strategy, but because that strategy was well implemented.

By the end of this chapter, you will understand how strategic leaders can manage the strategy-making process by formulating and implementing strategies that enable a company to achieve a competitive advantage and superior performance. Moreover, you will learn how the strategy-making process can sometimes go wrong, and what managers can do to make this process more effective.

1-2 Strategic Leadership and Superior Performance

Strategic leadership is concerned with managing the strategy-making process to increase the performance of a company, thereby increasing the value of the enterprise to its owners and its shareholders. As shown in Figure 1.1, to increase shareholder value, managers must pursue strategies that increase the *profitability* of the company and ensure that *profits grow* (for more details, see the Appendix to this chapter). To do this, a company must be able to outperform its rivals; it must have a competitive advantage.

1-2a Superior Performance

Shareholder value refers to the returns that shareholders earn from purchasing shares in a company. These returns come from two sources: (a) capital appreciation in the value of a company's shares and (b) dividend payments. For example, during 2021 the shares of the venerable U.S. consumer products company Procter & Gamble increased in price from $137.99 to $163.58. Each share of P&G also paid a dividend of $3.40 to its shareholders during 2021. Thus, in 2021, shareholders in P&G earned a total return of 21%, of which 18.54% came from capital appreciation in the value of the shares, and 2.46% in the form of a dividend payout.

Maximizing shareholder value is the primary goal of profit-making companies for two reasons. First, shareholders provide a company with the risk capital that enables managers to buy the resources needed to produce and sell goods and services. **Risk capital** is capital that cannot be recovered if a company fails and goes bankrupt.

shareholder value

Returns that shareholders earn from purchasing shares in a company.

risk capital

Equity capital invested with no guarantee that stockholders will recoup their cash or earn a decent return.

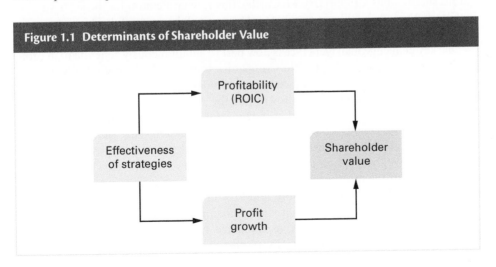

Figure 1.1 Determinants of Shareholder Value

Shareholders will not provide risk capital unless they believe that managers are committed to pursuing strategies that provide a good return on their capital investment. Second, shareholders own a stake in the corporation equal to the number of shares they hold as a percentage of the total shares outstanding. Shares represent a claim of their owners on the economic profits generated by a company. Thus, managers have an obligation to invest those profits back in the company or disperse them to shareholders (through dividends or stock buybacks) in a manner that is consistent with maximizing shareholder value.[1] However, as discussed later, an important caveat to this dictum is that managers should seek to maximize shareholder value *subject* to the constraint that they do so in a legal, ethical, and socially responsible manner (see Chapter 11).

As noted in Figure 1.1, increasing shareholder value requires strategies that boost the profitability of the enterprise, and enable it to attain greater profit growth. One way to measure the **profitability** of a company is by its return on the capital invested in the enterprise.[2] The **return on invested capital (ROIC)** that a company earns is defined as its net profit over the capital invested in the firm (profit/capital invested). By net profit, we mean net income after tax. By capital, we mean the sum of money invested in the company; that is, stockholders' equity plus debt owed to creditors. So defined, *profitability is the result of how efficiently and effectively managers use the capital at their disposal to produce goods and services that satisfy customer needs.* A company that uses its capital efficiently and effectively makes a positive return on invested capital. In 2021, for example, the investment service Morningstar calculated that Procter & Gamble earned a return on invested capital (ROIC) of 18.11%. Morningstar calculated P&G's cost of capital at about 8%, so that translates into a real economic return of 10.11%.

A company's **profit growth** can be measured by the increase in net profit over time. A company can grow its profits if it sells products in rapidly growing markets, gains market share from rivals, increases sales to existing customers, gets out of underperforming products and businesses, expands overseas, or diversifies profitably into new lines of business. For example, between 2017 and 2021, P&G increased its net profits from continuing operations from $10.19 billion to $14.35 billion, primarily by pursuing strategies to strengthening its existing consumer brands through product development and marketing, and by discontinuing or selling off products that were not performing well. This profit growth help to drive an increase in the value of P&G's shares from $84.17 to $163.58 over the same period.

Together, profitability and profit growth are the principal drivers of shareholder value (see the Appendix to this chapter for details). *To both boost profitability and grow profits over time, managers must formulate and implement strategies that give their company a competitive advantage over rivals.* Under the leadership of founder John Foley, and his successor as CEO, Barry McCarthy, this is what Peloton has been striving to do. Clearly the jury is still out on whether Peloton will be successful. The company is trying to establish a competitive advantage, but they have yet to do so.

One key challenge managers face is how best to simultaneously generate high profitability and increase profit growth. Companies that have high profitability, but no profit growth, will often be less valued by shareholders than companies that have both high profitability and rapid profit growth (see the Appendix for details). At the same time, managers need to be aware that if they grow profits but profitability declines, that too will be less highly valued by shareholders. In the long run, what shareholders want to see, and what managers must try to deliver through strategic leadership, is *profitable growth*; that is, high profitability and sustainable profit growth. This is not easy, but some of the most successful enterprises of our era have achieved it—companies such as Apple, Google, Microsoft, and Procter & Gamble.

It is important to remember that while maximizing shareholder value is the primary goal of for-profit enterprises, as explained later in this book, managers must behave in a legal, ethical, and socially responsible manner while working towards

profitability

The return a company makes on the capital invested in the enterprise.

return on invested capital (ROIC)

Return on invested capital is equal to net profit divided by capital invested in the company.

profit growth

The increase in net profit over time.

this goal. Moreover, an important theme in this book is that one of the best ways to increase shareholder value is to create value for your customers, treat your employees well, and respect the needs of the communities in which the company does business. There are good reasons for believing that in the long run companies that do not serve their customers well, exploit their employees, or degrade their communities, are unlikely to create value for their shareholders.[3] Satisfying customer needs, making sure that employees are fairly treated and work productively, and establishing a reputation for being a good corporate citizen typically translate into better financial performance and superior long-run returns for shareholders. Alternatively, ignoring customer needs, treating employees unfairly, and disrespecting the needs of communities may boost short-run profits and returns to shareholders, but it will also damage the long-run viability of the enterprise and ultimately depress shareholder value.

1-3 Competitive Advantage and a Company's Business Model

1.3 Explain what is meant by "competitive advantage."

Managers do not make strategic decisions in a competitive vacuum. Their company is competing against other companies for customers. Peloton competes against direct rivals such as Bowflex and Nordic Track, indirect rivals such as SoulCycle and Freewheel who offer spin classes in a boutique gym setting, and gyms in general. Competition is a rough-and-tumble process in which only the most efficient, effective companies win out. It is a race without end. To maximize long-run shareholder value, managers must formulate and implement strategies that enable their company to outperform rivals—that give it a competitive advantage. A company is said to have a **competitive advantage** over its rivals when its profitability and profit growth are greater than the average of other companies competing for the same set of customers. The higher its profitability and profit growth relative to rivals, the greater its competitive advantage will be. A company has a **sustained competitive advantage** when its strategies enable it to maintain above-average profitability and profit growth for a number of years. Clearly, Peloton is struggling to establish a sustained competitive advantage.

The key to understanding competitive advantage is appreciating how the different strategies managers pursue over time can create activities that fit together to make a company unique and able to consistently outperform the competition. A **business model** is managers' conception of how the set of strategies their company pursues work together as a congruent whole, enabling the company to gain a competitive advantage and achieve superior profitability and profit growth. In essence, a business model is a kind of mental model, or gestalt, of how the various strategies and capital investments a company makes fit together to generate above-average performance. A business model encompasses the totality of how a company will:

competitive advantage

The achieved advantage over rivals when a company's profitability is greater than the average profitability of firms in its industry.

sustained competitive advantage

A company's strategies enable it to maintain above-average profitability for a number of years.

business model

The conception of how strategies should work together as a whole to enable the company to achieve competitive advantage.

- Select its customers.
- Define and differentiate its product offerings.
- Create value for its customers.
- Acquire and keep customers.
- Produce goods or services.
- Increase productivity and lower costs.
- Deliver goods and services to the market.
- Organize activities within the company.
- Configure its resources.
- Achieve and sustain a high level of profitability.
- Grow the business over time.

The business model at discount stores such as Walmart, for example, is based on the idea that costs can be lowered by replacing a full-service retail format with a self-service format and a wider selection of products sold in a large-footprint store that contains minimal fixtures and fittings. These savings are passed on to consumers in the form of lower prices, which in turn grow revenues and help the company achieve further cost reductions from economies of scale. Over time, this business model has proved superior to the business models adopted by smaller, full-service, "mom-and-pop" stores, and by traditional, high-service department stores such as Sears. The business model—known as the self-service supermarket business model—was first developed by grocery retailers in the 1950s and later refined and improved on by general merchandisers such as Walmart in the 1960s and 1970s. Subsequently, the same basic business model was applied to toys (Toys "R" Us), office supplies (Staples, Office Depot), and home-improvement supplies (Home Depot and Lowe's).

1-3a Industry Differences in Performance

It is important to recognize that in addition to its business model and associated strategies, a company's performance is also determined by the characteristics of the industry in which it competes. Different industries are characterized by different competitive conditions. In some industries, demand is growing rapidly; in others, it is contracting. Some industries might be beset by excess capacity and persistent price wars; others by strong demand and rising prices. In some, technological change might be revolutionizing competition; others may be characterized by stable technology. In some industries, high profitability among incumbent companies might induce new companies to enter the industry, and these new entrants might subsequently depress prices and profits in the industry. In other industries, new entry might be difficult, and periods of high profitability might persist for a considerable time. Thus, the different competitive conditions prevailing in different industries may lead to differences in profitability and profit growth. For example, average profitability might be higher in some industries and lower in other industries because competitive conditions vary from industry to industry. Exactly how industries differ is discussed in detail in Chapter 2. For now, it is important to remember that the profitability and profit growth of a company are determined by two main factors: *its relative success in its industry and the overall performance of its industry relative to other industries.*[4]

1-3b Performance in Nonprofit Enterprises

A final point concerns the concept of superior performance in the nonprofit sector. Nonprofit enterprises such as government agencies, universities, and charities are not in "business" to make profits. Nevertheless, they are expected to use their resources efficiently and operate effectively, and their managers set goals to measure their performance. One performance goal for a business school might be to get its programs ranked among the best in the nation. A performance goal for a charity such as the Gates Foundation might be to eradicate malaria (see Strategy in Action 1.1 for details). A performance goal for a government agency might be to improve its services while reducing its need for taxpayer funds. The managers of nonprofits need to map out strategies to attain these goals. They also need to understand that nonprofits compete for scarce resources, just as businesses do. For example, charities compete for scarce donations, and their managers must plan and develop strategies that lead to high performance and demonstrate a track record of meeting performance goals. A successful strategy gives potential donors a compelling message about why they should contribute additional donations. Thus, planning and thinking strategically are as important for managers in the nonprofit sector as they are for managers in profit-seeking firms.

The Gates Foundation—Eradicating Malaria

In 2007, the Bill & Melinda Gates Foundation, the philanthropic foundation established by Microsoft founder Bill Gates and his wife, Melinda, announced an ambitious, long-term goal: to eradicate malaria worldwide, rather than just keeping it under control, as had been the prevailing policy for decades. Many thought the goal was overly ambitious. An earlier attempt to eradicate the disease in the late 1950s had failed. The call came at a challenging time. Malaria was killing more than 1 million people a year, most of them children. Deaths from malaria in Sub-Saharan Africa had doubled over the prior 20 years as the malaria parasite grew resistant to existing drugs, and as the mosquitos that carry the disease grew resistant to insecticides. The Gates Foundation backed up its call to arms with a commitment to invest $860 million to malaria programs, and another $650 million to support the Global Fund to Fight AIDS, tuberculosis, and malaria.

With a clear, long-term goal in place, the Gates Foundation needed to develop a set of strategies to attain this goal. The Foundation knew only too well that simply throwing money at the problem would not lead to a solution. Besides, even an organization like the Gates Foundation, which is the world's largest private charity, has limited resources and many different requests for funding. The foundation needed to make very clear choices about how it allocated its limited resources in order to have maximum effect and help win the war against malaria. To aid in this process, it hired scientists and public health experts to help evaluate requests for funding.

As it developed over the next few years, the foundation's strategy had several elements. First, it committed funds to promising efforts to develop a vaccine for malaria. Second, realizing that many malaria carriers are asymptomatic, the foundation backed efforts to developing better diagnostic tests that could be used quickly and efficiently in poor regions so that carriers in a population could be identified and treated. Third, it funded efforts to develop new drugs to treat those with malaria. These drugs represented an effort to respond to the rise of drug-resistant malaria parasites. Fourth, it sought to fund the development of more effective transmission control tools such as insecticide-treated bed nets and indoor spraying of walls and other surfaces with an insecticide. Finally, realizing that it could do far more with the support and cooperation of national governments and multinational institutions, the foundation used its resources to advocate for better funding and more effective policies, and it partnered proactively with national government in affected areas to help them develop more effective policies.

How much progress has the foundation made? In 2016, malaria claimed 429,000 lives. While that figure is still way too high, it represented a 50% reduction overall from the disease's peak in the early 2000s. The Gates Foundation's malaria strategy is evolving. Bill Gates is the first to admit that some of its goals were too ambitious. Early on, he thought we would have a malaria vaccine by now. While that hasn't happened, a promising vaccine is now in development. Equally notable, some low technology and inexpensive strategies have proved to be very successful, such as giving away insecticide-treated bed nets and placing mosquito traps in ventilation airways between the walls and rooks of buildings.

Sources: D. G. Blankinship, "Gates Foundation Looks to Fight Malaria," *Associated Press*, October 17, 2007; B. Gates, "Mosquito Wars," *gatesnotes*, August 15, 2017; Bill & Melinda Gates Foundation, "Malaria: Strategy Overview," April 2011; N. Kirsch, "Philanthropy King: Bill Gates Gives Away $4.6 Billion, Unveils New Campaign to Combat Malaria," *Forbes*, August 15, 2017.

1-4 Strategic Managers

Managers are the linchpin in the strategy-making process. Individual managers must take responsibility for formulating strategies to attain a competitive advantage and for putting those strategies into effect through implementation. They must lead the strategy-making process. The strategies that have resulted in the growth of Peloton were not chosen by some abstract entity known as "the company"; they were chosen by the company's founder and CEO, John Foley, and the managers he hired. Later in the chapter, we discuss strategic leadership, which is how managers can effectively lead the strategy-making process.

In most companies, there are two primary types of managers: **general managers**, who bear responsibility for the overall performance of the company or for one of its businesses or product lines, and **functional managers**, who are responsible for supervising a particular function; that is, a task, an activity, or an operation such as accounting, marketing, research and development (R&D), information technology,

> **1.4 Discuss the strategic role of managers at different levels within an organization.**
>
> **general managers**
>
> Managers who bear responsibility for the overall performance of the company or for one of its major self-contained subunits or divisions.
>
> **functional managers**
>
> Managers responsible for supervising a particular function; that is, a task, activity, or operation, such as accounting, marketing, research and development (R&D), information technology, or logistics.

or logistics. Put differently, general managers have profit-and-loss responsibility for a product, a business, or the company as a whole.

A company is a collection of functions or departments that work together to bring a particular good or service to the market. A company that operates in several different businesses often creates self-contained divisions for each business, with a general manager running each. The overriding concern of general managers is the success of the whole company or the divisions under their direction; they are responsible for deciding how to create a competitive advantage and achieve high profitability with the resources and capital at their disposal. Figure 1.2 shows the organization of a **multidivisional company** that competes in several different businesses and has created a separate, self-contained division to manage each. As you can see, there are three main levels of management: corporate, business, and functional. General managers are found at the first two of these levels, but their strategic roles differ depending on their sphere of responsibility.

multidivisional company

A company that competes in several different businesses and has created a separate, self-contained division to manage each.

1-4a Corporate-Level Managers

The corporate level of management consists of the chief executive officer (CEO), other senior executives, and corporate staff. These individuals occupy the apex of decision making within the organization. The CEO is the principal general manager. In consultation with other senior executives, the role of corporate-level managers is to oversee the development of strategies for the whole organization. This role includes defining the goals of the organization, determining what businesses it should be in, allocating resources among the different businesses, formulating and implementing strategies that span individual businesses, and providing leadership for the entire organization.

Consider 3M as an example. One of America's most venerable corporations, 3M is active in a wide range of businesses, including safety equipment (e.g., medical masks, protective glasses, and earmuffs), industrial products, electronics, reflective film for road signs, health care, water filtration systems, abrasives, DIY products, office supplies, cleaning products, and consumer medical supplies.

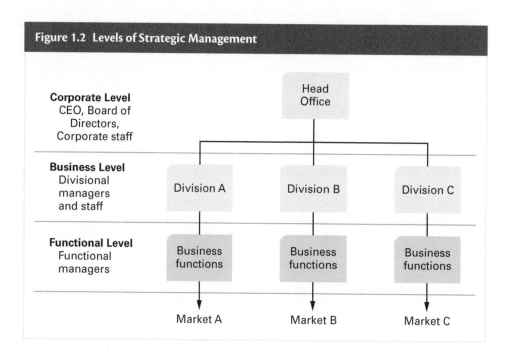

Figure 1.2 Levels of Strategic Management

Corporate Level
CEO, Board of Directors, Corporate staff

Head Office

Business Level
Divisional managers and staff

Division A | Division B | Division C

Functional Level
Functional managers

Business functions | Business functions | Business functions

Market A | Market B | Market C

The main strategic responsibilities of its CEO include setting overall strategic goals, monitoring the performance of the businesses, allocating resources among different business areas, deciding whether the firm should divest itself of any of its businesses, and determining whether it should acquire any new ones. In other words, it is up to the CEO to develop strategies that span individual businesses; the CEO is concerned with building and managing 3M's portfolio of businesses to maximize shareholder value.

It is not the CEO's specific responsibility to develop strategies for competing in individual business areas such as its health care products, masking tapes, Post-it Notes, or water filtration systems. The development of such strategies is the responsibility of the general managers in these different businesses, or business-level managers. However, it is the responsibility of the CEO to probe the strategic thinking of business-level managers to make sure that they are pursuing robust business models and strategies that will contribute to the maximization of 3M's long-run performance, to coach and motivate those managers, to reward them for attaining or exceeding goals, and to hold them accountable for poor performance.

Corporate-level managers also provide a link between the people who oversee the strategic development of a firm and those who own it (the shareholders). Corporate-level managers, particularly the CEO, can be viewed as the agents of shareholders. It is their responsibility to ensure that the corporate and business strategies that the company pursues are consistent with superior profitability and profit growth. If they are not, then the CEO may ultimately be called to account by the shareholders.

1-4b Business-Level Managers

A **business unit** is a self-contained division with its own functions (for example, finance, purchasing, production, and marketing departments) that provides a product or service for a particular market. The principal general manager at the business level, or the business-level manager, is the head of the division. The strategic role of these managers is to translate the general statements of direction and intent from the corporate level into concrete strategies for individual businesses. Whereas corporate-level general managers are concerned with strategies that span individual businesses, business-level general managers are concerned with strategies that are specific to a particular business. At 3M, a long-standing major corporate objective has been to generate a high percentage of revenues from new products. The general managers in each division work out for their business the strategies that are consistent with this objective.

business unit

A self-contained division that provides a product or service for a particular market.

1-4c Functional-Level Managers

Functional-level managers are responsible for the specific business functions or operations (human resources, purchasing, product development, logistics, production, customer service, and so on) found within a company or one of its divisions. Thus, a functional manager's sphere of responsibility is generally confined to one organizational activity, whereas general managers oversee the operation of an entire company or division. Although they are not responsible for the overall performance of the organization, functional managers nevertheless have a major strategic role: to develop functional strategies in their areas that help fulfill the strategic objectives set by business- and corporate-level general managers.

In 3M's safety equipment business, for instance, production and supply chain managers are responsible for developing strategies consistent with business unit and corporate objectives. Moreover, functional managers provide most of the information that makes it possible for business- and corporate-level general managers to formulate realistic and attainable strategies. Indeed, because they are closer to the customer than is the typical general manager, functional managers may generate important ideas that subsequently become major strategies for the company. Thus, it is important for general managers to listen closely to the ideas of their functional managers. An equally great responsibility for managers at the operational level is strategy implementation: the execution of corporate- and business-level plans.

1.5 Identify the primary steps in a strategic planning process.

1-5 The Strategic Planning Process

We can now turn our attention to the process by which managers formulate and implement strategies. Many writers have emphasized that strategy is the outcome of a formal planning process, and that top management plays the most important role in this process.[5] Although this view has some basis in reality, it is not the whole story. As we shall see later in the chapter, valuable strategies often emerge from deep within the organization without prior planning. Nevertheless, a consideration of formal, rational planning is a useful starting point for our journey into the world of strategy. Accordingly, we consider what might be described as a typical, formal strategic planning model.

1-5a A Model of the Strategic Planning Process

The formal strategic planning process has the following five main steps:

1. Select the corporate mission and major corporate goals.
2. Analyze the organization's external competitive environment to identify opportunities and threats.
3. Analyze the organization's internal operating environment to identify the organization's strengths and weaknesses.
4. Select strategies that build on the organization's strengths and correct its weaknesses to take advantage of external opportunities and counter external threats. These strategies should be consistent with the mission and major goals of the organization. They should be congruent and constitute a viable business model.
5. Implement the strategies.

The task of analyzing the organization's external and internal environments, and then selecting appropriate strategies, constitutes strategy formulation. In contrast, as noted earlier, strategy implementation involves putting the strategies (or plan) into action. This includes taking actions consistent with the selected strategies of the company at the corporate, business, and functional levels; allocating roles and responsibilities among managers (typically through the design of organizational structure); allocating resources (including capital and money); setting short-term objectives; and designing the organization's control and reward systems. These steps are illustrated in Figure 1.3 (which can also serve as a road map for the rest of this book).

Each step in Figure 1.3 constitutes a sequential step in the strategic planning process. At step 1, each round, or cycle, of the planning process begins with a statement of the corporate mission and major corporate goals. The mission statement is followed by the foundation of strategic thinking: external analysis, internal analysis, and strategic choice. The strategy-making process ends with the design of the organizational structure and the culture and control systems necessary to implement the organization's chosen strategy. This chapter discusses how to select a corporate mission and

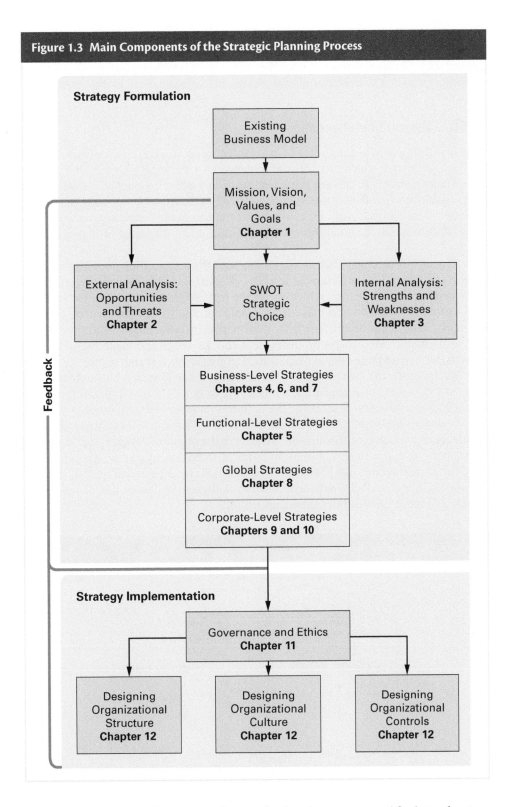

Figure 1.3 Main Components of the Strategic Planning Process

Strategy Formulation

Existing Business Model

Mission, Vision, Values, and Goals
Chapter 1

External Analysis: Opportunities and Threats
Chapter 2

SWOT Strategic Choice

Internal Analysis: Strengths and Weaknesses
Chapter 3

Feedback

Business-Level Strategies
Chapters 4, 6, and 7

Functional-Level Strategies
Chapter 5

Global Strategies
Chapter 8

Corporate-Level Strategies
Chapters 9 and 10

Strategy Implementation

Governance and Ethics
Chapter 11

Designing Organizational Structure
Chapter 12

Designing Organizational Culture
Chapter 12

Designing Organizational Controls
Chapter 12

choose major goals. Other aspects of strategic planning are reserved for later chapters, as indicated in Figure 1.3.

Some organizations go through a new cycle of the strategic planning process every year. This does not necessarily mean that managers choose a new strategy each year. In many instances, the result is simply to modify and reaffirm a strategy and structure already in place. The strategic plans generated by the planning process generally project over a period of 1 to 5 years, and the plan is updated, or rolled forward, every year. The results of the annual strategic planning process should be used as input into the budgetary process for the coming year so that strategic planning shapes resource allocation within the organization.

1-5b Mission Statement

The first component of the strategic management process is crafting the organization's mission statement, which provides the framework—or context—within which strategies are formulated. A mission statement has four main components: a statement of the organization's reason for existence—normally referred to as *the mission*; a statement of some desired future state, usually referred to as *the vision*; a statement of the key *values* to which the organization is committed; and a statement of major *goals*.

mission

The purpose of the company, or a statement of what the company strives to do.

The Mission A company's **mission** describes what the organization does. For example, Google's mission is *to organize the world's information and make it universally accessible and useful.* Google's search engine is the method that is employed to "organize the world's information and make it accessible and useful." In the view of Google's founders, Larry Page and Sergey Brin, information includes not just text on websites, but also images, video, maps, products, news, books, blogs, and much more. You can search through all these information sources using Google's search engine.

According to the famous management writer, Peter Drucker, an important first step in the process of formulating a mission is to come up with a definition of the organization's business. Essentially, the definition answers these questions: "What is our business? What will it be? What should it be?"[6] The responses to these questions guide the formulation of the mission. To answer the question "What is our business?" a company should define its business in terms of three dimensions: who is being satisfied (what customer groups), what is being satisfied (what customer needs), and how customers' needs are being satisfied (by what skills, knowledge, or distinctive competencies).[7] Figure 1.4 illustrates these dimensions.

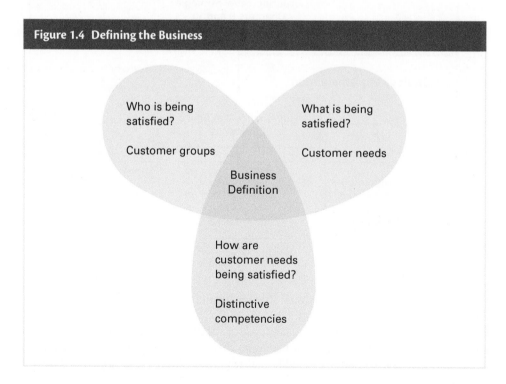

Figure 1.4 Defining the Business

Who is being satisfied?

Customer groups

What is being satisfied?

Customer needs

Business Definition

How are customer needs being satisfied?

Distinctive competencies

Drucker's approach stresses the need for a *customer-oriented* rather than a *product-oriented* business definition. A product-oriented business definition focuses on the characteristics of the products sold and the markets served, not on the customer needs the products satisfy. Such an approach obscures the company's true mission because a product is only the physical or service manifestation of applying a particular skill to satisfy a particular need for a particular customer group. In practice, that need may be satisfied in many different ways, and a broad, customer-oriented business definition that identifies these ways can safeguard companies from being caught unaware by major shifts in demand.

Google's mission statement is customer oriented. Google's product is its search engine. Its production technology involves the development of complex search algorithms and vast databases that archive information. But Google does not define itself as a search engine company. Rather, it sees itself as organizing information to make it accessible and useful *to customers*.

The need to take a customer-oriented view has often been ignored. History is peppered with the ghosts of once-great corporations that did not define their businesses, or defined them incorrectly, and so ultimately declined. In the 1950s and 1960s, many office equipment companies such as Smith Corona and Underwood defined their businesses as being the production of typewriters. This product-oriented definition ignored the fact that they were really in the business of satisfying customers' needs for information processing. Unfortunately for those companies, when a new form of technology appeared that better served customer needs for information processing (personal computers), demand for typewriters plummeted. The last great typewriter company, Smith Corona, went bankrupt in 1996, a victim of the success of personal computers equipped with word-processing technology.

In contrast, the *New York Times* correctly foresaw what its business would be (see Strategy in Action 1.2). In the 1990s the *New York Times* was the leading high-quality print newspaper in America with over 1 million daily subscribers. However, the *Times* did not see itself as being in the "newspaper" business; rather, it was in the "news" business with a mission to *seek truth and help people understand the world*. This customer-focused mission led the company to rapidly transform itself into the largest subscription-based digital news source in America, with 10 million subscribers as of early 2022.[8]

Vision The **vision** of a company defines a desired future state; it articulates, often in bold terms, what the company would like to achieve. In its early days, Microsoft operated with a very powerful vision of *a computer on every desk and in every home*. To transform this vision into a reality, Microsoft focused on producing computer software that was cheap and useful to businesses and consumers. In turn, the availability of powerful, inexpensive software such as Windows and Office helped to drive the penetration of personal computers into homes and offices. Similarly, the vision of the *New York Times* in the digital era is *to become the essential subscription for every curious, English-speaking person seeking to understand and engage with the world* (see Strategy in Action 1.2).

vision
The articulation of a company's desired achievements or future state.

Values The **values** of a company state how managers and employees should conduct themselves, how they should do business, and what kind of organization they should build. Insofar as they help drive and shape behavior within a company, values are commonly seen as the bedrock of a company's organizational culture: the set of values, norms, and standards that control how employees work to achieve an organization's mission and goals. An organization's culture is commonly seen as an important source of its competitive advantage.[9] (We discuss the issue of organizational culture in depth in Chapter 12.) For example, Nucor Steel is one of the most productive and profitable steel firms in the world. Its competitive advantage is based, in part, on the

values
A statement of how employees should conduct themselves and their business to help achieve the company mission.

The Digital Transformation on the *New York Times*

The 21st century has been a difficult one for the newspaper business. The growth of news content on the internet has cut sharply into the subscription and advertising revenues of traditional newspapers, transforming what was once a highly profitable business into a landscape scattered with the bones of dead publications. In 1990, some 62 million newspapers were produced every day in the United States, all of them print. By 2020, the number of dailies had declined to just 24 million, of which a significant share was digital. Industry advertising revenues peaked at $49 billion in 2006, before declining to under $10 billion in 2020. Subscription revenues have been flat at between $10–$11 billion since 2003, although this aggregate figure hides a dramatic decline in subscription revenues for print newspapers and growing digital subscriptions.

One company that has managed to navigate the transformation taking place in the newspaper industry has been the *New York Times*. Early in the century, management at the *Times* recognized that digitalization was inevitable, and that it offered both and a threat and an opportunity for the company. Management decided to commit the company to digitalization, and to build a digital-first, subscription-first business, centered on journalism worth paying for. In essence, the *Times* recognized that lucrative print subscription revenue stream from its roughly 1.1 million daily subscribers would go away, and that advertising revenue would decline as a result. Management decided that there was no alternative but to go all in on digital.

A milestone in the company's digital transformation was a decision to create a digital paywall in 2011. Readers would get three free articles a month, and then to read more they would have to purchase a subscription. To make that shift easier, the *Times* offered different tiers of subscriptions; basic access (news); all access (news plus the NYT crossword and NYT cooking); and all-access plus print. The *Times* also offered a low subscription price for the first year to entice readers to try the product, and then gave itself the task of making the content so compelling that they would pay more for a subscription after the first year.

Consistent with this strategy, the company committed itself to maintaining its tradition of strong fact-based journalism and continued to invest in its newsroom and reporters. Management believed that in a digital landscape populated by untrustworthy and shallow publications, the strong brand of the *Times*, if supported by continued investment in the very best journalism, would start to stand out. At the same time, recognizing its own weaknesses, the company hired more staff with expertise in digital production to produce the best online offering, and to help develop complementary products, such as the NYT Daily Podcast, which has become an increasingly popular news source.

The *Times* also came to the realization that its potential audience was bigger than just the United States. Its research suggests that there are more than 135 million adults worldwide who are paying, or willing to pay, for one or more subscriptions to English-language news and opinion, sports journalism, puzzles, recipes, expert shopping advice, or podcasting. The *Times* characterizes this core demographic as curious readers, lifelong learners, independent thinkers, who are interested in other cultures, perspectives, and experiences. This is the core demographic that the *Times* is going after. The company's vision is *to become the essential subscription for every curious, English-speaking person seeking to understand and engage with the world.*

Ten years after the *Times* created it digital paywall, the strategy is clearly working. In early 2022, the company passed a milestone that once seemed impossible; more than 10 million digital subscriptions, up from 3 million in 2018 (and more than double that of its nearest digital rival, the *Washington Post*). Meanwhile, print subscriptions had fallen to just 300,00 by 2022, down from over a million a decade earlier. Even though the revenue per subscriber is significantly lower for the digital product, so are costs of production and distribution. As a result, in 2021 the *Times* reported that its revenues exceeded $2 billion for the first time, up from $1.56 billion in 2016. Operating profits were $270 million, up from $120 million in 2015. Now the company's goal is to grow its digital subscriber base to 15 million by the end of 2027.

Sources: Howard Tiersky, "The New York Times Is Winning at Digital," *CIO.com*, June 8, 2017; "Newspapers Fact Sheet," *Pew Research Center*, June 29, 2001; "Our Strategy," *New York Times*, March 24, 2022; D. Mastrangelo, "New York Times Adds 455K Subscriptions in Latest Quarter," *The Hill*, November 3, 2021.

extremely high productivity of its workforce, which the company maintains is a direct result of its cultural values, which in turn determine how it treats its employees. These values are as follows:

- "Management is obligated to manage Nucor in such a way that employees will have the opportunity to earn according to their productivity."
- "Employees should be able to feel confident that if they do their jobs properly, they will have a job tomorrow."
- "Employees have the right to be treated fairly and must believe that they will be."
- "Employees must have an avenue of appeal when they believe they are being treated unfairly."[10]

At Nucor, values emphasizing pay for performance, job security, and fair treatment for employees help to create an atmosphere within the company that leads to high employee productivity. In turn, this has helped Nucor achieve one of the lowest cost structures in its industry, and it helps to explain the company's profitability in a very price-competitive business.

In one study of organizational values, researchers identified a set of values associated with high-performing organizations that help companies achieve superior financial performance through their impact on employee behavior.[11] These values included respect for the interests of key organizational stakeholders: individuals or groups that have an interest, claim, or stake in the company, in what it does, and in how well it performs.[12] They include stockholders, bondholders, employees, customers, the communities in which the company does business, and the general public. The study found that deep respect for the interests of customers, employees, suppliers, and shareholders was associated with high performance. The study also noted that the encouragement of leadership and entrepreneurial behavior by mid- and lower-level managers, and a willingness to support change efforts within the organization, contributed to high performance. The same study identified the attributes of poorly performing companies—as might be expected, these are not articulated in company mission statements: (1) arrogance, particularly in response to ideas from outside the company; (2) lack of respect for key stakeholders; and (3) a history of resisting change efforts and "punishing" mid- and lower-level managers who showed "too much leadership."

1-5c Major Goals

Having stated the mission, vision, and key values, strategic managers can take the next step in the formulation of a mission statement: establishing major goals. A goal is a precise, measurable, desired future state that a company attempts to realize. In this context, the purpose of goals is to specify with precision what must be done if the company is to attain its mission or vision.

Well-constructed goals have four main characteristics:[13]

- They are precise and measurable. Measurable goals give managers a yardstick or standard against which they can judge their performance.
- They address crucial issues. To maintain focus, managers should select a limited number of crucial or important goals to assess the performance of the company.
- They are challenging but realistic. They give all employees an incentive to look for ways of improving the operations of the organization. If a goal is unrealistic in the challenges it poses, employees may give up; a goal that is too easy may fail to motivate managers and other employees.[14]
- They specify, when appropriate, a time in which the goals should be achieved. Time constraints tell employees that success requires a goal to be attained by a given date, not after that date. Deadlines can inject a sense of urgency into goal attainment and act as a motivator. However, not all goals require time constraints.

Well-constructed goals also provide a means by which the performance of managers can be evaluated.

As noted earlier, although most companies operate with a variety of goals, the primary goal of most corporations is to maximize shareholder returns. Doing this requires both high profitability and sustained profit growth. Thus, most companies operate with goals for profitability and profit growth. However, it is important that top managers do not make the mistake of overemphasizing current profitability to the detriment of long-term profitability and profit growth.[15] The overzealous pursuit of current profitability to maximize short-term ROIC can encourage such misguided managerial actions as cutting expenditures judged to be nonessential in the short run—for instance, expenditures for research and development, marketing, and new capital investments. Although cutting current expenditures increases current profitability, the resulting underinvestment, lack of innovation, and diminished marketing can jeopardize long-run profitability and profit growth.

To guard against short-run decision making, managers need to ensure that they adopt goals whose attainment will increase the long-run performance and competitiveness of their enterprise. Long-term goals are related to such issues as product development, customer satisfaction, and efficiency. They emphasize specific objectives or targets concerning such details as employee and capital productivity, product quality, innovation, customer satisfaction, and customer service.

1-5d External Analysis

The second component of the strategic management process is an analysis of the organization's external operating environment. The essential purpose of the external analysis is to identify strategic opportunities and threats within the organization's operating environment that will affect how it pursues its mission. Strategy in Action 1.2 describes how an analysis of opportunities and threats in the external environment resulted in a strategic shift at the *New York Times*.

Three interrelated environments should be examined when undertaking an external analysis: the industry environment in which the company operates, the country or national environment, and the wider socioeconomic or macroenvironment. Analyzing the industry environment requires an assessment of the competitive structure of the company's industry, including the competitive position of the company and its major rivals. It also requires analysis of the nature, stage, dynamics, and history of the industry. Because many markets are now global, analyzing the industry environment also means assessing the impact of globalization on competition within an industry. Such an analysis may reveal that a company should move some production facilities to another nation, that it should aggressively expand in emerging markets such as India, or that it should beware of new competition from emerging nations. Analyzing the macroenvironment consists of examining macroeconomic, social, governmental, legal, international, and technological factors that may affect the company and its industry. We look at external analysis in Chapter 2.

1-5e Internal Analysis

Internal analysis, the third component of the strategic planning process, focuses on reviewing the resources, capabilities, and competencies of a company to identify its strengths and weaknesses. For example, as described in Strategy in Action 1.2, an internal analysis at the *New York Times* revealed that although the company had a strong, well-known brand, it suffered from a lack of digital skills. To correct this deficiency, the *Times* hired people skilled in this area. We consider internal analysis in Chapter 3.

1-5f SWOT Analysis and the Business Model

The next component of strategic thinking requires the generation of a series of strategic alternatives, or choices of future strategies to pursue, given the company's internal strengths and weaknesses and its external opportunities and threats. The comparison of strengths, weaknesses, opportunities, and threats is normally referred to as a **SWOT analysis**.[16] The central purpose is to identify the strategies to exploit external opportunities, counter threats, build on and protect company strengths, and eradicate weaknesses.

As described in Strategy in Action 1.2, this is exactly what senior management at the *New York Times* did. They understood that digitalization represented both an

SWOT analysis

The comparison of strengths, weaknesses, opportunities, and threats.

opportunity and a threat, and they decided to embrace that opportunity by moving rapidly into the digital arena with a subscription-based offering targeted at a well-specified core demographic not just in America, but worldwide. Managers recognized that the well-known brand and strong reporting capabilities of the *New York Times* were *strengths* that would serve it well online, but that they needed to build digital publishing capabilities to fix a weakness in that area.

More generally, the goal of a SWOT analysis is to create, affirm, or fine-tune a company-specific business model that will best align, fit, or match a company's resources and capabilities to the demands of the environment in which it operates. Managers compare and contrast various alternative possible strategies, and then identify the set of strategies that will create and sustain a competitive advantage. These strategies can be divided into four main categories:

- *Business-level strategies*, which encompass the business's overall competitive theme, the way it positions itself in the marketplace to gain a competitive advantage, and the different positioning strategies that can be used in different industry settings— for example, cost leadership, differentiation, focusing on a particular niche or segment of the industry, or some combination of these. We review business-level strategies in Chapters 4, 6, and 7.
- *Functional-level strategies*, directed at improving the efficiency and effectiveness of operations within a company, such as manufacturing, marketing, materials management (logistics), product development, and customer service. We review functional-level strategies in Chapter 5.
- *Global strategies*, which address how to expand operations outside the home country in order to grow and prosper in a world where competitive advantage is determined at a global level. We review global strategies in Chapter 8.
- *Corporate-level strategies* answer the primary questions: What business or businesses should we be in to maximize the long-run profitability and profit growth of the organization, and how should we enter and increase our presence in these businesses to gain a competitive advantage? We review corporate-level strategies in Chapters 9 and 10.

The strategies identified through a SWOT analysis should be congruent with each other. Thus, functional-level strategies should be consistent with, or support, the company's business-level strategies and global strategies. Moreover, as we explain later in this book, corporate-level strategies should support business-level strategies. When combined, the various strategies pursued by a company should constitute a complete, viable business model. In essence, a SWOT analysis is a methodology for choosing between competing business models, and for fine-tuning the business model that managers choose. For example, when Microsoft entered the video-game market with its Xbox offering, it had to settle on the best business model for competing in this market. Microsoft used a SWOT-type analysis to compare alternatives and settled on a business model referred to as "razor and razor blades," in which the Xbox console is priced at cost to build sales (the "razor"), while profits are generated from royalties on the sale of games for the Xbox (the "blades").

1-5g Strategy Implementation

Once managers have chosen a set of congruent strategies to achieve a competitive advantage and increase performance, those strategies must be implemented. Strategy implementation involves taking actions at the functional, business, and corporate levels to execute a strategic plan. For example, implementation can include the following: putting quality improvement programs into place; changing the way a product is designed; positioning the product differently in the marketplace; segmenting the market and offering different versions of the product to different consumer groups; implementing price increases or decreases; expanding through mergers and acquisitions; downsizing the company by closing or selling off parts of the company; and much more. These and other topics are discussed in detail in Chapters 4 through 10.

Strategy implementation also entails designing the best organizational structure and the best culture and control systems to put a chosen strategy into action. In addition, senior managers need to put a governance system in place to make sure that everyone within the organization acts in a manner that is not only consistent with maximizing profitability and profit growth, but also legal and ethical. We look at the topic of governance and ethics in Chapter 11; in Chapter 12, we discuss the organizational structure, culture, and controls required to implement business-level strategies.

1-5h The Feedback Loop

The feedback loop in Figure 1.3 indicates that strategic planning is ongoing: it never ends. Once a strategy has been implemented, its execution must be monitored to determine the extent to which strategic goals and objectives are being achieved, and to what degree competitive advantage is being created and sustained. This information and knowledge are returned to the corporate level through feedback loops and becomes the input for the next round of strategy formulation and implementation. Top managers can then decide whether to reaffirm the existing business model and the existing strategies and goals or suggest changes for the future. For example, if a strategic goal proves too optimistic, a more conservative goal is set.

1.6 Examine the criticisms of strategic planning.

1-6 Strategy as an Emergent Process

The planning model suggests that a company's strategies are the result of a plan, that the strategic planning process is rational and highly structured, and that top management orchestrates the process. Several scholars have criticized the formal planning model for three main reasons: (1) the unpredictability of the real world; (2) the role that lower-level managers can play in the strategic management process; and (3) the fact that many successful strategies are often the result of serendipity, not rational strategizing. These scholars have advocated an alternative view of strategy making.[17]

1-6a Strategy Making in an Unpredictable World

Critics of formal planning systems argue that we live in a world in which uncertainty, complexity, and ambiguity dominate, and in which small, chance events can have a large, unpredictable impact on outcomes.[18] In such circumstances, they claim, even the most carefully thought-out strategic plans are prone to being rendered useless by rapid and unforeseen change. To paraphrase the 19th-century German General Helmuth von Moltke, "no plan survives contact with the enemy," or as the former heavyweight boxing champion Mike Tyson once said, "everyone has a plan until they get punched in the mouth." The point is that the future is inherently uncertain, and the only thing we know about it is that it is unknown. Major market-changing events often surprise us. Consider the unanticipated nature of major world events in this century, such as the COVID-19 pandemic; the September 11, 2001, attack on the World Trade Center; and the great financial crisis of 2008–2009. Who planned in advance for these?

In an unpredictable world, being able to respond quickly to changing circumstances, and to alter the strategies of the organization accordingly, is paramount.

The dramatic rise of Google, for example, with its business model based on revenues earned from advertising links associated with search results (the so-called "pay-per-click" business model), disrupted the business models of companies that made money from more traditional forms of online advertising. Nobody could foresee this development or plan for it, but companies had to respond to it, and rapidly. Companies with a strong online advertising presence, including Yahoo.com and Microsoft's MSN network, rapidly changed their strategies to adapt to the threat Google posed. Specifically, both companies developed their own search engines and copied Google's pay-per-click business model. According to critics of formal systems, such a flexible approach to strategy making is not possible within the framework of a traditional strategic planning process, with its implicit assumption that an organization's strategies only need to be reviewed during the annual strategic planning exercise.

1-6b Autonomous Action: Strategy Making by Lower-Level Managers

Another criticism leveled at the rational planning model of strategy is that too much importance is attached to the role of top management, particularly the CEO.[19] An alternative view is that individual managers deep within an organization can—and often do—exert a profound influence over the strategic direction of the firm.[20] Writing with Robert Burgelman of Stanford University, Andy Grove, the former CEO of Intel, noted that many important strategic decisions at Intel were initiated not by top managers but by the autonomous actions of lower-level managers deep within Intel who, on their own initiative, formulated new strategies and worked to persuade top-level managers to alter the strategic priorities of the firm.[21] These strategic decisions included the decision to exit an important market (the DRAM memory chip market) and to develop a certain class of microprocessors (RISC-based microprocessors) in direct contrast to the stated strategy of Intel's top managers.

Autonomous action may be particularly important in helping established companies deal with the uncertainty created by the arrival of a radical new technology that changes the dominant paradigm in an industry.[22] Top managers usually rise to preeminence by successfully executing the established strategy of the firm. Therefore, they may have an emotional commitment to the status quo and are often unable to see things from a different perspective. In this sense, they can be a conservative force that promotes inertia. Lower-level managers are less likely to have the same commitment to the status quo and have more to gain from promoting new technologies and strategies. They may be the first ones to recognize new strategic opportunities and lobby for strategic change. As described in Strategy in Action 1.3, this seems to have been the case at discount stockbroker Charles Schwab, which had to adjust to the arrival of the web in the 1990s.

1-6c Serendipity and Strategy

Business history is replete with examples of accidental events that helped push companies in new and profitable directions. These examples suggest that many successful strategies are not the result of well-thought-out plans, but of serendipity—stumbling across good outcomes unexpectedly. One such example occurred at 3M during the 1960s. At that time, 3M was producing fluorocarbons for sale as coolant liquid in air-conditioning equipment. One day, a researcher working with fluorocarbons in a 3M lab spilled some of the liquid on her shoes. Later that day when she spilled coffee over her shoes, she watched with interest as the coffee formed into little beads of liquid and then ran off her shoes without leaving a stain. Reflecting on this phenomenon, she realized that a fluorocarbon-based liquid might turn out to be useful for protecting fabrics from liquid stains, and so the idea for Scotchgard was born. Subsequently, Scotchgard

A Strategic Shift at Charles Schwab

In the mid-1990s, Charles Schwab was the most successful discount stockbroker in the world. Over 20 years, it had gained share from full-service brokers like Merrill Lynch by offering deep discounts on the commissions charged for stock trades. Although Schwab had a nationwide network of branches, most customers executed their trades through a telephone system, TeleBroker. Others used online proprietary software, Street Smart, which had to be purchased from Schwab. It was a business model that worked well—then along came E*TRADE.

Bill Porter, a physicist and inventor, started the discount brokerage firm E*TRADE in 1994 to take advantage of the opportunity created by the rapid emergence of the web. E*TRADE launched the first dedicated website for online trading: E*TRADE had no branches, no brokers, and no telephone system for taking orders, and thus it had a very-low-cost structure. Customers traded stocks over the company's website. Due to its low-cost structure, E*TRADE was able to announce a flat $14.95 commission on stock trades, a figure significantly below Schwab's average commission, which at the time was $65. It was clear from the outset that E*TRADE and other online brokers such as Ameritrade, which soon followed, offered a direct threat to Schwab. Not only were their cost structures and commission rates considerably lower than Schwab's, but the ease, speed, and flexibility of trading stocks over the web suddenly made Schwab's Street Smart trading software seem limited and its telephone system antiquated.

Deep within Schwab, William Pearson, a young software specialist who had worked on the development of Street Smart, immediately saw the transformational power of the web. Pearson believed that Schwab needed to develop its own web-based software, and quickly. Try as he might, though, Pearson could not get the attention of his supervisor. He tried a number of other executives but found little support. Eventually he approached Anne Hennegar, a former Schwab manager who now worked as a consultant to the company. Hennegar suggested that Pearson meet with Tom Seip, an executive vice president at Schwab known for his ability to think outside the box. Hennegar approached Seip on Pearson's behalf, and Seip responded positively, asking her to set up a meeting. Hennegar and Pearson arrived, expecting to meet only Seip, but to their surprise in walked Charles Schwab, Chief Operating Officer David Pottruck, and the vice presidents in charge of strategic planning and electronic brokerage.

As the group watched Pearson's demo, which detailed how a web-based system would look and work, they became increasingly excited. It was clear to those in the room that a web-based system using real-time information, personalization, customization, and interactivity all advanced Schwab's commitment to empowering customers. By the end of the meeting, Pearson had received a green light to start work on the project. A year later, Schwab launched its own web-based offering, eSchwab, which enabled Schwab clients to execute stock trades for a low, flat-rate commission. eSchwab went on to become the core of the company's offering, enabling it to stave off competition from deep discount brokers like E*TRADE.

Sources: J. Kador, *Charles Schwab: How One Company Beat Wall Street and Reinvented the Brokerage Industry* (New York: John Wiley Sons, 2002); E. Schonfeld, "Schwab Puts It All Online," *Fortune* (December 7, 1998): 94–99.

became one of 3M's most profitable products and took the company into the fabric protection business, an area within which it had never planned to participate.[23]

Serendipitous discoveries and events can open all sorts of profitable avenues for a company. But some companies have missed profitable opportunities because serendipitous discoveries or events were inconsistent with their prior (planned) conception of their strategy. In one classic example of such myopia, in the 19th century, the telegraph company Western Union turned down an opportunity to purchase the rights to an invention by Alexander Graham Bell. The invention was the telephone—the technology that subsequently made the telegraph obsolete.

1-6d Intended and Emergent Strategies

Henry Mintzberg's model of strategy development provides a more encompassing view of strategy.[24] According to this model, illustrated in Figure 1.5, a company's realized strategy is the product of whatever planned strategies are put into action (the company's *deliberate* strategies) and any unplanned, or *emergent*, strategies. In Mintzberg's view, many planned strategies are not implemented because of unpredicted changes in the environment (they are unrealized). Emergent strategies are the unplanned responses to

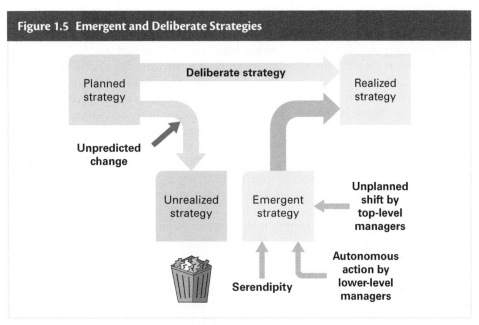

Figure 1.5 Emergent and Deliberate Strategies

Source: Adapted from H. Mintzberg and A. McGugh, *Administrative Science Quarterly* 30:2 (June 1985).

unforeseen circumstances. They arise from autonomous action by individual managers deep within the organization, from serendipitous discoveries or events, or from an unplanned strategic shift by top-level managers in response to changed circumstances. They are not the product of formal, top-down planning mechanisms.

Mintzberg maintains that emergent strategies are often successful and may be more appropriate than intended strategies. In a classic example of this process from business history, Richard Pascale described the entry of Honda Motor Co. into the U.S. motorcycle market.[25] When a number of Honda executives arrived in Los Angeles from Japan in 1959 to establish a U.S. operation, their original aim (intended strategy) was to focus on selling 250-cc and 350-cc machines to confirmed motorcycle enthusiasts, rather than the 50-cc Honda Cub, which was a big hit in Japan. Their instincts told them that the Honda 50s were not suitable for the U.S. market, where everything was bigger and more luxurious than in Japan.

However, sales of the 250-cc and 350-cc bikes were sluggish, and the bikes were plagued by mechanical failure. It looked as if Honda's strategy was going to fail. At the same time, the Japanese executives who were using the Honda 50s to run errands around Los Angeles were attracting a lot of attention. One day, they got a call from a Sears, Roebuck and Co. buyer who wanted to sell the 50-cc bikes to a broad market of Americans who were not necessarily motorcycle enthusiasts. The Honda executives were hesitant to sell the small bikes for fear of alienating serious bikers, who might then associate Honda with "wimpy" machines. In the end, however, they were pushed into doing so by the failure of the 250-cc and 350-cc models.

Honda had stumbled onto a previously untouched market segment that would prove huge: the average American who had never owned a motorbike. Honda had also found an untried channel of distribution: general retailers, rather than specialty motorbike stores. By 1964, nearly one out of every two motorcycles sold in the United States was a Honda.

The conventional explanation for Honda's success is that the company redefined the U.S. motorcycle industry with a brilliantly conceived intended strategy. The fact was that Honda's intended strategy was a near-disaster. The strategy that emerged did so not through planning but through unplanned action in response to unforeseen circumstances. Nevertheless, credit should be given to Honda's management for recognizing the strength of the emergent strategy and for pursuing it with vigor.

The critical point demonstrated by the Honda example is that successful strategies can often emerge within an organization without prior planning and in response to unforeseen circumstances. As Mintzberg has noted, strategies can take root wherever people have the capacity to learn and the resources to support that capacity.

In practice, the strategies of most organizations are likely a combination of the intended and the emergent. The message is that management needs to recognize the process of emergence and to intervene when appropriate, relinquishing bad emergent strategies and nurturing potentially good ones.[26] To make such decisions, managers must be able to judge the worth of emergent strategies. They must be able to think strategically. Although emergent strategies arise from within the organization without prior planning—that is, without completing the steps illustrated in Figure 1.3 in a sequential fashion—top management must still evaluate them. Such evaluation involves comparing each emergent strategy with the organization's goals, external environmental opportunities and threats, and internal strengths and weaknesses. The objective is to assess whether the emergent strategy fits the company's needs and capabilities. In addition, Mintzberg stresses that an organization's capability to produce emergent strategies is a function of the kind of corporate culture that the organization's structure and control systems foster. In other words, the different components of the strategic management process are just as important from the perspective of emergent strategies as they are from the perspective of intended strategies.

1.7 **Review the practice of strategic planning.**

1-7 Strategic Planning in Practice

Despite criticisms, research suggests that formal planning systems do help managers make better strategic decisions. A study that analyzed the results of 26 previously published studies came to the conclusion that, on average, strategic planning has a positive impact on company performance.[27] Another study of strategic planning in 656 firms found that formal planning methodologies and emergent strategies both form part of a good strategy-formulation process, particularly in an unstable environment.[28] For strategic planning to work, it is important that top-level managers plan not only within the context of the current competitive environment but also within the context of the future competitive environment. To try to forecast what that future will look like, managers can use scenario-planning techniques to project different possible futures. They can also involve operating managers in the planning process and seek to shape the future competitive environment by emphasizing strategic intent.

1-7a Scenario Planning

One reason that strategic planning may fail over longer time periods is that strategic managers, in their initial enthusiasm for planning techniques, may forget that the future is entirely unpredictable. As noted earlier, even the best-laid plans can fall apart if unforeseen contingencies occur, and that happens all the time. The recognition that uncertainty makes it difficult to forecast the future accurately led planners at Royal Dutch Shell to pioneer the scenario approach to planning.[29] **Scenario planning** involves formulating plans that are based upon "what-if" scenarios about the future. In the typical scenario-planning exercise, some scenarios are optimistic, some pessimistic. Teams of managers are asked to develop specific strategies to cope with each scenario. A set of indicators is chosen as signposts to track trends and identify the probability that any particular scenario is coming to pass. The idea is to allow managers to understand the dynamic and complex nature of their environment, to think through

scenario planning

Formulating plans that are based upon "what-if" scenarios about the future.

problems in a strategic fashion, and to generate a range of strategic options that might be pursued under different circumstances.[30] The scenario approach to planning has spread rapidly among large companies. One survey found that over 50% of the *Fortune 500* companies use some form of scenario-planning methods.[31]

Royal Dutch Shell has, perhaps, done more than most companies to pioneer the concept of scenario planning, and its experience demonstrates the power of the approach.[32] Shell has been using scenario planning since the 1980s. For example, in the early 2000s, it used two primary scenarios to anticipate future demand for oil and refine its strategic planning. The first scenario, called "Dynamics as Usual," predicted a gradual shift from carbon fuels (such as oil) to natural gas, and, eventually, to renewable energy. The second scenario, "The Spirit of the Coming Age," looked at the possibility that a technological revolution will lead to a rapid shift to new energy sources.[33] Shell made investments to ensure profitability for the company, regardless of which scenario comes to pass, and it is carefully tracking technological and market trends for signs of which scenario is becoming more likely over time.

The great virtue of the scenario approach to planning is that it pushes managers to think outside the box, to anticipate what they might need to do in different situations. It reminds managers that the world is complex and unpredictable, and to place a premium on flexibility rather than on inflexible plans based on assumptions about the future (which may or may not be correct). As a result of scenario planning, organizations might pursue one dominant strategy related to the scenario that is judged to be most likely, but they make investments that will pay off if other scenarios come to the fore (see Figure 1.6).

1-7b Decentralized Planning

Some companies constructing a strategic planning process erroneously treat planning exclusively as a top-management responsibility. This "ivory tower" approach can result in strategic plans formulated in a vacuum by top managers who may be disconnected from current operating realities. Consequently, top managers may formulate suboptimal strategies. For example, when demographic data indicated that houses and families were shrinking, planners at GE's appliance group concluded that smaller appliances were the wave of the future. Because they had little contact with

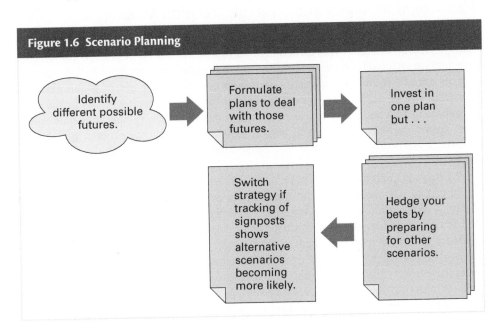

Figure 1.6 Scenario Planning

Identify different possible futures. → Formulate plans to deal with those futures. → Invest in one plan but . . .

Switch strategy if tracking of signposts shows alternative scenarios becoming more likely. ← Hedge your bets by preparing for other scenarios.

homebuilders and retailers, they did not realize that kitchens and bathrooms were the two rooms that were not shrinking. Nor did they appreciate that two-income families wanted large refrigerators to cut down on trips to the supermarket. GE wasted a lot of time designing small appliances for which there was limited demand.

The ivory tower concept of planning can also lead to tensions between corporate-, business-, and functional-level managers. The experience of GE's appliance group is again illuminating. Many of the corporate managers in the planning group were recruited from consulting firms or top-flight business schools. Many of the functional managers took this pattern of recruitment to mean that the corporate managers did not believe they were smart enough to think through strategic problems. They felt shut out of the decision-making process, which they believed to be unfairly constituted. From this perceived lack of procedural justice sprang an us-versus-them mindset that quickly escalated into hostility. As a result, even when the planners were correct, operating managers would not listen to them. Furthermore, ivory tower planning ignores both the important, strategic role of autonomous action by lower-level managers and the role of serendipity.

Correcting the ivory tower approach to planning requires recognizing that successful strategic planning encompasses managers at all levels of the corporation. Much of the best planning can and should be done by business and functional managers who are closest to the facts. In other words, planning should be decentralized. Corporate-level planners should be facilitators who help business and functional managers do the planning by setting the broad strategic goals of the organization and providing the resources necessary to identify the strategies required to attain those goals.

1.8 Explain strategic decision making and the cognitive biases that might lead to poor strategic decisions.

1-8 Strategic Decision Making

Even the best-designed strategic-planning systems will fail to produce the desired results if managers do not effectively use the information at their disposal. Consequently, it is important that strategic managers use that information to understand why they sometimes make poor decisions. One important way to do so is to understand how common cognitive biases can result in poor decision making.[34]

1-8a Cognitive Biases and Strategic Decision Making

The rationality of decision making is bound by one's cognitive capabilities.[35] Humans are not supercomputers—it is difficult for us to absorb and process large amounts of information effectively. As a result, when we make decisions, we tend to fall back on certain rules of thumb, or heuristics, that help us make sense out of a complex and uncertain world. Sometimes these rules lead to severe, systematic errors in the decision-making process.[36] Systematic errors are those that appear time and time again. They seem to arise from a series of **cognitive biases** in the way we process information and reach decisions. Cognitive biases cause many managers to make poor strategic decisions.

Numerous cognitive biases have been verified repeatedly in laboratory settings, so we can be reasonably sure that these biases exist and that all people are prone to them.[37] **Confirmation bias** refers to the fact that decision makers who have strong prior beliefs tend to make decisions on the basis of these beliefs, even when presented with evidence that their beliefs are incorrect. Moreover, they tend to seek and use information that is consistent with their prior beliefs while ignoring information that contradicts these beliefs. To place this bias in a strategic context, it suggests that a CEO who has a strong prior belief that a certain strategy makes sense might continue to pursue that strategy despite evidence that it is inappropriate or failing.

cognitive biases

Systematic errors in decision making that arise from the way people process information.

confirmation bias

Refers to the fact that decision makers who have strong prior beliefs tend to make decisions on the basis of these beliefs, even when presented with evidence that their beliefs are wrong.

Another well-known cognitive bias, **escalating commitment**, occurs when decision makers, having already committed significant resources to a project, commit even more resources even if they receive feedback that the project is failing.[38] A more logical response would be to abandon the project and move on (that is, to cut one's losses and exit), rather than escalate commitment.

A third bias, **reasoning by analogy**, involves the use of simple analogies to make sense out of complex problems. The problem with this heuristic is that the analogy may not be valid. A fourth bias, **representativeness**, is rooted in the tendency to generalize from a small sample or even a single, vivid anecdote. This bias violates the statistical law of large numbers, which states that it is inappropriate to generalize from a small sample, let alone from a single case. In many respects, the dot-com boom of the late 1990s was based on reasoning by analogy and representativeness. Prospective entrepreneurs saw some early dot-com companies such as Amazon and Yahoo! achieve rapid success, at least as judged by some metrics. Reasoning by analogy from a very small sample, they assumed that any dot-com could achieve similar success. Many investors reached similar conclusions. The result was a massive wave of start-ups that attempted to capitalize on perceived internet opportunities. The vast majority of these companies subsequently went bankrupt, proving that the analogy was wrong and that the success of the small sample of early entrants was no guarantee that all dot-coms would succeed.

A fifth cognitive bias is referred to as **overconfidence** or the **illusion of control**, refers to the tendency to overestimate one's ability to control events. General or top managers seem to be particularly prone to this bias: having risen to the top of an organization, they tend to be overconfident about their ability to succeed. According to Richard Roll, such overconfidence leads to what he has termed the *hubris hypothesis of takeovers*.[39] Roll argues that top managers are typically overconfident about their ability to create value by acquiring other companies. Hence, they make poor acquisition decisions, often paying far too much for the companies they acquire. Subsequently, servicing the debt taken on to finance such acquisitions makes it all but impossible to profit from them.

Availability error, another common bias, arises from our predisposition to estimate the probability of an outcome based on how easy the outcome is to imagine. For example, more people seem to fear a plane crash than a car accident, yet statistically one is far more likely to be killed in a car on the way to the airport than in a plane crash. People overweigh the probability of a plane crash because the outcome is easier to imagine, and because plane crashes are more vivid events than car crashes, which affect only small numbers of people at one time. As a result of availability error, managers might allocate resources to a project with an outcome that is easier to imagine, rather than to one that might have the highest return.

1-8b Techniques for Improving Decision Making

The existence of cognitive biases raises a question: How can critical information affect the decision-making mechanism so that a company's strategic decisions are realistic and based on thorough evaluation? Two techniques known to enhance strategic thinking and counteract cognitive biases are devil's advocacy and dialectic inquiry.[40]

Devil's advocacy requires the generation of a plan and a critical analysis of that plan. One member of the decision-making group acts as the devil's advocate, emphasizing all the reasons that might make the proposal unacceptable. In the process, decision makers become aware of the possible perils of recommended courses of action.

Dialectic inquiry is more complex because it requires the generation of a plan (a thesis) and a counterplan (an antithesis) that reflect plausible but conflicting courses of action.[41] Strategic managers listen to a debate between advocates of the plan and counterplan and

escalating commitment

A cognitive bias that occurs when decision makers, having already committed significant resources to a project, commit even more resources after receiving feedback that the project is failing.

reasoning by analogy

Use of simple analogies to make sense out of complex problems.

representativeness

A bias rooted in the tendency to generalize from a small sample or even a single ,vivid anecdote.

illusion of control

A cognitive bias rooted in the tendency to overestimate one's ability to control events.

availability error

A bias that arises from our predisposition to estimate the probability of an outcome based on how easy the outcome is to imagine.

devil's advocacy

A technique in which one member of a decision-making team identifies all the considerations that might make a proposal unacceptable.

dialectic inquiry

The generation of a plan (a thesis) and a counterplan (an antithesis) that reflect plausible but conflicting courses of action.

then decide which plan will lead to higher performance. The purpose of the debate is to reveal problems with the definitions, recommended courses of action, and assumptions of both plans. As a result of this exercise, strategic managers are able to form a new and more encompassing conceptualization of the problem, which then becomes the final plan (a synthesis). Dialectic inquiry can promote strategic thinking.

Another technique for countering cognitive biases is the outside view, which has been championed by Nobel Prize Winner Daniel Kahneman and his associates.[42] The **outside view** requires planners to identify a reference class of analogous past strategic initiatives, determine whether those initiatives succeeded or failed, and evaluate the project at hand against those prior initiatives. According to Kahneman, this technique is particularly useful for countering biases such as illusion of control (hubris), reasoning by analogy, and representativeness. For example, when considering a potential acquisition, planners should look at the track record of acquisitions made by other enterprises (the reference class), determine if they succeeded or failed, and objectively evaluate the potential acquisition against that reference class. Kahneman argues that such a reality check against a large sample of prior events tends to constrain the inherent optimism of planners and produce more realistic assessments and plans.

outside view

Identification of past successful or failed strategic initiatives to determine whether those initiatives will work for the project at hand.

1-9 Strategic Leadership

1.9 Discuss the characteristics of strategic leaders.

One key strategic role of both general and functional managers is to use all their knowledge, energy, and enthusiasm to provide strategic leadership for their subordinates and develop a high-performing organization. Several authors have identified key characteristics of strong strategic leaders that lead to high performance: (1) vision, eloquence, and consistency; (2) articulation of a business model; (3) commitment; (4) being well informed; (5) willingness to delegate and empower; (6) astute use of power; and (7) emotional intelligence.[43]

1-9a Vision, Eloquence, and Consistency

One key task of leadership is to give an organization a sense of direction. Strong leaders have a clear, compelling vision of where the organization should go, eloquently communicate this vision to others within the organization in terms that energize people, and consistently articulate their vision until it becomes part of the organization's culture.[44]

In the political arena, John F. Kennedy, Winston Churchill, Martin Luther King Jr., and Margaret Thatcher are regarded as visionary leaders. Think of the impact of Kennedy's summons, "Ask not what your country can do for you, ask what you can do for your country"; of King's "I have a dream" speech; of Churchill's declaration that "we will never surrender"; and of Thatcher's statement that "the problem with socialism is that you eventually run out of other peoples' money." Kennedy and Thatcher used their political office to push for governmental actions that were consistent with their visions. Churchill's speech galvanized a nation to defend itself against an aggressor. King pressured the government from outside to make changes within society.

Historical examples of strong business leaders include Microsoft's Bill Gates; Jack Welch, the former CEO of General Electric; and Sam Walton, Walmart's founder. For years, Bill Gates's vision of a world in which there would be a Windows-based personal computer on every desk was a driving force at Microsoft. At GE, Jack Welch was responsible for articulating the simple but powerful vision that GE should be first or second in every business in which it competed, or it should exit from that business. Similarly, Walmart founder Sam Walton established and articulated the vision that has been central to Walmart's success: passing on cost savings from suppliers and operating efficiencies to customers in the form of everyday low prices.

1-9b Articulation of the Business Model

Another key characteristic of good strategic leaders is their ability to identify and articulate the business model the company will use to attain its vision. A business model is the managers' conception of how the various strategies that the company pursues fit together into a congruent whole. At Dell, for example, Michael Dell identified and articulated the basic business model of the company: the direct sales business model. The various strategies that Dell has pursued over the years have refined this basic model, creating one that is very robust in terms of its efficiency and effectiveness. Although individual strategies can take root in many different places in an organization, and although their identification is not the exclusive preserve of top management, only strategic leaders have the perspective required to make sure that the various strategies fit together into a congruent whole and form a valid, compelling business model. If strategic leaders lack a clear conception of the company's business model (or what it should be), it is likely that the strategies the firm pursues will not fit together, and the result will be lack of focus and poor performance.

1-9c Commitment

Strong leaders demonstrate their commitment to their visions and business models by actions and words, and they often lead by example. For illustration, consider Nucor's former CEO, Ken Iverson. Nucor is a very efficient steelmaker with perhaps the lowest cost structure in the steel industry. It has achieved 50 years of profitable performance in an industry where most other companies have lost money due to a relentless focus on cost minimization. In his tenure as CEO, Iverson set the example: he answered his own phone, employed only one secretary, drove an old car, flew coach class, and was proud of the fact that his base salary was the lowest of the *Fortune* 500 CEOs (Iverson made most of his money from performance-based pay bonuses). This commitment was a powerful signal to employees that Iverson was serious about doing everything possible to minimize costs. It earned him the respect of Nucor employees and made them more willing to work hard. Although Iverson has retired, his legacy lives on in Nucor's cost-conscious organizational culture. Like all great leaders, his impact will last beyond his tenure.

1-9d Being Well Informed

Effective strategic leaders develop a network of formal and informal sources who keep them well informed about what is going on within the company. At T-Mobile, one way former CEO John Legere stayed well informed was by listening in on customer calls to the company's help desks.[45] Similarly, Herb Kelleher, the founder of Southwest Airlines, was able to gauge the health of his company by dropping in unannounced on aircraft maintenance facilities and helping workers perform their tasks. Kelleher would also often help airline attendants on Southwest flights, distributing refreshments and talking to customers. One frequent flyer on Southwest Airlines reported sitting next to Kelleher three times in 10 years. Each time, Kelleher asked him (and others sitting nearby) how Southwest Airlines was doing in a number of areas, in order to spot trends and inconsistencies.[46]

Using informal and unconventional ways to gather information is wise because formal channels can be captured by special interests within the organization or by gatekeepers—managers who may misrepresent the true state of affairs to the leader. People like Legere and Kelleher, who constantly interact with employees at all levels, are better able to build informal information networks than leaders who closet themselves and never interact with lower-level employees.

1-9e Willingness to Delegate and Empower

High-performance leaders are skilled at delegation. They recognize that unless they learn how to delegate effectively, they can quickly become overloaded with responsibilities. They also recognize that empowering subordinates to make decisions is a good motivational tool and often results in decisions being made by those who must implement them. At the same time, astute leaders recognize that they need to maintain control over certain key decisions. Although they will delegate many important decisions to lower-level employees, they will not delegate those that they judge to be of critical importance to the future success of the organization, such as articulating the company's vision and business model.

1-9f The Astute Use of Power

In a now-classic article on leadership, Edward Wrapp noted that effective leaders tend to be very astute in their use of power.[47] He argued that strategic leaders must often play the power game with skill and attempt to build consensus for their ideas rather than use their authority to force ideas through; they must act as members of a coalition or its democratic leaders rather than as dictators. Jeffery Pfeffer articulated a similar vision of the politically astute manager who gets things done in organizations through the intelligent use of power.[48] In Pfeffer's view, power comes from control over resources that are important to the organization: budgets, capital, positions, information, and knowledge. Politically astute managers use these resources to acquire another critical resource: critically placed allies who can help them attain their strategic objectives. Pfeffer stresses that one need not be a CEO to assemble power in an organization. Sometimes junior functional managers can build a surprisingly effective power base and use it to influence organizational outcomes.

1-9g Emotional Intelligence

Emotional intelligence, a term coined by Daniel Goleman, describes a bundle of psychological attributes that many strong, effective leaders exhibit:[49]

- Self-awareness—the ability to understand one's own moods, emotions, and drives, as well as their effect on others.
- Self-regulation—the ability to control or redirect disruptive impulses or moods; that is, to think before acting.
- Motivation—a passion for work that goes beyond money or status, and a propensity to pursue goals with energy and persistence.
- Empathy—the ability to understand the feelings and viewpoints of subordinates and to take those into account when making decisions.
- Social skills—friendliness with a purpose.

According to Goleman, leaders who exhibit a high degree of emotional intelligence tend to be more effective than those who lack these attributes. Their self-awareness and self-regulation help elicit the trust and confidence of subordinates. In Goleman's view, people respect leaders who, because they are self-aware, recognize their own limitations and, because they are self-regulating, consider decisions carefully. Goleman also argues that self-aware, self-regulating individuals tend to be more self-confident and therefore are better able to cope with ambiguity and are more open to change. A strong motivation exhibited in a passion for work can be infectious, persuading others to join together in pursuit of a common goal or organizational mission. Finally, strong empathy and social skills help leaders earn the loyalty of subordinates. Empathetic, socially adept individuals tend to be skilled at remedying disputes between managers and are better able to find common ground and purpose among diverse constituencies. They are better able to move people in a desired direction compared to leaders who lack these skills. In short, Goleman argues that the psychological makeup of a leader matters.

Key Terms

strategy 4
strategic leadership 4
strategy formulation 4
strategy implementation 4
shareholder value 5
risk capital 5
profitability 6
return on invested
   capital 6

profit growth 6
competitive advantage 7
sustained competitive
   advantage 7
business model 7
general managers 9
functional managers 9
multidivisional company 10
business unit 11

mission 14
vision 15
values 15
SWOT analysis 18
scenario planning 24
cognitive biases 26
confirmation bias 26
escalating
   commitment 27

reasoning by analogy 27
representativeness 27
overconfidence
illusion of control 27
availability error 27
devil's advocacy 27
dialectic inquiry 27
outside view 28

Takeaways for Strategic Managers

1. The major goal of for-profit companies is to maximize the returns that shareholders receive from holding shares in the company. To maximize shareholder value, managers must pursue strategies that result in high and sustained profitability and also in profit growth.

2. The profitability of a company can be measured by the return that it makes on the capital invested in the enterprise. The profit growth of a company can be measured by the growth in earnings per share. Profitability and profit growth are determined by the strategies managers adopt.

3. A company has a competitive advantage over its rivals when it is more profitable and has greater profit growth than the average for all firms in its industry. It has a sustained competitive advantage when it is able to maintain above-average performance over a number of years.

4. General managers are responsible for the overall performance of the organization, or for one of its major self-contained divisions. Their overriding strategic concern is for the health of the total organization under their direction.

5. Functional managers are responsible for a particular business function or operation. Although they lack general management responsibilities, they play a very important strategic role.

6. Formal strategic planning models stress that an organization's strategy is the outcome of a rational planning process.

7. The major components of the strategic management process are defining the mission, vision, and major goals of the organization; analyzing the external and internal environments of the organization; choosing a business model and strategies that align an organization's strengths and weaknesses with external environmental opportunities and threats; and adopting organizational structures and control systems to implement the organization's chosen strategies.

8. Strategy can emerge from deep within an organization in the absence of formal plans as lower-level managers respond to unpredicted situations.

9. Strategic planning may fail because executives do not plan for uncertainty and because ivory tower planners lose touch with operating realities.

10. In spite of systematic planning, companies may adopt poor strategies if cognitive biases are allowed to intrude into the decision-making process.

11. Devil's advocacy, dialectic inquiry, and the outside view are techniques for enhancing the effectiveness of strategic decision making.

12. Good leaders of the strategy-making process have a number of key attributes: vision, eloquence, and consistency; ability to craft a business model; commitment; being well informed; willingness to delegate and empower; political astuteness; and emotional intelligence.

Discussion Questions

1. What do we mean by strategy? How does a business model differ from a strategy?
2. What do you think are the sources of sustained superior profitability?
3. What are the strengths of formal strategic planning? What are its weaknesses?
4. Can you think of an example in your own life where cognitive biases resulted in you making a poor decision? How might that mistake have been avoided?

5. Discuss the accuracy of the following statement: Formal strategic planning systems are irrelevant for firms competing in high-technology industries where the pace of change is so rapid that plans are routinely made obsolete by unforeseen events.
6. Pick the current or a past president of the United States and evaluate his performance against the leadership characteristics discussed in the text. Based on this comparison, do you think that the president was/is a good strategic leader? Why or why not?

Closing Case

When John Legere joined T-Mobile as CEO in September 2012, the number four U.S. wireless service provider was in trouble. The company would lose $7.2 billion in 2012. The market was saturated, and growth was slow. Verizon and AT&T dominated the business with almost 80% of the market between them. T-Mobile had just 10%. Verizon and AT&T enjoyed cost advantages that came from significant economies of scale. Both companies had better network coverage and fewer dropped calls than T-Mobile. Moreover, unlike its larger rivals, T-Mobile did not offer the best-selling iPhone to its customers. To compound matters, AT&T had tried to acquire T-Mobile, but the deal fell apart after opposition from the Justice Department who thought that the merger would reduce competition in the industry. Employee morale had taken a hit during the merger talks and had yet to recover.

Legere saw things differently. Although employee morale was beaten down, he thought that the overall culture was intact and had the potential to be a powerful driver of growth. The average age of field employees was just 27. They were looking for somebody to energize them, and Legere meant to deliver. He did so by providing a clear strategic direction, eliminating bureaucratic rules and procedures that stifled motivation and initiative taking, and creating a sense of excitement. Legere also realized that customers hated industry practices. They hated being locked into contracts. They hated being gouged by extra fees they couldn't understand or couldn't fully control, such as data and roaming charges. They also thought wireless phones were cheap, whereas the wireless carriers were in fact subsidizing the phone manufacturers and recouping the cost of selling cheap handsets by charging high service fees. To Legere's way of thinking, customer dissatisfaction with industry practices created an opportunity for T-Mobile. He believed that the best way to succeed in the industry was to do things differently from existing carriers—to do the complete opposite—and so was born T-Mobile's strategy of being the "Un-carrier."

First though, Legere had to fix some obvious problems. T-Mobile wasn't selling the iPhone, so he went to Apple and made a deal. T-Mobile's network coverage had been terrible, so the company began buying up all of the wireless spectrum they could and investing heavily in upgrading their network to improve both the coverage and speed of service. Next, Legere and his team started to make dramatic changes to the company's offering aimed at making the experience better for customers. T-Mobile eliminated long-term contracts and replaced them with a transparent pricing model. They made it easier to upgrade to a new smartphone and stopped charging for global roaming. They offered to pay the early termination fees for customers who wanted to switch from other carriers to T-Mobile. The company was also the first to offer unlimited data plans. In 2017, it upped the ante by offering free Netflix streaming to customers with two or more lines. Legere backed up all of this with flashy marketing, including creative use of his Twitter account to promote T-Mobile and lambast industry rivals (Legere has an impressive 5.3 million followers on Twitter).

The strategy has produced some noticeable results. The total number of subscribers at T-Mobile increased from 33 million in late 2012 to 70 million by late 2017, making the company number one in terms of customer growth. Market share expanded from 10% to 17% over the same period. Monthly churn rates, a key metric of customer satisfaction, fell from 2.7% in 2011 to 1.3% in 2017, close to the 1% achieved by industry leader Verizon.

However, T-Mobile still faced big challenges. Its profitability measured by ROIC was still relatively low at 6.37%. It continued to lack the economies of scale and coverage of its larger rivals. T-Mobile also has poor retail distribution in one-third of the United States, a deficiency it started to fix by rapidly expanding its retail presence. It added more than 3,000 retail stores in 2017 alone. Most worrying of all, the implementation of 5G technology was on the horizon

(5G technology offered the promise of much faster speeds for wireless devices than the existing 4G technology, and was widely predicted to be a game changer, enabling high-speed streaming of videos, mobile games, and the like). Rolling out 5G would be very expensive, and Legere rightly worried that T-Mobile lacked the scale to effectively compete with industry leaders Verizon and AT&T in 5G.

Legere's solution was to merge with rival Sprint in a $26 billion all-stock transaction. The addition of Sprint, which was number four in the industry, bought another 30 million customers to T-Mobile, giving the combined company a 29% share of the retail subscriber market, ahead of AT&T's 27% share (Verizon continued to lead the market with a 42% share). More importantly, the merger gave T-Mobile the scale it needed to commit to an aggressive rollout of 5G technology. The merger agreement was announced in April 2018, and finally approved after 2 years of regulatory review on April 1, 2020. On that day, John Legere retired, passing the CEO reins over to his long-time second in command, Mike Sievert.

Sievert, who stuck with the Legere's un-carrier strategy, oversaw the rapid rollout of 5G technology at T-Mobile, enabling the company to leap ahead of Verizon and AT&T in 5G coverage. At the end of 2021 T-Mobile's mid-band 5G technology covered about 210 million people, and the company plans to cover 300 million by the end of 2023. In contrast, Verizon's 5G service is forecasted to cover 175 million people by the end of 2022. Although T-Mobile's mid-band version of 5G has somewhat less bandwidth than the versions now being rolled out by Verizon and AT&T, it is less expensive to implement and perhaps good enough for most subscribers. In any event, the Sprint merger helped T-Mobile to achieve greater economies of scale, and its profitability, measured by ROIC, improved to 12.37% in 2021.

Sources: J. Legere, "T-Mobile's CEO on Winning Market Share by Trash Talking Rivals," *Harvard Business Review* (January–February 2017); B. Ranj, "How the Unlimited Data Plans from AT&T, Verizon, T-Mobile and Sprint All Stack Up," *Business Insider*, June 29, 2017; I. Fried, "T-Mobile COO Explains Why the 'Uncarrier' Strategy Is Working," *Axios*, September 11, 2017; M. Dano, "US Wireless Snapshot: Subscribers, Market Share and Q3 Estimates," *Light Reading*, October 16, 2020; M. Sievert, "A New Era of Un-carrier," *T-Mobile Blog*, April 1, 2022; M. Alleven, "T-Mobile Claims 5G Mid-Band PoP Star Status," *Fierce Wireless*, March 9, 2022.

Case Discussion Questions

1. What challenges was T-Mobile facing before John Legere became CEO in 2014? Without a change in strategy, what do you think the future looked like for T-Mobile?
2. How did Legere's un-carrier strategy change the nature of competition in the industry? What opportunities did the strategy seek to capitalize upon? How did T-Mobile's strengths play into this strategy? Why was T-Mobile able to gain subscribers from its rivals?
3. What weaknesses do you think the merger with Sprint addressed? Why do you think it took 2 years for regulators to approve the merger? What does this tell you about the role of government in regulating competition? Do strategists need to take government into account when formulating strategy?
4. Does T-Mobile now have a source of competitive advantage? How sustainable is its advantage?

Appendix to Chapter 1: Enterprise Valuation, ROIC, and Growth

A primary goal of strategy is to maximize the value of a company to its shareholders (subject to the important constraints that this is done in a legal, ethical, and socially responsible manner). The two main drivers of enterprise valuation are return on invested capital (ROIC) and the growth rate of profits, g.[50]

ROIC is defined as net operating profits less adjusted taxes (NOPLAT) over the invested capital of the enterprise (IC), where IC is the sum of the company's equity and debt (the method for calculating adjusted taxes need not concern us here). That is:

$$ROIC = NOPLAT/IC$$

where

NOPLAT = revenues − cost of goods sold
  − operating expenses − depreciation charges
  − adjusted taxes
IC = value of shareholders' equity + value of debt

The growth rate of profits, g, can be defined as the percentage increase in net operating profits (NOPLAT) over a given time period. More precisely:

$$g = [(NOPLAT_{t+1} − NOPLAT_t)/NOPLAT_t] \times 100$$

Note that if NOPLAT is increasing over time, earnings per share will also increase so long as (a) the number of shares stays constant, or (b) the number of shares outstanding increases more slowly than NOPLAT.

The valuation of a company can be calculated using discounted cash flow analysis and applying it to future expected free cash flows (free cash flow in a period is defined as NOPLAT − net investments). It can be shown that the valuation of a company so calculated is related to the company's weighted average cost of capital (WACC), which is the cost of the equity and debt that the firm uses to finance its business, and the company's ROIC. Specifically:

- If ROIC > WACC, the company is earning more than its cost of capital and is creating value.
- If ROIC = WACC, the company is earning its cost of capital, and its valuation will be stable.
- If ROIC < WACC, the company is earning less than its cost of capital, and it is therefore destroying value.

Table A1 ROIC, Growth, and Valuation

NOPLAT Growth, g	ROIC 7.5%	ROIC 10.0%	ROIC 12.5%	ROIC 15.0%	ROIC 20%
3%	887	1000	1058	1113	1170
6%	708	1000	1117	1295	1442
9%	410	1000	1354	1591	1886

A company that earns more than its cost of capital is even more valuable if it can grow its net operating profits less adjusted taxes (NOPLAT) over time. Conversely, a firm that is not earning its cost of capital destroys value if it grows its NOPLAT. This critical relationship between ROIC, g, and value is shown in Table A1.

In Table A1, the figures in the cells of the matrix represent the discounted present values of future free cash flows for a company that has a starting NOPLAT of $100, invested capital of $1,000, a cost of capital of 10%, and a 25-year time horizon after which ROIC = cost of capital.

The important points revealed by this exercise are as follows:

1. A company with an already high ROIC can create more value by increasing its profit growth rate rather than pushing for an even higher ROIC. Thus, a company with an ROIC of 15% and a 3% growth rate can create more value by increasing its profit growth rate from 3% to 9% than it can by increasing ROIC to 20%.
2. A company with a low ROIC destroys value if it grows. Thus, if ROIC = 7.5%, a 9% growth rate for 25 years will produce less value than a 3% growth rate. This is because unprofitable growth requires capital investments, the cost of which cannot be covered. Unprofitable growth destroys value.
3. The best of both worlds is high ROIC and high growth.

Very few companies are able to maintain an ROIC > WACC and grow NOPLAT over time, but there are notable examples including Dell, Microsoft, and Walmart. Because these companies have generally been able to fund their capital investment needs from internally generated cash flows, they have not had to issue more shares to raise capital. Thus, growth in NOPLAT has translated directly into higher earnings per share for these companies, making their shares more attractive to investors and leading to substantial share-price appreciation. By successfully pursuing strategies that result in a high ROIC and growing NOPLAT, these firms have maximized shareholder value.

[1] This view is known as "agency theory." See M. C. Jensen and W. H. Meckling, "Theory of the Firm: Managerial Behavior, Agency Costs and Ownership Structure," *Journal of Financial Economics* 3 (1976): 305–360; E. F. Fama, "Agency Problems and the Theory of the Firm," *Journal of Political Economy* 88 (1980): 375–390.

[2] There are several different ratios for measuring profitability, such as return on invested capital, return on assets, and return on equity. Although these different measures are highly correlated with each other, finance theorists argue that the return on invested capital is the most accurate measure of profitability. See T. Copeland, T. Koller, and J. Murrin, *Valuation: Measuring and Managing the Value of Companies* (New York: Wiley, 1996).

[3] J. B. Barney, "Why resource-based theory's model of profit appropriation must incorporate a stakeholder perspective," *Strategic Management Journal* 39 (2018): 305–325.

[4] Trying to estimate the relative importance of industry effects and firm strategy on firm profitability has been one of the most important areas of research in the strategy literature during the past decade. See Y. E. Spanos and S. Lioukas, "An Examination of the Causal Logic of Rent Generation," *Strategic Management* 22:10 (October 2001): 907–934; R. P. Rumelt, "How Much Does Industry Matter?" *Strategic Management* 12 (1991): 167–185. See also A. J. Mauri and M. P. Michaels, "Firm and Industry Effects Within Strategic Management: An Empirical Examination," *Strategic Management* 19 (1998): 211–219.

[5] K. R. Andrews, *The Concept of Corporate Strategy* (Homewood, Ill.: Dow Jones Irwin, 1971); H. I. Ansoff, *Corporate Strategy* (New York: McGraw-Hill, 1965); C. W. Hofer and D. Schendel, *Strategy Formulation: Analytical Concepts* (St. Paul, Minn.: West, 1978). See also P. J. Brews and M. R. Hunt, "Learning to Plan and Planning to Learn," *Strategic Management* 20 (1999): 889–913; R. W. Grant, "Planning in a Turbulent Environment," *Strategic Management* 24 (2003): 491–517; A. G. Lafley and R. L. Martin, *Playing to Win* (Harvard Business Review Press, 2013).

[6] P. F. Drucker, *Management: Tasks, Responsibilities, Practices* (New York: Harper & Row, 1974), pp. 74–94.

[7] D. F. Abell, *Defining the Business: The Starting Point of Strategic Planning* (Englewood Cliffs, N.J.: Prentice-Hall, 1980).

[8] "Our Strategy," *New York Times*, March 24, 2022.

[9] J. C. Collins and J. I. Porras, "Building Your Company's Vision," *Harvard Business Review* (September–October 1996): 65–77.

[10] www.nucor.com.

[11] See J. P. Kotter and J. L. Heskett, *Corporate Culture and Performance* (New York: Free Press, 1992); Collins and Porras, "Building Your Company's Vision."

[12] E. Freeman, *Strategic Management: A Stakeholder Approach* (Boston: Pitman Press, 1984).

[13] M. D. Richards, *Setting Strategic Goals and Objectives* (St. Paul, Minn.: West, 1986).

[14] E. A. Locke, G. P. Latham, and M. Erez, "The Determinants of Goal Commitment," *Academy of Management Review* 13 (1988): 23–39.

[15] R. E. Hoskisson, M. A. Hitt, and C. W. L. Hill, "Managerial Incentives and Investment in R&D in Large Multiproduct Firms," *Organization Science* 3 (1993): 325–341.

[16] Andrews, *Concept of Corporate Strategy;* Ansoff, *Corporate Strategy;* Hofer and Schendel, *Strategy Formulation.*

[17] For details, see R. A. Burgelman, "Intraorganizational Ecology of Strategy Making and Organizational Adaptation: Theory and Field Research," *Organization Science* 2 (1991): 239–262; H. Mintzberg, "Patterns in Strategy Formulation," *Management Science* 24 (1978): 934–948; S. L. Hart, "An Integrative Framework for Strategy Making Processes," *Academy of Management Review* 17 (1992): 327–351; G. Hamel, "Strategy as Revolution," *Harvard Business Review* 74 (July–August 1996): 69–83; R. W. Grant, "Planning in a Turbulent Environment," *Strategic Management Journal* 24 (2003): 491–517; G. Gavetti, D. Levinthal, and J. W. Rivkin, "Strategy Making in Novel and Complex Worlds: The Power of Analogy," *Strategic Management Journal* 26 (2005): 691–712; R. A. Burgelman et al., "Strategy Processes and Practices: Dialogs and Intersections," *Strategic Management Journal* (2018): 531–558.

[18] This is the premise of those who advocate that complexity and chaos theory should be applied to strategic management. See S. Brown and K. M. Eisenhardt, "The Art of Continuous Change: Linking Complexity Theory and Time-Based Evolution in Relentlessly Shifting Organizations," *Administrative Science Quarterly* 29 (1997): 1–34; R. Stacey and D. Parker, *Chaos, Management and Economics* (London: Institute for Economic Affairs, 1994). See also H. Courtney, J. Kirkland, and P. Viguerie, "Strategy Under Uncertainty," *Harvard Business Review* 75 (November–December 1997): 66–79; N.N. Taleb, *The Black Swan: The Impact of the*

Highly Improbable (New York: Random House, 2007)

[19]R. A. Burgelmen et al., "Strategy Processes and Practices: Dialogs and Intersections," *Strategic Management Journal* 39 (2018): 531–558.

[20]See Burgelman, "Intraorganizational Ecology," and Mintzberg, "Patterns in Strategy Formulation."

[21]R. A. Burgelman and A. S. Grove, "Strategic Dissonance," *California Management Review* (Winter 1996): 8–28.

[22]C. W. L. Hill and F. T. Rothaermel, "The Performance of Incumbent Firms in the Face of Radical Technological Innovation," *Academy of Management Review* 28 (2003): 257–274.

[23]Personal communication to the author by George Rathmann, former head of 3M's research activities.

[24]H. Mintzberg, "Patterns in Strategy Formulation," *Management Science* 24 (1978): 934–948.

[25]R. T. Pascale, "Perspectives on Strategy: The Real Story Behind Honda's Success," *California Management Review* 26 (1984): 47–72.

[26]This viewpoint is strongly emphasized by Burgelman and Grove, "Strategic Dissonance."

[27]C. C. Miller and L. B. Cardinal, "Strategic Planning and Firm Performance: A Synthesis of More Than Two Decades of Research," *Academy of Management Journal* 37 (1994): 1649–1665. See also P. R. Rogers, A. Miller, and W. Q. Judge, "Using Information Processing Theory to Understand Planning/Performance Relationships in the Context of Strategy," *Strategic Management* 20 (1999): 567–577; R. J. Shea-Van Fossen, H. R. Rothstein, and H. J. Korn, "Thirty Years of Strategic Planning and Firm Performance Research: A Meta-analysis," *Academy of Management Proceedings*, (2006): 24–36.

[28]P. J. Brews and M. R. Hunt, "Learning to Plan and Planning to Learn," *Strategic Management Journal* 20 (1999): 889–913.

[29]P. Cornelius, A. Van de Putte, and M. Romani, "Three Decades of Scenario Planning at Shell," *California Management Review* 48 (2005): 92–110.

[30]H. Courtney, J. Kirkland, and P. Viguerie, "Strategy Under Uncertainty," *Harvard Business Review* 75 (November–December 1997): 66–79.

[31]P. J. H. Schoemaker, "Multiple Scenario Development: Its Conceptual and Behavioral Foundation," *Strategic Management Journal* 14 (1993): 193–213.

[32]P. Schoemaker, P. J. H. van der Heijden, and A. J. M. Cornelius, "Integrating Scenarios into Strategic Planning at Royal Dutch Shell," *Planning Review* 20:3 (1992): 41–47; I. Wylie, "There Is No Alternative to…," *Fast Company* (July 2002): 106–111.

[33]"The Next Big Surprise: Scenario Planning," *The Economist* (October 13, 2001): 71.

[34]See C. R. Schwenk, "Cognitive Simplification Processes in Strategic Decision Making," *Strategic Management* 5 (1984): 111–128; K. M. Eisenhardt and M. Zbaracki, "Strategic Decision Making," *Strategic Management* 13 (Special Issue, 1992): 17–37. D. Kahneman, *Thinking Fast and Slow* (New York: Farrar, Strauss and Giroux, 2011).

[35]H. Simon, *Administrative Behavior* (New York: McGraw-Hill, 1957).

[36]The original statement of this phenomenon was made by A. Tversky and D. Kahneman, "Judgment Under Uncertainty: Heuristics and Biases," *Science* 185 (1974): 1124–1131. See also D. Lovallo and D. Kahneman, "Delusions of Success: How Optimism Undermines Executives' Decisions," *Harvard Business Review* 81 (July 2003): 56–67; J. S. Hammond, R. L. Keeny, and H. Raiffa, "The Hidden Traps in Decision Making," *Harvard Business Review* 76 (September–October 1998): 25–34.

[37]Schwenk, "Cognitive Simplification Processes," pp. 111–128.

[38]B. M. Staw, "The Escalation of Commitment to a Course of Action," *Academy of Management Review* 6 (1981): 577–587.

[39]R. Roll, "The Hubris Hypotheses of Corporate Takeovers," *Journal of Business* 59 (1986): 197–216. For another argument in this vein, see C. Camerer and D. Lovallo, "Overconfidence and Excess Entry," *American Economic Review* 89 (1999): 306–318.

[40]See R. O. Mason, "A Dialectic Approach to Strategic Planning," *Management Science* 13 (1969): 403–414; R. A. Cosier and J. C. Aplin, "A Critical View of Dialectic Inquiry in Strategic Planning," *Strategic Management Journal* 1 (1980): 343–356; I. I. Mintroff and R. O. Mason, "Structuring III—Structured Policy Issues: Further Explorations in a Methodology for Messy Problems," *Strategic Management Journal* 1 (1980): 331–342.

[41]Mason, "A Dialectic Approach," pp. 403–414.

[42]Lovallo and Kahneman, "Delusions of Success."

[43]For a summary of research on strategic leadership, see D. C. Hambrick, "Putting Top Managers Back into the Picture," *Strategic Management Journal* 10 (Special Issue, 1989): 5–15; D. Goldman, "What Makes a Leader?" *Harvard Business Review* (November–December 1998): 92–105; H. Mintzberg, "Covert Leadership," *Harvard Business Review* (November–December 1998): 140–148; R. S. Tedlow, "What Titans Can Teach Us," *Harvard Business Review* (December 2001): 70–79; S. Finkelstein, D. Hambrick, and A. A. Cannella, *Strategic Leadership: Theory and Research on Executives, Top Management Teams and Boards*, (New York: Oxford University Press, 2009).

[44]N. M. Tichy and D. O. Ulrich, "The Leadership Challenge: A Call

for the Transformational Leader," *Sloan Management Review* (Fall 1984): 59–68; F. Westley and H. Mintzberg, "Visionary Leadership and Strategic Management," *Strategic Management Journal* 10 (Special Issue, 1989): 17–32.

[45]"T-Mobile's CEO on Winning Market Share by Trash Talking Rivals," *Harvard Business Review*, January–February 2017.

[46]B. McConnell and J. Huba. *Creating Customer Evangelists* (Chicago: Dearborn Trade Publishing, 2003).

[47]E. Wrapp, "Good Managers Don't Make Policy Decisions," *Harvard Business Review* (September–October 1967): 91–99.

[48]J. Pfeffer, *Managing with Power* (Boston: Harvard Business School Press, 1992).

[49]D. Goleman, "What Makes a Leader?" *Harvard Business Review* (November–December 1998): 92–105.

[50]C. Y. Baldwin, *Fundamental Enterprise Valuation: Return on Invested Capital*, Harvard Business School Note 9-801-125, July 3, 2004; T. Copeland et al., *Valuation: Measuring and Managing the Value of Companies* (New York: Wiley, 2000).

synto/Shutterstock.com

Part

2

External
and Internal
Analysis

Chapter 2

External Analysis:
The Identification of
Opportunities and Threats

Chapter 3

Internal Analysis:
Resources and
Competitive Advantage

2

External Analysis: The Identification of Opportunities and Threats

Learning Objectives

2.1 Define industry and industry environment.

2.2 Review the primary technique used to analyze competition in an industry environment: the Five Forces model.

2.3 Explore the concept of strategic groups, including the implications for industry analysis.

2.4 Discuss how industries evolve over time, with reference to the industry life-cycle model.

2.5 Discuss limitations of models for industry analysis.

2.6 Summarize the ways in which the macroenvironment can shape the nature of competition in an industry.

Opening Case

The Streaming Wars

Back in 2007, Netflix—which had got its start renting out DVDs by mail—launched its streaming video on demand service. It was an idea whose time had come. What made streaming possible was the development of two complementary technologies: high-bandwidth connections into the home through cable and fiber-optic conduits, and the emergence of cloud computing infrastructure, most notably by Amazon Web Services (AWS). Netflix contracted with AWS to store its vast video library of films and TV shows "on the cloud," sold access to consumers for a monthly subscription fee, and the streaming video on-demand market was born.

Netflix's innovation unlocked rapid subscriber growth. Revenues grew from $3.61 billion in 2012 to almost $30 billion in 2021 as the company's subscriber base expanded to over 200 million in the United States and elsewhere. Along the way Netflix started to invest in developing its own content, which was streamed exclusively through its service. The political drama *House of Cards* was one of the first fruits of these investments. When the first season was released in 2013, it became an instant hit and helped to attract more subscribers. Over six seasons, *House of Cards* garnered 33 Primetime Emmy Award nominations, establishing Netflix as a major force in the content creation business. Netflix followed its *House of Cards* success with other hits, including *Stranger Things* and *The Crown*. As demand for streaming content grew, people began to cancel their cable TV service, "cutting the cord" and disrupting the long-established and once-profitable cable TV business. When the COVID-19 pandemic hit in early 2020, people found themselves spending more time at home and demand for streaming video on-demand content jumped again.

Nothing attracts imitators like success, and before long Netflix had to deal with several rivals. Early entrants included Hulu and Amazon with its Prime Video service. Both companies followed Netflix's lead and started to create their own content in addition to offering access to a substantial library of films and TV shows. As the "cord-cutting" phenomenon gained steam, a slew of established companies started to enter the industry. Entrants included Disney+ (owned by Disney, which also owns TV broadcaster ABC and is the majority owner of Hulu), HBO Max (owned by AT&T's Warner Media division), Peacock (owned by Comcast, which also owns the TV broadcaster NBC), Paramount+ (owned by Paramount, which also owns TV broadcaster CBS), and Apple TV+. Clearly, the owners of legacy TV networks saw it as necessary to get into the streaming business. Of these new entrants, Disney+, which was launched in November 2019, has been by far the most successful. Disney had the advantage of a huge library of popular films from Disney, Pixar, and the Marvel and Star Wars franchises. By early 2020, Disney+ had 130 million subscribers, making it second only to Netflix.

Sources: D. Gallagher, "Netflix Isn't Looking Up," *Wall Street Journal*, January 20, 2022; B. Mullin and D. Marcelis, "Disney+, HBO Max and Other Streamers Get Waves of Subscribers from Must See Content. Keeping Them Is Hard," *Wall Street Journal*, January 3, 2022; "Disney, Netflix, Apple: Is Anyone Winning the Streaming Wars," *The Economist*, February 12, 2022.

The new entries led to increased competition for subscribers. Even though the average American household now subscribes to more than three streaming services, customer churn rates have increased, along with the proliferation of competitive offerings.

One noticeable phenomenon is that while the release of high-profile original content might attract a lot of new subscribers to a service, as many as half of these new subscribers leave the service within six months. Apple TV+ has the most serious churn problem, with more than 10% of its customers leaving the service every month at the end of 2021. The monthly churn rate at HBO Max was around 5.5% in December 2021, while Netflix had the lowest churn rate at just 2.5% a month. The monthly churn rate at Disney+ was a little over 4%.

To try and reduce churn and build their subscriber base, streaming companies have increased their investments in original exclusive programming and are spending more on expanding their library of film and TV content. According to a *Wall Street Journal* report, spending on the production of original content surged from less than $1 billion in 2017 to around $12 billion in 2021, while film and TV acquisition costs doubled from $10 billion to $20 billion. A related strategy has been to offer a wider array of content that is bundled into a subscription. Disney, for example, offers a bundle that includes Disney+, Hulu, and ESPN+ (the sports broadcaster owned by Disney). The thinking is that by offering a compelling bundle of exclusive content, Disney will be able to build customer loyalty and hold on to its subscribers. Apple and Amazon also both package their streaming offering with other services.

To complicate matters, there were clear signs that, in the core U.S. market at least, by early 2022 subscriber growth was starting to slow significantly. After a decade of rapid growth, the market is starting to mature, new subscribers are harder to come by, and the intensity of competition seems set to increase. A post-pandemic slump in demand as people start to spend more time outside the home is another factor here. How this all plays out remains to be seen, but several analysts now believe that the streaming business might be less profitable for providers than the cable TV business that it is displacing.

Overview

Strategy formulation begins with an analysis of the forces that shape competition within the industry in which a company is based. The goal is to understand the opportunities and threats confronting the firm, and to use this understanding to identify strategies that will enable the company to outperform its rivals. **Opportunities** arise when a company can take advantage of conditions in its industry environment to formulate and implement strategies that enable it to become more profitable. For example, as discussed in the Opening Case, Netflix took advantage of the *opportunities* presented by the emergence of high-bandwidth pipes into American homes, and new storage technology "on the cloud," to offer a new service to consumers—streaming video on demand. **Threats** arise when conditions in the external environment endanger the integrity and profitability of the company's business. As explained in the Opening Case, the creation of the streaming video on-demand market constituted a *threat* for established cable TV providers, who have seen their subscriber base shrink as households "cut the cord" and move to streaming services. The rapid entry of multiple players into the streaming video on demand market during the last few years also constitutes a *threat* for the early incumbents such as Netflix, Amazon, and Hulu since it has increased the intensity of competition and made it more difficult to build a profitable business in the industry.

This chapter begins with an analysis of the external industry environment. First, it examines concepts and tools for analyzing the competitive structure of an industry and identifying industry opportunities and threats. Second, it analyzes the competitive implications that arise when groups of companies within an industry pursue similar or different kinds of competitive strategies. Third, it explores the way an industry evolves over time, and the changes present in competitive conditions. Fourth, it looks at the way in which forces in the macroenvironment affect industry structure and influence opportunities and threats. By the end of the chapter, you will understand that, in order to succeed, a company must either fit its strategy to the external environment in which it operates or be able to reshape the environment to its advantage through its chosen strategy.

opportunities

Elements and conditions in a company's environment that allow it to formulate and implement strategies that enable it to become more profitable.

threats

Elements in the external environment that could endanger the integrity and profitability of the company's business.

2-1 Defining an Industry

2.1 Define industry and industry environment.

An **industry** can be defined as a group of companies offering products or services that are close substitutes for each other—that is, products or services that satisfy the same basic customer needs. A company's closest competitors—its rivals—are those that serve the same basic customer needs. For example, carbonated drinks, fruit punches, and bottled water can be viewed as close substitutes for each other because they serve the same basic customer needs for refreshing, cold, nonalcoholic beverages. Thus, we can talk about the soft-drink industry, whose major players are Coca-Cola, PepsiCo, and Cadbury Schweppes. Similarly, desktop and laptop computers and tablets satisfy the same basic need that customers have for computer hardware devices on which

industry

A group of companies offering products or services that are close substitutes for each other.

to run personal productivity software; browse the internet; send e-mail; play games, music, and video; and store, display, or manipulate digital images. Thus, we can talk about the computer hardware device industry, whose participants include Apple, Dell, Hewlett-Packard, Lenovo, Microsoft, and Samsung.

External analysis begins by identifying the industry within which a company competes. To do this, managers must start by looking at the basic customer needs their company is serving—that is, they must take a customer-oriented view of their business rather than a product-oriented view (see Chapter 1). The basic customer needs that are served by a market define an industry's boundaries. It is very important for managers to realize this, for if they define industry boundaries incorrectly, they may be caught off-guard by the rise of competitors that serve the same basic customer needs but with different product offerings. For example, Coca-Cola long saw itself as part of the soda industry—meaning carbonated soft drinks—whereas it actually was part of the soft-drink industry, which includes noncarbonated soft drinks. In the mid-1990s, the rise of customer demand for bottled water and fruit drinks began to cut into the demand for sodas, which caught Coca-Cola by surprise. Coca-Cola moved quickly to respond to these threats, introducing its own brand of water, Dasani, and acquiring several other beverage companies, including Minute Maid and Glaceau (the owner of the Vitamin Water brand). By defining its industry boundaries too narrowly, Coke almost missed the rapid rise of noncarbonated soft drinks within the soft-drinks market.

It is important to realize that industry boundaries can change over time as customer needs evolve, or as emerging new technologies enable companies in unrelated industries to satisfy established customer needs in new ways. During the 1990s, consumers of soft drinks began to develop a taste for bottled water and noncarbonated, fruit-based drinks. As a consequence, Coca-Cola found itself in direct competition with the manufacturers of bottled water and fruit-based soft drinks: All were in the same industry.

For another example of how technological change can alter industry boundaries, consider the convergence that has taken place between the computer and telecommunications industries. Historically, the telecommunications equipment industry has been considered an entity distinct from the computer hardware industry. However, as telecommunications equipment moved from analog technology to digital technology, this equipment increasingly resembled computers. The result is that the boundaries between these once-distinct industries has been blurred. A smartphone such as Apple's iPhone is nothing more than a small, handheld computer with a wireless connection and telephone capabilities. Thus, Samsung and HTC, which manufacture wireless phones, are now competing directly with traditional computer companies such as Apple and Dell.

2-2 Porter's Competitive Forces Model

2.2 Review the primary technique used to analyze competition in an industry environment: the Five Forces model.

Once the boundaries of an industry have been identified, managers face the task of analyzing competitive forces within the industry environment in order to identify opportunities and threats. Michael E. Porter's well-known framework, the Five Forces model, helps managers with this analysis.[1] An extension of his model, shown in Figure 2.1, focuses on *six* forces that shape competition within an industry: (1) the risk of entry by potential competitors, (2) the intensity of rivalry among established companies within an industry, (3) the bargaining power of buyers, (4) the bargaining power of suppliers, (5) the closeness of substitutes to an industry's products, and (6) the power of complement providers (Porter did not recognize this sixth force).

As each of these forces grows stronger, it limits the ability of established companies to raise prices and earn greater profits. Within this framework, a strong competitive force can be regarded as a threat because it depresses profits. A weak competitive force can be viewed as an opportunity because it allows a company to earn greater profits.

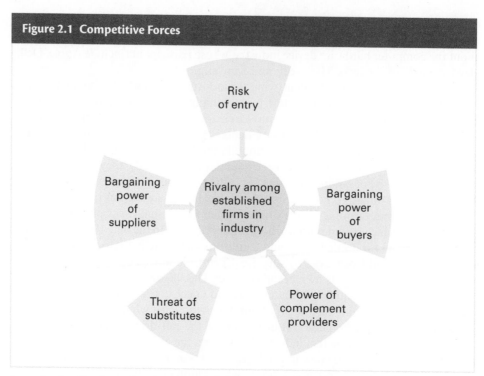

Figure 2.1 Competitive Forces

Risk of entry

Bargaining power of suppliers

Rivalry among established firms in industry

Bargaining power of buyers

Threat of substitutes

Power of complement providers

Source: Based on "How Competitive Forces Shape Strategy," by Michael E. Porter, *Harvard Business Review*, March/April 1979.

The strength of the six forces may change over time as industry conditions change. Managers face the task of recognizing how changes in the six forces give rise to new opportunities and threats, and formulating appropriate strategic responses. In addition, it is possible for a company, through its choice of strategy, to alter the strength of one or more of the forces to its advantage. This is discussed in the following chapters.

2-2a Risk of Entry by Potential Competitors

potential competitors

Companies that are currently not competing in the industry but have the potential to do so if they choose.

Potential competitors are companies that are not currently competing in an industry but have the capability to do so if they choose. For example, as discussed in the Opening Case, streaming video on-demand companies such as Netflix, Amazon, and Hulu created the market for streaming video on-demand services in the 2010s. New digital technologies allowed these streaming companies to enter the home entertainment market and take customers away from traditional cable TV providers. Moreover, as they developed their own original content, they started to take share away from long-established production companies. But the established companies were always potential entrants into the streaming market. It is no surprise then, that companies such as Disney, Paramount, Warner Communications, and Comcast have leveraged their own brands, customer relationships, and extensive library of film and TV content to enter the streaming market and offer their own competing services. The potential competitors of the 2010s have now entered the market and become rivals to Netflix, Amazon, and Hulu in the 2020s.

Established companies already operating in an industry often attempt to discourage potential competitors from entering the industry because their entry makes it more difficult for the established companies to protect their share of the market and generate profits. A high risk of entry by potential competitors represents a threat to the profitability of established companies. The risk of entry by potential competitors is a function of how attractive the industry is (for example, how profitable or growing the industry is), and the height of **barriers to entry** (that is, those factors that make it costly for companies to enter an industry).

barriers to entry

Factors that make it costly for companies to enter an industry.

The greater the costs potential competitors must bear to enter an industry, the greater the barriers to entry and the weaker this competitive force. High entry barriers may keep potential competitors out of an industry even when industry profits are high. Important barriers to entry include economies of scale, brand loyalty, absolute cost advantages, customer switching costs, and government regulation.[2] An important strategy is building barriers to entry (in the case of incumbent firms) or finding ways to circumvent those barriers (in the case of new entrants). We discuss this topic in more detail in subsequent chapters.

Economies of Scale   **Economies of scale** arise when unit costs fall as a firm expands its output. Sources of scale economies include: (1) cost reductions gained through mass-producing a standardized output; (2) discounts on bulk purchases of raw material inputs and component parts; (3) the advantages gained by spreading fixed production costs over a large production volume; and (4) the cost savings associated with distributing, marketing, and advertising costs over a large volume of output. For example, the economies of scale enjoyed by incumbent firms in the airline industry are fairly large and include the ability to cover the fixed costs of purchasing aircraft. This constitutes a barrier to new entry into the market. More generally, if the cost advantages from economies of scale are significant, a new company that enters the industry and produces on a small scale suffers a significant cost disadvantage relative to established companies. If the new company decides to enter on a large scale in an attempt to obtain these economies of scale, it must raise the capital required to build large-scale production facilities and bear the high risks associated with such an investment. In addition, an increased supply of products will depress prices and result in vigorous retaliation by established companies, which constitutes a further risk of large-scale entry. For these reasons, the threat of entry is reduced when established companies achieve economies of scale.

economies of scale

Reductions in unit costs attributed to large output.

Brand Loyalty   **Brand loyalty** exists when consumers have a preference for the products of established companies. A company can create brand loyalty by continuously advertising its brand-name products and company name, protecting the patents of its products, achieving product innovation through company research and development (R&D) programs, and emphasizing high-quality products and exceptional after-sales service. Significant brand loyalty makes it difficult for new entrants to take market share away from established companies. Thus, it reduces the threat of entry by potential competitors; they may see the task of breaking down well-established customer preferences as too costly. In the smartphone business, for example, Apple generated such strong brand loyalty with its iPhone offering and related products that Microsoft found it very difficult to attract customers away from Apple and build demand for its Windows phone, introduced in late 2011. Despite its financial might, 5 years after launching the Windows phone, Microsoft's U.S. market share remained mired at under 4%, and in 2016 it exited the market.[3]

brand loyalty

Preference of consumers for the products of established companies.

Absolute Cost Advantages   Sometimes established companies have an **absolute cost advantage** relative to potential entrants, meaning that entrants cannot expect to match the established companies' lower cost structure. Absolute cost advantages arise from three main sources: (1) superior production operations and processes due to accumulated experience, patents, or trade secrets; (2) control of particular inputs required for production, such as labor, materials, equipment, or management skills, that are limited in supply; and (3) access to cheaper funds because existing companies represent lower risks than new entrants. If established companies have an absolute cost advantage, the threat of entry as a competitive force weakens.

absolute cost advantage

A cost advantage that is enjoyed by incumbents in an industry and that new entrants cannot expect to match.

Customer Switching Costs Switching costs arise when a customer invests time, energy, and money switching from the products offered by one established company to the products offered by a new entrant. When switching costs are high, customers can be locked into the product offerings of established companies, even if new entrants offer better products.[4] A familiar example of switching costs concerns the costs associated with switching from one computer operating system to another. If a person currently uses Microsoft's Windows operating system and has a library of related software applications and document files, it is expensive for that person to switch to another computer operating system, such as Apple's iOS operating system. To effect the change, this person would need to purchase a new set of software applications and convert all existing document files to the new system's format. Faced with such a commitment of money and time, most people are unwilling to make the switch unless the competing operating system offers a substantial leap forward in performance. Thus, the higher the switching costs, the higher the barrier to entry for a company attempting to promote a new computer operating system.

Government Regulations Government regulations can constitute a major entry barrier for many industries. For example, until the mid-1990s, U.S. government regulations prohibited providers of long-distance telephone service from competing for local telephone service, and vice versa. Other potential providers of telephone service, including cable television service companies such as Time Warner and Comcast (which could have used their cables to carry telephone traffic as well as TV signals), were prohibited from entering the market altogether. These regulatory barriers to entry significantly reduced the level of competition in both the local and long-distance telephone markets, enabling telephone companies to earn higher profits than they might have otherwise. All this changed in 1996 when the government significantly deregulated the industry. In the months that followed, local, long-distance, and cable TV companies all announced their intention to enter each other's markets, and a host of new players entered the market as well. The competitive forces model predicts that falling entry barriers due to government deregulation will result in significant new entry, an increase in the intensity of industry competition, and lower industry profit rates, and that is what occurred here.

Summary In summary, if established companies have built brand loyalty for their products, have an absolute cost advantage over potential competitors, have significant scale economies, are the beneficiaries of high switching costs, or enjoy regulatory protection, the risk of entry by potential competitors is greatly diminished; it is a weak competitive force. Consequently, established companies can charge higher prices, and industry profits are therefore higher. Evidence from academic research suggests that the height of barriers to entry is an important determinant of profit rates within an industry.[5] Clearly, it is in the interest of established companies to pursue strategies consistent with raising entry barriers to secure these profits. Additionally, potential new entrants must find strategies that allow them to circumvent barriers to entry. For an example of a company that did this, see Strategy in Action 2.1, which looks at how the Cott Corporation circumvented barriers to entry in the soft-drink industry.

2-2b Rivalry Among Established Companies

The second competitive force is the intensity of rivalry among established companies within an industry. Rivalry refers to the competitive struggle between companies within an industry to gain market share. The competitive struggle can be fought using price, product design, advertising and promotional spending, direct-selling efforts, and after-sales service and support. Intense rivalry implies lower prices or more spending on non-price-competitive strategies, or both. Because intense rivalry lowers prices and

2.1 Strategy in Action

Circumventing Entry Barriers into the Soft-Drink Industry

Two companies have long dominated the carbonated soft-drink industry: Coca-Cola and PepsiCo. By spending large sums of money on advertising and promotion, these two giants have created significant brand loyalty and made it very difficult for new competitors to enter the industry and take away market share. When new competitors have tried to enter, both companies have responded by cutting prices, forcing new entrants to curtail expansion plans.

However, in the early 1990s, the Cott Corporation, then a small Canadian bottling company, worked out a strategy for entering the carbonated soft-drink market. Cott's strategy was deceptively simple. The company initially focused on the cola segment of the market. Cott struck a deal with Royal Crown (RC) Cola for exclusive global rights to its cola concentrate. RC Cola was a small player in the U.S. cola market. Its products were recognized as high quality, but RC Cola had never been able to effectively challenge Coke or Pepsi. Next, Cott entered an agreement with a Canadian grocery retailer, Loblaw, to provide the retailer with its own, private-label brand of cola. The Loblaw private-label brand, known as "President's Choice," was priced low, became very successful, and took shares from both Coke and Pepsi.

Emboldened by this success, Cott tried to convince other retailers to carry private-label cola. To retailers, the value proposition was simple because, unlike its major rivals, Cott spent almost nothing on advertising and promotion. This constituted a major source of cost savings, which Cott passed on to retailers in the form of lower prices. Retailers found that they could significantly undercut the price of Coke and Pepsi colas and still make better profit margins on private-label brands than on branded colas.

Despite this compelling value proposition, few retailers were willing to sell private-label colas for fear of alienating Coca-Cola and Pepsi, whose products were a major draw for grocery store traffic. Cott's breakthrough came when it signed a deal with Walmart to supply the retailing giant with a private-label cola, "Sam's Choice" (named after Walmart founder Sam Walton). Walmart proved to be the perfect distribution channel for Cott. The retailer was just beginning to appear in the grocery business, and consumers shopped at Walmart not to buy branded merchandise, but to get low prices. As Walmart's grocery business grew, so did Cott's sales. Cott soon added other flavors to its offerings, such as lemon-lime soda, which would compete with 7-Up and Sprite. Moreover, by the late 1990s, other U.S. grocers pressured by Walmart had also started to introduce private-label sodas and often turned to Cott to supply their needs.

By 2017, Cott's private-label customers included Walmart, Kroger, Costco, and Safeway. Cott had revenues of $3.8 billion and accounted for 60% of all private-label sales of carbonated beverages in the United States, and 6 to 7% of overall sales of carbonated beverages in grocery stores, its core channel. Although Coca-Cola and PepsiCo remain dominant, they have lost incremental market share to Cott and other companies that have followed Cott's strategy. In 2018, Cott sold its bottling operations to Refresco, a large independent bottler for established soft drink brands in Europe and North America.

Sources: A. Kaplan, "Cott Corporation," *Beverage World*, June 15, 2004, p. 32; J. Popp, "2004 Soft Drink Report," *Beverage Industry*, March 2004, pp. 13–18; L. Sparks, "From Coca-Colonization to Copy Catting: The Cott Corporation and Retailers Brand Soft Drinks in the UK and US," *Agribusiness* 13:2 (March 1997): 153–167; E. Cherney, "After Flat Sales, Cott Challenges Pepsi, Coca-Cola," *Wall Street Journal*, January 8, 2003, pp. B1, B8; "Cott Corporation: Company Profile," *Just Drinks*, August 2006, pp. 19–22; Cott Corp. 2016 Annual Report, www.cott.com.

raises costs, it squeezes profits out of an industry. Thus, intense rivalry among established companies constitutes a strong threat to profitability. Alternatively, if rivalry is less intense, companies may have the opportunity to raise prices or reduce spending on non-price-competitive strategies, leading to higher industry profits. Four factors have a major impact on the intensity of rivalry among established companies within an industry: (1) industry competitive structure, (2) demand conditions, (3) cost conditions, and (4) the height of exit barriers in the industry.

Industry Competitive Structure The competitive structure of an industry refers to the number and size distribution of companies within it. Strategic managers determine the competitive structure at the beginning of an industry analysis. Industry structures vary, and different structures have different implications for the intensity of rivalry. A fragmented industry consists of a large number of small or medium-sized companies, none of which is in a position to determine industry price. A consolidated industry is dominated by a small number of large companies (an oligopoly) or, in extreme cases, by just one company (a monopoly), and such companies often are in a position to determine industry prices. Examples of fragmented industries are agriculture, dry cleaning, health clubs, real estate brokerage, and sun-tanning salons. Consolidated industries include the aerospace, soft-drink, wireless service, and small-package express delivery industries. In the small-package express delivery industry, two firms, United Parcel Service (UPS) and FedEx, account for over 85% of industry revenues in the United States.

Low-entry barriers and commodity-type products that are difficult to differentiate characterize many fragmented industries. This combination tends to result in boom-and-bust cycles as industry profits rapidly rise and fall. Low-entry barriers imply that new entrants will flood the market, hoping to profit from the boom that occurs when demand is strong and profits are high. The number of video stores, health clubs, and tanning salons that exploded onto the market during the 1980s and 1990s exemplifies this situation.

Often, the flood of new entrants into a booming, fragmented industry creates excess capacity, and consequently companies cut prices. The difficulty of differentiating their products from those of competitors can exacerbate this tendency. The result is a price war, which depresses industry profits, forces some companies out of business, and deters potential new entrants. For example, after two decades of expansion and booming profits, many health clubs are now finding that they have to offer large discounts in order to maintain their memberships. In general, the more commodity-like an industry's product, the more vicious the price war will be. The bust phase of this cycle continues until overall industry capacity is brought into line with demand (through bankruptcies), at which point prices may stabilize again.

A fragmented industry structure, then, constitutes a threat rather than an opportunity. Economic boom times in fragmented industries are often relatively short-lived because the ease of new entry can soon result in excess capacity, which in turn leads to intense price competition and the failure of less-efficient enterprises. Because it is often difficult to differentiate products in these industries, minimizing costs is the best strategy for a company that strives to be profitable in a boom and survive any subsequent bust. Alternatively, companies might try to adopt strategies that change the underlying structure of fragmented industries and lead to a consolidated industry structure in which the level of industry profitability is increased. (We shall consider how companies can do this in later chapters.)

In consolidated industries, companies are interdependent because one company's competitive actions (for instance, changes in price or quality) directly affect the market share of its rivals and thus their profitability. One company making a move can force a response from its rivals, and the consequence of such competitive interdependence can be a dangerous competitive spiral. Rivalry increases as companies attempt to undercut each other's prices or offer customers more value, pushing industry profits down in the process.

Companies in consolidated industries sometimes seek to reduce this threat by matching the prices set by the dominant company in the industry.[6] However, care must be taken, for explicit, face-to-face, price-fixing agreements are illegal. (Tacit, indirect agreements, arrived at without direct or intentional communication, are legal.) For the most part, though, companies set prices by watching, interpreting, anticipating, and responding to one another's strategies. However, tacit price-leadership agreements often break down under adverse economic conditions, as occurred in the breakfast cereal industry, profiled in Strategy in Action 2.2.

Industry Demand   The level of industry demand is another determinant of the intensity of rivalry among established companies. Growing demand from new customers or additional purchases by existing customers tend to moderate competition by providing greater scope for companies to compete for customers. Growing demand tends to reduce rivalry because all companies can sell more without taking market share away from other companies. High industry profits are often the result. Conversely, stagnant, or declining, demand results in increased rivalry as companies fight to maintain market share and revenues (see Strategy in Action 2.2). Demand stagnates when the market is saturated and replacement demand is not enough to offset the lack of first-time

2.2 Strategy in Action

Price Wars in the Breakfast Cereal Industry

For decades, the breakfast cereal industry was one of the most profitable in the United States. The industry has a consolidated structure dominated by Kellogg's, General Mills, and Kraft Foods with its Post brand. Strong brand loyalty, coupled with control over the allocation of supermarket shelf space, helped to limit the potential for new entry. Meanwhile, steady demand growth of about 3% per annum kept industry revenues expanding. Kellogg's, which accounted for over 40% of the market share, acted as the price leader in the industry. Every year, Kellogg's increased cereal prices, its rivals followed, and industry profits remained high.

This favorable industry structure began to change in the 1990s, when growth in demand slowed—and then stagnated—as a latte and bagel or muffin replaced cereal as the American morning fare. Then came the rise of powerful discounters such as Walmart (which entered the grocery industry in 1994) that began to aggressively promote their own cereal brands and priced them significantly below the brand-name cereals. As the decade progressed, other grocery chains such as Kroger's started to follow suit, and brand loyalty in the industry began to decline as customers realized that a $2.50 bag of wheat flakes from Walmart tasted about the same as a $3.50 box of cornflakes from Kellogg's. As sales of cheaper, store-brand cereals began to take off, supermarkets, no longer dependent on brand names to bring traffic into their stores, began to demand lower prices from the branded cereal manufacturers.

For several years, manufacturers of brand-name cereals tried to hold out against these adverse trends, but in the mid-1990s, the dam broke. In 1996, Kraft (then owned by Philip Morris) aggressively cut prices by 20% for its Post brand in an attempt to gain market share. Kellogg's soon followed with a 19% price cut on two-thirds of its brands, and General Mills quickly did the same. The decades of tacit price collusion were officially over.

If breakfast cereal companies were hoping that price cuts would stimulate demand, they were wrong. Instead, demand remained flat while revenues and margins followed price decreases, and operating margins at Kellogg's dropped from 18% in 1995 to 10.2% in 1996—a trend also experienced by the other brand-name cereal manufacturers.

By 2000, conditions had worsened. Private-label sales continued to make inroads, gaining over 10% of the market. Moreover, sales of breakfast cereals started to contract at 1% per annum. To cap it off, an aggressive General Mills continued to launch expensive price-and-promotion campaigns in an attempt to take away share from the market leader. Kellogg's saw its market share slip to just over 30% in 2001, behind the 31% now held by General Mills. For the first time since 1906, Kellogg's no longer led the market. Moreover, profits at all three major producers remained weak in the face of continued price discounting.

In mid-2001, General Mills finally blinked and raised prices a modest 2% in response to its own rising costs. Competitors followed, signaling—perhaps—that after a decade of costly price warfare, pricing discipline might once more emerge in the industry. Both Kellogg's and General Mills tried to move further away from price competition by focusing on brand extensions, such as Special K containing berries and new varieties of Cheerios. Efforts with Special K helped Kellogg's recapture market leadership from General Mills and, more important, the renewed emphasis on non-price competition halted years of damaging price warfare.

After a decade of relative peace, price wars broke out in 2010 once more in this industry. The trigger, yet again, appears to have been falling demand for breakfast cereals due to substitutes such as a quick trip to the local coffee shop. In the third quarter of 2010, prices fell by 3.6% and unit volumes by 3.4%, leading to falling profit rates at Kellogg's. Both General Mills and Kellogg's introduced new products to boost demand and raise prices.

Sources: G. Morgenson, "Denial in Battle Creek," *Forbes*, October 7, 1996, p. 44; J. Muller, "Thinking out of the Cereal Box," *Business Week*, January 15, 2001, p. 54; A. Merrill, "General Mills Increases Prices," *Star Tribune*, June 5, 2001, p. 1D; S. Reyes, "Big G, Kellogg's Attempt to Berry Each Other," *Brandweek*, October 7, 2002, p. 8; M. Andrejczak, "Kellogg's Profit Hurt by Cereal Price War," *Market Watch*, November 2, 2010.

---

buyers. Demand declines when customers exit the marketplace, or when each customer purchases less. When demand is stagnating or declining, a company can grow only by taking market share away from its rivals. Stagnant or declining demand constitutes a threat because it increases the extent of rivalry between established companies.

Cost Conditions The cost structure of firms in an industry is a third determinant of rivalry. In industries where fixed costs are high, profitability tends to be highly leveraged to sales volume, and the desire to grow volume can spark intense rivalry. Fixed costs are costs that must be paid before the firm makes a single sale. For example, to offer express courier service, a company such as FedEx must first invest in planes, package-sorting facilities, and delivery trucks—all fixed costs that require significant capital investment. In industries where the cost of production is high, firms cannot cover their fixed costs and will not be profitable if sales volume is low. Thus, they have an incentive to cut their prices and/or increase promotional spending to drive up sales volume in order to cover fixed costs. In situations where demand is not rapidly growing and many companies are simultaneously engaged in the same pursuits, the result can be intense rivalry and lower profits. Research suggests that the weakest firms in an industry often initiate such actions precisely because they are struggling to cover their fixed costs.[7]

exit barriers

Economic, strategic, and emotional factors that prevent companies from leaving an industry.

Exit Barriers Exit barriers are economic, strategic, and emotional factors that prevent companies from leaving an industry.[8] If exit barriers are high, companies become locked into an unprofitable industry where overall demand is static or declining. The result is often excess productive capacity, leading to even more intense rivalry and price competition as companies cut prices, attempting to obtain the customer orders needed to use their idle capacity and cover their fixed costs.[9] Common exit barriers include:

- Investments in assets such as specific machines, equipment, or operating facilities that are of little or no value in alternative uses, or cannot be later sold. If the company wishes to leave the industry, it must write off the book value of these assets.
- High fixed costs of exit such as severance pay, health benefits, or pensions that must be paid to workers who are laid off when a company ceases to operate.
- Emotional attachments to an industry, such as when a company's owners or employees are unwilling to exit an industry for sentimental reasons or because of pride.
- Economic dependence because a company relies on a single industry for its entire revenue and all profits.
- The need to maintain an expensive collection of assets at or above a minimum level in order to participate effectively in the industry.
- Bankruptcy regulations, particularly in the United States, where Chapter 11 bankruptcy provisions allow insolvent enterprises to continue operating and to reorganize under this protection. These regulations can keep unprofitable assets in the industry, result in persistent excess capacity, and lengthen the time required to bring industry supply in line with demand.

As an example of exit barriers and effects in practice, consider the small-package express mail and parcel delivery industry. Key players in this industry, such as FedEx and UPS, rely entirely upon the delivery business for their revenues and profits. They must be able to guarantee their customers that they will deliver packages to all major localities in the United States, and much of their investment is specific to this purpose. To meet this guarantee, they need a nationwide network of air routes and ground routes, an asset that is required in order to participate in the industry. If excess capacity develops in this industry, as it does from time to time, FedEx cannot incrementally reduce or minimize its excess capacity by deciding not to fly to and deliver packages in Miami, for example, because that portion of its network is underused. If it did, it would no longer be able to guarantee to its customers that packages could be delivered to all major locations in the United States, and its customers would switch to another carrier. Thus, the need to maintain a nationwide network is an exit barrier that can result in persistent excess capacity in the air-express industry during periods of weak demand.

2-2c The Bargaining Power of Buyers

The third competitive force is the bargaining power of buyers. An industry's buyers may be the individual customers who consume its products (end-users) or the intermediary companies that distribute an industry's products to end-users such as retailers and wholesalers. For example, although soap powder made by Procter & Gamble (P&G) and Unilever is consumed by end users, the principal buyers of soap powder are supermarket chains and discount stores, which resell the product to end users. The bargaining power of buyers refers to their ability to bargain down prices charged by companies in the industry, or to raise the costs of companies in the industry by demanding better product quality and service. By lowering prices and raising costs, powerful buyers can squeeze profits out of an industry. Powerful buyers, therefore, should be viewed as a threat. Alternatively, when buyers are in a weak bargaining position, companies in an industry can raise prices and perhaps reduce their costs by lowering product quality and service, thus increasing the level of industry profits. Buyers are most powerful in the following circumstances:

- When buyers have a choice. If the industry is a monopoly, buyers obviously lack a choice. If there are two or more companies in the industry, buyers clearly have a choice.
- When buyers purchase in large quantities, they can use their purchasing power as leverage to bargain for price reductions.
- When the supply industry depends upon buyers for a large percentage of its total orders.
- When switching costs are low and buyers can pit the supplying companies against each other to force down prices.
- When it is economically feasible for buyers to purchase an input from several companies at once, they can pit one company in the industry against another.
- When buyers can threaten to enter the industry and independently produce the product, thus supplying their own needs, they can force down industry prices.

The automobile component supply industry, whose buyers are large manufacturers such as General Motors (GM), Ford, Honda, and Toyota, is a good example of an industry in which buyers have strong bargaining power and thus pose a strong competitive threat. Why? The suppliers of auto components are numerous and typically smaller in scale; their buyers, the auto manufacturers, are large in size and few in number. Additionally, to keep component prices down, historically automobile manufacturers have used the threat of manufacturing a component themselves rather than buying it from a supplier. The automakers use their powerful position to pit suppliers against one another, forcing down the prices for component parts, and to demand better quality. If a component supplier objects, the automaker can use the threat of switching to another supplier as a bargaining tool.

2-2d The Bargaining Power of Suppliers

The fourth competitive force is the bargaining power of suppliers—the organizations that provide inputs—such as materials, services, and labor, which may be individuals, organizations such as labor unions, or companies that supply contract labor—into the industry. The bargaining power of suppliers refers to their ability to raise input prices, or to raise the costs of the industry in other ways—for example, by providing poor-quality inputs or poor service. Powerful suppliers squeeze profits out of an industry by raising the costs of companies in the industry. Thus, powerful suppliers are a threat. Conversely, if suppliers are weak, companies in the industry have the opportunity to force down input prices and demand higher-quality inputs (such as more productive labor). As with buyers, the ability of suppliers to make demands on a company depends on their power relative to that of the company. Suppliers are most powerful in these situations:

- The product that suppliers sell has few substitutes and is vital to the companies in an industry.
- The profitability of suppliers is not significantly affected by the purchases of companies in a particular industry; in other words, when the industry is not an important customer to the suppliers.
- Companies in an industry would experience significant switching costs if they moved to the product of a different supplier because a particular supplier's

products are unique. In such cases, the company depends upon a particular supplier and cannot pit suppliers against each other to reduce prices.

- Suppliers can threaten to enter their customers' industry and use their inputs to produce products that would compete directly with those of companies already in the industry.
- Companies in the industry cannot threaten to enter their suppliers' industry and make their own inputs as a tactic for lowering the price of inputs.

An example of an industry in which companies are dependent upon a powerful supplier is the PC industry. Personal computer (PC) firms have long been dependent on Intel, the world's largest supplier of microprocessors for PCs. Intel's microprocessor chips are the industry standard for personal computers. Intel's competitors, such as Advanced Micro Devices (AMD), must develop and supply chips that are compatible with Intel's standard. Although AMD has developed competing chips, as of 2022 Intel still supplied around 64% of the chips used in desktop and laptop PCs, primarily because only Intel has the manufacturing capacity required to serve a large share of the market. It is beyond the financial resources of Intel's competitors to match the scale and efficiency of its manufacturing systems. This means that although PC manufacturers can purchase some microprocessors from Intel's rivals, most notably AMD, they still must turn to Intel for the bulk of their supply. Because Intel is in a powerful bargaining position, it can charge higher prices for its microprocessors than if its competitors were stronger and more numerous (that is, if the microprocessor industry were fragmented).

2-2e Substitute Products

The final force in Porter's model is the threat of substitute products: the products of different businesses or industries that can satisfy similar customer needs. For example, companies in the coffee industry compete indirectly with those in the tea and soft-drink industries because all three serve customer needs for nonalcoholic, caffeinated drinks. The existence of close substitutes is a strong competitive threat because it limits the price that companies in one industry can charge for their product, which also limits industry profitability. If the price of coffee rises too much relative to that of tea or soft drinks, coffee drinkers may switch to those substitutes.

If an industry's products have few close substitutes (making substitutes a weak competitive force), then companies in the industry have the opportunity to raise prices and earn additional profits. There is no close substitute for microprocessors, which thus gives companies like Intel and AMD the ability to charge higher prices than if there were available substitutes.

2-2f Complementors

Andrew Grove, the former CEO of Intel, has argued that Porter's original formulation of competitive forces ignored a sixth force: the power, vigor, and competence of complementors.[10] Complementors are companies that sell products that add value to (complement) the products of companies in an industry because, when used together, the combined products better satisfy customer demands. For example, the complementors to the PC industry are the companies that make software applications. The greater the supply of high-quality software applications running on these machines, the greater the value of PCs to customers, the greater the demand for PCs, and the greater the profitability of the PC industry.

Grove's argument has a strong foundation in economic theory, which has long argued that both substitutes and complements influence demand in an industry.[11] Research has emphasized the importance of complementary products in determining demand and profitability in many high-technology industries, such as the computer industry, where Grove made his mark.[12] When complements are an important determinant of demand for an industry's products, industry profits critically depend upon an adequate supply of complementary products. When the number of complementors is increasing and producing attractive complementary products, demand increases and profits in the industry can broaden opportunities for creating value.

Conversely, if complementors are weak and not producing attractive complementary products, they can become a threat, slowing industry growth, and limiting profitability. For example, one factor limiting the demand for the electric vehicles produced by companies such as Tesla is "range anxiety," which is the fear that people have that they will run out of battery power far away from a charging station. To reduce this fear, Tesla and others are investing in establishing a dense nationwide network of charging stations (a complementary product) to reduce range anxiety and boost demand for electric vehicles. Indeed, in 2014 Tesla placed its charging technology in the public domain to encourage the adoption of its technology as the industry standard for charging stations. It is also possible for complementors to gain so much power that they are able to extract profit from the industry to which they provide complements. Complementors this strong can be a competitive threat. For another example of this, and how it has shaped strategy in an industry, see Strategy in Action 2.3.

2.3 Strategy in Action

Why Does Microsoft Want to Acquire Activision Blizzard?

In January 2022, Microsoft announced its intention to acquire Activision Blizzard for $68 billion. Activision is the second-largest videogame company in the world, and the developer of several popular franchises including *Overwatch, Call of Duty,* and *World of Warcraft.* Microsoft, of course, has long participated in the industry with its Xbox console, and does have a history of developing and/or publishing some video games in house, including its immensely popular *Halo* series and the *Gears of War* franchise. But why would Microsoft want to increase its involvement in the game development side of the business, particularly given the high development costs, which can exceed over $100 million for top-tier games, and the risks involved if the game flops in the market? To understand the reasoning behind the strategy, one must dig a little into the history of the industry.

In the videogame industry, for a long time it was the companies that produced the consoles—Nintendo, Microsoft (Xbox), and Sony (PS5)—that made the most money. They have done so by charging game-development companies (the providers of the *complementary product*) a royalty fee for every game sold that runs on their consoles. For example, Nintendo used to charge third-party game developers a 20% royalty fee for every game they sold that was written to run on a Nintendo console. This made Nintendo a fabulously profitable company. Sony pursued a similar strategy when it launched its original PlayStation in the 1990s.

However, things have changed over the last two decades. In the 1980s and 1990s, a single console dominated the industry. First it was Nintendo, then Sega, then Sony. This meant that game developers had little choice but to pay a high royalty fee if they wanted access to the market. But in the last two decades, the market has been large enough to support three consoles simultaneously—Nintendo, Xbox, and PlayStation. Game developers now have choices. They can, for example, decide to write for Microsoft Xbox first and for Sony PS5 a year later. Second, some game franchises are now so popular that consumers will purchase whichever platform runs the most recent version of the game. *Madden NFL,* produced by Electronic Arts, has an estimated 5 to 7 million dedicated fans that will purchase each new release. The game is in such demand that Electronic Arts can bargain for lower royalty fees from Microsoft and Sony in return for writing it to run on their gaming platforms. Put differently, Electronic Arts has gained bargaining power over the console producers, and it uses this to extract profit from the console industry in the form of lower royalty rates paid to console manufacturers.

The console manufacturers have responded by trying to develop powerful franchises that are exclusive to their platforms, thereby driving greater demand and higher profitability for their offerings. Nintendo has been successful here with its long-running *Super Mario* series, and Microsoft has had a major franchise hit with its *Halo* series. Sony, too, has invested in its own in-house game development studios to reduce its reliance on powerful complement suppliers. Viewed in this way, Microsoft's acquisition of Activision Blizzard makes good strategic sense (at the time of writing, the acquisition still has to be approved by regulators). It will give Microsoft exclusive control over some very popular franchises and, by publishing those franchises on its Xbox platform, including its online game streaming platform Xbox network, Microsoft will put itself in the position of being able to capture significant economic value both from its Xbox platform, and from the sales of games that can be accessed through that platform.

2-2g Summary: Why Industry Analysis Matters

The analysis of competition in the industry environment using the competitive forces framework is a powerful tool that helps managers think strategically. It is important to recognize that one competitive force often affects others, and all forces need to be considered when performing industry analysis. For example, new entries due to low entry barriers increase competition in the industry and drive down prices and profit rates, other things being equal (this may now be occurring in the streaming video on-demand industry—see the Opening Case). If buyers are powerful, they may take advantage of the increased choice resulting from new entry to further bargain down prices, increasing the intensity of competition and making it more difficult to make a decent profit in the industry. Thus, it is important to understand how one force might impact another.

Industry analysis inevitably leads managers to think systematically about strategic choices. For example, if entry barriers are low, managers might ask themselves, "How can we raise entry barriers into this industry, thereby reducing the threat of new competition?" The answer often involves trying to achieve economies of scale, build brand loyalty, create switching costs, and so on, so that new entrants are at a disadvantage and find it difficult to gain traction in the industry. Or they could ask, "How can we modify the intensity of competition in our industry?" They might do this by emphasizing brand loyalty to differentiate their products, or by creating switching costs that reduce buyer power in the industry. For example, to try and reduce customer churn, wireless service providers have historically required new customers to sign a 2-year contract with early termination fees that may run into hundreds of dollars whenever they upgrade their phone equipment. This action effectively increased the costs of switching to a different wireless provider, thus making it more difficult for new entrants to gain traction in the industry. The increase in switching costs also moderates the intensity of rivalry in the industry by making it less likely that consumers will switch from one provider to another to lower the price they pay for their service.

For another example, consider what happened when Coca-Cola looked at its industry environment in the early 2000s. It noticed a disturbing trend—per capita consumption of carbonated beverages had started to decline as people switched to noncarbonated soft drinks. In other words, substitute products were becoming a threat. This realization led to a change in the strategy at Coca-Cola. The company started to develop and offer its own noncarbonated beverages, effectively turning the threat into a strategic opportunity. Similarly, in the 2000s, demand for traditional newspapers began to decline as people increasingly started to consume news content online. In other words, the threat from a substitute product was increasing. Several traditional newspapers such as the *New York Times* and *Wall Street Journal* responded by rapidly developing their own online content.

In all these examples, an analysis of industry opportunities and threats led directly to a change in strategy by companies within the industry. This, of course, is the crucial point—analyzing the industry environment to identify opportunities and threats leads logically to a discussion of what strategies should be adopted to exploit opportunities and counter threats. We will return to this issue again in Chapters 4, 5, 6, and 7 when we look at the different strategies firms can pursue, and how they can match strategy to the conditions prevailing in their industry environment.

2-3 Strategic Groups within Industries

2.3 Explore the concept of strategic groups, including the implications for industry analysis.

Companies in an industry often differ significantly from one another regarding the way they strategically position their products in the market. Factors such as the distribution channels they use, the market segments they serve, the quality of their products, technological leadership, customer service, pricing policy, advertising policy, and promotions all affect product position. As a result of these differences, within most industries it is possible to observe groups of companies in which each company follows a strategy similar to that pursued by other companies in the group, but different from the strategy pursued by companies in other groups. These different groups of companies are known as strategic groups.[13]

For example, the commercial aerospace industry has traditionally had two main strategic groups: the manufacturers of regional jets and the manufacturers of large commercial jets (see Figure 2.2). Bombardier and Embraer are the standouts in the regional jet industry, whereas Boeing and Airbus have long dominated the market for large commercial jets. Regional jets have less than 100 seats and limited range. Large jets have anywhere from 100 to 550 seats, and some models are able to fly across the Pacific Ocean. Large jets are sold to major airlines, and regional jets to small, regional carriers. Historically, the companies in the regional jet group have competed against each other but not against Boeing and Airbus (the converse is also true).

Normally, the basic differences between the strategies that companies in different strategic groups use can be captured by a relatively small number of factors. In the case of commercial aerospace, the differences are primarily in terms of product attributes (seat capacity and range) and customer set (large airlines versus smaller regional airlines). For another example, consider the pharmaceutical industry. Here, two primary strategic groups stand out.[14] One group, which includes such companies as Merck, Eli Lilly, and Pfizer, is characterized by a business model based on heavy R&D spending and a focus on developing new, proprietary, blockbuster drugs. The companies in this proprietary strategic group are pursuing a high-risk, high-return strategy because basic drug research is difficult and expensive. Bringing a new drug to market can cost up to $800 million in R&D funding and a decade of research and clinical trials. The risks are high because the failure rate in new drug development is very high: only one out of every five drugs entering clinical trials is eventually approved by the U.S. Food and Drug Administration (FDA). However, this strategy has the potential for a high return because a single successful drug can be patented, giving the innovator a monopoly on the production and sale of the drug for the life of the patent (patents are issued for 20 years). This allows proprietary companies to charge a high price for the drug, earning them millions, if not billions, of dollars over the lifetime of the patent.

The second strategic group might be characterized as the generic-drug strategic group. This group of companies, which includes Teva Pharmaceutical Industries, Sun

Figure 2.2 Strategic Groups in the Commercial Aerospace Industry

Pharmaceutical, and Mylan Inc., focuses on the manufacture of generic drugs: low-cost copies of drugs that were developed by companies in the proprietary group, which now have expired patents. Low R&D spending, production efficiency, and an emphasis on low prices characterize the business models of companies in this strategic group. They are pursuing a low-risk, low-return strategy: low risk because these companies are not investing millions of dollars in R&D and low return because they cannot charge high prices for their products.

2-3a Implications of Strategic Groups

The concept of strategic groups has a number of implications for the identification of opportunities and threats within an industry. First, because all companies in a strategic group are pursuing a similar strategy, customers tend to view the products of such enterprises as direct substitutes for each other. Thus, a company's closest competitors are those in its strategic group, not those in other strategic groups in the industry. The most immediate threat to a company's profitability comes from rivals within its own strategic group. For example, in the retail industry, there is a group of companies that might be characterized as general merchandise discounters. Included in this group are Walmart, Target, and Fred Meyer. These companies compete vigorously with each other, rather than with other retailers in different groups, such as Nordstrom or Gap. The general merchandise retailer K-Mart, for example, was driven into bankruptcy in the early 2000s, not because Nordstrom or Gap took its business, but because Walmart and Target gained share in the discounting group by virtue of their superior strategic execution of the discounting business model for general merchandise.

A second competitive implication is that different strategic groups can have different relationships to each of the competitive forces; thus, each strategic group may face a different set of opportunities and threats. Each of the following can be a relatively strong or weak competitive force depending on the competitive positioning approach adopted by each strategic group in the industry: the risk of new entry by potential competitors; the degree of rivalry among companies within a group; the bargaining power of buyers; the bargaining power of suppliers; and the competitive force of substitute and complementary products. For example, in the pharmaceutical industry, companies in the proprietary group historically have been in a very powerful position in relation to buyers because their products are patented and there are no substitutes. Also, rivalry based on price competition within this group has been low because competition in the industry depends upon which company is first to patent a new drug ("patent races"), not on drug prices. Thus, companies in this group are able to charge high prices and earn high profits. In contrast, companies in the generic group have been in a much weaker position because many companies are able to produce different versions of the same generic drug after patents expire. Thus, in this strategic group, products are close substitutes, rivalry is high, and price competition has led to lower profits than for the companies in the proprietary group.

2-3b The Role of Mobility Barriers

It follows from these two issues that some strategic groups are more desirable than others because competitive forces open greater opportunities and present fewer threats for those groups. Managers, after analyzing their industry, might identify a strategic group where competitive forces are weaker and higher profits can be made. Sensing an opportunity, they might contemplate changing their strategy and move to compete in that strategic group. However, taking advantage of this opportunity may be difficult because of mobility barriers between strategic groups.

Mobility barriers are within-industry factors that inhibit the movement of companies between strategic groups. They include the barriers to entry into a group and the barriers to exit from an existing group. For example, attracted by the promise of higher returns, Forest Labs might want to enter the proprietary strategic group in the pharmaceutical industry, but it might find doing so difficult because it lacks the requisite R&D skills, and building these skills would be an expensive proposition. Over time, companies in different groups develop different cost structures, skills, and competencies that allow them different pricing options and choices. A company contemplating entry into another strategic group must evaluate whether it can imitate, and outperform, its potential competitors in that strategic group. Managers must determine if it is cost-effective to overcome mobility barriers before deciding whether the move is worthwhile.

At the same time, managers should be aware that companies based in another strategic group within their industry might ultimately become their direct competitors if they can overcome mobility barriers. This now seems to be occurring in the commercial aerospace industry, where two regional jet manufacturers, Bombardier and Embraer, have started to move into the large commercial jet business with the development of narrow-bodied aircraft in the 100- to 150-seat range. This implies that Boeing and Airbus will be seeing more competition in the years ahead, and their managers need to prepare for this. Indeed, in 2017, Airbus entered into a partnership with Bombardier to co-opt them, and in 2018, Boeing considered acquiring Embraer, although it backed out of the deal in 2020 due to the impact of the COVID-19 pandemic on demand for commercial jet aircraft.

2-4 Industry Life-Cycle Analysis

2.4 Discuss how industries evolve over time, with reference to the industry life-cycle model.

Changes that take place in an industry over time are an important determinant of the strength of the competitive forces in the industry (and of the nature of opportunities and threats). The similarities and differences between companies in an industry often become more pronounced over time, and its strategic group structure frequently changes. The strength and nature of each competitive force also changes as an industry evolves, particularly the two forces of risk of entry by potential competitors and rivalry among existing firms.[15]

A useful tool for analyzing the effects of industry evolution on competitive forces is the industry life-cycle model. This model identifies five sequential stages in the evolution of an industry that represent five distinct kinds of industry environment: embryonic, growth, shakeout, mature, and decline (see Figure 2.3). The task managers

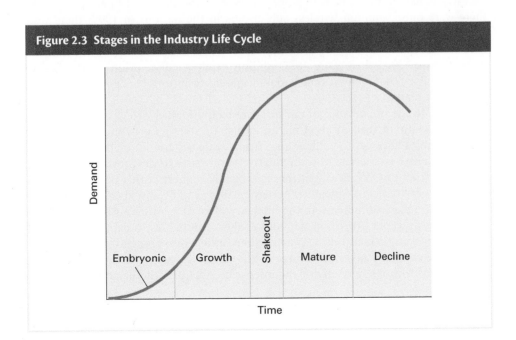

Figure 2.3 Stages in the Industry Life Cycle

face is to anticipate how the strength of competitive forces will change as the industry environment evolves, and to formulate strategies that take advantage of opportunities as they arise and that counter emerging threats.

2-4a Embryonic Industries

An embryonic industry is one that is just beginning to develop (for example, personal computers and biotechnology in the 1970s, wireless communications in the 1980s, online retailing in the mid-1990s, cloud computing in the 2000s, and nanotechnology today). Growth at this stage is slow because of factors such as buyers' unfamiliarity with the industry's product, high prices due to the inability of companies to leverage significant scale economies, and poorly developed distribution channels. Barriers to entry tend to be based on access to key technological know-how rather than cost economies or brand loyalty. If the core know-how required to compete in the industry is complex and difficult to grasp, barriers to entry can be quite high, and established companies will be protected from potential competitors. Rivalry in embryonic industries is based not so much on price as on educating customers, opening distribution channels, and perfecting the design of the product. Such rivalry can be intense, and the company that is the first to solve design problems often can develop a significant market position. An embryonic industry may also be the creation of one company's innovative efforts, as happened with microprocessors (Intel), vacuum cleaners (Hoover), photocopiers (Xerox), small-package express delivery (FedEx), and internet search engines (Google). In such circumstances, the developing company has a major opportunity to capitalize on the lack of rivalry and build a strong hold on the market.

2-4b Growth Industries

Once demand for an industry's products begins to increase, it develops the characteristics of a growth industry. In a growth industry, first-time demand is expanding rapidly as many new customers enter the market. Typically, an industry grows when customers become familiar with a product, prices fall because scale economies have been attained, and distribution channels develop. The U.S. wireless telephone industry remained in the growth stage for most of the 1985–2012 period. In 1990, there were only 5 million wireless subscribers in the nation. In 1997, there were 50 million. By 2014, this figure had increased to about 360 million, or roughly 1.08 accounts per person, implying that the market was now saturated and the industry mature. As of 2022 there were 468.9 million wireless subscriptions in the United States, implying that many people had multiple subscriptions (e.g. a personal phone and a work phone).

Normally, the importance of control over technological knowledge as a barrier to entry has diminished by the time an industry enters its growth stage. Because few companies have yet to achieve significant scale economies or built brand loyalty, other entry barriers tend to be relatively low early in the growth stage. Thus, the threat from potential competitors is typically highest at this point. Paradoxically, high growth usually means that new entrants can be absorbed into an industry without a marked increase in the intensity of rivalry. Thus, rivalry tends to be relatively low. Rapid growth in demand enables companies to expand their revenues and profits without taking market share away from competitors. A strategically aware company takes advantage of the relatively benign environment of the growth stage to prepare itself for the intense competition of the coming industry shakeout.

2-4c Industry Shakeout

Rapid growth cannot be maintained indefinitely. Sooner or later, the rate of growth slows, and the industry enters the shakeout stage. In the shakeout stage, demand approaches saturation levels: more and more of the demand is limited to replacement because fewer potential first-time buyers remain.

As an industry enters the shakeout stage, rivalry between companies can build. Typically, companies that have become accustomed to rapid growth continue to add capacity at rates consistent with past growth. However, demand is no longer growing at historic rates, and the consequence is excess productive capacity. This condition is illustrated in Figure 2.4, where the solid curve indicates the growth in demand over time and the broken curve indicates the growth in productive capacity over time. As you can see, past time t_1, demand growth slows as the industry matures. However, capacity continues to grow until time t_2. The gap between the solid and broken lines signifies excess capacity. In an attempt to use this capacity, companies often cut prices. The result can be a price war that drives inefficient companies into bankruptcy and deters new entry.

2-4d Mature Industries

The shakeout stage ends when the industry enters its mature stage: The market is totally saturated, demand is limited to replacement demand and demand growth is low or zero. Typically, the growth that remains comes from population expansion, bringing new customers into the market or increasing replacement demand.

As an industry enters maturity, barriers to entry increase, and the threat of entry from potential competitors decreases. As growth slows during the shakeout, companies can no longer maintain historic growth rates merely by holding on to their market share. Competition for market share develops, driving down prices and often producing a price war, as has happened in the airline and PC industries. To survive the shakeout,

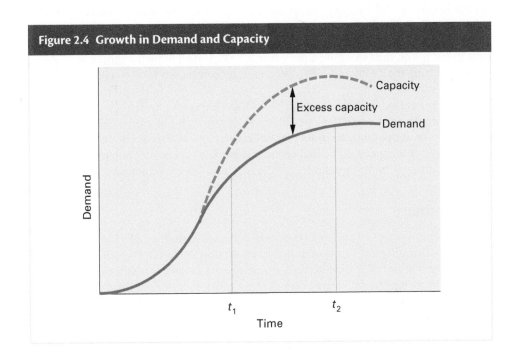

Figure 2.4 Growth in Demand and Capacity

companies begin to focus on minimizing costs and building brand loyalty. The airlines, for example, tried to cut operating costs by hiring nonunion labor, and to build brand loyalty by introducing frequent-flyer programs. PC computer companies have sought to build brand loyalty by providing excellent after-sales service and working to lower their cost structures. By the time an industry matures, the surviving companies are those that have secured brand loyalty and efficient, low-cost operations. Because both of these factors constitute a significant barrier to entry, the threat of entry by potential competitors is often greatly diminished. High entry barriers in mature industries can give companies the opportunity to increase prices and profits, although this does not always occur.

As a result of the shakeout, most industries in the maturity stage consolidate and become oligopolies. Examples include the beer industry, breakfast cereal industry, and wireless service industry. In mature industries, companies tend to recognize their interdependence and try to avoid price wars. Stable demand gives them the opportunity to enter into tacit price-leadership agreements. The net effect is to reduce the threat of intense rivalry among established companies, thereby allowing greater profitability. Nevertheless, the stability of a mature industry is always threatened by further price wars. A general slump in economic activity can depress industry demand. As companies fight to maintain their revenues in the face of declining demand, price-leadership agreements break down, rivalry increases, and prices and profits fall. The periodic price wars that occur in the airline industry appear to follow this pattern.

2-4e Declining Industries

Eventually, most industries enter a stage of decline: growth becomes negative for a variety of reasons, including technological substitution (air travel instead of rail travel), social changes (greater health consciousness impacting tobacco sales), demographics (the declining birth rate constricting the market for products for babies and children), and international competition (low-cost, foreign competition pushing the U.S. steel industry into decline). Within a declining industry, the degree of rivalry among established companies usually increases. Depending on the speed of the decline and the height of exit barriers, competitive pressures can become as fierce as in the shakeout stage.[16] The largest problem in a declining industry is that falling demand leads to the emergence of excess capacity. In trying to use this capacity, companies begin to cut prices, thus sparking a price war. The U.S. steel industry experienced these problems during the 1980s and 1990s because steel companies tried to use their excess capacity despite falling demand. The same problem occurred in the airline industry in the 1990–1992 period, in 2001–2005, in 2008–2009, and again in 2020–2021 as companies cut prices to ensure that they would not be flying with half-empty planes (that is, they would not be operating with substantial excess capacity). Exit barriers play a part in adjusting excess capacity. The higher the exit barriers, the harder it is for companies to reduce capacity and the greater the threat of severe price competition.

2-4f Summary

A third task of industry analysis is to identify the opportunities and threats that are characteristic of different kinds of industry environments to develop effective strategies. Managers must tailor their strategies to changing industry conditions. They must also learn to recognize the crucial points in an industry's development, so they can forecast when the shakeout stage of an industry might begin or when an industry might be moving into decline. This is also true at the level of strategic groups, for new, embryonic groups may emerge because of shifts in customer needs and tastes, or because some groups may grow rapidly due to changes in technology, whereas others will decline as their customers defect.

2-5 Limitations of Models for Industry Analysis

2.5 Discuss limitations of models for industry analysis.

The competitive forces, strategic groups, and life-cycle models provide useful ways of thinking about and analyzing the nature of competition within an industry to identify opportunities and threats. However, each has its limitations, and managers must be aware of them.

2-5a Life-Cycle Issues

It is important to remember that the industry life-cycle model is a generalization. In practice, industry life cycles do not always follow the pattern, as illustrated in Figure 2.3. In some cases, growth is so rapid that the embryonic stage is skipped altogether. In others, industries fail to get past the embryonic stage. Industry growth can be revitalized after long periods of decline through innovation or social change. For example, the health boom brought the bicycle industry back to life after a long period of decline.

The time span of these stages can vary significantly from industry to industry. Some industries can remain mature almost indefinitely if their products are viewed as necessities, as is the case for the auto industry. Other industries skip the mature stage and go straight into decline, as in the case of the vacuum-tube industry. Transistors replaced vacuum tubes as a major component in electronic products even though the vacuum-tube industry was still in its growth stage. Still other industries may go through several shakeouts before they enter full maturity, as appears to have been occurring in the telecommunications industry.

2-5b Innovation and Change

Over any reasonable length of time, in many industries competition can be viewed as a process driven by innovation.[17] Innovation is frequently the major factor in industry evolution and propels a company's movement through the industry life cycle. Innovation is attractive because companies that pioneer new products, processes, or strategies often earn enormous profits. Consider the explosive growth periods enjoyed for a time by Netflix, Dell, and Walmart. In a variety of ways, all these companies were innovators. Netflix pioneered a new way of offering videos to customers (streaming video on demand); Dell pioneered an entirely new way of selling personal computers (directly via telephone, and then online); and Walmart pioneered the low-price, discount superstore concept.

Successful innovation can transform the nature of industry competition. In recent decades, one frequent consequence of innovation has been to lower the fixed costs of production, thereby reducing barriers to entry and allowing new, smaller enterprises to compete with large, established organizations. Five decades ago, large, integrated steel companies such as U.S. Steel, LTV, and Bethlehem Steel dominated the steel industry. The industry was an oligopoly, with a small number of large producers, in which tacit price collusion was practiced. Then along came a series of efficient, mini-mill producers such as Nucor and Chaparral Steel. They used a new technology: electric arc furnaces. Over the past 50 years, they have revolutionized the structure of the industry. What was once a consolidated industry is now fragmented and price competitive. U.S. Steel now has only a 12% market share, down from 55% in the mid-1960s. In contrast, the mini-mills as a group now hold around 60% of the market, up from 5% 40 years ago.[18] Thus, the mini-mill innovation has reshaped the nature of competition in the steel industry.[19] A competitive forces model applied to the industry in 1970 would look very different from a competitive forces model applied in 2022.

Michael Porter sees innovation as "unfreezing" and "reshaping" industry structure. He argues that, after a period of turbulence triggered by innovation, the structure of an industry once more settles into a fairly stable pattern and the competitive forces and strategic group concepts can once more be applied.[20] This view of the evolution of industry structure, often referred to as "punctuated equilibrium,"[21] holds that long periods of equilibrium (refreezing), when an industry's structure is stable, are punctuated by periods of rapid change (unfreezing), when industry structure is revolutionized by innovation.

Figure 2.5 depicts punctuated equilibrium for a key dimension of industry structure: competitive structure. From time t_0 to t_1, the competitive structure of the industry is a stable oligopoly, and few companies share the market. At time t_1, a major new innovation is pioneered either by an existing company or a new entrant. The result is a period of turbulence between t_1 and t_2. Afterward, the industry settles into a new state of equilibrium, but now the competitive structure is far more fragmented. Note that the opposite could have happened: the industry could have become more consolidated, although this seems to be less common. In general, innovation seems to lower barriers to entry, allow more companies into the industry, and, as a result, lead to fragmentation rather than consolidation.

During a period of rapid change when industry structure is being revolutionized by innovation, value typically migrates to business models based on new positioning strategies.[22] In the stockbrokerage industry, value migrated from the full-service broker model to the online trading model. In the steel industry, electric arc technology led to a migration of value away from large, integrated enterprises and toward small mini-mills. In the bookselling industry, value has migrated first away from small, boutique "brick-and-mortar" booksellers toward large bookstore chains like Barnes & Noble, and toward online bookstores such as Amazon.com. Because the competitive forces and strategic group models are static, they cannot adequately capture what occurs during periods of rapid change in the industry environment when value is migrating.

2-5c Company Differences

Another criticism of industry models is that they overemphasize the importance of industry structure as a determinant of company performance and underemphasize the importance of variations or differences among companies within an industry or a strategic group.[23] As we discuss in the next chapter, the profit rates of individual companies within an industry can vary enormously. Research by Richard Rumelt and his associates suggests that industry structure explains only about 10% of the variance in profit rates across companies.[24] This implies that individual company differences account for much of the remainder. Other studies have estimated the explained variance at closer to 20%.[25] Similarly, several studies have found only weak evidence linking strategic group membership

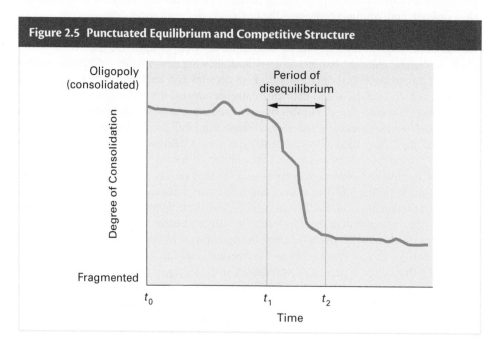

Figure 2.5 Punctuated Equilibrium and Competitive Structure

and company profit rates, even though the strategic group model predicts a strong link.[26] Collectively, these studies suggest that a company's individual resources and capabilities may be more important determinants of its profitability than the industry or strategic group of which the company is a member. In other words, there are strong companies in tough industries where average profitability is low (Nucor in the steel industry), and weak companies in industries where average profitability is high.

Although these findings do not invalidate the competitive forces and strategic group models, they do imply that the models are imperfect predictors of enterprise profitability. A company will not be profitable just because it is based in an attractive industry or strategic group. As we will discuss in subsequent chapters, much more is required.

2-6 The Macroenvironment

2.6 Summarize the ways in which the macroenvironment can shape the nature of competition in an industry.

Just as the decisions and actions of strategic managers can often change an industry's competitive structure, so too can changing conditions or forces in the wider macroenvironment; that is, the broader economic, global, technological, demographic, social, and political context in which companies and industries are embedded (see Figure 2.6). Changes in the forces within the macroenvironment can have a direct impact on any or all the forces in Porter's model, thereby altering the relative strength of these forces as well as the attractiveness of an industry.

2-6a Macroeconomic Forces

Macroeconomic forces affect the general health and well-being of a nation and the regional economy of an organization, which in turn affect companies' and industries'

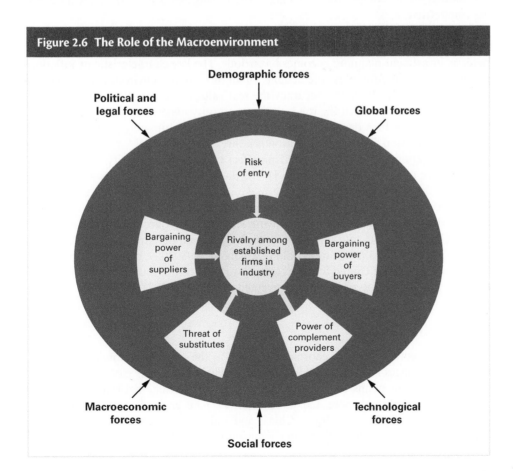

Figure 2.6 The Role of the Macroenvironment

ability to earn an adequate rate of return. The four primary macroeconomic forces are the growth rate of the economy, interest rates, currency exchange rates, and inflation (or deflation) rates. Economic growth, because it leads to an expansion in customer expenditures, tends to ease competitive pressures within an industry. This gives companies the opportunity to expand their operations and earn higher profits. Because economic decline (a recession) leads to a reduction in customer expenditures, it increases competitive pressures. Economic decline frequently causes price wars in mature industries that produce commodity products.

Interest rates can determine the demand for a company's products and thus are important whenever customers routinely borrow money to finance their purchase of these products. The most obvious example is the housing market, where mortgage rates directly affect demand. Interest rates also have an impact on the sale of autos, appliances, and capital equipment, to give just a few examples. For companies in such industries, rising interest rates are a threat and falling rates an opportunity. Interest rates are also important because they influence a company's cost of capital, and therefore its ability to raise funds and invest in new assets. The lower the interest rate, the lower the cost of capital for companies and the more potential investment.

Currency exchange rates define the comparative value of different national currencies. Movement in currency exchange rates has a direct impact on the competitiveness of a company's products in the global marketplace. For example, when the value of the dollar is low compared to the value of other currencies, products made in the United States are relatively inexpensive, and products made overseas are relatively expensive. A low or declining dollar reduces the threat from foreign competitors while creating opportunities for increased sales overseas. The fall in the value of the dollar against several major currencies during 2004–2008 helped to make the U.S. steel industry more competitive, whereas its rise during 2012–2014 made the industry less competitive.

Price inflation can destabilize the economy, producing slower economic growth, higher interest rates, and volatile currency movements. If inflation continues to increase, investment planning becomes hazardous. The key characteristic of inflation is that it makes the future less predictable. In an inflationary environment, it may be impossible to predict with any accuracy the real value of returns that can be earned from a project 5 years down the road. Such uncertainty makes companies less willing to invest, which in turn depresses economic activity and ultimately pushes the economy into a recession. Thus, high inflation is a threat to companies.

Price deflation also has a destabilizing effect on economic activity. If prices fall, the real price of fixed payments rises. This is damaging for companies and individuals with a high level of debt who must make regular, fixed payments on that debt. In a deflationary environment, the increase in the real value of debt consumes more household and corporate cash flows, leaving less for other purchases and depressing the overall level of economic activity. Although significant deflation has not been seen since the 1930s, in the 1990s it took hold in Japan; in 2008–2009, concerns grew that it might re-emerge in the United States as the country plunged into a deep recession (and although that did not occur, inflation remained muted until 2021–2022).

2-6b Global Forces

The last half-century has seen enormous changes in the world's economic system. We review these changes in some detail in Chapter 8, where we discuss global strategy. For now, the important points to note are that barriers to international trade and investment have tumbled, and more and more countries have enjoyed sustained economic growth. Economic growth in Brazil, China, and India has created new, large markets for companies' goods and services and is giving companies an opportunity to grow their profits faster by entering these markets. Falling barriers to international trade and investment have made it much easier to enter foreign nations. For example, 30 years ago, it was almost impossible for a Western company to set up operations in China. Until the COVID-19 pandemic derailed a lot of cross-border investment into China, Western and Japanese companies were investing over $100 billion annually in China. By the same token, falling barriers to international trade and investment have made it easier for foreign enterprises to enter the domestic markets of many companies (by lowering barriers to entry), thereby increasing the intensity of competition, and lowering profitability. Because of these changes, many formerly isolated domestic markets have now become part of a much larger, more competitive global marketplace, creating both threats and opportunities for companies. Interestingly, although barriers to cross-border trade and investment have been falling for 60 years, the decision by the United Kingdom to leave the European Union (Brexit), and the protectionist instincts of the Trump Administration in the United States, and the reluctance of the Biden Administration to remove many of Trump's trade barriers, particularly those on China, may indicate that for now at least, the tide may be turning.

2-6c Technological Forces

Over the last few decades, the pace of technological change has accelerated.[27] This has unleashed a process that has been called a "perennial gale of creative destruction."[28] Technological change can render established products obsolete overnight and simultaneously create a host of new product possibilities. Thus, technological change is both creative and destructive—both an opportunity and a threat.

Most important, the impacts of technological change can affect the height of barriers to entry and therefore radically reshape industry structure. For example, the internet lowered barriers to entry into the news industry. Providers of financial news must now compete for advertising dollars and customer attention with new, online media organizations that developed during the 1990s and 2000s, such as TheStreet.com, The Motley Fool, Yahoo Finance, Business Insider, and Google News. Advertisers now have more choices due to the resulting increase in rivalry, enabling them to bargain down the prices that they must pay to media companies.

2-6d Demographic Forces

Demographic forces result from changes in the characteristics of a population such as age, gender, ethnic origin, race, sexual orientation, and social class. Like the other forces in the general environment, demographic forces present managers with opportunities and threats and can have major implications for organizations. Change in the age distribution of a population is an example of a demographic force that affects managers and organizations. Currently, most industrialized nations are experiencing the aging of their populations because of falling birth and death rates and the aging of the Baby Boom generation. As the population ages, opportunities for organizations that cater to older people are increasing; the home-healthcare and recreation industries, for example, are seeing an upswing in demand for their services. As the Baby Boom generation from the late 1950s to the early 1960s has aged, it has created a host of opportunities and threats. During the 1980s, many Baby Boomers were getting married and creating an upsurge in demand for the customer appliances normally purchased by couples marrying for the first time. Companies such as Whirlpool Corporation and General Electric (GE) capitalized on the resulting upsurge in demand for washing machines, dishwashers, dryers, and the like. In the 1990s, many of these same Baby Boomers began to save for retirement, creating an inflow of money into mutual funds and creating a surge in the mutual fund industry. Today, many Baby Boomers are retiring, creating a surge in retirement communities.

2-6e Social Forces

Social forces refer to the way in which changing social mores and values affect an industry. Like other macroenvironmental forces, social change creates opportunities and threats. One major social movement of recent decades has been the trend toward greater health consciousness. Its impact has been immense, and many companies that recognized the opportunities early on have reaped significant gains. Philip Morris, for example, capitalized on the growing health consciousness trend when it acquired Miller Brewing Company, and then redefined competition in the beer industry with its introduction of low-calorie beer (Miller Lite). Similarly, PepsiCo was able to gain market share from its rival, Coca-Cola, by being the first to introduce diet colas and fruit-based soft drinks. At the same time, the health trend has created a threat for many industries. The tobacco industry, for example, is in decline as a direct result of greater customer awareness of the health implications of smoking.

2-6f Political and Legal Forces

Political and legal forces are outcomes of changes in laws and regulations, and they significantly affect managers and companies. Political processes shape a society's laws, which constrain the operations of organizations and managers and thus create both opportunities and threats.[29] For example, throughout much of the industrialized world, there has been a strong trend toward deregulation of industries previously controlled by the state, and privatization of organizations once owned by the state. In the United States, deregulation in 1979 allowed 29 new airline companies to enter the industry between 1979 and 1993. The increase in passenger-carrying capacity after deregulation led to excess capacity on many routes, intense competition, and fare wars. To respond to this more competitive environment, airlines needed to look for ways to reduce operating costs. The development of hub-and-spoke systems, the rise of nonunion airlines, and the introduction of no-frills, discount service are all responses to increased competition in the airlines' task environment. Despite these innovations, the airline industry still experiences intense fare wars, which have lowered profits and caused numerous airline company bankruptcies. The global telecommunications service industry is now experiencing the same kind of turmoil following the deregulation of that industry in the United States and elsewhere.

Key Terms

opportunities 42	potential competitors 44	brand loyalty 45	switching costs 46
threats 42	barriers to entry 45	absolute cost	exit barriers 50
industry 42	economies of scale 45	advantage 45	

Takeaways for Strategic Managers

1. An industry is a group of companies offering products or services that are close substitutes for each other. Close substitutes are products or services that satisfy the same basic customer needs.
2. The main technique used to analyze competition in the industry environment is the competitive forces model.

The forces are: (1) the risk of new entry by potential competitors, (2) the extent of rivalry among established firms, (3) the bargaining power of buyers, (4) the bargaining power of suppliers, (5) the threat of substitute products, and (6) the power of complement providers. The stronger each force is, the more competitive the industry and the lower the rate of return that can be earned.

3. The risk of entry by potential competitors is a function of the height of barriers to entry. The higher the barriers to entry are, the lower the risk of entry and the greater the potential profits in the industry.

4. The extent of rivalry among established companies is a function of an industry's competitive structure, demand conditions, cost conditions, and barriers to exit. Strong demand conditions moderate the competition among established companies and create opportunities for expansion. When demand is weak, intensive competition can develop, particularly in consolidated industries with high exit barriers.

5. Buyers are most powerful when a company depends on them for business, but they are not dependent on the company. In such circumstances, buyers are a threat.

6. Suppliers are most powerful when a company depends on them for business but they are not dependent on the company. In such circumstances, suppliers are a threat.

7. Substitute products are the products of companies serving customer needs similar to the needs served by the industry being analyzed. When substitute products are very similar to one another, companies can charge a lower price without losing customers to the substitutes.

8. The power, vigor, and competence of complementors represent a sixth competitive force. Powerful, vigorous complementors may have a strong, positive impact on demand in an industry.

9. Most industries are composed of strategic groups of companies pursuing the same or a similar strategy. Companies in different strategic groups pursue different strategies.

10. The members of a company's strategic group constitute its immediate competitors. Because different strategic groups are characterized by different opportunities and threats, a company may improve its performance by switching strategic groups. The feasibility of doing so is a function of the height of mobility barriers.

11. Industries go through a well-defined life cycle: from an embryonic stage through growth, shakeout, and maturity, and eventually decline. Each stage has different implications for the competitive structure of the industry, and each gives rise to its own opportunities and threats.

12. The competitive forces, strategic group, and industry life-cycles models all have limitations. The competitive forces and strategic group models present a static picture of competition that de-emphasizes the role of innovation. Yet innovation can revolutionize industry structure and completely shift the strength of different competitive forces. The competitive forces and strategic group models have been criticized for de-emphasizing the importance of individual company differences. A company will not be profitable just because it is part of an attractive industry or strategic group; much more is required. The industry life-cycle model is a generalization that is not always followed, particularly when innovation revolutionizes an industry.

13. The macroenvironment affects the intensity of rivalry within an industry. Included in the macroenvironment are the macroeconomic environment, the global environment, the technological environment, the demographic and social environment, and the political and legal environment.

Discussion Questions

1. Under what environmental conditions are price wars most likely to occur in an industry? What are the implications of price wars for a company? How should a company try to deal with the threat of a price war?

2. Discuss the competitive forces model with reference to what you know about the U.S. market for streaming video on demand (see the Opening Case). What does the model tell you about the current nature and intensity of competition in this industry?

3. Identify a growth industry, a mature industry, and a declining industry. For each industry, identify the following: (a) the number and size distribution of companies, (b) the nature of barriers to entry, (c) the height of barriers to entry, and (d) the extent of product differentiation. What do these factors tell you about the nature of competition in each industry? What are the implications for the company in terms of opportunities and threats?

4. Birth rates have fallen below replacement rates across much of the developed world, including in Europe, North America, China, and Japan. If this does not turn around soon, by mid-century the population will be falling across much of the world outside of Africa (where birth rates remain high). What are the long-term implications of this trend for the nature of competition in established markets for consumer and industrial products? Illustrate your answer by analyzing the likely consequences of a falling population for competition in a market that you think might be significantly impacted by these shifting demographics.

Prior to 1978, the U.S. airline industry was tightly regulated in a way that made it difficult for new airlines to enter. Deregulation lowered the floodgates and allowed a swarm of new players to enter the industry, with 29 new airlines being established between 1978 and 1993. Among these new entrants was Southwest, which pioneered the low-cost business model in the industry. Other low-cost entrants included Jet Blue and Air Tran. The low-cost players offered a bare-bones service, without the expensive frills of traditional carriers (those frills included in-flight meals, ample business and first-class seating, and lounges in airports for premium travelers). The new entrants had lower labor costs due to a flexible, nonunion workforce—a crucially important factor in an industry where labor costs account for one-third of operating costs. They flew point to point (which customers preferred), rather than routing passengers through hubs and requiring them to change planes. They further lowered costs by standardizing their fleet around one model of aircraft (the Boeing 737 in the case of Southwest).

The incumbents responded to new entrants by trying to lower their own costs, not always successfully. Prices tumbled, load factors declined (load factor refers to the average percentage of seats occupied on a flight), and high profits prior to 1978 were replaced by ongoing price wars and periods of heavy financial losses. Between 1980 and 2016, the average price for a round-trip flight in the United States tumbled from $653 to $367 when adjusted for inflation. As prices fell between 2001 and 2009, U.S. airlines lost $65 billion in net income as they struggled to lower their costs and fill their planes.

The price wars were amped up by several factors. First, consumers increasingly came to see airline travel as a commodity product. The development of online price comparison sites in the 1990s, such as Expedia and Priceline, contributed to this trend. Second, Chapter 11 bankruptcy laws allowed bankrupt airlines to continue operating as they reorganized their capital structure. Among the big carriers, United, Delta, and America have all operated under bankruptcy for a time since 2001. By allowing bankrupt airlines to continue to fly, Chapter 11 regulations continue to keep unprofitable capacity in the industry, making it difficult for all airlines to get the load factors to cover their fixed costs. Third, adverse macroeconomic events, such as the 2001–2002 and 2008–2009 recessions, periodically exacerbated the excess capacity situation in the industry and intensified price competition.

However, after 40 years of transformation, the industry does seem to have achieved some degree of stability. Many of the smaller players have exited the industry. A wave of mergers between larger airlines has resulted in a more concentrated competitive structure. By 2021, four airlines—American, Delta, United, and Southwest—captured 75% of all traffic. Although prices remained low, until the COVID-19 pandemic hit in 2020, they were no longer falling. Moreover, under the protection of bankruptcy reorganization, the legacy airlines have made improvements in lowering their cost structure. The airlines have also been helped by a decline in fuel costs since 2010 and the introduction of more fuel-efficient aircraft (although fuel prices spiked again in 2022). As a result, the breakeven load factor had fallen to 71% by 2019 from 81% during the 2001–2010 period. Meanwhile, demand for airline travel continued to expand until the COVID-19 pandemic hit in 2020, and now seems to be rebounding strongly after two soft years. Between 1980 and 2016, the number of passengers flying in the United States increased from 400 million to 824 million. Higher demand and reduced competition have resulted in fuller aircraft. Load factors reached 84% in 2019, up from 70% in 2001. As a result, profitability returned to the industry. Between 2010 and 2019, U.S. airlines made $104 billion in net profit, making up for the losses of the 2001–2009 period.

Sources: Airlines for America, *Presentation: Industry Review and Outlook*, April 10, 2022, airlines.org; K. Huschelrath and K. Muller, "Low Cost Carriers and the Evolution of the U.S. Airline Industry," *ZEW Discussion Paper No 11–051*, 2017; J. Mouawad, "The Challenge of Starting an Airline," *New York Times*, May 25, 2012.

Unfortunately for the airlines, the COVID-19 pandemic hit the industry particularly hard. As demand slumped, load factors fell to 58.8% in 2020; prices came under pressure, falling by 18% from their 2019 level; and the industry lost an estimated $35 billion in 2020 alone. However, demand surged in early 2022 as the pandemic started to fade, suggesting that the industry might soon return to the good times.

Case Discussion Questions

1. Was the flood of new entrants into the airline industry that followed deregulation in 1978 good for customers? Was it good for the airlines?
2. Apart from government regulations, what are the other barriers to entry into the U.S. airline industry? How have these entry barriers changed over time? To what extent have these entry barriers been shaped by the strategy of the airlines themselves?
3. Why do you think it took the legacy airlines so long to adjust to the entry of low-cost carriers such as Southwest and Jet Blue?
4. What does this case tell you about the role of strategy in (a) changing the competitive structure of an industry and (b) enterprise success and failure?
5. What events trigger price wars in this industry? What is it about the structure of this industry that results in periods of intense price competition? What can the airlines do strategically to avoid future price wars?

Notes

[1] M. E. Porter, *Competitive Strategy* (New York: Free Press, 1980).

[2] J. E. Bain, *Barriers to New Competition* (Cambridge: Harvard University Press, 1956). For a review of the modern literature on barriers to entry, see R. J. Gilbert, "Mobility Barriers and the Value of Incumbency," in R. Schmalensee and R. D. Willig (eds.), *Handbook of Industrial Organization,* vol. 1 (Amsterdam: North-Holland, 1989). See also R. P. McAfee, H. M. Mialon, and M. A. Williams, "What Is a Barrier to Entry?"

American Economic Review 94 (May 2004): 461–468.

[3]R. Molla, "Closing the Books on Microsoft's Windows Phone," Recode, July 17, 2017.

[4]A detailed discussion of switching costs can be found in C. Shapiro and H. R. Varian, *Information Rules: A Strategic Guide to the Network Economy* (Boston: Harvard Business School Press, 1999).

[5]Most information on barriers to entry can be found in the industrial organization economics literature. See especially Bain, *Barriers to New Competition;* M. Mann, "Seller Concentration, Barriers to Entry and Rates of Return in 30 Industries," *Review of Economics and Statistics* 48 (1966): 296–307; W. S. Comanor and T. A. Wilson, "Advertising, Market Structure and Performance," *Review of Economics and Statistics* 49 (1967): 423–440; Gilbert, "Mobility Barriers"; K. Cool, L. H. Roller, and B. Leleux, "The Relative Impact of Actual and Potential Rivalry on Firm Profitability in the Pharmaceutical Industry," *Strategic Management Journal* 20 (1999): 1–14.

[6]For a discussion of tacit agreements, see T. C. Schelling, *The Strategy of Conflict* (Cambridge: Harvard University Press, 1960).

[7]M. Busse, "Firm Financial Condition and Airline Price Wars," *Rand Journal of Economics* 33 (2002): 298–318.

[8]For a review, see F. Karakaya, "Market Exit and Barriers to Exit: Theory and Practice," *Psychology and Marketing* 17 (2000): 651–668.

[9]P. Ghemawat, *Commitment: The Dynamics of Strategy* (Boston: Harvard Business School Press, 1991).

[10]A. S. Grove, *Only the Paranoid Survive* (New York: Doubleday, 1996).

[11]In standard microeconomic theory, the concept used for assessing the strength of substitutes and complements is the cross elasticity of demand.

[12]For details and further references, see Charles W. L. Hill, "Establishing a Standard: Competitive Strategy and Technology Standards in Winner Take All Industries," *Academy of Management Executive* 11 (1997): 7–25; Shapiro and Varian, *Information Rules.*

[13]The development of strategic group theory has been a strong theme in the strategy literature. Important contributions include R. E. Caves and M. E. Porter, "From Entry Barriers to Mobility Barriers," *Quarterly Journal of Economics* (May 1977): 241–262; K. R. Harrigan, "An Application of Clustering for Strategic Group Analysis," *Strategic Management Journal* 6 (1985): 55–73; K. J. Hatten and D. E. Schendel, "Heterogeneity Within an Industry: Firm Conduct in the U.S. Brewing Industry, 1952–71," *Journal of Industrial Economics* 26 (1977): 97–113; M. E. Porter, "The Structure Within Industries and Companies' Performance," *Review of Economics and Statistics* 61 (1979): 214–227. See also K. Cool and D. Schendel, "Performance Differences Among Strategic Group Members," *Strategic Management Journal* 9 (1988): 207–233; A. Nair and S. Kotha, "Does Group Membership Matter? Evidence from the Japanese Steel Industry," *Strategic Management Journal* 20 (2001): 221–235; G. McNamara, D. L. Deephouse, and R. A. Luce, "Competitive Positioning Within and Across a Strategic Group Structure," *Strategic Management Journal* 24 (2003): 161–180.

[14]For details on the strategic group structure in the pharmaceutical industry, see K. Cool and I. Dierickx, "Rivalry, Strategic Groups, and Firm Profitability," *Strategic Management Journal* 14 (1993): 47–59.

[15]C. W. Hofer argued that life-cycle considerations may be the most important contingency when formulating business strategy. See Hofer, "Towards a Contingency Theory of Business Strategy," *Academy of Management Journal* 18 (1975): 784–810. For empirical evidence to support this view, see C. R. Anderson and C. P. Zeithaml, "Stages of the Product Life Cycle, Business Strategy, and Business Performance," *Academy of Management Journal* 27 (1984): 5–24; D. C. Hambrick and D. Lei, "Towards an Empirical Prioritization of Contingency Variables for Business Strategy," *Academy of Management Journal* 28 (1985): 763–788. See also G. Miles, C. C. Snow, and M. P. Sharfman, "Industry Variety and Performance," *Strategic Management Journal* 14 (1993): 163–177; G. K. Deans, F. Kroeger, and S. Zeisel, "The Consolidation Curve," *Harvard Business Review* 80 (December 2002): 2–3.

[16]The characteristics of declining industries have been summarized by K. R. Harrigan, "Strategy Formulation in Declining Industries," *Academy of Management Review* 5 (1980): 599–604. See also J. Anand and H. Singh, "Asset Redeployment, Acquisitions and Corporate Strategy in Declining Industries," *Strategic Management Journal* 18 (1997): 99–118.

[17]This perspective is associated with the Austrian school of economics, which goes back to Schumpeter. For a summary of this school and its implications for strategy, see R. Jacobson, "The Austrian School of Strategy," *Academy of Management Review* 17 (1992): 782–807; C. W. L. Hill and D. Deeds, "The Importance of Industry Structure for the Determination of Industry Profitability: A Neo-Austrian Approach," *Journal of Management Studies* 33 (1996): 429–451. R. R. Nelson, G. Dosi, C. E. Helfat, et al, *Modern Evolutionary Economics:*

An Overview (Cambridge: Cambridge University Press, 2018).

[18] N. Tolomeo, M. Fitzgerald, and J. Eckelman, "US Steel Sector Thrives as Mills Move up the Quality Ladder," *S&P Global Commodity Insights*, May 9, 2019.

[19] D. F. Barnett and R. W. Crandall, *Up from the Ashes* (Washington, D.C.: Brookings Institution, 1986); N. Tolomeo, M. Fitzgerald, and J. Eckelman, "US Steel Sector Thrives as Mills Move up the Quality Ladder," *S&P Global Commodity Insights*, May 9, 2019.

[20] M. E. Porter, *The Competitive Advantage of Nations* (New York: Free Press, 1990).

[21] The term *punctuated equilibrium* is borrowed from evolutionary biology. For a detailed explanation of the concept, see M. L. Tushman, W. H. Newman, and E. Romanelli, "Convergence and Upheaval: Managing the Unsteady Pace of Organizational Evolution," *California Management Review* 29:1 (1985): 29–44; C. J. G. Gersick, "Revolutionary Change Theories: A Multilevel Exploration of the Punctuated Equilibrium Paradigm," *Academy of Management Review* 16 (1991): 10–36; R. Adner and D. A. Levinthal, "The Emergence of Emerging Technologies," *California Management Review* 45 (Fall 2002): 50–65.

[22] A. J. Slywotzky, *Value Migration: How to Think Several Moves Ahead of the Competition* (Boston: Harvard Business School Press, 1996).

[23] Hill and Deeds, "Importance of Industry Structure."

[24] R. P. Rumelt, "How Much Does Industry Matter?" *Strategic Management Journal* 12 (1991): 167–185. See also A. J. Mauri and M. P. Michaels, "Firm and Industry Effects Within Strategic Management: An Empirical Examination," *Strategic Management Journal* 19 (1998): 211–219.

[25] R. Schmalensee, "Inter-Industry Studies of Structure and Performance," in Schmalensee and Willig (eds.), *Handbook of Industrial Organization*. Similar results were found by A. N. McGahan and M. E. Porter, "How Much Does Industry Matter, Really?," *Strategic Management Journal* 18 (1997): 15–30.

[26] For example, see K. Cool and D. Schendel, "Strategic Group Formation and Performance: The Case of the U.S. Pharmaceutical Industry, 1932–1992," *Management Science* (September 1987): 1102–1124.

[27] See M. Gort and J. Klepper, "Time Paths in the Diffusion of Product Innovations," *Economic Journal* (September 1982): 630–653. Looking at the history of 46 products, Gort and Klepper found that the length of time before other companies entered the markets created by a few inventive companies declined from an average of 14.4 years for products introduced before 1930 to 4.9 years for those introduced after 1949. For more recent research on this issue, see A. Singh, G. Triulzi and C. L. Magee, "Technological Improvement Rate Predictions for All Technologies," *Research Policy*, 50 (2021): 9.

[28] The phrase was originally coined by J. Schumpeter, *Capitalism, Socialism and Democracy* (London: Macmillan, 1950), p. 68.

[29] For a detailed discussion of the importance of the structure of law as a factor explaining economic change and growth, see D. C. North, *Institutions, Institutional Change, and Economic Performance* (Cambridge: Cambridge University Press, 1990).

Internal Analysis: Resources and Competitive Advantage

Opening Case

Competitive Advantage at IKEA

IKEA, the privately held furniture retailer, is a global colossus. The world's largest furniture retailer, in 2022, IKEA had 420 stores in 50 countries around the globe, 225,000 employees, and revenues of €42 billion. The company started out with a single store in Sweden in 1958. The vision of the company's founder, Ingvar Kamprad, was to "democratize furniture," making stylish, functional furniture available at a low cost.

Kamprad's vision was a reaction to the existing market for furniture. Furniture was either seen as an expensive heirloom, which typically had to be ordered from the manufacturer after the consumer had made a purchase decision in a retail store, and might take 3 months to deliver, or was poorly designed, low-quality, cheap furniture sold in discount stores. As IKEA's strategy evolved, its core target market became young professionals looking to furnish their first apartments or homes with stylish but inexpensive furniture that could be disposed of when they were able to buy more traditional, heirloom-style furniture.

Over the years, Kamprad assembled a world-class team that designed stylish, quality furniture that emphasized clean, "Swedish" lines. An important goal was to make IKEA offerings 30% cheaper than comparable items produced by rivals. To drive down costs, Kamprad and his associates worked out ways to reduce the costs of making and delivering this furniture. They cooperated closely with long-term suppliers to drive down material and manufacturing costs. They designed furniture that could be flat packed, which reduced transportation and storage costs. They pushed assembly onto the consumer but gave them lower prices as part of the bargain. They even made the consumer responsible for pulling inventory out of the warehouse, which was typically placed between the product-display areas and the cash registers. As a result of these actions, all taken at the functional level within the company, IKEA was able to offer more value to its target customers

Source: C. W. L. Hill, "IKEA in 2013: Furniture Retailer to the World," in C.W. L. Hill, G. R. Jones, and M. Shilling, *Strategic Management*, 11th ed. (Boston: Cengage, 2015).

Tooykrub/Shutterstock.com

than rivals, and to do so at a lower cost. Through astute market segmentation and a well-thought-out strategy, IKEA redefined the furniture market not just in Sweden but in countries around the globe; in the process becoming the world's largest furniture retailer and making Ingvar Kamprad one of the world's richest people.

Overview

Why, within a particular industry or market, do some companies outperform others? What is the basis of their sustained competitive advantage? The Opening Case provides some clues. For decades, IKEA has outperformed rivals in the business of selling furniture and household accessories. IKEA has been able to do this because it is *responsive to the needs of its core customers*, upwardly mobile young professionals who desired stylishly designed but inexpensive furniture. Moreover, IKEA is extremely *efficient* in the way in which it designs, manufactures, and sells furniture and other products, thereby lowering both costs and prices. As you will see in this chapter, responding to customer needs by offering them more *value* and doing so efficiently, are common themes seen in many enterprises that have established a sustainable competitive advantage over their rivals.

This chapter focuses on internal analysis, which is concerned with identifying the strengths and weaknesses of a company. At IKEA, for example, product design, manufacturing capabilities, and logistics are all significant strengths. Internal analysis, coupled with an analysis of the company's external environment, gives managers the information they need to choose the strategy that will enable their company to attain a sustained competitive advantage.

As explained in this chapter, internal analysis is a three-step process. First, managers must understand the role of rare, valuable, and hard-to-imitate resources in the establishment of competitive advantage. Second, they must appreciate how such resources lead to superior efficiency, innovation, quality, and customer responsiveness. Third, they must be able to analyze the sources of their company's competitive advantage to identify what drives the profitability of their enterprise and, just as importantly, where opportunities for improvement might lie. In other words, they must be able to identify how the strengths of the enterprise boost its profitability, how its weaknesses result in lower profitability, and what steps can be taken to build upon and protect strengths and fix weaknesses.

After reading this chapter, you will understand the nature of competitive advantage and why managers need to perform internal analysis (just as they must conduct industry analysis) to achieve superior performance and profitability.

3.1 Discuss the source of competitive advantage.

3-1 Competitive Advantage

A company has a *competitive advantage* over its rivals when its profitability is greater than the average profitability of all companies in its industry. It has a *sustained competitive advantage* when it is able to maintain above-average profitability over a number of years (as IKEA appears to have done). The primary objective of strategy is to achieve a sustained competitive advantage, which in turn results in superior profitability and profit growth. What are the sources of competitive advantage, and what is the link between strategy, competitive advantage, and profitability?

3-1a Distinctive Competencies

distinctive competencies

Firm-specific strengths that allow a company to differentiate its products and/or achieve substantially lower costs to achieve a competitive advantage.

It has long been argued that competitive advantage is based upon the possession of distinctive competencies. **Distinctive competencies** are firm-specific strengths that allow a company to differentiate its products from those offered by rivals and/or achieve substantially lower costs than its rivals. Apple, for example, has a distinctive competence in design. Customers want to own the devices that Apple markets. Similarly, it can be argued that Toyota, which historically has been the standout performer in the automobile industry, has distinctive competencies in the development and operation of manufacturing processes. Toyota pioneered an entire range of manufacturing techniques such as just-in-time inventory systems, self-managing teams, and reduced setup times for complex equipment. These competencies, collectively known as the "Toyota lean production system," helped the company attain superior efficiency and product quality as the basis of its competitive advantage in the global automobile industry.[1]

3-1b Resources

Distinctive competencies also can be rooted in one or more of a company's resources.[2] **Resources** refer to the factors of production that a company uses to transform inputs into outputs that it can sell in the marketplace. Resources include basic factors of production such as labor, land, management, physical plant, and equipment.

However, any enterprise is more than just a combination of the basic factors of production. Another important factor of production is **process knowledge** about how to develop, produce, and sell a company's output. Also often referred to as **capabilities**, process knowledge can be thought of as the organizational equivalent of human skills. Process knowledge resides in the rules, routines, and procedures of an organization; that is, in the style or way managers make decisions and utilize the company's internal processes to achieve organizational objectives.[3] Process knowledge is accumulated by the organization over time and through experience. Organizations, like people, learn by doing, often through trial and error. Process knowledge is often **socially complex**, which means that it is diffused among many different individuals, teams, departments, and functions within the company, not one of which possesses all the knowledge required to develop, produce, and sell its products. Process knowledge also often has an important **tacit** component, meaning that some of it is not documented or codified, but instead is learned by doing and is transmitted to new employees through the culture of the organization.[4]

The organizational architecture of a company is another very important factor of production. By **organizational architecture** we mean the combination of the organizational structure of a company, its control systems, its incentive systems, its organizational culture, and the human capital strategy of the enterprise, particularly regarding its hiring and employee development and retention strategies. We will explore the concept of organizational architecture in depth in Chapter 12. For now, it is important to understand that companies with well-designed organizational architecture generally outperform those with poorly designed organizational architecture. Getting the organizational structure, control systems, incentives, culture, and human capital strategy of a company right is extremely important. Differences in the efficacy of organizational architecture are a major reason for performance differentials across companies.

The codified **intellectual property** that a company has created over time represents another important factor of production. Intellectual property takes many forms, such as engineering blueprints, the molecular structure of a new drug, proprietary software code, and brand logos. Companies establish ownership rights over their intellectual property through patents, copyrights, and trademarks. For example, Apple has built a powerful brand based on its reputation for high-quality, elegantly designed computing devices. The Apple logo displayed on its hardware products symbolizes that brand. That logo is Apple's intellectual property. It assures the consumer that this is a genuine Apple product. It is protected from imitation by trademark law.

In sum, a company's resources include not just *basic* factors of production such as land, labor, managers, property, and equipment. They also include more *advanced* factors of production such as process knowledge (capabilities), organizational architecture, and intellectual property. For example, Coca-Cola has been very successful over a prolonged period in the carbonated beverage business. Coca-Cola's factors of production include not just labor, land, management, plants, and equipment, but also the *process knowledge* about how to develop, produce, and sell carbonated beverages. Coca-Cola is, in fact, a very strong marketing company—it really knows how to sell its

resources
Assets of a company.

process knowledge
Knowledge of the internal rules, routines, and procedures of an organization that managers can leverage to achieve organizational objectives.

capabilities
Another term for "process knowledge."

socially complex
Something that is characterized by, or is the outcome of, the interaction of multiple individuals.

tacit
A characteristic of knowledge or skills such that they cannot be documented or codified but may be understood through experience or intuition.

organizational architecture
The combination of the organizational structure of a company, its control systems, its incentive systems, its organizational culture, and its human-capital strategy.

intellectual property
Knowledge, research, and information that is owned by an individual or organization.

product. Furthermore, Coca-Cola has an *organizational architecture* that enables it to manage its functional processes well. Coca-Cola also has valuable *intellectual property* such as the recipes for its leading beverages (which Coca-Cola keeps secret) and its brand, which is protected from imitation by trademark law.

Similarly, Apple is more than just a combination of land, labor, management, plants, and equipment. Apple has world-class *process knowledge* when it comes to developing, producing, and selling its products. Most notably, Apple probably has the best industrial-design group in the computer business. This design group is ultimately responsible for the format, features, look, and feel of Apple's innovative products, including the iPod, iPhone, and iPad, and its striking line of desktop and laptop computers. Apple also has a strong *organizational architecture* that enables it to manage the enterprise productively. In particular, the industrial-design group has a very powerful position within Apple's organizational structure. It initiates and coordinates the core product development processes. This includes ensuring that hardware engineering, software engineering, and manufacturing all work to achieve the product specifications mapped out by the design group. Apple is probably unique among computing-device companies in terms of the power and influence granted to its design group. Furthermore, Apple has created extremely valuable *intellectual property*, including the patents underlying its products and the trademark that protects the logo symbolizing the Apple brand.

Thus, as in the Coca-Cola and Apple examples, the resources (or factors of production) of any enterprise include not just **basic factors of production** but also **advanced factors of production**. The important point to understand is that advanced factors of production are not endowments; they are human creations. Skilled managers can and do create these advanced factors of production, often out of little more than thin air, vision, and drive. Apple founder and longtime CEO Steve Jobs, in combination with his handpicked head of industrial design, Jonny Ive, created the process knowledge that underlies Apple's world-class skills in industrial design, and he built an organizational structure that gave the design group a powerful central role.

To summarize, an expanded list of resources includes labor, land, management, plants, equipment, process knowledge, organizational architecture, and intellectual property. As shown in Figure 3.1, a company is in effect a bundle of resources (factors

basic factors of production

Resources such as land, labor, management, plant, and equipment.

advanced factors of production

Resources such as process knowledge, organizational architecture, and intellectual property that contribute to a company's competitive advantage.

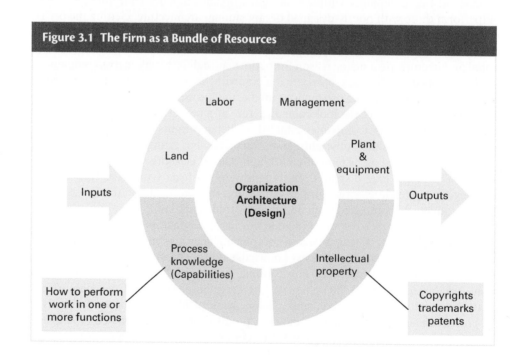

Figure 3.1 The Firm as a Bundle of Resources

of production) that transforms inputs (e.g., raw materials) into outputs (goods or services). The efficiency and effectiveness with which a company performs this transformation process depends critically upon the *quality* of its resources, and most significantly, upon the quality of its advanced factors of production—process knowledge, organizational architecture, and intellectual property. This insight gives rise to other, very important questions. What determines the quality of a company's resources? How do we know if its resources constitute a strength or a weakness?

3-2 Resource Quality: The VRIO Framework

Jay Barney and Bill Hesterly have developed a framework that represents a useful way for managers to think about the quality of resources.[5] They refer to this framework as the **VRIO framework**, where *V* stands for value, *R* for rarity, *I* for inimitability, and *O* for organization. They encourage managers to ask themselves the following questions when performing an internal analysis.

First, are the company's resources *valuable* in the sense that they enable the enterprise to exploit opportunities and counter threats in the external environment? For example, Apple's product-design skills constitute a valuable resource that has helped the company exploit opportunities to develop new product categories in the computer-device industry with its touchscreen iPhone and iPad offerings. At the same time, those skills have also enabled Apple to keep rivals at bay, thereby countering threats. More generally, resources can be judged as valuable if they (a) enable a company to create strong demand for its products and/or (b) lower the costs of producing those products.

Second, are those resources *rare*? If they are not rare and rivals also have access to them, they cannot be a source of competitive advantage. For a company to gain a competitive advantage, it must have a resource that is superior to that possessed by its rivals. It cannot be a commodity; it must be uncommon. Thus, the process knowledge that underlies Apple's design skills is rare; no other enterprise in its industry has a similar high-quality skill set.

Third, are the valuable and rare resources of the company *inimitable*? Put differently, are they easy or hard to copy? If they are easy to copy, rivals will quickly do so, and the company's competitive advantage will erode. However, if those resources are hard to copy—if they are inimitable–the company's competitive advantage is more likely to be sustainable. Apple's design skills appear to be difficult to imitate.

Fourth, is the company *organized* and managed in a way that enables it to exploit its rare, valuable, and inimitable resources and capture the value they produce? In other words, does the firm have the broader *organizational architecture* required to make the most out of its unique strengths? Apple has been successful not just because of its design skills, but because those skills reside within an organization that is well managed and has the capability to take superbly designed products, produce them efficiently, and market and distribute them to customers. Without the correct organization and management systems, even firms with valuable, rare, inimitable resources will be at a competitive disadvantage. As noted previously, we return to the question of organizing in Chapter 12.

3-2a Resources and Sustained Competitive Advantage

This discussion leads logically to another very important question: Which valuable resources are most likely to result in a long-term, *sustainable* competitive advantage? The quick answer is process knowledge, organizational architecture, and intellectual property. As we shall explain, these resources or advanced factors of production are more likely to be rare and are, in general, more difficult for rivals to imitate.

3.2 Utilize the VRIO model to assess the quality of resources.

VRIO framework

A framework managers use to determine the quality of a company's resources, where *V* is value, *R* is rarity, *I* is inimitability, and *O* is for organization.

Rare Resources   Consider the issue of rareness or scarcity with regard to basic factors of production. In general, land, labor, management, plants, and equipment are purchased on the open market. Of course, these resources are not homogenous; some employees are more productive than others, some land has more value, and some managers have better skills. Over time, however, this becomes evident, and the more productive resources will command a higher price for their services. You simply must pay more for the best land, employees, managers, and equipment. Indeed, in a free market, the price of such resources will be bid up to reflect their economic value, and the sellers of those resources, as opposed to the firm, will capture much of that value.

Now consider process knowledge and organizational architecture. These are likely to be heterogeneous. No two companies are the same. Each has its own history, which impacts the way activities are organized and processes managed within the enterprise. The way in which product development is managed at Apple, for example, differs from the way it is managed at Microsoft or Samsung. Marketing at Coca-Cola might differ in subtle but important ways from marketing at PepsiCo. The human resource function at Nucor Steel might be organized in such a way that it raises employee productivity above the level achieved by U.S. Steel. Each organization has its own culture; its own way of doing certain things. As a result of strategic vision, systematic process-improvement efforts, trial and error, or just blind luck, some companies will develop process knowledge and organizational architecture that is of higher quality than that of their rivals. Such resources will be rare, since they are a *path-dependent* consequence of the history of the company. Moreover, the firm "owns" its process knowledge and organizational architecture. It does not buy these from a provider, so it is able to capture the full economic value of these resources.

Intellectual property that is protected by patents, copyrights, or trademarks is also by definition rare. You can only patent something that no one else has patented. A copyright protects the *unique* creation of an individual, or a company, and prevents anyone from copying it. The software code underlying Microsoft Windows, for example, is copyrighted, so no one else can use the same code without express permission from Microsoft. Similarly, a trademark protects the *unique* symbols, names, or logos of a company, preventing them from being copied and in effect making them rare. Rivals cannot use the Apple logo; it is Apple's unique property—thus it is rare.

Barriers to Imitation   Now let us consider the issue of inimitability. If a company develops a rare, valuable resource that enables it to create more demand, charge a higher price, and/or lower its costs, how easy will it be for rivals to copy that resource? Put differently, what are the **barriers to imitation?**[6]

Consider first intellectual property. The ability of rivals to copy a firm's intellectual property depends foremost upon the efficacy of the intellectual property regime in a nation-state. In advanced nations such as the United States or the member states of the European Union, for example, where there is a well-established body of intellectual property law, direct imitation is outlawed, and violators are likely to be sued for damages. This legal protection prevents most enterprises from engaging in direct copying of intellectual property. However, in developing nations with no well-established body of intellectual property law, copying may be widespread given the absence of legal sanctions. This used to be the case in China, for example, but it is becoming less common as the Chinese legal system adopts international norms regarding patents, copyrights, and trademarks.

Even though direct copying is outlawed, it is certainly possible for companies to invent a way around their rivals' intellectual property through reverse engineering, producing a functionally similar piece of technology that works in a slightly different way to produce the same result. This seems to be a particular problem with patented knowledge. Patents accord the inventor 20 years of legal protection from direct

barriers to imitation

Factors or characteristics that make it difficult for another individual or company to replicate something.

imitation, but research suggests that rivals invent their way around 60% of patent innovations within 4 years.[7] On the other hand, trademarks are initially protected from imitation for 10 years but can be renewed every 10 years. Moreover, it is almost impossible for a rival to copy a company's trademark protected logo and brand name without violating the law. This is important because logos and brand names are powerful symbols. As such, trademarks can insulate a company's brand from direct attack by rivals, which builds something of an economic moat around companies with strong brands.

A company's rare and valuable process knowledge can be very hard for rivals to copy; the barriers to imitation are high. There are two main reasons for this. First, process knowledge is often (1) partly tacit, (2) hidden from view within the firm, and (3) socially complex. As such, it is difficult for outsiders to identify with precision the nature of a company's rare and valuable process knowledge. We refer to this problem as **causal ambiguity**.[8] Moreover, the socially complex nature of such knowledge means that hiring individual employees away from a successful firm to gain access to its process knowledge may be futile, because each individual only has direct experience with part of the overall knowledge base.

causal ambiguity
When the way that one thing, A, leads to an outcome (or "causes"), B, is not clearly understood.

Second, even if a rival were able to identify with precision the form of a company's valuable and rare process knowledge, it still has to implement that knowledge within its own organization. This is not easy to do; it requires changing the way the imitating company currently operates. Such change can be stymied by organizational inertia. We discuss organizational inertia in more detail in Chapter 12, but for now note that organizational structure, routines, and culture are notoriously hard to change. The reasons include opposition from organizational members whose power and influence will be reduced as a result of the change, and the difficulties associated with changing the culture of an organization, particularly old habits, old ways of doing things, and old ways of perceiving the world. Typically, process change takes a sustained effort over several years, during which time the company that is the target of the imitation efforts may have accumulated new knowledge and moved on.

An inability to imitate valuable process knowledge seems to have been a problem in the U.S. automobile industry, where attempts by Ford and GM to imitate Toyota's lean production systems were held back for years, if not decades, by their own internal inertia. These included objections from unions to proposals to change work practices, the legacy of decades of investment in factories configured to mass production rather than lean production, and an organizational culture that resisted change that altered the balance of power and influence within the company.

Organizational architecture that is rare and valuable can also be very hard for rivals to imitate, for many of the same reasons that process knowledge is hard to imitate. Specifically, even if the would-be imitator can identify with precision the features of a successful company's value-creating organizational architecture, adopting that architecture might require wholesale organizational change, which is both risky and difficult to do given internal inertia.

Implications In sum, we have demonstrated how *advanced* factors of production such as intellectual property, process knowledge, and organizational architecture are more likely to be rare, and will be harder to imitate due to high barriers to imitation, than more basic factors of production. Put differently, advanced factors of production are more likely to constitute the unique strengths of an organization. Several implications flow from this insight.

First, it is clearly important for managers to vigorously protect their intellectual property from imitation both by establishing their intellectual property rights (e.g., by filing for patent, copyright or trademark protection), and by asserting those rights, legally challenging rivals who try to violate them. This said, it is sometimes best not to patent valuable technology but instead keep it as a trade secret, because that can make imitation more difficult. Coca-Cola, for example, has never patented the recipe underlying its core Coke brand, because filing a patent would reveal valuable information about the recipe.

Second, given that process knowledge is often an important source of sustainable competitive advantage, managers would be well advised to devote considerable attention to optimizing their processes. They might, for example, invest time and effort in process improvement methodologies such as Six Sigma (which we shall discuss in Chapter 5). Similarly, given the importance of organizational architecture, it is crucial for managers to assure that their company's organization is optimal. Thinking critically and proactively about organizational design becomes a very important task (as we discuss in Chapter 12).

Third, it is important to protect knowledge about superior processes and practices from leaking out. For example, Intel, long a very efficient manufacturer of microprocessors, has developed valuable technology to improve its manufacturing processes but has chosen not to patent it. Instead, it treats the underlying knowledge as a trade secret. Intel's reasoning is that if the technology were patented, the patent filing would make available crucial information about the technology, making imitation by rivals more likely.

Fourth, if a company has developed rare and valuable process knowledge in core functional activities of the firm, it would be unwise for the firm to outsource those activities to a third-party producer in pursuit of a perceived short-term cost saving or other transitory benefit. Some observers believed that Boeing made this mistake when it decided to outsource production of horizontal stabilizers for its 737 aircraft to Chinese subcontractors. Horizontal stabilizers are the horizontal winglets on the tail section of an aircraft. Historically, Boeing designed and built these, and consequently it accumulated rare and valuable design and manufacturing process knowledge. In the late 1990s, Boeing outsourced production of horizontal stabilizers in exchange for the tacit promise of more orders from Chinese airlines. Although this benefited Boeing in the short run, it gave Chinese manufacturers the chance to develop their own process knowledge, while Boeing stopped accumulating important process knowledge. Today, Chinese aircraft manufacturers are building a competitor to Boeing's 737 aircraft, and Boeing may well have helped them do that through outsourcing decisions that diminished the company's long-run competitive advantage.

3-3 Value Creation and Profitability

3.3 Understand the link between competitive advantage and profitability.

We have discussed how competitive advantage based upon valuable, rare, inimitable resources that reside within a well-organized, well-managed firm constitute unique strengths that lead to a sustained competitive advantage. In this section, we take a deeper look at how such resources (strengths) translate into superior profitability.

At the most basic level, a company's profitability depends on three factors: (1) the value customers place on the company's products, (2) the price that a company charges for its products, and (3) the costs of creating those products. The value customers place on a product reflects the *utility* they derive from it, or the happiness or satisfaction gained from consuming or owning it. Value must be distinguished from price. Value is something that customers receive from a product. It is a function of the attributes of the product such as its performance, design, quality, and point-of-sale and after-sale service. For example, most customers would place a much higher value on a top-end BMW than on a low-end, basic economy car from Kia, precisely because they perceive BMW to have better performance and superior design, quality, and service. A company that strengthens the value of its products in the eyes of customers enhances its brand and has more pricing options: It can raise prices to reflect that value or keep prices lower to induce more customers to purchase its products, thereby expanding unit sales volume.

Regardless of the pricing option a company chooses, that price is typically less than the value placed upon the good or service by the customer. This is because the customer captures some of that value in the form of what economists call a *consumer surplus.*

This occurs because it is normally impossible to segment the market to such a degree that the company can charge each customer a price that reflects that individual's unique assessment of the value of a product—what economists refer to as a customer's *reservation price.* In addition, because the company is competing against rivals for customers, it must charge a lower price than it could were it a monopoly. For these reasons, the point-of-sale price tends to be less than the value placed on the product by many customers. Nevertheless, remember this basic principle: The more value that consumers derive from a company's goods or services, the more pricing options that company has.

These concepts are illustrated in Figure 3.2. V is the *average* value per unit of a product to a customer, P is the average price per unit that the company decides to charge for that product, and C is the average unit cost of producing that product (including actual production costs and the cost of capital investments in production systems). The company's average profit per unit is equal to $P - C$, and the consumer surplus is equal to $V - P$. In other words, $V - P$ is a measure of the value the consumer captures, and $P - C$ is a measure of the value the company captures. The company makes a profit so long as P is more than C, and its profitability will be greater the lower C is relative to P. Bear in mind that the difference between V and P is in part determined by the intensity of competitive pressure in the marketplace; the lower the competitive pressure's intensity, the higher the price that can be charged relative to V, but the difference between V and P is also determined by the company's pricing choice.[9]

As we shall see, a company may choose to keep prices low relative to volume because lower prices enable the company to sell more products, attain scale economies, and boost its profit margin by lowering C relative to P.

Also, note that the *value created by a company* is measured by the difference between the value or utility a consumer gets from the product (V) and the costs of production (C); that is, $V - C$. A company creates value by converting inputs that cost C into a good or service from which customers derive a value of V. A company can create more value for its customers by lowering C or making the product more attractive through superior design, performance, quality, service, and other factors. When customers assign a greater value to the product (V increases), they are willing to pay a higher price (P increases). This discussion suggests that a company has a competitive advantage and high profitability when it creates more value for its customers than rivals.[10]

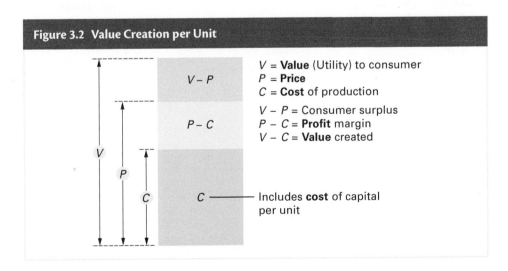

Figure 3.2 Value Creation per Unit

$V - P$

$P - C$

C

V

P

C

V = **Value** (Utility) to consumer
P = **Price**
C = **Cost** of production

$V - P$ = Consumer surplus
$P - C$ = **Profit** margin
$V - C$ = **Value** created

C —— Includes **cost** of capital per unit

The company's pricing options are captured in Figure 3.3. Suppose a company's current pricing option is the one pictured in the middle column of Figure 3.3. Imagine that the company decides to pursue strategies to increase the utility of its product offering from V to V^* in order to boost its profitability. Increasing value initially raises production costs because the company must spend money in order to increase product performance, quality, service, and other factors. Now there are two different pricing options that the company can pursue. Option 1 is to raise prices to reflect the higher value: the company raises prices more than its costs increase, and profit per unit $(P - C)$ increases. Option 2 involves a very different set of choices: The company lowers prices in order to expand unit volume. Generally, customers recognize that they are getting a great bargain because the price is now much lower than the value (the consumer surplus has increased), so they rush out to buy more (demand increases). As unit volume expands due to increased demand, the company is able to realize scale economies and reduce its average unit costs. Although creating the extra value initially costs more, and although margins are initially compressed by aggressive pricing, ultimately profit margins widen because the average per-unit cost of production falls as volume increases and scale economies are attained.

Managers must understand the dynamic relationships among value, pricing, demand, and costs in order to make decisions that will maximize competitive advantage and profitability. Option 2 in Figure 3.3, for example, may not be a viable strategy if demand did not increase rapidly with lower prices, or if few economies of scale will result by increasing volume. Managers must understand how value creation and pricing decisions affect demand, as well as how unit costs change with increases in volume. In other words, they must clearly comprehend the demand for their company's product and its cost structure at different levels of output if they are to make decisions that maximize profitability.

The most beneficial position for a company occurs when it can utilize its valuable, rare, inimitable resources and capabilities to deliver a product offering that consumers value more highly than that of rivals (that is, they derive more utility from it), and which can be produced at a lower cost than that of rivals. This is an outcome that many companies strive to achieve. Consider again the example of Apple and its

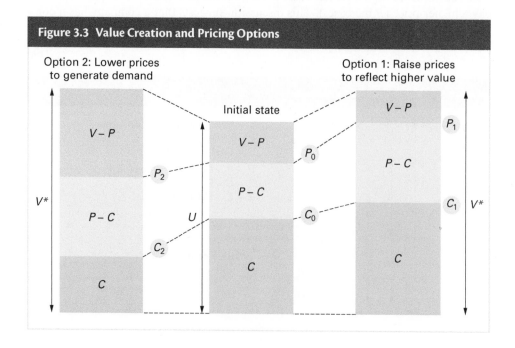

Figure 3.3 Value Creation and Pricing Options

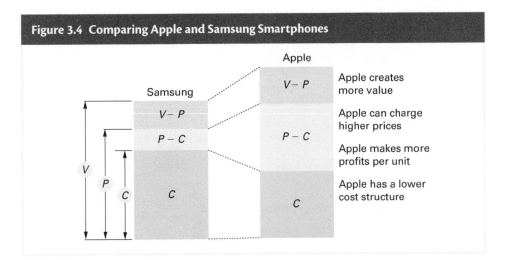

Figure 3.4 Comparing Apple and Samsung Smartphones

Apple

Samsung

$V - P$ Apple creates more value

$V - P$

$P - C$ Apple can charge higher prices

$P - C$

Apple makes more profits per unit

C

C Apple has a lower cost structure

successful iPhone offering (see Figure 3.4). Apple creates value for consumers with the elegance of its design for the iPhone, its intuitive, easy-to-use interface, its onboard applications (apps) such as iTunes and iCloud, and the fact that Apple has encouraged a healthy ecosystem of developers to write third-party applications that run on the phone. Apple has been so successful at differentiating its product along these dimensions that it is able to charge a premium price for its iPhone relative to offerings from Samsung, HTC, and the like. At the same time, it sells so many iPhones that the company has been able to achieve enormous economies of scale in production and the purchasing of components, which have driven down the average unit cost of the iPhone. Thus, even though the iPhone makes use of expensive materials such as brushed aluminum casing and a gorilla-glass screen, Apple has been able to charge a higher price *and* has lower costs than its rivals. Hence, although Samsung sold more units than Apple in 2021, Apple was able to capture 75% of all profit and 40% of revenues in the global smartphone industry for that year, even though it accounted for only 13% of global handset shipments!

3-4 The Value Chain

All functions of a company—production, marketing, product development, service, information systems, materials management, and human resources—have a role in lowering the cost structure and increasing the perceived value of products through differentiation. To explore this idea, consider the concept of the value chain illustrated in Figure 3.5.[11] The term **value chain** refers to the idea that a company is a chain of functional activities that transforms inputs into outputs. The transformation process involves both primary activities and support activities. Value is added to the product at each stage in the chain. *Valuable, rare, inimitable resources can be found within one or more of a company's value-chain activities.*

3-4a Primary Activities

Primary activities include the design, creation, and delivery of the product, the product's marketing, and its support and after-sales service. In the value chain illustrated in Figure 3.5, the primary activities are broken down into four functions: research and development, production, marketing and sales, and customer service.

3.4 Explain the concept of the value chain.

value chain

The concept that a company consists of a chain of activities that transforms inputs into outputs.

primary activities

Activities related to the design, creation, and delivery of the product, its marketing, and its support and after-sales service.

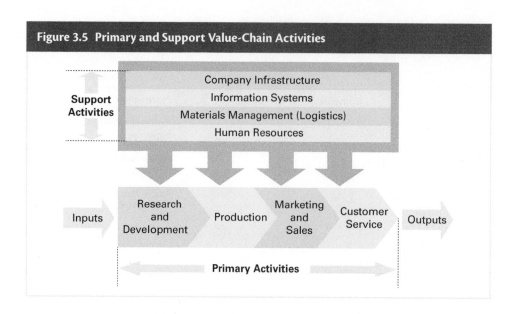

Figure 3.5 Primary and Support Value-Chain Activities

Research and Development Research and development (R&D) refers to the design of products and production processes. We may think of R&D as being associated with the design of physical products, such as an iPhone or a Toyota, and/or the production processes in manufacturing enterprises; however, service companies also undertake R&D. For example, banks compete by developing new financial products and new ways of delivering those products to customers. Online banking and smart debit cards are examples of the fruits of new-product development in the banking industry. Earlier innovations in the banking industry include ATM machines, credit cards, and debit cards.

By creating superior product design, R&D can increase the functionality of products, making them more attractive to customers and thereby adding value. Alternatively, R&D may result in more efficient production processes, thereby lowering production costs. Either way, R&D can lower costs or raise a product's value, thus permitting a company to charge higher prices. At semiconductor companies such as Intel and Taiwan Semiconductor Manufacturing Company, R&D creates value by developing ever-more powerful microprocessors and pioneering ever-more efficient manufacturing processes (in conjunction with equipment suppliers).

It is important to emphasize that R&D is not just about enhancing the features and functions of a product; it is also about the elegance of product design, which can create an impression of superior value in the minds of consumers. Apple's success with the iPhone is based upon the elegance and appeal of the iPhone design, which has turned an electronic device into a fashion accessory. For another example of how design elegance can create value, see Strategy in Action 3.1, which discusses value creation at the fashion house Burberry.

Production Production refers to the creation of a good or service. For tangible products, this generally means manufacturing. For services such as banking or retail operations, "production" typically takes place while the service is delivered to the customer. For a retailer like IKEA, production occurs every time a customer makes a purchase. By performing its activities efficiently, the production function of a company helps to lower its cost structure. The production function can also perform its activities in a way that is consistent with high product quality, which leads to differentiation (and higher value) and lower costs.

Marketing and Sales There are several ways in which the marketing and sales functions of a company can create value. Through brand positioning and advertising, the

Value Creation at Burberry

When Rose Marie Bravo, the highly regarded president of Saks Fifth Avenue, announced in 1997 that she was leaving to become CEO of ailing British fashion house Burberry, people thought she was crazy. Burberry, best known as a designer of raincoats with a trademark tartan lining, had been described as an outdated, stuffy business with a fashion cachet of almost zero. When Bravo stepped down in 2006, she was heralded in Britain and the United States as one of the world's best managers. In her tenure at Burberry, she had engineered a remarkable turnaround, leading a transformation of Burberry into what one commentator called an "achingly hip" high-end fashion brand whose famous tartan bedecks everything from raincoats and bikinis to handbags and luggage in a riot of color from pink to blue to purple. In less than a decade, Burberry had become one of the most valuable luxury fashion brands in the world.

When asked how she achieved the transformation, Bravo explained that there was hidden value in the brand, which was unleashed by constant creativity and innovation. Bravo hired world-class designers to redesign Burberry's tired fashion line and bought in Christopher Bailey, one of the very best, to lead the design team. The marketing department worked closely with advertisers to develop hip ads that would appeal to a younger, well-heeled audience. The ads featured supermodel Kate Moss promoting the line, and Burberry hired a top fashion photographer to shoot Moss in Burberry. Burberry exercised tight control over distribution, pulling its products from stores whose image was not consistent with the Burberry brand, and expanding its own chain of Burberry stores.

Bravo also noted that "creativity doesn't just come from designers ... ideas can come from the sales floor, the marketing department, even from accountants, believe it or not. People at whatever level they are working have a point of view and have something to say that is worth listening to." Bravo emphasized the importance of teamwork: "One of the things I think people overlook is the quality of the team. It isn't one person, and it isn't two people. It is a whole group of people—a team that works cohesively toward a goal—that makes something happen or not." She notes that her job is to build the team and then motivate the team, "keeping them on track, making sure that they are following the vision."

Sources: Quotes from S. Beatty, "Bass Talk: Plotting Plaid's Future," *Wall Street Journal*, September 9, 2004, p. B1; C. M. Moore and G. Birtwistle, "The Burberry Business Model," *International Journal of Retail and Distribution Management* 32 (2004): 412–422; M. Dickson, "Bravo's Legacy in Transforming Burberry," *Financial Times*, October 6, 2005, p. 22.

marketing function can increase the value that customers perceive to be contained in a company's product (and thus the utility they attribute to the product). Insofar as these help to create a favorable impression of the company's product in the minds of customers, they increase utility. For example, the French company Perrier persuaded U.S. customers that slightly carbonated, bottled water was worth $2.50 per bottle rather than a price closer to the $1.00 that it cost to collect, bottle, and distribute the water. Perrier's marketing function increased the perception of value that customers ascribed to the product. Similarly, by helping to rebrand the company and its product offering, the marketing department at Burberry helped create value (see Strategy in Action 3.1). Marketing and sales can also create value by discovering customer needs and communicating them back to the R&D function, which can then design products that better match those needs.

Customer Service   The role of the service function of an enterprise is to provide after-sales service and support. This function can create superior utility by solving customer problems and supporting customers after they have purchased the product. For example, Caterpillar, the U.S.-based manufacturer of heavy earth-moving equipment, can ship spare parts to any location in the world within 24 hours, thereby minimizing the amount of downtime its customers face if their Caterpillar equipment malfunctions. This is an extremely valuable support capability in an industry where downtime is very expensive. The extent of customer support has helped to increase the utility that customers associate with Caterpillar products, and therefore the price that Caterpillar can charge for them.

3-4b Support Activities

support activities

Activities that provide inputs that allow the primary activities to take place

The **support activities** of the value chain provide inputs that allow the primary activities to take place. These activities are broken down into four functions: materials management (or logistics), human resources, information systems, and company infrastructure (see Figure 3.5).

Materials Management (Logistics) The materials-management (or logistics) function controls the transmission of physical materials through the value chain, from procurement through production and into distribution. The efficiency with which this is carried out can significantly lower cost, thereby generating profit. A company that has benefited from very efficient materials management, the Spanish fashion company Zara, is discussed in Strategy in Action 3.2.

Human Resources There are numerous ways in which the human resource function can help an enterprise create more value. This function ensures that the company has the right combination of skilled people to perform its value creation activities effectively. It is also the job of human resources to ensure that people are adequately trained, motivated, and compensated to perform their value creation tasks. If the human resources are functioning well, employee productivity rises (which lowers costs) and customer service improves (which raises value to consumers), thereby enabling the company to create more value.

3.2 Strategy in Action

Competitive Advantage at Zara

Fashion retailer Zara is one of Spain's fastest-growing and most successful companies, with sales of some $10 billion and a network of 6,500 stores in 88 countries. Zara's competitive advantage centers around one thing: speed. Whereas it takes most fashion houses 6 to 9 months to go from design to delivering merchandise to a store, Zara can complete the entire process in just 5 weeks. This competitive advantage enables Zara to quickly respond to changing fashion trends.

Zara achieves this by breaking many of the rules of operation in the fashion business. Whereas most fashion houses outsource production, Zara has its own factories and keeps approximately half of its production in-house. Zara also has its own designers and its own stores. Its designers, who are in constant contact with the stores, track what is selling on a real-time basis through information systems and talk to store managers weekly to get their impressions of what is "hot." This information supplements data gathered from other sources such as fashion shows.

Drawing on this information, Zara's designers create approximately 40,000 new designs a year, 10,000 of which are selected for production. Zara then purchases basic textiles from global suppliers, but performs capital-intensive production activities in its own factories. These factories use computer-controlled machinery to cut pieces for garments. Zara does not produce in large volumes to attain economies of scale; instead, it produces in small lots. Labor-intensive activities such as sewing are performed by subcontractors located close to Zara's factories. Zara makes a practice of retaining more production capacity than necessary, so that when a new fashion trend emerges it can quickly respond by designing garments and ramping up production.

Completed garments are delivered to one of Zara's own warehouses, and then shipped to its own stores once a week. Zara deliberately underproduces products, supplying small batches of products in hot demand before quickly shifting to the next fashion trend. Often, its merchandise sells out quickly. The empty shelves in Zara stores create a scarcity value—which helps to generate demand. Customers quickly snap up products they like because they know these styles may soon be out of stock and never produced again.

As a result of this strategy, which is supported by competencies in design, information systems, and logistics management, Zara carries less inventory than its competitors (Zara's inventory equals about 10% of sales, compared to 15% at rival stores such as Gap and Benetton). This means fewer price reductions to move products that haven't sold, and higher profit margins.

Sources: "Shining Examples," *The Economist: A Survey of Logistics,* June 17, 2006, pp. 4–6; K. Capell et al., "Fashion Conquistador," *Business Week,* September 4, 2006, pp. 38–39; K. Ferdows et al., "Rapid Fire Fulfillment," *Harvard Business Review* 82 (November 2004): 101–107; "Inditex Is a Leader in the Fast Fashion Industry," *Morningstar,* December 15, 2009; "Pull Based Centralized Manufacturing Yields Cost Efficiencies for Zara," *Morningstar,* June 19, 2014.

Information Systems   Information systems are, primarily, the digital systems for managing inventory, tracking sales, pricing products, selling products, dealing with customer service inquiries, and so on. Modern information systems, coupled with the communications features of the internet, have enabled many enterprises to significantly improve the efficiency and effectiveness with which they manage their other value creation activities. World-class information systems are an aspect of Zara's competitive advantage (see Strategy in Action 3.2).

Company Infrastructure   Company infrastructure is the company-wide context within which all the other value creation activities take place. This includes organizational structure, control systems, incentive systems, and organizational culture—what we refer to as the organizational architecture of a company. The company infrastructure also includes corporate-level legal, accounting, and finance functions. Because top management can exert considerable influence upon shaping all of these aspects of a company, top management should also be viewed as part of the infrastructure. Indeed, through strong leadership, top management can shape the infrastructure of a company and, through that, the performance of all other value creation activities that take place within it. A good example of this process is given in Strategy in Action 3.1, which looks at how Rose Marie Bravo helped to engineer a turnaround at Burberry.

3-4c Value-Chain Analysis: Implications

The concept of the value chain is useful because, when performing an internal analysis, managers can look at the different value-chain activities of the firm, identifying which activities result in the creation of the most value and which are not performing as well as they might be. In other words, value-chain analysis is a useful tool that helps managers identify the company's strengths and weaknesses. Furthermore, it helps managers pinpoint where valuable, rare, and inimitable resources reside within the company.

If managers are to perform a rigorous value-chain analysis, they need to do several things. First, they must analyze how efficiently and effectively each activity is being performed. This should go beyond a qualitative assessment to include an in-depth analysis of quantitative data. For example, the efficiency of the materials-management function might be measured by inventory turnover, the effectiveness of the customer service function might be measured by the speed with which customer complaints are satisfactorily resolved, and the ability of the enterprise to deliver reliable products might be measured by customer returns and warranty costs. Managers need to identify those quantitative measures that are important for their business, collect data on them, and assess how well the firm is performing.

Second, as an aid to this process, whenever possible managers should benchmark each activity against a similar activity performed by rivals to see how well the company is doing. **Benchmarking** requires a company to measure how well it is performing against other enterprises using strategically relevant data. An airline, for example, can benchmark its activities against rivals by using publicly available data that covers important aspects of airline performance such as departure and arrival delays, revenue per seat mile, and cost per seat mile. Government agencies, industry associations, or third-party providers may collect such data. The Department of Transportation and the Air Transport Industry Association collect a wealth of valuable information on the airline industry. Similarly, the market research company J.D. Power provides important information on product quality and customer satisfaction for companies operating in several industries, including automobiles and wireless telecommunications. Regarding online businesses, comScore.com collects a trove of valuable information on internet traffic, search-engine performance, advertising conversions, and so on.

benchmarking

Measuring how well a company is doing by comparing it to another company, or to itself, over time.

Third, in addition to benchmarking performance against rivals, it can be valuable to benchmark performance against best-in-class companies in other industries. For example, Apple is known for excellent customer services in its stores. Comcast has a reputation for poor customer service. Thus, managers at Comcast might want to benchmark their customer service activities against Apple. Although Apple and Comcast are very different organizations, the comparison might yield useful insights that could help Comcast improve its performance.

Fourth, there are several process improvement methodologies that managers can and should use to analyze how well value creation activities are performing, and to identify opportunities for improving the efficiency and effectiveness of those activities. One of the most famous process improvement tools, *Six Sigma*, is discussed in more detail in Chapter 5. Finally, whenever there is potential for improvement within a value-chain activity, leaders within the company need to (a) empower managers to take the necessary actions, (b) measure performance improvements over time against goals, (c) reward managers for meeting or exceeding improvement goals, and (d) when goals are not met, analyze why this is so and take corrective action if necessary.

3.5 Identify and explore the role of efficiency, quality, innovation, and customer responsiveness in building and maintaining a competitive advantage.

3-5 The Building Blocks of Competitive Advantage

Four factors help a company build and sustain competitive advantage: superior efficiency, quality, innovation, and customer responsiveness. We call these factors the building blocks of competitive advantage. Each factor is the *result* of the way the various value-chain activities within an enterprise are performed. By performing value-chain activities to achieve superior efficiency, quality, innovation, and customer responsiveness, a company can (1) differentiate its product offering, and hence offer more value to its customers; and (2) lower its cost structure (see Figure 3.6). Although each factor is discussed sequentially below, all are highly interrelated, and the important ways in which these building blocks affect each other should be noted. For example, superior quality can lead to superior efficiency, and innovation can enhance efficiency, quality, and responsiveness to customers.

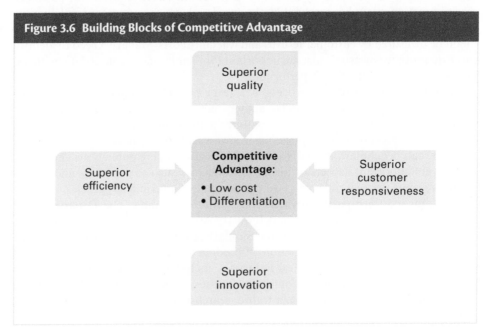

Figure 3.6 Building Blocks of Competitive Advantage

Superior quality

Superior efficiency

Competitive Advantage:
• Low cost
• Differentiation

Superior customer responsiveness

Superior innovation

3-5a Efficiency

The simplest measure of efficiency is the quantity of inputs required to produce a given output; that is, efficiency = outputs/inputs. The more efficient a company is, the fewer inputs it requires to produce a particular output, and the lower its costs.

One common measure of efficiency is employee productivity. **Employee productivity** refers to the output produced per employee. For example, if it takes General Motors 30 hours of employee time to assemble a car, and it takes Ford 25 hours, we can say that Ford has higher employee productivity than GM and is more efficient. If other factors such as wage rates are equal, we can assume from this information that Ford will have a lower cost structure than GM. Thus, employee productivity helps a company attain a competitive advantage through a lower cost structure.

Another important measure of efficiency is capital productivity. **Capital productivity** refers to the output produced by a dollar of capital invested in the business. Firms that use their capital very efficiently and don't waste it on unproductive assets or activities will have higher capital productivity. For example, a firm that adopts just-in-time inventory systems to reduce both its inventory and its need for warehouse facilities will use less working capital (have less capital tied up in inventory) and less fixed capital (have less capital tied up in warehouses). Consequently, its capital productivity will increase.

employee productivity
The output produced per employee.

capital productivity
The sales produced by a dollar of capital invested in the business.

3-5b Quality as Excellence and Reliability

A product can be thought of as a bundle of attributes.[12] The attributes of many physical products include their form, features, performance, durability, reliability, style, and design.[13] A product is said to have *superior quality* when customers perceive that its attributes provide them with higher utility than the attributes of products sold by rivals. For example, a Rolex watch has attributes such as design, styling, performance, and reliability that customers perceive as being superior to the same attributes in many other watches. Thus, we can refer to a Rolex as a high-quality product: Rolex has differentiated its watches by these attributes.

When customers evaluate the quality of a product, they commonly measure it against two kinds of attributes: those related to *quality as excellence* and those related to *quality as reliability*. From a quality-as-excellence perspective, the important attributes are a product's design and styling, its aesthetic appeal, its features and functions, the level of service associated with delivery of the product, and so on. For example, customers can purchase a pair of imitation-leather boots for $20 from Walmart, or they can buy a handmade pair of butter-soft, leather boots from Nordstrom for $500. The boots from Nordstrom will have far superior styling, feel more comfortable, and look much better than those from Walmart. The value consumers get from the Nordstrom boots will in all probability be much greater than the value derived from the Walmart boots, but of course they will have to pay far more for them. That is the point: When excellence is built into a product offering, consumers must pay more to own or consume it.

Regarding quality as reliability, a product can be said to be reliable when it consistently performs the function it was designed for, performs it well, and rarely, if ever, breaks down. As with excellence, reliability increases the value (utility) a consumer derives from a product, and thus affects the price the company can charge for that product and/or the demand for that product.

The concept of quality applies whether we are talking about Toyota automobiles, clothes designed and sold by Zara, Verizon's wireless service, the customer service department of Citibank, or the ability of airlines to arrive on time. Quality is just as relevant to services as it is to goods.[14]

The impact of high product quality on competitive advantage is twofold.[15] First, providing high-quality products increases the value (utility) those products provide to customers, which gives the company the option of charging a higher price for the products. In the automobile industry, for example, Toyota has historically been able to charge a higher price for its cars because of the higher quality of its products.

Second, when products are reliable, less employee time is wasted making defective products, or providing substandard services, and less time has to be spent fixing mistakes—which means higher employee productivity and lower unit costs. Thus, high product quality not only enables a company to differentiate its product from that of rivals, but, if the product is reliable, it also lowers costs.

The importance of reliability in building competitive advantage has increased dramatically over the past 30 years. The emphasis many companies place on reliability is so crucial to achieving high product reliability that it can no longer be viewed as just one way of gaining a competitive advantage. In many industries, it has become an absolute imperative for a company's survival.

3-5c Innovation

product innovation

Development of products that are new to the world or have superior attributes to existing products.

process innovation

Development of a new process for producing and delivering products to customers.

There are two main types of innovation: product innovation and process innovation. **Product innovation** is the development of products that are new to the world or have superior attributes to existing products. Examples are Intel's invention of the microprocessor in the early 1970s; Cisco's development of the router for routing data over the internet in the mid-1980s; and Apple's development of the iPod, iPhone, and iPad in the 2000s. **Process innovation** is the development of a new process for producing and delivering products to customers. Examples include Toyota, which developed a range of new techniques collectively known as the "Toyota lean production system" for making automobiles: just-in-time inventory systems, self-managing teams, and reduced setup times for complex equipment.

Product innovation generates value by creating new products, or enhanced versions of existing products, that customers perceive as having more value, thus increasing the company's pricing options. Process innovation often allows a company to create more value by lowering production costs. Toyota's lean production system helped boost employee productivity, thus giving Toyota a cost-based competitive advantage.[16] Similarly, Staples dramatically lowered the cost of selling office supplies by applying the supermarket business model to retail office supplies. Staples passed on some of this cost savings to customers in the form of lower prices, which enabled the company to increase its market share rapidly.

In the long run, innovation of products and processes is perhaps the most important building block of competitive advantage.[17] Competition can be viewed as a process driven by innovations. Although not all innovations succeed, those that do can be a major source of competitive advantage because, by definition, they give a company something unique that its competitors lack (at least until they imitate the innovation). Uniqueness can allow a company to differentiate itself from its rivals and charge a premium price for its product, or, in the case of many process innovations, reduce its unit costs far below those of competitors.

3-5d Customer Responsiveness

To achieve superior responsiveness to customers, a company must be able to do a better job than competitors of identifying and satisfying its customers' needs. Customers will then attribute more value to its products, creating a competitive advantage based on differentiation. Improving the quality of a company's product offering is consistent with achieving responsiveness, as is developing new products with features that existing products lack. In other words, achieving superior quality and innovation is integral to achieving superior responsiveness to customers.

Another factor that stands out in any discussion of responsiveness to customers is the need to customize goods and services to the unique demands of individuals or groups. For example, the proliferation of soft drinks and beers can be viewed partly as a response to this trend. An aspect of responsiveness to customers that has drawn increasing attention is **customer response time**: the time that it takes for a good to be delivered or a service to be performed.[18] For a manufacturer of machinery, response time is the time it takes to fill customer orders. For a bank, it is the time it takes to process a loan, or the time that a customer must stand in line to wait for a free teller. For a supermarket, it is the time that customers must stand in checkout lines. For a fashion retailer, it is the time required to take a new product from design inception to placement in a retail store (see Strategy in Action 3.2 for a discussion of how the Spanish fashion retailer Zara minimizes this). Customer survey after customer survey has shown slow response time to be a major source of customer dissatisfaction.[19]

customer response time

Time that it takes for a good to be delivered or a service to be performed.

Other sources of enhanced responsiveness to customers are superior design, superior service, and superior after-sales service and support. All of these factors enhance responsiveness to customers and allow a company to differentiate itself from its less responsive competitors. In turn, differentiation enables a company to build brand loyalty and charge a premium price for its products. Consider how much more people are prepared to pay for next-day delivery of Express Mail, compared to delivery in 3 to 4 days. In 2022, a two-page letter sent by overnight Express Mail within the United States cost about $25, compared to $0.58 for regular U.S. Postal Service mail. Thus, the price premium for express delivery (reduced response time) was $24.42, or a premium of 4,200% over the regular price!

3-6 Analyzing Competitive Advantage and Profitability

3.6 Explain the relationship between competitive advantage and profitability.

To perform a solid internal analysis and dig into how well different value-chain activities are performed, managers must be able to analyze the financial performance of their company, identifying how its strategies contribute (or not) to profitability. To identify strengths and weaknesses effectively, they must be able to compare, or benchmark, the performance of their company against competitors, as well as against the historic performance of the company itself. This will help them determine whether they are more or less profitable than competitors and whether the performance of the company has been improving or deteriorating through time, whether their company strategies are maximizing the value being created, whether their cost structure is out of alignment compared to competitors, and whether they are using the company resources to the greatest effect.

As we noted in Chapter 1, the key measure of a company's financial performance is its profitability, which captures the return that a company is generating on its investments. Although several different measures of profitability exist, such as return on assets and return on equity, many authorities on the measurement of profitability argue that return on invested capital (ROIC) is the best measure because "it focuses on the true operating performance of the company."[20] (However, return on assets is very similar in formulation to return on invested capital.)

ROIC is defined as net profit over invested capital, or ROIC = net profit/invested capital. Net profit is calculated by subtracting the total costs of operating the company from its total revenues (total revenues − total costs). *Net profit* is what is left over after the government takes its share in taxes. *Invested capital* is the amount that is invested in the operations of a company: property, plant, equipment, inventories, and other assets. Invested capital comes from two main sources: interest-bearing debt and shareholders' equity. *Interest-bearing debt* is money the company borrows from banks and those who purchase its bonds. *Shareholders' equity* is money raised from selling shares to the public; plus earnings that the company has retained in prior years (and that are available to fund current investments). ROIC measures the effectiveness with which a company is using the capital funds that it has available for investment. As such, it is recognized to be an excellent measure of the value a company is creating.[21]

A company's ROIC can be algebraically divided into two major components: return on sales and capital turnover.[22] Specifically:

$$ROIC = \text{net profits/invested capital}$$
$$= \text{net profits/revenues} \times \text{revenues/invested capital}$$

where net profits/revenues is the return on sales, and revenues/invested capital is capital turnover. Return on sales measures how effectively the company converts revenues into profits. Capital turnover measures how effectively the company employs its invested capital to generate revenues. These two ratios can be further divided into some basic accounting ratios, as shown in Figure 3.7 and defined in Table 3.1.[23]

Figure 3.7 notes that a company's managers can increase ROIC by pursuing strategies that increase the company's return on sales. To increase the company's return on sales, they can pursue strategies that reduce the cost of goods sold (COGS) for a given level of sales revenues (COGS/sales); reduce the level of spending on sales force, marketing, general, and administrative expenses (SG&A) for a given level of sales revenues (SG&A/sales); and reduce R&D spending for a given level of sales revenues (R&D/sales). Alternatively, they can increase return on sales by pursuing strategies

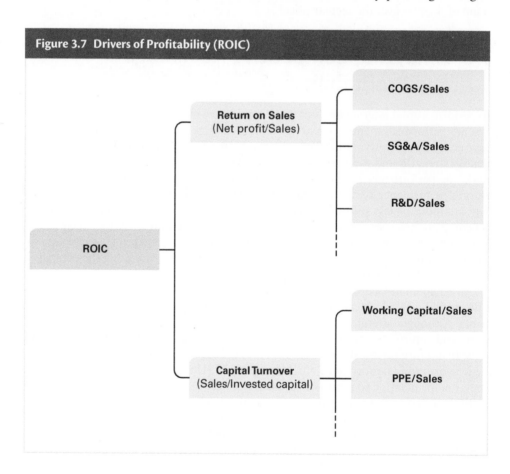

Figure 3.7 Drivers of Profitability (ROIC)

Table 3.1 Definitions of Basic Accounting Terms

Terms	Definitions	Sources
Cost of goods sold (COGS)	Total costs of producing products	Income statement
Sales, general, and administrative expenses (SG&A)	Costs associated with selling products and administering the company	Income statement
Research and development (R&D) expenses	Research and development expenditure	Income statement
Working capital	The amount of money the company has to "work" with in the short term: Current assets − current liabilities	Balance sheet
Property, plant, and equipment (PPE)	The value of investments in the property, plant, and equipment that the company uses to manufacture and sell its products; also known as *fixed capital*	Balance sheet
Return on sales (ROS)	Net profit expressed as a percentage of sales; measures how effectively the company converts revenues into profits	Ratio
Capital turnover	Revenues divided by invested capital; measures how effectively the company uses its capital to generate revenues	Ratio
Return on invested capital (ROIC)	Net profit divided by invested capital	Ratio
Net profit	Total revenues minus total costs before tax	Income statement
Invested capital	Interest-bearing debt plus shareholders' equity	Balance sheet

that increase sales revenues more than they increase the costs of the business as measured by COGS, SG&A, and R&D expenses. That is, they can increase the return on sales by pursuing strategies that lower costs or increase value through differentiation, and thus allow the company to increase its prices more than its costs.

Figure 3.7 also tells us that a company's managers can boost the profitability of their company by obtaining greater sales revenues from their invested capital, thereby increasing capital turnover. They do this by pursuing strategies that reduce the amount of working capital, such as the amount of capital invested in inventories, needed to generate a given level of sales (working capital/sales) and then pursuing strategies that reduce the amount of fixed capital that they have to invest in property, plant, and equipment (PPE) to generate a given level of sales (PPE/sales). That is, they pursue strategies that reduce the amount of capital that they need to generate every dollar of sales, and therefore reduce their cost of capital. Recall that cost of capital is part of the cost structure of a company (see Figure 3.2), so strategies designed to increase capital turnover also lower the cost structure.

To see how these basic drivers of profitability help us understand what is going on in a company and identify its strengths and weaknesses, let us compare the financial performance of two high-profile specialty retailers: lululemon and Gap Inc. Lululemon, which sells high-quality athleisure wear, has been a standout performer in the North American specialty retail market for almost two decades. The company has grown rapidly, built a brand around stylishly designed, high quality, athleisure wear, and boasts the highest sales per square foot among apparel retailers in North America (in 2021 its sales per square foot were $1,443, surpassed in the entire retail space only by the jeweler Tiffany's and The Apple Store). Gap Inc. is a long-established apparel retailer that owns four major retail brands: Gap, Banana Republic, Old Navy, and Athleta (which is a direct competitor of lululemon). While lululemon has soared, in recent years Gap Inc. has stumbled. We will compare the performance of the two companies for fiscal 2020 (which for both entities ended on January 31, 2020). We have chosen this date because it avoids the distorting effect of the COVID-19 pandemic, which started to sweep around the world in February 2020.

3-6a Comparing lululemon and Gap Inc.

For the financial year ending January 2020, lululemon earned an impressive ROIC of 25.4%, whereas the ROIC of Gap Inc. was only 3.5%, significantly below its cost of capital (which was around 10%), suggesting that Gap Inc. was destroying economic value, while lululemon was clearly creating economic value. Lululemon's higher profitability can be understood in terms of the impact of its strategies on the various ratios identified in Figure 3.7 and summarized in Figure 3.8.[24] The most obvious difference is that lululemon earned a return on sales of 16.3%, compared to Gap Inc. which only managed 2.1%. The primary reason for this difference is that lululemon has a much lower COGS/Sales ratio than Gap Inc.—44.2% versus 62.6%. Put differently, lululemon has a much higher gross margin because it can charge a much high price markup for its apparel than Gap Inc. This difference is a result of the fact that lululemon has a much more powerful brand! Lululemon's customers are prepared to pay a premium price for its athleisure wear because they see it as being better designed, and of significantly higher quality, than anything offered by Gap Inc. For example, a pair of yoga pants sold by lululemon typically sell for $30 more than pants offered by Gap Inc.'s Athleta stores. In the language of this chapter, lululemon's *brand* (which is protected by its trademark) is a valuable, rare, and difficult-to-imitate resource. In contrast, the financial analysis suggests that Gap Inc.'s brands are relatively weak and that the company needs to take action to correct this.

Of course, this analysis begs the question of why lululemon's brand is so powerful. The quick answer is that the company has invested heavily in both product design and the development of high-quality performance fabrics (some of which are themselves trademarked). Its apparel is designed to be bacterial and smell resistant and survive

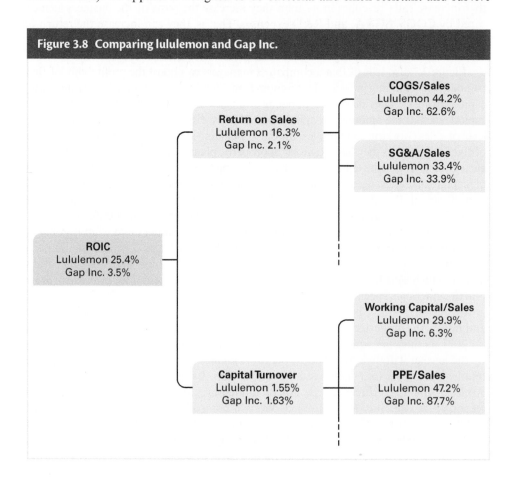

Figure 3.8 Comparing lululemon and Gap Inc.

many washes. And while the fabric is more expensive than traditional athletic fabric, such as that used by Athleta, lululemon's customers value it and are prepared to pay significantly more for it. Unlike most apparel retailers, including Gap Inc., lululemon has substantial design and fabric research activities in-house. It has accumulated valuable, rare, and difficult-to-imitate *process knowledge*, which enables the company to produce apparel that its customers value highly, and which underpins its valuable trademark and brand. In contrast, Gap Inc. lacks a powerful brand that can support a premium pricing strategy and high gross margins.

What is perhaps not clear from Figure 3.8, is that while the two companies have roughly the same SG&A to sales ratio, there is a difference in the composition of SG&A spending (a more detailed financial ratio analysis would reveal this). Lululemon spends far less on general marketing to consumers than Gap Inc., and more on in-house design and material research activities. This strategy has helped lululemon to build a competitive advantage, whereas Gap Inc. has clearly lost the advantage it once had. Put differently, there is nothing distinctive about much of the apparel sold by Gap Inc., while lululemon's apparel is more distinctive.

If we look at capital turnover in Figure 3.8, we see that both companies have a similar performance. Lululemon generates $1.55 for every dollar of capital invested in the business, while Gap Inc. generates $1.63. However, this figure masks a big difference, which we can see when we look at the working capital/sales and PPE/sales ratios. Lululemon has more working capital as a percentage of sales, and significantly less PPE as a percentage of sales. Lululemon's low PPE/sales ratio (47.2% versus 87.7% at Gap Inc.) reflects the fact that its stores are far more productive at generating sales than those owned by Gap Inc. This, too, is a function of strategy. Not only is lululemon's apparel well designed and of high quality, but the company also has short product life cycles for individual items of 9–12 weeks. If you go into a lululemon store and see an item that has the styling and color you want, you might want to buy it right away because that item may vanish from the shelves in a few weeks. By training customers to make impulse buys, and having short product life cycles, lululemon typically does not have to hold discount sales to sell excess inventory; hence, the high gross margins and high sales per square foot, which are reflected in the low PPE/sales ratio. In contrast, Gap Inc. relies far more on discounting to shift unsold inventory, and therefore has lower gross margins and a higher PPE/sales ratio.

Finally, we should ask why lululemon has a higher working capital to sales ratio. One possibility is that this may reflect a difference in buying power and payment terms. With 2020 revenues of over $16 billion, Gap Inc. is more than four times as large as lululemon. This may mean that Gap is able to extract more favorable payment terms from contract manufacturers (both companies outsource the manufacture of their apparel to factories, mostly in Asia). If Gap can do a better job of selling inventory before it must pay for it, even if it must deeply discount some of that inventory and accept lower gross margins, this will explain the lower working capital/sales ratio (for example, due to its larger volume, Gap may be able to pay some suppliers net 60 days, whereas lululemon may be net 30 days). Is this a weakness for lululemon relative to Gap Inc.? Perhaps, and, if it is, the company may want to take steps to fix it by improving its logistics and supply chain functions. Alternatively, the higher working capital ratio at lululemon may simply reflect the fact that it has inventory in its system to which a higher value is assigned, but which it knows it will sell without having to discount.

In sum, we can see how lululemon's high profitability is a function of its strategy, and the rare, valuable, and inimitable resources that its strategic investments have built over the years, particularly in product design and quality, whereas Gap's weak performance is due to the lack of a powerful brand that supports higher pricing and greater gross margins. As in this example, the methodology described in this section can be very useful for analyzing why and how well a company is achieving and sustaining a competitive advantage (or why it is not). It highlights a company's strengths and weaknesses, showing where there is room for improvement and where a company is excelling. As such, it can drive strategy formulation. Moreover, the same methodology can be used to analyze the performance of competitors and gain a greater understanding of their strengths and weakness, which in turn can inform strategy.

Key Terms

distinctive competencies 74
resources 75
process knowledge 75
capabilities 75
socially complex 75
tacit 75
organizational architecture 75

intellectual property 75
basic factors of production 76
advanced factors of production 76
VRIO framework 77
barriers to imitation 78
causal ambiguity 79

value chain 83
primary activities 83
Research and development (R&D) 84
support activities 86
benchmarking 87
employee productivity 89

capital productivity 89
product innovation 90
process innovation 90
customer response time 91

Takeaways for Strategic Managers

1. Distinctive competencies are the firm-specific strengths of a company. Valuable, distinctive competencies enable a company to earn a profit rate that is above the industry average.
2. The distinctive competencies of an organization arise from its resources. Resources include land, labor, management, plant, equipment, process knowledge, intellectual property, and organizational architecture.
3. Resources are likely to result in a competitive advantage when they are valuable, rare, and inimitable, and when the firm is organized to exploit them.
4. Advanced factors of production (resources) such as intellectual property, process knowledge, and organizational architecture are most likely to result in a sustained competitive advantage. Valuable advanced resources are more likely to be rare and inimitable.
5. In order to achieve a competitive advantage, a company needs to pursue strategies that build on its existing resources and formulate strategies that create additional resources (and thus develop new competencies).

6. The amount of value a company creates is measured by the difference between the value (utility) consumers derive from its goods or services and the cost of creating that value.
7. To create more value, a company must lower its costs or differentiate its product so that it creates more utility for consumers and can charge a higher price, or do both simultaneously.
8. The four building blocks of competitive advantage are efficiency, quality, innovation, and responsiveness to customers. Superior efficiency enables a company to lower its costs; superior quality allows it to charge a higher price and lower its costs; and superior customer service lets it charge a higher price. Superior innovation can lead to higher prices in the case of product innovations, or lower unit costs in the case of process innovations.
9. To perform a solid internal analysis, managers need to be able to analyze the financial performance of their company, identifying how the strategies of the company relate to its profitability as measured by the return on invested capital.

Discussion Questions

1. What are the primary implications of the material discussed in this chapter for strategy formulation?
2. When is a company's competitive advantage most likely to be sustained over time?
3. It is possible for a company to be the lowest-cost producer in its industry and simultaneously have an output that is the most valued by customers. Discuss this statement.

4. Why is it important to understand the drivers of profitability as measured by the return on invested capital?
5. Which is more important in explaining the success and failure of companies: strategizing to create valuable resources or luck?

Nordstrom is one of American's most successful department store fashion retailers. John Nordstrom, a Swedish immigrant, established the company in 1901 with a single shoe store in Seattle. From the start, Nordstrom's approach to business was to provide exceptional customer service and product selection, quality, and value. This approach remains Nordstrom's hallmark today.

The modern Nordstrom is a fashion specialty chain with more than 100 high-end "full-price" department stores across the United States, and another 250 "off-price" Nordstrom Rack stores. Nordstrom generated almost $15 billion in sales in 2022. Between 2012 and 2022, Nordstrom's returns on invested capital averaged 14% annually (which is good for a retailer), even though the company was hit hard by the COVID-19 pandemic in 2020 and 2021. Nordstrom returned to profitability in fiscal 2022 and seems set to return to its long-term history of outperformance.

Nordstrom is a niche company. Its core department store business focuses on a relatively affluent customer base that is looking for affordable luxury. Its department stores are in upscale areas and have expensive fittings and fixtures that convey an impression of luxury. The stores invite browsing. Touches such as live music played on a grand piano help create an appealing atmosphere. The merchandise is fashionable and of high quality. What truly differentiates Nordstrom from many of its rivals, however, is its legendary excellence in customer service.

Nordstrom's salespeople are typically well groomed and dressed, polite and helpful, and known for their attention to detail. They are selected for their ability to interact with customers in a positive way. During the interview process for new employees, one of the most important questions asked of candidates is their definition of good customer service. Thank-you cards, home deliveries, personal appointments, and access to personal shoppers are the norm at Nordstrom. There is a no-questions-asked returns policy, with no receipt required. Nordstrom's philosophy is that the customer is always right. The company's salespeople are well compensated, with good benefits and commissions on sales that range from 6.75% to 10% depending on the department. Top salespeople at Nordstrom can earn over $100,000 a year, mostly in commissions.

The customer service ethos is central to the culture and organization of Nordstrom. The organization chart is an inverted pyramid, with salespeople on the top and executive management at the bottom. According to former Co-president Blake Nordstrom, this is because

Sources: A. Martinez, "Tale of Lost Diamond Adds Glitter to Nordstrom's Customer Service," *Seattle Times*, May 11, 2011 (www .seattletimes.com); C. Conte, "Nordstrom Built on Customer Service," *Jacksonville Business Journal*, September 7, 2012 (www. bizjournals.com/Jacksonville); W. S. Goffe, "How Working as a Stock Girl at Nordstrom Prepared Me for Being a Lawyer," *Forbes*, December 3, 2012; B. Welshaar, "Nordstrom Inc," Morningstar, April 5, 2022, www .Morningstar.com.

"I work for them. My job is to make them as successful as possible." Management constantly shares anecdotes emphasizing the primacy of customer service at Nordstrom to reinforce the culture. One story relates that when a customer in Fairbanks, Alaska, wanted to return two tires (which Nordstrom does not sell), bought some time ago from another store once on the same site, a salesclerk looked up their price and gave him his money back!

Despite its emphasis on quality and luxury, Nordstrom has not neglected operating efficiency. Sales per square foot are around $500 despite the large, open-plan nature of the stores, and inventory turns exceed 5 times per year, up from 3.5 times a decade ago. These are good figures for a high-end department store (by comparison, inventory turns at Macy's and Kohl's are around three times per year). Management constantly seeks ways to improve efficiency and customer service. For example, in 2016, it put mobile checkout devices into the hands of 5,000 salespeople, eliminating the need for customers to wait in a checkout line.

Nordstrom also has a strong presence in the discount apparel market through its Nordstrom Rack stores. The off-price Rack business has grown from one clearance store in Seattle in 1973 to about 250 stores today. Nordstrom believes that its Rack stores do not cannibalize its full-price department store business since Rack attracts a somewhat younger (average age under 40), less affluent customer than the full-price stores. Nordstrom claims that Rack is the company's number-one source of new customers and that one-third of off-price customers become full-price customers over time. Further, the company reports that customers who shop at both full-price and off-price stores spend four times as much as customers who only shop at one or the other. Nordstrom uses Rack to sell lower-priced apparel items of popular brands, to sell private-label apparel, and to clear merchandise from full-price stores (about 10% of merchandise sold).

E-commerce sales have also been growing at a rapid clip. Nordstrom was an early mover in the e-commerce space. The company's main site, Nordstrom.com, was launched in 1998 and was integrated into the rest of the business from the outset, which includes both the department stores and the Rack format. The physical stores play an important role in online sales, acting as a display site for items that can be ordered online; a pickup location for customers if they wish to do that; and, perhaps most importantly, a location where customers can return merchandise purchased online. Key to Nordstrom's online success has been its ability to leverage its brand to boost online sales, which increased from 14% to 40% of total revenues between 2012 and 2022, making Nordstrom one of the leading e-commerce companies in the United States. Nordstrom's approach contrasts with that adopted by many other traditional retailers, who kept their online offering separate from the rest of their business and outsource implementation to third parties.

Case Discussion Questions

1. What resources underlie Nordstrom's historically strong position among apparel retailers in the United States?
2. How do these resources enable Nordstrom to improve one or more of the following: efficiency, quality, customer responsiveness, and innovation?
3. Apply the VRIO framework and describe to what extent these resources can be considered valuable, rare, inimitable, and well organized.
4. How do Nordstrom's Rack and e-commerce offerings fit into the big picture? Do these offerings benefit from Nordstrom's well-established resources and capabilities?
5. What must Nordstrom do to maintain its competitive advantage going forward?

Notes

[1] M. Cusumano, *The Japanese Automobile Industry* (Cambridge: Harvard University Press, 1989); S. Spear and H. K. Bowen, "Decoding the DNA of the Toyota Production System," *Harvard Business Review* (September–October 1999): 96–108.

[2] The material in this section relies on the resource-based view of the company. For summaries of this perspective, see J. B. Barney,

"Company Resources and Sustained Competitive Advantage," *Journal of Management* 17 (1991): 99–120; J. T. Mahoney and J. R. Pandian, "The Resource-Based View Within the Conversation of Strategic Management," *Strategic Management Journal* 13 (1992): 63–380.

[3]R. Amit and P. J. H. Schoemaker, "Strategic Assets and Organizational Rent," *Strategic Management Journal* 14 (1993): 33–46; M. A. Peteraf, "The Cornerstones of Competitive Advantage: A Resource-Based View," *Strategic Management Journal* 14 (1993): 179–191; B. Wernerfelt, "A Resource-Based View of the Company," *Strategic Management Journal* 15 (1994): 171–180; K. M. Eisenhardt and J. A. Martin, "Dynamic Capabilities: What Are They?," *Strategic Management Journal* 21 (2000): 1105–1121; D. G. Sirmon and M. A. Hitt, "Contingenecies with Dynamic Managerial Capabilities: Interdependent Effects of Resource Investment and Deployment on Firm Performance," *Strategic Management Journal*, 30 (2009): 1375–1394.

[4]For a discussion of organizational capabilities, see R. R. Nelson and S. Winter, *An Evolutionary Theory of Economic Change* (Cambridge: Belknap Press, 1982).

[5]J. B. Barney and W. S. Hesterly, *Strategic Management and Competitive Advantage* (Boston: Pearson, 2005).

[6]The concept of barriers to imitation is grounded in the resource-based view of the company. For details, see R. Reed and R. J. DeFillippi, "Causal Ambiguity, Barriers to Imitation, and Sustainable Competitive Advantage," *Academy of Management Review* 15 (1990): 88–102.

[7]E. Mansfield, "How Economists See R&D," *Harvard Business Review* (November–December 1981): 98–106.

[8]R. Reed and R. J. DeFillippi, "Causal Ambiguity, Barriers to Imitation, and Sustainable Competitive Advantage," *Academy of Management Review* 15 (1990): 88–102.

[9]However, $P = V$ only in the special case when the company has a perfect monopoly and can charge each customer a unique price that reflects the utility of the product to that customer (i.e., where perfect price discrimination is possible). More generally, except in the limiting case of perfect price discrimination, even a monopolist will see most customers capture some of the value of a product in the form of a consumer surplus.

[10]This point is central to the work of Michael Porter. See M. E. Porter, *Competitive Advantage* (New York: Free Press, 1985). See also P. Ghemawat, *Commitment: The Dynamic of Strategy* (New York: Free Press, 1991), Chapter 4.

[11]Porter, *Competitive Advantage*.

[12]This approach goes back to the pioneering work by K. Lancaster, *Consumer Demand: A New Approach* (New York: Columbia University Press, 1971).

[13]D. Garvin, "Competing on the Eight Dimensions of Quality," *Harvard Business Review* (November-December 1987): 101–119; P. Kotler, *Marketing Management* (Millennium Ed.) (Upper Saddle River: Prentice-Hall, 2000).

[14]C. K. Prahalad and M. S. Krishnan, "The New Meaning of Quality in the Information Age," *Harvard Business Review* (September–October 1999): 109–118.

[15]See D. Garvin, "What Does Product Quality Really Mean?" *Sloan Management Review* 26 (Fall 1984): 25–44; P. B. Crosby, *Quality Is Free* (New York: Mentor, 1980); A. Gabor, *The Man Who Discovered Quality* (New York: Times Books, 1990).

[16]M. Cusumano, *The Japanese Automobile Industry* (Cambridge: Harvard University Press, 1989); S. Spear and H. K. Bowen, "Decoding the DNA of the Toyota Production System," *Harvard Business Review* (September–October 1999): 96–108.

[17]W. C. Kim and R. Mauborgne, "Value Innovation: The Strategic Logic of High Growth," *Harvard Business Review* (January–February 1997): 102–115.

[18]G. Stalk and T. M. Hout, *Competing Against Time* (New York: Free Press, 1990).

[19]Ibid.

[20]T. Copeland, T. Koller, and J. Murrin, *Valuation: Measuring and Managing the Value of Companies* (New York: Wiley, 1996). See also S. F. Jablonsky and N. P. Barsky, *The Manager's Guide to Financial Statement Analysis* (New York: Wiley, 2001).

[21]Copeland, Koller, and Murrin, *Valuation*.

[22]This is done as follows. Signifying net profit by $=$, invested capital by K, and revenues by R, then ROIC $= =/K$. If we multiply through by revenues, R, this becomes $R = (K) = (= = R)/(K = R)$, which can be rearranged as $=/R = R/K$, where $=/R$ is the return on sales and R/K is capital turnover.

[23]Figure 3.7 is a simplification that ignores other important items that enter the calculation, such as depreciation/sales (a determinant of ROS) and other assets/sales (a determinant of capital turnover).

[24]Figure 3.8 was constructed from financial accounts reported by the investment service Morningstar. For retailers, PPE includes not just physical stores, warehouses, and equipment that the company owns, but also long-term capital lease obligations. The SG&A figures may include some other expenses that are not strictly SG&A, such as a 50-person team at lululemon that undertakes applied research into different fabrics.

Michal Sanca/Shutterstock.com

Part

3

Strategies

Chapter 4

Business-Level Strategy

Learning Objectives

4.1 Define business-level strategy.

4.2 Explain the difference between low-cost and differentiation strategies.

4.3 Summarize the process of market segmentation.

4.4 Identify the generic business-level strategic choices.

4.5 Explain the relationship between business-level strategies and competitive advantage.

4.6 Explain how a company executes its business-level strategy through functional-level strategies and organizational arrangements.

4.7 Discuss the concept of blue ocean strategy and value innovation.

Opening Case

Rivian

Founded in 2009 by California entrepreneur R.J. Scaringe, Rivian is an early leader in the market for all-electric pickup trucks. Their initial offering, the R1T pickup, rolled off the assembly line at the factory in Normal, Illinois, in late 2021, making Rivian the first company to deliver an electric pickup. Rivian is riding strong tailwinds in the electric vehicle market. With concerns about climate change on the rise, and governments around the world taking action to encourage electrification of transportation, demand seems set to rise. While electric vehicle industry leader Tesla has focused most of its efforts so far on the car market, until now the pickup truck market has lagged.

Rivian's truck is not your father's pickup. It is a high-priced luxury vehicle, with an entry price of $67,500, aimed at the well-healed outdoor enthusiast. Some of the features are mindboggling. The R1T can go from 0 to 60 mph in 3 seconds. It can climb a 45-degree grade hill and wade through 3 feet of water, something that most pickups can do only once. The R1T's platform has a low center of gravity comprising of four motors (one for each wheel), half shafts, brakes, and hubs; a floor-mounted battery pack and power electronics; and a chassis with four-corner air springs with adaptive dampening and an electrohydraulic anti-roll system. The low-slung, highly ridged frame allows for innovative features, such as a huge front trunk. One optional feature is a pullout kitchen with an induction stovetop and a sink, designed for cooking at campsites. The cabin is spacious, well isolated against wind and tire noise, comfortable and full of high-end features, including a 16-inch touch-screen control panel. The Rivian can even increase its ground clearance by 8 inches at the touch of a virtual button to wade through water or drive over rough ground.

Rivian also has two other vehicles in late-stage development, an SUV, the R1S, and a delivery truck. The delivery truck is the result of a deal with Amazon, which owns around 18% of Rivian. Amazon is planning to convert its entire fleet of delivery trucks to electric vehicles and has contracted with Rivian to deliver 100,000 trucks by the end of 2025. To finance all of this, Rivian has raised $20 billion from investors, including $13.7 billion from a November 2021 IPO. The factory in Illinois has the capacity to produce 150,000 vehicles a year. In December 2021, it announced plans to invest $5 billion in a second plant in Georgia that will have a peak annual capacity of 400,000 vehicles. The goal is to rapidly ramp up production, achieve economies of scale, and achieve profitability. It is an audacious strategy, but with over 70,000 preorders in hand for the R1T and R1S models, in addition to that 100,000 preorder from Amazon, Rivian has some solid reasons for believing that its strategy might work.

Tada Images/Shutterstock.com

Sources: C. Domonoske, "The Electric Automaker Rivian Soared in Its Stock Debut," *NPR: Business*, November 10, 2021; M. Colias, "Rivian Automotive Curtails Production in 2022 Due to Supply-Chain Disruptions," *Wall Street Journal*, March 10, 2022; D. Neil, "2022 Rivian R1T: Much Anticipated, Still a Work in Progress," *Wall Street Journal*, December 9, 2021; B. Foldy, "Electric Truck Startup Rivian Plans New $5 Billion Factory Complex in Georgia," *Wall Street Journal*, December 16, 2021.

Rivian will not have the market space all to itself. The competition is heating up. GM began delivery of its Hummer electric truck in 2022, and Ford plans to start delivering its electric F-150 Lightning in 2023. Tesla, too, will start producing its own futuristic "Cybertruck" at high volumes in 2023. Tesla claims to have around a million reservations for the Cybertruck, while Ford's F-150 Lightning has 200,000 reservations and is now backordered for 3 years. The Lightning is priced significantly below Rivian's R1T, suggesting that Ford is targeting a different demographic.

To complicate matters for Rivian, supply chain problems related to the COVID-19 pandemic have hit automobile production hard. Due to supply chain issues, including shortages of critical electronics components and batteries, in March 2022 Rivian announced that it would only be able to produce 25,000 vehicles in 2022, down from an initial forecast of 40,000, and pushing off into the future that point where substantial economies of scale start to kick in and the company will become profitable.

4-1 Business-Level Strategy

In this chapter, we look at the formulation of **business-level strategy**. As you may recall from Chapter 1, business-level strategy refers to the overarching competitive theme of a company in a market. At its most basic, business-level strategy is about *whom* a company decides to serve (its customer segments), what customer *needs* and *desires* the company is trying to satisfy, and *how* the company decides to satisfy those needs and desires.[1] If this sounds familiar, it is because we have already discussed this in Chapter 1 when we considered how companies construct a mission statement.

The electric vehicle manufacturer Rivian provides us with an illustration of how this works (see the Opening Case). Rivian's target demographic are upper-income outdoor enthusiasts who *desire* a vehicle that is eye catching, powerful, environmentally conscious, and has strong off-road capabilities. Rivian is striving to meet the needs of this *segment* by building a well-designed, powerful, high-quality, electric pickup truck. Through design and engineering, it is trying to *differentiate* its offering from other electric pickup trucks that will soon enter the market, such as Ford's F-150 Lightning. To make up for the higher quality of its offering, Rivian is charging a premium price. To help in its quest to make a profit, Rivian is also seeking to lower costs through mass production and the attainment of economies of scale. Whether Rivian succeeds or not will depend upon how well it implements its strategy and solves unanticipated problems (such as the supply chain disruptions resulting from the COVID-19 pandemic). If it can do these things, it might be able to gain a competitive advantage over its emerging rivals such as Ford, GM, and Tesla.

In this chapter, we will look at how managers decide what business-level strategy to pursue, and how they go about executing that strategy to attain a sustainable competitive advantage. We start by looking at the two basic ways that companies compete in a marketplace—by *lowering costs* and by *differentiating* their goods or services from those offered by rivals so that they create more value. Next, we consider the issue of *customer choice* and *market segmentation* and discuss the decisions that managers must make when it comes to their company's segmentation strategy. Then, synthesizing this, we discuss the various business-level strategies that an enterprise can adopt, and what must be done to successfully implement those strategies. This chapter closes with a discussion of how managers can think about formulating an innovative, business-level strategy that gives their company a unique and defendable position in the marketplace.

4-2 Low-Cost and Differentiation Strategies

Strategy is about the search for competitive advantage. As we saw in Chapter 3, at the most fundamental level, a company has a competitive advantage if it can lower costs relative to rivals and/or if it can differentiate its product offering from those of rivals, thereby creating more value. We will look at lowering costs first, and then at differentiation.[2]

4-2a Lowering Costs

Imagine that all enterprises in an industry offer products that are very similar in all respects except for price, and that each company is small relative to total market demand, so that they are unable to influence the prevailing price. This situation exists in commodity markets such as those for oil, wheat, aluminum, and steel. In the global oil market, for example, prices are set by the interaction of supply and demand. Even the world's largest private oil producer, ExxonMobil, only produces around 3.5% of world output and cannot influence the prevailing price.

In commodity markets, competitive advantage goes to the company that has the lowest costs. Low costs enable a company to make a profit at price points where its rivals are losing money. Low costs can also allow a company to undercut rivals on price, gain market share, and maintain or even increase profitability. Being the low-cost player in an industry can be a very advantageous position.

Although lowering costs below those of rivals is a particularly powerful strategy in a pure commodity industry, it can also have great utility in other settings. General merchandise retailing, for example, is not a classic commodity business. Nevertheless, Walmart has built a very strong competitive position in the U.S. market by being the low-cost player in its segment. Because its costs are so low, Walmart can cut prices, grow its market share, and still make profits at price points where its competitors lose money. The same is true in the airline industry, where Southwest Airlines has established a low-cost position. Southwest's operating efficiencies have enabled it to make money in an industry that has been hit by repeated bouts of price warfare, and where many of its rivals have been forced into bankruptcy.

4-2b Differentiation

Now let us look at the differentiation side of the equation. Differentiation involves distinguishing your company from its rivals by offering something that they find hard to match. As we saw in the Opening Case, Rivian is trying to *differentiate* itself from rivals by offering a high-quality electric pickup truck that is a cut above those offered by rivals in terms of its power, styling, design, and features. Whether Rivian will succeed remains to be seen, but it does have a clear business-level strategy. A company can differentiate itself from rivals in many ways. A product can be differentiated by superior reliability (it breaks down less often, or not at all), better design, superior functions and features, better point-of-sale service, better after-sales service and support, better branding, and so on. A Rolex watch is differentiated from a Timex watch by superior design, materials, and reliability; a Toyota car is differentiated from a GM car by superior reliability (historically, new Toyota models have had fewer defects than new GM models); Apple differentiates its iPhone from rival offerings through superior product design, ease of use, excellent customer service at its Apple stores, and easy synchronization with other Apple products such as computers, tablets, Apple Music, Apple TV, and iCloud.

Differentiation gives a company two advantages. First, it can allow the company to charge a premium price for its good or service should it choose to do so. Second, it can help the company grow overall demand and capture market share from its rivals. In the case of the iPhone, Apple has reaped both benefits through its successful differentiation strategy. Apple charges more for its iPhone than people pay for rival smartphone offerings, and the differential appeal of Apple products has led to strong demand growth.

It is important to note that differentiation often (but not always) raises the cost structure of the firm. It costs Rivian more to produce a top-of-the-line electric pickup truck. It is often the case that companies pursuing a differentiation strategy have a higher cost structure than companies pursuing a low-cost strategy. On the other hand, somewhat counterintuitively, there are situations where successful differentiation, because it increases primary demand so much, can actually lower costs. Apple's iPhone is a case in point. Apple uses very expensive materials in the iPhone—Gorilla Glass for the screen and brushed aluminum for the case. It could have used cheaper plastic, but then the product would not have looked as good and would have scratched easily. Although these decisions about materials originally raised the unit cost of the iPhone, the fact is that Apple has sold so many iPhones that it now enjoys economies of scale in purchasing and can effectively bargain down the price it pays for expensive materials. The result for Apple—successful differentiation of the iPhone—not only has allowed the company to charge a premium price, but it has also grown demand to the point where Apple can lower costs through the attainment of scale economies, thereby widening profit margins. This is why Apple captured 75% of all profits in the global smartphone business in 2021 despite only having a 13% market share.

The Apple example points to an essential truth: Successful differentiation gives managers options. One option is to raise the price to reflect the differentiated nature of the product offering and cover any incremental increase in costs (see Figure 4.1). Many firms pursue this option, which can by itself enhance profitability if prices increase more than costs. For example, Four Seasons hotels are very luxurious—and it is costly to provide that luxury—but it also charges very high prices for its rooms, and the firm is profitable as a result.

However, the Apple example also suggests that increased profitability and profit growth can come from the increased demand associated with successful differentiation, which enables the firm to use its assets more efficiently and thereby realize *lower costs* from scale economies. This leads to another option: The successful differentiator can hold prices constant, or only increase them slightly, sell more, and boost profitability through the attainment of scale economies (see Figure 4.1).[3]

For another example, consider Starbucks. The company has successfully differentiated its product offering from that of rivals by the excellent quality of its coffee-based drinks; by the quick, efficient, friendly service that its baristas offer customers; by the comfortable atmosphere created by the design of its stores; and by its strong brand image. This differentiation increases traffic volume in each Starbucks store, thereby increasing the productivity of employees (they are always busy) and the productivity

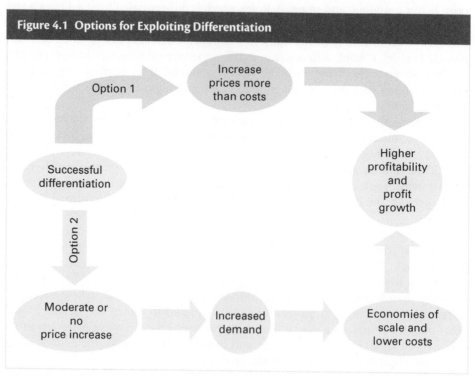

Figure 4.1 Options for Exploiting Differentiation

Source: Charles W.L. Hill © Copyright 2013.

of the capital invested in the store. Thus, each store realizes scale economies from greater volume, which lowers the average unit costs at each store. Spread across the 34,000 stores that Starbucks operates worldwide, this represents potentially huge cost savings that translate into higher profitability. Add this to the enhanced demand that comes from successful differentiation—which in the case of Starbucks not only enables the firm to sell more from each store, but also to open more stores—and profit growth will also accelerate.

4-2c The Differentiation–Low-Cost Trade-Off

The thrust of our discussion so far is that a low-cost position and a differentiated position are two very different ways of gaining a competitive advantage. The enterprise striving for the lowest costs does everything it can to be productive and drive down its cost structure, whereas the enterprise striving for differentiation necessarily has to bear higher costs to achieve that differentiation. Put simply, one cannot be both Walmart and Nordstrom, Porsche and Kia, Rolex and Timex. Managers must choose between these two basic ways of attaining a competitive advantage.

However, presenting the choice between differentiation and low costs in these terms is something of a simplification. As we have already noted, the successful differentiator might be able to subsequently reduce costs if differentiation leads to significant demand growth and the attainment of scale economies. But the relationship between low cost and differentiation is subtler than this. Strategy is not so much about making discrete choices as it is about achieving the right balance between differentiation and low costs.

To understand these issues, see Figure 4.2. The convex curve in Figure 4.2 illustrates what is known as an *efficiency frontier* (also known in economics as a production possibility frontier).[4] The efficiency frontier shows all of the different positions that a company can adopt with regard to differentiation and low cost, *assuming* that its internal functions and organizational arrangements are configured efficiently to support a particular position (note that the horizontal axis in Figure 4.2 is reverse scaled—moving along the axis to the right implies lower costs). The efficiency frontier

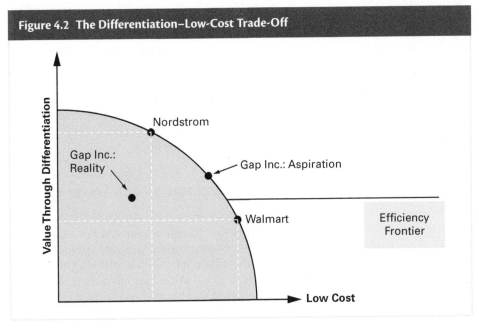

Figure 4.2 The Differentiation–Low-Cost Trade-Off

Source: Charles W.L. Hill © Copyright 2022.

has a convex shape because of diminishing returns. Diminishing returns imply that when an enterprise already has significant differentiation built into its product offering, increasing differentiation by a relatively small amount requires significant additional costs. The converse also holds: A company that already has a low-cost structure must relinquish much differentiation in its product offering to achieve additional cost reductions.

The efficiency frontier shown in Figure 4.2 is for the U.S. retail apparel business (Walmart sells more than apparel, but that need not concern us here). As you can see, the high-end retailer Nordstrom and the low-cost retailer Walmart are both shown to be on the frontier, implying that both organizations have configured their internal functions and organizations efficiently. However, they have adopted very different positions; Nordstrom has high differentiation and high costs, whereas Walmart has low costs and low differentiation. These are not the only viable positions in the industry, however. As shown in Figure 4.2, Gap Inc. *aspires* to position itself on the frontier between Nordstrom and Walmart. Gap offers higher-quality apparel merchandise than does Walmart, sold in a more appealing environment, but its offering is nowhere near as differentiated as that of Nordstrom; it is positioned between Walmart and Nordstrom. This mid-level position, offering moderate differentiation at a higher cost than Walmart, makes sense because there are enough consumers demanding this option. They do not want to look as if they purchased their clothes at Walmart; they want fashionable, casual clothes that are more affordable than those available at Nordstrom. Unfortunately for Gap, in recent years it has not executed well, and as a result, it finds itself inside the efficiency frontier; its costs are higher, and the quality of its offering is lower, than the company aspires to. Consequently, as we saw in Chapter 3, its profitability is lower than many other specialty retailers, such as lululemon.

The essential point is that *there are often multiple positions on the differentiation–low-cost continuum that are viable in the sense that they have enough demand to support an offering*. The task for managers is to identify a position in the industry that is viable and then configure the functions and organizational arrangements of the enterprise so that they are run as efficiently and effectively as possible and enable the firm to reach the frontier. Not all companies are able to do this. Only those that can get to the frontier have a competitive advantage. Getting to the frontier requires excellence in strategy implementation. As has been suggested already in this chapter, business-level strategy is implemented through function and organization. Therefore, *to successfully implement a business-level strategy and reach the efficiency frontier, a company must pursue the right functional-level strategies and be appropriately organized; business-level strategy, functional-level strategy, and organizational arrangement must all be in alignment*.

It should be noted that not all positions on an industry's efficiency frontier are equally attractive. For some positions, there may not be sufficient demand to support a product offering. For other positions, there may be too many competitors going after the same basic position—the competitive space might be too crowded—and the resulting competition might drive prices below acceptable levels.

4-2d Value Innovation: Greater Differentiation at a Lower Cost

The efficiency frontier is not static; it is continually being pushed outward by the efforts of managers to improve their firm's performance through innovation. For example, in the mid-1990s, Dell pushed out the efficiency frontier in the personal computer (PC) industry (see Figure 4.3). Dell pioneered the online sale of PCs, allowing customers to build their own machines and effectively creating value through customization. In other words, the strategy of selling online allowed Dell to *differentiate* itself from rivals that sold PCs through retail outlets. At the same time, Dell used order information submitted online to efficiently coordinate and manage the global supply chain, driving

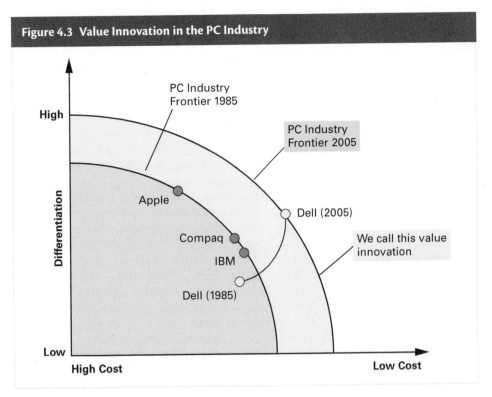

Figure 4.3 Value Innovation in the PC Industry

Source: Charles W.L. Hill © Copyright 2013.

down production costs in the process. The net result was that Dell was able to offer more value (through superior *differentiation*) at a *lower cost* than its rivals. Through its process innovations, it redefined the frontier of what was possible in the industry.

We use the term **value innovation** to describe what happens when innovation pushes out the efficiency frontier in an industry, allowing for greater value to be offered through superior differentiation at a lower cost than was previously thought possible.[5] When a company pioneers process innovations that lead to value innovation, it effectively changes the game in an industry and may be able to outperform its rivals for a long period of time. This is what happened to Dell. After harnessing the power of the internet to sell PCs online and coordinate the global supply chain, Dell outperformed its rivals in the industry for over a decade while they scrambled to catch up with the industry leader.

Toyota, too, has benefitted from value innovation. As we discussed in Chapter 3, Toyota pioneered lean production systems that improved the quality of automobiles while simultaneously lowering costs. Toyota *redefined what was possible in the automobile industry*, effectively pushing out the efficiency frontier and enabling the company to better differentiate its product offering at a cost level that its rivals couldn't match. The result was a competitive advantage that persisted for over two decades.

value innovation

When innovations push out the efficiency frontier in an industry, allowing for greater value to be offered through superior differentiation at a lower cost than was previously thought possible.

4-3 Who Are Our Customers? Market Segmentation

4.3 Summarize the process of market segmentation.

As noted in the introduction to this chapter, business-level strategy begins with deciding *who* the company is going to serve, what *needs* or *desires* it is trying to satisfy, and *how* it is going to satisfy those needs and desires. Answering these questions is not straightforward because customers in a market are not homogenous. They often differ in fundamental ways. Some are wealthy, some are not; some are old, some are young; some are women, some are men; some are influenced by popular culture, some never watch TV; some live in cities, some in the suburbs; some care deeply about status symbols, others do not; some place a high value on luxury, others on value for money; some exercise every day, others have never seen the inside of a gym; some speak English most of the time, while for others Spanish is their first language; and so on.

One fundamental decision that every company faces is whether to recognize such differences in customers, and if so, how to tailor its approach depending on which customer segment or segments it decides to serve. The first step toward answering these questions is to segment the market according to differences in customer demographics, needs, and desires.

Market segmentation refers to the process of subdividing a market into clearly identifiable groups of customers with similar needs, desires, and demand characteristics. Customers within these segments are relatively homogenous, whereas they differ in important ways from customers in other segments of the market. For example, Nike segments the athletic shoe market according to sport and gender because it believes that people participating in different sports expect different things from an athletic shoe (a shoe designed for running is not suitable for playing basketball), and that men and women desire different shoe styling and construction (most men do not want to wear pink shoes). Similarly, in the market for colas, Coca-Cola segments the market by needs—regular Coke for the average consumer, and diet cola for consumers concerned about their weight. In 2005, the diet cola segment was further subdivided when the company introduced Coke Zero, a sugar-free, caffeine-free cola. Diet Coke was targeted more at women, while Coke Zero targeted men looking for a "healthy" alternative to traditional Coke (Coke Zero cans were colored black to communicate a more "masculine" look).

4-3a Three Approaches to Market Segmentation

Companies adopt one of three basic approaches to market segmentation. The first is to *not* tailor different offerings to different segments and instead produce and sell a standardized product that is targeted at the average customer in that market. This was the approach adopted by Coca-Cola until the early 1980s, before the introduction of Diet Coke and flavored cola drinks such as Cherry Cola. In those days, Coke was *the* drink for everyone. Coke was differentiated from the offerings of rivals, particularly Pepsi Cola, by lifestyle advertising that positioned Coke as the iconic American drink, the "Real Thing." Some network broadcast news programs adopt this approach today. The coverage offered by ABC News, for example, is tailored toward the average American viewer. The giant retailer Walmart targets the average customer in the market, although, unlike Coca-Cola, Walmart's goal is to drive down costs so that it can charge everyday low prices, give its customers value for money, and still make a profit.

A second approach is to recognize differences between segments and create different product offerings for each segment. Coca-Cola has adopted this approach since the 1980s. In 1982, it introduced Diet Coke, targeting the drink at those who were weight and health conscious. As noted, in 2005 it introduced Coke Zero, also a diet cola, but targeted at men because company research found that men tended to associate Diet Coke with women. Since 2005, Diet Coke has been repositioned as more of a women's diet drink. Similarly, in the apparel retail industry, Gap Inc. has brands that address several different market segments; Old Navy and The Gap are aimed at the average consumer looking for casual clothing, Banana Republic is positioned to serve a somewhat higher income demographic seeking more stylish clothing, while Athleta is aimed at the exercise market. In the automobile market, Toyota sells under the Toyota brand to a wide spread of the market but uses the Lexus brand to target

---

market segmentation

The way a company decides to group customers, based on important differences in their needs, in order to gain a competitive advantage.

the luxury end of the market. In each segment, Toyota tries to differentiate itself from rivals in the segment by the excellent reliability and high quality of its offerings.

A third approach is to target only a limited number of market segments, or just one, and to become the very best at serving that segment. In the automobile market, Porsche focuses exclusively on the very top end of the market, targeting wealthy, middle-aged, male consumers who have a passion for the speed, power, and engineering excellence associated with its range of sports cars. Porsche is clearly pursuing a differentiation strategy regarding this segment, although it emphasizes a different type of differentiation than Toyota. Alternatively, Kia of South Korea got its start by positioning itself as low-cost player in the industry, selling vehicles that were aimed at value-conscious buyers in the middle- and lower-income brackets. In the network broadcasting news business, Fox News and MSNBC have also adopted a focused approach. Fox tailors its content toward viewers on the right of the political spectrum, whereas MSNBC is differentiated toward viewers on the left.

When managers decide to ignore different segments and produce a standardized product for the average consumer, we say they are pursuing a **standardization strategy**. When they decide to serve many segments, or even the entire market, producing different offerings for different segments, we say they are pursuing a **segmentation strategy**. When they decide to serve a limited number of segments, or just one segment, we say they are pursuing a **focus strategy**. Today, Walmart is pursuing a standardization strategy, Toyota a segmentation strategy, and lululemon a focus strategy.

4-3b Market Segmentation, Costs, and Revenues

It is important to understand that these different approaches to market segmentation have different implications for costs and revenues. Consider first the comparison between a standardization strategy and a segmentation strategy.

A standardization strategy, which is typically associated with lower costs than a segmentation strategy, involves the company producing one basic offering and trying to attain economies of scale by achieving high-volume sales. Walmart pursues a standardization strategy and achieves enormous economies of scale in purchasing, driving down its cost of goods sold.

In contrast, a segmentation strategy requires that the company customize its product offering to different segments, producing multiple offerings, one for each segment. Customization can drive up costs for two reasons; first, the company may sell less of each offering, making it harder to achieve economies of scale; second, products targeted at segments at the higher-income end of the market may require more functions and features, which can raise the costs of production and delivery.

On the other hand, it is important not to lose sight of the fact that advances in production technology, and particularly lean production techniques, have allowed for *mass customization*—that is, the production of more product variety without a large cost penalty (see Chapter 5 for details). In addition, by designing products that share common components, some manufacturing companies achieve substantial economies of scale in component production while still producing a variety of end products aimed at different segments. This approach is adopted by large automobile companies, which try to utilize common components and platforms across a wide range of models. To the extent that mass customization and component sharing is possible, the cost penalty borne by a company pursuing a segmentation strategy may be limited.

Although a standardization strategy may have lower costs than a segmentation strategy, a segmentation strategy has one big advantage. It allows the company to capture incremental revenues by customizing its offerings to the needs of different groups of consumers and thus selling more in total. A company pursuing a

standardization strategy

When a company decides to ignore different segments and produces a standardized product for the average consumer.

segmentation strategy

When a company decides to serve many segments, or even the entire market, producing different offerings for different segments.

focus strategy

When a company decides to serve a limited number of segments, or just one segment.

standardization strategy where a product is aimed at the average consumer may lose sales from customers who desire more functions and features and are prepared to pay more for them. Similarly, it may lose sales from customers who cannot afford to purchase the average product but might enter the market if a more basic offering was available.

This reality was first recognized in the automobile industry back in the 1920s. The early leader in the automobile industry was Ford with its Model T offering. Henry Ford famously said that consumers could have it in "any color as long as it's black." Ford was, in essence, pursuing a standardization strategy. However, in the 1920s, Ford rapidly lost market share to GM, a company that pursued a segmentation strategy and offered a range of products aimed at different customer groups.

For a focus strategy, the impact on costs and revenues is subtler. Companies that focus on the higher-income or higher-value end of the market will tend to have a higher cost structure for two reasons. First, they have to add features and functions to their products that appeal to higher-income consumers, and this raises costs. For example, luxury retailer Nordstrom locates its department stores in areas where real estate is expensive; its stores have costly fittings and fixtures and a wide-open store plan with lots of room to browse; the merchandise is expensive and does not turn over as quickly as the basic clothes and shoes sold at stores like Walmart. Second, the relatively limited nature of demand associated with serving a given segment of the market may make it hard to attain economies of scale. Offsetting this, however, is the fact that the customization and exclusivity associated with a strategy of focusing on the high-income end of the market may enable a firm to charge significantly higher prices than enterprises pursuing standardization and segmentation strategies.

For companies focusing on the lower-income end of the market, or a segment that desires value for money, a different calculus comes into play. First, such companies tend to produce a more basic offering that is relatively inexpensive to produce and deliver. This may help them to drive down their cost structure. The retailer Costco, for example, focuses on consumers who seek value for money and are less concerned about brand than they are about price. Costco sells a limited range of merchandise in large, warehouse-like stores. A Costco store has about 3,750 stock-keeping units (SKUs), compared to 142,000 SKUs at the average Walmart superstore. Products are stored on pallets stacked on utilitarian metal shelves. Costco offers consumers the opportunity to purchase basic goods such as breakfast cereal, dog food, and paper towels in bulk quantities and at lower prices than found elsewhere. It turns over inventory rapidly, typically selling it before it has to pay its suppliers and thereby reducing its working capital needs. Thus, by tailoring its business to the needs of a segment, Costco is able to undercut the cost structure and pricing of a retail giant such as Walmart, even though it lacks Walmart's enormous economies of scale in purchasing. The drawback, of course, is that Costco offers much less choice than you will find at a Walmart superstore; so, for customers looking for one-stop shopping at a low price, Walmart is likely to be the store of choice.

generic business-level strategy

A strategy that gives a company a specific form of competitive position and advantage vis-à-vis its rivals, resulting in above-average profitability.

4.4 Identify the generic business-level strategic choices.

4-4 Business-Level Strategy Choices

We now have enough information to identify the basic, business-level strategy choices that companies make. These basic choices, sometimes collectively called the generic business-level strategy, are illustrated in Figure 4.4.

Companies that pursue a standardized or segmentation strategy both target a broad market. However, those pursuing a segmentation strategy recognize different

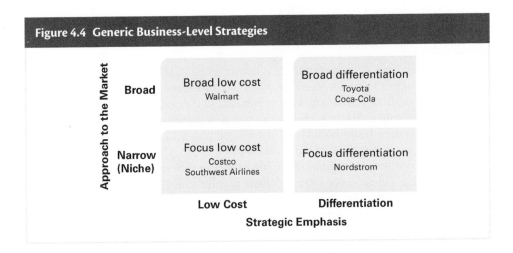

Figure 4.4 Generic Business-Level Strategies

	Low Cost	Differentiation
Broad	Broad low cost Walmart	Broad differentiation Toyota Coca-Cola
Narrow (Niche)	Focus low cost Costco Southwest Airlines	Focus differentiation Nordstrom

Approach to the Market (vertical axis)

Strategic Emphasis (horizontal axis)

segments and tailor their offering accordingly, whereas those pursuing a standardization strategy focus on serving the average consumer. Companies that target the broad market can either concentrate on lowering their costs so that they can lower prices and still make a profit, in which case they are pursuing a **broad low-cost strategy**, or they can try to differentiate their product in some way, in which case they are pursuing a **broad differentiation strategy**. Companies that decide to recognize different segments and offer different product to each one are, by default, pursuing a broad differentiation strategy. It is possible, however, to pursue a differentiation strategy while not recognizing different segments, as Coca-Cola did prior to the 1980s. Today, Walmart pursues a broad low-cost strategy, whereas Toyota and Coca-Cola pursue a broad differentiation strategy.

Companies that target a few segments, or more typically just one, are pursuing a focus or niche strategy. These companies can either try to be the low-cost player in that niche, as Costco has done, in which case we say they are pursuing a **focus low-cost strategy**, or they can try to customize their offering to the needs of their segment through the addition of features and functions, as Nordstrom has done, in which case we say they are pursuing a **focus differentiation strategy**.

It is important to understand that there is often no one best way to compete in an industry. Different strategies may be equally viable. Walmart, Costco, and Nordstrom are all in the retail industry; all three compete in different ways and all three have done very well financially. The important thing is that managers are confident in their business-level strategy, have clear logic for pursuing that strategy, have an offering that matches their strategy, and have aligned functional activities and organizational arrangements with that strategy to execute it well.

Michael Porter, the originator of the concept of generic business-level strategies, has argued that companies must make a clear choice between the different options outlined in Figure 4.4.[6] If they don't, he argues, they may become "stuck in the middle" and experience relatively poor performance. Central to Porter's thesis is the assertion that it is not possible to be both a differentiated company and a low-cost enterprise. According to Porter, differentiation by its very nature raises costs and makes it impossible to attain the low-cost position in an industry. By the same token, to achieve a low-cost position, companies necessarily must limit spending on product differentiation.

There is certainly considerable value in this perspective. As we have noted, one company cannot be both Nordstrom and Walmart, Timex and Rolex, or Porsche and Kia. Low cost and differentiation are very different ways of competing—they require

broad low-cost strategy

When a company lowers costs so that it can lower prices and still make a profit.

broad differentiation strategy

When a company differentiates its product in some way, such as by recognizing different segments or offering different products to each segment.

focus low-cost strategy

When a company targets a certain segment or niche and tries to be the low-cost player in that niche.

focus differentiation strategy

When a company targets a certain segment or niche and customizes its offering to the needs of that particular segment through the addition of features and functions.

different functional strategies and different organizational arrangements. Trying to do both at the same time may not work. On the other hand, there are important caveats to this argument.

First—as we have already seen in this chapter when we discussed value innovation through improvements in process and product—a company can push out the efficiency frontier in its industry, redefining what is possible, and deliver more differentiation at a lower cost than its rivals. In such circumstances, a company might find itself in the fortunate position of being both the differentiated player in its industry and having a low-cost position. Ultimately its rivals might catch up, in which case it may well have to make a choice between emphasizing low cost and differentiation, but as we have seen from the case histories of Dell and Toyota, value innovators can gain a competitive advantage that lasts for years.

Second, it is important for the differentiated company to recognize that it cannot waver in its focus on efficiency. Similarly, the low-cost company cannot ignore product differentiation. The task facing a company pursuing a differentiation strategy is to be as efficient as possible given its choice of strategy. The differentiated company should not cut costs so deeply that it harms its capability to differentiate its offering from that of rivals. At the same time, it cannot let costs get out of control. Nordstrom, for example, is very efficient given its choice of strategic position. It is not a low-cost company by any means but given its choice of how to compete it operates as efficiently as possible. Similarly, the low-cost company cannot totally ignore key differentiators in its industry. Walmart does not provide the high level of customer service found at Nordstrom, but Walmart cannot simply ignore customer service. Even though Walmart has a self-service business model, employees are on hand to help customers with questions if needed. The task for low-cost companies such as Walmart is to be "good enough" regarding key differentiators. For another example of how this plays out, see Strategy in Action 4.1, which examines the competition between Google and Microsoft in the market for office-productivity software.

4.5 Explain the relationship between business-level strategies and competitive advantage.

4-5 Business-Level Strategy and Competitive Advantage

Properly executed, a well-chosen, well-crafted business-level strategy can give a company a competitive advantage over actual and potential rivals. More precisely, it can put the company in an advantageous position relative to each of the competitive forces that we discussed in Chapter 2—specifically, the threat of entrants, the power of buyers and suppliers, the threat posed by substitute goods or services, and the intensity of rivalry between companies in the industry.

Consider first the low-cost company; by definition, the low-cost enterprise can make profits at price points that its rivals cannot profitably match. This makes it very hard for rivals to enter its market. In other words, the low-cost company can build an entry barrier into its market; it can, in effect, erect an economic moat around its business that thwarts higher-cost rivals. Amazon has done this in the online retail business. Through economies of scale and other operating efficiencies, Amazon has attained a very-low-cost structure that effectively constitutes a high entry barrier into this business. Rivals with less volume and fewer economies of scale than Amazon cannot match it on price without losing money—not a very appealing proposition.

A low-cost position and the ability to charge low prices and still make profits also protect a company against substitute goods or services. Low costs can help a company absorb cost increases that may be passed on downstream by powerful suppliers. Low

Microsoft Office versus Google Workspace

Microsoft has long been the dominant player in the market for office productivity software with its Office suite of programs, which includes word processing, spreadsheet, and presentation software, and an e-mail client. Microsoft's rise to dominance in this market was the result of an important innovation—in 1989, Microsoft was the first company to bundle word processing, spreadsheet, and presentation programs together into a single offering that was interoperable. At the time, the market leader in word-processing software was WordPerfect; in spreadsheet software it was Lotus; and in presentation software it was Harvard Graphics. Microsoft was number two in each of these markets. However, by offering a bundle and pricing it below the price of each program purchased on its own, Microsoft grabbed shares from its competitors, none of which had a full suite of offerings. In effect, Microsoft Office offered consumers more value (interoperability), at a lower price, than could be had from rivals.

As demand for Office expanded, Microsoft was able to spread the fixed costs of product development over a much larger volume than its rivals, and unit costs fell, giving Microsoft the double advantage of a differentiated product offering and a low-cost position. The results included the creation of a monopoly position in office-productivity software and two decades of extraordinary high returns for Microsoft in this market.

The landscape shifted in 2006, when Google introduced Google Apps, an online suite of office productivity software that was aimed squarely at Microsoft's profitable Office franchise. Unlike Office at the time, Google Apps was an online service. The basic programs reside on the cloud, and documents are saved on the cloud. At first, Google lacked a full suite of programs, and traction was slow, but since 2010, adoption of Google Apps has accelerated. In 2020, Google rebranded Google Apps as Google Workspace. Today, Google Workspace offers the same basic programs as Office—word processing, spreadsheet, and presentation software, and an e-mail client—but far fewer features. Google's approach is not to match Office on features, but to *be good enough* for most users. This helps to reduce development costs. Google was also first to distribute Google Workspace exclusively online, which is a very-low-cost distribution model.

In sum, Google is pursuing a low-cost strategy with Google Workspace. Consistent with this, Google Workspace is priced significantly below Microsoft's offering. Initially, Google Apps was targeted at small businesses and start-ups, but more recently, Google seems to be gaining traction in the enterprise space, which is Microsoft's core market for Office. Estimates suggest that Google has a 10–12% share of the office suite market. Microsoft is still the clear leader with 88% of the market, and the product remains Microsoft's most profitable business, but Microsoft cannot ignore Google's offering. Indeed, in 2012, Microsoft rolled out its own cloud-based Office offering, Office 365, which now accounts for most installs around the world. Microsoft argues that Google cannot match the quality of the enterprise experience that Microsoft can provide in areas like privacy, security, and data handling. Microsoft's message is clear—it still believes that Office is the superior product offering, differentiated by features, functions, privacy, data handling, and security. Whether Office 365 will keep Google Workspace in check, however, remains to be seen.

Sources: Author interviews at Microsoft and Google; Q. Hardy, "Google Apps Moving onto Microsoft's Business Turf," *New York Times*, December 26, 2012; A. R. Hickey, "Google Apps: A $1-Billion Business?" *CRN*, February 3, 2012, www.crn.com; M. Foley, "Microsoft now has $120 million Business Users for Office 365," *ZDNet*, October 26, 2017; Matthew Finnegan, "As Google Moves to Reshape Workspace, Barriers to Business Adoption Remain," *Computerworld*, October 18, 2021.

---

costs can also enable the company to respond to demands for deep price discounts from powerful buyers and still make money. The low-cost company is often best positioned to survive price rivalry in its industry. Indeed, a low-cost company may deliberately initiate a price war in order to grow volume and drive its weaker rivals out of the industry. Dell did this during its glory days in the early 2000s, when it repeatedly cut prices for PCs to drive up sales volume and force marginal competitors out of the business. This strategy enabled Dell to become the largest computer company in the world by the mid-2000s.

Now let us consider the differentiated company. The successful differentiator is also protected against each of the competitive forces we discussed in Chapter 2. The brand loyalty associated with differentiation can constitute an important entry barrier, protecting the company's market from potential competitors. The brand loyalty enjoyed by Apple in the smartphone business has set a very high hurdle for any new entrant to match, and effectively acts as a deterrent to entry. Because the successful differentiator sells on non-price factors such as design or customer service, it is also less exposed to pricing pressure from powerful buyers. Indeed, the opposite may be the case—the successful differentiator may be able to implement price increases without encountering much, if any, resistance from buyers. The differentiated company can also fairly easily absorb price increases from powerful suppliers and pass them on downstream in the form of higher prices for its offerings, without suffering much, if any, loss in market share. The brand loyalty enjoyed by the differentiated company also protects it from substitute goods and service.

The differentiated company is protected from intense price rivalry within its industry by its brand loyalty, and by the fact that non-price factors are important to its customer set. At the same time, the differentiated company often does have to invest significant effort and resources in non-price rivalry, such as brand building through marketing campaigns or expensive product development efforts, but to the extent that it is successful, it can reap the benefits of these investments in the form of stable or higher prices.

This being said, it is important to note that focused companies often have an advantage over their broad market rivals in the segment or niche in which they compete in. For example, although Walmart and Costco are both low-cost companies, Costco has a cost advantage over Walmart in the segment that it serves. This primarily is due to the fact that Costco carries far fewer SKUs, and those it does are sold in bulk. However, if Costco tried to match Walmart and serve the broader market, the need to carry a wider product selection (Walmart has over 140,000 SKUs) means that its cost advantage would be lost.

The same can be true for a differentiated company. By focusing on a niche, and customizing the offering to that segment, a differentiated company can often outsell differentiated rivals that target a broader market. Thus, Porsche can outsell broad market companies like Toyota or GM in the high-end sports car niche of the market, in part because the company does not sell outside of its core niche. Porsche creates an image of exclusivity that appeals to its customer base. Were Porsche to start moving down the market, it would lose this exclusive appeal and become just another broad market differentiator.

4-6 Implementing Business-Level Strategy

4.6 Explain how a company executes its business-level strategy through functional-level strategies and organizational arrangements.

As we have already suggested in this chapter, for a company's business-level strategy to translate into a competitive advantage, it must be well implemented. This means that actions taken at the functional level should support the business-level strategy, as should the organizational arrangements of the enterprise. There must, in other words, be *alignment* or *fit* between business-level strategy, functional strategy, and organization (see Figure 4.5). We will discuss functional strategy in Chapter 5; a detailed discussion of organizational arrangements is postponed until Chapter 12. Notwithstanding, we will make some basic observations about the functional strategies and organizational arrangements required to implement the business-level strategies of low cost and differentiation.

4-6a Lowering Costs Through Functional Strategy and Organization

Companies achieve a low-cost position primarily by pursuing functional-level strategies that result in *superior efficiency* and *superior product reliability*, which we discussed

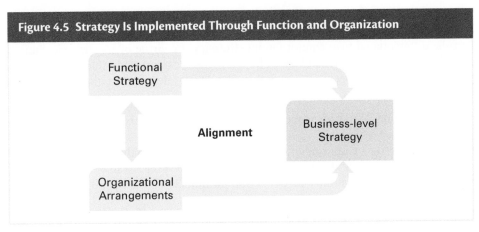

Figure 4.5 Strategy Is Implemented Through Function and Organization

Source: Charles W.L. Hill © Copyright 2013.

in Chapter 3 when we looked at the building blocks of competitive advantage. As you will see in the next chapter, when we discuss functional strategies in greater detail, the following are clearly important:

- Achieving economies of scale and learning effects
- Adopting lean production and flexible manufacturing technologies
- Implementing quality improvement methodologies to ensure that the goods or services the company produces are reliable, so that time, materials, and effort are not wasted by producing and delivering poor-quality products that must be scrapped, reworked, or reproduced from scratch
- Streamlining processes to take out unnecessary steps
- Using information systems and technology to automate business process
- Implementing just-in-time inventory control systems
- Designing products that can be produced and delivered at as low a cost as possible
- Taking steps to increase customer retention and reduce customer churn

In addition, to lower costs, the firm must be *organized* in such a way that the structure, control systems, incentive systems, and culture of the company all emphasize and reward employee behaviors and actions that are consistent with, or lead to, higher productivity and greater efficiency. As will be explained in detail in Chapter 12, the kinds of organizational arrangements that are favored in such circumstances include a flat structure with very few levels in the management hierarchy, clear lines of accountability and control, and measurement and control systems that focus on productivity and cost containment. Incentive systems encourage employees to work in as productive a manner as possible, and that empower them to suggest and pursue initiatives that are consistent with productivity improvements. A frugal culture emphasizes the need to control costs. Companies that operate with these organizational arrangements include Amazon and Walmart.

4-6b Differentiation Through Functional-Level Strategy and Organization

As with low costs, to successfully differentiate itself, a company must pursue the right actions at the functional level and organize itself appropriately. Pursuing functional-level strategies that enable the company to achieve *superior quality* in terms of both reliability and excellence are important, as is an emphasis upon *innovation* in the product offering, and high levels of *customer responsiveness*. You will recall from Chapter 3 that superior quality, innovation, and customer responsiveness are three of the four building blocks of competitive advantage, the other being *efficiency*. Remember, too, that the differentiated firm cannot ignore efficiency; by virtue of its strategic choice, the differentiated company is likely to have a higher cost structure than the low-cost player in its industry. Specific functional-level strategies designed to improve differentiation include:

- Customization of the product offering and marketing mix to different market segments
- Designing product offerings that have high perceived quality in terms of their functions, features, and performance, in addition to being reliable
- A well-developed customer-care function for quickly handling and responding to customer inquiries and problems
- Marketing efforts focused on brand building and perceived differentiation from rivals
- Hiring and employee development strategies designed to ensure that employees act in a manner that is consistent with the image that the company is trying to project to the world

For example, Apple has an excellent customer care function, as demonstrated by its in-store employees who are available to help customers with inquiries and problems and provide tutorials to help them get the best value out of their purchases. Apple has also been very successful at building a brand that differentiates it from rivals such as Microsoft (for example, the long-running TV advertisements that featured "Mac," a very hip guy, and "PC," a short, overweight man in a shabby gray suit).

In regards to organization, creating the right structure, controls, incentives, and culture can all help a company differentiate itself. In a differentiated enterprise, one key issue is to make sure that marketing, product design, customer service, and customer care functions all play a key role. Again, consider Apple. Following his return to the company in 1997, Steve Jobs reorganized the company to give the industrial design group the lead on all new product-development efforts. Under this arrangement, industrial design, headed by Johnny Ive, reported directly to Jobs, and engineering reported to industrial design for purposes of product development. This meant that designers rather than engineers specified the look and feel of a new product, and engineers then had to design according to the parameters imposed by the design group. This contrasts with almost all other companies in the computer and smartphone business, where engineering typically takes the lead on product development. Jobs felt that this organizational arrangement was necessary to ensure that Apple produced beautiful products that not only worked well, but also looked and felt elegant. Because Apple under Jobs was differentiating by design, design was given a pivotal position in the organization.[7]

Making sure that control systems, incentive systems, and culture are aligned with the strategic thrust is also extremely important for differentiated companies. We will return to, and expand upon, these themes in Chapter 12.

4.7 Discuss the concept of blue ocean strategy and value innovation.

4-7 The Blue Ocean Strategy and Value Innovation

We have already suggested in this chapter that sometimes companies can fundamentally shift the game in their industry by figuring out ways to offer more value through differentiation at a lower cost than their rivals. We referred to this as *value innovation*, a term first coined by Chan Kim and Renee Mauborgne.[8] Kim and Mauborgne developed their ideas further in their best-selling book *Blue Ocean Strategy*.[9] Their basic proposition is that many successful companies have built their competitive advantage by redefining their product offering through value innovation and, in essence, creating a new market space. They describe the process of thinking through value innovation as searching for the blue ocean—which they characterize as a wide-open market space where a company can chart its own course.

One of their examples of a company that found its blue ocean is Southwest Airlines. From its conception, Southwest competed differently than other companies in the U.S. airline industry. Most important, Southwest saw its main competitors not as other airlines but as people who would typically drive or take a bus to travel. For Southwest, the focus was to reduce travel time for its customer set and do so in a way that was cheap, reliable, and convenient, so that they would prefer to fly rather than drive.

The first route that Southwest operated was between Houston and Dallas. To reduce total travel time, it decided to fly into the small, downtown airports in both cities, Hobby in Houston, and Love Field in Dallas, rather than the large, intercontinental airports located an hour's drive outside of both cities. The goal was to reduce total travel time by eliminating the need to drive to reach a major airport outside the city before even beginning one's journey. Southwest put as many flights a day on the route as possible to make it convenient, and did everything possible to drive down operating costs so that it could charge low prices and still make a profit.

As the company grew and opened more routes, it followed the same basic strategy. Southwest always flew point to point, never routing passengers through hubs. Changing planes in a hub adds to total travel time and can hurt reliability, measured by on-time departures and arrivals, if connections are slow arriving or departing a hub due to adverse events such as bad weather delaying traffic somewhere in an airline's network. Southwest also dispensed with in-flight meals, only offers coach-class seating, does not have lounges in airports for business-class passengers, and has standardized on one type of aircraft, the Boeing 737, which helps to raise reliability. The net result is that Southwest delivers more value *to its customer set* and does so at a lower cost than its rivals, enabling it to price tickets lower than others and still make a profit. Southwest is a value innovator.

Kim and Mauborgne use the concept of a *strategy canvas* to map out how value innovators differ from their rivals. The strategy canvas for Southwest, shown in Figure 4.6, shows that Southwest charges a low price and does not provide meals or lounges in airports, business-class seating, or connections through hubs (it flies point to point), but does provide friendly, quick, convenient, reliable low-cost service, *which is its customer set values*.

The whole point of the Southwest example, and other business case histories Kim and Mauborgne review, is to illustrate how many successful enterprises compete differently than their less successful rivals: They carve out a unique market space for themselves through value innovation. When thinking about how a company might redefine its market and craft a new business-level strategy, Kim and Mauborgne suggest that managers ask themselves the following questions:

1. **Eliminate**: Which factors that rivals take for granted in our industry can be eliminated, thereby reducing costs?
2. **Reduce**: Which factors should be reduced well below the standard in our industry, thereby lowering costs?
3. **Raise**: Which factors should be raised above the standard in our industry, thereby increasing value?
4. **Create**: What factors can we create that rivals do not offer, thereby increasing value?

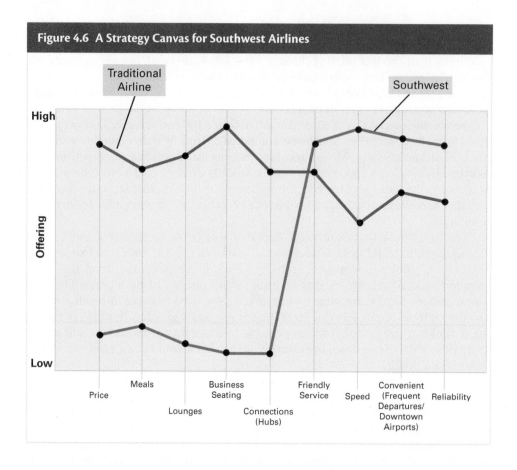

Figure 4.6 A Strategy Canvas for Southwest Airlines

Southwest *eliminated* lounges, business seating, and meals in flight; it *reduced* inflight refreshment to be well below industry standards; and by flying point-to-point it *raised* speed (reducing travel time), convenience, and reliability. Southwest also *created* value by flying between smaller, downtown airports whenever possible—something that other airlines did not typically do.

This is a useful framework, and it directs managerial attention to the need to think differently than rivals in order to create an offering and strategic position that are unique. If such efforts are successful, they can help a company build a sustainable advantage.

One great advantage of successful value innovation is that it can catch rivals off guard and make it difficult for them to catch up. For example, when Dell Computer started to sell directly to customers online, it was very difficult for rivals to respond because they had already invested in a different way of doing business—selling though a physical retail channel. Dell's rivals could not easily adopt the Dell model without alienating their channel, which would have resulted in lost sales. The prior strategic investment of Dell's rivals in distribution channels—which, at the time they were made, seemed reasonable—became a source of inertia that limited their ability to rapidly respond to Dell's innovations. The same holds true in the airline industry, where the prior strategic investments of traditional airlines have made it very difficult for them to respond to the threat posed by Southwest.

In sum, value innovation, because it shifts the basis of competition, can result in a sustained competitive advantage for the innovating company due to the relative inertia of rivals and their inability to respond in a timely manner without breaking prior strategic commitments.

Key Terms

business-level
    strategy 102
value innovation 109
market
    segmentation 110

standardization
    strategy 111
segmentation
    strategy 111
focus strategy 111

generic business-level
    strategy 112
broad low-cost strategy 113
broad differentiation
    strategy 113

focus low-cost
    strategy 113
focus differentiation
    strategy 113

Takeaways for Strategic Managers

1. Business-level strategy refers to the overarching competitive theme of a company in a given market.
2. At the most basic level, a company has a competitive advantage if it can lower costs relative to rivals and/or differentiate its product offering from those of rivals.
3. A low-cost position enables a company to make money at price points where its rivals are losing money.
4. A differentiated company can charge a higher price for its offering, and/or it can use superior value to generate growth in demand.
5. There are often multiple viable market positions along the differentiation–low-cost continuum.
6. Value innovation occurs when a company develops new products, processes, or strategies that enable it to offer more value through differentiation at a lower cost than its rivals.
7. Formulating a business-level strategy starts with deciding who the company is going to serve, what needs or desires it is trying to satisfy, and how it is going to satisfy those needs and desires.

8. Market segmentation is the process of subdividing a market into clearly identifiable groups of customers that have similar needs, desires, and demand characteristics.
9. A company's approach to market segmentation is an important aspect of its business-level strategy.
10. There are four generic business-level strategies: broad low cost, broad differentiation, focus low cost, and focus differentiation.
11. Business-level strategy is executed through actions taken at the functional level and through organizational arrangements.
12. Many successful companies have built their competitive advantage by redefining their product offering through value innovation and creating a new market space. The process of thinking through value innovation has been described as searching for a "blue ocean"—a wide-open market space where a company can chart its own course.

Discussion Questions

1. What are the main differences between a low-cost strategy and a differentiation strategy?
2. Why is market segmentation such an important step in the process of formulating a business-level strategy?
3. How can a business-level strategy of (a) low cost and (b) differentiation offer some protection against competitive forces in a company's industry?
4. What is required to transform a business-level strategy from a concept to a reality?
5. What is meant by the term *value innovation*? Can you identify a company not discussed in the text that has established a strong competitive position through value innovation?

Verizon is the leading company in the U.S. wireless telecommunications business, from which it derives nearly 80% of its $133 billion in annual revenue and nearly all of its operating income (the remaining revenues come from its fixed line business, which is primarily based on fiber optics into businesses and homes). Verizon serves about 93 million postpaid and 24 million prepaid customers. Postpaid customers are more lucrative; they have better credit ratings, purchase more premium services, and are less likely to leave the service. Of Verizon's wireless revenue, around 70% comes from consumers, and 30% from business customers. Verizon's market share of postpaid customers is around 40%, about one-third greater than the share of its two main rivals, AT&T and T-Mobile. Verizon has also been persistently more profitable than its rivals. Its 5-year average return on invested capital (ROIC) between 2016 and 2021 was just shy of 14%, compared to around 9% for AT&T and 8% for T-Mobile. However, T-Mobile has been growing faster than both Verizon and AT&T, capturing about 75% of the 27 million new postpaid customers that entered the market between 2013 and 2019.

Verizon's advantages come from several sources. The company has long excelled in network quality. It has the most extensive coverage of the big three wireless companies, so very few calls are dropped, and the quality of its connections is high. In the last decade, Verizon invested heavily in 4G technology, enabling fast downloads of streaming music and video. Now, Verizon is rolling out its high-bandwidth 5G service, which has much faster download speeds and significantly less latency. While T-Mobile took an early lead in rolling out 5G technology in the United States, Verizon spent some $50 billion acquiring higher-bandwidth C-band 5G spectrum in government auctions, which it is rolling out nationwide starting in early 2022. The higher quality of Verizon's 5G networks is expected to attract more consumer and business subscribers. Moreover, C-band 5G will potentially support many new applications associated with the Internet of Things that require high bandwidth and very low latency (for example, autonomous vehicles). Significantly, Verizon's own research has found that customers with 5G phones are 2.5 times more likely to subscribe to the company's premium unlimited plans. As customers adopt 5G handsets, this should drive up the average revenue per account.

Verizon has leveraged its reputation for having a high-quality network into a strong brand identity. According to a ranking by Kantar, Verizon was the 10th most valuable brand in the United States in 2020 (AT&T was number 9, while T-Mobile came in at 39). In addition, Verizon has the lowest customer churn rate in the industry. In 2021, just 1.1% of Verizon's customers left the service, compared with 1.7% at AT&T and 2.2% at T-Mobile (the churn rate refers to the average percentage of customers who terminate their monthly subscription to a company's services). Lower churn not only signifies greater customer loyalty, it also means lower customer acquisition costs since less must be invested to acquire customers to replace those leaving the service.

Verizon's other great advantage comes from economies of scale. Many of the infrastructure costs of providing a wireless service are fixed, such as cell towers, backbone fibers, and switches. As the market leader, Verizon can spread its fixed costs over a larger subscriber base than either AT&T or T-Mobile. This drives down the average cost of serving a customer. Verizon also enjoys economies of scale in advertising. For example, while Verizon historically spent more on advertising than T-Mobile, on a per customer basis T-Mobile has spent about 30% more.

None of this means that Verizon's position is secure. T-Mobile has been gaining share with its aggressive "uncarrier" strategy (see the closing case on T-Mobile in Chapter 1), although T-Mobile still lacks Verizon's economies of scale and strong brand. In addition, there is a disruptive technology on the horizon: low earth orbit satellite internet. Both Space X and

Amazon are putting up thousands of low earth orbit satellites, and a wireless satellite service might cut into at least some of Verizon's customer base. Plus, the wireless phone market is now mature, which implies significant competition for market share going forward.

Sources: S. Krouse, "Verizon's Quest for 5G Revenue," *Wall Street Journal*, March 24, 2021; C. Wilson, "Does the Drop in Verizon Provide a Buying Opportunity?," *Seeking Alpha*, April 11, 2022; "BrandZ Top 100 Most Valuable US Brands," SyncForce, https://www.rankingthebrands.com/The-Brand-Rankings; M. Hodel, "Verizon Offers a Cautious 2022 Outlook, but Our Long Term View Is Unchanged," *Morningstar*, April 22, 2022.

Case Discussion Questions

1. What is Verizon's segmentation strategy? Who does the company serve?
2. Regarding its core segment, or segments, what does Verizon offer to its customers?
3. Using the Porter model, which generic business-level strategy is Verizon pursuing?
4. What resources underlie Verizon's strong competitive position? How difficult is it for rivals to match Verizon's resources? Does Verizon have a sustainable competitive advantage?
5. What do you think Verizon needs to do to maintain its competitive advantage going forward?

Notes

[1] D. F. Abell, *Defining the Business: The Starting Point of Strategic Planning* (Englewood Cliffs, NJ: Prentice-Hall, 1980).

[2] M. E. Porter, *Competitive Advantage* (New York: Free Press, 1985); M. E. Porter, *Competitive Strategy* (New York: Free Press, 1980).

[3] C. W. L. Hill, "Differentiation Versus Low Cost or Differentiation and Low Cost: A Contingency Framework," *Academy of Management Review* 13 (1988): 401–412.

[4] M. E. Porter, "What Is Strategy?" *Harvard Business Review,* On-point Enhanced Edition Article, February 1, 2000.

[5] W. C. Kim and R. Mauborgne, "Value Innovation: The Strategic Logic of High Growth," *Harvard Business Review* (January–February 1997).

[6] Porter, *Competitive Advantage* and *Competitive Strategy*.

[7] The story was related to author Charles Hill by an executive at Apple.

[8] Kim and Mauborgne, "Value Innovation: The Strategic Logic of High Growth."

[9] W. C. Kim and R. Mauborgne, *Blue Ocean Strategy* (Boston: Harvard Business School Press, 2005).

Building Competitive Advantage and Executing Business-Level Strategy Through Functional Strategy

Opening Case

Colgate Palmolive

Established in 1806, Colgate Palmolive (Colgate) is one of the oldest continually operating business enterprises in the world. Today, it is a leading global consumer products organization best known for its market leading position in oral care products including toothpaste, toothbrushes, mouthwash, and dental floss. Globally, the firm maintains a nearly 40% share in the market for toothpaste – over 2.5 times more than its next largest competitor. For example, in India its share is 40%, versus the 14% share held by the local Indian company, Dabur. In Brazil, it holds 67% versus 10% for Procter & Gamble, and in China it has a 27% share, while second-place P&G has only 13% of the market. Colgate is also perennially profitable. Returns on invested capital averaged nearly 30% annually between 2012 and 2022, far above the company's estimated cost of capital, which is around 7%.

How does Colgate achieve such consistently strong performance? The company has long had a very strong brand recognition in the oral care market. The foundation of Colgate's brand equity is the close relationships it has built over decades with industry professionals around the world. Colgate boasts that it is the most recommended brand by dentists around the world. The company sees professional endorsements as crucial for building brand equity, and the company devotes considerable attention to providing scientific support and recommendations for Colgate's oral care products. These activities include attending and presenting at dental conventions to explain the scientific research behind Colgate's products, as well as offering free samples to dentists (which they then give to their patients) and obtaining seals of approval from dental associations. Colgate touts its professional endorsements in its consumer-focused campaigns, which emphasize the bright, white, beautiful "Colgate Smile" that comes from using Colgate products.

There are also targeted educational campaigns in different countries to build brand awareness. In India, for example, Colgate has worked closely with the Indian Dental Association to build awareness of oral health and provide free dental screening to children across the country through a school dental education program known as "Bright Smile, Bright Futures." Similar programs have been introduced in other countries. Colgate claims that since 1991 these programs have brought oral health education to more than half a billion children around the world.

To further support its strong brand equity, Colgate devotes significant attention to product innovation, so that it can respond quickly to evolving customer needs. The company spends some $300 million a year, or 2% of sales, on R&D. While it may not always be the first to introduce new products, it responds quickly to market shifts. For example, when a rival introduced toothpaste

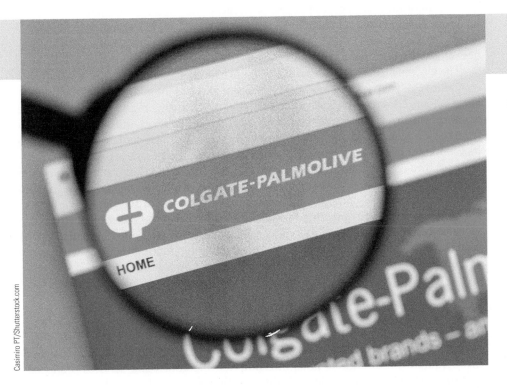

Casimiro PT/Shutterstock.com

Sources: Colgate Palmolive, *Annual Report*, 2020; "Colgate Palmolive in Beauty and Personal Care," *Euromonitor International*, December 2021; E. Lash, "Colgate Prudently Working to Steady Its Competitive Position Even as Unrelenting Headwinds Swirl," *Morningstar*, March 21, 2022; D. Kum, "Colgate: Regaining Leadership in India's Sensitive Teeth Market," *Ivey Publishing*, December 16, 2015.

that gave long-lasting relief to tooth sensitivity, Colgate quickly brought its own offering to the market and captured 75% of a $1 billion global market for sensitive toothpaste. Similarly, when the start-up Sonicare developed its electric toothbrushes, Colgate responded by developing its own electric toothbrushes to protect its market position, and when rival Procter & Gamble introduced "whitening" mouthwash, Colgate responded by bringing its own whitening mouthwash to the market. Through better management of the product development process, Colgate claims that it has reduced the time it takes to bring new products to the market from 18 to 36 months down to 6 to 12 months, significantly enhancing its ability to respond to market shifts.

Colgate's strong brand equity supports premium pricing, and this, taken together with its broad product portfolio, makes the company an attractive partner for retailers, who give its products significant shelf space. In turn, the company's high market share and strong retail presence translates into economies of scale, giving Colgate a cost advantage relative to its smaller rivals in the oral healthcare market. Analysts believe that Colgate can operate with lower unit and distribution costs, as well as greater supply chain efficiency and an enhanced ability to leverage brand spending, than smaller peers.

5-1 Overview

In Chapter 3, we saw how valuable, rare, inimitable resources that are well organized within an enterprise form the foundation of competitive advantage. In Chapter 4, we discussed business-level strategy and explained how the development of valuable, rare, inimitable resources underpin a company's business-level strategy. In this chapter, we shall take a closer look at how a company can use strategic investments at the functional level to build valuable resources that enable it to attain superior efficiency, quality, innovation, and customer responsiveness (see Figure 5.1), thereby executing its business-level strategy. We refer to these investments as **functional-level strategies**, which are the are actions that managers take to improve the efficiency and effectiveness of one or more value creation activities (see Figure 3.5 in Chapter 3).

functional-level strategies

Actions that managers take to improve the efficiency and effectiveness of one or more of value creation activities.

The Opening Case illustrates some of these relationships. Colgate has a sustainable competitive advantage in the oral care business and has long been the global market share leader. The company's advantage is based upon strong brand equity, a valuable resource, which supports a *differentiation* strategy. In addition, the company benefits from the *low costs* that flow from economies of scale. The company is *efficient* (due to its economies of scale), responds to evolving customer preferences (*customer responsiveness*) through rapid product development (*innovation*), and has a strong reputation among industry professionals and consumers for developing *high-quality* products. In other words, over the years, Colgate has made investments at the functional level in the building blocks of competitive advantage that have enabled the company to create valuable resources (including its brand equity and economies of scale) and build a sustainable competitive advantage-based product differentiation that can be delivered cost efficiently.

5-2 Achieving Superior Efficiency

A company is a device for transforming inputs (such as labor, land, capital, management, equipment, and know-how) into outputs (the goods and services produced). The simplest measure of efficiency is the quantity of inputs that it takes to produce a given output; that is, efficiency = outputs/inputs. The more efficient a company, the fewer the inputs required to produce a given output, and therefore the lower its cost structure. Put another way, an efficient company has higher productivity and therefore lower costs than its rivals. Here, we review the steps that companies can take at the functional level to increase efficiency and lower its cost structure.

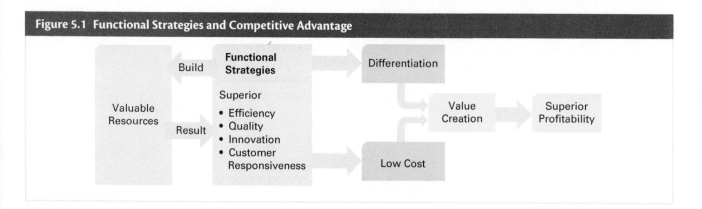

Figure 5.1 Functional Strategies and Competitive Advantage

5-2a Efficiency and Economies of Scale

Economies of scale are unit cost reductions associated with large-scale output. You will recall from the Chapter 3 that it is very important for managers to understand how the cost structure of their enterprise varies with output, because this understanding should help to drive strategy. For example, if unit costs fall significantly as output is expanded—that is, if there are significant economies of scale—a company may benefit by keeping prices down and increasing volume.

One source of economies of scale is the ability to spread fixed costs over a large production volume. **Fixed costs** are costs that must be incurred to produce a product regardless of the level of output; examples are the costs of purchasing machinery, setting up machinery for individual production runs, building facilities, advertising, and R&D. For example, Microsoft spent approximately $5 billion to develop its Windows operating system, Windows 10. It realized substantial scale economies by spreading the fixed costs associated with developing the new operating system over the enormous unit sales volume it expects for this system (over 75% of the world's 2 billion desktop and laptop PCs use Windows). These scale economies are significant because of the trivial incremental (or marginal) cost of producing additional copies of Windows 10. For example, once the master copy has been produced, original equipment manufacturers (OEMs) can install copies of Windows 10 on new PCs for zero marginal cost to Microsoft. The key to Microsoft's efficiency and profitability in the operating system business has long been to increase sales rapidly enough that fixed costs can be spread out over a large unit volume and substantial scale economies realized.

Another source of scale economies is the ability of companies producing in large volumes to achieve a greater division of labor and specialization. Specialization is said to have a favorable impact on productivity, primarily because it enables employees to become very skilled at performing a particular task. The classic example of such economies is Ford's Model T automobile. The Model T Ford, introduced in 1923, was the world's first mass-produced car. Until 1923, Ford had made cars using an expensive, hand-built, craft production method. Introducing mass-production techniques allowed the company to achieve greater division of labor (it split assembly into small, repeatable tasks) and specialization, which boosted employee productivity. Ford was also able to distribute the fixed costs of developing a car and setting up production machinery over a large volume of output. As a result of these economies, the cost of manufacturing a car at Ford fell from $3,000 to less than $900 (in 1958 dollars).

The concept of scale economies is depicted in Figure 5.2, which illustrates that, as a company increases its output, unit costs decrease. This process comes to an end at an output of Q1, where all scale economies are exhausted. Indeed, at outputs of greater than Q1, the company may encounter **diseconomies of scale**, which are the unit cost increases associated with a large scale of output. Diseconomies of scale occur primarily because of the increased bureaucracy associated with large-scale enterprises and the managerial inefficiencies that can result.[1] Larger enterprises have a tendency to develop extensive managerial hierarchies in which dysfunctional political behavior is commonplace. Information about operating matters can accidentally and/or deliberately be distorted by the number of managerial layers through which the information must travel to reach top decision makers. The result is poor decision making. Therefore, past a specific point—such as Q1 in Figure 5.2—inefficiencies that result from such developments outweigh any additional gains from economies of scale. As output expands, unit costs begin to rise.

Managers must know the extent of economies of scale, and where diseconomies of scale begin to occur. At Nucor Steel, for example, the realization that diseconomies of scale exist has led to the company's decision to build plants that employ only

economies of scale

Reductions in unit costs attributed to larger output.

fixed costs

Costs that must be incurred to produce a product regardless of level of output.

diseconomies of scale

Unit cost increases associated with a large scale of output.

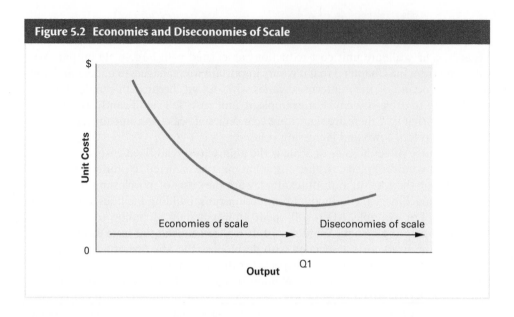

Figure 5.2 Economies and Diseconomies of Scale

Unit Costs

$

0

Economies of scale

Diseconomies of scale

Output

Q1

300 individuals or fewer. The belief is that it is more efficient to build two plants, each employing 300 people, than one plant employing 600 people. Although the larger plant may theoretically make it possible to reap greater scale economies, Nucor's management believes that larger plants would suffer from the diseconomies of scale associated with large organizational units.

5-2b Efficiency and Learning Effects

learning effects

Cost savings that come from learning by doing.

Learning effects are cost savings that result from "learning by doing." Labor, for example, learns by repetition how to best carry out a task. Therefore, labor productivity increases over time, and unit costs decrease as individuals learn the most efficient way to perform a particular task. Equally important, management in a new manufacturing facility typically learns over time how best to run the new operation. Hence, production costs decline because of increasing labor productivity and management efficiency. Put differently, over time, management and labor accumulate valuable process knowledge that leads to higher productivity. Japanese automobile company Toyota is known for making the accumulation of process knowledge central to its operating philosophy.

Learning effects tend to be more significant when a technologically complex task is repeated because there is more to learn. Thus, learning effects will be more significant in an assembly process that has 1,000 complex steps than in a process with 100 simple steps. Although learning effects are normally associated with the manufacturing process, there is substantial evidence that they are just as important in-service industries. One famous study of learning in the healthcare industry discovered that more-experienced medical providers posted significantly lower mortality rates for a number of common surgical procedures, suggesting that learning effects are at work in surgery.[2] The authors of this study used the evidence to argue in favor of establishing regional referral centers for the provision of highly specialized medical care. These centers would perform many specific surgical procedures (such as heart surgery), replacing local facilities with lower volumes and presumably higher mortality rates. Strategy in Action 5.1 looks at the determinants of differences in learning effects across a sample of hospitals performing cardiac surgery.

Another recent study found strong evidence of learning effects in a financial institution. This study looked at a newly established document-processing unit with 100 staff members and found that, over time, documents were processed much more

Learning Effects in Cardiac Surgery

Researchers at the Harvard Business School carried out a study to estimate the importance of learning effects in the case of a new technology for minimally invasive heart surgery that was approved by federal regulators. The researchers looked at 16 hospitals and obtained data on operations for 660 patients who underwent surgery using the new technology. They examined how the time required to undertake the procedure varied with cumulative experience. Across the 16 hospitals, they found that average time decreased from 280 minutes for the first procedure with the new technology to 220 minutes once a hospital had performed 50 procedures (note that not all hospitals performed 50 procedures, and the estimates represent an extrapolation based on the data).

Next, the study observed differences across hospitals; here they found evidence of very large differences in learning effects. One hospital, in particular, stood out. This hospital, called "Hospital M," reduced its net procedure time from 500 minutes on case 1 to 132 minutes by case 50. Hospital M's 88-minute procedure time advantage over the average hospital at case 50 meant a cost savings of approximately $2,250 per case, which allowed surgeons at the hospital to complete one more revenue-generating procedure per day.

The researchers inquired into factors that made Hospital M superior. They noted that all hospitals had similar, state-of-the-art operating rooms; all used the same devices, approved by the Food and Drug Administration (FDA); all surgeons who adopted the new technology

completed the same training courses; and all surgeons came from highly respected training hospitals. Follow-up interviews, however, suggested that Hospital M differed in how it implemented the new procedure. The adopting surgeon handpicked the team that would perform the surgery. Members of the team had significant prior experience working together, which was a key criterion for member selection, and the team trained together to perform the surgery with the new technology. Before undertaking the surgery, the entire team met with the operating room nurses and anesthesiologists to discuss it. In addition, the adopting surgeon mandated that no changes would be made to either the team or the procedure in the early stages of using the technology. The initial team completed 15 procedures before members were added or substituted and completed 20 cases before the procedure was modified. The adopting surgeon also insisted that the team meet prior to each of the first 10 cases, and after the first 20 cases, to debrief.

The picture that emerges is a core team selected and managed to maximize gains from learning, unlike other hospitals where team members and procedures were less consistent, and where there was not the same attention to briefing, debriefing, and learning. Thus, surgeons at Hospital M learned much faster and ultimately achieved higher productivity than their peers in other institutions. Clearly, differences in the implementation of the new procedure were very significant.

Source: G. P. Pisano, R. M. J. Bohmer, and A. C. Edmondson, "Organizational Differences in Rates of Learning: Evidence from the Adoption of Minimally Invasive Cardiac Surgery," *Management Science* 47 (2001): 752–768.

rapidly as the staff learned the process. Overall, the study concluded that unit costs decreased every time the cumulative number of documents processed doubled.[3]

In terms of the unit cost curve of a company, economies of scale imply a movement along the curve (say, from A to B in Figure 5.3). The realization of learning

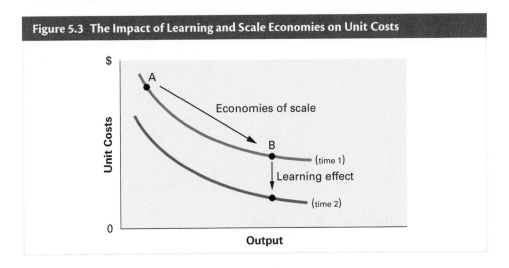

Figure 5.3 The Impact of Learning and Scale Economies on Unit Costs

effects implies a downward shift of the entire curve (B to C in Figure 5.3) as both labor and management become more efficient over time at performing their tasks at every level of output. In accounting terms, learning effects in a production setting reduce the cost of goods sold as a percentage of revenues, enabling the company to earn a higher return on sales and return on invested capital.

No matter how complex the task, learning effects typically diminish in importance after a period of time. Indeed, it has been suggested that they are most important during the start-up period of a new process and become trivial after a few years.[4] When a company's production system changes—as a result of the use of new information technology, for example—the learning process must begin again.

5-2c Efficiency and the Experience Curve

experience curve

The systematic lowering of the cost structure and consequent unit cost reductions that have been observed to occur over the life of a product.

The **experience curve** refers to the systematic lowering of the cost structure, and consequent unit-cost reductions, that have been observed to occur over the life of a product.[5] According to the experience-curve concept, per-unit production costs for a product typically decline by some characteristic amount each time accumulated output of the product is doubled (accumulated output is the total output of a product since its introduction). This relationship was first observed in the aircraft industry, where it was found that each time the accumulated output of airframes doubled, unit costs declined to 80% of their previous level.[6] As such, the fourth airframe typically cost only 80% of the second airframe cost to produce, the eighth airframe only 80% of the fourth, the sixteenth only 80% of the eighth, and so on. The outcome of this process is a relationship between unit manufacturing costs and accumulated output similar to the illustration in Figure 5.3. Both economies of scale and learning effects underlie the experience-curve phenomenon. Put simply, as a company increases the accumulated volume of its output over time, it is able to realize both economies of scale (as volume increases) and learning effects. Consequently, unit costs and cost structure fall with increases in accumulated output.

The strategic significance of the experience curve is clear: Increasing a company's product volume and market share will lower its cost structure relative to its rivals. In Figure 5.4, Company B has a cost advantage over Company A because of its lower cost structure, and because it is farther down the experience curve. This concept is

Figure 5.4 The Experience Curve

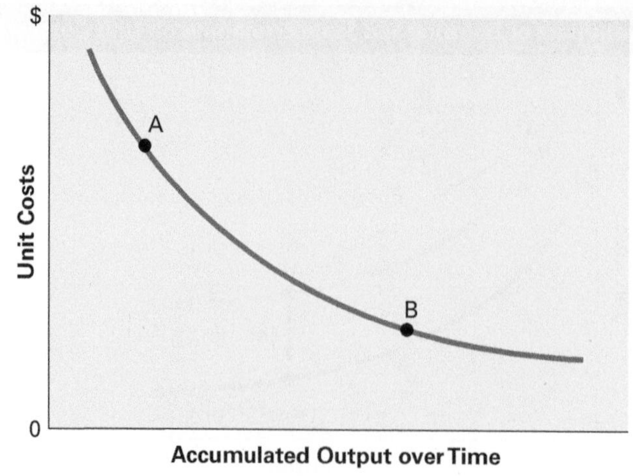

very important in industries that mass-produce a standardized output—for example, the manufacture of semiconductor chips. A company that wishes to become more efficient and lower its cost structure must try to move down the experience curve as quickly as possible. This means constructing manufacturing facilities that are scaled for efficiency even before the company has generated demand for its product, and aggressively pursuing cost reductions from learning effects. It might also need to adopt an aggressive marketing strategy, cutting prices drastically and stressing heavy sales promotions and extensive advertising in order to build up demand and accumulated volume as quickly as possible. A company is likely to have a significant cost advantage over its competitors because of its superior efficiency once it is down the experience curve. It has been argued that Intel and, more recently, TSCM use such tactics to ride down the experience curve and gain a competitive advantage over rivals in the micro-processor market.[7]

It is worth emphasizing that this concept is just as important outside of manufacturing. For example, as it invests in its distribution network, online retailer Amazon is trying to both realize economies of scale (spreading the fixed costs of its distribution centers over a large sales volume) and improve the efficiency of its inventory-management and order-fulfillment processes at distribution centers (a learning effect). Together, these two sources of cost savings should enable Amazon to ride down the experience curve ahead of its rivals, thereby gaining a low-cost position that enables it to make greater profits at lower prices than its rivals.

Managers should not become complacent about efficiency-based cost advantages derived from experience effects. First, because neither learning effects nor economies of scale are sustained forever, the experience curve will bottom out at some point; it must do so by definition. When this occurs, further unit-cost reductions from learning effects and economies of scale will be difficult to attain. Over time, other companies can lower their cost structures and match the cost leader. Once this happens, many low-cost companies can achieve cost parity with each other. In such circumstances, a sustainable competitive advantage must rely on strategic factors other than the minimization of production costs by using existing technologies—factors such as better responsiveness to customers, product quality, or innovation.

Second, cost advantages gained from experience effects can be rendered obsolete by the development of new technologies. For example, the large, "big-box" bookstores Borders and Barnes & Noble may have had cost advantages that were derived from economies of scale and learning. However, those advantages diminished when Amazon, utilizing web technology, launched its online bookstore in 1994. By selling online, Amazon was able to offer a larger selection at a lower cost than established rivals with physical storefronts. When Amazon introduced its Kindle digital reader in 2007 and started to sell eBooks, it changed the basis of competition once more, effectively nullifying the experience-based advantage enjoyed by Borders and Barnes & Noble. By 2022, Borders was bankrupt, and Barnes & Noble was in financial trouble and closing stores. Amazon, in the meantime, has gone from strength to strength.

5-2d Efficiency, Flexible Production Systems, and Mass Customization

Central to the concept of economies of scale is the idea that a lower cost structure, attained through the mass production of a standardized output, is the best way to achieve high efficiency. There is an implicit trade-off in this idea between unit costs and product variety. Wide product variety shipped from a single factory implies shorter production runs, which implies an inability to realize economies of scale and thus higher costs. That is, greater product variety makes it difficult for a company to increase its production efficiency and reduce its unit costs. According to this logic, the way to increase efficiency and achieve a lower cost structure is to limit product variety and produce a standardized product in large volumes (see Figure 5.5a).

This view of production efficiency has been challenged by the rise of flexible production technologies. The term **flexible production technology** covers a range of technologies designed to reduce setup times for complex equipment, increase the use of individual machines through better scheduling, and improve quality control at all stages of the manufacturing process.[8] Flexible production technologies allow the company to produce a wider variety of end products at a unit cost that at one time could be achieved only through the mass production of a standardized output (see Figure 5.5b). Research suggests that the adoption of flexible production technologies may increase efficiency and lower unit costs relative to what can be achieved by the mass production of a standardized output, while at the same time enabling the company to customize its product offering to a much greater extent than was once thought possible. The term **mass customization** describes a company's ability to use flexible manufacturing technology to reconcile two goals that were once thought to be incompatible: low cost and differentiation through product customization.[9]

Dell Technologies originally rose to prominence by being the first in the personal computer industry to pursue a mass customization strategy, by enabling its customers to build their own machines online. Dell kept costs and prices under control by allowing customers to make choices within a limited menu of options (different amounts of memory, hard-drive capacity, video card, microprocessor, and so on). The result was to create more value for customers than was possible for rivals that sold a limited range of PC models through retail outlets. Similarly, Mars offers a service, My M&Ms, that enables customers to design personalized M&Ms online. Customers can pick different colors and have messages or pictures printed on their M&Ms. Another example of mass customization is the online radio service Pandora, which is discussed in Strategy in Action 5.2.

The effects of installing flexible production technology on a company's cost structure can be dramatic. Over the last two decades, the Ford Motor Company has been

flexible production technology

A range of technologies designed to reduce setup times for complex equipment, increase the use of machinery through better scheduling, and improve quality control at all stages of the manufacturing process.

mass customization

The use of flexible manufacturing technology to reconcile two goals that were once thought to be incompatible: low cost and differentiation through product customization.

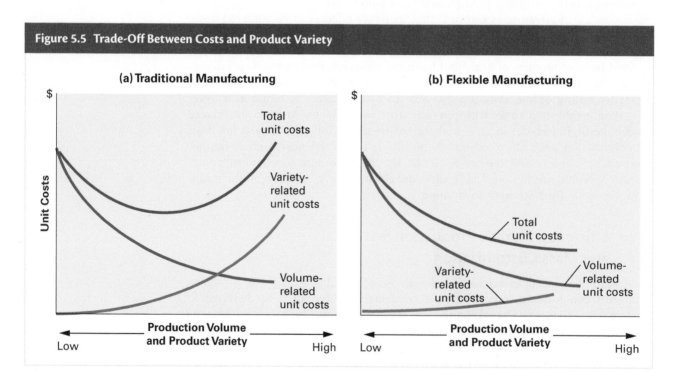

Figure 5.5 Trade-Off Between Costs and Product Variety

(a) Traditional Manufacturing

$

Unit Costs

Total unit costs

Variety-related unit costs

Volume-related unit costs

Production Volume and Product Variety

Low   High

(b) Flexible Manufacturing

$

Total unit costs

Variety-related unit costs

Volume-related unit costs

Production Volume and Product Variety

Low   High

Pandora: Mass Customizing Internet Radio

Pandora Media streams music to PCs and mobile devices. Customers start by typing in the kind of music that they want to listen to. With a database of over 100,000 artists, there is a good chance that Pandora has something for you, however particular your tastes. Customers can then rate the music that Pandora plays for them (thumbs up or down). Pandora takes this feedback and refines the music it streams to a customer. The company also uses sophisticated predictive statistical analysis (what do other customers who also like this song listen to?) and product analysis (what Pandora calls its Music Genome, which analyzes songs and identifies similar songs) to further customize the experience for the individual listener. The Music Genome has the added benefit of introducing listeners to new songs they might like based on an analysis of their listening habits. The result is a radio station attuned to each individual's unique listening preferences. This is mass customization at its most pure.

Launched in 2000, by late 2017 Pandora's annualized revenue run rate was $1.7 billion. There were 250 million registered users and 78 million active users, giving Pandora a 69% share of the online radio market in the United States. Pandora's revenue comes primarily from advertising, although premium subscribers can pay $109 a year and get commercial-free music.

Despite its rapid growth—a testament to the value of mass customization—Pandora does have its problems. Pandora pays more than half of its revenue in royalties to music publishers. By comparison, satellite-radio company Sirius-XM pays out only 7.5% of its revenue in the form of royalties, and cable companies that stream music pay only 15%. The different royalty rates are due to somewhat arcane regulations under which three judges who serve on the Copyright Royalty Board, an arm of the Library of Congress, set royalty fees for radio broadcasters. This method of setting royalty rates has worked against Pandora, although the company is lobbying hard to change the law. Pandora is also facing growing competition from Spotify and Rdio, two customizable music-streaming services that have sold equity stakes to recording labels in exchange for access to their music libraries. There are also reports that Apple will soon be offering its own customizable music-streaming service. Regardless of what happens to Pandora in the long run, it would seem that the mass customization of Internet radio is here to stay.

Sources: A. Fixmer, "Pandora Is Boxed in by High Royalty Fees," Bloomberg Businessweek, December 24, 2012; E. Smith and J. Letzing, "At Pandora Each Sales Drives up Losses," Wall Street Journal, December 6, 2012; E. Savitz, "Pandora Swoons on Weak Outlook," Forbes.com, December 5, 2012; G. Peoples, "Pandora Revenue Up 40 percent, Listening Growth Softens," Billboardbiz, October 23, 2014; Craig Smith, "80 Interesting Pandora Statistics and Facts," DMR, February 3, 2018.

---

introducing such technologies in its automotive plants around the world. These technologies have enabled Ford to produce multiple models from the same line, and to switch production from one model to another much more quickly than in the past.[10]

5-2e Efficiency, Automation, and Artificial Intelligence

One of the most notable developments of the last decade has been the rapid rise of robotics and the growing sophistication of artificial intelligence. We seem to be entering the age of robots.[11] Adoption of robots is growing rapidly. In China, the number of robots per 10,000 employees increased from 25 units in 2013 to 150 units per 10,000 employees by 2020. In the United States, there were 189 robots per 10,000 employees in 2016, and robot installations are growing at 15% per year. In South Korea, the world leader in robot adoption, there are 631 robots per 10,000 employees.

The resulting automation of manufacturing and service activities is reducing labor costs and increasing productivity in a wide range of industries. For example, robots are taking over the tasks of drilling holes and putting fasteners in Boeing's commercial jet aircraft. Other robots are building carbon-fiber wings automatically with minimal human involvement, transforming what used to be a very labor-intensive process into one that is highly automated. By speeding up production activities, Boeing can increase the output of its factories without adding any labor or floor space. For example, the output at Boeing's Renton factory near Seattle, where it builds 737 jets, doubled between 2005 and 2018, primarily because of automation, while the labor force increased only 30%. The consequences of such striking gains in efficiency are lower variable costs for Boeing and higher profit margins.

For another example, consider how autonomous trucks can potentially transform the trucking industry. In the United States, trucks carry more than 70% of domestic freight, and the trucking industry generates $800 billion in annual revenues. With numerous companies from Google and Uber to Daimler Benz and Tesla investing heavily in autonomous vehicles, it seems to be only a matter of time before self-driving trucks are a standard sight on American roads. By eliminating the costs associated with human labor, which include not only wages but also the enforced breaks that drivers must take, and by optimizing driving routes based on a real-time analysis of traffic flows, autonomous vehicles could take a significant slice out of logistics costs, and lead to significant improvements in efficiency for a wide range of industries. Obvious beneficiaries include delivery companies such as United Parcel Service (UPS), FedEx, and Amazon (all of which are now testing autonomous vehicles).

5-2f Marketing and Efficiency

The marketing strategy that a company adopts can have a major impact on its efficiency and cost structure. **Marketing strategy** refers to the position that a company takes regarding market segmentation, pricing, promotion, advertising, product design, and distribution. Some of the steps leading to greater efficiency are obvious. For example, moving down the experience curve to achieve a lower cost structure can be facilitated by aggressive pricing, promotion, and advertising—all of which are tasks of the marketing function. Other aspects of marketing strategy have a less obvious—but no less important—impact on efficiency. One important aspect is the relationship of customer defection rates, cost structure, and unit costs.[12]

Customer defection (or "churn rate") is the percentage of a company's customers who defect every year to competitors. Defection rates are determined by customer loyalty, which in turn is a function of the ability of a company to satisfy its customers. Because acquiring a new customer often entails one-time fixed costs, there is a direct relationship between defection rates and costs. For example, when a wireless service company signs up a new subscriber, it must bear the administrative cost of opening a new account and the cost of a subsidy that it pays to the manufacturer of the handset the new subscriber chooses. There are also the costs of advertising and promotions designed to attract new subscribers. The longer a company retains a customer, the greater the volume of customer-generated unit sales that can be set against these fixed costs, and the lower the average unit cost of each sale. Thus, lowering customer defection rates allows a company to achieve a lower cost structure.

One consequence of the defection–cost relationship is illustrated in Figure 5.6. Because of the relatively high fixed costs of acquiring new customers, serving customers who stay with the company only for a short time before switching to competitors often leads to a loss on the investment made to acquire those customers. The longer a customer stays with the company, the more the fixed costs of acquiring that customer can be distributed over repeat purchases, boosting the profit per customer. Thus, there is a positive relationship between the length of time that a customer stays with a company and profit per customer. A company that can reduce customer defection rates can make a much better return on its investment in acquiring customers, and thereby boost its profitability.

marketing strategy

The position that a company takes with regard to pricing, promotion, advertising, product design, and distribution.

customer defection

The percentage of a company's customers who defect every year to competitors.

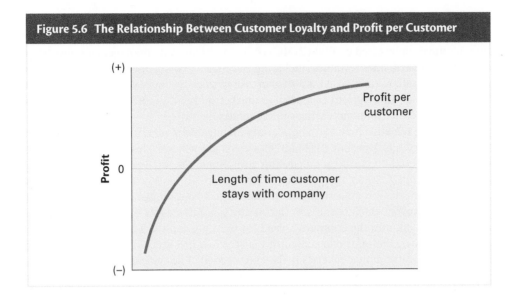

Figure 5.6 The Relationship Between Customer Loyalty and Profit per Customer

For example, consider the credit card business.[13] Most credit card companies spend an average of $80 per customer for recruitment and new account setup. These costs accrue from the advertising required to attract new customers, the credit checks required for each customer, and the mechanics of setting up an account and issuing a card. These one-time fixed costs can be recouped only if a customer stays with the company for at least 2 years. Moreover, when customers stay a second year, they tend to increase their use of the credit card, which raises the volume of revenues generated by each customer over time. As a result, although the credit card business loses $80 per customer in year 1, it makes a profit of $44 in year 3 and $55 in year 6. Another economic benefit of long-time customer loyalty is the free advertising that customers provide for a company. Loyal customers can dramatically increase the volume of business through referrals.

The key message, then, is that reducing customer defection rates and building customer loyalty can be major sources of a lower cost structure. One study has estimated that a 5% reduction in customer defection rates leads to the following increases in profits per customer over average customer life: 75% in the credit card business, 50% in the insurance brokerage industry, 45% in the industrial laundry business, and 35% in the computer software industry.[14]

A central component of developing a strategy to reduce defection rates is to identify customers who have defected, find out why they defected, and act on that information so that other customers do not defect for similar reasons in the future. To take these measures, the marketing function must have information systems capable of tracking customer defections.

5-2g Materials Management, Just-in-Time Systems, and Efficiency

The contribution of materials management (logistics) to boosting the efficiency of a company can be just as dramatic as the contribution of production and marketing. Materials management encompasses the activities necessary to get inputs and components to a production facility (including the costs of purchasing inputs), through the production process, and out through a distribution system to the end user.[15] Because there are so many sources of cost in this process, the potential for reducing costs through more efficient materials-management strategies is enormous. For a typical manufacturing company, materials and transportation costs account for 50 to 70%

of its revenues, so even a small reduction in these costs can have a substantial impact on profitability. According to one estimate, for a company with revenues of $1 million, a return on invested capital (ROIC) of 5% and materials-management costs that amount to 50% of sales revenues (including purchasing costs), increasing total profits by $15,000 would require either a 30% increase in sales revenues or a 3% reduction in materials costs.[16] In a typical competitive market, reducing materials costs by 3% is usually much easier than increasing sales revenues by 30%.

Improving the efficiency of the materials-management function typically requires the adoption of a **just-in-time (JIT) inventory system**, which is designed to economize on inventory holding costs by scheduling components to arrive at a manufacturing plant just in time to enter the production process, or to have goods arrive at a retail store only when stock is almost depleted. The major cost saving comes from increasing inventory turnover, which reduces both inventory-holding costs, such as warehousing and storage costs, and the company's need for working capital. For example, through efficient logistics, Walmart can replenish the stock in its stores at least twice a week; many stores receive daily deliveries if they are needed. The typical competitor replenishes its stock every 2 weeks, so it must carry a much higher inventory, which requires more working capital per dollar of sales. Compared to its competitors, Walmart can maintain the same service levels with a lower investment in inventory—a major source of its lower cost structure. Thus, faster inventory turnover has helped Walmart achieve an efficiency-based competitive advantage in the retailing industry.[17]

More generally, in terms of the profitability model developed in Chapter 3, JIT inventory systems reduce the need for working capital (because there is less inventory to finance) and the need for fixed capital to finance storage space (because there is less to store), which reduces capital needs, increases capital turnover, and, by extension, boosts ROIC.

The drawback of JIT systems is that they leave a company without a buffer stock of inventory. Although buffer stocks are expensive to store, they can help a company prepare for shortages on inputs brought about by disruption among suppliers (e.g., a labor dispute at a key supplier, or as we saw during 2020–2022, a global pandemic), and can help a company respond quickly to increases in demand. However, there are ways around these limitations. For example, to reduce the risks linked to dependence on just one supplier for an important input, a company might decide to source inputs from multiple suppliers located in multiple countries.

Recently, the efficient management of materials and inventory has been recast in terms of **supply chain management**: the task of managing the flow of inputs and components from suppliers into the company's production processes to minimize inventory holding and maximize inventory turnover.

5-2h Research and Development Strategy and Efficiency

The role of superior R&D in helping a company achieve a greater efficiency and a lower cost structure is twofold. First, the R&D function can boost efficiency by designing products that are easy to manufacture. By cutting down on the number of parts that make up a product, R&D can dramatically decrease the required assembly time, which results in higher employee productivity, lower costs, and higher profitability. For example, after Texas Instruments redesigned an infrared sighting mechanism that it supplies to the Pentagon, it found that it had reduced the number of parts from 47 to 12, the number of assembly steps from 56 to 13, the time spent fabricating metal from 757 minutes per unit to 219 minutes per unit, and unit assembly time from 129 minutes to 20 minutes. The result was a substantial decline in production costs. Design for manufacturing requires close coordination between the production and R&D functions of the company. Cross-functional teams that contain production and R&D personnel who work jointly can best achieve this.

just-in-time (JIT) inventory system
System of economizing on inventory-holding costs by scheduling components to arrive just in time to enter the production process or only as stock is depleted.

supply chain management
The task of managing the flow of inputs and components from suppliers into the company's production processes to minimize inventory holding and maximize inventory turnover.

Pioneering process innovations is the second way in which the R&D function can help a company achieve a lower cost structure. A **process innovation** is a new, unique way that production processes can operate more efficiently. Process innovations are often a major source of competitive advantage. Toyota's competitive advantage is based partly on the company's invention of new, flexible manufacturing processes that dramatically reduced setup times. This process innovation enabled Toyota to obtain efficiency gains associated with flexible manufacturing systems years ahead of its competitors.

process innovation

A process innovation is a new, unique way that production processes can operate more efficiently.

5-2i Human Resource Strategy and Efficiency

Employee productivity is a key determinant of an enterprise's efficiency, cost structure, and profitability.[18] Productive manufacturing employees can lower the cost of goods sold as a percentage of revenues; a productive sales force can increase sales revenues for a given level of expenses; and productive employees in the company's R&D function can boost the percentage of revenues generated from new products for a given level of R&D expenses. Thus, productive employees lower the costs of generating revenues, increase the return on sales, and, by extension, boost the company's ROIC. The challenge for a company's human resource function is to devise ways to increase employee productivity. Among its choices are using strategic hiring strategies, training employees, organizing the workforce into self-managing teams, and linking pay to performance.

Hiring Strategy   Many companies that are well known for their productive employees devote considerable attention to hiring. Southwest Airlines hires people who have a positive attitude and who work well in teams because it believes that people who have a positive attitude will work hard and interact well with customers, therefore helping to create customer loyalty. Nucor Steel hires people who are self-reliant and goal-oriented because its employees, who work in self-managing teams, require these skills to perform well. As these examples suggest, it is important to assure that the hiring strategy of the company is consistent with its internal organization, culture, and strategic priorities. A company's hires should have attributes that match its strategic objectives.

Employee Training   Employees are a major input into the production process. Those who are highly skilled can perform tasks faster and more accurately and are more likely to learn the complex tasks associated with many modern production methods than are individuals with lesser skills. Training upgrades employee skill levels, bringing the company productivity-related efficiency gains from learning and experimentation.[19]

Self-Managing Teams   The use of **self-managing teams,** whose members coordinate their own activities and make their own hiring, training, work, and reward decisions, has been spreading rapidly. The typical team comprises 5 to 15 employees who produce an entire product or undertake an entire task. Team members learn all team tasks and rotate from job to job. Because a more flexible workforce is one result, team members can fill in for absent coworkers and take over managerial duties such as scheduling work and vacation, ordering materials, and hiring new members. The greater responsibility delegated to team members, and the empowerment that it implies, are seen as motivators. (*Empowerment* is the process of giving lower-level employees decision-making power.) People often respond well to being given greater autonomy and responsibility. Performance bonuses linked to team production and quality targets work as an additional motivator.

   The effect of introducing self-managing teams is reportedly an increase in productivity of 30% or more and a substantial increase in product quality. Further cost savings arise from eliminating supervisors and creating a flatter organizational hierarchy, which lowers the cost structure of the company. In manufacturing companies, perhaps the most potent way to lower the cost structure is to combine self-managing

self-managing teams

Teams where members coordinate their own activities and make their own hiring, training, work, and reward decisions.

teams with flexible manufacturing cells. For example, after the introduction of flexible manufacturing technology and work practices based on self-managing teams, a General Electric (GE) plant in Salisbury, North Carolina, increased productivity by 250% compared with GE plants that produced the same products 4 years earlier.[20]

Still, teams are no panacea. In manufacturing companies, self-managing teams may fail to live up to their potential unless they are integrated with flexible manufacturing technology. Also, many management responsibilities are placed upon team members, and helping them cope with these responsibilities often requires substantial training—a fact that many companies often forget in their rush to drive down costs. Haste can result in teams that don't work out as well as planned.[21]

Pay for Performance It is hardly surprising that linking pay to performance can help increase employee productivity, but the issue is not quite as simple as just introducing incentive pay systems. It is also important to define what kind of job performance is to be rewarded and how. Some of the most efficient companies in the world, mindful that cooperation among employees is necessary to realize productivity gains, link pay to group or team (rather than individual) performance. Nucor Steel divides its workforce into teams of about 30, with bonus pay, which can amount to 30% of base pay, linked to the ability of the team to meet productivity and quality goals. This link creates a strong incentive for individuals to cooperate in pursuit of team goals; that is, it facilitates teamwork.

5-2j Information Systems and Efficiency

With the rapid spread of computers and digital devices such as smartphones and tablets, the ubiquity of the internet and corporate intranets, and the spread of high-bandwidth fiber-optics and digital wireless technology, the information systems function has moved to center stage in the quest for operating efficiencies and a lower cost structure.[22] The impact of information systems on productivity is wide ranging and potentially affects all other activities of a company. For example, Cisco Systems was able to realize significant cost savings by moving its ordering and customer service functions online. The company found it could operate with just 300 service agents handling all of its customer accounts, compared to the 900 it would need if sales were not handled online. The difference represented an annual savings of $20 million a year. Moreover, without automated customer service functions, Cisco calculated that it would need at least 1,000 additional service engineers, at a cost of close to $75 million.[23]

Like Cisco, many companies are using web-based information systems to reduce the costs of coordination between the company and its customers and the company and its suppliers. By using web-based programs to automate customer and supplier interactions, they can substantially reduce the staff required to manage these interfaces, thereby reducing costs. This trend extends beyond high-tech companies. Banks and financial-service companies have found that they can substantially reduce costs by moving customer accounts and support functions online. Such a move reduces the need for customer service representatives, bank tellers, stockbrokers, insurance agents, and others. For example, it costs an average of about $1.07 to execute a transaction using a teller at a bank, such as shifting money from one account to another; executing the same transaction over the Internet costs $0.01.[24]

Similarly, the concept behind online-based retailers such as Amazon.com is that replacing physical stores and their supporting personnel with an online, virtual store and automated ordering and checkout processes allows a company to eliminate significant costs from the retailing system. Cost savings can also be realized by using online-based information systems to automate many internal company activities, from managing expense reimbursements to benefits planning and hiring processes, thereby reducing the need for internal support personnel.

5-2k Infrastructure and Efficiency

A company's infrastructure—including its organizational structure, culture, style of strategic leadership, and control system—determines the context within which all other value creation activities take place. It follows that improving infrastructure can help a company increase efficiency and lower its cost structure. Above all, an appropriate infrastructure can help foster a company-wide commitment to efficiency and promote cooperation among different functions in pursuit of efficiency goals. These issues are addressed at length in Chapter 12.

For now, it is important to note that strategic leadership is especially important in building a company-wide commitment to efficiency. The leadership task is to articulate a vision that recognizes the need for all functions of a company to focus on improving efficiency. It is not enough to improve the efficiency of production, or of marketing, or of R&D in a piecemeal fashion. Achieving superior efficiency requires a company-wide commitment to this goal that must be articulated by general and functional managers. A further leadership task is to facilitate the cross-functional cooperation needed to achieve superior efficiency. For example, designing products that are easy to manufacture requires that production and R&D personnel communicate; integrating JIT systems with production scheduling requires close communication between materials management and production; and designing self-managing teams to perform production tasks requires close cooperation between human resources and production.

5-2l Summary

Table 5.1 summarizes the primary roles of various functions in achieving superior efficiency. Keep in mind that achieving superior efficiency is not something that can be tackled on a function-by-function basis. It requires organization-wide commitment and the ability to ensure close cooperation among functions. Top management, by exercising leadership and influencing the infrastructure, plays a significant role in this process.

Table 5.1 Primary Roles of Value Creation Functions in Achieving Superior Efficiency	
Value Creation Function	**Primary Role**
Infrastructure (leadership)	1. Provide company-wide commitment to efficiency. 2. Facilitate cooperation among functions.
Production	1. Where appropriate, pursue economies of scale and learning economics. 2. Implement flexible manufacturing systems.
Marketing	1. Where appropriate, adopt aggressive marketing to ride down the experience curve. 2. Limit customer defection rates by building brand loyalty.
Materials management	1. Implement JIT systems. 2. Implement supply chain coordination.
R&D	1. Design products for ease of manufacture. 2. Seek process innovations.
Information systems	1. Use information systems to automate processes. 2. Use information systems to reduce costs of coordination.
Human resources	1. Institute training programs to build skills. 2. Implement self-managing teams. 3. Implement pay for performance.

5-3 Achieving Superior Quality

In Chapter 3, we noted that quality can be thought of in terms of two dimensions: *quality as reliability* and *quality as excellence*. High-quality products are reliable, do the job well for which they were designed, and are perceived by consumers to have superior attributes. We also noted that superior quality provides a company with two advantages. First, a strong reputation for quality allows a company to differentiate its products from those offered by rivals, thereby creating more value in the eyes of customers and giving the company the option of charging a premium price for its products. Second, eliminating defects or errors from the production process reduces waste, increases efficiency, lowers the cost structure of the company, and increases its profitability. For example, reducing the number of defects in a company's manufacturing process will lower the cost of goods sold as a percentage of revenues, thereby raising the company's return on sales and ROIC. In this section, we look in more depth at what managers can do to enhance the reliability and other attributes of the company's product offering.

5-3a Attaining Superior Reliability

total quality management (TQM)
Increasing product reliability so that it consistently performs as it was designed to and rarely breaks down.

The principal tool that most managers now use to increase the reliability of their product offering is the Six Sigma quality improvement methodology. Six Sigma is a direct descendant of the **total quality management (TQM)** philosophy that was widely adopted, first by Japanese companies and then by American companies, during the 1980s and early 1990s.[25] The TQM concept was developed by a number of American management consultants, including W. Edwards Deming, Joseph Juran, and A. V. Feigenbaum.[26]

Originally, these consultants won few converts in the United States. However, managers in Japan embraced their ideas enthusiastically, and even named their premier annual prize for manufacturing excellence after Deming. Underlying TQM, according to Deming, are five factors:

1. Improved quality means that costs decrease because of less rework, fewer mistakes, fewer delays, and better use of time and materials.
2. As a result, productivity improves.
3. Better quality leads to higher market share and allows the company to raise prices.
4. Higher prices increase the company's profitability and allow it to stay in business.
5. Thus, the company creates more jobs.[27]

Deming identified several steps that should be part of any quality improvement program:

1. Management should embrace the philosophy that mistakes, defects, and poor-quality materials are not acceptable and should be eliminated.
2. Quality of supervision should be improved by allowing more time for supervisors to work with employees, and training employees in appropriate skills for the job.
3. Management should create an environment in which employees will not fear reporting problems or recommending improvements.
4. Work standards should not only be defined as numbers or quotas, but should also include some notion of quality to promote the production of defect-free output.
5. Management is responsible for training employees in new skills to keep pace with changes in the workplace.
6. Achieving better quality requires the commitment of everyone in the company.

Western businesses were blind to the importance of the TQM concept until Japan rose to the top rank of economic powers in the 1980s. Since that time, quality

5.3 Strategy in Action

General Electric's Six Sigma Quality Improvement Process

Six Sigma, a quality and efficiency program adopted by many major corporations, including Motorola, General Electric, and AlliedSignal, aims to reduce defects, boost productivity, eliminate waste, and cut costs throughout a company. "Sigma" refers to the Greek letter that statisticians use to represent a standard deviation from a mean: the higher the number of sigmas, the smaller the number of errors. At Six Sigma, a production process would be 99.99966% accurate, creating just 3.4 defects per million units. Although it is almost impossible for a company to achieve such precision, several companies strive toward that goal.

General Electric (GE) is perhaps the most well-known adopter of the Six Sigma program. One of the first products designed using Six Sigma processes was a $1.25-million diagnostic computed tomography (CT) scanner, the LightSpeed VCT, which produces rapid, three-dimensional images of the human body. The new scanner captured multiple images simultaneously, requiring only 20 seconds to do full-body scans that once took 3 minutes—important because patients must remain perfectly still during the scan. GE spent $50 million to run 250 separate Six Sigma analyses designed to improve the reliability and lower the manufacturing cost of the new scanner. Its efforts were rewarded when LightSpeed VCT's first customers soon noticed that it ran without downtime between patients—a testament to its reliability.

Achieving that reliability took immense work. GE's engineers deconstructed the scanner into its basic components and tried to improve the reliability of each one through a detailed, step-by-step analysis. For example, the most important components of CT scanners are vacuum tubes that focus x-ray waves. The tubes that GE used in previous scanners, which cost $60,000 each, suffered from low reliability. Hospitals and clinics wanted the tubes to operate for 12 hours a day for at least 6 months, but typically they lasted only half that long. Moreover, GE was scrapping some $20 million in tubes each year because they failed preshipping performance tests, and disturbing numbers of faulty tubes were slipping past inspection, only to prove dysfunctional upon arrival.

To try to solve the reliability problem, the Six Sigma team disassembled the tubes. They knew that one problem was a petroleum-based oil used in the tubes to prevent short circuits by isolating the anode (which has a positive charge) from the negatively charged cathode. The oil often deteriorated after a few months, leading to short circuits, but the team did not know why. Using statistical "what-if" scenarios on all parts of the tube, the researchers discovered that the lead-based paint on the inside of the tube was contaminating the oil. Acting on this information, the team developed a paint that would preserve the tube and protect the oil.

By pursuing this and other improvements, the Six Sigma team was able to extend the average life of a vacuum tube in the CT scanner from 3 months to over 1 year. Although the improvements increased the cost of the tube from $60,000 to $85,000, the increased cost was outweighed by the reduction in replacement costs, making it an attractive proposition for customers.

Sources: C. H. Deutsch, "Six-Sigma Enlightenment," *New York Times*, December 7, 1998, p. 1; J. J. Barshay, "The Six-Sigma Story," *Star Tribune*, June 14, 1999, p. 1; D. D. Bak, "Rethinking Industrial Drives," *Electrical/Electronics Technology*, November 30, 1998, p. 58; G. Eckes, *The Six-Sigma Revolution* (New York: Wiley, 2000); General Electric, "What Is Six Sigma?" http://www.ge.com/en/company/companyinfo/quality/whatis.htm.

improvement programs have spread rapidly throughout Western industries. Strategy in Action 5.3 describes one of the most successful implementations of a quality improvement process, GE's Six Sigma program.

5-3b Implementing Reliability Improvement Methodologies

Among companies that have successfully adopted quality improvement methodologies, certain imperatives stand out. These are discussed in the following sections in the order in which they are usually tackled in companies implementing quality improvement programs. However, it is essential to understand that improvement in product reliability is a cross-functional process. Its implementation requires close cooperation among all functions in the pursuit of the common goal of improving quality; it is a process that works across functions. The roles played by the different functions in implementing reliability improvement methodologies are summarized in Table 5.2.

First, it is important that senior managers agree to a quality improvement program and communicate its importance to the organization. Second, if a quality improvement program is to be successful, individuals must be identified to lead the program. Under the Six Sigma methodology, exceptional employees are identified and put through

Table 5.2 Roles Played by Different Functions in Implementing Reliability Improvement Methodologies

Infrastructure (leadership)	1. Provide leadership and commitment to quality.
	2. Find ways to measure quality.
	3. Set goals and create incentives.
	4. Solicit input from employees.
	5. Encourage cooperation among functions.
Production	1. Shorten production runs.
	2. Trace defects back to the source.
Marketing	1. Focus on the customer.
	2. Provide customer feedback on quality.
Materials management	1. Rationalize suppliers.
	2. Help suppliers implement quality improvement methodologies.
	3. Trace defects back to suppliers.
R&D	1. Design products that are easy to manufacture.
Information systems	1. Use information systems to monitor defect rates.
Human resources	1. Institute quality improvement training programs.
	2. Identify and train black belts.
	3. Organize employees into quality teams.

a "black belt" training course on the Six Sigma methodology. The black belts are taken out of their normal job roles and assigned to work solely on Six Sigma projects for 2 years. In effect, the black belts become internal consultants *and* project leaders. Because they are dedicated to Six Sigma programs, the black belts are not distracted from the task at hand by day-to-day operating responsibilities. To make a black belt assignment attractive, many companies now endorse the program as an advancement in a career path. Successful black belts might not return to their prior job after 2 years but could instead be promoted and given more responsibility.

Third, quality improvement methodologies preach the need to identify defects that arise from processes, trace them to their source, find out what caused the defects, and make corrections so that they do not recur. Production and materials management are primarily responsible for this task. To uncover defects, quality improvement methodologies rely upon the use of statistical procedures to pinpoint variations in the quality of goods or services. Once variations have been identified, they must be traced to their respective sources and eliminated.

One technique that helps greatly in tracing defects to the source is reducing lot sizes for manufactured products. With short production runs, defects show up immediately. Consequently, they can quickly be sourced, and the problem can be rectified. Reducing lot sizes also means that defective products will not be produced in large lots, thus decreasing waste. Flexible manufacturing techniques can be used to reduce lot sizes without raising costs. JIT inventory systems also play a part. Under a JIT system, defective parts enter the manufacturing process immediately. They are not warehoused for several months before use. Hence, defective inputs can be quickly spotted. The problem can then be traced to the supply source and corrected before more defective parts are produced. Under a more traditional system, the practice of warehousing parts for months before they are used may mean that suppliers deliver large quantities of parts with defects before they are detected in the production process.

Fourth, another key to any quality improvement program is to create a metric that can be used to measure quality. In manufacturing companies, quality can be measured by criteria such as defects per million parts. In service companies, suitable metrics can be devised with a little creativity. For example, one of the metrics Florida Power & Light uses to measure quality is meter-reading errors per month.

Fifth, once a metric has been devised, the next step is to set a challenging quality goal and create incentives for reaching it. Under Six Sigma programs, the goal is 3.4 defects per million units. One way of creating incentives to attain such a goal is to link rewards such as bonus pay and promotional opportunities to the goal.

Sixth, shop floor employees can be a major source of ideas for improving product quality, so these employees must participate and be incorporated into a quality improvement program.

Seventh, a major source of poor-quality finished goods is poor-quality component parts. To decrease product defects, a company must work with its suppliers to improve the quality of the parts they supply.

Eighth, the more assembly steps a product requires, the more opportunities there are for mistakes. Thus, designing products with fewer parts is often a major component of any quality improvement program.

Finally, implementing quality improvement methodologies requires organization-wide commitment and substantial cooperation among functions. R&D must cooperate with production to design products that are easy to manufacture; marketing must cooperate with production and R&D so that customer problems identified by marketing can be acted on; and human resource management must cooperate with all the other functions of the company in order to devise suitable quality-training programs.

5-3c Improving Quality as Excellence

As we stated in Chapter 3, a product is comprised of different attributes. Reliability is just one attribute, albeit an important one. Products can also be *differentiated* by attributes that collectively define product excellence. These attributes include the form, features, performance, durability, and styling of a product. In addition, a company can create quality as excellence by emphasizing attributes of the service associated with the product. Dell Inc., for example, differentiates itself on ease of ordering (via online), prompt delivery, easy installation, and the ready availability of customer support and maintenance services. Differentiation can also be based on the attributes of the people in the company with whom customers interact when making a purchase, such as competence, courtesy, credibility, responsiveness, and communication. Singapore Airlines enjoys an excellent reputation for quality service, largely because passengers perceive their flight attendants as competent, courteous, and responsive to their needs. Thus, we can talk about the product attributes, service attributes, and personnel attributes associated with a company's product offering (see Table 5.3).

To be regarded as being high in the excellence dimension, a company's product offering must be seen as superior to that of rivals. Achieving a perception of high quality on any of these attributes requires specific actions by managers. First, it is important for managers to collect marketing intelligence, indicating which attributes are most important to customers. For example, consumers of PCs may place a low weight on durability because they expect their PCs to be made obsolete by technological advances within 3 years, but they may place a high weight on features and performance. Similarly, ease of ordering and timely delivery may be very important

Table 5.3 Attributes Associated with a Product Offering		
Product Attributes	**Service Attributes**	**Associated Personnel Attributes**
Form	Ordering ease	Competence
Features	Delivery	Courtesy
Performance	Installation	Credibility
Durability	Customer training	Reliability
Reliability	Customer consulting	Responsiveness
Style	Maintenance and repair	Communication

attributes for customers of online booksellers (as indeed they are for customers of Amazon.com), whereas customer training and consulting may be very important attributes for customers who purchase complex, business-to-business software to manage their relationships with suppliers.

Second, once the company has identified the attributes that are important to customers, it needs to design its products (and the associated services) in such a way that those attributes are embodied in the product. It also needs to train personnel in the company so that the appropriate attributes are emphasized during design creation. This requires close coordination between marketing and product development (the topic of the next section) and the involvement of the human resource management function in employee selection and training.

Third, the company must decide which significant attributes to promote and how best to position them in the minds of consumers; that is, how to tailor the marketing message so that it creates a consistent image in the minds of customers.[28] At this point, it is important to recognize that although a product might be differentiated on the basis of six attributes, covering all of those attributes in the company's communications may lead to an unfocused message. Many marketing experts advocate promoting only one or two central attributes. For example, Volvo consistently emphasizes the safety and durability of its vehicles in all marketing messages, creating the perception in the minds of consumers (backed by product design) that Volvos are safe and durable. Volvos are also very reliable and have high performance, but the company does not emphasize these attributes in its marketing messages. In contrast, Porsche emphasizes performance and styling in all of its marketing messages; thus, a Porsche is positioned differently in the minds of consumers than a Volvo. Both are regarded as high-quality products because both have superior attributes, but each company differentiates its models from the average car by promoting distinctive attributes.

Finally, it must be recognized that competition is not stationary, but instead continually produces improvement in product attributes, and often the development of new-product attributes. This is obvious in fast-moving high-tech industries where product features that were considered leading edge just a few years ago are now obsolete—but the same process is also at work in more stable industries. For example, the rapid diffusion of microwave ovens during the 1980s required food companies to build new attributes into their frozen-food products: they had to maintain their texture and consistency while being cooked in the microwave; a product could not be considered high quality unless it could do that. This speaks to the importance of a strong R&D function within the company that can work with marketing and manufacturing to continually upgrade the quality of the attributes that are designed into the company's product offerings. Exactly how to achieve this is covered in the next section.

5-4 Achieving Superior Innovation

5.4 Define multiple ways an enterprise can make strategic investments to increase its innovation.

In many ways, innovation is the most important source of competitive advantage. This is because innovation can result in new products that better satisfy customer needs, can improve the quality (attributes) of existing products, or can reduce the costs of making products that customers want. The ability to develop innovative new products or processes gives a company a major competitive advantage that allows it to: (1) differentiate its products and charge a premium price, and/or (2) lower its cost structure below that of its rivals. Competitors, however, attempt to imitate successful innovations and often succeed. Therefore, maintaining a competitive advantage requires a continuing commitment to innovation.

Successful new-product launches are major drivers of superior profitability. Robert Cooper reviewed more than 200 new-product introductions and found that of those classified as successes, some 50% achieve a return on investment in excess of 33%, half have a payback period of 2 years or less, and half achieve a market share in excess of 35%.[29] Many companies have established a track record for successful innovation. Among them are Apple, whose successes include the iPod, iPhone, and iPad; Pfizer, a drug company that during the 1990s and early 2000s produced eight new blockbuster drugs; and 3M, which has applied its core competency in tapes and adhesives to developing a wide range of new products.

5-4a The High Failure Rate of Innovation

Although promoting innovation can be a source of competitive advantage, the failure rate of innovative products is high. Research evidence suggests that only 10 to 20% of major R&D projects give rise to commercial products.[30] Well-publicized product failures include Apple's Newton, an early, hand-held computer that flopped in the marketplace; Sony's Betamax format in the videocassette recorder segment; Sega's Dreamcast videogame console; and Windows Mobile, an early smartphone operating system created by Microsoft that was made obsolete in the eyes of consumers by the arrival of Apple's iPhone. Although many reasons have been advanced to explain why so many new products fail to generate an economic return, five explanations for failure repeatedly appear.[31]

First, many new products fail because the demand for innovation is inherently uncertain. It is impossible to know prior to market introduction whether the new product has tapped an unmet customer need, and if there is sufficient market demand to justify manufacturing the product. Although good market research can reduce the uncertainty about likely future demand for a new technology, that uncertainty cannot be fully eradicated; a certain failure rate is to be expected.

Second, new products often fail because the technology is poorly commercialized. This occurs when there is definite customer demand for a new product, but the product is not well adapted to customer needs because of factors such as poor design and poor quality. For instance, the failure of Microsoft to establish an enduring, dominant position in the market for smartphones, even though phones using the Windows Mobile operating system were introduced in 2003—4 years before Apple's iPhone hit the market—can be traced to its poor design. Windows Mobile phones had a physical keyboard, and a small, cluttered screen that was difficult to navigate, which made the product unattractive to many consumers. In contrast, the iPhone's large touch screen and associated keyboard appealed to many consumers, who rushed out to buy it in droves.

Third, new products may fail because of poor positioning strategy. **Positioning strategy** is the specific set of options a company adopts for a product based upon four main dimensions of marketing: price, distribution, promotion and advertising, and product features. Apart from poor design, another reason for the failure of Windows Mobile phones was poor positioning strategy. They were targeted at business users, whereas Apple developed a mass market by targeting the iPhone at retail consumers.

positioning strategy

The specific set of options a company adopts for a product based upon four main dimensions of marketing: price, distribution, promotion and advertising, and product features.

Fourth, many new-product introductions fail because companies make the mistake of marketing a technology for which there is not enough demand. A company can become blinded by the wizardry of a new technology and fail to determine whether there is sufficient customer demand for it. A classic example is the Segway two-wheeled personal transporter. Even though its gyroscopic controls were highly sophisticated, and that the product introduction was accompanied by massive media hype, sales fell well below expectations when it transpired that most consumers had no need for such a conveyance.

Finally, companies fail when products are slowly marketed. The more time that elapses between initial development and final marketing—the slower the "cycle time"—the more likely it is that a competitor will beat the company to market and gain a first-mover advantage.[32] In the car industry, GM long suffered from being a slow innovator. Its typical product development cycle used to be about 5 years, compared with 2 to 3 years at Honda, Toyota, and Mazda, and 3 to 4 years at Ford. Because GM's offerings were based on 5-year-old technology and design concepts, they were already out of date when they reached the market.

5-4b Reducing Innovation Failures

One of the most important things that managers can do to reduce the high failure rate associated with innovation is to make sure that there is tight integration between R&D, production, and marketing.[33] Tight, cross-functional integration can help a company ensure that:

1. Product development projects are driven by customer needs.
2. New products are designed for ease of manufacture.
3. Development costs are not allowed to spiral out of control.
4. The time it takes to develop a product and bring it to market is minimized.
5. Close integration between R&D and marketing is achieved to ensure that product development projects are driven by the needs of customers.

Customers can be a primary source of new-product ideas. The identification of customer needs, particularly unmet needs, can set the context within which successful product innovation takes place. As the point of contact with customers, the marketing function can provide valuable information. Moreover, integrating R&D and marketing is crucial if a new product is to be properly commercialized—otherwise, a company runs the risk of developing products for which there is little or no demand.

Integration between R&D and production can help a company ensure that products are designed with manufacturing requirements in mind. Design for manufacturing lowers manufacturing costs and leaves less room for error. Thus, it can lower costs and increase product quality. Integrating R&D and production can help lower development costs and speed products to market. If a new product is not designed with manufacturing capabilities in mind, it may prove too difficult to build with existing manufacturing technology. In that case, the product will need to be redesigned, and both overall development costs and time to market may increase significantly. Making design changes during product planning can increase overall development costs by 50% and add 25% to the time it takes to bring the product to market.[34]

One of the best ways to achieve cross-functional integration is to establish cross-functional product development teams composed of representatives from R&D, marketing, and production. The objective of a team should be to oversee a product development project from initial concept development to market introduction. Specific attributes appear to be important for a product development team to function effectively and meet all of its development milestones.[35]

First, a project manager who has high status within the organization and the power and authority required to secure the financial and human resources that the team needs to succeed should lead the team and be dedicated primarily, if not entirely, to the project. The leader should believe in the project (be a champion for the project) and be skilled at integrating the perspectives of different functions and helping personnel from different functions work together for a common goal. The leader should also act as an advocate of the team to senior management.

Second, the team should be composed of at least one member from each key function or position. Individual team members should have a number of attributes, including an ability to contribute functional expertise, high standing within their function, a willingness to share responsibility for team results, and an ability to put functional advocacy aside. It is generally preferable if core team members are 100% dedicated to the project for its duration. This ensures that their focus is on the project, not on their ongoing, individual work.

Third, team members work in proximity to one another to create a sense of camaraderie and facilitate communication. Fourth, the team should have a clear plan and clear goals, particularly with regard to critical development milestones and development budgets. The team should have incentives to attain those goals; for example, bonuses paid when major development milestones are attained. Fifth, each team needs to develop its own processes for communication, as well as conflict resolution. For example, one product development team at Quantum Corporation, a California-based manufacturer of disk drives for PCs, mandated that all major decisions would be made and conflicts resolved during meetings that were held every Monday afternoon. This simple rule helped the team meet its development goals.[36]

Finally, there is substantial evidence that developing competencies in innovation requires managers to proactively learn from their experience with product development, and to incorporate the lessons from past successes and failures into future new-product development processes.[37] This is easier said than done. To learn, managers need to undertake an objective assessment after a product development project has been completed, identifying key success factors and the root causes of failures, and allocating resources to repairing failures. Leaders also must admit their own failures if they are to encourage other team members to responsibly identify what they did wrong.

The primary role that the various functions play in achieving superior innovation is summarized in Table 5.4. The table makes two matters clear. First, top management must bear primary responsibility for overseeing the entire development process. This entails both managing the development process and facilitating cooperation among the functions. Second, the effectiveness of R&D in developing new products and processes depends upon its ability to cooperate with marketing and production.

Table 5.4 Functional Roles for Achieving Superior Innovation	
Value Creation Function	**Primary Role**
Infrastructure (leadership)	1. Manage overall project (i.e., manage the development function). 2. Facilitate cross-functional cooperation.
Production	1. Cooperate with R&D on designing products that are easy to manufacture. 2. Work with R&D to develop process innovations.
Marketing	1. Provide market information to R&D. 2. Work with R&D to develop new products.
Materials management	No primary responsibility.
R&D	1. Develop new products and processes. 2. Cooperate with other functions, particularly marketing and manufacturing, in the development process.
Information systems	1. Use information systems to coordinate cross-functional, cross-company product development.
Human resources	2. Hire talented scientists and engineers.

5-5 Achieving Superior Customer Responsiveness

To achieve superior customer responsiveness, a company must give customers what they want, when they want it, and at a price they are willing to pay—and not compromise the company's long-term profitability in the process. Customer responsiveness is an important differentiating attribute that can help build brand loyalty. Strong product differentiation and brand loyalty give a company more pricing options; it can charge a premium price for its products, or keep prices low to sell more goods and services to customers. Whether prices are at a premium or kept low, the company that is most responsive to customers' needs will gain the competitive advantage.

Achieving superior responsiveness to customers means giving customers value for their money, and steps taken to improve the efficiency of a company's production process and the quality of its products should be consistent with this aim. In addition, giving customers what they want may require the development of new products with new features. In other words, achieving superior efficiency, quality, and innovation are all part of achieving superior responsiveness to customers. There are two other prerequisites for attaining this goal. First, a company must develop a competency in listening to its customers, focusing on its customers, and investigating and identifying their needs. Second, it must constantly seek better ways to satisfy those needs.

5-5a Focusing on the Customer

A company cannot respond to its customers' needs unless it knows what those needs are. Thus, the first step to building superior customer responsiveness is to motivate the entire company to focus on the customer. The means to this end are demonstrating leadership, shaping employee attitudes, and using mechanisms for making sure that customer needs are well known within the company.

5-5b Demonstrating Leadership

Customer focus must emanate from the top of the organization on down. A commitment to superior responsiveness to customers brings attitudinal changes throughout a company that can only be built through strong leadership. A mission statement that puts customers first is one way to send a clear message to employees about the desired focus. Another avenue is top management's own actions. For example, Tom Monaghan, the founder of Domino's Pizza, stayed close to the customer by eating Domino's pizza regularly, visiting as many stores as possible every week, running some deliveries himself, and insisting that top managers do the same.[38]

5-5c Shaping Employee Attitudes

Leadership alone is not enough to attain superior customer responsiveness. All employees must see the customer as the focus of their activity and be trained to concentrate on the customer—whether their function is marketing, manufacturing, R&D, or accounting. The objective should be to put employees in customers' shoes, a perspective that enables them to become better able to identify ways to improve the quality of a customer's experience with the company.

To reinforce this mindset, incentive systems should reward employees for satisfying customers. For example, senior managers at the Four Seasons hotel chain, who pride themselves on customer focus, tell the story of Roy Dyment, a doorman in Toronto who neglected to load a departing guest's briefcase into his taxi. The doorman called the guest, a lawyer, in Washington, D.C., and found that he desperately needed the briefcase for a morning meeting. Dyment hopped on a plane to Washington and returned it—without first securing approval from his boss. Far from punishing Dyment for not checking with management before going to Washington, Four Seasons responded by naming Dyment Employee of the Year.[39] This sent a powerful message to Four Seasons employees, stressing the importance of satisfying customer needs.

5-5d Knowing Customer Needs

"Know thy customer" is one of the keys to achieving superior responsiveness to customers. Knowing the customer not only requires that employees think like customers; it also demands that they listen to what customers have to say. This involves communicating customers' opinions by soliciting feedback from customers on the company's goods and services, and by building information systems that disseminate the feedback to the relevant people.

For an example, consider clothing retailer Lands' End. Through its catalog, online, and customer-service telephone operators, Lands' End actively solicits comments about the quality of its clothing and the kind of merchandise customers want Lands' End to supply. Indeed, it was customer insistence that initially prompted the company to move into the clothing segment. Lands' End formerly supplied equipment for sailboats through mail-order catalogs. However, it received so many requests from customers to include outdoor clothing in its offering that it responded by expanding the catalog to fill this need. Soon, clothing became its main business, and Lands' End ceased selling sailboat equipment. Today, the company continues to pay close attention to customer requests. Every month, data on customer requests and comments is reported to managers. This feedback helps the company fine-tune the merchandise it sells; new lines of merchandise are frequently introduced in response to customer requests.

5-5e Satisfying Customer Needs

Once customer focus is integral to the organization, the next requirement is to satisfy those customer needs that have been identified. As already noted, efficiency, quality, and innovation are crucial competencies that help a company satisfy customer needs. Beyond that, companies can provide a higher level of satisfaction if they differentiate their products by (1) customizing them, where possible, to the requirements of individual customers, and (2) reducing the time it takes to respond to, or satisfy, customer needs.

Customization Customization involves varying the features of a good or service to tailor it to the unique needs or tastes of a group of customers, or—in the extreme case—individual customers. Although extensive customization can raise costs, the development of flexible manufacturing technologies has made it possible to customize products to a greater extent than was feasible 10 to 15 years ago, without experiencing a prohibitive rise in cost structure (particularly when flexible manufacturing technologies are linked with online information systems). For example, online retailers such as Amazon.com have used web-based technologies to develop a home page customized for each individual user. When a customer accesses Amazon.com, they are offered a list of recommended products to purchase based on an analysis of prior buying history—a powerful competency that gives Amazon.com a competitive advantage.

The trend toward customization has fragmented many markets, particularly customer markets, into ever-smaller niches. An example of this fragmentation occurred in Japan in the early 1980s, when Honda dominated the motorcycle market there. Second-place Yamaha was determined to surpass Honda's lead. It announced the opening of a new factory that, when operating at full capacity, would make Yamaha the world's largest manufacturer of motorcycles. Honda responded by proliferating its product line and increasing its rate of new-product introduction. At the start of what became known as the "Motorcycle Wars," Honda had 60 motorcycles in its product line. Over the next 18 months thereafter, it rapidly increased its range to 113 models, customizing them to ever-smaller niches. Because of its competency in flexible manufacturing, Honda accomplished this without bearing a prohibitive cost penalty. The flood of Honda's customized models pushed Yamaha out of much of the market, effectively stalling its bid to overtake Honda.[40]

Response Time To gain a competitive advantage, a company must often respond to customer demands very quickly, whether the transaction is a furniture manufacturer's completion of an order, a bank's processing of a loan application, an automobile manufacturer's delivery of a spare part, or the wait in a supermarket checkout line. We live in a fast-paced society where time is a valuable commodity. Companies that can satisfy customer demands for rapid response build brand loyalty, differentiate their products, and can charge higher prices for products.

Increased speed often lets a company opt for premium pricing, as the mail delivery industry illustrates. The air-express niche of the mail delivery industry is based on the notion that customers are often willing to pay substantially more for overnight express mail than for regular mail. Another exemplar of the value of rapid response is Caterpillar, the manufacturer of heavy-earthmoving equipment, which can deliver a spare part to any location in the world within 24 hours. Downtime for heavy-construction equipment is very costly, so Caterpillar's ability to respond quickly in the event of equipment malfunction is of prime importance to its customers. As a result, many customers have remained loyal to Caterpillar despite the aggressive, low-price competition from Komatsu of Japan.

In general, reducing response time requires: (1) a marketing function that can quickly communicate customer requests to production, (2) production and materials-management functions that can quickly adjust production schedules in response to unanticipated customer demands, and (3) information systems that can help production and marketing in this process.

Table 5.5 summarizes the steps different functions must take if a company is to achieve superior responsiveness to customers. Although marketing plays a critical role

Table 5.5 Primary Roles of Different Functions in Achieving Superior Customer Responsiveness

Value Creation Function	Primary Role
Infrastructure (leadership)	• Through leadership by example, build a company-wide commitment to responsiveness to customers
Production	• Achieve customization through implementation of flexible manufacturing • Achieve rapid response through flexible manufacturing
Marketing	• Know the customer • Communicate customer feedback to appropriate functions
Materials management	• Develop logistics systems capable of responding quickly to unanticipated customer demands (JIT)
R&D	• Bring customers into the product development process
Information systems	• Use online information systems to increase responsiveness to customers
Human resources	• Develop training programs that get employees to think like customers

in helping a company attain this goal (primarily because it represents the point of contact with the customer), Table 5.5 shows that the other functions also have major roles. Achieving superior responsiveness to customers requires top management to lead in building a customer orientation within the company.

Key Terms

functional-level
  strategies   126
economies of scale   127
fixed costs   127
diseconomies of
  scale   127

learning effects   128
experience curve 130
flexible production
  technology   132
mass customization   132
marketing strategy   134

customer defection   134
just-in-time (JIT) inventory
  system   136
supply chain
  management   136
process innovation 137

self-managing teams   137
total quality management
  (TQM)   140
positioning strategy   145

Takeaways for Strategic Managers

1. A company can increase efficiency through a number of steps: exploiting economies of scale and learning effects, adopting flexible manufacturing technologies, reducing customer defection rates, implementing just-in-time systems, getting the R&D function to design products that are easy to manufacture, upgrading the skills of employees through training, introducing self-managing teams, linking pay to performance, building a company-wide commitment to efficiency through strong leadership, and designing structures that facilitate cooperation among different functions in pursuit of efficiency goals.

2. Superior quality can help a company lower its costs, differentiate its product, and charge a premium price.

3. Achieving superior quality demands an organization-wide commitment to quality and a clear focus on the customer. It also requires metrics to measure quality goals and incentives that emphasize quality, input from employees regarding ways in which quality can be improved, a methodology for tracing defects to their source and correcting the problems that produce them, a rationalization of the company's supply base, cooperation with approved suppliers to implement total quality management programs, products that are designed for ease of manufacturing, and substantial cooperation among functions.

4. The failure rate of new-product introductions is high because of factors such as uncertainty, poor commercialization, poor positioning strategy, slow cycle time, and technological shortsightedness.

5. To achieve superior innovation, a company must build skills in basic and applied research; design good processes for managing development projects; and achieve close integration between the different functions of the company, primarily through the adoption of cross-functional product development teams and partly parallel development processes.

6. Achieving superior customer responsiveness often requires that the company achieve superior efficiency, quality, and innovation.

7. Furthermore, to achieve superior customer responsiveness, a company must give customers what they want, when they want it. It must ensure a strong customer focus, which can be attained by emphasizing customer focus through leadership, training employees to think like customers, bringing customers into the company through superior market research, customizing products to the unique needs of individual customers or customer groups, and responding quickly to customer demands.

Discussion Questions

1. How are the four building blocks of competitive advantage related to each other?

2. What role can top management play in helping a company achieve superior efficiency, quality, innovation, and responsiveness to customers?

3. Over time, will the adoption of Six Sigma quality improvement processes give a company a competitive advantage, or will it be required only to achieve parity with competitors?

4. What is the relationship between innovation and competitive advantage?

Closing Case

When Jeff Bezos founded Amazon.com in 1995, the online retailer focused solely on selling books. Music and videos were soon added to the mix. Today, one can purchase a vast range of products from Amazon, which is now the world's largest online retailer, with $470 billion in annual sales in 2021. According to Bezos, Amazon's success is based on three core factors: a relentless focus on delivering value to customers, operating efficiencies, and a willingness to innovate.

Amazon offers customers a much wider selection of merchandise than they can find in a physical store and does so at a low price. Amazon both stocks and sells merchandise directly, and acts as an online marketplace for third-party sellers (who accounted for close to 60% of Amazon's retail sales in 2021). Online shopping and purchasing are made easy with a user-friendly interface, product recommendations, customer wish lists, and a one-click purchasing option for repeat customers. The percentage of traffic that Amazon gets from search engines such as Google has been falling for several years, whereas other online retailers are becoming more dependent on third-party search engines. This indicates that Amazon is increasingly becoming the starting point for online purchases and has developed its own powerful search capabilities. As a result, its active customer base in 2022 numbered around 310 million, some 200 million of which are Amazon Prime members who pay $139 a year for a variety of services, such as free next-day shipping on a wide range of products and access to Amazon's streaming services. According to Jeff Bezos, while a typical trip to a brick-and-mortar store may take an hour, a purchase on Amazon takes 15 minutes. Without having to take the time to go to a physical store, Bezos estimates that the average Prime customer saves 75 hours a year.

To deliver products to customers quickly and accurately, Amazon has been investing heavily in a network of distribution centers. In the United States alone, there are now over 100 such centers. Sophisticated software analyzes customer purchasing patterns and informs the company what to order, where to store it in the distribution network, what to charge for it, and when to mark it down to shift it. The goal is to reduce inventory holding costs while always having product in stock. The increasingly dense network of distribution centers enables Amazon to reduce the time it takes to deliver products to consumers and to cut down on delivery costs. As Amazon grows, it can support a denser distribution network, which in turn enables it to fulfill customer orders more rapidly and at a lower cost, thereby solidifying its competitive advantage over smaller rivals.

To make its distribution centers even more efficient, Amazon is embracing automation. Until recently, most picking and packing of products at Amazon distribution centers was done by hand, with employees walking as much as 20 miles per shift to pick merchandise off shelves and bring it to packing stations. Although walking 20 miles a day may be good for the physical health of employees, it represents much wasted time and hurts productivity. In 2012, Amazon purchased Kiva, a leading manufacturer of robots that service warehouses. Post-acquisition, Kiva announced that, for the next 2 to 3 years, it would take no external orders and instead focus on automating Amazon's distribution centers. Kiva robots pick products from shelves and deliver them to packing stations. This reduces the staff needed per distribution center by 30 to 40%, and boosts productivity accordingly. Today, Amazon has more than 500,000 mobile robots operating in its warehouses.

On the innovation front, Amazon has been a leader in pushing the digitalization of media. Its invention of the Kindle digital reader, and the ability of customers to use that reader either on a dedicated Kindle device or on a general-purpose device, such as an iPad, turbocharged the digital distribution of books—a market segment where Amazon is the clear leader. Digitalization of books is disrupting the established book-retailing industry and strengthening

Amazon's advantage in this segment. To store digital media, from books to films and music, and to enable rapid customer download, Amazon has built huge server farms. Its early investment in "cloud-based" infrastructure has turned it into a leader in this field. It is now leveraging its expertise and infrastructure to build another business, Amazon Web Services (AWS), which hosts websites, data, and associated software for other companies. In 2021, AWS generated $62 billion in revenues, making Amazon the leader in the rapidly emerging field of cloud computing. Jeff Bezos is on record as stating that he believes AWS will ultimately match Amazon's online retail business in sales volume.

Sources: "Amazon to Add 18 New Distribution Centers," *Supply Chain Digest*, August 7, 2012; A. Lashinsky, "Jeff Bezos: The Ultimate Disrupter," *Fortune*, December 3, 2012, pp. 34–41; S. Banker, "The New Amazon Distribution Model," *Logistics Viewpoints*, August 6, 2012; G. A. Fowler, "Holiday Hiring Call: People Vs Robots," *Wall Street Journal*, December 10, 2010, p. B1; D. Romanoff, "Amazon's Profitability Hit by Inflation, Excess Capacity," *Morningstar*, April 28, 2022; D. Howley, "Amazon Prime Now Has 200 Million Members," *Yahoo News*, April 15, 2021.

Case Discussion Questions

1. What functional-level strategies has Amazon pursued to boost its efficiency?
2. What functional-level strategies has Amazon pursued to boost its customer responsiveness?
3. What does product quality mean for Amazon? What functional-level strategies has Amazon pursued to boost its product quality?
4. How has innovation helped Amazon improve its efficiency, customer responsiveness, and product quality?
5. Do you think that Amazon has any rare and valuable resources? In what value creation activities are these resources located?
6. How sustainable is Amazon's competitive position in the online retail business?
7. How would you characterize Amazon's business-level strategy in its retail operations? How do functional-level strategies at Amazon help the company to execute its business-level strategy?

Notes

[1]G. J. Miller, *Managerial Dilemmas: The Political Economy of Hierarchy* (Cambridge: Cambridge University Press, 1992).

[2]H. Luft, J. Bunker, and A. Enthoven, "Should Operations Be Regionalized?" *New England Journal of Medicine* 301 (1979): 1364–1369.

[3]S. Chambers and R. Johnston, "Experience Curves in Services," *International Journal of Operations and Production Management* 20 (2000): 842–860.

[4]G. Hall and S. Howell, "The Experience Curve from an Economist's Perspective," *Strategic Management Journal* 6 (1985):

197–212; M. Lieberman, "The Learning Curve and Pricing in the Chemical Processing Industries," *RAND Journal of Economics* 15 (1984): 213–228; R. A. Thornton and P. Thompson, "Learning from Experience and Learning from Others," *American Economic Review* 91 (2001): 1350–1369.

[5]Boston Consulting Group, *Perspectives on Experience* (Boston: Boston Consulting Group, 1972); Hall and Howell, "The Experience Curve," pp. 197–212; W. B. Hirschmann, "Profit from the Learning Curve," *Harvard Business Review* (January–February 1964): 125–139.

[6]A. A. Alchian, "Reliability of Progress Curves in Airframe Production," *Econometrica* 31 (1963): 679–693.

[7]M. Borrus, L. A. Tyson, and J. Zysman, "Creating Advantage: How Government Policies Create Trade in the Semi-Conductor Industry," in P. R. Krugman (ed.), *Strategic Trade Policy and the New International Economics* (Cambridge: MIT Press, 1986); S. Ghoshal and C. A. Bartlett, "Matsushita Electrical Industrial (MEI) in 1987," Harvard Business School Case #388-144 (1988).

[8]See P. Nemetz and L. Fry, "Flexible Manufacturing Organi-

zations: Implications for Strategy Formulation," *Academy of Management Review* 13 (1988): 627–638; N. Greenwood, *Implementing Flexible Manufacturing Systems* (New York: Halstead Press, 1986); J. P. Womack, D. T. Jones, and D. Roos, *The Machine That Changed the World* (New York: Rawson Associates, 1990); R. Parthasarthy and S. P. Seith, "The Impact of Flexible Automation on Business Strategy and Organizational Structure," *Academy of Management Review* 17 (1992): 86–111.

[9]B. J. Pine, *Mass Customization: The New Frontier in Business Competition* (Boston: Harvard Business School Press, 1993); S. Kotha, "Mass Customization: Implementing the Emerging Paradigm for Competitive Advantage," *Strategic Management Journal* 16 (1995): 21–42; J. H. Gilmore and B. J. Pine II, "The Four Faces of Mass Customization," *Harvard Business Review* (January–February 1997): 91–101.

[10]P. Waurzyniak, "Ford's Flexible Push," *Manufacturing Engineering*, September 1, 2003, pp. 47–50.

[11]M. Ford, *Rise of the Robots* (New York: Basic Books, 2015). International Federation of Robotics, "Robot Density Rises Globally," February 7, 2018.

[12]F. F. Reichheld and W. E. Sasser, "Zero Defections: Quality Comes to Service," *Harvard Business Review* (September–October 1990): 105–111.

[13]Ibid.

[14]The example comes from Reichheld and Sasser.

[15]R. Narasimhan and J. R. Carter, "Organization, Communication and Coordination of International Sourcing," *International Marketing Review* 7 (1990): 6–20.

[16]H. F. Busch, "Integrated Materials Management," *IJDP & MM* 18 (1990): 28–39.

[17]G. Stalk and T. M. Hout, *Competing Against Time* (New York: Free Press, 1990).

[18]See P. Bamberger and I. Meshoulam, *Human Resource Strategy: Formulation, Implementation, and Impact* (Thousand Oaks: Sage, 2000); P. M. Wright and S. Snell, "Towards a Unifying Framework for Exploring Fit and Flexibility in Human Resource Management," *Academy of Management Review* 23 (October 1998): 756–772.

[19]A. Sorge and M. Warner, "Manpower Training, Manufacturing Organization, and Work Place Relations in Great Britain and West Germany," *British Journal of Industrial Relations* 18 (1980): 318–333; R. Jaikumar, "Postindustrial Manufacturing," *Harvard Business Review* (November–December 1986): 72–83.

[20]J. Hoerr, "The Payoff from Teamwork," *Business Week,* July 10, 1989, pp. 56–62.

[21]"The Trouble with Teams," *The Economist,* January 14, 1995, p. 61.

[22]T. C. Powell and A. Dent Micallef, "Information Technology as Competitive Advantage: The Role of Human, Business, and Technology Resource," *Strategic Management Journal* 18 (1997): 375–405; B. Gates, *Business @ the Speed of Thought* (New York: Warner Books, 1999).

[23]"Cisco@speed," *The Economist,* June 26, 1999, p. 12; S. Tully, "How Cisco Mastered the Net," *Fortune,* August 17, 1997, pp. 207–210; C. Kano, "The Real King of the Internet," *Fortune,* September 7, 1998, pp. 82–93.

[24]Gates, *Business @ the Speed of Thought.*

[25]See the articles published in the special issue of the *Academy of Management Review on Total Quality Management* 19:3 (1994). The following article provides a good overview of many of the issues involved from an academic perspective: J. W. Dean and D. E.

Bowen, "Management Theory and Total Quality," *Academy of Management Review* 19 (1994): 392–418. See also T. C. Powell, "Total Quality Management as Competitive Advantage," *Strategic Management Journal* 16 (1995): 15–37.

[26]For general background information, see "How to Build Quality," *The Economist,* September 23, 1989, pp. 91–92; A. Gabor, *The Man Who Discovered Quality* (New York: Penguin, 1990); P. B. Crosby, *Quality Is Free* (New York: Mentor, 1980).

[27]W. E. Deming, "Improvement of Quality and Productivity Through Action by Management," *National Productivity Review* 1 (Winter 1981–1982): 12–22.

[28]A. Ries and J. Trout, *Positioning: The Battle for Your Mind* (New York: Warner Books, 1982).

[29]R. G. Cooper, *Product Leadership* (Reading: Perseus Books, 1999).

[30]See Cooper, *Product Leadership*; A. L. Page "PDMA's New Product Development Practices Survey: Performance and Best Practices," presentation at PDMA 15th Annual International Conference, Boston, MA, October 16, 1991; E. Mansfield, "How Economists See R&D," *Harvard Business Review* (November–December 1981): 98–106.

[31]S. L. Brown and K. M. Eisenhardt, "Product Development: Past Research, Present Findings, and Future Directions," *Academy of Management Review* 20 (1995): 343–378; M. B. Lieberman and D. B. Montgomery, "First Mover Advantages," *Strategic Management Journal* 9 (Special Issue, Summer 1988): 41–58; D. J. Teece, "Profiting from Technological Innovation: Implications for Integration, Collaboration, Licensing and Public Policy," *Research Policy* 15 (1987): 285–305; G. J. Tellis and P. N. Golder, "First to Market, First to Fail?" *Sloan Management Review,* Winter 1996, pp. 65–75; G. A. Stevens and J. Bur-

ley, "Piloting the Rocket of Radical Innovation," *Research Technology Management* 46 (2003): 16–26.

[32]G. Stalk and T. M. Hout, *Competing Against Time* (New York: Free Press, 1990).

[33]K. B. Clark and S. C. Wheelwright, *Managing New Product and Process Development* (New York: Free Press, 1993); M. A. Schilling and C. W. L. Hill, "Managing the New Product Development Process," *Academy of Management Executive* 12:3 (August 1998): 67–81.

[34]O. Port, "Moving Past the Assembly Line," *Business Week* (Special Issue, "Reinventing America," 1992): 177–180.

[35]K. B. Clark and T. Fujimoto, "The Power of Product Integrity," *Harvard Business Review* (November–December 1990): 107–118; Clark and Wheelwright, *Managing New Product and Process Development*; Brown and Eisenhardt, "Product Development"; Stalk and Hout, *Competing Against Time.*

[36]C. Christensen, "Quantum Corporation—Business and Product Teams," Harvard Business School Case #9-692-023.

[37]H. Petroski, *Success Through Failure: The Paradox of Design* (Princeton: Princeton University Press, 2006). See also A. C. Edmondson, "Learning from Mistakes Is Easier Said Than Done," *Journal of Applied Behavioral Science* 40 (2004): 66–91.

[38]S. Caminiti, "A Mail Order Romance: Lands' End Courts Unseen Customers," *Fortune,* March 13, 1989, pp. 43–44.

[39]Sellers, "Getting Customers to Love You."

[40]Stalk and Hout, *Competing Against Time.*

Business-Level Strategy and the Industry Environment

Learning Objectives

6.1 Identify the strategies managers can develop to increase profitability in fragmented industries.

6.2 Discuss the special problems that exist in embryonic and growth industries.

6.3 Describe strategies enterprises can use to effectively compete in both embryonic and growth industries.

6.4 Describe competitive dynamics in mature industries.

6.5 Compare strategies managers can develop to increase profitability when competition is intense.

6.6 Outline the different strategies that companies in declining industries can use to support their business models and profitability.

Opening Case

The Online Food Delivery Business Is Getting Bigger, but the Playing Field Is Getting Smaller. *Much* Smaller.

In 1993, a company called Mosaic introduced the first graphical user interface for the internet, unleashing a frenzy of activity aimed at harnessing the "world wide web." One such effort was the world's first online restaurant delivery website, World Wide Waiter (which later became Waiter.com). The platform served the Bay Area in San Francisco, California, and was modestly successful. Soon similar sites were showing up in cities around the world, and as the internet grew in terms of number of users, so too did sales for the newly emergent online food delivery industry. Worldwide sales grew to over $150 billion by 2019. Then when the COVID-19 pandemic forced restaurants to close their doors to would-be diners, online food delivery surged to new record highs, doubling global online delivery revenues to over $300 billion by 2022. More than 50% of U.S. consumers were using online food delivery by 2022, and globally the number of users was more than 1.8 billion.

The strong growth in nearly every year and every geography attracted a wide range of national and regional players. However, that crowding put heavy pressure on the prices charged to both consumers and restaurants, making it increasingly hard to successfully compete in the industry. Scale became an important weapon: Delivery services that represented a large number of restaurants attracted more consumers, and could invest in sophisticated information technology, and achieve a streamlined cost structure that amortized that investment over a very large number of transactions. Furthermore, the services with the largest customer bases had bargaining power to negotiate larger fees from restaurants, protecting their profit margins even in the wake of strong competition. Smaller delivery services were either bought, dissolved, or clung to niche markets that had not yet attracted the attention of the dominant players.

From 2015 to 2022, the consolidation of the market was particularly acute. Grubhub swallowed up Delivered Dish, Eat24, and Foodler.[1] Germany-based Delivery Hero bought up Baedaltong (South Korea), Yemeksepeti (Turkey), Foodora (Germany), and Foodpanda (Singapore), but ultimately closed several of these businesses and exited the German market. DoorDash acquired Caviar. Amsterdam-based Takeaway acquired London-based Just Eat in 2019, forming Just Eat Takeaway. Then in 2020, Uber attempted to acquire Grubhub, but when it became clear that U.S. federal regulators were likely to block the deal due to the high concentration that was emerging in the U.S. online delivery industry, Uber backed away and Just Eat Takeaway bought Grubhub instead. Uber, not wanting to be outdone, bought Postmates.[2] In 2021, DoorDash, which had thus far generated nearly all of its revenues in the United States, bought Finland-based Wolt, bringing its service into 22 European countries.

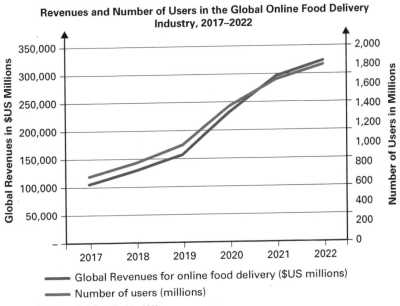

Revenues and Number of Users in the Global Online Food Delivery Industry, 2017–2022

Global Revenues in $US Millions

Number of Users in Millions

— Global Revenues for online food delivery ($US millions)
— Number of users (millions)

Source: Data compiled from Statista, 2022.

The major online delivery services also began to look for ways to differentiate their services. One way was through exclusive partnerships with major restaurant chains. For example, DoorDash officially teamed up with Little Caesars, Chipotle, and The Cheesecake Factory, and Grubhub had deals with KFC and Taco Bell.[3] It was not always clear, however, that such relationships boosted revenues—the exclusive deals often included provisions for the restaurants to pay lower delivery fees.

Several delivery services also attempted to differentiate themselves by launching "ghost kitchens" (kitchens built for delivery only in rented or mobile locations). By locating kitchens near demand, ghost kitchens could reduce delivery time and costs, and because the kitchens had no permanent brick-and-mortar presence, many branding and staffing expenses could be avoided. While it could be difficult to establish a relationship with customers in absence of a physical restaurant, several companies overcame this by partnering with known restaurant brands. For example, DoorDash formed a partnership with Burma Superstar to open a delivery-only location called Burma Bites,[4] Uber partnered with SushiYaa to develop ghost kitchens called Poke Station, and Deliveroo acquired ghost kitchen Maple.[5] By the end of 2020, India-based Swiggy was operating over 1,000 ghost kitchens.

Other delivery services were trying to fuel revenue growth by expanding the range of products they delivered. For example, Just Eat Takeaway, Deliveroo, and Uber Eats expanded into grocery delivery,[6] Uber Eats also expanded into alcohol delivery by buying Drizly,[7] prescription delivery through a partnership with Nimble, and same-day delivery of home products through a partnership with Costco. DoorDash expanded into household essentials (but not prescriptions) through a partnership with giant drugstore chain CVS.[8]

By May of 2022, most of the major online food delivery markets were heavily consolidated. In the United States, almost 99% of the food delivery market was controlled by just three players: DoorDash (with 59% market share), Uber Eats (with 27% market share), and Grubhub (with 13% market share). Most of Europe was similarly controlled by three players, with Uber Eats, Just Eat Takeaway, and Deliveroo controlling over 80% of the market. Most of Southeast Asia was dominated by just two players: Grab (with roughly 50% of the market across the area overall) and Foodpanda (which had a share as high as 49% in some Southeast Asian countries). Latin America is even more consolidated, with iFood controlling over 80% of the market, though Rappi, Glovo, and Uber Eats keep the pricing pressure intense in the Latin American market. With new customer acquisition slowing and fierce competition between sophisticated players to maintain or expand their share, it was getting harder to see how the delivery giants would continue to fuel the growth investors had come to expect.

Overview

In Chapter 2, we learned that industries go through a life cycle. Some industries are young and dynamic, with rapidly growing demand. Others are mature and relatively stable, whereas still other industries, like newspapers and many categories of brick-and-mortar retailers, are in decline.

We will see that each stage in the evolution of its industry raises interesting challenges for a business. Managers must adopt the appropriate strategies to deal with these challenges.

For example, as illustrated in the Closing Case, cable television providers that once held near monopolies in the regions they served are now under intense pressure from streaming services. Both numbers of subscribers and subscription revenues are in precipitous decline and many (perhaps most) of the services are likely to disappear. However, paradoxically, there is often still good money to be made in a declining industry if managers can figure out the right strategy. A niche strategy of focusing on market segments where demand remains strong is one way. Firms in a declining industry may also possess valuable assets or customer relationships that can be leveraged in a new industry. For example, cable service operators became the internet providers for many of their former cable subscribers, slowing their overall decline in revenues.

Before we look at the different stages of an industry life cycle, we first consider strategy in a fragmented industry because fragmented industries can offer unique opportunities for enterprises to pursue strategies that result in the consolidation of those industries, often creating significant wealth for the consolidating enterprise and its owners.

6.1 Identify the strategies managers can develop to increase profitability in fragmented industries.

fragmented industry
An industry composed of a large number of small- and medium-sized companies.

6-1 Strategy in a Fragmented Industry

A **fragmented industry** is composed of many small- and medium-sized companies. Examples of fragmented industries include the dry-cleaning, hair salon, restaurant, health club, massage, and legal services. There are several reasons that an industry may consist of many small companies rather than a few large ones.[9]

6-1a Reasons for Fragmentation

There are three reasons for fragmentation. First, a lack of scale economies may mean that there are few, if any, cost advantages to large size. There are no obvious scale economies in landscaping and massage services, for example, which helps explain why these industries remain highly fragmented. In some industries, customer needs are so specialized that only a small amount of a product is required. Hence, there is no scope for a large, mass-production operation to satisfy the market. Custom-made jewelry and catering are examples. In some industries, there may even be diseconomies of scale. In the restaurant business, for example, customers often prefer the unique food and style of a popular, local restaurant rather than the standardized offerings of a national chain. This diseconomy of scale places a limit on the ability of large restaurant chains to dominate the market.

Second, brand loyalty in the industry may primarily be local. It may be difficult to build a brand through differentiation that transcends a particular location or region. Many homebuyers, for example, prefer dealing with independent local real estate agents, whom they perceive as having better local knowledge than agents with national chains. Similarly, there are few large chains in the massage services industry because differentiation and brand loyalty are primarily driven by differences in the skill sets of individual massage therapists.

Third, the lack of scale economies and national brand loyalty often implies low entry barriers. When this is the case, a steady stream of new entrants may keep the industry fragmented. The massage services industry exemplifies this situation. Due to the absence of scale requirements, the costs of opening a massage services business can be shouldered by a single entrepreneur. The same is true of landscaping services, which helps to keep that industry fragmented.

In industries that have these characteristics, focus strategies tend to work best. Companies may specialize by customer group, customer need, or geographic region. Many small, specialty companies may operate in local or regional markets. All kinds of specialized or custom-made products fall into this category, as do all small, service operations that cater to personalized customer needs.

6-1b Consolidating a Fragmented Industry Through Value Innovation

Business history is full of examples of entrepreneurial organizations that have pursued strategies to create meaningful scale economies and national brands where none previously existed. In the process, they have consolidated industries that were once fragmented, reaping enormous gains for themselves and their shareholders in the process.

For example, until the 1980s, the office-supply business was a highly fragmented industry composed of many small, "mom-and-pop" enterprises that served local markets. The typical office-supply enterprise in those days had a limited selection of products, low inventory turnover, limited operating hours, and a focus on providing personal service to local businesses. Customer service included having a small sales force, which visited businesses and took orders, along with several trucks that delivered merchandise to larger customers. Then along came Staples, started by executives who had cut their teeth in the grocery business; they opened a big-box store with a wide product selection, long operating hours, and a self-service business model. They implemented computer information systems to track product sales and make sure that inventory was replenished just before it was out of stock, which drove up inventory turnover. True, Staples did not initially offer the same level of personal service that established office-supply enterprises did, but the managers of Staples made a bet that small-business customers were more interested in value from a wide product selection, long opening hours, and low prices—and they were right. Put differently, the managers at Staples had a different view of what was important to their customer set than did the established enterprises. Today, Staples and Office Depot OfficeMax dominate the office-supply industry. Though they face considerable competition from Amazon, most of their small rivals have gone out of businesses.

You may recognize in the Staples story a theme that we discussed in Chapter 5: Staples is a *value innovator*.[10] The company's founders figured out a way to offer more value to their customer set, and at a lower cost. Companies like Walmart and Carrefour did a similar thing in general merchandise retail, as did Home Depot, Lowes, Kingfisher, and others in building materials and home improvement. In the restaurant sector, McDonald's, Taco Bell, Kentucky Fried Chicken, and, more recently, Starbucks, have all followed a similar course. Although the restaurant industry remains extremely fragmented, overall, in each case, these enterprises succeeded in achieving consolidation advantages in once-fragmented industries.

The lesson is clear: Fragmented industries are wide-open market spaces—blue oceans—just waiting for entrepreneurs to transform them through the pursuit of value innovation. A key to understanding this process is to recognize that, in each case, the value innovator defines value differently than do established companies, and it finds a way to offer value that lowers costs through the creation of scale economies. In fast food, for example, McDonald's offers reliable, quick, convenient fast food at a low cost. The low cost has two sources—first, the standardization of processes within each store, which boosts labor productivity; second, the attainment of scale economies on the input side due to McDonald's considerable purchasing power (which grew over time as the McDonald's chain grew). McDonald's was a value innovator in its day, and through its choice of strategy it helped to drive consolidation in the fast-food segment of the restaurant industry.

6-1c Chaining and Franchising

In many fragmented industries that have been consolidated through value innovation, the transforming company often starts with a single location, or just a few locations. This was true for Best Buy, which started as a single store (called Sound of Music) in St. Paul, Minnesota, and Starbucks, which had just three stores in Seattle, Washington, when Howard Shultz took over and started to transform the business. The key is to get the strategy right at the first few locations, and then expand as rapidly as possible to build a national brand and realize scale economies before rivals move into the market. If this is done right, the value innovator can build formidable barriers to new entry by establishing strong brand loyalty and enjoying the scale economies that come from large size (often, these scale economies are associated with purchasing power). Enterprises use two strategies to *replicate* their offering once they get it right: chaining and franchising.[11]

chaining

A strategy designed to obtain the advantages of cost leadership by establishing a network of linked merchandising outlets interconnected by information technology that functions as one large company.

Chaining involves opening additional locations that adhere to one basic formula *that the company owns*. Thus, Staples pursued a chaining strategy when it quickly opened additional stores after perfecting its formula at its first location in Boston. Today, Staples has approximately 1,338 stores worldwide. Starbucks, too, has pursued a chaining strategy, offering the same basic formula in every store that it opens. Its store count now exceeds 34,000 around the world. Best Buy, Walmart, and Home Depot have also all pursued a chaining strategy.

By expanding through chaining, a value innovator can quickly build a national brand. This may be of significant value in a mobile society such as the United States, where people move and travel frequently, and when in a new town or city they look for familiar offerings. At the same time, by rapidly opening locations, and by knitting those locations together through good information systems, the value innovator can realize many of the cost advantages that come from large size. Walmart, for example, uses a hub-and-spoke distribution system monitored in real time through a satellite-based information system that enables it to tightly control the flow of inventory through its stores. This tight control allows it to customize inventory for particular regions based on sales patterns and maximize inventory turnover (a major source of cost savings). In addition, as Walmart grew, it was able to exercise more and more bargaining power over suppliers, driving down the price for the goods that it resold in its stores.

Franchising is similar in many respects to chaining, except that in the case of franchising the founding company—the franchisor—licenses the right to open and operate a new location to another enterprise—the franchisee—in return for a fee. Typically, franchisees must adhere to strict rules that require them to adopt the same basic business model and operate in a certain way. Thus, a McDonald's franchisee must have the same basic look, feel, offerings, pricing, and business processes as other restaurants in the system, and must report standardized financial information to McDonald's on a regular basis.

franchising

A strategy in which the franchisor grants to its franchisees the right to use the franchisor's name, reputation, and business model in return for a franchise fee and, often, a percentage of the profits.

There are advantages to using a franchising strategy. First, normally the franchisee puts up some or all of the capital to establish their operation. This helps to finance the growth of the system and can result in rapid expansion. Second, because franchisees invest capital and own their operations, they have a strong incentive to run them as efficiently and effectively as possible—which is good for the franchisor.

Third, franchisees often have a deep knowledge of the local market that enables them to develop new offerings and/or processes suited to their customers' preferences. Typically, the franchisor will give franchisees some latitude, as long as they do not deviate too much from the basic business model. Ideas developed in this way may then be transferred to other locations, improving the performance of the entire system. For example, McDonald's changed the design and menu of its restaurants in the United States based on ideas first pioneered by a franchisee in France.

The drawbacks of a franchising strategy are threefold. First, it may allow less control than can be achieved through a chaining strategy because, by definition, a franchising strategy delegates some authority to the franchisee. Early in Starbucks' history, for example, Howard Shultz decided to expand primarily via a chaining strategy rather than a franchising strategy because he felt that franchising would not give Starbucks the necessary control over customer service in each store. Later, licensing agreements were used to enter venues where the store could not otherwise operate (e.g., in airports) and international markets. Second, in a franchising system, the franchisee captures some of the economic profit from a successful operation, whereas in a chaining strategy it all flows to the company. Third, because franchisees are small relative to the founding enterprise, they may face a higher cost of capital, which raises system costs and lowers profitability. Given these various pros and cons, the choice between chaining and franchising depends on managers evaluating which strategy is best given the circumstances facing the founding enterprise.

6-1d Horizontal Mergers

Another way of consolidating a fragmented industry is to merge with or acquire competitors, combining them into a single, large enterprise that is able to realize scale economies and build a compelling national brand. The online food delivery industry is a great example of this—markets once crowded with dozens of competitors have now been consolidated into oligopolies with a few powerful players that can leverage significant scale economies and bargaining power over restaurants and well-known brands. This consolidation is a double-edged sword for restaurants. On the one hand, consolidation means that restaurants only have to work with a few platforms to reach nearly all of the market, which streamlines their processes for taking orders. Restaurants also benefit by the market reach of the platforms (enabling them to cast a wider net for customers than they could on their own), and well-developed transaction and review systems provided by the online platforms.

On the other hand, the bargaining power of the large and powerful platforms enables them to negotiate higher fees from the restaurants—sometimes up to 30% of the prices charged by the restaurants!

It is worth noting that although mergers and acquisitions can help a company consolidate a fragmented industry, the road to success when pursuing this strategy is littered with failures. Some companies pay too much for the businesses they acquire. Others find out after the acquisition that they have bought a "lemon" that is nowhere as efficient as they thought prior to the acquisition. Still others discover that the gains envisaged for an acquisition are difficult to realize due to a clash between the culture of the acquiring and acquired enterprises. We will consider the benefits, costs, and risks associated with a strategy of horizontal mergers and acquisitions in Chapters 9 and 10 when we look at corporate-level strategy.

6-2 Strategies in Embryonic and Growth Industries

6.2 Discuss the special problems that exist in embryonic and growth industries.

As Chapter 2 discussed, an embryonic industry is one that is just beginning to develop, and a growth industry is one in which first-time demand is rapidly expanding as many new customers enter the market. Choosing the strategies needed to succeed in such industries poses special challenges because new groups of customers with different needs enter the market. Managers must be aware of the way competitive forces in embryonic and growth industries change over time because they frequently need to develop new competencies and refine their business strategy to effectively compete in the future.

Most embryonic industries emerge when a technological innovation creates a new product opportunity. For example, in 1975, the personal computer (PC) industry was born after Intel developed the microprocessor technology that allowed companies to build the world's first PCs; this spawned the growth of the PC software industry that took off after Microsoft developed an operating system for IBM.[12] Similarly, the development of the internet gave rise to the e-commerce and social media industries, and advances in broadband and smartphones gave rise to the music and video streaming industries.

Customer demand for the products of an embryonic industry is initially limited for a variety of reasons, including: (1) the limited performance and poor quality of the first products; (2) customer unfamiliarity with what the new product can do for them; (3) poorly developed distribution channels to get the product to customers; (4) a lack of complementary products that might increase the value of the product for customers; and (5) high production costs because of small volumes of production. For this reason, first movers in an embryonic industry are often at a disadvantage to later entrants; they must bear greater development costs to work out how to produce the technology and make it desirable to customers, and they bear greater "missionary" costs of educating customers about the product's benefits.

Customer demand for the first cars, for example, was limited by their poor performance (they were no faster than a horse, far noisier, and frequently broke down), a lack of important complementary products (such as a network of paved roads and gas stations), and high production costs that made these cars an expensive luxury (before Ford invented the assembly line, cars were built by hand in a craft-based production setting). Similarly, demand for electric cars has been limited because many customers are unfamiliar with the technology and its implications for service and resale value. Customers also worry about whether there are charging stations along routes they will drive, or worry that charging will take too long. Because of such concerns, early demand for the products of embryonic industries typically comes from a small set of technologically savvy customers willing and able to tolerate, and even enjoy, the imperfections in their new purchase.[13] Early adopters of electric cars, for example, tend to have higher-than-average incomes and are highly motivated to buy a car that is environmentally friendly.[14]

An industry moves from the embryonic stage to the growth stage when a mass market starts to develop for its product. A **mass market** is one in which large numbers of customers enter the market. Mass markets emerge when three things happen: (1) ongoing technological progress makes a product easier to use, and increases its value for the average customer; (2) complementary products are developed that also increase its value; and (3) companies in the industry work to find ways to reduce the costs of producing the new products so they can lower their prices and stimulate high demand.[15] For example, the mass market for cars emerged and the demand for cars surged when: (1) technological progress increased the performance of cars; (2) a network of paved roads and gas stations was established; and (3) Henry Ford began to mass-produce cars using an assembly-line process, dramatically reducing production costs and enabling him to decrease prices and build consumer demand. Similarly, the mass market for PCs emerged when technological advances made computers easier to use, a supply of complementary software (such as spreadsheet and word-processing programs) was developed, and companies in the industry (such as Dell) began to use mass production to build PCs at low cost.

mass market

A market into which large numbers of customers enter.

6-2a The Changing Nature of Market Demand

Managers who understand how the demand for a product is affected by the changing needs of customers can focus on developing new strategies that will protect and strengthen their competitive position, such as building competencies to lower production costs or speed product development. In most product markets, the changing needs of customers lead to the S-shaped growth curve in Figure 6.1.[16] This illustrates how different groups of customers with different needs enter the market over time. The curve is S-shaped because adoption is initially slow when an unfamiliar technology is introduced to the market. Adoption accelerates as the technology becomes better understood and utilized by the mass market, and eventually the market is saturated.

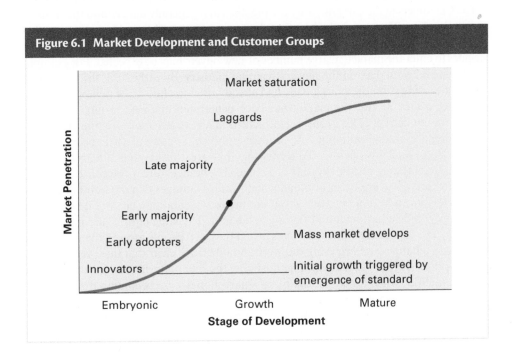

Figure 6.1 Market Development and Customer Groups

The rate of new adoptions then declines as demand is increasingly limited to replacement demand.[17] For instance, electronic calculators were adopted upon their introduction by a relatively small pool of scientists and engineers. This group had previously used slide rules. Then, the calculator began to penetrate the larger markets of accountants and commercial users, followed by the still-larger market that included students and the general public. After these markets had become saturated, fewer opportunities remained for new adoptions. This curve has major implications for a company's differentiation, cost, and pricing decisions.

The first group of customers to enter the market is referred to as *innovators*. Innovators are often technophiles who are delighted to be the first to purchase and experiment with a product based on a new technology—even if it is imperfect and expensive. Frequently, innovators have technical talents and interests, which drive them to "own" and develop new technology. They tend to be less risk averse than other customer groups, and often have greater resources to spare. Though they are not always well integrated into social networks, they are influential in new-product adoption because they are the first to bring a new idea into the social system. In the PC market, the first customers were software engineers and computer hobbyists who wanted to write computer code at home.[18]

Early adopters are the second group of customers to enter the market; they understand that the technology may have important future applications and are willing to experiment with it to see if they can pioneer new uses for the technology. They are comfortable with technical information and will adopt products that seem appealing even if none of their peers have purchased those products. Early adopters often envision how the technology may be used in the future, and they try to be the first to profit from its use. Early adopters often have significant social influence and will actively promote new technologies, making them particularly important for the diffusion of new innovations. Jeff Bezos, the founder of Amazon.com, was an early adopter of Web technology. In 1994, before anyone else, he saw that the Web could be used in innovative ways to sell books.

Innovators and early adopters alike enter the market while the industry is in its embryonic stage. The next group of customers, the *early majority*, forms the leading wave or edge of the mass market. Their entry into the market signifies the beginning of the growth stage. Customers in the early majority are practical and generally understand the value of new technology. They weigh the benefits of adopting new products against the costs, and wait to enter the market until they are confident they will benefit. When the early majority decides to enter the market, a large number of new buyers may be expected. For example, see Figure 6.2 with data on the music streaming industry. By early 2022, the number of music streaming subscriptions globally had already risen to almost 524 million.

When about 50% of the market has been penetrated, the next group of customers enters the market. This group is characterized as the *late majority*, the customers who purchase a new technology or product only when many of their peers already have done so and it is obvious the technology has great utility and is here to stay. A typical late majority customer group is a somewhat "older" and more conservative set of customers. They are often unfamiliar with the advantages of new technology. The late majority can be a bit nervous about buying new technology but will do so if they see many people adopting it and finding value in it. The late majority did not start to enter the PC market until the mid-1990s, when they saw people around them engaging in e-mail exchanges and browsing the Web, and it became clear that these technologies were here to stay. In the smartphone business, the late majority started to enter the market in 2012, when it became clear that smartphones were becoming the dominant mobile-phone technology.

Laggards, the last group of customers to enter the market, are inherently conservative and unappreciative of the uses of new technology. Laggards frequently refuse

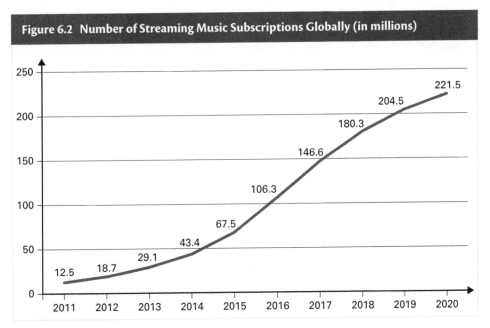

Figure 6.2 Number of Streaming Music Subscriptions Globally (in millions)

Source: MIDiA research, 2018.

to adopt new products even when the benefits are obvious, or unless they are forced to do so by circumstances—for example, due to work-related reasons. People who use typewriters rather than computers to write letters and books are laggards. In the United States, people who do not use smartphones are laggards, and given the fast rate of adoption of music streaming, it will not be long before the only people not in the music streaming market are laggards.

In Figure 6.3, the bell-shaped curve represents the total market, and the divisions in the curve show the average percentage of buyers who fall into each of these customer groups. Note that early adopters are a very small percentage of the market;

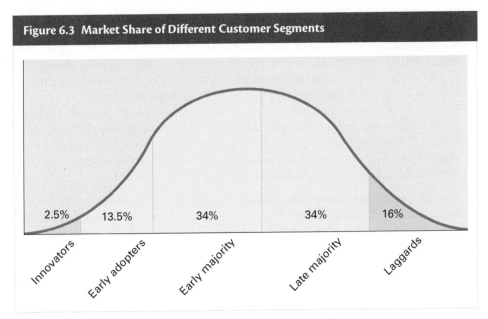

Figure 6.3 Market Share of Different Customer Segments

Source: Adapted from Rogers, EM. 2010. *Diffusion of Innovations*. New York: Simon and Schuster.

hence, the figure illustrates a vital competitive dynamic—the highest market demand and industry profits arise when the early and late majority groups enter the market. Additionally, research has found that although early pioneering companies succeed in attracting innovators and early adopters, many of these companies often *fail* to attract a significant share of early and late majority customers, and ultimately go out of business.[19]

6.3 Describe strategies enterprises can use to effectively compete in both embryonic and growth industries.

6-3 Strategic Implications: Crossing the Chasm

Why are pioneering companies often unable to create a business model that allows them to be successful over time and remain as market leaders? *Innovators and early adopters have very different customer needs from the early majority.* In an influential book, Geoffrey Moore argues that because of the differences in customer needs between these groups, the business-level strategies required for companies to succeed in the emerging mass market are quite different from those required to succeed in the embryonic market.[20] Pioneering companies that do not change the strategies they use to pursue their business model will therefore lose their competitive advantage to those companies that implement new strategies aimed at best serving the needs of the early and late majority. New strategies are often required to strengthen a company's business model as a market develops over time for the following reasons:

- Innovators and early adopters are technologically sophisticated customers willing to tolerate the limitations of the product. The early majority, however, values ease of use and reliability. Companies competing in an embryonic market typically pay more attention to increasing the performance of a product than to its ease of use and reliability. Those competing in a mass market need to make sure that the product is reliable and easy to use. Thus, the product development strategies required for success vary as a market develops over time.
- Innovators and early adopters are typically reached through specialized distribution channels, and products are often sold by word of mouth. They are active consumers of technical information. Reaching the early majority requires mass-market distribution channels and mass-media advertising campaigns that require a different set of marketing and sales strategies.
- Because innovators and the early majority are relatively few in number and are not particularly price sensitive, companies serving them typically pursue a focus model, produce small quantities of a product, and price high. To serve the rapidly growing mass market, large-scale mass production may be critical to ensure that a high-quality product can be reliably produced at a low price point.
- The spread of new technologies is often a social process: people typically find out about new technologies from their friends and colleagues. Mass market customers often will not adopt a product until they see it widely in use and perceive it as ubiquitous.[21] This can create a chicken-and-egg problem: until enough people have adopted the product, the mass market will be reluctant to adopt it.

In sum, the business models and strategies required to compete in an embryonic market populated by early adopters and innovators are very different from those required to compete in a high-growth, mass market populated by the early majority. As a consequence, the transition between the embryonic market and the mass market is not a smooth, seamless one. Rather, it represents a *competitive chasm* or gulf that companies must cross. According to Moore, many companies do not or cannot develop the right business model; they fall into the chasm and go out of business. Thus, although embryonic markets are typically populated by numerous small companies, once the mass market begins to develop, the number of companies sharply decreases.[22] For a detailed example of how this unfolds, see Strategy in Action 6.1, which explains how Microsoft and Research in Motion fell into the chasm in the smartphone market, whereas Apple leaped across it with its iPhone, a product designed for the early majority.

The implication is clear: To cross the chasm successfully, managers must correctly identify the needs of the first wave of early majority users—the leading edge of the

Crossing the Chasm in the Smartphone Market

The first smartphones appeared in the early 2000s. Early market leaders included Research in Motion (RIM), with its Blackberry line of smartphones, and Microsoft, whose Windows Mobile operating system powered a number of early smartphone offerings made by companies such as Motorola. These phones were sold to business users and marketed as business productivity tools. They had small screens and a physical keyboard crammed onto a relatively small device. Although they had the ability to send and receive e-mails, browse online, and so on, there was no independent applications market, and consequently the utility of the phones was very limited. Nor were they always easy to use. System administrators were often required to set up basic features such as corporate e-mail access. They were certainly not consumer-friendly devices. Their customers at this time were primarily innovators and early adopters.

The market changed dramatically after the introduction of the Apple iPhone in 2007 (Figure 6.4). First, this phone was aimed not at power business users, but at a broader consumer market. Second, the phone was easy to use, with a large, touch-activated screen and a virtual keyboard that vanished when not in use. Third, the phone was stylishly designed, with an elegance that appealed to many consumers. Fourth, Apple made it very easy for independent developers to write applications that could run on the phone, and they set up their App Store, which made it easy for developers to market their apps. Very quickly, new applications appeared, adding value to the phone. These included mapping applications, news feeds, stock information, and a wide array of games, several of which soon became big hits. Clearly, the iPhone was a device squarely aimed not at business users but at consumers. The ease of use and utility of the iPhone quickly drew the early majority into the market, and sales surged. Meanwhile, sales of Blackberry devices and Windows Mobile phones spiraled downward.

Both Microsoft and Blackberry were ultimately forced to abandon their existing phone platforms and strategies, and to reorient. Both developed touch-activated screens similar to those on the iPhone, launched app stores, and targeted consumers. However, it may have been too late for them. By early 2015, both former market leaders had market shares in the single digits, whereas Apple's iPhone and Google's Android (which imitated many of the design and technical features of the iPhone) dominated the market.

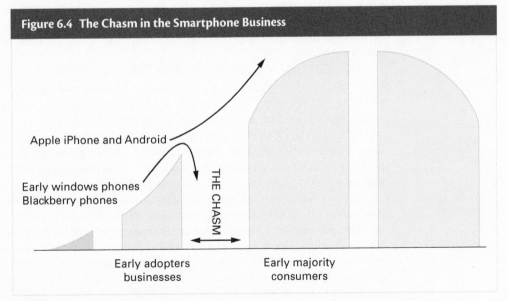

Figure 6.4 The Chasm in the Smartphone Business

Apple iPhone and Android

Early windows phones
Blackberry phones

THE CHASM

Early adopters
businesses

Early majority
consumers

Source: Adapted from Moore, GA. 2009. *Crossing the Chasm: Marketing and Selling High Tech Products to Mainstream Customers*. New York: Harper Collins.

Sources: Anonymous, "iPhone Tops 1 Millionth Sale," *Information Today* 24(9): (2007): 27; Anonymous, "The Battle for the Smart-phone's Soul," *The Economist*, November 22, 2008, pp. 76–77; L. Dignan, "Android, Apple iOS Flip Consumer, Corporate Market Share," *Between the Lines*, February 13, 2013; IDC: Smartphone OS Market Share, Q1, 2015, www.idc.com.

mass market. Then they must adjust their business models by developing new strategies to redesign products and create distribution channels and marketing campaigns to satisfy the needs of the early majority. They must have a suitable product available at a reasonable price to sell to the early majority when they begin to enter the market in large numbers. At the same time, industry pioneers must abandon outdated, focused business models directed at the needs of innovators and early adopters. Focusing on an outdated model leads managers to ignore the needs of the early majority—and the need to develop the strategies necessary to pursue a differentiation or cost-leadership business model in order to remain a dominant industry competitor.

6-3a Strategic Implications of Differences in Market Growth Rates

Managers must understand a final, important issue in embryonic and growth industries: Different markets develop at different rates. The speed at which a market develops can be measured by its growth rate, that is, the rate at which customers in that market purchase the industry's product. A number of factors explain the variation in market growth rates for different products, and thus the speed with which a particular market develops. It is important for managers to understand the source of these differences because their choice of strategy can accelerate or retard the rate at which a market grows.[23]

The first factor that accelerates customer demand is a new product's *relative advantage*; that is, the degree to which a new product is perceived as being better at satisfying customer needs than the product it supersedes. For example, the early growth in demand for cell phones was partly driven by their economic benefits. Studies showed that because business customers could always be reached by cell phone, they made better use of their time—for example, by not showing up at a meeting that had been canceled at the last minute—and saved 2 hours per week in time that would otherwise have been wasted. For busy executives—the early adopters—the productivity benefits of owning a cell phone outweighed the costs. Cell phones also rapidly diffused for social reasons, in particular, because they conferred glamour or prestige upon their users (something that also drives demand for today's most advanced smartphones).

A second factor of considerable importance is *complexity*. Products that are viewed by consumers as being complex and difficult to master will diffuse more slowly than products that are easy to master. The early PCs diffused quite slowly because many people saw the archaic command lines needed to operate a PC as being very complex and intimidating. PCs did not become a mass-market device until graphical user interfaces with onscreen icons became widespread, enabling users to open programs and perform functions by pointing and clicking with a mouse. In contrast, the first cell phones were simple to use and quickly adopted.

Another factor driving growth in demand is *compatibility*, the degree to which a new product is perceived as being consistent with the current needs or existing values of potential adopters. Demand for cell phones grew rapidly because their operation was compatible with the prior experience of potential adopters who used traditional, landline phones. A fourth factor is *trialability*, the degree to which potential customers can experiment with a new product during a hands-on trial basis. Many people first used cell phones by borrowing them from colleagues to make calls, and their positive experiences helped accelerate growth rates. In contrast, early PCs were more difficult to experiment with because they were rare and expensive, and because some training was needed in how to use them. These complications led to slower growth rates for

PCs. A final factor is *observability*, the degree to which the results of using and enjoying a new product can be seen and appreciated by other people. Originally, iPhone and Android phones diffused rapidly because it was easy to observe people using them for many purposes, including phone calls, playing music, sending e-mail, mapping, and more.

Thus, managers must devise strategies that educate customers about the value of their new products if they are to grow demand over time. They need to design their products to overcome barriers to adoption by making them less complex and intimidating, easy to use, and by showcasing their relative advantage over prior technology. This is exactly what Apple did with the iPhone, which helps explain the rapid diffusion of smartphones after Apple introduced its first iPhone in 2007.

When a market is growing rapidly and social processes are driving the spread of a product, companies can take advantage of viral diffusion by identifying and aggressively courting opinion leaders (customers whose views command respect) in a particular market. For example, when the manufacturers of new, high-tech medical equipment such as magnetic resonance imaging (MRI) scanners market a new product, they try to get well-known doctors at major research and teaching hospitals to use the product first. Companies may give these opinion leaders (the doctors) free machines for research purposes, and work closely with the doctors to further develop the technology. Once these opinion leaders commit to the product and give it their stamp of approval, doctors at other hospitals often follow.

In sum, understanding competitive dynamics in embryonic and growth industries is an important strategic issue. The ways in which different customer groups emerge and the ways in which customer needs change are important determinants of the strategies that need to be pursued to make a business model successful over time. Similarly, understanding the factors that affect a market's growth rate allows managers to tailor their business model to a changing industry environment. (Competition in high-tech industries is discussed further in the Chapter 7.)

6-4 Strategy in Mature Industries

6.4 Describe competitive dynamics in mature industries.

A mature industry is commonly dominated by a small number of large companies. Although a mature industry may also contain many medium-sized companies and a host of small, specialized companies, the large companies often determine the nature of competition in the industry because they can influence the six competitive forces. Indeed, these large companies hold their leading positions because they have developed the most successful business models and strategies in an industry.

By the end of the shakeout stage, companies have learned how important it is to analyze each other's business models and strategies. They also know that if they change their strategies, their actions are likely to stimulate a competitive response from industry rivals. For example, a differentiator that starts to lower its prices because it has adopted a more cost-efficient technology not only threatens other differentiators, but may also threaten cost leaders that see their competitive advantage being eroded. Hence, by the mature stage of the life cycle, companies have learned the meaning of competitive interdependence.

As a result, in mature industries, business-level strategy revolves around understanding how established companies *collectively* attempt to moderate the intensity of industry competition to preserve both company and industry profitability. Interdependent companies can protect their competitive advantage and profitability by adopting strategies and tactics, first, to deter entry into an industry, and second, to reduce the level of rivalry within an industry.

6-5 Strategies to Deter Entry

In mature industries, successful enterprises have normally gained substantial economies of scale and established strong brand loyalty. As we saw in Chapter 2, the economies of scale and brand loyalty enjoyed by incumbents in an industry constitute strong barriers to entry. However, there may be cases in which scale and brand, although significant, are not sufficient to deter entry. In such circumstances, companies can pursue other strategies to make new entry less likely. These strategies include product proliferation, limit pricing, technology upgrading, and strategic commitments.[24]

Product Proliferation   One way in which companies try to enter a mature industry is by looking for market segments or niches that are poorly served by incumbent enterprises. This strategy involves entering these segments, gaining experience, scale, and brand in that segment, and then progressively moving upmarket. This is how Japanese automobile companies first entered the U.S. market in the late 1970s and early 1980s. They targeted segments at the bottom end of the market for small, inexpensive, fuel-efficient cars. These segments were not well served by large American manufacturers such as Ford Motor Company (Ford) and General Motors Company (GM). Once companies like Toyota and Honda had gained a strong position in these segments, they started to move upmarket with larger offerings, and ultimately entered the pickup truck and SUV markets, which historically had been the most profitable segments of the automobile industry for American companies.

product proliferation strategy

The strategy of "filling the niches" or catering to the needs of customers in all market segments to deter entry by competitors.

A **product proliferation strategy** involves incumbent companies attempting to forestall entry by making sure that *every* niche or segment in the marketplace is well served. Had U.S. automobile companies pursued product proliferation in the 1970s and early 1980s, and produced lines of smaller, fuel-efficient cars, it may have been more difficult for Japanese automobile companies to enter the U.S. market. Another example is provided by breakfast cereal companies, which are famous for pursuing a product proliferation strategy. Typically, they produce many different types of cereal, so that they can cater to all likely consumer needs. The net result is that the four biggest breakfast cereal companies—General Mills, Post, PepsiCo (which owns Quaker), and Kellogg— have been able to occupy all of the valuable real estate in the industry (i.e., shelf space in supermarkets) by filling it with a multiplicity of offerings and leaving very little room for new entrants. Moreover, when new entry does occur—as happened when smaller companies selling granola and organic cereals entered the market—the big four have moved rapidly to offer their own versions of these products, effectively foreclosing entry. A product proliferation strategy can thus effectively deter entry because it gives new entrants very little opportunity to find an unoccupied niche in an industry.

limit price strategy

Charging a price that is lower than that required to maximize profits in the short run to signal to new entrants that the incumbent has a low-cost structure that the entrant likely cannot match.

Limit Price   A limit price strategy may be used to deter entry when incumbent companies in an industry enjoy economies of scale, but the resulting cost advantages are *not* enough to keep potential rivals out of the industry. A **limit price strategy** involves charging a price that is lower than that required to maximize profits in the short run to signal to a potential entrant that the incumbent could price the new entrant out of the market, thereby deterring entry. Though limit pricing may not be sustainable in the long run for the incumbent, new entrants often do not have full information about the incumbent's costs and thus do not know how long the incumbent can keep prices low.

Consider Figure 6.5, which shows that incumbent companies have a unit cost structure that is lower than that of potential entrants. However, if incumbents charge the price that the market will bear (Figure 6.5a), this will be above the unit cost structure of new entrants (Figure 6.5b), allowing them to enter and still make a profit under the pricing umbrella set by incumbents. In this situation, the best option for incumbents might be to charge a price that is still above their own cost structure but just below the cost structure

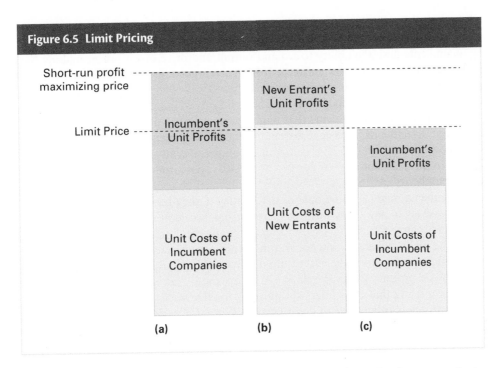

Figure 6.5 Limit Pricing

of any potential new entrants (Figure 6.5c). Now there is no incentive for companies to attempt to enter the market, because at the lower limit price they cannot make a profit. Thus, because it deters entry, the limit price might be thought of as the long-run, profit-maximizing price. For example, in the U.S. cable industry, incumbents such as Time Warner Cable (now Spectrum) and Comcast (dba Xfinity) often had near-monopolies over the regions they served. However, when new competitors attempted to enter their markets, the incumbents often engaged in limit pricing to deter entry. Research by Robert Seamans showed that when new entrants came from outside industries—and thus were unlikely to have full information on the incumbent's costs (e.g., telecom companies such as Verizon FIOS)—incumbent cable companies often used limit pricing to deter their entry. On the other hand, when new entrants were city-owned and thus less sensitive to profit margins, incumbents would use large investments in technology upgrading (discussed below) that city-owned operators had difficulty matching.[25]

Technology Upgrading   If an incumbent is limited in its pricing strategies or faces potential entrants that may be willing to match its pricing, it can deter entry through investments in **technology upgrading** that the new entrant has difficulty matching. For example, though municipal cable TV entrants may be relatively insensitive to profit margins (as described previously), they may have difficulty matching investments that a large incumbent can make in state-of-the-art technologies. Thus, when incumbent cable companies were threatened by potential, city-owned entrants, they invested in upgrading their cable infrastructure to provide the two-way communication needed to provide internet service, thereby slowing municipal entry.[26]

Strategic Commitments   Incumbent companies can deter entry by engaging in strategic commitments that send a signal to potential new entrants that entry will be difficult. **Strategic commitments** are investments that signal an incumbent's long-term commitment to a market or market segment.[27] As an entry-deterring strategy, strategic commitments involve raising the perceived costs of entering a market, thereby reducing the likelihood of entry. To the extent that such actions are successful, strategic commitments can protect an industry and lead to greater long-run profits for those already in the industry.

technology upgrading

Incumbent companies deterring entry by investing in costly technology upgrades that potential entrants have trouble matching.

strategic commitments

Investments that signal an incumbent's long-term commitment to a market or market segment.

One example of strategic commitment occurs when incumbent companies invest in excess productive capacity. The idea is to signal to potential entrants that if they do enter, the incumbents have the ability to expand output and drive down prices, making the market less profitable for new entrants. It has been argued, for example, that chemical companies may overinvest in productive capacity as a way of signaling their commitment to a particular market and indicating that new entrants will find it difficult to compete.[28]

Other strategic commitments that might act as an entry deterrent include making significant investments in basic research, product development, or advertising beyond those necessary to maintain a company's competitive advantage over its existing rivals.[29] In all cases, for such actions to deter entry, potential rivals must be aware of what incumbents are doing, and the investments must be sufficient to deter entry.

Incumbents might also be able to deter entry if they have a history of responding aggressively to new entry through price cutting, accelerating product development efforts, increasing advertising expenditures, or some combination of these. For example, in the 1990s, when a competitor announced a new software product Microsoft would often attempt to make entry difficult by quickly announcing that it had a similar software product under development that would work well with Windows (the implication being that consumers should wait for the Microsoft product). The term "vaporware" was often used to describe such aggressive product preannouncements. Many observers believe that the practice did succeed on occasion in forestalling entry.[30]

A history of such actions sends a strong signal to potential rivals that market entry will not be easy and that the incumbents will respond vigorously to any encroachment on their turf. When established companies succeed in signaling this position to potential rivals through past actions, they have established a *credible commitment* to respond to new entry.

Note that, when making strategic commitments, a company must be careful not to fall afoul of antitrust law. For example, it is illegal to engage in predatory pricing, or pricing a good or service below the cost of production with the express intent of driving a rival out of business and monopolizing a market. In the late 1990s, Microsoft violated antitrust laws when it informed PC manufacturers that they had to display Internet Explorer on the PC desktop if they wanted to license the company's Windows operating system. Because Windows was the only viable operating system for PCs at the time, this was basically viewed as strong-arming PC makers. The intent was to give Internet Explorer an edge over rival browsers, particularly one produced by Netscape. The U.S. Justice Department ruled that Microsoft's actions were predatory, and it was forced to pay fines and change its practices.

6-5a Strategies to Manage Rivalry

Beyond seeking to deter entry, companies may wish to develop strategies to manage their competitive interdependence and decrease price rivalry. Unrestricted competition over prices reduces both company and industry profitability. Companies use several strategies to manage industry rivalry. The most important are price signaling, price leadership, non-price competition, and capacity control.

Price Signaling   A company's ability to choose the price option that leads to superior performance is a function of several factors, including the strength of demand for a product and the intensity of competition between rivals. **Price signaling** is a method whereby companies attempt to control rivalry among competitors to allow the *industry* to choose the most favorable pricing option. In this process, companies increase or decrease product prices to convey their intentions to other companies and influence the way other companies price their products. Companies use price signaling to improve industry profitability.

price signaling

The process whereby companies increase or decrease product prices to convey their intentions to other companies and influence the price of an industry's products.

Companies may use price signaling to communicate that they will vigorously respond to hostile, competitive moves that threaten them. For example, they may signal that if one company starts to aggressively cut prices, they will respond in kind. A *tit-for-tat strategy* is a well-known price signaling maneuver in which a company exactly mimics its rivals: If its rivals cut prices, the company follows; if they raise prices, the company follows. By consistently pursuing this strategy over time, a company sends a clear signal to its rivals that it will mirror any pricing moves they make; sooner or later, rivals learn that the company will always pursue a tit-for-tat strategy. Because rivals know that it will match any price reductions and thus reduce profits, price cutting becomes less common in the industry. Moreover, a tit-for-tat strategy also signals to rivals that price increases will be imitated, growing the probability that rivals will initiate price increases to raise profits. Thus, a tit-for-tat strategy can be a useful way of shaping pricing behavior in an industry.[31]

The airline industry is a good example of the power of price signaling when prices typically rise and fall depending upon the current state of customer demand. If one carrier signals the intention to lower prices, a price war frequently ensues as carriers copy one another's signals. If one carrier feels demand is strong, it tests the waters by signaling an intention to increase prices, and price signaling becomes a strategy to obtain uniform price increases. Nonrefundable tickets or charges for a second bag—a strategy adopted to allow airlines to charge higher prices—originated as a market signal by one company that was quickly copied by all other companies in the industry (it is estimated that extra bag charges have so far allowed U.S. airlines to make over $5 billion annually)[32]. Carriers have recognized that they can stabilize their revenues and earn interest on customers' money if they collectively act to force customers to assume the risk of buying airline tickets in advance.

In essence, price signaling allows companies to exchange information that enables them to understand each other's competitive product or market strategy and make coordinated, price-competitive moves.

Price Leadership   When one company assumes the responsibility for setting the pricing option that maximizes industry profitability, that company assumes the position of price leader—a second tactic used to reduce price rivalry between companies in a mature industry. Explicit price leadership, when companies jointly set prices, is illegal under antitrust laws. Therefore, the process of **price leadership** is often very subtle. In the car industry, for example, prices are set by imitation. The price set by the weakest company—that is, the company with the highest cost structure—is often used as the basis for competitors' pricing. Thus, in the past, U.S. carmakers set their prices and Japanese carmakers then set their prices in response. The Japanese were happy to do this because they had lower costs than U.S. carmakers and still made higher profits without having to compete on price. Pricing is determined by market segment. The prices of different auto models in a particular range indicate the customer segments that the companies are targeting, and the price range the companies believe each segment can tolerate. Each manufacturer prices a model in the segment with reference to the prices charged by its competitors, not with reference to competitors' costs. Price leadership also allows differentiators to charge a premium price.

Although price leadership can stabilize industry relationships by preventing head-to-head competition and raising the level of profitability within an industry, it has its dangers. It allows companies with high cost structures to survive without needing to implement strategies to become more efficient, although in the long term such behavior makes them vulnerable to new entrants that have lower costs because they have developed low-cost production techniques. This happened in the U.S. car industry. After decades of tacit price fixing, and GM as the price leader, U.S. carmakers were threatened by growing, low-cost, overseas competition. In 2009, the U.S. government bailed out Chrysler and GM, loaning them billions of dollars while forcing them to

price leadership

When one company assumes responsibility for determining the pricing strategy that maximizes industry profitability.

enter, and then emerge from, bankruptcy. This dramatically lowered the cost structures of these companies and has made them more competitive today. (This also applies to Ford, which obtained similar benefits while managing to avoid bankruptcy.)

Non-Price Competition   A third very important aspect of product and market strategy in mature industries is the use of **non-price competition** to manage rivalry within an industry. The use of strategies to try to prevent costly price cutting and price wars does not preclude competition by product differentiation. In many industries, product differentiation strategies are the principal tools companies use to deter potential entrants and manage rivalry.

Product differentiation allows industry rivals to compete for market share by offering products with different or superior features, such as smaller, more powerful, or more sophisticated computer chips, as AMD, Intel, and NVIDIA compete to offer, or by applying different marketing techniques, as Procter & Gamble, Colgate, and Unilever do. In Figure 6.6, product and market segment dimensions are used to identify four non-price competitive strategies based on product differentiation: market penetration, product development, market development, and product proliferation. (Note that this model applies to new market *segments*, *not* new markets.)

Market Penetration   When a company concentrates on expanding market share in its existing product markets, it is engaging in a *market penetration* strategy. Market penetration involves heavy advertising to promote and build product differentiation. For example, Intel has actively pursued penetration with its aggressive marketing campaign of "Intel Inside." In a mature industry, advertising aims to influence customers' brand choice and create a brand-name reputation for the company and its products. In this way, a company can increase its market share by attracting its rival's customers. Because brand-name products often command premium prices, building market share in this situation can be very profitable.

In some mature industries—for example, soap and detergent, disposable diapers, and beer brewing—a market-penetration strategy becomes a long-term strategy. In these industries, all companies engage in intensive advertising as they battle for market share. Each company fears that if it does not advertise it will lose market share to rivals who do. Consequently, the consumer products giant Procter & Gamble (P&G) spends roughly 11% of sales revenues on advertising,[33] with the aim of maintaining, and perhaps building, market share. These huge advertising outlays constitute a barrier to entry for prospective competitors.

Product Development   **Product development** is the creation of new or improved products to replace existing ones. The wet-shaving industry depends on product

Figure 6.6 Four Non-Price Competitive Strategies

		Products	
		Existing	New
Marketing Segments	Existing	Market penetration	Product development
	New	Market development	Product proliferation

non-price competition

The use of product differentiation strategies to deter potential entrants and manage rivalry within an industry.

product development

The creation of new or improved products to replace existing products.

replacement to create successive waves of customer demand, which then create new sources of revenue for companies in the industry. Gillette, for example, periodically unveils a new, improved razor such as those that incorporate lubricating shave gel or trimmers to reach hard-to-reach places, to try to boost its market share. Similarly, in the car industry, each major car company replaces its models every 3 to 5 years to encourage customers to trade in old models and purchase new ones.

Product development is crucial for maintaining product differentiation and building market share. For instance, the laundry detergent Tide has gone through more than 50 changes in formulation during the past 40 years to improve its performance. The product is always advertised as Tide, but it is a different product each year. Refining and improving products is a crucial strategy companies use to fine-tune and improve their business models in a mature industry, but this kind of competition can be as vicious as a price war because it is very expensive and can dramatically increase a company's cost structure. This occurred in the videogame console industry, where intense competition to make the fastest or most powerful console and become the market leader has dramatically increased the cost structure of Sony, Microsoft, and Nintendo, constraining their profitability.

Market Development   Market development seeks new market segments for a company's products. A company pursuing this strategy seeks to capitalize on the brand name it has developed in one market segment by locating new market segments in which to compete—as Mattel and Nike do by entering many different segments of the toy and shoe markets, respectively. In this way, a company can leverage the product differentiation advantages of its brand name. Japanese auto manufacturers provide an interesting example of the use of market development. When each manufacturer entered the market, it offered a car model aimed at the economy segment of the auto market, such as the Toyota Corolla and the Honda Accord. These companies upgraded each model over time to target a more expensive market segment. The Honda Accord is a leading contender in the mid-sized car segment, and the Toyota Corolla fills the small-car segment. By redefining their product offerings, Japanese manufacturers have profitably developed their market segments and successfully attacked their U.S. rivals, wresting market share from them. Although the Japanese once competed primarily as cost leaders, market development has allowed them to become differentiators as well. In fact, as we noted in the previous chapter, Toyota has used market development to become a broad differentiator. Over time, it has used market development to create a vehicle for almost every segment of the car market, a tactic discussed in Strategy in Action 6.2.

Product Proliferation   We have already seen how product proliferation can deter entry into an industry. The same strategy can be used to manage rivalry within an industry. As noted earlier, product proliferation generally means that large companies in an industry have a product in each market segment (or niche). If a new niche develops, such as SUVs, designer sunglasses, or online shoe stores, the leader gets a first-mover advantage—but soon thereafter, all the other companies catch up. Once again, competition is stabilized, and rivalry within the industry is reduced. Product proliferation thus allows the development of stable industry competition based on product differentiation, not price—that is, non-price competition based on the development of new products. The competitive battle is over a product's perceived uniqueness, quality, features, and performance, not its price. Nike, for example, was founded as a running shoe company, and early in its history it shunned markets for gear for sports such as golf, soccer, basketball, tennis, and skateboarding. However, when its sales declined, Nike realized that using marketing to increase sales in a particular market segment (market penetration) could only grow sales and profits so much. The company thus directed its existing design and marketing competencies to the crafting of new lines of shoes for those market segments and others.

market development
When a company searches for new market segments for its existing products in order to increase sales.

Toyota Uses Market Development to Become the Global Leader

The car industry has always been one of the most competitive in the world because of the huge revenues and profits at stake. Given difficult economic conditions in the late-2000s, it is hardly surprising that rivalry has increased as global carmakers struggle to develop new models that better satisfy the needs of particular groups of buyers. Toyota is at the competitive forefront.

Toyota produced its first car 40 years ago—an ugly, boxy vehicle that was, however, cheap. As the quality of its products became apparent, sales increased. Toyota, which was then a focused cost leader, reinvested its profits into improving the styling of its vehicles, and into efforts to continually reduce production costs. Over time, Toyota has taken advantage of its low-cost structure to make an ever-increasing range of reasonably priced vehicles tailored to different segments of the car market. The company's ability to begin with the initial design stage and move to the production stage in 2 to 3 years allowed it to make new models available more rapidly than its competitors, and to capitalize on the development of new market segments.

Toyota has been a leader in positioning its entire range of vehicles to take advantage of new, emerging market segments. In the SUV segment, for example, its first offering was the expensive Toyota Land Cruiser, priced at over $35,000. Realizing the need for SUVs in lower price ranges, it next introduced the 4Runner, priced at $20,000 and designed for the average SUV customer; the RAV4, a small SUV in the low $20,000 range, followed; then came the Sequoia, a bigger, more powerful version of the 4Runner in the upper $20,000 range. Finally, drawing on technology from its Lexus division, it introduced the luxury Highlander SUV in the $30,000 range. Today, it sells six SUV models, each offering a particular combination of price, size, performance, styling, and luxury to appeal to a particular customer group within the SUV segment of the car market. In a similar way, Toyota positions its sedans to appeal to the needs of different sets of customers. For example, the Camry is targeted at the middle of the market to customers who can afford to pay between $26,000–32,000 and want a balance of luxury, performance, safety, and reliability.

Toyota's broad-differentiation business model is geared toward making a range of vehicles that optimizes the amount of value it can create for different groups of customers. At the same time, the number of models it makes is constrained by the need to keep costs under strict control so that its pricing options that will generate maximum revenues and profits. Competition in every car market segment is now intense, so all carmakers must balance the advantages of showcasing more cars to attract customers against the increasing costs that result when their line of models expands to suit different customers' needs.

Capacity Control   Although non-price competition helps mature industries avoid the cutthroat price cutting that reduces company and industry levels of profitability, price competition does periodically occur when excess capacity exists in an industry. Excess capacity arises when companies collectively produce too much output; to dispose of it, they cut prices. When one company cuts prices, others quickly do the same because they fear that the price cutter will be able to sell its entire inventory and leave them with unwanted goods. The result is a developing price war.

Excess capacity may be caused by a shortfall in demand, as when a recession lowers the demand for cars and causes automakers to offer customers price incentives to purchase new cars. In this situation, companies can do nothing but wait for better times. By and large, however, excess capacity results from companies within an industry simultaneously responding to favorable conditions; they all invest in new plants to take advantage of the predicted upsurge in demand. Paradoxically, each individual company's effort to outperform the others means that, collectively, they create industry overcapacity—which hurts them all. Although demand is rising, the consequence of each company's decision to increase capacity is a surge in industry capacity, which drives down prices. To prevent the accumulation of costly excess capacity, companies must devise strategies that enable them to control—or at least benefit from—capacity-expansion programs. Before we examine these strategies, however, we need to consider in greater detail the factors that cause excess capacity.[34]

Factors Causing Excess Capacity   Excess capacity often derives from technological developments. New, low-cost technology sometimes can create an issue because all companies invest in it simultaneously to prevent being left behind. Excess capacity occurs as the new technology produces more efficiently than the old. In addition, new technology is often introduced in large increments, which generates overcapacity. For instance, an airline that needs more seats on a route must add another plane, thereby adding hundreds of seats even if only 50 are needed. To take another example, a new chemical process may efficiently operate at the rate of only 1,000 gallons per day, whereas the previous process was efficient at 500 gallons per day. If all companies within an industry change technologies, industry capacity may double, and enormous problems can ensue.

Competitive factors within an industry can cause overcapacity. Entry into an industry is one such factor. The economic recession of 2008–2009 caused global overcapacity, and the price of steel plunged; with global recovery, the price has increased. Sometimes the age of a company's physical assets is the source of the problem. For example, in the hotel industry, given the rapidity with which the quality of hotel room furnishings decline, customers are always attracted to new hotels. When new hotel chains are built alongside the old chains, excess capacity can result. Often, companies are simply making simultaneous competitive moves based on industry trends—but these moves lead to head-to-head competition. Most fast-food chains, for instance, establish new outlets whenever demographic data show population increases. However, companies seem to forget that all other chains use the same data—they do not anticipate their rivals' actions. Thus, a certain locality that has few fast-food outlets may suddenly have several new outlets being built at the same time. Whether all the outlets survive depends upon the growth rate of customer demand, but often the least popular outlets close.

Choosing a Capacity-Control Strategy   Given the various ways in which capacity can expand, companies clearly need to find means of controlling it. Companies that are always plagued by price cutting and price wars will be unable to recoup their investments in generic strategies. Low profitability caused by overcapacity forces not only the weakest companies but also sometimes major players to exit the industry. In general, companies have two strategic choices: (1) each company must try to preempt its rivals and seize the initiative, or (2) the companies must collectively find indirect means of coordinating with each other so that they are all aware of the mutual effects of their actions.

To *preempt* rivals, a company must forecast a large increase in demand in the product market and then move rapidly to establish large-scale operations that will be able to satisfy the predicted demand. By achieving a first-mover advantage, the company may deter other firms from entering the market because the preemptor will usually be able to move down the experience curve, reduce its costs, and therefore reduce its prices as well—and threaten a price war if necessary.

This strategy is extremely risky, for it involves investing resources before the extent and profitability of the future market are clear. A preemptive strategy is also risky if it does not deter competitors that decide to enter the market. If competitors can develop a stronger generic strategy or have more resources (as do Google and Microsoft), they can make the preemptor suffer. Thus, for the strategy to succeed, the preemptor must generally be a credible company with enough resources to withstand a possible advertising/price war.

To *coordinate* with rivals as a capacity-control strategy, caution must be exercised because collusion on the timing of new production capacity investments is illegal under antitrust law. However, tacit coordination is practiced in many industries as companies attempt to understand and forecast one another's competitive moves. Generally, companies use market signaling to secure coordination. They make announcements about their future investment decisions in trade journals and newspapers. In addition, they share information about their production levels and their forecasts of demand within an industry to bring supply and demand into equilibrium. Thus, a coordination strategy reduces the risks associated with investment in the industry. This is common in the chemical refining and oil businesses, where new capacity investments frequently cost hundreds of millions of dollars.

6.6 Outline the different strategies that companies in declining industries can use to support their business models and profitability.

6-6 Strategies in Declining Industries

Sooner or later, many industries enter into a decline stage in which the size of the total market begins to shrink. Examples are the railroad industry, the tobacco industry, the steel industry, and the newspaper business. Industries decline for many reasons, including technological change, social trends, and demographic shifts. The railroad and steel industries began to decline when technological changes brought viable substitutes for their products. The advent of the internal combustion engine drove the railroad industry into decline, the steel industry fell into decline with the rise of plastics and composite materials, and the newspaper industry is in decline because of the rise of news sites online. As for the tobacco industry, changing social attitudes and warnings about the health effects of smoking have caused the decline.

6-6a The Severity of Decline

Competition tends to intensify in a declining industry, and profit rates tend to fall. The intensity of competition in a declining industry depends on the four critical factors depicted in Figure 6.7. First, the intensity of competition is greater in industries in which decline is rapid, as opposed to industries such as tobacco in which decline is slow and gradual.

Second, the intensity of competition is greater in declining industries in which exit barriers are high. Recall from Chapter 2 that high exit barriers keep companies locked into an industry, even when demand is falling. The result is excess productive capacity and hence an increased probability of fierce price competition.

Third, and related to the previous point, the intensity of competition is greater in declining industries in which fixed costs are high (as in the steel industry). The reason is that the need to cover such fixed costs as the costs of maintaining productive capacity can drive companies to try to use excess capacity by slashing prices, which can trigger a price war.

Finally, the intensity of competition is greater in declining industries in which the product is perceived as a commodity (as it is in the steel industry) in contrast to

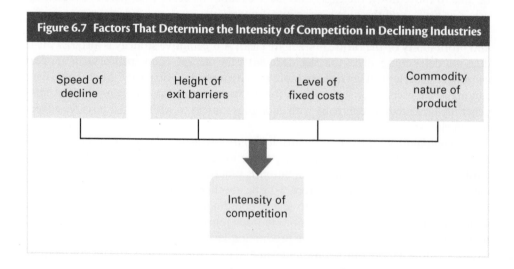

Figure 6.7 Factors That Determine the Intensity of Competition in Declining Industries

industries in which differentiation gives rise to significant brand loyalty, as was true (until very recently) of the declining tobacco industry.

Not all segments of an industry typically decline at the same rate. In some segments, demand may remain reasonably strong despite decline elsewhere. The steel industry illustrates this situation. Although bulk steel products such as sheet steel have suffered a general decline, demand has actually risen for specialty steels such as those used in high-speed machine tools. Vacuum tubes provide another example. Although demand for the tubes collapsed when transistors replaced them as a key component in many electronics products, vacuum tubes still had limited applications in radar equipment for years afterward. Consequently, demand in this one segment remained strong despite the general decline in demand for vacuum tubes. The point is that there may be pockets of demand in an industry in which demand is declining more slowly than in the industry as a whole—or where demand is not declining at all. Price competition may be far less intense among companies serving pockets of demand than within the industry as a whole.

6-6b Choosing a Strategy

Companies can adopt four main strategies to deal with decline: (1) a **leadership strategy**, by which a company seeks to become the dominant player in a declining industry; (2) a **niche strategy**, which focuses on pockets of demand that are declining more slowly than the industry as a whole; (3) a **harvest strategy**, which optimizes cash flow; and (4) a **divestment strategy**, by which a company sells the business to others.[35] Figure 6.8 provides a simple framework for guiding strategic choice. Note that the intensity of competition in the declining industry is measured on the vertical axis, and a company's strengths relative to remaining pockets of demand are measured on the horizontal axis.

Leadership Strategy A leadership strategy aims at growing in a declining industry by picking up the market share of companies that are leaving it. This strategy makes most sense when (1) the company has distinctive strengths that allow it to capture market share

leadership strategy
When a company develops strategies to become the dominant player in a declining industry.

niche strategy
When a company focuses on pockets of demand that are declining more slowly than the industry as a whole in order to maintain profitability.

harvest strategy
When a company reduces to a minimum the assets it employs in a business to reduce its cost structure and extract ("milk") maximum profits from its investment.

divestment strategy
When a company exits an industry by selling its business assets to another company.

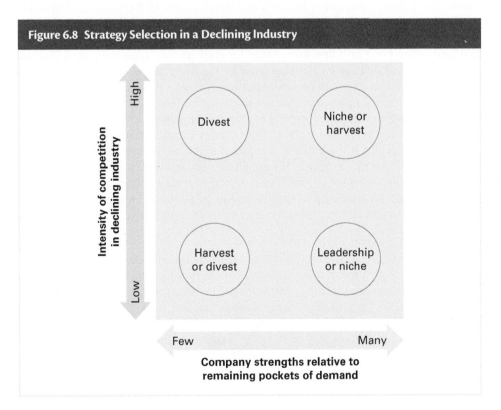

Figure 6.8 Strategy Selection in a Declining Industry

in a declining industry, and (2) the speed of decline and the intensity of competition in the declining industry are moderate. Philip Morris used this strategy in the tobacco industry. While other cigarette companies were responding to slumping demand by cutting costs or exiting the market, Philip Morris increased its advertising, and subsequently its market share, in the declining industry. It earned enormous profits in the process.

The tactical steps companies might use to achieve a leadership position include using aggressive pricing and marketing to build market share; acquiring established competitors to consolidate the industry; and raising the stakes for other competitors, for example by making new investments in productive capacity. Such competitive tactics signal to rivals that the company is willing and able to stay and compete in the declining industry. These signals may persuade other companies to exit the industry, which would further enhance the competitive position of the industry leader.

Niche Strategy A niche strategy focuses on pockets of demand in the industry in which demand is stable or declining less rapidly than the industry as a whole. This strategy makes sense when the company has unique strengths relative to those niches in which demand remains relatively strong. For example, in response to the introduction of digital cameras, sales of traditional film cameras and film spiraled toward zero. A number of competitors declared bankruptcy (e.g., Ilford, Agfaphoto, Polaroid, Ferrania, Eastman Kodak), while others diversified out of the industry (e.g., Fujifilm), or exited by other means (e.g., Konica-Minolta). However, Ilford and Eastman Kodak ultimately survived by targeting the much narrower markets of specialty film photography, which continues to be used by photography enthusiasts.[36]

Harvest Strategy As noted earlier, a harvest strategy is the best choice when a company wishes to exit a declining industry and optimize cash flow in the process. This strategy makes the most sense when the company foresees a steep decline and intense future competition, or when it lacks strengths relative to remaining pockets of demand in the industry. A harvest strategy requires the company to halt all new investments in capital equipment, advertising, research and development (R&D), and so forth. The inevitable result is that the company will lose market share, but because it is no longer investing in the business, initially its positive cash flow will increase. Essentially, the company is accepting cash flow in exchange for market share. Ultimately, cash flow will decline, and when that occurs, it makes sense for the company to liquidate the business.

Although this strategy can be very appealing in theory, it can be somewhat difficult to put into practice. Employee morale in a declining business may suffer. Furthermore, if customers realize what the company is doing, they may rapidly defect, and market share may decline much faster than the company expects. Research by Professors Daniel Elfenbein and Anne Marie Knott found that U.S. banks often delayed exiting the market well past the time when it would have been rational to do so based on their profits. Elfenbein and Knott argue that banks appear to exit late in part because of rational demand uncertainty, and in part because of irrational optimism or escalating commitment that results in management overweighting positive signals that profits might rebound.[37]

Divestment Strategy A divestment strategy rests on the idea that a company can recover most of its investment in an underperforming business by selling it early, before the industry has entered into a steep decline. This strategy is appropriate when the company has few strengths relative to whatever pockets of demand are likely to remain in the industry, and when the competition in the declining industry is likely to be intense. The best option may be to sell to a company that is pursuing a leadership strategy in the industry. The drawback of the divestment strategy is that its success depends upon the ability of the company to spot industry decline before it becomes detrimental, and to sell while the company's assets are still valued by others.

Key Terms

fragmented industry   158
chaining   160
franchising   161
mass market   163
product proliferation
    strategy   170

limit price strategy   170
technology
    upgrading   171
strategic
    commitments   171
price signaling   172

price leadership   173
non-price
    competition   174
product development   174
market development   175
leadership strategy   179

niche strategy   179
harvest strategy   179
divestment strategy   179

Takeaways for Strategic Managers

1. In fragmented industries composed of many small- and medium-sized companies, the principal forms of competitive strategy are chaining, franchising, and horizontal merger.

2. In embryonic and growth industries, strategy is partly determined by market demand. Innovators and early adopters have different needs than the early and the late majority, and a company must have the right strategies in place to cross the chasm and survive. Similarly, managers must understand the factors that affect a market's growth rate so that they can tailor their business model to a changing industry environment.

3. Mature industries are composed of a few large companies whose actions are so highly interdependent that the success of one company's strategy depends upon the responses of its rivals.

4. The principal strategies used by companies in mature industries to deter entry are product proliferation, price cutting, and maintaining excess capacity.

5. The principal strategies used by companies in mature industries to manage rivalry are price signaling, price leadership, non-price competition, and capacity control.

6. In declining industries, in which market demand has leveled off or is decreasing, companies must tailor their price and non-price strategies to the new competitive environment. Companies also need to manage industry capacity to prevent the emergence of capacity-expansion problems.

7. The four main strategies a company can pursue when demand is falling are leadership, niche, harvest, and divestment. The strategic choice is determined by the severity of industry decline and the company's strengths relative to the remaining pockets of demand.

Discussion Questions

1. Why are industries fragmented? What are the primary ways in which companies can turn a fragmented industry into a consolidated industry?

2. What are the key problems in maintaining a competitive advantage in embryonic and growth industry environments? What are the dangers associated with being the leader in an industry?

3. What investment strategies should be made by: (a) differentiators in a strong competitive position, and (b) differentiators in a weak competitive position, while managing a company's growth through the life cycle?

4. Discuss how companies can use: (a) product differentiation and (b) capacity control to manage rivalry and increase an industry's profitability.

5. What strategies might these enterprises use to strengthen their business models: (a) a small pizzeria operating in a crowded college market and (b) a detergent manufacturer seeking to unveil new products in an established market?

Closing Case

For more than three decades, customers in most television markets had become increasingly reliant upon cable television operators to access television content, movies, internet service, and more. Many television markets were controlled by only one or a few cable operators, giving the companies near monopoly power. Furthermore, for much of that period, cable TV was the consumer's primary source for news, network programming, specialized programming such as sports channels and foreign language programming, and movie services such as HBO and Showtime.

However, the emergence of internet streaming alternatives such as Netflix, Roku, Hulu, YouTube, Amazon Prime Video, and other online services had led many customers to begin "cutting the cord" with their cable companies. Cable operators required customers to commit to expensive, lengthy contracts. To make matters worse, they had historically provided very poor customer satisfaction. Customers complained of long wait times for customer service, hidden fees, and difficulty in changing or cancelling service. Internet-based streaming services are usually much cheaper (sometimes free), and allow more flexible terms like month-to-month contracts or payment for individual shows. Many have also proven they can develop successful original content that attracts subscribers to their service. As Laura Martin, media analyst with Needham & Co., notes: "There's never been more types of premium video content. And the consumer has never had more screens to watch all that content."[38]

Though globally the number of people paying for television content was still increasing and was expected to continue to increase until at least 2023, in markets where pay TV was more mature subscriber numbers were declining. Between 2016 and 2021, cable lost more than 25% of all U.S. households and overall cable TV subscriptions had dropped below 50% of U.S. households.[39] Furthermore, revenues for companies providing television content were decreasing even faster because of the pricing pressure created by the streaming alternatives. Many customers now paid only for less expensive, internet-only services rather than expensive TV channel bundles.

According to a study by Digital TV Research, global revenues for pay TV peaked in 2016 at $205 billion but then began to drop yearly, falling to $161 billion in 2021. The geographic differences in revenue and subscriber patterns are stark; between 2017 and 2023, China is expected to gain nearly $1 billion in pay TV revenues, and India is expected to gain $1.6 billion. North American pay TV revenues, on the other hand, are expected to fall by $22 billion over the same time frame.[40]

Cable companies attempted to staunch their losses by consolidating through acquisitions, negotiating exclusive contracts with content providers, offering their own online video-on-demand services, and incorporating services like Netflix and Hulu into their offerings in a gamble that customers would value being able to access all of the services without the awkwardness of changing applications and remotes. In the short run, cable companies still have the upper hand because they provide the internet service that consumers were using to stream video, making it difficult to truly "cut the cord." A 2018 survey by Deloitte, for example, found that 56% of pay TV subscribers say they had kept their service because it was bundled with their internet access.[41] In the long run, however, most analysts agreed that much of the power that cable companies had wielded in the past would inevitably shift to consumers and producers of highly differentiated and valued content.

Case Discussion Questions

1. How does the ability to stream content change consumers' behaviors?
2. Most consumers had a single cable subscription, but many now have multiple streaming subscriptions. Do you think this is the new normal (i.e., will consumers continue to subscribe to multiple streaming services), or will there be pressure to consolidate content so that consumers will not have to have multiple subscriptions?
3. Will traditional cable service providers survive? If so, how?
4. What would you recommend cable service providers do?

Notes

[1] J. Guszkowski, "Delivery Consolidation Puts Restaurants in a Tight Spot," Restaurantbusiness online.com, December 7, 2020.

[2] R. Padhi, "Food Delivery: The Consolidation Saga Continues," *Mergersight*, July 26, 2020.

[3] J. Perri, "Which Company Is Winning the Restaurant Food Delivery War?" *Bloomberg*, June 15, 2022.

[4] J. Guszkowski, "Delivery Consolidation Puts Restaurants in a Tight Spot," Restaurantbusinessonline.com, December 7, 2020.

[5] R. Padhi, "Food Delivery: The Consolidation Saga Continues," *Mergersight*, July 26, 2020.

[6] T. Sterling, "Analysis – Eat or Be Eaten? Food Delivery Apps Have Knives out as Pandemic Boom Fades," *Reuters*, March 31, 2021.

[7] M. Cheng, "Consolidation Is Coming for US Food Delivery Unless the Government Stops It First," *Quartz*, August 12, 2021.

[8] J. Perri, "Which Company Is Winning the Restaurant Food Delivery War?" *Bloomberg*, June 15, 2022.

[9] M. E. Porter, *Competitive Strategy: Techniques for Analyzing Industries and Competitors* (New York: Free Press, 1980), pp. 191–200.

[10] W. C. Kim and R. Mauborgne, "Value Innovation: The Strategic Logic of High Growth," *Harvard Business Review* (January–February 1997): pp. 103–112.

[11] S. A. Shane, "Hybrid Organizational Arrangements and Their Implications for Firm Growth and Survival: A Study of New Franchisors," *Academy of Management Journal* 1 (1996): 216–234.

[12] Microsoft is often accused of not being an innovator, but the fact is that Bill Gates and Paul Allen wrote the first commercial software program for the first commercially available personal computer. Microsoft was the first mover in its industry. See P. Freiberger and M. Swaine, *Fire in the Valley* (New York: McGraw-Hill, 2000).

[13] J. M. Utterback, *Mastering the Dynamics of Innovation* (Boston: Harvard Business School Press, 1994).

[14] E. M. Rogers, *Diffusion of Innovations,* 5th ed. (Free Press, 2003).

[15] Ibid.

[16] R. Brown "Managing the 'S' Curves of Innovation, *"Journal of Consumer Marketing* 9 (1992): 61–72; P. A. Geroski. "Models of Technology Diffusion," *Research Policy* 29 (2000): 603–25.

[17] Freiberger and Swaine, *Fire in the Valley*.

[18] Utterback, *Mastering the Dynamics of Innovation*.

[19] G. A. Moore, *Crossing the Chasm* (New York: HarperCollins, 1991).

[20] Utterback, *Mastering the Dynamics of Innovation*.

[21] E. Rogers, *Diffusion of Innovations* (New York: Free Press, 1995).

[22] R. J. Gilbert, "Mobility Barriers and the Value of Incumbency," in R. Schmalensee and R. D. Willig (eds.), *Handbook of Industrial Organization* (Elsevier Science Publishers, 1989).

[23]R. Seamans, "Threat of Entry, Asymmetric Information, and Pricing," *Strategic Management Journal* 34 (2013): 426–44.

[24]R. Seamans. "Fighting City Hall: Entry Deterrence and Technology Upgrades in Cable TV Markets," *Management Science* 58 (2012): 461–75.

[25]P. Ghemawat, *Commitment: The Dynamic of Strategy* (Harvard Business School Press, 1991).

[26]M. B. Lieberman, "Excess Capacity as a Barrier to Entry: An Empirical Appraisal," *Journal of Industrial Economics* 35 (1987): 607–27.

[27]R. Lukach, P. M. Kort, and J. Plasmans, "Optimal R&D Investment Strategies Under the Threat of New Technology Entry," *International Journal of Industrial Organization* 25 (February 2007): 103–19.

[28]W. B. Arthur, "Increasing Returns and the New World of Business," *Harvard Business Review* (July 1996): 100–109.

[29]R. Axelrod, *The Evolution of Cooperation* (New York: Basic Books, 1984).

[30]The next section draws heavily on Marvin B. Lieberman, "Strategies for Capacity Expansion," *Sloan Management Review* 8 (1987): 19–27; Porter, *Competitive Strategy*, 324–38.

[31]K. R. Harrigan, "Strategy Formulation in Declining Industries," *Academy of Management Review* 5 (1980): 599–604.

[32]https://upgradedpoints.com/travel/airlines/us-airlines-highest-baggage-fees/

[33]https://www.global cosmeticsnews.com/procter-gamble-ups-ad-spend-to-us8-2-billi-on/#:~:text=Procter%20%26%20Gamble%20increased%20its%20spend,report%20published%20by%20PR%20Week.

[34]D. W. Elfenbein and A. W. Knott. "Time to Exit: Rational, Behavioral, and Organizational Delays," *Strategic Management Journal* (June 2014): 957–75.

[35]E. M. Rogers, *Diffusion of Innovations*, 5th ed. (New York: Simon & Schuster, 2003).

[36]F. Schlagwein, "Analog Photography Makes a Comeback," DW, February 10, 2021; A. Gold, "Going Back to Film? Here's What's Changed," PopPhoto, March 19, 2022; "*Why Kodak Died and Fujifilm Thrived: A Tale of Two Film Companies*," *PetaPixel*. 19 October 2018.

[37]*Overcoming the Barriers to Electric Vehicle Deployment.* (National Academies Press).

[38]R. Crum, "Why Streaming TV Choices Are Cutting Away Cable Subscriber Levels," *Mercury News*, October 31, 2017.

[39]Hoffman, C. Hoffman, "Cable TV Subscriptions Set to Drop Below 50% of All US House-holds," Martech, March 17, 2022.

[40]Briel, R, "Global Pay-TV Revenues to Fall by 11%," Broadband TV News, April 16, 2018.

[41]Ramachandran, 2018.

Opening Case

An Arms Race in Cryptocurrency

As of June 2022, there were more than 19,000 cryptocurrencies[1] that were collectively worth just over $1.1 trillion. Cryptocurrencies are not issued, regulated, or backed by a central authority like a bank or government, and they do not exist in a physical form like paper or coins.[2] Instead, they are entirely virtual, and exist (and are used in transactions) on a distributed ledger (blockchain) that is replicated on thousands of independent computers around the world.

In 2009, Satoshi Nakamoto (believed to be a pseudonym) invented Bitcoin, a digital currency that is independent of any government or central bank, and the blockchain ledger on which Bitcoin exists. Before Bitcoin was invented, the only way to use money was to exchange physical money directly in a transaction, or to exchange digital money through an intermediary like a bank or PayPal. The money used in those transactions was controlled by governments, and thus considered a centrally controlled currency or "fiat currency," i.e., its value was determined by fiat of the government. Bitcoin, by contrast, is a digital currency that individuals can trade directly (without an intermediary), and that is not controlled by a government. Each transaction is validated through a peer-to-peer network of thousands of independent computers, making the system nearly impossible to shut down, manipulate, or control.

The system that performs this validation and confirmation is the decentralized ledger system known as *blockchain*. Instead of individual banks keeping their own spreadsheets of transactions, there is just one global spreadsheet of every transaction made using a given cryptocurrency—a "ledger." But this ledger is also decentralized in that though everything is on the same ledger, there are many copies of that ledger being maintained and updated. This is why blockchain is considered decentralized finance, or "defi." Cryptocurrency mining, or "Bitcoin mining," is when an individual sets up a computer to crunch through transactions on their copy of this ledger, earning some Bitcoin (or other cryptocurrency) as compensation for their work. There are over a million Bitcoin miners around the world, and all these decentralized miners are verifying all the transactions on the network in real time. This makes it very difficult to change the entries inappropriately—a discrepancy would be instantly visible to thousands of miners.

The idea of blockchain was to create a world with open, traceable transactions without centralized intermediaries like banks and governments. Each transaction is associated with a public key, so while there are no names visible to others, the transaction is a public record. Money transfers that used to take days or even weeks can be completed almost instantly with blockchain. International payments can be made in minutes, with no exchange rates and much lower transaction fees than those charged by traditional intermediaries.

Bitcoin enabled blockchain, but blockchain can be used for more than just transactions using Bitcoin. By 2011, new competitors were adopting the blockchain to launch their own cryptocurrencies, launching a race to see which currency could attain the most value, legitimacy, and widespread adoption. Thousands of different cryptocurrencies emerged over the next decade, each with slightly different features, and many of them taking advantage of more complex functionality enabled by blockchain than had been utilized by Bitcoin. In 2022, Bitcoin was still by far the biggest cryptocurrency, but its biggest challenger was Ether, a currency based on the Ethereum blockchain platform (see Table 7.1 below). Ethereum was first proposed in 2013 by Vitalik Buterin, co-founder of *Bitcoin Magazine*. Ethereum enables more complex transactions than those done with Bitcoin. It executes and verifies application code called smart contracts. Using Ethereum's Solidity scripting language and Ethereum Virtual machine, developers can create a wide range of applications on the platform—similar to how the Android and iOS operating systems enable developers to create apps for phones. These applications could enable decentralization of many types of transactions that are currently controlled by centralized organizations, like voting, real estate transfers, providing insurance, lending, and more.

Like many new technologies, cryptocurrencies came with some problems to work out. One of the chief problems was the volatility in its value. As thousands of individuals and companies began producing cryptocurrencies and millions of investors rushed into the market, the value of cryptocurrencies became very volatile. From early November 2021 to mid-June 2022, for example, Bitcoin's value dropped more than 70%—from over $67,000 to around $20,000. Over the same time frame, Ethereum fell from over $4,800 to about $1,000, an almost 80% drop, and the overall market capitalization of the crypto market dropped by about 66%, from a peak of $3 trillion to less than $1 trillion in mid-June. Needless to say, this drop shook many crypto investors. Critics have also been quick to point out that all of that processing required by thousands of computers to verify cryptocurrency transactions uses a lot of electricity. By one estimate, the processing of Bitcoin alone consumes 127 terawatt-hours of energy a year—more than the annual electricity consumption of Norway.[3]

The potential for decentralized finance (and other transactions) holds tremendous promise, particularly in regions or contexts in which centralized control is prone to corruption or is expensive. It is thus probably fair to conclude that some version of the blockchain is here to stay. However, which cryptocurrency or platform will have staying power, or become dominant in the long run, is still anyone's guess. The nascent cryptocurrency market is clearly still in an era of ferment, and we may not yet have seen the product or market architecture that will become the dominant design.

Table 7.1 Top 10 Cryptocurrencies by Market Capitalization, August 16th 2022[i]			
	Cryptocurrency	Price	Market Capitalization
	1. Bitcoin	$24,034	$459,388,930,913
	2. Ether	$1899	$231,387,128,723
	3. Tether	$1	$67,569,580,989
	4. USD Coin	$1	$53,472,832,592
	5. BNB	$318	$51,356,773,982
	6. Cardano	$.58	$19,408,871,762
	7. XRP	$.39	$19,189,079,073
	8. Binance	$1	$17,982,583,656
	9. Solana	$44	$15,330,791,972
	10. Dogecoin	$.1	$11,416,913,217

[i] www.coinmarketcap.com, retrieved August 16, 2022.

7-1 Overview

7.1 Explain the components of high-technology industries.

In industries where standards and compatibility are important strategic levers, a technology that gains an initial advantage can sometimes rise to achieve a nearly insurmountable position. Such industries can thus become "winner-take-all" markets. Being successful in such industries can require very different strategies than those used in more traditional industries. Firms may aggressively subsidize adoption of their preferred technology (including sometimes giving away products for free) in order to win the standards battle.

In this chapter, we will take a close look at the nature of competition and strategy in high-technology industries. Technology refers to the body of scientific knowledge used in the production of goods or services. High-technology (high-tech) industries are those in which the underlying scientific knowledge that companies in the industry use is rapidly advancing and, by implication, so are the attributes of the products and services that result from its application. The computer industry is often thought of as the quintessential example of a high-technology industry. Other industries often considered high tech are telecommunications, where new technologies based on wireless and the internet have proliferated in recent years; pharmaceuticals, where new technologies based on cell biology, recombinant DNA, and genomics are revolutionizing the process of drug discovery; power generation, where new technologies based on fuel cells and renewable energy may change the economics of the industry; and aerospace, where the combination of new composite materials, electronics, and more efficient jet engines is giving birth to a new era of superefficient commercial jet aircraft and electric vertical take-off and landing vehicle (evtols).

This chapter focuses on high-technology industries for a number of reasons. First, technology is accounting for an ever-larger share of economic activity. Data from the U.S. Bureau of Labor Statistics indicates that information technology accounts for roughly 10% of U.S. gross domestic product. This figure actually underestimates the true impact of technology on the economy, because it ignores technology in health care, transportation, and consumer electronics. Moreover, as technology advances, many low-technology industries are becoming more high tech. For example, the development of biotechnology and genetic engineering transformed the production of seed corn, long considered a low-tech business, into a high-technology business. The rise of "fintech" (financial technologies) has transformed many sectors of the financial industry, in many cases replacing roles once played by humans with services provided by computers. Retailing was once considered a low-tech business, but the shift to online retailing, led by companies like Amazon.com, has changed this. In addition, high-tech products are making their way into a wide range of businesses; today, most automobiles contain more computing power than the multimillion-dollar mainframe computers used in the *Apollo* space program, and the competitive advantage of physical stores such as Walmart is based on their use of information technology. The circle of high-technology industries is both large and expanding, and technology is revolutionizing aspects of the product or production system even in industries not typically considered high tech.

Although high-tech industries may produce very different products, when developing a business model and strategies that will lead to a competitive advantage and superior profitability and profit growth, they often face a similar situation. For example, "winner-take-all" format wars are common in many high-tech industries such as the consumer electronics and computer industries. In payments, for example, it is possible that one of the growing mobile payment systems will displace Visa, MasterCard, and American Express as the dominant firms for managing payment transactions worldwide. This could result in a tremendous windfall for the firm(s) controlling the new standard (and a tremendous loss for Visa, MasterCard, and

American Express). Firms are thus carefully forging alliances and backing standards they believe will best position them to capture the billions of dollars in transactions fees that are at stake. This chapter examines the competitive features found in many high-tech industries and the kinds of strategies that companies must adopt to build business models that will allow them to achieve superior profitability and profit growth.

7.2 Summarize technical standardization and its role in competition.

technical standards

A set of technical specifications that producers adhere to when making a product or component.

format wars

Battles to control the source of differentiation, and thus the value that such differentiation can create for the customer.

7-2 Technical Standards and Format Wars

Especially in high-tech industries, ownership of **technical standards**—a set of technical specifications that producers adhere to when making the product, or a component of it—can be an important source of competitive advantage.[4] Indeed, in many cases, product differentiation is based on a technical standard. Often, only one standard will dominate a market, so many battles in high-tech industries involve companies that compete to set the standard. For example, for the last four decades, Microsoft has controlled the market as the dominant operating system for personal computers (PCs), sometimes exceeding a 90% market share. Notably, however, Microsoft held less than 1% of the smartphone and tablet operating system markets in 2022, suggesting turbulent times ahead for the firm (see Strategy in Action 7.1).

Battles to set and control technical standards in a market are referred to as **format wars**—essentially, battles to control the source of differentiation, and thus the value that such differentiation can create for the customer. Because differentiated products often command premium prices and are often expensive to develop, the competitive stakes are enormous. The profitability and survival of a company may depend on the outcome of the battle.

7-2a Examples of Standards

A familiar example of a standard is the layout of a computer keyboard. No matter what keyboard you purchase, the letters are all arranged in the same pattern.[5] The reason is obvious. Imagine if each computer maker changed the ways keys were arranged—if some had QWERTY on the top row of keys (which is indeed the format used, known as the QWERTY format), some had YUHGFD, and some had ACFRDS. If you learned to type on one layout, it would be irritating and time consuming to relearn on a YUHGFD layout. The standard QWERTY format makes it easy for people to move from computer to computer because the input medium, the keyboard, is standardized.

Another example of a technical standard can be seen in the dimensions of containers used to transport goods on trucks, railcars, and ships. All have the same basic dimensions of height, length, and width, and all make use of the same locking mechanisms to secure them to a surface or to bolt together. Having a standard ensures that containers can easily be moved from one mode of transportation to another—from trucks, to railcars, to ships, and back to railcars. If containers lacked standard dimensions and locking mechanisms, it would become much more difficult to deliver containers around the world. Shippers would need to make sure that they had the right kind of container to go on the ships, trucks, and railcars scheduled to carry a particular container around the world—a very complicated process.

Consider, finally, PCs. Most share a common set of features: an Intel or Intel-compatible microprocessor, random access memory (RAM), an operating system, an internal hard drive, a DVD drive, a keyboard, a monitor, a mouse, a modem, and so on. We call this set of features the dominant design for personal computers. **Dominant design** refers to a common set of features or design characteristics. Embedded in this

dominant design

Common set of features or design characteristics.

"Segment Zero"—A Serious Threat to Microsoft?

From 1980 to 2013, Microsoft's Windows was entrenched as the dominant PC operating system, giving it enormous influence over many aspects of the computer hardware and software industries. Although competing operating systems had been introduced during that time (e.g., Unix, Geoworks, NeXTSTEP, Linux, and the Mac OS), Microsoft's share of the PC operating system market held stable at roughly 85% throughout most of that period. By 2018, however, Microsoft's position in the computing industry was under greater threat than it had ever been. A high-stakes race for dominance over the next generation of computing was well under way, and Microsoft was not in the front pack.

"Segment Zero"

As Andy Grove, former CEO of Intel, noted in 1998, in many industries—including microprocessors, software, motorcycles, and electric vehicles—technologies improve faster than customer demands of those technologies increase. Firms often add features such as speed and power to products more quickly than customers' capacity to absorb them. Why would firms provide higher performance than that required by the bulk of their customers? The answer appears to lie in the market segmentation and pricing objectives of a technology's providers. As competition in an industry drives prices and margins lower, firms often try to shift sales into progressively higher tiers of the market. In these tiers, high-performance and feature-rich products can command higher margins. Although

customers may also expect to have better-performing products over time, their ability to fully utilize such performance improvements is slowed by the need to learn how to use new features and adapt their work and lifestyles accordingly. Thus, both the trajectory of technology improvement and the trajectory of customer demands are upward sloping, but the trajectory for technology improvement is steeper.

In Figure 7.1, the technology trajectory begins at a point where it provides performance close to that demanded by the mass market, but over time it increases faster than the expectations of the mass market as the firm targets the high-end market. As the price of the technology rises, the mass market may feel it is overpaying for technological features it does not value. In Figure 7.1 the low-end market is not being served; it either pays far more for technology that it does not need, or it goes without. It is this market that Andy Grove, former CEO of Intel, refers to as segment zero.

For Intel, segment zero was the market for low-end personal computers (those less than $1,000). Although segment zero may seem unattractive in terms of margins, if it is neglected, it can become the breeding ground for companies that provide lower-end versions of the technology. As Grove notes, "The overlooked, underserved, and seemingly unprofitable end of the market can provide fertile ground for massive competitive change."

As the firms serving low-end markets with simpler technologies ride up their own trajectories (which are also steeper than the slope

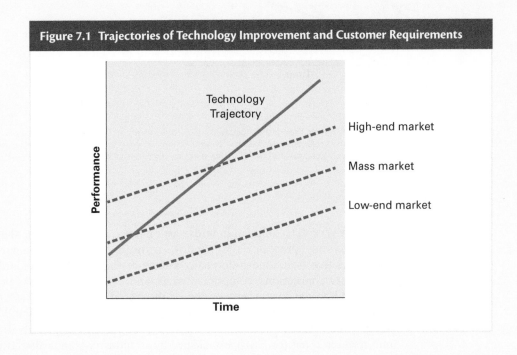

Figure 7.1   Trajectories of Technology Improvement and Customer Requirements

of the trajectories of customer expectations), they can eventually reach a performance level that meets the demands of the mass market while offering a much lower price than the premium technology (see Figure 7.2). At this point, firms offering premium technology may suddenly find they are losing the bulk of their sales revenue to industry contenders that do not look so low-end anymore. For example, by 1998, the combination of rising microprocessor power and decreasing prices enabled PCs priced under $1,000 to capture 20% of the market.

The Threat to Microsoft

So where was the segment zero that could threaten Microsoft? Look in your pocket. In 2018, Apple's iPhone operating system (iOS) and Google's Android collectively controlled over 99% of the worldwide market for smartphones. The iOS and Android interfaces offered a double whammy of beautiful aesthetics and remarkable ease of use. The applications business model used for the phones was also extremely attractive to both developers and customers, and quickly resulted in enormous libraries of applications that ranged from ridiculous to indispensable.

From a traditional economics perspective, the phone operating system market should not be that attractive to Microsoft—people do not spend as much on the applications, and the carriers have too much bargaining power, among other reasons. However, those smartphone operating systems soon became tablet operating systems, and tablets were rapidly becoming fully functional computers. Suddenly, all of the mindshare that Apple and Google had achieved in smartphone operating systems was transforming into mindshare in PC operating systems. Despite years of masterminding the computing industry, Microsoft's dominant position was at risk of evaporating.

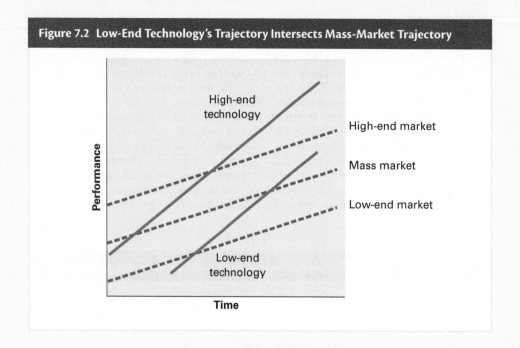

Figure 7.2 Low-End Technology's Trajectory Intersects Mass-Market Trajectory

Sources: Adapted from M. A. Schilling, "'Segment Zero': A Serious Threat to Microsoft?" Conceptual Note, New York University, 2013; A. S. Grove, "Managing Segment Zero," *Leader to Leader* 11 (1999); L. Dignan, "Android, Apple iOS Flip Consumer, Corporate Market Share," *Between the Lines*, February 13, 2013; J. Edwards, "The iPhone 6 Had Better Be Amazing and cheap, Because Apple Is Losing the War to Android," *Business Insider*, May 31, 2014; M. Hachman, "Android, iOS Gobble Up Even More Global Smartphone Share," *PC World*, August 14, 2014. IDC 2018.

design are several technical standards (see Figure 7.3). For example, the combination of an Intel microprocessor and Windows software became so dominant in personal computers that it became colloquially known as the "Wintel" standard. Developers of software applications, component parts, and peripherals such as printers adhere to this ad hoc standard when developing their products because this guarantees that they will work well with a PC based on Intel microprocessors and the Windows operating system. Another technical standard for connecting peripherals to the PC is the universal serial bus (or USB), established by an industry-standards-setting board. No one owns it; the standard is in the public domain. A third technical standard is for

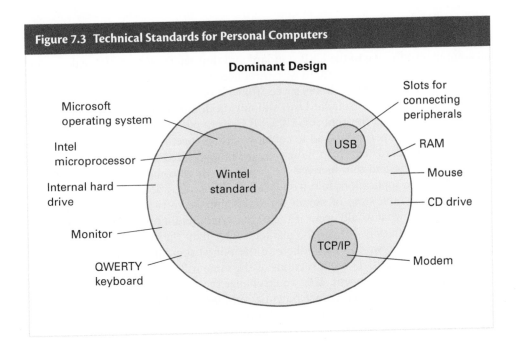

Figure 7.3 Technical Standards for Personal Computers

Dominant Design

- Microsoft operating system
- Intel microprocessor
- Internal hard drive
- Monitor
- QWERTY keyboard
- Wintel standard
- USB
- TCP/IP
- Slots for connecting peripherals
- RAM
- Mouse
- CD drive
- Modem

communication between a PC and the Internet via a modem. Known as TCP/IP, this standard was also set by an industry association and is in the public domain. Thus, as with many other products, the PC is based on several technical standards. It is also important to note that when a company owns a standard, as Microsoft and Intel do with the Wintel standard, it may be a source of competitive advantage and high profitability.

7-2b Benefits of Standards

Standards emerge because there are economic benefits associated with them. First, a technical standard helps to guarantee compatibility between products and their complements. For example, containers are used with railcars, trucks, and ships, and PCs are used with software applications. Compatibility has the tangible economic benefit of reducing the costs associated with making sure that products work well with each other.

Second, a standard can help reduce confusion in the minds of consumers. For example, when Blu-ray was first launched it was competing against HD-DVD to be the dominant video standard. Players based on the different standards were incompatible; a disc designed to run on a Blu-ray player would not run on a HD-DVD player, and vice versa. The companies feared that selling these incompatible versions of the same technology would produce confusion in the minds of consumers, who would not know which version to purchase and might decide to wait and see which technology would dominate the marketplace. With lack of demand, both technologies might fail to gain traction in the marketplace and be unsuccessful. After Toshiba conceded the defeat of the HD-DVD standard, Blu-ray sales grew rapidly.

Third, a standard can help reduce production costs. Once a standard emerges, products that are based on the standard design can be mass produced, enabling the manufacturers to realize substantial economies of scale while lowering their cost structures. For example, the USB standard for connecting peripheral devices was introduced in the late 1990s and rapidly became a dominant standard. The fact that nearly all computers used the USB standard for the next two decades helped to make it simpler to mass produce computers and peripheral devices that would work together. A manufacturer of computer speakers, for example, could mass produce speakers for all computers adhering to the USB standard and thus realize substantial scale economies. In 2014, the USB C standard was introduced and slowly began to make inroads into the market, becoming initially successful with phones (other than iPhone). However, because the USB C standard was still not yet dominant by 2020, manufacturers had to decide whether to support USB, USB C, or to put both kinds of ports on their devices, and consumers often had to cobble solutions together with adapters.

Fourth, standards can help reduce the risks associated with supplying complementary products, and thus increase the supply for those complements. For instance, writing software applications to run on PCs is a risky proposition, requiring the investment of considerable sums of money for developing the software before a single unit is sold. Imagine what would occur if there were ten different operating systems in use for PCs, each with only 10% of the market, rather than the current situation, where roughly 76% of the world's PCs adhere to the Wintel standard. Software developers would need to write 10 different versions of the same software application, each for a much smaller market segment. This would change the economics of software development, increase its risks, and reduce potential profitability. Moreover, because of their higher cost structure and fewer economies of scale, the price of software programs would increase.

Thus, although many people complain about the consequences of Microsoft's near-monopoly of PC operating systems, that dominance does have at least one good effect: It substantially reduces the risks facing the makers of complementary products and the costs of those products. In fact, standards lead to both low-cost and differentiation advantages for individual companies and can help raise the level of industry profitability.

7-2c Establishment of Standards

Standards emerge in an industry in three primary ways. First, when the benefits of establishing a standard are recognized, companies in an industry might lobby the government to mandate an industry standard. In the United States, for example, the Federal Communications Commission (FCC), after detailed discussions with broadcasters and consumer electronics companies, mandated a single technical standard for digital television broadcasts (DTV) and required analog television broadcasts to be terminated in 2009. The FCC took this step because it believed that without government action to set the standard, the DTV rollout would be very slow.

Second, technical standards are often set by cooperation among businesses, without government help, and often through the medium of an industry association, as the example of the DVD forum illustrates. Companies cooperate in this way when they decide that competition to create a standard might be harmful because of the uncertainty that it would create in the minds of consumers or the risk it would pose to manufacturers and distributors.

public domain

Government- or association-set standards of knowledge or technology that any company can freely incorporate into its product.

Government- or association-set standards fall into the **public domain**, meaning that any company can freely incorporate the knowledge and technology upon which the standard is based into its products. For example, no one owns the QWERTY format, and therefore no company can profit from it directly. Similarly, the language that underlies the presentation of text and graphics online, hypertext markup language (HTML), is in the public domain; it is free for all to use. The same is true for TCP/IP, the communications standard used for transmitting data on the internet.

Often, however, the industry standard is selected competitively by the purchasing patterns of customers in the marketplace—that is, by market demand. In this case, the strategy and business model a company has developed for promoting its technological standard are of critical importance because ownership of an industry standard that is protected from imitation by patents and copyrights is a valuable asset—a source of sustained competitive advantage and superior profitability. Microsoft and Intel, for example, both owe their competitive advantage to their ownership of a specific technological standard or format. As noted earlier, format wars occur when two or more companies compete to get their designs adopted as the industry standard. Format wars are common in high-tech industries where standards are important. The Wintel standard became the dominant standard for PCs only after Microsoft and Intel won format wars against Apple's proprietary system, and later against IBM's OS/2 operating system. There is an ongoing standards battle within the smartphone business, as Apple and Google battle for dominance in the smartphone operating system market (see Strategy in Action 7.1).

7-2d Network Effects, Positive Feedback, and Lockout

There has been a growing realization that when standards are set by competition between companies promoting different formats, network effects are a primary determinant of how standards are established.[6] **Network effects** arise in industries where the size of the "network" of compatible products is a primary determinant of demand for an industry's product. For example, the demand for automobiles early in the 20th century was an increasing function of the network of paved roads and gas stations. Similarly, the demand for early telephones was an increasing function of the multitude of numbers that could be called; that is, of the size of the telephone network (the telephone network being the complementary product). When the first telephone service was introduced in New York City, only 100 numbers could be dialed. The network was very small because of the limited number of wires and telephone switches, which made the telephone a relatively useless piece of equipment. But, as an increasing number of people acquired telephones and the network of wires and switches expanded, the telephone connection gained value. This led to an upsurge in demand for telephone lines, which further increased the value of owning a telephone, setting up a positive feedback loop.

network effects

The network of complementary products as a primary determinant of the demand for an industry's product.

To understand why network effects are important in the establishment of standards, consider the classic example of a format war: the battle between Sony and Matsushita to establish their respective technologies for videocassette recorders (VCRs) as the standard in the marketplace. Sony was first to market with its Betamax technology, followed by JVC with its VHS technology. Both companies sold VCR recorder-players, and movie studios issued films prerecorded on VCR tapes for rental to consumers. Initially, all tapes were issued in Betamax format to play on Sony's machine. Sony did not license its Betamax technology, preferring to make all player-recorders itself. Because Japan's Ministry of International Trade and Industry (MITI) appeared poised to select Sony's Betamax as a standard for Japan, JVC decided to liberally license its format and turned to Matsushita (now Panasonic) for support. Matsushita was the largest Japanese electronics manufacturer at that time. JVC and Matushita realized that to make the VHS format players valuable to consumers, they would need to encourage movie studios to issue movies for rental in VHS format. The only way to do that, they reasoned, was to increase the installed base of VHS players as rapidly as possible. They believed that the greater the installed base of VHS players, the greater the incentive for movie studios to issue films in VHS format for rental. As more prerecorded VHS tapes were made available for rental, VHS players became more valuable to consumers and demand for them increased. JVC and Matsushita wanted to exploit a positive feedback loop.

JVC and Matsushita chose a licensing strategy under which any consumer electronics company could manufacture VHS-format players under license. This strategy worked. A large number of companies signed on to manufacture VHS players, and soon far more VHS players were available for purchase in stores than Betamax players. As sales of VHS players grew, movie studios issued more films for rental in VHS format, and this stoked demand. Before long, it was clear to anyone who entered a video rental store that there were more VHS tapes available for rent than Betamax tapes. This served to reinforce the positive feedback loop, and ultimately Sony's Betamax technology was shut out of the market. The pivotal difference between the two companies was strategy: JVC and Matsushita chose a licensing strategy; Sony did not. As a result, JVC's VHS technology became the de facto standard for VCRs.

Network effects can be divided into *direct* (or "same-side") *network effects*, such as in the case of QWERTY, where the greater the use of QWERTY the more it benefits users of QWERTY, and *indirect* (or "cross-side") *network effects*, where much of the value of network benefits comes from one side's ability to attract the other. The VHS story illustrates such indirect network effects: the larger the installed base of VHS players, the more movie producers were motivated to record movies in the VHS format. The more movies available in the VHS format, the more potential buyers were attracted to the VHS player format. The video game industry also exhibits indirect network effects: The greater the installed base of a videogame console, the more developers want to produce games for that console. The more games available for a particular console, the more likely users are to buy that console. The two sides create a self-reinforcing cycle (see Figure 7.4). Platforms that create indirect network effects by mediating such complementary relationships—like videogame consoles do for third-party games and end consumers, or universities do for recruiters and students—are often called "multisided platforms."

The general principle that underlies this example is that when two or more companies compete to get technology adopted as an industry standard, and when network effects and positive feedback loops are important, *the company whose strategy best exploits positive feedback loops wins the format war*. This is a very important strategic principle in many high-technology industries, particularly computer hardware, software, telecommunications, and consumer electronics.

Network externalities and positive feedback loops are also important in a number of industries that would not typically be considered particularly high tech, including newspapers (where the number of readers attracts advertisers), online retail (the sites with the most customers attract the most vendors and the sites with the greatest product variety attracts the most customers), and lodging sharing or ride sharing platforms. For example, consider Uber or DiDi Chuxing ride sharing services. Drivers only want to work for services that have many riders because otherwise they will spend too much time idle and will not make enough income. Riders only want to ride with services that have

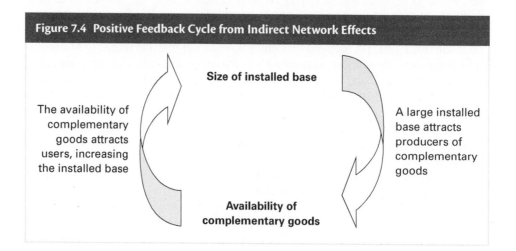

Figure 7.4 Positive Feedback Cycle from Indirect Network Effects

Size of installed base

The availability of complementary goods attracts users, increasing the installed base

A large installed base attracts producers of complementary goods

Availability of complementary goods

many drivers because a service with few drivers will have very long waits for rides. Thus, services with many drivers attract more riders, and services with many riders attract more drivers. The indirect network effects cause the services to become more valuable as they grow, and can lead to one service becoming dominant in a geographical region.

One of the ways a firm can exploit a positive feedback loop is to use strategies that accelerate the growth of one or both sides of the feedback loop. Dolby provides a great example. When Ray Dolby invented a technology for reducing the background hiss in professional tape recording, he adopted a licensing model that charged a very modest fee. He knew his technology was valuable, but he also understood that charging a high fee would encourage manufacturers to develop their own noise-reduction technology. He also decided to license the technology for use on prerecorded tapes for free, collecting licensing fees on the players only. This set up a powerful, positive feedback loop: Growing sales of prerecorded tapes encoded with Dolby technology created a demand for tape players that contained Dolby technology, and as the installed base of tape players with Dolby technology grew, the proportion of prerecorded tapes that were encoded with Dolby technology surged—further boosting demand for players incorporating Dolby technology. By the mid-1970s, virtually all prerecorded tapes were encoded with Dolby noise-reduction technology.

There is another important consideration for exploiting positive feedback cycles: switching costs. A dominant computer platform tends to stay dominant for a long time because there are high switching costs. Changing operating systems, for example, requires customers to learn new ways of navigating around the computer, and they may have incompatibility problems with their existing files. There are also switching costs for manufacturers of hardware and software. For the producer of a software application, for example, to redesign their program to work on a different operating system requires considerable effort and investment. Switching costs thus bind both customers and complementary goods producers to a particular standard, making it harder for a competing standard to overtake a dominant standard.

Some systems, however, have network externalities yet low switching costs. This can make it harder to sustain a dominant position. For example, while consumers prefer an online retailer with many vendors, they can switch to another online retailer quickly and with little or no cost. It might be somewhat more complicated for product suppliers to switch retailers, but the costs are usually not prohibitive. A new retailer that offers great features or better prices can thus enter the market and attract customers and suppliers relatively easily. More generally, the lack of high switching costs means a dominant position is less sticky and more prone to being overturned. The preceding implies that one way that firms can leverage positive feedback cycles is to create switching costs that bind customers or suppliers to the firm's platform. For example, consider the ride sharing industry. As of 2022, drivers of most ride sharing platforms can drive for multiple ride sharing platforms, and customers routinely have multiple ride sharing applications on their phones. This enables both riders and drivers to choose which ride they take at any given moment based on timing and price. If, however, ride sharing companies that were dominant in a region created loyalty incentives for drivers and riders, or made drivers sign exclusivity agreements, they could make a dominant position stickier, and potentially locking out competitors.

This is illustrated well by Microsoft's long-held dominance in the personal computer operating system industry. Consumers choose PCs not for their operating system but for the applications that run on the operating system. A new operating system initially has a very small installed base, so few developers are willing to take the risks involved in writing word-processing programs, spreadsheets, games, and other applications for a new operating system. If a new operating system has very few applications available, consumers who make the switch would have to bear the switching costs associated with giving up some of their applications, which they might be unwilling to do. Moreover, even if applications were available for the new operating system, consumers would have to bear the costs of purchasing those applications—another source of switching costs. In addition, as noted previously, they would have to bear the costs associated with learning to use the new operating system, yet another source of switching costs. Thus, many consumers are unwilling to switch even if they perceive that an alternative operating system performs better than Windows, and companies promoting alternative operating systems have largely been locked out of the market.

However, consumers will bear switching costs if the benefits of adopting the new technology outweigh the costs of switching. For example, in the late 1980s and early 1990s, millions of people switched from analog record players to digital CD players despite the fact that switching costs were significant: Consumers had to purchase the new player technology, and many people purchased CD versions of favorite musical recordings that they already owned. Nevertheless, people made the switch because, for many, the perceived benefit—the incredibly better sound quality associated with CDs—outweighed the costs of switching.

As this switching process continued, a positive feedback loop developed. The installed base of CD players grew, leading to an increase in the number of musical recordings issued on CD as opposed to, or in addition to, vinyl records. The installed base of CD players got so big that mainstream music companies began to issue recordings only in CD format. Once this occurred, even those who did not want to switch to the new technology were required to do so if they wished to purchase new music recordings. The industry standard had shifted: new technology had locked in as the standard and the old technology was locked out.

Extrapolating from this example, it can be argued that despite its dominance, the Wintel standard for PCs could one day be superseded if a competitor finds a way of providing sufficient benefits that enough consumers are willing to bear the switching costs associated with moving to a new operating system. Indeed, there are signs that Apple and Google are chipping away at the dominance of the Wintel standard, primarily by using elegant design and ease of use as tools to get people to bear the costs of switching from Wintel computers.

7.3 Describe the strategies that firms can use to establish their technology as the standard in a market.

7-3 Strategies for Becoming the Dominant Standard

From the perspective of a company pioneering a new technological standard in a marketplace where network effects and positive feedback loops operate, the key question becomes: "What strategy should we pursue to establish our format as the dominant one?"

The various strategies that companies should adopt in order to win format wars are centered upon *finding ways to make network effects work in their favor and against their competitors*. Winning a format war requires a company to build the installed base for its standard as rapidly as possible, thereby leveraging the positive feedback loop, inducing consumers to bear switching costs and ultimately locking the market to its technology. It requires the company to jump-start and then accelerate demand for its technological standard or format such that it becomes established as quickly as possible as the industry standard, thereby locking out competing formats. A number of key strategies and tactics can be adopted to try to achieve this.[7]

7-3a Ensure a Supply of Complements

It is important for a company to make sure that there is an adequate supply of complements for its product. For example, no one will purchase the Sony PS5 unless there is an adequate supply of games to run on that machine. Companies typically take two steps to ensure an adequate supply of complements.

First, they may diversify into the production of complements and seed the market with sufficient supply to help jump-start demand for their format. Before Sony produced the original PlayStation in the early 1990s, for example, it established its own in-house unit to produce videogames for the console. When it launched PlayStation, Sony also simultaneously released 16 games to run on it, giving consumers a reason to purchase the format. Tesla is similarly constructing its own network of supercharging stations at which customers can charge its electric vehicles for free.

Second, companies may create incentives or make it easy for independent companies to produce complements. Sony also licensed the right to produce games to a number of independent game developers, charged the developers a lower royalty rate than they had to pay to competitors such as Nintendo and Sega, and provided them with software tools that made it easier for them to develop games (Apple and Google do the same thing with their smartphone operating systems). Thus, the launch of the Sony PlayStation was accompanied by the simultaneous launch of approximately 30 games, which quickly helped to stimulate demand for the machine.

7-3b Leverage Killer Applications

Killer applications are applications or uses of a new technology or product that are so compelling that they persuade customers to adopt the new format or technology in droves, thereby "killing" demand for competing formats. Killer applications often help to jump-start demand for the new standard. For example, the killer applications that induced consumers to sign up for online services such as AOL in the 1990s were e-mail, chat rooms, and Web browsers. Some of the killer applications that drove consumers to adopt smartphones despite their considerably higher price tag compared to feature phones include texting and mapping applications.

Ideally, the company promoting a technological standard will also want to develop its own killer applications—that is, develop the appropriate complementary products so that they can limit the compatibility of the killer application to their own platform. However, sometimes companies are also able to leverage applications that others develop. For example, the early sales of the IBM PC following its 1981 introduction were primarily driven by IBM's decision to license two important software programs for the PC: VisiCalc (a spreadsheet program) and EasyWriter (a word-processing program), both developed by independent companies. IBM saw that they were driving rapid adoption of rival personal computers, such as the Apple II, so it quickly licensed software, produced versions that would run on the IBM PC, and sold these programs as complements to the IBM PC, a very successful strategy.

In video games, console producers such as Microsoft, Nintendo, and Sony often help to transform a game into a killer application by endorsing it and promoting it. For example, PlayStation designates the best games for each console generation with the award "Platinum: The Best of PlayStation." Nintendo similarly has a "Nintendo Selects" endorsement, and Microsoft has a "Greatest Hits for Xbox One" endorsement. These endorsements signal potential customers about the quality of the game and help to generate "buzz" about the game and the console. Endorsing a complement in this way can help to turn the complement into a blockbuster, which in turn fuels more sales of the platform.[8]

7-3c Aggressive Pricing and Marketing

A common tactic used to jump-start demand is to adopt a **razor and blade strategy**: pricing the product (razor) low to stimulate demand and increase the installed base,

killer applications
Applications or uses of a new technology or product that are so compelling that customers adopt them in droves, killing competing formats.

razor and blade strategy
Pricing the product low in order to stimulate demand, and pricing complements high.

and then trying to make high profits on the sale of complements (razor blades), which are priced relatively high. This strategy owes its name to Gillette, the company that pioneered this strategy to sell its razors and blades. Many other companies have followed this strategy—for example, Hewlett-Packard typically sells its printers at cost but makes significant profits on the subsequent sales of replacement cartridges. In this case, the printer is the "razor" and is priced low to stimulate demand and induce consumers to switch from their existing printer, while the cartridges are the "blades," which are priced high to make profits. The inkjet printer represents a proprietary technological format because only HP cartridges can be used with HP printers; cartridges designed for competing inkjet printers such as those sold by Canon will not work in HP printers. A similar strategy is used in the videogame industry: manufacturers price videogame consoles at cost to induce consumers to adopt their technology, while they make profits on royalties from the sales of games that run on the system.

Aggressive marketing is also a key factor in jump-starting demand to get an early lead in an installed base. Substantial upfront marketing and point-of-sales promotion techniques are often used to try to attract potential early adopters who will bear the switching costs associated with adopting the format. If these efforts are successful, they can be the start of a positive feedback loop. Again, the Sony PlayStation provides a good example. Sony co-linked the introduction of the PlayStation with nationwide television advertising aimed at its primary demographic (18- to 34-year-olds) and in-store displays that allowed potential buyers to play games on the machine before making a purchase.

7-3d Cooperate with Competitors

Companies have been close to simultaneously introducing competing and incompatible technological standards a number of times. A good example is the compact disc. Initially, four companies—Sony, Philips, JVC, and Telefunken—were developing CD players using different variations of the underlying laser technology. If this situation had persisted, they might have introduced incompatible technologies into the marketplace; a CD made for a Philips CD player would not play on a Sony CD player. Understanding that the nearly simultaneous introduction of such incompatible technologies can create significant confusion among consumers, and often lead them to delay their purchases, Sony and Philips decided to join forces and cooperate on developing the technology. Sony contributed its error-correction technology, and Philips contributed its laser technology. The result of this cooperation was that momentum among other players in the industry shifted toward the Sony–Philips alliance; JVC and Telefunken were left with little support. Most important, recording labels announced that they would support the Sony–Philips format but not the Telefunken or JVC format.

Telefunken and JVC subsequently abandoned their efforts to develop CD technology. The cooperation between Sony and Philips was important because it reduced confusion in the industry and allowed a single format to rise to the fore, which accelerated adoption of the technology. The cooperation was a win-win situation for both Philips and Sony, which eliminated competitors and enabled them to share in the success of the format.

7-3e License the Format

Licensing the format to other enterprises so that they too can produce products based on the format is another strategy often adopted. The company that pioneered the format gains from the licensing fees that return to it, as well as from the enlarged supply of the product, which can stimulate demand and help accelerate market adoption. As illustrated previously, this was the strategy that JVC and Matsushita adopted with the VHS format for the VCR, and the strategy that Dolby used with its noise reduction technology.

The correct strategy to pursue in a particular scenario requires that the company consider all of these different strategies and tactics and pursue those that seem most appropriate given the competitive circumstances prevailing in the industry and the likely strategy of rivals. Although there is no single best combination of strategies and tactics, the company must keep the goal of rapidly increasing the installed base of products based on its standard at the forefront of its endeavors. By helping to jump-start demand for its format, a company can induce consumers to bear the switching costs associated with adopting its technology and leverage any positive feedback process that might exist. It is also important not to pursue strategies that have the opposite effect. For example, pricing high to capture profits from early adopters, who tend not to be as price sensitive as later adopters, can have the unfortunate effect of slowing demand growth and allowing a more aggressive competitor to pick up share and establish its format as the industry standard.

7-4 Costs in High-Technology Industries

7.4 Explain the cost structure of many high-technology firms, including the strategic implications of this structure.

In many high-tech industries, the *fixed costs* of developing the product are very high, but the costs of producing one extra unit (the *marginal costs*) of the product are very low. This is most obvious in the case of software. For example, it reportedly cost Microsoft $1.5 billion to develop Windows in 2015, but the cost of producing one more copy of Windows 10 is virtually zero. Once the Windows 10 program was complete, Microsoft duplicated its master disks and sent the copies to PC manufacturers, such as Dell Computer, which then installed a copy of Windows 10 onto every PC sold. Microsoft's cost was, effectively, zero, and yet the company receives a significant licensing fee for each copy of Windows Vista installed on a PC.[9]

Many other high-technology products have similar cost economics: very high fixed costs and very low marginal costs. Most software products share these features, although if the software is sold through stores, the costs of packaging and distribution will raise the marginal costs, and if it is sold by a sales force direct to end users, this too will raise the marginal costs. Many consumer electronics products have the same basic economics. The fixed costs of developing a DVD player or a videogame console can be very expensive, but the costs of producing an incremental unit are very low. Similarly, the fixed costs of developing a new drug are typically estimated to be at least $1.6 billion (and potentially much more if one factors in the cost of all the failed drug development efforts),[10] but the marginal cost of producing each additional pill is at most a few cents.

7-4a Comparative Cost Economics

To grasp why this cost structure is strategically important, a company must understand that, in many industries, marginal costs rise as a company tries to expand output (economists call this the *law of diminishing returns*). To produce more of a good, a company must hire more labor and invest in more plant and machinery. At the margin, the additional resources used are not as productive, so this leads to increasing marginal costs. However, the law of diminishing returns often does not apply in many high-tech settings such as the production of software or sending data through a digital telecommunications network.

Consider two companies, α and β (see Figure 7.5). Company α is a conventional producer and faces diminishing returns, so as it tries to expand output, its marginal costs rise. Company β is a high-tech producer, and its marginal costs do not rise at

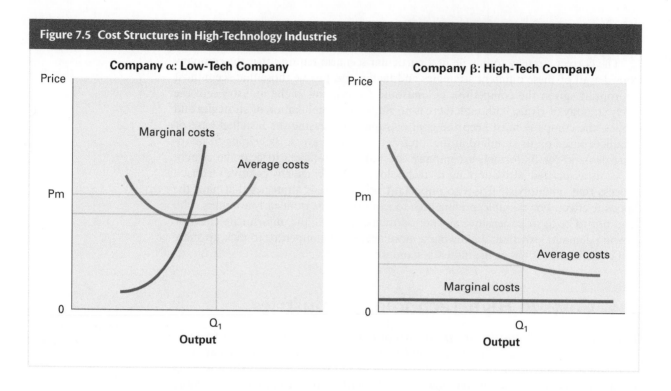

Figure 7.5 Cost Structures in High-Technology Industries

Company α: Low-Tech Company

Price

Marginal costs

Average costs

Pm

0

Q₁

Output

Company β: High-Tech Company

Price

Pm

Average costs

Marginal costs

0

Q₁

Output

all as output is increased. Note that in Figure 7.5, company β's marginal cost curve is drawn as a straight line near to the horizontal axis, implying that marginal costs are close to zero and do not vary with output, whereas company α's marginal costs rise as output is expanded, illustrating diminishing returns. Company β's flat, low marginal cost curve means that its average cost curve will continuously fall over all ranges of output as it spreads its fixed costs out over greater volume. In contrast, the rising marginal costs encountered by company α mean that its average cost curve is the U-shaped curve familiar from basic economics texts. For simplicity, assume that both companies sell their product at the same price, Pm, and both sell exactly the same quantity of output, $0 - Q_1$. Figure 7.5 shows that, at an output of Q_1, company β has much lower average costs than company α and as a consequence is making far more profit (profit is the shaded area in Figure 7.5).

7-4b Strategic Significance

If a company can shift from a cost structure where it encounters increasing marginal costs to one where fixed costs may be high but marginal costs are much lower, its profitability may increase. In the consumer electronics industry, such a shift has been playing out for five decades. Musical recordings were once based on analog technology where marginal costs rose as output expanded due to diminishing returns (as in the case of company α in Figure 7.5). In the 1980s and 1990s, digital systems such as CD players replaced analog systems. Digital systems are software based, and this implies much lower marginal costs of producing one more copy of a recording. As a result, music companies were able to lower prices, expand demand, and see their profitability increase (their production system has more in common with company β in Figure 7.5).

This process, however, was still unfolding. The latest technology for copying musical recordings is based on distribution over the internet (e.g., streaming platforms such as Spotify). Here, the marginal costs of making one more copy of a recording are basically zero, and do not increase with output. The only problem is that the low costs of copying and distributing music recordings can lead to widespread illegal file sharing, which ultimately leads to a very large decline in overall revenues in recorded music. According to the International Federation of the Phonographic Industry, worldwide revenues for CDs, vinyl, cassettes, and digital downloads dropped from about $25 billion in 1999 to about $15 billion in 2010. Fortunately, increases in music streaming revenues eventually reversed that loss, and global recorded music revenues for 2021 were almost $26 billion.[11] We discuss copyright issues in more detail shortly when we consider intellectual property rights.

When a high-tech company faces high fixed costs and low marginal costs, its strategy should emphasize the low-cost structure option: deliberately drive down prices in order to increase volume. Figure 7.5 shows that the high-tech company's average costs fall rapidly as output expands. This implies that prices can be reduced to stimulate demand, and as long as prices fall less rapidly than average costs, per-unit profit margins will expand as prices fall. This is a consequence of low marginal costs that do not rise with output. This strategy of pricing low to drive volume and reap wider profit margins is central to the business model of some very successful high-tech companies, including Microsoft.

7-5 Capturing First-Mover Advantages

7.5 Evaluate the pros and cons of first-mover advantage in high-technology industries.

In high-technology industries, companies often compete by striving to be the first to develop revolutionary new products, that is, to be a **first mover**. By definition, the first mover that creates a revolutionary product is in a monopoly position. If the new product satisfies unmet consumer needs and demand is high, the first mover can capture significant revenues and profits. Such revenues and profits signal to potential rivals that imitating the first mover makes money. Figure 7.6 implies that in the absence of strong barriers to imitation, imitators will rush into the market created by the first mover, competing away the first mover's monopoly profits and leaving all participants in the market with a much lower level of returns.

first mover

A firm that pioneers a particular product category or feature by being first to offer it to market.

Despite imitation, some first movers have the ability to capitalize on and reap substantial first-mover advantages—the advantages of pioneering new technologies and products that lead to an enduring competitive advantage. Intel introduced the world's

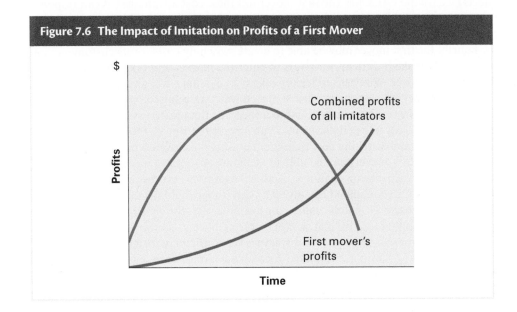

Figure 7.6 The Impact of Imitation on Profits of a First Mover

first microprocessor in 1971. Today, it still dominates the microprocessor segment of the semiconductor industry. Xerox introduced the world's first photocopier and for a long time enjoyed a leading position in the industry. Cisco introduced the first Internet protocol network router in 1986, and is still a leader in the market for networking equipment today. Microsoft introduced the world's first software application for a personal computer in 1979, Microsoft BASIC, and it remains a dominant force in PC software.

Some first movers can reap substantial advantages from their pioneering activities that lead to an enduring competitive advantage. They can, in other words, limit or slow the rate of imitation.

But there are plenty of counterexamples suggesting that first-mover advantages might not be easy to capture and, in fact, that there might be **first-mover disadvantages**— the competitive disadvantages associated with being first. For example, Apple was the first company to introduce a handheld computer, the Apple Newton, but the product failed; a second mover, Palm, succeeded where Apple had failed. In the market for commercial jet aircraft, DeHavilland was first to market with the Comet, but it was the second mover, Boeing, with its 707 jetliner, that went on to dominate the market.

Clearly, being a first mover does not by itself guarantee success. As we shall see, the difference between innovating companies that capture first-mover advantages and those that fall victim to first-mover disadvantages in part incites the strategy that the first mover pursues. Before considering the strategy issue, however, we need to take a closer look at the nature of first-mover advantages and disadvantages.[12]

7-5a First-Mover Advantages

There are five primary sources of first-mover advantages.[13] First, the first mover has an opportunity to exploit network effects and positive feedback loops, locking consumers into its technology.

Second, the first mover may be able to establish significant brand loyalty, which is expensive for later entrants to break down. Indeed, if the company is successful in this endeavor, its name may become closely associated with the entire class of products, including those produced by rivals. People still talk of "Xeroxing" when making a photocopy, or "FedExing" when they will be sending a package by overnight mail.

Third, the first mover may be able to increase sales volume ahead of rivals and thus reap cost advantages associated with the realization of scale economies and learning effects (see Chapter 4). Once the first mover has these cost advantages, it can respond to new entrants by cutting prices to retain its market share and still earn significant profits.

Fourth, the first mover may be able to create switching costs for its customers that subsequently make it difficult for rivals to enter the market and take customers away from the first mover. Wireless service providers, for example, will give new customers a "free" cell phone, but customers must sign a contract agreeing to pay for the phone if they terminate the service contract within a specified time period such as 1 or 2 years. Because the real cost of a cell phone may run anywhere from $100 to $1,200, this represents a significant switching cost that later entrants must overcome.

Finally, the first mover may be able to accumulate valuable knowledge related to customer needs, distribution channels, product technology, process technology, and so on. Knowledge so accumulated can give it an advantage that later entrants might find difficult or expensive to match. Sharp, for example, was the first mover in the commercial manufacture of active matrix liquid crystal displays used in laptop computers. The process for manufacturing these displays is very difficult, with a high rejection rate for flawed displays. Sharp accumulated such an advantage with regard to production processes that it was very difficult for later entrants to match it on product quality, and therefore on costs.

7-5b First-Mover Disadvantages

Balanced against these first-mover advantages are a number of disadvantages.[14] First, the first mover has to bear significant pioneering costs that later entrants do not. The first mover must pioneer the technology, develop distribution channels, and educate customers about the nature of the product. This can be expensive and time consuming. Later entrants, by way of contrast, might be able to free-ride on the first mover's investments in pioneering the market and customer education. That is, they do not have to bear the pioneering costs of the first mover. Generic drug makers, for example, spend very little on research and development (R&D) compared to the costs borne by the developer of an original drug because they can replicate the finished chemical or biological product (that is, they do not have to explore many alternative paths to a solution), and they can bypass most of the clinical testing process.[15]

Related to this, first movers are more prone to make mistakes because there are so many uncertainties in a new market. Later entrants may learn from the mistakes made by first movers, improve on the product or the way in which it is sold, and come to market with a superior offering that captures significant market share from the first mover. For example, one reason that the Apple Newton failed was that the software in the handheld computer failed to recognize human handwriting. The second mover in this market, Palm, learned from Apple's error. When it introduced the PalmPilot, it used software that recognized letters written in a particular way, graffiti style, and then persuaded customers to learn this method of inputting data into the handheld computer.

Third, first movers run the risk of building the wrong resources and capabilities because they focus on a customer set that is not characteristic of the mass market. This is the "crossing the chasm" problem that we discussed in the previous chapter. You will recall that the customers in the early market—those we categorized as innovators and early adopters—have different characteristics from the first wave of the mass market, the early majority. The first mover runs the risk of directing its resources and capabilities to the needs of innovators and early adopters, and not being able to switch when the early majority enters the market. As a result, first movers run a greater risk of plunging into the chasm that separates the early market from the mass market.

Finally, the first mover may invest in inferior or obsolete technology. This can happen when its product innovation is based on underlying technology that is rapidly advancing. Basing its product on an early version of a technology may lock a company into a resource that rapidly becomes obsolete. In contrast, later entrants may be able to leapfrog the first mover and introduce products that are based on later versions of the underlying technology. This happened in France during the 1980s when, at the urging of the government, France Telecom introduced the world's first consumer online service, Minitel. France Telecom distributed free terminals to consumers, which connected to the phone line and could be used to browse phone directories. Other simple services were soon added, and before long the French could shop, bank, make travel arrangements, and check weather and news "online"—years before the Web was invented. The problem was that by the standards of the Web, Minitel was very crude and inflexible, and France Telecom, as the first mover, suffered. The French were very slow to adopt personal computers and the internet primarily because Minitel had such a presence. In 1998, only one-fifth of French households had a computer, compared with two-fifths in the United States, and only 2% of households were connected to the internet, compared to over 30% in the United States. As the result of a government decision, both France Telecom and the entire nation of France were slow to adopt a revolutionary new online medium—the Web—because they were the first to invest in a more primitive version of the technology.[16]

7-5c Strategies for Exploiting First-Mover Advantages

First movers must strategize and determine how to exploit their lead and capitalize on first-mover advantages to build a sustainable, long-term competitive advantage while simultaneously reducing the risks associated with first-mover disadvantages. There are three basic strategies available: (1) develop and market the innovation; (2) develop and market the innovation jointly with other companies through a strategic alliance or joint venture; and (3) license the innovation to others and allow them to develop the market.

The optimal choice of strategy depends on the answers to three questions:

1. Does the innovating company have the complementary assets to exploit its innovation and capture first-mover advantages?
2. How difficult is it for imitators to copy the company's innovation? In other words, what is the height of barriers to imitation?
3. Are there capable competitors that could rapidly imitate the innovation?

Complementary Assets   Complementary assets are required to exploit a new innovation and gain a competitive advantage.[17] Among the most important complementary assets are competitive production and distribution capabilities that can handle rapid growth in customer demand while maintaining high product and service quality. State-of-the-art manufacturing facilities, for example, enable the first mover to quickly move down the experience curve without encountering production bottlenecks or problems with the quality of the product. The inability to satisfy demand because of these problems, however, creates the opportunity for imitators to enter the marketplace. For example, in 1998, Immunex was the first company to introduce a revolutionary biological treatment for rheumatoid arthritis. Sales for this product, Enbrel, very rapidly increased, reaching $750 million in 2001. However, Immunex had not invested in sufficient manufacturing capacity. In mid-2000, it announced that it lacked the capacity to satisfy demand and that bringing additional capacity online would take at least 2 years. This manufacturing bottleneck gave the second mover in the market, Johnson & Johnson, the opportunity to rapidly expand demand for its product, which by early 2002 was outselling Enbrel. Immunex's first-mover advantage had been partly eroded because it lacked an important complementary asset, the manufacturing capability required to satisfy demand.

Complementary assets also include marketing knowhow, an adequate sales force, access to distribution systems, and an after-sales service and support network. All of these assets can help an innovator build brand loyalty and more rapidly achieve market penetration.[18] In turn, the resulting increases in volume facilitate more rapid movement down the experience curve and the attainment of a sustainable, cost-based advantage due to scale economies and learning effects. EMI, the first mover in the market for computed tomography (CT) scanners, ultimately lost out to established medical equipment companies such as GE Medical Systems because it lacked the marketing knowhow, sales force, and distribution systems required to effectively compete in the world's largest market for medical equipment, the United States.

Developing complementary assets can be very expensive, and companies often need large infusions of capital for this purpose. That is why first movers often lose out to late movers that are large, successful companies in other industries with the resources to quickly develop a presence in the new industry. For example, though online grocery ordering and delivery was pioneered by start-up firms, Amazon's entry into this market in 2007 with its Amazon Fresh service threatened to displace the smaller companies due to Amazon's far greater brand awareness, distribution capabilities, and bargaining power with suppliers.

Height of Barriers to Imitation   Recall from Chapter 3 that barriers to imitation are factors that prevent rivals from imitating a company's distinctive competencies and innovations. Although any innovation can be copied, the higher the barriers are, the longer it takes for rivals to imitate the innovation, and the more time the first mover has to build an enduring competitive advantage.

Barriers to imitation give an innovator time to establish a competitive advantage and build more enduring barriers to entry in the newly created market. Patents, for example, are among the most widely used barriers to imitation. By protecting its photocopier technology with a thicket of patents, Xerox was able to delay any significant imitation of its product for 17 years. However, patents are often easy to "invent around." For example, one study found that this happened to 60% of patented innovations within 4 years.[19] If patent protection is weak, a company might try to slow imitation by developing new products and processes in secret. The most famous example of this approach is Coca-Cola, which has kept the formula for Coke a secret for generations.

Capable Competitors   Capable competitors are companies that can move quickly to imitate the pioneering company. Competitors' capability to imitate a pioneer's innovation depends primarily on two factors: (1) R&D skills; and (2) access to complementary assets. In general, the greater the number of capable competitors with access to the R&D skills and complementary assets needed to imitate an innovation, the more rapid imitation is likely to be.

In this context, R&D skills refer to the ability of rivals to reverse-engineer an innovation to find out how it works and quickly develop a comparable product. As an example, consider the CT scanner. GE bought one of the first CT scanners produced by EMI, and its technical experts reverse-engineered the machine. Despite the product's technological complexity, GE developed its own version, which allowed it to quickly imitate EMI and replace it as the major supplier of CT scanners.

Complementary assets—the access that rivals have to marketing, sales knowhow, and manufacturing capabilities—are key determinants of the rate of imitation. If would-be imitators lack critical complementary assets, not only will they have to imitate the innovation, but they may also need to imitate the innovator's complementary assets. This is expensive, as AT&T discovered when it tried to enter the PC business in 1984. AT&T lacked the marketing assets (sales force and distribution systems) necessary to support personal computer products. The lack of these assets and the time it takes to build the assets partly explain why: Four years after it entered the market, AT&T had lost $2.5 billion and still had not emerged as a viable contender. It subsequently exited this business.

Three Innovation Strategies   The way in which these three factors—complementary assets, height of barriers to imitation, and the capability of competitors—influence the choice of innovation strategy is summarized in Table 7.1. The competitive strategy of developing and marketing the innovation alone makes most sense when: (1) the innovator has the complementary assets necessary to develop the innovation, (2) the barriers to imitating a new innovation are high, and (3) the capability of competitors is limited. Complementary assets allow rapid development and promotion of the innovation. High barriers to imitation give the innovator time to establish a competitive advantage and build enduring barriers to entry through brand loyalty or experience-based cost advantages. The fewer capable competitors there are, the less likely it is that any one of them will succeed in circumventing barriers to imitation and quickly imitating the innovation.

The competitive strategy of developing and marketing the innovation jointly with other companies through a strategic alliance or joint venture makes most sense when:

Table 7.2 Strategies for Profiting from Innovation

Strategy	Does the Innovator Have the Required Complementary Assets?	Likely Height of Barriers to Imitation	Existence of Capable Competitors
Going it alone	Yes	High	Very few
Entering into an alliance	No	High	Moderate number
Licensing the innovation	No	Low	Many

(1) the innovator lacks complementary assets, (2) barriers to imitation are high, and (3) there are several capable competitors. In such circumstances, it makes sense to enter into an alliance with a company that already has the complementary assets—in other words, with a capable competitor. Theoretically, such an alliance should prove to be mutually beneficial, and each partner can share in high profits that neither could earn on its own. Moreover, such a strategy has the benefit of coopting a potential rival. For example, had EMI teamed with a capable competitor to develop the market for CT scanners, such as GE Medical Systems, instead of going it alone, the company might have been able to build a more enduring competitive advantage and also co-opt a powerful rival into its camp.

The third strategy, licensing, makes most sense when: (1) the innovating company lacks the complementary assets, (2) barriers to imitation are low, and (3) there are many capable competitors. The combination of low barriers to imitation and many capable competitors makes rapid imitation almost certain. The innovator's lack of complementary assets further suggests that an imitator will soon capture the innovator's competitive advantage. Given these factors, because rapid diffusion of the innovator's technology through imitation is inevitable, the innovator can at least share in some benefits of this diffusion by licensing out its technology.[20] Moreover, by setting a relatively modest licensing fee, the innovator may be able to reduce the incentive that potential rivals have to develop their own competing, and possibly superior, technology. As described previously, Dolby adopted this strategy to get its technology established as the standard for noise reduction in the music and film businesses.

7-6 Technological Paradigm Shifts

7.6 Explain the nature of technological paradigm shifts and their implications for enterprise strategy.

technological paradigm shifts

Shifts in new technologies that revolutionize the structure of the industry, dramatically alter the nature of competition, and require companies to adopt new strategies in order to survive.

Technological paradigm shifts occur when new technologies revolutionize the structure of the industry, dramatically alter the nature of competition, and require companies to adopt new strategies in order to survive. Digitization and online platforms are dramatically shifting the levers of competition in industries as diverse as real estate, lodging, stock trading, retail commerce, music and movie distribution, and many more. Many once-dominant firms in these industries have been displaced by new "born digital" competitors. A classic example of a paradigm shift was mentioned in Chapter 6: the evolution of photography from chemical to digital printing processes. For over half a century, the large, incumbent enterprises in the photographic industry such as Kodak and Fujifilm generated most of their revenues from selling and processing film using traditional silver halide technology. The rise of digital photography was a huge disruptive threat to their business models. Digital cameras do not use film, the mainstay of Kodak's and

Fuji's business. In addition, these cameras are more like specialized computers than conventional cameras, and are therefore based on scientific knowledge in which Kodak and Fuji have little expertise. Although both Kodak and Fuji have heavily invested in the development of digital cameras, they faced intense competition from companies such as Sony, Canon, and Hewlett-Packard, which developed their own digital cameras; from software developers such as Adobe and Microsoft, which make software for manipulating digital images; and from printer companies such as Hewlett-Packard and Canon, which make printers that consumers use to print high-quality pictures from home. As time passed, these companies also faced disruption. As the quality of cameras integrated into smartphones improved, a large portion of the market that would have previously purchased digital cameras and printed pictures at home now took pictures on their smartphone and shared them electronically —foregoing most printing altogether.

Examples such as these raise four questions:

1. When do paradigm shifts occur, and how do they unfold?
2. Why do so many incumbents go into decline following a paradigm shift?
3. What strategies can incumbents adopt to increase the probability that they will survive a paradigm shift and emerge on the other side of the market abyss created by the arrival of new technology as a profitable enterprise?
4. What strategies can new entrants into a market adopt to profit from a paradigm shift?
5. We shall answer each of these questions in the remainder of this chapter.

7-6a Paradigm Shifts and the Decline of Established Companies

Paradigm shifts appear to be more likely to occur in an industry when one, or both, of the following conditions are in place.[21] First, the established technology in the industry is mature, and is approaching or at its "natural limit." Second, a new "disruptive technology" has entered the marketplace and is taking root in niches that are poorly served by incumbent companies using established technology.

Natural Limits to Technology   Richard Foster has formalized the relationship between the performance of a technology and time in terms of what he calls the technology S-curve (see Figure 7.7).[22] This curve shows the relationship over time of cumulative investments in R&D and the performance (or functionality) of a given technology.

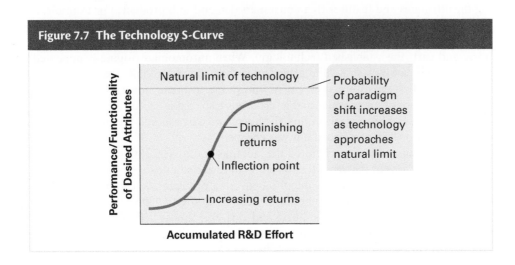

Figure 7.7 The Technology S-Curve

Early in its evolution, R&D investments in a new technology tend to yield rapid improvements in performance as basic engineering problems are solved. After a time, diminishing returns to cumulative R&D begin to set in, the rate of improvement in performance slows, and the technology starts to approach its natural limit, where further advances are not possible. For example, one can argue that there was more improvement in the first 50 years of the commercial aerospace business following the pioneering flight by the Wright Brothers than there has been in the second 50 years. Indeed, the venerable Boeing 747 is based on a 1960s' design. In commercial aerospace, therefore, we are now in the region of diminishing returns and may be approaching the natural limit to improvements in the technology of commercial aerospace.

Similarly, it can be argued that we are approaching the natural limit to technology in the performance of silicon-based semiconductor chips. Over the past three decades, the performance of semiconductor chips has increased dramatically; companies can now manufacture a larger amount of transistors in a single, small silicon chip. This process helped to increase the power of computers, lower their cost, and shrink their size. But we are starting to approach limits to the ability to shrink the width of lines on a chip and therefore pack ever more transistors onto a single chip. The limit is imposed by the natural laws of physics. Light waves are used to etch lines onto a chip, and one cannot etch a line that is smaller than the wavelength of light being used. Semiconductor companies are already using light beams with very small wavelengths, such as extreme ultraviolet, to etch lines onto a chip, but there are limits to how far this technology can be pushed, and many believe that we will reach those limits within the decade. Does this mean that our ability to make smaller, faster, cheaper computers is coming to an end? Probably not. It is more likely that we will find another technology to replace silicon-based computing and enable us to continue building smaller, faster, cheaper computers.

What does all of this have to do with paradigm shifts? According to Foster, when a technology approaches its natural limit, research attention turns to possible alternative technologies, and sooner or later one of those alternatives might be commercialized and replace the established technology. That is, the probability that a paradigm shift will occur increases. Thus, sometime in the next decade or two, another paradigm shift might shake up the foundations of the computer industry as an alternative technology replaces silicon-based computing. If history is any guide, if and when this happens, many incumbents in today's computer industry will go into decline, and new enterprises will rise to dominance.

Foster pushes this point a little further, noting that, initially, the contenders for the replacement technology are not as effective as the established technology in producing the attributes and features that consumers demand in a product. For example, in the early years of the 20th century, automobiles were just beginning to be produced. They were valued for their ability to move people from place to place, but so was the horse and cart (the established technology). When automobiles originally appeared, the horse and cart was still quite a bit better than the automobile (see Figure 7.8). After all, the first cars were slow, noisy, and prone to break down. Moreover, they needed a network of paved roads and gas stations to be really useful, and that network didn't yet exist. For most applications, the horse and cart was still the preferred mode of transportation—in part because it was cheaper.

However, this comparison ignored the fact that in the early 20th century, automobile technology was at the very start of its S-curve and about to experience dramatic improvements in performance as major engineering problems were solved (and those paved roads and gas stations were built). In contrast, after 3,000 years of continuous improvement and refinement, the horse and cart was almost definitely at the end of its technological S-curve. The result was that the rapidly improving automobile soon replaced the horse and cart as the preferred mode of transportation. At time T_1 in

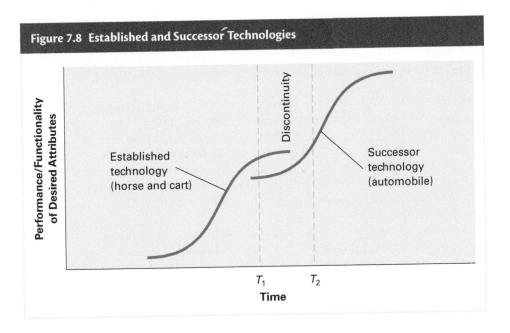

Figure 7.8 Established and Successor Technologies

Figure 7.8, the horse and cart was still superior to the automobile. By time T_2, the automobile had surpassed the horse and cart.

Foster notes that because successor technology is initially less efficient than established technology, established companies and their customers often make the mistake of dismissing it, only to be surprised by its rapid performance improvement. Many people are betting that this is the process unfolding in the electric vehicle industry. Although electric vehicles still have technical disadvantages to internal combustion vehicles (e.g., limited range, time spent recharging), and cost significantly more than comparable internal combustion vehicles, it is possible that dramatic improvements in battery technology could simultaneously address technical disadvantages while reducing the costs of the vehicles.

A final point is that often there is not a single potential successor technology but a swarm of potential successor technologies, only one of which might ultimately rise to the fore (see Figure 7.9). When this is the case, established companies are put at a

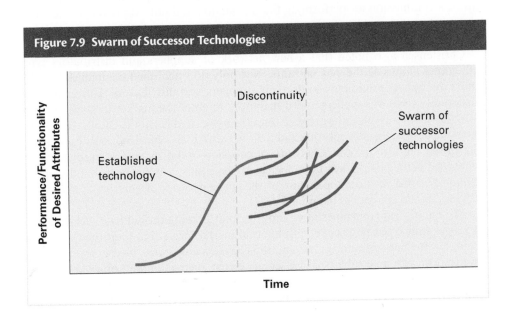

Figure 7.9 Swarm of Successor Technologies

disadvantage. Even if they recognize that a paradigm shift is imminent, companies may not have the resources to invest in all the potential replacement technologies. If they invest in the wrong one—which is easy to do, given the uncertainty that surrounds the entire process—they may be locked out of subsequent development.

Disruptive Technology   Clayton Christensen built on Foster's insights and his own research to develop a theory of disruptive technology that has become very influential in high-technology circles.[23] Christensen used the term *disruptive technology* to refer to a new technology that originates away from the mainstream of a market and then, as its functionality improves over time, invades the main market. Such technologies are disruptive because they revolutionize industry structure and competition, often causing the decline of established companies. They cause a technological paradigm shift.

Christensen's greatest insight was that established companies are often aware of the new technology but do not invest in it because they listen to their customers, and their customers do not want it. Of course, this arises because the new technology is early in its development and only at the beginning of the S-curve for that technology. Once the performance of the new technology improves, customers will want it, but by this time it is new entrants, as opposed to established companies, that have accumulated the required knowledge to bring the new technology into the mass market.

In addition to listening too closely to their customers, Christensen also identified a number of other factors that make it very difficult for established companies to adopt a new disruptive technology. He noted that many established companies decline to invest in new disruptive technologies because initially they serve such small market niches that it seems unlikely there would be an impact on the company's revenues and profits. As the new technology starts to improve in functionality and invade the main market, their investment can often be hindered by the difficult implementation of a new business model required to exploit the new technology.

Both of these points can be illustrated by reference to one more example: the rise of online discount stockbrokers during the 1990s such as Ameritrade and E*TRADE, which made use of a new technology—the internet—to allow individual investors to trade stocks for a very low commission fee, whereas full-service stockbrokers such as Merrill Lynch, which required that orders be placed through a stockbroker who earned a commission for performing the transaction, did not. Many full-service brokerages survived by adding low-cost online trading as a service for their customers, but not before losing significant share to new competitors.

Christensen also noted that a new network of suppliers and distributors typically grows alongside the new entrants. Not only do established companies initially ignore disruptive technology, so do their suppliers and distributors. This creates an opportunity for new suppliers and distributors to enter the market to serve the new entrants. As the new entrants grow, so does the associated network. Ultimately, Christensen suggested, the new entrants and their network may replace not only established enterprises, but also the entire network of suppliers and distributors associated with established companies. Taken to its logical extreme, this view suggests that disruptive technologies may result in the demise of the entire network of enterprises associated with established companies in an industry.

The established companies in an industry that is being rocked by a technological paradigm shift often must cope with internal inertia forces that limit their ability to adapt, but the new entrants do not and thus have an advantage. New entrants do not have to deal with an established, conservative customer set and an obsolete business model. Instead, they can focus on optimizing the new technology, improving its performance, and riding the wave of disruptive technology into new market segments until they invade the main market and challenge the established companies. By then, they may be well equipped to surpass the established companies.

7-6b Strategic Implications for Established Companies

Although Christensen uncovered an important tendency, it is by no means written in stone that all established companies are doomed to fail when faced with disruptive technologies, as we have seen with IBM and Merrill Lynch. Established companies must meet the challenges created by the emergence of disruptive technologies.[24]

First, having access to the knowledge about how disruptive technologies can revolutionize markets is a valuable strategic asset. Many of the established companies that Christensen examined failed because they took a myopic view of the new technology and asked their customers the wrong question. Instead of asking: "Are you interested in this new technology?" they should have recognized that the new technology was likely to improve rapidly over time and instead have asked: "Would you be interested in this new technology if it improves its functionality over time?" If established enterprises had done this, they may have made very different strategic decisions.

Second, it is clearly important for established enterprises to invest in newly emerging technologies that may ultimately become disruptive technologies. Companies have to hedge their bets about new technology. As we have noted, at any time, there may be a swarm of emerging technologies, any one of which might ultimately become a disruptive technology. Large, established companies that are generating significant cash flows can, and often should, establish and fund central R&D operations to invest in and develop such technologies. In addition, they may wish to acquire emerging companies that are pioneering potentially disruptive technologies, or enter into alliances with others to jointly develop the technology. The strategy of acquiring companies that are developing potentially disruptive technology is one that Cisco Systems, a dominant provider of internet network equipment, is famous for pursuing. At the heart of this strategy must be recognition on behalf of the incumbent enterprise that it is better for the company to develop disruptive technology, and then cannibalize its established sales base, than to have the sales base taken away by new entrants.

However, Christensen made a very important point: Even when established companies undertake R&D investments in potentially disruptive technologies, they often fail to commercialize those technologies because of internal forces that suppress change. For example, managers who are currently generating the most cash in one part of the business may claim that they need the greatest R&D investment to maintain their market position, and may lobby top management to delay investment in a new technology. This can be a powerful argument when, early in the S-curve, the long-term prospects of a new technology are very unclear. The consequence, however, may be that the company fails to build competence in the new technology, and suffers accordingly.

In addition, Christensen argued that the commercialization of new disruptive technology often requires a radically different value chain with a completely different cost structure—a new business model. For example, it may require a different manufacturing system, a different distribution system, and different pricing options, and may involve very different gross margins and operating margins. Christensen argued that it is almost impossible for two distinct business models to coexist within the same organization. When companies try to implement both models, the already established model will almost inevitably suffocate the model associated with the disruptive technology.

The solution to this problem is to create an autonomous operating division devoted solely to the new technology. For example, during the early 1980s, HP built a very successful laserjet printer business. Then inkjet technology was invented. Some employees at HP believed that inkjet printers would cannibalize sales of laserjet printers, and consequently argued that HP should not produce inkjet printers. Fortunately for HP, senior management saw inkjet technology for what it was: a potential disruptive technology. Instead of choosing to not invest in inkjet technology, HP allocated significant R&D funds toward its commercialization. Furthermore, when the technology was ready for market introduction, HP established an autonomous inkjet division at a different geographical location, including manufacturing, marketing, and distribution departments. HP senior managers accepted that the inkjet division might take sales away from the laserjet division and decided that it was better for an HP division to cannibalize the sales of another HP division, than allow those sales to be cannibalized by another company. Happily for HP, inkjets cannibalize sales of laserjets only on the margin, and both laserjet and inkjet printers have profitable market niches. This felicitous outcome, however, does not detract from the message of this example: If a company is developing a potentially disruptive technology, the chances for success will be enhanced if it is placed in a stand-alone product division and given its own mandate.

7-6c Strategic Implications for New Entrants

Christensen's work also holds implications for new entrants. The new entrants, or attackers, have several advantages over established enterprises. Pressures to continue the existing, out-of-date business model do not hamstring new entrants, which do not need to worry about product cannibalization issues. They need not worry about their established customer base or about relationships with established suppliers and distributors. Instead, they can focus all their energies on the opportunities offered by the new disruptive technology, move along the S-curve of technology improvement, and rapidly grow with the market for that technology. This does not mean that the new entrants do not have problems to solve. They may be constrained by a lack of capital or must manage the organizational problems associated with rapid growth; most important, they may need to find a way to take their technology from a small, out-of-the-way niche into the mass market.

Perhaps one of the most important issues facing new entrants is choosing whether to partner with an established company or go it alone in an attempt to develop and profit from a new disruptive technology. Although a new entrant may enjoy all the advantages of the attacker, it may lack the resources required to fully exploit them. In such a case, the company might want to consider forming a strategic alliance with a larger, established company to gain access to those resources. The main issues here are the same as those discussed earlier when examining the three strategies that a company can pursue to capture first-mover advantages: go it alone, enter into a strategic alliance, or license its technology.

Key Terms

Takeaways for Strategic Managers

1. Technical standards are important in many high-tech industries. They guarantee compatibility, reduce confusion in the minds of customers, allow for mass production and lower costs, and reduce the risks associated with supplying complementary products.
2. Network effects and positive feedback loops often determine which standard will dominate a market.
3. Owning a standard can be a source of sustained competitive advantage.
4. Establishing a proprietary standard as the industry standard may require the company to win a format war against a competing and incompatible standard. Strategies for doing this include producing complementary products, leveraging killer applications, using aggressive pricing and marketing, licensing the technology, and cooperating with competitors.
5. Many high-tech products are characterized by high fixed costs of development but very low or zero marginal costs of producing one extra unit of output. These cost economics create a presumption in favor of strategies that emphasize aggressive pricing to increase volume and drive down average total costs.
6. It is very important for a first mover to develop a strategy to capitalize on first-mover advantages. A company can choose from three strategies: develop and market the technology itself, do so jointly with another company, or license the technology to existing companies. The choice depends on the complementary assets required to capture a first-mover advantage, the height of barriers to imitation, and the capability of competitors.
7. Technological paradigm shifts occur when new technologies emerge that revolutionize the structure of the industry, dramatically alter the nature of competition, and require companies to adopt new strategies in order to succeed.
8. Technological paradigm shifts are more likely to occur when progress in improving the established technology is slowing because of diminishing returns and when a new disruptive technology is taking root in a market niche.
9. Established companies can deal with paradigm shifts by investing in technology or setting up a stand-alone division to exploit technology.

Discussion Questions

1. What is different about high-tech industries? Were all industries once high-tech?
2. Why are standards so important in high-tech industries? What are the competitive implications of this?
3. You work for a small company that has the leading position in an embryonic market. Your boss believes that the company's future is ensured because it has a 60% share of the market, the lowest cost structure in the industry, and the most reliable and highest-valued product. Write a memo to your boss outlining why the assumptions posed might be incorrect.
4. You are working for a small company that has developed an electric scooter that is lower cost, lighter, and has longer battery range than most existing electric scooters on the market. What strategies might your company pursue to try to increase your company's success?
5. Reread the Strategy in Action 7.1 on Microsoft's "segment zero" threat. Do you think one operating system for smartphones or tablets will become dominant? If so, which one and why?

Closing Case

Tencent was founded in 1998 by Ma Huateng, Zhang Zhidong, Xu Chenye, Chen Yidan, and Zeng Liqing. Though the company was incorporated in the Cayman Islands, it was physically located in Shenzhen, China. Its first product was a messaging service called OICQ, released in 1999, and then renamed QQ after being threatened with a lawsuit by AOL who already had a messaging product called ICQ. Tencent grew rapidly by investing in a range of information technology and media products—most notably video games and e-commerce businesses. Between 2013 and 2018, Tencent bought stakes in 277 tech companies, making it one of the world's largest and most active technology investors.[25] It launched China's first online-only bank, WeBank, created a gaming platform called WeGame, offered a mobile payment system called WeChat Pay, operated a film production company and music streaming service, an internet browser, a search engine, and more. By mid-year 2022, it had a market capitalization of $375 billion, putting its valuation at just over one-fourth that of Amazon ($1.46 trillion) and significantly ahead of Alibaba Group ($251 billion).

One of Tencent's better-known products is WeChat, a multipurpose messaging, social media, and mobile payment application launched in 2011. It has grown to become one of the world's largest stand-alone mobile applications with over 1 billion monthly active users. WeChat is primarily used as a social networking site like Facebook or Instagram, but it also provides news, access to e-commerce sites, a portal for government agencies, a form of payment (WeChat Pay), and serves as an identity card. Unlike U.S.–based applications that tend to specialize in individual functions, WeChat has aggressively expanded the range of services it can bring to its large and growing installed base of users.[26] The program is used for everything from connecting with friends, to booking train tickets, ordering food, and applying for government services.

Though the application has close ties to the Chinese government and is known for being monitored and censored, privacy concerns have not prevented the application from becoming the most ubiquitously used smartphone program in China.[27] According to data from eMarketer, WeChat's penetration rate as of 2022 was a staggering 80% of all smartphone users in China and accounted for nearly 30% of smartphone users' mobile app usage. In fact, some analysts noted that for many in China, WeChat was their entire smartphone experience, and thus those consumers had no loyalty to any particular smartphone device or operating system so long as it had WeChat. As described by Ben Thompson:

> The fundamental issue is this: unlike the rest of the world, in China the most important layer of the smartphone stack is *not* the phone's operating system. Rather, it is WeChat... every aspect of a typical Chinese person's life, not just online but also off is conducted through a single app (and, to the extent other apps are used, they are often games promoted through WeChat).
>
> There is *nothing* in any other country that is comparable, particularly the Meta Platforms (Facebook) properties (Messenger, and WhatsApp) to which WeChat is commonly compared. All of those are about communication or wasting time: WeChat is that, but it is also for reading news, for hailing taxis, for paying for lunch (try and pay with cash for lunch, and you'll look like a luddite), for accessing government resources, for business. For all intents and purposes WeChat *is* your phone, and to a far greater extent in China than anywhere else, your phone is everything.[28]

Government barriers help to ensure that Tencent's biggest rivals are other Chinese firms like Alibaba and Baidu, but the big question is what will happen when WeChat starts to seriously target non-Chinese users. Though WeChat was estimated to have less than 100 million users outside of China by the end of 2022, analysts predicted that the firm could soon become a threat to Silicon Valley. First, the scale of the Chinese market meant that WeChat's dominance there gave it access to an impressive capital base that it could invest in R&D and promoting adoption outside of China. To get a sense of that scale, consider the competition in mobile payment systems: By mid-year 2022, Tencent's WeChat Pay and Alibaba's Alipay had over 900 million and 700 million active users, respectively. These numbers dwarfed the leading U.S.–based mobile payment systems, PayPal (with 392 million users) and Apple Pay (with just over 500 million users). According to David Chao, co-founder of DCM Ventures, "China is at least three or four years ahead on mobile payments," and, "That's igniting a whole new economy."[29]

Second, Tencent's scale and breadth also helped it to attract the best talent in fields such as software engineering and artificial intelligence (AI). In 2016, Tencent opened an AI lab with a vision to "Make AI Everywhere," and it began to invest heavily in developing machine learning, speech recognition, and natural language processing capabilities that would enable it to deploy AI applications across its businesses. The company also opened an AI lab in Bellevue, Washington (near Microsoft's home base of Redmond, Washington) so that it could tap the Seattle area talent.[30] As noted by Connie Chan, a general partner at the venture capital firm Andreessen Horowitz, "The market opportunity in China is so large, these companies can go toe-to-toe on salary with Google."[31]

WeChat's ubiquitous presence in people's lives also meant that Tencent was gathering massive amounts of data it could leverage in its machine-learning algorithms. Because of Tencent's capital, talent, and data many analysts in high-tech industries speculated that it was not just a question of *whether* Tencent would become a threat to stalwarts like Google and Amazon, but *when*.

Case Discussion Questions

1. What are some of the factors that led WeChat to attain an 80% market share in China? Do you think it could replicate that in other countries? If so, which ones?
2. Why do you think mobile payment systems are more ubiquitous in China than in Europe and the United States?
3. How does the dominance of WeChat and WePay in China help Tencent to become stronger in artificial intelligence?

Notes

[1]A. Kharpal, "Crypto Firms Say Thousands of Digital Currencies Will Collapse, Compare Market to Dot-com Days," *Davos*, June 3, 2022.

[2]C. Tardi, "Understanding the Different Types of Cryptocurrency," *SoFi Learn*, July 12, 2022.

[3]J. Schmidt, "Why Does Bitcoin Use So Much Energy?" *Forbes*, May 18, 2022.

[4]J. M. Utterback, *Mastering the Dynamics of Innovation* (Boston: Harvard Business School Press, 1994); C. Shapiro and H. R. Varian, *Information Rules: A Strategic Guide to the Network Economy* (Boston: Harvard Business School Press, 1999); M. A. Schilling, "Technology Success and Failure in Winner-take-all Markets: Testing a Model of Technological Lock Out,"

Academy of Management Journal 45 (2002): 387–398.

[5]The layout is not universal, although it is widespread. The French, for example, use a different layout.

[6]For details, see C. W. L. Hill, "Establishing a Standard: Competitive Strategy and Technology Standards in Winner Take All Industries," *Academy of Management Executive* 11 (1997): 7–25; Shapiro and Varian, *Information Rules;* B. Arthur, "Increasing Returns and the New World of Business," *Harvard Business Review,* July–August 1996, pp. 100–109; G. Gowrisankaran and J. Stavins, "Network Externalities and Technology Adoption: Lessons from Electronic Payments," *Rand Journal of Economics* 35 (2004): 260–277; V. Shankar and B. L. Bayus, "Network Effects and Competition: An Empirical Analysis of the Home Video Game Industry," *Strategic Management Journal* 24 (2003): 375–394; R. Casadesus-Masanell and P. Ghemawat, "Dynamic Mixed Duopoly: A Model Motivated by Linux vs Windows," *Management Science* 52 (2006): 1072–1085.

[7]See Shapiro and Varian, *Information Rules;* Hill, "Establishing a Standard"; M. A. Schilling, "Technological Lockout: An Integrative Model of the Economic and Strategic Factors Driving Technology Success and Failure," *Academy of Management Review* 23:2 (1998): 267–285.

[8]J. Reitveld, C. Bellavitus, and M. A. Schilling, "Relaunch and Reload: Platform Governance and the Creation and Capture of Value in Ecosystems," New York University Working Paper, 2015.

[9]Microsoft does not disclose the per-unit licensing fee that it receives from original equipment manufacturers, although media reports speculate that it is around $50 a copy.

[10]M. Herper, "The Truly Staggering Costs of Inventing New Drugs," *Forbes,* February 10, 2012; Pharmaceutical Industry 2008, *Standard & Poor's Industry Surveys;* J. A. DiMasi and H. G. Grabowski, "R&D Costs and Returns to New Drug Development: A Review of the Evidence," in P. M. Danzon and S. Nicholson (ed.), *The Oxford Handbook of the Economics of the Bio-pharmaceutical Industry* (Oxford, UK: Oxford University Press, 2012), chapter 2, pp. 21–46; Innovation.org, 2007; *Drug Discovery and Development: Understanding the R&D Process* (Washington, DC: PhRMA, February), www.phrma.org (accessed August 1, 2015).

[11]F. Richter, "2022. Streaming Drives Global Music Industry," *Statista,* April 8, 2022.

[12]Much of this section is based on C. W. L. Hill, M. Heeley, and J. Sakson, "Strategies for Profiting from Innovation," in *Advances in Global High Technology Management* (3rd ed.). (Greenwich, CT: JAI Press, 1993), pp. 79–95.

[13]M. Lieberman and D. Montgomery, "First Mover Advantages," *Strategic Management Journal* 9 (Special Issue, Summer 1988): 41–58.

[14]W. Boulding and M. Christen, "Sustainable Pioneering Advantage? Profit Implications of Market Entry Order?" *Marketing Science* 22 (2003): 371–386; C. Markides and P. Geroski, "Teaching Elephants to Dance and Other Silly Ideas," *Business Strategy Review* 13 (2003): 49–61.

[15]M. A. Schilling, "Towards Dynamic Efficiency: Innovation and Its Implications for Antitrust," *Antitrust Bulletin,* forthcoming.

[16]J. Borzo, "Aging Gracefully," *Wall Street Journal,* October 15, 2001, p. R22.

[17]The importance of complementary assets was first noted by D. J. Teece. See D. J. Teece, "Profiting from Technological Innovation," in D. J. Teece (ed.), *The Competitive Challenge* (New York: Harper & Row, 1986), pp. 26–54.

[18]M. J. Chen and D. C. Hambrick, "Speed, Stealth, and Selective Attack: How Small Firms Differ from Large Firms in Competitive Behavior," *Academy of Management Journal* 38 (1995): 453–482.

[19]E. Mansfield, M. Schwartz, and S. Wagner, "Imitation Costs and Patents: An Empirical Study," *Economic Journal* 91 (1981): 907–918.

[20]This argument has been made in the game theory literature. See R. Caves, H. Cookell, and P. J. Killing, "The Imperfect Market for Technology Licenses," *Oxford Bulletin of Economics and Statistics* 45 (1983): 249–267; N. T. Gallini, "Deterrence by Market Sharing: A Strategic Incentive for Licensing," *American Economic Review* 74 (1984): 931–941; C. Shapiro, "Patent Licensing and R&D Rivalry," *American Economic Review* 75 (1985): 25–30.

[21]M. Christensen, *The Innovator's Dilemma* (Boston: Harvard Business School Press, 1997); R. N. Foster, *Innovation: The Attacker's Advantage* (New York: Summit Books, 1986).

[22]Ray Kurzweil, *The Age of the Spiritual Machines: When Computers Exceed Human Intelligence* (New York: Penguin Books, 1999).

[23]See Christensen, *The Innovator's Dilemma;* C. M. Christensen and M. Overdorf, "Meeting the Challenge of Disruptive Change," *Harvard Business Review* (March–April 2000): pp. 66–77.

[24]C. W. L. Hill and F. T. Rothaermel, "The Performance of Incumbent Firms in the Face of Radical Technological Innovation," *Academy of Management Review* 28 (2003): 257–274; F. T. Rothaermel and Charles W. L. Hill, "Technological Discontinuities and Complementary Assets: A Longitudinal

Study of Industry and Firm Performance," *Organization Science* 16:1 (2005): 52–70.

[25]L. Lin and J. Steinberg, "How China's Tencent Uses Deals to Crowd Out Tech Rivals," *Wall Street Journal*, May 15, 2018.

[26]B. O'Keefe, "Why China Will Soon Challenge Silicon Valley," *Fortune*, July 18, 2018.

[27]L. Chen, "Why China's Tech-Savvy Millennials Are Quitting WeChat," *The Star Online*, July 23, 2018.

[28]B. Thompson, "Apple's China Problem," *Stratechery*, May 2017.

[29]O'Keefe "Why China Will Soon Challenge Silicon Valley," What's going to happen when China innovation goes around the world?

[30]B. Marr, "Artificial Intelligence in China: The Amazing Ways Tencent Is Driving Its Adoption," *Forbes*, June, 2018.

[31]O'Keefe, "Why China Will Soon Challenge Silicon Valley."

Strategy in the Global Environment

Opening Case

Emirates Global Strategy

Emirates is one of the world's largest airlines. As of January 2022, they provided service to more than 150 cities in 80 countries across the globe through a fleet of 270 aircraft. Emirates ranks fourth in the world by total scheduled passenger kilometers flown. The airline is also the second-largest cargo airline in the world behind Federal Express. Emirates was incorporated in 1985 in Dubai, the most populous city in the United Arab Emirates and the capital of the Emirate of Dubai. The airline, which is state owned, started its operations with just two aircraft.

If Emirates had followed the standard pattern on smaller start-up airlines, it perhaps would have established a number of short-haul routes, serving other locations in the Middle East. In fact, it pursued a radically different global strategy. Using Dubai as a hub, Emirates positioned itself as a long-haul, low-cost global carrier, with ambitions to connect the world through Dubai. Dubai's location on the Persian Gulf was strategically valuable because it was ideally positioned to connect the West and East. Still, it was an audacious strategy. Emirates' business model was focused purely on purchasing wide-bodied long-haul aircraft that would be able to link any two points on the globe through its 24-hour hub in Dubai. To support this strategy, Emirates emerged as the largest operator of Airbus' A380 superjumbo jets. Indeed, Emirates operates nearly half of all A380s ever delivered. The company also has the world's largest fleet of long-haul Boeing 777 aircraft.

This strategy has given Emirates a cost advantage that comes from several sources. First, if it can fill its fuel-efficient wide-bodied jets, the operating cost per passenger mile will be lower than for airlines that operate a mixed fleet of long-haul and short-haul jets, as do all other major airlines. Short-haul networks tend to be more expensive to operate, with higher costs per passenger mile. Second, as a relatively new airline, Emirates does not have the legacy costs associated with high labor costs, pension requirements, union work rules, and the like that burden many long-established airlines (to say nothing of the fact that unions are rare in Dubai). Third, the corporate tax rate in Dubai is zero, which is another source of cost advantage.

Despite its relatively low operating costs, it would be incorrect to think of Emirates as a low-cost airline in the mode of Southwest or Ryanair. Far from it, Emirates offers a full complement of first- and business-class seating, premium in-flight service, and lounges in airports for business and first-class travelers. In 2019, Emirates was 10th out of 80 global airlines ranked by AirHelp by on-time performance, service quality, and claim processing. Measured on service quality alone, Emirates was ranked number one in the world by AirHelp. The double advantage of being able to offer high-quality service at a low cost goes a long way to explaining Emirates' emergence as one

ZGPhotography/Shutterstock.com

Sources: AirHelp Score 2019, www.airhelp. com/en/airhelp-score/airlineranking; S. Nataraj and A. Al-Aali, "The Exceptional Performance Strategies of Emirate Airlines," *Journal of Global Competitiveness*, October 2011; Anonymous, "Emirates: The Long-Haul Low-Cost Carrier," *Aviation Strategy*, May 2005; "What's an A380 Worth?" *The Economist*, August 13, 2020; A. Cornwell, "Emirates Will Have to Review Strategy after Coronavirus Pandemic," *Reuters*, June 25, 2020.

of the world's major airlines. Its strong global brand helped to drive demand, which resulted in full aircraft and lower operating costs.

Another interesting aspect of its strategy concerns its partnership with the Dubai government to promote Dubai as a leisure destination for tourists, as well as for business and professional conventions. The city has many luxury hotels, restaurants, clubs, beaches, amusement parks, shopping malls, and so on, turning it into a destination, rather than just a hub. This strategy creates more demand and helps to fill incoming and outbound aircraft, which further lowers Emirates' operating costs.

Despite all its advantages, however, Emirates has been particularly hard hit by the sharp decline in airline travel resulting from the COVID-19 global pandemic. As airline travel slumped in 2020, Emirates could no longer fill its A380s and 777 aircraft, operating costs surged, and losses mounted. The company has canceled orders for additional A380s, and in anticipation of several years of depressed demand due to the pandemic, for the first time it is adding some smaller aircraft to its long-haul mix. To shore up demand, the airline is also looking to boost its strategy of bringing more travelers to Dubai for vacations and conventions, hoping this will help to fill its aircraft.

Overview

One striking development during the last five decades has been the globalization of markets. As a result of declining barriers to cross-border trade and investment, along with the rapid economic development of countries like Brazil, India, and China, segmented national markets have increasingly merged into much larger global markets. In this chapter, we discuss the implications of this phase shift in the global competitive environment for strategic management. We will also discuss recent countertrends that suggest something of a retreat from globalization may be underway.

The chapter begins with a discussion of ongoing changes in the global competitive environment. Next, it discusses the various ways in which global expansion can increase a company's profitability and profit growth. We then discuss the advantages and disadvantages of the different strategies companies can pursue to gain a competitive advantage in the global marketplace. This is followed by a discussion of two related strategic issues: (1) how managers decide which foreign markets to enter, when to enter them, and on what scale; and (2) what kind of vehicle or method a company should use to expand globally and enter a foreign country.

The overview of the strategy of Emirates presented in the Opening Case illustrates some of the issues we will touch on in this chapter. Over the last 30 years, Emirates has emerged as one of the world's largest airlines by pursuing a *global strategy*, efficiently connecting the world through its hub in Dubai. The fact that Emirates is now struggling with the impact of the COVID-19 pandemic on its revenues and costs does not invalidate its established strategy, but it does point to the need for strategic adaptation to respond to unanticipated changes in the macro environment.

8-1 Global and National Environments

8.1 Describe the process of globalization and how it impacts a company's strategy.

Fifty years ago, most national markets were isolated from one another by significant barriers to international trade and investment. In those days, managers could focus on analyzing only those national markets in which their company competed. They did not need to pay much attention to entry by global competitors, for there were few and entry was difficult. Nor did they need to pay much attention to entering foreign markets because that was often prohibitively expensive. Over the last half-century, much of this has changed. Barriers to international trade and investment have tumbled; huge global markets for goods and services have been created; and companies from different nations are entering each other's home markets on an unprecedented scale, increasing the intensity of competition. Rivalry can no longer be understood merely in terms of what happens within the boundaries of a nation; managers now need to consider how globalization is impacting the environment in which their company competes, and what strategies their company should adopt to exploit the unfolding opportunities and counter competitive threats. In this section, we look at the changes ushered in by falling barriers to international trade and investment, and we discuss a model for analyzing the competitive situation in different nations.

8-1a The Globalization of Production and Markets

The past half-century has seen a dramatic lowering of barriers to international trade and investment. For example, the average tariff rate on manufactured goods traded between advanced nations has fallen from around 40 to under 4%. For some goods, such as information technology, tariff rates have approached zero. Similarly, in nation after nation, regulations prohibiting foreign companies from entering domestic markets and establishing production facilities, or acquiring domestic companies, have been removed. As a result, there has been a surge in both the volume of international trade and the value of foreign direct investment (FDI). Indeed, the volume of world trade and foreign direct investment has been growing faster than the global economy for decades. Between 1960 and 2022, the value of the world economy (adjusted for inflation) increased nine times, while the value of international trade in merchandised goods increased more than 20 times. This underestimates the growth in trade, because trade in services has also been growing rapidly in recent decades. By 2021, the value of world trade in merchandised goods was $22.2 trillion, while the value of trade in services was $5.7 trillion. Although international trade slumped by as much as 20% in 2020 due to the COVID-19 pandemic, trade in goods bounced back strongly in 2021, hitting record levels.[1] As for foreign direct investment, between 1990 and 2021, the total flow of foreign direct investment from all countries increased from $250 billion to $1.85 trillion as companies invested in each other's markets (as with trade, there was a big slump in FDI in 2020 due to the COVID-19 pandemic, but investment flows bounced back in 2021).[2] These trends have led to the globalization of production and the globalization of markets.[3]

The globalization of production has been increasing as companies take advantage of lower barriers to international trade and investment to disperse important functions of their production processes around the globe. Doing so enables them to exploit national differences in the cost and quality of factors of production such as labor, energy, land, and capital, which allows companies to lower their cost structures and boost profits. For example, foreign companies build nearly 65% by value of Boeing's 787 commercial jet aircraft. Three Japanese companies build 35% of the 787, and another 20% is allocated to companies located in Italy, Singapore, and the United Kingdom.[4] Part of Boeing's rationale for outsourcing so much production to foreign suppliers is that these suppliers are the best in the world at performing their activity. Therefore, the result of having foreign suppliers build specific parts is a better final product and higher profitability for Boeing. Apple has had a similar experience. Strategy in Action 8.1 describes how it has configured its global supply chain in order to gain a competitive advantage in the smartphone business.

As for the globalization of markets, it has been argued that the world's economic system is moving from one in which national markets are distinct entities, isolated from each other by trade barriers and barriers of distance, time, and culture, toward a system in which national markets are merging into one huge, global marketplace. Increasingly, customers around the world demand and use the same basic product offerings. Consequently, in many industries, it is no longer meaningful to talk about the German market, the U.S. market, or the Chinese market; there is only the global market. The global acceptance of Coca-Cola, Citigroup credit cards, Starbucks, McDonald's hamburgers, Samsung and Apple smartphones, IKEA furniture, and Microsoft's Windows operating system are examples of this trend.[5]

The trend toward the globalization of production and markets has several important implications for competition within an industry. First, industry boundaries do not stop at national borders. Because many industries are becoming global in scope, competitors and potential future competitors exist not only in a company's home market but also in international markets. Managers who analyze only their home market can be caught unprepared by the entry of efficient foreign competitors. The globalization of markets and production implies that companies around the globe are finding their home markets under attack from foreign competitors. For example, in Japan, American financial institutions such as J.P. Morgan have been making inroads against Japanese financial service institutions. In the United States, South Korea's Samsung has been battling Apple for a share of the smartphone market. In the European Union (EU), the once-dominant Dutch company Philips has seen its market share in the customer electronics industry diminished by Japan's Panasonic and Sony, and Samsung of South Korea.

Making the Apple iPhone

In its early days, Apple usually didn't look beyond its own backyard to manufacture its devices. A few years after Apple started to make the Macintosh computer back in 1983, Steve Jobs bragged that it was "a machine that was made in America." As late as the early 2000s, Apple still manufactured many of its computers at the company's iMac plant in Elk Grove, California. Jobs often said that he was as proud of Apple's manufacturing plants as he was of its devices.

By 2004, however, Apple had largely turned to foreign manufacturing. The shift to offshore manufacturing reached its peak with the iconic iPhone, which Apple first introduced in 2007. All iPhones contain hundreds of parts, an estimated 90% of which are manufactured abroad. Advanced semiconductors come from Germany and Taiwan, memory from Korea and Japan, display panels and circuitry from Korea and Taiwan, chip sets from Europe, and rare metals from Africa and Asia. Apple's major subcontractor, the Taiwanese multinational firm Foxconn, performs final assembly in China.

Apple still employs some 80,000 people in the United States, and it has kept important activities at home, including product design, software engineering, and marketing. Furthermore, Apple claims that its business supports another 450,000 jobs at suppliers in the United States. For example, the glass for the iPhone is manufactured at Corning's U.S. plants in Kentucky and New York. An additional 1.2 million people are involved in the engineering, building, and final assembly of its products *outside* of the United States, and most of them work at subcontractors like Foxconn.

When explaining its decision to assemble the iPhone in China, Apple cites a number of factors. While it is true that labor costs are much lower in China, Apple executives point out that labor costs only account for a very small proportion of the total value of its products and are not the main driver of location decisions. Far more important, according to Apple, is the ability of its Chinese subcontractors to respond very quickly to requests from Apple to scale production up and down. In a famous illustration of this capability back in 2007, Steve Jobs demanded that a glass screen replace the plastic screen on his prototype iPhone. Jobs didn't like the look and feel of plastic screens, which at the time were standard in the industry, nor did he like the way they scratched easily. This last-minute change in the design of the iPhone put Apple's market introduction date at risk. Apple had selected Corning to manufacture large panes of strengthened glass, but finding a manufacturer that could cut those panes into millions of iPhone screens wasn't easy. Then a bid arrived from a Chinese factory. When the Apple team visited the factory, they found that the plant's owners were already constructing a new wing and installing equipment to cut the glass. "This is in case you give us the contract," the manager said. The plant also had a warehouse full of glass samples for Apple, and a team of engineers available to work with Apple. They had built on-site dormitories so that the factory could run three shifts 7 days a week in order to meet Apple's demanding production schedule. The Chinese company won the bid.

Another critical advantage of China for Apple was that it was much easier to hire engineers there. Apple calculated that about 8,700 industrial engineers were needed to oversee and guide the 200,000 assembly-line workers involved in manufacturing the iPhone. The company had estimated that it would take as long as 9 months to find that many engineers in the United States. In China, it took 15 days. Also important is the clustering together of factories in China. Many of the factories providing components for the iPhone are located close to Foxconn's assembly plant. As one executive noted, "The entire supply chain is in China. You need a thousand rubber gaskets? That's the factory next door. You need a million screws? That factory is a block away. You need a screw made a little bit different? That will take 3 hours."

However, there are drawbacks to outsourcing to China. Several of Apple's subcontractors have been targeted for their poor working conditions. Criticisms include low pay of line workers, long hours, mandatory overtime for little or no additional pay, and poor safety records. Some former Apple executives say there is an unresolved tension within the company: Executives want to improve working conditions within the factories of subcontractors, such as Foxconn, but that dedication falters when it conflicts with crucial supplier relationships or the fast delivery of new products. Furthermore, Apple's outsourcing decisions have been criticized by former President Trump, who argues that the company is guilty of moving U.S. jobs overseas. While Apple disagrees with this assessment, it has responded by increasing its investment in U.S. facilities. In 2018, for example, the company announced it would invest $30 billion over 5 years to create 20,000 new Apple jobs in the United States. Most of these jobs, however, are expected to be in software development and data center operations, not manufacturing and assembly. Finally, in late 2019, a new risk associated with a globally dispersed supply chain emerged when a highly infectious novel coronavirus, COVID-19, emerged in China, forcing a temporary shutdown of many suppliers, limiting production of the iPhone in China and threatening to depress the company's global revenues and profits.

Sources: "Where Is the iPhone Made?" *Lifewire*, July 14, 2018; D. Barboza, "How China Built iPhone City with Billions in Perks for Apple's Partner," *New York Times*, December 29, 2016; G. Huini, "Human Costs Are Built into iPad in China," *New York Times*, January 26, 2012; C. Jones, "Apple's $350 Billion US Contribution Was Already in the Cards," *Forbes*, January 19, 2018.

Second, the shift from national to global markets has intensified competitive rivalry in many industries. National markets that once were consolidated oligopolies dominated by three or four companies and subjected to relatively little foreign competition, have been transformed into segments of fragmented, global industries in which many companies battle each other for market share in many countries. This rivalry has threatened to drive down profitability and made it more critical for companies to maximize their efficiency, quality, customer responsiveness, and innovative ability. The painful restructuring and downsizing that has been occurring at companies such as the once-dominant photographic company Kodak is as much a response to the increased intensity of global competition as it is to any other factor. However, not all global industries are fragmented. Many remain consolidated oligopolies, except that now they are consolidated, global (rather than national) oligopolies. In the videogame industry, for example, three companies are battling for global dominance: Microsoft from the United States and Nintendo and Sony from Japan. In the market for smartphones, Apple is in a global battle with Samsung from South Korea and Huawei Technologies from China.

Finally, although globalization has increased both the threat of entry and the intensity of rivalry within many formerly protected national markets, it has also created enormous opportunities for companies based in those markets. The steady decline in barriers to cross-border trade and investment has opened many once-protected national markets to companies based outside these nations. Thus, for example, Western European, Japanese, and U.S. companies have accelerated their investment in the nations of Eastern Europe, Latin America, and Southeast Asia as they try to take advantage of growth opportunities in those areas.

8-2 Countertrends to Globalization

8.2 Summarize different countertrends to globalization.

Despite the half-century shift towards greater globalization, it should be noted that, since 2016, there have been some notable countertrends to the march toward globalization. First, in June 2016, the United Kingdom voted to exit from the EU, the world's largest and in many ways most successful trading block. The EU has removed barriers to cross-border trade and investment between its 28 member countries, and it has been strongly in support of lowering those barriers globally. The so-called "Brexit" seems to signify a shift away from what has been a consensus that greater globalization is a good thing. Britain's exit from the EU was finalized in 2020, and since then the United Kingdom has been struggling to adjust to a different trading environment.

Then, in November 2016, Donald Trump—who articulated explicitly protectionist views—was elected to the presidency of the United States. After assuming office, Trump withdrew the United States from the proposed Transpacific Partnership, which would have lowered tariff barriers between 12 Pacific Rim nations (excluding China), renegotiated the North American Free Trade Agreement (NAFTA) between Canada, Mexico, and the United States (replacing it with the United States-Mexico-Canada Agreement that went into effect in 2020), raised tariffs on imports of solar panels, washing machines, steel, and aluminum into the United States, and imposed tariffs of 25% on a wide range of imports from China. China, it should be noted, responded in kind, raising tariffs on a wide range of U.S. imports into China. Similarly, many other countries impacted by the tariffs on steel and aluminum imports into the United States imposed retaliatory tariffs on American exports to their markets. This was a striking development. Since the end of World War II, America has been a leader on the international stage pushing for lower barriers to cross-border trade and investment, but under Trump's leadership it seemed to be taking the opposite tack. The election of Joe Biden to the presidency in 2021 does not appear to have resulted in a fundamental shift back to the post-Trump era. As of mid-2022, the tariffs on China were still in place, although the Biden administration had reduced some of the tariffs placed on imports of steel and aluminum from the EU.

To further complicate matters, we are witnessing something of a geopolitical realignment that may constrain globalization going forward. Russia's invasion of Ukraine in February 2022 has, at a minimum, recast relationships between that country and the West. Russia, once seen as a partner in the global economy and a vibrant emerging market offering a host of opportunities for international businesses, is now effectively closed off from much of the rest of the world by prohibitive sanctions. Many Western businesses have exited that country entirely, writing off billions in investments. The Russian economy itself is set to shrink significantly due to these sanctions. Unless there is a significant change in regime in Russia, history suggests that this situation could persist for some time.

Finally, under the leadership of Xi Jinping, China has also slipped back into greater authoritarianism and state control of economic activity, which could have a potentially chilling effect on private enterprise in that nation. This would jeopardize China's position as a major source of global production and exports, and a major market opportunity for international businesses. There is also a risk that an authoritarian China will take aggressive action to bring Taiwan, once a Chinese province, back under its control. If that happens, it seems highly probably that the West will respond with significant economic sanctions (as they did with Russia's invasion of Ukraine), which would result in a major disruption of trade and investment flows.

Although these policy shifts and geopolitical developments are still unfolding at the time of writing, there is no doubt that if this countertrend continues it will significantly alter the environment within which international businesses have been operating for the last quarter-century, and it may require many enterprises to make major shifts in their global strategy.

8.3 Describe the components of a national competitive advantage.

8-3 National Competitive Advantage

Despite the globalization of production and markets, many of the most successful companies in certain industries are still clustered in a small number of countries. For example, many of the world's most successful biotechnology and computer companies are based in the United States, and many of the most successful consumer electronics companies are based in Japan, Taiwan, South Korea, and China. Germany is the base for many successful chemical and engineering companies. These facts suggest that the nation-state within which a company is based may have an important bearing on the competitive position of that company in the global marketplace.

In a study of national competitive advantage, Michael Porter identified four attributes of a national or country-specific environment that have an important impact on the global competitiveness of companies located within that nation:[6]

- *Factor endowments*: A nation's position in factors of production such as skilled labor or the infrastructure necessary to compete in each industry
- *Local demand conditions*: The nature of home demand for the industry's product or service
- *Related and supporting industries*: The presence or absence in a nation of supplier industries and related industries that are internationally competitive
- *Firm strategy, structure, and rivalry*: The conditions in the nation governing how companies are created, organized, and managed, and the nature of domestic rivalry

Porter speaks of these four attributes as constituting the "diamond," arguing that companies from a given nation are most likely to succeed in industries or strategic groups in which the four attributes are favorable (see Figure 8.1). He also argues that the diamond's attributes form a mutually reinforcing system in which the effect of one attribute is dependent on the state of others.

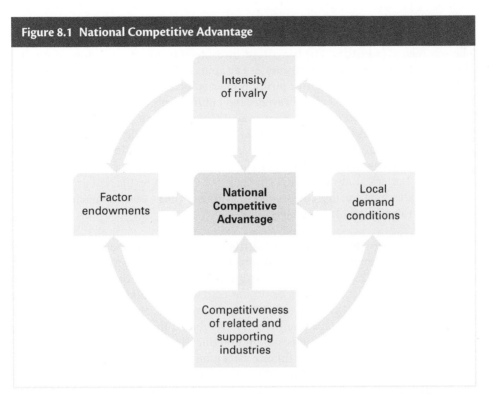

Figure 8.1 National Competitive Advantage

Intensity
of rivalry

Factor
endowments

**National
Competitive
Advantage**

Local
demand
conditions

Competitiveness
of related and
supporting
industries

Source: Adapted from M. E. Porter, "The Competitive Advantage of Nations," *Harvard Business Review*, March–April 1990, p. 77.

Factor Endowments   Factor endowments—the cost and quality of factors of production—are a prime determinant of the competitive advantage that certain countries might have in certain industries. Factors of production include basic factors such as land, labor, capital, and raw materials, and advanced factors such as technological know-how, managerial sophistication, and physical infrastructure (roads, railways, and ports). The competitive advantage that the United States enjoys in biotechnology might be explained by the presence of certain advanced factors of production—for example, technological know-how—in combination with some basic factors, such as a pool of relatively low-cost venture capital that can be used to fund risky start-ups in industries such as biotechnology.

Local Demand Conditions   Home demand plays an important role in providing the impetus for "upgrading" competitive advantage. Companies are typically most sensitive to the needs of their closest customers. Thus, the characteristics of home demand are particularly important in shaping the attributes of domestically made products and creating pressures for innovation and quality. A nation's companies gain competitive advantage if their domestic customers are sophisticated and demanding, and if they pressure local companies to meet high standards of product quality and produce innovative products. Japan's sophisticated, knowledgeable buyers of cameras helped stimulate the Japanese camera industry to improve product quality and introduce innovative models. A similar example can be found in the cellphone equipment industry, where sophisticated, demanding local customers in Scandinavia helped push Nokia of Finland and Ericsson of Sweden to invest in cellular phone technology long before demand for cellular phones increased in other developed nations. As a result, Nokia, and Ericsson, together with Motorola, became significant players in the global cellular telephone equipment industry.

Competitiveness of Related and Supporting Industries   The third broad attribute of national advantage in an industry is the presence of internationally competitive suppliers or related industries. The benefits of investment in advanced factors of production by related and supporting businesses can spill over into a given industry and help it to achieve a strong competitive position internationally. Swedish strength in fabricated steel products such as ball bearings and cutting tools has drawn on strengths in Sweden's specialty-steel industry. Switzerland's success in pharmaceuticals is closely related to its previous international success in the technologically related dye industry. One consequence of this process is that successful industries within a country tend to be grouped into clusters of related industries. Indeed, this is one of the most pervasive findings of Porter's study. One such cluster is the German textile and apparel sector, which includes high-quality cotton, wool, synthetic fibers, sewing-machine needles, and a wide range of textile machinery.

Intensity of Rivalry   The fourth broad attribute of national competitive advantage in Porter's model is the intensity of rivalry of firms within a nation. Porter makes two important points. First, different nations are characterized by different management ideologies, which either help them or do not help them to build national competitive advantage. For example, Porter noted the predominance of engineers in top management at German and Japanese firms. He attributed this to these firms' emphasis on improving manufacturing processes and product design. In contrast, Porter noted a predominance of people with finance backgrounds leading many U.S. firms. He linked this to U.S. firms' lack of attention to improving manufacturing processes and product design. He argued that the dominance of finance led to an overemphasis on maximizing short-term financial returns. According to Porter, one consequence of these different management ideologies was a relative loss of U.S. competitiveness in those engineering-based industries where manufacturing processes and product design issues are all-important (such as the automobile industry).

Porter's second point is that there is a strong association between vigorous domestic rivalry and the creation and persistence of competitive advantage in an industry. Rivalry compels companies to look for ways to improve efficiency, which makes them better international competitors. Domestic rivalry creates pressures to innovate, improve quality, reduce costs, and invest in upgrading advanced factors. All of this helps to create world-class competitors.

Using the Framework   The framework just described can help managers identify where their most significant global competitors are likely to originate. For example, a cluster of computer service and software companies in Bangalore, India, includes two of the largest information technology companies in the world, Infosys and Wipro. These companies have emerged as aggressive competitors in the global market. Both companies have offices in the EU and United States so they can better compete against Western rivals such as IBM and Hewlett Packard, and both are gaining share in the global marketplace.

The framework can also be used to help managers decide where they might want to locate certain productive activities. Seeking to take advantage of U.S. expertise in biotechnology, many foreign companies have set up research facilities in San Diego, Boston, and Seattle, where U.S. biotechnology companies tend to cluster. Similarly, to take advantage of Japanese success in consumer electronics, many U.S. electronics companies have set up research and production facilities in Japan, often in conjunction with Japanese partners.

Finally, the framework can help a company assess how tough it might be to enter certain national markets. If a nation has a competitive advantage in certain industries, it might be challenging for foreigners to enter those industries. For example, the highly competitive retailing industry in the United States has proved to be a very difficult industry for foreign companies to enter. Successful foreign retailers such as Britain's Tesco have found it tough going into the United States because the U.S. retailing industry is the most competitive in the world.

8-4 Motives for Global Expansion

8.4 Discuss the motives for expanding internationally.

Expanding globally allows firms to increase their profitability and rate of profit growth in ways not available to purely domestic enterprises.[7] Firms that operate internationally are able to:

1. Expand the market for their domestic product offerings by selling those products in international markets.
2. Realize location economies by dispersing individual value creation activities to those locations around the globe where they can be performed most efficiently and effectively.
3. Realize greater cost economies from experience effects by serving an expanded global market from a central location, thereby reducing the costs of value creation.
4. Earn a greater return by leveraging valuable skills developed in foreign operations and transferring them to other entities within the firm's global network of operations.

As we will see, however, a firm's ability to increase its profitability and profit growth by pursuing these strategies is constrained by the need to customize its product offering, marketing strategy, and business strategy to differing national or regional conditions—that is, by the imperative of localization.

8-4a Expanding the Market: Leveraging Products

A company can increase its growth rate by taking goods or services developed at home and selling them internationally; almost all multinationals started out doing this. Procter & Gamble (P&G), for example, developed most of its bestselling products at home and then sold them around the world. Similarly, from its earliest days, Microsoft has focused on selling its software worldwide. Automobile companies such as Ford, Volkswagen, and Toyota Motor Corporation also grew by developing products at home and then selling them in international markets. The returns from such a strategy are likely to be greater if indigenous competitors in the nations a company enters lack comparable products. Thus, Toyota has grown its profits by entering the large automobile markets of North America and Europe and offering products differentiated from those offered by local rivals (Ford and GM) by superior quality and reliability.

The success of many **multinational companies** that expand in this manner is based not just on the goods or services that they sell in foreign nations, but also upon the distinctive competencies (i.e., unique resources) that underlie the production and marketing of those goods or services. Thus, Toyota's success is based on its distinctive competency in manufacturing automobiles. International expansion can be seen as a way for Toyota to generate greater returns from this competency. Similarly, P&G's global success was based on more than its portfolio of consumer products; it was also based on the company's competencies in mass marketing consumer goods. P&G grew rapidly in international markets between 1950 and 1990 because it was one of the most skilled mass-marketing enterprises in the world and could "out-market" indigenous competitors in the nations it entered. Global expansion was, therefore, a way of generating higher returns from its valuable, rare, and inimitable resources in marketing.

multinational companies
Companies that do business in two or more national markets.

The same can be said of companies engaged in the service sectors of an economy, such as financial institutions, retailers, restaurant chains, and hotels. Expanding the market for their services often means replicating their business model in foreign nations (albeit with some changes to account for local differences, which we will discuss in more detail shortly). Starbucks, for example, has expanded globally by taking the basic business model it developed in the United States and using that as a blueprint for establishing international operations.

8-4b Realizing Cost Economies from Global Volume

In addition to growing profits more rapidly, a company can realize cost savings from economies of scale, thereby boosting profitability, by expanding its sales volume through international expansion. Such scale economies come from several sources. First, by spreading the fixed costs associated with developing a product and setting up production facilities over its global sales volume, a company can lower its average unit cost. Thus, Microsoft garnered significant scale economies by spreading the $5- to $10-billion cost of developing Windows 10 over global demand.

Second, by serving a global market, a company can potentially utilize its production facilities more intensively, which leads to higher productivity, lower costs, and greater profitability. For example, if Intel sold microprocessors solely in the United States, it might be able to keep its factories open only for one shift, 5 days a week. But by serving a global market from the same factories, it might be able to utilize those assets for two shifts, 7 days a week. In other words, the capital invested in those factories is used more intensively if Intel sells to a global—as opposed to a national—market, which translates into higher capital productivity and a higher return on invested capital.

Third, as global sales increase the size of the enterprise, its bargaining power with suppliers increases, which may allow it to bargain down the cost of key inputs and boost profitability that way. For example, Walmart uses its enormous sales volume as a lever to bargain down the price it pays to suppliers for merchandise sold through its stores.

In addition to the cost savings that come from economies of scale, companies that sell to a global rather than a local marketplace may be able to realize further cost savings from learning effects. We first discussed learning effects in Chapter 5, where we noted that employee productivity increases with cumulative increases in output over time. (For example, it costs considerably less to build the 100th aircraft from a Boeing assembly line than the 10th, because employees learn how to perform their tasks more efficiently over time.) Selling to a global market may enable a company to increase its sales volume more rapidly—and thus increase the cumulative output from its plants—which in turn should result in accelerated learning, higher employee productivity, and a cost advantage over competitors that are growing more slowly because they lack international markets.

8-4c Realizing Location Economies

Earlier in this chapter, we discussed how countries differ along several dimensions, including differences in the cost and quality of factors of production. These differences imply that some locations are more suited than others for producing certain goods and services.[8] **Location economies** are the economic benefits that arise from performing a value creation activity in the optimal location for that activity, wherever in the world that might be (transportation costs and trade barriers permitting). Thus, if the best designers for a product live in France, a firm should base its design operations in France. If the most productive labor force for assembly operations is in Mexico, assembly operations should be based in Mexico. If the best marketers are in the United States, the marketing strategy should be formulated in the United States—and

location economies

The economic benefits that arise from performing a value creation activity in an optimal location.

so on. Apple, for example, designs the iPhone and develops the associated software in California, but undertakes final assembly in China precisely because the company believes that these are the best locations in the world for carrying out these different value creation activities.

Locating a value creation activity in the optimal location for that activity can have one of two effects: (1) it can lower the costs of value creation, helping the company achieve a low-cost position; or (2) it can enable a company to differentiate its product offering, which gives it the option of charging a premium price or keeping prices low and using differentiation as a means of increasing sales volume. Thus, efforts to realize location economies are consistent with the business-level strategies of low cost and differentiation.

In theory, a company that realizes location economies by dispersing each of its value creation activities to the optimal location for that activity should have a competitive advantage over a company that bases all of its value creation activities at a single location. It should be able to better differentiate its product offering and lower its cost structure more than its single-location competitor. In a world where competitive pressures are increasing, such a strategy may well become an imperative for survival.

Introducing transportation costs and trade barriers can complicate the process of realizing location economies. New Zealand might have a comparative advantage for low-cost auto-assembly operations, but high transportation costs make it an uneconomical location from which to serve global markets. Factoring transportation costs and trade barriers into the cost equation helps explain why some U.S. companies have shifted production from Asia to Mexico. Mexico has three distinct advantages over many Asian countries as a location for value creation activities: Mexico's low labor costs and its proximity to the large U.S. market reduces transportation costs. Also, the United States-Mexico-Canada Agreement (USMCA), which is the successor to the North American Free Trade Agreement (NAFTA), has removed many trade barriers between Mexico, the United States, and Canada, increasing Mexico's appeal as a production site for the North American market. Thus, although the relative costs of value creation are important, transportation costs and trade barriers also must be considered in location decisions.

8-4d Leveraging the Competencies of Global Subsidiaries

You will recall from Chapter 3 that competitive advantage is based upon valuable, rare, and inimitable resources, in particular process knowledge, intellectual property, and organizational architecture. Initially, many multinational companies develop the valuable resources and competencies that underpin their competitive advantage in their home nation and then expand internationally, primarily by selling products and services based on those competencies. However, for more mature multinational enterprises that have already established a network of subsidiary operations in foreign markets, the development of valuable resources and competencies can just as well occur in foreign subsidiaries.[9] Competencies can be created anywhere within a multinational's global network of operations, wherever people have the opportunity and incentive to try new ways of doing things. The creation of resources and competencies—such as unique process knowledge that helps to lower the costs of production or enhance perceived value and support higher product pricing—is not the monopoly of the corporate center.

Leveraging the valuable resources created within subsidiaries and applying them to other operations within the firm's global network may create value. For example, McDonald's is increasingly finding that its foreign franchisees are a source of valuable new ideas. Faced with slow growth in France, its local franchisees have begun to experiment with the menu, as well as the layout and theme of restaurants. Gone are the ubiquitous golden arches; gone too are many of the utilitarian chairs and tables and other plastic features of the fast-food giant. Many McDonald's restaurants in France now have hardwood floors, exposed brick walls, and even armchairs. Half of the outlets in France have been upgraded to a level that would make them unrecognizable to an American. The menu, too, has been changed to include premier sandwiches, such as chicken on focaccia bread, priced some 30% higher than the average hamburger. In France, this strategy seems to be working. Following these changes, increases in same-store sales rose from 1% annually to 3.4%. Impressed with the impact, McDonald's executives implemented similar changes at other restaurants in markets where same-store sales growth was sluggish, including the United States.[10]

For the managers of a multinational enterprise, this phenomenon creates important new challenges. First, managers must have the humility to recognize that valuable resources can arise anywhere within the firm's global network, not just at the corporate center. Second, they must establish an incentive system that encourages local employees to acquire and build new resources and competencies. This is not easy: Creating new competencies involves a degree of risk, and not all new skills add value. For every valuable idea created by a McDonald's subsidiary in a foreign country, there may be several failures. The management of the multinational must install incentives that encourage employees to take necessary risks and reward them for successes, and not sanction them for taking risks that did not pan out. Third, managers must have a process for identifying when valuable new resources and competencies have been created in a subsidiary. Finally, they need to act as facilitators, helping to transfer valuable resources and competencies within the firm.

8-5 Strategies for Competing in the Global Marketplace

Companies that compete in the global marketplace typically face two types of competitive pressures: *pressures for cost reductions* and *pressures to be locally responsive* (see Figure 8.2).[11] These competitive pressures place conflicting demands on a company.

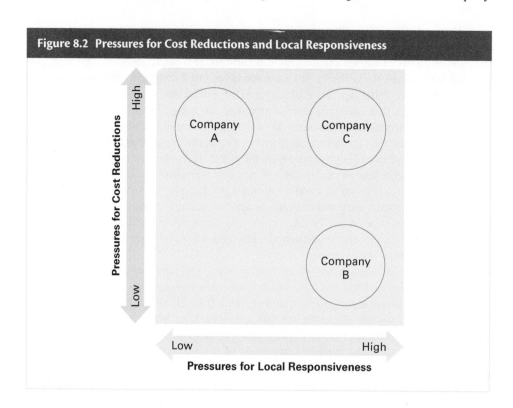

Figure 8.2 Pressures for Cost Reductions and Local Responsiveness

Responding to pressures for cost reductions requires that a company attempt to minimize its unit costs. To attain this goal, it may have to base its productive activities at the most favorable low-cost location. It may also need to offer a standardized product to the global marketplace to realize the cost savings that come from economies of scale and learning effects. On the other hand, responding to pressures to be locally responsive requires that a company differentiate its product offering and marketing strategy from country to country to accommodate the diverse demands arising from national differences in consumer tastes and preferences, business practices, distribution channels, competitive conditions, and government policies. Because differentiation across countries can involve significant duplication and a lack of product standardization, it may raise costs.

Whereas some companies, such as Company A in Figure 8.2, face high pressures for cost reductions and low pressures for local responsiveness, and others, such as Company B, face low pressures for cost reductions and high pressures for local responsiveness, many companies are in the position of Company C. They face high pressures for both cost reductions and local responsiveness. Dealing with these conflicting and contradictory pressures is a difficult strategic challenge, primarily because local responsiveness tends to raise costs.

8-5a Pressures for Cost Reductions

In competitive global markets, international businesses often face pressures for cost reductions. To respond to these pressures, a firm must try to lower the costs of value creation. A manufacturer, for example, might mass-produce a standardized product at an optimal site to realize economies of scale and location economies. Alternatively, it might outsource certain functions to low-cost foreign suppliers to reduce costs. Thus, many computer companies have outsourced their telephone-based customer-service functions to India, where qualified technicians who speak English can be hired for a lower wage rate than in the United States. In the same vein, Walmart pushes its suppliers (which are manufacturers) to also lower their prices. In fact, the pressure that Walmart has placed on its suppliers to reduce prices has been cited as a major cause of the trend among North American manufacturers to shift production to China.[12] A service business such as a bank might move back-office functions such as information processing to developing nations where wage rates are lower.

Cost-reduction pressures can be particularly intense in industries producing commodity-type products where meaningful differentiation on non-price factors is difficult and price is the main competitive weapon. This tends to be the case for products that serve universal needs. Universal needs exist when the tastes and preferences of consumers in different nations are similar, if not identical, such as for bulk chemicals, petroleum, steel, sugar, and similar products. Pressures for cost reductions also exist for many industrial and consumer products—for example, semiconductor chips, personal computers, Android smart phones, and liquid crystal display screens. Pressures for cost reductions are also intense in industries where major competitors are based in low-cost locations, where there is persistent excess capacity, and where consumers are powerful and face low switching costs. Many commentators have argued that the liberalization of the world trade and investment environment in recent decades, by facilitating greater international competition, has generally increased cost pressures.[13]

8-5b Pressures for Local Responsiveness

Pressures for local responsiveness arise from differences in consumer tastes and preferences, infrastructure and traditional practices, distribution channels, and host government demands. Responding to pressures to be locally responsive requires that a company differentiate its products and marketing strategy from country to country to accommodate these factors, all of which tend to raise a company's cost structure.

Differences in Customer Tastes and Preferences   Strong pressures for local responsiveness emerge when customer tastes and preferences differ significantly between countries, as they may for historic or cultural reasons. In such cases, a multinational company's products and marketing message must be customized to appeal to the tastes and preferences of local customers. The company is then typically pressured to delegate its production and marketing responsibilities and functions to overseas subsidiaries.

For example, the automobile industry in the 1980s and early 1990s moved toward the creation of "world cars." The idea was that global companies such as General Motors, Ford, and Toyota would be able to sell the same basic vehicle globally, sourcing it from centralized production locations. If successful, the strategy would have enabled automobile companies to reap significant gains from global-scale economies. However, this strategy frequently ran aground upon the hard rocks of consumer reality. Consumers in different automobile markets have historically had different tastes and preferences, and these require different types of vehicles. North American consumers show a strong demand for pickup trucks. This is particularly true in the South and West, where many families have a pickup truck as a second or third vehicle. But in European countries, pickup trucks are seen purely as utility vehicles and are purchased primarily by firms rather than individuals. Consequently, the product mix and marketing message need to be tailored to take into account the different nature of demand in North America and Europe.

Some commentators have argued that customer demands for local customization are on the decline worldwide.[14] According to this argument, modern communications and transport technologies have created the conditions for a convergence of the tastes and preferences of customers from different nations. The result is the emergence of enormous global markets for standardized consumer products. The worldwide acceptance of McDonald's hamburgers, Coca-Cola, Zara clothes, and the Apple iPhone, all of which are sold globally as standardized products, is often cited as evidence of the increasing homogeneity of the global marketplace.

However, this argument may not hold in many consumer-goods markets. Significant differences in consumer tastes and preferences still exist across nations and cultures. Managers in international businesses do not yet have the luxury of being able to ignore these differences, and they may not for a long time to come.

Differences in Infrastructure and Traditional Practices   Pressures for local responsiveness also arise from differences in infrastructure or traditional practices among countries, creating a need to customize products accordingly. To meet this need, companies may have to delegate manufacturing and production functions to foreign subsidiaries. For example, in North America, consumer electrical systems are based on 110 volts, whereas in some European countries 240-volt systems are standard. Thus, domestic electrical appliances must be customized to take this difference in infrastructure into account. Traditional social practices also often vary across nations. In Britain, people drive on the left-hand side of the road, creating a demand for right-hand-drive cars, whereas in France and the rest of Europe, people drive on the right-hand side of the road (and therefore want left-hand-drive cars).

Differences in Distribution Channels   A company's marketing strategies may have to be responsive to differences in distribution channels among countries, which may necessitate delegating marketing functions to national subsidiaries. In the pharmaceutical industry, for example, the British and Japanese distribution system is radically different from the U.S. system. British and Japanese doctors will not accept or respond favorably to a U.S.-style, high-pressure sales force. Thus, pharmaceutical companies must adopt different marketing practices in Britain and Japan compared with the United States—soft sell versus hard sell.

Similarly, Poland, Brazil, and Russia are all considered emerging markets, but there are big differences in distribution systems across the three countries. For example, supermarkets account for a higher percentage of food sales in Brazil than either Poland or Russia.[15] These differences in channels require that companies adapt their own distribution and sales strategies.

Host Government Demands Finally, economic and political demands imposed by host country governments may require local responsiveness. For example, pharmaceutical companies are subject to local clinical testing, registration procedures, and pricing restrictions, all of which make it necessary that the manufacturing and marketing of a drug meet local requirements. Moreover, because governments and government agencies control a significant portion of the healthcare budget in most countries, they are in a powerful position to demand a high level of local responsiveness. More generally, threats of protectionism, economic nationalism, and local content rules (which require that a certain percentage of a product be manufactured locally) can dictate that international businesses manufacture locally.

The Rise of Regionalism Typically, we think of pressures for local responsiveness as deriving from *national* differences in tastes and preferences, infrastructure, and the like. While this is still often the case, there is also a tendency toward the convergence of tastes, preferences, infrastructure, distribution channels, and host government demands within a broader *region* that is composed of two or more nations.[16] We sometimes see this when there are strong pressures for convergence due to, for example, a shared history and culture, or the establishment of a trading block in a deliberate attempt to harmonize trade policies, infrastructure, regulations, and the like.

The most obvious example of a region is the EU, and particularly the eurozone countries within that trade block, where institutional forces are pushing toward convergence. The creation of a single EU market, with a single currency, common business regulations, standard infrastructure, and so on, cannot help but result in the reduction of certain national differences between countries within the EU, and the creation of one regional rather than several national markets. Indeed, at the economic level at least, that is the explicit intent of the EU.

Another example of regional convergence is North America, which includes the United States, Canada, and to some extent in some product markets, Mexico. Canada and the United States share history, language, and much of their culture, and both are members of the new USMCA agreement negotiated by the Trump administration. Mexico is clearly different in many regards, but its proximity to the United States, along with its membership in USMCA, implies that for some product markets (e.g., automobiles) it might be reasonable to consider it part of a relatively homogenous regional market. In the Latin America region, shared Spanish history, cultural heritage, and language (with the exception of Brazil, which was colonized by the Portuguese) mean that national differences are somewhat moderated. One can argue that Greater China, which includes the city-states of Hong Kong and Singapore, along with Taiwan, is a coherent region, as is much of the Middle East, where a strong Arab culture and shared history may limit national differences. Similarly, Russia and some former states of the Soviet Union, such as Belarus and Ukraine, might be considered part of a larger regional market, at least for some products.

Taking a regional perspective is important because it may suggest that localization at the regional rather than the national level is the appropriate strategic response. For example, rather than produce cars for each national market within Europe or North America, it makes far more sense for car manufacturers to build cars for the European or North

American regions. The ability to standardize a product offering within a region allows for the attainment of greater scale economies, and hence lower costs, than if each nation required its own offering. At the same time, one should be careful to not push this perspective too far. There are still deep, profound, cultural differences between the United Kingdom, France, Germany, and Italy—all members of the EU—which may require some degree of local customization at the national level. Managers must thus make a judgment call about the appropriate level of aggregation given (1) the product market they are looking at and (2) the nature of national differences and trends for regional convergence. What might make sense for automobiles might not be appropriate for packaged food products.

8.6 Outline the different global entry strategies.

8-6 Choosing a Global Strategy

Pressures for local responsiveness imply that it may not be possible for a firm to realize the full benefits from economies of scale and location economies. It may not be possible to serve the global marketplace from a single, low-cost location, producing a globally standardized product, and marketing it worldwide to achieve economies of scale. In practice, the need to customize the product offering to local conditions may work against the implementation of such a strategy. For example, automobile firms have found that Japanese, American, and European consumers demand different kinds of cars, and this necessitates producing products that are customized for local markets (although using common global platforms—see the Opening Case). In response, firms such as Honda, Ford, and Toyota are pursuing a strategy of establishing top-to-bottom design and production facilities in each region so that they can better serve local demands. Although such customization brings benefits, it also limits the ability of a firm to realize significant scale economies and location economies.

In addition, pressures for local responsiveness imply that it may not be possible to leverage skills and products associated with a firm's distinctive competencies wholesale from one nation to another. Concessions often must be made to local conditions. Despite being depicted as "poster child" for the proliferation of standardized, global products, even McDonald's has found that it must customize its product offerings (its menu) in order to account for national differences in tastes and preferences.

Given the need to balance the cost and differentiation (value) sides of a company's business model, how do differences in the strength of pressures for cost reductions versus those for local responsiveness affect the choice of a company's strategy? Companies typically choose among four main strategic postures when competing internationally: a global standardization strategy, a localization strategy, a transnational strategy, and an international strategy.[17] The appropriateness of each strategy varies with the extent of pressures for cost reductions and local responsiveness. Figure 8.3 illustrates the conditions under which each strategy is most appropriate.

8-6a Global Standardization Strategy

global standardization strategy
A business model based on pursuing a low-cost strategy on a global scale.

Companies that pursue a **global standardization strategy** focus on increasing profitability by reaping the cost reductions that come from economies of scale and location economies; that is, they pursue a low-cost strategy on a global scale. The production, marketing, and R&D activities of companies pursuing a global strategy are concentrated in a few favorable locations. These companies try not to customize their product offerings and marketing strategy to local conditions because customization, which involves shorter production runs and the duplication of functions, can raise costs. Instead, they prefer to market a standardized product worldwide so that they can reap the maximum benefits from economies of scale. They also tend to use their cost advantage to support aggressive pricing in world markets.

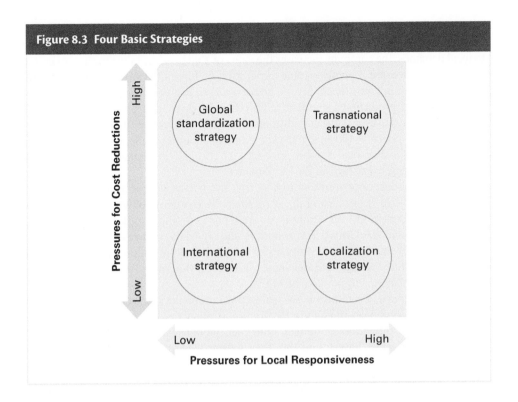

Figure 8.3 Four Basic Strategies

Pressures for Cost Reductions — High / Low

- Global standardization strategy
- Transnational strategy
- International strategy
- Localization strategy

Pressures for Local Responsiveness — Low / High

A global standardization strategy makes obvious sense when there are strong pressures for cost reductions and when demands for local responsiveness are minimal. Increasingly, these conditions prevail in many industrial goods industries, whose products often serve universal needs. In the semiconductor industry, for example, global standards have emerged, creating enormous demands for standardized global products. However, these conditions are not always found in many consumer goods markets, where demands for local responsiveness remain high. The strategy is inappropriate when demands for local responsiveness can remain high.

It is important to note that while a global standardization strategy helps to lower costs, the firm may not present itself as a low-cost competitor to its customers. Indeed, it may also do certain things that raise its costs in pursuit of superior brand equity. As we saw in the Opening Case, Emirates Airline based in Dubai is essentially pursuing a global standardization strategy, offering only long-haul service through its Dubai hub. While this strategy helps to fill its planes and lower costs, the airline also overlays this with superior inflight customer service, which has created an image of quality and a superior global brand. What the management of Emirates realized is that long-haul international travelers have the same basic needs wherever they come from; they desire an efficient, affordable, comfortable flight with high-quality preflight and inflight service to make the experience of spending 4 to 18 hours in an aircraft as pleasant as possible. Emirates has built a global brand around these attributes. While this raises some costs (in-flight quality can be expensive to provide), it also helps to drive demand, fill its aircraft, and lower operating costs per mile. So long as the *cost reduction* from filling its aircraft outweigh the *additional costs* of providing superior customer service, such a strategy can boost revenues and profits.

8-6b Localization Strategy

A **localization strategy** focuses on increasing profitability by customizing the company's goods or services so that they provide a favorable match to tastes and preferences in different national or regional markets. Localization is most appropriate when there are

localization strategy
A strategy focused on increasing profitability by customizing a company's goods or services so that they provide a favorable match to tastes and preferences in different national markets.

substantial differences across nations or regions regarding consumer tastes and preferences, and where cost pressures are not too intense. By customizing the product offering to local demands, the company increases the value of that product in the local market. On the downside, because it involves some duplication of functions and smaller production runs, customization limits the ability of the company to capture the cost reductions associated with mass-producing a standardized product for global consumption. The strategy may make sense, however, if the added value associated with local customization supports higher pricing—which would enable the company to recoup its higher costs—or if it leads to substantially greater local demand, enabling the company to reduce costs through the attainment of scale economies in the local market.

MTV is a good example of a company that has had to pursue a localization strategy. MTV localizes its programming to match the demands of viewers in different nations. For example, in India it has a program based on the popular sport of cricket, a game that few in the United States understand. If MTV hadn't done this, it would have lost market share to local competitors, its advertising revenues would have fallen, and its profitability would have declined. Thus, even though it raised costs, localization became a strategic imperative at MTV.

At the same time, it is important to realize that companies like MTV still must closely monitor costs. Companies pursuing a localization strategy need to be efficient and, whenever possible, capture scale economies from their global reach. As noted earlier, many automobile companies have found that they have to customize some of their product offerings to local market demands—for example, by producing large pickup trucks for U.S. consumers and small, fuel-efficient cars for European and Japanese consumers. At the same time, these companies try to achieve scale economies from their global volume by using common vehicle platforms and components across many different models and by manufacturing those platforms and components at efficiently scaled factories that are optimally located. By designing their products in this way, these companies have localized their product offerings and simultaneously capture some scale economies.

8-6c Transnational Strategy

We have argued that a global standardization strategy makes most sense when cost pressures are intense and demands for local responsiveness limited. Conversely, a localization strategy makes most sense when demands for local responsiveness are high, but cost pressures are moderate or low. What happens, however, when the company simultaneously faces both strong cost pressures and strong pressures for local responsiveness? How can managers balance out such competing and inconsistent demands? According to some researchers, pursuing a transnational strategy is the answer.

Two of these researchers, Christopher Bartlett and Sumantra Ghoshal, argue that, in today's global environment, competitive conditions are so intense that, to survive, companies must do all they can to respond to pressures for both cost reductions and local responsiveness. They must try to realize location economies and economies of scale from global volume, transfer distinctive competencies and skills within the company, and simultaneously pay attention to pressures for local responsiveness.[18]

Moreover, Bartlett and Ghoshal note that, in the modern, multinational enterprise, valuable competencies and resources do not reside just in the home country but can develop in any of the company's worldwide operations. Thus, they maintain that the flow of skills and product offerings should not be all one way, from home company to foreign subsidiary. Rather, the flow should also be from foreign subsidiary to home country, and from foreign subsidiary to foreign subsidiary. Transnational companies, in other words, must focus on leveraging subsidiary skills.

In essence, companies that pursue a **transnational strategy** are trying to develop a strategy that simultaneously achieves low costs, differentiates the product offering across

transnational strategy

A business model that simultaneously achieves low costs, differentiates the product offering across geographic markets, and fosters a flow of skills between different subsidiaries in the company's global network of operations.

geographic markets, and fosters a flow of resources such as process knowledge between different subsidiaries in the company's global network of operations. As attractive as this may sound, the strategy is not easy to pursue because it places conflicting demands on the company. Differentiating the product to respond to local demands in different geographic markets raises costs, which runs counter to the goal of reducing costs. Companies such as 3M and ABB (a Swiss-based multinational engineering conglomerate) have tried to implement a transnational strategy and found it difficult.

Indeed, how best to implement a transnational strategy is one of the most complex questions that large, global companies grapple with today. It may be that few, if any, companies have perfected this strategic posture. But some clues to the right approach can be derived from a number of companies. Consider, for example, the case of Caterpillar. The need to compete with low-cost competitors such as Komatsu of Japan forced Caterpillar to look for greater cost economies. However, variations in construction practices and government regulations across countries meant that Caterpillar also had to be responsive to local demands. Therefore, it confronted significant pressures for cost reductions and for local responsiveness.

To deal with cost pressures, Caterpillar redesigned its products to use many identical components and invested in a few large-scale, component-manufacturing facilities, sited at favorable locations, to fill global demand and realize scale economies. At the same time, the company augments the centralized manufacturing of components with assembly plants in each of its major global markets. At these plants, Caterpillar adds local product features, tailoring the finished product to local needs. Thus, Caterpillar realizes many of the benefits of global manufacturing while reacting to pressures for local responsiveness by differentiating its product among national markets.[19] Caterpillar started to pursue this strategy in the 1980s. By the 2000s, it had succeeded in doubling output per employee, significantly reducing its overall cost structure in the process. Meanwhile, Komatsu and Hitachi, which are still wedded to a Japan-centric global strategy, have seen their cost advantages evaporate and have been steadily losing market share to Caterpillar.

However, building an organization capable of supporting a transnational strategy is a complex, challenging task. Indeed, some would say it is too complex because the strategy implementation problems of creating a viable organizational structure and set of control systems to manage this strategy are immense. We return to this issue in Chapter 12.

8-6d International Strategy

Sometimes it is possible to identify multinational companies that find themselves in the fortunate position of being confronted with low-cost pressures and low pressures for local responsiveness. Typically, these enterprises sell a product that serves universal needs, but because they do not face significant competitors, they are not confronted with pressures to reduce their cost structure. Xerox found itself in this position in the 1960s, after its invention and commercialization of the photocopier. Strong patents protected the technology comprising the photocopier, so for several years Xerox did not face competitors—it had a monopoly. Because the product was highly valued in most developed nations, Xerox was able to sell the same basic product all over the world and charge a relatively high price for it. At the same time, because it did not face direct competitors, the company did not have to deal with strong pressures to minimize its costs.

Historically, companies like Xerox have followed a similar pattern as they developed their international operations. They tend to centralize product development functions such as R&D at home. However, companies also tend to establish manufacturing and marketing functions in each major country or geographic region in which they do business. Although they may undertake some local customization of product offering and marketing strategy, this tends to be rather limited in scope. Ultimately, in most international companies, the head office retains tight control over marketing and product strategy.

Other companies that have pursued this strategy include P&G, which had historically always developed innovative new products in Cincinnati and thereafter transferred them wholesale to local markets. Microsoft has followed a similar strategy. The bulk of Microsoft's product development work takes place in Redmond, Washington, where the company is headquartered. Although some localization work is undertaken elsewhere, it is limited to producing foreign-language versions of popular Microsoft programs such as Office 365.

8-6e Changes in Strategy over Time

The Achilles heel of the international strategy is that, over time, competitors inevitably emerge, and if managers do not take proactive steps to reduce their cost structure, their company may be rapidly outflanked by efficient, global competitors. This is exactly what happened to Xerox. Japanese companies such as Canon ultimately invented their way around Xerox's patents, produced their own photocopying equipment in very efficient manufacturing plants, priced the machines below Xerox's products, and rapidly took global market share from Xerox. Xerox's demise was not due to the emergence of competitors, for ultimately that was bound to occur, but rather to its failure to proactively reduce its cost structure in advance of the emergence of competitors. The message here is that an international strategy may not be viable in the long term, and to survive, companies that are able to pursue it need to shift toward a global standardization strategy, or perhaps a transnational strategy, ahead of competitors (see Figure 8.4).

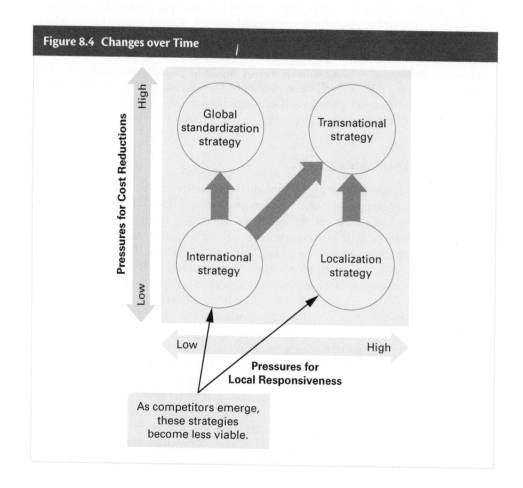

Figure 8.4 Changes over Time

The same can be said about a localization strategy. Localization may give a company a competitive edge, but if it is simultaneously facing aggressive competitors, the company will also need to reduce its cost structure—and the only way to do that may be to adopt a transnational strategy. Thus, as competition intensifies, international and localization strategies tend to become less viable, and managers need to orientate their companies toward either a global standardization strategy or a transnational strategy.

8-7 The Choice of Entry Mode

8.7 Summarize the five primary modes of entry into global markets.

Any firm contemplating entering a different national market must determine the best mode or vehicle for such entry. There are five primary choices of entry mode: exporting, licensing, franchising, entering into a joint venture with a host-country company, and setting up a wholly owned subsidiary in the host country. Each mode has advantages and disadvantages, and managers must weigh these carefully when deciding which mode to use.[20]

8-7a Exporting

Most manufacturing companies begin their global expansion as exporters and only later switch to one of the other modes for serving a foreign market. Exporting has two distinct advantages: It avoids the costs of establishing manufacturing operations in the host country, which are often substantial, and it may be consistent with scale economies and location economies. By manufacturing the product in a centralized location and then exporting it to other national markets, a company may be able to realize substantial scale economies from its global sales volume. That is how many Japanese auto companies originally made inroads into the U.S. auto market, and how Samsung gained share in the market for computer memory chips.

There are several drawbacks to exporting. First, exporting from the company's home base may not be appropriate if there are lower-cost locations for manufacturing the product abroad (that is, if the company can achieve location economies by moving production elsewhere). Thus, particularly in the case of a company pursuing a global standardization or transnational strategy, it may pay to manufacture in a location where conditions are most favorable from a value creation perspective and then export from that location to the rest of the globe. This is not so much an argument against exporting as it is an argument against exporting from the company's home country. For example, many U.S. electronics companies have moved some manufacturing to Asia because low-cost but highly skilled labor is available there. They export from Asia to the rest of the globe, including the United States (as Apple does with the iPhone).

Another drawback is that high transport costs can make exporting uneconomical, particularly in the case of bulk products. One way of alleviating this problem is to manufacture bulk products on a regional basis, thereby realizing some economies from large-scale production while limiting transport costs. Many multinational chemical companies manufacture their products on a regional basis, serving several countries in a region from one facility.

A third drawback is that tariff barriers can make exporting uneconomical. Similarly, the threat of tariff barriers by the host-country government can make it very risky. In the world we now live in, many countries are becoming more and more nationalistic, which means that they are increasing trade barriers (e.g., the United States) or renegotiating their partnerships (e.g., the United Kingdom). The largely unknown standing of international trade barriers in some countries—due to nationalistic, political strategies—can be a detriment to exporting across country borders.

Finally, a common practice among companies that are just beginning to export also poses risks. A company may delegate marketing activities in each country in which it does business to a local agent, but there is no guarantee that the agent will act in the company's best interest. Often, foreign agents also carry the products of competing companies and thus have divided loyalties. Consequently, agents may not perform as well as the company would if it managed marketing itself. One way to solve this problem is to set up a wholly owned subsidiary in the host country to handle local marketing. In this way, the company can reap the cost advantages that arise from manufacturing the product in a single location and exercise tight control over marketing strategy in the host country.

8-7b Licensing

International licensing is an arrangement whereby a foreign licensee purchases the rights to produce a company's product in the licensee's country for a negotiated fee (normally, royalty payments on the number of units sold). The licensee then provides most of the capital necessary to open the overseas operation.[21] The advantage of licensing is that the company does not have to bear the development costs and risks associated with opening up a foreign market. Licensing therefore can be a very attractive option for companies that lack the capital to develop operations overseas. It can also be an attractive option for companies that are unwilling to commit substantial financial resources to an unfamiliar or politically volatile foreign market where political risks are particularly high.

Licensing has some serious drawbacks, however. First, it does not give a company the tight control over manufacturing, marketing, and strategic functions in foreign countries that it needs to have in order to realize scale economies and location economies—as companies pursuing both global standardization and transnational strategies try to do. Typically, each licensee sets up its manufacturing operations. Hence, the company stands little chance of realizing scale economies and location economies by manufacturing its product in a centralized location. When these economies are likely to be important, licensing may not be the best way of expanding overseas.

Second, competing in a global marketplace may make it necessary for a company to coordinate strategic moves across countries so that the profits earned in one country can be used to support competitive attacks in another. Licensing, by its very nature, severely limits a company's ability to coordinate strategy in this way. A licensee is unlikely to let a multinational company take its profits (beyond those due in the form of royalty payments) and use them to support an entirely different licensee operating in another country.

Third, there is risk associated with licensing technological know-how to foreign companies. For many multinational companies, technological know-how forms the basis of their competitive advantage, and they want to maintain control over how this competitive advantage is put to use. By licensing its technology, a company can quickly lose control over it. RCA, for instance, once licensed its color television technology to a number of Japanese companies. The Japanese companies quickly assimilated RCA's technology and then used it to enter the U.S. market, where they soon gained a larger share of the U.S. market than the RCA brand holds.

There are ways of reducing this risk. One way is by entering into a cross-licensing agreement with a foreign firm. Under a cross-licensing agreement, a firm might license some valuable, intangible property to a foreign partner and, in addition to a royalty payment, also request that the foreign partner license some of its valuable know-how to the firm. Such agreements are reckoned to reduce the risks associated with licensing technological know-how, as the licensee realizes that if it violates the spirit of a licensing contract (by using the knowledge obtained to compete directly with the licensor), the licensor can do the same to it. Put differently, cross-licensing agreements enable firms to hold each other hostage, thereby reducing the probability that they will behave opportunistically toward each other.[22] Such cross-licensing agreements are increasingly common in high-technology industries. For example, the U.S. biotechnology firm Amgen licensed one of its key drugs, Neupogen, to Kirin, the Japanese pharmaceutical company. The license gives Kirin the right to sell Neupogen in Japan. In return, Amgen receives a royalty payment, and through a licensing agreement it gains the right to sell certain Kirin products in the United States.

Finally, a licensee can degrade or damage the brand of the company that it is licensing from if it pursues strategies that are not in the best interests of the licensee. For example, the luxury apparel company Burberry licensed Sanyo Shokai of Japan to sell its branded products in Japan. However, Sanyo Shokai ultimately started to damage Burberry's global brand by charging a much lower price for Burberry branded products in Japan than elsewhere in the world (see Strategy in Action 8.2 for details). Burberry responded to the "Japan problem" by terminating its licensing arrangement with Sanyo Shokai in 2015 and setting up its own wholly owned stores in the country.

8-7c Franchising

In many respects, franchising is similar to licensing, although franchising tends to involve longer-term commitments than licensing. Franchising is basically a specialized form of licensing in which the franchiser not only sells intangible property to

8.2 Strategy in Action

Burberry Shifts Its Strategy in Japan

Burberry, the iconic British luxury apparel company best known for its high-fashion outerwear, has been operating in Japan for nearly half a century. Until recently, its branded products were sold under a licensing agreement with Sanyo Shokai. The Japanese company had considerable discretion as to how it utilized the Burberry brand. It sold everything from golf bags to miniskirts and Burberry-clad Barbie dolls in its 400 stores around the country, typically at prices significantly below those Burberry charged for its high-end products in the United Kingdom.

For a long time, it looked like a good deal for Burberry. Sanyo Shokai did all of the market development in Japan, generating revenues of around $800 million a year and paying Burberry $80 million in annual royalty payments. However, by 2007, Burberry CEO Angela Ahrendts was becoming increasingly dissatisfied with the Japanese licensing deal and 22 others like it in countries around the world. In Ahrendts's view, the licensing deals were diluting Burberry's core brand image. Licensees such as Sanyo Shokai were selling a wide range of products at a much lower price point than Burberry charged for products in its own stores. "In luxury, "Ahrendts once remarked, "ubiquity will kill you—it means that you're not really luxury anymore." Moreover, with an increasing number of customers buying Burberry products online and on trips to Britain, where the brand was considered very upmarket, Ahrendts felt that it was crucial for Burberry to tightly control its global brand image.

Ahrendts was determined to rein in licensees and regain control of Burberry's sales in foreign markets, even if it meant taking a short-term hit to sales. She started off the process of terminating licensees before leaving Burberry to run Apple's retail division in 2014. Her hand-picked successor as CEO, Christopher Bailey, who rose through the design function at Burberry, has continued to pursue this strategy.

In Japan, the license was terminated in 2015. Sanyo Shokai was required to close nearly 400 licensed Burberry stores. Burberry is not giving up on Japan, however. After all, Japan is the world's second-largest market for luxury goods. Instead, the company will now sell products through a limited number of wholly owned stores. Burberry's goal was to have 35 to 50 stores in the most exclusive locations in Japan by 2018. They would offer only high-end products such as Burberry's classic $1,800 trench coat. In general, the price point will be 10 times higher than was common for most Burberry products in Japan. The company realizes the move is risky and fully expects sales to initially fall before rising again as it rebuilds its brand, but CEO Bailey argues that the move is necessary if Burberry is to have a coherent global brand image for its luxury products.

Sources: K. Chu and M. Fujikawa, "Burberry Gets a Grip on Brand in Japan," *Wall Street Journal*, August 15–16, 2015; A. Ahrendts, "Burberry's CEO on Turning an Aging British Icon into a Global Luxury Brand," *Harvard Business Review*, January–February 2013; T. Blanks, "The Designer Who Would be CEO," *Wall Street Journal Magazine*, June 18, 2015.

the franchisee (normally a trademark), but also insists that the franchisee abide by strict rules governing how it does business. They normally provide training, operating systems, marketing support, and require franchisees to use specific vendors. The franchiser will often assist the franchisee to run the business on an ongoing basis. As with licensing, the franchiser typically receives a royalty payment, which amounts to a percentage of the franchisee revenues. Depending on the franchise, there are additional fees such as marketing or a monthly percentage of sales.

Whereas licensing is a strategy pursued primarily by manufacturing companies, franchising, which resembles it in some respects, is a strategy employed chiefly by service companies. McDonald's provides a good example of a firm that has grown by using a franchising strategy. McDonald's has set down strict rules as to how franchisees should operate a restaurant. These rules extend to controlling the menu, cooking methods, staffing policies, and restaurant design and location. McDonald's also organizes the supply chain for its franchisees and provides management training.[23]

The advantages of franchising are similar to those of licensing. Specifically, the franchiser does not need to bear the development costs and risks associated with opening up a foreign market on its own, for the franchisee typically assumes those costs and risks. Thus, using a franchising strategy, a service company can build up a global presence quickly and at a low cost.

The disadvantages of franchising are less pronounced than in licensing. Because service companies often use franchising, there is no reason to consider the need for coordination of manufacturing to achieve experience curve and location economies. But franchising may inhibit the firm's ability to take profits out of one country to support competitive attacks in another. A more significant disadvantage of franchising is quality control. The foundation of franchising arrangements is that the firm's brand name conveys a message to consumers about the quality of the firm's product. Thus, a business traveler checking in at a Four Seasons hotel in Hong Kong can reasonably expect the same quality of room, food, and service that would be received in New York, Hawai'I, or Ontario, Canada. The Four Seasons name is assumed to guarantee consistent product quality. This presents a problem in that foreign franchisees may not be as concerned about quality as they are supposed to be, and the result of poor quality can cascade beyond lost sales in a particular foreign market to a decline in the firm's worldwide reputation. For example, if a business traveler has a bad experience at the Four Seasons in Hong Kong, he or she may never go to another Four Seasons hotel, and may urge colleagues to avoid the chain as well. The geographical distance of the firm from its foreign franchisees can make poor quality difficult to detect. In addition, the numbers of franchisees—in the case of McDonald's, tens of thousands—can make quality control difficult.

To reduce these problems, a company can set up a subsidiary in each country or region in which it is expanding. The subsidiary, which might be wholly owned by the company or a joint venture with a foreign company, then assumes the rights and obligations to establish franchisees throughout that particular country or region. The combination of proximity and the limited number of independent franchisees that need to be monitored reduces the quality control problem. Because the subsidiary is at least partly owned by the company, it can place its own managers in the subsidiary to ensure the level of quality monitoring it demands. This organizational arrangement has proved very popular in practice; it has been used by McDonald's, KFC, and Hilton Worldwide to expand international operations, to name just three examples.

8-7d Joint Ventures

Establishing a joint venture with a foreign company has long been a favored mode for entering a new market. The most typical form of joint venture is a 50/50 joint venture, in which each party takes a 50% ownership stake and a team of managers from both parent companies shares operating control. Some companies seek joint ventures wherein they become the majority shareholder (for example, a 51 to 49% ownership split), which permits tighter control by the dominant partner.[24]

Joint ventures have several advantages. First, a company may feel that it can benefit from a local partner's knowledge of a host country's competitive conditions, culture, language, political systems, and business systems. Second, when the development costs and risks of opening up a foreign market are high, a company might gain by sharing these costs and risks with a local partner. Third, in some countries, political considerations make joint ventures the only feasible entry mode. For example, historically, many U.S. companies found it much easier to obtain permission to set up operations in Japan if they joined with a Japanese partner than if they tried to enter on their own. The same has been true in China.

Despite the advantages, there are major disadvantages with joint ventures. First, as with licensing, a firm that enters into a joint venture may risk yielding control of its technology to its partner. Thus, a proposed joint venture in 2002 between Boeing and Mitsubishi Heavy Industries to build Boeing's wide-body jet (the 787) raised fears that Boeing might unwittingly give its commercial airline technology to the Japanese. However, joint-venture agreements can be constructed to minimize this risk. One option is to hold majority ownership in the venture. This allows the dominant partner to exercise great control over its technology—but it can be difficult to find a foreign partner who is willing to settle for minority ownership. Another option is to "wall off" from a partner technology that is central to the core competence of the firm while sharing other technology.

A second disadvantage is that a joint venture does not give a firm the tight control over subsidiaries that it might need to realize experience-curve or location economies. Nor does it give a firm the control over a foreign subsidiary it might need for engaging in coordinated, global attacks against its rivals. Consider the entry of Texas Instruments (TI) into the Japanese semiconductor market. When TI established semiconductor facilities in Japan, it did so for the dual purpose of checking Japanese manufacturers' market share and limiting the cash they had available for invading TI's global market. In other words, TI was engaging in global strategic coordination. To implement this strategy, TI's subsidiary in Japan had to be prepared to take instructions from corporate headquarters regarding competitive strategy. The strategy also required the Japanese subsidiary to run at a loss if necessary. Few, if any, potential joint-venture partners would have been willing to accept such conditions, as it would have necessitated a willingness to accept a negative return on investment. Indeed, many joint ventures establish a degree of autonomy that would make such direct control over strategic decisions all but impossible to establish.[25] Thus, to implement this strategy, TI set up a wholly owned subsidiary in Japan.

8-7e Wholly Owned Subsidiaries

A wholly owned subsidiary is one in which the parent company owns 100% of the subsidiary's stock. To establish a wholly owned subsidiary in a foreign market, a company can either set up a completely new operation in that country or acquire an established host-country company to promote its products in the host market.

Setting up a wholly owned subsidiary offers three advantages. First, when a company's competitive advantage is based on its control of a technological competency, a wholly owned subsidiary will normally be the preferred entry mode because it reduces the company's risk of losing this control. Consequently, many high-tech companies prefer wholly owned subsidiaries to joint ventures or licensing arrangements. Wholly owned subsidiaries tend to be the favored entry mode in the semiconductor, computer, electronics, and pharmaceutical industries.

Second, a wholly owned subsidiary gives a company the kind of tight control over operations in different countries that it needs if it is going to engage in global strategic coordination—taking profits from one country to support competitive attacks in another.

Third, a wholly owned subsidiary may be the best choice if a company wants to realize location economies and the scale economies that flow from producing a standardized output from a single or limited number of manufacturing plants. When pressures on costs are intense, it may pay a company to configure its value chain in such a way that value added at each stage is maximized. Thus, a national subsidiary may specialize in manufacturing only part of the product line, or certain components of the end product, exchanging parts and products with other subsidiaries in the company's global system. Establishing such a global production system requires a high degree of control over the operations of national affiliates. Different national operations must be prepared to accept centrally determined decisions as to how they should produce, how much they should produce, and how their output should be priced for transfer between operations. A wholly owned subsidiary would have to comply with these mandates, whereas licensees or joint-venture partners would most likely shun such a subservient role.

On the other hand, establishing a wholly-owned subsidiary is generally the costliest method of serving a foreign market. The parent company must bear all the costs and risks of setting up overseas operations—in contrast to joint ventures, where the costs and risks are shared, or licensing, where the licensee bears most of the costs and risks. But the risks of learning to do business in a new culture diminish if a company acquires an established host-country enterprise. Acquisitions, however, raise a set of additional problems, such as trying to marry divergent corporate cultures, and these may more than offset the benefits. (The problems associated with acquisitions are discussed in Chapter 10.)

8-7f Pros and Cons of Entry Modes

The advantages and disadvantages of the various entry modes are summarized in Table 8.1. Inevitably, there are trade-offs in choosing one entry mode over another. For example, when considering entry into an unfamiliar country with a track record of nationalizing foreign-owned enterprises, a company might favor a joint venture with a local enterprise. Its rationale might be that the local partner will help it establish operations in an unfamiliar environment and speak out against nationalization should the possibility arise. But if the company's distinctive competency is based on proprietary technology, entering into a joint venture might mean risking loss of control over that technology to the joint venture partner, which would make this strategy unattractive. Despite such hazards, some generalizations can be offered about the optimal choice of entry mode.

Distinctive Competencies and Entry Mode   When companies expand internationally to earn greater returns from their differentiated product offerings, entering markets where indigenous competitors lack comparable products, the companies are pursuing an international strategy. The optimal entry mode for such companies depends to some degree upon the nature of their distinctive competency. In particular, we need to distinguish between companies with a distinctive competency in technological know-how and those with a distinctive competency in management know-how.

If a company's competitive advantage—its distinctive competency—derives from its control of proprietary technological know-how (i.e., intellectual property), licensing and joint-venture arrangements should be avoided, if possible, to minimize the

Table 8.1 The Advantages and Disadvantages of Different Entry Modes

Entry Mode	Advantages	Disadvantages
Exporting	• Ability to realize location- and scale-based economies	• High transport costs • Trade barriers • Problems with local marketing agents
Licensing	• Low development costs and risks	• Inability to realize location- and scale-based economies • Inability to engage in global strategic coordination • Lack of control over technology
Franchising	• Low development costs and risks	• Inability to engage in global strategic coordination • Lack of control over quality
Joint ventures	• Access to local partner's knowledge • Shared development costs and risks • Political dependency	• Inability to engage in global strategic coordination • Inability to realize location- and scale-based economies • Lack of control over technology
Wholly owned subsidiaries	• Protection of technology • Ability to engage in global strategic coordination • Ability to realize location- and scale-based economies	• High costs and risks

risk of losing control of that technology. Thus, if a high-tech company is considering setting up operations in a foreign country in order to profit from a distinctive competency in technological know-how, it should probably do so through a wholly owned subsidiary.

However, this should not be viewed as a hard-and-fast rule. For instance, a licensing or joint-venture arrangement might be structured in such a way as to reduce the risks that licensees or joint-venture partners will expropriate a company's technological know-how. (We consider this kind of arrangement in more detail later in the chapter when we discuss the issue of structuring strategic alliances.) Or consider a situation where a company believes its technological advantage will be short lived and expects rapid imitation of its core technology by competitors. In this situation, the company might want to license its technology as quickly as possible to foreign companies in order to gain global acceptance of its technology before imitation occurs.[26] Such a strategy has some advantages. By licensing its technology to competitors, the company may deter them from developing their own, possibly superior, technology. It also may be able to establish its technology as the dominant design in the industry, ensuring a steady stream of royalty payments. Such situations aside, however, the attractions of licensing are probably outweighed by the risks of losing control of technology, and therefore licensing should be avoided.

The competitive advantage of many service companies such as McDonald's or Hilton Worldwide is based on management know-how (i.e., process knowledge). For such companies, the risk of losing control of their management skills to franchisees or joint-venture partners is not that great. The reason is that the valuable asset of such companies is their brand name, and brand names are generally well protected by intellectual property laws pertaining to trademarks. Given this fact, many issues that arise in the case of technological know-how do not arise in the case of management know-how. As a result, many service companies favor a combination of franchising and subsidiaries to control franchisees within a particular country or region. The subsidiary may be wholly owned or a joint venture. In most cases, however, service companies have found that entering into a joint venture with a local partner in order to set up a controlling subsidiary in a country or region works best because a joint venture is often politically more acceptable and brings a degree of local knowledge to the subsidiary.

Pressures for Cost Reduction and Entry Mode   The greater the pressures for cost reductions, the more likely that a company will want to pursue some combination of exporting and wholly owned subsidiaries. By manufacturing in the locations where factor conditions are optimal and then exporting to the rest of the world, a company may be able to realize substantial location economies and substantial scale economies. The company might then want to export the finished product to marketing subsidiaries based in various countries. Typically, these subsidiaries would be wholly owned and have the responsibility for overseeing distribution in a particular country. Setting up wholly owned marketing subsidiaries is preferable to a joint-venture arrangement or using a foreign marketing agent because it gives the company the tight control over marketing that might be required to coordinate a globally dispersed value chain. In addition, tight control over a local operation enables the company to use the profits generated in one market to improve its competitive position in another market. Hence companies pursuing global or transnational strategies prefer to establish wholly owned subsidiaries.

8-8 Global Strategic Alliances

8.8 Discuss how an enterprise would benefit from a global strategic alliance.

global strategic alliances
Cooperative agreements between companies from different countries that are actual or potential competitors.

Global strategic alliances are cooperative agreements between companies from different countries that are actual or potential competitors. Strategic alliances range from formal joint ventures in which two or more companies have an equity stake, to short-term contractual agreements in which two companies may agree to cooperate on a particular problem (such as developing a new product).

8-8a Advantages of Strategic Alliances

Companies enter into strategic alliances with competitors to achieve a number of strategic objectives.[27] First, strategic alliances may facilitate entry into a foreign market. For example, many firms feel that if they are to successfully enter the Chinese market, they need a local partner who understands business conditions and has good connections. Thus, Warner Brothers entered into a joint venture with two Chinese partners to produce and distribute films in China. As a foreign film company, Warner found that if it wanted to produce films on its own for the Chinese market, it had to go through a complex approval process for every film. It also had to farm out distribution to a local company, which made doing business in China very difficult. Due to the participation of Chinese firms, however, the joint-venture films will merit a streamlined approval process, and the venture can distribute any films it produces. Moreover, the joint venture is able to produce films for Chinese TV, something that foreign firms are not allowed to do.[28]

Second, strategic alliances allow firms to share the fixed costs (and associated risks) of developing new products or processes. An alliance between Boeing and a number of Japanese companies to build Boeing's latest commercial jetliner, the 787, was motivated by Boeing's desire to share the estimated $8-billion investment required to develop the aircraft.

Third, an alliance is a way to bring together complementary skills and assets that neither company could easily develop on its own.[29] In 2011, for example, Microsoft and Nokia established an alliance aimed at developing and marketing smartphones that used Microsoft's Windows 8 operating system. Microsoft contributed its software engineering skills, particularly with regard to the development of a version of its Windows operating system for smartphones, and Nokia contributed its design, engineering, and marketing know-how. The first phones resulting from this collaboration reached the market in late 2012. Microsoft subsequently purchased Nokia's mobile phone business in 2013.

Fourth, it can make sense to form an alliance that will help firms establish technological standards for the industry that will benefit them. This was also a goal of the alliance between Microsoft and Nokia. The idea was to establish Windows 8 as the de facto operating system for smartphones in the face of strong competition from Apple, with its iPhone, and Google, whose Android operating system was the most widely used smartphone operating system in the world in 2012. Unfortunately for Microsoft, the Nokia Windows phone failed to gain sufficient market share, primarily because by the time the phone reached the market, the iPhone and Android phones already dominated the market and consumers did not want to switch to a new offering.

8-8b Disadvantages of Strategic Alliances

The advantages we have discussed can be very significant. Despite this, some commentators have criticized strategic alliances on the grounds that they give competitors a low-cost route to new technology and markets.[30] For example, some commentators argued that many strategic alliances between U.S. and Japanese firms were part of an implicit Japanese strategy to keep high-paying, high-value-added jobs in Japan while gaining the project engineering and production process skills that underlie the competitive success of many U.S. companies.[31] They argued that Japanese success in the machine tool and semiconductor industries was built on U.S. technology acquired through strategic alliances. And they argued that U.S. managers were aiding the Japanese by entering alliances that channel new inventions to Japan and provide a U.S. sales and distribution network for the resulting products. Although such deals may generate short-term profits, the argument goes, in the long term, the result is to "hollow out" U.S. firms, leaving them with no competitive advantage in the global marketplace. The same point could be made about many alliances between Western companies and Chinese enterprises.

These critics have a point; alliances have risks. Unless a firm is careful, it can give away more than it receives. But there are so many examples of apparently successful alliances between firms—including alliances between U.S. and Japanese firms—that this position appears extreme. It is difficult to see how the Boeing–Mitsubishi alliance for the 787, or the long-term Fuji–Xerox alliance, fit the critics' thesis. In these cases, both partners seem to have gained from the alliance. Why do some alliances benefit both firms, while others benefit one firm and hurt the other? The next section provides an answer to this question.

8-8c Making Strategic Alliances Work

The failure rate for international strategic alliances is quite high. For example, one study of 49 international strategic alliances found that two-thirds run into serious managerial and financial troubles within 2 years of their formation, and that although many of these problems are ultimately solved, 33% are rated as failures by the parties involved.[32] The success of an alliance seems to be a function of three main factors: partner selection, alliance structure, and the manner in which the alliance is managed.

Partner Selection One key to making a strategic alliance work is selecting the right partner. A good partner has three principal characteristics. First, a good partner helps the company accomplish strategic goals such as achieving market access, sharing the costs and risks of new-product development, or gaining access to critical core competencies. In other words, the partner must have capabilities that the company lacks and that it values. Second, a good partner shares the firm's vision for the purpose of the alliance. If two companies approach an alliance with radically different agendas, the chances are great that the relationship will not be harmonious, and the partnership will end.

Third, a good partner is unlikely to try to exploit the alliance for its own ends—that is, to expropriate the company's technological know-how while giving away little in return. In this respect, firms with reputations for fair play probably make the best partners. For example, IBM is involved in so many strategic alliances that it would not pay for the company to trample over its individual alliance partners.[33] This would tarnish IBM's reputation of being a good ally and would make it more difficult for it to attract alliance partners. Because IBM attaches great importance to its alliances, it is unlikely to engage in the kind of opportunistic behavior that critics highlight. Similarly, their reputations make it less likely (but by no means impossible) that such Japanese firms as Sony, Toshiba, and Fuji, which have histories of alliances with non-Japanese firms, would exploit an alliance partner.

To select a partner with these three characteristics, a company needs to conduct comprehensive research on potential alliance candidates. To increase the probability of selecting a good partner, the company should collect as much pertinent, publicly available information about potential allies as possible; collect data from informed third parties, including companies that have had alliances with the potential partners, investment bankers who have had dealings with them, and former employees; and get to know potential partners as well as possible before committing to an alliance. This last step should include face-to-face meetings between senior managers (and perhaps middle-level managers) to ensure that the chemistry is right.

Alliance Structure Having selected a partner, the alliance should be structured so that the company's risk of giving too much away to the partner is reduced to an acceptable level. First, alliances can be designed to make it difficult (if not impossible) to transfer technology not meant to be transferred. Specifically, the design, development, manufacture, and service of a product manufactured by an alliance can be structured to "wall off" sensitive technologies to prevent their leakage to the other participant. In the alliance between General Electric and Snecma to build commercial aircraft engines (now known as Safran), for example, GE reduced the risk of "excess transfer" by walling off certain steps of the production process. The modularization effectively cut off the transfer of what GE regarded as key competitive technology while permitting Snecma access to final assembly. First established in the 1970s, this alliance has proved to be remarkably enduring and is still operating today. Similarly, in the alliance between Boeing and the Japanese to build the 787, Boeing walled off research, design, and marketing functions considered central to its competitive position, while allowing the Japanese to share in production technology. Boeing also walled off new technologies not required for 787 production.[34]

Second, contractual safeguards can be written into an alliance agreement to guard against the risk of **opportunism** by a partner. For example, the auto parts supplier TRW had three strategic alliances with large Japanese auto component suppliers to produce seat belts, engine valves, and steering gears for sale to Japanese-owned auto assembly plants in the United States. TRW had clauses in every alliance contract that barred the Japanese firms from competing with TRW to supply U.S.-owned auto companies with component parts. TRW thus protected itself against the possibility that the Japanese companies were entering into the alliances merely as a means of gaining access to the North American market to compete with TRW in its home market.

opportunism

Seeking one's own self-interest, often through the use of guile.

Third, both parties in an alliance can agree in advance to exchange skills and technologies that the other covets, thereby ensuring a chance for equitable gain. Cross-licensing agreements are one way to achieve this goal.

Fourth, the risk of opportunism by an alliance partner can be reduced if the firm extracts a significant, credible commitment from its partner in advance. A nearly 60-year alliance between Xerox and Fuji to build photocopiers for the Asian market perhaps best illustrates this. Rather than enter into an informal agreement or a licensing arrangement (which Fujifilm initially preferred), Xerox insisted that Fuji invest in a 50/50 joint venture to serve Japan and East Asia. This venture constituted such a significant investment in people, equipment, and facilities that Fujifilm was committed from the outset to making the alliance work in order to earn a return on its investment. By agreeing to the joint venture, Fuji essentially made a credible commitment to the alliance. In turn, Xerox felt secure in transferring its photocopier technology to Fuji. The alliance was widely regarded as very successful and endured until 2021.

Managing the Alliance   Once a partner has been selected and an appropriate alliance structure agreed upon, the task facing the company is to maximize benefits from the alliance. One important ingredient of success appears to be sensitivity to cultural differences. Many variations in management style are attributable to cultural differences, and managers need to make allowances for these when dealing with their partners. Beyond this, maximizing benefits from an alliance seems to involve building trust between partners and learning from partners.[35]

Managing an alliance successfully requires building interpersonal relationships between the firms' managers, or what is sometimes referred to as *relational capital*.[36] This is one lesson that can be drawn from the strategic alliance between Ford and Mazda, which lasted from 1974 until 2015. Ford and Mazda set up a framework of meetings within which their managers not only discuss matters pertaining to the alliance, but also have time to get to know one another. The belief is that the resulting friendships help build trust and facilitate harmonious relations between the two firms. Personal relationships also foster an informal management network between the firms. This network can then be used to help solve problems arising in more formal contexts (such as in joint committee meetings between personnel from the two firms).

Academics have argued that a major determinant of how much knowledge a company acquires from an alliance is its ability to learn from its alliance partner.[37] For example, in a study of 15 strategic alliances between major multinationals, Gary Hamel, Yves Doz, and C. K. Prahalad focused on a number of alliances between Japanese companies and Western (European or American) partners.[38] In every case in which a Japanese company emerged from an alliance stronger than its Western partner, the Japanese company had made a greater effort to learn. Few of the Western companies studied seemed to want to learn from their Japanese partners. They tended to regard the alliance purely as a cost-sharing or risk-sharing arrangement, rather than an opportunity to learn how a potential competitor does business.

For an example of an alliance in which there was a clear learning asymmetry, consider the agreement between GM and Toyota to build the Chevrolet Nova. This alliance was structured as a formal joint venture, New United Motor Manufacturing, in which both parties had a 50% equity stake. The venture owned an auto plant in Fremont, California. According to one of the Japanese managers, Toyota achieved most of its objectives from the alliance: "We learned about U.S. supply and transportation. And we got the confidence to manage U.S. workers." All that knowledge was then quickly transferred to Georgetown, Kentucky, where Toyota opened a plant of its own in 1986. Today, Toyota has 12 plants in the United States (although the Fremont plant was closed in 2010 and sold to Tesla). By contrast, although GM got a new product (the Nova), some GM managers complained that their new knowledge was never put to good use inside GM. They say that they should have been kept together as a team to educate GM's engineers and workers about the Japanese system. Instead, they were dispersed to different GM subsidiaries.

When entering an alliance, a company must take measures to ensure that it learns from its alliance partner and then embeds that knowledge within its own organization. One suggested approach is to educate all operating employees about the partner's strengths and weaknesses, and to make clear to them how acquiring particular skills will bolster their company's competitive position. For such learning to be of value, the knowledge acquired from an alliance must be diffused throughout the organization—which did not happen at GM. To spread knowledge, the managers involved in an alliance should be used as a resource to educate others within the company about the skills of the alliance partner.

Key Terms

Takeaways for Strategic Managers

1. For some companies, international expansion represents a way of earning greater returns by transferring the skills and product offerings derived from their distinctive competencies to markets where indigenous competitors lack those skills. As barriers to international trade have fallen, industries have expanded beyond national boundaries and domestic competition, and opportunities have increased.

2. Because of national differences, it pays for a company to base each value creation activity it performs at the location where factor conditions are most conducive to the performance of that activity. This strategy is known as focusing on the attainment of location economies.

3. By building sales volume more rapidly, international expansion can help a company gain a cost advantage through the realization of scale economies and learning effects.

4. The best strategy for a company to pursue depends on the pressures it must cope with: pressures for cost reductions or for local responsiveness. Pressures for cost reductions are greatest in industries producing commodity-type products, where price is the main competitive weapon. Pressures for local responsiveness arise from differences in consumer tastes and preferences, as well as from national infrastructure and traditional practices, distribution channels, and host government demands.

5. Companies pursuing an international strategy transfer the skills and products derived from distinctive competencies to foreign markets, while undertaking some limited local customization.

6. Companies pursuing a localization strategy customize their product offerings, marketing strategies, and business strategies to national conditions.

7. Companies pursuing a global standardization strategy focus on reaping the cost reductions that come from scale economies and location economies.

8. Many industries are now so competitive that companies must adopt a transnational strategy. This involves a simultaneous focus upon reducing costs, transferring skills and products, and being locally responsive. Implementing such a strategy may prove difficult.

9. There are five different ways of entering a foreign market: exporting, licensing, franchising, entering into a joint venture, and setting up a wholly owned subsidiary. The optimal choice among entry modes depends on the company's strategy.

10. Strategic alliances are cooperative agreements between actual or potential competitors. The advantages of alliances are that they facilitate entry into foreign markets, enable partners to share the fixed costs and risks associated with new products and processes, facilitate the transfer of complementary skills between companies, and help companies establish technical standards.

11. The drawbacks of a strategic alliance are that the company risks giving away technological know-how and market access to its alliance partner, while getting very little in return.

12. The disadvantages associated with alliances can be reduced if the company selects partners carefully, paying close attention to reputation, and structures the alliance in order to avoid unintended transfers of know-how.

Discussion Questions

1. Plot the position of the following companies on Figure 8.3: Microsoft, Google, Coca-Cola, Dow Chemicals, Pfizer, and McDonald's. In each case, justify your answer.

2. Are the following global standardization industries, or industries where localization is more important: bulk chemicals, pharmaceuticals, branded food products, moviemaking, television manufacture, personal computers, airline travel, fashion retailing?

3. Discuss how the need for control over foreign operations varies with the strategy and distinctive competencies of a company. What are the implications of this relationship for the choice of entry mode?

4. Licensing proprietary technology to foreign competitors is the best way to give up a company's competitive advantage. Discuss.

5. What kind of companies stand to gain the most from entering into strategic alliances with potential competitors? Why?

6. Reread Strategy in Action 8.1 on how the iPhone is made, and then answer the following questions:
   a) What are the benefits to Apple of outsourcing the assembly of the iPhone to foreign countries, and particularly China? What are the potential costs and risks to Apple?
   b) In addition to Apple, who else benefits from Apple's decision to outsource assembly to China? Who are the potential losers here?
   c) What are the potential ethical problems associated with outsourcing assembly jobs to Foxconn in China? How might Apple deal with these?
   d) On balance, do you think that the kind of outsourcing undertaken by Apple is a good thing or a bad thing for the American economy? Explain your reasoning.
   e) How can a company like Apple, with a global supply chain, hedge against the risks of significant supply chain disruptions due to the SARS virus that appeared in 2003 or the COVID-19 virus that appeared in 2019?

Closing Case

Zhejiang Geely Holding Group Co. Ltd—or Geely, for short—is a Chinese auto manufacturer that started in 1986 as a manufacturer of refrigerators. Founded by Li Shufu, an energetic entrepreneur and car enthusiast, the Hangzhou-based company did not enter the automobile business until 1997. By 2019, it was the second-largest private automobile manufacturer in China, selling 1.36 million cars.

Li Shufu reportedly has a great appreciation for design. He scrapped three batches of poorly designed and built models before finally arriving at one that met his expectations: a four-door subcompact sedan introduced in 2002 and known as the Ziyoujian (*Free Cruiser* in English). In a clear sign that Geely had yet to develop its own design and engineering skills, the car was designed by the South Korean firm Daewoo Motors.

It was around this time that Li started to think about owning Volvo, his personal favorite carmaker. Based in Sweden, Volvo had been acquired by Ford Motor Company in 1999 for $6.45 billion. In 2009, Li got his chance when Ford, battered by the Great Recession that had hammered the auto market in the United States and Europe, announced it would sell many of its specialty car brands, including Volvo. In 2010, Geely reached an agreement to purchase Volvo for $1.8 billion. At the time, this was the largest overseas acquisition by a Chinese automaker.

Many observers had low expectations for the acquisition, but they have been proved wrong. The marriage of Volvo's brand and engineering design skills with Geely's manufacturing capabilities has proved to be a winning combination. Today, Volvo cars are still engineered, designed, and tested in Gothenburg, Sweden, and they still retain their Swedish character, but they are assembled at two new plants in China and a new plant in South Carolina, all built after the acquisition.

Geely has big plans for the South Carolina plant. It is now producing Volvo S60 sedans for sale in the United States, and for export to China. In a few years, the plant is expected to be expanded to produce Volvo SUVs for the U.S. market, increasing output to 150,000 units a year, and doubling the number of U.S. employees to almost 4,000. According to Katarina Fjording, Volvo's vice president of manufacturing and logistics for the Americas, the U.S. plant required a bigger commitment than those in China, where Geely was already building cars and where it had an established logistics and supplier base. In South Carolina, the company has had to do everything from scratch.

Geely and Volvo executives admit it has not all been plain sailing. There have been some cultural clashes along the way. In 2012, for example, when Li visited Sweden to discuss plans for a Chinese version of Volvo's S90 executive sedan, he was horrified by the designs for the back seats. In a Swedish car, "the back seat is where the dog goes," said Volvo's CEO. "Our engineers don't pay much attention to the back seats." "But you guys don't get it," countered Li. "In China, the guy who's paying for the car is sitting in the back!"

Since the acquisition, China has emerged as a major market for Volvo cars, where the brand is valued for its safety and elegance. The company's aim is to produce the safest car on the road that handles well under any road conditions. Geely has pledge to produce a "death-proof" car, with a commitment that no one should be seriously injured or killed in a new Volvo. The technologies required to achieve this include auto steering, adaptive cruise control, and pedestrian and animal detection for collision warnings and avoidance, all technologies that are being developed in Gothenburg.

The proof of the strategy is in the sales figures. In 2018, sales of Geely's Volvo brand rose 12.4% year-on-year to a new record high for the 92-year-old brand. All regions contributed to the 642,000 Volvo cars sold. Sales in China grew by 14%, and sales in the United States grew by 20%. China is now the largest market for the Volvo brand, with 171,676 units sold in 2021, followed by the United States, where 122.173. units were sold.

Since the acquisition, Geely and Volvo have continued to be managed as separate companies. Both Geely and Volvo are owned by Li's investment fund, Zhejiang Geely Holding Group. In February 2020, Li announced that the companies were in talks to combine the two entities into a single integrated operation, but those talks were shelved in 2021.

In other developments, emboldened by its success with Volvo, Geely is now making more foreign investments. In 2017, it acquired a controlling stake in the British sports car manufacturer Lotus Cars; a 49.9% stake in Proton, Malaysia's largest car company; and minority stakes in the Swedish Truck Company, the Volvo Group (the one-time parent of Volvo Cars), and Daimler-Benz (where it took a 10% stake and is now the company's largest shareholder).

Sources: P. Ambler, "Volvo and Geely: The Unlikely Marriage of Swedish Tech and Chinese Manufacturing," *Forbes*, January 23, 2018; S.-L. Wee, "Geely Buys Stake in Volvo Trucks," *New York Times*, December 27, 2017; "Volvo Cars Sets New Global Sales Record in 2018," Volvo Car Group, January 4, 2019; B. Gruley and J. Butler, "How China's 36th Best Car Company Saved Volvo," *Bloomberg Businessweek*, May 24, 2018; T. Moss, "How China's Geely Turned a Disassembled Mercedes into a Global Car Company," *Wall Street Journal*, March 4, 2018; W. Boston, "Chinese Auto Tycoon Aims to Merge Volvo and Geely," *Wall Street Journal*, February 10, 2020.

Case Discussion Questions

1. Which of the strategies described in the chapter is Geely pursuing with Volvo? How might this strategy create value for Geely, enabling it to make a positive return on its investments in Volvo?
2. What are the risks associated with Geely's strategy for Volvo? How might internal company factors and macro-environmental changes impact Geely's ability to maximize its return on investment? What should Geely do to mitigate such risks?
3. In 2017, Geely doubled down on its international expansion with its acquisition of Lotus, a manufacturer of luxury sports cars. What do you think is Geely's objective here? What strategy do you expect Geely to pursue with Lotus? Does this strategy make sense?

Notes

[1] World Trade Organization (WTO), *International Trade Statistics 2022* (Geneva: WTO, 2022).

[2] Ibid.; *United Nations World Investment Report 2022* (New York and Geneva: United Nations, 2022). OECD Data Base on FDI Flows, *OECD.org*, accessed May 2022.

[3] P. Dicken, *Global Shift* (New York: Guilford Press, 1992).

[4] D. Pritchard, "Are Federal Tax Laws and State Subsidies for Boeing 7E7 Selling America Short?" *Aviation Week*, April 12, 2004, pp. 74–75.

[5] T. Levitt, "The Globalization of Markets," *Harvard Business Review*, May–June 1983, pp. 92–102.

[6] M. E. Porter, *The Competitive Advantage of Nations* (New York: Free Press, 1990). See also R. Grant, "Porter's Competitive Advantage of Nations: An Assessment," *Strategic Management Journal* 7 (1991): 535–548.

[7] Empirical evidence does seem to indicate that, on average, international expansion is linked to greater firm profitability. For examples, see M. A. Hitt, R. E. Hoskisson, and H. Kim, "International Diversification, Effects on Innovation and Firm Performance," *Academy of Management Journal* 40 (4) (1997): 767–798; S. Tallman and J. Li, "Effects of International Diversity and Product Diversity on the Performance of Multinational Firms," *Academy of Management Journal* 39:1: (1996): 179–196.

[8] Porter, *Competitive Advantage of Nations*.

[9] See J. Birkinshaw and N. Hood, "Multinational Subsidiary Evolution: Capability and Charter Change in Foreign Owned Subsidiary Companies," *Academy of Management Review* 23 (October 1998): 773–795; A. K. Gupta and V. J. Govindarajan, "Knowledge Flows Within Multinational Corporations," *Strategic Management Journal* 21 (2000): 473–496; V. J. Govindarajan and A. K. Gupta, *The Quest for Global Dominance* (San Francisco: Jossey-Bass, 2001); T. S. Frost, J. M. Birkinshaw, and

P. C. Ensign, "Centers of Excellence in Multinational Corporations," *Strategic Management Journal* 23 (2002): 997–1018; U. Andersson, M. Forsgren, and U. Holm, "The Strategic Impact of External Networks," *Strategic Management Journal* 23 (2002): 979–996.

[10]S. Leung, "Armchairs, TVs and Espresso: Is It McDonald's?" *Wall Street Journal,* August 30, 2002, pp. A1, A6.

[11]C. K. Prahalad and Y. L. Doz, *The Multinational Mission: Balancing Local Demands and Global Vision* (New York: Free Press, 1987). See also J. Birkinshaw, A. Morrison, and J. Hulland, "Structural and Competitive Determinants of a Global Integration Strategy," *Strategic Management Journal* 16 (1995): 637–655.

[12]J. E. Garten, "Walmart Gives Globalization a Bad Name," *Business Week*, March 8, 2004, p. 24.

[13]Prahalad and Doz, *Multinational Mission*. Prahalad and Doz actually talk about local responsiveness rather than local customization.

[14]Levitt, "Globalization of Markets."

[15]W. W. Lewis. *The Power of Productivity* (Chicago: University of Chicago Press, 2004).

[16]For an extended discussion, see G. S. Yip and G. T. M. Hult, *Total Global Strategy* (Boston: Pearson, 2012); A. M. Rugman and A. Verbeke, "A Perspective on Regional and Global Strategies of Multinational Enterprises," *Journal of International Business Studies* 35:1: (2004): 3–18.

[17]Bartlett and Ghoshal, *Managing Across Borders.*

[18]Ibid.

[19]T. Hout, M. E. Porter, and E. Rudden, "How Global Companies Win Out," *Harvard Business Review* (September–October 1982): 98–108.

[20]This section draws on numerous studies, including C. W. L. Hill, P. Hwang, and W. C. Kim, "An Eclectic Theory of the Choice of International Entry Mode," *Strategic Management Journal* 11 (1990): 117–128; C. W. L. Hill and W. C. Kim, "Searching for a Dynamic Theory of the Multinational Enterprise: A Transaction Cost Model," *Strategic Management Journal* 9 (Special Issue on Strategy Content, 1988): 93–104; E. Anderson and H. Gatignon, "Modes of Foreign Entry: A Transaction Cost Analysis and Propositions," *Journal of International Business Studies* 17 (1986): 1–26; F. R. Root, *Entry Strategies for International Markets* (Lexington, MA: D. C. Heath, 1980); A. Madhok, "Cost, Value and Foreign Market Entry: The Transaction and the Firm," *Strategic Management Journal* 18 (1997): 39–61; K. D. Brouthers and L. B. Brouthers, "Acquisition or Greenfield Start-Up?" *Strategic Management Journal* 21:1: (2000): 89–97; X. Martin and R. Salmon, "Knowledge Transfer Capacity and Its Implications for the Theory of the Multinational Enterprise," *Journal of International Business Studies,* July 2003, p. 356; A. Verbeke, "The Evolutionary View of the MNE and the Future of Internalization Theory," *Journal of International Business Studies,* November 2003, pp. 498–515. J. F. Hennart, "Down with the MNC centric theories!" *Journal of International Business Studies*, 40 (2009): 1432–1454. Christian G. Asmussen, and Nicolai J. Foss, "Strategizing and Economizing in Global Strategy," *Global Strategy Journal*, May 16, 2022.

[21]F. J. Contractor, "The Role of Licensing in International Strategy," *Columbia Journal of World Business,* Winter 1982, pp. 73–83.

[22]A. E. Serwer, "McDonald's Conquers the World," *Fortune,* October 17, 1994, pp. 103–116.

[23]For an excellent review of the basic theoretical literature of joint ventures, see B. Kogut, "Joint Ventures: Theoretical and Empirical Perspectives," *Strategic Management Journal* 9 (1988): 319–332. More recent studies include T. Chi, "Option to Acquire or Divest a Joint Venture," *Strategic Management Journal* 21:6: (2000): 665–688; H. Merchant and D. Schendel, "How Do International Joint Ventures Create Shareholder Value?" *Strategic Management Journal* 21:7: (2000): 723–737; H. K. Steensma and M. A. Lyles, "Explaining IJV Survival in a Transitional Economy Through Social Exchange and Knowledge Based Perspectives," *Strategic Management Journal* 21:8: (2000): 831–851; J. F. Hennart and M. Zeng, "Cross Cultural Differences and Joint Venture Longevity," *Journal of International Business Studies,* December 2002, pp. 699–717.

[24]J. A. Robins, S. Tallman, and K. Fladmoe-Lindquist, "Autonomy and Dependence of International Cooperative Ventures," *Strategic Management Journal,* October 2002, pp. 881–902.

[25]C. W. L. Hill, "Strategies for Exploiting Technological Innovations," *Organization Science* 3 (1992): 428–441.

[26]See K. Ohmae, "The GlobalLogic of Strategic Alliances," *Harvard Business Review*, March–April 1989, pp. 143–154; G. Hamel, Y. L. Doz, and C. K. Prahalad, "Collaborate with Your Competitors and Win!" *Harvard Business Review,* January–February 1989, pp. 133–139; W. Burgers, C. W. L. Hill, and W. C. Kim, "Alliances in the Global Auto Industry," *Strategic Management Journal* 14 (1993): 419–432; P. Kale, H. Singh, and H. Perlmutter, "Learning and Protection of Proprietary Assets in Strategic Alliances: Building Relational Capital," *Strategic Management Journal* 21 (2000): 217–237.

[27]L. T. Chang, "China Eases Foreign Film Rules," *Wall Street Journal,* October 15, 2004, p. B2.

[28]B. L. Simonin, "Transfer of Marketing Knowhow in International Strategic Alliances," *Journal*

of *International Business Studies,* 30:3 (1999): 463–91; J. W. Spencer, "Firms' Knowledge Sharing Strategies in the Global Innovation System," *Strategic Management Journal* 24 (2003): 217–233.

[29]Kale et al., "Learning and Protection of Proprietary Assets."

[30]R. B. Reich and E. D. Mankin, "Joint Ventures with Japan Give Away Our Future," *Harvard Business Review,* March–April 1986, pp. 78–90.

[31]J. Bleeke and D. Ernst, "The Way to Win in Cross-Border Alliances," *Harvard Business Review,* November–December 1991, pp. 127–135.

[32]E. Booker and C. Krol, "IBM Finds Strength in Alliances," *B to B,* February 10, 2003, pp. 3, 27.

[33]W. Roehl and J. F. Truitt, "Stormy Open Marriages Are Better," *Columbia Journal of World Business,* Summer 1987, pp. 87–95.

[34]See T. Khanna, R. Gulati, and N. Nohria, "The Dynamics of Learning Alliances: Competition, Cooperation, and Relative Scope," *Strategic Management Journal* 19 (1998): 193–210; Kale et al., "Learning and Protection of Proprietary Assets."

[35]Kale et al., "Learning and Protection of Proprietary Assets."

[36]Hamel et al., "Collaborate with Competitors"; Khanna et al., "The Dynamics of Learning Alliances"; E. W. K. Tang, "Acquiring Knowledge by Foreign Partners from International Joint Ventures in a Transition Economy: Learning by Doing and Learning Myopia," *Strategic Management Journal* 23 (2002): 835–854.

[37]Hamel et al., "Collaborate with Competitors."

[38]B. Wysocki, "Cross Border Alliances Become Favorite Way to Crack New Markets," *Wall Street Journal,* March 4, 1990, p. A1.

Corporate-Level Strategy: Horizontal Integration, Vertical Integration, and Strategic Outsourcing

Opening Case

Volkswagen Invests $20 billion in Developing Its Own Batteries for Electric Vehicles

In July 2022, Volkswagen announced that it would invest over $20 billion to build the capacity to build its own batteries for electric vehicles. The battery manufacturing operations would be overseen by a new Volkswagen spinout called PowerCo. PowerCo would be responsible for managing the entire Volkswagen battery supply chain, from mining raw materials and developing new battery technologies, to manufacturing, and recycling batteries at their end of life.

In the race to build electric vehicles many automakers had found it difficult to secure enough batteries to meet demand. Furthermore, many new battery technologies with better performance characteristics or lower cost were widely expected to displace lithium-ion batteries within the next 5–10 years, spurring many auto manufacturers to invest heavily in battery technology development. The battery of an electric vehicle contributed a huge portion of both its performance and cost; thus, an electric vehicle with a better battery could have a significant competitive advantage in attracting sales over other electric vehicles. Automakers that wanted to compete in electric vehicles could not afford to be left behind in the competition to have a better battery.

Volkswagen had already revealed in 2021 plans to build six battery cell production plants in Europe by 2030, and other plants planned for North America thereafter. The company had also signed contracts with two major battery producers, Samsung and CATL, and had made a major investment in Silicon Valley battery start-up Quantumscape.

PowerCo was expected to employ over 20,000 people and to generate annual sales of over €20 billion. The first plant, at Salzgitter in Germany, was expected to reach an annual capacity of 40 GWh—enough for approximately 500,000 electric vehicles. As the other five European plants came online, that capacity would rise to a total volume of about 240 GWh. Furthermore, PowerCo CEO Frank Blome noted that each factory would be operated 100% on electricity from regenerative sources and would be designed for future closed-loop recycling. PowerCo was also expected to develop major storage systems for the energy grid.[1] Though senior management at Volkswagen was conspicuously silent about whether PowerCo would be able to sell batteries to other automotive manufacturers, industry insiders believed that Volkswagen would likely maintain majority ownership of the company and that its automotive batteries would be sold exclusively to Volkswagen.[2]

Volkswagen was not the first automaker to announce a plan to move into battery manufacturing. Tesla had led the way in July 2016 when it opened its Gigafactory 1—a giant lithium-ion battery factory built near Reno, Nevada, with its partner Panasonic. Tesla CEO Musk justified the vertical integration move by arguing that the Gigafactory 1 would ultimately drive battery production costs down by as

much as 30%.[3] Until recently, however, most automakers had been reluctant to integrate into battery production. Developing and manufacturing batteries required a different set of capabilities from those typically possessed by automakers, and it was seen as risky to make major investments in a technology that was expected to undergo massive change. Instead, automakers had relied on suppliers, largely based in Asia. However, in 2020, General Motors launched a partnership with LG Chem to build batteries for electric vehicles, followed by announcements in 2021 by Stellantis (formerly Fiat Chrysler), Ford, Toyota, and Honda that they would all enter battery production (Stellantis would do so through a joint venture with LG Chem; Ford through a joint venture with SK Innovation). As noted by Arun Kumar, managing director in the automotive and industrial practice at AlixPartners, "There's the rapid electrification that's going to happen, plus the COVID-19 semiconductor shortage has really taught us that we need to do more than just rely on battery as a commodity…You're going to see this accelerate even more, in our viewpoint, primarily because localization becomes an important factor, if you really think about producing batteries at scale."[4]

As stated by Herbert Diess, CEO of Volkswagen, "The battery cell business is one of the cornerstones of our New Auto Strategy which will make Volkswagen a leading provider of the sustainable, software-driven mobility of tomorrow. Establishing our own cell factory is a megaproject in technical and economic terms. It shows that we are bringing the leading-edge technology of the future to Germany!"[5]

Thomas Schmall, Board Member of Volkswagen AG and Supervisory Board Chairman of PowerCo added, "In building our first in-house cell factory, we are consistently implementing our technology roadmap. PowerCo will become a global battery player. The company's major strength will be vertical integration from raw materials and the cell right through to recycling. In the future, we will handle all the relevant activities in-house and will gain a strategic competitive advantage in the race to take the lead in e-mobility. We have secured a top team for this great undertaking."

9-1 Overview

The overriding goal of managers is to maximize the value of a company for its shareholders. The Opening Case about Volkswagen's move into producing its own batteries shows how a company might seek to vertically integrate to have more control over its supply chain and to ensure that it stays on the leading edge of technology. The Closing Case, on Netflix, shows how a firm can create value by leveraging its expertise into adjacent fields, increasing customer loyalty, and increasing bargaining power over suppliers. Often, however, the potential value from vertical or horizontal integration is overestimated; it is thus crucial to be able to understand what the sources of value are, what the probability of harvesting that value is, and the costs and trade-offs involved.

Corporate-level strategy defines the boundaries and scope of the firm, including the businesses and industries in which the firm will compete, which of the value creation activities the firm will perform for those businesses, and how the businesses should be entered, combined, or exited to maximize long-term profitability.

Formulating a strong corporate-level strategy requires discipline, and a very in-depth understanding of when and how different activities and businesses contribute to each other's value creation—and when they do not. It is easy to be seduced by the prospect of growth through expanding the firm's scope, yet many scope expansion moves can increase top-line growth at the expense of profitability. If, for example, a firm with a return on invested capital of 12% invests in assets to enter a new line of business that will increase its revenues but will do so at a return on invested capital of 9%, investors are likely to be (rightfully) angry even if both the revenues and absolute income are increased—the dollars invested in those assets could have instead been paid out to shareholders (or reinvested in the firm's existing higher return activities) rather than invested in assets that earn a lower rate of return.

Chasing revenue growth has led many managers to make decisions that erode a firm's value creation. Good strategic management requires a careful consideration of how investments create value for the firm, whether and why those investments are better than the next best use of its resources, and how such investments create a sustainable advantage for the firm.

When formulating corporate-level strategy, managers must adopt a long-term perspective and consider how changes taking place in an industry and in its products, technology, customers, and competitors will affect their company's current business model and its future strategies. They then decide how to implement specific corporate-level strategies that redefine their company's business model to allow it to increase its competitive advantage in a changing industry environment by taking advantage of opportunities and countering threats. Thus, the principal goal of corporate-level strategy is to enable a company to sustain or promote its competitive advantage and profitability in its present business—*and in any new businesses or industries that it chooses to enter*.

This chapter is the first of two that describe the role of corporate-level strategy in repositioning and redefining a company's business model. We discuss three corporate-level strategies—horizontal integration, vertical integration, and strategic outsourcing—that are primarily directed toward improving a company's competitive advantage and profitability in its current business or industry. Diversification, which entails entry into new kinds of businesses or industries, is examined in the next chapter, along with guidelines for choosing the most profitable way to enter new businesses or industries, or to exit others. By the end of this chapter and the next, you will understand how the different levels of strategy contribute to the creation of a successful, profitable business or multibusiness model. You will also be able to distinguish between the types of corporate strategies managers use to maximize long-term company profitability.

9-2 Corporate-Level Strategy and the Multibusiness Model

9.2 Discuss how corporate-level strategy can be used to strengthen a company's business model and business-level strategies.

The choice of corporate-level strategies is the final part of the strategy-formulation process. Corporate-level strategies drive a company's business model over time and determine which types of business- and functional-level strategies managers will choose to maximize long-term profitability. The relationship between business-level strategy and functional-level strategy was discussed in Chapter 5. Strategic managers develop a business model and strategies that use their company's distinctive competencies to strive for a cost-leadership position and/or to differentiate its products. Chapter 8 described how global strategy is an extension of these basic principles.

In this chapter and the next, we repeatedly emphasize that, to increase profitability, a corporate-level strategy should enable a company or one or more of its business divisions or units *to perform value-chain functional activities (1) at a lower cost and/or (2) in a way that results in increased differentiation.* In addition, corporate-level strategy can increase profitability if it helps a company reduce industry rivalry by reducing the threat of damaging price competition. In sum, a company's corporate-level strategies should be chosen to promote the success of its business-level strategies, which allows it to achieve a sustainable competitive advantage, leading to higher profitability.

Many companies choose to expand their business activities beyond one market or industry and enter others. When a company decides to expand into new industries, it must construct its business model at two levels. First, it must develop a business model and strategies for each business unit or division in every industry in which it competes. Second, it must develop a higher-level *multibusiness model* that justifies its entry into different businesses and industries. This multibusiness model should explain how and why entering a new industry will allow the company to use its existing functional competencies and business strategies to increase its overall profitability. Any time that multiple businesses are integrated into one firm they should pass the "better-off test" and "cost-of-entry test."

The **better-off test** asks "Is additional value created by having these businesses under one roof and does it achieve more value than these businesses could achieve under any non-ownership configuration?" Notably, this test requires managers to think about whether and how the value could be achieved through a market contract, collaboration or other means that might be less costly or more flexible compared to ownership. For example, in the 2000 merger between AOL and Time Warner, managers argued that some of the sources of value of the merger would be to use Time Warner's magazines to advertise AOL's service, and to use AOL's platform to advertise Time Warner's movies. However, neither of these sources of value requires ownership—both companies were already in the business of selling advertising to others and could do so very efficiently. These sources of value should have been excluded from consideration in the assessment of the merger.

better-off test

Is additional value created by having these businesses under one roof and does it achieve more value than these businesses could achieve under any non-ownership configuration?

The **cost-of-entry test** asks, "Can the better-off test be met even after accounting for the cost of entering these businesses?" For example, when Microsoft bought LinkedIn in 2016, they noted that there was the potential to integrate the functionality of Microsoft Word and LinkedIn to create a résumé-building tool. However, Microsoft paid $26.2 billion for LinkedIn, a 50% premium over the market valuation of LinkedIn at that time. For this move to pass the cost-of-entry test, the combination of Microsoft and LinkedIn has to create additional value (over what the companies are worth separately) that exceeds the premium Microsoft paid.

cost-of-entry test

Can the better-off test be met even after accounting for the cost of entering these businesses?

The "better-off test" and "cost-of-entry test" are challenging hurdles to meet, and highlight the complexity of creating value through corporate-level strategy. Managers must have a deep understanding of how businesses create value separately and in combination, what the absolute amount of that value is likely to be, and how much it will cost (in both time and money) to realize that value.

This chapter first focuses on the advantages of staying inside one industry by pursuing horizontal integration. It then looks at why companies use vertical integration and expand into new industries that are in the same value chain as its current businesses. In the next chapter, we examine two principal corporate strategies companies use to enter new industries to increase their profitability—related and unrelated diversification—and several other strategies companies use to enter and compete in new industries.

9.3 Discuss the primary advantages and disadvantages associated with the corporate-level strategy of horizontal integration.

9-3 Horizontal Integration: Single-Industry Corporate Strategy

Managers use corporate-level strategy to identify industries in which their company should compete in order to maximize its long-term profitability. For many companies, profitable growth and expansion often entail finding ways to successfully compete within a single market or industry over time. In other words, a company confines its value creation activities to just one business or industry. Examples of such single-business companies include McDonald's, with its focus on the global fast-food business, and Walmart, with its focus on global discount retailing.

Staying within one industry allows a company to focus all of its managerial, financial, technological, and functional resources and capabilities on competing successfully in one area. This is important in fast-growing, changing industries in which demands on a company's resources and capabilities are likely to be substantial, but where the long-term profits from establishing a competitive advantage are also likely to be substantial.

A second advantage of staying within a single industry is that a company "sticks to the knitting," meaning that it stays focused on what it knows and does best. A company that stays within a single industry does not make the mistake of entering new industries in which its existing resources and capabilities create little value and/or where a whole new set of competitive industry forces—new competitors, suppliers, and customers—present unanticipated threats. Coca-Cola, like many other companies, has committed this strategic error in the past. Coca-Cola once decided to expand into the movie business and acquired Columbia Pictures in 1982; it also acquired Taylor Wine Company in 1977, a large California winemaker. It soon found it lacked the competencies to successfully compete in these new industries, and it had not foreseen the strong competitive forces that existed in these industries from movie companies such as Paramount and winemakers such as Gallo. Coca-Cola concluded that entry into these new industries had reduced rather than created value, and had lowered its profitability; it divested, or sold off, Columbia Pictures to Sony in 1989 and the wine business in 1983 to Joseph E. Seagram & Sons Inc., both at a significant loss.

Even when a company stays in one industry, sustaining a successful business model over time can be difficult because of changing conditions in the environment, such as advances in technology that allow new competitors into the market, or because of changing customer needs. Four decades ago, the strategic issue facing telecommunications providers was how to shape their landline phone services to best meet customer needs in local and long-distance telephone service. However, when wireless telephone service emerged and quickly gained in popularity, landline providers like Verizon and AT&T had to quickly change their business models, lower the price of landline service, merge with wireless companies, and offer broadband services to ensure their survival.

Even within one industry, it is very easy for strategic managers to fail to see the "forest" (the changing nature of the industry, which results in new product/market opportunities) for the "trees" (focusing only on how to position current products). A focus on corporate-level strategy can help managers anticipate future trends and then change their business models to position their companies to compete successfully in a changing environment. Strategic managers must not become so committed to improving their company's *existing* product or service lines that they fail to recognize *new* product or service opportunities and threats. Apple has been so successful because it recognized the increasing number of product opportunities offered by digital entertainment, leading them to move into digital audio devices (iPods), smartphones and watches with a robust ecosystem of applications (iPhone and Apple Watch), and video streaming devices (Apple TV). The task for corporate-level managers is to analyze how emerging technologies will impact their business models, how and why these technologies might change customer needs and customer groups in the future, and what kinds of new, distinctive competencies will be needed to respond to these changes.

One corporate-level strategy that has been widely used to help managers strengthen their company's business model is **horizontal integration**, the process of acquiring or merging with industry competitors to achieve the competitive advantages that arise from a large size and scope of operations. An **acquisition** occurs when one company uses capital resources such as stock, debt, or cash, to purchase another company. A **merger** is an agreement between equals to pool their operations and create a new entity.

Mergers and acquisitions are common in most industries. In the aerospace industry, Boeing merged with McDonnell Douglas in 1996 to create the world's largest aerospace company; in 2000, in the pharmaceutical industry, Pfizer acquired Warner-Lambert to become the largest pharmaceutical firm; and in 2022, Jet Blue and Spirit announced they would merge, enabling them to pool their complementary fleets and serve a larger network of routes while eliminating redundancies and reducing competition for low-fare air travel.[6] Horizontal integration often significantly improves the competitive advantage and profitability of companies whose managers choose to stay within one industry and focus on managing its competitive position to keep the company at the value creation frontier.

horizontal integration
The process of acquiring or merging with industry competitors to achieve the competitive advantages that arise from a large size and scope of operations.

acquisition
When a company uses its capital resources to purchase another company.

merger
An agreement between two companies to pool their resources and operations and join together to better compete in a business or industry.

9-3a Benefits of Horizontal Integration

In pursuing horizontal integration, managers invest their company's capital resources to purchase the assets of industry competitors to increase the profitability of its single-business model. Profitability increases when horizontal integration (1) lowers the cost structure, (2) increases product differentiation, (3) leverages a competitive advantage more broadly, (4) reduces rivalry within the industry, and (5) increases bargaining power over suppliers and buyers.

Lower Cost Structure   Horizontal integration can lower a company's cost structure because it creates increasing *economies of scale*. Suppose five major competitors in the same industry operate manufacturing plants in a given region of the world, but none of the plants operate at full capacity. If one competitor buys another and closes that plant, it can operate its own plant at full capacity and reduce its manufacturing costs. Achieving economies of scale is very important in industries that have a high-fixed-cost structure. In such industries, large-scale production allows companies to spread their fixed costs over a large volume, and in this way drive down average unit costs.

In the telecommunications industry, for example, the fixed costs of building advanced 4G and LTE broadband networks that offered tremendous increases in speed are enormous, and to make such an investment profitable requires a large volume of customers. Thus, AT&T and Verizon purchased other telecommunications companies to acquire their customers, increase their customer base, increase utilization rates, and reduce the cost of servicing each customer. Similar considerations were involved in the hundreds of acquisitions that have taken place in the pharmaceutical industry in the last two decades because of the need to realize scale economies in research and development (R&D) and sales and marketing. The fixed costs of building a nation-wide pharmaceutical sales force are enormous, and pharmaceutical companies such as Pfizer and Merck must possess a wide portfolio of drugs to sell to effectively make use of their sales forces.

A company can also lower its cost structure when horizontal integration allows it to *reduce the duplication of resources* between two companies, such as by eliminating the need for two sets of corporate head offices, two separate sales teams, and so forth. Notably, however, these cost savings are often overestimated. If two companies are operating a function such as a call center, for example, and both are above the minimum efficient scale for operating such a center, there may be few economies from consolidating operations. If each center was already optimally utilized, the consolidated call center could require just as many service people, computers, phone lines, and real estate as the two call centers previously required. Similarly, one justification made for banks consolidating during the late 1990s was that they could save by consolidating their information technology (IT) resources. Ultimately, however, most merged banks realized that their potential savings were meager at best, and the costs of attempting to harmonize their information systems were high; thus, most of them continued to run the separate legacy systems they had prior to merging.

Increased Product Differentiation   Horizontal integration may also increase profitability when it increases product differentiation; for example, by increasing the flow of innovative products that a company's sales force can sell to customers at premium prices. Desperate for new drugs to fill its pipeline, for example, Eli Lilly paid $6.5 billion to ImClone Systems in 2008 to acquire its new, cancer-preventing drugs (and simultaneously prevent its rival, Bristol-Myers Squibb from acquiring ImClone instead). Similarly, Netflix dramatically expanded the range of content it offers to its large subscriber base (both through internal development of original content and acquisition of rights to other's content) in order to increase customer loyalty.

Horizontal integration may also increase differentiation when it allows a company to combine the product lines of merged companies so that it can offer customers a wider range of products that can be bundled together. **Product bundling** involves offering customers the opportunity to purchase a range of products at a single, combined price. Customers may value this if it is more efficient to deal with one company and its representatives, if the brand of a single component offers important signaling about the quality of other components, and if customers can get the bundle at a discount to the price of obtaining the goods individually. This can be valuable to the company by inducing customers to buy the full range of goods from a single company and increasing customer loyalty. It is important to note, however, that product bundling often does not require joint ownership—it can often be achieved through contracts between producers of complementary goods.

A similar way to increase product differentiation is through **cross-selling**, which is when a company takes advantage of or leverages its established relationship with customers by way of acquiring additional product lines or categories that it can sell to them. In this way, a company increases differentiation because it can provide a "total solution" and satisfy all of a customer's specific needs. Cross-selling and becoming a total solution provider is an important rationale for horizontal integration in the computer sector, where IT companies attempt to increase the value of their offerings by satisfying all of the hardware and service needs of corporate customers. Providing a total solution saves customers time and money because they do not have to work with several suppliers, and a single sales team can ensure that all the components of a customer's IT seamlessly work together. When horizontal integration increases the

product bundling

Offering customers the opportunity to purchase a range of products at a single, combined price; this increases the value of a company's product line because customers often obtain a price discount when purchasing a set of products at one time, and customers become used to dealing with only one company and its representatives.

cross-selling

When a company takes advantage of or leverages its established relationship with customers by way of acquiring additional product lines or categories that it can sell to them. In this way, a company increases differentiation because it can provide a "total solution" and satisfy all of a customer's specific needs.

Walmart's Expansion into Other Retail Formats

In 2022, Walmart was one of the world's largest firms (by revenues), with sales of over $570 billion, and employing 2.3 million people. However, as the U.S. discount retail market was mature (where Walmart earned 70% of its revenues), it looked for other opportunities to apply its exceptional retailing power and expertise. In the United States, it had expanded into supercenters that sold groceries in addition to general merchandise and even-lower-priced warehouse store formats (Sam's Club), both of which were doing well. These stores could directly leverage Walmart's bargaining power over suppliers (for many producers of general merchandise, Walmart accounted for more than 70% of their sales, giving it unrivaled power to negotiate prices and delivery terms), and benefitted from its exceptionally efficient system for transporting, managing, and tracking inventory. Walmart had invested relatively early in advanced information technology: it adopted radio frequency identification (RFID) tagging well ahead of its competitors, and satellites tracked inventory in real time. Walmart knew where each item of inventory was at all times and when it was sold, enabling it to simultaneously minimize its inventory holding costs while optimizing the inventory mix in each store. As a result, it had higher sales per square foot and inventory turnover than either Target or Kmart. It handled inventory through a massive, hub-and-spoke distribution system that included more than 140 distribution centers that each served approximately 150 stores within a 150-mile radius. As supercenters and Sam's Clubs were also approaching saturation, however, growth had become harder and harder to sustain. Walmart began to pursue other types of expansion opportunities. It expanded into smaller-format neighborhood stores, international stores (many of which were existing chains that were acquired), and was considering getting into organic foods and trendy fashions. While expansion into contiguous geographic regions (e.g., Canada and Mexico) had gone well, its success at overseas expansions was spottier. Walmart's forays into Germany and South Korea, for example, resulted in large losses, and it ultimately exited the markets. Walmart's entry into Japan was also not as successful as hoped, resulting in many years of losses and never gaining a large share of the market. The challenge was that many of these markets already had tough competitors by the time Walmart entered—they weren't the sleepy, underserved markets that had initially helped it grow in the United States. Furthermore, Walmart's IT and logistics advantages could not easily be leveraged into overseas markets—they would require massive, upfront investments to replicate, and it would be hard to break even on those investments without achieving massive scale in those markets. This raised important questions such as: "Which of Walmart's advantages could be leveraged overseas and to which markets?" "Was Walmart better off trying to diversify its product offerings within North America?" "Should it perhaps reconsider its growth objectives altogether?"

Source: www.walmart.com.

differentiated appeal and value of the company's products, the total solution provider gains market share.

Leveraging a Competitive Advantage More Broadly   For firms that have resources or capabilities that could be valuably deployed across multiple market segments or geographies, horizontal integration may offer opportunities to become more profitable. In the retail industry, for example, Walmart's enormous bargaining power with suppliers and its exceptional efficiency in inventory logistics enabled it to have a competitive advantage in other discount retail store formats, such as its chain of Sam's Clubs (an even-lower-priced warehouse segment). It also expanded the range of products it offers customers when it entered the supermarket business and established a nationwide chain of Walmart supercenters that sell groceries as well as all the clothing, toys, and electronics sold in regular Walmart stores. It has also replicated its business model globally, although not always with as much success as it has had in the United States because many of its efficiencies in logistics (such as its hub-and-spoke distribution system and inventory tracked by satellite) employ fixed assets that are geographically limited (see the Strategy in Action 9.1 for more on this).

Reduced Industry Rivalry   Horizontal integration can help to reduce industry rivalry in two ways. First, acquiring or merging with a competitor helps to *eliminate excess* *capacity* in an industry, which, as we discussed in Chapter 6, often triggers price wars. By taking excess capacity out of an industry, horizontal integration creates a more benign environment in which prices might stabilize—or even increase.

Second, by reducing the number of competitors in an industry, horizontal integration often makes it easier to implement *tacit price coordination* between rivals; that is, coordination reached without communication (explicit communication to fix prices is illegal in most countries). In general, the larger the number of competitors in an industry, the more difficult it is to establish informal pricing agreements—such as price leadership by the dominant company—which increases the possibility that a price war will erupt. By increasing industry concentration and creating an oligopoly, horizontal integration can make it easier to establish tacit coordination among rivals.

Both of these motives seem to have been behind Oracle's many software acquisitions. There was significant excess capacity in the corporate software industry, and major competitors were offering customers discounted prices that had led to a price war and falling profit margins. Oracle hoped to eliminate excess industry capacity, which would reduce price competition.

Increased Bargaining Power Finally, horizontal integration allows some companies to obtain bargaining power over suppliers or buyers and increase profitability at their expense. By consolidating the industry through horizontal integration, a company becomes a much larger buyer of suppliers' products and uses this as leverage to bargain down the price it pays for its inputs, thereby lowering its cost structure. Walmart, for example, is well known for pursuing this strategy. Consolidation among competitors also gives companies more bargaining power over customers: By gaining control over a greater percentage of an industry's product or output, a company can increase its power to raise prices and profits because customers have less choice of suppliers and are more dependent on the company for their products. When a company has greater ability to raise prices to buyers or bargain down the price paid for inputs, it has obtained increased market power.

All five of these motives for horizontal integration can be seen in the case of airline mergers. Mergers in the airline industry are frequently suspected of being anticompetitive; it is often assumed the primary purpose of the mergers is to reduce rivalry and increase market power over customers so that prices can be increased. Consistent with this, researchers have frequently shown the air travel prices of a merged airline rise after the merger. For example, Professors Kwoka and Shumilkina showed that after the merger of US Air and Piedmont in 1987, prices rose between 9 and 10.2% on routes in which the two firms overlapped, and between 5 to 6% on the routes in which one competed and the other firm was a potential entrant.[7] Professors Hüschelrath and Müller similarly found that when Delta Airlines and Northwest Airlines merged in 2009, prices on their previously shared routes went up 11%.[8] However, prices alone paint an incomplete picture of the motives for mergers and their consequences.[9]

The Delta-Northwest merger involved an intense integration effort. The two companies had to negotiate a new common contract with pilots and flight attendants. They merged 1,100 computer systems into about 600, and replaced more than 140,000 electronic devices, including printers, kiosks, and more.[10] By 2010, all of Northwest's bookings had been cancelled and transferred to newly created Delta flights, a feat that required computer engineers to perform 8,856 separate steps. Parts inventory and maintenance processes also had to be merged, and Northwest's assets had to be rebranded as Delta, including painting the planes—a task that was not completed until 2011.[11] It was a costly, lengthy process, but managers of the companies anticipated that the deal would result in significant savings.[12]

The two airlines had route systems that were highly complementary—they had only 12 overlapping routes prior to the merger, accounting for just 2% of Northwest's seats and 3% of Delta's seats.[13] Not surprisingly, then, the savings of the merger were not premised on layoffs or hub closures. Furthermore, on eight of the overlapping routes there were at least two other competing carriers, restricting the ability of the airlines to raise prices. Overall, low-cost carriers were growing 10% annually and accounted for almost one-third of domestic flights, so competition—domestically at least—was still high.

The bigger gains appear to have been upside potential in the quality of service (i.e., product differentiation) and customer loyalty. Delta and Northwest had complementary international footprints: Delta was stronger in Europe and Latin America; Northwest had a stronger presence in Asia and a hub in Tokyo. After the merger, flights formerly branded as Northwest began to offer Delta's higher-quality international service, including free alcoholic drinks on international flights, meals created by Delta's celebrity chefs, a better in-flight entertainment system, and higher-grade amenities in bathrooms and onboard kits. In the decade prior to the merger, Northwest's customer satisfaction rating was consistently below the industry average, and Delta's rating hovered around the industry average. After the merger, Delta's Customer Service rating initially fell for 2 years, and then climbed consistently from 2012 to 2017, achieving a 19% total improvement. Similarly, United, which merged with Continental in 2010, had significant gains in its customer service rating after its merger, achieving a 17% total improvement by 2017. Furthermore, for frequent business travelers, having a single airline with a more comprehensive global footprint and better business-class services made customers willing to bear moderate price increases, and enhanced customer loyalty.

Collectively, this suggests that perhaps the mergers were not intended to achieve monopolistic pricing power, but rather to help them to invest in customer service improvements that would help them to achieve parity with low-cost competitors on customer satisfaction, while also increasing their differentiation from low-cost competitors through larger global footprints and enhanced service features.[14] That differentiation would enable them to charge higher ticket prices.

9-3b Problems with Horizontal Integration

Although horizontal integration can strengthen a company's business model in several ways, there are problems, limitations, and dangers associated with pursuing this corporate-level strategy. Implementing a horizontal integration strategy is no easy task for managers. As discussed in Chapter 10, there are several reasons why mergers and acquisitions may fail to result in higher profitability: problems associated with merging very different company cultures; high management turnover in the acquired company when the acquisition is a hostile one; and a tendency of managers to overestimate the potential benefits from a merger or acquisition and underestimate the challenges involved in merging their operations.[15]

When a company uses horizontal integration to become a dominant industry competitor in the United States, it may come into conflict with the Federal Trade Commission (FTC) or the Department of Justice (DOJ), two government agencies that help to enforce antitrust laws. Antitrust authorities are concerned about the potential for abuse of market power; more competition is generally better for consumers than less competition. Antitrust authorities are likely to intervene when a few companies within one industry try to make acquisitions that will allow them to raise consumer prices above the level that would exist in a more competitive situation, and thus abuse their market power. The FTC and DOJ try to prevent dominant companies from using their market power to crush potential competitors; for example, by cutting prices when a new competitor enters the industry and forcing the competitor out of business, then raising prices after the threatening company has been eliminated.

Because of these concerns, any merger or acquisition the FTC perceives as creating too much consolidation, and the *potential* for future abuse of market power, may, for antitrust reasons, be blocked. The proposed merger between the two dominant satellite radio companies Sirius and XM was blocked for months until it became clear that customers had many other options to obtain high-quality radio programming—for example, through their computers and cell phones—so substantial competition would still exist in the industry. Similarly, in 2015, the DOJ signaled its intention to block the Comcast/Time Warner merger, leading the firms to abandon the deal.

9-4 Vertical Integration: Entering New Industries to Strengthen the "Core" Business Model

Many companies that use horizontal integration to strengthen their business model and improve their competitive position also use the corporate-level strategy of vertical integration for the same purpose. When pursuing vertical integration, however, a company is entering new industries to support the business model of its "core" industry, that is, the industry which is the primary source of its competitive advantage and profitability. At this point, therefore, a company must formulate a multibusiness model that explains how entry into a new industry using vertical integration will enhance its long-term profitability. The model that justifies the pursuit of vertical integration is based on a company entering industries that *add value* to its core products because this increases product differentiation and/or lowers its cost structure, thus increasing its profitability.

vertical integration

When a company expands its operations either backward into an industry that produces inputs for the company's products (backward vertical integration) or forward into an industry that uses, distributes, or sells the company's products (forward vertical integration).

A company pursuing a strategy of **vertical integration** expands its operations either backward into an industry that produces inputs for the company's products (*backward vertical integration*), or forward into an industry that uses, distributes, or sells the company's products (*forward vertical integration*). To enter an industry, it may establish its own operations and build the value chain needed to compete effectively, or it may acquire a company that is already in the industry. A steel company that supplies its iron ore needs from company-owned iron ore mines illustrates backward integration. An auto manufacturer that operates its own dealerships illustrates forward integration. For example, Tesla sells its cars primarily through its own network of retail outlets, often located in high-traffic locations such as shopping malls. IBM is a highly vertically integrated company; it integrated backward into the chip and memory disk industry to produce the components that work inside its mainframes and servers, and integrated forward into the computer software and consulting services industries.

Figure 9.1 illustrates four *main* stages in a typical raw-materials-to-customer value-added chain. For a company based in the final assembly stage, backward integration

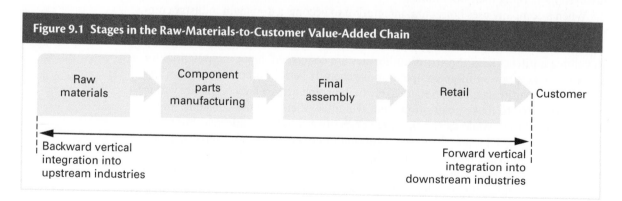

Figure 9.1 Stages in the Raw-Materials-to-Customer Value-Added Chain

Raw materials → Component parts manufacturing → Final assembly → Retail → Customer

Backward vertical integration into upstream industries

Forward vertical integration into downstream industries

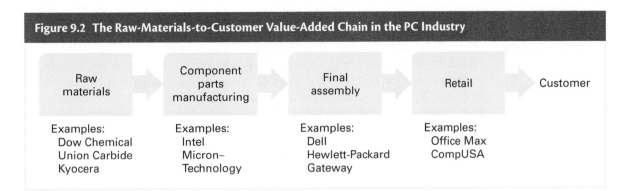

Figure 9.2 The Raw-Materials-to-Customer Value-Added Chain in the PC Industry

Raw materials → Component parts manufacturing → Final assembly → Retail → Customer

Examples:
Dow Chemical
Union Carbide
Kyocera

Examples:
Intel
Micron–Technology

Examples:
Dell
Hewlett-Packard
Gateway

Examples:
Office Max
CompUSA

means moving into component parts manufacturing and raw materials production. Forward integration means moving into distribution and sales (retail). At each stage in the chain *value is added* to the product, transforming it in such a way that it is worth more to the company at the next stage in the chain and, ultimately, to the customer. It is important to note that each stage of the value-added chain involves a separate industry, or industries, in which many different companies compete. Moreover, within each industry, each company has a value chain composed of the value creation activities we discussed in Chapter 3: R&D, production, marketing, customer service, and so on. In other words, we can think of a value chain that runs *across* industries, and embedded within that are the value chains of companies *within* each industry.

As an example of the value-added concept, consider how companies in each industry involved in the production of a PC contribute to the final product (Figure 9.2). The first stage in the chain includes raw-materials companies that make specialty ceramics, chemicals, and metal, such as Kyocera of Japan, which manufactures the ceramic substrate for semiconductors. Companies at the first stage in the chain sell their products to the makers of PC component products, such as Intel and AMD, which transform the ceramics, chemicals, and metals they purchase into PC components such as microprocessors, disk drives, and memory chips. In the process, companies *add value* to the raw materials they purchase. At the third stage, the manufactured components are sold to PC makers such as Apple, Dell, and HP, and these companies decide which components to purchase and assemble to *add value* to the finished PCs (that they make or outsource to a contract manufacturer). At stage four, the finished PCs are then either sold directly to the final customer over the Internet or sold to retailers such as Best Buy and Staples, which distribute and sell them to the final customer. Companies that distribute and sell PCs also *add value* to the product because they make the product accessible to customers and provide customer service and support.

Thus, companies in different industries add value at each stage in the raw-materials-to-customer chain. Viewed in this way, vertical integration presents companies with a choice about within which industries in the raw-materials-to-customer chain to operate and compete. This choice is determined by the degree to which establishing operations at a given stage in the value chain will increase product differentiation or lower costs—and therefore increase profitability—as we discuss in the following section.

9-5 Advantages and Disadvantages of Vertical Integration

9.5 Review the advantages and disadvantages of vertical integration.

As noted earlier, a company pursues vertical integration to strengthen the business model of its original or core business and improve its competitive position.[16] Vertical integration increases product differentiation, lowers costs, or reduces industry competition when it (1) facilitates investments in efficiency-enhancing, specialized assets, (2) protects product quality, and (3) results in improved scheduling.

Facilitating Investments in Specialized Assets　A specialized asset is one designed to perform a specific task, and the value of which is significantly reduced in its next-best use.[17] The asset may be a piece of equipment that has a firm-specific use or the knowhow or skills that a company or employees have acquired through training and experience. Companies invest in specialized assets because these assets allow them to lower their cost structure or to better differentiate their products, which facilitates premium pricing. A company might invest in specialized equipment to lower manufacturing costs, as Toyota does, for example; or it might invest in an advanced technology that allows it to develop better-quality products than its rivals, as Apple does. Thus, specialized assets can help a company achieve a competitive advantage at the business level.

Just as a company invests in specialized assets in its own industry to build competitive advantage, it is often necessary that suppliers invest in specialized assets to produce the inputs that a specific company needs. By investing in these assets, a supplier can make higher-quality inputs that provide its customers with a differentiation advantage, or inputs at a lower cost so it can charge its customers a lower price to keep their business. However, it is often difficult to persuade companies in adjacent stages of the value chain to invest in specialized assets. Often, to realize the benefits associated with such investments, a company must vertically integrate and enter into adjacent industries and invest its own resources. Why does this happen?

Imagine that Panasonic has developed a ceramic coating for metal pans that enabled you to bake a cake in its microwaves using a special cooking setting. The ability to bake would be a strong differentiating feature for Panasonic microwaves. Panasonic has to decide whether to make the coated pans in-house (vertical integration) or contract with a specialist outsourcing manufacturer to make the pans. Manufacturing these new pans requires a substantial investment in equipment that can be used only for this purpose.. Thus, this is an investment in specialized assets.

Consider this situation from the perspective of the outside supplier deciding whether or not to make this investment. The supplier might reason that once it has made the investment, it will become dependent on Panasonic for business because *Panasonic is the only microwave maker that has developed the baking technique in its microwaves.* The supplier realizes that this puts Panasonic in a strong bargaining position, and that Panasonic might use its buying power to demand lower prices for the pans. Given the risks involved, the supplier declines to make the investment in specialized equipment.

Now consider Panasonic's position. Panasonic might reason that if it outsources production of these pans to an outside supplier, it might become too dependent on that supplier for a vital input. Because specialized equipment is required to produce the pans, Panasonic cannot quickly switch its order to other suppliers. Panasonic realizes that this increases the bargaining power of the supplier, which then might demand higher prices.

The situation of *mutual dependence* that would be created by the investment in specialized assets makes Panasonic hesitant to allow outside suppliers to make the product and makes suppliers hesitant to undertake such a risky investment. The problem is a lack of trust—neither Panasonic nor the supplier can trust the other to operate fairly in this situation. The lack of trust arises from the risk of **holdup**—that is, being taken advantage of by a trading partner *after* the investment in specialized assets has been made.[18] Because of this risk, Panasonic reasons that the only cost-effective way to get the new pans is to invest in specialized assets and manufacture the pans in-house.

holdup

When a company is taken advantage of by another company it does business with after it has made an investment in expensive specialized assets to better meet the needs of the other company.

To generalize from this example, if achieving a competitive advantage requires one company to make investments in specialized assets so it can trade with another, *the risk of holdup* may serve as a deterrent, and the investment may not take place. Consequently, the potential for higher profitability from specialization will be lost. To prevent such loss, companies vertically integrate into adjacent stages in the value chain. Historically, the problems surrounding specific assets have driven automobile companies to vertically integrate backward into the production of component parts, steel companies to vertically integrate backward into the production of iron, computer companies to vertically integrate backward into chip production, and aluminum companies to vertically integrate backward into bauxite mining. Often such firms practice **tapered integration**, whereby the firm makes some input and buys some input. Purchasing part or most of its needs for a given input from suppliers enables the firm to tap the advantages of the market (e.g., choosing from suppliers that are competing to improve quality or lower the cost of the product). At the same time, meeting some of its needs for input through internal production improves the firm's bargaining power by reducing the likelihood of holdup by its supplier. A firm that is engaged in production of an input is also better able to evaluate the cost and quality of external suppliers of that input.[19]

tapered integration
When a firm uses a mix of vertical integration and market transactions for a given input. For example, a firm might operate limited semiconductor manufacturing while also buying semiconductor chips on the market. Doing so helps to prevent supplier holdup (because the firm can credibly commit to not buying from external suppliers) and increases its ability to judge the quality and cost of purchased supplies.

Enhancing Product Quality By entering industries at other stages of the value-added chain, a company can often enhance the quality of the products in its core business and strengthen its differentiation advantage. For example, the ability to control the reliability and performance of complex components such as engine and transmission systems may increase a company's competitive advantage in the luxury-sedan market and enable it to charge a premium price. Conditions in the banana industry also illustrate the importance of vertical integration in maintaining product quality. Historically, a problem facing food companies that import bananas has been the variable quality of delivered bananas, which often arrive on the shelves of U.S. supermarkets too ripe or not ripe enough. To correct this problem, major U.S. food companies such as Del Monte Fresh Produce and Dole Food Company have integrated backward and now own banana plantations, sea transportation, and ripening facilities, putting them in control of the banana supply. As a result, they can distribute and sell bananas of a standard quality at the optimal time to better satisfy customers. Knowing they can rely on the quality of these brands, customers are willing to pay more for them. Thus, by vertically integrating backward into plantation ownership, banana companies have built customer confidence, which has in turn enabled them to charge a premium price for their product.

The same considerations can promote forward vertical integration. Ownership of retail outlets may be necessary if the required standards of after-sales service for complex products are to be maintained. For example, in the 1990s, McDonald's faced a problem: After decades of rapid growth, the fast-food market was beginning to show signs of saturation. McDonald's responded to the slowdown by rapidly expanding abroad. However, McDonald's U.S. success was built on a formula of close relations with suppliers, nationwide marketing, and tight control over store-level operating procedures. It proved to be far more difficult replicating these sources of success in other countries. For example, one of the keys to McDonald's consistency and quality control was very rigorous specifications for all the raw ingredients it uses. Outside of the United States, however, McDonald's has found suppliers far less willing to make the investments required to meet its specifications. In Great Britain, for example, McDonald's had problems getting local bakeries to produce the hamburger bun. After experiencing quality problems with two local bakeries, McDonald's had to vertically integrate backward and build its own bakeries to supply its British stores. When McDonald's first entered Russia, it found that local suppliers lacked the capability to produce ingredients of the quality it demanded. It was then forced to vertically integrate through the local food industry on an epic scale, importing potato seeds and bull semen and indirectly managing dairy farms, cattle ranches, and vegetable plots. It also needed to construct the world's largest food-processing plant, at great cost. In South America, McDonald's purchased huge ranches in Argentina upon which it could raise its own cattle. In short, vertical integration has allowed McDonald's to protect product quality and reduce its global cost structure.[20]

Improved Scheduling   Sometimes important strategic advantages can be obtained when vertical integration makes it quicker, easier, and more cost-effective to plan, coordinate, and schedule the transfer of a product such as raw materials or component parts between adjacent stages of the value-added chain.[21] Such advantages can be crucial when a company wants to realize the benefits of just-in-time (JIT) inventory systems. For example, in the 1920s, Ford profited from the tight coordination and scheduling that backward vertical integration made possible. Ford integrated backward into steel foundries, iron ore shipping, and iron ore production—it owned mines in Upper Michigan. Deliveries at Ford were coordinated to such an extent that iron ore unloaded at Ford's steel foundries on the Great Lakes was turned into engine blocks within 24 hours, which lowered Ford's cost structure.

9-5a   Problems with Vertical Integration

Vertical integration can often be used to strengthen a company's business model and increase profitability. However, the opposite can occur when vertical integration results in (1) an increasing cost structure, (2) disadvantages that arise when technology is changing fast, (3) disadvantages that arise when demand is unpredictable, and (4) mismatches in optimal scale. Sometimes these disadvantages are so great that vertical integration, rather than increasing profitability, may actually reduce it—in which case a company engages in **vertical disintegration** and exits industries adjacent to its core industry in the industry value chain. For example, Ford, which was highly vertically integrated, sold all its companies involved in mining iron ore and making steel when more efficient and specialized steel producers emerged that were able to supply lower-priced steel.

Increasing Cost Structure   Although vertical integration is often undertaken to lower a company's cost structure, it can raise costs if, over time, a company makes mistakes such as continuing to purchase inputs from company-owned suppliers when low-cost independent suppliers that can supply the same inputs exist. For decades, for example, GM's company-owned suppliers made more than 60% of the component parts for its vehicles; this figure was far higher than that for any other major carmaker, which is why GM became such a high-cost carmaker. In 1990s, it vertically disintegrated by selling off many of its largest component operations, such as Delphi Automotive Systems, its electrical components supplier. Thus, vertical integration can be a major disadvantage when company-owned suppliers develop a higher cost structure than those of independent suppliers. Why would a company-owned supplier develop such a high cost structure?

In this example, company-owned or in-house suppliers know that they can always sell their components to the car-making divisions of their company—they have a "captive customer." Because company-owned suppliers do not have to compete with independent, outside suppliers for orders, they have much less *incentive* to look for new ways to reduce operating costs or increase component quality. Indeed, in-house suppliers simply pass on cost increases to the car-making divisions in the form of higher **transfer prices**, the prices one division of a company charges other divisions for its products. Unlike independent suppliers, which constantly need to increase their efficiency to protect their competitive advantage, in-house suppliers face no such competition, and the resulting rising cost structure reduces a company's profitability.

vertical disintegration

When a company decides to exit industries, either forward or backward in the industry value chain, to its core industry to increase profitability.

transfer prices

The prices that one division of a company charges another division for its products, which are the inputs the other division requires to manufacture its own products.

The term *bureaucratic costs* refers to the costs of solving the transaction difficulties that arise from managerial inefficiencies and the need to manage the handoffs or exchanges between business units to promote increased differentiation, or to lower a company's cost structure. Bureaucratic costs become a significant component of a company's cost structure because considerable managerial time and effort must be spent to reduce or eliminate managerial inefficiencies such as those that result when company-owned suppliers lose their incentive to increase efficiency or innovation.

Technological Change   When technology is changing fast, vertical integration may lock a company into an old, inefficient technology and prevent it from changing to a new one that would strengthen its business model.[22] Consider Sony, which had integrated backward to become the leading manufacturer of now-outdated cathode ray tubes (CRTs) used in TVs and computer monitors. Because Sony was locked into the outdated CRT technology, it was slow to recognize that the future was in liquid crystal display (LCD) flat screens and it did not exit the CRT business. Sony's resistance to change in technology forced it to enter into a strategic alliance with Samsung to supply the LCD screens that were used in its BRAVIA TVs. As a result, Sony lost its competitive advantage and experienced a major loss in TV market share. Thus, vertical integration can pose a serious disadvantage when it prevents a company from adopting new technology, or changing its suppliers or distribution systems to match the requirements of changing technology.

Demand Unpredictability   Suppose the demand for a company's core product, such as cars or washing machines, is predictable, and the company knows how many units it needs to make each month or year. Under these conditions, vertical integration allows a company to schedule and coordinate efficiently the flow of products along the industry value-added chain, which may result in major cost savings. However, suppose the demand for cars or washing machines wildly fluctuates and is unpredictable. If demand for cars suddenly plummets, the carmaker may find itself burdened with warehouses full of component parts it no longer needs, which is a major drain on profitability—something that has hurt major carmakers during the recent recession. Thus, vertical integration can be risky when demand is unpredictable because it is hard to manage the volume or flow of products along the value-added chain.

For example, a PC maker might vertically integrate backward to acquire a supplier of memory chips so that it can make exactly the number of chips it needs each month. However, if demand for PCs falls because of the popularity of mobile computing devices, the PC maker finds itself locked into a business that is now inefficient because it is not producing at full capacity, and therefore its cost structure starts to rise. In general, high-speed environmental change (e.g., technological change, changing customer demands, and major shifts in institutional norms or competitive dynamics) provides a disincentive for integration, as the firm's asset investments are at greater risk of rapid obsolescence.[23] It is clear that strategic managers must carefully assess the advantages and disadvantages of expanding the boundaries of their company by entering adjacent industries, either backward (upstream) or forward (downstream), in the industry value-added chain. Moreover, although the decision to enter a new industry to make crucial component parts may have been profitable in the past, it may make no economic sense today because so many low-cost, global, component parts suppliers exist that compete for the company's business. The risks and returns on investing in vertical integration must be continually evaluated, and companies should be as willing to vertically disintegrate as to vertically integrate to strengthen their core business model.

Mismatches in Optimal Scale   Even in situations where it appears that vertical integration might improve product quality or provide other benefits, it can be inefficient to vertically integrate if the new business has a higher minimum efficient scale than could be reasonably utilized by the current business. Consider, for example, a company like Lime, which operates a dockless electric scooter sharing service. Lime leaves electric scooters in locations where it believes customers want to use them, and customers use an application on their smartphone to unlock the scooter and pay for the rental. The battery on a typical Lime electric scooter has about a 25-mile range, and requires many hours to fully charge. Lime pays "juicers"—people who sign up to be independent contractors—to pick up the scooters, charge them overnight, and drop them off in locations designated by Lime. Because many people are riding Lime's scooters during the day, often for commuting purposes, their batteries are discharged much more quickly than the average consumer's scooter. Thus, many scooters spend a large portion of the day sitting idle because their batteries are dead. For Lime, a scooter with a fast-charging battery with a longer range would significantly enhance the value of service while also streamlining its operations. However, it is not feasible for Lime to backward vertically integrate into manufacturing scooters or battery production because both have very large fixed costs, and their minimum efficient scale (i.e., the size at which they could compete efficiently against competitors) is very large. A minimum, efficient, scale scooter manufacturing plant, for example, would produce more scooters than Lime needs, meaning that it would have to find other buyers of its longer-range scooters, which would likely include competing electric scooter services. Instead, Lime opts to buy scooters that are not optimized for its purposes.

9-6 Alternatives to Vertical Integration: Cooperative Relationships

9.6 Discuss the best conditions for using cooperative relationships.

Is it possible to obtain the differentiation and cost-savings advantages associated with vertical integration without having to bear the problems and costs associated with this strategy? In other words, is there another corporate-level strategy that managers can use to obtain the advantages of vertical integration while allowing other companies to perform upstream and downstream activities? Today, companies have found that they can realize many of the benefits associated with vertical integration by entering into *long-term cooperative relationships* with companies in industries along the value-added chain, also known as **quasi integration**. Such moves could include, for example, sharing the expenses of investment in production assets or inventory, or making long-term supply or purchase guarantees.

quasi integration

The use of long-term relationships, or investment in some activities normally performed by suppliers or buyers, in place of full ownership of operations that are backward or forward in the supply chain.

9-6a Short-Term Contracts and Competitive Bidding

Many companies use short-term contracts that last for a year or less to establish the price and conditions under which they will purchase raw materials or components from suppliers or sell their final products to distributors or retailers. A classic example is the carmaker that uses a *competitive bidding strategy*, in which independent component suppliers compete to be chosen to supply a particular component, such as brakes, made to agreed-upon specifications, at the lowest price. For example, GM typically solicits bids from global suppliers to produce a particular component and awards a 1-year contract to the supplier that submits the lowest bid. At the end of the year, the contract is once again put out for competitive bid, and once again the lowest-cost supplier is most likely to win the bid.

The advantage of this strategy for GM is that suppliers are forced to compete over price, which drives down the cost of its components. However, GM has no long-term commitment to outside suppliers—and it drives a hard bargain. For this reason, suppliers are sometimes unwilling to make the expensive, long-term investments in specialized assets that are required to produce higher-quality or better-designed component parts over time.

As a result, short-term contracting might not result in the specialized investments that are required to realize differentiation and cost advantages *because it signals a company's lack of long-term commitment to its suppliers*. Of course, this is not a problem when there is minimal need for cooperation, and specialized assets are not required to improve scheduling, enhance product quality, or reduce costs. In this case, competitive bidding may be optimal. However, when there is a need for cooperation—something that is becoming increasingly significant today—the use of short-term contracts and competitive bidding can be a serious drawback.

9-6b Strategic Alliances and Long-Term Contracting

Unlike short-term contracts, **strategic alliances** between buyers and suppliers are long-term, cooperative relationships; both companies agree to make specialized investments and work jointly to find ways to lower costs or increase product quality so that they both gain from their relationship. A strategic alliance becomes a *substitute* for vertical integration because it creates a relatively stable, long-term partnership that allows both companies to obtain the same kinds of benefits that result from vertical integration. However, it also avoids the problems (bureaucratic costs) that arise from managerial inefficiencies that result when a company owns its own suppliers, such as those that arise because of a lack of incentives, or when a company becomes locked into an old technology even when technology is rapidly changing.

strategic alliances
Long-term agreements between two or more companies to jointly develop new products or processes that benefit all companies that are a part of the agreement.

Consider the cooperative relationships that many Japanese carmakers have with their component suppliers (the *keiretsu* system), often established decades ago. Japanese carmakers and suppliers cooperate to find ways to maximize the value added they can obtain from being a part of adjacent stages of the value chain; for example, by jointly implementing JIT inventory system or sharing future component-parts designs to improve quality and lower assembly costs. As part of this process, suppliers make substantial investments in specialized assets to better serve the needs of a particular carmaker, and the cost savings that result are shared. Thus, Japanese carmakers have been able to capture many of the benefits of vertical integration without having to enter the component industry.

Similarly, component suppliers also benefit because their business and profitability grow as the companies they supply grow, and they can invest their profits in investing in ever more specialized assets.[24] An interesting example of this is the computer chip outsourcing giant Taiwan Semiconductor Manufacturing Company (TSMC), which makes chips for many companies such as NVIDIA, Acer, and AMD. The cost of investing in the machinery necessary to build a state-of-the-art chip factory can exceed $10 billion. TSMC is able to make this huge and risky investment because it has developed cooperative, long-term relationships with its computer-chip partners. All parties recognize that they will benefit from this outsourcing arrangement, which does not preclude hard bargaining between TSMC and the chip companies, because all parties want to maximize their profits and reduce their risks.

9-6c Modularity and Platform Competition

As noted in Chapter 7, in many industries, a product is only valuable if there are a range of complements available for it. A smartphone operating system, for example, is only as good as the applications available, and a music streaming service is only as valuable as the number and quality of tracks it offers. A firm must decide which of these to produce itself (treating them as features), which to buy and include with the product (treating them as supplies), and which to count on the market providing (treating them as third-party complements). This is often a difficult decision; it may be impractical for a firm to attempt to meet these needs itself, but if the market does not provide adequate complements, its product may fail. In such a case, firms will often use *modularity* and contracts with third-party complements providers to create a *platform ecosystem* where many different firms contribute to the product system.[25]

To understand **modularity**, consider a product like a bicycle: A bicycle is a bundle of components that includes a frame, a gear shifting system, a headset, and more. Some of these components can be bought separately and assembled by the user, and some are typically bought preassembled. Products may be made increasingly modular both by expanding the range of compatible components (increasing the range of possible product configurations), and by uncoupling integrated functions within components (making the product modular at a finer level) (see Figure 9.3). For example, smartphone manufacturers might originally only offer proprietary phones where they have produced both the hardware and software, and integrate them tightly into a single product configuration (Figure 9.3, panel A). However, greater market demand for flexibility might induce manufacturers to start offering phones with a few different configurations. If customers prefer to be able to combine phones with accessories or applications from other producers, smartphone makers may "open" their systems up, creating a **standardized interface** that enables other developers to create products that are compatible with the phones (Figure 9.3, panel B). Smartphone makers may even decide to uncouple their operating systems from the hardware so that consumers can use the operating system on devices made by other manufacturers, as Google does with Android (Figure 9.3, panel C). In each of these stages, the product has become increasingly modular.

The majority of products are modular at some level. For example, when you buy a car, you can often choose an engine size, upholstery options, automatic steering or transmission, stereo system, tires, roof racks, security systems, etc., but the automaker assembles the configuration for you.

Tightly integrated (i.e., nonmodular) product systems and modular systems have different advantages. A tightly integrated product system might have components that are customized to work together, which may enable a level of performance that more standardized components cannot achieve. The producer of a tightly integrated system also has more control over the end product, which can enable it to better monitor quality and reliability. For years, this was the reason Steve Jobs gave for not making Apple computers as modular as Windows-based computers—he believed that by controlling all of the components and most of the software, Apple computers could achieve greater functionality and reliability.[26] An integrated product may also be more attractive to a customer that does not want to choose or assemble components.

Modular products, on the other hand, often offer more choices over function, design, scale, and other features, enabling the customer to choose a product system that more closely suits their needs and preferences.[27] Second, because components are re-used in different combinations, this can achieve product variety while still allowing scale economies in manufacturing the individual components. This is known as "economies of substitution."[28]

Modularity becomes increasingly valuable in a product system when there are diverse technological options available to be recombined and heterogeneous customer preferences.[29] For example, there is a very wide range of applications available for smartphones, and customers are very heterogeneous in the applications they want on their smartphones. This increases the value of being able to pick and choose your own customized mix of applications that go on your smartphone. This example also reveals how pressure for modularity can lead to platform ecosystems.

In a **platform ecosystem**, some core part of a product (such as a videogame console or music streaming service) mediates the relationship between a wide range of

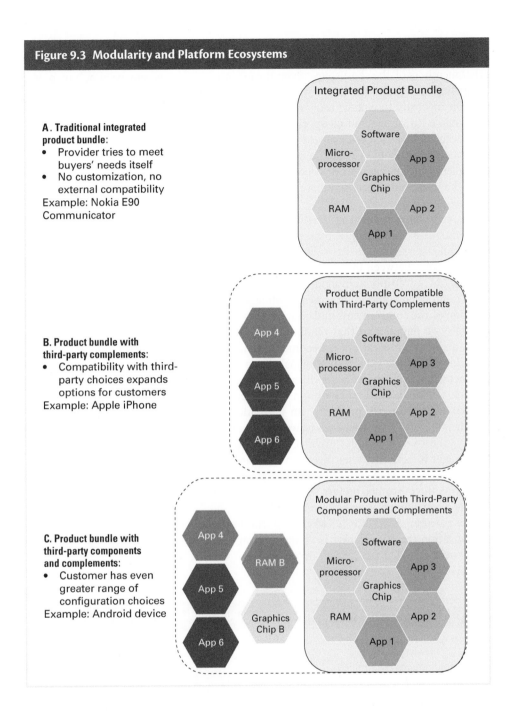

Figure 9.3 Modularity and Platform Ecosystems

A. Traditional integrated product bundle:
- Provider tries to meet buyers' needs itself
- No customization, no external compatibility

Example: Nokia E90 Communicator

Integrated Product Bundle

Software, Micro-processor, App 3, Graphics Chip, RAM, App 2, App 1

B. Product bundle with third-party complements:
- Compatibility with third-party choices expands options for customers

Example: Apple iPhone

Product Bundle Compatible with Third-Party Complements

App 4, App 5, App 6

Software, Micro-processor, App 3, Graphics Chip, RAM, App 2, App 1

C. Product bundle with third-party components and complements:
- Customer has even greater range of configuration choices

Example: Android device

Modular Product with Third-Party Components and Complements

App 4, RAM B, App 5, Graphics Chip B, App 6

Software, Micro-processor, App 3, Graphics Chip, RAM, App 2, App 1

other components or complements (such as video games or music) and prospective end users.[30] A platform ecosystem's boundaries can be well defined, with a stable set of members dedicated wholly to that platform, or they can be amorphous and changing, with members entering and exiting freely, and participating in multiple platforms simultaneously. For example, consider the difference between the television/movie streaming services HBO On Demand and Amazon Prime. HBO On Demand exists to serve only HBO content up to consumers. The shows available are tightly controlled, and there is limited entry and exit of show producers. The Amazon Prime ecosystem is much more open. In fact, just about any content producer—including individual, independent filmmakers—can make their content available on Amazon Prime.

Because it is the overall appeal of the ecosystem that attracts end-users to the platform, the success of individual members depends, at least in part, upon the success of other members of the ecosystem—even those with which they may be simultaneously competing. Furthermore, in many platforms there are switching costs that make it difficult or costly to change ecosystems. Platforms and their complements providers often make investments in co-specialization or sign exclusivity agreements that bind them into stickier, longer-term relationships than the market contracts used in typical reseller arrangements. A video game that has been made for the Microsoft Xbox, for example, cannot be played on a PlayStation console unless a new version of it is made (and the game producer may have signed a contract with Microsoft that prohibits this).

A platform ecosystem is thus characterized by relationships that are neither as independent as arms-length market contracts, nor as dependent as those within a hierarchical organization. It is, in essence, a hybrid organizational form.[31] It strikes a compromise between the loose coupling of a purely modular system, and the tight coupling of a traditional integrated product. It enables customers to mix-and-match some components and complements, while still enabling some co-specialization and curation of the complements and components available for the system (see Figure 9.4).

Once we understand that platforms are like a compromise between pure modularity and pure integration, it becomes easier to understand when platforms will be desirable in a market. First, platforms will be more valuable than a tightly integrated product when (a) customers are diverse and want more choices than a single firm can provide, (b) when third-party options are diverse and high quality, (c) when compatibility with third-party products can be made seamless without integration, and/or (d) when the platform sponsor is powerful enough that it can retain control over quality and the overall product architecture without producing the complements itself. Looking at it from the other direction, platforms will be more valuable than a purely modular system when (a) complements are nonroutine purchases with uncertainty (and thus the customer prefers to have some shepherding by the platform sponsor), (b) when some integration between the platform and its complements provides performance advantages, and/or (c) when important components of the ecosystem require subsidization (i.e., the market is unlikely to provide all the complements the end customer needs at adequate quality or value).

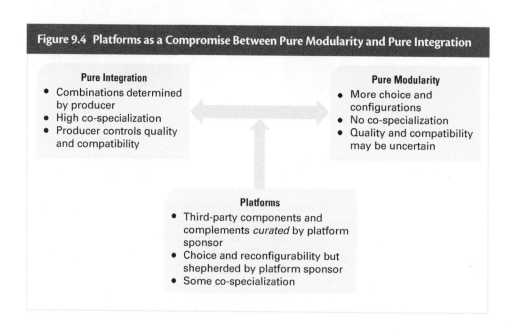

Figure 9.4 Platforms as a Compromise Between Pure Modularity and Pure Integration

Pure Integration
- Combinations determined by producer
- High co-specialization
- Producer controls quality and compatibility

Pure Modularity
- More choice and configurations
- No co-specialization
- Quality and compatibility may be uncertain

Platforms
- Third-party components and complements *curated* by platform sponsor
- Choice and reconfigurability but shepherded by platform sponsor
- Some co-specialization

Videogame systems are an iconic example of platform ecosystems. Consoles need to launch with high-quality games. Since it is difficult to induce game developers to make games for a console that has not yet been widely adopted, most game console producers must produce games themselves (or subsidize their production) to ensure that high-quality games are available when the console launches. On the other hand, end users want more games than just those produced by the console producer, so console producers like Microsoft, Sony, and Nintendo also license third-party developers to produce games for their consoles. They carefully screen the licensed games for quality and compatibility, and they may require the game developers to sign exclusivity agreements or to customize the games for the console. The console maker may also manage the end users' awareness and perception of the games in the ecosystem by giving "Best of" awards to particular games, by bundling particular games with the console at point of purchase, or by featuring particular games in its marketing. These strategies enable the console producer to actively manage the overall value created by its ecosystem.[32]

9-6d Building Long-Term Cooperative Relationships

How does a company create a long-term strategic alliance with another company when the fear of holdup exists, and the possibility of being cheated arises if one company makes a specialized investment with another company? How do companies such as GM or Nissan manage to develop profitable, enduring relationships with their suppliers?

There are several strategies companies can adopt to promote the success of a long-term, cooperative relationship and lessen the chance that one company will renege on its agreement and cheat the other. One strategy is for the company that makes the specialized investment to demand a *hostage* from its partner. Another is to establish a *credible commitment* from both companies that will result in a trusting, long-term relationship.[33]

Hostage Taking Hostage taking is essentially a means of guaranteeing that each partner will keep its side of the bargain. The cooperative relationship between Boeing and Northrop Grumman illustrates this type of situation. Northrop is a major subcontractor for Boeing's commercial airline division, providing many components for its aircraft. To serve Boeing's special needs, Northrop made substantial investments in specialized assets, and, in theory, because of this investment, has become dependent on Boeing—which can threaten to change orders to other suppliers as a way of driving down Northrop's prices. In practice, Boeing is highly unlikely to change suppliers because it is, in turn, a major supplier to Northrop's defense division and provides many parts for its Stealth aircraft; it also has made major investments in specialized assets to serve Northrop's needs. Thus, the companies are *mutually dependent*; each company holds a hostage—the specialized investment the other has made. Thus, Boeing is unlikely to renege on any pricing agreements with Northrop because it knows that Northrop would respond the same way.

Credible Commitments A credible commitment is a believable promise or pledge to support the development of a long-term relationship between companies. Consider the way GE and IBM developed such a commitment in 1987. GE was a major supplier of advanced semiconductor chips to IBM, and many of the chips were customized to IBM's requirements. To meet IBM's specific needs, GE had to make substantial investments in specialized assets that had little value outside of the IBM relationship. As a consequence, GE was dependent on IBM and faced a risk that IBM would take advantage of this dependence to demand lower prices. In theory,

hostage taking
A means of exchanging valuable resources to guarantee that each partner to an agreement will keep its side of the bargain.

credible commitment
A believable promise or pledge to support the development of a long-term relationship between companies.

eBay's Changing Commitment to Its Sellers

Since its founding in 1995, eBay has cultivated good relationships with the millions of sellers that advertise their goods for sale on its website. Over time, however, to increase its revenues and profits, eBay has steadily increased the fees it charges sellers to list their products on its sites, to insert photographs, to use its PayPal online payment service, and for other additional services. Although this has caused grumbling among sellers because it reduces their profit margins, eBay increasingly engages in extensive advertising to attract millions more buyers to its website, so sellers can receive better prices and increase their total profits. As a result, they remained largely satisfied with eBay's fee structure.

These policies changed when a new CEO, John Donohue, took the place of eBay's long-time CEO, Meg Whitman, who had built the company into a dot.com giant. By 2008, eBay's profits had not increased rapidly enough to keep its investors happy, and its stock price plunged. To increase performance, one of Donohue's first moves was to announce a major overhaul of eBay's fee structure and feedback policy. The new fee structure would reduce upfront seller listing costs but increase back-end commissions on completed sales and payments. For smaller sellers that already had thin profit margins, these fee hikes were painful. In addition, in the future, eBay announced it would block sellers from leaving negative feedback about buyers—feedback such as buyers didn't pay for the goods they purchased, or buyers took too long to pay for goods. The feedback system that eBay had originally developed had been a major source of its success; it allowed buyers to be certain they were dealing with reputable sellers, and vice versa. All sellers and buyers have feedback scores that provide them with a reputation as good—or bad—individuals with whom to do business, and these scores helped reduce the risks involved in online transactions. Donohue claimed this change was implemented in order to improve the buyer's experience because many buyers had complained

that if they left negative feedback on a seller, the seller would in turn leave negative feedback for the buyer.

Together, however, throughout 2009, these changes resulted in conflict between eBay and its millions of sellers, who perceived they were being harmed by these changes. Their bad feelings resulted in a revolt. Blogs and forums all over the Internet were filled with messages claiming that eBay had abandoned its smaller sellers and was pushing them out of business in favor of high-volume "powersellers" who contributed more to eBay's profits. Donohue and eBay received millions of hostile e-mails, and sellers threatened they would do business elsewhere, such as on Amazon.com and Yahoo!, two companies that were both trying to break into eBay's market. Sellers also organized a 1-week boycott of eBay during which they would list no items with the company to express their dismay and hostility! Many sellers did shut down their eBay online storefronts and moved to Amazon. com, which claimed in 2011 that its network of sites had overtaken eBay in monthly unique viewers or "hits" for the first time. The bottom line was that the level of commitment between eBay and its sellers had fallen dramatically; the bitter feelings produced by the changes eBay had made were likely to result in increasing problems that would hurt its future performance.

Realizing that his changes had backfired, Donohue reversed course and eliminated several of eBay's fee increases and revamped its feedback system; sellers and buyers can now respond to one another's comments in a fairer way. These changes did improve hostility and smooth over the bad feelings between sellers and eBay, but the old "community relationship" it had enjoyed with sellers in its early years largely disappeared. As this example suggests, finding ways to maintain cooperative relationships—such as by testing the waters in advance and asking sellers for their reactions to fee and feedback changes—could have avoided many of the problems that arose.

Source: www.ebay.com.

IBM could have backed up its demand by threatening to switch its business to another supplier. However, GE reduced this risk by having IBM enter into a contractual agreement that committed IBM to purchase chips from GE for a 10-year period. In addition, IBM agreed to share the costs of the specialized assets needed to develop the customized chips, thereby reducing the risks associated with GE's investment. Thus, by publicly committing itself to a long-term contract and putting money into the chip development process, IBM made a *credible commitment* that it would continue to purchase chips from GE. When a company violates a credible commitment with its partners, the results can be dramatic, as discussed in Strategy in Action 9.2.

Maintaining Market Discipline   Just as a company pursuing vertical integration faces the problem that its company-owned suppliers might become inefficient, a company that forms a strategic alliance with an independent component supplier runs the risk that its alliance partner might become inefficient over time, resulting in higher component costs or lower quality. This also happens because the outside supplier knows it does not need to compete with other suppliers for the company's business. Consequently, a company seeking to form a mutually beneficial, long-term, strategic alliance needs to possess some kind of power that it can use to discipline its partner should the need arise.

A company holds two strong cards over its supplier partner. First, all contracts, including long-term contracts, are periodically renegotiated, usually every 3 to 5 years, so the supplier knows that if it fails to live up to its commitments, its partner may refuse to renew the contract. Second, many companies that form long-term relationships with suppliers use a **parallel sourcing policy**—that is, they enter into long-term contracts with at least *two* suppliers for the *same* component (this is Toyota's policy, for example).[34] This arrangement protects a company against a supplier that adopts an uncooperative attitude, because the supplier knows that if it fails to comply with the agreement, the company can switch *all* its business to its other supplier partner. When both the company and its suppliers recognize that the parallel sourcing policy allows a supplier to be replaced at short notice, most suppliers behave because the policy brings market discipline into their relationship.

The growing importance of JIT inventory systems as a way to reduce costs and enhance quality and differentiation is increasing the pressure on companies to form strategic alliances in a wide range of industries. The number of strategic alliances formed each year—especially global strategic alliances—is increasing, and the popularity of vertical integration is falling because so many low-cost global suppliers exist in countries such as Malaysia, Korea, and China.

parallel sourcing policy

A policy in which a company enters into long-term contracts with at least two suppliers for the same component to prevent any incidents of opportunism.

9-7 Strategic Outsourcing

9.7 Explain the strategic reasons for outsourcing.

Vertical integration and strategic alliances are alternative ways of managing the value chain *across industries* to strengthen a company's core business model. However, just as low-cost suppliers of component parts exist, today many *specialized companies* exist that can perform one of a company's *own value-chain activities* in a way that contributes to a company's differentiation advantage or that lowers its cost structure. For example, Apple found that using Foxconn factories in China to assemble its iPhones enabled it to not only benefit from lower costs, but to also much more rapidly incorporate design changes and scale up production.

Strategic outsourcing is the decision to allow one or more of a company's value-chain activities or functions to be performed by independent specialist companies that focus all their skills and knowledge on just one kind of function, such as the manufacturing function, or on just one kind of activity that a function performs. For example, many companies outsource the management of their pension systems while keeping other human resource management (HRM) activities within the company. When a company chooses to outsource a value-chain activity, it is choosing to focus on a *fewer* number of value creation activities to strengthen its business model.

There has been a clear move among many companies to outsource activities that managers regard as being "noncore" or "nonstrategic," meaning they are not a source of a company's distinctive competencies and competitive advantage.[35] The vast majority of companies outsource manufacturing or some other value-chain activity to domestic or overseas companies. Some well-known companies that outsource include Nike, which does not make its athletic shoes; Gap Inc., which does not make its jeans and clothing; and Microsoft, which does not make its Xbox consoles. These products

strategic outsourcing

The decision to allow one or more of a company's value-chain activities to be performed by independent, specialist companies that focus all their skills and knowledge on just one kind of activity to increase performance.

are made under contract at low-cost, global locations by contract manufacturers that specialize in low-cost assembly.

Although manufacturing is the most common form of strategic outsourcing, as we noted earlier, many other kinds of noncore activities are also outsourced. Microsoft has long outsourced its entire customer technical support operation to an independent company, as does Dell. Both companies have extensive customer support operations in India staffed by skilled operatives who are paid a fraction of what their U.S. counterparts earn. British Petroleum outsourced almost all of its human resource function to Exult, a San Antonio company, in a 5-year deal worth $600 million; a few years later, Exult won a 10-year, $1.1-billion contract to handle HRM activities for Bank of America's 150,000 employees. Similarly, American Express outsourced its entire IT function to IBM in a 7-year deal worth $4 billion.

Companies engage in strategic outsourcing to strengthen their business models and increase their profitability. The process of strategic outsourcing typically begins with strategic managers identifying the value-chain activities that form the basis of a company's competitive advantage; these are obviously kept within the company to protect them from competitors. Managers then systematically review noncore functions to assess whether independent companies that specialize in those activities can perform them more effectively and efficiently. Because these companies specialize in particular activities, they can perform them in ways that lower costs or improve differentiation. If managers determine that there are differentiation or cost advantages, these activities are outsourced to those specialists.

This is illustrated in Figure 9.5, which shows the primary value-chain activities and boundaries of a company before and after it has pursued strategic outsourcing. In this example, the company decided to outsource its production and customer service functions to specialist companies, leaving only R&D and marketing and sales within the company. Once outsourcing has been executed, the relationships between the company and its specialists are then often structured as long-term, contractual relationships, with rich information sharing between the company and the specialist organization to which it has contracted the activity. The term

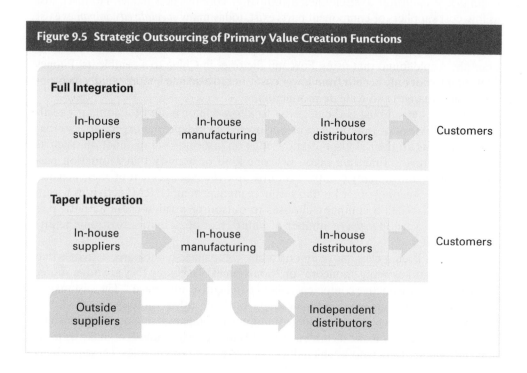

Figure 9.5 Strategic Outsourcing of Primary Value Creation Functions

Full Integration

In-house suppliers → In-house manufacturing → In-house distributors → Customers

Taper Integration

In-house suppliers → In-house manufacturing → In-house distributors → Customers

Outside suppliers   Independent distributors

virtual corporation has been coined to describe companies that have pursued extensive strategic outsourcing.[36]

virtual corporation

When companies pursued extensive strategic outsourcing to the extent that they only perform the central value creation functions that lead to competitive advantage.

9-7a Benefits of Outsourcing

Strategic outsourcing has several advantages. It can help a company (1) lower its cost structure, (2) increase product differentiation,[37] and (3) focus on the distinctive competencies that are vital to its long-term competitive advantage and profitability.

Lower Cost Structure   Outsourcing will reduce costs when the price that must be paid to a specialist company to perform a particular value-chain activity is less than what it would cost the company to perform that activity in-house. Specialists are often able to perform an activity at a lower cost than the company because they are able to realize scale economies or other efficiencies not available to the company. For example, performing human resource management (HRM) activities such as managing benefit and pay systems requires a significant investment in sophisticated HRM IT; purchasing these IT systems represents a considerable fixed cost for a single company. But, by aggregating the HRM IT needs of many individual companies, companies that specialize in HRM such as ADP and Paychex can obtain huge economies of scale in IT that no single company could hope to achieve. Some of these cost savings are then passed to the client companies in the form of lower prices, which reduces their cost structure.

A similar dynamic is at work in the contract manufacturing business. Manufacturing specialists like Foxconn, Flex, and Jabil make large capital investments to build efficient-scale manufacturing facilities, but then are able to spread those capital costs over a huge volume of output and drive down unit costs so that they can make a specific product—an Apple iPhone, for example—at a lower cost than the company.

Specialists are also likely to obtain the cost savings associated with learning effects much more rapidly than a company that performs an activity just for itself (see Chapter 4 for a review of learning effects). For example, because Flexis manufacturing similar products for several different companies, it is able to build up *cumulative* volume more rapidly, and it learns how to manage and operate the manufacturing process more efficiently than any of its clients could. This drives down the specialists' cost structure and also allows them to charge client companies a lower price for a product than if they made that product in-house.

Specialists are also often able to perform activities at lower costs than a specific company because of lower wage rates in those locations. Moving production of iPhones to the United States would, according to estimates, raise the cost of an iPhone by $65.[38] Similarly, Nike outsources the manufacture of its running shoes to companies based in China because of much lower wage rates. Even though wages in China have risen significantly over the last decade, a Chinese-based specialist can assemble shoes (a very labor-intensive activity) at a much lower cost than could be done in the United States. Although Nike could establish its own operations in China to manufacture running shoes, it would require a major capital investment and limit its ability to switch production to an even lower-cost location later—for example, Vietnam; many companies are moving to Vietnam because wage rates are lower there. So, for Nike and most other consumer goods companies, outsourcing manufacturing activities lowers costs and gives companies the flexibility to switch to a more favorable location if labor costs change and is the most efficient way to handle production.

Enhanced Differentiation   A company may also be able to differentiate its final products better by outsourcing certain noncore activities to specialists. For this to occur, the *quality* of the activity performed by specialists must be greater than if that same activity was performed by the company. On the reliability dimension of quality, for example, a specialist may be able to achieve a lower error rate in performing an activity precisely because it focuses solely on that activity and has developed a strong, distinctive competency in it. Again, this is one advantage claimed for contract manufacturers. Companies like Flex have adopted Six Sigma methodologies (see Chapter 4) and driven down the defect rate associated with manufacturing a product. This means they can provide more reliable products to their clients and differentiate their products on the basis of their superior quality.

A company can also improve product differentiation by outsourcing to specialists when they stand out on the excellence dimension of quality. For example, the excellence of Dell's U.S. customer service is a differentiating factor, and Dell outsources its PC repair and maintenance function to specialist companies. A customer who has a problem with a product purchased from Dell can get excellent help over the phone, and if there is a defective part in the computer, a maintenance person will be dispatched to replace the part within a few days. The excellence of this service differentiates Dell and helps to guarantee repeat purchases, which is why HP has worked hard to match Dell's level of service quality. In a similar way, carmakers often outsource specific vehicle component design activities such as microchips or headlights, to specialists that have earned a reputation for design excellence in this particular activity.

Focus on the Core Business   A final advantage of strategic outsourcing is that it allows managers to focus their energies and their company's resources on performing the core activities that have the most potential to create value and competitive advantage. In other words, companies can enhance their core competencies and are able to push out the value frontier and create more value for their customers. For example, Cisco Systems remains a dominant competitor in the Internet router industry because it has focused on building its competencies in product design, marketing and sales, and supply-chain management. Companies that focus on the core activities essential for competitive advantage in their industry are better able to drive down the costs of performing those activities and thus better differentiate their final products.

9-7b Risks of Outsourcing

Although outsourcing noncore activities has many benefits, there are also risks associated with it such as holdup and the possible loss of important information when an activity is outsourced. Managers must assess these risks before they decide to outsource a particular activity, although, as we discuss in the following section, these risks can be reduced when the appropriate steps are taken.

Holdup   In the context of outsourcing, holdup refers to the risk that a company will become too dependent upon the specialist provider of an outsourced activity, and that the specialist will use this fact to raise prices beyond some previously agreed-upon rate. As with strategic alliances, the risk of holdup can be reduced by outsourcing to several suppliers and pursuing a parallel sourcing policy, as Toyota and Cisco do. Moreover, when an activity can be performed well by any one of several different providers, the threat that a contract will not be renewed in the future is normally sufficient to keep the chosen provider from exercising bargaining power over the company. For example, although IBM enters into long-term contracts to provide IT services to a wide range of companies, it would be unadvisable for those companies to attempt to raise prices after the contract has been signed because it knows full well that such an action would reduce its chance of getting the contract renewed in the future. Moreover, because IBM has many strong competitors in the IT services business, such as Accenture, Capgemini, and HP, it has a very strong incentive to deliver significant value to its clients.

Increased Competition As firms employ contract manufacturers for production, they help to build an industry-wide resource that lowers barriers to entry in that industry. In industries that have efficient, high-quality contract manufacturers, large firms may find that their size no longer affords them protection against competitive pressure; their high investments in fixed assets can become a constraint rather than a source of advantage.[39] Furthermore, firms that use contract manufacturing pay, in essence, for the contract manufacturer to progress down its own learning curve. Over time, the contract manufacturer's capabilities improve, putting it at a greater manufacturing advantage over the firm. Contract manufacturers in many industries increase the scope of their activities over time, adding a wider range of services (e.g., component purchasing, redesign-for-manufacturability, testing, packaging, and after-sales service) and may eventually produce their own end products in competition with their customers. Contracts to manufacture goods for U.S. and European electronics manufacturers, for example, helped to build the electronics manufacturing giants that exist today in Japan and Korea.

Loss of Information and Forfeited Learning Opportunities A company that is not careful can lose important competitive information when it outsources an activity. For example, many computer hardware and software companies have outsourced their customer technical support function to specialists. Although this makes good sense from a cost and differentiation perspective, it may also mean that a critical point of contact with the customer, and a source of important feedback, is lost. Customer complaints can be useful information and valuable inputs into future product design, but if those complaints are not clearly communicated to the company by the specialists performing the technical support activity, the company can lose the information. Similarly, a firm that manufactures its own products also gains knowledge about how to improve design in order to lower the costs of manufacturing or produce more reliable products. Thus, a firm that forfeits the development of manufacturing knowledge could unintentionally forfeit opportunities for improving its capabilities in product design. The firm risks becoming "hollow."[40] These are not arguments against outsourcing; rather, they are arguments for ensuring that there is appropriate communication between the outsourcing specialist and the company. At Dell, for example, a great deal of attention is paid to making sure that the specialist responsible for providing technical support and on-site maintenance collects and communicates all relevant data regarding product failures and other problems to Dell, so that Dell can design better products.

Key Terms

Takeaways for Strategic Managers

1. A corporate strategy should enable a company, or one or more of its business units, to perform one or more of the value creation functions at a lower cost or in a way that allows for differentiation and a premium price.

2. The corporate-level strategy of horizontal integration is pursued to increase the profitability of a company's business model by (a) reducing costs, (b) increasing the value of the company's products through differentiation, (c) replicating the business model, (d) managing rivalry within the industry to reduce the risk of price warfare, and (e) increasing bargaining power over suppliers and buyers.

3. There are two drawbacks associated with horizontal integration: (a) the numerous pitfalls associated with making mergers and acquisitions and (b) the fact that the strategy can bring a company into direct conflict with antitrust authorities.

4. The corporate-level strategy of vertical integration is pursued to increase the profitability of a company's "core" business model in its original industry. Vertical integration can enable a company to achieve a competitive advantage by helping build barriers to entry, facilitating investments in specialized assets, protecting product quality, and helping to improve scheduling between adjacent stages in the value chain.

5. The disadvantages of vertical integration include (a) increasing bureaucratic costs if a company-owned or in-house supplier becomes lazy or inefficient, (b) potential loss of focus on those resources and capabilities that create the most value for the firm, and (c), reduced flexibility to adapt to a fast-changing environment. Entering into a long-term contract can enable a company to realize many of the benefits associated with vertical integration without having to bear the same level of bureaucratic costs. However, to avoid the risks associated with becoming too dependent upon its partner, it needs to seek a credible commitment from its partner or establish a mutual hostage-taking situation.

6. Firms whose products require a wide range of high-quality complements may induce complements to be made by third-party complements providers. Complements providers may enter into a contract with the platform provider (e.g., a license agreement), and the platform provider manages the overall ecosystem to help ensure it creates value for the end customer.

7. The strategic outsourcing of noncore value creation activities may allow a company to lower its costs, better differentiate its products, and make better use of scarce resources, while also enabling it to respond rapidly to changing market conditions. However, strategic outsourcing may have a detrimental effect if the company outsources important value creation activities or becomes too dependent upon the key suppliers of those activities.

Discussion Questions

1. Under what conditions might horizontal integration be inconsistent with the goal of maximizing profitability?

2. What is the difference between a company's internal value chain and the industry value chain? What is the relationship between vertical integration and the industry value chain?

3. Why was it profitable for GM and Ford to integrate backward into component-parts manufacturing in the past, and why are both companies now buying more of their parts from outside suppliers?

4. When will an industry tend to become dominated by platform ecosystems? What will determine which platform ecosystems are more successful in an industry than others?

5. What value creation activities should a company outsource to independent suppliers? What are the risks involved in outsourcing these activities?

6. What steps would you recommend that a company take to build mutually beneficial, long-term, cooperative relationships with its suppliers?

In 2022, Netflix had over 222 million subscribers worldwide. It had earned almost $30 billion in revenues in 2021, with an operating profit of $5.1 billion (an 85% increase year over year). Rapid growth in both domestic and international subscribers had fueled intense investor enthusiasm, causing its market capitalization to reach over $300 billion by late 2021, though it had fallen with the rest of the stock market in the first part of 2022, settling at about $80 billion.

When Netflix was founded in 1997, its business model was to rent and sell movies on DVDs by mail. Customers could browse and select movies online, and those movies would be mailed out to the customer, who would then mail the movies back after watching. Though it initially started with a per-movie rental fee like its largest brick-and-mortar rival, Blockbuster, it soon moved to a subscription fee. Customers could choose among plans with different prices based on how many movies they wanted to rent simultaneously, and they could keep movies out as long as they wanted without late fees. The subscription plan was a hit, and by 2005 the company was shipping out over a million DVDs a day.[41]

One of the most compelling features of the Netflix site was its recommender system. As people rented movies, Netflix prompted them to review the movies they had already seen. It thus steadily accrued a massive database about correlations among movie preferences that it could use to make movie suggestions to users. For example, if a user gave a five-star rating to *Journey to the Center of the Earth*, the system would suggest they might also like *The Mummy*, *Indiana Jones and the Kingdom of the Crystal Skull*, and *Inkheart*.

The service turned out to be enormously popular and soon sounded a death knell for brick-and-mortar video stores. By having centralized inventory and shipping movies to people, Netflix could offer a much wider selection than physical stores could offer, and its scale meant it could both negotiate better prices on content, and invest in value-added services for customers like the review and recommender systems mentioned previously, online movie trailers, and more. Importantly, Netflix was also a key channel for films by small, independent filmmakers to reach audiences, enabling the company to forge relationships that would prove to be increasingly valuable as time passed.

In 2007, Netflix began offering movie streaming, which rapidly grew to be the preferred mode of movie consumption. Then, in 2011, the company began acquiring original content for exclusive distribution on Netflix, starting with the series *House of Cards* and *Lilyhammer*. By 2013, it had moved into co-producing original content with production houses such as Marvel Television, DreamWorks, and others. In 2017, it opened Netflix Studios and began recruiting some of television's most successful writers and producers to produce original content in house.[42]

For a movie rental service to vertically integrate into developing its own content seemed a peculiar move. Making films and television shows required fundamentally different technology, equipment, personnel, and expertise than distributing films and television shows. What could a specialist in media distribution know about media production? A lot, it turns out.

Netflix's rapidly growing data sets meant that it knew which customers liked which films, which genres were growing, which new stars were gaining followings, which new production houses were gaining traction, and more. The relationships it had cultivated with independent filmmakers and budding actors helped ensure the firm's access to a pipeline of new creative talent and helped build goodwill toward the company. Sean Fennessey, a writer for pop-culture website *The Ringer*, explained how important Netflix was to frustrated filmmakers who could not raise enough support to get a major studio movie off the ground, "To the creators stifled by the rise of Hollywood's all-or-nothing focus on franchise films, Netflix felt like salve on an open wound."[43]

Netflix also used its massive distribution reach to promote its original content, building audiences for its series and crafting its reputation as a first-tier production house. As put by Ted Sarandos, Netflix chief content officer, "the way we can secure those shows is having a great reputation with talent, having a brand people want to be associated with, and a good track record of delivering."

Furthermore, while most film studios needed to profit directly from their films, Netflix profited in multiple ways from its content: Having popular, exclusive shows helped attract and retain subscribers, and having both a large audience and a powerful library of original content gave it more bargaining power when negotiating license fees for content produced by others. Collectively, it was a powerful advantage.

Netflix spent $5.2 billion on original content in 2021, and by 2022 had produced over 2,400 original titles, including about 150 original films in 2021 alone, making it one of the largest film producers in the world.

Notes

[1] Volkswagen Press Release, July 7, 2022.

[2] Interview with Michael Liedtke, Chief Commercial Officer of Zeta Energy, July 12, 2022.

[3] F. Lambert, "Tesla Is Now Claiming 35% Battery Cost Reduction at 'Gigafactory 1' – Hinting at Breakthrough Cost Below $125/kWh," *Electrek*, February 18, 2017.

[4] M. Wayland, "Automakers Are Spending Billions to Produce Battery Cells for EVs in the U.S.," CNBC, October 19, 2021.

[5] "Volkswagen to Invest $20 bln in Building Own EV Batteries," Nasdaq RTTNews, July 7, 2022.

[6] http://mediaroom.jetblue.com/investor-relations/press-releases/2022/07-28-2022-113040248.

[7] J Kwoka and E. Shumilkina, "The Price Effect of Eliminating Potential Competition: Evidence from an Airline Merger," *Journal of Industrial Economics* 58 (2010): 767.

[8] K. Hüschelrath and K Müller, "Market Power, Efficiencies, and Entry Evidence from an Airline Merger," *Managerial and Decision Economics* 36 (2015): 239.

[9] M. A. Schilling, "Potential Sources of Value in Mergers and Their Indicators," *Antitrust Bulletin* 26 (2018): 183–197.

[10] J. Mouawad, "Delta-Northwest Merger's Long and Complex Path," *New York Times,* May 18, 2011.

[11] Ibid.

[12] J. Bailey, "Delta and Northwest Promote Benefits of Merger," *New York Times,* April 15, 2008.

[13] D. Reed and M. Adams, "Delta, Northwest Executives Tout Merger," *USA Today*, April 16, 2008.

[14] Schilling, "Potential Sources of Value in Mergers and Their Indicators."

[15] M. A. Schilling, "The Top 4 Reasons Most Acquisitions Fail," *Inc.*, May 18, 2018.

[16] M. Ceccagnoli, C. Forman, P. Huang, and D. J. Wu, "Cocreation of Values in a Platform Ecosystem: The Case of Enterprise Software," *MIS Quart* 36:1 (2012): 263–290; A. Gawer, "Bridging Differing Perspectives on Technological Platforms: Toward an Integrative Framework," *Res Pol* 43:7 (2014): 1239–1249; M. G. Jacobides, T. Knudsen,

and M. Augier, "Benefiting From Innovation: Value Creation, Value Appropriation and the Role of Industry Architectures," *Res Pol* 35:8 (2006): 1200–1221; J. Rietveld, M. A. Schilling, and C. Bellavitis, *Platform Strategy: Managing Ecosystem Value Through Selective Promotion of Complements*. New York University working paper, 2018; M. A. Schilling, "Towards a General Modular Systems Theory and Its Application to Interfirm Product Modularity," *Academy of Management Review* 25 (2000): 312–334.

[17] M. A. Schilling, "Quirky: The Remarkable Story of the Traits, Foibles, and Genius of Breakthrough Innovators Who Changed the World," New York: Public Affairs, 2018.

[18] Schilling, "Towards a General Modular Systems Theory and Its application to Interfirm Product Modularity."

[19] R. Garud and A. Kumaraswamy, "Technological and Organizational Designs for Realizing Economies of Substitution," *Strategic Management Journal* 16 (1995): 93–109.

[20]Rietveld, Schilling, and Bellavitis, *Platform Strategy: Managing Ecosystem Value Through Selective Promotion of Complements.*

[21]M. A. Schilling, *Strategic Management of Technological Innovation*, 6th ed. (Boston: McGraw Hill, 2019).

[22]This is the essence of Chandler's argument. See A. D. Chandler, *Strategy and Structure* (Cambridge: MIT Press, 1962). The same argument is also made by J. Pfeffer and G. R. Salancik, *The External Control of Organizations* (New York: Harper & Row, 1978). See also K. R. Harrigan, *Strategic Flexibility* (Lexington: Lexington Books, 1985); K. R. Harrigan, "Vertical Integration and Corporate Strategy," *Academy of Management Journal* 28 (1985): 397–425; F. M. Scherer, *Industrial Market Structure and Economic Performance* (Chicago: Rand McNally, 1981).

[23]O. E. Williamson, *The Economic Institutions of Capitalism* (New York: Free Press, 1985). For another empirical work that uses this framework, see L. Poppo and T. Zenger, "Testing Alternative Theories of the Firm: Transaction Cost, Knowledge Based, and Measurement Explanations for Make or Buy Decisions in Information Services," *Strategic Management Journal* 19 (1998): 853–878.

[24]Williamson, *Economic Institutions of Capitalism.*

[25]J. M. deFigueiredo and B. S. Silverman, "Firm Survival and Industry Evolution in Vertically Related Populations," *Management Science* 58 (2012): 1632–1650; D. He and J. A. Nickerson, "Why Do Firms Make and Buy? Efficiency, Appropriability and Competition in the Trucking Industry," *Strategic Organization* 4 (2006): 43–69.

[26]www.mcdonalds.com.

[27]Ibid.

[28]A. D. Chandler, *The Visible Hand* (Cambridge: Harvard University Press, 1977).

[29]Harrigan, *Strategic Flexibility*, pp. 67–87. See also A. Afuah, "Dynamic Boundaries of the Firm: Are Firms Better Off Being Vertically Integrated in the Face of a Technological Change?" *Academy of Management Journal* 44 (2001): 1121–1228.

[30]K. M. Gilley, J. E. McGee, and A. A. Rasheed, "Perceived Environmental Dynamism and Managerial Risk Aversion as Antecedents of Manufacturing Outsourcing: The Moderating Effects of Firm Maturity," *Journal of Small Business Management* 42 (2004): 117–134; M. A. Schilling and H. K. Steensma, "The Use of Modular Organizational Forms: An Industry-Level Analysis," *Academy of Management Journal* 44 (2001): 1149–1169.

[31]X. Martin, W. Mitchell, and A. Swaminathan, "Recreating and Extending Japanese Automobile Buyer-Supplier Links in North America," *Strategic Management Journal* 16 (1995): 589–619; C. W. L. Hill, "National Institutional Structures, Transaction Cost Economizing, and Competitive Advantage," *Organization Science* 6 (1995): 119–131.

[32]Williamson, *Economic Institutions of Capitalism.* See also J. H. Dyer, "Effective Inter-Firm Collaboration: How Firms Minimize Transaction Costs and Maximize Transaction Value," *Strategic Management Journal* 18 (1997): 535–556.

[33]Richardson, "Parallel Sourcing."

[34]W. H. Davidow and M. S. Malone, *The Virtual Corporation* (New York: Harper & Row, 1992).

[35]J. Krane, "American Express Hires IBM for $4 Billion," *Columbian*, February 26, 2002, p. E2; www.ibm.com.

[36]Ibid.; see also H. W. Chesbrough and D. J. Teece, "When Is Virtual Virtuous? Organizing for Innovation," *Harvard Business Review* (January–February 1996): 65–74; J. B. Quinn, "Strategic Outsourcing: Leveraging Knowledge Capabilities," *Sloan Management Review*, Summer 1999, pp. 9–21.

[37]C. Duhigg and K. Bradsher, "How the U.S. Lost Out on iPhone Work," *New York Times*, January 21, 2012, p. 1.

[38]Schilling and Steensma, "The Use of Modular Organizational Forms."

[39]R. Venkatesan, "Strategic Sourcing: To Make or Not to Make," *Harvard Business Review* (November–December 1992): 98–107.

[40]G. McDermott, R. Mudambi, and R. Parente, "Strategic Modularity at the Architecture of Multinational Firms," *Global Strategy Journal* 3 (2013): 1–7; and MC Becker and F. Zirpoli, "Organizing New Product Development: Knowledge Hollowing-Out and Knowledge Integration—the FIAT Auto Case," *International Journal of Operations & Production Management* 23 (2003): 1033–1061.

[41]S. Ramachandran and I. Moise, "Netflix Subscriber Growth Tops Expectations," *The Wall Street Journal*, April 16, 2018.

[42]"Movies to Go," *The Economist*, July 7, 2005.

[43]L. Shaw, "Netflix Aims to Make the Next Great Hollywood Studio," *Chicago Tribune*, September 15, 2017.

Corporate-Level Strategy: Related and Unrelated Diversification

Opening Case

The Transformation of United Technologies into Raytheon Technologies

United Technologies was an American multinational conglomerate with businesses in commercial aircraft, military aerospace and defense, elevators, heating and cooling systems, security products, and other commercial building systems. With most of its businesses clustered near Farmington, Connecticut, it was long considered one of the few U.S. firms to have successfully practiced unrelated diversification even as investors began to demand that conglomerates be broken apart. All of that changed in 2018, when the CEO of United Technology, Gregory Hayes, announced that he believed United Technologies might be more valuable as separate, more specialized companies.

United Technologies Founding and Growth

The origin story of United Technologies is a unique one. In the 1930s, an investigation revealed that the major airlines in the United States were colluding to control the delivery of mail. The scandal and ensuing *Air Mail Act of 1934* resulted in the splitting apart of the vertically integrated United Aircraft and Transport Corporation (UATC) into three companies: its airline interests became United Air Lines Transportation Company (which later became known simply as United Airlines), its manufacturing interests east of the Mississippi River (notably Pratt & Whitney, Chance Vought and Sikorsky) became United Aircraft Manufacturing Company (what would ultimately become known as United Technologies), and its manufacturing interests west of the Mississippi became Boeing Aircraft Company.

The United Aircraft Manufacturing Company grew rapidly during the 1940s by serving the near-limitless demand for aircraft and aircraft engines for the military. It remained, however, relatively undiversified until 1974, when Harry Gray became CEO. Gray began diversifying the company into numerous high-technology fields, primarily through acquisition. He renamed the company United Technologies. Gray's diversification strategy was in part an attempt to build up the company's civilian businesses in order to not be overly reliant on military contracts. United Technologies acquired Otis Elevator in 1976, and then Carrier Refrigeration in 1979. The company spent the next four decades getting bigger and broader, becoming one of the world's most well-known conglomerates.

Most of United Technologies' businesses were in two main groups: aerospace and building systems. Over the years, its aerospace group included Sikorsky aircraft, Pratt & Whitney Engines, and UTC Aerospace systems, which was formed through the merger of Hamilton Sundstrand and Goodrich. Its building systems group included Otis elevators and escalators; Carrier and NORESCO

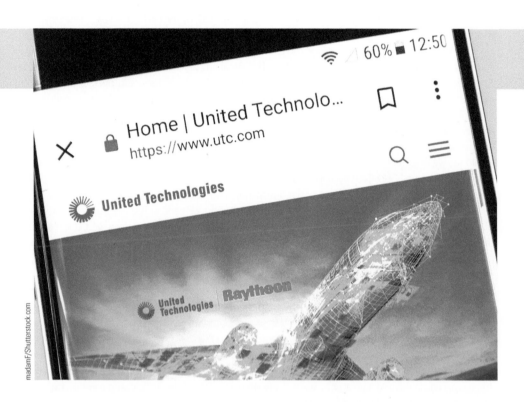

madamF/Shutterstock.com

heating and air-conditioning solutions; fire-detection and security businesses that include Chubb, Kidde, Edwards, Fenwal, Marioff, Supra, and Interlogix; and businesses that develop business automation systems (such as automatically controlled lighting and temperature) including Automated Logic, Onity, Lenel, and UTEC.

Throughout that long period of diversification, management justified the moves by pointing to efficiencies in capital allocation across the businesses and a shared Total Quality Management program called "Achieving Competitive Excellence" (ACE). ACE was a set of tasks and procedures used across the company to analyze all aspects of how its products were made, with an eye toward improving quality and reliability while reducing costs. It was similar, at least in principle, to the Six Sigma system used by companies such as Motorola, Honeywell, and General Electric. Notably, Jack Welch had made Six Sigma central to his diversification strategy at General Electric.

As investors became more sophisticated and capital markets became more robust at allocating capital to businesses, however, the conglomerate model came increasingly under fire. Investors began to question whether cross-subsidization of businesses in the corporation could really compete with the efficiency of the external capital market, and whether different kinds of businesses really had to be jointly owned to implement quality control processes. Separating the businesses, many argued, could allow them to operate more flexibly and create greater transparency into each business' value. The units of United Technologies did not share customers, manufacturing assets, or even similar business models. Activist investor Dan Loeb noted that a "sum-of-the-parts" analysis of the company (as of mid-2018) suggested that the company was trading at a significant discount to peer firms—$124 per share versus the $190–$210 implied value per share.[1] Finally, in 2018, CEO Gregory Hayes conceded his agreement. At a *Fortune* conference he noted that the board and investors had been asking, "Will these businesses be better as a part of United Technologies as a conglomerate, or better as stand-alone, focused business? ... My view is: Focus ultimately leads to success."[2] By the end of the year, management had actively begun planning the process to break the conglomerate into more specialized companies.

On April 1, 2020, United Technology merged with the electronics and radar company Raytheon, and spun out its elevator and cooling businesses. The remaining aerospace company included Collins Aerospace Systems, the Pratt & Whitney unit, and Raytheon. This business would operate under the name Raytheon Technologies. A now separate company, Otis Worldwide Corporation, would continue to manufacture elevators and escalators. The third, Carrier Global Corporation, would primarily focus on manufacturing heating and cooling equipment and take along the fire and security equipment. The re-organization was a tax-free transaction to shareholders whereby for each UTX share owned, shareholders would receive one share of RTX (Raytheon), one half share of OTIS, and one share off CARR (Carrier).[3] United Technologies' CEO, Gregory Hayes, noted, "Our decision to separate United Technologies is a pivotal moment in our history and will best position each independent company to drive sustained growth."

The stock market reacted to the merger and breakup announcement with some skepticism. At the end of 2017, before any hint of breaking up UTC or merging with Raytheon had emerged, the market capitalization of United Technologies was roughly $102 billion and the market capitalization of Raytheon Company was roughly $54 billion for a total value of $156 billion. At the end of 2021, after the merger, the market capitalization of Raytheon Technologies, Otis, and Carrier were, respectively, $129 billion, $37 billion, and $47 billion, for a combined valuation of $213 billion. Notably, however, the entire stock market rose at an even faster pace during this time period. Furthermore, Raytheon Technologies suffered heavily in 2020 due to the COVID-19 pandemic, leading to several periods of reporting losses.[4]

The benefits of the merger of United Technologies and Raytheon were anticipated to be long-term gains due to greater scale economies and bargaining power in aerospace and defense. The gains in splitting off Otis and Carrier were expected to be long-term performance improvement due to specialization, and a greater investor transparency. None of the anticipated gains, therefore, were quick fixes that could be expected to show up on the bottom line in the near term, and there would be restructuring effort and expenses to be borne. The market would thus have to wait several years to see how the transformation of United Technologies affected its performance.

<table>
<tr><td>10.1 Define diversification as a strategy.</td></tr>
</table>

10-1 Overview

Diversification can create, and destroy, value. As shown in the Opening Case, investors expect diversification to yield gains over and above what those businesses could earn on their own—if businesses do not create *additional* value by being under one roof, then the loss of focus and transparency is a losing proposition. The chapter's Closing Case illustrates how Google realized gains of diversification by leveraging its strength in general online search into online travel booking. Google's unique position gave it a large competitive advantage in flight search. However, as we shall see, diversification can also lead a firm away from its key strengths, reduce the firm's transparency in reporting its results, and make it more difficult for managers to provide adequate oversight within the organization. Diversification can be very alluring to managers, and it is easy to overestimate potential synergies. It is much harder to realize them.[5]

In this chapter, we continue to discuss both the challenges and opportunities created by corporate-level strategies of related and unrelated diversification. A diversification strategy is based upon a company's decision to enter one or more new industries to take advantage of its existing distinctive competencies and business model. We examine the different kinds of multibusiness models upon which related and unrelated diversification are based. Then, we discuss three different ways companies can implement a diversification strategy: internal new ventures, acquisitions, and joint ventures. In the last section, we will discuss how firms exit businesses when it no longer creates additional value to have them under one roof or when more value can be reaped by enabling the businesses to operate on their own. By the end of this chapter, you will understand the advantages and disadvantages of diversification, and you will understand how managers enter and exit markets and industries.

10-2 Ways Diversification Can Increase Profitability

10.2 Explain the five primary ways in which diversification can increase company profitability.

Diversification is the process of entering new industries, distinct from a company's core or original industry, to make new kinds of products that can be sold profitably to customers in these new industries. A multibusiness model based on diversification aims to find ways to use a company's existing strategies and distinctive competencies to make products that are highly valued by customers in the new industries it enters. A **diversified company** is one that makes and sells products in two or more different or distinct industries (industries *not* in adjacent stages of an industry value chain, as in vertical integration). As in the case of the corporate strategies discussed in Chapter 9, a diversification strategy should enable a company or its individual business units to perform one or more value-chain functions: (1) at a lower cost, (2) in a way that allows for greater differentiation and gives the company better pricing options, or (3) in a way that helps the company manage industry rivalry better—*in order to increase profitability*.

diversification

The process of entering new industries, distinct from a company's core or original industry, to make new kinds of products for customers in new markets.

diversified company

A company that makes and sells products in two or more different or distinct industries.

Most companies consider diversification when they are generating *free cash flow;* that is, cash in excess of that required to fund new investments in the company's current business and meet existing debt commitments.[6] In other words, free cash flow is cash beyond that needed to make profitable new investments in the existing business. When a company's successful business model is generating free cash flow and profits, managers must decide whether to return that cash to shareholders in the form of higher dividend payouts or to invest it in diversification.

The free cash flow of a firm technically belongs to the company's owners—its shareholders. So, for diversification to create value, a company's return on investing free cash flow to pursue diversification opportunities—that is, its future ROIC—*must exceed* the value shareholders would reap by returning the cash to them. When a firm does not pay out its free cash flow to its shareholders, the shareholders bear an opportunity cost equal to their next best use of those funds (i.e., another investment that pays a similar return at a similar risk, an investment that pays a higher return at a higher risk, or an investment that pays a lower return but at a lower risk). Thus, as noted in Chapter 9, a diversification strategy must pass the "better-off" test: The firm must be more valuable than it was before the diversification, and that value must not be fully capitalized by the cost of the diversification move (i.e., the cost of entry into the new industry must be taken into account when assessing the value created by the diversification). Thus, managers might defer paying dividends now to invest in diversification, but they should do so only when this is expected to create even greater cash flow (and thus higher dividends) in the future.

There are four primary ways in which pursuing a multibusiness model based on diversification can increase company profitability. Diversification can increase profitability when strategic managers (1) transfer competencies between business units in different industries, (2) leverage competencies to create business units in new industries, (3) share resources between business units to realize synergies or economies of scope, or (4) utilize *general* organizational competencies that increase the performance of *all* a company's business units.

10-2a Transferring Competencies Across Businesses

transferring competencies

The process of taking a distinctive competency developed by a business unit in one industry and implanting it in a business unit operating in another industry.

Transferring competencies involves taking a distinctive competency developed by a business unit in one industry and implanting it in a business unit operating in another industry. The second business unit is often one a company has acquired. Companies that base their diversification strategy on transferring competencies aim to use one or more of their existing distinctive competencies in a value-chain activity—for example, in manufacturing, marketing, materials management, or research and development (R&D)—to significantly strengthen the business model of the acquired business unit or company. For example, over time, Philip Morris developed distinctive competencies in product development, consumer marketing, and brand positioning that had made it a leader in the tobacco industry. Sensing a profitable opportunity, it acquired Miller Brewing in 1969, which at the time was a relatively small player in the brewing industry. Then, to create valuable new products in the brewing industry, Philip Morris transferred some of its best marketing experts to Miller, where they applied the skills acquired at Philip Morris to turn around Miller's lackluster brewing business (see Figure 10.1). The result was the creation of Miller Light, the first "light" beer in 1972, and a marketing campaign that helped to push Miller from number 6 to number 2 in market share in the brewing industry.

commonality

A skill or competency that, when shared by two or more business units, allows them to operate more effectively and create more value for customers.

Companies that base their diversification strategy on transferring competencies tend to acquire new businesses *related* to their existing business activities because of commonalities between one or more of their value-chain functions. A **commonality** is a skill or attribute that, when shared or used by two or more business units, allows both businesses to operate more effectively and efficiently and create more value for customers.

For example, Miller Brewing was related to Philip Morris's tobacco business because it was possible to create important marketing commonalities; both beer and tobacco are mass-market consumer goods in which brand positioning, advertising, and product development skills are crucial to create successful new products. In general, such competency transfers increase profitability when they either (1) lower the cost structure of one or more of a diversified company's business units or (2) enable one or more of its business units to better differentiate their products, both of which give business-unit pricing options to lower a product's price to increase market share, or to charge a premium price.

To increase profitability, transferred competencies must involve value-chain activities that become an important source of a specific business unit's competitive advantage in the future. In other words, the distinctive competency being transferred must

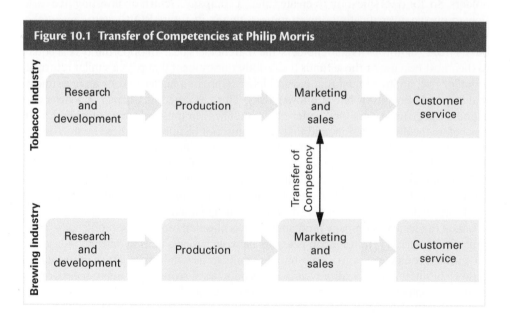

Figure 10.1 Transfer of Competencies at Philip Morris

have real strategic value. However, all too often, companies assume that *any* commonality between their value chains is sufficient for creating value. When they attempt to transfer competencies, they find the anticipated benefits are not forthcoming because the different business units did not share some important attribute in common. For example, Coca-Cola acquired Minute Maid in 1960, the fruit juice maker, to take advantage of commonalities in global distribution and marketing, and this acquisition has proved to be highly successful. On the other hand, in 1982 Coca-Cola acquired the movie studio Columbia Pictures because it believed it could use its marketing prowess to produce blockbuster movies. This acquisition was a disaster that cost Coca-Cola billions in losses, and Columbia was sold to Sony in 1989, which was then able to base many of its successful PlayStation games on the hit movies the studio produced.

10-2b Leveraging Competencies to Create a New Business

By **leveraging competencies**, a company can develop a new business in a different industry. For example, Apple leveraged its competencies in personal computer (PC) hardware and software to enter the smartphone industry. Once again, the multibusiness model is based on the premise that the set of distinctive competencies that are the source of a company's competitive advantage in one industry might be applied to create a differentiation or cost-based competitive advantage for a new business unit or division in a different industry. For example, Canon used its distinctive competencies in precision mechanics, fine optics, and electronic imaging to produce laserjet printers, which, for Canon, was a new business in a new industry. Its competencies enabled it to produce high-quality (differentiated) laser printers that could be manufactured at a low cost, which created its competitive advantage, and made Canon a leader in the printer industry.

Many companies base their diversification strategy on leveraging their competencies to create new business units in different industries. Microsoft leveraged its long-time experience and relationships in the computer industry, skills in software development, and its expertise in managing industries characterized by network externalities to create new business units in industries such as videogames (with its Xbox videogame consoles and game), online portals and search engines (e.g., MSN and Bing), and tablet computers (the Surface).

leveraging competencies
The process of taking a distinctive competency developed by a business unit in one industry and using it to create a new business unit in a different industry.

10-2c Sharing Resources and Capabilities

A third way in which two or more business units that operate in different industries can increase a diversified company's profitability is when the shared resources and capabilities result in economies of scope, or synergies.[7] **Economies of scope** arise when one or more of a diversified company's business units are able to realize cost-saving or differentiation synergies because they can more effectively pool, share, and utilize expensive resources or capabilities such as skilled people, equipment, manufacturing facilities, distribution channels, advertising campaigns, and R&D laboratories. If business units in different industries can share a common resource or function, they can collectively lower their cost structure; the idea behind synergies is that 2 + 2 = 5, not 4, in terms of value created.[8] For example, Louis Vuitton Moet Hennessy (LVMH) found that it could realize benefits of owning many different luxury clothing and accessory brands such as Christian Dior, Fendi, Givenchy, Marc Jacobs, Stella McCartney, Loro Piana, Kenzo, Celine, and others. It could utilize its distribution channels for nearly all of them, and it could use its influence with fashion editors to help newer brands reach a global market more quickly and cost effectively. Similarly, GE can leverage its expertise and industrial relationships across its wide range of energy and electronics businesses, including power generation, aviation, medical imaging and patient monitoring systems, and more.

economies of scope
The synergies that arise when one or more of a diversified company's business units are able to lower costs or increase differentiation because they can more effectively pool, share, and utilize expensive resources or capabilities.

There are two major sources of cost reductions. First, when companies can share resources or capabilities across business units, it lowers their cost structure compared to a company that operates in only one industry and bears the full costs of developing resources and capabilities. For example, P&G makes disposable diapers, toilet paper, and paper towels, which are all paper-based products that customers value for their ability to absorb fluids without disintegrating. Because these products need the same attribute—absorbency—P&G can share the R&D costs associated with developing and making even more advanced absorbent, paper-based products across the three distinct businesses (only two are shown in Figure 10.2). Similarly, because all of these products are sold to retailers, P&G can use the same sales force to sell its whole array of products (see Figure 10.2). In contrast, P&G competitors that make only one or two of these products cannot share these costs across industries, so their cost structures are higher. As a result, P&G has lower costs; it can use its marketing function to better differentiate its products, and it achieves a higher ROIC than companies that operate only in one or a few industries—which are unable to obtain economies of scope from the ability to share resources and obtain synergies across business units.

Similarly, Nike, which began strictly as a maker of running shoes, realized that its brand image, and its relationships with athletes and sports events, could be profitably leveraged into other types of athletic footwear, athletic apparel, and accessories such as sunglasses and headphones. Those products were more differentiated because of the Nike brand name and had better exposure because Nike was able to place them in suitable endorsement spots via its relationships with athletes and events, and Nike is able to amortize the cost of its brand-building activities across a wider range of products, thus achieving economies of scope.

To reiterate, diversification to obtain economies of scope is possible only when there are *significant* commonalities between one or more value-chain functions in a company's different business units or divisions that result in synergies which increase profitability. In addition, managers must be aware that the costs of coordination necessary to achieve synergies or economies of scope within a company may sometimes be *higher* than the value that can be created by such a strategy.[9] For example, from 1990 to 2010, Citibank transitioned from being wholly focused on retail consumer banking to a "financial supermarket" by diversifying into insurance, mortgage banking, stock brokering, and more, believing that it would achieve major cost savings from consolidating operations across its acquisitions, and revenue-increasing opportunities from cross-selling. In reality, the

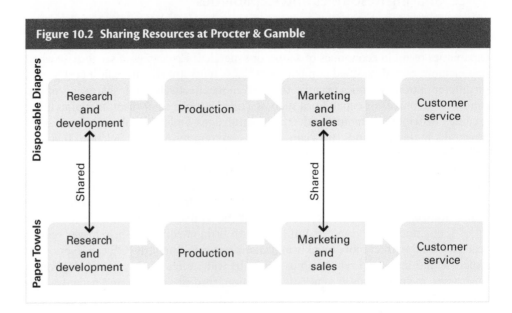

Figure 10.2 Sharing Resources at Procter & Gamble

coordination costs that Citi bore (in the form of massive losses due to inadequate oversight over its investment activities) vastly exceeded the synergies it gained, and proved devastating for the firm. Citibank subsequently dismantled its financial supermarket, selling off Smith Barney, Phibro, Diner's Club, Primerica, and more. The Citi example illustrates that diversification based on obtaining economies of scope should be pursued only when the sharing of competencies will result in *significant* synergies that will achieve a competitive advantage for one or more of a company's new or existing business units, and when those advantages will exceed the costs and risks created.

Citi also illustrates that one of the sources of economies of scope that firms seek through diversification is through product bundling. Product bundling allows a company to satisfy customers' needs for a complete package of related products, potentially leveraging the advantage the firm has in one part of the bundle to other parts of the bundle while achieving economies of scope in building and maintaining the customer relationship. Customers often want the convenience and reduced price of a bundle of related products. For example, end consumers may prefer to buy their internet, cable television, and phone service from a single provider that will give them a single point of contact for customer service and a discount for buying a bundled package. Industrial customers similarly prefer to deal with fewer suppliers. For example, in the medical equipment industry, many companies that in the past made one kind of product such as operating theater equipment, ultrasound devices, or magnetic imaging or X-ray equipment, have now merged with or been acquired by other companies to allow a larger, diversified company to provide hospitals with a complete range of medical equipment. This industry consolidation has also been driven by hospitals and health maintenance organizations (HMOs) that wish to obtain the convenience and lower prices that often follow from forming a long-term contract with a single supplier.

It is important to note, however, that product bundling often does not require joint ownership. In many instances, bundling can be achieved through market contracts. For example, McDonald's does not need to manufacture toys in order to bundle them into Happy Meals—it can buy them through a supply contract. Disney does not need to own airline services to offer a package deal on a vacation—an alliance contract will serve just as well. For product bundling to serve as a justification for diversification, there must be a strong need for coordination between the producers of the different products that cannot be overcome through market contracts.

10-2d Utilizing General Organizational Competencies

General organizational competencies transcend individual functions or business units and are found at the top or corporate level of a multibusiness company. Typically, **general organizational competencies** are the result of the skills of a company's top managers and functional experts. When these general competencies are present—and many times they are not—they help each business unit within a company perform at a higher level than it could if it operated as a separate or independent company. This increases the profitability of the entire corporation.[10] Three general organizational competencies help a company increase its performance and profitability: (1) entrepreneurial capabilities, (2) organizational design capabilities, and (3) strategic capabilities.

Entrepreneurial Capabilities A company that generates significant excess cash flow can take advantage of it only if its managers are able to identify new opportunities and act on them to create a stream of new and improved products, in its current industry and in new industries. Companies such as Apple, 3M, Google, and Samsung are able to promote entrepreneurship because they have an organizational culture that stimulates managers to act entrepreneurially.[11] As a result, they create new, profitable business units more quickly than do other companies, and this allows them to take advantage of profitable opportunities

general organizational competencies
Competencies that result from the skills of a company's top managers and that help every business unit within a company perform at a higher level than it could if it operated as a separate or independent company.

for diversification. We discuss one of the strategies required to generate new, profitable businesses later in this chapter: internal new venturing. For now, it is important to note that, to promote entrepreneurship, a company must (1) encourage managers to take risks, (2) give managers the time and resources to pursue novel ideas, (3) not punish managers when a new idea fails, and (4) make sure that the company's free cash flow is not wasted in pursuing too many risky ventures that have a low probability of generating a profitable return on investment. Strategic managers face a significant challenge in achieving all four of these objectives. On the one hand, a company must encourage risk taking; on the other hand, it must limit the number of risky ventures in which it engages.

Companies that possess strong entrepreneurial capabilities achieve this balancing act. For example, 3M's goal of generating 40% of its revenues from products introduced within the past 4 years focuses managers' attention on the need to develop new products and enter new businesses. 3M's long-standing commitment to help its customers solve problems also ensures that ideas for new businesses are customer focused. The company's celebration of employees who have created successful new businesses reinforces the norm of entrepreneurship and risk taking. Similarly, there is a norm that failure should not be punished but instead viewed as a learning experience.

Capabilities in Organizational Design   Organizational design skills are a result of managers' ability to create a structure, culture, and control systems that motivate and coordinate employees to perform at a high level. Organizational design is a major factor that influences a company's entrepreneurial capabilities; it is also an important determinant of a company's ability to create the functional competencies that give it a competitive advantage. The way strategic managers make organizational design decisions, such as how much autonomy to give to managers lower in the hierarchy, what kinds of norms and values should be developed to create an entrepreneurial culture, and even how to design its headquarters to encourage the free flow of ideas, is an important determinant of a diversified company's ability to profit from its multibusiness model. Effective organizational structure and controls create incentives that encourage business-unit (divisional) managers to maximize the efficiency and effectiveness of their units. Moreover, good organizational design helps prevent strategic managers from missing out on profitable new opportunities, as happens when employees become so concerned with protecting their company's competitive position in *existing* industries that they lose sight of new or improved ways to do business and gain profitable opportunities to enter new industries.

Chapters 11 and 12 of this book look at organizational design in depth. To profit from pursuing the corporate-level strategy of diversification, a company must be able to continuously manage and change its structure and culture to motivate and coordinate its employees to work at a high level and develop the resources and capabilities upon which its competitive advantage depends. The need to align a company's structure with its strategy is a complex, never-ending task, and only top managers with superior organizational design skills can do it.

Superior Strategic Management Capabilities   For diversification to increase profitability, a company's top managers must have superior capabilities in strategic management. They must possess the intangible, hard-to-define governance skills that are required to manage different business units in a way that enables these units to perform better than they would if they were independent companies.[12] These governance skills are a rare and valuable capability. However, certain CEOs and top managers seem to have them; they have developed the aptitude of managing multiple businesses simultaneously and encouraging the top managers of those business units to devise strategies that achieve superior performance. Examples of CEOs famous for their superior strategic management capabilities include Abigail Johnson at Fidelity, Warren Buffet at Berkshire Hathaway, and Sundar Pichai at Google.

organizational design skills

The ability of a company's managers to create a structure, culture, and control systems that motivate and coordinate employees to perform at a high level.

An especially important governance skill in a diversified company is the ability to diagnose the underlying source of the problems of a poorly performing business unit, and then to understand how to proceed to solve those problems. This might involve recommending new strategies to the existing top managers of the unit, or knowing when to replace them with a new management team that is better able to fix the problems. Top managers who have such governance skills tend to be very good at probing business-unit managers for information and helping them think through strategic problems.

Related to strategic management skills is the ability of the top managers of a diversified company to identify inefficient, poorly managed companies in other industries and then acquire and restructure them to improve their performance—and thus the profitability of the total corporation. This is known as a **turnaround strategy**.[13] There are several ways to improve the performance of an acquired company. First, the top managers of the acquired company are replaced with a more aggressive top-management team. Second, the new top-management team sells off expensive assets such as underperforming divisions, executive jets, and elaborate corporate headquarters; it also terminates staff to reduce the cost structure. Third, the new management team devises new strategies to improve the performance of the operations of the acquired business and improve its efficiency, quality, innovativeness, and customer responsiveness.

Fourth, to motivate the new top-management team and the other employees of the acquired company to work toward such goals, a companywide, pay-for-performance bonus system linked to profitability is introduced to reward employees at all levels for their hard work. Fifth, the acquiring company often establishes "stretch" goals for employees at all levels; these are challenging, hard-to-obtain goals that force employees at all levels to work to increase the company's efficiency and effectiveness. The members of the new top-management team clearly understand that if they fail to increase their division's performance and meet these stretch goals within some agreed-upon amount of time, they will be replaced. In sum, corporate managers of the acquiring company establish a system of rewards and sanctions that incentivize new top managers of the acquired unit to develop strategies to improve their unit's operating performance.

turnaround strategy
When managers of a diversified company identify inefficient, poorly managed companies in other industries and then acquire and restructure them to improve their performance—and thus the profitability of the total corporation.

10-3 Related and Unrelated Diversification

The last section discussed five principal ways in which companies use diversification to transfer and implant their business models and strategies into other industries and so increase their long-term profitability. The two corporate strategies of *related diversification* and *unrelated diversification* can be distinguished by how they attempt to realize the five profit-enhancing benefits of diversification.[14]

10.3 Differentiate between multibusiness models based on related and unrelated diversification.

10-3a Related Diversification

Related diversification is a corporate-level strategy based on the goal of establishing a business unit (division) in a new industry that is *related* to a company's existing business units by some form of commonality or linkage between the value-chain functions of the existing and new business units. As you might expect, the goal of this strategy is to obtain benefits from transferring competencies, leveraging competencies, sharing resources, and bundling products, as just discussed.

The multibusiness model of related diversification is based on taking advantage of strong technological, manufacturing, marketing, and sales commonalities between new and existing business units that can be successfully "tweaked" or modified to increase the competitive advantage of one or more business units. Figure 10.3 illustrates the commonalities or linkages possible among the different functions of three different business units or divisions. The greater the number of linkages that can be

related diversification
A corporate-level strategy based on the goal of establishing a business unit in a new industry that is related to a company's existing business units by some form of commonality or linkage between their value-chain functions.

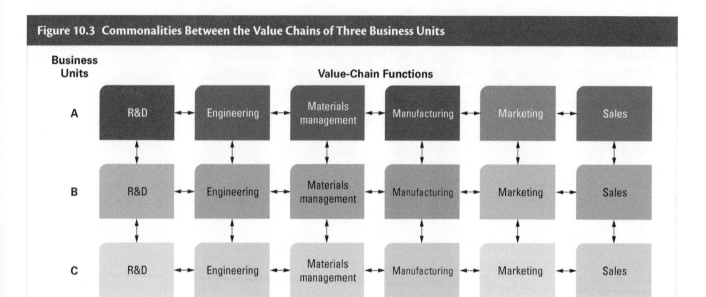

Figure 10.3 Commonalities Between the Value Chains of Three Business Units

formed among business units, the greater the potential to realize the profit-enhancing benefits of the five reasons to diversify discussed previously.

Another advantage of related diversification is that it can allow a company to use any general organizational competency it possesses to increase the overall performance of *all* its different industry divisions. For example, strategic managers may strive to create a structure and culture that encourages entrepreneurship across divisions, as Google/Alphabet Inc., Apple, and 3M have done; beyond these general competences, these companies all have a set of distinctive competencies that can be shared among their different business units and that they continuously strive to improve.

10-3b Unrelated Diversification

unrelated diversification

A corporate-level strategy based on a multibusiness model that uses general organizational competencies to increase the performance of all the company's business units.

internal capital market

A corporate-level strategy whereby the firm's headquarters assesses the performance of business units and allocates money across them. Cash generated by units that are profitable but have poor investment opportunities within their business is used to cross-subsidize businesses that need cash and have strong promise for long-run profitability.

Unrelated diversification is a corporate-level strategy whereby firms own unrelated businesses and attempt to increase their value through an internal capital market, the use of general organizational competencies, or both. Business organizations that operate in many diverse industries are often called *conglomerates*. An **internal capital market** refers to a situation whereby corporate headquarters assesses the performance of business units and allocates money across them. Cash generated by units that are profitable but have poor investment opportunities within their business is used to cross-subsidize businesses that need cash and have strong promise for long-run profitability. A large, diverse firm may have free cash generated from its internal businesses, or readier access to cheap cash on the external capital market, than an individual business unit might have. For example, GE's large capital reserves and excellent credit rating enable it to provide funding to advanced-technology businesses within its corporate umbrella (e.g., solar power stations, subsea oil-production equipment, avionics, photonics) that would otherwise pay a high price (either in interest payments or equity shares) for funding due to their inherent uncertainty.

The benefits of an internal capital market are limited, however, by the efficiency of the external capital market (banks, stockholders, venture capitalists, angel investors, and so on). If the external capital market were perfectly efficient, managers could not create additional value by cross-subsidizing businesses with internal cash. An internal capital market is, in essence, an arbitrage strategy whereby managers make money by making better investment decisions within the firm than the external capital market would, often because they possess superior information. The amount of value that can be created through an internal capital market is thus directly proportional to the inefficiency of the external capital market. In the United States, where capital markets have become fairly efficient due to (1) reporting requirements mandated by the Securities and Exchange Commission (SEC), (2) large numbers of research analysts, (3) an extremely large and active investment community, (4) strong communication systems, and (5) strong contract law, it is not common to see firms create significant value through an internal capital market. As a result, few large conglomerates have survived, and many of those that do survive trade at a discount (that is, their stock is worth less than the stock of more specialized firms operating in the same industries). On the other hand, in a market with a less efficient capital market, conglomerates may create significant value. Tata Group, for example, is an extremely large, diverse, business-holding group in India. Founded during the 1800s, it took on many projects that its founders felt were crucial to India's development (for example, developing a rail transportation system, hotels, and power production). The lack of a well-developed investment community and poor contract law to protect investors and bankers meant that funds were often unavailable to entrepreneurs in India, or were available only at a very high cost. Tata Group was thus able to use cross-subsidization to fund projects much more cheaply than independent businesses could. Furthermore, the reputation of the company served as a strong guarantee that it would fulfill its promises (which was particularly important in the absence of strong contract law), and its long, deep relationships with the government gave it an advantage in securing licenses and permits.

Companies pursuing a strategy of unrelated diversification have *no* intention of transferring or leveraging competencies between business units or sharing resources other than cash and general organizational competencies. If the strategic managers of conglomerates have the special skills needed to manage many companies in diverse industries, the strategy can result in superior performance and profitability; often they do not have these skills, as is discussed later in the chapter.

10-4 The Limits and Disadvantages of Diversification

10.4 Discuss the disadvantages of diversification.

Many companies, such as 3M, Samsung, and Cisco, have achieved the benefits of pursuing either or both of the two diversification strategies just discussed, and they have sustained their profitability over time. On the other hand, GM, Tyco, Textron, and Philips failed miserably and became unprofitable when they pursued diversification. There are three principal reasons why a business model based on diversification may lead to a loss of competitive advantage: (1) changes in the industry or inside a company that occur over time, (2) diversification pursued for the wrong reasons, and (3) excessive diversification that results in increasing bureaucratic costs.

10-4a Changes in the Industry or Company

Diversification is a complex strategy. To pursue it, top managers must have the ability to recognize profitable opportunities to enter new industries and implement the strategies necessary to make diversification profitable. Over time, a company's top-management team often changes; sometimes its most able executives join other companies and become CEOs, and sometimes successful CEOs retire or step down. When the managers who possess the hard-to-define skills leave, they often take their vision with them. A company's new leaders may lack the competency or commitment necessary to pursue diversification successfully over time; thus, the cost structure of the diversified company increases and eliminates any gains the strategy may have produced.

In addition, the environment often changes rapidly and unpredictably over time. When new technology blurs industry boundaries, it can destroy the source of a company's competitive advantage. For example, by 2011, it was clear that Apple's iPhone and iPad had become a direct competitor with Nintendo's and Sony's mobile gaming consoles. When such a major technological change occurs in a company's core business, the benefits it has previously achieved from transferring or leveraging distinctive competencies disappear. The company is then saddled with a collection of businesses that have all become poor performers in their respective industries because they are not based on the new technology. Thus, a major problem with diversification is that the future success of a business is hard to predict when this strategy is used. For a company to profit from it over time, managers must be as willing to divest business units as they are to acquire them. Research suggests managers do not behave in this way, however.

10-4b Diversification for the Wrong Reasons

As we have discussed, when managers decide to pursue diversification, they must have a clear vision of how their entry into new industries will allow them to create new products that provide more value for customers and increase their company's profitability. Over time, however, a diversification strategy may result in falling profitability for reasons noted earlier, but managers often refuse to recognize that their strategy is failing. Although they know they should divest unprofitable businesses, managers "make up" reasons to keep their collection of businesses together.

In the past, for example, one widely used (and false) justification for diversification was that the strategy would allow a company to obtain the benefits of risk pooling. The idea behind risk pooling is that a company can reduce the risk of its revenues and profits rising and falling sharply (something that sharply lowers its stock price) if it acquires and operates companies in several industries that have different business cycles. The business cycle is the tendency for the revenues and profits of companies in an industry to rise and fall over time because of "predictable" changes in customer demand. For example, even in a recession, people still need to eat—the profits earned by supermarket chains will be relatively stable; sales at Safeway, Kroger, and also at "dollar stores," rise as shoppers attempt to get more value for their dollars. At the same time, a recession can cause demand for cars and luxury goods to plunge. Many CEOs argue that diversifying into industries that have different business cycles would allow the sales and revenues of some of their divisions to rise, while sales and revenues in other divisions would fall. A more stable stream of revenue and profits is the net result over time. An example of risk pooling occurred when U.S. Steel diversified into the oil and gas industry in an attempt to offset the adverse effects of cyclical downturns in the steel industry.

This argument ignores two important facts. First, stockholders can eliminate the risk inherent in holding an individual stock by diversifying their own portfolios, and they can do so at a much lower cost than a company can. Thus, for a publicly held firm, attempts to pool risks through diversification represent an unproductive use of resources; instead, profits should be returned to shareholders in the form of increased dividends. Second, research suggests that corporate diversification is not an effective way to pool risks because the business cycles of different industries are *inherently difficult to predict,* so it is likely that a diversified company will find that an economic downturn affects *all* its industries simultaneously. If this happens, the company's profitability plunges.[15]

When a company's core business is in trouble, another mistaken justification for diversification is that entry into new industries will rescue the core business and lead to long-term growth and profitability. However, when a company diversifies into industries in which it has no competitive advantage, it is likely to multiply the number and range of problems, leading to even worse performance rather than improving its performance. In fact, a very long line of empirical research on diversification has found that diversification often reduces value instead of creating it.[16]

10-4c The Bureaucratic Costs of Diversification

A major reason why diversification often fails to boost profitability is that, very often, the *bureaucratic costs* of diversification exceed the benefits created by the strategy (that is, the increased profit that results when a company makes and sells a wider range of differentiated products and/or lowers its cost structure). As we mentioned in the previous chapter, **bureaucratic costs** are the costs associated with solving the transaction difficulties that arise between a company's business units and between business units and corporate headquarters, as the company attempts to obtain the benefits from transferring, sharing, and leveraging competencies. They also include the costs associated with using general organizational competencies to solve managerial and functional inefficiencies. The level of bureaucratic costs in a diversified organization is a function of two factors: the number of business units in a company's portfolio, and the degree to which coordination is required between these different business units to realize the advantages of diversification.

bureaucratic costs
The costs associated with solving the transaction difficulties between business units and corporate headquarters as a company obtains the benefits from transferring, sharing, and leveraging competencies.

Number of Businesses   The greater the number of business units in a company's portfolio, the more difficult it is for corporate managers to remain informed about the complexities of each business. Managers simply do not have the time to assess the business model of each unit. This problem occurred at GE in the 1970s, when its growth-hungry CEO, Reg Jones, acquired many new businesses. As he commented:

> I tried to review each plan [of each business unit] in great detail. This effort took untold hours and placed a tremendous burden on the corporate executive office. After a while I began to realize that no matter how hard we would work, we could not achieve the necessary in-depth understanding of the 40-odd business unit plans.[17]

The inability of top managers in extensively diversified companies to maintain control over their multibusiness models over time often leads them to base important resource-allocation decisions on a superficial analysis of each business unit's competitive position. For example, a promising business unit may be starved of investment funds, while other business units receive far more cash than they can profitably reinvest in their operations. Furthermore, because they are distant from the day-to-day operations of the business units, corporate managers may find that business-unit managers try to hide information on poor performance to save their own jobs. For example, business-unit managers might blame poor performance on difficult competitive conditions, even when it is the result of their inability to craft a successful business model. As such organizational problems increase, top managers must spend an enormous amount of time and effort to solve them. This increases bureaucratic costs and cancels out the profit-enhancing advantages of pursuing diversification, such as those obtained from sharing or leveraging competencies.

Coordination Among Businesses   The amount of coordination required to realize value from a diversification strategy based on transferring, sharing, or leveraging competencies is a major source of bureaucratic costs. The bureaucratic mechanisms needed to oversee and manage the coordination and handoffs between units, such as cross-business-unit teams and management committees, are a major source of these costs. A second source of bureaucratic costs arises because of the enormous amount of managerial time and effort required to accurately measure the performance and unique profit contribution of a business unit that is transferring or sharing resources with another. Consider a company that has two business units, one making household products (such as liquid soap and laundry detergent) and another making packaged food products. The products of both units are sold through supermarkets. To lower the cost structure, the parent company pools the marketing and sales functions of each business unit, using an organizational structure similar to that illustrated in Figure 10.4. The company is organized into three divisions: a household products division, a food products division, and a marketing division.

Although such an arrangement may significantly lower operating costs, it can also give rise to substantial control problems, and hence bureaucratic costs. For example, if the performance of the household products business begins to slip, identifying who is to be held accountable—managers in the household products division or managers in the marketing division—may prove difficult. Indeed, each may blame the other for poor performance. Although such problems can be resolved if corporate management performs an in-depth audit of both divisions, the bureaucratic costs (managers' time and effort) involved in doing so may once again cancel out any value achieved from diversification. The need to reduce bureaucratic costs is evident from the experience of Pfizer, as discussed in Strategy in Action 10.1.

In sum, although diversification can be a highly profitable strategy to pursue, it is also the most complex and difficult strategy to manage because it is based on a complex, multibusiness model. Even when a company has pursued this strategy successfully in the past, changing conditions both in the industry environment and within a company can quickly reduce its profit-creating advantages. For example, such changes may result in one or more business units losing their competitive advantage. Or, changes may cause the bureaucratic costs associated with pursuing diversification to rise sharply and cancel out its advantages. Thus, the existence of bureaucratic costs places a limit on the amount of diversification that a company can profitably pursue. It makes sense for a company to diversify only when the profit-enhancing advantages of this strategy exceed the bureaucratic costs of managing the increasing number of business units required when a company expands and enters new industries.

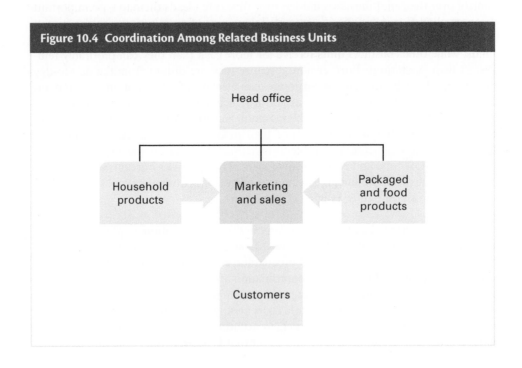

Figure 10.4 Coordination Among Related Business Units

How Bureaucratic Costs Rose Then Fell at Pfizer

Pfizer is one of the largest global pharmaceuticals companies in the world, with sales of over $80 billion in 2021. Its research scientists have innovated some of the most successful, profitable drugs in the world, such as the first cholesterol reducer, Lipitor. In the 2000s, however, Pfizer encountered major problems in its attempt to innovate new blockbuster drugs while its current blockbuster drugs, such as Lipitor, lost their patent protection. Whereas Lipitor once earned $13 billion in profits per year, its sales were now fast declining. By 2012, Lipitor was only bringing in $3.9 billion. Pfizer desperately needed to find ways to make its product development pipeline work. One manager, Martin Mackay, believed he knew how to do it.

When Pfizer's R&D chief retired, Mackay, his deputy, made it clear to CEO Jeffrey Kindler that he wanted the job. Kindler made it equally clear he thought the company could use some new talent and fresh ideas to solve its problems. Mackay realized he had to quickly devise a convincing plan to change the way Pfizer's scientists worked to develop new drugs, gain Kindler's support, and get the top job. He created a detailed plan for changing the way Pfizer's thousands of researchers made decisions, ensuring that the company's resources, talent, and funds would be put to their best use. After Kindler reviewed the plan, he was so impressed he promoted Mackay to the top R&D position. What was Mackay's plan?

As Pfizer had grown over time as a result of mergers with two large pharmaceutical companies, Warner-Lambert and Pharmacia, Mackay noted how decision-making problems and conflict between the managers of Pfizer's different drug divisions had increased. As it grew, Pfizer's organizational structure had become taller and taller, and the size of its headquarters staff grew. With more managers and levels in the company's hierarchy there was a great need for committees to integrate across activities. However, in meetings, different groups of managers fought to promote the development of the drugs in which they had the most interest, and increasingly came into

conflict with one another in efforts to ensure they got the resources needed to develop these drugs. In short, Mackay felt that too many managers and committees were resulting in too much conflict, and that the company's performance was suffering as a result. In addition, Pfizer's success depended upon innovation, but conflict had resulted in a bureaucratic culture that reduced the quality of decision making, creating more difficulty when identifying promising new drugs—and increasing bureaucratic costs.

Mackay's bold plan to reduce conflict and bureaucratic costs involved slashing the number of management layers between top managers and scientists from 14 to 7, which resulted in the layoff of thousands of Pfizer's managers. He also abolished the product development committees whose wrangling he believed was slowing down the process of transforming innovative ideas into blockbuster drugs. After streamlining the hierarchy, he focused on reducing the number of bureaucratic rules scientists had to follow, many of which were unnecessary and promoted conflict. He and his team eliminated every kind of written report that was slowing the innovation process. For example, scientists had been in the habit of submitting quarterly and monthly reports to top managers explaining each drug's progress; Mackay told them to choose one report or the other.

As you can imagine, Mackay's efforts caused enormous upheaval in the company, as managers fought to keep their positions and scientists fought to protect the drugs they had in development. However, a resolute Mackay pushed his agenda through with the support of the CEO, who defended his efforts to create a new R&D product development process that empowered Pfizer's scientists and promoted innovation and entrepreneurship. Pfizer's scientists reported that they felt "liberated" by the new workflow; the level of conflict decreased, and they felt hopeful that new drugs would be produced more quickly.

Source: www.pfizer.com.

10-5 Choosing a Strategy

10-5a Related Versus Unrelated Diversification

Because related diversification involves more sharing of competencies, one might think it can boost profitability in more ways than unrelated diversification, and is therefore the better diversification strategy. However, some companies can create as much or more value from pursuing unrelated diversification, so this strategy must also have some substantial benefits. An unrelated company does *not* need to achieve coordination between business units; it must cope only with the bureaucratic costs that arise from the number of businesses in its portfolio. In contrast, a related company must achieve coordination *among* business units if it is to realize the gains that come from utilizing its distinctive competencies. Consequently, it has to cope with the bureaucratic costs that arise *both* from the

> **10.5** Examine why companies choose related or unrelated diversification.

number of business units in its portfolio *and* from coordination among business units. Although it is true that related diversified companies can create value and profit in more ways than unrelated companies, they also have to bear higher bureaucratic costs to do so. These higher costs may cancel out the greater benefits, making the strategy no more profitable than one of unrelated diversification.

How, then, does a company choose between these strategies? The choice depends upon a comparison of the benefits of each strategy against the bureaucratic costs of pursuing it. It pays for a company to pursue related diversification when (1) the company's competencies can be applied across a greater number of industries and (2) the company has superior strategic capabilities that allow it to keep bureaucratic costs under close control—perhaps by encouraging entrepreneurship, or by developing a value-creating organizational culture.

Using the same logic, it pays for a company to pursue unrelated diversification when (1) each business unit's functional competencies have few useful applications across industries, but the company's top managers are skilled at raising the profitability of poorly run businesses and (2) the company's managers use their superior strategic management competencies to improve the competitive advantage of their business units and keep bureaucratic costs under control. Well-managed companies have managers who can successfully pursue unrelated diversification and reap its rewards.

10.6 Discuss the advantages and disadvantages of internal new venturing.

10-6 Entering New Industries: Internal New Ventures

We have discussed the sources of value managers seek through corporate-level strategies of related and unrelated diversification (and the challenges and risks these strategies also impose). Now we turn to the three main methods managers employ to enter new industries: internal new ventures, acquisitions, and joint ventures. In this section, we consider the pros and cons of using internal new ventures. In the following sections, we look at acquisitions and joint ventures.

10-6a The Attractions of Internal New Venturing

Internal new venturing is typically used to implement corporate-level strategies when a company possesses one or more distinctive competencies in its core business model that can be leveraged or recombined to enter a new industry. **Internal new venturing** is the process of transferring resources to, and creating a new business unit or division in, a new industry. Internal venturing is used often by companies that have a business model based upon using their technology or design skills to innovate new kinds of products and enter related markets or industries. Thus, technology-based companies that pursue related diversification—for example, DuPont, which has created new markets with products such as cellophane, nylon, Freon, and Teflon—are most likely to use internal new venturing. 3M has a near-legendary knack for creating new or improved products from internally generated ideas, and then establishing new business units to create the business model that enables it to dominate a new market. Similarly, HP entered into the computer and printer industries by using internal new venturing.

A company may also use internal venturing to enter a newly emerging or embryonic industry—one in which no company has yet developed the competencies or business model to give it a dominant position in that industry. For example, in 2016, Tesla announced it was developing solar roof tiles—miniature solar panels that would replace shingles. As described by Elon Musk, "It's not a thing on the roof. It is the roof."[18] Musk believed this was the next obvious evolution of residential solar power (an industry that Tesla entered with its acquisition of Solar City earlier that same year), and no other company had made

internal new venturing

The process of transferring resources to, and creating a new business unit or division in, a new industry to innovate new kinds of products.

significant headway on it yet. Musk set a goal of achieving 1,000 solar roof installations a week. However, developing successful solar roof tiles turned out to be more difficult than Musk had anticipated and, by 2022, the company's installation rate was about 4% of that goal. As explained by Musk, "We basically made some significant mistakes in assessing the difficulty of certain roofs. . . . You can't just have a one-size-fits-all situation."[19]

10-6b Pitfalls of New Ventures

As the Tesla roof example above highlights, internal new venturing has a high risk of failure. Though statistics vary widely across industries, time periods, and sources, it is generally accepted that a very large percentage of new ventures fail to generate an economic return. Three reasons are often put forward to explain the relatively high failure rate of internal new ventures: (1) market entry on too small a scale, (2) poor commercialization of the new-venture product, and (3) poor corporate management of the new-venture division.[20]

Scale of Entry   Research suggests that large-scale entry into a new industry is often a critical precondition for the success of a new venture. In the short run, this means that a substantial capital investment must be made to support large-scale entry; thus, there is a risk of major losses if the new venture fails. But, in the long run—which can be as long as 5 to 12 years (depending on the industry)—such a large investment results in far greater returns than if a company chooses to enter on a small scale to limit its investment and reduce potential losses.[21] Large-scale entrants can more rapidly realize scale economies, build brand loyalty, and gain access to distribution channels in the new industry, all of which increase the probability of new-venture success. In contrast, small-scale entrants may find themselves handicapped by high costs due to lack of scale economies and lack of market presence, which limits the entrant's ability to build brand loyalty and gain access to distribution channels. These scale effects are particularly significant when a company is entering an established industry in which incumbent companies possess scale economies, brand loyalty, and access to distribution channels. In that case, the new entrant must make a major investment to succeed.

Figure 10.5 plots the relationship between scale of entry and profitability over time for successful small-scale and large-scale ventures. The figure shows that successful small-scale entry is associated with lower initial losses, but in the long term, large-scale entry generates

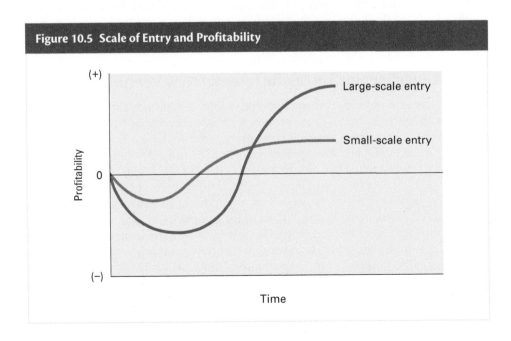

Figure 10.5 Scale of Entry and Profitability

greater returns. However, because of the high costs and risks associated with large-scale entry, many companies make the mistake of choosing a small-scale entry strategy, which often means they fail to build the market share necessary for long-term success.

Commercialization   Many internal new ventures are driven by the opportunity to use a new or advanced technology to make better products and outperform competitors in a market. To succeed commercially, the products under development must be tailored to meet the needs of customers. New ventures often fail because the company ignores these needs; its managers become so focused on the technological possibilities of the new product that customer requirements are forgotten.[22] Thus, a new venture may fail because it is marketing a product based on a technology for which there is no demand, or the company fails to correctly position or differentiate the product in the market to attract customers.

Poor Implementation   Managing the new-venture process, and controlling the new-venture division, creates many difficult managerial and organizational problems.[23] For example, one common mistake companies make to try to increase their chances of introducing successful products is to establish too many internal new-venture divisions at the same time. Managers attempt to spread the risks of failure by having many divisions, but this places enormous demands upon a company's cash flow. Sometimes companies are forced to reduce the funding each division receives to keep the entire company profitable, and this can result in the most promising ventures being starved of the cash they need in order to succeed.[24] Another common mistake is when corporate managers fail to do the extensive advanced planning necessary to ensure that the new venture's business model is sound and contains all the elements that will be needed later if it is to succeed. Sometimes corporate managers leave this process to the scientists and engineers championing the new technology. Focused on the new technology, managers may innovate new products that have little strategic or commercial value. Corporate managers and scientists must work together to clarify how and why a new venture will lead to a product that has a competitive advantage, and jointly establish strategic objectives and a timetable to manage the venture until the product reaches the market.

The failure to anticipate the time and costs involved in the new-venture process constitutes a further mistake. Many companies have unrealistic expectations regarding the time frame and expect profits to flow in quickly. Research suggests that some companies operate with a philosophy of killing new businesses if they do not turn a profit by the end of the third year, which is unrealistic given that it can take 5 years or more before a new venture generates substantial profits.

10-6c Guidelines for Successful Internal New Venturing

To avoid these pitfalls, a company should adopt a well-thought-out, structured approach to manage internal new venturing. New venturing is based on R&D. It begins with the *exploratory research* necessary to advance basic science and technology (the "R" in R&D) and *development research* to identify, develop, and perfect the commercial applications of a new technology (the "D" in R&D). Companies with strong track records of success at internal new venturing excel at both kinds of R&D; they help to advance basic science and discover important commercial applications for it.[25] To advance basic science, it is important for companies to have strong links with universities, where much of the scientific knowledge that underlies new technologies is discovered. It is also important to make sure that research funds are being controlled by scientists who understand the importance of both "R" and "D" research. If the "D" is lacking, a company will probably generate few successful commercial ventures no matter how well it does basic research. Companies can take several steps to ensure that good science ends up with good, commercially viable products.

First, many companies must place the funding for research into the hands of business-unit managers who have the skill or knowhow to narrow down and then select the optimal set of research projects—those that have the best chance of a significant commercial payoff. Second, to make effective use of its R&D competency, top managers must work with R&D scientists to continually develop and improve the business model and strategies that guide their efforts, and make sure that all its scientists and engineers understand what they have to do to make it succeed.[26]

Third, a company must foster close links between R&D and marketing to increase the probability that a new product will be a commercial success in the future. When marketing works to identify the most important customer requirements for a new product and then communicates these requirements to scientists, it ensures that research projects meet the needs of their intended customers. Fourth, a company should also foster close links between R&D and manufacturing to ensure that it has the ability to make a proposed new product in a cost-effective way. Many companies successfully integrate the activities of the different functions by creating cross-functional project teams to oversee the development of new products from their inception to market introduction. This approach can significantly reduce the time it takes to bring a new product to market. For example, while R&D is working on design, manufacturing is setting up facilities, and marketing is developing a campaign to show customers how much the new product will benefit them.

Finally, because large-scale entry often leads to greater long-term profits, a company can promote the success of internal new venturing by "thinking big." A company should construct efficient-scale manufacturing facilities and allocate marketing a large budget to develop a future product campaign that will build market presence and brand loyalty quickly and well in advance of that product's introduction. Also, corporate managers should not panic when customers are slow to adopt the new product; they need to accept the fact there will be initial losses and recognize that as long as market share is expanding, the product will eventually succeed.

10-7 Entering New Industries: Acquisitions

10.7 Discuss the advantages and disadvantages of acquisitions as a way to enter new industries.

In Chapter 9, we explained that acquisitions are the main vehicle that companies use to implement a horizontal integration strategy. Acquisitions are also a principal way companies enter new industries to pursue vertical integration and diversification, so it is necessary to understand both the benefits and risks associated with using acquisitions to implement a corporate-level strategy.

10-7a The Attraction of Acquisitions

In general, acquisitions are used to pursue vertical integration or diversification when a company lacks the distinctive competencies necessary to compete in a new industry, and so uses its financial resources to purchase an established company that has those competencies. A company is particularly likely to use acquisitions when it needs to move rapidly to establish a presence in an industry, commonly an embryonic or growth industry. Entering a new industry through internal venturing is a relatively slow process; acquisition is a much quicker way for a company to establish a significant market presence. A company can purchase a leading company with a strong competitive position in months, rather than waiting years to build a market leadership position by engaging in internal venturing. Thus, when speed is particularly important, acquisition is the favored entry mode. Intel, for example, used acquisitions to build its communications chip business because it sensed that the market was developing very quickly, and that it would take too long to develop the required competencies.

In addition, acquisitions are often perceived as being less risky than internal new ventures because they involve less commercial uncertainty. Because of the risks of failure associated with internal new venturing, it is difficult to predict its future success and profitability. By contrast, when a company makes an acquisition, it gains a company with an already established reputation, and it knows the magnitude of the company's market share and profitability.

Finally, acquisitions are an attractive way to enter an industry that is protected by high barriers to entry. Recall from Chapter 2 that barriers to entry arise from factors such as product differentiation, which leads to brand loyalty, and high market share, which leads to economies of scale. When entry barriers are high, it may be very difficult for a company to enter an industry through internal new venturing because it will have to construct large-scale manufacturing facilities and invest in a massive advertising campaign to establish brand loyalty—difficult goals that require huge capital expenditures. In contrast, if a company acquires another company already established in the industry, possibly the market leader, it can circumvent most entry barriers because that company has already achieved economies of scale and obtained brand loyalty. In general, the higher the barriers to entry, the more likely it is that acquisitions will be the method used to enter the industry.

10-7b Acquisition Pitfalls

For these reasons, acquisitions have long been the most common method that companies use to pursue diversification. Numerous research studies have been conducted to assess whether, on average, acquisitions create or destroy shareholder value. These studies have used a wide range of methodological approaches (e.g., event studies, large panel analyses, case studies), samples (e.g., acquisitions in particular industries, acquisitions where both the acquirer and target are publicly held U.S. firms, acquisitions that vary in the share that is taken by the acquirer), and performance measures (e.g., stock price reactions, long-run cumulative abnormal returns, accounting performance, productivity, patenting outcomes). The research falls well short of a consensus on the effect of acquisitions; however, a very large number of studies conclude that many acquisitions fail to increase the profitability of the acquiring company and may result in losses. For example, one study of 700 large acquisitions found that although 30% of these resulted in higher profits, 31% led to losses, and the remainder had little impact.[27,28] Another study of the postacquisition performance of acquired companies found that their profitability and market share often decline, suggesting that many acquisitions destroy rather than create value.[29]

Acquisitions may fail to raise the performance of the acquiring companies for four reasons:[30] (1) companies frequently experience management problems when they attempt to integrate a different company's organizational structure and culture into their own; (2) companies often overestimate the potential economic benefits from an acquisition; (3) acquisitions tend to be so expensive that they do not increase future profitability; (4) companies are often negligent in screening their acquisition targets and fail to recognize important problems with their business models; and (5) managers may have incentives to make acquisitions even when they do not increase shareholder value (i.e., "agency problems").

Integrating the Acquired Company   Once an acquisition has been made, the acquiring company must integrate the acquired company and combine it with its own organizational structure and culture. Integration involves the adoption of common management and financial control systems, the joining together of operations from the acquired and the acquiring company, the establishment of bureaucratic mechanisms to share information and personnel, and the need to create a common culture.[31] Experience has shown that many problems can occur as companies attempt to integrate their activities. When the processes and cultures of two companies are very different, integration can be extremely challenging. For example, when Daimler Benz acquired Chrysler in 1998, the two companies discovered that the more formal and hierarchical culture at

Daimler chafed Chrysler employees, who were used to a looser, more entrepreneurial culture. Furthermore, though Daimler had hoped to benefit from Chrysler's more rapid new-product development processes, they soon realized that to do so they would have to adopt a more modular approach to developing cars, for instance by re-using platforms across different car models. This contrasted sharply with Daimler's historic emphasis on holistic "ground up" development of car designs. In the end, few of the anticipated advantages of the acquisition materialized. After paying roughly $36 billion for Chrysler (through a stock swap), Daimler ended up having to *pay out* another $650 million to Cerberus Capital Management to shed the Chrysler group in 2007.[32]

Many acquired companies experience high management turnover because their employees do not like the acquiring company's way of operating—its structure and culture.[33] Research suggests that the loss of management talent and expertise, and the damage from constant tension between the businesses, can materially harm the performance of the acquired unit.[34] Moreover, companies often must take on an enormous amount of debt to fund an acquisition, and they are frequently unable to pay it once the management problems (and sometimes the weaknesses) of the acquired company's business model surface.

Overestimating Economic Benefits   Even when companies find it easy to integrate their activities, they often overestimate the combined businesses' future profitability. Managers often overestimate the competitive advantages that will derive from the acquisition and so pay more for the acquired company than it is worth. One reason is that top managers typically overestimate their own general competencies to create valuable new products from an acquisition (this is known as the "hubris hypothesis").[35] The very fact that they have risen to the top of a company gives some managers an exaggerated sense of their own capabilities and a self-importance that distorts their strategic decision making. Coca-Cola's acquisition of several midsized winemakers illustrates this. Reasoning that a beverage is a beverage, Coca-Cola's then-CEO decided he would be able to mobilize his company's talented marketing managers to develop the strategies needed to dominate the U.S. wine industry. After purchasing three wine companies and enduring 7 years of marginal profits because of failed marketing campaigns, he subsequently decided that wine and soft drinks are very different products; in particular, they have different kinds of appeal, pricing systems, and distribution networks. Coca-Cola eventually sold the wine operations to Joseph E. Seagram & Sons, Inc. and took a substantial loss.[36]

The Expense of Acquisitions   Perhaps the most important reason for the failure of acquisitions is that acquiring a company with stock that is publicly traded tends to be very expensive—and the expense of the acquisition can more than wipe out the value of the stream of future profits that are expected from the acquisition. One reason is that the top managers of a company that is "targeted" for acquisition are likely to resist any takeover attempt unless the acquiring company agrees to pay a substantial premium above its current market value. These premiums are often 30 to 50% above the usual value of a company's stock. Similarly, the stockholders of the target company are unlikely to sell their stock unless they are paid major premiums over market value prior to a takeover bid. Collectively, this means that it is far easier to overpay for an acquisition target than to "get a bargain," and research shows that managers do regularly overpay for acquisitions.[37]

To pay such high premiums, the acquiring company must be certain it can use its acquisition to generate the stream of future profits that justifies the high price of the target company. This is frequently difficult to do given how fast the industry environment can change and other problems discussed earlier such as integrating the acquired company. This is a major reason why acquisitions are frequently unprofitable for the acquiring company.

The reason why the acquiring company must pay such a high premium is that the stock price of the acquisition target increases enormously during the acquisition process as investors speculate on the final price the acquiring company will pay to capture it. In the case of a contested bidding contest, where two or more companies simultaneously bid to acquire the target company, its stock price may surge. Also, when many acquisitions are occurring in one industry, investors speculate that the value of the remaining industry companies that have *not* been acquired has increased, and that a bid for these companies will be made at some future point. This also drives up their stock price and increases the cost of making acquisitions. This happened in the telecommunications sector when, to make sure they could meet the needs of customers who were demanding leading-edge equipment, many large companies went on acquisition "binges." Nortel and Alcatel-Lucent engaged in a race to purchase smaller, innovative companies that were developing new telecommunications equipment. The result was that the stock prices for these companies were bid up by investors, and they were purchased at a hugely inflated price. When the telecommunications boom turned to bust, the acquiring companies found that they had vastly overpaid for their acquisitions and had to take enormous accounting write-downs. Nortel was forced to declare bankruptcy and sold off all its assets, and the value of Alcatel-Lucent's stock plunged almost 90%.

Inadequate Pre-acquisition Screening   As the problems of these companies suggest, top managers often do a poor job of pre-acquisition screening—that is, evaluating how much a potential acquisition may increase future profitability. Researchers have discovered that one important reason for the failure of an acquisition is that managers make the decision to acquire other companies without thoroughly analyzing potential benefits and costs.[38] In many cases, after an acquisition has been completed, many acquiring companies discover that instead of buying a well-managed business with a strong business model, they have purchased a troubled organization. Obviously, the managers of the target company may manipulate company information or the balance sheet to make their financial condition look much better than it is. The acquiring company must be wary and complete extensive research. In 2009, IBM was in negotiations to purchase chip-maker Sun Microsystems. After spending 1 week examining its books, IBM reduced its offer price by 10% when its negotiators found its customer base was not as solid as they had expected. Sun Microsystems was eventually sold to Oracle in 2010 for $7.4 billion.

Agency Problems   It is important to note that managers may make acquisitions for reasons that have nothing to do with shareholder value. This is called an "agency problem," and will be discussed further in Chapter 11. It is well established, for example, that the pay, perquisites, and other benefits managers receive are strongly related to firm size.[39] Furthermore, managers often have a very large portion of their personal wealth tied to the firm they manage. This means they may be extremely underdiversified. Their solution might be to diversify the firm, even if that is not in the interests of other shareholders (who may more easily and inexpensively diversify by holding shares in other firms).

10-7c Guidelines for Successful Acquisition

To avoid these pitfalls and make successful acquisitions, companies need to follow an approach to targeting and evaluating potential acquisitions that is based on four main steps: (1) target identification and pre-acquisition screening, (2) bidding strategy, (3) integration, and (4) learning from experience.[40]

Identification and Screening   Thorough pre-acquisition screening increases a company's knowledge about a potential takeover target and lessens the risk of purchasing a problem company—one with a weak business model. It also leads to a more realistic assessment of the problems involved in executing an acquisition so that a company can plan how to integrate the new business and blend organizational structures and cultures. The screening process should begin with a detailed assessment of the strategic rationale for making the acquisition, an identification of the kind of company that would make an ideal acquisition candidate, and an extensive analysis of the strengths and weaknesses of the prospective company's business model compared to other possible acquisition targets.

Indeed, an acquiring company should select a set of top potential acquisition targets and evaluate each company using a set of criteria that focus on revealing (1) its financial position, (2) its distinctive competencies and competitive advantage, (3) changing industry boundaries, (4) its management capabilities, and (5) its corporate culture. Such an evaluation helps the acquiring company perform a detailed strength, weakness, opportunities, and threats (SWOT) analysis that identifies the best target, for example, by measuring the potential economies of scale and scope that can be achieved between the acquiring company and each target company. This analysis also helps reveal potential problems that might arise when it is necessary to integrate the corporate cultures of the acquiring and acquired companies. For example, managers at Microsoft and SAP, the world's leading provider of enterprise resource planning (ERP) software, met to discuss a possible acquisition by Microsoft. Both companies decided that despite the strong, strategic rationale for a merger—together they could dominate the software computing market, satisfying the need of large global companies—they would have challenges to overcome. The difficulties of creating an organizational structure that could successfully integrate their hundreds of thousands of employees throughout the world, and blend two very different cultures, were insurmountable.

Once a company has reduced the list of potential acquisition candidates to the most favored one or two, it needs to consult expert third parties such as investment bankers like Goldman Sachs and Merrill Lynch. These companies provide valuable insights about the attractiveness of a potential acquisition, assess current industry competitive conditions, and handle the many other issues surrounding an acquisition such as how to select the optimal bidding strategy for acquiring the target company's stock and keep the purchase price as low as possible.

Bidding Strategy   The objective of the bidding strategy is to reduce the price that a company must pay for the target company. The most effective way a company can acquire another is to make a friendly takeover bid, which means the two companies decide upon an amicable way to merge the two companies, satisfying the needs of each company's stockholders and top managers. A friendly takeover prevents speculators from bidding up stock prices. By contrast, in a hostile bidding environment, such as existed between Oracle and PeopleSoft in 2005, which took 18 months and drove the stock price to $26.50 per share until Oracle was successful. The price of the target company often gets bid up by speculators who expect that the offer price will be raised by the acquirer, or by another company with a higher counteroffer.

Integration   Despite good screening and bidding, an acquisition will fail unless the acquiring company possesses the essential organizational-design skills needed to integrate the acquired company into its operations and quickly develop a viable multibusiness model. Integration should center upon the source of the potential strategic advantages of the acquisition; for instance, opportunities to share marketing, manufacturing, R&D, financial, or management resources. Integration should also involve steps to eliminate any duplication of facilities or functions. In addition, any unwanted business units of the acquired company should be divested.

Learning from Experience   Research suggests that organizations that acquire many companies over time become expert in this process and can generate significant value from their experience of the acquisition process.[41] Their experience enables them to develop a "playbook" they can follow to execute an acquisition efficiently and effectively. For example, Tyco International never made hostile acquisitions. It audited the accounts of the target companies in detail; acquired companies to help it achieve a critical mass in an industry; moved quickly to realize cost savings after an acquisition; promoted managers one or two layers down to lead the newly acquired entity; and introduced profit-based, incentive-pay systems in the acquired unit.[42] Over time, however, Tyco became too large and diversified, leading both investors and management to suspect it was not generating as much value as it could. In 2007, Tyco's healthcare and electronics divisions were spun off. In 2012, Tyco was split again into three parts that would each have their own stock: Tyco Fire and Security, ADT (which provided residential and small-business security installation), and Flow Control (which sold water and fluid valves and controls).[43] Tyco Fire and Security was then merged with Johnson Controls in 2016, creating a larger company focused on building systems.

| 10.8 | Discuss the advantages and disadvantages of joint ventures as a method companies use to enter new industries. |

10-8 Entering New Industries: Joint Ventures

Joint ventures, where two or more companies agree to pool their resources to create new business, are most commonly used to enter an embryonic or growth industry. Suppose a company is contemplating the creation of a new-venture division in an embryonic industry. Such a move involves substantial risks and costs because the company must make the huge investment necessary to develop the set of value-chain activities required to make and sell products in the new industry. On the other hand, an acquisition can be a dangerous proposition because there is rarely an established leading company in an emerging industry; even if there is, it will be extremely expensive to purchase.

In this situation, a joint venture frequently becomes the most appropriate method to enter a new industry because it allows a company to share the risks and costs associated with establishing a business unit in the new industry with another company. This is especially true when the companies share *complementary* skills or distinctive competencies, because this increases the probability of a joint venture's success. Consider the 50/50 equity joint venture formed between UTC and Dow Chemical to build plastic-based composite parts for the aerospace industry. UTC was already involved in the aerospace industry (it builds Sikorsky helicopters), and Dow Chemical had skills in the development and manufacture of plastic-based composites. The alliance called for UTC to contribute its advanced aerospace skills, and for Dow to contribute its skills in developing and manufacturing plastic-based composites. Through the joint venture, both companies became involved in new product markets. They were able to realize the benefits associated with related diversification without having to merge their activities into one company or bear the costs and risks of developing new products on their own. Thus, both companies enjoyed the profit-enhancing advantages of entering new markets without having to bear the increased bureaucratic costs.

Although joint ventures usually benefit both partner companies, under some conditions they may result in problems. First, although a joint venture allows companies to share the risks and costs of developing a new business, it also requires that they share in the profits if it succeeds. So, if one partner's skills are more important than the other partner's skills, the partner with more valuable skills will have to "give away" profits to the other party because of the 50/50 agreement. This can create conflict and sour the working relationship as time passes. Second, the joint-venture partners may have different business models or time horizons, and problems can arise if they start to come into conflict about how to run the joint venture; these kinds of problems can disintegrate a business and result in failure.

Third, while one advantage of joint ventures is that they allow frequent and close contact between companies, which facilitates learning and transfer of knowledge, this also creates a risk that a joint venture can lead to the unintentional leak of proprietary information across companies.[44] Even when collaboration agreements have extensive contractual clauses designed to protect the proprietary knowledge possessed by each partner or developed through the collaboration, it is still very difficult to prevent that knowledge from being expropriated. Secrecy clauses are very difficult to enforce when knowledge is dispersed over a large number of employees.[45] A company that enters into a joint venture thus runs the risk of giving away important, company-specific knowledge to its partner, which might then use it to compete with its other partner in the future. For example, having gained access to Dow's expertise in plastic-based composites, UTC might have dissolved the alliance and produced these materials on its own. As the previous chapter discussed, this risk could be minimized if Dow got a *credible commitment* from UTC, which is what it did. UTC had to make an expensive, asset-specific investment to make the products the joint venture was formed to create.

10-9 De-Diversification: Sell-Offs, Spinoffs, Carve-Outs, and Split-Offs

10.9 Explain the four ways a company can de-diversify.

Many managers invest considerable effort and energy in assessing opportunities to expand the scope of the firm while overlooking a key part of a strong corporate-level strategy: exiting businesses and activities that no longer make sense to have under joint ownership. Divestiture can be important both for upside opportunities, such as when a business can unlock higher value on the stock market or operate more flexibly as an independent company, and for addressing downside threats, such as when assets need to be sold off to rescue the firm from financial crisis or capacity needs to be reduced in an industry due to falling demand.

There is often a strong bias against divestiture. A study of the 200 largest corporations conducted in 2002 showed that companies bought 40% more businesses than they sold and tended to sell only reactively in response to some kind of pressure.[46] This is an unfortunate mistake, as waiting until the firm is in an emergency situation dramatically limits the firm's options and reduces the amount of value the firm is likely to harvest from divestiture. Instead, managers should recognize that divestiture is a crucial part of value creation. Holding onto businesses just because they have been part of the corporation for a long time or because they provide stable revenues, for example, can lead to an inflexible and risk averse culture that does not attract investors or top talent.[47] Furthermore, keeping the wrong mix of businesses together can lead to a drain on management time and investor funds that could otherwise go into creating new businesses with stronger growth prospects. Divesting businesses that are no longer core to the firm's strategy, even if they are strong cash generators, can release resources the firm needs to pursue its strategy more vigorously.

Managers that take a disciplined and proactive approach to divestiture not only sharpen the focus of the corporation, but also create much more value for shareholders. A study by Bain & Company of 7,315 divestitures completed by 742 companies over a 20-year period found that an investment of $100 in the average company in 1987 would have been worth about $1,000 at the end of 2007, but the same investment made in a portfolio of the "best divestors" would have increased in value to over $1,800.[48]

In the last few decades, there has been mounting pressure to break apart conglomerates because the stock market has valued their stock at a *diversification discount*, meaning that the stock of highly diversified companies is valued lower, relative to their earnings, than the stock of less-diversified companies.[49] Investors see highly diversified companies as less attractive investments for four reasons. First, as we discussed earlier, investors often feel these companies no longer have multibusiness models that justify their participation in many different industries. Second, the complexity of the financial statements of highly diversified enterprises disguises the performance of individual business units; thus, investors cannot determine if their multibusiness models are succeeding. The result is that investors perceive the company as being riskier than companies that operate in one industry, whose competitive advantage and financial statements are more easily understood. Given this situation, **restructuring** can be seen as an attempt to boost returns to shareholders by splitting up a multibusiness company into separate, independent parts.

The third reason for the diversification discount is that many investors have learned from experience that managers often have a tendency to pursue too much diversification or diversify for the wrong reasons: Their attempts to diversify *reduce* profitability.[50] For example, some CEOs pursue growth for its own sake; they are empire builders who expand the scope of their companies to the point where fast-increasing bureaucratic costs become greater than the additional value that their diversification strategy creates. Restructuring thus becomes a response to declining financial performance brought about by overdiversification.

A final factor leading to restructuring is that innovations in strategic management have diminished the advantages of vertical integration or diversification. For example, a few decades ago, there was little understanding of how long-term cooperative relationships or strategic alliances between a company and its suppliers could be a viable alternative to vertical integration. Most companies considered only two alternatives for managing the supply chain: vertical integration or competitive bidding. As we discussed in Chapter 9, in many situations, long-term cooperative relationships can create the most value, especially because they avoid the need to incur bureaucratic costs or dispense with market discipline. As this strategic innovation has spread throughout global business, the relative advantages of vertical integration have declined.

Pressure to break up conglomerates helped make 2021 a record year for corporate divestitures—roughly $1.36 trillion worth, according to Refinitv, representing a 35% increase over corporate divestitures in 2020. Corporate giants such as Johnson & Johnson, Toshiba, and General Electric were just a few of the companies that announced they would break themselves up into several smaller companies. As stated by Keith Campbell of West Monroe consulting firm, "With all the new players being created in so many different markets, and the Amazons out there, you have to really continue to change and reinvent yourself. And you can only do that in so many core operating businesses. Which is kind of why we think the conglomerates, the cross-vertical conglomerates, are a little bit of a thing of the past."[51]

Managers can break apart a conglomerate into separate, more specialized, businesses through sell-offs, spinoffs, and carve-outs, each of which is described below.

10-9a Sell-Offs

One of the most straightforward ways for a firm to exit businesses or assets is to sell them to a buyer. For example, in 2008, when Ford Motor Company was at risk of bankruptcy and needed to raise cash fast, it sold Jaguar and Land Rover together to Tata Motors for $2.3 billion (about half what it had paid for the brands in 1999 and

2000, respectively). Ford also had to pay Tata $600 million to make up for shortfalls in the two brands' pension plans, meaning that the sale netted Ford $1.7 billion.[52] Despite the loss, the sale was necessary: It not only helped to rescue Ford's balance sheet, but transferred the brands to a company that could afford the scale of investment that both brands badly needed.[53]

In some cases, businesses or assets might be sold to a private equity firm that believes it can unleash more value in the business through an alternative ownership configuration or new management. For example, in January 2022, Citrix Systems, a cloud computing company that provides software that enables individuals to work and collaborate remotely, announced that it would be acquired by private equity firms Vista Equity Partners and Evergreen Coast Capital. The private equity firms paid $16.5 billion for Citrix—a 30% premium over the company's prior market value. Vista and Evergreen planned to combine Citrix's operations with those of another of Vista's portfolio companies, TIBCO Software. TIBCO software was an enterprise data management company that focused on providing data transfers and communication between machines with otherwise incompatible software. Bob Calderonia, chairman of the board and interim CEO at Citrix, argued that the deal would provide both strategic and financial benefits: "Together with TIBCO, we will be able to operate with greater scale and provide a larger customer base with a broader range of solutions to accelerate their digital transformations and enable them to deliver the future of hybrid work. As a private company, we will have increased financial and strategic flexibility to invest in high-growth opportunities, such as DaaS, and accelerate its ongoing cloud transition."[54]

10-9b Spinoffs

Another popular method of paring down the scope of the firm is a spinoff. A **spinoff** is when a corporation makes a division or subsidiary of the firm into a separate legal entity. Spinning off a business can give it the independence it needs to be more successful, while also enabling its stock to trade separately from the corporate parent's stock. This can be especially important when the spinoff is in an industry that has better growth prospects or is more attractive than the overall corporate portfolio—the now-independent stock may rise faster in value than the corporate parent's stock value. Spinning off a business can also allow it to raise additional funds by selling shares. When the spinoff occurs, owners of shares in the corporate parent receive shares in the spinoff. The parent company itself, however, receives no cash for spinning off the division. The corporation may also choose to spinoff only a portion of the division's shares. In the United States, a spinoff is generally a tax-free transaction to the company and its shareholders only if the corporation spins off at least 80% of the voting and non-voting shares in the new business. For example, in 2014, Baxter International spun off its biopharmaceuticals business, Baxalta Incorporated. Baxter kept a 19.5% stake in Baxalta and distributed the remaining 80.5% in the form of shares distributed to Baxter shareholders.[55]

Note, spinoffs are often confused with **spinouts** due to the similarities of the words, but these terms refer to different events. Whereas a spinoff is an intentional divestment decision by the managers of the corporation, a *spinout* is an independent decision made by employees of the firm that decide to leave to start a new venture. Neither the parent company nor its shareholders receive shares or other consideration in the spinout. Parent companies often try to challenge the spinout through patent litigation, enforcement of non-compete agreements or non-disclosure agreements, or other means.[56]

A very famous case of a spinout occurred when the "traitorous eight" (a group of eight employees) left Shockley Semiconductor Laboratory to found Fairchild Semiconductor. William Shockley had founded Shockley Semiconductor in

spinoff
A spinoff is when a corporation makes a division or subsidiary a separate legal entity.

spinout
A spinout is when employees decide to leave the firm and form their own venture.

Mountain View, California, in 1955 with transistor technology he had brought from Bell Labs in New Jersey. Shockley was brilliant, but also had a violent temper, was extremely paranoid, and had extreme views, including supporting eugenics. He even advocated that people with an IQ below 100 should undergo voluntary sterilization.[57] He was also an authoritarian manager who was difficult to work for. Eight scientists thus left Shockley Semiconductor and, with the backing of New York industrialist Sherman Fairchild, founded Fairchild Semiconductor in 1957. Shockley was stunned by the betrayal and would refer to them the rest of his life as the "traitorous eight."[58] Fairchild Semiconductor went on to become a global leader in the semiconductor industry and is accredited with leading to the emergence of Silicon Valley through the dozens of businesses that spun out of it, including Intel, Kleiner Perkins Caufield & Byers, LSI Logic, Signetics (now Philips Semiconductor), and AMD.[59]

10-9c Carve-outs

carve-out

A carve-out is a partial divestiture of a business where a parent company sells some portion of a business unit to outside investors, such as to a strategic buyer or to the public in an initial public offering.

split-off

A split-off can occur after a carve-out and is when shareholders in the parent company are offered the opportunity to hold shares in the subsidiary instead of some or all of their shares in the parent company (i.e., they can trade some or all of their shares in the parent for shares in the subsidiary according to an exchange ratio based on the value of the two stocks).

A **carve-out** is a partial divestiture of a business where a parent company sells some portion of a business unit to outside investors, such as to a strategic buyer or to the public in an initial public offering. Unlike a spinoff, a carve-out results in a cash inflow to the corporate parent. Sometimes a carve-out is used to establish a market value of the subsidiary—funds raised in a public offering provide a market-based assessment of what the subsidiary is worth. A carve-out is sometimes followed by a **split-off**, where shareholders in the parent company are offered the opportunity to hold shares in the subsidiary instead of some or all of their shares in the parent company (i.e., they can trade some or all of their shares in the parent for shares in the subsidiary according to an exchange ratio based on the value of the two stocks). For example, in 1998, DuPont Co. sold off 30% of Conoco through an initial public offering that raised $4.4 billion—one of the largest initial public offerings in the world at that time. In the following year, DuPont split off the remaining 70% in a split-off, giving shareholders the option to take shares in Conoco or to keep their shares in DuPont.[60]

Often, a plan to reorganize a major conglomerate into separate businesses includes a combination of sell-offs and spinoffs. For example, in 2022, Toshiba underwent a massive reorganization that included separating into two stand-alone companies and selling off other assets deemed "non-core," including its joint venture stake in Toshiba Carrier (which was sold to Carrier group), Toshiba Elevator and Building Systems, and Toshiba Lighting & Technology Corporation. Buyers for the latter two businesses had not yet been identified as of July 2022. Toshiba also said it intended to spin off Toshiba Device Company, which included its semiconductor, integrated circuits, and disk drive manufacturing operations (a name for the new company had yet to be announced in 2022). The remaining business, Toshiba Infrastructure Service, would include Toshiba's Energy Systems and Solutions, Infrastructure Systems & Solutions, and Digital Solutions and Battery businesses.[61]

Key Terms

Takeaways for Strategic Managers

1. Strategic managers often pursue diversification when their companies are generating free cash flow; that is, financial resources they do not need to maintain a competitive advantage in their company's core industry and so can be used to fund new, profitable, business ventures.

2. A diversified company can create value by (a) transferring competencies among existing businesses, (b) leveraging competencies to create new businesses, (c) sharing resources to realize economies of scope, (d) using product bundling, (e) taking advantage of general organizational competencies that enhance the performance of all business units within a diversified company, and (f) operating an internal capital market. The bureaucratic costs of diversification rise as a function of the number of independent business units within a company and the extent to which managers must coordinate the transfer of resources between those business units.

3. Diversification motivated by a desire to pool risks or achieve greater growth often results in falling profitability.

4. The three methods companies use to enter new industries are internal new venturing, acquisition, and joint ventures.

5. Internal new venturing is used to enter a new industry when a company has a set of valuable competencies in its existing businesses that can be leveraged or recombined to enter a new business or industry.

6. Many internal ventures fail because of entry on too small a scale, poor commercialization, and poor corporate management of the internal new venturing process. Guarding against failure involves a carefully planned approach to project selection and management, integration of R&D, and marketing to improve the chance new products will be commercially successful, and entry on a scale large enough to result in competitive advantage.

7. Acquisitions are often the best way to enter a new industry when a company lacks the competencies required to compete in the new industry, and it can purchase a company that does have those competencies at a reasonable price. Acquisitions are also the method chosen to enter new industries when there are high barriers to entry and a company is unwilling to accept the time frame, development costs, and risks associated with pursuing internal new venturing.

8. Acquisitions are unprofitable when strategic managers (a) underestimate the problems associated with integrating an acquired company, (b) overestimate the profit that can be created from an acquisition, (c) pay too much for the acquired company, and (d) perform inadequate pre-acquisition screening to ensure the acquired company will increase the profitability of the whole company. Guarding against acquisition failure requires careful pre-acquisition screening, a carefully selected bidding strategy, effective organizational design to successfully integrate the operations of the acquired company into the whole company, and managers who develop a general managerial competency by learning from their experience of past acquisitions.

9. Joint ventures are used to enter a new industry when (a) the risks and costs associated with setting up a new business unit are more than a company is willing to assume on its own and (b) a company can increase the probability that its entry into a new industry will result in a successful new business by teaming up with another company with skills and assets that complement its own.

10. Restructuring is often required to correct the problems that result from (a) a business model that no longer creates competitive advantage, (b) the inability of investors to assess the competitive advantage of a highly diversified company from its financial statements, (c) excessive diversification because top managers desire to pursue empire building that results in growth without profitability, and (d) innovations in strategic management, such as strategic alliances and outsourcing, that reduce the advantages of vertical integration and diversification.

11. Managers should routinely assess when it makes sense to exit businesses that no longer benefit from joint ownership. Common methods of divestiture include spinoffs, sell-offs and carve outs.

Discussion Questions

1. When is a company likely to choose (a) related diversification and (b) unrelated diversification?

2. What factors make it most likely that (a) acquisitions or (b) internal new venturing will be the preferred method to enter a new industry?

3. Imagine that IBM has decided to diversify into the telecommunications business to provide online cloud-computing data services and broadband access for businesses and individuals. What method would you recommend that IBM pursue to enter this industry? Why?

4. Under which conditions are joint ventures a useful way to enter new industries?

5. Identify Honeywell's portfolio of businesses, which can be found at its website (www.honeywell.com). In how many different industries is Honeywell involved? Would you describe Honeywell as a related or an unrelated diversification company? Has Honeywell's diversification strategy increased profitability over time?

On July 10, 2010, Google announced it would be making a big move into travel search by acquiring ITA Software, a Cambridge, Massachusetts–based flight information software company, for about $700 million. ITA's flight search, pricing, and reservation programs were considered the most advanced in the industry, and ITA was licensing its software to major travel search companies like Orbitz, Kayak, TripAdvisor, and Bing Travel.

Travel search companies like Expedia and Orbitz enable direct booking through their sites and charge a referral fee to the airlines. Other sites (like Kayak) just provide search and refer customers to other sites to book. These companies make their revenues from paid advertising from hotels and other travel services. Airlines naturally preferred customers to book directly on their own sites so that they could avoid paying fees, and discount airlines who refused to pay fees often would not be included in search results from direct booking sites like Expedia and Orbitz. Google's flight search, like Kayak's, would direct customers directly to airline reservation sites; it would charge no booking fees.

At the time of the announcement Google was not competing in flight search—this represented an extension to its core internet search business. However, Google had a tremendous advantage in customer reach. Google had the number 1 search engine in the world, and many people began their travel planning by searching destinations on Google, putting Google in a prime position to be the first stop for flight search.

In the announcement, Google noted, "The acquisition will benefit passengers, airlines and online travel agencies by making it easier for users to comparison shop for flights and airfares and by driving more potential customers to airlines' and online travel agencies' websites. Google won't be setting airfare prices and has no plans to sell airline tickets to consumers." Google also promised to continue to honor the existing relationships ITA Software had to provide flight search information to other travel search companies.

The deal underwent intense regulatory scrutiny because even though Google did not compete in flight searches at the time of the acquisition, the deal would pair the world's largest internet search company with the dominant flight software company. Other online travel agencies were rightfully worried. On April 8, 2011, however, the U.S. Department of Justice said the deal would be permitted so long as Google agreed to continue licensing ITA's QPX software (software that gathers pricing data from airlines) to other airfare websites on "commercially reasonable terms" for at least 5 years.

Google launched Google Flights on September 13, 2011. They also announced that in the long run, they planned to create a system that organizes your entire travel experience (e.g., book your trip, deliver your bags to your hotel, reroute you automatically if there is a problem with your connection). For Google, knowing more about your travel plans and experiences enables them to serve up more targeted advertising. Together, the companies could develop a flight search service that surpassed what either could do alone; however, it required investments and exchange of proprietary information.

By 2017, Google's travel advertising revenue exceeded that of Expedia, and by August of 2018 the share of referrals to major airlines that came from Google exceeded those that came from Kayak. Initially Google's flight search gains were primarily in the U.S. market, while companies like Momondo and Skyscanner dominated in other markets. However, by 2018, the reach of Google Flights was being felt everywhere. As noted by Hugo Burge, CEO of UK-headquartered Momondo Group, "Certainly, we have always seen Google—after the purchase of ITA—as having its best product in the USA, which might explain its faster growth there." Burge adds, "However, Google has been playing catch-up with its product rollout in the rest

Sources: Google press announcement, July 10, 2010; A. Efrati and G. Chon, , "Google's Empire Expands to Travel," *Wall Street Journal*, July 2, 2010; H. Grigonis, "Google Pulls Flight API Search, Putting Its Competition in a Tight Spot," *Digital Trends*, November 1, 2017; D. Schaal, "Google Flights Is Making Gains with Consumers," *Skift*, January 31, 2017; K. May, "Google Breathes Down the Neck of Kayak in Clicks Sent to Airlines," *Phocuswire*, September 5, 2017; D. Sevitt, " Google Flights Continued: Closing the Delta," *Market Intelligence Insights*, August 28, 2018; S. O'Neill, "Google Is One Step Closer to Its User-Centric Vision of Travel Booking," February 6, 2018; M. A. Schilling, "Potential Sources of Value in Mergers and Their Indicators," *Antitrust Bulletin* (2018) 26: 183–197.

of the world and now has made significant gains in Europe with strong ongoing momentum ... Google should be seen as one of the key global players within online travel—it has the advantage of global reach, an unparalleled traffic base and access to enormous amounts of data."

Could Google and ITA have developed these services through a market relationship like a license or strategic alliance? Not likely. The asymmetry in size, power, and what each partner contributed would have put ITA at risk: In a partnership, Google might have been able to assimilate ITA's proprietary technology and over time developed its own competing alternative. ITA, on the other hand, could not credibly threaten to counter Google's advantage in capturing buyers. The benefits of collaborating were potentially large, but the risk of doing so via an arm's-length contract were even larger. Thus, ITA agreed to be acquired by Google so that their interests would be irrevocably aligned.

Case Discussion Questions

1. What are the key resources or competencies Google can leverage in flight searches?
2. Why do you think ITA agreed to the deal? What are the advantages and disadvantages to ITA of being owned by Google?
3. Since Google doesn't charge booking fees, what do you think is its business model for its entry into flight searches? If you were a manager at another flight search company (e.g., Expedia), how would you compete against Google?

Notes

[1] L. Samaha, "Why This Billionaire Hedge Fund Manager Wants to Break Up United Technologies," *The Motley Fool*, May 21, 2018.

[2] N. Kitroeff, "United Technologies to Split into 3 Companies, Each with a Sharper Focus," *New York Times*, November 26, 2018.

[3] B. Rishel, "The Break-up of Raytheon & United Technologies," Tufton Capital, October 23, 2020.

[4] A. Gregg, "Coronavirus Opens a Stark Divide in America's Aerospace Industry," *Washington Post*, November 3, 2020.

[5] M. A. Schilling, "Potential Sources of Value in Mergers and Their Indicators," *Antitrust Bulletin* (2018) 26: 183–197.

[6] This resource-based view of diversification can be traced to Edith Penrose's seminal book, *The Theory of the Growth of the Firm* (Oxford: Oxford University Press, 1959).

[7] D. J. Teece, "Economies of Scope and the Scope of the Enterprise," *Journal of Economic Behavior and Organization* 3 (1980): 223–247. For more recent empirical work on this topic, see C. H. St. John and J. S. Harrison, "Manufacturing Based Relatedness, Synergy and Coordination," *Strategic Management Journal* 20 (1999): 129–145.

[8] Teece, "Economies of Scope." For more recent empirical work on this topic, see St. John and Harrison, "Manufacturing Based Relatedness, Synergy and Coordination."

[9] For a detailed discussion, see C. W. L. Hill and R. E. Hoskisson, "Strategy and Structure in the Multiproduct Firm," *Academy of Management Review* 12 (1987): 331–341.

[10] See, for example, G. R. Jones and C. W. L. Hill, "A Transaction Cost Analysis of Strategy Structure Choice," *Strategic Management Journal* 2 (1988): 159–172; O. E. Williamson, *Markets and Hierarchies, Analysis and Antitrust Implications* (New York: Free Press, 1975), pp. 132–175.

[11] R. Buderi, *Engines of Tomorrow* (New York: Simon & Schuster, 2000).

[12] See, for example, Jones and Hill, "A Transaction Cost Analysis," and Williamson, *Markets and Hierarchies*.

[13] C. A. Trahms, H. A. Ndofor, and D. G. Sirmon, "Organizational Decline and Turnaound: A Review and Agenda for Future Research," *Journal of Management*, 39 (2013): 1277–1307.

[14] The distinction goes back to R. P. Rumelt, *Strategy, Structure and Economic Performance* (Cambridge: Harvard Business School Press, 1974).

[15] For evidence, see C. W. L. Hill, "Conglomerate Performance over the Economic Cycle," *Journal of Industrial Economics* 32 (1983): 197–212; D. T. C. Mueller, "The Effects of Conglomerate Mergers," *Journal of Banking and Finance* 1 (1977): 315–347.

[16] P. G Berger and E Ofek, "Bust-up Takeovers of Value Destroying Diversified Firms," *Journal of Finance* 49:4 (1996):1175–1200; L. Daley, V. Mehrotra, and R. Sivakumar, "Corporate Focus and Value Creation: Evidence from Spinoffs," *Journal of Financial Economics* 45 (1977): 257–281; H. Desai and P. C. Jain, "Firm Performance and Focus: Long-Run Stock Market Performance Following Spinoffs," *Journal of Financial Economics* 54 (1999): 75–101; K. John and E. Ofek, "Asset Sales and Increase in Focus," *Journal of Financial Economics* 37 (1995): 105–126; S. N. Kaplan and M. S. Weisbach, "The Success of Acquisitions: Evidence from Divestitures," *Journal of Finance* 47 (1992): 107–138; O. Lamont and C. Polk, "Does Diversification Destroy Value? Evidence from Industry Shocks." Unpublished paper. The Center for Research in Securities Prices, No. 521 (July 2000); L. H. P. Lang and R. M. Stulz, "Tobin's q, Corporate Diversification, and Firm Performance," *Journal of Political Economy* 102 (1994): 1248–1280; M. E. Porter, "From Competitive Advantage to Corporate Strategy," *Harvard Business Review* (May–June 1987): 43–59; H. Servaes, "The Value of Diversification During the Conglomerate Merger Wave," *Journal of Finance* 51 (1996): 1201–1226; B. Wernerfelt and C. A. Montgomery, "Tobin's q and the Importance of Focus in Firm Performance," *American Economic Review* 78 (1988): 246–250.

[17] C. R. Christensen et al., *Business Policy Text and Cases* (Homewood: Irwin, 1987), p. 778.

[18] H. Weber,"Tesla Reportedly Nowhere Near Goal of Installing 1,000 Solar Roofs a Week," Techcrunch, July 7, 2022.

[19] H. Weber,"Tesla Reportedly Nowhere Near Goal of Installing 1,000 Solar Roofs a Week," *Techcrunch*, July 7, 2022.

[20] See R. Biggadike, "The Risky Business of Diversification," *Harvard Business Review* (May–June 1979): 103–111; R. A. Burgelman, "A Process Model of Internal Corporate Venturing in the Diversified Major Firm," *Administrative Science Quarterly* 28 (1983): 223–244; Z. Block and I. C. MacMillan, *Corporate Venturing* (Boston: Harvard Business School Press, 1993).

[21] Biggadike, "The Risky Business of Diversification"; Block and Macmillan, *Corporate Venturing*.

[22] Buderi, *Engines of Tomorrow*; S. Jain, "Time Inconsistency and Product Design: A Strategic

Analysis of Feature Creep," *Marketing Science* (Sept–Oct 2019): 733–912; G. Marzi, "On the Nature, Origins and Outcomes of Over Featuring in the New Product Development Process," *Journal of Engineering and Technology Management* 64 (2022).

[23]I. C. MacMillan and R. George, "Corporate Venturing: Challenges for Senior Managers," *Journal of Business Strategy* 5 (1985): 34–43.

[24]See R. A. Burgelman, M. M. Maidique, and S. C. Wheelwright, *Strategic Management of Technology and Innovation* (Chicago: Irwin, 1996), pp. 493–507. See also Buderi, *Engines of Tomorrow*.

[25]Buderi, *Engines of Tomorrow*.

[26]See Block and Macmillan, *Corporate Venturing*; Burgelman et al., *Strategic Management of Technology and Innovation,* and Buderi, *Engines of Tomorrow*.

[27]For evidence on acquisitions and performance, see R. E. Caves, "Mergers, Takeovers, and Economic Efficiency," *International Journal of Industrial Organization* 7 (1989): 151–174; M. C. Jensen and R. S. Ruback, "The Market for Corporate Control: The Scientific Evidence," *Journal of Financial Economics* 11 (1983): 5–50; R. Roll, "Empirical Evidence on Takeover Activity and Shareholder Wealth," in J. C. Coffee, L. Lowenstein, and S. Rose (eds.), *Knights, Raiders and Targets* (Oxford: Oxford University Press, 1989), pp. 112–127; A. Schleifer and R. W. Vishny, "Takeovers in the 60s and 80s: Evidence and Implications," *Strategic Management Journal* 12 (Special Issue, Winter 1991): 51–60; T. H. Brush, "Predicted Changes in Operational Synergy and Post Acquisition Performance of Acquired Businesses," *Strategic Management Journal* 17 (1996): 1–24; T. Loughran and A. M. Vijh, "Do Long-Term Shareholders Benefit from Corporate

Acquisitions?" *Journal of Finance* 5 (1997): 1765–1787.

[28]Ibid.

[29]D. J. Ravenscraft and F. M. Scherer, *Mergers, Sell-offs, and Economic Efficiency* (Washington, DC: Brookings Institution, 1987).

[30]M. A. Schilling, "The Top 4 Reasons Most Acquisitions Fail," *Inc.*, May 1, 2018

[31]F. Bauer and K. Matzler, "Antecedents of M&A Success: The Role of Strategic Complementarity, Cultural Fit, and Degree and Speed of Integration," *Strategic Management Journal* 35 (2014): 269–291.

[32]C. Isidore, "Daimler Pays to Dump Chrysler," *CNNMoney* (May 14, 2007).

[33]See J. P. Walsh, "Top Management Turnover Following Mergers and Acquisitions," *Strategic Management Journal* 9 (1988): 173–183.

[34]See A. A. Cannella and D. C. Hambrick, "Executive Departure and Acquisition Performance," *Strategic Management Journal* 14 (1993): 137–152.

[35]R. Roll, "The Hubris Hypothesis of Corporate Takeovers," *Journal of Business* 59 (1986): 197–216.

[36]"Coca-Cola: A Sobering Lesson from Its Journey into Wine," *Business Week* (June 3, 1985): 96–98.

[37]J. Harford, M. Humphery-Jenner, and R. Powell, "The Sources of Value Destruction in Acquisitions by Entrenched Managers," *Journal of Financial Economics* 106 (2012): 247–161; F. Fu, L. Lin, and M. C. Officer, "Acquisitions Driven by Stock Overvaluation: Are They Good Deals?" *Journal of Financial Economics* 109 (2013): 24–39.

[38]P. Haspeslagh and D. Jemison, *Managing Acquisitions* (New York: Free Press, 1991).

[39]M. C. Jensen and K. J. Murphy, "Performance Pay and Top-Management Incentives," *Journal of Political Economy* (1990) 98: 225–264.

[40]For views on this issue, see L. L. Fray, D. H. Gaylin, and J. W. Down, "Successful Acquisition Planning," *Journal of Business Strategy* 5 (1984): 46–55; C. W. L. Hill, "Profile of a Conglomerate Takeover: BTR and Thomas Tilling," *Journal of General Management* 10 (1984): 34–50; D. R. Willensky, "Making It Happen: How to Execute an Acquisition," *Business Horizons* (March–April 1985): 38–45; Haspeslagh and Jemison, *Managing Acquisitions*; and P. L. Anslinger and T. E. Copeland, "Growth Through Acquisition: A Fresh Look," *Harvard Business Review* (January–February 1996): 126–135.

[41]M. L. A. Hayward, "When Do Firms Learn from Their Acquisition Experience? Evidence from 1990–1995," *Strategic Management Journal* 23 (2002): 21–39; K. G. Ahuja, "Technological Acquisitions and the Innovation Performance of Acquiring Firms: A Longitudinal Study," *Strategic Management Journal* 23 (2001): 197–220; H. G. Barkema and F. Vermeulen, "International Expansion Through Startup or Acquisition," *Academy of Management Journal* 41 (1998): 7–26.

[42]Hayward, "When Do Firms Learn from Their Acquisition Experience?"

[43]N. Zieminski, "Tyco Shareholders Approve Three-Way Break-Up," Reuters, September 17, 2012.

[44]A. C. Inkpen and S. C. Currall, "The Coevolution of Trust, Control, and Learning in Joint Ventures," *Organization Science* 15 (2004): 586–599; D. C. Mowery, J. E. Oxley, and B. S. Silverman, "Strategic Alliances and Interfirm Knowledge Transfer," *Strategic Management* 17 (1996): 77–91.

[45]M. A. Schilling, "Technology Shocks, Technological Collaboration, and Innovation Outcomes," *Organization Science* 26: 668–686.

[46]L. Dranikoff, T. Koller, and A. Schneider,"Divestiture: Strategy's Missing Link," *Harvard Business Review*, May 2002.

[47]L. Dranikoff, T. Koller, and A. Schneider, "Divestiture: Strategy's Missing Link," *Harvard Business Review*, May 2002.

[48]M. Mankins, D. Harding, and R. M. Weddigan, "How the Best Divest," *Harvard Business Review*, October 2008.

[49]A. Lamont and C. Polk, "The Diversification Discount: Cash Flows Versus Returns," *Journal of Finance* 56 (October 2001): 1693–1721; R. Raju, H. Servaes, and L. Zingales, "The Cost of Diversity: The Diversification Discount and Inefficient Investment," *Journal of Finance* 55 (2000): 35–80.

[50]For example, see Schleifer and Vishny, "Takeovers in the '60s and '80s." M. A. Schilling "Potential Sources of Value in Mergers and Their Indicators," *Antitrust Bulletin* (2018) 26: 183–197; P. André, M. Kooli, and J. L'Her. "The Long-Run Performance of Mergers: Evidence from the Canadian Stock Market" *Financial Management* 33:4 (2004): 27– 43; M. Bradley, A. Desai, and E. H. Kim. "Synergistic Gains from Corporate Acquisitions and Their Division Between the Stockholders of Target and Acquiring Firms," *Journal of Financial Economics* 21 (1988): 3–40; M. Cloodt, J. Hagedoorn, and H. Van Kranenburg, "Mergers and Acquisitions: Their Effect on The Innovative Performance of Companies In High-Tech Industries," *Research Policy* 35 (2006): 642–654; M. Danzon, A. Epstein, and S. Nicholson, "Mergers and Acquisitions in the Pharmaceutical and Biotech Industries," *Managerial and Decision Economics* 28 (2007): 307–328; D. R. King, D. R. Dalton, C. M. Daily, and J. G. Covin, "Meta-Analyses of Post-Acquisition Performance: Indications of Unidentified Moderators," *Strategic Management Journal* 25 (2003): 187–200; V. M. Papadakis and I. C. Thanos, "Measuring the Performance of Acquisitions: An Empirical Investigation Using Multiple Criteria," *British Journal of Management 21* (2010): 859–873; 36 (1987): 147–156; D. J. Ravenscraft and F. M. Scherer, "The Profitability of Mergers," *International Journal of Industrial Organization* 7 (1989): 101–116.

[51]K. Dowd, "With Divestitures on the Rise, Dealmakers Adjust to a New Reality," *Forbes*, December 5, 2021.

[52]H. Timmons, "Ford Sells Land Rover and Jaguar to Tata," *New York Times*, March 26, 2008.

[53]E. Mullen, "JLR Would Have Ruined Ford, Says Former Chief," *Business Live*, July 10, 2014.

[54]Citrix Press Release. "Citrix to Be Acquired by Affiliates of Vista Equity Partners and Evergreen Coast Capital for $16.5 Billion," January 31, 2022.

[55]Baxter Press Release. "Baxter Announces Plans to Create Two Separate Leading Global Healthcare Companies," 2014.

[56]https://entrepreneurshiptheories.blogspot.com/2018/12/spinout-versus-spinoff-whats-difference.html.

[57]E. J. Boyer, "Controversial Nobel Laureate Shockley Dies," *Los Angeles Times*, August 14, 1989.

[58]M. A. Hiltzik, "The Twisted Legacy of William Shockley," Los Angeles Times, December 2, 2001.

[59]"Fairchild's Offspring," *BusinessWeek,* December 25, 1997.

[60]"Dupont Sets Conor Terms," *CNNMoney*, July 9, 1999.

[61]"Toshiba Now Plans to Split into 2 Companies, not Three," *Nasdaq Markets*, RTT News, February 7, 2022.

Part

4

Implementing Strategy

Chapter 11

Corporate Governance, Social Responsibility, and Ethics

Chapter 12

Implementing Strategy Through Organization

Chapter

11

Corporate Governance, Social Responsibility, and Ethics

Opening Case

Purdue Pharma and the Opioid Crisis

In 1995, Purdue Pharma, a privately held firm owned by the Sackler family, launched OxyContin, an extended-release form of oxycodone (an opioid). The drug was hailed as a medical breakthrough that could help patients suffering from moderate to severe pain. OxyContin rapidly became a blockbuster and would go on to earn roughly $35 billion in revenue for Purdue.[1]

Physicians had long been wary of prescribing opioids because of the long-standing (and well founded) fear of their addictive properties. As put by David Kessler, former commissioner of the U.S. Food and Drug Administration (FDA), "Few drugs are as dangerous as the opioids."[2] Purdue set out to change that sentiment. OxyContin was launched with an exceptionally vigorous marketing campaign that sought to convince patients and doctors that concerns about opioid addiction were overblown. The company sponsored all-expense-paid trips for medical education courses for physicians and paid large bonuses to sales representatives—as much as $240,000—for high OxyContin sales in their territories. Purdue also used a "patient starter coupon" that provided patients with a free limited-time prescription for a 7- to 30-day supply of OxyContin.[3] In all these marketing activities Purdue enthusiastically described OxyContin as safe, effective, and with a low potential for addiction. The company even convinced the FDA to approve labeling for the drug that indicated that addiction was very rare if opioids were used correctly, and that the delayed absorption of OxyContin reduced the abuse liability of the drug. Notably, the FDA examiner who oversaw the approval of the labeling left the agency shortly thereafter and took a job at Purdue.

Millions of patients found the drug helped their pain, at least initially. Soon, however, trouble began. Patients began to complain that their prescribed dose of OxyContin was not sufficing to relieve their pain. Opioids, it turns out, are not very effective for long-term pain treatment because people develop a tolerance to them and become even more sensitive to pain. OxyContin also turned out to be *very* addictive. The drug was also prone to abuse by crushing and inhaling or injecting it, enabling a much more intense high. Purdue's own testing had, in 1995, demonstrated that 68% of the oxycodone in an OxyContin tablet could be extracted by crushing the tablet.[4] This meant that the drug was a risk for "diversion" (i.e., when prescription products are intentionally used for drug abuse). Purdue was well aware of the risk of "diversion" and abuse of such prescription opioids because one of its previous products, an extended-release morphine pill called MS Contin, had been one of the most widely abused prescription opioids in the 1980s.

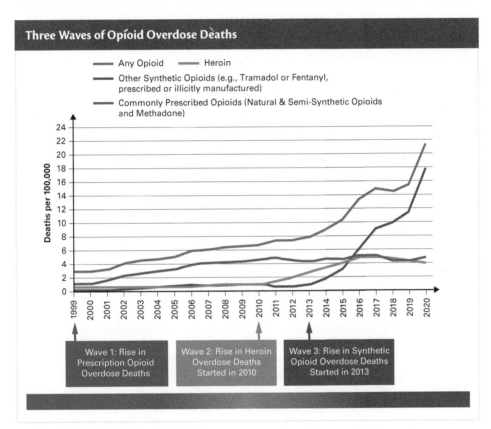

Three Waves of Opioid Overdose Deaths

Legend:
- Any Opioid
- Heroin
- Other Synthetic Opioids (e.g., Tramadol or Fentanyl, prescribed or illicitly manufactured)
- Commonly Prescribed Opioids (Natural & Semi-Synthetic Opioids and Methadone)

Y-axis: Deaths per 100,000

Wave 1: Rise in Prescription Opioid Overdose Deaths

Wave 2: Rise in Heroin Overdose Deaths Started in 2010

Wave 3: Rise in Synthetic Opioid Overdose Deaths Started in 2013

Source: U.S. Centers for Disease Control and Prevention

The Opioid Crisis

"The current opioid crisis ranks as one of the most devastating public health catastrophes of our time." – Dr. Howard Koh, Professor of the Practice of Public Health and Leadership, Harvard University[5]

From 1999–2021, the number of drug overdose deaths per year in the United States quintupled, from 16,849 in 1999 to over 100,000 in 2021.[6] Of the nearly 92,000 drug overdose deaths in 2020, nearly 75% involved an opioid. A report from the U.S. Centers for Disease Control and Prevention shows that the opioid crisis escalated in three waves (see figure on previous page).[7] First, in the late 1990s, there was a wave of deaths due to abuse of legal prescription opioids, most prominently among those was OxyContin. Andrew Kolodny, the co-director of the Opioid Policy Research Collaborative at Brandeis University notes that though many fatal overdoses have resulted from opioids other than OxyContin, the real expansion in prescriptions was engineered by Purdue: "If you look at the prescribing trends for all the different opioids, it's in 1996 that prescribing really takes off." He adds, "It's not a coincidence. That was the year Purdue launched a multifaceted campaign that misinformed the medical community about the risks." Eventually, however, many of the people addicted to OxyContin found that keeping up with their addiction with prescription drugs was too expensive or difficult, so they turned to heroin. This led to a second wave of deaths from the heroin market that rapidly expanded in response to people addicted to OxyContin. A third wave of deaths began in 2013, with the rise of cheaper—and more potent—synthetic opioids like fentanyl.

The Investigations Begin

A series of investigations revealed that the Sackler family knew that OxyContin was being abused. In 1999, one of Purdue's legal secretaries logged into online forums and message boards devoted to recreational drug use to catalog the way people were using OxyContin. Her report detailed that people were easily bypassing the drug's extended-release coating by crushing the tablets and snorting or injecting them. She circulated her findings in a memo to all the Sacklers involved in running the company, but that report mysteriously disappeared from Purdue's files. Reports of misuse of the drug were also flooding into the company from its salesforce, who by now realized that the drug was being resold on the street for as much as $80 for an 80 mg pill. Richard Sackler, then president of Purdue, responded by turning the blame on drug abusers, arguing that the company simply manufactured and sold a legal drug approved by the FDA, and that if anyone was a criminal, it was those who became addicted and "abused" their drug. In a February 1, 2001, e-mail, Sackler wrote, "Abusers aren't victims. They are the victimizers."[8]

Despite growing public awareness that OxyContin was extremely addictive and being widely abused, Sackler and the management team at Purdue refused to pull the drug from shelves. Salespeople were told to ignore the abuse reports and continue to promote the drug. Purdue had access to data about which doctors were prescribing unusually high amounts of OxyContin, and rather than intervening to stop potential abuse, Purdue referred to heavy prescribers as "whales," the term Las Vegas casinos use to denote their most prized gamblers.

In 2006, Purdue spent $75 million to settle a lawsuit representing 5,000 patients who said they had become addicted to OxyContin after receiving a doctor's prescription. In 2007, federal prosecutors in Virginia brought a case against Purdue and its executives for intent to defraud or mislead. The company pleaded guilty and three senior executives (but not Sackler) were ordered to collectively pay nearly $35 million in fines, and the company was ordered to pay $600 million. Following the 2007 fine, the Sacklers continued to deny having any knowledge of the connection between OxyContin and the exponential increase in opioid overdose deaths. However, perhaps sensing the impending threat of thousands of liability suits, the Sackler family began pulling money out of the company. From 2008 to 2017, the Sackler family withdrew approximately $10 billion from Purdue, presumably so that it could not be awarded to civil liability claimants.[9]

In 2010, Purdue quietly replaced its regular formulation of OxyContin—for which the patent was soon to expire—with a new version that could not be crushed into a dissolvable powder. This reformulation made it harder to abuse the drug and sales of OxyContin plummeted 40%. Tragically, however, rather than helping to alleviate the opioid crisis, the reformulation prompted a large portion of the addicted OxyContin customer base to turn to heroin, leading to the second wave of overdose deaths discussed previously. The crisis OxyContin had brought to millions of people now no longer relied on—nor could be managed by—OxyContin or its producers.

On November 24th, 2020, Purdue pleaded guilty to three felony offenses. First, it admitted to defrauding the Drug Enforcement Agency by claiming that it maintained an effective anti-diversion program when, in fact, Purdue continued to market its opioid products to more than 100 healthcare providers whom the company had good reason to believe were diverting opioids. It also admitted that it had facilitated the dispensing of OxyContin without a legitimate medical purpose. Finally, it admitted that the company had paid kickbacks to doctors for prescribing its extended-release opioid products, in violation of the Federal Anti-Kickback Statute. At the trial, U.S. Attorney Christina Nolan stated, "As today's plea to felony charges shows, Purdue put opioid profits ahead of people and corrupted the sacred doctor-patient relationship."[10]

Under the terms of the plea agreement, Purdue was charged a $3.5 billion criminal fine, and an additional $2 billion in criminal forfeiture—the largest penalty ever imposed on a pharmaceutical firm. The firm was also required to pay $2.8 billion to resolve civil liability cases that were pending against the firm. The Sackler family that owned the firm was also required to relinquish its ownership of Purdue. However, though there were years of court cases against the company, as of August 2022, none of Purdue Pharma's executives or members of the Sackler family had been required to serve prison time, and no member of the Sackler family had ever acknowledged blame for the addiction and deaths caused by OxyContin.

Overview

We open this chapter with a discussion of the different types of stakeholders the firm serves, including stockholders, employees, suppliers and customers, and others. Good governance requires addressing the impact of the firm's activities on all stakeholders and incorporating this into the firm's strategies and incentives. In fact, in recent years, there has been a rise in "ESG investing" where investors and analysts take the firm's performance on social and environmental issues into account. We also discuss agency problems, i.e., problems that arise due to the separation of ownership and control, such as when senior managers seek to grow the company into an empire that serves their own interest rather than the interests of other stakeholders. Finally, we will also discuss ethical issues that arise in the process of making strategic decisions, and discuss how managers can make sure that their strategic decisions are founded upon strong ethical principles.

11-1 Organization Stakeholders

A company's **stakeholders** are individuals or groups with an interest, claim, or stake in the company, in what it does, and in how well it performs.[11] They include stockholders, creditors, employees, customers, suppliers, government agencies, the communities in which the company does business, and the general public. Stakeholders can be divided into two groups: internal stakeholders and external stakeholders (see Figure 11.1). **Internal stakeholders** are stockholders and employees, including executive officers, other managers, and board members. **External stakeholders** are all other individuals and groups that have some claim on the company. Typically, this group comprises customers, suppliers, creditors (including banks and bondholders), governments, unions, local communities, and the public.

All stakeholders are in an exchange relationship with their company. Each stakeholder group listed in Figure 11.1 supplies the organization with important resources (or contributions), and in exchange each expects its interests to be satisfied (by inducements).[12] Stockholders provide the enterprise with risk capital and expect management to attempt to maximize the return on their investment. Creditors, particularly bondholders, also provide the company with capital, in the form of

11.1 Identify the multiple stakeholders in an organization.

stakeholders

Individuals or groups with an interest, claim, or stake in the company—in what it does and in how well it performs.

internal stakeholders

Stockholders and employees, including executive officers, other managers, and board members.

external stakeholders

All other individuals and groups that have some claim on the company.

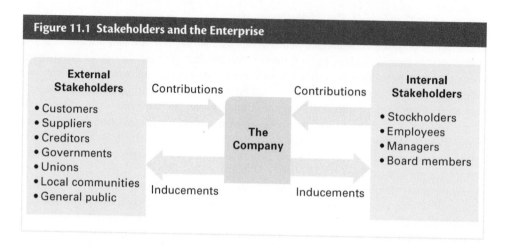

Figure 11.1 Stakeholders and the Enterprise

External Stakeholders
- Customers
- Suppliers
- Creditors
- Governments
- Unions
- Local communities
- General public

Contributions

The Company

Contributions

Internal Stakeholders
- Stockholders
- Employees
- Managers
- Board members

Inducements

Inducements

debt, and they expect to be repaid on time, with interest. Employees provide labor and skills and in exchange expect commensurate income, job satisfaction, job security, and good working conditions. Customers provide a company with its revenues, and in exchange want high-quality, reliable products that represent value for money. Suppliers provide a company with inputs and in exchange seek revenues and dependable buyers. Governments provide a company with rules and regulations that govern business practice and maintain fair competition. In exchange, they want companies to adhere to these rules. Unions help to provide a company with productive employees, and in exchange they want benefits for their members in proportion to their contributions to the company. Local communities provide companies with local infrastructure, and in exchange want companies that are responsible citizens. The general public provides companies with national infrastructure and, in exchange, seeks some assurance that the quality of life will be improved as a result of the company's existence.

A company must take these claims into account when formulating its strategies, or stakeholders may withdraw their support. For example, stockholders may sell their shares, bondholders may demand higher interest payments on new bonds, employees may leave their jobs, and customers may buy elsewhere. Suppliers may seek more dependable buyers, and unions may engage in disruptive labor disputes. Government may take civil or criminal action against the company and its top officers, imposing fines and, in some cases, jail terms. Communities may oppose the company's attempts to locate its facilities in their area, and the general public may form pressure groups, demanding action against companies that impair the quality of life. Any of these reactions can have a damaging impact on an enterprise. A study by Henisz, Dorobantu, and Nartey on the impact of stakeholder opposition to gold mines, for example, found that the value of cooperative relationships with external stakeholders was worth twice as much as the market value of the gold itself.[13] As articulated by Yani Roditis, former COO of Gabriel Resources, "It used to be that the value of a gold mine was based on three variables: the amount of gold in the ground, the cost of extraction, and the world price of gold. Today, I can show you two mines identical on these three variables that differ in their valuation by an order of magnitude. Why? Because one has local support and the other doesn't."

11-1a Stakeholder Impact Analysis

A company cannot always satisfy the claims of all stakeholders. The goals of different groups may conflict, and, in practice, few organizations have the resources to manage all stakeholders.[14] For example, union claims for higher wages can conflict with consumer demands for lower prices and stockholder demands for continued returns. Often, the company must make choices, and to do so it must identify the most important stakeholders and give highest priority to pursuing strategies that satisfy their needs. Stakeholder impact analysis can provide such identification. Typically, stakeholder impact analysis follows these steps:

1. Identify stakeholders.
2. Identify stakeholders' interests and concerns.
3. As a result, identify the claims stakeholders are likely to make on the organization.
4. Identify the stakeholders who are most important from the organization's perspective.
5. Identify the resulting strategic challenges.[15]

Such an analysis enables a company to identify the stakeholders most critical to its survival and to make sure that the satisfaction of their needs is paramount. Most companies that have gone through this process quickly conclude that three stakeholder groups must be satisfied above all others if a company is to survive and prosper: stockholders, customers, and employees.

11-1b The Unique Role of Stockholders

A company's stockholders are usually put in a different class from other stakeholder groups, and for good reason. Stockholders are the legal owners and the providers of **risk capital**, a major source of the capital resources that allow a company to operate. The capital that stockholders provide to a company is considered risk capital because there is no guarantee that stockholders will recoup their investments and/or earn a decent return.

Recent history demonstrates all too clearly the nature of risk capital. For example, many investors who bought shares in Washington Mutual, the large, Seattle-based bank and home loan lender, believed that they were making a low-risk investment. The company had been around for decades and paid a solid dividend, which it increased every year. It had a large branch network and billions in deposits. However, during the 2000s, Washington Mutual was also making increasingly risky mortgage loans, reportedly giving mortgages to people without properly verifying if they had the funds to pay back those loans on time. By 2008, many borrowers were beginning to default on their loans, and Washington Mutual had to take multibillion-dollar write-downs on the value of its loan portfolio, effectively destroying its once-strong balance sheet. The losses were so large that customers with deposits at the bank started to worry about its stability, and they withdrew nearly $16 billion in November 2008 from accounts at Washington Mutual. The stock price collapsed from around $40 at the start of 2008 to under $2 a share, and with the bank teetering on the brink of collapse, the federal government intervened, seized the bank's assets, and engineered a sale to J.P. Morgan. Washington Mutual's shareholders got absolutely nothing: They were wiped out.

Over the past decade, maximizing returns to stockholders has taken on significant importance as an increasing number of employees have become stockholders in the companies for which they work through employee stock ownership plans (ESOPs). At Publix, a grocery store chain with more than 225,000 employees, all employees who have worked for more than 1 year receive stock at no cost to them and are eligible to buy more.[16] Under an ESOP, employees are given the opportunity to purchase stock in the company, sometimes at a discount or less than the market value of the stock. The company may also contribute a certain portion of the purchase price to the ESOP. By making employees stockholders, ESOPs tend to increase the already strong emphasis on maximizing returns to stockholders, for they now help to satisfy two key stakeholder groups: stockholders and employees.

risk capital
Capital that cannot be recovered if a company fails and goes bankrupt.

11-2 Stakeholder Management and Performance

Because of the unique position assigned to stockholders, managers normally seek to pursue strategies that maximize the returns that stockholders receive from holding shares in the company. As we noted in Chapter 1, stockholders receive a return on their investment in a company's stock in two ways: from dividend payments and from capital appreciation in the market value of a share (that is, by increases in stock market prices). The best way for managers to generate the funds for future dividend payments and keep the stock price appreciating is to pursue strategies that maximize the company's long-term profitability (as measured by the return on invested capital, ROIC) and grow the profits of the company over time.[17]

As we saw in Chapter 3, ROIC is an excellent measure of the profitability of a company. It tells managers how efficiently they are using the capital resources of the company (including the risk capital provided by stockholders) to generate profits. A company that is generating a positive ROIC is covering its ongoing expenses and has money left over, which is then added to shareholders' equity, thereby increasing the value of a company and thus the value of a share of stock in the company. The value of each share will increase further if a company can grow its profits over time, because then the profit that is attributable to every share (that is, the company's earnings per share) will also grow. As we have seen in this book, to grow profits, companies must do one or more of the following: (a) increase the margins earned on their products and services, (b) maintain margins and share while participating in a market that is growing, (c) maintain margins while taking market share from competitors, or (d) develop new markets through innovation, geographic expansion, or diversification.

Although managers should strive for profit growth if they are trying to maximize shareholder value, the relationship between profitability and profit growth is a complex one because attaining future profit growth may require investments that reduce the current rate of profitability. The task of managers is to find the right balance between profitability and profit growth.[18] Too much emphasis on current profitability at the expense of future profitability and profit growth can make an enterprise less attractive to shareholders. Too much emphasis on profit growth can reduce the current profitability of the enterprise and have the same effect. In an uncertain world where the future is unknowable, finding the right balance between profitability and profit growth is as much art as it is science, but it is something that managers must try to do.

In addition to maximizing returns to stockholders, boosting a company's profitability and profit growth rate is consistent with satisfying the claims of several other key stakeholder groups. When a company is profitable and its profits continue to grow, it can pay higher salaries to productive employees and afford benefits such as health insurance coverage, all of which help to satisfy employees. In addition, companies with a high level of profitability and profit growth have no problem meeting their debt commitments, which provides creditors, including bondholders, with a measure of security. Profitable organizations are also better able to undertake philanthropic investments, which can help to satisfy some of the claims that local communities and the public place on a company. Pursuing strategies that maximize long-term profitability and profit growth is therefore generally consistent with satisfying the claims of various stakeholder groups.

Stakeholder management requires consideration of how the firm's practices affect the cooperation of stakeholders in the short term, the benefits of building trust and a knowledge-sharing culture with stakeholders in the long run, and the firm's profitability and growth that will enable it to serve stakeholder interests in the future.[19] The company that overpays its employees in the current period, for example, may have very happy employees for a short while, but such action will raise the company's cost structure and limit its ability to attain a competitive advantage in the marketplace, thereby depressing its long-term profitability and hurting its ability to award future pay increases. As far as employees are concerned, the way many companies deal with this situation is to make future pay raises contingent upon improvements in labor productivity. If labor productivity increases, labor costs as a percentage of revenues will fall, profitability will rise, and the company can afford to pay its employees more and offer greater benefits.

Of course, not all stakeholder groups want the company to maximize its long-run profitability and profit growth. Suppliers are more comfortable selling goods and services to profitable companies because they can be assured that the company will have the funds to pay for those products. Similarly, customers may be more willing to purchase from profitable companies because they can be assured that those companies will be around in the long term to provide after-sales services and support. But neither suppliers nor customers want the company to maximize its profitability at their expense. Rather, they would like to capture some of these profits from the company in the form of higher prices for their goods and services (in the case of suppliers), or lower prices for the products they purchase from the company (in the case of customers). Garcia-Castro and Aguilera capture this dynamic nicely by breaking the traditional explanation of value creation and value capture (discussed in Chapter 3) down into more fine-grained categories that show how value is created and captured by multiple stakeholders, similar to Figure 11.2.[20] As shown, the total value that is created is the spread between the opportunity costs of the resources it employs and the willingness to pay of its customers. However, value is created and captured by different stakeholders. Suppliers create and capture value in the form of goods and services they sell to the firm. Employees and management create value through their labor and capture value in the form of salaries and other benefits. Government creates value in the form of providing the broad infrastructure in which the firm operates and captures value in the form of taxes. Debt providers and stockholders create value by providing capital to the firm that it can use to finance its operations, and they capture value in the form of interest, dividends, and capital gains. Finally, customers capture value in the form of consumer surplus—the difference between the price they pay for goods and their true willingness-to-pay.

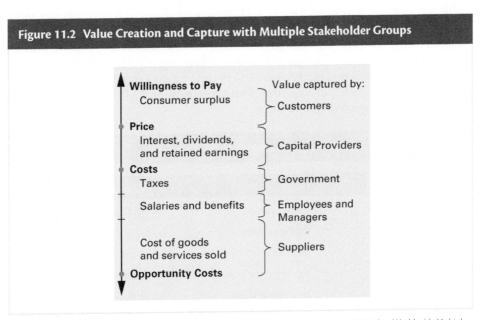

Figure 11.2 Value Creation and Capture with Multiple Stakeholder Groups

Source: Adapted from R. Garcia-Castro and R. Aguilera, "Increasing Value Creation and Appropriation in a World with Multiple Stakeholders," *Strategic Management Journal*, 36 (2015): 137–147.

Figure 11.3 Commitments of the PRI

1. We will incorporate ESG issues into investment analysis and decision-making processes.

2. We will be active owners and incorporate ESG issues into our ownership policies and practices.

3. We will seek appropriate disclosure on ESG issues by the entities in which we invest.

4. We will promote acceptance and implementation of the Principles within the investment industry.

5. We will work together to enhance our effectiveness in implementing the Principles.

6. We will each report on our activities and progress towards implementing the Principles.

11-2a The Rise of Environmental, Social, and Governance (ESG) Investing

In early 2005, The United Nations invited a group of the world's largest institutional investors to develop a set of "Principles for Responsible Investment" (PRI). This group published a report in 2006 that laid out a mission statement that said "We believe that an economically efficient, sustainable global financial system is a necessity for long-term value creation. Such a system will reward long-term, responsible investment and benefit the environment and society as a whole." The report laid out a set of principles the group would commit to (see Figure 11.3), and a set of steps for becoming a signatory to the PRI group.

The group also provided examples of ESG factors that should be included in investment analysis and shown in Figure 11.4.

At the time of the report, 63 investment companies with a total of $6.5 trillion in assets under management became signatories to the Principles for Responsible Investment. Major accounting firms such as Deloitte, PwC, KPMG, and Ernst & Young began working on creating standardized measures for companies to report their ESG performance, and ratings organizations such as MSCI and Sustainalytics began to emerge to score firms on ESG issues. The U.S. Securities and Exchange Commission also decided to create an ESG disclosure framework to help ensure consistent comparisons across firms. By end of March 2021, there were almost 4,000 signatories to the Principles of Responsible Investing, comprising over $120 trillion in assets under management (see Figure 11.5).[21] Though there remains some controversy around the clarity and/or consistency of ratings and there has been some political backlash against governments or firms that use ESG criteria in their funding or investment decisions,[22] most studies have indicated that firms that score high on ESG criteria also tend to exhibit higher returns and lower risk.[23]

Figure 11.4 The United Nations' Examples of ESG Factors

Environmental	Social	Governance
Climate change	Human rights	Bribery and corruption
Resource depletion	Modern slavery	Executive pay
Waste	Child labor	Board diversity and structure
Pollution	Working conditions	Political lobbying and donations
Deforestation	Employee relations	Tax strategy

Source: United Nations Principles for Responsible Investment, 2021

Figure 11.5 Principles for Responsible Investment Signatories and Assets Under Management

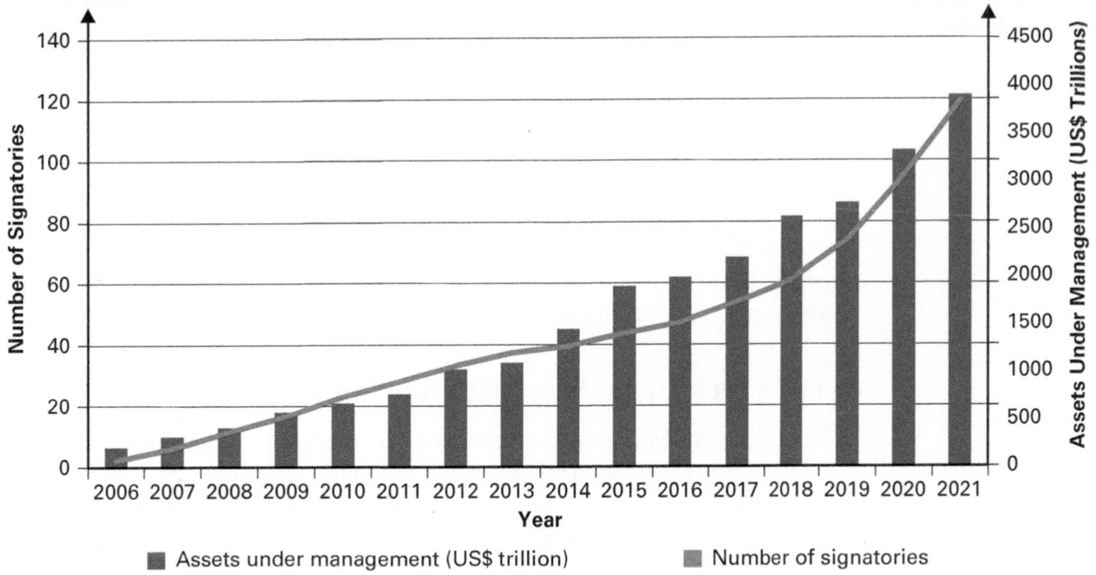

Source: https://www.unpri.org/about-us/about-the-pri

11.1   Strategy in Action

Price Fixing at Sotheby's and Christie's

Sotheby's and Christie's are the two largest fine-art auction houses in the world. In the mid-1990s, the two companies controlled 90% of the fine-art auction market, which at the time was worth approximately $4 billion annually. Traditionally, auction houses earn their profits by the commissions they charge on auction sales. In good times, these commissions can be as high as 10% on some items, but in the early 1990s, the auction business was in a slump, with the supply of art for auction shriveling. With Sotheby's and Christie's desperate for works of art, sellers played the two houses against each other, driving commissions down to 2%, or sometimes lower.

To try to control this situation, Sotheby CEO Dede Brooks met with Christie CEO Christopher Davidge in a series of clandestine meetings held in parking lots that began in 1993. Brooks claimed that she was acting on behalf of her boss, Alfred Taubman, the chairman and controlling shareholder of Sotheby's. According to Brooks, Taubman had agreed with the chairman of Christie's, Anthony Tennant, to work together in the weak auction market and limit price competition. In their meetings, Brooks and Davidge agreed to a fixed and nonnegotiable commission structure. Based on a sliding scale, the commission structure would range from 10% on a $100,000 item to 2% on a $5-million item. In effect, Brooks and Davidge were agreeing

to eliminate price competition between them, thereby guaranteeing both auction houses higher profits. The price-fixing agreement began in 1993 and continued unabated for 6 years, until federal investigators uncovered the arrangement and brought charges against Sotheby's and Christie's.

With the deal out in the open, lawyers filed several class-action lawsuits on behalf of the sellers that had been defrauded. Ultimately, at least 100,000 sellers signed on to the class-action lawsuits, which the auction houses settled with a $512-million payment. The auction houses also pleaded guilty to price fixing and paid $45 million in fines to U.S. antitrust authorities. As for the key players, the chairman of Christie's, as a British subject, was able to avoid prosecution in the United States (price fixing is not an offense for which someone can be extradited). Davidge struck a deal with prosecutors and, in return for amnesty, turned over incriminating documents to the authorities. Brooks also cooperated with federal prosecutors and avoided jail (in April 2002, she was sentenced to 3 years of probation, 6 months of home detention, 1,000 hours of community service, and a $350,000 fine). Taubman, ultimately isolated by all his former coconspirators, was sentenced to 1 year in jail and fined $7.5 million.

Sources: S. Tully, "A House Divided," *Fortune*, December 18, 2000, pp. 264–275; J. Chaffin, "Sotheby's Ex CEO Spared Jail Sentence," *Financial Times*, April 30, 2002, p. 10; and T. Thorncroft, "A Courtroom Battle of the Vanities," *Financial Times*, November 3, 2001, p. 3.

11-3 Agency Theory

Agency theory looks at the problems that can arise in a business relationship when one person delegates decision-making authority to another. It offers a way of understanding why managers do not always act in the best interests of stakeholders and why they might sometimes behave unethically, and, perhaps, also illegally.[24] Although agency theory was originally formulated to capture the relationship between management and stockholders, the basic principles have also been extended to cover the relationship with other key stakeholders, such as employees, as well as relationships between different layers of management within a corporation.[25] Although the focus of attention in this section is on the relationship between senior management and stockholders, some of the same language can be applied to the relationship between other stakeholders and top managers, and between top management and lower levels of management.

11-3a Principal–Agent Relationships

The basic propositions of agency theory are relatively straightforward. First, an agency relationship is held to arise whenever one party delegates decision-making authority or control over resources to another. The principal is the person delegating authority, and the agent is the person to whom authority is delegated. The relationship between stockholders and senior managers is the classic example of an agency relationship. Stockholders, who are the principals, provide the company with risk capital but delegate control over that capital to senior managers, and particularly to the CEO, who, as their agent, is expected to use that capital in a manner consistent with the best interests of stockholders. As we have seen, this means using capital to maximize the company's long-term profitability and profit growth rate.

The agency relationship continues down the hierarchy within the company. For example, in a large, complex, multibusiness company, top managers cannot possibly make all the important decisions; therefore, they delegate some decision-making authority and control over capital resources to business-unit (divisional) managers. Thus, just as senior managers such as the CEO are the agents of stockholders, business-unit managers are the agents of the CEO (and in this context, the CEO is the principal). The CEO entrusts business-unit managers to use the resources over which they have control in the most effective manner in order to maximize the performance of their units. This helps the CEO ensure that they maximize the performance of the entire company, thereby discharging agency obligation to stockholders. More generally, whenever managers delegate authority to managers below them in the hierarchy and give them the right to control resources, an agency relationship is established.

11-3b The Agency Problem

Although agency relationships often work well, problems may arise if agents and principals have different goals, and if agents take actions that are not in the best interests of their principals. Sometimes this occurs because an **information asymmetry** exists between the principal and the agent: Agents almost always have more information about the resources they are managing than principals do. Unscrupulous agents can take advantage of such information asymmetry to mislead principals and maximize their own interests at the expense of principals.

In the case of stockholders, the information asymmetry arises because they delegate decision-making authority to the CEO, their agent, who, by virtue of their position inside the company, is likely to know far more than stockholders do about the company's operations. Indeed, there may be certain information about the company that the CEO is unwilling to share with stockholders because that information would also help competitors. In

information asymmetry

A situation where an agent has more information about the resources he or she is managing than the principal has.

such a case, withholding information from stockholders may be in the best interest of all. Generally, the CEO, involved in the day-to-day operations of the company, is bound to have an information advantage over stockholders, just as the CEO's subordinates may have an information advantage over the CEO with regard to the resources under their control.

The information asymmetry between principals and agents is not necessarily a bad thing, but it can make it difficult for principals to measure an agent's performance and thus hold the agent accountable for how well they are using the entrusted resources. There is a certain amount of performance ambiguity inherent in the relationship between a principal and agent. Principals cannot know for sure if the agent is acting in their best interest. They cannot know for sure if the agent is using the resources to which they have been entrusted as effectively and efficiently as possible. This ambiguity is amplified by the fact that agents must engage in behavior that has outcomes for different time horizons. For example, investing in research and development may lower profits today but help to ensure the firm is profitable in the future. Principals who reward only immediate performance outcomes could induce myopic ("short-sighted") behavior on the part of the agent. To an extent, principals must trust the agent to do the right thing.

Of course, this trust is not blind: principals do put mechanisms in place with the purpose of monitoring agents, evaluating their performance, and, if necessary, taking corrective action. As we shall see shortly, the board of directors is one such mechanism, for, in part, the board exists to monitor and evaluate senior managers on behalf of stockholders. In Germany, the codetermination law (*Mitbestimmungs-gesetz*) requires that firms with over 2,000 employees have boards of directors that represent the interests of employees—just under half of a firm's supervisory board members must represent workers. Other mechanisms serve a similar purpose. In the United States, publicly owned companies must regularly file detailed financial statements with the Securities and Exchange Commission (SEC) that are in accordance with generally agreed-upon accounting principles (GAAP). This requirement exists to give stockholders consistent, detailed information about how well management is using the capital with which it has been entrusted. Similarly, internal control systems within a company help the CEO ensure that subordinates are using the resources with which they have been entrusted to the best possible advantage.

Despite the existence of governance mechanisms and comprehensive measurement and control systems, a degree of information asymmetry will always remain between principals and agents, and there is always an element of trust involved in the relationship. Unfortunately, not all agents are worthy of this trust. A minority will deliberately mislead principals for personal gain, sometimes behaving unethically or breaking laws in the process, or engaging in behaviors that the principals would never condone.

The interests of principals and agents are not always the same; they diverge. For example, some authors argue that, like many other people, senior managers are motivated by desires for status, power, job security, and income.[26] By virtue of their position within the company, managers such as the CEO can use their authority and control over corporate funds to satisfy these desires at the cost of returns to stockholders. CEOs might use their position to invest corporate funds in various perks that enhance their status—executive jets, lavish offices, and expense-paid trips to exotic locales—rather than investing those funds in ways that increase stockholder returns. Economists have termed such behavior **on-the-job consumption**.[27]

Aside from engaging in on-the-job consumption, CEOs, along with other senior managers, might satisfy their desire for greater income by using their influence or control over the board of directors to persuade the compensation committee of the board to grant pay increases. Critics of U.S. industry claim that extraordinary pay has now become an endemic problem, and that senior managers are enriching themselves at the expense of stockholders and other employees. They point out that CEO pay has been increasing far more rapidly than the pay of average workers, primarily because of very liberal stock

on-the-job consumption

A term used by economists to describe the behavior of senior management's use of company funds to acquire perks (lavish offices, jets, and the like) that will enhance their status, instead of investing the funds to increase stockholder returns.

option grants that enable a CEO to earn huge pay bonuses in a rising stock market, even if the company underperforms the market and competitors.[28] In 1980, the average CEO in *Bloomberg Businessweek's* survey of CEOs of the largest 500 American companies earned 42 times what the average blue-collar worker earned. In 1990, this figure had increased to 85 times. By 2022, The Institute for Policy Studies found that the average American CEO earned 670 times what the median worker made.[29]

The size of some CEO pay packages, and their apparent lack of relationship to company performance, rankles critics.[30] In 2010, a study by Graef Crystal evaluating the relationship between CEO pay and performance concluded that there virtually is none. For example, if CEOs were paid according to shareholder return, the CEO of CBS Corporation, Leslie Moonves, who earned an impressive $43.2 million in 2009, should have gotten a $28 million pay cut, according to Crystal.[31] Critics argue that CEO compensation is disproportionate to achievement, representing a clear example of the agency problem. However, in response to shareholder pressure, in recent years more companies have begun adopting compensation practices that more closely tie CEO pay to performance. For example, at Air Products & Chemicals, when the earnings per share fell short of its 9% growth target in 2012, CEO John McGlade paid the price in the form of a 65% cut in his annual bonus. His stock grants and stock options decreased as well, reducing his total direct compensation 19%, to 9.1 million.[32]

A further concern is that in trying to satisfy a desire for status, security, power, and income, a CEO might engage in empire building—buying many new businesses in an attempt to increase the size of the company through diversification.[33] Although such growth may depress the company's long-term profitability and thus stockholder returns, it increases the size of the empire under the CEO's control and, by extension, the CEO's status, power, security, and income (there is a strong relationship between company size and CEO pay). Instead of trying to maximize stockholder returns by seeking the right balance between profitability and profit growth, some senior managers may trade long-term profitability for greater company growth via new business purchases. For example, in the mid-1970s, Compagnie Générale des Eaux was primarily a water utility and waste-management company, operating "near-monopolies" in local municipalities in France and generating strong, stable cash flows for its shareholders. However, a series of audacious, debt-funded acquisitions in the 1980s and 1990s, first by CEO Guy DeJouany and later by his successor, Jean-Marie Messier, rapidly transformed the company into one of the world's largest media and telecom empires, renamed Vivendi." Then, in the 2000s, as the tech, media, and telecom bubble burst, the Vivendi empire came crashing down under the weight of its debt burden. Jean-Marie Messier was investigated by both French and U.S. courts, and was accused of misleading shareholders, misappropriating funds, and worsening the company's precarious position. He was fined and forced to resign in 2002.[34]

Figure 11.6 graphs long-term profitability against the rate of growth in company revenues. A company that does not grow is likely missing out on profitable opportunities.[35] A moderate revenue growth rate of G^* allows a company to maximize long-term profitability, generating a return of π^*. Thus, a growth rate of $G1$ in Figure 11.6 is not consistent with maximizing profitability ($\pi1 < \pi^*$). By the same token, however, attaining growth in excess of $G2$ requires moving into market segments that earn lower profit margins or diversification into areas that the company knows little about. Consequently, it can be achieved only by sacrificing profitability; that is, past G^*, the investment required to finance further growth does not produce an adequate return, and the company's profitability declines. Yet $G2$ may be the growth rate favored by an empire-building CEO, for it will increase their power, status, and income. At this growth rate, profitability is equal only to $\pi2$. Because $\pi^* < \pi2$, a company growing at this rate is clearly not maximizing its long-run profitability or the wealth of its stockholders.

The magnitude of agency problems was emphasized in the early 2000s, when a series of scandals swept through the corporate world, many of which could be attributed to

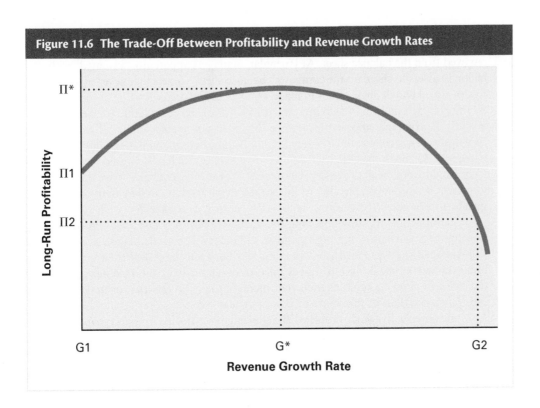

Figure 11.6 The Trade-Off Between Profitability and Revenue Growth Rates

self-interest-seeking senior executives and a failure of corporate governance mechanisms. In 2003, an investigation revealed that Hollinger CEO Conrad Black had used "tunneling" to divert over $400 million in company funds to his family and friends (see the Strategy in Action 11.2 for more details on Hollinger and Black). Between 2001 and 2004, accounting scandals unfolded at a number of major corporations, including Enron, WorldCom, Tyco, Computer Associates, HealthSouth, Adelphia Communications, Dynegy, Royal

11.2 Strategy in Action

Self-Dealing at Hollinger International Inc.

From 1999 to 2003, Conrad Black, CEO, and F. David Radler, COO, of Hollinger International Inc., illegally diverted cash and assets to themselves, family members, and other corporate insiders. Hollinger International, a global publishing empire, owned newspapers around the world, such as the *Chicago Sun-Times*, the *Daily Telegraph* (in London), the *National Post* (in Toronto), and the *Jerusalem Post* (in Israel), among others. According to Stephen Cutler, the director of the SEC's Division of Enforcement, "Black and Radler abused their control of a public company and treated it as their personal piggy bank. Instead of carrying out their responsibilities to protect the interest of public shareholders, the defendants cheated and defrauded these shareholders through a series of deceptive schemes and misstatements." In a practice known as "tunneling,"

Black and Radler engaged in a series of self-dealing transactions, such as selling some of Hollinger's newspapers at below-market prices to companies privately held by Black and Radler themselves—sometimes for as low as one dollar. They also directly channeled money out of the firm under the guise of "noncompetition payments." The managers abused corporate perks, using a company jet to fly to the South Pacific for a vacation and spending corporate funds on a swanky New York apartment on Park Avenue and a lavish $62,000 birthday party for Black's wife. Black's ill-gotten gains are thought to total more than $400 million, and fallout from the scandal resulted in a loss of $2 billion in shareholder value. Although Black was sentenced to 6½ years in jail, he ultimately only served 42 months.

Sources: S. Taub, "SEC Charges Hollinger, Two Executives," *CFO*, November 16, 2004; www.cfo.com, U.S. Department of Justice, "Former Hollinger Chairman Conrad Black and Three Other Executives Indicted in U.S.–Canada Corporate Fraud Schemes," indictment released November 17, 2005; "Ex-Media Mogul Black Convicted of Fraud," Associated Press, July 13, 2007; and A. Stern, "Ex-Media Mogul Conrad Black Sent Back to Prison," Reuters, June 24, 2011.

Dutch Shell, and Parmalat, a major Italian food company. At Enron, $27 billion in debt was hidden from shareholders, employees, and regulators in special partnerships that were removed from the balance sheet. At Parmalat, managers apparently "invented" $8 to $12 billion in assets to shore up the company's balance sheet—assets that never existed. In the case of Royal Dutch Shell, senior managers knowingly inflated the value of the company's oil reserves by one-fifth, which amounted to 4 billion barrels of oil that never existed, making the company appear much more valuable than it was. At the other companies, earnings were systematically overstated, often by hundreds of millions of dollars, or even billions of dollars in the case of Tyco and WorldCom, which understated its expenses by $3 billion in 2001. In all of these cases, the prime motivation seems to have been an effort to present a more favorable view of corporate affairs to shareholders than was the case, thereby securing senior executives significantly higher pay packets.[36]

It is important to remember that the agency problem is not confined to the relationship between senior managers and stockholders. It can also bedevil the relationship between the CEO and subordinates, and between them and their subordinates. Subordinates might use control over information to distort the true performance of their unit in order to enhance their pay, increase their job security, or make sure their unit gets more than its fair share of company resources.

Confronted with agency problems, the challenge for principals is to (1) shape the behavior of agents so that they act in accordance with the goals set by principals, (2) reduce information asymmetry between agents and principals, and (3) develop mechanisms for removing agents who do not act in accordance with the goals of principals and mislead them. Principals deal with these challenges through a series of governance mechanisms.

11.4 Describe the various governance mechanisms that are used to align the interests of stockholders and managers and why they do not always work.

11-4 Governance Mechanisms

Principals put governance mechanisms in place to align incentives between principals and agents, and to monitor and control agents. The purpose of governance mechanisms is to reduce the scope and frequency of the agency problem; that is, to help ensure that agents act in a manner that is consistent with the best interests of their principals. In this section, the primary focus is on governance mechanisms that exist to align the interests of senior managers (as agents) with their principals, stockholders. It should not be forgotten, however, that governance mechanisms also exist to align the interests of business-unit managers with those of their superiors, and likewise down the hierarchy within the organization.

Here we look at four main types of governance mechanisms for aligning stockholder and management interests: the board of directors, stock-based compensation, financial statements, and the takeover constraint. The section closes with a discussion of governance mechanisms within a company to align the interests of senior and lower-level managers.

11-4a The Board of Directors

The board of directors is the centerpiece of the corporate governance system. Board members are directly elected by stockholders, and under corporate law they represent the stockholders' interests in the company. Hence, the board can be held legally accountable for the company's actions. Its position at the apex of decision making within the company allows it to monitor corporate strategy decisions and ensure that they are consistent with stockholder interests. If the board believes that corporate strategies are not in the best interest of stockholders, it can take measures such as voting against management nominations to the board of directors, or submitting its own nominees. In addition, the board has the legal authority to hire, fire, and compensate corporate employees, including, most importantly, the CEO.[37] The board is also responsible for making sure that the company's audited financial statements present a true picture of its financial situation. Thus, the board exists to reduce the information asymmetry between stockholders and managers, and to monitor and control management actions on behalf of stockholders.

The typical board is composed of a mix of inside and outside directors. **Inside directors** are senior employees of the company, such as the CEO. They are required on the board because they have valuable information about the company's activities. Without such information, the board cannot adequately perform its monitoring function. But because insiders are full-time employees of the company, their interests tend to be aligned with those of management. Hence, outside directors are needed to bring objectivity to the monitoring and evaluation processes. **Outside directors** are not full-time employees of the company. Many of them are full-time, professional directors who hold positions on the boards of several companies. They need to maintain a reputation for competency, and so are motivated to perform their role as objectively and effectively as possible.[38]

There is little doubt that many boards perform their assigned functions admirably. For example, when the board of Sotheby's discovered that the company had been engaged in price fixing with Christie's, board members moved quickly to oust both the CEO and the chairman of the company (see Strategy in Action 11.1). But not all boards perform as well as they should. The board of now-bankrupt energy company Enron approved the company's audited financial statements, which were later discovered to be grossly misleading.

Critics of the existing governance system charge that inside directors often dominate the outsiders on the board. Insiders can use their position within the management hierarchy to exercise control over the company-specific information that the board receives. Consequently, they can present information in a way that puts them in a favorable light. In addition, because insiders have intimate knowledge of the company's operations, and because superior knowledge and control over information are sources of power, they may be better positioned than outsiders to influence boardroom decision making. The board may become the captive of insiders and merely rubber-stamp management decisions instead of guarding stockholder interests.

Some observers contend that many boards are dominated by the company CEO, particularly when the CEO is also the chairman of the board.[39] To support this view, they point out that both inside and outside directors are often the CEO's nominees. The typical inside director is subordinate to the CEO in the company's hierarchy and therefore unlikely to criticize the boss. Nor can outside directors nominated by the CEO be expected to evaluate the CEO objectively. Sometimes CEOs sit on each other's boards as outside directors, forming "interlocking directorates" that may induce them to act in each other's interests. Thus, the loyalty of the board may be biased toward the CEO, not the stockholders. Moreover, a CEO who is also chairman of the board may be able to control the agenda of board discussions in such a manner as to deflect criticisms of his or her leadership. Notably, although shareholders ostensibly vote on board members, board members are not legally required to resign if they do not receive a majority of the vote. The Council of Institutional Investors (which represents pension funds, endowments, and other large investors) regularly publishes a list of "zombie directors"—directors who were retained on boards despite being rejected by shareholders. In 2020, 54 directors of U.S. firms were considered zombie directors. For example, Netflix's lead director, Jay Hoag, received just 45.2% investor support in 2020. In 2019, all four of Netflix's board nominees received majority "no" votes, including Susan Rice, a national security adviser for President Barack Obama.[40]

In the aftermath of the wave of scandals that hit the corporate world in the early 2000s, there are clear signs that many corporate boards are moving away from merely rubber-stamping top-management decisions and are beginning to play a much more active role in corporate governance. In part, they have been prompted by legislation such as the 2002 Sarbanes–Oxley Act in the United States, which tightened rules regulating corporate reporting and corporate governance. A growing trend on the part of the courts to hold directors liable for corporate misstatements has also been important. Powerful

inside directors

Senior employees of the company, such as the CEO.

outside directors

Directors who are not full-time employees of the company, needed to provide objectivity to the monitoring and evaluation of processes.

institutional investors such as pension funds have also been more aggressive in exerting their power, often pushing for more outside representation on the board of directors and for a separation between the roles of chairman and CEO. An apt example is provided by the settlement reached in September 2018 between Tesla, Elon Musk, and the Securities Exchange Commission, requiring that Musk, who served in both the CEO and chairman of the board roles, would step down from his position as chairman. Musk had come under fire for tweeting that he intended to take the company private, and that funding was secured; the Securities and Exchange Commission believed the tweet was reckless and had the potential to mislead stockholders, and thus believed Musk needed more oversight.

In general, there has been growing pressure to have the chairman role go to an outsider rather than firm management. Partly as a result, 56% of firms on the Standard & Poor's 500 index split the chairman and CEO jobs as of 2022—up from 25% in 2002, and the percentage of companies with an independent board chair (i.e., not affiliated with the company) was 37% in 2022.[41] Separating the role of chairman and CEO limits the ability of corporate insiders, particularly the CEO, to exercise control over the board. Regardless, it must be recognized that boards of directors do not work as well as they should in theory, and other mechanisms are needed to align the interests of stockholders and managers.

11-4b Stock-Based Compensation

According to agency theory, one of the best ways to reduce the scope of the agency problem is for principals to establish incentives for agents to behave in the company's best interest through pay-for-performance systems. In the case of stockholders and top managers, stockholders can encourage top managers to pursue strategies that maximize a company's long-term profitability and profit growth, and thus the gains from holding its stock, by linking the pay of those managers to the performance of the stock price.

Giving managers **stock options**—the right to purchase the company's shares at a predetermined (strike) price at some point in the future, usually within 10 years of the grant date—has been the most common pay-for-performance system. Typically, the strike price is the price at which the stock was trading when the option was originally granted. Ideally, stock options will motivate managers to adopt strategies that increase the share price of the company, for in doing so managers increase the value of their stock options. Granting managers stock if they attain predetermined performance targets is another stock-based, pay-for-performance system.

Several academic studies suggested that stock-based compensation schemes such as stock options and stock grants can align executive and stockholder interests. For instance, one study found that managers were more likely to consider the effects of their acquisition decisions on stockholder returns if they were significant shareholders.[42] According to another study, managers who were significant stockholders were less likely to pursue strategies that would maximize the size of the company rather than its profitability.[43] More generally, it is difficult to argue with the proposition that the chance to get rich from exercising stock options is the primary reason for the 14-hour days and 6-day workweeks that many employees of fast-growing companies experience.

However, the practice of granting stock options has become increasingly controversial. Many top managers earn huge bonuses from exercising stock options that were granted several years prior. Critics claim that these options are often too generous but do not deny that they motivate managers to improve company performance. A particular cause for concern is that stock options are often granted at such low strike prices that the CEO can hardly fail to make a significant amount of money by exercising them, even if the company underperforms in the stock market by a significant margin. A serious example of the agency problem emerged in 2005 and 2006, when the SEC investigated several companies that had granted stock options to senior executives and apparently "backdated" the stock to a time when the price was lower, enabling executives to earn more money than if those options had simply been dated on the day they were granted.[44] By late 2006, the SEC had investigated nearly 130 companies for possible fraud related to stock-option backdating, including such major corporations as Apple, Jabil Circuit, United Healthcare, and Home Depot.[45]

Other critics of stock options, including the famous investor Warren Buffett, complain that huge stock-option grants increase the outstanding number of shares in a company and therefore dilute the equity of stockholders; accordingly, they should be shown in company accounts as an expense against profits. Under accounting regulations that were enforced until 2005, stock options, unlike wages and salaries, were not expensed. However, this has since changed, and as a result many companies are beginning to reduce their use of options. Microsoft, for example, which had long given generous stock-option grants to high-performing employees, replaced stock options with stock grants in 2005. Requiring senior management to hold large numbers of shares in the company also has its downside: Managers who hold a large portion of their personal wealth in the company they manage are likely to be underdiversified. This can lead to excessively risk-averse behavior, or overdiversification of the firm.

11-4c Financial Statements and Auditors

Publicly traded companies in the United States are required to file quarterly and annual reports with the SEC that are prepared according to GAAP. The purpose of this requirement is to give consistent, detailed, and accurate information about how efficiently and effectively the agents of stockholders—the managers—are running the company. To make sure that managers do not misrepresent financial information, the SEC also requires that the accounts be audited by an independent, accredited accounting firm. Similar regulations exist in most other developed nations. If the system works as intended, stockholders can have faith that the information contained in financial statements accurately reflects the state of affairs at a company. Among other things, such information can enable a stockholder to calculate the profitability (ROIC) of a company in which they invest and to compare its ROIC against that of competitors.

Unfortunately, this system has not always worked as intended in the United States. Despite the fact that the vast majority of companies do file accurate information in their financial statements, and although most auditors review that information accurately, there is substantial evidence that a minority of companies have abused the system, aided in part by the compliance of auditors. This was clearly an issue at bankrupt energy trader Enron, where the CFO and others misrepresented the true financial state of the company to investors by creating off-balance-sheet partnerships that hid the true state of Enron's indebtedness from public view. Enron's auditor, Arthur Andersen, was complicit with this deception and in direct violation of its fiduciary duty. Arthur Anderson had lucrative consulting contracts with Enron that it did not want to jeopardize by questioning the accuracy of the company's financial statements. The losers in this mutual deception were shareholders, who relied completely upon inaccurate information to make their investment decisions.

There have been numerous examples of managers' gaming of financial statements to present a distorted picture of their company's finances to investors. For example, in 2011, Hewlett Packard (HP) acquired Autonomy for $11 billion. However, after the acquisition, HP sued Autonomy's former CEO and former chief financial officer on the grounds that they had artificially inflated its revenues, revenue growth, and gross margins to increase the acquisition price. It became the United Kingdom's biggest civil fraud trial of all time, and in January of 2022 it was announced that HP had won the case.[46] The amount of damages to be paid to HP were not announced but were expected to be in the billions of dollars. The typical motive of misrepresenting financial statements is to inflate the earnings or revenues of a company, thereby generating investor enthusiasm and propelling the stock price higher, which gives managers an opportunity to cash in stock-option grants for huge personal gain, obviously at the expense of stockholders, who have been misled by the reports.

The gaming of financial statements by companies such as Enron raises serious questions about the accuracy of the information contained in audited financial statements. In response, Congress passed the Sarbanes–Oxley Act in 2002, representing the most far-reaching overhaul of accounting rules and corporate governance procedures since the 1930s. Among other things, Sarbanes–Oxley established an oversight board for accounting firms, required CEOs and CFOs to endorse their company's financial statements, and barred companies from hiring the same accounting firm for both auditing and consulting services.

11-4d The Takeover Constraint

Given the imperfections in corporate governance mechanisms, it is clear that the agency problem persists at some companies. However, stockholders do have residual power—they can always sell their shares. If stockholders sell in large numbers, the price of the company's shares will decline. If the share price falls far enough, the company might be worth less on the stock market than the actual value of its assets. At this point, the company may become an attractive acquisition target and runs the risk of being purchased by another enterprise, against the wishes of the target company's management.

The risk of being acquired by another company is known as the **takeover constraint**—it limits the extent to which managers can pursue strategies and take actions that put their own interests above those of stockholders. If they ignore stockholder interests and the company is acquired, senior managers typically lose their independence, and likely their jobs as well. Therefore, the threat of takeover can constrain management action and limit the worst excesses of the agency problem.

During the 1980s and early 1990s, the threat of takeover was often enforced by corporate raiders: individuals or corporations that purchase large blocks of shares in companies which appear to be pursuing strategies inconsistent with maximizing stockholder wealth. Corporate raiders argue that if these underperforming companies pursued different strategies, they could create more wealth for stockholders. Raiders purchase stock in a company either to take over the business and run it more efficiently, or to precipitate a change in top management, replacing the existing team with one more likely to maximize stockholder returns. Raiders are motivated not by altruism, but by gain. If they succeed in their takeover bid, they can institute strategies that create value for stockholders, including themselves. Even if a takeover bid fails, raiders can still earn millions, for their stockholdings will typically be bought out by the defending company for a hefty premium. Called **greenmail**, this source of gain has stirred much controversy and debate about its benefits. Whereas some claim that the threat posed by raiders has had a salutary effect on enterprise performance by pushing corporate management to run companies better, others counter that there is little evidence of this.[47]

Although the incidence of hostile takeover bids has fallen off significantly since the early 1990s, this should not imply that the takeover constraint has ceased to operate. Unique circumstances existed in the early 2000s that made it more difficult to execute hostile takeovers. The boom years of the 1990s left many corporations with excessive debt (corporate America entered the new century with record levels of debt on its balance sheets), limiting the ability to finance acquisitions, particularly hostile acquisitions, which are often particularly expensive. In addition, the market valuation of many companies became misaligned with underlying fundamentals during the stock market bubble of the 1990s, and after a substantial fall in certain segments of the stock market, such as the technology sector, present valuations are still high relative to historic norms—making the hostile acquisition of even poorly run and unprofitable companies expensive. However, takeovers tend to occur in cycles, and it seems likely that once excesses are worked out of the stock market and off corporate balance sheets, the takeover constraint will reassert itself. It should be remembered that the takeover constraint—the governance mechanism of last resort—is often invoked only when other governance mechanisms have failed.

takeover constraint

The risk of being acquired by another company.

greenmail

A source of gaining wealth whereby corporate raiders either push companies to change their corporate strategy to one that will benefit stockholders, or charge a premium for stock when the company wants to buy it back.

11-4e Governance Mechanisms Inside a Company

Thus far, this chapter has focused on the governance mechanisms designed to reduce the agency problem that potentially exists between stockholders and managers. Agency relationships also exist within a company, and the agency problem can arise between levels of management. In this section, we explore how the agency problem can be reduced within a company by using two complementary governance mechanisms to align the incentives and behavior of employees with those of upper-level management: strategic control systems and incentive systems.

Strategic Control Systems   Strategic control systems are the primary governance mechanisms established within a company to reduce the scope of the agency problem between levels of management. These systems are the formal, target-setting, measurement and feedback systems that allow managers to evaluate whether a company is executing the strategies necessary to maximize its long-term profitability. In particular, control systems are used to assess whether the company is achieving superior efficiency, quality, innovation, and customer responsiveness. They are discussed in more detail in Chapter 12.

The purpose of strategic control systems is to (1) establish standards and targets against which performance can be measured, (2) create systems for measuring and monitoring performance on a regular basis, (3) compare actual performance against the established targets, and (4) evaluate results and take corrective action if necessary. In governance terms, their purpose is to ensure that lower-level managers, as the agents of top managers, act in a way that is consistent with top managers' goals—which should be to maximize the wealth of stockholders, subject to legal and ethical constraints.

Employee Incentives   Control systems alone may not be sufficient to align incentives between stockholders, senior management, and the organization as a whole. To help do this, positive incentive systems are often put into place to motivate employees to work toward goals that are central to maximizing long-term profitability. As already noted, ESOPs are one form of positive incentive, as are stock-option grants. In the 1990s, ESOPs and stock-ownership grants were pushed down deep within many organizations, meaning that employees at many levels of the firm were eligible for the plans. The logic behind such systems is straightforward: Recognizing that the stock price, and therefore their own wealth, is dependent upon the profitability of the company, employees will work toward maximizing profitability.

In addition to stock-based compensation systems, employee compensation can be tied to goals that are linked to the attainment of superior efficiency, quality, innovation, and customer responsiveness. For example, the bonus pay of a manufacturing employee might depend upon attaining quality and productivity targets, which, if reached, will lower the costs of the company, increase customer satisfaction, and boost profitability. Similarly, a salesperson's bonus pay might depend upon surpassing sales targets, and an R&D employee's bonus pay may be contingent upon the success of new products he or she had worked on developing.

11-5 Ethical Issues and behavior

The term **ethics** refers to accepted principles of right or wrong that govern the conduct of a person, the members of a profession, or the actions of an organization. **Business ethics** are the accepted principles of right or wrong governing the conduct of businesspeople. Ethical decisions are in accordance with those accepted principles, whereas unethical decisions violate accepted principles. This is not as straightforward as it sounds. Managers may be confronted with **ethical dilemmas**, situations where

ethics

Accepted principles of right or wrong that govern the conduct of a person, the members of a profession, or the actions of an organization.

business ethics

Accepted principles of right or wrong governing the conduct of businesspeople.

ethical dilemmas

Situations where there is no agreement over exactly what the accepted principles of right and wrong are, or where none of the available alternatives seems ethically acceptable.

11.5 Summarize the main ethical issues that arise in businesses, including common causes of unethical behavior.

there is no agreement over the accepted principles of right and wrong, or where none of the available alternatives seems ethically acceptable.

In our society, many accepted principles of right and wrong are not only universally recognized but also codified into law. In the business arena, laws govern product liability (tort laws), contracts and breaches of contract (contract law), the protection of intellectual property (intellectual property law), competitive behavior (antitrust law), and the selling of securities (securities law). Not only is it unethical to break these laws, it is illegal.

Unfortunately, as we have already seen in this chapter, managers do break laws. Moreover, managers may take advantage of ambiguities and gray areas in the law, of which there are many in our common law system, to pursue actions that are at best legally suspect and, in any event, clearly unethical. It is important to realize, however, that behaving ethically surpasses staying within the bounds of the law.

Many nations have different laws and ethical norms, making issues of ethics and legality vastly more complicated when firms' activities span multiple national borders. Research by Surroca, Tribó, and Zahra on 110 multinational firms found that often multinational firms deal with stakeholder pressures and legal concerns in their home country by simply transferring their socially irresponsible practices to their overseas subsidiaries. The researchers found that this was particularly likely when it was not overtly apparent that the subsidiary had a connection to the multinational, suggesting that managers knew the behavior was unethical and did not want to be associated with it, yet continued the practice anyway.[48]

In this section, we take a closer look at the ethical issues that managers may confront when developing strategy, and at the steps they can take to ensure that strategic decisions are not only legal but also ethical.

11-5a Ethical Issues in Strategy

The ethical issues that strategic managers confront cover many topics, but most are due to a potential conflict between the goals of the enterprise, or the goals of individual managers, and the fundamental rights of important stakeholders, including stockholders, customers, employees, suppliers, competitors, communities, and the general public. Stakeholders have basic rights that must be respected; it is unethical to violate those rights.

Stockholders have the right to timely, accurate information about their investments (in accounting statements); it is unethical to violate that right. Customers have the right to be fully informed about the products and services they purchase, including the right to information about how those products might cause them harm, and it is unethical to restrict their access to such information. Employees have the right to safe working conditions, fair compensation for the work they perform, and just treatment by managers. Suppliers have the right to expect contracts to be respected, and the company should not take advantage of a power disparity between it and a supplier to opportunistically rewrite a contract. Competitors have the right to expect that the firm will abide by the rules of competition and not violate the basic principles of antitrust laws. Communities and the general public, including their political representatives in government, have the right to expect that a firm will not violate the basic expectations that society places on enterprises—for example, by dumping toxic pollutants into the environment, or overcharging for work performed on government contracts.

Those who take the stakeholder view of business ethics often argue that it is in the enlightened self-interest of managers to behave in an ethical manner that recognizes and respects the fundamental rights of stakeholders, because doing so will ensure the support of stakeholders and, ultimately, benefit the firm and its managers. Others go beyond this instrumental approach to ethics and argue that, in many cases, acting ethically is simply the right thing to do. They argue that businesses need to recognize their *noblesse oblige*—a French term that refers to honorable and benevolent behavior that is considered the responsibility of people of high (noble) birth—and give something back to the society that made their success possible. In a business setting, it is understood that benevolent behavior is the moral responsibility of successful enterprises.

Unethical behavior often arises in a corporate setting when managers decide to put the attainment of their own personal goals, or the goals of the enterprise, above the fundamental rights of one or more stakeholder groups (in other words, unethical behavior may arise from agency problems). The most common examples of such behavior involve self-dealing, information manipulation, anticompetitive behavior, opportunistic exploitation of other players in the value chain in which the firm is embedded (including suppliers, complement providers, and distributors), the maintenance of substandard working conditions, environmental degradation, and corruption.

Self-dealing occurs when managers find a way to feather their own nests with corporate monies, as we have already discussed in several examples in this chapter (such as Conrad Black at Hollinger). **Information manipulation** occurs when managers use their control over corporate data to distort or hide information in order to enhance their own financial situation or the competitive position of the firm; HP accused Autonomy of this in an example described earlier in the chapter. As we have seen, many accounting scandals have involved the deliberate manipulation of financial information. Information manipulation can also occur with nonfinancial data. An example is when managers at the tobacco companies suppressed internal research that linked smoking to health problems, violating the right of consumers to accurate information about the dangers of smoking. When this evidence came to light, lawyers filed class-action suits against the tobacco companies, claiming that they had intentionally caused harm to smokers—they had broken tort law by promoting a product that they knew was seriously harmful to consumers. In 1999, the tobacco companies settled a lawsuit brought by the states that sought to recover healthcare costs associated with tobacco-related illnesses; the total payout to the states was $260 billion.

Anticompetitive behavior covers a range of actions aimed at harming actual or potential competitors, most often by using monopoly power, and thereby enhancing the long-run prospects of the firm. For example, in the 1990s, the Justice Department claimed that Microsoft used its monopoly in operating systems to force PC makers to bundle Microsoft's Web browser, Internet Explorer, with the Windows operating system, and to display the Internet Explorer logo prominently on the computer desktop. Microsoft reportedly told PC makers that it would not supply them with Windows unless they did this. Because the PC makers needed Windows to sell their machines, this was a powerful threat. The alleged aim of the action, which exemplifies "tie-in sales"—which are illegal under antitrust laws—was to drive a competing browser maker, Netscape, out of business. The courts ruled that Microsoft was indeed abusing its monopoly power in this case and, under a 2001 consent decree, the company was forced to cease this practice.

Legality aside, the actions in which Microsoft managers allegedly engaged are unethical on at least three counts; first, by violating the rights of end users by unfairly limiting their choice; second, by violating the rights of downstream participants in the industry value chain—in this case, PC makers—by forcing them to incorporate a particular product in their design; and third, by violating the rights of competitors to free and fair competition.

Opportunistic exploitation of other players in the value chain in which the firm is embedded is another example of unethical behavior. Exploitation of this kind typically occurs when the managers of a firm seek to unilaterally rewrite the terms of a contract with suppliers, buyers, or complement providers in a way that is more favorable to the firm, often using their power to force a revision to the contract. For example, in the late 1990s, Boeing entered into a $2-billion contract with Titanium Metals Corporation to purchase certain amounts of titanium annually for 10 years. In 2000, after Titanium Metals had already spent $100 million to expand its production capacity to fulfill the contract, Boeing demanded that the contract be renegotiated, asking for

self-dealing
Managers using company funds for their own personal consumption.

information manipulation
When managers use their control over corporate data to distort or hide information in order to enhance their own financial situation or the competitive position of the firm.

anticompetitive behavior
A range of actions aimed at harming actual or potential competitors, most often by using monopoly power, and thereby enhancing the long-run prospects of the firm.

opportunistic exploitations
Unethical behavior sometimes used by managers to unilaterally rewrite the terms of a contract with suppliers, buyers, or complement providers in a way that favors to the firm.

lower prices and an end to minimum-purchase agreements. As a major purchaser of titanium, managers at Boeing probably thought they had the power to push this contract revision through, and Titanium's investment meant that it would be unlikely that the company walk away from the deal. Titanium promptly sued Boeing for breach of contract. The dispute was settled out of court, and under a revised agreement Boeing agreed to pay monetary damages to Titanium Metals (reported to be in the $60-million range) and entered into an amended contract to purchase titanium.[49] This action was arguably unethical because it violated the supplier's right to have a purchaser do business in a fair and open way, regardless of any issues of legality.

substandard working conditions

Arise when managers underinvest in working conditions, or pay employees below-market rates, to reduce their production costs.

Substandard working conditions arise when managers underinvest in working conditions, or pay employees below-market rates, in order to reduce their production costs. The most extreme examples of such behavior occur when a firm establishes operations in countries that lack the workplace regulations found in developed nations. For example, a 2020 study by the Australian Strategic Policy Institute linked 82 multinational firms such as BMW, Huawei, Nike, Apple, Microsoft, and Samsung to forced labor by Uighurs in factories across China. Uighurs, a persecuted ethnic minority from China's Xinjiang region, were transferred directly from internment camps to factories. There they live in segregated dormitories, are unable to go home, and are forced to undergo Mandarin and ideological training outside of work hours. Advertisements from organizations offering to supply Uighur workers claimed it could provide 1,000 Uighur workers between the ages of 16–18, and stated, "The advantages of Xinjiang workers are: semi-military style management, can withstand hardship, no loss of personnel!"[50] Is it ethical for companies to use such a supplier? Many would say it is not.

environmental degradation

Occurs when a company's actions directly or indirectly result in pollution or other forms of environmental harm.

Environmental degradation occurs when a company's actions directly or indirectly result in pollution or other forms of environmental harm. Environmental degradation can violate the right of local communities and the general public to clean air and water, land that is free from pollution by toxic chemicals, and properly managed forests. For example, IKEA's "fast furniture" business model (i.e., producing furniture that is inexpensive and not expected to last a long time) has led to the company becoming the world's largest consumer of wood. In fact, in 2020, IKEA used 1% of the world's wood. To address this, IKEA has committed to transitioning to 100% recycled materials by 2030.[51]

corruption

Can arise in a business context when managers pay bribes to gain access to lucrative business contracts.

Finally, **corruption** can arise in a business context when managers pay bribes to gain access to lucrative business contracts. For example, it was alleged that Halliburton was part of a consortium that paid nearly $180 million in bribes to win a lucrative contract to build a natural gas plant in Nigeria.[52] Similarly, between 2006 and 2009, Siemens was found guilty of paying hundreds of millions of dollars in bribes to secure sales contracts; the company was ultimately forced to pay hefty fines, and one Chinese executive who accepted $5.1 million in bribes was sentenced to death by Chinese courts.[53] Corruption is clearly unethical because it violates many rights, including the right of competitors to a level playing field when bidding for contracts, and, when government officials are involved, the right of citizens to expect that government officials will act in the best interests of the local community (or nation), and not in response to corrupt payments.

11-5b The Roots of Unethical Behavior

Why do some managers behave unethically? What motivates managers to engage in actions that violate accepted principals of right and wrong, trample on the rights of one or more stakeholder groups, or simply break the law? Although there is no simple answer to this question, a few generalizations can be made.[54] First, it is important to recognize that business ethics are not divorced from **personal ethics**, which are the generally accepted principles of right and wrong governing the conduct of individuals. As individuals, we are taught that it is wrong to lie and cheat, and that it is right to behave with integrity and honor, and to stand up for what we believe to be true. The personal ethical code that guides

personal ethics

Generally accepted principles of right and wrong governing the conduct of individuals.

behavior comes from many sources, including parents, schools, religion, and the media. A personal ethical code will exert a profound influence on the way an individual behaves as a businessperson. An individual with a strong sense of personal ethics is less likely to behave in an unethical manner in a business setting; in particular, they are less likely to engage in self-dealing and more likely to behave with integrity.

Second, many studies of unethical behavior in a business setting have come to the conclusion that businesspeople sometimes do not realize that they are behaving unethically, primarily because they simply fail to ask the relevant question: Is this decision or action ethical? Instead, they apply straightforward business calculus to what they perceive to be a business decision, forgetting that the decision may also have an important ethical dimension.[55] The fault here is within processes that do not incorporate ethical considerations into business decision making. This may have been the case at Nike and other textile companies when managers originally made subcontracting arrangements with contractors that operated factories as "sweatshops," with long hours, low pay, and poor working conditions. Those decisions were probably based upon good economic logic. Subcontractors were probably chosen on the basis of business variables such as cost, delivery, and product quality, and key managers simply failed to ask: "How does this subcontractor treat its workforce?" If managers pondered this question at all, they probably reasoned that it was the subcontractor's concern, not the company's.

Unfortunately, the climate in some businesses does not encourage people to think through the ethical consequences of business decisions. This brings us to the third cause of unethical behavior in businesses: an organizational culture that de-emphasizes business ethics and considers all decisions to be purely economic ones. Individuals may believe their decisions within the workplace are not subject to the same ethical principles that govern their personal lives, or that their decisions within the firm do not really "belong" to them, but rather that they are merely acting as agents of the firm. A related fourth cause of unethical behavior may be pressure from top management to meet performance goals that are unrealistic and can only be attained by cutting corners or acting in an unethical manner. Thus, the pressure to perform induces individuals to behave in ways they otherwise would not. This appears to have been the case at Volkswagen: Engineers were under extreme pressure to produce a diesel car that would be fuel efficient, powerful, and meet U.S. emission standards in order to meet then-CEO Winterkorn's goal of tripling U.S. sales. Documents from within the organization suggest that the company had a "culture of fear" that made employees so afraid of disappointing management they were willing to cheat even though they clearly knew it was both a legal and ethical violation.

An organizational culture can "legitimize" behavior that society would judge as unethical, particularly when this is mixed with a focus upon unrealistic performance goals such as maximizing short-term economic performance regardless of the costs. In such circumstances, there is a greater-than-average probability that managers will violate their own personal ethics and engage in behavior that is unethical. By the same token, an organization's culture can do just the opposite and reinforce the need for ethical behavior. Recreational Equipment Inc. (REI), for example, has a strong culture around valuing environmental sustainability, respect for individuals, and trustworthiness. The firm backs up this belief system with such policies as producing an annual environmental stewardship report and providing healthcare benefits for all workers (including part-time employees), a retirement plan that does not require individual contributions, and grants for employees to contribute to their communities or to buy gear to pursue personal outdoor challenges. The company has made *Fortune*'s "100 Best Companies to Work For" list from 1998 to 2020.

This brings us to a fifth root cause of unethical behavior: *unethical leadership.* Leaders help to establish the culture of an organization, and they set the example that others follow. Other employees in a business often take their cues from business leaders, and if those leaders do not behave in an ethical manner, employees may not either. It is not what leaders say that matters, but what they do. A good example is Elizabeth Holmes, whose meteoric rise to fame and wealth based on her start-up, Theranos, turned out to be fueled almost entirely by hopes and lies. Holmes wanted to revolutionize medical testing by inventing a machine that could perform dozens of tests from a single drop of blood. Unfortunately, the technology was never achieved. She raised money from investors and secured distribution agreements with retailers such as Safeway and Walgreens by showing them fraudulent results and secretly running tests with diluted blood samples on traditional machines. At one point, Theranos was valued at $9 billion.[56] However, in 2015 the truth began to come crashing down as professors wrote articles challenging the legitimacy of the technology and the *Wall Street Journal* published a scathing expose.[57] According to the articles, investors were being defrauded and patients were being put at risk. One patient had been told, based on a Theranos test, that she had miscarried her baby. She went through significant emotional distress before opting to get additional tests from a traditional lab and found out that she was still pregnant.[58] In court, Holmes claimed not to know about the fraudulent tests but multiple employees testified that she knew (and had significant control over) everything. On January 3, 2022, Holmes was found guilty of three counts of wire fraud and one count of conspiracy to commit wire fraud.[59]

11.6 Identify what managers can do to improve the ethical climate of their organization.

11-6 Improving the Ethical Climate

What is the best way for managers to ensure that ethical considerations are taken into account? In many cases, there is no easy answer to this question, for many of the most vexing ethical problems involve very real dilemmas and suggest no obvious right course of action. Nevertheless, managers can and should do at least seven things to ensure that basic ethical principles are adhered to, and that ethical issues are routinely considered when making business decisions. They can (1) favor hiring and promoting people with a well-grounded sense of personal ethics, (2) build an organizational culture that places a high value on ethical behavior, (3) make sure that leaders within the business not only articulate the rhetoric of ethical behavior but also act in a manner that is consistent with that rhetoric, (4) put decision-making processes in place that require people to consider the ethical dimension of business decisions, (5) use ethics officers, (6) put strong governance processes in place, and (7) act with moral courage.

Hiring and Promotion   It seems obvious that businesses should strive to hire people who have a strong sense of personal ethics and would not engage in unethical or illegal behavior. Similarly, you would rightly expect a business to not promote people, and perhaps fire people, whose behavior does not match generally accepted ethical standards. But doing this is actually very difficult.

Is there anything that businesses can do to ensure they do not hire people who have poor personal ethics, particularly given that people have an incentive to hide this from public view (indeed, unethical people may well lie about their nature)? Businesses can give potential employees psychological tests to try to discern their ethical predisposition, and they can check with prior employees regarding someone's reputation, such as by asking for letters of reference and talking to people who have worked with the prospective employee. The latter approach is not uncommon and does influence the hiring process. Promoting people who have displayed poor ethics should not occur in an organization that values ethical behavior, and where leaders act accordingly.

Organization Culture and Leadership   To foster ethical behavior, organizations must build a culture that places high value on ethical behavior. Three actions are particularly important. First, businesses must explicitly articulate values that place a strong emphasis on ethical behavior. Many companies now do this by drafting a **code of ethics,** a formal statement of the ethical priorities to which a business adheres—in fact, both the New York Stock Exchange and Nasdaq listing services require listed companies to have a code of ethics that identifies areas of ethical risk, provides guidance for recognizing and dealing with ethical issues, provides mechanisms for reporting unethical conduct, and notes procedures to ensure prompt action against violations.[60] Firms also sometimes incorporate ethical statements into documents that articulate the values or mission of the business. For example, the food and consumer products giant Unilever's code of ethics includes the following points: "We will not use any form of forced, compulsory or child labor" and "No employee may offer, give or receive any gift or payment which is, or may be construed as being, a bribe. Any demand for, or offer of, a bribe must be rejected immediately and reported to management."[61] Unilever's principles send a very clear message to managers and employees within the organization. Data from the National Business Ethics Survey, administered by the Ethics Resource Center, a U.S. nonprofit, has found that firms with strong, well-implemented ethics programs have significantly fewer cases of ethical misconduct.

Having articulated values in a code of ethics or some other document, it is important that business leaders give life and meaning to those words by repeatedly emphasizing their importance and then acting on them. This means using every relevant opportunity to stress the importance of business ethics and making sure that key business decisions not only make good economic sense but also are ethical. Many companies have gone a step further and hired independent firms to audit them and make sure that they are behaving in a manner consistent with their ethical codes. Nike, for example, has in recent years hired independent auditors to ensure that its subcontractors are adhering to Nike's code of conduct.

Finally, building an organizational culture that places a high value on ethical behavior requires incentive and reward systems, including promotional systems that reward people who engage in ethical behavior and sanction those who do not.

Decision-Making Processes   In addition to establishing the right kind of ethical culture in an organization, businesspeople must be able to think through the ethical implications of decisions in a systematic way. To do this, they need a moral compass, and beliefs about what determines individual rights and justice. Some experts on ethics have proposed a straightforward practical guide, or ethical algorithm, to determine whether a decision is ethical. A decision is acceptable on ethical grounds if a businessperson can answer "yes" to each of these questions:

1. Does my decision fall within the accepted values or standards that typically apply in the organizational environment (as articulated in a code of ethics or some other corporate statement)?
2. Am I willing to see the decision communicated to all stakeholders affected by it— for example, by having it reported in newspapers or on television?
3. Would the people with whom I have a significant personal relationship, such as family members, friends, or even managers in other businesses, approve of the decision?

Ethics Officers   To make sure that a business behaves in an ethical manner, a number of firms now have ethics officers. These individuals are responsible for making sure that all employees are trained to be ethically aware; that ethical considerations enter the business decision-making process; and that employees adhere to the company's code of ethics. Ethics officers may also be responsible for auditing decisions to ensure that they are consistent with this code. In many businesses, ethics officers act as an internal ombudsperson with responsibility for handling confidential inquiries from employees, investigating complaints from employees or others, reporting findings, and making recommendations for change.

Raytheon, a large aerospace company with worldwide revenues of about $60 billion, has had a formal code of ethics since 1990. They also established an ombudsperson program in 1986 that allowed employees to inquire anonymously about ethics issues.[62]

code of ethics

Formal statement of the ethical priorities to which a business adheres.

Strong Corporate Governance   Strong corporate governance procedures are needed to ensure that managers adhere to ethical norms—in particular, that senior managers do not engage in self-dealing or information manipulation. Strong corporate governance procedures require an independent board of directors that is willing to hold top managers accountable for self-dealing and can verify the information managers provide. If companies like Tyco, WorldCom, and Enron had had strong boards of directors, it is unlikely that they would have experienced accounting scandals, or that top managers would have been able to access the funds of these corporations as personal treasuries.

There are five cornerstones of strong governance. The first is a board of directors that is composed of a majority of outside directors who have no management responsibilities in the firm, are willing and able to hold top managers accountable, and have no business ties with important insiders. Outside directors should be individuals of high integrity whose reputation is based on their ability to act independently. The second cornerstone is a board where the positions of CEO and chairman are held by separate individuals and the chairman is an outside director. When the CEO is also chairman of the board of directors, they can control the agenda, thereby furthering their personal agenda (which may include self-dealing) or limiting criticism against current corporate policies. The third cornerstone is a compensation committee formed by the board that is composed entirely of outside directors. The compensation committee sets the level of pay for top managers, including stock-option grants and additional benefits. The scope of self-dealing is reduced by making sure that the compensation committee is independent of managers. Fourth, the audit committee of the board, which reviews the financial statements of the firm, should also be composed of outsiders, thereby encouraging vigorous, independent questioning of the firm's financial statements. Finally, the board should use outside auditors that are truly independent and do not have a conflict of interest. This was not the case in many recent accounting scandals, where outside auditors were also consultants to the corporation and therefore less likely to ask management hard questions for fear that doing so would jeopardize lucrative consulting contracts.

Moral Courage   It is important to recognize that sometimes managers and others need significant moral courage. Moral courage enables managers to walk away from a decision that is profitable but unethical, gives employees the strength to say no to superiors who instruct them to behave unethically, and gives employees the integrity to contact the media and "blow the whistle" on persistent unethical behavior in a company. Moral courage does not come easily; there are well-known cases where individuals have lost their jobs because they were whistleblowers on unethical corporate behaviors.

Companies can strengthen the moral courage of employees by making a commitment to refuse to seek retribution against employees who exercise moral courage, say no to superiors, or otherwise complain about unethical actions. For example, Unilever's code of ethics includes the following:

> Any breaches of the Code must be reported in accordance with the procedures specified by the Joint Secretaries. The Board of Unilever will not criticize management for any loss of business resulting from adherence to these principles and other mandatory policies and instructions. The Board of Unilever expects employees to bring to their attention, or to that of senior management, any breach or suspected breach of these principles. Provision has been made for employees to be able to report in confidence and no employee will suffer as a consequence of doing so.

This statement gives "permission" to employees to exercise moral courage. Companies can also set up an ethics hotline that allows employees to anonymously register a complaint with a corporate ethics officer.

Final Words   The steps discussed here can help to ensure that when managers make business decisions, they are fully cognizant of the ethical implications and do not violate basic ethical prescripts. At the same time, not all ethical dilemmas have a clean and obvious solution—that is why they are dilemmas. At the end of the day, there are things that a business should not do, and there are things that a business should do, but there are also situations that present managers with a true predicament. In these cases, a premium is placed upon the ability of managers to make sense out of complex, messy situations, and to make balanced decisions that are as just as possible.

Key Terms

stakeholders 329	inside directors 341	self-dealing 347	substandard working
internal stakeholders 329	outside directors 341	information	conditions 348
external stakeholders 329	stock options 342	manipulation 347	environmental
risk capital 331	takeover constraint 344	anticompetitive	degradation 348
information	greenmail 344	behavior 347	corruption 348
asymmetry 336	ethics 345	opportunistic	personal ethics 348
on-the-job	business ethics 345	exploitations 347	code of ethics 351
consumption 337	ethical dilemmas 345		

Takeaways for Strategic Managers

1. Stakeholders are individuals or groups that have an interest, claim, or stake in a company—in what it does and in how well it performs.
2. Stakeholders are in an exchange relationship with the company. They supply the organization with important resources (or contributions), and in exchange expect their interests to be satisfied (by inducements).
3. A company cannot always satisfy the claims of all stakeholders. The goals of different groups may conflict. The company must identify the most important stakeholders and give highest priority to pursuing strategies that satisfy their needs.
4. A company's stockholders are its legal owners and the providers of risk capital—a major source of capital resources that allow a company to operate its business. As such, they have a unique role among stakeholder groups.
5. Maximizing long-term profitability and profit growth is the route to maximizing returns to stockholders, and is also consistent with satisfying the claims of several other key stakeholder groups.
6. When pursuing strategies that maximize profitability, a company has the obligation to do so within the limits set by the law and in a manner consistent with societal expectations.
7. An agency relationship is said to exist whenever one party delegates decision-making authority or control over resources to another party.
8. The essence of the agency problem is that the interests of principals and agents are not always the same, and some agents may take advantage of information asymmetries to maximize their own interests at the expense of principals.
9. Numerous governance mechanisms serve to limit the agency problem between stockholders and managers. These include the board of directors, stock-based compensation schemes, financial statements and auditors, and the threat of a takeover.
10. The term *ethics* refers to accepted principles of right or wrong that govern the conduct of a person, the members of a profession, or the actions of an organization. Business ethics are the accepted principles of right or wrong governing the conduct of businesspeople. An ethical strategy is one that does not violate these accepted principles.
11. Unethical behavior is rooted in poor personal ethics; the inability to recognize that ethical issues are at stake; failure to incorporate ethical issues into strategic and operational decision making; a dysfunctional culture; and failure of leaders to act in an ethical manner.
12. To make sure that ethical issues are considered in business decisions, managers should (a) favor hiring and promoting people with a well-grounded sense of personal ethics, (b) build an organizational culture that places high value on ethical behavior, (c) ensure that leaders within the business not only articulate the rhetoric of ethical behavior but also act in a manner that is consistent with that rhetoric, (d) put decision-making processes in place that require people to consider the ethical dimension of business decisions, (e) use ethics officers, (f) have strong corporate governance procedures, and (g) be morally courageous and encourage others to be the same.

Discussion Questions

1. How prevalent has the agency problem been in corporate America during the last decade? During the late 1990s, there was a boom in initial public offerings of internet companies (dot.com companies), supported by sky-high valuations, often assigned to Internet start-ups that had no revenues or earnings. The boom ended abruptly in 2001, when the Nasdaq stock market collapsed, losing almost 80% of its value. Who do you think benefited most from this boom: investors (stockholders) in those companies, managers, or investment bankers?

2. Why is maximizing ROIC consistent with maximizing returns to stockholders?

3. How might a company configure its strategy-making processes to reduce the probability that managers will pursue their own self-interest at the expense of stockholders?

4. In a public corporation, should the CEO of the company also be allowed to be the chairman of the board (as allowed for by the current law)? What problems might this present?

5. Under what conditions is it ethically defensible to outsource production to companies in the developing world that have much lower labor costs when such actions involve laying off long-term employees in the firm's home country?

6. Is it ethical for a firm faced with a labor shortage to employ illegal immigrants to meet its needs?

Volkswagen, the "People's Car," was founded in 1937 as part of Adolf Hitler's vision to make an affordable car that German families could own. Hitler decreed that the car needed to be able to carry two adults and three children, travel at 60 miles per hour, and cost no more than a motorbike. The beetle-shaped car's design and price were immediately popular, and by 1938 roughly 336,000 people had signed up to buy them via a monthly savings plan. However, by the outbreak of World War II, few cars had been built and none delivered. During the war, the plant only produced military vehicles, and then it was destroyed by bombing. Under the Potsdam Agreement among the USSR, the USA, and the United Kingdom, what was left of the plant was slated for dismantling. However, a British officer named Major Ivan Hirst convinced his commanders that he should take charge of the plant to produce cars for the British army. The British military continued to run the company, successfully producing "beetles" until 1949 when it handed the company back over to the German State of Lower Saxony.

In the 1950s, production increased rapidly, and the company began to expand its product range by introducing the "Transporter" (pre-cursor to the VW Bus) and the Ghia Coupe.[63] In the 1960s Volkswagen took ownership of Audi and started producing its first luxury cars. It later expanded into a range of sporty cars such as the Golf, Polo, and Passat that helped fuel the brand's popularity with a wider market. Over time, Volkswagen also bought other luxury brands including Porsche, Lamborghini, Bugatti, and Bentley, and by 2015 was poised to become the largest automaker in the world.

Winterkorn's Plan

When Martin Winterkorn took the helm of Volkswagen in 2007, he created an aggressive plan for the company. One of his first initiatives was to dramatically increase the modularity of auto design at Volkswagen so that different models across its various brands could be produced with many components in common, reducing both development and manufacturing costs and speeding up new product design. He also set a target for Volkswagen to sell 10 million cars worldwide annually by 2018 at net margins of 8% or higher (at the time, Winterkorn assumed the CEO position, the company was selling 6.2 million cars annually at a net margin of 6%).

A key to hitting this ambitious target was Winterkorn's plan to triple U.S. sales, in part by introducing "clean diesel" technology. Heavy taxation on gasoline had made diesel cars very popular in Europe, where they accounted for about half of all vehicle purchases. However, historically, diesel cars had not been popular with Americans and accounted for only 2.6% of cars in the United States in 2011.[64] Early diesel cars produced more particulate emissions and an odorous exhaust, earning them the reputation in the United States of being dirty and smelly. Volkswagen aimed to change that. In 2009, Volkswagen launched a lineup of "Clean Diesel" cars to the United States that purported to both meet U.S. emission standards and offer greater power and efficiency by incorporating a new Volkswagen innovation: turbocharged direct injection (TDI).[65] The engines earned rave reviews, and TDI-based cars won the "Green Car of the Year" award from the *Green Car Journal* in both 2009 (Volkswagen Jetta 2.0-liter TDI clean diesel) and 2010 (Audi A3 TDI clean diesel).

The engines, however, would turn out to be too good to be true. In 2013, the International Council on Clean Transportation (ICCT) hired researchers from West Virginia University to do a standard emissions test on diesel cars. Since Volkswagen had been promoting its diesel cars as environmentally friendly and fuel efficient, it was a natural place to start. However, the researchers tested two Volkswagen models and found a huge difference in nitrogen oxide and dioxide (collectively referred to as NOx) emissions in lab tests versus actual driving conditions.

They contacted the U.S. Environmental Protection Agency (EPA) and the California Air Resources Board, which opened an investigation.[66]

Volkswagen agreed to a voluntary recall of 500,000 cars in December 2014, claiming that the emissions result was due to a technical problem that could be fixed with a software change. However, follow-up tests in July 2015 showed the cars were still failing emissions standards, and none of Volkswagen's arguments could explain the discrepancy. According to Stanley Young, spokesperson for the California Air Resources Board, "They basically ran out of excuses. They would say the tests weren't at the right temperature, or some other issue. We had them in [to our offices] several times."[67] On September 3, 2015, the company finally admitted to rigging the emissions tests.

On September 18, 2015, the U.S. EPA told the press that Volkswagen had used software called "defeating devices" in its TDI diesel engines to cheat the emission standards tests. These devices could sense emissions testing conditions by detecting the steering, throttle, and other inputs required during an emissions test drive cycle. During the test, the device would utilize NOx controls to make the car compliant, but when the car was on the road, the device turned off the controls

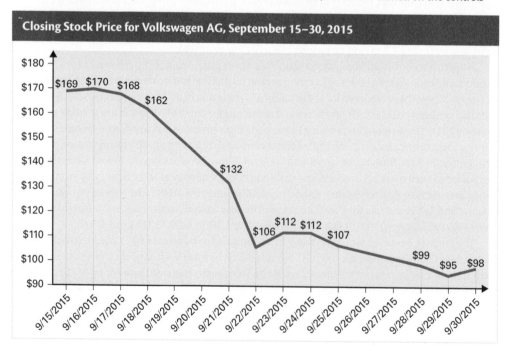

Closing Stock Price for Volkswagen AG, September 15–30, 2015

permitting higher mileage and power, but also causing the car to emit up to forty times the NOx permitted under U.S. law.[68] Two days later, Winterkorn issued a videotaped apology saying, "I personally am deeply sorry that we have broken the trust of our customers and the public," and he added, "We will cooperate fully with the responsible agencies, with transparency and urgency, to clearly, openly and completely establish all of the facts of this case."[69]

On September 22, 2015, Volkswagen revealed that roughly 11 million of its diesel vehicles worldwide had the emissions defeating devices, including Volkswagen, Audi, and Skoda cars. The company's stock price was reeling, dropping by almost 38% from September 15th through September 22nd. Under mounting pressure, Winterkorn announced his resignation on September 23, 2015, asserting that he was "stunned" by the events of "the past few days," and that he was "not aware of any wrongdoing on my part."[70]

Mueller Takes the Wheel

On September 25, 2015, Matthias Mueller, who had formerly headed Porsche, became the CEO of the Volkswagen Group. He promised he would "win back trust for the Volkswagen Group—by leaving no stone unturned and with maximum transparency, as well as drawing the right conclusions from the current situation."[71] The company immediately created a whistle-blower program for Volkswagen employees to provide information about how the tests were rigged, and promised employees that if they provided information before November 30, 2015, they would be absolved from dismissal and damages, though it could not guarantee that admitting involvement would prevent prosecution.[72] The Volkswagen Group of America returned three Cars.com awards it had won for its TDI diesel cars, and the Volkswagen Group was removed from the Dow Jones Sustainability Index, in which it had scored first place among auto manufacturers just one month prior. As the scandal continued to unfold, German newspapers revealed that internal memos within Volkswagen Group had alerted management to the emissions-defeating software in both 2007 and 2011. Volkswagen did not respond to the reports.

In October of 2015, Volkswagen Group outlined a five-step plan to address the crisis:[73]

1. It would conduct a worldwide probe to find out how the problem occurred and to hold the responsible parties accountable.
2. It would reassure the public that the vehicles were safe to drive.
3. It would develop fixes for all affected vehicles that used the 2.0-liter diesel engine.
4. It would review Volkswagen's compliance processes and standards and adopt preventative measures.
5. It would adopt regular and open communication systems with customers, dealers, employees, and the public, including a designated hotline, website, and letters to each customer.

Volkswagen would also attempt to repair all affected cars in Europe by the end of 2016, but it could not fix cars in the United States because it did not yet have a technology that would meet U.S. emission standards. Then, in November, things went from bad to worse. Volkswagen received notice from the U.S. EPA that some of its 3.0-liter engines were also found to have the defeat devices, including the 2014 Volkswagen Tuareg, 2015 Porsche Cayenne SUV, 2016 Audi A6 and A8 sedans, Audi A7 hatchback, and Audi QQ5 SUV. Furthermore, the CO_3 emissions and fuel efficiency of roughly 800,000 other Volkswagen models had been underreported.

An interview with U.S. National Public Radio in December 2015 demonstrated Mueller's uncertainty and ambivalence about how to address the crisis:

> **NPR:** You said this was a technical problem, but the American people feel this is not a technical problem, this is an ethical problem that's deep inside the company. How do you change that perception in the United States?
> **Mueller:** Frankly spoken, it was a technical problem. We made a default, we had a ... not the right interpretation of the American law. And we had some targets for our technical

engineers, and they solved this problem and reached targets with some software solutions which haven't been compatible to the American law. That is the thing. And the other question you mentioned—it was an ethical problem? I cannot understand why you say that.

NPR: Because Volkswagen, in the U.S., intentionally lied to EPA regulators when they asked them about the problem before it came to light.

Mueller: We didn't lie. We didn't understand the question first. And then we worked since 2014 to solve the problem. And we did it together and it was a default of VW that it needed such a long time.

NPR: And how do you fix the perception that's here in the U.S.—how do you change American thinking about Volkswagen. ...

Mueller: We don't want to change the American thinking. We have to make up our mind and we have to change our thinking. And we just do that.

NPR: How do we know when it's changed? How will we know when Volkswagen is different?

Mueller: How? So. ...

NPR: What's the proof?

Mueller: I'm CEO in three months, and I'm working day and night to make a change process within Volkswagen. We started this, and it needs some time. It needs, let me say, one year ... one to three years. ... For example, we have installed new board member for integrity and—Ms. [Christine] Hohmann-Dennhardt, she came from Daimler with a lot of other solutions within our company.

NPR: There were a lot of people in Congress and the [Obama] administration who are very angry with Volkswagen. What do you say to those people who are investigating and who feel like personally that the company lied to them?

Mueller: First of all, I have to apologize on behalf of Volkswagen. Second, I have to promise—and we will do the pledge—that we deliver appropriate solutions for our customers. As soon as possible.

NPR: How soon is soon?

Mueller: We have to discuss it with the EPA on Wednesday, and then we will see whether the time schedule is OK or not.

Over the next three years, prosecutors in the United States and Germany would trace responsibility for the scheme to more than 40 people spread out over at least four cities, working for three Volkswagen brands. They would also implicate supplier Robert Bosch. In the course of their investigation, they would hear evidence that, in July 2015, Winterkorn had been informed about the defeating devices by engineers and had authorized its concealment.

Numerous fines were levied, including a U.S. District Court settlement finalized on October 25, 2016, for $14.7 billion, requiring Volkswagen to notify all current owners and lessors of affected cars of a $10 billion buyback program whereby TDI owners could sell their cars back to Volkswagen for a value between $12,500 to $44,000 depending on the model, age, and trim level (lessees would receive $2,600 to $4,900). Owners who did not sell their cars back would receive between $5,100 to $10,000 to compensate them for diminished resale value, plus owners were entitled to have their emissions fixed for free. On January 11, 2017, the U.S. Department of Justice imposed an additional $4.3 billion in criminal and civil penalties to be paid by Volkswagen (in total the United States would extract roughly $25 billion in fines from Volkswagen). Canada and South Korea would also fine the company, and though the European governments were less aggressive in seeking financial penalties, eventually Germany fined the company approximately €1.2 billion. Perhaps more significantly, a total of eight executives of Volkswagen were charged with crimes in the United States, with several being assigned prison sentences, and Germany was investigating dozens more, leaving many wondering how far and how high up the Volkswagen hierarchy the punishments would go.[74]

Case Discussion Questions

1. What were some of the potential harms created by Volkswagen cheating the emissions test?
2. What missteps do you think Volkswagen's management team made in handling the scandal when the cheating was discovered?
3. What steps would you recommend for Volkswagen to take to rebuild its reputation with consumers and regulators?

Notes

[1]P. R. Keefe, "2017. The Family That Built an Empire of Pain," *New Yorker*, October 23, 2017.

[2]P. R. Keefe, "The Family That Built an Empire of Pain," *New Yorker*, October 23, 2017.

[3]A. Van Zee, "The Promotion and Marketing of OxyContin: Commercial Triumph, Public Health Tragedy," *American Journal of Public Health*, 99:2 (2009): 221–227.

[4]A. Van Zee, "The Promotion and Marketing of OxyContin: Commercial Triumph, Public Health Tragedy," *American Journal of Public Health*, 99:2 (2009): 221–227.

[5]Howard Koh, quoted in 2022 interview, "What Led to the Opioid Crisis—and How to Fix It," Harvard School of Public Health, February 9, 2022, https://www.hsph.harvard.edu/news/features/what-led-to-the-opioid-crisis-and-how-to-fix-it/

[6]Number of National Drug Overdose Deaths Involving Select Prescription and Illicit Drugs, National Institute of Health: National Institute on Drug Abuse, https://nida.nih.gov/research-topics/trends-statistics/overdose-death-rates. Retrieved August 12, 2022; https://www.cdc.gov/nchs/pressroom/nchs_press_releases/2021/20211117.htm

[7]https://www.cdc.gov/opioids/basics/epidemic.html

[8]Z. Siegel, "What Did the Sacklers Know?" *New Republic*, April 23, 2021.

[9]J. Hoffman, "Sacklers Face Furious Questions in Rare Testimony on Opioid Epidemic," *New York Times*, December 17, 2020.

[10]United States Department of Justice, "Opioid Manufacturer Purdue Pharma Pleads Guilty to Fraud and Kickback Conspiracies," November 24, 2020.

[11]E. Freeman, *Strategic Management: A Stakeholder Approach* (Boston: Pitman Press, 1984).

[12]C. W. L. Hill and T. M. Jones, "Stakeholder-Agency Theory," *Journal of Management Studies* 29 (1992): 131–154; J. G. March and H. A. Simon, *Organizations* (New York: Wiley, 1958).

[13]W. Henisz, S. Dorobantu, and L. Nartey, "Spinning Gold: The Financial Returns to Stakeholder Engagement," *Strategic Management Journal*, 35 (2014): 1727–1748.

[14]Hill and Jones, "Stakeholder-Agency Theory; C. Eesley and M. J. Lenox, "Firm Responses to Secondary Stakeholder Action," *Strategic Management Journal* 27 (2006): 13–24.

[15]I. C. Macmillan and P. E. Jones, *Strategy Formulation: Power and Politics* (St. Paul: West, 1986).

[16]https://corporate.publix.com/careers/why-publix/benefits.

[17]T. Copeland, T. Koller, and J. Murrin, *Valuation: Measuring and Managing the Value of Companies* (New York: Wiley, 1996).

[18]R. S. Kaplan and D. P. Norton, *Strategy Maps* (Boston: Harvard Business School Press, 2004).

[19]J. S. Harrison, D. A. Bosse, and R. A. Phillips, "Managing for Stakeholders, Stakeholder Utility Functions, and Competitive Advantage," *Strategic Management Journal* 31 (2010): 58–74.

[20]R. Garcia-Castro, and R. Aguilera, "Increasing Value Creation and Appropriation in a World with Multiple Stakeholders," *Strategic Management Journal*, 36 (2015): 137–147.

[21]F, Berg J. F. Kolbel, and R. Rigobon, "Aggregate Confusion: The Divergence of ESG Ratings," forthcoming in the *Review of Finance*.

[22]A. Ramkumar, "Some GOP States Push Back Against ESG Investing Trend," *Wall Street Journal*, August 30, 2022. "The ESG Investing Backlash Arrives," *Wall Street Journal*, August 15, 2022.

[23]B. Atkins, "Demystifying ESG: Its History & Current Status," *Forbes*, June 8, 2020; T., Whelan, U. Atz, T. Van Holt, and C. Clark, "ESG and Financial Performance: Uncovering the Relationship by Aggregating Evidence from 1,000 Plus Studies Published between 2015–2020." NYU Stern School of Business, Center for Sustainable Business.

[24]M. C. Jensen and W. H. Meckling, "Theory of the Firm: Managerial Behavior, Agency Costs and Ownership Structure," *Journal of Financial Economics* 3 (1976): 305–360, and E. F. Fama, "Agency Problems and the Theory of the Firm," *Journal of Political Economy* 88 (1980): 375–390.

[25]Hill and Jones, "Stakeholder-Agency Theory."

[26]For example, see R. Marris, *The Economic Theory of Managerial Capitalism* (London: Macmillan, 1964), and J. K. Galbraith, *The New Industrial State* (Boston: Houghton Mifflin, 1970).

[27]Fama, "Agency Problems and the Theory of the Firm."

[28]A. Rappaport, "New Thinking on How to Link Executive Pay with Performance," *Harvard Business Review*—March–April 1999, pp. 91–105.

[29]D. Rushe, "Wage Gap between CEOs and US Workers Jumped to 670-to-1 Last Year, Study Finds," *The Guardian*, June 7, 2022.

[30]For academic studies that look at the determinants of CEO pay, see M. C. Jensen and K. J. Murphy, "Performance Pay and Top Management Incentives," *Journal of Political Economy* 98 (1990): 225–264; Charles W. L. Hill and Phillip Phan, "CEO Tenure as a Determinant of CEO Pay," *Academy of Management Journal* 34 (1991): 707–717; H. L. Tosi and L. R. Gomez-Mejia, "CEO Compensation Monitoring and Firm Performance," *Academy of Management Journal* 37 (1994): 1002–1016; J. F. Porac, J. B. Wade, and T. G. Pollock, "Industry Categories and the Politics of the Comparable Firm in CEO Compensation," *Administrative Science Quarterly* 44 (1999): 112–144.

[31]J. Silver-Greenberg and A. Leondis, "CBS Overpaid Moonves $28 Million, Says Study of CEO Pay," *Bloomberg News*, May 6, 2010.

[32]"'Pay for Performance' No Longer a Punchline," *Wall Street Journal*, March 20, 2013.

[33]For research on this issue, see P. J. Lane, A. A. Cannella, and M. H. Lubatkin, "Agency Problems as Antecedents to Unrelated Mergers and Diversification: Amihud and Lev Reconsidered," *Strategic Management Journal* 19 (1998): 555–578.

[34]M. Saltmarsh and E. Pfanner, "French Court Convicts Executives in Vivendi Case," *New York Times*, January 21, 2011.

[35]E. T. Penrose, *The Theory of the Growth of the Firm* (London: Macmillan, 1958).

[36]G. Edmondson and L. Cohn, "How Parmalat Went Sour," *Bloomberg Businessweek*, January 12, 2004, pp. 46–50; and "Another Enron? Royal Dutch Shell," *Economist*, March 13, 2004, p. 71.

[37]O. E. Williamson, *The Economic Institutions of Capitalism* (New York: Free Press, 1985).

[38]Fama, "Agency Problems and the Theory of the Firm."

[39]S. Finkelstein and R. D'Aveni, "CEO Duality as a Double-Edged Sword," *Academy of Management Journal* 37 (1994): 1079–1108; and B. Ram Baliga and R. C. Moyer, "CEO Duality and Firm Performance," *Strategic Management Journal* 17 (1996): 41–53; M. L. Mace, *Directors: Myth and Reality* (Cambridge: Harvard University Press, 1971); and S. C. Vance, *Corporate Leadership: Boards of Directors and Strategy* (New York: McGraw-Hill, 1983).

[40]P. Temple-West, "Zombie Invasion Stalks US Boardrooms," *Financial Times*, November 1, 2020.

[41]A. Kidwai, "The Dual CEO-Chairman Role Is Losing Favor on Public Boards," *Fortune*, July 15, 2022.

[42]W. G. Lewellen, C. Eoderer, and A. Rosenfeld, "Merger Decisions and Executive Stock Ownership in Acquiring Firms," *Journal of Accounting and Economics* 7 (1985): 209–231.

[43]C. W. L. Hill and S. A. Snell, "External Control, Corporate Strategy, and Firm Performance," *Strategic Management Journal* 9 (1988): 577–590.

[44]The phenomenon of back dating stock options was uncovered by academic research, and then picked up by the SEC. See Erik Lie, "On the Timing of CEO Stock Option Awards," *Management Science* 51 (2005): 802–812.

[45]G. Colvin, "A Study in CEO Greed," *Fortune*, June 12, 2006, pp. 53–55.

[46]J. Rogerson, J. Rennie, and W. Corbett-Graham, "HP v Autonomy: The 'Fake It 'till We Make It' Start-up Culture on Trial." White & Case, May 2022.

[47]J. P. Walsh and R. D. Kosnik, "Corporate Raiders and Their Disciplinary Role in the Market for Corporate Control," *Academy of Management Journal* 36 (1993): 671–700.

[48]J. Surroca, J. A. Tribó, and S. A. Zahr, "Stakeholder Pressure on MNEs and the Transfer of Socially Irresponsible Practices to Subsidiaries," *Academy of Management Journal*, 56 (2015): 549–572.

[49]"Timet, Boeing Settle Lawsuit," *Metal Center News* 41 (June 2001): 38–39.

[50]S. Mistreanu, "Study Links Nike, Adidas and Apple to Forced Uighur Labor," *Forbes*, March 2, 2020; V. Xu, D. Cave, J. Leibold, K. Munro, and N. Ruser, "Uyghurs for Sale," Australian Strategic Policy Institute, March 1, 2020.

[51]J. Marsh, "7 Companies Facing Environmental Issues in 2020," www.environment.co April 13, 2020.

[52]N. King, "Halliburton Tells the Pentagon Workers Took Iraq Deal Kickbacks," *Wall Street Journal*, 2004, p. A1; "Whistleblowers Say Company Routinely Overcharged," *Reuters*, February 12, 2004; and R. Gold and J. R. Wilke, "Data Sought in Halliburton Inquiry," *Wall Street Journal*, 2004, p. A6.

[53]L. Jieqi and Z. Hejuan, "Siemens Bribery Scandal Ends in Death Sentence," *Caixin Online*, June 30, 2011.

[54]S. W. Gellerman, "Why Good Managers Make Bad Ethical Choices," *Ethics in Practice: Managing the Moral Corporation*, ed.

K. R. Andrews (Harvard Business School Press, 1989).

[55]Ibid.

[56]"Wounded Unicorn: Sentiment Analysis Highlights How Badly Theranos Has Been Destroyed in the Press," CBInsights, October 16, 2015.

[57]J. Carreyrou, "Hot Startup Theranos Has Struggled with Its Blood-Test Technology," *Wall Street Journal*, April 6, 2015; L. F. Friedman and K. Loria, "A Scientist Just Raised 4 Serious Questions about a Blood Test That Made Elizabeth Holms a Billionaire," *Insider*, June 26, 2021.

[58]K. Briquelet, "Theranos Tests Told Her She'd Miscarried—But She Was Still Pregnant," *The Daily Beast*, September 21, 2021.

[59]B. Allyn, "Elizabeth Holmes Verdict: Former Theranos CEO Is Found Guilty on 4 Counts," NPR, All Things Considered, January 3, 2022.

[60]S. Hopkins, "How Effective Are Ethics Codes and Programs?," *Financial Executive*, March 2013.

[61]www.unilever.com/company /ourprinciples/.

[62]www.utc.com/governance/ethics.

[63]"History," www.volswagenag .com, accessed October 12, 2018.

[64]S. Glinton, "Automakers Give Disregarded Diesels a Second Look," National Public Radio, All Things Considered, January 30, 2012.

[65]M. Schuetz, "Dieselgate— Heavy Fumes Exhausting the Volkswagen Group," Asia Case Research Centre, case #HK1089, 2016.

[66]S. Glinton, "How a Little Lab in West Virginia Caught Volkswagen's Big Cheat," National Public Radio, Morning Edition, September 24, 2015.

[67]P. Whoriskey and J, Warrick, "Anatomy of Volkswagen's Deception: The Recall That Never Fixed Any Cars," *The Washington Post*, September 22, 2015.

[68]C. Atiyeh, "Everything You Need to Know About the VW Diesel-Emissions Scandal," *Car and Driver*, October 9, 2018.

[69]B. Visnic, "As CEO Apologizes for Emissions Cheating, VW Halts Sales of Some Diesels in U.S.," *Forbes*, September 20, 2015.

[70]R. Parloff "How VW Paid $25 Billion for 'Dieselgate'—And Got Off Easy," *Fortune*, February 6, 2014.

[71]K. Mays, "VW Diesel Crisis: Timeline of Events," Cars.com, September 23, 2015.

[72]A. Cremer "Volkswagen sets end-November deadline for scandal whistleblowers," Reuters, November 13, 2015.

[73]Schuetz, "Dieselgate—Heavy Fumes Exhausting the Volkswagen Group."

[74]R. Parloff,, "How VW Paid $25 Billion for 'Dieselgate'—And Got Off Easy," *Fortune*, February 6, 2018.

Chapter

12

Implementing Strategy Through Organization

Learning Objectives

12.1 Explain the concept of organizational architecture.

12.2 Discuss the different dimensions of a company's organizational structure, including centralization and decentralization, integrating mechanisms, and the various structural forms a company can use.

12.3 Discuss the various control systems and incentive mechanisms that a company can use.

12.4 Review the concept of organization culture and explain why it is important for strategy implementation.

12.5 Explain the importance of organizational processes for strategy implementation.

12.6 Discuss how the appropriate organization design enables a company to better implement its business and corporate-level strategies.

Opening Case

Amazon's Agile Team-Based Structure

In 2017 Amazon's founder and then CEO, Jeff Bezos, asked a basic question in his letter to shareholders; "What does Day 2 (in the life of a company) look like?" According to Bezos, Day 2 is stasis. It is the beginning of the end. It is followed by irrelevance, then decline, then death. And that, says Bezos, is why at Amazon it is always Day 1. Bezos point is that for Amazon to survive, it must create a culture, and an organization, where there is always a "Day 1" start-up mentality. In his view, customer focus, quick decision making, and constant innovation are required to avoid becoming a Day 2 company. Bezos has a point. Recent research has documented how companies that were in the *Fortune* 500 between 2000 and 2009 had only a 63% chance of survival. The high failure rate of established corporations was found to derive from inflexible, non-agile business models and a lack of innovation.

So how does a behemoth like Amazon—with $470 billion in revenues and 1.6 million employees in 2021—organize for customer focus, quick decision making, and innovation? How does the company avoid becoming a rigid bureaucracy with a formal reporting structure that inhibits innovation? How does it avoid becoming a Day 2 company? An answer can be found in Amazon's reliance on an agile team structure and adaptive practices to innovate on behalf of customers.

At Amazon, teams emerge when an employee sees an opportunity. The opportunity can be big—such as Amazon's Alexa, Kindle reader, Fire Tablet, Fire TV, or Prime application for the iPhone—or it can be one of numerous smaller opportunities. The employee then must recruit other team members, and an executive sponsor. The employee can go outside of their existing team, or division, to find other employees interested in their idea. They can also shop their idea around until they find a senior manager to sponsor their project. If their immediate boss declines to sponsor the idea, there is nothing to stop the employee pitching it to other senior managers within Amazon. Thus, in a Darwinian process, proto teams compete for sponsorship and resources.

When building a team, there are several key principles that must be adhered to. First, the team must be kept small. This is Amazon's famous "Two Pizza" rule, where a team can be no bigger than the number of people who can consume two pizzas, or 8–10 people. If the problem becomes too big for one team to handle, it is broken down into components and other "Two Pizza" teams are created. Second, each team must have a "Single Thread Owner," or STO. This is a senior manager, often the sponsor, who is responsible for that team, protects it from competing priorities, and helps to get resources (an STO can "own" several teams at the same time, although for important projects, the STO might be focused on just that team). Third, each team must be "open" in the sense that other teams within Amazon can access its data electronically. This open access is an important mechanism for enabling teams to connect with each other, providing coordination between teams

©Mike Kane/Bloomberg/Getty Images

Sources: Robin Gaster, "How Amazon Uses Agile Teams to Secure Its Rise to Power," *Business Insider*, April 14, 2021; Beth Galetti, John Golden, and Stephen Brozovich, "Insider Day 1: How Amazon Uses Agile Team Structures and Adaptive Practices to Innovate on Behalf of Customers," *SHRM Executive Network*, Spring 2019; Janson del Rey, "The Amazonification of the American Workforce," *Vox*, April 21, 2022.

without establishing formal hierarchical mechanisms or liaison roles—that is, without putting a Day 2 bureaucracy in place.

Fourth, each team must adopt a "working backward" process to product development. The notion is that every idea starts by thinking about how to delight customers, and teams must work backward from that to create an offering. As part of Amazon's working backward process, each team must write a detailed press release, describing the new features, products, or services, and what they do for customers, *before* work begins on developing the offering. Put differently, the end point must be defined before the development work begins. In addition to the press release, there must be a document addressing Frequently Asked Questions. This is also written *before* development work starts. The FAQ document is meant to flesh out how the new offering will work and how Amazon will execute.

Amazon has an annual strategic and operational planning process for teams that lays out their goals, investments, and resource requirements for the coming year. STOs then audit the performance of teams against goals on a regular basis throughout the year, often monthly and sometimes weekly, updating plans as they go along. This process provides senior leadership with visibility on the progress of teams and allows for adjustments as needed.

As a project develops, and an offering reaches customers, teams may evolve into fully independent entities within Amazon's organization, each with their own marketing, sales, engineering, and finance functions, and each with their own profit and loss statements, so that they have both autonomy and accountability.

Overview

Earlier in this book, we noted that strategy is implemented through the organizational arrangements of a firm and through actions taken at the functional level. We discussed the functional actions required to implement different *business-level strategies* in Chapter 5. In this chapter, we look at how organizational arrangements are used to implement the business-, corporate-, and global-level strategies of an enterprise.

The Opening Case illustrates some of the issues that we shall be discussing in this chapter. Amazon has grown into one of the largest organizations in the world by continuing to innovate—constantly developing new goods and services for its customers that improve the efficiency and effectiveness of its operations. It is a large company that has maintained a small company start-up mentality. It has been able to do this by organizing in a particular way that allows for the autonomous formation of agile customer-focused product development teams within Amazon. Put differently, its organization is explicitly designed to encourage innovation, to empower teams created by employees, and to discourage the formation of a rigid bureaucracy that can inhibit the pursuit of new initiatives. Amazon's strategy of continuous innovation to keep customers happy is executed through its organization.

12-1 Organizational Architecture

12.1 Explain the concept of organizational architecture.

In this chapter, we use the term **organizational architecture** to refer to the totality of a firm's organizational arrangements, including its formal organizational structure, control systems, incentive systems, organizational culture, organizational

organizational architecture

The totality of a firm's organizational arrangements, including its formal organizational structure, control systems, incentive systems, organizational culture, organizational processes, and human capital.

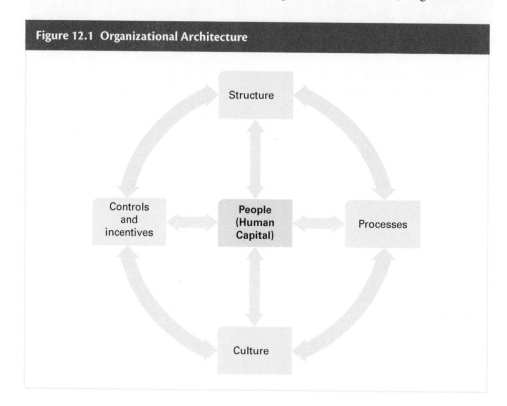

Figure 12.1 Organizational Architecture

processes, and people (or human capital).[1] Figure 12.1 illustrates these different elements.

By **organizational structure**, we mean three things: First, the location of decision-making responsibilities in the firm (e.g., centralized or decentralized); second, the formal division of the organization into subunits such as functions, product divisions, and national operations; and third, the establishment of integrating mechanisms to coordinate the activities of subunits.

Controls are the metrics used to measure the performance of subunits and make judgments about how well managers are running those subunits. **Incentives** are the devices used to encourage desired employee behavior. Incentives are very closely tied to performance metrics. For example, the incentives of a manager in charge of 3M's office supplies business might be linked to the performance of that division.

Organizational processes refer to the way decisions are made, and work is performed within the organization. Examples include the processes for formulating strategy, for deciding how to allocate resources within a firm, for developing new products, and for evaluating the performance of managers and giving feedback. Processes are conceptually distinct from the location of decision-making responsibilities within an organization, although both involve decisions. For example, while the CEO might have the ultimate responsibility for deciding on the firm's strategy (that is, the decision-making responsibility is centralized), the *process* they use to make that decision might include the solicitation of ideas and criticism from lower-level managers and employees.

Organizational culture refers to the norms and value systems that are shared among the employees of an organization. Just as societies have cultures, so do organizations. Organizations are societies of individuals who come together to perform collective tasks. They have their own distinctive patterns of culture and subculture.[2] As we shall see, organizational culture can have a profound impact on a firm's performance. As noted in the Opening Case, for example, Amazon has a customer-focused culture. This culture is reinforced through a process that require team members to work backward from an assessment of customer needs when developing new products.

Finally, by **people** we mean not just the employees of the organization, but also the strategy used to recruit, compensate, motivate, and retain those individuals, as well as the type of people that they are in terms of their skills, values, and orientation. Collectively, the people within an organization, the employees, constitute the human capital of an enterprise. We have already discussed the role of human resources in recruiting, training, developing, and compensating employees to execute the strategy of the firm in Chapters 3 and 5. We will not repeat that discussion here. However, it is important to note that the value of an organization's human capital is more than the sum of each individual employee's skills and capabilities. Much of the value is *contextual* in the sense that employees can achieve things within an organization that would not be possible if they were working as independent contractors. Put differently, the other elements of the architecture of an organization may create an environment within which it is possible for people to do extraordinary things.

For example, Johnny Ive, who was the head of product design at Apple from 1997 to 2019, is clearly a remarkably skilled individual. However, Ive probably could not have had the impact that he has without the benefit of working within Apple, where the structure, control systems, incentives, decision-making processes, and culture all supported what he was trying to do in terms of developing elegantly designed digital devices that are as much a fashion statement as they are a computing tool. Much of Ive's human capital, in other words, was the result of the *combination* of his skills and Apple's organizational architecture.

As suggested by this example, and as illustrated by the arrows in Figure 12.1, the various components of organization architecture are not independent of each other: Each component shapes, and is shaped by, other components of architecture. Again, an obvious example is the strategy regarding people. Human resources can proactively hire individuals whose internal values are consistent with those that the firm emphasizes in its

organizational structure

The combination of the location of decision-making responsibilities, the formal division of the organization into subunits, and the establishment of integrating mechanisms to coordinate the activities of the subunits.

controls

The metrics used to measure the performance of subunits and make judgments about how well managers are running them.

incentives

The devices used to encourage desired employee behavior.

organizational processes

The manner in which decisions are made and work is performed within the organization.

organizational culture

The norms and value systems that are shared among the employees of an organization.

people

The employees of an organization, as well as the strategy used to recruit, compensate, motivate, and retain those individuals; also refers to employees' skills, values, and orientation.

organizational culture. The people component of architecture can be used to reinforce the prevailing culture of the organization. A business enterprise endeavoring to attain a competitive advantage and maximize its performance must pay close attention to achieving internal consistency between the various components of its architecture, and the architecture must support the strategy and functional activities of the enterprise.

12-2 Organizational Structure

12.2 Discuss the different dimensions of a company's organizational structure, including centralization and decentralization, integrating mechanisms, and the various structural forms a company can use.

Organizational structure can be thought of in terms of three dimensions. The first is **vertical differentiation**, which refers to the location of decision-making responsibilities within a structure (that is, centralization or decentralization), and also to the number of layers in a hierarchy (that is, whether the organizational structure is tall or flat). The second is **horizontal differentiation**, which refers to the formal division of the organization into subunits. The third is the establishment of **integrating mechanisms** for coordinating subunits. We will discuss each in turn.

12-2a Centralization and Decentralization

vertical differentiation

The location of decision-making responsibilities within a structure, referring to centralization or decentralization, and also the number of layers in a hierarchy, referring to whether the organizational structure is tall or flat.

horizontal differentiation

The formal division of the organization into subunits.

integrating mechanisms

Processes and procedures used for coordination subunits.

centralization

Structure in which decision-making authority is concentrated at a high level in the management hierarchy.

decentralization

Structure in which decision-making authority is distributed to lower-level managers or other employees.

A firm's vertical differentiation determines where in its hierarchy decision-making power is concentrated.[3] Are production and marketing decisions centralized in the offices of upper-level managers, or are they decentralized to lower-level managers? Where does the responsibility for R&D decisions lie? Are important strategic and financial decisions pushed down to operating units, or are they concentrated in the hands of top management? And so on. There are arguments for centralization, and other arguments for decentralization. **Centralization** is a condition where decision-making authority is concentrated at a high level in a management hierarchy. **Decentralization** is a condition where decision-making authority is vested in lower-level managers or other employees.

Arguments for Centralization   There are four main arguments for centralization. First, it can facilitate coordination. For example, consider a firm that that has a component manufacturing operation in California and a final assembly operation in Seattle. The activities of these two operations need to be coordinated to ensure a smooth flow of products from the component operation to the assembly operation. This might be achieved by centralizing production scheduling at the firm's head office.

Second, centralization can help ensure that decisions are consistent with organizational objectives. When decisions are decentralized to lower-level managers, those managers may make decisions at variance with top management's goals. Centralization of important decisions minimizes the chance of this occurring. Major strategic decisions, for example, may be centralized in an effort to make sure that the entire organization is pulling in the same direction. In this sense, centralization is a way of controlling the organization.

Third, centralization can avoid the duplication of activities that occurs when similar activities are carried on by various subunits within the organization. For example, some firms centralize their R&D functions at one or two locations to ensure that R&D work is not duplicated. Similarly, production activities may be centralized at key locations to eliminate duplication, attain economies of scale, and lower costs. The same may also be true of purchasing decisions. Walmart, for example, has centralized all purchasing decisions at its Bentonville headquarters in Arkansas. By wielding its enormous bargaining power, purchasing managers at the head office can drive down the costs that Walmart pays for the goods it sells in its stores. It then passes on those savings to consumers in the form of lower prices, which enables the company to grow its market share and profits.

Fourth, by concentrating power and authority in one individual or a management team, centralization can give top-level managers the means to bring about needed major organizational changes. Often, firms seeking to transform their organizations centralize power and authority in a key individual (or group), who then sets the new strategic direction for the firm and redraws organizational architecture. Once the new strategy and architecture have been decided upon, however, greater decentralization of decision making normally follows. Put differently, the *temporary* centralization of decision-making power is often an important step in organizational change.

Arguments for Decentralization   There are five main arguments for decentralization. First, top management can become overburdened when decision-making authority is centralized. Centralization increases the amount of information that senior managers must process, and this can result in information overload and poor decision making.[4] Decentralization gives top management time to focus on critical issues by delegating more routine issues to lower-level managers and reducing the amount of information top managers must process.

Second, motivational research favors decentralization. Behavioral scientists have long argued that people are willing to give more to their jobs when they have a greater degree of individual freedom and control over their work. The idea behind employee empowerment is that if you give employees more responsibility for their jobs, they will work harder, increasing productivity and reducing costs.

Third, decentralization permits greater flexibility—more rapid response to environmental changes. In a centralized firm, the need to refer decisions up the hierarchy for approval can significantly impede the speed of decision making and inhibit the ability of the firm to adapt to rapid environmental changes.[5] This can put the firm at a competitive disadvantage. Managers deal with this by decentralizing decisions to lower levels within the organization. Thus, at Walmart, while purchasing decisions are centralized so that the firm can realize economies of scale in purchasing, routine pricing and stocking decisions are decentralized to individual store managers who have some control over pricing and decide upon the products to stock depending on local conditions. This enables store managers to respond quickly to changes in their local environment, such as a drop in demand or actions by a local competitor. Similarly, as described in the Opening Case, Amazon has decentralized responsibility for identifying and developing new product opportunities to autonomous teams within its organization. Amazon argues that these autonomous teams make it more agile than corporations where product development decisions are centralized.

Fourth, decentralization can result in better decisions. In a decentralized structure, decisions are made closer to the spot by individuals who (presumably) have better information than managers several levels up a hierarchy. It might make little sense for the CEO of Procter & Gamble to make marketing decisions for the detergents business in Germany because they are unlikely to have the relevant expertise and information. Instead, those decisions are decentralized to local marketing managers, who are far more likely to be in tune with the German market.

Fifth, decentralization can increase control and be used to establish relatively autonomous, self-contained subunits within an organization. An **autonomous subunit** is one that has all the resources and decision-making power required to run the operation on a day-to-day basis. Managers of autonomous subunits can be held accountable for subunit performance. The more responsibility subunit managers have for decisions that impact subunit performance, the fewer excuses they have for poor performance and the more accountable they are. Thus, by giving store managers the ability to hire local employees, set some prices and make merchandising decisions, Walmart's top managers can hold local store managers accountable for the performance of their stores. This increases the ability of top managers to control the organization. Just as centralization is one way of maintaining control in an organization, decentralization is another.

autonomous subunit

A subunit that has all the resources and decision-making power required to run the operation on a day-to-day basis.

The Choice Between Decentralization and Centralization   The choice between centralization and decentralization is not absolute. Frequently, it makes sense to centralize some decisions and decentralize others, depending on the type of decision and the firm's strategy. We have already noted how Walmart centralized purchasing decisions and decentralized pricing and stocking decisions. Similarly, Microsoft has centralized major development activities for its Windows operating system at its Redmond corporate campus but has decentralized responsibility for marketing and sales to local managers in each country and region where it does business. Although the choice between centralization and decentralization depends upon the circumstances being considered, a few important generalizations can be made.

First, decisions regarding overall firm strategy, major financial expenditures, financial objectives, and legal issues are centralized at the senior-management level in most organizations. Functional decisions relating to production, marketing, R&D, and human resource management may or may not be centralized depending on the firm's strategy and environmental conditions.

Second, when the realization of economies of scale is an important factor, there tends to be greater centralization. Purchasing and manufacturing decisions are often centralized to eliminate duplication and realize scale economies. In contrast, sales decisions tend to be more decentralized because economies of scale are less of a consideration here.

Third, when local adaptation is important, decentralization is typically favored. When there are substantial differences between conditions in local markets, marketing and sales decisions will often be decentralized to local marketing and sales managers. Multinational, consumer products firms such as Unilever centralize decisions about manufacturing and purchasing to realize scale economies but decentralize marketing and sales decisions to local brand managers in different countries precisely because competitive conditions differ from country to country and local adaptation is required.[6]

Finally, decentralization is favored in environments characterized by high uncertainty and rapid change. When competitive conditions in a firm's market are changing rapidly, with new technologies and competitors emerging in ways that are difficult to anticipate, centralization, because it slows down decision making, can put a firm at a competitive disadvantage. Due to this, many high-tech firms operate with a greater degree of decentralization than firms operating in more predictable environments.[7] At Amazon, for example, lower-level employees are given the ability to develop new business ideas and the right to lobby top managers for the funds to develop those ideas (see the Opening Case). Such decentralization of strategy making might not be found in firms operating in a more stable environment such as the automobile industry. For a vivid example of the costs of making the wrong choice between centralization and decentralization, see Strategy in Action 12.1 on FEMA and Hurricane Katrina.

12-2b Tall Versus Flat Hierarchies

A second aspect of vertical differentiation refers to the number of levels in an organization hierarchy. **Tall hierarchies** have many layers of management, while **flat hierarchies** have very few layers (see Figure 12.2). Most firms start out small, often with only one or at most two layers in the hierarchy. As they grow, management finds that there is a limit to the amount of information they can process and the control they can exert over day-to-day operations. To avoid being stretched too thin and losing control, they tend to add another layer to the management hierarchy, hiring more managers and delegating some decision-making authority to them. In other words, as an organization gets larger it tends to become taller. In addition, growing

tall hierarchies

An organizational structure with many layers of management.

flat hierarchies

An organizational structure with very few layers of management.

FEMA and Hurricane Katrina

A vivid example of the costs of making the wrong choice between centralization and decentralization occurred in 2005, when the Federal Emergency Management Agency (FEMA) responded to the devastating impact that Hurricane Katrina had on New Orleans. The hurricane flooded much of the city and resulted in a mandatory evacuation. However, FEMA, the Federal agency responsible for disaster relief, was widely criticized for being very slow to respond to the plight of the hundreds of thousands of mostly poor people who had been made homeless. For several days, while thousands of homeless people huddled in the New Orleans Superdome, lacking food and adequate sanitary facilities, FEMA was nowhere to be seen.

A postmortem revealed that one reason for FEMA's slow response was that the once-autonomous agency had been placed under the direct supervision of the Department of Homeland Security after September 11, 2001. FEMA officials apparently felt that they had to discuss relief efforts with their superiors before proceeding. This cost the agency crucial time in the early hours of the disaster and significantly slowed its response, meaning that the relief effort was less effective than it might have been. In addition, FEMA was poorly managed. Its head, Mike Brown, a political appointee, had no experience in disaster relief. Moreover, the agency had been gutted by budget cuts.

In a report that was highly critical of FEMA, a U.S. Senate committee that was charged with reviewing the response to Katrina cited a "failure of agility" and concluded that response plans at all levels of government lacked flexibility and adaptability, which often delayed response. In other words, decision making was too centralized, bureaucratic, and inflexible. Decentralization would have helped enormously in this case.

Sources: "A Failure to Innovate: Final Report of the Select Bipartisan Committee to Investigate the Preparation for and Response to Hurricane Katrina," United States Government Printing Office, February 17, 2006; *The Economist*, "When Government Fails—Katrina's Aftermath," September 2005, p. 25.

organizations often undertake more activities, expanding their product line, diversifying into adjacent activities, vertically integrating, or expanding into new regional or national markets. This too creates problems of coordination and control, and once again the organization's response often is to add another management layer. Adding levels in the hierarchy is a problem that mounts when managers have too much work to do. The number of layers added is also partly determined by the span of control that managers can effectively handle.

Figure 12.2 Tall Versus Flat Hierarchies

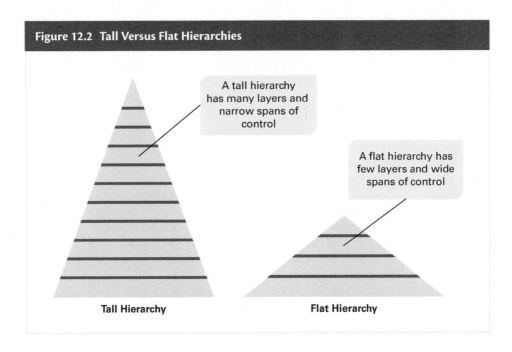

A tall hierarchy has many layers and narrow spans of control

A flat hierarchy has few layers and wide spans of control

Tall Hierarchy

Flat Hierarchy

span of control

The number of a manager's direct reports.

Span of Control The term span of control refers to the number of direct reports that a manager has. At one time, it was thought that the optimal span of control was six subordinates.[8] The argument was that, if a manager was responsible for more than six subordinates, they would soon lose track of what was going on and control loss would occur. Now we recognize that the relationship is not this simple. The number of direct reports a manger can handle depends upon (1) the nature of the work being supervised, (2) the extent to which the performance of subordinates is visible, and/or (3) the extent of decentralization within the organization. Generally, if the work being performed by subordinates is routine, their performance is visible and easy to measure, and/or they are empowered to make many decisions and need not refer up the hierarchy for approval or consultation, managers can operate with a wide span of control. How wide is the subject of debate, but it does seem as if managers can effectively handle as many as 20 direct reports if the circumstances permit.

In sum, as organizations grow and undertake more activities, the management hierarchy tends to be come taller, but how tall depends upon the span of control that is feasible, and that in turn depends upon the nature of the work being performed, the visibility of subordinate performance, and the extent of decentralization within the organization. It is important to note that managers can influence the visibility of subunit performance and the extent of decentralization through organization design, thereby limiting the impact of organization size and diversity on the size of a management hierarchy. This is significant, because we know that while adding layers to an organization can reduce the workload of higher-level managers and attenuate control loss, tall hierarchies have their own problems.

Problems in Tall Hierarchies Several problems can occur in tall hierarchies that may result in lower organizational efficiency and effectiveness. First, there is a tendency for information to get *accidentally distorted* as it passes through layers in a hierarchy. The phenomenon is familiar to anyone who has played the game "telephone," in which players sit in a circle and each whispers a message to the person sitting next to them, who then whispers the message to the next person, and so on around the room. Often, by the time the message has been transmitted through all the players, it has become distorted, and its meaning has changed (this can have amusing consequences, which of course is the point of the game). Human beings are not adept at transmitting information; we tend to embellish or omit data. In a management context, if critical information must pass through many layers in a tall hierarchy before it reaches critical decision makers, it may well get distorted in the process, resulting in a message that differs from the one originally sent. As a result, decisions may be made based on inaccurate information, and poor performance may result.

In addition to the accidental distortion of information as it travels through a management hierarchy, there is also the problem of *deliberate distortion* by midlevel managers trying to curry favor with their superiors or pursue a personal agenda. For example, the manager of a division might suppress negative information while exaggerating positive information to "window dress" the performance of the unit under their control to higher-level managers and win their approval. By doing so, they may gain access to more resources, earn performance bonuses, or avoid sanctions for poor performance. All things being equal, the more layers in a hierarchy, the more opportunities exist for people to deliberately distort information. To the extent that information is distorted, once again it implies that senior managers will be making important decisions based on inaccurate information, which can result in poor performance. Economists refer to the loss of efficiency that arises from deliberate information distortions for personal gain within an organization as **influence costs**, which they argue can be a major source of low efficiency within organizations.[9]

influence costs

The loss of efficiency that arises from deliberate information distortions for personal gain within an organization.

An interesting case of information distortion in a hierarchy concerned the quality of prewar intelligence information on weapons of mass destruction in Iraq prior to the 2003 invasion by the United States and allied forces. The information on biological weapons that was used to help justify the invasion of Iraq was derived from a single Iraqi defector, code named "Curveball," who was an alcoholic and, in the view of the one person who had interviewed him, a Pentagon analyst, "utterly useless as a source." However, higher-level personnel in the intelligence community took the information provided by Curveball, stripped out the reservations expressed by the Pentagon analyst, and passed it on as high-quality intelligence to U.S. Secretary of State Colin Powell, who included the information in a speech he made to the United Nations to justify the war. Powell was apparently unaware of the highly questionable nature of the data. He stated later that had he been aware of this he would not have included it in his speech. Apparently, gatekeepers who stood between Powell and the Pentagon analyst deliberately distorted the information, presumably to further their own agenda or the agenda of other parties whose favor they were trying to curry.[10]

A third problem with tall hierarchies is that they are expensive. The salaries and benefits of multiple layers of midlevel managers can add up to significant overhead, which can increase the cost structure of the firm. Unless there is a commensurate benefit, a tall hierarchy can put a firm at a competitive disadvantage.

A final problem concerns the inherent inertia associated with a tall hierarchy. Organizations are inherently inert—that is, they are difficult to change. One cause of inertia in an organization is that, to protect their turf, and perhaps their jobs, managers often argue for the maintenance of the status quo. In tall hierarchies there is more turf, more centers of power and influence, and more voices arguing against change. Thus, tall hierarchies tend to be slow to change.

Delayering–Reducing the Size of a Hierarchy Many firms attempt to limit the size of the management hierarchy. **Delayering** to reduce the number of levels in a management hierarchy has become a standard component of many attempts to boost a firm's performance.[11] Delayering assumes that when times are good, many firms tend to expand their management hierarchies beyond the point at which it is efficient to do so. However, the bureaucratic inefficiencies associated with a tall hierarchy become evident when the competitive environment becomes tougher, at which time managers seek to delayer the organization. Delayering, and simultaneously widening spans of control, is also seen as a way of enforcing greater decentralization within an organization and reaping the associated efficiency gains.

delayering
The process of reducing the number of levels in a management hierarchy.

The process of delayering was a standard feature of Jack Welch's tenure at General Electric, during which time he laid off 150,000 people and reduced the number of layers in the hierarchy from nine to five, while simultaneously growing GE's profits and revenues. Welch believed that GE had become too top heavy during the tenure of his successors. A key element of his strategy was to transform GE into a leaner, faster-moving organization, which required delayering. Welch himself had a wide span of control, with some 20 subordinates reporting directly to him, including the heads of GE's 15 top businesses. Similarly, Jeffery Immelt, the head of GE's medical-systems business under Welch, had 21 direct reports (Immelt eventually replaced Welch as CEO).[12]

12-2c Structural Forms

Most firms begin with no formal structure and are run by a single entrepreneur or a small team of individuals. As they grow, the demands of management become too great for one individual or a small team to handle. At this point, the organization is split into functions that represent different aspects of the firm's value chain (see Chapter 3).

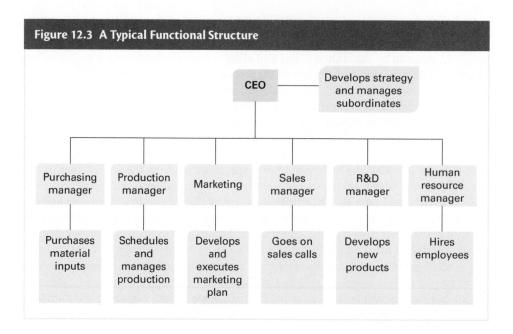

Figure 12.3 A Typical Functional Structure

Functional Structure In a **functional structure**, the structure of the organization follows the obvious *division of labor* within the firm with different functions focusing on different tasks. There might be a production function, an R&D function, a marketing function, a sales function, and so on (see Figure 12.3). A top manager, such as the CEO, or a small top-management team oversees these functions. Most single businesses of any scale are organized along functional lines.

While a functional structure can work well for a firm that is active in a single line of business, problems develop once the firm expands into different businesses. Google began as a search company but has expanded into operating systems (Android and Chrome), software applications (Google Docs), digital media distribution (Google Play), and social products (Google Plus, Blogspot). Trying to manage these different businesses within the context of a functional structure created problems of accountability, coordination, and control, so in 2015 Google transformed into Alphabet Inc. and placed each one into its own product division.[13]

Regarding control, it becomes difficult to identify the profitability of each distinct business when the activities of those businesses are scattered across various functions. It is hard to assess whether a business is performing well or poorly. Moreover, because no one individual or management team is responsible for the performance of each business, there is a lack of accountability within the organization, and this too can result in poor control. As for coordination, when the different activities that constitute a business are embedded in different functions, such as production and marketing, that are simultaneously managing multiple businesses, it can be difficult to achieve the tight coordination between functions needed to effectively run the business. Moreover, it is difficult to run a functional department if it is supervising the value creation activities of several business areas.

Multidivisional Structure The problems that we have just discussed were first recognized in the 1920s by one of the pioneers of American management thinking, Alfred Sloan, who at the time was CEO of GM, then the largest company in the world.[14] Under Sloan, GM had diversified into multiple businesses. In addition to making cars under several distinct brands, it made trucks, airplane engines, and refrigerators. After struggling to run these different businesses within the framework of a functional structure, Sloan realized that a fundamentally different structure was required. His

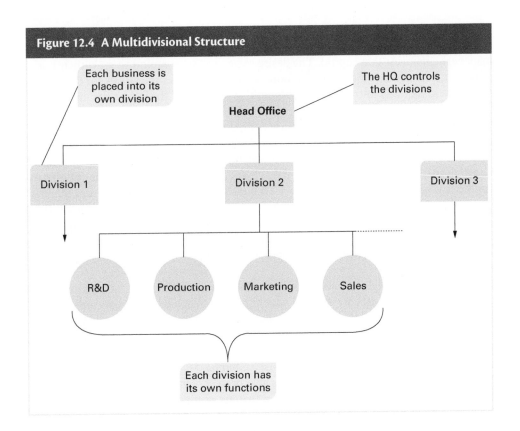

Figure 12.4 A Multidivisional Structure

Each business is placed into its own division

The HQ controls the divisions

Head Office

Division 1   Division 2   Division 3

R&D   Production   Marketing   Sales

Each division has its own functions

solution, which has since become the classic way to organize a diversified, multibusiness enterprise, was to adopt a multidivisional structure (see Figure 12.4).

In a **multidivisional structure**, the firm is divided into different divisions, each responsible for a distinct business area. The multidivisional structure has become the standard structural form for managing a diversified enterprise. In most multidivisional enterprises, each division is set up as a self-contained, largely autonomous entity with its own functions. Responsibility for functional decisions and business-level strategy is typically decentralized to the divisions, which are then held accountable for their performance. Headquarters is responsible for the overall strategic development of the firm (corporate-level strategy), for control of the various divisions, for allocating capital between divisions, for supervising and coaching the managers who run each division, and for transferring valuable knowledge between divisions.

The divisions are generally left alone to run day-to-day operations if they hit performance targets, which are typically negotiated on an annual basis between the head office and divisional management. Headquarters, however, will often help divisional managers think through their strategy. Thus, while the CEO of 3M does not develop strategy for the various businesses within 3M's portfolio (that is decentralized to divisional managers), they do probe the thinking of divisional managers to see if they have thought through their strategy. In addition, they devote effort to getting managers to share best practices across divisions, and to the formulation and implementation of strategies that span multiple businesses.

One great virtue claimed for the multidivisional structure is that it creates an internal environment where divisional managers focus on efficiency.[15] Because each division is a self-contained entity, its performance is highly visible. The high level of responsibility and accountability implies that divisional managers have few alibis for poor performance. This motivates them to focus on improving efficiency. Base pay, bonuses, and promotional opportunities for divisional managers can be tied to how

multidivisional structure

An organizational structure in which a firm is divided into divisions, each of which is responsible for a distinct business area.

well the division does. Capital is also allocated by top management between the competing divisions depending upon how effectively top management thinks the division managers can invest that capital. The desire to get access to capital to grow their businesses, and to gain pay increases and bonuses, creates further incentives for divisional managers to focus on improving the competitive position of the businesses under their control.

On the other hand, too much pressure from the head office on divisional managers to improve performance can result in some of the worst practices of management. These can include cutting necessary investments in plant, equipment, and R&D to boost short-term performance, even though such action can damage the long-term competitive position of the enterprise.[16] To guard against this possibility, top managers need to develop a good understanding of each division, set performance goals that are attainable, and acquire personnel who can regularly audit the accounts and operations of divisions to ensure that they are not being managed for short-term results or in a way that destroys their long-term competitiveness.

Matrix Structure High-technology firms based in rapidly changing environments sometimes adopt a **matrix structure** in which they try to achieve tight coordination between functions, particularly R&D, production, and marketing.[17] Tight coordination is required so that R&D designs products that (a) can be manufactured efficiently, and (b) are designed with customer needs in mind—both of which increase the probability of successful product commercialization (see Chapter 5). Tight coordination between R&D, manufacturing, and marketing has also been shown to result in a quicker product development effort, which can enable a firm to gain an advantage over its rivals.[18] As illustrated in Figure 12.5, in such an organization an employee might belong to two subunits within the firm. For example, a manager might be a member of the manufacturing function and a product development team.

A matrix structure looks nice on paper, but the reality can be very different. Unless this structure is managed very carefully it may not work well.[19] In practice, the matrix

matrix structure

An organizational structure in which managers try to achieve tight coordination between functions, particularly R&D, production, and marketing.

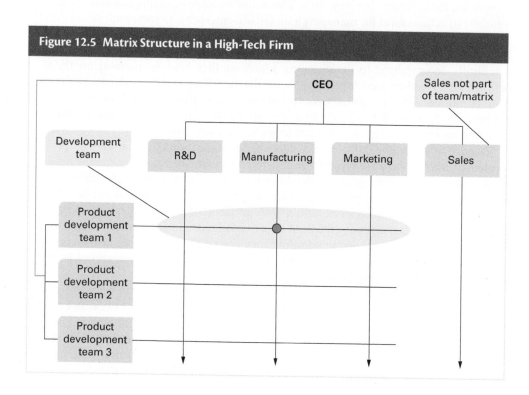

Figure 12.5 Matrix Structure in a High-Tech Firm

can be clumsy and bureaucratic. It can require so many meetings that it is difficult to get any work done. The dual-hierarchy structure can lead to conflict and perpetual power struggles between the different sides of the hierarchy. In one high-tech firm, for example, the manufacturing manager was reluctant to staff a product development team with his best people because he felt that would distract them from their functional work. The result was that the product development team did not work as well as it might have.

To make matters worse, it can prove difficult to ascertain accountability in a matrix structure. When all critical decisions are the product of negotiation between different hierarchies, one side can always blame the other when things go wrong. As a manager in one high-tech matrix structure said to the author when reflecting on a failed product launch, "Had the engineering [R&D] group provided our development team with decent resources, we would have got that product out on time, and it would have been successful." For his part, the head of the engineering group stated that "We did everything we could to help them succeed but the project was not well managed. They kept changing their requests for engineering skills, which was very disruptive." The result of such finger pointing can be that accountability is compromised and conflict escalated, and senior management can lose control over the organization.

Despite these problems, there is evidence that a matrix structure can work.[20] Making a matrix work requires clear lines of responsibility. Normally this means that one side of the matrix must be given the primary role, while the other is given a support role. In a high-tech firm, for example, the product development teams might be given the primary role, because getting good products to market as quickly as possible is a key to competitive success. Despite taking such steps, managing within a matrix structure is difficult. Considering these problems, managers sometimes try to build "flexible" matrix structures based more on enterprise-wide management knowledge networks, and a shared culture and vision, than on a rigid, hierarchical arrangement. Within such companies, the informal structure plays a greater role than the formal structure. We discuss this issue when we consider informal integrating mechanisms in the next section.

12-2d Formal Integrating Processes

There is often a need to coordinate the activities of different functions and divisions within an organization to achieve strategic objectives. For example, at the *business level*, effective new product development requires tight integration between R&D, production, and marketing functions. Similarly, at the *corporate level*, implementing a related diversification strategy requires integration between divisions to realize economies of scope and to transfer or leverage rare, valuable resources such as knowledge across divisions.

The formal integrating mechanisms used to coordinate subunits vary in complexity from simple, direct contact and liaison roles, to teams, to a matrix structure (see Figure 12.6). In general, the greater the need for coordination between subunits (functions or divisions), the more complex the formal integrating mechanisms need to be.[21]

Direct contact between subunit managers is the simplest integrating mechanism: Managers of the various subunits simply contact each other whenever they have a common concern. Direct contact may not be effective, however, if the managers have differing orientations that impede coordination, partly because they have different tasks. For example, production managers are typically concerned with issues such as capacity utilization, cost control, and quality control, whereas marketing managers are concerned with issues such as pricing, promotions, distribution, and market share. These differences can inhibit communication between managers. Managers from different functions often do not "speak the same language." Managers can also become entrenched in their own "functional silos," and this can lead to a lack of respect

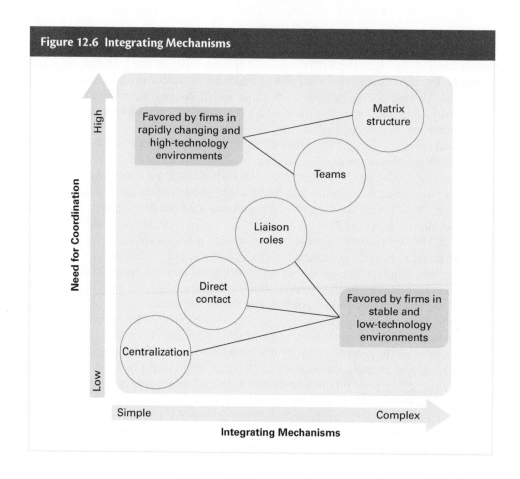

Figure 12.6 Integrating Mechanisms

between subunits (for example, marketing managers "looking down on" production managers, and vice versa). This further inhibits the communication required to achieve cooperation and coordination. For these reasons, direct contact is rarely sufficient to achieve coordination between subunits when the need for integration is high.

Liaison roles are a bit more complex than direct contact. As the need for coordination between subunits increases, integration can be improved by giving one individual in each subunit responsibility for coordinating with other subunits on a regular basis. Through these roles, the employees involved establish a permanent relationship, which helps attenuate the impediments to coordination discussed above.

When the need for coordination is greater still, firms often use temporary or permanent teams composed of individuals from the subunits that need to achieve coordination. Teams are often used to coordinate product development efforts, but they can be useful when any aspect of operations or strategy requires the cooperation of two or more subunits. Product development teams are typically composed of personnel from R&D, production, and marketing. The resulting coordination aids the development of products that are tailored to consumer needs and can be produced at a reasonable cost (through design for manufacturing).

When the need for integration is very high, firms may institute a matrix structure in which all roles are viewed as integrating roles. The structure is designed to facilitate maximum integration among subunits. However, as we have already noted, matrix structures can quickly become bogged down in a bureaucratic tangle that creates as many problems as it solves. If not well managed, matrix structures can become bureaucratic, inflexible, and characterized by conflict rather than the hoped-for cooperation. For such a structure to work, it needs to be somewhat flexible and be supported by informal integrating mechanisms.[22]

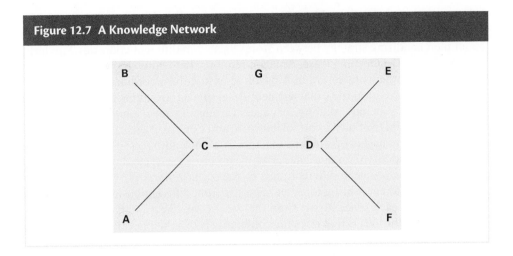

Figure 12.7 A Knowledge Network

12-2e Informal Integrating Mechanisms

In attempting to alleviate or avoid the problems associated with formal integrating mechanisms in general, and matrix structures in particular, firms with a high need for integration have been experimenting with an informal integrating mechanism: knowledge networks that are supported by an organization culture that values teamwork and cross-unit cooperation.[23] A **knowledge network** is a system for transmitting information within an organization that is based not on formal organizational structure but on informal contacts between managers within an enterprise.[24] The great strength of such a network is that it can be used as a nonbureaucratic conduit for knowledge flow within an enterprise.[25] For a network to exist, managers at different locations within the organization must be linked to each other, at least indirectly. For example, Figure 12.7 shows the simple network relationships between seven managers within a multinational firm. Managers A, B, and C all know each other personally, as do Managers D, E, and F. Although Manager B does not know Manager F personally, they are linked through common acquaintances (Managers C and D). Thus, Managers A through F are all part of the network; Manager G is not.

Imagine Manager B, a marketing manager in Spain, needs to know the solution to a technical problem to better serve an important European customer. Manager F, an R&D manager in the United States, has the solution to Manager B's problem. Manager B mentions their problem to all their contacts, including Manager C, and asks if they know of anyone who might be able to provide a solution. Manager C asks Manager D, who tells Manager F, who then calls Manager B with the solution. In this way, coordination is achieved informally through the network, rather than by formal integrating mechanisms such as teams or a matrix structure.

For such a network to function effectively, it must embrace as many managers as possible. For example, if Manager G had a problem like manager B's, they would not be able to utilize the informal network to find a solution; they would have to resort to more formal mechanisms. Establishing firmwide knowledge networks is difficult. Although network enthusiasts speak of networks as the "glue" that binds complex organizations together, it is far from clear how successful firms have been at building companywide networks. The techniques that have been used to establish knowledge networks include information systems, management development policies, and conferences.

Firms are using their distributed computer and telecommunications information systems to provide the foundation for informal knowledge networks.[26] E-mail, video-conferencing, intranets, and web-based search engines make it much easier for managers scattered over the globe to get to know each other, identify contacts who might

knowledge network

A network for transmitting information within an organization that is based not on formal organization structure but on informal contacts between managers within an enterprise and on distributed-information systems.

help to solve a particular problem, and publicize and share best practices within the organization. Walmart, for example, uses its intranet system to communicate ideas about merchandising strategy between stores located in different countries. Similarly, as described in the Opening Case, Amazon requires that teams share their data electronically with other entities within Amazon to ensure that coordination can occur.

Firms are also using their management development programs to build informal networks. Tactics include rotating managers through various subunits on a regular basis, so they build their own informal network, and using management education programs to bring managers of subunits together in a single location so they can become acquainted. In addition, some science-based firms use internal conferences to establish contacts between people in different units of the organization. At 3M, regular, multidisciplinary conferences bring together scientists from different business units and get them talking to each other. Apart from the benefits of direct interaction in the conference setting, the idea is that once the conference is over, the scientists may continue to share ideas, and this will increase knowledge flows within the organization. 3M has many stories of product ideas that were the result of such knowledge flows, including the ubiquitous Post-it Notes, whose inventor, Art Fry, first learned about the adhesive that he would use on the product from a colleague working in another division of 3M, Spencer Silver, who had spent several years shopping his adhesive around 3M.[27]

Knowledge networks alone may not be sufficient to achieve coordination if subunit managers persist in pursuing subgoals that are at variance with firmwide goals. For a knowledge network to function properly—and for a formal matrix structure to work as well—managers must share a strong commitment to the same goals. To appreciate the nature of the problem, consider again the case of Manager B and Manager F. As before, Manager F hears about Manager B's problem through the network. However, solving Manager B's problem would require Manager F to devote considerable time to the task. Insofar as this would divert Manager F away from their regular tasks—and the pursuit of subgoals that differ from those of Manager B—they may be unwilling to do it. Thus, Manager F may not call Manager B, and the informal network would fail to provide a solution to Manager B's problem.

To eliminate this flaw, an organization's managers must adhere to a common set of norms and values that override differing subunit orientations.[28] In other words, the firm must have a strong organizational culture that promotes teamwork and cooperation. When this is the case, a manager is willing and able to set aside the interests of their subunit when doing so benefits the firm as a whole. If Manager B and Manager F are committed to the same organizational norms and value systems, and if these organizational norms and values place the interests of the firm as a whole above the interests of any individual subunit, Manager F should be willing to cooperate with Manager B on solving their subunit's problems.

<table>
<tr><td>12.3</td><td>Discuss the various control systems and incentive mechanisms that a company can use.</td></tr>
</table>

12-3 Organization Controls and Incentives

One critical management task is to control an organization's activities. Controls are an integral part of an enterprise's organizational architecture. They are necessary to ensure that an organization is operating efficiently and effectively, and in a manner that is consistent with its intended strategy. Without adequate controls, *control loss* occurs, and the organization's performance will suffer.

12-3a Control Systems

Control can be viewed as the process through which managers *regulate* the activities of individuals and units so that they are consistent with the goals and standards of the

control

The process through which managers regulate the activities of individuals and units so that they are consistent with the goals and standards of the organization.

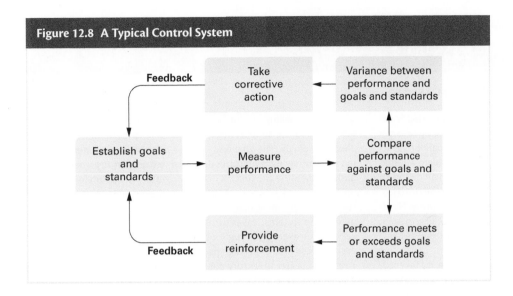

Figure 12.8 A Typical Control System

organization.[29] A **goal** is a desired future state that an organization attempts to realize. A **standard** is a performance requirement that the organization is meant to attain on an ongoing basis. Managers can regulate the activities of individuals and units in several different ways to assure that they are consistent with a firm's goals and standards. Before considering these, we need to review the workings of a typical control system. As illustrated in Figure 12.8, this system has five main elements; establishing goals and standards, measuring performance, comparing performance against goals and standards, taking corrective action, and/or providing reinforcement.[30]

Most organizations operate with a hierarchy of goals. In the case of a business enterprise, the major goals at the top of the hierarchy are normally expressed in terms of profitability and profit growth. These major goals are typically translated into subgoals that can be applied to individuals and units within the organization. A **subgoal** is an *objective*, the achievement of which helps the organization attain or exceed it major goals. Goals and subgoals should be precise, measurable, address important issues, be challenging but realistic, and specify a time period.

To illustrate the concept of a goal hierarchy, suppose that the retailer Nordstrom has a goal of attaining a 15% return on invested capital (ROIC) in the coming year. This is the company's major profitability goal. One way of achieving it is to reduce the amount of capital needed to generate a dollar's worth of sales, and a good way of doing that is to reduce the amount of capital that Nordstrom has tied up in inventory. How does the company do that? By turning over inventory more rapidly. Thus, Nordstrom might operate with a subgoal of turning over inventory five times in the next year. If it hits that subgoal, which is precise, measurable, challenging, and must be achieved within a prespecified time period, the company's profitability, measured by ROIC, will increase. In fact, as explained in Strategy in Action 12.2, Nordstrom has done something very much along these lines.

Standards are like goals but tend to be objectives that the organization is expected to achieve as a part of its routine operations, rather than a challenging goal it is striving to attain. For example, an organization might operate with standards specifying that vendors should be paid within 30 days of submitting an invoice, that customer inquiries should be answered within 24 hours, that all employees should have a formal performance review and be given written feedback once a year, that safety checks should be performed on production equipment every 6 months, or that employees should fly coach when traveling on business trips.

goal

A desired future state that an organization attempts to realize.

standard

A performance requirement that the organization is meant to attain on an ongoing basis.

subgoal

An objective, the achievement of which helps the organization attain or exceed its major goals.

Goal Setting and Controls at Nordstrom

A few years ago, Nordstrom, the venerable, high-end department store, was facing some challenges. Despite industry-leading sales per square foot, profits had fallen short of the company's goals for 3 years in a row and were down some 35%. The root of the problem was that poor inventory controls meant that Nordstrom either had too much merchandise that was in low demand, or too little of the merchandise that consumers wanted. To get rid of excess inventory, Nordstrom held frequent sales, marking down items and selling them at a lower profit margin. Moreover, the failure to stock popular items meant that Nordstrom was losing high-margin sales.

To correct this problem, Nordstrom revamped its inventory-control systems. The company invested heavily in information technology so that it could track its inventory on a real-time basis. It also built electronic links to provide suppliers with visibility of what was selling at Nordstrom and what the reorder pattern would be, so the suppliers could adjust their production schedules accordingly. The goal was to stock only what consumers demanded by having inventories delivered to stores on an as-needed basis. To measure the success of this program, Nordstrom focused on two metrics—inventory turnover and average inventory per square foot of selling space. When the company began to implement these systems, it was turning over its inventory 3.73 times a year, and on average throughout the year had $60 of inventory for every square foot of selling space in a store. Three years later, as a result of better inventory controls, inventory was turning over 4.51 times a year, and the company held $52.46 of inventory for every square foot of selling space. Due to improved operating efficiency, net profits tripled over this time period.[31]

Sources: J. Batsell, "Cost Cutting, Inventory Control Help Boost Nordstrom's Quarterly Profit," *Knight Ridder Tribune News*, February 22, 2002, p. 1; Nordstrom's 2004 10K statement.

A key element in the control process is generating the right goals, subgoals, and standards. Managers need to choose goals and standards carefully to avoid motivating the wrong behavior. There is a saying, "You get what you measure." If you chose the wrong goals and standards, you get the wrong behavior. Dysfunctional controls will generate dysfunctional behavior. A few years ago, a placement agency decided to start evaluating and rewarding its staff based on how many job seekers they sent to job interviews. This productivity measure seemed to produce the desired results; over the next few months, more job seekers got interviews. However, after a while the numbers started to drop off quite alarmingly. When management investigated the issue, they found that several prospective employers would no longer interview people referred to them by the placement agency. The problem: To hit their numbers, staff members had been sending people to interview for jobs for which they were not qualified. This had damaged the reputation of the placement agency among prospective employers and led to a fall-off in business for the agency—the opposite of what managers had been trying to achieve. Managers subsequently changed the measure to reflect the number of job seekers who were hired.

The next step in the control process is to compare actual performance against goals and standards. If performance is in line with goals or standards, that is good. However, the point made earlier still holds: Management needs to make sure that the reported performance is being achieved in a manner that is consistent with the values of the organization. If reported performance falls short of goals and standards, management needs to start digging to find out the reason for the variance. This typically requires collecting more information, much of which might be qualitative data gleaned from face-to-face meetings and detailed probing to get behind the numbers. The same is true if reported performance *exceeds* goals or standards. Management needs to find out the reason for such favorable variance and doing so requires collecting more information.

Variances from goals (and standards) require that managers take corrective action. When actual performance easily exceeds the goal, corrective action might include raising the goal. When actual performance falls short of the goal, depending on what further investigation reveals, management might make changes in strategy, operations, or personnel. Radical adjustment is not always the appropriate response when an organization fails to hit a major goal. Investigation might reveal that the original goal was too aggressive, or that changes in market conditions outside the control of management accounted for the poor performance. In such cases, the response to a shortfall might be to adjust the goal downward.

If the goals and standards are met, or exceeded, management needs to provide timely, positive reinforcement to those responsible. This can run from congratulations for a job well done, to awards, pay increases, bonuses, and enhanced career prospects for those responsible. Providing positive reinforcement is every bit as import an aspect of a control system as is taking corrective action. Behavioral scientists have long known that positive reinforcement increases the probability that those being acknowledged will continue to pursue the rewarded behavior in the future.[32] Without positive reinforcement, people become discouraged, feel underappreciated, may not be willing to work as hard, and might look for other employment opportunities where they are better appreciated.

12-3b Methods of Control

There are several main ways of achieving control within an organization including personal controls, bureaucratic controls, output controls, incentive controls, market controls, and control through culture (which we consider in the next section on organizational culture).[33]

Personal Controls   As the term suggests, **personal control** is control by personal contact with and direct supervision of subordinates. Personal control consists of making sure, through personal inspection and direct supervision, that individuals and units behave in a way that is consistent with the goals of the organization. Personal control can be very subjective, with the manager assessing how well subordinates are performing by observing and interpreting their behavior. As an overarching philosophy for control within an organization, personal control tends to be found primarily in small firms where the activities of a few people might be regulated through direct oversight. By its very nature, personal control tends to be associated with the centralization of power and authority in a key manager, who is often the owner of the small business. Personal control may work best when this key manager is a charismatic individual who can command the personal allegiance of subordinates.

Personal control has several serious limitations. For one thing, excessive supervision can be demotivating. Employees may resent being closely supervised and may perform better if given a greater degree of personal freedom. Moreover, the subjective nature of personal control can lead to a feeling that there is a lack of objectivity and procedural justice in the performance review process. Subordinates may feel that favoritism, personal likes and dislikes, and individual idiosyncrasies may be as important in performance reviews as actual performance. Personal control is also costly in that managers must devote considerable time and attention to the direct supervision of subordinates, which takes their attention away from other important issues. The real Achilles heel of personal control, however, is that it starts to break down as an overarching control philosophy when an organization grows in size and complexity. As this occurs, the key manager has no choice but to decentralize decision making to others within the hierarchy if the enterprise is to continue growing. Doing so effectively requires the adoption of different control philosophies.

Bureaucratic Control   **Bureaucratic control** is defined as control through a formal system of written rules and procedures.[34] As a strategy for control, bureaucratic control

personal control
Control by personal contact with and direct supervision of subordinates.

bureaucratic control
Control through a formal system of written rules and procedures.

methods rely on prescribing what individuals and units can and cannot do; that is, on establishing bureaucratic standards. At the University of Washington, for example, there is a bureaucratic standard specifying that faculty members can perform no more than 1 day a week of outside work. Other standards articulate the steps to be taken when hiring faculty and promoting faculty, purchasing computer equipment for faculty, and so on.

Almost all organizations use bureaucratic controls. Familiar examples are budgetary controls and controls over capital spending. Budgets are essentially a set of rules for allocating an organization's financial resources. A subunit's budget specifies with some precision how much the unit may spend, and how that spending should be allocated across different areas. Senior managers in an organization use budgets to control the behavior of subunits. For example, an R&D budget might specify how much cash an R&D unit may spend on product development in the coming year. R&D managers know that if they spend too much on one project, they will have less to spend on other projects, so they modify their behavior to stay within the budget. Most budgets are set by negotiation between headquarters management and subunit management. Headquarters management can encourage the growth of certain subunits and restrict the growth of others by manipulating their budgets.

Although the term "bureaucratic" often has negative connotations, bureaucratic control methods can be very useful in organizations. They allow managers to decentralize decision making within the constraints specified by formal rules and procedures. However, too great a reliance on bureaucratic rules can lead to problems. Excessive formal rules and procedures can be stifling, limiting the ability of individuals and units to respond in a flexible way to specific circumstances. This can result in poor performance and sap the motivation of those who value individual freedom and initiative. As such, extensive bureaucratic control methods are not well suited to organizations facing dynamic, rapidly changing environments, or to organizations that employ skilled individuals who value autonomy. The costs of monitoring the performance of individuals and units to make sure that they comply with bureaucratic rules can also be significant and may outweigh the benefits of establishing extensive rules and standards.

Bureaucratic standards can also lead to unintended consequences if employees try to find ways around rules that they think are unreasonable. An interesting and controversial case in point concerns rules on forced school busing in the United States. In the 1970s, school districts around America started to bus children to schools outside of their immediate neighborhood to achieve a better racial mix. This well-intentioned bureaucratic rule was designed to speed racial integration in a society characterized by significant racial discrimination. Unfortunately, the rule had unintended consequences. Parents of all races objected to their children being bused to distant schools to comply with a bureaucratic rule. In many large cities where forced busing was practiced, white families with children responded by fleeing to the suburbs, where there were few minorities and busing was not practiced, or by sending their children to expensive, private schools within the city. The result: Far from advancing racial integration, busing had the opposite effect. A case in point was Seattle, where the percentage of white students in city schools dropped from 60% to 41% over the 20 years during which forced busing was enforced.[35] In the 1990s, most school districts ended forced busing.

Output Controls Output controls can be used when managers can identify tasks that are complete in the sense of having a measurable output or meeting a criterion of overall achievement.[36] For example, the overall achievement of an automobile factory might be measured by the number of employee hours it takes to build a car (a measure of productivity) and the number of defects found per 100 cars produced by the factory (a measure of quality). Nordstrom measures the overall achievement of the unit responsible for inventory management by the number of inventory turns per year. FedEx measures the "output" of each of its local stations in its express delivery network by the percentage of packages delivered before 10:30 a.m. In a multibusiness company such as 3M, senior management might measure the "output" of a product division in terms of that division's profitability, profit growth, and market share.

When complete tasks can be identified, **output controls** involve setting goals for units or individuals, and monitoring performance against those goals. The performance of unit managers is then judged by their ability to achieve the goals.[37] If goals are met or exceeded, unit managers will be rewarded (an act of reinforcement). If goals are not met, senior management will normally intervene to find out why and take corrective action. Thus, as in a classic control system, control is achieved by comparing actual performance against targets, providing reinforcement, and intervening selectively to take corrective action.

output controls

Setting goals for units or individuals and monitoring performance against those goals.

The goals assigned to units depend on the unit's role in the firm. Self-contained product divisions are typically given goals for profitability and profit growth. Functions are more likely to be given goals related to their activity. Thus, R&D will be given product development goals, production will be given productivity and quality goals, marketing will be given market-share goals, and so on.

The great virtue of output controls is that they facilitate decentralization and give individual managers within units much greater autonomy then either personal or bureaucratic controls. This autonomy enables managers within a unit to configure their own work environment in a way that best matches the contingencies they face, rather than having a work environment imposed upon them from above. Thus, output controls are useful when units must respond rapidly to changes in the markets they serve. Output controls also involve less extensive monitoring than either bureaucratic or personal controls. Senior managers can achieve control by comparing actual performance against targets and intervening selectively. As such, they reduce the workload on senior executives and allow them to manage a larger, more diverse organization with relative ease. Thus, many large, multiproduct, multinational enterprises rely heavily upon output controls to manage their various product divisions and foreign subsidiaries.

Output controls have limitations. Senior managers need to look behind the numbers to make sure that unit managers are not only achieving goals but are doing so in a way that is consistent with the values of the organization. Managers also need to make sure that they choose the right criteria to measure output. Failure to select the right criteria might result in dysfunctional behavior. Moreover, output controls do not always work well when extensive interdependencies exist between units.[38]

The performance of a unit may be ambiguous if it is based upon cooperation with other units. For example, if the performance of a unit is declining, it may be because of poor management within that unit, or it may be because a unit with which it is cooperating is not doing its part. In general, interdependence between units within an organization can create performance ambiguities that make output controls more difficult to interpret. Resolving these ambiguities requires managers to collect more information, which places more demands on top management and raises the monitoring costs associated with output controls. It also increases the possibility that managers will become overloaded with information and, as a result, make poor decisions.

Market Controls **Market controls** involve regulating the behavior of individuals and units within an enterprise by setting up an *internal market* for valuable resources such as capital.[39] Market controls are usually found within diversified enterprises organized into product divisions, where the head office might act as an internal investment bank, allocating capital funds between the competing claims of the different product

market controls

The regulation of the behavior of individuals and units within an enterprise by setting up an internal market for valuable resources such as capital.

divisions based upon an assessment of their likely future performance. Within this internal market, all cash generated by the divisions is viewed as belonging to the head office. The divisions must compete for access to the capital resources controlled by the head office. Insofar as they need that capital to grow their divisions, the assumption is that this internal competition will drive divisional managers to find ways to improve the efficiency of their units. One of the first companies in the world to establish an internal capital market was Japanese electronics manufacturer Matsushita, which introduced such a system in the 1930s.[40]

In addition, in some enterprises divisions compete for the right to develop and sell new products. Again, Japan's Matsushita has a long history of letting different divisions develop similar new products, and then assigning overall responsibility for producing and selling the product to the division that seems to be furthest along in the commercialization process. While some might view such duplication of product development effort as wasteful, Matsushita's legendary founder, Konosuke Matsushita, believed that the creation of an internal market for the right to commercialize technology drove divisional managers to maximize the efficiency of product development efforts within their unit. Similarly, within Samsung, the Korean electronics company, senior management will often set up two different teams within different units to develop new products such as memory chips. The purpose of the internal competition between the two teams is to accelerate the product development process, with the winning team earning significant accolades and bonuses.[41]

The main problem with market controls is that fostering internal competition between divisions for capital and the right to develop new products can make it difficult to establish cooperation between divisions for mutual gain.[42] If two different divisions are racing against each other to develop very similar new products, and are competing against each other for limited capital resources, they may be unwilling to share technological knowhow with each other, perhaps to the detriment of the entire corporation. Companies like Samsung deal with this problem by using integrating mechanisms such as liaison roles, and by assigning the responsibility for leveraging technological know-how across divisions to key individuals.

Incentives Control Incentives are the devices used to encourage and reward appropriate employee behavior. Many employees receive incentives in the form of annual bonus pay. Incentives are usually closely tied to the performance metrics used for output controls. For example, setting targets linked to profitability might be used to measure the performance of a subunit such as a product division. To create positive incentives for employees to work hard to exceed those targets, they may be given a share of any profits over above those targeted. If a subunit has set a goal of attaining a 15% ROIC and attains a 20% return, unit employees may be given a share in the profits generated in excess of the 15% target in the form of bonus pay.

The idea is that giving employees incentives to work productively reduces the need for other control mechanisms. Control through incentives is designed to facilitate *self-control*. Employees regulate their own behavior in a manner consistent with organizational goals to maximize their chance of earning incentive-based pay. Although paying out bonuses and the like costs the organization money, well-designed incentives pay for themselves. That is, the increase in performance due to incentives more than offsets the costs of financing them.

The type of incentive used may vary depending on the employees and their tasks. Incentives for employees working on the factory floor may be very different from the incentives for senior managers. The incentives must be matched to the type of work being performed. The employees on the factory floor of a manufacturing plant may be broken into teams of 20 to 30 individuals, and they may have their bonus pay tied to the ability of their team to hit or exceed targets for output and product quality.

In contrast, the senior managers of the plant may be rewarded according to metrics linked to the output of the entire operation. The basic principle is to make sure the incentive scheme for an individual employee is linked to an output target that they have some control over and can influence. Individual employees on the factory floor may not be able to exercise much influence over the performance of the entire operation, but they can influence the performance of their team, so their incentive pay is tied to output at this level.

When incentives are tied to team performance, as is often the case, they have the added benefit of encouraging cooperation between team members and fostering a degree of peer control. **Peer control** occurs when employees pressure others within their team or work group to perform up to or in excess of the expectations of the organization.[43] Thus, if the incentive pay of a 20-person team is linked to team output, members can be expected to pressure those in the team who are perceived as slacking off and freeloading on the efforts of others, urging them to pick up the pace and make an equal contribution to team effort. Well-functioning peer control within an organization reduces the need for direct supervision of a team and can facilitate attempts to move toward a flatter management hierarchy.

In sum, incentives can reinforce output controls, induce employees to practice self-control, increase peer control, and lower the need for other control mechanisms. Like all other control methods discussed here, controls through incentives have limitations. Because incentives are typically linked to the metrics used in output controls, the points made regarding output controls also apply here. Specifically, managers need to make sure that incentives are not tied to output metrics that result in unintended consequences or dysfunctional behavior.

peer control

The pressure that employees exert on others within their team or work group to perform up to or in excess of the expectations of the organization.

12-4 Organizational Culture

12.4 Review the concept of organization culture and explain why it is important for strategy implementation.

Organizational culture refers to the values, norms, and assumptions that are shared among employees of an organization. By **values** we mean abstract ideas about what a group believes to be good, right, and desirable. Put differently, values are shared assumptions about how things ought to be. By **norms**, we mean social rules and guidelines that prescribe the appropriate behavior in particular situations.

Culture can exert a profound influence on the way people behave within an organization, on the decisions that are made, on the things that the organization pays attention to, and ultimately, on the firm's strategy and performance.

An organization's culture has several sources. There seems to be wide agreement that founders or important leaders can have a profound impact on organizational culture, often imprinting their own values upon it. In addition, the culture of an enterprise can be shaped by landmark events in its history. Culture is maintained and transmitted over time through formal and informal socialization mechanisms. These include hiring practices, procedures regarding rewards, pay, and promotions, and the informal rules of behavior that employees are expected to adopt if they want to fit in and succeed within the organization.[44]

Microsoft, for example, has a strong culture that was influenced by the company's founder and long-time CEO, Bill Gates. Gates always placed a high value on technical brilliance, competitiveness, and a willingness to work long hours—something that he himself did. Gates hired and promoted people who shared these characteristics, and he led by example. He also tended to dismiss the opinions of people who lacked technical brilliance. Talented engineers often "walked taller" within Microsoft, and they had a disproportionate impact on strategic decisions. The employees who gained Gates's confidence themselves hired and promoted individuals who were technically strong, competitive, and hardworking. The culture of the company was thus transmitted and enforced throughout

values

The ideas or shared assumptions about what a group believes to be good, right, and desirable.

norms

Social rules and guidelines that prescribe the appropriate behavior in particular situations.

the organization. As a result, Microsoft became a company where technical brilliance, competitiveness, and working long hours were highly valued attributes of behavior. New employees were socialized into these norms by coworkers who themselves had been similarly socialized. Interestingly, many Microsoft employees will point out that Satya Nadella, who became CEO in 2014, has ushered in some major changes in culture at Microsoft. Specifically, the emphasis on competition between employees has been replaced by a focus on collaboration and cooperation.

History also shaped the culture at Microsoft. Most notably, it took three versions and 6 years before sales of Windows started to take off with the introduction of Windows 3.1 (Windows 1.0 and 2.0 did not do well). The lesson that Microsoft gained from this was that persistence can pay off. "We will get it right by version 3" is a phrase that is still used at Microsoft. This culturally embedded value influences strategic decisions regarding investments such as Microsoft's long-running commitment to its money-losing Bing search business. Reflecting the culture of Microsoft, many employees believed that if the company stuck with Bing for long enough, it would eventually turn profitable (as seems to have occurred).

Culture as a Control Mechanism   Given that organizational culture shapes behavior, culture can be viewed as a control mechanism that mandates expected behaviors. At Microsoft, under the leadership of Gates, staff worked long hours not because bureaucratic rules told them to do so, and not because supervisors explicitly required them to do so, but because that was the cultural norm. In this sense, culture shaped behavior, thereby reducing the need for bureaucratic and personal controls. The company could trust people to work hard and behave in a competitive manner because those norms were such a pervasive aspect of the culture.

Although cultural controls can mitigate the need for other controls, thereby reducing monitoring costs, they are not universally beneficial. Cultural controls can have dysfunctional aspects. The hard-driving, competitive aspect of Microsoft's culture was arguably a contributing factor in the antitrust violations that the company was found to have made in the 1990s (the U.S. Justice Department, which brought the antitrust case against Microsoft in the United States, used as evidence internal e-mails where one senior manager stated that Microsoft would "cut off a competitor's air supply"). Moreover, Microsoft's culture of working long hours clearly had a downside: Many good employees burned out and left the company. In the post-Gates era, the company has become attuned to this. As its workforce has aged and started families, it has become more accommodating, stressing that the output produced is more important than the hours worked.

Implementing Strategy Through Culture   Given that culture can have such a profound impact upon the way in which people behave within organizations, it is important for managers to get culture right. The right culture can help a company execute its strategy; the wrong culture can hinder strategy execution.[45] In the 1980s, when IBM was performing very well, several authors sang the praises of its culture, which among other things placed a high value on consensus-based decision making.[46] These authors argued that such a decision-making process was appropriate given the substantial financial investments that IBM routinely made in new technology. However, this process turned out to be a weakness in the fast-moving computer industry of the late 1980s and 1990s. Consensus-based decision making was slow, bureaucratic, and not particularly conducive to corporate risk taking. While this was fine in the 1970s, IBM needed rapid decision making and entrepreneurial risk taking in the 1990s, but its culture discouraged such behavior. IBM was outflanked by then-small enterprises such as Microsoft, almost went bankrupt, and went through a massive change to shift its organizational culture.

One academic study concluded that firms that exhibited high performance over a prolonged period tended to have strong but adaptive cultures. According to this study, in an adaptive culture most managers care deeply about and value customers, stockholders, and employees. They also strongly value people and processes that create useful change in a firm.[47] While this is interesting, it does reduce the issue to a very high level of abstraction; after all, what company would say that it doesn't care deeply about customers, stockholders, and employees? A somewhat different perspective is to argue that the culture of the firm must match the rest of its architecture, its strategy, and the demands of the competitive environment for superior performance to be attained. All of these elements must be consistent with each other. Lincoln Electric provides a useful example (see Strategy in Action 12.3). Lincoln competes in a business that is very competitive, where cost minimization is a key source of competitive advantage. Its culture and incentive systems both encourage employees to strive for high levels of productivity, which translates into the low costs that are critical for its success. These aspects of Lincoln's organizational architecture are aligned with its low-cost strategy.

12-5 Organization Processes

12.5 Explain the importance of organizational processes for strategy implementation.

Processes, defined as the way decisions are made and work is performed within an organization,[48] are found at many different levels within an organization. There are processes for formulating strategy, allocating resources, evaluating new-product ideas, handling customer inquiries and complaints for improving product quality, evaluating employee performance, and so on. Often, a firm's core competencies or valuable,

12.3 Strategy in Action

Organizational Culture at Lincoln Electric

Lincoln Electric is one of the leading companies in the global market for arc welding equipment. Lincoln's success has been based on extremely high levels of employee productivity. The company attributes its productivity to a strong organizational culture and an incentive scheme based on piecework. Lincoln's organizational culture dates back to James Lincoln. Lincoln had a strong respect for the ability of the individual and believed that, correctly motivated, ordinary people could achieve extraordinary performance. He emphasized that Lincoln should be a meritocracy where people were rewarded for their individual effort. Strongly egalitarian, Lincoln removed barriers to communication between "workers" and "managers," practicing an open-door policy. He made sure that all who worked for the company were treated equally; for example, everyone ate in the same cafeteria, there were no reserved parking places for "managers," and so on. Lincoln also believed that gains in productivity should be shared with consumers in the form of lower prices, with employees in the form of higher pay, and with shareholders in the form of higher dividends.

The organizational culture that grew out of Lincoln's beliefs was reinforced by the company's incentive system. Production workers receive no base salary but are paid according to the number of pieces they produce. The piecework rates at the company enable an employee working at a normal pace to earn an income equivalent to the average wage for manufacturing workers in the area where a factory is based. Workers have responsibility for the quality of their output and must repair defects spotted by quality inspectors before the pieces are included in the piecework calculation. Production workers are awarded a semiannual bonus based on merit ratings. These ratings are based on objective criteria (such as an employee's level and quality of output) and subjective criteria (such as an employee's attitudes toward cooperation and his or her dependability). These systems give Lincoln's employees an incentive to work hard and generate innovations that boost productivity, for doing so influences their level of pay. Lincoln's factory workers have been able to earn a base pay that often exceeds the average manufacturing wage in the area by more than 50%, and they receive a bonus on top of this which, in good years, could double their base pay. Despite high employee compensation, its workers are so productive that Lincoln has a lower cost structure than its competitors.[49]

Sources: J. O'Connell, "Lincoln Electric: Venturing Abroad," Harvard Business School Case No. 9-398-095, April 1998; www.lincolnelectric.com.

knowledge-based resources are embedded in its processes (see Chapter 3). Efficient, effective processes can lower the costs of value creation and add additional value to a product. For example, the global success of many Japanese manufacturing enterprises in the 1980s was based in part on their early adoption of processes for improving product quality and operating efficiency, including total quality management and just-in-time inventory systems. Today, the competitive success of GE Healthcare's medical equipment business can in part be attributed to a number of processes that have been widely promoted within the company. These include the company's Six Sigma process for quality improvement, its process for "digitalization" of business (using corporate intranets and the Internet to automate activities and reduce operating costs), and its process for idea generation, referred to within the company as "workouts," where managers and employees gather for intensive sessions over several days to identify and commit to ideas for improving productivity.

An organization's processes can be summarized by means of a flowchart, which illustrates the various steps and decision points involved in performing work. A detailed consideration of the nature of processes and strategies for process improvement and reengineering is beyond the scope of this book. However, it is important to make two basic remarks about managing processes, particularly in the context of an international business.[50]

First, many processes cut across functions, or divisions, and require cooperation between individuals in different subunits. For example, product development processes require employees from R&D, manufacturing, and marketing to work in a cooperative manner to make sure new products are developed with market needs in mind and designed in such a way that they can be manufactured at a low cost. Because they cut across organizational boundaries, performing processes effectively often require the establishment of formal integrating mechanisms and incentives for cross-unit cooperation.

Second, it is particularly important for an enterprise to recognize that valuable new processes that might lead to a competitive advantage can be developed anywhere within the organization's network of operations.[51] Valuable and rare new processes may be developed within a team, function, product division, or foreign subsidiary. Those processes might then be valuable to other parts of the enterprise. The ability to create valuable processes matters, but it is also important to leverage those processes, and this requires both formal and informal integrating mechanisms such as knowledge networks.

12.6 Discuss how the appropriate organization design enables a company to better implement its business and corporate-level strategies.

12-6 Implementing Strategy Through Organizational Architecture

We are now able to make observations about the kind of organizational arrangements required to implement different strategies. Rather than construct an exhaustive list, we will focus on a limited number of business- and corporate-level strategies. We start by considering strategy and organization within the single-business firm. Then we look at strategy and organization within the diversified firm.

12-6a Strategy and Organization in the Single-Business Enterprise

As noted earlier, single-business enterprises are typically organized along functional lines (see Figure 12.3). However, the need for integration between functions will vary depending upon (1) the business-level strategy of the firm, and (2) the nature of the environment in which the firm competes (see Figure 12.9).

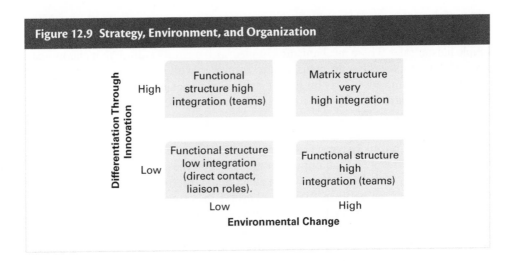

Figure 12.9 Strategy, Environment, and Organization

Differentiation Through Innovation

High — Functional structure high integration (teams) | Matrix structure very high integration

Low — Functional structure low integration (direct contact, liaison roles). | Functional structure high integration (teams)

Low — High
Environmental Change

Strategy, Environment, and the Need for Integration   In general, the need for integration between functions is greater for firms that are competing through product development and innovation.[52] This is typically the case when an organization's business-level strategy involves differentiation through the introduction of new and/or improved product offerings. Apple, Google, Ford, Microsoft, Tesla, and Toyota, for example, all try to differentiate themselves through product development and innovation. As discussed earlier, in such organizations there is an ongoing need to coordinate the R&D, production, and marketing functions of the firm to ensure that (1) new products are developed in a timely manner, (2) that they can be efficiently produced and delivered, and (3) that they match consumer demands. We saw that a matrix structure is one way of achieving such coordination (see Figure 12.5). Another, more common, solution is to form temporary teams to oversee the development and introduction of a new product. Once the new product has been introduced, the team is disbanded, and employees return to their functions or move to another team.

Firms that face an uncertain, highly turbulent, competitive environment, where rapid adaptation to changing market conditions is required, need coordination to survive.[53] Environmental change, such as that which occurs when an industry is disrupted by radical innovations, may require a change in product, process, business model, and strategy. In such cases, it is critical to make sure that the different functions of the firm all pull in the same direction, so that the firm's response to a changing environment is coherent and organization wide. Temporary teams are often used to achieve such coordination.

For example, in the mid-1990s, the World Wide Web emerged with stunning speed and in a way that almost no one anticipated. The rise of the Web produced a profound change in the environment facing computer software firms such as Microsoft, where managers quickly shifted their strategy so as to make their products Web enabled and position their marketing and sales activities to compete in this new landscape. This shift required very tight coordination between different software engineering groups, such as those working on the software code for Windows, Office and MSN, so that all products not only were Web enabled but also worked seamlessly with each other. Microsoft achieved this by forming cross-functional teams.

In addition to using formal integrating mechanisms such as cross-functional teams, firms with a crucial need for coordination between subunits—for instance, those based in turbulent, high-tech environments—would do well to foster informal knowledge networks, for they too can facilitate coordination between subunits.

In contrast, if the firm is based in a stable environment characterized by little or no change, and if developing new products is not a central aspect of the firm's business strategy, the need for coordination between functions may be less. In such cases, a firm may be able to function with basic integrating mechanisms such as direct contact or simple liaison roles. These mechanisms, coupled with a strong culture that encourages employees to pursue the same goals, and to cooperate with each other for the benefit of the entire organization, may be all that is required to achieve coordination between functions. Walmart and Costco, for example, utilize basic integrating mechanisms such as liaison roles.

Integration and Control Systems: Low Integration   The extent of integration required to implement a strategy has an important impact upon the control systems that management can use. Consider a firm with a functional structure where there are no integrating mechanisms between functions beyond direct contact and simple liaison roles. The environment facing the firm is stable, so the need for integration is minimal. Within such a firm, *bureaucratic controls* in the form of budgets are used to allocate financial resources to each function and control spending by the functions. *Output controls* will then be used to assess how well a function is performing. Different functions will be assigned different output targets, depending on their specific tasks. The procurement function might be assigned an output target based on procurement costs as a percentage of sales; a manufacturing function might be given productivity and product quality targets such as output per employee and defects per thousand products; the logistics function might be given an inventory turnover target; the marketing and sales function might be given sales-growth and market-share goals; and the success of the service function might be measured by the time it takes to resolve a customer problem. To the extent that each function hits these targets, the overall performance of the firm will improve and its profitability increase.

Output controls might also be pushed further down within functions. A production process might be subdivided into discrete tasks, each of which has a measurable output. Employee teams might be formed and empowered to take ownership over each discrete task. Each team will be assigned an output target. To the extent that functions can be divided into teams, and output controls applied to those teams, this will facilitate (1) decentralization within the organization, (2) wider spans of control (because it is relatively easy to control a team by monitoring its outputs, as opposed to regulating behavior through bureaucratic rules), and (3) a flatter organization structure.

Within such a structure, the CEO will monitor the functional heads. They in turn will exercise control over units or teams within their function. There may also be some degree of *personal control,* with the CEO using personal supervision to influence the behavior of functional heads; they in turn do the same for their direct reports. *Incentives* will be tied to output targets. The incentive pay of the head of manufacturing might be linked to the attainment of predetermined productivity and quality targets for the manufacturing function; the incentive pay of the head of logistics might be linked to increases in inventory turnover; the pay of the head of marketing and sales to gains in market share, and so on. Incentives might also be pushed further down within the organization, with members of teams within functions being rewarded based on the ability of their team to hit or exceed predetermined targets. A portion of the incentive pay for managers—and perhaps all employees—might be tied to the overall performance of the enterprise to encourage cooperation and knowledge sharing within the organization.

Finally, it is possible for such an enterprise to have strong *cultural controls*. Cultural controls may reduce the need for personal controls and bureaucratic rules. Individuals might be trusted to behave in the desired manner because they "buy into" the prevailing culture. Thus, cultural controls might allow the firm to operate with a flatter organization structure and wider spans of control, and generally increase the effectiveness of output controls and incentives, because employees may buy into the underlying philosophy upon which such controls are based.

Integration and Control Systems: High Integration A functional structure where the strategy and/or environment requires a high degree of integration presents managers with a complex control problem. The problem is particularly severe if the firm adopts a matrix structure. As noted earlier, a firm based in a dynamic environment where competition centers on product development might adopt such a structure. Within such an enterprise, *bureaucratic controls* will again be used for financial budgets and, as before, *output controls* will be applied to the different functions. *Output controls* will also be applied to cross-functional product development teams. Thus, a team might be assigned output targets covering development time, production costs of the new product, and the features the product should incorporate. For functional managers, *incentive controls* might be linked to output targets for their functions, whereas for the members of a product development team, incentives will be tied to team performance.

The problem with such an arrangement is that the performance of the product development team is dependent upon the support it gets from the various functions. The support needed includes people and information from production, marketing, and R&D. Consequently, significant performance ambiguity might complicate the process of using output controls to assess the performance of a product development team. **Performance ambiguity** arises when it is difficult to identify with precision the reason for the high (or low) performance of a subunit such as a function or team. In this context, the failure of a cross-functional product development team to hit predetermined output targets might be due to the poor performance of team members, but it could just as well be due to the failure of the functions to provide an appropriate level of support to the team. Senior management cannot determine which explanation is correct simply by observing output controls tied to team performance, because such outputs are not an unambiguous indicator of performance. Identifying the true cause of performance variations requires senior managers to collect information, much of it subjective, which increases the time and energy they must devote to the control process, diverts their attention from other important issues, and hence increases the costs of monitoring and controlling the organization. Other things being equal, this reduces the span of control that senior managers can handle, suggesting the need for a taller hierarchy which, as we saw earlier, gives rise to all kinds of additional problems.

The nature of the performance ambiguity problem in such an enterprise raises the question of whether there is a better solution to the control problem. In fact, there is. One step is to make sure that the incentives of all key personnel are aligned; that is, to use *incentive controls* in a discriminating way. The classic way of doing this is to tie incentives to a higher level of organization performance. Thus, in addition to being rewarded based on the performance of their function, functional heads might also be rewarded based on the overall performance of the firm. Insofar as the success of product development teams increases firm performance, this gives functional heads an incentive to make sure that the product development teams receive adequate support from the functions. In addition, strong *cultural controls* can be very helpful in establishing companywide norms and values that emphasize the importance of cooperation between functions and teams for their mutual benefit.

12-6b Strategy and Organization in the Multibusiness Enterprise

As discussed earlier, multibusiness enterprises typically organize themselves along divisional lines (see Figure 12.4). Within each division, there will be a functional organization. The extent of integration between functions *within divisions* may differ from division to division depending upon the business-level strategy and the nature of the environment. The need for integration *between divisions*, on the other hand, depends upon the specific corporate strategy the firm is pursuing. This will have an impact not only on the integrating mechanisms used, but also on the type of control and incentive systems employed.[54]

performance ambiguity
The difficulty of identifying with precision the reason for the high (or low) performance of a subunit such as a function or team.

If the firm is pursuing a strategy of related diversification and trying to realize economies of scope by sharing inputs across product divisions or is trying to boost profitability by transferring or leveraging valuable competencies across divisions, it will have a need for integrating mechanisms to coordinate the activities of the different product divisions. Liaison roles, temporary teams, and permanent teams can all be used to ensure such coordination. On the other hand, if top management is focusing primarily on boosting profitability through superior internal governance, and if each division is managed on a stand-alone basis, with no attempt to leverage competencies or realize economies of scope, as is the case in firms pursuing a strategy of unrelated diversification, the firm may well operate well with minimal or no integrating mechanisms between divisions.

Controls in the Diversified Firm with Low Integration In firms that focus primarily on boosting performance through superior internal governance where the strategy is one of unrelated diversification, the need for integration between divisions is low. Firms pursuing a strategy of unrelated diversification are not trying to share resources or leverage core competencies across divisions, so there is no need for complex integrating mechanisms, such as cross-divisional teams, to coordinate the activities of different divisions. In these enterprises, the head office typically controls the divisions in four main ways.[55]

First, they use *bureaucratic controls* to regulate the financial budgets and capital spending of the divisions. Typically, each division will have to have its financial budgets approved for the coming year by the head office. In addition, capital expenditures more than a certain amount must be approved by the head office; for example, any item of spending by a division in excess of $50,000 might have to be approved by the head office.

Second, the head office will use *output controls*, assigning each division output targets that are normally based on measurable financial criteria such as the profitability, profit growth, and cash flow produced by each division. Typically targets for the coming year are set by negotiation between divisional heads and senior managers at the head office. As long as the divisions hit their targets, they are left alone to run their own operations. If performance falls short of targets, however, top managers will normally audit a division to discover why this occurred, and take corrective action if necessary by instituting a change in strategy and/or personnel.

Third, *incentive controls* will be used, with the incentives for divisional managers being tied to the financial performance of their divisions. To earn pay bonuses, divisional managers must hit or exceed the performance targets previously negotiated between the head office and the divisions. To make sure that divisional managers do not try to "talk down" their performance targets for the year, making it easy for them to hit their targets and earn bonuses, the head office will normally benchmark a product division against its competitors, take a close look at industry conditions, and use this information to establish performance targets that are challenging but attainable.

Fourth, the head office will use *market controls* to allocate capital resources between different divisions.[56] As noted earlier, in multidivisional enterprises the cash generated by product divisions is normally viewed as belonging to the head office, which functions as an internal capital market, reallocating cash flows between the competing claims of different divisions based on an assessment of likely future performance. The competition between divisions for access to capital, which they need to grow their businesses, is assumed to create further incentives for divisional managers to run their operations as efficiently and effectively as possible. In addition, the head office might use market controls to allocate the right to develop and commercialize new products between divisions.

Within divisions, the control systems used will be those found within single-business enterprises. It should also be noted that head office managers might utilize some *personal controls* to influence the behavior of divisional heads. In particular, the CEO might exercise control over divisional heads by meeting with them on a regular basis and probing them to get rich feedback about the operations of the entity for which they are responsible.

Controls in the Diversified Firm with High Integration   The control problem is more complex in diversified firms pursuing a strategy of related diversification where they are trying to improve performance not only through superior internal governance, but also proactively attempting to leverage competencies across product divisions and realize economies of scope. Consider, for example, 3M, a highly diversified enterprise with multiple product divisions. The company devotes great effort trying to leverage core technology across divisions (for instance, by establishing internal knowledge networks). In addition, 3M tries to realize economies of scope, particularly in the areas of marketing and sales, where a marketing and sales division might sell the products of several 3M divisions. More generally, when a multidivisional enterprise tries to improve performance through the attainment of economies of scope, and via the leveraging of core competencies across divisions, the need for integration between divisions is high.

In such organizations, top managers use the standard repertoire of control mechanisms discussed in the last section (e.g., bureaucratic, output, incentive, and market controls). However, in addition, they must deal with two control problems that are not found in multidivisional firms pursuing a strategy of unrelated diversification where there is no cooperation and integration between divisions. First, they must find a control mechanism that induces divisions to cooperate with each other for mutual gain. Second, they need to find a way to deal with the performance ambiguities that arise when divisions are tightly coupled with each other, share resources, and the performance of one cannot be understood in isolation but depends upon how well it cooperates with others.

The solution to both problems is in essence the same as that adopted by single-business firms with high integration between functions. Specifically, the firm needs to adopt incentive controls for divisional managers that are linked to higher-level performance; in this case, the performance of the entire enterprise. Insofar as improving the performance of the entire firm requires cooperation between divisions, such incentive controls should facilitate that cooperation. In addition, strong cultural controls can be helpful in creating values and norms that emphasize the importance of cooperation between divisions for mutual gain. At 3M there is a long-established cultural norm that, while products belong to the divisions, the technology underlying those products belongs to the entire company. Thus, the surgical tape business might utilize adhesive technology developed by the office supply business to improve its own products.

Despite such solutions to control problems, there is no question that top managers in firms where divisions are tightly integrated must deal with greater performance ambiguities than top managers in less complex multidivisional organizations. Integration between various product divisions means that it is hard for top managers to judge the performance of each division just by monitoring objective output criteria. To accurately gauge performance and achieve adequate controls, they probably have to spend time auditing the affairs of operating divisions, and talking to divisional managers to get a comprehensive, qualitative picture of performance than can help them "dig behind" objective output numbers. Other things being equal, this might limit the span of control managers can effectively handle, and thus the scope of the enterprise.[57]

Key Terms

Takeaways for Strategic Managers

1. Strategy is implemented through the organizational architecture of the enterprise.
2. It is useful to think of organizational architecture as a system that encompasses structure, controls, incentives, processes, culture, and human capital.
3. In general, a flat organizational structure where the performance of each subunit is visible, unambiguous, and can be measured by objective output controls is preferable.
4. Implementing strategy may require cooperation between functions and product divisions. The need for cooperation requires integrating mechanisms. Extensive use of integrating

mechanisms may lead to performance ambiguity, and may require more complex and varied control mechanisms.
5. At the business level, the need for integrating mechanisms to coordinate functional activities is greater for firms whose business-level strategy requires ongoing product development efforts and product innovation, and for firms based in rapidly changing market environments.
6. At the corporate level, the need for integrating mechanisms to coordinate the activities of different divisions is greater for companies pursuing a strategy of related diversification than for those pursuing a strategy of unrelated diversification.

Discussion Questions

1. What is the relationship among organizational structure, control systems, incentives, and culture? Give some examples of when and under what conditions a mismatch among these components might arise.
2. What kind of structure best describes the way your (a) business school and (b) university operate? Why is the structure appropriate? Would another structure be better?
3. When would a company choose a matrix structure? What are the problems associated with managing this type of structure? How might these problems be mitigated?
4. What kind of structure, controls, incentives, and culture would you be likely to find in (a) a small manufacturing company based in a stable environment, (b) a high-tech company based in a rapidly changing market, and (c) a major accounting firm?
5. When would a company decide to change from a functional to a multidivisional structure?
6. How would you design structure, controls, incentives, processes, and culture to encourage entrepreneurship in a large, established corporation? How might the desire to encourage entrepreneurship influence your hiring and management development strategy?

As is often the case with many start-ups, in its early days Microsoft's organization developed organically. Initially, when the company's main product was its MS-DOS operating system (the forerunner to Windows), the company had a functional organization. The two main functions were engineering, which was responsible for developing software products, and marketing and sales, which sold those products to computer manufacturers, business users, and consumers. The engineering function was initially headed by founder and CEO Bill Gates, while Steve Ballmer (who would ultimately succeed Gates as CEO), ran the marketing and sales function. Support functions included finance, human relations, and legal.

As the company grew and developed new products such as Office, Windows server software, development tools, Xbox, and Internet search, Microsoft developed into a de facto matrix organization. Each major product category was put into its own business division, while the engineering and sales functions cut across these divisions. The rational for the matrix structure was that it encouraged close coordination between the different businesses. This was seen as a key imperative at Microsoft, where various software products needed to work well with each other. For example, on the engineering side, Office needed to be optimized to run well on Windows; Xbox used a customized version of the Windows operating system, so development had to be synchronized; and the Windows operating system for desktop and laptop computers had to communicate seamlessly with the Windows server software that ran on servers. On the sales and marketing side, coordination was important to ensure that business users had one main point of contact with Microsoft, which was far preferable to having multiple salespeople from different divisions contact the company.

While the matrix organization achieved its main objectives of facilitating coordination between divisions and presenting a main point of contact for businesses, it did create some problems for the organization. There was a chronic lack of accountability within Microsoft. When things went wrong, it could be unclear whether this was due to management problems within the business divisions, or due to a lack of execution by the engineering function, or by sales and marketing. It was also the case that engineering was viewed as the premier cultural function within the organization. Most importantly, engineering took the lead in developing new products. This didn't always serve the company well because its engineers, isolated from customers, were not as focused on the market as they should have been. Over time, the company also became increasingly bureaucratic and slow to respond to innovation by rivals such as Apple and Google.

When Satya Nadella became CEO of Microsoft in January 2014, one of his priorities was to increase accountability within the organization and make Microsoft more agile. By mid-2017, he had reorganized into three main business segments—Productivity and Business Processes (which included Office 365, Dynamics, and LinkedIn), Intelligent Cloud (public, private, and hybrid server products and cloud services), and More Personal Computing (Windows, Xbox, Surface, and search advertising). The heads of each segment report directly to Nadella, and they have primary profit-and-loss responsibility for their segments. The different product offerings within each segment are also profit centers, and the heads of those product divisions report to the head of each segment. Sales continues to operate as a separate function, but engineering and marketing responsibilities are now embedded in each segment, and the product groups within each segment. In other words, Microsoft has moved significantly away from its de facto matrix structure. The articulated goal of these changes is to align structure with strategy, drive accountability, and eliminate obstacles to innovation. Judged by Microsoft's financial results and the rapid growth of its cloud offerings since Nadella took over, so far this seems to be working.

Sources: Discussions with Microsoft personnel by the author.

Case Discussion Questions

1. What were the advantages of Microsoft's matrix organization?
2. What were the disadvantages of Microsoft's matrix organization? How might this organizational form have negatively impacted the company?
3. What was Satya Nadella trying to achieve when he reorganized Microsoft after becoming CEO in 2014? How successful has he been?
4. Is there still a need for coordination between businesses at Microsoft? How do you think the company achieves this?

Notes

[1] D. Naidler, M. Gerstein, and R. Shaw, *Organization Architecture* (San Francisco: Jossey-Bass, 1992).

[2] G. Morgan, *Images of Organization* (Beverly Hills, CA: Sage Publications, 1986).

[3] The material in this section draws on J. Child, *Organizations* (London: Harper & Row, 1984). Recent work addressing the issue includes J. R. Baum and S. Wally, "Strategic Decision Speed and Firm Performance," *Strategic Management Journal* 24 (2003): 1107–1120; D. I. Jung and B. J. Avolio, "Effects of Leadership Style and Followers Cultural Orientation on Performance in Groups and Individual Task Conditions," *Academy of Management Journal* 42 (1999): 208–218.

[4] This is a key tenet of the information-processing view of organizations. See J. Galbraith. *Designing Complex Organizations* (Reading, MA: Addison-Wesley, 1972).

[5] J. Kim and R. M. Burton, "The Effects of Uncertainty and Decentralization on Project Team Performance," *Computational & Mathematical Organization Theory* 8 (2002): 365–384.

[6] J. Birkinshaw, N. Hood, and S. Jonsson, "Building Firm Specific Advantages in Multinational Corporations: The Role of Subsidiary Initiatives," *Strategic Management Journal* 19 (1998): 221–241.

[7] K. M. Eisenhardt, "Making Fast Strategic Decisions in High Velocity Environments," *Academy of Management Journal* 32 (1989): 543–575.

[8] G. P. Hattrup and B. H. Kleiner, "How to Establish a Proper Span of Control for Managers," *Industrial Management* 35 (1993): 28–30.

[9] The classic statement was made by P. Milgrom and J. Roberts, "Bargaining Costs, Influence Costs and the Organization of Economic Activity," in J. E. Alt and K. A. Shepsle (eds.), *Perspectives in Positive Political Economy* (Cambridge: Cambridge University Press, 1990). Also see R. Inderst, H. M. Muller, and K. Warneryd, "Influence Costs and Hierarchy," *Economics of Governance* 6 (2005): 177–198.

[10] D. Priest and D. Linzer, "Panel Condemns Iraq Prewar Intelligence," *The Washington Post*, July 10, 2004, page A1; D. Jehl, "Senators Assail CIA Judgments of Iraq's Arms as Deeply Flawed," *New York Times,* July 10, 2004, page A1; M. Isikoff, "The Dots Never Existed," *Newsweek*, July 19, 2004, pp. 36–40.

[11] C. R. Littler, R. Wiesner and R. Dunford, "The Dynamics of Delayering," *Journal of Management Studies* 40 (2003): 225–240.

[12] J. A. Byrne, "Jack: A Close-up Look at How America's #1 Manager Runs GE," *Business Week*, June 8, 1998, pp 90–100. Also see *Harvard Business School Press*, "GE's Two Decade Transformation."

[13] A. D. Chandler, *Strategy and Structure: Chapters in the History of the Industrial Enterprise* (Cambridge, MA: MIT Press, 1962). Also see O. E. Williamson, *Markets and Hierarchies: Analysis and Anti-Trust Implications* (New York: Free Press, 1975).

[14] A. P. Sloan, *My Years at General Motors* (New York: Bantum Books, 1996). Originally published in 1963.

[15] C. W. L. Hill, M. A. Hitt, and R. E. Hoskisson. "Cooperative versus Competitive Structures in Related and Unrelated Firms," *Organization Science* 45 (1992): 501–521; O. E. Williamson, *Markets and Hierarchies: Analysis and Anti-Trust Implications* (New York: Free Press, 1975).

[16] C. W. L. Hill, M. A. Hitt, and R. E. Hoskisson, "Declining U.S. Competitiveness: Reflections on a Crisis," *Academy of Management Executives* 2 (1988): 51–60.

[17] P. R. Lawrence and J. Lorsch, *Organization and Environment* (Boston, MA: Harvard University Press, 1967).

[18] K. B. Clark and S. C. Wheelwright, *Managing New Product and Process Development* (New York: Free Press, 1993); M. A. Schilling and C. W. L. Hill, "Managing the New Product Development Process," *Academy of Management Executive* 12:3 (August 1998): 67–68; S. L. Brown and K. M.

Eisenhardt, "Product Development: Past Research, Present Findings, and Future Directions," *Academy of Management Review* 20 (1995): 343–378.

[19] L. R. Burns and D. R. Whorley, "Adoption and Abandonment of Matrix Management Programs: Effects of Organizational Characteristics and Interorganizational Networks," *Academy of Management Journal* (February 1993), pp. 106–138; C. A. Bartlett and S. Ghoshal, "Matrix Management: Not a Structure, a Frame of Mind," *Harvard Business Review* (July–August 1990): 138–145.

[20] S. Thomas and L. S. D'Annunizo, "Challenges and Strategies of Matrix Organizations," *HR Human Resource Planning* 28 (2005): 39–49.

[21] See J. R. Galbraith, *Designing Complex Organizations* (Reading, MA: Addison-Wesley, 1977).

[22] M. Goold and A. Campbell, "Structured Networks: Towards the Well Designed Matrix," *Long Range Planning* (October 2003): 427–460.

[23] Bartlett and Ghoshal, *Managing across Borders*; F. V. Guterl, "Goodbye, Old Matrix," *Business Month* (February 1989): 32–38; I. Bjorkman, W. Barner-Rasussen, and L. Li, "Managing Knowledge Transfer in MNCs: The Impact of Headquarters Control Mechanisms," *Journal of International Business* 35 (2004): 443–460.

[24] M. S. Granovetter, "The Strength of Weak Ties," *American Journal of Sociology* 78 (1973): 1360–1380.

[25] A. K. Gupta and V. J. Govindarajan, "Knowledge Flows within Multinational Corporations," *Strategic Management Journal* 21 (4) (2000): 473–496; V. J. Govindarajan and A. K. Gupta, *The Quest for Global Dominance* (San Francisco: Jossey-Bass, 2001); U. Andersson, M. Forsgren, and U. Holm, "The Strategic Impact of External Networks: Subsidiary Performance and Competence Development in the Multinational Corporation," *Strategic Management Journal* 23 (2002): 979–996.

[26] For examples, see W. H. Davidow and M. S. Malone, *The Virtual Corporation* (New York: Harper Collins, 1992).

[27] 3M. A Century of Innovation, the 3M Story. 3M, 2002. www.3m.com/about3m/century/index.jhtml.

[28] W. G. Ouchi, "Markets, Bureaucracies, and Clans," *Administrative Science Quarterly* 25 (1980): 129–144.

[29] J. Child, *Organization: A Guide to Problems and Practice* (Harper & Row: London, 1984).

[30] S. G. Green and M. A. Welsh. "Cybernetics and Dependence: Reframing the Control Concept," *Academy of Management Review* 13 (2) (1988): 287–301.

[31] J. Batsell, "Cost Cutting, Inventory Control Help Boost Nordstrom's Quarterly Profit," *Knight Ridder Tribune News* (February 22, 2002): 1; Nordstrom 2004 10K statement.

[32] For a recent summary, see D. M. Wiegand and E. S. Geller. "Connecting Positive Psychology and Organization Behavior Management," *Journal of Organization Behavior Management* 24 (12) (2004/2005): 3–20.

[33] J. Child, "Strategies of Control and Organization Behavior," *Administrative Science Quarterly* 18 (1973): 1–17; K. Eisenhardt, "Control: Organizational and Economic Approaches," *Management Science* 31 (1985): 134–149; S. A. Snell, "Control Theory in Human Resource Management," *Academy of Management Review* 35 (1992): 292–328; W. G. Ouchi, "The Transmission of Control Through Organizational Hierarchy," *Administrative Science Quarterly* 21 (1978): 173–192.

[34] J. Child, *Organization: A Guide to Problems and Practice* (Harper & Row: London, 1984).

[35] R. Teichroeb, "End to Forced Busing Creates New Problems for Seattle's Schools," *Seattle Post Intelligencer*, June 3, 1999, online edition. www.seattlepi.com

[36] J. Child, *Organization: A Guide to Problems and Practice* (Harper & Row: London, 1984).

[37] Hill, Hitt, and Hoskisson, "Cooperative versus Competitive Structures in Related and Unrelated Diversified Firms."

[38] J. D. Thompson, *Organizations in Action* (New York: McGraw Hill, 1967).

[39] O. E. Wiliamson. *The Economic Institutions of Capitalism* (New York: Free Press: 1985).

[40] C. Bartlett. "Philips versus Matsushita: A New Century, a New Round," *Harvard Business School Press* Case No. 9–302–049, 2005.

[41] L. Kim. "The Dynamics of Samsung's Technological Learning in Semiconductors," *California Management Review* 39:3 (1997): 86–101.

[42] Hill, Hitt, and Hoskisson, "Cooperative versus Competitive Structures in Related and Unrelated Diversified Firms."

[43] Peer control has long been argued to be a characteristic of many Japanese organizations. See M. Aoki, *Information, Incentives and Bargaining in the Japanese Economy* (Cambridge, UK: Cambridge University Press, 1988).

[44] E. H. Schein, *Organizational Culture and Leadership,* 2nd ed. (San Francisco: Jossey-Bass, 1992).

[45] J. P. Kotter and J. L. Heskett, *Corporate Culture and Performance* (New York: Free Press, 1992); M. L. Tushman and C. A. O'Reilly, *Winning through Innovation* (Boston, MA: Harvard Business School Press, 1997).

[46] The classic song of praise was produced by T. Peters and R. H. Waterman, *In Search of Excellence* (New York: Harper & Row, 1982). Ironically, IBM's decline

began shortly after their book was published.

[47] Kotter and Heskett, *Corporate Culture and Performance.*

[48] J. O'Connell, "Lincoln Electric: Venturing Abroad," Harvard Business School Press Case No. 9–398–095, April 1998, and www.lincolnelectric.com.

[49] M. Hammer and J. Champy, *Reengineering the Corporation* (New York: Harper Business, 1993).

[50] T. Kostova, "Transnational Transfer of Strategic Organizational Practices: A Contextual Perspective," *Academy of Management Review* 24:2 (1999): 308–324.

[51] Andersson, Forsgren, and Holm, "The Strategic Impact of External Networks: Subsidiary Performance and Competence Development in the Multinational Corporation."

[52] Ulf Anderson, Mats Forsgren, and Ulf Holm, "The strategic impact of external networks: Subsidiary performance and competence development in the multinational corporation," *Strategic Management Journal* 23:11 (2002): pp. 979–996.

[53] P. R Lawrence and J. Lorsch, *Organization and Environment.* (Boston, MA: Harvard University Press, 1967).

[54] Hill, Hitt, and Hoskisson, "Cooperative versus Competitive Structures in Related and Unrelated Firms."

[55] Ibid.

[56] C. W. L. Hill, "The Role of Corporate Headquarters in the Multidivisional Firm," in R. Rumelt, D. J. Teece, and D. Schendel (eds.), *Fundamental Issues in Strategy Research.* (Cambridge, MA: Harvard Business School Press, 1994), pp. 297–321.

[57] C. W. L. Hill and R. E. Hoskisson. "Strategy and Structure in the Multiproduct Firm," *Academy of Management Review* 12 (1988): 331–341.

Chatchai.b/Shutterstock.com

Part 5

Cases in Strategic Management

Cases

Cases					
	Chapter 1	**Chapter 2**	**Chapter 3**	**Chapter 4**	**Chapter 5**
Long Cases	**Introduction**	**External Analysis**	**Internal Analysis**	**Business Level Strategy**	**Functional Level Strategy**
1 Google: The Rise of an Internet Monopoly	X	X	X	X	X
2 Toyota: The Rise of the Lean Machine	X		X	X	X
3 Tesla Inc. in 2022			X		X
4 Zeta Energy: The Collaboration Decision		X	X		
5 Staples		X	X	X	X
6 Walmart Stores	X	X	X	X	X
7 IKEA	X	X	X	X	X
8 Coca Cola	X	X	X	X	
9 Jose Cuervo: The making of a legendary tequila brand		X	X	X	X
10 Boeing Commercial Aircraft		X	X	X	X
11 Charles Schwab 2022	X	X	X	X	X
12 Uber 2022		X	X	X	X
13 Uber Elevate Failure to Launch					
14 Microsoft (A) - The Gates and Ballmer Years	X	X	X	X	X
15 Microsoft (B) - Satya Nadella and the Push into Cloud Compouting		X	X	X	X
16 Consol Wars		X		X	
17 Space X: Disrupting the Space Industry				X	
18 Alibaba: The Rise of a Platform Giant					
19 Upside Foods: Changing the World Through Cultivated Meat					
20 3M	X		X	X	
21 General Electric	X		X	X	

Chapter 6	Chapter 7	Chapter 8	Chapter 9	Chapter 10	Chapter 11	Chapter 12
Business Level Strategy and Industry Environment	Strategy and Technology	Strategy in the Global Environment	Corporate Level Strategy	Corporate Level Strategy	Corporate Governance	Implementing Strategy
X	X		X			X
X			X	X		
	X		X			
		X				X
X		X				
X						
			X	X		
		X				
X	X					
	X		X			
X	X					X
X	X					X
X	X					
	X		X			
	X		X	X		
	X				X	
		X		X		X
				X		X

	Short Cases	Chapter 1 Introduction	Chapter 2 External Analysis	Chapter 3 Internal Analysis	Chapter 4 Business Level Strategy	Chapter 5 Functional Level Strategy
22	Competition in the Wireless Telecom Industry		X			
23	The Rise of Lululemon			X	X	X
24	Southwest Airlines		X	X	X	X
25	Virgin America		X	X	X	X
26	McDonald's			X	X	X
27	Starbucks: Expanding Globally			X	X	X
28	Starbbucks: taking a Stand on Social Issues					
29	JCB in India					
30	Organization Change at Google					
31	Battle for Dominance in Mobile Payments			X		
32	Proposed Merger of Comcast and Time Warner					
33	HP's Acquisition of Autonomy					
34	Louis Vuitton					

Chapter 6	Chapter 7	Chapter 8	Chapter 9	Chapter 10	Chapter 11	Chapter 12
Business Level Strategy and Industry Environment	Strategy and Technology	Strategy in the Global Environment	Corporate Level Strategy	Corporate Level Strategy	Corporate Governance	Implementing Strategy
		X				
					X	
		X				
						X
	X					
			X	X		
				X	X	
			X	X		

Anna Om/Shutterstock.com

Introduction

Analyzing a Case Study and Writing a Case Study Analysis

What Is Case Study Analysis?

Case study analysis is an integral part of a course in strategic management. The purpose of a case study is to provide students with experience of the strategic management problems that actual organizations face. A case study presents an account of what happened to a business or industry over a number of years. It chronicles the events that managers had to deal with, such as changes in the competitive environment, and charts the managers' response, which usually involved changing the business- or corporate-level strategy. The cases in this book cover a wide range of issues and problems that managers have had to confront. Some cases are about finding the right business-level strategy to compete in changing conditions. Some are about companies that grew by acquisition, with little concern for the rationale behind their growth, and how growth by acquisition affected their future profitability. Each case is different because each organization is different. The underlying thread in all cases, however, is the use of strategic management techniques to solve business problems.

Cases prove valuable in a strategic management course for several reasons. First, cases provide you, the student, with experience of organizational problems that you probably have not had the opportunity to experience firsthand. In a relatively short period of time, you will have the chance to appreciate and analyze the problems faced by many different companies and to understand how managers tried to deal with them.

Second, cases illustrate the theory and content of strategic management. The meaning and implications of this information are made clearer when they are applied to case studies. The theory and concepts help reveal what is going on in the companies studied and allow you to evaluate the solutions that specific companies adopted to deal with their problems. Consequently, when you analyze cases, you will be like a detective who, with a set of conceptual tools, probes what happened and what or who was responsible and then marshals the evidence that provides the solution. Top managers enjoy the thrill of testing their problem-solving abilities in the real world. It is important to remember that no one knows what the right answer is. All that managers can do is to make the best guess. In fact, managers say repeatedly that they are happy if they are right only half the time in solving strategic problems. Strategic management is an uncertain game, and using cases to see how theory can be put into practice is one way of improving your skills of diagnostic investigation.

Third, case studies provide you with the opportunity to participate in class and to gain experience in presenting your ideas to others. Instructors may sometimes call on students as a group to identify what is going on in a case, and through classroom discussion the issues in and solutions to the case problem will reveal themselves. In such a situation, you will have to organize your views and conclusions so that you can present them to the class. Your classmates may have analyzed the issues differently from you, and they will want you to argue your points before they will accept your conclusions, so be prepared for debate. This mode of discussion is an example of the dialectical approach to decision making. This is how decisions are made in the actual business world.

Instructors also may assign an individual, but more commonly a group, to analyze the case before the whole class. The individual or group probably will be responsible for a 30 to 40 minute presentation of the case to the class. That presentation must cover the issues posed, the problems facing the company, and a series of recommendations for resolving the problems. The discussion then will be thrown open to the class, and you will have to defend your ideas. Through such discussions and presentations, you will experience how to convey your ideas effectively to others. Remember that a great deal of managers' time is spent in these kinds of situations: presenting their ideas and engaging in discussion with other managers who have their own views about what is going on. Thus, you will experience in the classroom the actual process of strategic management, and this will serve you well in your future career.

If you work in groups to analyze case studies, you also will learn about the group process involved in working as a team. When people work in groups, it is often difficult to schedule time and allocate responsibility for the case analysis. There are always group members who shirk their responsibilities and group members who are so sure of their own ideas that they try to dominate the group's analysis. Most of the strategic management takes place in groups, however, and it is best if you learn about these problems now.

Analyzing a Case Study

The purpose of the case study is to let you apply the concepts of strategic management when you analyze the issues facing a specific company. To analyze a case study, therefore, you must examine closely the issues confronting the company. Most often you will need to read the case several times—once to grasp the overall picture of what is happening to the company and then several times more to discover and grasp the specific problems.

Generally, detailed analysis of a case study should include eight areas:

1. The history, development, and growth of the company over time
2. The nature of the external environment surrounding the company
3. The identification of the company's internal strengths and weaknesses, and whether it has sources of sustainable competitive advantage
4. A SWOT analysis
5. The kind of corporate-level strategy that the company is pursuing
6. The nature of the company's business-level strategy
7. The company's structure and control systems and how they match its strategy
8. Recommendations

To analyze a case, you need to apply the concepts taught in this course to each of these areas. To help you further, we next offer a summary of the steps you can take to analyze the case material for each of the eight points we just noted:

1. *Analyze the company's history, development, and growth.* A convenient way to investigate how a company's past strategy and structure affect it in the present is to chart the critical incidents in its history—that is, the events that were the most unusual or the most essential for its development into the company it is today. Some of the events have to do with its founding, its initial products, how it makes new-product market decisions, and how it developed and chose functional competencies to pursue. Its entry into new businesses and shifts in its main lines of business are also important milestones to consider.

2. *Analyze the external environment.* To identify environmental opportunities and threats, apply all the concepts on industry and macroenvironments to analyze the environment the company is confronting. Of particular importance at the industry level are the Competitive Forces Model, adapted from Porter's Five Forces Model and the stage of the life-cycle model. Which factors in the macroenvironment will appear salient depends on the specific company being analyzed. Use each factor in turn (e.g., demographic factors) to see whether it is relevant for the company in question.

3. *Identify the company's internal strengths and weaknesses.* Once the historical profile is completed, you can begin the SWOT analysis. Use all the incidents you have charted to develop an account of the company's strengths and weaknesses as they have emerged historically. Examine each of the value creation functions of the company, and identify the functions in which the company is currently strong and currently weak. Some companies might be weak in marketing; some might be strong in research and development. Make lists of these strengths and weaknesses. The SWOT Checklist (Table 1) gives examples of what might go in these lists.

   Having done this analysis, you will have generated both an analysis of the company's environment and a list of opportunities and threats. The SWOT Checklist table also lists some common environmental opportunities and threats that you may look for, but the list you generate will be specific to your company.

4. *Evaluate the SWOT analysis.* Having identified the company's external opportunities and threats as well as its internal strengths and weaknesses, consider what your findings mean. You need to balance strengths and weaknesses against opportunities and threats. Is the company in an overall strong competitive position? Can it continue to pursue its current business- or corporate-level strategy profitably? What can the company do to turn weaknesses into strengths and threats into opportunities? Can it develop new functional, business, or corporate strategies to accomplish this change? *Never merely generate the SWOT analysis and then put it aside.* Because it provides a succinct summary of the company's condition, a good SWOT analysis is the key to all the analyses that follow.

5. *Analyze corporate-level strategy.* To analyze corporate-level strategy, you first need to define the company's mission and goals. Sometimes the mission and goals are stated explicitly in the case; at other times, you will have to infer them from available information. The information you need to collect to find out the company's corporate strategy includes such factors as its lines of business and the nature of its subsidiaries and acquisitions. It is important to analyze the relationship among the company's businesses. Do they trade or exchange resources? Are there gains to be achieved from synergy? Alternatively, is the company just running a portfolio of investments? This analysis should enable you to define the corporate strategy that the company is pursuing (e.g., related or unrelated diversification, or a combination of both) and to conclude whether the company operates in just one core business. Then, using your SWOT analysis, debate the merits of this strategy. Is it appropriate given the environment the company is in? Could a change in corporate strategy provide the company with new opportunities or transform a weakness into a strength? For example, should the company diversify from its core business into new businesses?

   Other issues should be considered as well. How and why has the company's strategy changed over time? What is the claimed rationale for any changes? Often, it is a good idea to analyze the company's businesses or products to assess its situation and identify which divisions contribute the most to or detract from its competitive advantage. It is also useful to explore how the company has built its portfolio over time. Did it acquire new businesses, or did it internally venture its own? All of these factors provide clues about the company and indicate ways of improving its future performance.

Table 1 A SWOT Checklist

Potential Internal Strengths	Potential Internal Weaknesses
Many product lines?	Obsolete, narrow product lines?
Broad market coverage?	Rising manufacturing costs?
Manufacturing competence?	Decline in R&D innovations?
Good marketing skills?	Poor marketing plan?
Good materials management systems?	Poor material management systems?
R&D skills and leadership?	Loss of customer good will?
Information system competencies?	Inadequate human resources?
Human resource competencies?	Inadequate information systems?
Brand name reputation?	Loss of brand name capital?
Portfolio management skills?	Growth without direction?
Cost of differentiation advantage?	Bad portfolio management?
New-venture management expertise?	Loss of corporate direction?
Appropriate management style?	Infighting among divisions?
Appropriate organizational structure?	Loss of corporate control?
Appropriate control systems?	Inappropriate organizational
Ability to manage strategic change?	structure and control systems?
Well-developed corporate strategy?	High conflict and politics?
Good financial management?	Poor financial management?
Others?	Others?
Potential Environmental Opportunities	Potential Environment Threats
Expand core business(es)?	Attacks on core business(es)?
Exploit new market segments?	Increases in domestic competition?
Widen product range?	Increase in foreign competition?
Extend cost or differentiation advantage?	Change in consumer tastes?
Diversify into new growth businesses?	Fall in barriers to entry?
Expand into foreign markets?	Rise in new or substitute products?
Apply R&D skills in new areas?	Increase in industry rivalry?
Enter new related businesses?	New forms of industry competition?
Vertically integrate forward?	Potential for takeover?
Vertically integrate backward?	Existence of corporate raiders?
Enlarge corporate portfolio?	Increase in regional competition?
Overcome barriers to entry?	Changes in demographic factors?
Reduce rivalry among competitors?	Changes in economic factors?
Make profitable new acquisitions?	Downturn in economy?
Apply brand name capital in new areas?	Rising labor costs?
Seek fast market growth?	Slower market growth?
Others?	Others?

6. *Analyze business-level strategy.* Once you know the company's corporate-level strategy and have done the SWOT analysis, the next step is to identify the company's business-level strategy. If the company is in many businesses, each business will have its own business-level strategy. You will need to identify the company's generic competitive strategy—differentiation, low-cost, or focus—and its investment strategy, given its relative competitive position and the stage of the life cycle. The company also may market different products using different business-level strategies. For example, it may offer a low-cost product range and a line of differentiated products. Be sure to give a full account of a company's business-level strategy to show how it competes.

Identifying the functional strategies that a company pursues to build competitive advantage through superior efficiency, quality, innovation, and customer responsiveness and to achieve its business-level strategy is very important. The SWOT analysis will have provided you with information on the company's functional competencies. You should investigate its production, marketing, or research and development strategy further to gain a picture of where the company is going. For example, pursuing a low-cost or a differentiation strategy successfully requires very different sets of competencies. Has the company developed the right ones? If it has, how can it exploit them further? Can it pursue both a low-cost and a differentiation strategy simultaneously?

The SWOT analysis is especially important at this point if the industry analysis, particularly Porter's model, has revealed threats to the company from the environment. Can the company deal with these threats? How should it change its business-level strategy to counter them? To evaluate the potential of a company's business-level strategy, you must first perform a thorough SWOT analysis that captures the essence of its problems.

Once you complete this analysis, you will have a full picture of the way the company is operating and be in a position to evaluate the potential of its strategy. Thus, you will be able to make recommendations concerning the pattern of its future actions. However, first you need to consider strategy implementation, or the way the company tries to achieve its strategy.

7. *Analyze structure and control systems.* The aim of this analysis is to identify what structure and control systems the company is using to implement its strategy and to evaluate whether that structure is the appropriate one for the company. Different corporate and business strategies require different structures. You need to determine the *degree of fit between the company's strategy and structure.* For example, does the company have the right level of vertical differentiation (e.g., does it have the appropriate number of levels in the hierarchy or decentralized control?) or horizontal differentiation (e.g., does it use a functional structure when it should be using a product structure?)? Similarly, is the company using the right integration or control systems to manage its operations? Are managers being appropriately rewarded? Are the right rewards in place for encouraging cooperation among divisions? These are all issues to consider.

In some cases, there will be little information on these issues, whereas in others there will be a lot. In analyzing each case, you should gear the analysis toward its most salient issues. For example, organizational conflict, power, and politics will be important issues for some companies. Try to analyze why problems in these areas are occurring. Do they occur because of bad strategy formulation or because of bad strategy implementation?

Organizational change is an issue in many cases because the companies are attempting to alter their strategies or structures to solve strategic problems. Thus, as part of the analysis, you might suggest an action plan that the company in question could use to achieve its goals. For example, you might list in a logical sequence the steps the company would need to follow to alter its business-level strategy from differentiation to focus.

8. *Make recommendations.* The quality of your recommendations is a direct result of the thoroughness with which you prepared the case analysis. Recommendations are directed at solving whatever strategic problem the company is facing and increasing its future profitability. Your recommendations should be in line with your analysis; that is, they should follow logically from the previous discussion. For example, your recommendation generally will center on the specific ways of changing functional, business, and corporate strategies and organizational structure and control to improve business performance. The set of recommendations will be specific to each case, and so it is difficult to discuss these recommendations here. Such recommendations might include an increase in spending on specific research and development projects, the divesting of certain businesses, a change from a strategy of unrelated to related diversification, an increase in the level of integration among divisions by using task forces and teams, or a move to a different kind of structure to implement a new business-level strategy. Make sure your recommendations are mutually consistent and written in the form of an action plan. The plan might contain a timetable that sequences the actions for changing the company's strategy and a description of how changes at the corporate level will necessitate changes at the business level and subsequently at the functional level.

After following all these stages, you will have performed a thorough analysis of the case and will be in a position to join in class discussion or present your ideas to the class, depending on the format used by your professor. Remember that you must tailor your analysis to suit the specific issue discussed in your case. In some cases, you might completely omit one of the steps in the analysis because it is not relevant to the situation you are considering. You must be sensitive to the needs of the case and not apply the framework we have discussed in this section blindly. The framework is meant only as a guide, not as an outline.

Writing a Case Study Analysis

Often, as part of your course requirements, you will need to present a written case analysis. This may be an individual or a group report. Whatever the situation, there are certain guidelines to follow in writing a case analysis that will improve the evaluation your work will receive from your instructor. Before we discuss these guidelines and before you use them, make sure that they do not conflict with any directions your instructor has given you.

The structure of your written report is critical. Generally, if you follow the steps for analysis discussed in the previous section, *you already will have a good structure for your written discussion.* All reports begin with an *introduction* to the case. In it, outline briefly what the company does, how it developed historically, what problems it is experiencing, and how you are going to approach the issues in the case write-up. Do this sequentially by writing, for example, "First, we discuss the environment of Company. . . . Third, we discuss Company X's business-level strategy. . . . Last, we provide recommendations for turning around Company X's business."

In the second part of the case write-up, the *strategic analysis* section, do the SWOT analysis, analyze and discuss the nature and problems of the company's business-level and corporate strategies, and then analyze its structure and control systems. Make sure you use plenty of headings and subheadings to structure your analysis. For example, have separate sections on any important conceptual tool you use. Thus, you might have a section on the Competitive Forces Model as part of your analysis of the environment. You might offer a separate section on portfolio techniques when analyzing a company's corporate strategy. Tailor the sections and subsections to the specific issues of importance in the case.

In the third part of the case write-up, present your *solutions and recommendations*. Be comprehensive, and make sure they are in line with the previous analysis so that the recommendations fit together and move logically from one to the next. The recommendations section is very revealing because your instructor will have a good idea of how much work you put into the case from the quality of your recommendations.

Following this framework will provide a good structure for most written reports, though it must be shaped to fit the individual case being considered. Some cases are about excellent companies experiencing no problems. In such instances, it is hard to write recommendations. Instead, you can focus on analyzing why the company is doing so well, using that analysis to structure the discussion. Following are some minor suggestions that can help make a good analysis even better:

1. Do not repeat in summary form large pieces of factual information from the case. The instructor has read the case and knows what is going on. Rather, use the information in the case to illustrate your statements, defend your arguments, or make salient points. Beyond the brief introduction to the company, you must avoid being *descriptive*; instead, you must be *analytical*.
2. Make sure the sections and subsections of your discussion flow logically and smoothly from one to the next. That is, try to build on what has gone before so that the analysis of the case study moves toward a climax. This is particularly important for group analysis, because there is a tendency for people in a group to split up the work and say, "I'll do the beginning, you take the middle, and I'll do the end." The result is a choppy, stilted analysis; the parts do not flow from one to the next, and it is obvious to the instructor that no real group work has been done.
3. Avoid grammatical and spelling errors. They make your work look sloppy.
4. In some instances, cases dealing with well-known companies end in 1998 or 1999 because no later information was available when the case was written. If possible, do a search for more information on what has happened to the company in subsequent years.

Many libraries now have comprehensive web-based electronic data search facilities that offer such sources as *ABI/Inform, The Wall Street Journal Index,* the *F&S Index,* and the *Nexis-Lexis* databases. These enable you to identify any article that has been written in the business press on the company of your choice within the past few years. A number of nonelectronic data sources are also useful. For example, *F&S Predicasts* publishes an annual list of articles relating to major companies that appeared in the national and international business press. *S&P Industry Surveys* is a great source for basic industry data, and *Value Line Ratings and Reports* can contain good summaries of a firm's financial position and future prospects. You will also want to collect full financial information on the company. Again, this can be accessed from web-based electronic databases such as the *Edgar* database, which archives all forms that publicly quoted companies have to file with the Securities and Exchange Commission (SEC; e.g., 10-K filings can be accessed from the SEC's *Edgar* database). Most SEC forms for public companies can now be accessed from Internet-based financial sites, such as Yahoo's finance site (http://finance.yahoo.com/).

5. Sometimes instructors hand out questions for each case to help you in your analysis. Use these as a guide for writing the case analysis. They often illuminate the important issues that have to be covered in the discussion.

If you follow the guidelines in this section, you should be able to write a thorough and effective evaluation.

The Role of Financial Analysis in Case Study Analysis

An important aspect of analyzing a case study and writing a case study analysis is the role and use of financial information. A careful analysis of the company's financial condition immensely improves a case write-up. After all, financial data represent the concrete results of the company's strategy and structure. Although analyzing financial statements can be quite complex, a general idea of a company's financial position can be determined through the use of ratio analysis. Financial performance ratios can be calculated from the balance sheet and income statement. These ratios can be classified into five subgroups: profit ratios, liquidity ratios, activity ratios, leverage ratios, and shareholder-return ratios. These ratios should be compared with the industry average or the company's prior years of performance. It should be noted, however, that deviation from the average is not necessarily bad; it simply warrants further investigation. For example, young companies will have purchased assets at a different price and will likely have a different capital structure than older companies do. In addition to ratio analysis, a company's cash flow position is of critical importance and should be assessed. Cash flow shows how much actual cash a company possesses.

Profit Ratios

Profit ratios measure the efficiency with which the company uses its resources. The more efficient the company, the greater is its profitability. It is useful to compare a company's profitability against that of its major competitors in its industry to determine whether the company is operating more or less efficiently than its rivals. In addition, the change in a company's profit ratios over time tells whether its performance is improving or declining.

A number of different profit ratios can be used, and each of them measures a different aspect of a company's performance. Here, we look at the most commonly used profit ratios.

Return on Invested Capital (ROIC) This ratio measures the profit earned on the capital invested in the company. It is defined as follows:

$$\text{Return on invested capital (ROIC)} = \frac{\text{Net profit}}{\text{Invested capital}}$$

Net profit is calculated by subtracting the total costs of operating the company away from its total revenues (total revenues − total costs). Total costs are the (1) costs of goods sold, (2) sales, general, and administrative expenses, (3) R&D expenses, and (4) other expenses. Net profit can be calculated before or after taxes, although many financial analysts prefer the before-tax figure. Invested capital is the amount that is invested in the operations of a company—that is, in property, plant, equipment, inventories, and other assets. Invested capital comes from two main sources: interest-bearing debt and shareholders' equity. Interest-bearing debt is money the company borrows from banks and from those who purchase its bonds. Shareholders' equity is the money raised from selling shares to the public, *plus* earnings that have been retained by the company in prior years and are available to fund current investments. ROIC measures the effectiveness with which a company is using the capital funds that it has available for investment. As such, it is recognized to be an excellent measure of the value a company is creating.[1] Remember that a company's ROIC can be decomposed into its constituent parts.

Return on Total Assets (ROA)   This ratio measures the profit earned on the employment of assets. It is defined as follows:

$$\text{Return on total assets} = \frac{\text{Net profit}}{\text{Total assets}}$$

Return on Stockholders' Equity (ROE)   This ratio measures the percentage of profit earned on common stockholders' investment in the company. It is defined as follows:

$$\text{Return on stockholders Equity} = \frac{\text{Net profit}}{\text{Stockholders Equity}}$$

If a company has no debt, this will be the same as ROIC.

Liquidity Ratios

A company's liquidity is a measure of its ability to meet short-term obligations. An asset is deemed liquid if it can be readily converted into cash. Liquid assets are current assets such as cash, marketable securities, accounts receivable, and so on. Two liquidity ratios are commonly used.

Current Ratio   The current ratio measures the extent to which the claims of short-term creditors are covered by assets that can be quickly converted into cash. Most companies should have a ratio of at least 1 because failure to meet these commitments can lead to bankruptcy. The ratio is defined as follows:

$$\text{Current ratio} = \frac{\text{Current assets}}{\text{Current liabilities}}$$

Quick Ratio   The quick ratio measures a company's ability to pay off the claims of short-term creditors without relying on selling its inventories. This is a valuable measure since in practice the sale of inventories is often difficult. It is defined as follows:

$$\text{Quick ratio} = \frac{\text{Current assets} - \text{Inventory}}{\text{Current liabilities}}$$

Activity Ratios

Activity ratios indicate how effectively a company is managing its assets. Two ratios are particularly useful.

Inventory Turnover   This measures the number of times inventory is turned over. It is useful in determining whether a firm is carrying excess stock in inventory. It is defined as follows:

$$\text{Inventory turnover} = \frac{\text{Cost of goods sold}}{\text{Inventory}}$$

Cost of goods sold is a better measure of turnover than sales because it is the cost of the inventory items. Inventory is taken at the balance sheet date. Some companies choose to compute an average inventory, beginning inventory, and ending inventory, but for simplicity, use the inventory at the balance sheet date.

Days Sales Outstanding (DSO) or Average Collection Period   This ratio is the average time a company has to wait to receive its cash after making a sale. It measures how effective the company's credit, billing, and collection procedures are. It is defined as follows:

$$\text{DSO} = \frac{\text{Accounts receivable}}{\text{Total sales}/360}$$

Accounts receivable is divided by average daily sales. The use of 360 is the standard number of days for most financial analysis.

Leverage Ratios

A company is said to be highly leveraged if it uses more debt than equity, including stock and retained earnings. The balance between debt and equity is called the *capital structure*. The optimal capital structure is determined by the individual company. Debt has a lower cost because creditors take less risk; they know they will get their interest and principal. However, debt can be risky to the firm because if enough profit is not made to cover the interest and principal payments, bankruptcy can result. Three leverage ratios are commonly used.

Debt-to-Assets Ratio The debt-to-assets ratio is the most direct measure of the extent to which borrowed funds have been used to finance a company's investments. It is defined as follows:

$$\text{Debt-to-assets ratio} = \frac{\text{Total debt}}{\text{Total assets}}$$

Total debt is the sum of a company's current liabilities and its long-term debt, and total assets are the sum of fixed assets and current assets.

Debt-to-Equity Ratio The debt-to-equity ratio indicates the balance between debt and equity in a company's capital structure. This is perhaps the most widely used measure of a company's leverage. It is defined as follows:

$$\text{Debt-to-equity ratio} = \frac{\text{Total debt}}{\text{Total equity}}$$

Times-Covered Ratio The times-covered ratio measures the extent to which a company's gross profit covers its annual interest payments. If this ratio declines to less than 1, the company is unable to meet its interest costs and is technically insolvent. The ratio is defined as follows:

$$\text{Times-covered ratio} = \frac{\text{Profit before interest and tax}}{\text{Total interest charges}}$$

Shareholder-Return Ratios

Shareholder-return ratios measure the return that shareholders earn from holding stock in the company. Given the goal of maximizing stockholders' wealth, providing shareholders with an adequate rate of return is a primary objective of most companies. As with profit ratios, it can be helpful to compare a company's shareholder returns against those of similar companies as a yardstick for determining how well the company is satisfying the demands of this particularly important group of organizational constituents. Four ratios are commonly used.

Total Shareholder Returns Total shareholder returns measure the returns earned by time $t + 1$ on an investment in a company's stock made at time t. (Time t is the time at which the initial investment is made.) Total shareholder returns include both dividend payments and appreciation in the value of the stock (adjusted for stock splits) and are defined as follows:

$$\text{Total shareholder returns} = \frac{\begin{array}{c}\text{Stock price } (t+1) - \text{stock price}(t) \\ + \text{ sum of annual dividends per share}\end{array}}{\text{Stock price } (t)}$$

If a shareholder invests $2 at time t and at time $t + 1$ the share is worth $3, while the sum of annual dividends for the period t to $t + 1$ has amounted to $0.20, total shareholder returns are equal to $(3 - 2 + 0.2)/2 = 0.6$, which is a 60% return on an initial investment of $2 made at time t.

Price-Earnings Ratio   The price-earnings ratio measures the amount investors are willing to pay per dollar of profit. It is defined as follows:

$$\text{Price-earnings ratio} = \frac{\text{Market price per share}}{\text{Earnings per share}}$$

Market-to-Book Value   Market-to-book value measures a company's expected future growth prospects. It is defined as follows:

$$\text{Market-to-book value} = \frac{\text{Market price per share}}{\text{Earnings per share}}$$

Dividend Yield   The dividend yield measures the return to shareholders received in the form of dividends. It is defined as follows:

$$\text{Dividend} = \frac{\text{Dividend per share}}{\text{Market price per share}}$$

Market price per share can be calculated for the first of the year, in which case the dividend yield refers to the return on an investment made at the beginning of the year. Alternatively, the average share price over the year may be used. A company must decide how much of its profits to pay to stockholders and how much to reinvest in the company. Companies with strong growth prospects should have a lower dividend payout ratio than mature companies. The rationale is that shareholders can invest the money elsewhere if the company is not growing. The optimal ratio depends on the individual firm, but the key decider is whether the company can produce better returns than the investor can earn elsewhere.

Cash Flow

Cash flow position is cash received minus cash distributed. The net cash flow can be taken from a company's statement of cash flows. Cash flow is important for what it reveals about a company's financing needs. A strong positive cash flow enables a company to fund future investments without having to borrow money from bankers or investors. This is desirable because the company avoids paying out interest or dividends. A weak or negative cash flow means that a company has to turn to external sources to fund future investments. Generally, companies in strong-growth industries often find themselves in a poor cash flow position (because their investment needs are substantial), whereas successful companies based in mature industries generally find themselves in a strong cash flow position.

A company's internally generated cash flow is calculated by adding back its depreciation provision to profits after interest, taxes, and dividend payments. If this figure is insufficient to cover proposed new investments, the company has little choice but to borrow funds to make up the shortfall or to curtail investments. If this figure exceeds proposed new investments, the company can use the excess to build up its liquidity (i.e., through investments in financial assets) or repay existing loans ahead of schedule.

Conclusion

When evaluating a case, it is important to be *systematic*. Analyze the case in a logical fashion, beginning with the identification of operating and financial strengths and weaknesses and environmental opportunities and threats. Move on to assess the value of a company's current strategies only when you are fully conversant with the SWOT analysis of the company. Ask yourself whether the company's current strategies make sense given its SWOT analysis. If they do not, what changes need to be made? What are your recommendations? Above all, link any strategic recommendations you may make to the SWOT analysis. State explicitly how the strategies you identify take advantage of the company's strengths to exploit environmental opportunities, how they rectify the company's weaknesses, and how they counter environmental threats. Also, do not forget to outline what needs to be done to implement your recommendations.

Note

[1] Tom Copeland, Tim Koller, and Jack Murrin, *Valuation: Measuring and Managing the Value of Companies* (New York: Wiley, 1996).

Case 1

Google: The Rise of an Internet Monopoly

Charles W. L. Hill School of Business University of Washington, Seattle, 98195 July 2022

C1-1 Introduction

In the early 2000s, many Internet users started to gravitate towards a new search engine. It was called Google, and it delivered remarkable results. Put in a keyword, and in a blink of an eye the search engine would return a list of links, with the most relevant links appearing at the top of the page. People quickly realized that Google was an amazing tool, enabling users to quickly find almost anything they wanted on the web—to effortlessly sort through the vast sea of information contained in billions of web pages and retrieve the precise information they desired. It seemed like magic. Before long, "to Google" became a verb (in June 2006, the verb Google was added to the Oxford English Dictionary). To find out more about a person, you would "Google them." To find out more about a subject, you would "Google it." If you wanted to find a good or service, enter a key word in Google, and a list of relevant links would be returned in an instant. For many users, Google quickly became the "go to" page every time they wanted information about anything.

What captured the attention of the business community, however, was Google's ability to monetize its search results. Google's core business model was the essence of simplicity. The company auctioned off the keywords used in searches to advertisers. The highest bidders would have links to their sites placed on the right-hand side of a page returning search results (nowadays the links appear at the top of the page). The advertisers would then pay Google every time someone clicked on a link and was directed to their site. Thus, when bidding for a keyword, advertisers would bid for the price per click. Interestingly, Google did not necessarily place the advertiser who bid the highest amount per click at the top of the page. Rather, the top spot was determined by the amount per click multiplied by Google's statistical estimate of the likelihood that someone would click on the advertisement. This refinement maximized the revenue that Google got from its valuable real estate.

By 2022, Google dominated the online search market with an 80% plus global share of all searches (desktop and mobile), via which it generates strong revenue growth and profits. In 2021 Google's parent company, Alphabet, recorded revenues of $258 billion, net income of $75 billion, $103 billion in free cash flow, and a return on invested capital (ROIC) of 28.4%. Alphabet derives nearly all its revenue and all its profit from the Google search engine business (although its Google Cloud Platform business is now growing rapidly and earned revenues of $19.2 billion in 2021).[1]

In the United States, which is the most competitive of all major markets in which Google competes, in 2021 Google processes three times and four times as many desktop search requests as Bing (Microsoft) and Yahoo (Verizon), respectively. Microsoft's Bing has been gaining share in desktop searches, where it had 26.8% of the market in early 2022, up from 19.6% in 2014. Google had a 61.4% share of U.S. desktop searches in 2021, down from 67% in 2014. However, Google completely dominates the mobile search market with a 95%+ global share and 93% in the United States. Microsoft, which does not have a viable mobile phone operating system, has less than 2% of this market (Apple, which has a 55% share of mobile phone operating systems with iOS, uses Google as the default search engine).[2]

C1-2 Search Engines[3]

A search engine connects the keywords that users enter (queries) to a database it has created of web pages (an index). It then produces a list of links to pages (and summaries of content) that it believes are most relevant to a query.

Search engines consist of four main components—a web crawler, an index, a runtime index, and a query processor (the interface that connects users to the index). The web crawler is a piece of software that goes from link to link on the web, collecting the pages it finds and sending them back to the index. Once in the index, sophisticated algorithms that look for statistical patterns analyze web pages. Among other variables, for example, Google's page rank algorithm looks at the links on a page, the text around those links, and the popularity of the pages that link to that page, to determine how relevant a page is to a particular query (in total, Google's algorithm looks at more than 100 factors to determine a page's relevance to a query term).

Once analyzed, pages are tagged. The tag contains information about the pages, for example, whether it is porn, or spam, written in a certain language, or updated infrequently. Tagged pages are then dumped into a runtime index, which is a database that is ready to serve users. The runtime index forms a bridge between the back end of an engine, the web crawler and index, and the front end, the query processor and user interface. The query processor takes a keyword inputted by a user, transports it to the runtime index, where an algorithm matches the keyword to pages, ranking them by relevance, and then transports the results back to the user, where they are displayed on the user interface.

The computing and data storage infrastructure required to support a search engine is significant. It must scale with the continued growth of the web and with demands on the search engine. In 2021, Google had $56 billion in information technology assets on its balance sheet, and another $59 billion tied up in land and buildings. A significant chunk of these assets were in 23 data centers, each of which contained up to 1 million servers, each configured in large-scale clusters dedicated to the job of running its search engine.[4]

C1-3 The Early Days of Search

The first Internet search engine was Archie. Created in 1990 at McGill University in Montreal, Canada, before the World Wide Web had burst onto the scene, Archie connected users through queries to the machines on which documents they wanted were stored. The users then had to dig through the public files on those machines to find what they wanted. The next search engine, Veronica, developed in 1992 at the University of Nevada, Reno, improved on Archie insofar as it did allow searchers to connect directly to the document they had queried. Veronica was the primary search engine for Gopher Protocol, an alternative system to the World Wide Web.

The web started to take off after 1993, with the number of websites expanding from 130 to more than 600,000 by 1996. As this expansion occurred, the problem of finding the information you wanted on the web became more difficult. The first web-based search engine was the WWW Wanderer, developed by Matthew Gray at MIT. This was soon surpassed by Web Crawler, which was a search engine developed by

Brian Pinkerton of the University of washington. Web Crawler was the first search engine to index the full text of web pages, as opposed to just the title. Web Crawler was sold to AOL for $1 million in 1995. This marked the first time anyone had ascribed an economic value to a search engine.

In December 1995, the next search engine appeared on the scene, AltaVista. Developed by an employee at Digital Equipment Corporation (DEC), Louis Monier, like Web Crawler, AltaVista indexed the entire text of a web page. Unlike Web Crawler, AltaVista sent out thousands of web crawlers, which enabled it to build the most complete index of the web to date. Avid web users soon came to value the service. However, two things handicapped the search engine. First, it was a stepchild within DEC, which saw itself as a hardware-driven business and didn't really know what to do with AltaVista. Second, there was no obvious way for AltaVista to make much money, which meant that it was difficult for Monier to get the resources required for AltaVista to keep up with the rapid growth of the web. Ultimately in 1998 Compaq Computer acquired DEC. Compaq then sold AltaVista and related Internet properties to an Internet firm, CMGI, at the height of the Internet boom in 1999 for $2.3 billion in CMGI stock. CMGI did have plans to spin off AltaVista in an Initial Public Offering, but it never happened. The NASDAQ stock market collapsed in 2000, taking CMGI's stock down with it, and the market had no appetite for another dot.com IPO. In early 2003, AltaVista was purchased by Overture Services Inc. who later that year was acquired by Yahoo.

Around the same time that AltaVista was gaining traffic, two other companies introduced search engines, Lycos and Excite. Both search engines represented further incremental improvement. Lycos was the first search engine to use algorithms to try and determine the relevance of a web page for a search query. Excite utilized similar algorithms. However, neither company developed a way of making money directly from search. Instead, they saw themselves as portal companies, like Yahoo, AOL, and MSN. Search was just a tool to increase the value of their portal as a destination site, enabling them to capture revenues from banner ads, ecommerce transactions, and the like. Both Lycos and Excite went public and then squandered much of the capital raised on acquiring other Internet properties, before seeing their value implode as the Internet bubble burst in 2000-2001.

Another company that tried to make sense out of the web for users was Yahoo, but Yahoo did not use a search engine. Rather, it created a hierarchical directory of web pages. This helped drive traffic to its site. Yahoo emerged as one of the most popular portals on the web. In contrast to many of its smaller competitors, Yahoo's industry-leading scale allowed it to make good money from advertising on its site. Yahoo did add a search engine to its offering, but until 2003 it always did so through a partner. At one time, AltaVista powered Yahoo's search function, then Inktomi, and ultimately Google. Yahoo's managers did consider developing their own search engine, but they saw it as too capital intensive—search required a lot of computing power, storage, and bandwidth. Besides, there was no business model for monetizing search. That, however, was all about to change, and it wasn't Google that pioneered the way, it was a serial entrepreneur called Bill Gross.

C1-4 GoTo.com: A Business Model Emerges[5]

Bill Gross made his first million with Knowledge Adventure, which developed software to help kids learn. After he sold Knowledge Adventure to Cendant for $100 million, Gross created IdeaLab, a business incubator that subsequently generated a number of Internet startups including GoTo.com.

GoTo.com was born of Gross' concern that a growing wave of spam was detracting from the value of search engines such as AltaVista. Spam arose because publishers of websites realized that they could drive traffic to their sites by including commonly used search key words such as "used cars" or "airfares" on their sites. Often the words were in the same color as the background of the website (e.g., black words on a black background) so that web users, who would suddenly wonder why their search for used cars had directed them to a porn site, could not see them.

Gross also wanted a tool that would help drive good traffic to the websites of a number of Internet businesses being developed by IdeaLab. In Gross' view, much of the traffic arriving at websites was undifferentiated—people who had come to a site because of spam, bad portal real estate deals, or poor search engine results. Gross established GoTo.com to build a better search engine, one that would defeat spam, produce highly relevant results, and eliminate bad traffic.

Gross concluded that a way to limit spam was to charge for search. He realized that it was unworkable to charge the Internet user, so why not charge the advertiser? This led to his key insight—the keywords that Internet users typed into a search engine were inherently valuable to the owners of websites. They drove traffic to their sites, and many sites made money from that traffic, so why not charge for the keywords? Moreover, Gross realized that if a search engine directed higher quality traffic to a site, it would be possible to charge more for relevant keywords.

By this time, GoTo.com had decided to license search engine technology from Inktomi and focus its efforts on developing the paid search model. However, GoTo.com faced a classic chicken and egg problem—to launch a service the company needed both audience and advertisers, but it had neither.

To attract advertisers, GoTo.com adopted two strategies.[6] First, GoTo.com would only charge advertisers when somebody clicked on a link and was directed to their website. To Gross' way thinking, for merchants this pay-per-click model would be more efficient than advertising through traditional media, or through banner ads on web pages. Second, GoTo.com initially priced keywords low—as low as $0.01 a click (although they could of course be bid above that).

To capture an audience a website alone would not be enough. GoTo.com needed to tap into the traffic already visiting established websites. One approach was to pay the owners of high traffic websites to place banner ads that would direct traffic to GoTo.com's website. A second approach, which ultimately became the core of GoTo.com's business, was to syndicate its service, allowing affiliates to place a co-branded GoTo.com search box on their site, or to use GoTo.com's search engine and identify the results as "partner results." GoTo.com would then split the revenues from search with them. GoTo.com had to pay an upfront fee to significant affiliates, who viewed their websites as valuable real estate. For example, in late 2000, GoTo.com paid AOL $50 million to syndicate GoTo.com's listings on its sites, which included AOL, CompuServe, and Netscape.

To finance its expansion, GoTo.com raised some $53 million in venture capital funding—a relatively easy proposition in the heady days of the dot.com boom. In June 1999, GoTo.com raised another $90 million through an initial public offering.[7]

GoTo.com launched its service in June 1998 with just 15 advertisers. Initially GoTo.com was paying more to acquire traffic than it was earning from click through ad revenue. According to its initial IPO filing, in its first year of operation, GoTo.com was paying 5.5 cents a click to acquire traffic from Microsoft's MSN sites, and around 4 cents a click to acquire traffic from Netscape. The average yield from this traffic, however, was still less than the cost of acquisition, resulting in red ink, not an unusual situation for a dot.com in the 1990s.

However, the momentum was beginning to shift towards the company. As traffic volumes grew, and as advertisers began to understand the value of keywords, yields improved. By early 1999, the price of popular keywords was starting to rise. The highest bidder for the keyword "software" was $0.59 a click, "books" was $0.38 a click, "vacations" was $0.36 a click, and "porn," the source of so much spam, $0.28 a click.[8]

The turning point was the AOL syndication deal signed in September 2000. Prior to signing with AOL, GoTO.com was reaching 24 million users through its affiliates.

After the deal, it was reaching 60 million unique users, or some 75% of the United States Internet audience (AOL itself had 23 million subscribers, CompuServe 3 million, and Netscape—which was owned by AOL—another 31 million registered users).[9] With over 50,000 advertisers now in its network and a large audience pool, both keyword prices and click through rates increased. GoTo.com turned profitable shortly after the AOL deal was put into effect. In 2001, the company earned net profits $20.2 million on revenues of $288 million. In 2002 it earned $73.1 million on revenues of $667.7 million, making it one of the few dot.com companies to break into profitability.

In 2001, GoTo.com changed its name to Overture Services. The name change reflected the results of a strategic shift. By 2001, the bulk of revenues were coming from affiliate sites, with the GoTo.com website only garnering 5% of the company's total traffic.[10] Still, the fact that GoTo.com had its own website that was in effect competing with traffic going to affiliates created potential channel conflict. Many in the company feared that channel conflict might induce key affiliates, such as AOL, to switch their allegiance. After much internal debate, the company decided to phase out the GoTo.com website, focusing all of its attention on the syndication network.

Around the same time, Bill Gross talked to the founders of another fast-growing search engine, Google, about whether they would be interested in merging the two companies. At the time Google had no business model. Gross was paying attention to the fast growth of traffic going to Google's website. He saw a merger as an opportunity to join a superior search engine with Overture's advertising and syndication network. The talks stalled, however, reportedly because Google's founders stated that they would never be associated with a company that mixed paid advertising with organic results.[11]

Within months, Google had introduced its own advertising service, using a pay-for-click model that looked very similar in conception to Overture's. Overture sued Google for patent infringement. To make matters worse, in 2002, AOL declined to renew its deal with Overture, and instead switched to Google for search services.

By 2003, it was clear that although still growing and profitable, Overture was losing traction to Google (Overture's revenues were on track to hit $1 billion in 2003 and the company had 80,000 advertisers in its network).[12] Moreover, Overture was invisible to many of its users, who saw the service as a part of the offering of affiliates, many of whom were powerful brands, including Yahoo and Microsoft's MSN. Yahoo and Microsoft were also waking up to the threat posed by Google. Realizing that paid search was becoming a highly profitable market, both began to eye Overture to jumpstart their own paid search services. While Microsoft decided to build its own search engine and ad service from scratch, Yahoo decided to bid for Overture. In June 2003, a deal was announced, with Overture being sold to Yahoo for $1.63 billion in cash. The payday was a bittersweet one for Bill Gross. IdeaLab had done very well out of Overture, but Gross couldn't help but feel that a bigger opportunity had slipped through his fingers and into the palms of Google's founders.

As for the patent case, this settled in 2004 when Google agreed to hand over 2.7 million shares to Yahoo. This represented about 1% of the outstanding stock, which at the time was valued at $330. After Google's IPO the value of those shares was closer to $1 billion.[13]

C1-5 The Genesis of Google

Google started as a research project undertaken by Larry Page while he was a computer science PhD student at Stanford in 1996. Called BackRub, the goal of the project was to document the link structure of the web. Page had observed that while it was easy to follow links from one page to another, it was much more difficult to discover links *back*. Put differently, just by looking at a page, it was impossible to know who was linking to that page. Page reasoned that this might be very important information. Specifically, one might be able to rank to value of a web page by discovering which pages were linking to it, and if those pages were themselves linked to by many other pages.

To rank pages, Page knew that he would have to send out a web crawler to index pages and archive links. At this point, another PhD student, Sergey Brin became involved in the project. Brin, a gifted mathematician, was able to develop an algorithm that ranked web pages according not only to the number of links into that site, but also the number of links into each of the linking sites. This methodology had the virtue of discounting links from pages that themselves had few if any links into them.

Brin and Page noticed that the search results generated by this algorithm were superior to those returned by AltaVista and Excite, both of which often returned irrelevant results, including a fair share of spam. They had stumbled onto the key ingredient for a better search engine—rank search results according to their relevance using a back link methodology. Moreover, they realized that the bigger the web got, the better the results would be.

With the basic details of what was now a search engine worked out, Brin and Page released it on the Stanford website in August 1996. They christened their new search engine Google after googol, the term for the number 1 followed by 100 zeros. Early on, Brin and Page talked to several companies about the possibility of licensing Google. Executives at Excite looked but passed, as did executives at Infoseek and Yahoo. Many of these companies were embroiled in the portal wars–and portals were all about acquiring traffic, not about sending it away via search. Search just didn't seem central to their mission.

By late 1998, Google was serving some 10,000 queries a day and was rapidly outgrowing the computing resources available at Stanford. Brin and Page realized that to get the resources required to keep scaling Google they needed capital, and that meant starting a company. Here Stanford's deep links into Silicon Valley came in useful. Before long, they found themselves sitting together with Andy Bechtolsheim, one of the founders of another Stanford start-up, Sun Microsystems. Bechtolsheim watched a demo of Google, and wrote a check on the spot for $100,000.

Google was formally incorporate on September 7th, 1998, with Page as CEO and Brin as president. From this point on, things began to accelerate rapidly. Traffic was growing by nearly 50% a month, enough to attract the attention of several angle investors (including Amazon founder Jeff Bezos), who collectively put in another million.

That was not enough; search engines have a veracious appetite for computing resources. To run its search engine, Brin and Page had custom designed a low-cost, Linux-based server architecture that was modular and could be scaled rapidly. But to keep up with the growth of the web and return answers to search queries in a fraction of second, they needed ever more machines (by late 2005, the company was using over 250,000 Linux servers to handle more than 3,000 searches a second).[14]

To finance growth of their search engine, in early 1999, Brin and Page started to look for venture capital funding. It was the height of the dot.com boom and money was cheap. Never mind that there was no business model, Google's growth was enough to attract considerable interest. By June 1999, the company had closed its first round of venture capital financing, raising $25 million from two of the premier firms in Silicon Valley, Sequoia Capital, and Kleiner Perkins Caufield & Byers. Just as importantly perhaps, the legendary John Doerr, one of Silicon Valley's most successful investors and a Kleiner Perkins partner, took a seat on Google's board.

By late 1999, Google had grown to around 40 employees, and it was serving some 3.5 million searches a day. However, the company was burning through $500,000 a month and there was still no business model. They had some licensing deals with companies that used Google as their search technology, but they were not bringing in enough money to stem the flow of red ink. At this point, Google started to experiment with ads, but they were not yet pay-per-click ads. Rather, Google began selling text-based ads to clients that were interested in certain keywords. The ads would then appear on the page returning search results, but *not* in the list of relevant sites. For example, if someone typed in "Toyota Corolla," an ad would appear at the top of the page, above the list of links for Toyota Corolla cars. These ads were sold on a "cost per thousand impressions" basis, or CPM (the M being the Roman numeral for thousand). In other words, the cost of an ad was determined by how many people were estimated to have viewed it—not how many clicked on it. It didn't work very well.

The management team also started to ponder placing banner ads on Google's website as a way of generating additional revenue, but before they made that decision the dot.com boom imploded, the NASDAQ crashed, and the volume of online advertising dropped precipitously. Google clearly needed to figure out a different way to make money.

C1-6 Google Gets a Business Model

Brin and Page now looked closely at the one search company that seemed to be making good money, GoTo.com. They could see the value of the pay-per-click model, and of auctioning off keywords, but there were things about GoTo.com that they did not like. GoTo.com would give guarantees that websites would be included more frequently in web crawls, making sure they were updated, provided that the owners were prepared to pay more. Moreover, the purity of GoTo.com's search results was biased by the desire to make money from advertisers, with those who paid the most being ranked highest. Brin and Page were ideologically attached to the idea of serving up the best possible search results to users, uncorrupted by commercial considerations. At the same time, they needed to make money.

Although Bill Gross pitched the idea of GoTo.com teaming up with Google, Brin and Page decided to go it alone. They believed they could do as good a job as GoTo.com, so why share revenues with the company?[15]

The approach that Google ultimately settled on combined the innovations of GotTo.com with Google's superior relevance-based search engine. Brin and Page had always believed that Google's web page should be kept as clean and elegant as possible—something that seemed to appeal to users. Moreover, they knew that users valued the fact that Google served up relevant search results that were unbiased by commercial considerations. The last thing they wanted to do was alienate their rapidly growing user base. So, they decided to place text-based ads on the right-hand side of a page, clearly separated from search results by a thin line.

Like GoTo.com, they decided to adopt a pay-per-click model. Unlike GoTo.com, Brin and Page decided that in addition to the price an advertiser had paid for a keyword, ads should also be ranked according to relevance. Relevance was measured by how frequently users clicked on ads. More popular ads rose to the top of the list, less popular ones fell. In other words, Google allowed their users to rank ads. This had a nice economic advantage for Google, since an ad that is generating $1.00 a click, but is being clicked on three times as much as an ad generating $1.50 a click would make significantly more money for Google. It also motivated advertisers to make sure that their ads were appealing.

The system that Google used to auction off keywords was also different in detail from that used by GoTo.com. Google used a *Vickery second price auction* methodology. Under this system, the winner pays only one cent more than the bidder below them. Thus if there are bids of $1, $0.50 and $0.25 for a keyword, the winner of the top place pays just $0.51 cents, not $1, the winner of the second place $0.26, and so on. The auction is nonstop, with the price for a keyword rising or falling depending upon bids at each moment in time. Although the minimum bid for a keyword was set at $0.05, most were above that, and the range was wide. One of the most expensive search terms was reputed to be "mesothelioma," a type of cancer caused by exposure to asbestos. Bids were around $30 per click! They came from lawyers vying for a chance to earn lucrative fees by representing clients in suits against asbestos producers.[16]

While developing this service, Google continued to grow like wildfire. In mid-2000, the service was dealing with 18 million search queries a day and the index surpassed one billion documents, making it by far the largest search engine on the web. By late 2000, when Google introduced the first version of its new service, which it called AdWords, the company was serving up 60 million search queries a day—giving it a scale that GoTo.com never came close to achieving. In February 2002, Google introduced a new version of AdWords that included for the first time the full set of pay-per-click advertising, keyword auctions, and advertising links ranked by relevance. Ad sales immediately started to accelerate. Google had hit on the business model that would propel the company into the big league.

In 2003, Google introduced a second product, AdSense. AdSense allowed third-party publishers large and small to access Google's massive network of advertisers on a self-service basis. Publishers could sign up for AdSense in a matter of minutes. AdSense would then scan the publisher's site for content, and place contextually relevant ads next to that content. As with AdWords, this is a pay per click service, but with AdSense Google splits the revenues with the publishers. In addition to large publishers, such as online news sites, AdSense has been particularly appealing to many small publishers, such as web bloggers. Small publishers found that by adding a few lines of code to their site, they could suddenly monetize their content. However, many advertisers felt that AdSense is not as effective as AdWords in driving traffic to their sites. Google allowed advertisers to opt out of AdSense in 2004. Despite this, AdSense soon grew into a respectable business, accounting for 15% of Google's revenues in 2005, or close to $1 billion.

C1-7 Google Grows Up

Between 2001 and 2022, Google changed in a number of ways. First, in mid-2001 the company hired a new CEO to replace Larry Page, Eric Schmidt. Schmidt had been the chief technology officer of Sun Microsystems, and then CEO of Novell. Schmidt was brought on to help manage the company's growth with the explicit blessing of Brin and Page. Both Brin and Page were still in their twenties, and the board felt they needed a "grown-up" who had run a large company to help Google transition to the next stage (Google turned a profit the month after Schmidt joined). Brin and Page became the presidents of technology and products, respectively. When Schmidt was hired, Google had over 200 employees and was handling over 100 million searches a day.

According to knowledgeable observers, Schmidt, Brin, and Page acted as a triumvirate, with Brin and Page continuing to exercise strong influence over strategies and policies at Google. Schmidt may have been CEO, but Google was still very much Brin and Page's company.[17] Working closely together, the three drove the development of a set of values and an organization that would come to define the uniquely Google way of doing things. In January 2011, Schmidt retired from the CEO position, passing the reins back to Larry Page. Schmidt remained chairman, while Brin turned his attention to overseeing Google's experimental technologies division, Google X.

C1-7a Vision and Values

As Google's growth started to accelerate, there was concern that rapid hiring would quickly dilute the vision, values, and principles of the founders. In mid-2001, Brin and Page gathered a core group of early employees and asked them to come up with a policy for ensuring that the company's culture did not fracture as the company added employees. From this group, and subsequent discussions, emerged a vision and list of values that have continued to shape the evolution of the company. These were not new; rather, they represented the formalization of principles that Brin and Page felt they had always adhered to.

The central vision of Google is to *organize the world's information and make it universally acceptable and useful.*[18] The team also articulated a set of 10 core philosophies (values), which are now listed on its website.[19] Perhaps the most significant and certainly the most discussed of these values is captured by the phrase *"don't be evil."* The central message underlying this phrase was that Google should never compromise the integrity of its search results. Google would never let commercial considerations bias its rankings. Don't be evil, however, has become more than that at Google; it has become a central organizing principle of the company, albeit one that is far from easy to implement. Google got positive press from libertarians when it refused to share its search data with the U.S. government, which wanted the data to help fight child porn. However, the same constituency reacted with dismay when the company caved into the Chinese government and removed from its Chinese service offending results for search terms such as "human rights" and "democracy"! Brin justified the Chinese decision by saying that "it will be better for Chinese web users, because ultimately they will get more information, though not quite all of it."[20]

Another core value at Google is *"focus on the user, and all else will follow."* In many ways, this value captures what Brin and Page initially did. They focused on giving the user the best possible search experience—highly relevant results, delivered with lightning speed to an uncluttered and elegant interface. The value also reflects a belief at Google that it is okay to deliver value to users first, and then figure out the business model for monetizing that value. This belief seems to reflect Google's own early experience.

Yet another key principle, although it is not one that is written down anywhere, is captured by the phrase *"launch early and often."* This seems to underpin Google's approach to product development. Google has introduced a stream of new products over the years, not all of which were initially that compelling, but through rapid upgrades, it has subsequently improved the efficacy of many of these products.

Google also prides itself on being a company where decisions are *data driven*. Opinions are said to count for nothing unless they are backed up by hard data. It is not the loudest voice that wins the day in arguments over strategy, it is the data. In some meeting, people are not allowed to say, "I think..." but instead "The data suggests...."[21]

Finally, Google devotes considerable resources to making sure that its employees are working in a supportive and stimulating environment. To quote from the company's website:

> Google Inc. puts employees first when it comes to daily life in our Googleplex headquarters. There is an emphasis on team achievements and pride in individual accomplishments that contribute to the company's overall success. Ideas are traded, tested, and put into practice with an alacrity that can be dizzying. Meetings that would take hours elsewhere are frequently little more than a conversation in line for lunch and few walls separate those who write the code from those who write the checks. This highly communicative environment fosters a productivity and camaraderie fueled by the realization that millions of people rely on Google results. Give the proper tools to a group of people who like to make a difference, and they will.[22]

C1-7b Organization

Google has always operated with a flat organization. By the mid-2000s, Google had one manager for every 20 line employees. At times, the ratio has been as high as 1:40. For a while, one manager had 180 direct reports.[23] Until 2011, the structure was organized around five main functions: engineering, products, sales, legal, and finance. Within and across functions there were numerous teams. Big projects were (and still are) broken down and allocated to small tightly focused teams. Hundreds of projects could be going on at the same time. Teams often throw out new software in 6 weeks or less and look at how users respond hours later. Google can try a new user interface, or some other tweak, with just 0.1% of its users and get massive feedback very quickly, letting it decide a projects fate in weeks.[24]

In 2011, shortly after assuming the CEO position, Larry Page modified the organization, creating a structure with six product groups, each with its own functions, and each headed by a senior VP who reported directly to him. The product groups were mobile, social (e.g., Google+), Chrome browser and operating system, YouTube, Search, and Ads.[25] Another division, Google X, was created to oversee the exploration and development of experimental technologies. Sergey Brin leads this division until his retirement in 2019.

The reorganization was undertaken to increase accountability and control, speed up innovation, and reduce bureaucracy. Prior to the reorganization, there were reports that the company's freewheeling culture had led to an anarchic resource allocation process, extensive duplication, with multiple teams working on the same project, and increasingly dysfunctional political behavior.[26] There were also reports that Google's organization was not scaling that well, that the firm's personnel department was "collapsing," and that "absolute chaos reigns." One former employee noted that when she was hired, nobody knew when or where she was supposed to work.[27] Larry Page has remarked that he is very pleased with the way the reorganization has worked out, and believes it has helped Google to scale.

One aspect of Google's organization that has garnered considerable attention is the company's approach towards product development. Employees are expected to spend 20% of their time on something that interests them, away from their main jobs. Seemingly based on 3M's famous 15% rule, Google's 20% rule is designed to encourage creativity. The company has set up forums on its internal network where anyone can post ideas, discuss them, and solicit help from other employees. As a natural part of this process, talent tends to gravitate to those projects that seem most promising, giving those who post the most interesting ideas the ability to select a talented team to take them to the next level.

Like 3M, Google set up a process by which projects coming out of 20% time can be evaluated, receive feedback from peers, and ultimately garner funding. Until 2011, Marissa Myer, one of Google's early employees and now CEO of Yahoo, acted as a gatekeeper. She helped decide when projects were ready to be pitched to Brin and Page. Once in front of the founders, advocates have 20 minutes, and no more, to make their pitch.[28] Myer articulated several other principles that guide product development at Google.[29] These include:

1. Ideas come from everywhere: Set up a system where good ideas rise to the top.
2. Focus on users, not money: Money follows consumers. Advertisers follow consumers. If you amass a lot of consumers, you will find ways to monetize your ideas.
3. Innovation, not instant perfection: Put products on the market, learn and iterate.
4. Don't kill projects, morph them: If an idea has managed to make its way out of the door, there is usually some kernel of truth to it. Don't walk away from ideas, think of ways to replace or rejuvenate them.

One of the early products to come out 20% time was Google News, which returns news articles ranked by relevance in response to a keyword query. Put the term "oil prices" into Google News, for example, and the search will return news dealing with changes in oil prices, with the most relevant at the top of the list. A sophisticated algorithm determines relevance on a real-time basis by looking at the quality of the news source (e.g., the *New York Times* rates higher than local newspapers), publishing date, the number of other people who click on that source, and numerous other factors. Krishna Bharat, a software engineer from India, who in response to the events of September 11, 2001, had a desire to learn what was being written and said around the world, initiated the project. Two other employees worked with Bharat to construct a demo that was released within Google. Positive reaction soon got Bharat in front on Brin and Page, who were impressed and gave the project a green light, and Bharat started to work full time on the project.[30] Other products to come out of 20% time include Google Maps, Gmail, and AdSense.

Another feature of Google's organization is its hiring strategy. Like Microsoft, Google has made a virtue out of hiring people with a high IQ. The hiring process is very rigorous. Each prospect must take an "exam" to test their conceptual abilities. This is followed by interviews with eight or more people, each of whom rate the applicant on a 1 to 4 scale (4 being "I would hire this person"). Applicants also undergo detailed background checks to find out what they are like to work with. Reportedly, some brilliant prospects don't get hired when background checks find out that they are difficult to work with. In essence, all hiring at Google is by committee, and while this can take considerable time, the company insists that the effort yields dividends.

While accounts of Google's organization and culture tend to emphasize their positive aspects, not everyone has such a sanguine view. Brain Reid, who was recruited into senior management at Google in 2002, and fired 2 years later, told author John Battelle "Google is a monarchy with two kings, Larry and Sergey. Eric is a puppet. Larry and Sergey are arbitrary, whimsical people…they run the company with an iron hand … Nobody at Google from what I could tell had any authority to do anything of consequence except Larry and Sergey."[31] According to Battelle, several other former employees made similar statements to him. Some former employees have noted the in practice 20% time can turn out to be 120% time, since people still have their regular workload. There are also complaints that the culture is one of long workdays and 7-day workweeks, with little consideration for family issues.

C1-7c The IPO

As Google's growth started to accelerate, the question of when to undertake an IPO became more pressing. There were two obvious reasons for doing an IPO—gaining access to capital and providing liquidity for early backers and the large number of employees who had equity positions. On the other hand, from 2001 onwards, the company was profitable, generating significant cash flows, and could fund its expansion internally. Moreover, management felt that the longer they could keep the details of what was turning out to be an extraordinarily successful business model private, the better. In the end, the company's hand was forced by an obscure SEC regulation that required companies that give stock options to employees to report as if they were public company by as early as April 2004. Realizing that the cat would be out of the bag anyway, Google told its employees in early 2004 that it would go public.

The IPO gave the first public glimpse of Google's financials, which were contained in the offering document. They were jaw dropping. The company had generated revenues of $1.47 billion in 2003, an increase of 230% over 2002. Google earned net profits of $106 million in 2003, but accountants soon figured out that the number was depressed by certain one-time accounting items, and that cash flow in 2003 had exceeded $500 million!

Google's went public on August 19th, 2004, at $85 a share. The company's first quarterly report showed sales doubling over the prior year, and by November the price was $200. In September 2005, with the stock close to $300 a share, Google undertook a secondary offering, selling 14 million shares to raise $4.18 billion. With positive cash flow adding to this, by June 2008 Google was sitting on $12.8 billion in cash and short-term investments, prompting speculation as to the company's strategic intentions.

C1-7d Strategy

Since 2001, Google has endeavored to keep enhancing the efficacy of its search engine, continually improving the search algorithms, and investing heavily in computing resources. The company has branched out from being a text-based search engine.

One strategic thrust has been to extend search to as many digital devices as possible. Google started out on PCs, but its fastest-growing revenue stream is now on mobile devices. A second strategy has been to widen the scope of search to include different sorts of information. Google quickly pushed beyond text into indexing and offered up searches of images, news reports, books, maps, apps, scholarly papers, a blog search, a shopping network, and videos.

Not all of this has gone smoothly. Book publishers were angered by Google's book project, which seeks to create the world's largest searchable digital library of books by systematically scanning books from the libraries of major universities (e.g., Stanford). The publishers argued that Google had no right to do this without first getting permission from the publishers and was violating copyright. Several publishers filed a complaint with the U.S. District Court in New York. Google responded that users would not be able to download entire books, and that in any event, creating an easy-to-use index of books is fair use under copyright law and will increase the awareness and sales of books, directly benefiting copyright holders. On another front, the World Association of News Paper Publishers formed a task force to examine the exploitation of content by search engines.[32]

Since going public, Google has introduced a rash of product offerings, many of which seem to represent diversification away from the company's core search business. Most of these products grew out of the company's new product development process. They have included Gmail, Google Workspace, Blogger, Google+ social networking site, the Chrome browser and operating system, the Android operating system for mobile devices (smartphones and tablets), citywide fiber-optic networks (Google Fiber), and Google Cloud. Not all of these were successful. Google+, for example, failed to gain any traction against Facebook and was shut down. However, several of them have been spectacular successes, most notably Android (the world top mobile operating system) and Chrome (the world's top web browser).

Google Workspace is a cloud-based offering that seems aimed squarely at Microsoft's Office franchise. Workspace includes word processing, spreadsheet, and presentation programs, along with Gmail and Google Drive (for cloud storage). Google Workspace is designed for online collaboration. Files can save files in formats used by Microsoft products, although they lack the full feature set of Microsoft's Office. Google has stated that the company is not trying to match the features of office, and that "90% of users don't necessarily need 90% of the functions that are in there."[33] Google offers Workspace to business customers for a licensing fee of between $6 and $18 a month per person.

In late 2007, Google announced a suite of software for smartphones that includes an operating system, Android, and applications that work with it. Android was aimed squarely at Apple's iPhone and Research in Motion's Blackberry, which at the time were the leaders in the smartphone space. Apple's iPhone had been introduced in 2007, and it was redefining the market for smartphones. Like Apple's iPhone, Android phones had a touch screen, a virtual keyboard, apps displayed as onscreen icons, and an ability to download third-party apps from an App store that Google established. The attraction for Google was that advertising was increasingly being inserted into content viewed on mobile handsets. Google decided to give away Android to device manufacturers for free, aiming instead to make money through mobile search traffic.

The free model turned out to be remarkably successful. Android was very appealing to smartphone manufacturers such as Samsung, HTC, and Motorola, all of whom needed an operating system that would help them to build phones that could compete with Apple's iPhone. When Apple introduced the iPad in 2010, Google quickly followed with a version of Android that could run tablets.

By 2022, Android was the dominant operating system for smartphones with a worldwide market share of 72%. Apple was second with a 27% share for its iOS operating system. As noted earlier, however, Google had a 95%+ share of mobile searches in 2021. This is occurring because Apple used Google as the default search engine on all iOS devices (mobile and desktop). According to news reports, by 2020, Apple received an estimated $8–12 billion in annual payments from Google in exchange for building Google's search engine into its products.[34] One calculation suggests that Google paid Apple $15 billion in 2021.[35]

In October 2010, Google reported that its mobile advertising revenues were growing strongly due to the adoption of Android and that it now had hit an annualized run rate of $1 billion.[36] By 2014, estimates suggest that Google was generating more than $13 billion from mobile search. It's share of mobile ad revenues stood at 41%. Facebook was second in the mobile space with 18% of the market.[37]

Google's App store was renamed Google Play in 2012. Like Apple's iTunes, Google Play allows users to download applications and digital media including music, video (movies, TV programs, etc.), and books. By mid-2013 Google Play had 1.3 million apps available and registered over 50 billion downloads. Google Play is now the second-largest distribution channel in the world for apps and digital media by revenues behind Apple's App store.[38] Estimates suggest that Google Play generated gross revenues of around $48 billion in 2021. Apple's App store had gross revenues of $80–85 billion in 2021.[39]

Another remarkable successful new product offering from Google has been its Chrome browser. Released at the end of 2008, Chrome has steadily gained share on both desktop and mobile devices. By June 2022, it had a 66% global market share, followed by Safari with 18.6%, and Microsoft's Edge browser with 4%.[40]

On the acquisition front, until 2006, Google stuck to purchasing small technology firms. This changed in October 2006 when Google announced that it would purchase YouTube for $1.64 billion in stock. YouTube is a simple, fun website to which anybody can upload video clips to share them. In October 2006, some 65,000 video clips were being uploaded every day and 100 million were being watched. Like Google in its early days, YouTube initially had no business model. The thinking was that Google would find ways to sell advertising that is linked to video clips on YouTube.[41]

By 2022, YouTube had more than 2.6 billion monthly active users who watched around 1 billion hours of video every day, which helped to generate an estimated $30 billion in annual advertising revenue.[42]

Another notable Google acquisition was its $3.1 billion purchase of DoubleClick in 2007. Double-Click is a specialist on online display advertising, such as banner ads that are targeted at building brand awareness. Internet publishers pay DoubleClick to insert display ads on their websites as users visit their websites. While display advertising has not grown as rapidly as search-based advertising, it is a big business accounting for around a quarter of all Internet advertising revenue with significant upside potential as companies begin to apply demographic technology to increase the effectiveness of Internet display ads.[43] The DoubleClick deal was criticized by Google's rivals, including Microsoft, on antitrust grounds, but regulators in the United States and the EU approved the deal, which closed in 2008. By 2021, estimates suggested that Google generated about 30% of its advertising from display ads, and the rest from search-generated ads. Facebook, however, earned more from display ad revenues.[44]

Critics argue that as Google moves into these additional areas, its profit margins will be compressed. One analyst argued that in its core pay-for-click search business, Google makes profit margins of about 60%. In its more recent business of placing advertisements on web pages belonging to other people, such as bloggers, its profit margins are 10–20%, because it is harder to make the advertisements as relevant to the audience and it must share the resulting revenues. Display advertising also offers lower returns. Google, not surprisingly, does not see things this way. The company argues that since its costs are mostly fixed and incremental revenues are profit, it makes good sense to push into other markets, even if its average revenue per viewer is only 1 cent (compared with 50 cents for each click on the web).[45]

C1-8 The Online Advertising Market in 2022

There is an old adage in advertising that half of all the money spent on advertising is wasted—advertisers just don't know which half. Estimates in the early 2000s suggest that around half of worldwide advertising spend was wasted because the wrong message was sent to the wrong audience.[46] The problem was that traditional media advertising was indiscriminate. Consider a 30-second ad spot on broadcast TV. Advertisers pay a rate for such a spot called CPM (costs per thousand). The CPM is based on estimates of how many people are watching a show. There are numerous problems with this system. The estimates of audience numbers are only approximations at best. The owners of the TV may have left the room while the commercials are airing. They may channel surf during the commercial break, be napping, or talking on the telephone. The viewer may not be among the intended audience—a high-end sports car commercial might be dismissed by a high school student, for example.

By contrast, newer digital advertising models based on pay-for-click are more discriminating. Rather than sending out ads to a large audience, only a few of whom will be interested in the products being advertised, consumers select into search-based ads. They do this twice, first, by entering a keyword in a search engine, and second, by scanning the search results as well as the sponsored links, and clicking on a link. In effect, potential purchasers pull the ads towards them through the search process. Advertisers only pay when someone clicks on their ad. Consequently, the conversion rate for search-based ads is far higher than the conversion rate for traditional media advertising. Put differently, less advertising money is wasted.

Moreover, traditional advertising was so wasteful that most firms only advertised 5% –10% of their products in the mass media, hoping that other products would benefit from a halo effect. In contrast, the targeted nature of search-based advertising makes it cost effective to advertise products that only sell in small quantities. In effect, search-based Internet advertising allows producers to exploit the economics of the long tail. Pay-for-click models also make it economical for small merchants to advertise their wares on the Internet to a bigger audience than they could ever reach through traditional channels.

C1-8a The Growth Story

Powered by the rapid growth of search-based pay-for-click advertising, and the increasing amount of time people spend online, total advertising spending on the Internet has expanded rapidly over the last two decades. In 2000, Internet advertising revenues were valued at $8 billion. In 2013, Internet ad revenues hit $117 billion, and they were forecasted to reach $195 billion by 2018.[47] By 2021, some 65% of the $700 billion spent on advertising globally was on the Internet, or around $450 billion, and that share is expected to continue to grow over time.[48]

C1-8b Google's Competitors

Historically, Google's most significant competitors include Microsoft and Yahoo in search, and Meta (the owner of Facebook, Instagram, and WhatsApp) in display advertising. Both Yahoo and Microsoft spent several years and hundreds of millions in R&D spending trying to improve their search engine technology and gain market share at the expense of Google. Yahoo failed, their share declined, and Yahoo was bought by Verizon in 2017. Microsoft recorded moderate but steady market share gains after it launched its Bing search engine in 2008, reaching a 26% share of the U.S. desktop search market in 2021. However, following the failure of its Windows phone to gain share in the 2010s, and the discontinuation of that offering in 2020, Microsoft has almost no presence in the large and fast-growing mobile search market that now accounts for more than 50% of total search-based advertising spend.

Microsoft has long struggled to make profits in the search business, even as revenues have grown. In 2021, Bing generated $8.53 billion in revenue for Microsoft, but the search engine is believed to be only marginally profitable on an operating basis, and on an investment basis it is probably still deep in the red. Reports suggest that in its first decade, Microsoft racked up cumulative losses of over $15 billion in search, and it seems unlikely that it will recouped those any time soon, even though the unit finally started to become profitable in 2017.[49] The problem for Microsoft is that because its search traffic is far lower than Google's, the price that it can get for auctioning keywords is significantly lower too, which results in lower revenue per click. For Microsoft to challenge Google, it must have a significant presence in mobile search, and it does not.

While Microsoft is struggling to gain traction in search after two decades of trying, another company has been gaining ground—Amazon. Amazon's search business is linked to its sprawling ecommerce site and primarily exists to promoting products in its online marketplace, the world's largest. Like Google, it uses a pay-for-click model. When many people consider purchasing physical goods, they search on Amazon first. By one estimate, nearly 75% of American consumers begin their product search on Amazon. This strong buyer intent drives up keyword prices and enables Amazon to make higher revenues per click. Due to its rapidly growing search business, which some estimates suggest accounts for 19% of all U.S. searches in early 2022, Amazon became the third-largest digital advertising company behind Google and Facebook with $31.2 billion in 2021 revenues (roughly the same as the entire global newspaper industry).[50]

Finally, in digital display advertising, Meta is a powerful competitor. Founded in 2004 as Facebook, its three leading platforms—Facebook, Instagram, and WhatsApp—make it the largest social network in the world with nearly 3 billion active users. Two decades of growth in users and user engagement, along with the valuable data that they generate, makes Meta's platforms attractive to advertisers. With more user interaction among friends and family, and the sharing of videos and pictures, Meta has compiled ever more social data, which the company and advertising clients then use to launch online advertising campaigns targeting specific users, thereby increasing the ROI for every advertising dollar spent. For fiscal 2021, this dynamic helped to drive Meta's revenues to $118 billion and net income to $39.4 billion, almost all of which comes from targeted digital display advertising.[51]

Notes

[1]A. Mogharabi, "Alphabet Missed Q2 Expectations, but Cloud Growth Impressive and Advertising Intact," *Morningstar*, July 26, 2022.

[2]"Search Engine Market Share Worldwide, June 2021-June 2022," *Statcounter*, gs.statcounter.com.

[3]This section draws heavily upon the excellent description of search given by John Battelle. See John Battelle, *The Search* (New York: Penguin Portfolio, 2005).

[4]Google 10K for 2021.

[5]The basic story of GoTo.com is related in John Battelle, *The Search* (New York: Penguin Portfolio, 2005).

[6]K. Greenberg, "Pay-for-Placement Search Services Offer Ad Alternatives," *Adweek*, September 25, 2000, p. 60.

[7]M. Gannon, "GoTo.com Inc." *Venture Capital Journal*, August 1, 1999, p. 1.

[8]T. Jackson, "Cash Is the Key to a True Portal," *Financial Times*, February 2, 1999, p. 16.

[9]K. Greenberg, "Pay-for-Placement Search Services Offer Ad Alternatives," *Adweek*, September 25, 2000, p. 60.

[10]Sarah Heim, "GoTo.com Changes to Overture Services, Launches Campaign," *Adweek*, September 10, 2001, p. 7.

[11]This little gem comes from John Battelle, *The Search* (New York: Penguin Portfolio, 2005). There is no independent confirmation of the story.

[12]Anonymous, "Yahoo to Acquire Overture Services for 2.44 Times Revenues," *Weekly Corporate Growth Service*, July 21, 2003, p. 8.

[13]R. Waters, "Google Settles Yahoo Case with Shares," *Financial Times*, August 19, 2004, p. 29.

[14]F. Vogelstein, "Gates vs Google: Search and Destroy," *Fortune*, May 2, 2005, pp. 72-82.

[15] This is according to David A. Vise, *The Google Story* (New York: Random House, 2004).

[16] D. A. Vise, *The Google Story* (New York: Random House, 2004).

[17] J. Battelle, *The Search* (New York: Penguin Portfolio, 2005). There is no independent confirmation of the story.

[18] http://www.google.com/corporate/index.html

[19] http://www.google.com/corporate/tenthings.html

[20] A. Kessler, "Sellout.com," *Wall Street Journal*, January 31, 2006, p. A14.

[21] Q. Hardy, "Google Thinks Small," *Fortune*, November 14, 2005, pp. 198–199.

[22] http://www.google.com/corporate/tenthings.html

[23] Q. Hardy, "Google Thinks Small," *Fortune*, November 14, 2005, pp. 198–199. D. A. Garvin, "How Google Sold Its Engineers on Management," Harvard Business Review, December 2013.

[24] Q. Hardy, "Google Thinks Small," *Fortune*, November 14, 2005, pp. 198–199.

[25] B. Ortutay, "Google CEO Larry Page Completes Major Reorganization," *Huffington Post*, January 30, 2015.

[26] B. Lashinsky and Y. W. Yen, "Where Does Google Go Next?," *Fortune*, May 26, 2008, pp. 104–110.

[27] *The Economist*, "Inside the Googleplex," September 1, 2007, pp. 53–56.

[28] B. Elgin, "Managing Google's Idea Factory," *Business Week*, October 3, 2005, pp. 88–90.

[29] M. Krauss, "Google's Mayer tells How Innovation Gets Done," *Marketing News*, April 1, 2007, pp. 7–8.

[30] D. A. Vise, *The Google Story* (New York: Random House, 2004).

[31] J. Battelle, *The Search* (New York: Penguin Portfolio, 2005), p. 233.

[32] J. Doherty, "In the Drink," *Barrons*, February 13, 2006, pp. 31–36.

[33] K. J. Delaney and R. A. Guth, "Google's Free Web Services will vie with Microsoft Office," *Wall Street Journal,* October 11, 2006, p. B1.

[34] D. Wakabayshi and J. Nicas, "Apple, Google and a Deal; That Ccontrols the Internet," *New York Times*, October 25, 2020.

[35] J. Moreno, "Google Estimated to Be Paying $15 Billion to Remain Default Search Engine on Safari," *Forbes*, August 27, 2021.

[36] Citigroup Global Markets. Google Inc, October 14, 2010.

[37] B. Womack, "Google Revenue Falls Short as Mobile Competition Intensifies," *Global and Mail*, January 29, 2015.

[38] S. M. Patterson, "Revenue from the Google Play Store Will Overtake Apple's App Store in 2018," *Quartz*, July 17, 2014.

[39] "Morgan Stanley: Apple's App Store revenue growth slowed in June," *Mac Daily News*, July 5, 2022.

[40] "Browser Market share Worldwide, June 2021-June 2022," *statcounter*, gs.statcounter.com.

[41] *The Economist,* "Two Kings Get Together; Google and YouTube," October 14, 2006, pp. 82–83.

[42] "YouTube by the Numbers," *Omnicore*, March 14, 2022.

[43] R. Hof, "Ad Wars: Google's Green Light," *Business Week*, March 3, 2008, p. 22.

[44] K. Likakasa, "Facebook Pulls Ahead of Google in US Digital Display Ad Revenues," Ad Exchanger, March 11, 2014.

[45] *The Economist*, "Inside the Googleplex", September 1, 2007, pp. 53–56.

[46] The Economist, "The Ultimate Marketing Machine," July 8, 2006, pp. 61–64. K. J. Delaney, "Google Push to Sell Ads on YouTube Hits Snag," *Wall Street Journal*, July 9, 2008, p. A1.

[47] PWC. "Global Entertainment and Media Outlook, 2014-2018," www.pwc.com

[48] B. Adgate, "Agencies Agree; 2021 Was a Record Year for Ad Spending, with More Growth Expected in 2022," *Forbes*, December 8, 2021.

[49] S. Cleland, "What If Microsoft Exited the Search Business?" *The Daily Caller*, January 14, 2013.

[50] T. Soper, "Here's Why Amazon's $30 Billion Advertising Business Is So Effective," *GeekWire,* February 3, 2022.

[51] A. Mogharabi, "Meta's Q2 Advertising Softness and Weak Q3 Guidance," *Morningstar*, July 27, 2022.

Case 2

Toyota: The Rise of the Lean Machine

This case was prepared by Charles W. L. Hill Foster School of Business University of Washington Seattle, WA 98185 July 2022

C2-1 Introduction

The growth of Toyota Motor Corporation (Toyota) has been one of the great success stories of Japanese industry during the last half century. In 1947, the company was a little-known domestic manufacturer producing around 100,000 vehicles a year. In 2021 Toyota supplanted Volkswagen as the largest automobile manufacturer in the world with global sales of 10.5 million units, or about 12% of the global market. This generated $270 billion in revenues for Toyota.[1] In its second-largest market, the United States, Toyota powered ahead of General Motors Company (GM) in 2021 to become the largest car company in the country for the first time with 15% of the U.S. market.

Toyota's global success in 2021 owed much to its ability to better manage its supply chain than rivals such as Volkswagen and GM. Modern cars contain a lot of electronics. There are about 100 electronic components in every car accounting for a staggering 40% of the cost of a new car. Each component contains multiple chips. By one estimate, on average each car contains around 1,400 individual semiconductor chips, with electric cars containing closer to 2,000 chips each.[2] When the COVID-19 pandemic hit and auto sales slumped, unlike its rivals, Toyota did not cut back on orders for semiconductor chips, but instead kept the flow going, storing them in warehouses. This put the company in a better position than its main rivals when auto sales rebounded sharply in 2021.

Although unusual events underlay Toyota's global success in 2021, the company has a long history of outperforming its rivals and gaining market share. In 1976, GM sold 8.6 million vehicles and was the dominant global automaker, while Toyota sold just 1.7 million cars globally. Then came rising oil prices and the need for fuel efficiency, and that was all Toyota needed to crack the U.S. market, then the world's largest. By 1996, Toyota was selling 4.8 million cars a year and GM 8.3 million, but Toyota was far more profitable, earning $3,700 gross profit per vehicle compared to GM's $2,700. By 2000, the Toyota Camry was the best-selling car in America. In 2014, with auto sales booming, Toyota continued to lead the industry in profitability, making an average net profit of $2,726 per vehicle, compared to $994 for Ford Motor Company (Ford) and $654 at GM. While no one factor explains Toyota's impressive rise, at the heart of its multidecade run is the philosophy of *kaizen*, or continuous improvement, and the rise of what is now known as the Toyota Production System, or lean production.[3]

C2-2 The Origins Of Toyota

The original idea behind the founding of the Toyota Motor Company came from the fertile mind of Toyoda Sakichi.[4] The son of a carpenter, Sakichi was an entrepreneur and inventor whose primary interest lay in the textile industry, but he had been intrigued by automobiles since a visit to the United States in 1910. Sakichi's principal achievement was the invention of an automatic loom that held out the promise of being able to lower the costs of weaving high-quality cloth. In 1926, Sakichi set up Toyoda Automatic Loom to manufacture this product. In 1930, Sakichi sold the patent rights to a British textile firm, Platt Brothers, for about 1 million yen, a considerable sum in those days. Sakichi urged his son, Toyoda Kiichiro, to use this money to study the possibility of manufacturing automobiles in Japan. A mechanical engineer with a degree from the University of Tokyo, in 1930 Kiichiro became managing director of loom production at Toyoda Automatic Loom.

Kiichiro was at first reluctant to invest in automobile production. The Japanese market was at that time dominated by Ford and GM both of which imported knock-down car kits from the United States and assembled them in Japan. Given this, the board of Toyoda Automatic Loom, including Kiichiro's brother-in-law and the company's president, Kodama Risaburo, opposed the investment on the grounds that it was too risky. Kiichiro probably would not have pursued the issue further had not his father made a deathbed request in 1930 that Kiichiro explore the possibilities of automobile production. Kiichiro had to push, but in 1933 he was able to get permission to set up an automobile department within Toyoda Automatic Loom.

Kiichiro's belief was that he would be able to figure out how to manufacture automobiles by taking apart U.S.-made vehicles and examining them piece by piece. He also felt that it should be possible to adapt U.S. mass-production technology to manufacture cost efficiently at lower volumes. His confidence was based in large part upon the already considerable engineering skills and capabilities at his disposal through Toyoda Automatic Loom. Many of the precision engineering and manufacturing skills needed in automobile production were similar to the skills required to manufacture looms.

Kiichiro produced his first 20 vehicles in 1935, and in 1936 the automobile department produced 1,142 vehicles—910 trucks, 100 cars, and 132 buses. At this time, however, the production system was essentially craft-based rather than a modern assembly line. Despite some progress, the struggle might still have been uphill had not fate intervened in the form of the Japanese military. Japan had invaded Manchuria in 1931 and quickly found American-made trucks useful for moving men and equipment. As a result, the military felt that it was strategically important for Japan to have its own automobile industry. The result was the passage of an automobile manufacturing law in 1936 that required companies producing more than 3,000 vehicles per year in Japan to get a license from the government. Moreover, to get a license, over 50% of the stock had to be owned by Japanese investors. The law also placed a duty on imported cars, including the knock-down kits that Ford and GM brought into Japan. As a direct result of this legislation, both GM and Ford exited from the Japanese market in 1939.

Once the Japanese government passed this law, Kodama Risaburo decided that the automobile venture could be profitable and switched from opposing to proactively supporting Kiichiro (in fact, Risaburo's wife, who was Kiichiro's elder sister, had been urging him to take this step for some time). The first priority was to attract the funds necessary to build a mass-production facility. In 1937, Risaburo and Kiichiro decided to incorporate the automobile department as a separate company in order to attract outside investors—which they were successful in doing. Kiichiro Toyoda was appointed president of the new company. The company was named the Toyota Motor

Company. (The founding family's name, "Toyoda," means "abundant rice field" in Japanese. The new name had no meaning in Japanese.)

Upon incorporation, Risaburo and Kiichiro's vision was that Toyota should expand its passenger car production as quickly as possible. However, once again fate intervened in the form of the Japanese military. Toyota had barely begun passenger car production when war broke out; in 1939, the Japanese government, on advice from the military, prohibited passenger car production and demanded that the company specialize in the production of military trucks.

C2-3 The Evolution of the Toyota Production System

After the end of World War II, Kiichiro was determined that Toyota should reestablish itself as a manufacturer of automobiles.[5] Toyota, however, faced several problems in doing this:

1. The Japanese domestic market was too small to support efficient-scale mass-production facilities such as those common in America by that time.
2. The Japanese economy was starved of capital, which made it difficult to raise funds to finance new investments.
3. New labor laws introduced by the American occupiers increased the bargaining power of labor and made it difficult for companies to lay off workers.
4. North America and Western Europe were full of large auto manufacturers eager to establish operations in Japan.

In response to the last point, in 1950, the new Japanese government prohibited direct foreign investment in the automobile industry and imposed high tariffs on the importation of foreign cars. This protection, however, did little to solve the other problems facing the company at this time.

C2-3a Limitations of Mass Production

At this juncture a remarkable mechanical engineer entered the scene: Ohno Taiichi. More than anyone else, it was Ohno who was to work out a response to the above problems. Ohno had joined Toyoda Spinning and Weaving in 1932 as a production engineer in cotton thread manufacture and entered Toyota when the former company was absorbed into the latter in 1943. Ohno worked in auto production for two years, was promoted and managed auto assembly and machine shops between 1945 and 1953, and in 1954 was appointed a company director.

When Ohno Taiichi joined Toyota the mass-production methods pioneered by Ford had become the accepted method of manufacturing automobiles. The basic philosophy behind mass production was to produce a limited product line in massive quantities to gain maximum economies of scale. The economies came from spreading the fixed costs involved in setting up the specialized equipment required to stamp body parts and manufacture components over as large a production run as possible. Since setting up much of the equipment could take a full day or more, the economies involved in long production runs were reckoned to be considerable. Thus, for example, Ford would stamp 500,000 right-hand door panels in a single production run and then store the parts in warehouses until they were needed in the assembly plant, rather than stamp just those door panels that were needed immediately and then change the settings and stamp out left-hand door panels, or other body parts.

A second feature of mass production was that each assembly worker should perform only a single task, rather than a variety of tasks. The idea here was that as the worker became completely familiar with a single task, they could perform it much faster, thereby increasing labor productivity. Assembly line workers were overseen by a foreman who did not perform any assembly tasks themselves, but instead ensured that the workers followed orders. In addition, several specialists were employed to perform non-assembly operations such as tool repair, die changes, quality inspection, and general "housecleaning."

After working in Toyota for 5 years and visiting Ford's U.S. plants, Ohno became convinced that the basic mass-production philosophy was flawed. He saw five problems with the mass-production system:

1. Long production runs created massive inventories that had to be stored in large warehouses. This was expensive both because of the cost of warehousing and because inventories tied up capital in unproductive uses.
2. If the initial machine settings were wrong, long production runs resulted in the production of a large number of defects.
3. The sheer monotony of assigning assembly line workers to a single task generated defects, since workers became lax about quality control. In addition, since assembly line workers were not responsible for quality control, they had little incentive to minimize defects.
4. The extreme division of labor resulted in the employment of specialists such as foremen, quality inspectors, and tooling specialists, whose jobs logically could be performed by assembly line workers.
5. The mass-production system was unable to accommodate consumer preferences for product diversity.

In addition to these flaws, Ohno knew that the small domestic market in Japan and the lack of capital for investing in mass-production facilities made the American model unsuitable for Toyota.

C2-3b Reducing Setup Times

Given these flaws and the constraints that Toyota faced, Ohno decided to take a fresh look at the techniques used for automobile production. His first goal was to try to make it economical to manufacture autobody parts in small batches. To do this, he needed to reduce the time it took to set up the machines for stamping out body parts. Ohno and his engineers began to experiment with several techniques to speed up the time it took to change the dies in stamping equipment. This included using rollers to move dies in and out of position along with several simple mechanized adjustment mechanisms to fine-tune the settings. These techniques were relatively simple to master, so Ohno directed production workers to perform the die changes themselves. This reduced the need for specialists and eliminated the idle time that workers previously had enjoyed while waiting for the dies to be changed.

Through a process of trial and error, Ohno succeeded in reducing the time required to change dies on stamping equipment from a full day to 15 minutes by 1962, and to as little as 3 minutes by 1971. By comparison, even in the early 1980s, many American and European plants required anywhere between 2 and 6 hours to change dies on stamping equipment. As a consequence, American and European plants found it economical to manufacture in lots equivalent to 10 to 30 days' supply and to reset equipment only every other day. In contrast, since Toyota could change the dies on stamping equipment in a matter of minutes, it manufactured in lots equivalent to just 1 day's supply, while resetting equipment three times per day.

Not only did these innovations make small production runs economical, but they also had the added benefit of reducing inventories and improving product quality. Making small batches eliminated the need to hold large inventories, thereby reducing warehousing costs and freeing up scarce capital for investment elsewhere. Small production runs and the lack of inventory also meant that defective parts were produced only in small numbers and entered the assembly process almost immediately. This had the added effect of making those in the stamping shops far more concerned about quality. In addition, once it became economical to manufacture small batches of components, much greater variety could be included into the final product at little or no cost penalty.

C2-3c Organization of the Workplace

One of Ohno's first innovations was to group the work force into teams. Each team was given a set of assembly tasks to perform, and team members were trained to perform each task that the team was responsible for. Each team had a leader who was himself an assembly line worker. In addition to coordinating the team, the team leader was expected to perform basic assembly line tasks and to fill in for any absent worker. The teams were given the job of housecleaning, minor tool repair, and quality inspection (along with the training required to perform these tasks). Time was also set aside for team members to discuss ways to improve the production process (the practice now referred to as "quality circles").

The immediate effect of this approach was to reduce the need for specialists in the workplace and to create a more flexible work force in which individual assembly line workers were not treated simply as human machines. All of this resulted in increased worker productivity.

None of this would have been possible, however, had it not been for an agreement reached between management and labor after a 1950 strike. The strike was brought on by management's attempt to cut the workforce by 25% (in response to a recession in Japan). After lengthy negotiations, Toyota and the union worked out a compromise. The workforce was cut by 25% as originally proposed, but the remaining employees were given two guarantees, one for lifetime employment and the other for pay graded by seniority and tied to company profitability through bonus payments. In exchange for these guarantees, the employees agreed to be flexible in work assignments. In turn, this allowed for the introduction of the team concept.

C2-3d Improving Quality

One of the standard practices in the mass-production automobile assembly plants was to fix any errors that occurred during assembly in a rework area at the end of the assembly line. Errors routinely occurred in most assembly plants either because bad parts were installed or because good parts were installed incorrectly. The belief was that stopping an assembly line to fix such errors would cause enormous bottlenecks in the production system. Thus, it was thought to be more efficient to correct errors at the end of the line.

Ohno viewed this system as wasteful for three reasons: (1) since workers understood that any errors would be fixed at the end of the line, they had little incentive to correct errors themselves; (2) once a defective part had been embedded in a complex vehicle, an enormous amount of rework might be required to fix it; and (3) since defective parts were often not discovered until the end of the line when the finished cars were tested, a large number of cars containing the same defect may have been built before the problem was found.

To get away from this practice, Ohno decided to look for ways to reduce the amount of rework at the end of the line. His approach involved two elements. First, he placed a cord above every workstation and instructed workers to stop the assembly line if a problem emerged that could not be fixed. It then became the responsibility of the whole team to come over and work on the problem. Second, team members were taught to trace every defect back to its ultimate cause and then to ensure that the problem was fixed so that it would not reoccur.

Initially, this system produced enormous disruption. The production line was stopping all the time and workers became discouraged. However, as team members began to gain experience in identifying problems and tracing them back to their root cause, the number of errors began to drop dramatically and stops in the line became much rarer, so that today in most Toyota plants the line virtually never stops.

C2-3e Developing the Kanban System

Once reduced setup times had made small production runs economical, Ohno began to look for ways to coordinate the flow of production within the Toyota manufacturing system so that the amount of inventory in the system could be reduced to a minimum. Toyota produced about 25% of its major components in-house (the rest were contracted out to independent suppliers). Ohno's initial goal was to arrange for components and/or subassemblies manufactured in-house to be delivered to the assembly floor only when they were needed, and not before (this goal was later extended to include independent suppliers).

To achieve this, in 1953, Ohno began experimenting with what came to be known as the kanban system. Under the kanban system, component parts are delivered to the assembly line in containers. As each container is emptied, it is sent back to the previous step in the manufacturing process. This then becomes the signal to make more parts. The system minimizes work in progress by increasing inventory turnover. The elimination of buffer inventories also means that defective components show up immediately in the next process. This speeds up the processes of tracing defects back to their source and facilitates correction of the problem before too many defects are made. Moreover, the elimination of buffer stocks, by removing all safety nets, makes it imperative that problems be solved before they become serious enough to jam up the production process, thereby creating a strong incentive for workers to ensure that errors are corrected as quickly as possible. In addition, by decentralizing responsibility for coordinating the manufacturing process to lower-level employees, the kanban system does away with the need for extensive centralized management to coordinate the flow of parts between the various stages of production.

After perfecting the kanban system in one of Toyota's machine shops, Ohno had a chance to apply the system broadly in 1960 when he was made general manager of the Motomachi assembly plant. Ohno already had converted the machining, body stamping, and body shops to the kanban system, but since many parts came from shops that had yet to adopt the system, or from outside suppliers, the impact on inventories was initially minimal. However, by 1962 he had extended the kanban to forging and casting, and between 1962 and 1965 he began to bring independent suppliers into the system.

C2-3f Organizing Suppliers

Assembly of components into a final vehicle accounts for only about 15% of the total manufacturing process in automobile manufacture. The remaining 85% of the process involves manufacturing more than ten thousand individual parts and assembling them into about one hundred major components, such as engines, suspension systems, transaxles, and so on. Coordinating this process so that everything comes together at the right time has always been a problem for auto manufacturers. Historically, the response at Ford and GM to this problem was massive vertical integration. The belief was that control over the supply chain would allow management to coordinate the flow of component parts into the final assembly plant. In addition, American firms held the view that vertical integration made them more efficient by reducing their dependence on other firms for materials and components and by limiting their vulnerability to opportunistic overcharging.

As a consequence of this philosophy, even as late as the mid-1990s, GM made 68% of its own components in-house, while Ford made 50% (in the late 1990s both GM and Ford de-integrated, spinning out much of their in-house supply operations as independent enterprises). For those products they did not make in-house, U.S. auto companies tried to reduce the procurement costs that remained through competitive bidding—asking a number of companies to submit contracts and giving orders to suppliers offering the lowest price.

Under the leadership of Kiichiro during the 1930s and 1940s, Toyota followed the American model and pursued extensive vertical integration into the manufacture of component parts. In fact, Toyota had little choice in this matter, since only a handful of Japanese companies were able to make the necessary components. However, the low volume of production during this period meant that the scale of integration was relatively small. In the 1950s, however, the volume of auto production began to increase dramatically. This presented Toyota with a dilemma: should the company increase its capacity to manufacture components in-house in line with the growth in production of autos, or should the company contract out?

In contrast to American practice, the company decided that while it should increase in-house capacity for essential subassemblies and bodies, it would do better to contract out for most components. Four reasons seem to bolster this decision:

1. Toyota wanted to avoid the capital expenditures required to expand capacity to manufacture a wide variety of components.
2. Toyota wanted to reduce risk by maintaining a low factory capacity in case factory sales slumped.
3. Toyota wanted to take advantage of the lower wage scales in smaller firms.
4. Toyota managers realized that in-house manufacturing offered few benefits if it was possible to find stable, high-quality, and low-cost external sources of component supply.

At the same time, Toyota managers felt that the American practice of inviting competitive bids from suppliers was self-defeating. While competitive bidding might achieve the lowest short-run costs, the practice of playing suppliers off against each other did not guarantee stable supplies, high quality, or cooperation beyond existing contracts to solve design or engineering problems. Ohno and other Toyota managers believed that real efficiencies could be achieved if the company entered into long-term relationships with major suppliers. This would allow them to introduce the kanban system, thereby further reducing inventory holding costs and realizing the same kind of quality benefits that Toyota was already beginning to encounter with its in-house supply operations. In addition, Ohno wanted to bring suppliers into the design process since he believed that suppliers might be able to suggest ways of improving the design of component parts based upon their own manufacturing experience.

As it evolved during the 1950s and 1960s, Toyota's strategy toward its suppliers had several elements. The company spun off some of its own in-house supply operations into quasi-independent entities in which it took a minority stake, typically holding between 20% and 40% of the stock. It then recruited several independent companies with a view to establishing a long-term relationship with them for the supply of critical components. Sometimes, but not always, Toyota took a minority stake in these companies as well. All these companies were designated as "first-tier suppliers." First-tier suppliers were responsible for working with Toyota as an integral part of the new product development team. Each first tier was responsible for the formation of a "second tier" of suppliers under its direction. Companies in the second tier were given the job of fabricating individual parts. Both first- and second-tier suppliers were formed into supplier associations.

By 1986, Toyota had three regional supply organizations in Japan with 62, 135, and 25 first-tier suppliers. A major function of the supplier associations was to share information regarding new manufacturing, design, or materials management techniques among themselves. Concepts such as statistical process control, total quality control, and computer-aided design were rapidly diffused among suppliers by this means.

Toyota also worked closely with its suppliers, providing them with management expertise, engineering expertise, and sometimes capital to finance new investments. A critical feature of this relationship was the incentives that Toyota established to encourage its suppliers to focus on realizing continuous process improvements. The basic contract for a component would be for 4 to 5 years, with the price being agreed on in advance. If by joint efforts the supplier and Toyota succeeded in reducing the costs of manufacturing the components, then the additional profit would be shared between the two. If the supplier by its own efforts came up with an innovation that reduced costs, the supplier would keep the additional profit that the innovation generated for the lifetime of the contract.

Because of this strategy, Toyota outsourced more production than almost any other major auto manufacturer. By the late 1980s, Toyota was responsible for only about 27% of the value going into a finished automobile, with the remainder coming from outside suppliers. In contrast, at the time, GM was responsible for about 70% of the value going into a finished automobile. Other consequences included long-term improvements in productivity and quality among Toyota's suppliers that were comparable to the improvements achieved by Toyota itself. In particular, the extension of the kanban system to include suppliers, by eliminating buffer inventory stocks, in essence forced suppliers to focus more explicitly on the quality of their product.

C2-3g Consequences

The consequences of Toyota's production system included a surge in labor productivity and a decline in the number of defects per car. Exhibit 1 compares the number of vehicles produced per worker at GM, Ford, Nissan, and Toyota between 1965 and 1983.

These figures are adjusted for the degree of vertical integration pursued by each company. As can be seen, in 1960, productivity at Toyota already outstripped that of Ford, GM, and its main Japanese competitor, Nissan. As Toyota refined its production system over the next 18 years, productivity doubled. In comparison, productivity essentially stood still at GM and Ford during the same period.

Exhibit 1 Vehicles Produced per Worker (adjusted for vertical integration), 1965–1983				
Year	General Motors	Ford	Nissan	Toyota
1965	5.0	4.4	4.3	8.0
1970	3.7	4.3	8.8	13.4
1975	4.4	4.0	9.0	15.1
1979	4.5	4.2	11.1	18.4
1980	4.1	3.7	12.2	17.8
1983	4.8	4.7	11.0	15.0

Source: M. A. Cusumano, The Japanese Automotive Industry (Cambridge, Mass.: Harvard University Press, 1989), Table 48, p. 197.

Exhibit 2 General Motors's Framingham Plant versus Toyota's Takaoka Plant, 1987

	GM Framingham	Toyota Takaoke
Assembly Hours per Car	31	16
Assembly defects per 100 Cars	135	45
Inventory of Parts	2 weeks	2 hours

Source: J. P. Womack, D. T. Jones, and D. Roos, The Machines That Changed the World (New York: Macmillan, 1990), Figure 4.2, p. 83.

Exhibit 2 provides another way to assess the superiority of Toyota's production system. Here, the performance of Toyota's Takaoka plant is compared with that of General Motors's Framingham plant in 1987. As can be seen, the Toyota plant was more productive, produced far fewer defects per 100 cars, and kept far less inventory on hand.

A further aspect of Toyota's production system is that the short setup times made it economical to manufacture a much wider range of models than is feasible at a traditional mass-production assembly plant. In essence, Toyota soon found that it could supply much greater product variety than its competitors with little in the way of a cost penalty. In 1990, Toyota was offering consumers around the world roughly as many products as GM (about 150), even though Toyota was still only half GM's size. Moreover, it could do this at a lower cost than GM.

C2-3h Distribution and Customer Relations

Toyota's approach to its distributors and customers as it evolved during the 1950s and 1960s was in many ways just as radical as its approach toward suppliers. In 1950, Toyota formed a subsidiary, Toyota Motor Sales, to handle distribution and sales. The new subsidiary was headed by Kaymiya Shotaro from its inception until 1975. Kaymiya's philosophy was that dealers should be treated as "equal partners" in the Toyota family. To back this up, he had Toyota Motor Sales provide a wide range of sales training and service training for dealership personnel.

Kaymiya then used the dealers to build long-term ties with Toyota's customers. The aim was to bring customers into the Toyota design and production process. To this end, through its dealers, Toyota Motor Sales assembled a huge database on customer preferences. Much of these data came from monthly or semiannual surveys conducted by dealers. These asked Toyota customers their preferences for styling, model types, colors, prices, and other features. Toyota also used these surveys to estimate the potential demand for new models. This information was then fed directly into the design process.

Kaymiya began this process in 1952 when the company was redesigning its Toyopet model. The Toyopet was primarily used by urban taxi drivers. Toyota Motor Sales surveyed taxi drivers to try to find out what type of vehicle they preferred. They wanted something reliable, inexpensive, and with good city fuel mileage, which Toyota engineers then set about designing. In 1956, Kaymiya formalized this process when he created a unified department for planning and market research whose function was to coordinate the marketing strategies developed by researchers at Toyota Motor Sales with product planning by Toyota's design engineers. From this time on, marketing information played a critical role in the design of Toyota's cars and in the company's strategy. In particular, it was the research department at Toyota Motor Sales that provided the initial stimulus for Toyota to start exporting during the late 1960s after predicting, correctly, that growth in domestic sales would slow down considerably during the 1970s.

C2-3i Expanding Internationally

Large-scale overseas expansion did not become feasible at Toyota until the late 1960s for one principal reason: Despite the rapid improvement in productivity, Japanese cars were still not competitive.[6] In 1957, for example, the Toyota Corona sold in Japan for the equivalent of $1,694. At the same time, the Volkswagen Beetle sold for $1,111 in West Germany, while Britain's Austin company was selling its basic model for the equivalent of $1,389 in Britain. Foreign companies were effectively kept out of the Japanese market, however, by a 40 %value-added tax and shipping costs.

Despite these disadvantages, Toyota tried to enter the U.S. market in the late 1950s. The company set up a U.S. subsidiary in California in October 1957 and began to sell cars in early 1958, hoping to capture the American small car market (which at that time was poorly served by the U.S. automobile companies). The result was a disaster. Toyota's cars performed poorly in road tests on U.S. highways. The basic problem was that the engines of Toyota's cars were too small for prolonged high-speed driving and tended to overheat and burn oil, while poorly designed chassis resulted in excessive vibration. Sales were slow and in 1964 Toyota closed down its U.S. subsidiary and withdrew from the market.

The company was determined to learn from experiencets U.S.experiencece and quickly redesigned several of its models based on feedback from American consumer surveys and U.S. road tests. As a result, by 1967, the picture had changed considerably. The quality of Toyota's cars was now sufficient to make an impact in the U.S. market, while production costs and retail prices had continued to fall and were now comparable with international competitors in the small car market.

In the late 1960s Toyota reentered the U.S. market. Although sales were initially slow, they increased steadily. Then the OPEC-engineered fourfold increase in oil prices that followed the 1973 Israeli/Arab conflict gave Toyota an unexpected boost. U.S. consumers began to turn to small, fuel-efficient cars in droves, and Toyota was one of the main beneficiaries. Driven primarily by a surge in U.S. demand, worldwide exports of Toyota cars increased from 157,882 units in 1967 to 856,352 units by 1974 and 1,800,923 units by 1984. Put another way, in 1967 exports accounted for 19% 'of Toyota's total output. By 1984, they accounted for 52.5%.

Success brought its own problems. By the early 1980s, political pressures and talk of local content regulations in the United States and Europe were forcing an initially reluctant Toyota to rethink its exporting strategy. Toyota already had agreed to "voluntary" import quotas with the United States in 1981. The consequence for Toyota was stagnant export growth between 1981 and 1984. Against this background, in the early 1980s, Toyota began to think seriously about setting up manufacturing operations overseas.

C2-3j Transplant Operations

Toyota's first overseas operation was a 50/50 joint venture with GM established in February 1983 under the name New United Motor Manufacturing, Inc. (NUMMI). NUMMI, which is based in Fremont, California, began producing Chevrolet Nova cars for GM in December 1984.[7] The maximum capacity of the Fremont plant is about 250,000 cars per year.

For Toyota, the joint venture provided a chance to find out whether it could build quality cars in the United States using American workers and American suppliers. It also provided Toyota with experience dealing with an American union (the United Auto Workers Union) and with a means of circumventing "voluntary" import restrictions. For GM, the venture provided an opportunity to observe in full detail the Japanese approach to manufacturing. While GM's role was marketing and distributing the plant's output, Toyota designed the product and designed, equipped, and operated the plant. At the venture's start, 34 executives were loaned to NUMMI by Toyota and 16 by GM. The chief executive and chief operating officer were both Toyota personnel.

By the fall of 1986, the NUMMI plant was running at full capacity and the early indications were that the NUMMI plant was achieving productivity and quality levels close to those achieved at Toyota's major Takaoka plant in Japan. For example, in 1987, it took the NUMMI plant 19 assembly hours to build a car, compared to 16 hours at Takaoka, while the number of defects per 100 cars was the same at NUMMI as at Takaoka—45.[8]

Encouraged by its success at NUMMI, in December 1985, Toyota announced that it would build an automobile manufacturing plant in Georgetown, Kentucky. The plant, which came on stream in May 1988, officially had the capacity to produce 200,000 Toyota Camrys a year. Such was the success of this plant, however, that by early 1990 it was producing the equivalent of 220,000 cars per year. This success was followed by an announcement in December 1990 that Toyota would build a second plant in Georgetown with a capacity to produce a further 200,000 vehicles per year.[9]

By 2012, Toyota had 14 vehicle assembly plants in North America, 10 of them in the United States, which collectively produced 7 out of every 10 Toyota cars sold in the region. In addition, the company had six other plants producing a range of components, including engines and transmissions. The company also has two R&D and design centers in the United States, its only such facilities outside of Japan. By 2012, Toyota's cumulative investment in the United States exceeded $19.5 billion. In April 2013, Toyota announced that it would move production of one of its luxury Lexus vehicles from Japan to the United States, marking the first time that the company had produced a luxury vehicle outside of Japan. At the same time, Toyota announced that it would invest another $2.5 billion to expand U.S. production capacity.[10]

In addition to its North American transplant operations, Toyota moved to set up production in Europe in anticipation of the 1992 lowering of trade barriers among the 12 members of the European Economic Community (now the EU). In 1989, the company announced that it would build a plant in England with the capacity to manufacture 200,000 cars per year by 1997. It opened a second plant in France in 2001, and by 2008, Toyota had four assembly plants in Europe with a total production capacity of 800,000 vehicles.

The company also expanded to China during the first decade of the 20th century. In China, it had three assembly plants by 2008 that were capable of producing over 440,000 vehicles a year. In the rest of Southeast Asia, Toyota had another 10 plants that could produce almost 1 million vehicles. There were also significant assembly plants in South Africa, Australia, and South America.

Despite Toyota's apparent commitment to expand global assembly operations, it was not all smooth sailing. One problem was building an overseas supplier network comparable to Toyota's Japanese network. For example, in a 1990 meeting of Toyota's North American supplier's association, Toyota executives informed their North American suppliers that the defect ratio for parts produced by 75 North American and European suppliers was 100 times greater than the defect ratio for parts supplied by 147 Japanese suppliers—1,000 defects per million parts versus 10 defects per million among Toyota's Japanese suppliers. Moreover, Toyota executives pointed out that parts manufactured by North American and European suppliers tend to be significantly more expensive than comparable parts manufactured in Japan.

Because of these problems, Toyota had to import many parts from Japan for its U.S. assembly operations. However, for political reasons Toyota was being pushed to increase the local content of cars assembled in North America. By the mid-2000s, the local content of cars produced in North America was over 70%. To improve the efficiency of its U.S.-based suppliers, Toyota embarked upon an aggressive supplier education process.

In 1992, it established the Toyota Supplier Support Center to teach its suppliers the basics of the Toyota production system. By the mid-2000s over 100 supplier companies had been through the center. Many have reportedly seen double- and triple-digit productivity growth as a result, as well as dramatic reductions in inventory levels.[11]

C2-3k Product Strategy

Toyota's initial production was aimed at the small car/basic transportation end of the automobile market. This was true both in Japan and of its export sales to North America and Europe. During the 1980s, however, Toyota progressively moved up the market and abandoned much of the lower end of the market to new entrants, such as the South Koreans. Thus, the company's Camry and Corolla models, which initially were positioned toward the bottom of the market, have been constantly upgraded and now are aimed at the middle-income segments of the market. This upgrading reflects two factors: (1) the rising level of incomes in Japan and the commensurate increase in the ability of Japanese consumers to purchase mid-range and luxury cars and (2) a desire to hold onto its U.S. consumers, many of whom initially purchased inexpensive Toyotas in their early twenties and who have since traded up to more expensive models.

The upgrading of Toyota's models reached a logical conclusion in September 1989 when the company's Lexus division began marketing luxury cars to compete with Jaguars, BMWs, and the like. Although the Lexus brand initially got off to a slow start–in large part due to an economic recession–by 2001, Toyota was selling over 200,000 Lexus models a year in the United States, making it the best-selling luxury brand in the country.

C2-4 Toyota in 2000–2022

The first decade of the 21st century were ones of solid growth for Toyota. In 2004, it overtook Ford to become the second-largest car company in the world. The company surpassed GM in 2008 globally and seemed on track to meet its goal of capturing 15% of the global automobile market by 2010. Toyota was now a truly international company. Its overseas operations had grown from 11 production facilities in 9 countries in 1980 to 48 production facilities in 26 countries around the world.[12] In the important U.S. market, the world's largest, Toyota held an 18.4% share of passenger car sales in mid-2008, up from 11% in 2000. Ford's share was 15.4% while GM held onto a 19.3% share.[13]

The company was very profitable. In the financial year ending March 2008, it earned $17.5 billion net profits on sales of $183 billion. Both GM and Ford lost money that year.

According to data from J.D. Power, Toyota was the quality leader in the U.S. market in 2008. For cars that had been on the market for over 3 years, Toyota's Lexus brand led the pack for the 14th consecutive year with 120 problems per 100 vehicles, compared to an industry average of 206 problems per 100 vehicles. The Toyota brand had 159 problems per 100 vehicles, compared to 177 for Honda, 204 for Ford, 226 for GM, 229 for Chrysler, and 253 for Volkswagen. Toyota also had a strong record in the industry when measured by problems reported in the first 90 days after a sale–99 problems per 100 cars for the Lexus brand and 104 for the Toyota brand versus an industry average of 118 problems per 100 cars.[14]

J.D. Power also found that Toyota led the market in Japan. A survey found that for vehicles purchased in 2002, Toyota had 89 problems per 100 vehicles compared to an industry average of 104. Honda was next with 91 problems per 100 vehicles, followed by Nissan with 108 problems per 100 vehicles.[15]

On the productivity front, Toyota's lead seemed to have narrowed. While it was clearly the productivity leader in the United States in 2003, where it took an average of 30.1 hours to make a car, compared to 35.2 hours at GM and 38.6 hours at Ford,

Exhibit 3 Total manufacturing productivity in the U.S. automobile industry (total labor hours per unit)

Company	2003	2007
Ford	38.6	33.88
Chrysler	37.42	30.37
General Motors	35.2	32.39
Nissan	32.94	32.96
Honda	32.36	31.33
Toyota	30.01	30.37

Note: Includes assembly, stamping, engine, and transmission plants.

Source: *Oliver Wyman's Harbour Report*, Oliver Wyman, June 2008.

by 2007 Toyota was taking 30.37 to build a car, compared to 32.29 at GM and 33.88 at Ford.[16] On the other hand, according to J.D. Power, Toyota has the three most efficient assembly plants in the world, all of which are located in Japan.[17]

Higher quality and greater productivity helped Toyota make far more money per car than its large rivals. In 2007, Toyota made a pretax profit of $922 per vehicle in the United States, compared with losses of $729 and $1,467 at GM and Ford, respectively. These losses also reflect the fact that Ford and GM still pay more for health care, pensions, and sales incentives than Toyota. Also, Ford and GM support more dealers relative to their market share than Toyota.[18]

C2-4a Further Productivity Gains: The Power of Kaizen

Toyota's ability to stay on top of productivity and quality rankings can be attributed to an ongoing company-wide obsession with continuing to improve the efficiency and effectiveness of its manufacturing operations, or *kaizen*. Another round of these was initiated in 2000 by Toyota President Fujio Cho. Cho, who worked for a while under Toyota's legendary engineer, Taichi Ohno, introduced an initiative known as "Construction of Cost Competitiveness for the 21st Century," or CCC21. The initiative had a goal of slashing component part costs by 30% on all new models. Attaining this goal necessitated Toyota working closely with suppliers, something it has long done.

By the mid-2000s Toyota was close to attaining its CCC21 goal. In implementing CCC21, no detail was too small. For example, Toyota took a close look at the grip handles mounted above the doors inside most cars. By working closely with suppliers, they managed to reduce the number of parts in these handles from 34 to 5, which cut procurement costs by 40% and reduced the time needed for installation from 12 seconds to 3 seconds.[19]

More generally, Toyota continued to refine its lean production system. For example, in die making, by 2004, Toyota had reduced the lead time to engineer and manufacture die sets for large body panels to 1.7 months, down from 3 months in 2002. By reducing lead-time, Toyota reduced the start-up costs associated with producing a new model, and the development time.[20]

In welding, Toyota developed and installed a simplified assembly process known as the "Global Body Line" or GBL. First developed in a low-volume Vietnamese assembly plant in 1996, and introduced into its first Japanese plant in 1998, by 2004 the GBL was operating in some 20 of the company's 50 assembly plants and was found in all plants by 2007. The GBL system replaced Toyota's Flexible Body Line assembly philosophy that had been in place since 1985. The GBL system was based upon a series of programmable robotic wielding tools. Under the old FBL system, each car required three pallets to hold body parts in place during the wielding process; each gripping either a major body side assembly or the roof assembly. The GBL system replaces these three pallets with a single pallet that holds all three major body panels in place from the inside as wielding proceeds.[21]

According to Toyota, the GBL system has the following consequences:

- 30% reduction in the time a vehicle spends in the body shop.
- 70% reduction in the time required to complete a major body change
- 50% cut in the cost to add or switch models
- 50% reduction in the investment to set up a line for a new model
- 50% reduction in assembly line footprint

The floor space freed up by the GBL allowed two assembly lines to be placed in the space traditionally required for one, effectively doubling plant capacity. Moreover, by using GBL technology, as many as eight different models can be produced on a single assembly line. To achieve this, Toyota has pushed for consistency in design across model ranges, particularly regarding the "hard points" that are grasped by the single master pallet.

Meanwhile, Toyota has also been accelerating the process of moving towards fewer vehicle platforms, the goal being to build a wide range of models on a limited range of platforms that use many of the same component parts or modules. The company is reportedly working towards a goal of having just 10 platforms, down from over 20 in 2000.[22]

While Toyota is undoubtedly making progress refining its manufacturing efficiency, the fact remains that the productivity and quality gap between Toyota and its global competitors has narrowed. GM and Ford have both made significant strides in improving their quality and productivity in recent years. Moreover, in the American market at least, Toyota has suffered from the perception that its product offerings lack design flair and are not always as well attuned to consumer tastes as they might be. Here too, however, there are signs that Toyota is improving matters, by listening more to its American designers and engineers.

A pivotal event in the changing relationship between Toyota and its American designers occurred in the late 1990s. Japanese managers had resisted their U.S. colleagues' idea that the company should produce a V8 pickup truck for the American market. To change their minds, the U.S. executives flew their Japanese counterparts over from Japan and took them to a Dallas Cowboys football game—with a pit stop in the Texas Stadium parking lot. There the Japanese saw row upon row of full-size pickups. Finally, it dawned on them that Americans see the pickup as more than a commercial vehicle, considering it primary transportation. The result of this was Toyota's best-selling V8 pickup truck, the Toyota Tundra.[23]

American designers also pushed Toyota to redesign the Prius, its hybrid car first introduced in Japan in 1997. The Americans wanted a futuristic design change so that people would notice the technology. The result, the new Prius, was a surprise hit, with Toyota hitting cumulative global sales of over 1 million vehicles in mid-2008. By 2010, Toyota was making more than 1 million hybrids a year.[24]

Toyota's Americanization runs deeper than just product design issues. On the sales front, the company now sells more cars and trucks in North American than it does in Japan, and 70–80% of Toyota's global profits come from North America. On the personnel front, President Cho himself made his reputation by opening Toyota's first U.S. production plant in Georgetown, Kentucky, in 1988. Another senior executive, Yoshi Inaba, spent 8 years in the United States and has an MBA from Northwestern University. American executives are also starting to make their way into Toyota's top ranks.[25]

C2-4b The 2008–2010 Global Financial Crisis and Its Aftermath

Starting in mid-2008, sales in the global automobile industry collapsed at unprecedented rates, falling by around 40%. The sales collapse was a direct consequence of the global financial crisis that started in the American mortgage market, and then spilled over into other sectors. A combination of tight credit and uncertainty about the future caused consumers to buy far fewer new cars. For an industry with high fixed costs, a sales decline of this level was catastrophic.

Toyota was caught flat-footed by the decline. Toyota had been adding to its production capacity in the United States, its largest market, and pushing into the full-sized pickup truck segment, when the storm hit. It had also been adding significant capacity elsewhere, a move that seemed sensible only 12 months earlier given that the company had been struggling to keep up with demand for its vehicles. Indeed, between 2001 and 2007, Toyota added about 500,000 cars worth of production capacity per year, a pace that now seems to be aggressive.[26]

By April 2009, Toyota's sales in the United States were down 42% compared to the same month a year earlier. Moreover, there were sales declines in all other major national markets as well, including China, where Toyota sales fell by 17% in the first quarter of 2009, even though that market was one of the few that continued to grow. Toyota's problems in China reflected a slow response to increasing demand outside of China's big cities for small affordable cars. Toyota exports from Japan were also hit hard by a rise in the value of the Japanese yen against the dollar and euro during 2008 and early 2009.

In the United States, Toyota responded to the recession by placing the planned addition of a new production plant in Mississippi on hold, and idling a production line in Texas. In Japan, production was cut by as much as 40% in some factories. These actions created a huge problem for Toyota, which adheres to a policy of lifetime employment, and has not made any significant workforce reductions since the 1950s. Toyota's initial response was to send underutilized employees to training sessions, and to have them work on identifying ideas for cost savings. However, the company did start to lay off temporary workers and many questioned whether Toyota would be able to stick to its commitment of lifetime employment, particularly if the recession dragged on.

Toyota also launched an "Emergency Profit Improvement Committee," whose job was to find $1.4 billion in savings in 2009. These cost savings came upon some $3.3 billion in cost reductions attained during the preceding few years. In typical Toyota style, no action seems too small. Employees were encouraged to take the stairs rather than use elevators to save electricity. The heat in the factories was turned down. Teams of workers were looking for any way to shave costs out of a production system that was already the world's most efficient.[27]

To try and boost sales in the United States, Toyota introduced 0% financing in late 2008, but sales continued to falter. Ironically, one of Toyota's best-selling cars in the United States during much of 2007 and 2008, the fuel-efficient Prius, which carried a relative high price sticker, also saw steep sales declines in early 2009 as gasoline prices fell, and consumers who did purchase switched to low-priced small cars from Kia and even Ford.

Meanwhile, Toyota was also going through a changing of senior management ranks. In June 2009, Akio Toyoda, grandson of the company's founder, succeeded outgoing CEO Katsuaki Watanabe. With an MBA from Babson College in the United States, and time working in both New York and London, Toyoda is without question the most cosmopolitan CEO to take the helm at Toyota. He did so at a particularly challenging time for the company. His major challenge was to weather the storm and return the company to its growth path.

By 2012, it looked as if he had succeeded in doing that. Toyota had regained the mantel of the world's largest automobile company. Its reputation for quality, which had been badly tarnished by the sudden acceleration problems in the United States, was again riding high. According to J.D. Power's annual Vehicle Dependency Study, after slipping in 2009 and 2010, Toyota brands regained the top spot in 2011 and 2012. Still, Toyota faced invigorated competitors who were fast closing in on the company. Most notably, Hyundai-Kia of South Korea had grown its output from just 2.4 million units in 2000 to 7.1 million in 2012, making it the fourth-largest automobile maker in the world. Hyundai was now more profitable than Toyota, and produced more vehicles per employee, suggesting that Toyota might be losing its crown as the most productive automobile company in the world. In addition, Volkswagen was investing aggressively in capacity, particularly in China, now the world's largest national automobile market, and was well positioned to challenge Toyota for global market share leadership. Rounding out the top four global automobile makers was GM, which had emerged from bankruptcy a smaller but stronger company. Indeed, on global measures of labor productivity, GM now surpassed Toyota. Moreover, GM was well positioned in the large and rapidly growing Chinese market, where Toyota had struggled due to anti-Japanese sentiment. The future thus presented numerous challenges for Toyota.[28]

C2-4c The Electric Future

Although 2021 was a very good year for Toyota, storm clouds were appearing on the horizon. The automobile industry appeared to be at the cusp of an epochal shift, away from the internal combustion engine and towards battery electric vehicles (BEVs). The rise of Tesla from gusty start-up to a rapidly growing mass producer of electric vehicles, and the most valuable automobile company in the world in terms of market valuation, had focused the attention of the world's established automobile companies on the need to make significant investments in electric vehicles. Ford had announced plans to invest $30 billion in BEVs by 2025. The company had also seized leadership in the market for electric pickup trucks, where it registered over 200,000 pre-orders for its all-electric F150 Lightening pickup truck, which entered production in 2022. GM announced plans to invest $35 billion in battery electric vehicles and become carbon neutral by 2040. Not to be outdone, Volkswagen invested $100 billion in electric vehicle development, and expects that 25% of its sales will be electric by the end of 2026.

These are huge numbers and reflect a widely held belief among business executives in the automobile industry and elsewhere that climate change will force the world to shift rapidly towards electrification, and that BEVs are the wave of the future. Toyota was an early investor in electric vehicles, with its hybrid Prius, first introduced in 1997 still leads the market in hybrid technology. In 2021, the company sold 584,000 hybrid vehicles, roughly 65% of the U.S. hybrid market, but the company has lagged the other major automobile producers in its investments in battery electric vehicles.

Toyota seems to be hedging its bets, continuing to invest in hybrid technology, and hydrogen fuel cells, in addition to the lithium-ion battery technology used in BEVs. As of mid-2021, Toyota had announced investments of around $35 billion in hybrid and hydrogen cell technology, and around $28 billion in BEVs. Given Toyota's scale, many analysts wondered if this was wise, particularly given Volkswagen's commitment to invest $100 billion in BEVs, and the rapid progress now being made in BEV range, production, and costs. Toyota's response is that diversity of offerings is the correct strategy for now, and that it is producing vehicles for a wide range of buyers, many of whom will continue to prefer internal combustion engines, or at least a hybrid solution. It also, somewhat quixotically, remains committed to investing in hydrogen fuel cells, even as the rest of the industry is increasingly their commitments to lithium-ion battery technology.[29]

If forecasts from other automobile manufacturers are correct, BEVs will make up half of all vehicle sales by 2030, up from 6% in 2021. By taking a go-slow approach, and hedging its bets in different technological solutions, Toyota risks being left behind in the race to ramp up BEV production. Perhaps in recognition of this, in December 2021 Toyota announced that it would increase its investment in BEVs to $35 billion and announced a target to sell 3.5 million BEVs by 2030, with 100% of its Lexus luxury cars being BEVs by that date.

Notes

[1] "Leading Motor Vehicle Manufacturers Worldwide in 2020 and 2021, Based on Sales Worldwide," *Statista,* July 27, 2022.

[2] S. Buchanan, "How Many Semiconductor Chips Are There in a Car?," *WordPress Blog, Economist Writing Every Day,* January 4, 2022.

[3] A. Root, "Toyota Is Trying to Catch up in a Crowded EV Race. It May Be Too Late," *Barron's,* May 7, 2022.

[4] This section is based primarily on the account given in M. A. Cusumano, *The Japanese Automobile Industry* (Cambridge, Mass: Harvard University Press, 1989).

[5] The material in this section is drawn from three main sources: M. A. Cusumano, *The Japanese Automobile Industry*; Ohno Taiichi, *Toyota Production System* (Cambridge, Mass.: Productivity Press, 1990; Japanese Edition, 1978); J. P. Womack, D. T. Jones, and D. Roos, *The Machine That Changed the World* (New York: Macmillan, 1990).

[6] The material in this section is based on M. A. Cusumano, The Japanese Automobile Industry.

[7] Niland Powell, "U.S.-Japanese Joint Venture: New United Motor Manufacturing, Inc.," *Planning Review,* January–February 1989, pp. 40–45.

[8] From J. P. Womack, D. T. Jones, and D. Roos, *The Machine That Changed the World.*

[9] J. B. Treece, "Just What Detroit Needs: 200,000 More Toyotas a Year," *Business Week,* December 10, 1990, p. 29.

[10] P. Eisensteon, "Toyota Investing over $500 Million to Launch US Lexus Production," *NBC News,* April 19, 2013.

[11] P. Strozniak, "Toyota Alters the Face of Production," *Industry Week,* August 13, 2001, pp. 46–48.

[12] Anonymous, "The Car Company out in Front," *The Economist,* January 29, 2005, pp. 65–67.

[13] R. Newman, "How Toyota Could Become the US Sales Champ," *US News and World Reports,* June 9, 2008.

[14] J.D. Power Press Release, August 7, 2008, "Lexus Ranks Highest in Vehicle Dependability for 14th Consecutive Year". J.D. Power Press Release, June 4, 2008, "Overall Initial Quality Improves Considerably."

[15] J.D. Power Press Release, "Toyota Ranks Highest in Japan's First Long Term Vehicle Dependability Study," September 2, 2004.

[16] *Oliver Wyman's Harbour Report,* Oliver Wyman, June 2008.

[17] *Oliver Wyman's Harbour Report,* Oliver Wyman, June 2008.

[18] *Oliver Wyman's Harbour Report,* Oliver Wyman, June 2008.

[19] B. Bremner and C. Dawson, "Can Anything Stop Toyota," *Business Week,* November 17, 2003, pp. 114–117.

[20] M. Hara, "Moving Target," *Automotive Industries,* June 2004, pp. 26–29.

[21] B. Visnic, "Toyota Adopts New Flexible Assembly Process," *Wards Auto World,* November 2002, pp. 30–31. M. Bursa, "A Review of Flexible Automotive Manufacturing," *Just Auto,* May 2004, p. 15.

[22] M. Hara, "Moving Target," *Automotive Industries,* June 2004, pp. 26–29.

[23] C. Dawson and L. Armstrong, "The Americanization of Toyota," *Business Week,* April 15, 2002, pp. 52–54.

[24] C. Squatriglia, "Prius Sales Top 1 Million," *Autopia,* May 15, 2008.

[25] A. Taylor, "The Americanization of *Toyota*," *Fortune,* December 8, 2004, p. 165.

[26] Y. Takahashi, "Toyota Record $7.74 Billion Quarterly Loss," *Wall Street Journal,* May 11, 2009, p. 3.

[27] I. Rowly, "Toyota's Cost Cutting Drive," *Business Week,* January 1, 2009, p. 15.

[28] S. Pearson et al., "Global Autos: A Clash of Titans," *Morgan Stanley Blue Paper,* January 22, 2013.

[29] A. Root, "Toyota Is Trying to Catch up in a Crowded EV Race. It May Be Too Late," *Barron's,* May 7, 2022.

Tesla, Inc. in 2022

Case written by Melissa A. Schilling

In 2022, Tesla was one of the most talked about companies in the world. What had been founded in 2003 as an unlikely and risky venture to produce an all-electric luxury sports car had grown into a company with over $50 billion in annual revenues that produced multiple car models, solar panels, and energy storage systems (e.g., Powerwall) (see select items and segment data in Table 1, and full financials in Exhibits 1 & 2). With a market capitalization of $943 billion in September of 2022, it was the sixth most valuable company in the world. It operated six huge vertically integrated factories around the globe (California, Nevada, New York, Shanghai, Grünheide, and Texas) and employed over 100,000 people. Tesla's growth and success was astonishing—no other auto manufacturing start-up had been successful in the United States since the 1920s.

The road leading up to Tesla's position in 2022 had been anything but smooth. From 2003 to 2019, the company had reported annual losses in every year. The year 2020 was the first in which the company reported a profit for the year. The company's CEO, Elon Musk, was also a near-constant source of controversy, much of which

Table 1 Select Items from Tesla Income Statement, in $US Millions					
USD Millions	2021	2020	2019	2018	2017
Sales/Revenue	53,823	31,536	24,578	21,461	11,759
Sales Growth	70.67%	28.31%	14.52%	82.51%	–
COGS excluding D&A	37,306	22,584	18,355	15,518	7,906
Gross Income	13,606	6,630	4,069	4,042	2,217
Gross Income Growth	105.22%	62.94%	0.67%	82.33%	–
Gross Profit Margin	25.28%	–	–	–	–
SG&A Expense	7,110	4,636	3,989	4,295	3,855
Research & Development	2,593	1,491	1,343	1,460	1,378
EBIT	6,496	1,994	–	−253	−1,638
Net Income	5,524	690	−870	−976	−1,961
Net Income Growth	700.58%	179.31%	10.87%	50.23%	–

Source: Tesla 10Ks

played out on Twitter. For example, on August 17, 2018, Musk got into hot water with the Securities and Exchange Commission (SEC) by posting on Twitter, "Am considering taking Tesla private at $420. Funding secured." Funding, however, was not secured, and Musk later revealed that the "$420" reference was a marijuana joke. The SEC did not think it was funny. The price of Tesla stock jumped up 11% within hours of the tweet, and Nasdaq halted trading of the stock. The SEC sued Musk and Tesla for "making false and misleading statements," and both Musk and Tesla were each ordered to pay a $20 million fine. Musk was further required to step down as chairman of the board at Tesla and had to agree to have his tweets reviewed by Tesla's legal department if they were material to the company. This didn't appear to have daunted Musk, however, who tweeted a few months later, "Just wanted to say that the Short-seller Enrichment Commission is doing incredible work. And the name change is so on point!" Musk also drew ire from many people when he protested the COVID-19 lockdown by tweeting on April 28, 2020, "FREE AMERICA NOW," and caused another stir with his May 1, 2020, tweet, "Tesla stock price is too high imo" that resulted in a $14 billion drop in market capitalization.

In an interesting twist, Musk announced on April 14, 2022, that he wanted to buy Twitter for $54.20 a share (with yet another 420 reference), a 38% premium over Twitter's share price at the time. Twitter accepted the offer, but by July 8th, Musk had changed his mind and wanted out of the deal, stating that Twitter had too many fake accounts. The news sent Twitter's stock price reeling downwards. Twitter sued Musk to force him to make good on his offer and after the court ruled in favor of Twitter, Musk bought the company on October 27th, 2022 for $44 billion.

C3-1 History of Tesla

In 2003, an engineer named Martin Eberhard was looking for his next big project. A tall, slim man with a mop of gray hair, Eberhard was a serial entrepreneur who had launched several start-ups, including NuvoMedia, which he sold to Gemstar in a $187-million deal. Eberhard was also looking for a sports car that would be environmentally friendly—he had concerns about global warming and U.S. dependence on the Middle East for oil. When he didn't find the car of his dreams on the market, he began contemplating building one himself, even though he had zero experience in the auto industry. Eberhard noticed that many of the driveways that had a Toyota Prius hybrid electric vehicle (or "dorkmobile" as he called it) also had expensive sports cars in them, making him speculate that there could be a market for a high-performance, environmentally friendly car. As Eberhard explained: "It was clear that people weren't buying a Prius to save money on gas. Gas was selling close to inflation-adjusted all-time lows. They were buying them to make a statement about the environment."[1]

Eberhard began to consider a range of alternative fuel options for his car: hydrogen fuel cells, natural gas, diesel. However, he soon concluded that the highest efficiency and performance would come from an entirely electric vehicle. Luckily for Eberhard, Al Cocconi (founder of AC Propulsion and one of the original engineers for GM's ill-fated EV-1) had concluded the same thing and produced a car called the tzero. The tzero could go from zero to 60 miles per hour in 4.1 seconds, but it was powered with extremely heavy lead-acid batteries, limiting its range to about 60 miles between charges. Eberhard approached Cocconi with the idea of using lighter, lithium ion batteries, which offered six times more energy per pound. Cocconi was eager to try out the idea (he had, in fact, been experimenting with lithium ion batteries), and the resulting lithium ion powered tzero accelerated to 60 miles per hour in 3.6 seconds and could travel more than 300 miles. Eberhard licensed the electric-drive-train technology from AC Propulsion, and founded his company, Tesla Motors (named after Nikola Tesla, a late 19th- and early 20th-century inventor who developed, among other things, the AC electrical system used in the United States today).[2]

Meanwhile, another entrepreneur—one with much deeper pockets—was also interested in developing electric vehicles based on the tzero: Elon Musk. In 2002, Musk was a 31-year-old South African living in California, who had founded a company that ultimately became PayPal. After selling PayPal to eBay in 2002 for $1.5 billion, he started a company called SpaceX with the ambitious goal of developing cheap, consumer space travel. (SpaceX's Dragon spacecraft ultimately made history in May 2012 by becoming the first commercial vehicle to launch and dock at the International Space Station.[3]) Musk's assertive style and astonishing record of high-tech entrepreneurship made him one of the inspirations for the Tony Stark character in Jon Favreau's *Iron Man* movies.

Like Eberhard, Musk thought electric cars were the key to the United States achieving energy independence, and he approached Cocconi about buying the tzero. Tom Gage, who was then AC Propulsion's CEO, suggested that Musk collaborate with Eberhard. After a 2-hour meeting in February 2004, Musk agreed to fund Eberhard's plan with $6.3 million. He would be the company's chairman; Eberhard would serve as CEO.

C3-1a The Roadster

The first Tesla prototype, the Roadster, was based on the $45,000 Lotus Elise, a fast, light sports car that seemed perfect for the creation of Eberhard and Musk's grand idea (see Figure 1). The car would have 400 volts of electric potential, liquid-cooled, lithium ion batteries, and a series of silicon transistors that would give the car acceleration so powerful the driver would be pressed back against the seat.[4] It would be nearly as fast as a Porsche 911 Turbo, would not create a single emission, and would get about

Figure 1 The Roadster

Charles Hill

220 miles on a single charge from the kind of outlet you would use to power a washing machine.[5] Furthermore, rather than creating new large-format batteries to power the car, they connected nearly 7,000 small, cylindrical 18650 lithium batteries together into a pack. 18650 batteries are the type used in many consumer devices, including laptops, and over a billion a year are manufactured. This meant that the Roadster was using a battery that had been thoroughly "debugged," that already had a good ratio of energy capacity to price, and for which there was already large production capacity.

While the men worked well together at first, personality clashes soon emerged. Both were technically savvy and vigorously addressed problems within the company. As described by Laurie Yoler, Eberhard was "just brilliant, and he has this tenacity that is unbelievable … He is the guy you want around in those early days when you have naysayers all around." However, Eberhard could also be abrasive and critical. Musk, in turn, was not content to just financially back the company. He began to get intimately involved in decisions about the car's design and the operation of the company. Soon, Musk and Eberhard were at odds over decision making. Eberhard preferred to stick with the fiberglass body panels used in the original Elise; Musk wanted to use the lighter, stronger, and more expensive carbon fiber. Eberhard had approved the hiring of PR professionals to build publicity for the car before its launch; Musk fired them, believing his own involvement and the car itself would generate enough publicity. Eberhard wanted to reap the cost savings of sticking with the Elise's original crash-tested, off-the-rack chassis; Musk wanted to lower the doorsills by 2 inches to make the car easier to enter and exit. Musk also wanted to redesign the headlights and door latches, and replace the Elise's seats with more comfortable—and again, more expensive—custom seats.[6]

In each case, Musk prevailed. He insisted that "you can't sell a $100,000 car that looks like crap." Musk's views were hard to ignore given that, by 2007, he had put $55 million of his own money into the company and had also raised money from wealthy friends, including eBay's second employee, Jeff Skoll, and Google founders Sergey Brin and Larry Page.

Musk's insistence on the best materials and parts, however, combined with Eberhard's inexperience as the manager of a major firm, resulted in delays and runaway costs. At a staff meeting in June 2007, Tom Colson, head of manufacturing, revealed a cost analysis suggesting that the average cost of the cars would be over $100,000 for the first 50, and would decline only slightly with increased volume. Eberhard could not answer the financial questions of the venture capitalists on Tesla's board, and their confidence in him was eroded even further by his defense: "In any other company it's the CFO that provides those numbers … I'm an engineer, not a finance guy." In August 2007, the board removed him as CEO and demoted him to president of technology. In October 2007, Musk arranged for Eberhard to be ousted from the company entirely. Furious, Eberhard started a blog detailing what he called the "Stealth Bloodbath" going on at Tesla, and he would later sue Musk for libel, slander, and breach of contract.[7]

Meanwhile, Eberhard's temporary replacement was Michael Marks, former CEO of Flextronics. Marks immediately created a priority list that identified items with the potential to delay the car. He mothballed any plans for side projects and focused the entire business on streamlining costs and launching the Roadster. Despite his efforts, the Roadster missed its deadline for beginning production at the Lotus facility, triggering a $4-million penalty built into the manufacturing contract Eberhard had signed with Lotus.

By the beginning of 2008, morale was at an all-time low. In March, however, production began on the Roadster, and by July 2008, most of the production problems had been forgotten as the first seven Roadsters (the "Founder's Series") hit the road. Enthusiasm for the cars was astonishing—an all-star list of celebrities made reservations to buy one, and everywhere a Roadster appeared, people stopped to stare.[8]

C3-1b The Model S

Musk's ambitions did not stop at a niche, high-end car. He wanted to build a major U.S. auto company, a feat that had not been successfully accomplished since the 1920s. To do so, he knew he needed to introduce a less expensive car that could attract a higher volume of sales, if not quite the mass market. In June 2008, Tesla announced the Model S, a high-performance, all-electric sedan that would sell for a price ranging from $57,400 to $77,400 and compete against cars like the BMW 5-series (see Figure 2). The car would have an all-aluminum body and a range of up to 300 miles per charge.[9] The Model S cost $500 million to develop; however, offsetting that cost was a $465-million loan Tesla received from the U.S. government to build the car, part of the U.S. government's initiative to promote the development of technologies that would help the United States achieve energy independence.

By May 2012, Tesla reported that it already had 10,000 reservations from customers hoping to buy the Model S, and Musk confidently claimed the company would soon be producing and selling 20,000 Model S cars per year. Musk also noted that after ramping up production, he expected to see "at least 10,000 units a year from demand in Europe and at least 5,000 in Asia."[10] The production of the Model S went more smoothly than that of the Roadster and, by June 2012, the first Model S cars rolled off the factory floor. The very first went to Jeff Skoll, eBay's first president and a major investor in Tesla. On the day of the launch, Skoll talked with Musk about whether it was harder to build a rocket or a car (referring to Musk's SpaceX company): "We decided it was a car. There isn't a lot of competition in space."[11]

To build the car, Tesla bought a recently closed automobile factory in Fremont, California, that had been used for the New United Motor Manufacturing Inc. (NUMMI) venture between Toyota and General Motors. The factory, which was capable of producing 1,000 cars a week, was far bigger than Tesla's immediate needs and would give the company room to grow. Furthermore, though the plant and the land it was on had been appraised at around $1 billion before NUMMI was shut down, Tesla was able

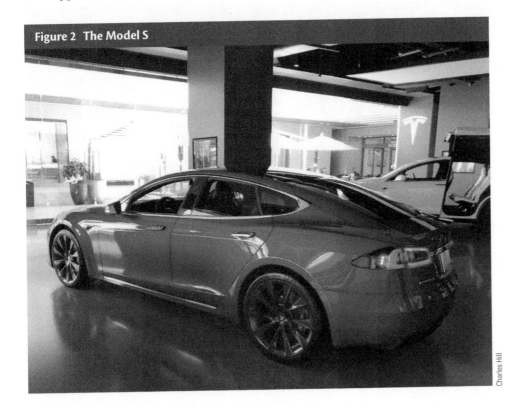

Figure 2 The Model S

Charles Hill

to snap up the idled factory for $42 million.[12] Tesla also used the factory to produce battery packs for Toyota's RAV4, and a charger for a subcompact Daimler AG electric vehicle. These projects would supplement Tesla's income while also helping it to build scale and learning-curve efficiencies in its technologies.

In the first quarter of 2013, Tesla announced its first quarterly profit. The company had taken in $562 million in revenues and reported an $11.2-million profit. Then more good news came: The Model S had earned *Consumer Reports'* highest rating, and had outsold similarly priced BMW and Mercedes models in the first quarter.[13] In May 2013, the company raised $1 billion by issuing new shares, and then surprised investors by announcing that it had paid back its government loan. After repaying the loan, Tesla had some $679 million in cash. Musk had announced confidently that he felt it was his obligation to pay back taxpayer money as soon as possible, and that the company had sufficient funds now to develop its next generation of automobiles without the loan and without issuing further shares.[14]

C3-1c Model X

The Model X, unveiled in 2015, was designed as a high-end sport utility vehicle (SUV) that seats seven. Several distinctive features set it apart from the crowded luxury SUV market. In addition to being all-electric and able to go from zero to 60 miles per hour in just 3.2 seconds, it featured a panoramic windshield and distinctive, gull-wing doors (that open upward rather than swinging out) that open automatically in response to the driver's approach (see Figure 3). "It will triangulate my position," Musk said; "It will open the front door without touching. When you sit down, it will close the door."[15] The Model X had a range of about 250 miles (like the Model S) but could tow 5,000 pounds. Its selling price would start at $70,000 but could exceed $100,000 depending on the options selected.

Figure 3 The Model X

Charles Hill

In the United States, the mid-size luxury SUV market was about five times the size of the high-end luxury sedan market, and the Model X rapidly attracted a long waiting list of people who placed deposits for the car. Musk projected a fast production ramp up, with goals of producing 85,000 to 90,000 Model X and S vehicles in 2017. Analysts at the time doubted that production could be ramped up so quickly, but despite several supplier parts shortages, Tesla's estimates ended up being very close to the mark: The company produced a total of 83,922 cars in 2017.[16]

Reviews of the car were mixed. *Consumer Reports* found the car disappointing, citing rear doors that were prone to pausing, the car's limited cargo capacity, and a ride that was "too firm and choppy for a $110,000 car."[17] *Car and Driver*'s review also expressed doubts about the wing doors, but gave the car overall a rating of five out of five stars, stating, "There are no other electric SUVs at the moment. And even against fossil-fuel-fed SUVs, the Tesla's effortless performance and efficiency can't be matched."[18]

By the end of 2016, the Model X had accumulated total sales of 25,524, ranking it seventh among the bestselling plug-in cars in the world (notably, cumulative sales of Tesla Model S reached 158,159 by the end of 2016, making it the second-bestselling plug-in car in the world, behind only the Nissan Leaf).[19] By the end of 2017, cumulative sales of the Model X reached approximately 72,059 units.[20]

C3-1d Model 3

To achieve Musk's goal of making a real dent in fossil fuel use, Tesla needed a truly mass-market car. Thus, in the fall of 2016, he announced the Model 3, a midsized, all-electric, four-door sedan with a range of 220 to 310 miles (depending on the battery option), and a base price of $35,000 (see Figure 4). Within a week, Tesla had received 325,000 reservations for the car, ranking it among the most sought-after cars in the world. A review in *Road and Track* said that the "Model 3 proves that

Figure 4 The Model 3

Charles Hill

Tesla is thinking far beyond the edges of the Model S and X. Stepping out of the 3, you realize that, as far as the S and X pushed the envelope, they were always meant as intermediaries, stepping stones designed to draw people away from comfortable convention and into the future of the automobile."[21] *Popular Mechanics* gave the car its 2018 Car of the Year award, and *Automobile Magazine* gave it the 2018 Design of the Year Award.

The company announced an extremely ambitious production ramp-up plan, with Musk claiming that the company would be able to produce 5,000 Model 3s a week by the end of 2017 and would reach 500,000 total cars (across all three models) by the end of 2018. This would require a massive expansion in production capacity that many experts viewed as unattainable in such a short time frame. The Model 3 would also incorporate new hardware and software to enable automated driving that created significant new design and production challenges. By early 2018, it was clear that Model 3 production was well behind Musk's initial ambitious projections, and criticism from analysts and the press was coming at a furious pace. As one analyst at Cowen and Co. noted, "Tesla needs to slow down and more narrowly focus its vision and come up for a breath of fresh air ... Elon Musk needs to stop over promising and under delivering."[22] Tesla's production ramp-up promises had become so newsworthy that *Bloomberg* created a website dedicated to tracking the number of Model 3 Vehicle Identification Numbers (VINs) on the road (see Figure 5).

By June 2018, however, Tesla was hitting its 5,000 Model 3s a week.[23] Tesla reached over 500,000 cars on the road by the end of 2018.[24]

C3-1e Model Y and Cybertruck

In March of 2019, Tesla unveiled its plan for a compact crossover vehicle that would be similar to the Model X but less expensive—the Model Y (see Figure 6). The cars began shipping in March 2020. Its larger size and heavier weight gave it a slightly lower range than the Model 3 but it had significantly more interior space (68 cubic feet compared to the 44 cubic feet in the Model 3), enabling it to accommodate an optional third row of seating. It was launched with a base price of $41,190 though most cars were sold

Figure 5 The Bloomberg "Tesla Model 3 Vin Tracker" website

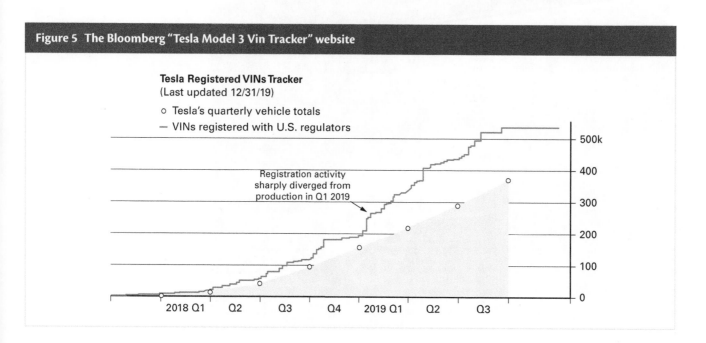

Figure 6 The Model Y

Roschetzky Photography/Shutterstock.com

with options that brought the price significantly higher. The Model Y quickly became the best-selling car in Tesla's lineup, and by 2021 was the best-selling electric vehicle in the United States, though globally it was still beaten out by its older sibling, the Model 3, with 501,000 units sold in the year.[25]

Tesla had also promised the world an electric light-duty truck called "Cybertruck." The truck was designed with an unusual angular wedge shape and was planned to have an exoskeleton of scratch- and dent-resistant stainless steel. However, its release date had been pushed back several times and as of 2022 it still did not have a firm timeline for beginning deliveries.

In total, by August 14, 2022, Tesla had produced over 3 million cars, with over 1 million of those coming from Tesla's Giga Shanghai factory.[26]

C3-2 Obstacles to the Adoption of Electric Vehicles

Numerous obstacles had slowed the adoption of electric vehicles by the mass market. The first was the price: Electric vehicles were, typically, significantly more expensive than comparable internal-combustion models. Complicating matters further, most consumers had a very difficult time estimating the cost of ownership of an electric car. How much would they pay to charge at home? How much would they pay to charge away from home? What would the maintenance and repairs of an electric vehicle cost? How long would the battery and/or car last? Would it have resale value?

To lessen these concerns, Elon Musk set out to make the cost of owning a Tesla as certain as possible. First, he created a "Supercharger" network that Model S owners could use for free, for the life of the car. As noted by Musk, "The clearest way to convey the message that electric cars are actually better than gasoline cars is to say charging is free."[27] The hitch was that a user had to be within range of a Supercharger station. Second, Musk announced an unprecedented price-protection guarantee that permitted a Model S owner to trade in the car for a designated residual value anytime within the first 3 years of the car's life. Musk also announced plans to offer free repairs, and a free replacement car while a customer's car was being repaired. Needless to say, analysts scratched their heads at the potential costs of these guarantees.

The second major obstacle to the adoption of electric vehicles was their limited range and the associated "range anxiety" (concerns about driving in places where owners were not sure they would be able to charge their cars). These concerns were not so much of an issue for Tesla cars due to their exceptionally long range. Other "mass-market" electric vehicles faced tougher hurdles. For example, though a Nissan Leaf could be charged at an ordinary, 110-volt household outlet, a full charge by this method could take 8 hours. Level 2 charging with a 220-volt outlet could shorten that time to 4 hours, but this was still completely impractical for recharging during a trip. DC Fast Chargers and Tesla's "Superchargers" promised to fully charge a vehicle in 30 minutes or less. While this is still significantly longer than the typical 6-minute gasoline fill-up, it meant that charging could be feasible if it were co-located with other services that drivers might appreciate, such as restaurants or coffee shops. DC Fast Chargers and Tesla's Supercharging stations were expensive to purchase and install—up to $250,000 depending on the location—and they had to be close to heavy-duty electricity transformers. By September 2022, Tesla had deployed over 35,000 Superchargers around the world.[28]

C3-3 The Global Electric Vehicle Market

In 2021, global sales of electric vehicles reached nearly 6.8 million vehicles—representing 9% of the global auto market—and were forecasted to hit over 8 million in 2022.[29] Plug-in electric passenger vehicles were expected to make up 23% of new passenger vehicle sales globally in 2025.[30] Globally, China led the pack in electric vehicle sales (see Figure 7). In 2021, there were 450 electric car companies in China, the largest of which was BYD which sold 593,743 electric cars in 2021 (see Table 2).[31]

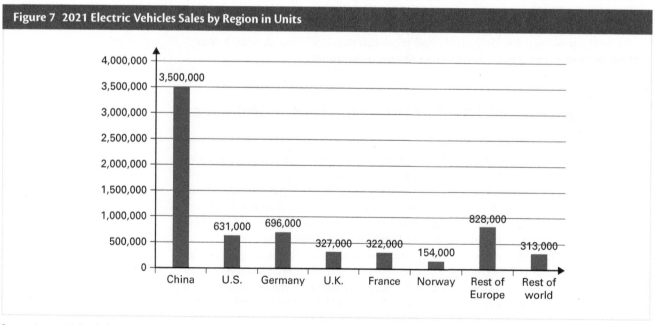

Figure 7 2021 Electric Vehicles Sales by Region in Units

Source: Argonne National Laboratories

Table 2	Global Deliveries of Electric Vehicles	
#1	Tesla, Inc.	936,172
#2	Toyota	674,450
#3	BYD	593,743
#4	General Motors	516,600
#5	Volkswagen Group	452,900
#6	SAIC-GM-Wuling Motors	400,000
#7	BMW	328,316
#8	Nissan	184,033
#9	Hyundai	160,000
#10	Ford	27,000
#11	NIO	25,000
#12	Li Auto	18,126
#13	XPENG Motors	16,000
#14	Rivian	920
#15	Lucid Motors	125

Source: https://history-computer.com/largest-ev-companies-in-the-world/ September 2022

C3-4 Tesla's Strategies

C3-4a Automated Manufacturing

Tesla's manufacturing process was highly automated, with extensive use of 8- to 12-foot-tall red robots (most produced by Kuka and Fanuc), reminiscent of Iron Man. The largest robots were each named after characters from the Marvel series *X-Men* and could lift entire cars and maneuver them into position in the plant. Each robot had a single, multijointed arm. While typical auto factory robots perform only one function, Tesla's robots perform up to four tasks: welding, riveting, bonding, and installing a component. Eight robots might work on a single car at each station of the assembly line in a choreographed pattern, like ballet. For a glimpse into this manufacturing process, see the video here: https://youtu.be/8_lfxPI5ObM.

C3-4b Distribution

Musk saw the franchise-dealership arrangements that U.S. car companies use to sell cars as an expensive, margin-killing model. Furthermore, selling an electric vehicle is more complicated than selling an internal combustion vehicle. Because consumers are less familiar with electric vehicles, they required more explanation about the electricity costs, service issues, potential resale value issues, and more. Musk thus chose to sell direct to consumers with boutique-like stores in upscale shopping malls where salespeople could provide high-touch service and answer customer questions without using high-pressure sales tactics. As of April 2022, the company operated 438 Tesla stores, 308 of which were outside of the United States. The company also sold direct to consumers on the Internet.

Musk's decision to own and operate Tesla dealerships himself was a controversial move that provoked the ire of dealership networks. In the 1950s, regulation had been passed in the United States to protect dealers from exploitation by what were then very powerful auto manufacturers. This regulation prohibited auto manufacturers from competing with their own dealers by directly selling cars to consumers. The industry, however, had become increasingly competitive due to globalization, thereby lowering the power of auto manufacturers. Though most economic analysis suggested that the industry would be more efficient if the dealership restrictions were removed, the regulation remained largely unchallenged until Tesla's entry.[32] Tesla was chipping away at them one by one. In 2022, at least 17 states still banned direct sales, making it extremely difficult for Tesla to enter.

C3-4c Marketing

Tesla spends no money on advertising, nor does it have any plans to hire advertising agencies or run ads in the future. General Motors, by contrast, spent $2.7 billion in advertising in the United States in 2021; Ford Motor ranked second, having spent roughly $2 billion in promoting its brands across the country. Stellantis, Toyota Motor, and Honda Motor each spent about $1 billion on advertising.[33] Tesla has relied wholly on free attention from the press and the visibility of its cars, charging stations, and stores, which are located in high-traffic, high-rent locations.

C3-5 Not Just a Motor Company...

In 2016, Tesla began dropping the "Motors" from its name, signaling it was no longer just an auto company. In July 2016, Tesla opened Gigafactory 1, a giant, lithium ion battery factory built near Reno, Nevada, with its partner Panasonic. Musk justified the vertical integration move by arguing that the Gigafactory 1 would ultimately drive battery production costs down by as much as 30%. In addition to producing batteries for Tesla automobiles, the factory would build Powerwall and Powerpack energy storage devices. The Powerwall was a device for consumers to store solar energy at home. The Powerpack enabled industrial users to manage variable energy needs and provided a source for backup power.

In August 2016, Tesla also finalized a plan to acquire SolarCity, a company that leases and installs solar panels, for $2.6 billion. Solar City was founded in 2006 by Peter and Lyndon Rive, Elon Musk's cousins. Musk had sketched out the concept for the company around the time of Tesla's founding and had helped his cousins start the company. He also served as its chairman of the board. The company had an innovative business model that enabled consumers to have solar panels installed on their roofs with no upfront costs, and to pay instead for the power generated by the panels at a price that was comparable to or less than the price they would normally pay for electricity.

In the same month that the Solar City acquisition plan was finalized, Musk announced that the company would begin producing house roofs made entirely from solar panels. "I think this is a really fundamental part of achieving differentiated product strategy, where you have a beautiful roof," Musk said. "It's not a thing on the roof.[34] It is the roof." At a launch event in October 2016, Musk noted, "The goal is to make solar roofs that look better than a normal roof, generate electricity, last longer, have better insulation, and actually have an installed cost that is less than a normal roof plus the cost of electricity. Why would you buy anything else?"[35]

By 2022, it appeared that Tesla was on track to be successful with its Powerwall energy storage systems. By the end of 2021, Tesla had sold 250,000 Powerwalls and had a significant backlog of orders. Its performance in solar panels, however, was more concerning. Despite significant global growth in demand for solar power systems, Tesla's residential solar and installations had dropped to about half of what Solar City was installing before the acquisition. Collectively, energy generation and storage accounted for roughly 5% of Tesla's revenues and was a loss-making segment (see Table 3).

In April of 2021, Musk admitted that Tesla had made "significant mistakes" in the solar rooftile project that had led to cost overruns and delays. The company had run into trouble "assessing the difficulty of certain roofs." As a result, the company had often presented customers with a cost that was two or three times what was estimated in the original proposal. Many customers balked at this increase in price and Tesla refunded their deposits.[36] Musk, however, still felt that solar power and energy storage were crucial parts of his master plan for Tesla, and felt strongly that it made sense to have the businesses under one roof. "We can't do this well if Tesla and SolarCity are different companies, which is why we need to combine and break down the barriers inherent to being separate companies," he wrote. "That they are separate at all, despite similar origins and pursuit of the same overarching goal of sustainable energy, is largely an accident of history. Now that Tesla is ready to scale Powerwall and SolarCity is ready to provide highly differentiated solar, the time has come to bring them together."[37]

Tesla's auto manufacturing operations had overcome long odds to become an unprecedented success, winning accolades around the world, and becoming an undisputed leader in electric vehicles. Many credited Tesla with creating the widespread demand for electric vehicles that spurred other automakers to launch their own electric vehicles. From that perspective, Tesla had truly changed the world. Now Tesla was trying to help consumers transition to generating and storing their own energy from the sun—arguably an even more ambitious goal. Some analysts believed Tesla was trying to do too much at once and was unlikely to be successful in both automaking and energy production and storage systems. Others were betting—and hoping—Musk could pull it off.

Table 3 Tesla's revenue and gross profit by segment 2021, in $US millions			
	2019	2020	2021
Automotive Sales and Leasing			
Revenues	20,821	27,236	45,767
Gross profit	4372.4	7081.4	13410
Energy Generation and Storage			
Revenues	1,531	1,994	2,789
Gross Profit	183.72	19.94	−128.3
Services and Other			
Revenues	2,226	2,306	3,802
Gross Profit	−543.1	−364.3	−102.7

Source: Tesla 10K

Exhibit 1 Tesla Income Statement, in $US millions

	2021	2020	2019	2018	2017
Sales/Revenue	53,823	31,536	24,578	21,461	11,759
COGS excluding D&A	37,306	22,584	18,355	15,518	7,906
Depreciation & Amortization Expense	2,911	2,322	2,154	1,901	1,636
Depreciation	1,910	–	–	–	–
Amortization of Intangibles	1,001	–	–	–	–
COGS Growth	61.48%	21.44%	17.74%	82.56%	–
Gross Income	13,606	6,630	4,069	4,042	2,217
Gross Profit Margin	25.28%	–	–	–	–
SG&A Expense	7,110	4,636	3,989	4,295	3,855
Research & Development	2,593	1,491	1,343	1,460	1,378
Other SG&A	–	3,145	2,646	2,834	2,477
EBIT	6,496	1,994	–	−253	−1,638
Unusual Expense	−40	36	189	114	−7
Non Operating Income/Expense	122	−86	85	0	−127
Non-Operating Interest Income	56	30	44	25	20
Interest Expense	371	748	685	663	471
Gross Interest Expense	424	796	716	718	596
Interest Capitalized	53	48	31	55	125
Pretax Income	6,343	1,154	−665	−1,005	−2,209
Pretax Margin	11.78%	–	–	–	–
Income Tax	699	292	110	58	32
Income Tax - Current Domestic	9	4	5	2	−8
Income Tax - Current Foreign	839	248	86	24	43
Income Tax - Deferred Domestic	–	–	−4	–	–
Income Tax - Deferred Foreign	−149	40	23	32	−4
Other After Tax Income (Expense)	5	−31	−8	–	–
Consolidated Net Income	5,649	831	−783	−1,063	−2,241
Minority Interest Expense	125	141	87	−86	−279
Net Income	5,524	690	−870	−976	−1,961
Net Margin	10.26%	–	–	–	–
Net Income After Extraordinaries	5,524	690	−870	−976	−1,961
Net Income Available to Common	5,524	690	−870	−976	−1,961
EPS (Basic)	1.63	0.21	−0.33	−0.38	−0.79
Basic Shares Outstanding	2,958	2,799	2,661	2,558	2,486
EPS (Diluted)	–	0.64	−0.98	−1.14	−2.37
Diluted Shares Outstanding	3,387	3,249	2,661	2,558	2,486
EBITDA	9,407	4,316	2,234	1,648	−2

Source: Tesla 10Ks

Exhibit 2 Tesla Balance Sheet, in $US Millions

Assets	2021	2020	2019	2018	2017
Cash & Short Term Investments	18,052	19,622	6,514	3,878	3,523
Cash Only	17,921	19,622	6,514	3,878	3,523
Cash & Short Term Investments Growth	−8.00%	201.23%	67.97%	10.07%	–
Total Accounts Receivable	1,913	1,886	1,324	949	515
Accounts Receivables, Net	1,913	1,886	1,324	949	515
Accounts Receivables, Gross	1,913	1,886	1,324	949	515
Accounts Receivable Turnover	28.14	16.72	18.56	22.61	22.82
Inventories	5,757	4,101	3,552	3,113	2,264
Finished Goods	1,277	1,666	1,356	1,582	1,014
Work in Progress	1,089	493	362	297	243
Raw Materials	3,391	1,942	1,834	1,235	1,006
Other Current Assets	1,378	1,108	713	366	268
Miscellaneous Current Assets	1,378	1,108	713	366	268
Total Current Assets	27,100	26,717	12,103	8,306	6,571
Net Property, Plant & Equipment	31,176	23,375	20,199	19,691	20,492
Property, Plant & Equipment - Gross	39,867	29,893	25,062	22,886	22,436
Buildings	4,675	3,662	3,024	4,047	2,517
Machinery & Equipment	2,188	1,811	1,493	1,398	1,256
Construction in Progress	5,559	1,621	764	807	2,542
Computer Software and Equipment	1,414	856	595	487	395
Leased Property	5,284	3,537	2,853	2,090	4,117
Other Property, Plant & Equipment	18,731	16,848	15,115	14,057	11,609
Accumulated Depreciation	8,691	6,518	4,863	3,195	1,944
Total Investments and Advances	223	279	270	398	442
Other Long-Term Investments	223	279	270	398	442
Long-Term Note Receivable	299	334	402	422	457
Intangible Assets	1,717	520	537	351	422
Net Goodwill	200	207	198	68	60
Net Other Intangibles	–	313	339	282	362
Other Assets	1,616	923	798	572	273
Tangible Other Assets	1,616	923	798	572	273
Total Assets	62,131	52,148	34,309	29,740	28,655
Return On Average Assets	9.67%	–	–	–	–

Source: Tesla 10Ks

(continued)

Exhibit 2 Tesla Balance Sheet, in $US Millions (continued)

Liabilities & Shareholders' Equity	2021	2020	2019	2018	2017
ST Debt & Current Portion LT Debt	1,957	2,459	2,070	2,711	979
Short Term Debt	–	286	228	–	–
Current Portion of Long Term Debt	1,589	2,173	1,842	2,711	979
Accounts Payable	10,025	6,051	3,771	3,404	2,390
Accounts Payable Growth	65.68%	60.46%	10.77%	42.43%	–
Income Tax Payable	1,122	777	611	349	186
Other Current Liabilities	6,601	4,961	4,215	3,528	4,120
Accrued Payroll	906	654	466	449	378
Miscellaneous Current Liabilities	5,695	4,307	3,749	3,079	3,742
Total Current Liabilities	19,705	14,248	10,667	9,992	7,675
Current Ratio	1.38	1.88	1.13	0.83	0.86
Quick Ratio	1.08	1.59	0.8	0.52	0.56
Cash Ratio	0.92	1.38	0.61	0.39	0.46
Long-Term Debt	6,916	10,888	12,627	11,116	11,152
Long-Term Debt excl. Capitalized Leases	4,254	8,513	10,402	8,410	8,829
Non-Convertible Debt	4,254	8,462	10,402	8,410	8,829
Convertible Debt	–	51	–	–	–
Capitalized Lease Obligations	991	1,121	1,269	2,706	2,323
Provision for Risks & Charges	133	519	581	413	2,309
Deferred Taxes	24	151	66	–	–
Deferred Taxes - Credit	24	151	66	–	–
Other Liabilities	3,770	2,663	2,258	1,905	1,887
Other Liabilities (excl. Deferred Income)	1,718	1,379	1,051	855	662
Deferred Income	2,052	1,284	1,207	1,050	1,225
Total Liabilities	30,548	28,469	26,199	23,426	23,023
Total Liabilities / Total Assets	49.17%	54.59%	76.36%	78.77%	80.34%
Common Equity (Total)	30,189	22,225	6,618	4,923	4,237
Common Stock Par/Carry Value	1	1	1	0	0
Additional Paid-In Capital/Capital Surplus	29,803	27,260	12,736	10,249	9,178
Retained Earnings	331	−5,399	−6,083	−5,318	−4,974
Other Appropriated Reserves	54	363	−36	−8	33
Common Equity / Total Assets	48.59%	42.62%	19.29%	16.55%	14.79%
Total Shareholders' Equity	30,189	22,225	6,618	4,923	4,237
Accumulated Minority Interest	1,394	1,454	1,492	1,390	1,395
Total Equity	31,583	23,679	8,110	6,314	5,632
Liabilities & Shareholders' Equity	62,131	52,148	34,309	29,740	28,655

Source: Tesla 10Ks

[1]M. V. Copeland, "Tesla's Wild Ride," *Fortune* 158:2 (2008): 82–94.

[2] Ibid.

[3]J. Boudreau, "In a Silicon Valley Milestone, Tesla Motors Begins Delivering Model S Electric Cars," *Oakland Tribune*, June 24, 2012, Breaking News Section. http://www.insidebayarea.com/oaklandtribune/localnews/ci_20919723/silicon-valley-milestone-tesla-motors-begins-delivering-model.

[4]Copeland, "Tesla's Wild Ride."

[5]A. Williams, "Taking a Tesla for a Status Check in New York," *New York Times*, July 19, 2009. ST.7. www.nytimes.com.

[6]Copeland, "Tesla's Wild Ride."

[7]J. Garthwaite, "Tesla Sues 'Top Gear,'" *New York Times*, April 3, 2011, AU.2. www.nytimes.com.

[8]A. Williams, "Taking a Tesla for a Status Check in New York."

[9]M. Ramsey, "Tesla Sets 300-Mile Range for Second Electric Car," *Wall Street Journal (Online)*, March 7, 2011.

[10]C. Sweet, "Tesla Posts Its First Quarterly Profit," *Wall Street Journal (Online)*, May 9, 2013.

[11]J. Boudreau, "In a Silicon Valley Milestone, Tesla Motors Begins Delivering Model S Electric Cars," *Oakland Tribune*, June 24, 2012, Breaking News Section. http://www.insidebayarea.com/oaklandtribune/localnews/ci_20919723/silicon-valley-milestone-tesla-motors-begins-delivering-model.

[12]Anonymous, "Idle Fremont Plant Gears Up for Tesla," *Wall Street Journal (Online)*, October 20, 2010.

[13]M. Levi, "How Tesla Pulled Ahead of the Electric-Car Pack," *Wall Street Journal*, June 21, 2013, p. A.11.

[14]J. B. White, "Corporate News: Electric Car Startup Tesla Repays U.S. Loan," *Wall Street Journal*, May 23, 2013, p. B.3.

[15]J. Hirsch and R. Mitchell, "Model X: Under the Hood of Tesla's SUV Strategy," *Los Angeles Times*, September 29, 2015.

[16]Tesla Q4 2016 production and delivery report, January 3.

[17]"Tesla Model X Review: Fast and Flawed." *Consumer Reports,* 2016.

[18]*Car and Driver.* "Tesla Model S," May 2016.

[19]J. Cobb, "Tesla Model S Is World's Best-selling Plug-in Car for Second Year in a Row," *Hybrid-Cars*, January 26, 2017.

[20]Estimate based on Tesla quarterly production and delivery reports for quarter 1-4 in 2017. In some years Tesla only provides rounded numbers for breakdown between Model X and Model S, thus only an approximate number can be given here.

[21]B. Sorokanich, "Tesla Model 3: The Road & Track Review," *Road and Track*, January 12, 2018.

[22]A. Panchadar, "Tesla Must Stop Overpromising, Could Need More Finance: Analysts." *Reuters Business News*, November 2, 2017

[23]S. Alvarez, "Tesla's Model 3 Production Ramp up Is Here, and the US Auto Market Is Starting to Feel It," *Teslarati*, August 13, 2018; K. Field, "Elon Musk Deconstructs Tesla's Production Ramp Timelines," *Cleantechnica*, February 22, 2019.

[24]F. Richter, "Tesla's Road to 1,000,000," *Statista*, March 10, 2020.

[25]"Best-Selling Plug-in Electric Vehicle Models Worldwide in 2021," *Statista*, February 2022.

[26]K. Leswing, "Elon Musk Says Tesla Has Made over 3 Million Cars," *CNBC*, August 14,2022.

[27]T. Woody, "Billionaire Car Wars," *Forbes*, December 10, 2012, pp. 90–98.

[28]www.Tesla.com/supercharger, retrieved September 16, 2022.

[29]M. Kane, "Global Plug-in Electric Car Sales Reached New Record in June 2022: Over 913,000," *Inside EVs*, August 1, 2022.

[30]"Electric Vehicle Outlook, 2022," *Bloomberg NEF* (https://about.bnef.com/electric-vehicle-outlook/)

[31]M. Descalsota, "Take a Look at Tesla's 4 Biggest Rivals in China's Booming, $124 Billion Electric-Vehicle Market," *Business Insider*, July 5, 2022.

[32]D. A. Crane, "Tesla and the Car Dealers Lobby," *Regulation* (Summer 2014), pp. 10–14.

[33]*Statista*, August 22, 2022.

[34]O. Milman, "Elon Musk Leads Tesla Effort to Build House Roofs Entirely Out of Solar Panels," *The Guardian,* August 19, 2017.

[35]L. Kolodny and J. Pettitt, "Why Tesla's Solar Business Has Not Yet Taken Off as Elon Musk Promised," *CNBC*, Oct 6, 2021.

[36]S.O'Kane, "Elon Musk Says Tesla Made "Significant Mistakes" with Solar Roof Project," *The Verge*, April 26, 2021.

[37]Ibid.

Zeta Energy and the Collaboration Decision

By Melissa A. Schilling

In 2022, Zeta Energy was a battery technology start-up in an enviable position: It had invented a way to make a low-cost, high-energy density and long-lived battery that could offer radically improved performance in products like electric vehicles, consumer electronics, drones, grid storage, and more. However, bringing a technology like this from the development stage to the manufacturing stage required high levels of funding and manufacturing expertise. Zeta Energy's management team knew they were at the precipice of a potentially world-changing opportunity, but they also knew that there were other competing technologies in similar positions, and it was a race to see who could rase the funding and other assets needed to make it across the finish line. The management team also knew that finding great collaboration partners–and forging well-structured collaboration relationships—could be key to Zeta's success.

C4-1 Betting on a Breakthrough

In 2014, Charles Maslin, a lawyer and investor with an avid interest in technology, decided to place a major bet on innovations in battery technology. Like many others, Maslin believed that the key to reducing environmental degradation and climate change was better batteries. Batteries that were lower cost, higher capacity, and sustainably manufactured could enable more people to use solar power in their homes and could make electric vehicles (that had the potential of being powered by renewable energy sources) competitive with vehicles that used fossil fuels. The market for rechargeable batteries was already growing quickly—analysts at McKinsey estimated that the demand for battery cells would grow by more than 20% per year through 2030, reaching at least $360 billion globally.[1] The *potential* market, i.e., the market that could exist if batteries were better and cheaper, was even larger.

Most analysts considered the electric vehicle market to be the largest market for rechargeable batteries, followed by grid storage (large-scale energy storage used within an electrical power grid) (see Figure 1). However, better cheaper batteries also had the potential to expand the markets for batteries in consumer electronics, industrial equipment, medical equipment, aviation, and more.

Maslin thus knew that a better battery technology could have enormous commercial potential. Maslin thus began funding and licensing research being done on lithium metal batteries at Rice University. The group Maslin supported was led by world-renown chemist and nanotechnologist Dr. James Tour, and was advancing the state of the art in carbon graphene nanotubes. Soon Maslin had hired two of the group's postdoctoral fellows, Abdul-Rahman Raji and Rodrigo Salvatierra, and founded the

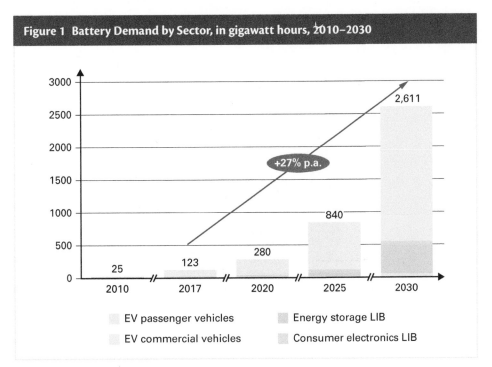

Figure 1 Battery Demand by Sector, in gigawatt hours, 2010–2030

Source: McKinsey, 2020

company Zeta Energy, LLC, with the intention of producing and selling extremely advanced lithium metal batteries.

C4-2 The Technology

By 2022, the lithium ion rechargeable battery technology that had come to dominate rechargeable applications like electric vehicles, laptops, smartphones, and more, was clearly mature.[2] The price per kilowatt hour had come down significantly since 2010, from $1,191 per kilowatt-hour in 2010 to $137 per kilowatt-hour. To put that into perspective, for a 50-kWh battery pack in an EV that was a cost change of $43,000 (see Figure 2).[3] However, further cost reductions were getting increasingly hard and unlikely as the bulk of the costs of the battery were now materials costs, i.e., the lithium, nickel, manganese, cobalt, etc. in the anode, cathode, and electrolyte (see Figure 3). Those costs were more likely to *increase* than decrease as production volumes scaled up.[4]

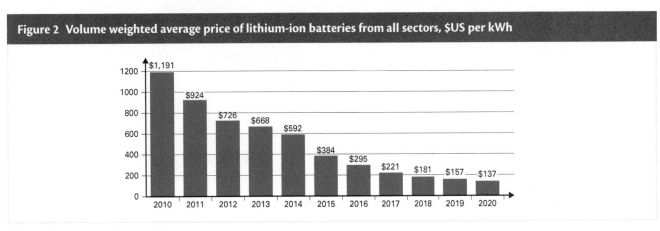

Figure 2 Volume weighted average price of lithium-ion batteries from all sectors, $US per kWh

Source: Based on Data from *BloombergNEF*

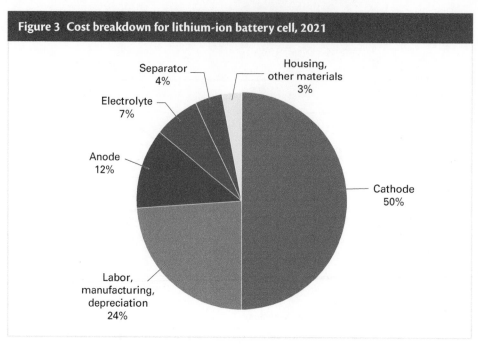

Figure 3 Cost breakdown for lithium-ion battery cell, 2021

- Separator 4%
- Housing, other materials 3%
- Electrolyte 7%
- Anode 12%
- Cathode 50%
- Labor, manufacturing, depreciation 24%

Source: Based on Data from *BloombergNEF*

There was widespread consensus that a breakthrough innovation in battery technology would be necessary to significantly advance applications in these and other markets. By this time, it was also already well understood that lithium *metal* batteries—those that contained lithium in metal form instead of just lithium ions in an electrolyte—offered significant potential advantages in terms of how much energy a battery could hold for a given volume or weight (see Figure 4).[5] However, lithium

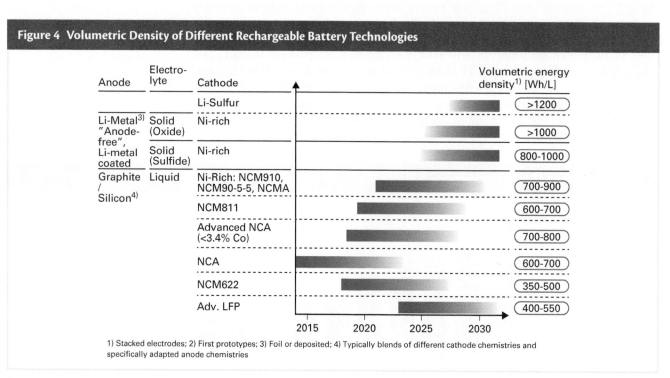

Figure 4 Volumetric Density of Different Rechargeable Battery Technologies

Anode	Electro-lyte	Cathode		Volumetric energy density[1] [Wh/L]
		Li-Sulfur		>1200
Li-Metal[3] "Anode-free", Li-metal coated	Solid (Oxide)	Ni-rich		>1000
	Solid (Sulfide)	Ni-rich		800-1000
Graphite / Silicon[4]	Liquid	Ni-Rich: NCM910, NCM90-5-5, NCMA		700-900
		NCM811		600-700
		Advanced NCA (<3.4% Co)		700-800
		NCA		600-700
		NCM622		350-500
		Adv. LFP		400-550

2015   2020   2025   2030

1) Stacked electrodes; 2) First prototypes; 3) Foil or deposited; 4) Typically blends of different cathode chemistries and specifically adapted anode chemistries

Source: Expert interviews, Roland Berger Integrated Battery Cost model C3

metal batteries had not been widely commercialized because they suffered from some serious problems that needed to first be solved.[3] One of the most significant of these was dendrites. In a lithium metal battery, dendrites (pointy projections of lithium particles) tended to form on the anode, similar to how a stalagmite forms on the floor of a cave. These projections could ultimately penetrate the separator between the anode and cathode, causing short circuits in the battery. Dendrites limited both the ability to recharge lithium metal batteries and created safety hazards. A short circuit in a battery could result in a fire or an explosion, for example.[6]

To overcome this problem, the Zeta Energy team had created anodes with a carbon nanotube structure. The nanotubes looked like a shag carpet of tiny tubes that could hold a tremendous amount of lithium while preventing the formation of dendrites (see Figure 5).[7] This would enable a lithium metal battery to simultaneously achieve both an extremely high energy density and have a low rate of degradation.

To realize the full potential of their anode, however, the team realized they also needed a better cathode. Sulfur cathodes had been of considerable interest in the scientific community because sulfur was cheap and abundant, and offered the theoretical potential of increasing the energy capacity of a battery up to 500% compared to conventional lithium-ion battery materials.[8] However, several challenges to realizing this potential had limited their use. Namely, sulfur cathodes suffered from a polysulfide shuttle effect that resulted in "leakage" of active material, leading to degradation of the battery.[9] Sulfur also expanded as it took on lithium ions, creating instability in the battery's structure. As a result of both of these effects, lithium sulfur batteries had a history of poor "cyclability," meaning that they could not be recharged very many times, making them commercially nonviable for most applications.[10] The Zeta Energy team, however, had developed a way of polymerizing sulfur that they believed solved these problems. The company held numerous patents (and had many more pending) on both the carbon nanotube anode and their polymerized sulfur cathode (Figure 6).

The combination of a high-density anode that was dendrite free, and a sulfur cathode with excellent "cyclability" achieved what *Forbes* termed "The Holy Grail"[11] in battery technology. As an added bonus, Zeta's battery did not use cobalt.

Figure 5 Anode with Vertically Aligned Carbon Nanotubes

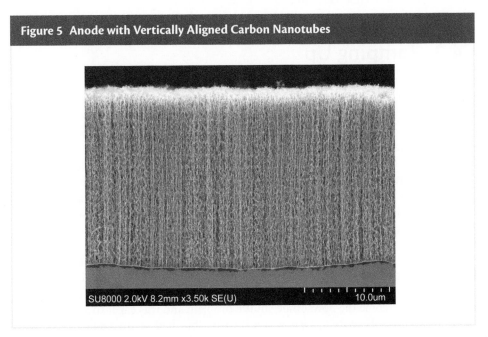

SU8000 2.0kV 8.2mm x3.50k SE(U)   10.0um

Source: Zeta Energy, 2022.

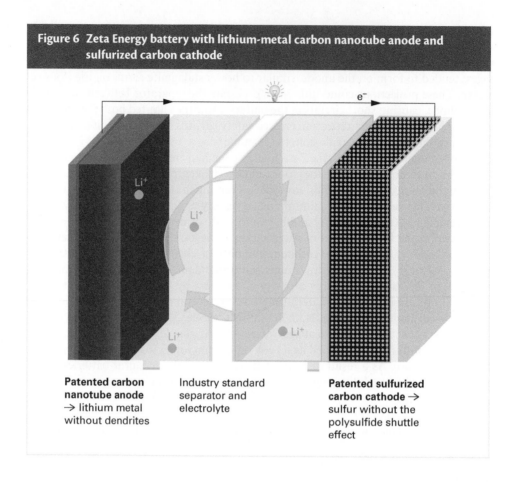

Figure 6 Zeta Energy battery with lithium-metal carbon nanotube anode and sulfurized carbon cathode

Patented carbon nanotube anode → lithium metal without dendrites

Industry standard separator and electrolyte

Patented sulfurized carbon cathode → sulfur without the polysulfide shuttle effect

Eliminating cobalt from the production of batteries was seen as highly desirable since cobalt was primarily mined in the Democratic Republic of Congo, a country that was notorious for using child labor in cobalt mines.[12]

C4-3 Ramping Up

Zeta Energy had received early funding from Maslin himself and investments from friends, family, and angel investors. However, to demonstrate the potential of Zeta's battery on a commercial scale required significant capital—on the order of $100 million—to build the required factory and equipment. Though early testing had shown Zeta's technology to be very promising, there were other potentially promising battery technologies also emerging in the market, including lithium silicon batteries, solid state batteries, and other lithium sulfur batteries. This made it challenging to secure sizeable investments; the future of battery technology appeared very uncertain to many would-be investors. To make matters more complicated, Maslin was reluctant to approach venture capitalists (VCs), because he knew venture capital firms would insist on taking significant control of the firm.

As of 2020, Maslin deliberated over a few options for continuing Zeta's progress. Each entailed difficult choices. First, another company, Oxis Energy, had approached Zeta about a potential collaboration. Oxis was also developing a lithium sulfur battery but had not overcome the polysulfide shuttle problem and was eager to gain access to Zeta's technology. Like Zeta, Oxis was a start-up, but had secured some early large investments from a European chemical firm called Arkema. Arkema produced (among other things) electrolytes, and was eager to see Oxis become successful both as a corporate venture capital investment, and because if successful, Oxis could become a large electrolyte customer. Zeta's management team, however, was reluctant to share their proprietary technology with another lithium sulfur startup. Second, Zeta had been approached by several potential customers of its battery, including BMW, Dyson, and the U.S. Army, but in all of those cases Zeta would have to find a way to first fund its own lab-scale factory to produce enough demonstration batteries for these companies to test. Third, Maslin could reverse his decision on VC funding and give more control of the company away in exchange for the funds and management support offered by VCs. Finally, Maslin also knew there was a potential to strike a joint venture with another major battery firm or automotive manufacturer, though Maslin worried that working with heavyweight companies in the close and frequent contact of a joint venture could put Zeta's proprietary technology at risk. He worried that a large and skillful partner might improve upon Zeta's technology in a way that helped them bypass Zeta's patents, ultimately leading to Zeta losing its technological edge.

C4-4 A Decision to Be Made

In January 2022, Zeta's team (which had now grown to a dozen people) felt a sense of urgency. The company was rapidly depleting its early funds and had made promises to several potential customers about producing demonstration units. It also knew that the longer it waited to bring its products to market, the greater the likelihood that advances by other battery start-ups would come to market, making it that much harder to get gain traction with investors and customers. Maslin had absolute faith that Zeta had a "holy grail" solution for batteries, but what was the best path to helping the company realize that potential?

Notes

[1] N. Campagnol , A. Pfeiffer, and C. Tryggestad, "Capturing the Battery Value-Chain Opportunity," January 7, 2022.

[2] https://www.spglobal.com/marketintelligence/en/news-insights/latest-news-headlines/as-battery-costsplummetlithium-ion-innovation-hits-limits-experts-say-58613238

[3] J. Frith, "EV Battery Prices Risk Reversing Downward Trend as Metals Surge," Bloomberg.com, September 14, 2021.

[4] Ibid.

[5] https://batteryuniversity.com/learn/article/experimental_rechargeable_batteries

[6] https://cen.acs.org/energy/energy-storage-/Video-Battery-scientists-tackle-dendrite/97/i48; https://spectrum.ieee.org/energy/renewables/less-fire-more-power-the-secret-to-safer-lithiumion-batteries; https://www.designnews.com/electronics-test/three-ways-lithium-dendrites-grow

[7] https://www.nature.com/articles/ncomms2234; https://pubs.acs.org/doi/abs/10.1021/acsnano; https://content.rolandberger.com/hubfs/07_presse/Roland%20Berger_The%20Lithium-Ion%20Battery%20Market%20and%20Supply%20Chain_2022_final.pdf

[8] https://en.wikipedia.org/wiki/Lithium%E2%80%93sulfur_battery

[9] https://www.electropages.com/blog/2020/01/why-lithium-sulphur-batteries-are-taking-so-long-beusedcommercially

[10] https://www.frontiersin.org/articles/10.3389/fenrg.2019.00123/full

[11] https://www.forbes.com/sites/rrapier/2019/05/16/the-holy-grail-of-lithiumbatteries/#55f989243d63

[12] https://www.ft.com/content/c6909812-9ce4-11e9-9c06-a4640c-9feebb

Staples

Charles W. L. Hill University of Washington July 2022

C5-1 Introduction

It was 1985, and a 36-year-old retailer called Tom Stemberg was being interviewed by the CEO of the Dutch-based warehouse club, Makro, for the top job at Makro's nascent U.S. operation. Stemberg didn't think Makro's concept would work in the United States, but he was struck by one thing as he toured Makro's first U.S. store in Langhorne, Pennsylvania: office supplies were flying off the shelves. "It was obvious that this merchandise was moving very fast," he later recalled. "That aisle (where the office supplies were located) was just devastated."[1] Stemberg began to wonder whether an office supplies supermarket would be a viable concept. He thought it might be possible that a supermarket selling just office supplies could do to the office supplies business what Toys "R" Us had done to the fragmented toy retailing industry: consolidate it and create enormous economic value in the process.

Within a year, Stemberg had founded Staples Inc. (Staples), the first office supplies supermarket. Thirty years later, Staples was the leading retailer in the office supplies business with 1,679 stores in the United States and Canada, and another 284 internationally in 23 countries. Although the company had performed well for most of its history, the 2008–2014 period proved to be extremely challenging. Demand fell in the face of a sharp economic pullback following the 2008–2009 global financial crisis. The period was characterized by intense price competition between Staples and its rivals, which depressed profitability. To compound matters, retailers such as Walmart, Costco, and Amazon.com had expanded their office supplies offerings, and were becoming increasingly tough competitors for Staples. In 2007, before the crisis hit, Staples' return on invested capital stood at 19.16%, but it declined to 9.11% by 2014. Staples' revenues peaked in 2013 at $25 billion. By 2014, they had fallen to $22.5 billion as Staples closed poor performing stores. Net income dropped from $974 million to $135 million over the same period.

Faced with an increasingly tough competitive environment, in early 2015, Staples announced that it had reached a deal to merge with its largest rival, Office Depot. Federal regulators had disallowed a similar proposed merger in 1997, but Staples and Office Depot believed that this time the merger would be approved given the significant change in market dynamics since then.[2]

C5-2 The Founding of Staples

C5-2a Tom Stemberg

Despite his young age, by 1985, Stemberg had assembled an impressive résumé in retailing. Stemberg had been born in Los Angeles but spent much of his teens in Austria, where his parents were originally from. He moved back to the United States to enter Harvard University, ultimately graduating with an MBA from Harvard Business School in 1973. Stemberg was hired out of Harvard by the Jewel Corporation, which put him to work at Star Market, the company's supermarket grocery division in the Boston area.

Henry Nasella, Stemberg's first boss at Jewel, who would later work for Stemberg at Staples, remembers meeting Stemberg on his first day at Jewel: "He came in 15 minutes late, his hair too long, his tie over his shoulder, his shirt hanging out over the back of his pants. I though, what in the world do I have here?"[3] What he had in the disheveled Stemberg, in turns out, was a brilliant marketer. Stemberg started out on the store floor, bagging groceries, stocking the aisle, and ringing up sales at the checkout counter. However, he rose rapidly. By the time he was 28, he had been named vice president of sales and marketing at Star Market, the youngest VP in the history of Jewel Corporation.

Stemberg became known as an aggressive marketer, competing vigorously on price and introducing generic brands (Stemberg developed and launched the first line of "generic" foods sold in the country).[4] According to Stemberg, "It was a nutso thing we were trying to do, and the fact that it worked out well was a miracle. We opened all these big stores, and we were trying to take market share away from people who were much better financed than we were. They retaliated and lowered prices.....I learnt to experience the challenges of rapid growth. There was no better experience to have been through. It taught me the necessity of having infrastructure and putting it in place."[5]

One of the supermarkets that Stemberg found himself battling with was Heartland Food Warehouse, the first successful deep-discount warehouse supermarket in the country. Leo Kahn, one of the country's leading supermarket retailers, ran Heartland. Kahn had started the Purity Supreme supermarket chain in the late 1940s, making him one of the founding fathers of the supermarket business. Stemberg and Kahn fought relentless marketing battles with each other. In a typical example of their tussles, at one point Kahn ran ads guaranteeing that his customers would get the best price on Thanksgiving turkeys. Stemberg responded with his own ads promising that Star would match the lowest advertised price on turkeys. Technically that made Kahn's claim incorrect, a point that Stemberg made to the Massachusetts attorney general's office, which told Kahn to pull his ad.

In 1982, Stemberg left Jewel to run the grocery division of another retailer, First National Supermarkets Inc. To build market share, he decided to take the company into the warehouse food business, imitating Leo Kahn's Heartland chain. Stemberg soon came into conflict with the CEO at First National. As he later admitted, "I probably didn't do a very good job, in a corporate political sense, of making sure he understood the risks in what we were trying to do. The situation was very stressful."[6] In January 1985, things came to a head and Stemberg was fired. It was probably the best thing that ever happened to him.

When Kahn heard that Stemberg had been fired, he quickly got in touch. Kahn had just sold his own business for $80 million and he was looking for investment opportunities. He had developed great respect for his old adversary, and wanted to back him in a new retailing venture. As Stemberg paraphrases it, Kahn said "I want to back you in a business kid, what have you got in mind?"[7] Kahn agreed to put up $500,000 in seed money to help Stemberg develop a new venture opportunity. He also took on the role of mentor, evaluating Stemberg's ideas.

Initially Kahn and Stemberg looked at the business they both knew best, supermarket grocery retailing. But they were put off by the intense competition now raging and the high price they would have to pay for properties. At this juncture, Bob Nakasone, then president of Toys "R" Us, stepped into the picture. Nakasone had worked at Jewel alongside Stemberg before moving to Toys "R" Us. It was Nakasone who urged Stemberg to "think outside of the food box." Nakasone told Stemberg that there were more similarities than differences across product categories, and that profit margins were much better outside of the grocery business.

While mulling over possible entrepreneurial opportunities, Stemberg continued to explore other options, including working for an established retailer. It was this parallel search that took him down to Makro for a job interview, and it was there that he suddenly realized there was a possible opportunity to be had in starting the Toys "R" Us of office supplies.

C5-3 The Founding of Staples

Hot on the heels of his trip to Makro, Stemberg started to think about his idea. The first thing was to get a handle on the nature of the market. Stemberg started by asking people if they knew how much they spent on office supplies. In his words: "There was this lawyer I knew in Hartford, which is where I lived then. If ever there was a cheap bastard in this world, he was a cheap bastard. And I said, 'Gee, how much do you spend on office supplies?' He said, "Oh I don't know, I guess about a couple of hundred bucks a person, 40 people in the office, I bet you we spend ten grand'. I said, 'Do me a favor will you? You've got good records. Go through your records and tell me exactly how much you spend: he calls me up the next day" 'Son of a bitch, I spend $1,000 apiece! But I'm getting a discount, I'm paying 10% of list: I said, 'Toys "R" Us' is paying 60% of list: He says, 'Are you kidding me? You mean I could save like half?' I could save like twelve grand? In his mind, this is the payment on his new Jaguar."[8]

Stemberg began to think that this idea had some potential. He reasoned that people want to save money, and in this case the money they could save might be substantial, but they didn't even know they were paying too much. Small businesses in particular, he though, might be a viable target market. While working on the idea, the printer ribbon on his printer ran out. It was a weekend. He drove down to the local office supply store in Hartford, and it was closed. Went to another, but that was also closed. He ended up going to BJ's Wholesale Club, a deep-discount warehouse club. BJ's was open, they sold office supplies at low prices, but the selection was limited and they didn't carry the type of ribbon Stemberg wanted. Stemberg immediately saw the opportunity.

Around the same time, Stemberg went to see another mentor of his, Walter Salmon, who taught retailing at Harvard Business School. Over lunch, they discussed the supermarket business and Stemberg's quest. Salmon asked Stemberg if he had thought of applying his retailing skills to a product category that was growing faster than the grocery business, and was not well served by modern retailers. Stemberg replied that he had been thinking about office supplies. Salmon's response: "Gee, this is a really big idea."

C5-3a Scoping Out the Opportunity

Stemberg ended up hiring a former teaching assistant of Salmon's for $20,000 to do some basic market research on the industry and validate the market. As he tells the story: "I never forget the night I went to her house and we went through the slide deck. I always want to jump ahead. And she puts her hand on my hand and says, 'Wait, we will walk though it: She's teasing us! Finally she said it was a $45 billion market growing at 15% per year. And it turns out she was lying. That was actually at the manufacturer level. It was actually more than $100 billion already if you looked at retail. She confirmed that the pricing umbrellas were as big as we though they were, and that small businesses were getting raped the way we had said they were. I was pretty damn excited during the long drive home."[9]

The market growth was being driven by some favorable demographic trends. The U.S. economy was recovering from the recessions of the late 1970s and early 1980s, and underlying economic growth was strong. A wave of new technology was finding its way into American businesses, including personal computers, printers, faxes, and small copiers, and this was driving demand for office supplies, including basic equipment along with consumables from paper and printer ink, to diskettes and copy toner.

The wave of downsizing that had swept corporate America in the early 1980s also had a beneficial side effect–unemployed people were starting their own businesses. The rate of new business formation was the highest in years. There were 11 million small businesses in the country, Stemberg's proposed target market, the vast majority of which had less than 20 employees. This sector was the engine of job growth in the economy – between 1980 and 1986, small enterprises had been responsible for a net increase of 10.5 million jobs. Many of these new jobs were in the service sector, which was a big consumer of office supplies. Each new white-collar job meant another $1,000 a year in office supplies.

Stemberg's research started to uncover an industry that was highly fragmented at the retail level, but had some huge participants. Upstream in the value chain were the manufacturers. This was a very diverse collection of companies including paper manufacturers such as Boise Cascade; office furniture makers; manufacturers of pencils, pens, and markets such as the Bic Corporation; companies like 3M that supplied Post-it Notes and a whole lot more besides; office equipment companies from Xerox and Canon (manufacturers of copiers and consumables); to manufacturers of personal computers, printers, and fax machines such as Apple, Compaq, and Hewlett Packard.

Then there were the wholesalers, some of which were very large such as United Stationers and McKesson. The wholesalers bought in bulk and sold to business clients and smaller retail establishments, either directly or through a network of dealers. The dealers often visited businesses to collect orders and arranged for delivery. The dealers themselves ranged in scale from small one-person enterprises to large firms that sold through central warehouses. Some dealers also had a retail presence, while other did not. Manufacturers and wholesalers would also sell directly to large business through catalogs, or a direct sales presence.

The retailers fell into two main categories. There were the local office supply retailers, generally small business themselves, and there were the general merchandise discounters, such As BJ's Wholesale and Walmart. The smaller retailers had an intrinsically high-cost structure. They were full-service retailers who purchased in small lots, and delivered in trucks or sold out of the store. The general merchandise discounters purchased from wholesalers, or direct from manufacturers, and their prices were much lower, but they did not carry a wide range of products.

On the consumer side, most large businesses had dedicated personnel for purchasing office supplies. They either bought from dealers, who purchased directly from manufacturers or through wholesalers, or bought direct from the manufacturer themselves. Large firms were able to negotiate on price and received discounts that could be as large as 80% of the list price on some items. Businesses of fewer than 100 people did not generally have someone dedicated to managing office supplies, and they tended to rely primarily on dealers. For these companies, product availability, not price, was viewed as key. In even smaller firms, it was the convenience of being able to get office supplies that seemed to matter more than anything else.

Consistent with his initial insight, Stemberg found that the big dealers ignored smaller firms. To verify this he called Boise Cascade, which operated as both a dealer and a manufacturer, to see what service they might offer. First, he called on behalf of Ivy Satellite Network, a small company that Stemberg owned that broadcasted events of Ivy League schools to alumni around the world. Boise couldn't even be bothered to send a catalog to this company. Then he called Boise back, this time representing the 100-person office of a friend of his who was a food broker. This time, Boise was happy to send a representative to the food broker. The representative offered the broker deep discounts. A Bic pen from Boise that cost Ivy $3.68 cents from the local stationary store was offered for just $0.85. More generally, Stemberg found that while an office manager in a company with more than 1,000 employees could often obtain discounts averaging 50% from dealers, small businesses with fewer than 20 employees were lucky to get a 10% discount, and often had to pay full price.[10]

Stemberg also found a study produced by researchers at the Wharton School that seemed to confirm his suspicions. "Essentially, they first asked dealers. 'What does the customer want?' Ninety percent of the dealers said, 'Better service' and '10% said, 'other'. Then they asked customers, and 90% of the customers said what they really wanted was lower prices. Ha! The dealers were totally out of touch. They were making 40% to 50%, the wholesalers were making 30%, and the manufacturers were making huge margins. Everybody's rich, fat, and happy, and they're all going: What's wrong with this?"[11]

C5-3b Creating the Company

Stemberg knows from experience that for Staples to succeed it would have to execute well, and do to that, it needed experienced management. Stemberg turned to people he knew, managers like him who had risen quickly through the ranks at the Jewel Corporation or other Boston-area retailers. From Jewel came Myra Hart, who was to become Staples' group vice president for growth and development; Todd Krasnow, who became vice president for marketing; Paul Korian, Staples' vice president of merchandising; and Henry Nasella, Stemberg's mentor at Star market who subsequently became president of Staples. The CFO was Bob Leombruno, who had bought Mammoth Mart, a failed retail operation, out of bankruptcy for a group of investors. Stemberg took on the CEO role, while Kahn became chairman. Most of these people started working full time on January 1, 1986. They gave up secure jobs, high salaries, and annual bonuses, for a salary cut, loss of bonuses, and 14-hour days.

According to Stemberg, the pitch to prospective managers was this: "I'm going to give you a big chunk of stock in this thing. This is your chance. We're all going to work our trials off. We're going to work crazy hours. But here you'll be part of a retailing revolution. If you own 2% of the company and it gets to be worth $100 million, you're going to make $2 million."[12] In the end, each member of the top management team got a 2.5% stake in the company.

By now, Stemberg had a name for this nascent company, Staples. Reflecting on how it came about years later, he noted; "I'm driving between Hartford and Boston. I'm thinking about names. Pencils? Pens? 8 ½ by 11? Staples? Staples! Staples the Office Superstore. That was it. The bad thing about the name was that when we started out, we had to explain to everybody what it was. Office Depot basically copied Home Depot and put the 'office' in front. It was Home Depot for the office, and it lived off the Home Depot name. Office Club was a Price Club for the office. It lived off the Price Club name. In the early days ours was actually a problem. But those other names aren't a brand. Ours is a brand."[13]

With the management team in place, the next steps were to refine the concept and raise capital. The concept itself was straightforward; implementing it would not be.

The plan was to offer a wide selection of merchandise in a warehouse type setting with prices deeply discounted from those found in smaller retailers. Because it was to be a supermarket, the idea was to move from full service to a self-service format. At the same time, they recognized the staff would need to be trained in office supplies so that they could provide advice when asked.

To make the concept viable, several issues had to be dealt with. They had to decide where to locate the stores. How big a population base would be needed to support a store? What kind of selection was required? How many Stock Keeping Units (SKUs) should the store offer? There was the problem of educating customers. If potential customers currently didn't know that they were paying excessive prices for office supplies, and consistently underestimated how much they spent on the category, what could Staples do to change this?

To get low prices, Staples would need to cut costs to the bone and be managed very efficiently. They would have to get manufacturers or wholesalers to deliver directly to Staples. How could this be done? Wouldn't wholesalers and manufacturers create channel conflict with dealers and established retailers by delivering straight to Staples? How was this to be resolved? Staples also needed to minimize its inventory, thereby reducing its working capital needs. Management knew that if they could turn inventory over 12 times a year, and delay payment to vendors for 30 days, then vendors would essentially finance Staples' inventory. Pulling that off would require state-of-the-art information systems, and the state of the art at the time in office supplies did not include bar coding on individual items. How was Staples to deal with this?

There was also the potential competition to worry about. Stemberg was sure that once Staples unveiled its concept, others would follow quickly. To preempt competitors, the plan called for rapid rollout of the concept, with sales ramping up from nothing to $42 million after three years. This would require a lot of capital. It also required that the concept be easy to replicate so that once the first store was opened, others could be opened in quick succession. This meant that the systems that were put in place for the first store had to be the right ones, and able to support rapid expansion. There wasn't much room for error here.

As the management team refined the concept, they came to the realization that the information systems were one of the keys to the entire venture. With the right information systems in place, Staples could track sales and inventory closely at the level of individual items and figure out its gross profit on each item sold, adjust its merchandising mix accordingly. This would be a departure from existing retailers, the majority of whom lacked the ability to calculate profit on each item sold and could only calculate the average gross profit across a range of items. The right information systems could also be used to collect data on customers at the point of sales, and this would assist greatly in market research and direct marketing to customers.

On the other hand, raising capital proved to be easier than they thought. Stemberg valued Staples at $8 million, even though it was still little more than a concept, a management team, and a business plan full of unanswered questions. He went looking for $4 million, which he would exchange for 50% of the company. The venture capitalists were initially reluctant. They seemed to hold back, waiting to see who would commit first. They also valued Staples at $6 million and wanted a 67% stake for the $4 million in first-round financing. Stemberg balked at that, and instead focused his efforts on one firm that seemed more willing to break away from the pack. The firm was Bain Venture Capital, whose managing general partner, Mitt Romney, later observed that: "A lot of retailing startups come by, but a lot of them are a twist on an old theme, or a better presentation.....Stemberg wasn't proposing just a chain of stores, but an entirely new retailing category. That really captures you attention. It slaps you in the face with the idea that this could be big." (Romney later became the governor of Massachusetts.)[14]

To validate the business concept, Romney's firm surveyed 100 small businesses after being urged to do so by Stemberg. In auditing the invoices from these companies for office supplies, Romney discovered what Stemberg already knew—the companies were spending about twice what they estimated. Romney then ran the numbers on his own company and found that his firm would save $117,000 a year by purchasing supplies at the discount that Stemberg promised. That was enough for Romney, and he committed to investing. Others followed and Staples raised $4.5 million in its first round of financing, which closed on January 23, 1986. This gave the company enough capital to go ahead with the first store. In return for the financing, Staples had to give the VCs a 54% stake in the company. To get the money, however, Staples had to commit to opening its first store on May 1, 1986, and to meet a plan for rolling out additional stores as quickly as possible.

C5-3c The First Store

With just 4 months to open their first store, the management team went into overdrive. They would meet every morning at about 7a.m. in a session that could run from 30 minutes to 2 hours. Someone would rush out to get sandwiches for lunch, and they would keep working. The workday came to a close at 9:00 p.m. or 10:00 p.m. Not only was there no template for what they were doing, they knew they had to put a system in place that would allow them to quickly roll out additional stores.

One of the most difficult tasks fell on the shoulders of Leombruno, the CFO. In addition to setting up an accounting system, he was put in charge of installing the entire information system for Staples. The system had to be able to track customer purchases so that Staples could reorder products. The cash registers, which were to be connected individually to the system, had to be easy to operate so that there would be no congestion at the checkout stands. Stemberg himself was adamant that the register receipts indicate the list price of each item, as well as a much lower Staples price, and an even lower price for customers who became Staples members. He also wanted the system to collect detailed demographics on each customer.

Leombruno insisted that the system be able to do two things: First, calculate the gross profit margin Staples made on each item sold. Most retailers at the time could only calculate the average profit margin across the mix of inventory. Second, Leombruno wanted to make sure that inventory turned over at least 12 times a year, and good information systems were the key. With most vendors requiring payment in 30 days, an inventory turnover of greater than 12 would allow Staples to cut its working capital requirements.

As the wish list for the information systems grew, it soon became apparent that it would not be possible to do everything in the allotted time span. No existing software package did what the management team wanted, and they had to hire consultants to customize existing packages. In the end, several proposed features were dropped. However, at Stemberg's insistence, the three-way price requirements remained. To track sales and inventory levels, Staples assigned a six-digit look-up code for each item. While entering the codes was a slower process than scanning items, most manufacturers in the office supplies business were still not marking their products with bar codes, which meant scanning was not feasible.

Another problem was to get suppliers to ship products to the first Staples store. The company was asking suppliers to bypass the existing distribution system, and risk alienating long time customers in the established channel of distribution. To get suppliers on board, Staples used several tactics. One was a visionary pitch. The company told suppliers that they were out to revolutionize the retail end of the industry. Staples would be very big, they said, and it was in the best interests of the suppliers to back the startup. Stemberg's punch line was simple: "I'm going to be very loyal to those who stick their necks out for us. But it's going to cost you a lot more to get in later."[15] Connections also helped to get suppliers to deliver to Staples. One of the VC backers of Staples, Bessemer Venture Partners, also owned a paper manufacturer, Ampad. Bessemer told Ampad to start selling to Staples, which they did, even though existing distributors complained bitterly about the arrangement.

Finding real estate also presented a problem. As an enterprise with no proven track record, Staples found it difficult to rent decent real estate large enough to stock and display the 5,000 SKUs that it was planning for its first store, and to do so at a decent price. Most landlords wanted sky-high rent from Staples. In the end, the best that Staples could do was a site in Brighton, Massachusetts, that was within site of a housing project and had failed as a site for several different retailers. The one redeeming feature of the site—it was smack in the middle of a high concentration of small businesses.

Despite all of the problems, Staples was able to open its first store on May 1, 1996. The opening day was busy, but only because everybody who worked at Staples had invited everybody they knew. On the second day, just 16 people came through the store. On the third day, it was the same number. A few weeks of this, and Staples would have to shut its doors. Desperate, Krasnow decided to bribe customers to get them into the store. The company sent $25 to each of 35 office managers, inviting them to shop in the store and pass along their reactions. According to Krasnow, "A week later we called them back. They had all taken the money, but none of them had come into the store. I was apoplectic."[16] In the end, nine of them finally came in, and they gave Staples rave reviews. Slowly the momentum started to build and by August lines were starting to form at the cash registers at lunchtime.

C5-4 The 1990s: Growth, Competition, and Consolidation

C5-4a Growth

Staples had set of target of $4 million in first-year sales from its Brighton store, but within a few months the numbers were tracking up toward a $6 million annual run rate. The concept was starting to work. The number of customers coming through the door every month was growing, but it was not only customers that were coming. One day, Joe Antonini, the CEO of K-Mart, was spotted walking around the Staples store. Around the same time, Stemberg heard from contacts that Staples had been mentioned at a Walmart board meeting. He realized that if other discount retailers were noticing Staples when it had just one store, competition could not be far behind.

Within 5 months of the opening of the first Staples store, a clone had appeared in the Southeast: Office Depot. Needing money fast to fund expansion and lock in Staples' territory, Stemberg went back to the venture capitalists. While the initial backers were only willing to value Staples at $15 million, Stemberg held out for and got a valuation of $22 million, raising another $14 million. He pulled this trick by finding institutional investors who were wiling to invest on a valuation of $22 million. He then went back to the original VCs and told them that the deal was closing fast, which persuaded them to commit.

By May 1987, Staples had three stores open and planned to increase the number to 20 by the end of 1988 (in the end, it opened 22). Sales were running at anywhere from $300 to $800 per square foot. In contrast, high-volume discount stores were lucky to get $300 per square foot. By mid-1989, 3 years after its first store opened, Staples had 27 stores open in the Northeast and an annual sales run rate of $120 million, way above the original 3-year target of $42 million. The stores now averaged 15,000 square feet and stocked 5,000 items.

Explaining the success, Stemberg noted; "From a value perspective, I think there is no question that we have been a friend to the entrepreneur. If you look at the average small-town merchant, we've lowered the costs of his office products–where he was once paying say $4,000 to $5,000 a year, now he's paying $2,000 or $3,000. We've made him more efficient."[17]

Helping to driving sales growth was the development of a direct marketing pitch. Every time Staples opened a store, it purchased a list of small businesses within 15 minutes' driving distance. A group of telemarketers would go to work, calling up the buyer of office supplies at the businesses. The telemarketers would tell them Staples was opening a store like Toys "R" Us for office supplies, ask them how much they spent on office supplies every year (often they did not know), cite typical cost savings at small businesses, and sent them a coupon for a free item, such as copy paper. Slowly at first, the customers would come in, but momentum would build up as customers realized the scale of the savings they were getting.

Every time a customer redeemed a coupon at a store, they were given a free Staples Card. This "membership" card entitled cardholders to even deeper discounts on select items. The card quickly became the lynchpin of Staples' direct marketing effort. From the card application, Staples gathered information about the customer—what type of business they were in, how many employees they had, and where they were located. This information was entered into a customer database and every time a card member used that card, the card number and purchases were logged into the database via the cash register. This gave Staples up-to-date information about what was being purchased and by whom. This information then allowed Staples to target promotions at certain customer groups—for example, card members who were not making purchases. The goal was to get existing customers to spend more at Staples, a goal that over time was attained.

Because Staples started to reach so many of its customers through direct marketing (about 80% of its sales were made to cardholders), it was able to spend less on media ads—in some areas it dropped media advertising altogether, saving on costs. This was an important source of cost savings in the Northeast where the media was expensive.

A problem that continued to bedevil Staples as it expanded was a shortage of good real estate locations that could be rented at a reasonable price, particularly in the Northeast. Finding a good site in the early days required flexibility; at various times Staples converted anything and everything from restaurants to massage parlors into Staples stores. As the company grew, its real estate strategy started to take a defensive aspect, with Staples bidding for prime sites to preempt competitors.

The high cost of real estate in the Northeast led Staples to establish its first distribution center in 1987 (today, it has some 65 "delivery fulfillment centers" and larger "distribution centers" in North America). This decision was hotly debated within the company and opposed by some of the investors who thought that the capital should be used to build more stores, but Stemberg prevailed. The distribution center was located off an interstate highway in an area of rural Connecticut where land was cheap. The facility cost $6 million to build and tied up a total of $10 million in working capital, almost $0.29 out of every dollar that the company had raised to that point. But Stemberg saw this as a necessary step. The inventory storage capacity at the distribution center enabled the company to operate with smaller stores than many of its rivals, but still offer the same variety of goods. By 1989, the average Staples store was 35% smaller than the Office Depot outlets that were then opening all over the Southeast, saving on real estate costs. The distribution center also helped save labor costs, since wages were lower in rural areas. Equally important, inventory storage at the distribution centers allowed the stores to remain fully stocked. A Stemberg noted: "In competition with the clones, it will come down to who has the lowest costs and the best in stock position.[18]"

The expansion strategy at Staples was very methodical. Stores were clustered together in a region, even to the extent that they cannibalized each other on the margin, so that Staples could become the dominant supplier in that market. The early focus was on major metropolitan areas such as Boston, New York, Philadelphia, and Los Angeles. Although high real estate and labor costs in these areas were a disadvantage, strong demand from local businesses helped compensate, as did the distribution centers. In 1990, Staples opened its second distribution center in California to support expansion there.

The expansion at Staples was fueled by the proceeds from a 1989 Initial Public Offering, which raised $61.7 million of capital—enough for Staples to accelerate its store openings. By mid-1991 Staples store count passed over 100.

C5-4b Competition

A rash of imitators to Staples soon appeared on the market. The first of those was Office Depot, focused in the Southeast. By the end of 1988, Office Depot had 26 stores, Office Club had opened 15, Biz Mart had established 10, and Office Max around a dozen. More than a dozen other office supplies superstores had sprung up. Venture capitalists looking to repeat the success with Staples financed some of these businesses. Others were financed by established retailers, or even started by them. For example, Ben Franklin started Office Station in 1987, but shut it down in 1989 as it failed to gain traction.

Initially, most of the competitors focused on unique regions—Office Depot on the Southeast, Office Club on California, Office Max on the Midwest, BizMart on the Southwest—but as the number of entrants increased, head-to-head competition started to become more frequent. Stemberg's belief had always been that competition was inevitable, and that the winners in the competitive race would not necessarily be those that grew the fastest, but those that executed best. It was this philosophy that underpinned Stemberg's insistence that the company should grow by focusing on key urban areas and achieving a critical mass of stores served by a central distribution system.

Not everyone agreed with this recipe for success. Office Depot did the opposite—the company grew as fast as possible, entering towns quickly to pre-empt competitors. Office Depot lacked the centralized distribution systems but made up for that by locating in less expensive areas than Staples, persuading suppliers to ship directly to stores and keeping more backup inventory on the premises. Although this meant larger stores, the lower rental costs in Office Depot's markets offset this.

What soon became apparent is that the rash of entrants included several companies that simply could not execute. Very quickly a handful of competitors emerged in the forefront of the industry—Staples, Office Depot, Office Max and Office Club. As the market leaders grew, they increasingly encountered each other. The result was price wars. These first broke out in California. Staples entered the market in 1990 and initially focused on pricing not against Office Club, but against Price Club. Although Price Club was a warehouse store selling food and general merchandise, it still had the largest share of the office supplies market in California. Staples positioned itself as having the same low prices as Price Club, but a wider selection of office supplies and no membership fee.

Todd Krasnow, the executive VP of marketing at Staples, described what happened next: "What we failed to realize was that Price Club was very worried about Office Club—and was pricing against Office Club. So when we went and matched Price Club, we were matching Office Club. And Office Club was saying: 'We are not going to let anybody have the same prices as us.'"[19] Office Club lowered its prices, causing Price Club to lower prices, and Staples followed. Not willing to be beat, Office Club cut prices again, and so they continued the spiral down. The price war drove profit margins down by as much as 8 percent.

Ultimately, Krasnow noted, "We realized that by engaging in this price war, we were focusing on our competitors, not our customers. Our customers weren't paying attention to this spat. So, we raised our prices a little. You feel like you're just doing absolutely the wrong thing, because your whole position is: We have the lowest price."[20] Be that as it may, Office Club and Price club followed suit, and prices started to rise again. Ultimately the three companies carved out different price niches, each unwilling to be undercut on about 20 or so top-selling items, but in general, they were not the same items.

What happened in California also occurred elsewhere. When Office Max entered the Boston market in 1992, a price war broke out. There was an unanticipated effect this time though; the price cuts apparently broadened the market by making buying from Staples attractive to customers with between 25 and 100 employees, who previously bought directly from mail order and retail stationers.[21]

Ultimately, Kransow noted, price wars such as those that started to break out in California and Boston started to moderate. "We finally realized that it's not in any company's self-interest to have a price war because you can get lots of market share without having a price war. And having a price war among low priced competitors doesn't get you more market share. It doesn't serve any purpose."[22] Other factors that may have contributed towards more rational pricing behavior in the market were the strong economy of the 1990s and industry consolidation.

C5-4c Industry Consolidation

At its peak in 1991, there were 25 chains in the office supply industry.[23] Industry consolidation started when some of the clones began to fall by the wayside, filing for bankruptcy. U.S. Office Supply, itself the result of a merger between two office supplies chains, filed for bankruptcy in 1991, as did Office Stop. Consolidation was also hastened by acquisitions. In 1991, Office Depot acquired Office Club, giving the primary rival of Staples more than twice the number of stores. For its part, Staples acquired HQ Office Supplies Warehouse in 1991, and in 1992 it purchased another smaller chain, Workplace.[24]

As these trends continued, by the mid-1990s it was apparent that three players were rising to dominance in the industry: Office Depot, Staples, and Office Max. By mid-1996, Office Depot led the industry with 539 stores, followed by Staples with 517, and Office Max with around 500 stores. In terms of revenues, Office Depot had a clear lead with $5.3 billion in 1996, Staples was second with $3.07 billion, and Office Max third with $2.6 billion. Staples remained concentrated in the Northeast and California, with many stores in dense urban areas. Office Depot's stores were concentrated in the South, and the company continued to stay clear of congested cities. Office Max was still strongest in the Midwest.[25]

The consolidation phase peaked in September 1996 when Staples announced an agreement to purchase its larger rival, Office Depot, for $3.36 billion. The executives of the two companies had apparently been talking about merger possibilities for years, while continuing to pursue their own independent growth strategies. If the merger went through, Tom Stemberg would step into the CEO role. The two companies sold the merger to the investment community on the basis of cost savings. The combined firm would have almost 1,100 stores and revenues of $8.5 billion. The combination, Stemberg argued, would attain terrific economies of scale that would allow it to significantly lower costs, saving an estimated $4.9 billion over 5 years, including $2.2 billion in product cost savings.

In a move to preempt a possible investigation by the Federal Trade Commission (FTC), the companies claimed that since their stores focused on different territories, the combination would not reduce competition. They also noted that Staples still faced intense competition not only from Office Max, but also from the likes of

Walmart, Circuit City, and mail-order outlets. Indeed, Stemberg claimed that the combined company would still only account for 5% of the total sales of office supplies in the nation.[26]

The FTC didn't buy the arguments, quickly started an investigation, and in May 1997 sought an injunction to block the deal. The FTC claimed that the deal would stifle competition and raise prices for office supplies, especially in those markets where the two firms competed head to head. To buttress its case, the FTC released a report of pricing data that showed that non-durable office supplies such as paper were 10% to 15% higher in markets where Staples faced no direct rivals. Staples claimed that the FTC's pricing surveys were done selectively and were biased.

In July 1997, a federal judge granted the FTC's request for an injunction to halt the merger. Staples realized that it was in a losing fight and pulled its bid for Office Depot. But the failure had a silver lining—not anticipating much interference from the FTC, Office Depot had put most of its expansion plans on hold, opening just two stores in 8 months. In comparison, Staples opened 43, allowing the company to close the gap between itself and its larger rival.

C5-5 Staples' Evolving Strategy

C5-5a Moving into Small Towns

Stemberg has described Staples' initial strategy to deal with the high costs of doing business in the Northeast as follows: "Establish superstores that were smaller than most, save on rent and operating costs, cluster them in densely populated areas to justify paying for expensive advertisements, and stock the stores from a distribution center."[27] The drawback with this strategy was that Staples ignored a lot of potentially lucrative markets in smaller towns. While Office Depot was barnstorming into towns with populations of just 75,000, Staples could not see how they made it pay. Surely towns of that size were just too small to support an office supply superstore?

It turned out they were not. The mistake Staples made was to assume that a store would serve customers within a 10- to 15-minute drive. But in smaller cities, customers would drive much further to get good prices. The revelation did not hit home until Staples opened its first store in Portland, Maine. With a population of 200,000, the town was smaller than most areas focused on by Staples, but within a few months the store was doing very well. To test the hypothesis, in 1992 and 1993, Staples opened stores in a number of smaller towns. The results were surprising. Many of the stores generated higher sales per square foot than those located in large cities. Sales were helped by the fact that in many of these small towns the only competitors were small "mom and pop" stationers, and that many small towns also lacked supermarket electronic retailers, such as Circuit City, selling low prices office equipment, allowing Staples to pick up a much larger share of that business. Moreover, the lower rent, labor costs, advertising costs, and shrinkage made these stores significantly more profitable.

From that point on, Staples moved into small towns and suburban locations, where the same economics applied. Stemberg has described not moving into small towns earlier as "one of the dumbest mistakes I made." In 1994, some 10% of Staples stores were in small towns; by 1998, that figure had risen to 28% and some of the most profitable stores in Staples' network were located in small towns.[28]

C5-5b Selling Direct

Established as a retailer, Staples initially turned its back on customer requests for delivery and mail or telephone order service. The reason for doing this was simple; Staples saw itself as a low-cost retailer, and a delivery service would probably raise costs. However, Staples competitors started to offer mail-order and delivery service, and customers continued to ask for the service, so in 1988 Staples began to experiment with this.

Initially, the experimentation was halfhearted. Store managers were not enthusiastic about supporting a delivery service that they believed decreased store sales, and Staples discouraged delivery by taking a 5% delivery charge onto the order price. Moreover, the company questioned whether it could generate the volume of business to cover the costs of a delivery service and make a decent return on capital.

What changed this was a study undertaken for Staples by a management-consulting firm. The study found that the customers who purchased via a catalog and required delivery were not always the same ones who brought directly from the store. While there was a lot of cross shopping, the mail-order customers tended to be bigger and somewhat more interested in service, whereas those buying from the store were often buying for home offices. Staples also could not help but notice that its major rivals were offering a delivery service, and that business seemed to be thriving.

In 1991, Staples set up an independent business unit within the company to handle the mail/telephone order and delivery service, known as Contract and Commercial. The core of this business unit was Staples Direct (now called Staples Business Delivery). The man put in charge of this business, Ronald Sargent, would ultimately replace Stemberg as CEO of Staples in 2003.

One issue that had to be dealt with was the potential conflict between Staples Direct and the stores. The stores didn't want to push business the way of Staples Direct because they would not get credit for the sale. As Sargent commented later, "We were like the bad guys inside Staples, because the feeling was that if customers got products delivered they wouldn't shop inside our stores."[29] To align incentives, Staples changed the compensation systems so that (a) the store would get credit if a delivery order was placed through the store, and (b) the annual bonus of store employees was partly based on how well they meet goals for generating delivery sales.

As Staples Direct started to grow, the company also discovered that the delivery infrastructure they put in place could be used to serve clients in addition to the company's established small business customers, which typically had less than 50 employees. Increasingly, medium sized business (with 50–100 employees), and larger businesses with more than 100 employees started to utilize Staples Direct. To support this new business, Staples started to grow by acquisition, purchasing a number of regional stationary companies with established customers and delivery systems. Typically, Staples kept the owners of these businesses on as Staples employees, often because they had long, established relationships with key accounts in large organizations such as Xerox, Ford, and Pepsi Cola. Staples, however, established a consistent product line, brand image, and computer and accounting systems across all the acquisitions.

Between 1991 and 1996, Staples Direct grew from a $30 million business to almost $1 billion. As sales volume ramped up, Staples was able to get greater efficiencies out of its distribution network, which helped to drive down the costs of doing business through this channel. Staples used a network of regional distribution centers to hold an inventory of some 15,000 SKUs for delivery, compared to 8,000 SKUs in a typical store. In 1998, a web-based element was added to Staples Direct, Staples. com. Through the web or catalog, Staples customers could get access to some 130,000 SKUs, many of which were shipped directly from manufacturers, with Staples acting as an intermediary and consolidator.

To continue building the direct business, in 1988, Staples acquired Quill Corporation for $685 million in Staples stock. Established in 1956, Quill is a direct-mail catalog business with a targeted approach to servicing the business products needs of around a million small and medium-sized businesses in the United States. Quill differentiated itself through excellent customer service. Staples decided to let Quill keep its own organization, setting it up as a separate division within the Contract and Commercial business unit, but integrated Quill's purchasing with those of the rest of Staples to gain economies of the input side. Quill now operates under two brands—Staples National Advantage, which focuses upon large multi-regional businesses, and Staples Business advantage, which focuses upon large and medium sized regional companies, and has the flexibility to handle smaller accounts (although these are mostly handled via Staples Direct). In justifying the acquisition of Quill, Stemberg noted that the direct business amounted to a $60 billion a year industry, but it was highly fragmented with the top eight players accounting for less than 20% of the market.[30]

By 2014, the combined North American delivery business had grown to represent 40% of total sales, with some two-thirds of the *Fortune* 100 being counted as customers of Staples delivery business.[31]

C5-5c Going International

Staples' first foray into international markets occurred in the early 1990s. A Canadian retailer, Jack Bingleman, who wanted to start a Staples-type chain north of the border, approached the company. Bingleman also approached Office Depot and Office Max but had a preference for Staples because of the close geographic proximity. Board members at Staples initially opposed any expansion into Canada, arguing that scarce resources should be dedicated towards growth in the much larger United States, but Stemberg liked Bingleman's vision, and pushed the idea. Ultimately, in 1991, Staples agreed to invest $2 million in Bingleman's start-up for a 16% equity stake.

Known as Business Depot, the Canadian venture expanded rapidly modeling itself after Staples. Between 1991 and 1994, the number of Canadian Business Depot stores expanded to 30 stores and the enterprise turned profitable in 1993. In 1994, Staples announced an agreement to purchase Business Depot outright for $32 million.[32] By 2014, there were 315 stores in Canada.

The Canadian venture was soon followed by investments in Europe. Staples entered the U.K. market in 1992, partnering with Kingfisher PLC, a large U.K. retailer that operated home improvement and consumer electronics stores among other things. The Canadian venture had taught Staples that a local partner was extremely valuable. As one Staples executive noted later: "You absolutely cannot do it yourself. There are too many cultural impediments for you to know where the booby traps lie. In a retail startup, the most important task is to generate locations. There's no way a U.S. national can go into any country and generate the real estate it needs. That person will be chasing his tail for a long time."[33]

On the heels of entry into the United Kingdom, Staples purchased MAXI-Papier, a German company that was attempting to copy what Staples had done in the United States. This was followed by entry into the Netherlands and Portugal. In late 2002, Staples purchased the mail order business of a French company, Guilbert, for nearly $800 million, which boosted delivery sales in Europe from $50 million a year to $450 million a year almost overnight.[34] In 2008, Staples purchased Corporate Express NV, a Dutch office supplies company with a substantial direct delivery business in Europe. By 2014, Staples had stores in 23 countries outside of North America, including 112 stores in the United Kingdom, 59 in Germany, 41 in the Netherlands, and 34 in Portugal. At this point, around 20% of total sales were generated by the international operations, with half of that total coming from direct delivery and the remainder from retail sales.

C5-5d Changing the Shopping Experience

By the 2000s, Staples started to realize that its stores looked very similar to those of its two main competitors, Office Depot and Office Max. As the number of markets where all three companies competed grew, head-to-head competition increased. Management then started to look for ways to differentiate their stores from those of competitors. What emerged was a new store design, known as "Dover." The core to "Dover" was a customer centric philosophy known as "Easy." Rolled out across the company in 2005, "Easy" is all about making the shopping experience for customers as easy as possible—through store design and layout, through a merchandising strategy that aims to ensure that items are never out of stock, and through superior in-store customer service. The idea is to help to get the customer in and out of the store as expeditiously as possible.

To execute Easy, Staples has had to redesign its store layout, invest in upgrading the knowledge level of its sales associates, and improve its supply chain management processes.[35] Staples started a big push to improve the efficiency of its supply chain management process in 2003, and that is still ongoing today. Elements of this push include better use of information systems to link Staples with its suppliers and extensive use of "cross-docking" techniques at distribution centers, so that merchandise spends less time in distribution centers. As a consequence of this strategy, Staples has increased inventory turnover, reduced inventory holdings, and improved its in stock experience for customers.

C5-6 Staples in the 21st Century

In February 2002, Tom Stemberg announced that he was stepping down as CEO and passing the baton on to Ron Sargent. Stemberg would remain on as chairman. Upon taking over as CEO, Sargent put the breaks on store expansion, declaring that Staples would open no more than 75 new stores a year, down from over 130 in 2000. He used the slowdown to refocus attention upon internal operating efficiencies. The product line within stores was rationalized, with Staples cutting back on the stocking of low-margin items such as personal computers. He also set up a task force to look for ways to take every excess cent out of the cost structure. As a result, operating margins at Staples stores came in at 5.9% of sales in 2002, the best in the industry, and up from 4.5% in 2000.

By 2003, Sargent was refocusing on attaining profitable growth for the company. Although by this point Staples or one of its competitors operated in all major markets in North America, the company's management decided that Staples was in a strong enough position to go head to head with major competitors. In 2005, Staples pushed into Chicago, a market previously served by just Office Depot and Office Max, where the company opened 25 stores. The Chicago experience proved to be a pivotal one for Staples. In the words of COO, Mike Miles, "What we found in Chicago was we can come into a two-player market and make it a three-player market successfully. There was a little trepidation about that because the model in the first 10 to 15 years was that office superstores were interchangeable."[36]

Outside of the retail market, Sargent turned his attention to the business where he made is name, the direct delivery business. He pointed out that although the number of independent office supplies dealers was down to 6,000 from 15,000 a decade earlier, the delivery market was still highly fragmented and very large. Ultimately, Sargent believed that direct delivery from warehouses could be as big a business as Staples office supplies stores. He also saw huge potential for growth in Europe, which was the second-largest office supplies market in the world and still years behind the United States in terms of consolidation.

At the same time, Staples continued to face strategic challenges. Additional expansion by Staples in North America was bringing it into head-to-head contact with Office Depot or Office Max. Staples also faced continued competition from Sam's Club and Costco, both of which were focusing on small businesses and continued to sell office supplies. In addition, FedEx Kinko's, which has a nation-wide network of 1,000 copying and printing stores, started to offer more office supplies in a new store layout.

The 2008–2009 global financial crisis triggered a deep economic recession in the United States and elsewhere. The U.S. Office Supplies industry was hit by price discounting which, resulting in much slower top line growth for Staples and a decline in net profit. Sargent responded by cutting back on expansion plans and reducing capital spending going forward. Staples however, continued to be the strongest of the big three office supplies retailers.

While the economy started to recover from the recession in 2010, Staples and its peers did not. The recession seemed to usher in a permanent change in buyer behavior. As Ron Sargent noted in 2014, "Our customers are using less office supplies, shopping less often in our stores and more often online, and the focus on value has made the marketplace even more competitive."[37] Amazon, Walmart, and Costco had all expanded their office supplies offerings since the mid-2000s, and online sales from all three were cutting into demand for product from physical stores. Staples, too, saw its online sales grow even as sales from its physical stores stagnated or declined. By 2015, over half of all of Staples' sales in North America were online.

Staples responded to this trend by announcing in March 2014 that it would close up to 225 of its North American stores by the end of 2015 as part of a corporate goal to reduce its annual operating costs by $500 million. At the same time, the company would continue to expand its online offerings. In 2013 and 2014, it increased the number of products it sold on its website, Staples.com, from 100,000 to 500,000. Ron Sargent expected this number to reach 1.5 million by the end of 2015. Most of these products were to be shipped directly from the manufacturer to the customer, with Staples acting as an intermediary, much as Amazon does.[38]

With their own sales also falling, Office Depot and Office Max completed a $1.2 billion merger in late 2013. When they announced the merger, the two companies cited the growth of Internet sales as a prime reason. The Federal Trade Commission, which had opposed the proposed merger between Staples and Office Depot in 1997, blessed this merger, noting that the deal "was unlikely to substantially lessen competition."[39] The merger was expected to reduce the costs of the combined entity by $400–$600 million per year, primarily by closing duplicate stores.

In late 2014, the hedge fund Starboard Value announced that it had taken a position in both Staples and Office Depot. Jeffrey Smith, the CEO of Starboard Value, had emerged as a powerful activist investor, taking large positions in companies, and then urging them to change their strategy. Smith urged Staples and Office Depot to merge, stating that if they did not, he would mount a proxy battle to get board seats in both companies, and push a merger through. As it turned out, neither company needed much encouragement. In February 2015, the two companies announced a $6.3 billion merger agreement. By merging the two companies, Smith hoped to create a company with $34 billion in revenues and 4,400 stores worldwide. Both Staples and Office Depot argue that the proposed merger was necessary to compete in a world where bigger store chains and online competitors had reduced prices and provided new competition. Ron Sargent noted: "I think Amazon just launched a business-to-business office products initiative, so I'm sure they are knocking on the door."[40]

However, in December 2015. the U.S. Federal Trade Commission filed a lawsuit seeking to prevent the merger on anti-competitive grounds. The FTC argued that the merger would monopolize the office supplies market, harming competition. In May 2017, a federal judge granted the FTC a preliminary injunction against the merger, and Staples called the merger off, paying a $250 million breakup fee to Office Depot.

With the merger now off the table, Staples looked for other options. The company announced that it would continue to pivot towards the business-to-business market, placing stronger emphasis on its delivery and e-commerce businesses. In August 2017, this was followed by the announcement that Staples would be purchased by the private equity firm, Sycamore Partners, for $6.9 billion, effectively taking Staples out of the public equity markets. In its filing documents, Sycamore stated that it would break Staples up into three main businesses—a U.S. retail operation, a Canadian retail business, and a North American e-commerce and delivery business focused on the business-to-business (B2B) market. Each business would be managed independently.[41]

In pursuing this strategy, Sycamore seemed to be positioning itself against growing competition from Amazon and staking out a position that the business-to-business delivery market would grow faster than the consumer-oriented retail store business. Most observers expected Sycamore to shrink the retail store count, while growing the delivery business. However, there were questions about how successful Staples would be in the B2B space against competition from Amazon. One survey found that in 2017, 56% of business purchasers had recently bought general office supplies from Amazon.

In 2021, Sycamore made one more try to broker a merger between Staples' retail business, and that of Office Depot, when it entered discussions with the owner of Office Depot's retail stores, ODP, to purchase Office Depot's retail stores. Discussions were terminated in June 2022, however, when ODP rejected the sales.[42] Staples' retail business, it seemed, would have to continue the struggle against growing competition on its own.

Notes

[1] S. D. Solomon, "Born to Be Big," Inc., June 1989, p. 94.

[2] M. de la Merced and D. Gelles, "Staples and Office Depot Say Merger Will Keep Them Competitive," New York Times, February 25, 2015.

[3] S. D. Solomon, "Born to Be Big," Inc., June 1989, p. 96.

[4] T. Stemberg. Staples for Success, Knowledge Exchange, Santa Monica, California, 1996

[5] M. Barrier, "Tom Stemberg Calls the Office," Nation's Business, July 1990, p. 42.

[6] M. Barrier, "Tom Stemberg calls the Office," Nation's Business, July 1990, p. 44.

[7] M. Barrier, "Tom Stemberg calls the Office," Nation's Business, July 1990, p. 44.

[8] T. Stemberg and D. Whiteford. "Putting a Stop to Mom and Pop," Fortune Small Business, October 2002, p. 39.

[9] T. Stemberg and D. Whiteford. "Putting a Stop to Mom and Pop," Fortune Small Business, October 2002, p. 40.

[10] T. Stemberg. Staples for Success, Knowledge Exchange, Santa Monica, California, 1996.

[11] T. Stemberg and D. Whiteford. "Putting a Stop to Mom and Pop," Fortune Small Business, October 2002, p. 40.

[12] Tom Stemberg. Staples for Success, Knowledge Exchange, Santa Monica, California, 1996, p. 17.

[13] T. Stemberg and D. Whiteford. "Putting a Stop to Mom and Pop," Fortune Small Business, October 2002, p. 41.

[14] S. D. Solomon, "Born to Be Big," Inc., June 1989, pp. 94–95.

[15] T. Stemberg. Staples for Success, Knowledge Exchange, Santa Monica, California, 1996, p. 24.

[16] T. Stemberg. Staples for Success, Knowledge Exchange, Santa Monica, California, 1996, p. 27.

[17] T. Stemberg and D. Whiteford. "Putting a Stop to Mom and Pop," Fortune Small Business, October 2002, p. 40.

[18] S. D. Solomon, "Born to Be Big," Inc., June 1989, p. 100.

[19] T. Stemberg. Staples for Success, Knowledge Exchange, Santa Monica, California, 1996, p. 97.

[20] T. Stemberg. Staples for Success, Knowledge Exchange, Santa Monica, California, 1996, p. 97.

[21] N. Alster. "Penney Wise," Forbes, February 1, 1993, pp. 48–51.

[22] T. Stemberg. Staples for Success, Knowledge Exchange, Santa Monica, California, 1996, p. 97.

[23] R. Covion Rouland. "And Then There Were Three," Discount Merchandiser, December 1994, p. 27.

[24]L. Montgomery, "Staples: Buy the Laggard," *Financial World*, November 9, 1993, p. 22. Anonymous, "The New Plateau in Office Supplies," *Discount Merchandiser*, November 1991, pp. 50–54.

[25]J. S. Hirsch and E. de Lisser, "Staples to Acquire Archrival Office Depot," *Wall Street Journal,* September 5, 1996, p. A3.

[26]J. Pereira and J. Wilke, "Staples Faces FTC in Antitrust Showdown on Merger," *Wall Street Journal,* May 19, 1997, p. B4.

[27]T. Stemberg. Staples for Success, Knowledge Exchange, Santa Monica, California, 1996, p. 128.

[28]W. M. Bulkeley. "Office Supplies Superstores Find Bounty in the Boonies," *Wall Street Journal,* September 1st, 1998, page B1.

[29]W. C. Symonds, "Thinking Outside the Big Box," *Business Week*, August 11, 2003, p. 62.

[30]W. M. Bulkeley, "Staples, Moving Beyond Superstores, Will Buy Quill for $685 Million in Stock," *Wall Street Journal*, April 8, 1998, p. A1.

[31]J. MacKay, "Staples Achieves Impressive Operating Margins Relative to Peers Due to Scale Advantages," *Morningstar Research Report*, May 19, 2011.

[32]S. Gelston. "Staples Goes on Buying Spree to Acquire Business Depot, National Office Supply Company," *Boston Herald*, January 25, 1994, p. 24.

[33]T. Stemberg, Staples for Success, Knowledge Exchange, Santa Monica, California, 1996, p. 90.

[34]W. C. Symonds, "Thinking Outside the Big Box," *Business Week,* August 11, 2003, pp. 62–64.

[35]M. Troy, "Office Supplies: Staples Positioned as the Architect of 'Easy,'" *Retailing Today*, August 7, 2006, p. 30.

[36]Anonymous, "Moving in on Major Markets," *DSN Retailing Today*, May 22, 2006, p. 10.

[37]Anonymous, "Citing Shift to Online Sales, Staples Says It Will Close up to 225 Stores by the End of 2015," *Reuters*, March 6, 2015.

[38]Anonymous, "Citing Shift to Online Sales, Staples Says It Will Close up to 225 Stores by the End of 2015," *Reuters*, March 6, 2015.

[39]M. de la Merced and D. Gelles, "Staples and Office Depot Say Merger Will Keep Them Competitive," *New York Times,* February 25, 2015.

[40]M. de la Merced and D. Gelles, "Staples and Office Depot Say Merger Will Keep Them Competitive," *New York Times,* February 25, 2015.

[41]B. Unglesbee, "Staples Spinning Off Retail Business," *Retail Drive*, August 17, 2017.

[42]B. Unglesbee, "After Much Mulling, Office Depot Owner Rejects Both Sale and Split," *Retail Drive*, June 22, 2022.

Case

6

Walmart Stores

Charles W. L. Hill Foster School of Business University of Washington Seattle, WA August 2022

C6-1 Introduction

In July 1962, Sam Walton opened his first Walmart discount store in Rogers, a small Arkansas town with a population of just 6,000. That same year, both Kmart Corporation (Kmart) and Target Corporation (Target) also opened their first stores, although unlike Sam Walton, they focused on large metropolitan areas. By 2022, Walmart had eclipsed its rivals to become the largest retailer in the world with annual revenues of around $575 billion. The company had 2.3 million employees and more than 10,500 stores in 24 countries including 4,735 in the United States that were served by more than 210 distribution centers. The company accounted for over 13.2% of all U.S. retail sales. More than 90% of the U.S. population now lived within 10 miles of a Walmart store.

Despite its success, in 2022, Walmart was facing significant challenges. In the warehouse store category, its Sam's Club offering was struggling against Costco Wholesale Corporation (Costco), the world's third-largest retailer. More troubling still, the online retailer Amazon.com Inc. (Amazon) was continuing to grow its share of U.S. retail sales. By 2021, Amazon's share of U.S. retail sales had increased to 10.8%, making it second only to Walmart both nationally and globally. Amazon's retail sales hit $468 billion in 2021, when it captured over 56% of all U.S. online retail sales. Amazon's 2017 acquisition of the Whole Foods Market IP, Inc. (Whole Foods) brick-and-mortar supermarket chain signaled that it was going after the grocery business, a category that Walmart had dominated since first expanding into the area back in 1988. In the wake of its August 2017 takeover of Whole Foods, Amazon cut grocery prices by as much as 40% on some products. In the months that followed, store traffic surged by 25%. Forecasts made in 2022 suggest that based on current growth trends, Amazon's share of the U.S. retail market could grow to 14.9% by 2026, while Walmart's share will slip to 12.7%, making Amazon the largest U.S. retailer.[1]

C6-2 Early History

The Walmart store in Rodgers was not Walton's first retailing venture. That was a Ben Franklin variety store in Newport, Arkansas, that Walton, an Arkansas native, took over in 1945 when he was just 27. Variety stores offered a selection of inexpensive items for household and personal use. This was a concept that had been pioneered by F.W. Woolworth in the late 19th century. By 1962, Walton was a well-established Ben Franklin franchisee running 15 variety stores in small towns across Arkansas and Kansas. It was a business where Walton had honed his skills, competing against other small town variety stores. From the outset, Walton focused relentlessly on reducing prices, cutting costs, and making a living on slim margins. His overarching philosophy was to sell stuff that people need every day just a little cheaper than everyone else, and to sell it at that low price all the time. He believed that if you offered *everyday low prices*, customers would flock to you. His experience in the variety store business had taught him the value of this approach. To make this strategy work, you had to control costs better than the next guy. By all accounts, Walton made a religion out of frugality by tightly controlling expenses. Moreover, while still a Ben Franklin franchisee, he had pushed the boundaries of what was possible in the retailing business. Walton was one of the first retailers in the country and the first in the South to adopt a self-service format.

Walton was fascinated by what other retailers were doing. He was known for visiting them and checking out their stores. He would walk into their headquarters, often unannounced, and ask to meet with senior managers. He would pepper them with questions, writing everything he saw and heard down on a yellow legal pad. When the discounting concept started to emerge in the mid-1950s in the Northeast, he made a point of visiting those stores, befriending their management, and gathering as much information as he could. These visits convinced Walton that large-footprint general merchandising discount stores would be the wave of the future. He believed that the wider range of products and better buying power of discount stores would ultimately put traditional small-town variety stores like his out of businesses. This led to the establishment of the first Walmart store.

Initially, Walton had wanted Ben Franklin to back his idea of building large discount stores in small towns. As Walton put it....

> I was used to franchising, and I liked the mindset, I generally liked my experience with Ben Franklin, and I didn't want to get involved in building a company with all that support apparatus.[2]

Ben Franklin turned him down. They didn't see the value in small towns. Walton's experience as a Ben Franklin franchisee, however, had taught him that there was money to be made in small towns.

The Rodgers store took 2 years to hit its stride, but by 1964 it was generating $1 million in annual revenues, three to five times what traditional variety stores made. This gave Walton the confidence to open two additional Walmarts in nearby towns, one in Harrison and one in Springdale. The Harrison Walmart was a basic affair. It was just 12,000 square feet with an 8-foot ceiling, a concrete floor, and bare-boned wooden plank fixtures. Walton called it ugly. David Glass, who would become CEO after Walton, said that it was the worst looking retail store he had ever seen. But as Walton noted...

> We were trying to find out if customers in a town of 6,000 people would come to our kind of barn and buy the same merchandise strictly because of price.[3]

By keeping costs as low as possible, Walton found he could keep prices 20% below those of nearby variety and specialty stores. He quickly discovered that his promise of everyday low prices attracted a lot of customers.

In Springdale, a town of close to 15,000, Walton was trying to learn something else, would a 35,000-square foot store work in a larger town? Here too, the answer was yes. The key was that these stores would draw in people from the surrounding small communities, who would drive an hour to the Walmart to gain price discounts. Although such discounts might be available at large suburban stores, those might be 3 hours' drive or more away. These early Walmart stores were open longer hours than rival merchants, had plenty of parking space, and utilized the self-service concept.

By the time Walton had three Walmarts up and running, he realized that the discounting formula was a success. The strategy that was emerging from these early experiences was to put a good-sized discount store into little one-horse towns that everyone else was ignoring. While rivals like Kmart wouldn't go into a town smaller than 50,000, Walton believed that towns as small as 5,000 could support one of his stores when you considered the population of the surrounding area. As noted by Ferold Arend, Walmart's first vice president....

> The truth is, we were working with a great idea. It was really easy to develop discounting in those small communities before things got competitive. There wasn't a lot of competition for us in the early days because nobody was discounting in the small communities.[4]

One of the problems of focusing on small towns, however, was that getting good deals from distributors and wholesalers was difficult. They would charge Walmart for the extra cost of delivering to a small-town store out in the sticks, something that irritated Sam Walton, whose obsession with controlling expenses knew no bounds. To make matters worse, large consumer product companies such as Procter & Gamble, Gillett, and Kodak would dictate how much they would sell to Walmart, and at what price. In the early days, the ordering of merchandise was also decentralized to individual store managers, so there was no opportunity to realize economies of scale from bulk purchasing.

Walton realized that this situation was untenable. The solution was to open the first Walmart distribution center, close to the company's headquarters in Bentonville, Arkansas. Buying was centralized in Bentonville to get discounts from bulk purchases. Suppliers would drop ship merchandise at the distribution centers. Then Walmart would truck them out to the stores in the area to replenish inventory. A cross docking system was developed in the distribution center to facilitate this process. It was at this point that Walmart started to build its own trucking fleet to transport the inventory.

For the distribution system to work efficiently, Walmart needed information to know what merchandise to order and when to replenish each store. This requirement drove Walmart to become an early adopter of computer-controlled inventory systems. Walton himself realized the need for better information systems early on and enrolled in an IBM school for retailers in 1966. Nevertheless, he was reluctant to spend the money on information technology and only relented in the 1970s after pressure from some of his managers. In retrospect, Walton acknowledged that Walmart was forced to be ahead of the times in distribution and information systems because the stores were situated in small towns.

During this period, Walton was also building a strong management team. In what would become a hallmark of Walton's approach, he would spot talented managers at other retailers and try to persuade them to come and work for him. Walton could be tenacious. He would keep pursuing talented managers until they agreed to join the company. For example, David Glass, who would eventually succeed Walton as CEO, was pursued by Walton for a decade before he agreed to join Walmart in 1976. Early recruits included Ferold Arend, the company's first chief operating officer; Bob Thornton, who was brought on to open Walmart's first distribution center; and Ron Mayer, who joined in 1968 as VP for finance and distribution. All three had experience at other retailers. It was Mayer who pushed Walton to invest in computer systems to improve distribution. Meyer hired the first data processing managers.

By the late 1960s, Walton had established the foundations for future growth: (1) The Walmart discounting concept had proved attractive, (2) the strategy of focusing on small towns was already paying dividends, (3) he had surrounded himself with a talented team of managers, and (4) with the opening of its first distribution center and the adoption of formal inventory control systems, the company was well placed to replicate its formula across America. At the same time the company was still small—Walmart only had 18 stores in 1969 and sales of $9 million, whereas Kmart had 250 stores and sales of $800 million (Kmart was owned by the well-established department store retailer Dayton Hudson). To grow, Walton needed capital.

Up to this point, Walton had financed Walmart's growth from a mix of cash flow and debt. By 1969, the company was not generating enough cash to fund Walton's growth ambitions and pay down the company's debt. Walton believed that he needed to grow the company rapidly before rivals figured out his small-town strategy. Initially, he tried to raise more debt but was turned down by several institutions who didn't buy into his strategy, and was "fleeced" by those who were prepared to lend him more. Walton was getting tired of owing other people money. He decided to take the company public. On October 1, 1970, Walmart had its initial public offering, selling 300,000 shares at $16.50 a share. After the IPO, the Walton family still held onto 61% of the stock. The IPO raised close to $5 million. This allowed Walton to pay down debt and fund the next stage of expansion.

C6-3 Building the Colossus

Walmart's growth strategy was very deliberate. While other discounters were leap frogging from large city to large city, for decades, Walmart remained focused on its small-town strategy. The company wanted stores to be within a day's return drive of distribution centers (about 300 miles) so that they could be restocked regularly. Regular replenishment reduced the need to store inventory in a dedicated space at the back of the store, which meant that more of the square footage could be devoted to selling merchandise, increasing sales per square foot. While rivals typically devoted 25% of their square footage to storing inventory, Walmart kept this figure down to 10%. As Walmart expanded its own trucking fleet, it also started to pick up merchandise from suppliers in the area, rather than have them drop ship goods off at the distribution centers. Trucks would replenish a store, then pick up goods from a supplier on the way back to the distribution centers so they had loads on the backhaul. When Walmart took logistics costs off suppliers, it negotiated lower prices, and then passed on those cost savings on to its customers in the form of lower selling prices.

Initially, Walton wanted stores to be situated close enough to each other so that they were within reach of management at Bentonville. Walton, a licensed pilot, would frequently fly his small plane from Bentonville to surrounding stores, often dropping in unannounced. As the company grew, he appointed regional vice presidents to oversee stores clustered in certain territories. Walmart started to invest in a fleet of small aircraft. The regional vice presidents were based in Bentonville. They would fly out on Monday morning to visit stores in their territory, returning Thursday. Walton insisted that they returned with at least one good idea to pay for the trip. As always, expenses were tightly controlled. When traveling, managers were expected to stay in cheap hotels, share rooms, and eat at budget restaurants. On buying trips to suppliers, managers were instructed to keep expenses below 1% of total purchases.

As it expanded, Walmart first saturated the area within a day's drive of Bentonville. Once an area was saturated, Walmart would build another distribution center in an adjacent area, go as far as possible from that center and put in a store, and then fill in the territory around the distribution center. As Walton described it,

> We would fill in the map of that territory, state by state, county seat by county seat, until we had saturated that market area. We saturated northwest Arkansas. We saturated Oklahoma. We saturated Missouri.....and so on.[5]

Walmart never planned to enter cities. Instead, the company would build stores in a ring around cities, some way out, and wait for the growth to come to the stores. The strategy seemed to work.

The saturation strategy had benefits beyond management control and distribution efficiencies. Walton never liked to spend much on advertising. The company found that when it went from small town to small town, filling in an area, word of mouth would get Walmart's everyday low pricing message out to customers, allowing Walmart to reduce advertising expenses. The clustering of stores also made it difficult for rivals to get traction in an area. For example, in the Springfield Missouri area Walmart had 40 stores within 100 miles. When Kmart finally entered the area with three stores, they had a hard time getting business.

Walton himself would spend a lot of time flying around an area scouting out possible store locations. From the air he could get a good idea of traffic flows, see which towns were growing, and evaluate the location of competitors, if there were any. He had a major hand in picking the first 150 store locations before being forced by the growing complexity of managing Walmart to delegate that task.

C6-3a Developing Information Systems and Logistics

Over time, one of the keys to Walmart's expansion was the introduction of state-of-the-art information systems and logistics. Walton had been interested in the potential of computers as far back as the mid-1960s, but the real push came with the hiring of David Glass in 1976 as executive vice president of finance. Glass convinced Walton to put mini-computers in every store to track sales. These were linked to the distribution centers and to the headquarters at Bentonville. Glass was also instrumental in persuading Walton to insist that suppliers place barcodes on every item so that they could be scanned at sale. Indeed, Walmart was the first retailer to mandate that suppliers barcode every item.

The company originally used phone lines to transmit data on sales, but as the volume of date grew, the phone lines became congested. In the days before the development of the Internet and high-capacity fiber-optic communications systems this was a major bottleneck. To deal with this problem, Walmart committed $24 million to build a communication system under which data would be uploaded via microwave dishes at every store to a satellite, which would then transmit the data to Bentonville and the distribution centers. Launched in 1983, the system was the first of its kind. The satellite system allowed Walmart to dive deep into its sales, tracking the history and real-time sales for every single item at every single store.

Glass also pushed for the development of highly automated distribution centers linked by computers and the satellite system to the stores and to suppliers. Walmart's first distribution center outside of Bentonville was built at Glass' insistence. Goods were bought into distribution centers, scanned, placed on laser guided conveyer belts, and then directed to the appropriate truck to deliver them to stores. By the early 1990s, Walmart had 20 of these distribution centers around the nation. Walmart was now directly replenishing about 85% of its in-store inventory from its own distribution centers, compared to only 50–65% for its rivals (today there are over 150 distribution centers in the United States). The internalization of logistics allowed Walmart to reduce to 2 days the gap between when stores placed a request for replenishment and when they received that inventory. This compared to a compared to 5-day gap for a lot of competitors. By the early 1990s, Walmart estimated that its logistics costs were running at about 3% of sales, compared to 4.5–5% of sales at rivals.

As Walmart added distribution centers, its trucking operation grew. Today, Walmart operates the largest private trucking company in the United States. This consists of over 12,000 drivers, 10,000 trucks, and 80,000 trailers. As a vital link in the company's logistics network, the trucking operations of Walmart have become progressively more efficient over time. For example, in 2005, Walmart set itself the goal of doubling the efficiency of its fleet by 2015. By 2014, the company reported that its trucks had delivered 830 million more cases while driving 300 million fewer miles than in 2005, an improvement of 84.2% over 2005. This had been achieved through more efficient loading and unloading of merchandise, better routing, GPS tracking, new tractor technologies, and so on.

One important innovation that Glass was responsible for was Walmart's Retail Link program. First introduced in 1985, this proprietary trend-forecasting software delivers important sales information to suppliers at no direct cost. Retail Link benefitted suppliers, enabling them to adjust their own production schedules and product plans to meet consumer demand as reviled by Walmart's sales data. At the same time, this software gave Walmart deep insight into a supplier's sales and profit margins, information that Walmart uses to bargain for lower prices from suppliers. As is the practice at Walmart with all cost reductions, those cost savings are then passed onto consumers in the form of lower selling prices.

One of the consequences of Walmart's investments in information systems and logistics has been better stock replenishment and faster inventory turnover. By 2016, Walmart was turning over its inventory 8.39 times per year, compared with 5.88 times per year at Target and 7.70 times at online rival Amazon.[6] Among other things, faster inventory turns can boost sales per square foot. On this measure, Walmart has long bested rivals such as Target. According to the National Retail Federation, Walmart registered sales per square foot of $535 in 2021, compared with $437 at Target.

Despite Walmart's prowess in information systems, not all its initiatives have succeeded. In 2003, for example, it announced that its top 100 suppliers would have to tag pallets and cases of goods with radio frequency identification (RFID) tags. The goal was to improve the efficiency of Walmart's logistics operation by passively tracking goods as they passed through the supply chain. In practice, technological problems resulted in spotty implementation and the initiative stumbled. But Walmart learned something from this—the company realized that RFID might have uses inside a store to maintain the right inventory mix. For instance, a shelf may look full of shirts, but what if they are only in sizes small and extra-large? RFID can help scan a shelf without the cost of tedious hand sorting of merchandise or bar code scanning to identify stocking shortages.

C6-3b Supplier Relations

As Walmart grew, its relationship with suppliers shifted. In the early days, powerful suppliers of branded products such as Procter & Gamble had dictated terms to Walmart. However, Walmart consolidated its buying in Bentonville and, as the company grew, its buying power began to increase. Today, Walmart is the largest distributor for many consumer products companies. For example, in 2015, Clorox earned 26% of its revenue from Walmart sales, Kellogg 21%, Campbell Soup 20%, and Procter & Gamble 14%.[7]

Walmart refers to its 60,000 plus suppliers as "partners," but there is little doubt who is the senior partner in this relationship. Walmart does work closely with its suppliers, providing them with detailed information through its Retail Link program that helps them to identify inefficiencies and improve their product planning and product offerings. Walmart also provides suppliers with the opportunity to attain tremendous sales volume, which can enable them to achieve economies of scale. Even if suppliers make very slim margins selling to Walmart, the information and economies of scale they get may enable them to make more money elsewhere. To take advantage of this relationship, many of Walmart's larger suppliers have established offices next to Walmart's headquarters in Bentonville. One of the first to do so was Procter & Gamble, which opened its Bentonville office in 1987 and now has a 250-person team dedicated to working with Walmart.

In return for its provision of data and volume, Walmart is relentless in demanding lower prices and better payment terms. Any cost savings achieved are then passed on to Walmart's customers in the form of lower prices (and to shareholders in the form of higher profits and dividend payouts). As David Glass once said...

We want everybody to be selling the same stuff, and we want to compete on a price basis, and they will go broke 5% before we will.[8]

Walmart's Bentonville buying center is legendary for its sparse fittings—conference rooms with no doors furnished with cheap tables and mismatched plastic chairs that Walmart was not able to sell—so it used them to furnish their offices instead. Some supplier representatives have reported having to sit on boxes because there were no chairs available. Suppliers were also required to give Walmart a toll-free number to call, or to take collect calls from Walmart buyers. The idea was to convey an impression of austerity. Walmart's buyers constantly push suppliers to lower their prices, often by 5% per year. After squeezing out all the efficiencies they can at home, many suppliers have only been able to achieve further cost reductions by moving production offshore to low-cost locations such as Mexico or China, leading to claims that Walmart has been a major reason for the hollowing out of U.S. manufacturing.

Walmart has also used its power to extract better payment terms from its suppliers. Suppliers may be paid net 60 days after Walmart takes ownership of a product, as opposed to the normal net 30 days. They may have to pay additional fees to cover the cost of their goods being transported through Walmart's logistics system. Since the early 2000s, Walmart has been pushing suppliers to agree to "pay on scan" contracts where Walmart does not take ownership of a good until it is scanned for sale at the checkout, effectively enabling Walmart to push off significant inventory costs onto suppliers.

Beginning in the early 1990s, Walmart has also developed its own store brand offerings. These include goods sold under the Sam's Choice and Great Value labels. Often priced 20–30% lower than national brands, the presence of private label offerings is another mechanism that can be used to pressure suppliers to reduce their prices. As a management consultant who worked with Walmart suppliers noted…

> Year after year, for any product that is the same as what you sold them last year, Wal-Mart is going to say, here's the price you gave me last year. Here's what I can get a competitor's product for; here's what I can get a private label version for. I want to see a better value that I can bring to my shopper this year. Or else I'm going to use that shelf space differently.[9]

C6-3c Managing the Business

Sam Walton believed in hard work, frugality, discipline, loyalty, and a restless effort at constant self-improvement. He described himself as a conservative, except when it came to business, where he was a champion of innovation and disruption. He believed in treating employees well, in giving them responsibility and a stake in the business through stock and profit sharing, but also in checking up on them. He was a numbers man, he wanted data on everything, and Walmart's information systems gave him that. In turn, the data gave him and his managers the raw material required to control his ever-expanding empire, to manage its merchandise offering, inventory turns, stores and employees.

He looked for the same values in the people he hired. If he saw a successful manager at another retailer who shared his values, he would do his best to hire them. If they said no, he would persist until he got his way. He would interview other applicants for management positions multiple times before making a hiring decision, trying to get a sense for who this person was and what their values were.

To this day, the consequences are easy to see. Walmart's headquarters' staff works relentlessly hard. Buyers and midlevel staffers get to work at 6:30 a.m., senior executives often arrive even earlier. Routine quitting time ranges from 5 p.m. to 7 p.m., depending on the job, the season, and the workload. All white-collar workers work from 7 a.m. to 1 p.m. on Saturday, including attending the legendary Saturday morning meeting. The meetings open with the Walmart cheer, an idea that Walton got from a visit to a South

Korean tennis ball factory in 1975. At the meetings, Walton and other managers would discuss the performance of the company, its stores, departments, and even individual items. There would also be entertainment —performances by well-known music stars and comedians, pep talks by NFL football players, competitions between top managers, light-hearted hazing of managers who had lost a bet with Walton. Walton himself once danced the Hula in a grass skirt on Wall Street after losing a bet with David Glass about sales. After losing a bet with Walton, another manager road a horse down the main street in Bentonville wearing a blond wig and pink tights.

The stores have their own version of the Saturday morning meeting. Associates meet before every shift to talk about the store's performance, describe their favorite in-store items, and perform the Walmart cheer.

Walmart centralizes much of its operations in Bentonville, including buying, logistics, and decisions about information systems. It even controls the temperature of its U.S. stores from Bentonville. However, it does give store managers discretion on merchandizing and some on pricing. Regarding merchandizing, Walmart understands that different locations require a different merchandizing mix, which is why Walton always stressed that store managers should be good merchants with a close eye on what sells in their community. Walmart's buyers are told to pay close attention to what the merchants in the store want. Through its information systems, Walmart also supplies store managers with detailed information on what is selling in their store, along with their monthly profit and loss statements, allowing them to fine-tune the merchandizing mix and compare their performance with other stores in Walmart's system. On pricing, store managers have long had the authority to match prices being offered at competing stores in their neighborhood if those prices are lower than Walmart's.

More generally, store managers are responsible for hiring and supervising employees, meeting financial goals, enforcing workplace regulations, delegating work, tracking inventory, analyzing sales data, processing payroll, and coordinating merchandising shipments. Store managers are supervised by regional vice presidents. Walmart does not have regional headquarters, which saves money. Instead, the regional VPs are based in Bentonville, but typically travel 3–4 days a week, visiting stores in their territory. Store managers earn between $50,000 and $175,000 a year. In addition, they earn bonuses tied to store performance and participate in Walmart's profit-sharing plans.

Walmart refers to its hourly paid employees as "associates." Sam Walton came up with the idea of calling employees "associates" after visiting retail stores in the United Kingdom where employees were called associates. It got him thinking about the importance of building a partnership with employees. Walton freely admits that in the early days, he was so cheap that he didn't want to pay hourly employees much. Over time, he came to the realization that if the company treated employees well, they would treat customers well, and happy customers would come back and buy more. Walmart had a profit-sharing plan in place for managers after it went public in 1970. The following year, he expanded the plan to include any associate who had been with the company for at least a year and worked at least 1,000 hours. Using a formula based on profit growth, Walmart contributed a percentage of every employee's eligible wage to a profit-sharing plan. Much of the money in that plan was invested in Walmart stock. When they left the company, employees could take the accumulated amount either in Walmart stock or cash. For many years, the annual contribution amounted to about 6% of an hourly employee's earnings. For those who got in early, the accumulated amount upon retirement could be hundreds of thousands of dollars in Walmart stock. To boost this still further, Walmart introduced an employee stock purchase plan, where employees could purchase Walmart stock through a payroll deduction at a 15% discount to the market value. Walmart changed the associate plan in 2010, replacing it with a 401k plan under which Walmart would match 100% of an employee's contribution up to 6% of their pay.

Walton also instituted an open-book policy at Walmart, sharing important information on a regular basis with associates, including store purchases, profits, sales, and markdowns. In Walton's view, it was important for associates to get to know the business, so that they could become better employees. The open book policy also fed into Walmart's strategy of promoting from within. Around 75% of store managers at Walmart today started as hourly paid associates. The company claims it now promotes around 160,000 associates each year. Associates can get promoted to supervisors, department managers, assistant managers, and finally store managers. Store managers move frequently, often every 18–24 months, a practice which Walmart uses to deepen their experience. Talented store managers can continue to move up in the organization becoming, for example, regional vice presidents.

C6-3d Criticisms of Walmart

While much has been written about Walton's ability to find, recruit and empower ordinary people to do extraordinary things, Walmart has also been the target of sustained political and legal criticism over its treatment of employees, particularly since the turn on the century. One class action lawsuit on behalf of 1.5 million women who have worked at Walmart alleged systematic sex discrimination in promotion and pay.[10] Other lawsuits have alleged that store managers routinely force hourly employees to punch out at the time clock, then return to work, putting in hours of unpaid labor. Walmart has also been cited for knowingly hiring illegal immigrant labor to clean its stores, and shockingly, locking them in the stores at night.[11]

Others have criticized Walmart for paying its hourly employees so little that they must rely upon state assistant such as food stamps to make ends meet, leading to the allegation that Walmart is indirectly subsidized by the state. Consistent with this, one academic study found that U.S. counties with more Walmart stores in 1987, and counties with more additions of stores between 1987 and 1998, experienced greater increases (or smaller decreases) in family poverty rates during the 1990s-economic boom.[12]

Another body of academic research suggests that the arrival of a Walmart store frequently puts other local retailers out of business. A classic study by Kenneth Stone of Walmart stores in Iowa found that while general merchandise sales grew 44% in the 5 years after Walmart arrived, competing grocery stores lost 5% of their business, specialty stores 14% and clothing stores 18%.[13] Stone also found that between 1983 and 1993, small Iowa towns with populations of between 500 and 1,000 lost 47% of retail sales as people simply drove to Walmart to shop. Data like this has resulted in some small towns blocking Walmart from locating in their area.

For its part, Walmart has countered these criticisms by taking steps to improve its image. It has instituted a diversity program to try and equalize opportunity and pay across gender and ethnicity. In 2016, it increased its minimum wage for new hires to $10 an hour. The company also points out that it does offer a healthcare plan for employees who work more than 30 hours a week. Regarding the negative impact on local communities, Walmart cites academic research that shows that long run price declines of 7–13% occur when Walmart enters an area, which increases the disposable income of residents. Research also shows that while competitors lose jobs, after accounting for both job losses at competing retailers, and job gains at Walmart, the establishment of a Walmart store in a county does lead to a small net gain in jobs.[14]

C6-4 Supercenters and Groceries

By the early 1990s, Walmart was starting to encounter limits to its growth. It's traditional market, small towns, was increasingly saturated. The company was relying on growth of suburban areas where competition was more intense. About this time,

Walmart decided to experiment with doubling the size of its stores to sell groceries alongside its general merchandise offerings in a format it called supercenters. At the time, the grocery business was dominated by long-established supermarket chains including Albertsons, Safeway, and Kroger.

In 1990, Walmart had just nine supercenters. By 2000, it had 888 and by 2017 it had more than 3,500 supercenters in the United States alone. Along the way, Walmart delivered a hammer blow to traditional grocery stores. By 2000, it was already the largest grocer in America. By 2020, Walmart and its Sam's Club subsidiary combined accounted for 21.3% of the food retail market in the United States; Kroger was second with at 9.9% and Costco third with 5.0%.[15] Walmart now generates more than half of its annual revenues from grocery sales.

One reason for Walmart's success in groceries: everyday low prices. Walmart's goal is for grocery prices to be 15% lower than that of its competitors 80% of the time. For a family of four that spends $500 a month on groceries, this can result in annual savings of $900 a year. The consequence for established grocery chains has been devastating. During its first decade in the grocery business, Walmart's dramatic rise in grocery sales pushed more than 30 supermarket chains into bankruptcy. Walmart was cited as a catalyst in 24 of those cases. The price pressure continues today, with Walmart driving down prices and pressuring margins at Kroger, Albertson's, and Target. To match Walmart, Kroger states that it spent more than $3.7 billion to lower prices between 2006 and 2016. Despite Kroger's attempts to match Walmart, in 2016, Kroger's food prices were still 4% above those of Walmart according to price checks. On non-perishable and frozen items, Kroger was charging 5.6% more than Walmart.[16] Due to the ongoing price war for grocery sales, year-to-year food prices fell by 1.3% in 2016.[17]

Keeping grocery prices low requires Walmart to do what it has always done, use its economies of scale in purchasing and its logistics knowhow to drive down the price it pays suppliers and maximize its supply chain efficiency. For example, Charles Fishman explained how Atlantic salmon that might have cost $20 a pound in 1990 was selling for just $4.84 a pound in 2006. The Atlantic salmon sold at Walmart was sourced from farms in Chile. Walmart's salmon use to come from Norway or Canada, but the constant quest for low prices drove Walmart to look for lower-cost supplies elsewhere. In turn, that helped to jump-start the growth of fish farms in Chile, which is now the world's second-largest salmon producer (the introduction of fish farms, and the "mechanization" of salmon production is one reason for the price drop). In Chile, fish is harvested early in the morning while it is still dark, taken to processing plants, processed, then put on a truck or plane to Santiago, and then on a plane to Miami. Fish harvested in Chile can be on a dining room table in Iowa within 48 hours. Multiply the salmon story across Walmart's product lines, and it becomes clear why grocery prices are so low at Walmart.[18]

C6-5 Sam's Club

Sam's Club is a deep discount warehouse type store selling a limited range of merchandise at wholesale prices to buyers who wish to make bulk purchases. To shop at Sam's Club, you must pay an annual membership fee ($45 in 2016). Wholly owned by Walmart, the first Sam's Club was established in 1983. Sam Walton got the idea from his friend and rival, Sol Price, who had pioneered the concept with his Price Club stores in California back in 1976. The original target market for Sam's Club was small business owners, but it was expanded to include general consumers who wished to make bulk purchases of household items. As of 2016, there were 650 Sam's Clubs in the United States and they generated $57 billion in annual revenues.

Sam's Club faces very tough competition from Costco, the world's second-largest retailer. Costco had 815 warehouse stores around the world and generated

$196 million in annual revenues in 2021. Costco benefits from a focus on higher-income households—Sam's Club estimates that the medium household income of its customers is around $80,000, compared to $120,000 for Costco. Costco also has very loyal customers, with about 90% renewing their annual membership. In addition to competition from Costco, Sam's Club has reported some cannibalization of sales from Walmart supercenters and growing direct competition from Amazon.

To try and deal with competition from Costco, Sam's Club started to shift its strategy in 2016.[19] First, the company aimed to open 8–10 new clubs each year in more affluent areas. Second, it decided to shutter underperforming stores. Third, it attempted to adjust its merchandising categories to appeal to more upscale customers. Finally, it continued to expand its private label offerings. Despite this strategic shift, Costco has continued to dominate the warehouse store market. In 2021, estimates suggest that Costco had a 56% market share in the United States, versus 36% at Sam's Club and 8.3% at BJ's Wholesale.[20]

C6-6 International Expansion

In 1991, Walmart started to expand internationally with the opening of its first stores in Mexico. The Mexican operation was established as a joint venture with Cifera, the largest local retailer. Initially, Walmart made several missteps. Walmart had problems replicating its efficient distribution system in Mexico. Poor infrastructure, crowded roads, and a lack of leverage with local suppliers, many of which could not or would not deliver directly to Walmart's stores or distribution centers, resulted in stocking problems and raised costs and prices. Initially, prices at Walmart in Mexico were some 20% above prices for comparable products in the company's U.S. stores, which limited Walmart's ability to gain market share. There were also problems with merchandise selection. Many of the stores in Mexico carried items that were popular in the United States. These included ice skates, riding lawn mowers, leaf blowers, and fishing tackle. Not surprisingly, these items did not sell well in Mexico, so managers would slash prices to move inventory, only to find that the company's automated information systems would immediately order more inventory to replenish the depleted stock.

By the mid-1990s, however, Walmart had learned from its early mistakes and adapted its operations in Mexico to match the local environment. A partnership with a Mexican trucking company dramatically improved the distribution system, and more careful stocking practices meant that the Mexican stores sold merchandise that appealed more to local tastes and preferences. As Walmart's presence grew, many of Walmart's suppliers built factories close by its Mexican distribution centers so that they could better serve the company, which helped to further drive down inventory and logistics costs. In 1998, Walmart acquired a controlling interest in Cifera. Today, Mexico is a leading light in Walmart's international operations, where the company is more than twice the size of its nearest rival.

The Mexican experience proved to Walmart that it could compete outside of the United States. It now has operations in 24 other countries. In Canada, Britain, Germany, and Japan, Walmart entered by acquiring existing retailers and then transferring its information systems, logistics, and management expertise. In Puerto Rico, Brazil, Argentina, and China, Walmart established its own stores (although it added to its Chinese operations with a major acquisition in 2007). Due to these moves, in 2022, the company had some 5,100 stores outside the United States, 550,000 foreign employees on the payroll, and generated international revenues of $100 billion.

In addition to greater growth, expanding internationally has brought Walmart two other major benefits. First, Walmart has also been able to reap significant economies of scale from its global buying power. Many of Walmart's key suppliers have long been international companies; for example, GE (appliances), Unilever (food products), and P&G (personal care products) are all major Walmart suppliers that have long had their own global operations. By building international reach, Walmart has been able to use its enhanced size to demand deeper discounts from the local operations of its global suppliers, increasing the company's ability to lower prices to consumers, gain market share, and ultimately earn greater profits. Second, Walmart has found that it is benefiting from the flow of ideas across the countries in which it now competes. For example, Walmart's Argentina team worked with Walmart's Mexican management to replicate a Mexico's Walmart store format and to adopt their best practices in human resources and real estate.. Other ideas, such as wine departments in its stores in Argentina, have now been integrated into layouts worldwide.

Moreover, Walmart realized that if it didn't expand internationally, other global retailers would beat it to the punch. In fact, Walmart faces significant global competition from Carrefour of France, Ahold of Holland, and Tesco from the United Kingdom. Carrefour is perhaps the most global of the lot. The pioneer of the hypermarket concept now operates in 26 countries and generates more than 50% of its sales outside France. Compared to this, Walmart is a laggard with just 18% of its sales in 2021 generated from international operations.

For all its success, Walmart has hit significant problems in its drive for global expansion. The overall profit rate of its international business is lower than its U.S. business. In 2006, the company pulled out of two markets, South Korea—where it failed to decode the shopping habits of local customers—and Germany, where it could not beat incumbent discount stores on price. In 2016, Walmart closed 115 underperforming stores in Brazil and several other Latin American countries in response to depressed local economic conditions. It also struggled in Japan, where the company did not seem to be able to grasp the market's cultural nuances. In one example, Walmart decided to sell lower-priced gift fruits at Japanese holidays, which failed because customers felt spending less would insult the recipient! In 2020, Walmart admitted defeat and sold its majority stake in Walmart Japan to its joint venture partner, Seiyu. Walmart also exited the United Kingdom in 2020, after 21 years, selling its ASDA grocery stores to a group of private equity investors for $8.8 billion. The British grocery market turned out to be fiercely competitive, and Walmart struggled against two well-run local retailers, Tesco and Sainsbury's. When a proposed merger with Sainsbury was blocked by local competition authorities, Walmart decided to exit the market entirely. As a result of these various moves, Walmart's international sales fell from a peak of $137 billion in 2013 to $101 billion by 2021.

The markets where Walmart has struggled most were all developed markets that it entered through acquisitions, where it faced long-established and efficient local competitors, and where shopping habits were very different than in the United States (Germany, South Korea, and the United Kingdom, for example). In contrast, many of those markets where it has done better have been developing nations that lacked strong local competitors, and where Walmart has built operations from the ground up (e.g., Mexico, Brazil, and, increasingly, China).

C6-7 Looking Forward: The E-Commerce Revolution

Walmart's biggest challenge going forward may be holding off competition from e-commerce retailers, and particularly Amazon.com. Walmart first established an online presence back in 2000 when it created Walmart.com. This subsidiary is headquartered not in Bentonville, but near San Francisco where the company has access to the world's deepest pool of Internet executive and technical talent. For years, Walmart.com lagged the sales growth achieved by Amazon. In 2021, Walmart generated nearly $55 billion in e-commerce sales, representing about 13% of its total sales. Amazon, in contrast, registered $468 billion in e-commerce sales in 2021.

In 2016, Walmart shifted its e-commerce strategy, buying the fast-growing e-commerce retailer, Jet.com, for $3.3 billion. Jet.com went online in mid-2015, and by 2016, was already on track for $500 million in revenue. With the acquisition, Walmart gained access to Marc Lore, the founder of Jet.com, considered by many to be one of the sharpest minds in e-commerce. Lore stated that under his direction, Walmart would move "at the speed of a startup." In January 2017 Lore announced that Walmart.com would offer free 2-day delivery on orders over $35, putting Walmart on a par with Amazon. Walmart's online inventory also grew rapidly from just 10 million items in 2016 to at least 67 million in late 2017. The expansion was helped by several other acquisitions of fashion and apparel e-commerce retailers, including Bonobos and ModCloth in apparel and Moosejaw in outdoor goods. These brands give Walmart the opportunity to sell upscale brands to online consumers who wouldn't normally shop at Walmart.[21] In May of 2020, however, Walmart decided to shut down the Jet.com banner in favor of a continued focus on Walmart.com, which management decided was the more powerful brand. Marc Lore would run Walmart.com.

Since 2016, Walmart has made concerted efforts to better leverage its brick-and-mortar stores and distribution systems. By the fall of 2017, it had expanded its grocery pickup service to more than 1,000 stores and launched a service offering discounts on items ordered online that are picked up at the stores. The company also installed pick-up towers in some stores to make in-store pickups easier. The company also added products to its website and expanded its third-party marketplace, increasing the number of products offered through Walmart.com from 10 million in 2017 to 240 million by 2022.

The early results of this strategic shift were dramatic, with online revenues surging by more than 60% in the first year after the Jet.com acquisition. However, Amazon.com did not stand still. In June 2017, Amazon acquired Whole Foods for $13.7 billion, a deal that catapulted Amazon into hundreds of physical stores and fulfilled a long-held goal of selling more groceries. With the Whole Foods acquisition, Amazon got a network of physical stores where it can implement decades worth of experience in how people pick, pay for, and get groceries delivered. Amazon was quick to signal its own commitment to price discounting, cutting prices of select items at Whole Foods by 40% immediately after the acquisition closed in August of 2017. As of 2022, however, Walmart was outperforming Amazon in the online grocery market by a wide margin. By mid-2022 Walmart's U.S. online grocery market share, which included pickup and delivery services, rose to 55%. Amazon's share stood at 7%, while the online grocery delivery platform Instacart had a 27% share. Walmart has been gaining share in this segment from its rivals. The company also noted that three quarters of its gains in online grocery market share were coming from higher-income shoppers with incomes over $100,000.[22]

Additional References

- R. Abrams, "Walmart, with Amazon in Its Cross Hairs, Posts E-Commerce Gains," *New York Times*, May 18, 2017.
- C. Fishman, *The Wal-Mart Effect* (Penguin Books, 2006, 2011).
- L. dePhillis, "This Walmart Worker Went from Temp to Store Manager," *Washington Post*, January 31, 2014.

- M. Malone, "Did Wal-Mart Love RFID to Death?," *ZDNet*, February 14, 2012.
- S. Nassauer and S. Terlep, "Wal-Mart and P&G: A $10 Billion Marriage under Strain," *Wall Street Journal*, June 14, 2016.
- S. Walton, *Made in America* (Bantam Books, 1993).
- Staff Reporter, "A Long Way from Bentonville," *The Economist*, September 20, 2006, pp. 38–39.

Notes

[1]R. Redman, "Amazon to Hurdle Walmart as Biggest U.S. Retailer by 2024," *Supermarket News*, July 2, 2022.

[2]S. Walton, *Made in America* (Bantam Books, 1993), p. 55.

[3]S. Walton, *Made in America* (Bantam Books, 1993), p. 59.

[4]S. Walton, *Made in America* (Bantam Books, 1993), pp. 152–153.

[5]Sam Walton, *Made in America* (Bantam Books, 1993), p. 141.

[6]Data from https://www. stock-analysis-on.net/NYSE/ Company/Wal-Mart-Stores-Inc/ Ratios/Short-term-Operating -Activity

[7]Data from S. Nassauer and S. Terlep, "Wal-Mart and P&G: A $10 Billion Marriage under Strain," *Wall Street Journal*, June 14, 2016.

[8]C. Fishman, *The Wal-Mart Effect* (Penguin Books, 2006), p. 68.

[9]C. Fishman, *The Wal-Mart Effect* (Penguin Books, 2006), p. 89.

[10]A. Norman, "Sex Discrimination at Wal-Mart: The 'Bitches' Story That Won't Go Away," *Huffington Post*, July 20, 2016.

[11]S. Greenhouse, "Workers Assail Night Lock-ins by Wal-Mart," *New York Times*, January 18, 2004.

[12]S. J. Goetz and H. Swaminathan, "Wal-Mart and County Wide Poverty," *Social Science Quarterly*, 87:2 (2006), 211–226.

[13]G. M. Artz and K.E.Stone, "Revisiting Wal-Mart's Impact on Iowa Small Town Retail," *Economic Development Quarterly*, October 4, 2012, pp. 298–310.

[14]E. Basker, "The Causes and Consequences of Wal-Mart's Growth," *Journal of Economic Perspectives*, 21:3 (2007), 177–198.

[15]H. Peterson, "The Grocery Wars Are Intensifying with Walmart and Kroger in the Lead," *Business Insider*, January 30, 2020.

[16]H. Peterson, "Walmart Is Crushing Kroger and Making Food History," *Business Insider*, April 20, 2017.

[17]H. Haddon and S. Nassauer, "Wal-Mart Brings Price War to Groceries, Boosting Pressure on Big Food Retailers," *Wall Street Journal*, April 20, 2017.

[18]C. Fishman, *The Wal-Mart Effect* (Penguin Books, 2006).

[19]Trefis Team, "How Wal-Mart Is Revamping Sam's Club to Take on Competition?," *Forbes*, March 1, 2016.

[20]Dumas, "Costco Killing It in Market Against Rivals," *Fox Business,* September 14, 2021.

[21]R. Abrams, "Walmart, with Amazon in Its Cross Hairs, Posts E-Commerce Gains," *New York Times*, May 18, 2017.

[22]S. Cavale, "Walmart.com Drew Higher Income Shoppers Looking to Buy Food," *Reuters*, August 17, 2022.

IKEA in 2022: Furniture Retailer to the World

By Charles W. L. Hill School of Business University of Washington Seattle, WA 98105

C7-1 Introduction

IKEA is one of the world's most successful global retailers. By 2022, IKEA had 420 home furnishing superstores stores in 50 countries, 225,000 employees and revenues of €42 billion, up from €4.4 billion in 1994. The founder, Ingvar Kamprad, died in early 2018 at the ripe old age of 91. At the time, he was one of the world's richest people with a net worth of $58.7 billion.

C7-2 Company Background

IKEA was established by Ingvar Kamprad in Sweden in 1943 when he was 17 years old. The fledgling company sold fish, Christmas magazines, and seeds from his family farm. It wasn't his first business—that had been selling matches which the enterprising Kamprad had purchased wholesale in 100 box lots (with help from his grandmother who financed the enterprise) and then resold individually at a higher mark-up. The name IKEA was an acronym, I and K being his initials, while E stood for Elmtaryd, the name of the family farm, and A stood for Agunnaryd, the name of the village in Southern Sweden where the farm was located. Before long Kamprad had added ball-point pens to his list and was selling his products via mail order. His warehouse was a shed on the family farm. The customer fulfillment system utilized the local milk truck, which picked up goods daily and took them to the train station.

In 1948, Kamprad added furniture to his product line and in 1949 he published his first catalog, distributed then as now, for free. In 1953, Kamprad found himself struggling with another problem, the milk truck had changed its route and he could no longer use it to take goods to the train station. Kamprad's solution was to buy an idle factory in nearby Almhult and convert it into his warehouse. With business now growing rapidly, Kamprad hired a 22-year-old designer, Gillis Lundgren. Lundgren originally helped Kamprad to do photo shoots for the early IKEA catalogs, but over time he started to design more and more furniture for IKEA, eventually designing as many as 400 pieces, including many best sellers.

IKEA's goal as it emerged over time was to provide stylish functional designs with minimalist lines that could be manufactured cost efficiently under contract by suppliers and priced low enough to allow most people to afford them. Kamprad's theory was that "good furniture could be priced so that the man with that flat wallet would make a place for it in his spending and could afford it."[1] Kamprad was struck by the fact that furniture in Sweden was expensive at the time, something that he attributed to a fragmented industry dominated by small retailers. Furniture was also often considered a family heirloom, passed down across the generations. He wanted to change this: to make it possible for people of modest means to buy their own furniture. Ultimately, this led to the concept of what IKEA calls "democratic design"—a design that, according to Kamprad, "was not just good, but also from the start adapted to machine production and thus cheap to assemble."[2] Gillis Lundgren was instrumental in the implementation of this concept. Time and time again he would find ways to alter the design of furniture to save on manufacturing costs.

Gillis Lundgren also stumbled on what was to become a key feature of IKEA furniture: self-assembly. Trying to efficiently pack and ship a long-legged table, he hit upon the idea of taking the legs off and mailing them packed flat under the tabletop. Kamprad quickly noticed that flat packed furniture reduced transport and warehouse costs, and also reduced damage (IKEA had been having a lot of problems with furniture damaged during the shipping process). Moreover, customers seemed willing to take on the task of assembly in return for lower prices. By 1956, self-assembly was integral to the IKEA concept.

In 1957, IKEA started to exhibit and sell its products at home furnishing fairs in Sweden. By cutting retailers out of the equation and using the self-assembly concept, Kamprad could undercut the prices of established retail outlets, much to their chagrin. Established retailers responded by prohibiting IKEA from taking orders at the annual furniture trade exhibit/show in Stockholm. Established outlets claimed that IKEA was imitating their designs. This was to no avail however, so the retailers went further, pressuring furniture manufacturers not to sell to IKEA. This had two unintended consequences. First, without access to the designs of many manufacturers, IKEA was forced to design more of its products in house. Second, Kamprad looked for a manufacturer who would produce the IKEA designed furniture. Ultimately, he found one in Poland.

To his delight, Kamprad discovered that furniture manufactured in Poland was as much as 50% cheaper than furniture made in Sweden, allowing him to cut prices even further. Kamprad also found that doing business with the Poles required the consumption of considerable amounts of vodka to celebrate business transactions, and for the next 40 years his drinking was legendary. Alcohol consumption apart, the relationship that IKEA established with the Poles was to become the archetype for future relationships with suppliers. According to one of the Polish managers, there were three advantages of doing business with IKEA: "One concerned the decision making; it was always one man's decision, and you could rely upon what had been decided. We were given long-term contracts, and were able to plan in peace and quiet....A third advantage was that IKEA introduced new technology. One revolution for instance, was a way of treating the surface of wood. They also mastered the ability to recognize cost savings that could trim the price."[3] By the early 1960s, Polish made goods were to be found on over half of the pages of the IKEA catalog.

By 1958, an expanded facility at the Almhult location became the first IKEA store. The original idea behind the store was to have a location where customers could come and see IKEA furniture set up. It was a supplement to IKEA's main mail-order business; but it very quickly became an important sales point in its own right. The store soon started to sell car roof racks so that customers could leave with flat-packed furniture loaded on top. Noticing that a trip to an IKEA store was something of an outing for many shoppers (Almhult was not a major population center, and people often drove in from long distances), Kamprad experimented with adding a restaurant to the Almhult store so that customers could relax and refresh themselves while shopping. The restaurant was a hit and it became an integral feature of all IKEA stores.

The response of IKEA's competitors to its success was to argue that IKEA products were of low quality. In 1964, just after 800,000 IKEA catalogs had been mailed to Swedish homes, the widely read Swedish magazine *Allt i Hemmet* (*Everything for the Home*) published a comparison of IKEA furniture to that sold in traditional Swedish retailers. The furniture was tested for quality in a Swedish design laboratory. The magazine's analysis, detailed in a 16-page spread, was that not only was IKEA's quality as good if not better than that from other Swedish furniture manufacturers, the prices were much lower. For example, the magazine concluded that a chair bought at IKEA for 33 kroner ($4) was better than a virtually identical one bought in a more expensive store for 168 kroner ($21). The magazine also showed how a living room furnished with IKEA products was as much as 65% less expensive than one furnished with equivalent products from four other stores. This publicity made IKEA acceptable in middle-class households, and sales began to take off.

In 1965, IKEA opened its first store in Stockholm, Sweden's capital. By now, IKEA was generating the equivalent of €25 million and had already opened a store in neighboring Norway. The Stockholm store, its third, was the largest furniture store in Europe and had an innovative circular design that was modeled on the famous Guggenhiem Art Museum in New York. The location of the store was to set the pattern at IKEA for decades. The store was situated on the outskirts of the city, rather than downtown, and there was ample space for parking and good access roads. The new store generated a large amount of traffic, so much so that employees could not keep up with customer orders, and long lines formed at the checkouts and merchandise pickup areas. To try and reduce the lines, IKEA experimented with a self-service pickup solution, allowing shoppers to enter the warehouse, load flat-packed furniture onto trolleys, and then take them through the checkout. It was so successful that this soon became the norm in all stores.

C7-3 International Expansion

By 1973, IKEA was the largest furniture retailer in Scandinavia with nine stores. The company enjoyed a market share of 15% in Sweden. Kamprad, however, felt that growth opportunities were limited. Starting with a single store in Switzerland over the next 15 years the company expanded rapidly in Western Europe. IKEA was met with considerable success, particularly in West Germany where it had 15 stores by the late 1980s. As in Scandinavia, Western European furniture markets were largely fragmented and served by high-cost retailers located in expensive downtown stores and selling relatively expensive furniture that was not always immediately available for delivery. IKEA's elegant functional designs with their clean lines, low prices, and immediate availability were a breath of fresh air, as was the self-service store format. The company was met with almost universal success even though, as one former manager put it: "We made every mistake in the book, but money nevertheless poured in. We lived frugally, drinking now and again, yes perhaps too much, but we were on our feet bright and cheery when the doors were open for the first customers, competing in good Ikean spirit for the cheapest solutions."[4]

The man in charge of the European expansion was Jan Aulino, Kamprad's former assistant, who was just 34 years old when the expansion started. Aulino surrounded himself with a young team. Aulino recalled that the expansion was so fast paced that the stores were rarely ready when IKEA moved in. Moreover, it was hard to get capital out of Sweden due to capital controls, so the trick was to make a quick profit and get a positive cash flow going as soon as possible. In the haste to expand, Aulino and his team did not always pay attention to detail, and he reportedly clashed with Kamprad on several occasions and considered himself fired at least four times, although he never was. Eventually the European business was reorganized, and tighter controls were introduced.

IKEA was slow to expand in the United Kingdom where the locally grown company Habitat had built a business that was similar in many respects to IKEA, offering stylish furniture and at a relatively low price. IKEA also entered North America, opening up seven stores in Canada between 1976 and 1982. Emboldened by this success, in 1985 the company entered the United States. It proved to be a challenge of an entirely different nature.

On the face of it, America looked to be fertile territory for IKEA. As in Western Europe, furniture retailing was a very fragmented business in the United States. At the low end of the market were the general discount retailers, such as Walmart, Costco, and Office Depot, who sold a limited product line of basic furniture, often at a very low price. This furniture was very functional, lacked the design elegance associated with IKEA, and was generally of a fairly low quality. Then there were higher-end retailers, such as Ethan Allen, who offered high-quality, well-designed, and high-priced furniture. They sold this furniture in full-service stores staffed by knowledgeable sales people. High-end retailers would often sell ancillary services as well, such as interior design. Typically, these retailers would offer home delivery service, including setup in the home, either for free or for a small additional charge. Since it was expensive to keep large inventories of high-end furniture, much of what was on display in stores was not readily available, and the client would often have to wait a few weeks before it was delivered.

IKEA opened its first U.S. store in 1985 in Philadelphia. The company had decided to locate on the coasts. Surveys of American consumers suggested that IKEA buyers were more likely to be people who had traveled abroad, who considered themselves risk takers, and who liked fine food and wine. These people were concentrated on the coasts. As one manager put it, "There are more Buicks driven in the middle than on the coasts."[5]

Although IKEA initially garnered favorable reviews, and enough sales to persuade it to start opening additional stores, by the early 1990s it was clear that things were not going well in America. The company found that its European-style offerings didn't always resonate with American consumers. Beds were measured in centimeters, not the king, queen, and twin sizes with which Americans are familiar. American sheets didn't fit on IKEA beds. Sofas weren't big enough, wardrobe drawers were not deep enough, glasses were too small, curtains too short, and kitchens didn't fit U.S. size appliances. In a story often repeated at IKEA, managers noted that customers were buying glass vases and using them to drink out of, rather than the small glasses for sale at IKEA. The glasses were apparently too small for Americans who like to add liberal quantities of ice to their drinks. To make matters worse, IKEA was sourcing many of the goods from overseas and they were priced in Swedish Kroner, which was strengthening against the U.S. dollar. This drove up the price of goods in IKEA's American stores. Moreover, some of the stores were poorly located, and the stores were not large enough to offer the full IKEA experience familiar to Europeans.

Turning around its American operations required IKEA to take some decisive actions. Many products had to be redesigned to fit with American needs. Newer and larger store locations were chosen. To bring prices down, goods were sourced from lower cost locations and priced in dollars. IKEA also started to source some products from factories in the United States to reduce both transport costs and dependency on the value of the dollar. At the same time, IKEA was noticing a change in American culture. Americans were becoming more concerned with design, and more open to the idea of disposable furniture. It used to be said that Americans changed their spouses about as often as they changed their dining room table, about 1.5 times in a lifetime, but something was shifting in American culture. Younger people were more open to risks and more willing to experiment, and there was a thirst for design elegance and quality. Starbucks was tapping into this, as was Apple Computer, and so did IKEA. According to one manager at IKEA, "ten or 15 years ago, travelling in the United States, you couldn't eat well. You couldn't get good coffee. Now you can get good bread in the supermarket, and people think that is normal. I like that very much. That is more important to good life than the availability of expensive wines. That is what IKEA is about."[6]

To tap into America's shifting culture, IKEA reemphasized design, and it started promoting itself with a series of quirky hip advertisements aimed at a younger demographic; young married couples, college students, and twenty- to thirty-something singles. One IKEA commercial, called "Unboring," made fun of the reluctance of Americans to part with their furniture. One famous ad featured a discarded lamp, forlorn and forsaken in some rainy American city. A man turns to the camera sympathetically. "Many of you feel bad for this lamp," he says in thick Swedish accent, "That is because you are crazy". Hip people, the commercial implied, bought furniture at IKEA. Hip people didn't hang onto their furniture either; after a while they discarded it, and replaced it with something else from IKEA.

The shift in tactics worked. IKEA's revenues doubled in a 4-year period to $1.27 billion in 2001, up from $600 million in 1997. By 2017, the United States was IKEA's largest market after Germany, with 48 stores accounting for 14% of the global total revenues.

Having learned vital lessons about competing in foreign countries outside of continental Western Europe, IKEA continued to expand internationally in the 1990s and 2000s. It entered the UK in 1987 and by 2018 had 18 stores in the country. IKEA also acquired Britain's Habitat in the early 1990s and continued to run it under the Habitat brand name. In 1998, IKEA entered China, where it had 24 stores by 2016, followed by Russia in 2000 (14 stores by 2012), and in 2006 Japan, a country where it had failed miserably 30 years earlier (by 2012 IKEA had 6 stores in Japan). In total, by 2017, there were 355 IKEA stores in 29 countries. The company's plans call for continued global expansion, opening 20–25 stores per year, funded by an investment of around €20 billion.

As with the United States, some local customization has been the order of the day. In China, for example, the store layout reflects the layout of many Chinese apartments, and since many Chinese apartments have balconies, IKEA's Chinese stores include a balcony section. IKEA also had to adapt its locations in China, where car ownership was not as widespread as in Europe or the United States. In the West, IKEA stores are generally located in suburban areas and have lots of parking space. In China, stores are located near public transportation, and IKEA offers delivery services so that Chinese customers can get their purchases home. IKEA also found that prices that were considered low in Europe and North America were higher than average in China. Local furniture makers had access to cheap labor and raw materials, and their design costs were usually nil since they simply copied the furniture designs of other companies, including IKEA. IKEA also had to deal with relatively high tariffs on furniture imported into China. To deal with these problems, IKEA built a number of factories in China and increased local sourcing of materials, raising local sourcing from 30% to 65%. These moves enabled IKEA to cut its prices on many items by up to 60%.

In something of a shift from its typical mass market approach, IKEA also worked hard in China to position itself as an aspirational Western brand for young middle-class Chinese. This demographic is benefiting from China's rapid economic development, has relatively high incomes, is better educated, and is more aware of Western styles and more open to IKEA's product.

The other decision IKEA had to make in China was how to respond to local competitors copying its designs, which occurred frequently. The company concluded that Chinese intellectual property laws were not yet strong enough to deter such activities, so it decided not to react with lawsuits. Instead, the company stepped up its marketing, using Chinese social media and the micro-blogging website Weibo to target the young, upwardly mobile middle class and build demand for the IKEA brand.[7] All of these moves seem to be bearing fruit. IKEA's sales in China have been growing at a robust pace. For fiscal 2017, IKEA reported a 14% increase in sales in China to $1.98 billion on the back of an 11% increase in store traffic. The company also announced plans to open another three Chinese stores.[8]

In 2018, IKEA entered India, where it planned to invest €1.5 billion and ultimately open 40 stores. With a population of 1.4 billion people, a rapidly growing economy, and a middle class approaching 350 million—100 million of whom enjoy living standards similar to those in the West—India was a market that was becoming just too big to ignore.[9] In late 2012, India's foreign investment board approved IKEA's plans to open stores in the country. However, the approval came with strings attached. The board denied IKEA to offer products in areas that the government thinks are politically sensitive, and where it wants to protect local retailers. These include food and beverage outlets, which are a standard feature of its stores around the world, and 18 of the 30 product categories it had initially applied for. Those 18 categories include gift items, fabrics, books, toys, and consumer electronics.[10] The government also required a significant amount of local sourcing. Adapting to these demands took time. After years of preparation, IKEA opened its first Indian store in Hyderabad in July 2018.[11] The company hopes to have 30 stores open in India by 2025.

As in other countries, in India IKEA had to adjust its offering to fit local tastes, conditions, and practices.[12] IKEA employees visited about 1,000 homes in various cities to understand how people lived and what they needed. The company then customized its offering to local conditions. For example, in the hot humid climate of Southern India, untreated pine furniture, which might work well in cooler climates, would swell and warp, so different materials had to be used. In addition, metal or wooden furniture made for India need small risers to lift it off the floor, since people frequently clean their tile floors with water. Indian women are also shorter on average than Europeans or Americans, so IKEA decided to offer cabinets and countertops at a lower height. Given Indian's lower income levels, IKEA also rejigged in store merchandise to feature hundreds of products—from dolls to spice jars—priced at less than 100 rupees, or $1.45. When visiting homes, IKEA employees noticed that Indian families spent a lot of time together, with relatives frequently popping in, so the company added more folding chairs and stools that could serve as flexible seating. Even the cafeteria caters to Indian tastes, with biryani, samosas, and vegetarian Swedish meatballs on the menu and 1,000 available seats, more than any other IKEA in the world, to accommodate the more leisurely dining style of Indian families.

Another problem that IKEA had to deal with in India were import tariffs that increased the cost of some standard IKEA furniture items such as chairs and cabinets by 30–50%. The Indian government also requires that foreign-owned single-brand retailers such as IKEA to source at least 30% of the value of the goods that they buy from local manufacturers. In its quest to keep prices low and comply with local regulations, IKEA has been expanding its network of suppliers in India.

One thing that IKEA has refused to adapt to, however, are business practices that clash with its values. The company prides itself on its "clean" image and is willing to halt investment in order to protect that. In the mid-2000s it put investment in Russia on hold as a protest against endemic corruption. It subsequently fired two senior executives in the country for allegedly turning a bribe to a subcontractor to secure electricity supply for its St. Petersburg outlets.[13]

Senior executives at IKEA have been known to complain that they could expand the business faster, were it not for administrative "red tape" in many countries that slows down the rate of expansion. According to the current CEO, Mikael Ohlsson, the amount of time it takes to open a store has roughly doubled to 5 or 6 years since the 1990s. Ohlsson singled out German local authorities as having planning restrictions designed to protect local city center shops that are detrimental to IKEA's expansion plans. Ohlsson argues that such regulations are holding back investment by IKEA, and thus job creation, across the European Union.[14]

C7-4 The IKEA Concept and Business Model

IKEA's target market is the young upwardly mobile global middle class who are looking for low-priced but attractively designed furniture and household items. This group is targeted with somewhat wacky offbeat advertisements that help to drive traffic into the stores. The stores themselves are large warehouses festooned in the blue and yellow colors of the Swedish flag that offer 8,000 to 10,000 items, from kitchen cabinets to candlesticks. There is plenty of parking outside, and the stores are located with good access to major roads.

The interior of the stores is configured almost as a maze that requires customers to pass through each department to get to the checkout. The goal is simple; to get customers to make more impulse purchases as they wander through the IKEA wonderland. Customers who enter the store planning to buy a $40 coffee table can end up spending $500 on everything from storage units to kitchenware. The flow of departments is constructed with an eye to boosting sales. For example, when IKEA managers noticed that men would get bored while their wives stopped in the home textile department, they added a tool section just outside the textile department, and sales of tools skyrocketed. At the end of the maze, just before the checkout, is the warehouse where customers can pick up their flat-packed furniture. IKEA stores also have restaurants (located in the middle of the store) and child-care facilities (located at the entrance for easy drop off) so that shoppers stay as long as possible.

Products are designed to reflect the clean Swedish lines that have become IKEA's trademark. IKEA has a product strategy council, which is a group of senior managers who establish priorities for IKEA's product lineup. Once a priority is established, product developers survey the competition, and then set a price point that is 30–50% below that of rivals. As IKEA's website states, "We design the price tag first, then the product." Once the price tag is set, designers work with a network of suppliers to drive down the cost of producing the unit. The goal is to identify the appropriate suppliers and least costly materials, a trial-and-error process that can take as long as 3 years. In 2008, IKEA had 1,380 suppliers in 54 countries. The top sourcing countries were China (21% of supplies), Poland (17%), Italy (8%), Sweden (6%), and Germany (6%). Some suppliers have been with IKEA for a long time and work closely with the company on cost and quality issues. IKEA is often their major customer.

IKEA devotes considerable attention to finding the right supplier for each item. Consider the company's best-selling Klippan love seat. Designed in 1980, the Klippan, with its clean lines, bright colors, simple legs, and compact size, had sold over 1.5 million units by 2010. IKEA originally manufactured the product in Sweden but soon transferred production to lower-cost suppliers in Poland. As demand for the Klippan grew, IKEA then decided that it made more sense to work with suppliers in each of the company's big markets to avoid the costs associated with shipping the product all over the world. In 2010, there were five suppliers of the frames in Europe, plus three in the United States and two in China. To reduce the cost of the cotton slipcovers, IKEA concentrated production in four core suppliers in China and Europe. The resulting efficiencies from these global sourcing decisions enabled IKEA to reduce the price of the Klippan by some 40% between 1999 and 2005.

Price declines over time such as those seen with the Klippan love seat are the norm at IKEA. The company's signature Poang chair, 1.5 million of which are sold every year, has gotten dramatically cheaper over time. In 1988, this chair cost $350 (in 2016 dollars). By 2016, the price had fallen to just $79. Other IKEA mainstays have followed a similar path. The venerable Lack table sold for $56 in 1985 (in 2016 dollars) but goes for just $10 today. The Billy bookcase costs 30% less in real terms than it did when introduced in 1978. In general, long-running products seem to drop in price by 1% per year, primarily due to constant tweaking of design, technological advances in production, and sheer economies of scale. Indeed, if IKEA can't figure out how to reduce prices over time, the product is often discontinued.[15]

For insight on how IKEA achieves this, consider the iconic Bang mug, some 25 million of which are sold every year. IKEA changed the height of the mug when it realized is could make slightly better use of the space in its supplier's kiln in Romania. Tweaking the handle design made them stack more compactly, doubling the number that could be placed on a pallet, which halved the cost of getting them from the kiln in Romania to shelves in the shop. Initially IKEA asked its Romanian supplier to price up to a million units in the first year. Then it asked, "What if we commit to 5 million a year for 3 years?" That cut costs by another 10%. Then there is the Billy bookcase. The factory in Sweden that produces this bookcase makes 37 times as many bookcases per year as it did in the 1980s, yet the number of employees has only doubled thanks to automation. The factory employees never actually touch a bookshelf—their job is to tend the machines, imported from Germany and Japan, which work constantly to cut, glue, drill, and pack the various components of the Billy bookcase. There are now 60 million Billy bookcases in the world, nearly 1 for every 100 people. Along the way IKEA and its supplier have clearly learned a lot about how to produce the bookcase more efficiently.[16]

Although IKEA contracts out manufacturing for most of its products, since the early 1990s, a certain proportion of goods have been made internally (today around 90% of all products are sourced from independent suppliers, with 10% being produced internally). The integration into manufacturing was born out of the collapse of communist governments in Eastern Europe after the fall of the Berlin Wall in 1989. By 1991, IKEA was sourcing some 25% of its goods from Eastern European manufacturers. It had invested considerable energy in building long-term relationships with these suppliers and had often helped them to develop and purchase new technology so that they could make IKEA products at a lower cost. As communism collapsed and new bosses came into the factories, many did not feel bound by the relationships with IKEA. They effectively tore up contracts, tried to raise prices, and under invested in new technology.

With its supply base at risk, IKEA purchased a Swedish manufacturer, Swedwood. IKEA then used Swedwood as the vehicle to buy and run furniture manufacturers across Eastern Europe, with the largest investments being made in Poland. IKEA invested heavily in its Swedwood plants, equipping them with the most modern technology. Beyond the obvious benefits given to IKEA of a low-cost source of supply, Swedwood has also enabled IKEA to acquire knowledge about manufacturing processes that are useful both in product design and in relationships with other suppliers, giving IKEA the ability to help suppliers adopt new technology and drive down their costs.

For illustration, consider IKEA's relationship with suppliers in Vietnam. IKEA has expanded its supply base here to help support its growing Asian presence. IKEA was attracted to Vietnam by the combination of low-cost labor and inexpensive raw materials. IKEA drives a tough bargain with its suppliers, many of whom say that they make thinner margins on their sales to IKEA than they do to other foreign buyers. IKEA demands high quality at a low price. But there is an upside; IKEA offers the prospect of forging a long-term, high-volume business relationship. Moreover, IKEA regularly advises its Vietnamese suppliers on how to seek out the best and cheapest raw materials, how to set up and expand factories, what equipment to purchase, and how to boost productivity through technology investments and management process.

For all its efficiency, the COVID-19 pandemic exposed some limitations in IKEA's global network of suppliers. In 2021, IKEA stated that a significant number of its products were missing from shelves around the world due to supply chain problems. These included a lack of manufacturing capacity due to lockdowns, shortages of raw materials, and a shortage of transportation. In the United Kingdom, for example, a shortage of truck drivers meant that at one point in 2021 about 10% of the normal in-store product offering was not available.[17]

C7-5 Organization and Management

In many ways IKEA's organization and management practices reflect the personal philosophy of its founder. A 2004 article in *Fortune* described Kamprad, then one of the world's richest men, as an informal and frugal man who "insists on flying coach, takes the subway to work, drives a ten-year-old Volvo, and avoids suits of any kind. It has long been rumored in Sweden that when his self-discipline fails, and he drinks an overpriced Coke out of a hotel mini bar, he will go down to a grocery store to buy a replacement."[18] Kamprad's thriftiness was attributed to his upbringing in Smaland, a traditionally poor region of Sweden. Kamprad's frugality is now part of IKEA's DNA. Managers are forbidden to fly first class and expected to share hotel rooms.

Under Kamprad, IKEA became mission driven. He had a cause, and those who worked with him adopted it too. It was to make life better for the masses, to democratize furniture. Kamprad's management style was informal, non-hierarchical, and team based. Titles and privileges are taboo at IKEA. There are no special perks for senior managers. Pay is not particularly high, and people generally work there because they like the atmosphere. Suits and ties have always been absent, from the head office to the loading docks. The culture is egalitarian. Offices are open plan, furnished with IKEA furniture, and private offices are rare. Everyone is called a "co-worker," and first names are used throughout. IKEA regularly stages anti-bureaucracy weeks during which executives work on the store floor or tend the registers. In a *Business Week* article, then CEO Andres Dahlvig, described how he spent time earlier in the year unloading trucks and selling beds and mattresses.[19] Creativity is highly valued, and the company is replete with stories of individuals taking the initiative; from Gillis Lundgren's pioneering of the self-assemble concept to the store manager in the Stockhom store who lets customers go into the warehouse to pick up their own furniture. To solidify this culture, IKEA had a preference for hiring younger people who had not worked for other enterprises, and then promoting from within. IKEA has historically tended to shy away from hiring the highly educated status-oriented elite because they often adapted poorly to the company.

Kamprad seems to have viewed his team as extended family. Back in 1957, he bankrolled a weeklong trip to Spain for all 80 employees and their families as a reward for hard work. The early team of employees all lived near each other. They worked together, played together, drank together, and talked about IKEA around the clock. When asked by an academic researcher what was the fundamental key to good leadership, Kamprad replied "love." Recollecting the early days, he noted that "when we were working as a small family in Aluhult, we were as if in love. Nothing whatsoever to do with eroticism. We just liked each other so damn much."[20] Another manager noted that "we who wanted to join IKEA did so because the company suits our way of life. To escape thinking about status, grandeur and smart clothes."[21]

As IKEA grew, the question of taking the company public arose. While there were obvious advantages associated with doing so, including access to capital, Kamprad decided against it. His belief was that the stock market would impose short-term pressures on IKEA that would not be good for the company. The constant demands to produce profits, regardless of the business cycle, would in Kamprad's view, make it more difficult for IKEA to take bold decisions. At the same time, as early as 1970, Kamprad started to worry about what would happen if he died. He decided that he did not want his sons to inherit the business. His worry was that they would either sell the company, or they might squabble over control of the company, and thus destroy it. All three of his sons, it should be noted, went to work at IKEA as managers.

The solution to this dilemma created one of the most unusual corporate structures in the world. In 1982, Kamprad transferred his interest in IKEA to a Dutch-based charitable foundation, Stichting Ingka Foundation. This is a tax-exempt, non-profit making legal entity that in turn owns Ingka Holding, a private Dutch firm that is the legal owner of IKEA. A five-person committee chaired by Kamprad that included his wife, runs the foundation. In addition, the IKEA trademark and concept was transferred to IKEA Systems, another private Dutch company, whose parent company, Inter-IKEA, is based in Luxembourg. The Luxembourg company is in turn owned by an identically named company in the Netherlands Antilles, whose beneficial owners remain hidden from public view, but they are almost certainly the Kamprad family. Inter-IKEA earns its money from a franchise agreement it has with each IKEA store. The largest franchisee is none other than Ingka Holdings. IKEA states that franchisees pay 3% of sales to Inter-IKEA. Thus, Kamprad has effectively moved ownership of IKEA out of Sweden, although the company's identity and headquarters remains there, and established a mechanism for transferring funds to himself and his family from the franchising of the IKEA concept. Kamprad himself moved to Switzerland in the 1980s to escape Sweden's high taxes. He lived there until his death in 2018.

In 1986, Kamprad gave up day-to-day control of IKEA to Andres Moberg, a 36-year-old Swede who had dropped out of college to join IKEA's mail-order department. Despite relinquishing management control, Kamprad continued to exert influence over the company as an advisor to senior management and an ambassador for IKEA, a role he was still pursuing with vigor well into his 80s.

C7-6 Looking Forward

IKEA had established an enviable position for itself. It had become one of the most successful retail establishments in the world. It had expanded into numerous foreign markets, learning from its failures and building on its successes. It had bought affordable, well-designed, functional furniture to the masses, helping them to, in Kamprad's words, achieve a better everyday life. IKEA's goal is to continue to grow opening 10–15 new stores a year. Achieving that growth would mean continued expansion into non-Western markets, including most notably China and India. Could the company continue to do so? Was its competitive advantage secure?

Additional Sources

1. Anonymous, "Furnishing the World," *The Economist*, November 19, 1995, pp. 79–80.
2. Anonymous. "Flat Pack Accounting," *The Economist*, May 13, 2006, pp. 69–70.
3. K. Capell, A. Sains, C. Lindblad, and A.T. Palmer, "IKEA," *Business Week*, November 14, 2005, pp. 96–101.
4. K. Capell, et al., "What a Sweetheart of a Love Seat," *Business Week*, November 14, 2005, p. 101.

5. C. Daniels, "Create IKEA, Make Billions, Take Bus," *Fortune*, May 3, 2004, p. 44.
6. J. Flynn and L. Bongiorno, "IKEA's New Game Plan," *BusinessWeek*, October 6, 1997, pp. 99–102.
7. R. Heller, "Folk Fortune," *Forbes*, September 4, 2000, p. 67.
8. IKEA Documents at www.ikea.com
9. J. Leland, "How the Disposable Sofa Conquered America," *New York Times Magazine*, October 5, 2005, pp. 4–50.
10. P. M. Miller, "IKEA with Chinese Characteristics," *Chinese Business Review*, July–August 2004, pp 36–69.
11. B. Torekull, *Leading by Design: The IKEA Story* (New York: Harper Collins, 1998).
12. Anonymous, "The Secret of IKEA's Success," *The Economist*, February 24, 2011.

Notes

[1] Quoted in R. Heller, "Folk Fortune," *Forbes*, September 4, 2000, p. 67.

[2] B. Torekull, *Leading by Design: The IKEA Story* (New York: Harper Collins, 1998), p. 53.

[3] B. Torekull, *Leading by Design: The IKEA Story* (New York: Harper Collins, 1998), pp. 61–62.

[4] B. Torekull, *Leading by Design: The IKEA Story* (New York: Harper Collins, 1998), p. 109.

[5] J. Leland, "How the Disposable Sofa Conquered America," *New York Times Magazine*, October 5, 2005, p. 45.

[6] J. Leland, "How the Disposable Sofa Conquered America," *New York Times Magazine*, October 5, 2005, p. 45.

[7] V. Chu, A. Girdhar, and R. Sood, "Couching Tiger Tames the Dragon," *Business Today*, July 21, 2013.

[8] W. Zhuoqiong, "Buoyant IKEA Gears up for More Store Expansion in China," *China Daily*, July 18, 2017.

[9] R. Kochhar, "In the Pandemic, India's Middle Class Shrinks," *Pew Research Center*, March 18, 2021.

[10] M. Kaushik, "Conditions Apply," *Business Today*, December 23, 2010.

[11] Anonymous, "IKEA to Open its First India Store in Hyderabad on July 19th," *Livemint*, July 8, 2018.

[12] V. Goel, "IKEA Opens First Indian Store, Tweaking Products but Not the Vibe," *New York Times*, August 7, 2018.

[13] Anonymous, "The Secret of IKEA's Success," *The Economist*, February 24, 2011.

[14] R. Milne, "Red Tape Frustrates IKEA's Plans for Growth," *Financial Times*, January 25, 2013.

[15] O. Roeder, "The Weird Economics of IKEA," *Five Thirty-Eight*, October 21, 2016.

[16] T. Harford, "How IKEA's Billy Bookcase Took Over the World," *BBC News*, February 27, 2017.

[17] T. Moss, "IKEA Struggles to Stock Shelves Amid Supply Chain Woes," *Wall Street Journal*, October 14, 2021.

[18] C. Daniels and A. Edstrom, "Create IKEA, Make Billions, Take a Bus," *Fortune*, May 3, 2006, p. 44.

[19] K. Capell, et al., "Ikea," *BusinessWeek*, November 14, 2005, pp. 96–106.

[20] B. Torekull, *Leading by Design: The IKEA Story* (New York: Harper Collins, 1998), p. 82.

[21] B. Torekull, *Leading by Design: The IKEA Story* (New York: Harper Collins, 1998), p. 83.

Coca-Cola

By Charles W. L. Hill Foster School of Business University of Washington Seattle, 98105 August 2022

C8-1 Introduction

On May 1, 2017, James Quincey became CEO of The Coca-Cola Company (Coca-Cola). The 52-year-old British businessman had worked at Coca-Cola since 1996. He had held leadership positions in Coke's operations in Latin America and Europe before being made COO in 2015. He lost no time in signaling that he would push for a major shift in Coca-Cola's strategy. He stated that the 130-year-old company must speed up the development of products beyond soda to become a "total beverage company," and that the company "needs to be bigger than the core brand." To do that he has said, the company must not be afraid to make mistakes.[1]

Quincey became CEO at a challenging time for Coca-Cola. Consumption of carbonated soft drinks (CSD), which still accounted for 70% of Coca-Cola's business, had been declining. In 2000, Americans drank 53 gallons of CSDs per capita, up from 23 gallons per capita in 1970. By 2016 consumption had fallen back to 38.5 gallons per capita.[2] Similar declines were occurring elsewhere in the world. Sales of Coca-Cola's core Coke mega brand (which included Coke and all its variants) had fallen by 5% over the last three years in the United States and 1% worldwide. Overall, CSDs accounted for about 24% of all non-alcoholic beverage consumption in the United States in 2017, down from around 37% in 2000. Sugary drinks were being attacked as a major source of obesity. In a possible harbinger of things to come, several national and local governments had placed "sin taxes" on sugary drinks in an effort to reduce their consumption. Coca-Cola's core brands were also being pressured by its perennial rival, Pepsi-Cola, and by numerous boutique beverage companies who had found it easier to bring new niche products to market. Some of these newer brands were using stevia, a natural plant-based zero-calorie sweetener, as an alternative to the synthetic sweetener aspartame that is widely used in diet CSD. The growth of such alternatives may have played a role in a sharp decline in consumption of diet CSD, such as Diet Coke, which has seen its U.S. sales volume fall every year since 2006. Paralleling the fall in CSD consumption, in the United States consumption of bottled water has grown dramatically from 13.2 gallons per capita in 2000 to 39.3 gallons per capita in 2016 when for the first time, Americans consumed more bottled water than CSDs.

Complicating matters, Coca-Cola was in the midst of a major reorganization of its bottling network. In 2010, Coca-Cola bought North American bottling operations from its minority owned bottler, Coca-Cola Enterprises. It did the same with hundreds of bottlers around the world. Now it was refranchising those bottling plants under terms aimed at making the asset heavy bottling and distribution operations more efficient, while freeing Coca-Cola to focus on marketing and product development.[3]

One of Quincey's first actions as CEO was to announce the company would eliminate 1,200 jobs at its headquarters in Atlanta, reducing the number of corporate positions by 20%. The cuts were part of a plan to save $800 million by 2019. Quincey's objective was to use about half of those cost savings to increase investments in new products and marketing. His goal was to raise Coca-Cola's revenue and profit growth to 4–6% per year. That was a challenging target—Coke's net profits had peaked at $12 billion in 2010 and had steadily fallen to $6.5 billion by 2016.

C8-2 An Overview of Coca-Cola's Business[4]

Coca-Cola is the world's largest beverage company with annual sales of $39 billion in 2021. Coca-Cola owns, or licenses, more than 500 non-alcoholic beverages grouped into five "category clusters": (1) sparkling (carbonated) soft drinks; (2) water, enhanced water, and sports drinks; (3) juice, dairy, and plant-based beverages; (4) tea and coffee; and (5) energy drinks. Coca-Cola's sparkling soft drinks (CSDs) account for 69% of volume. Coca-Cola owns four of the five top selling CSDs in the world: Coca-Cola, Diet Coke, Fanta, and Sprite. Estimates suggest that Coca-Cola and its archrival Pepsi-Cola. account for about 70% of global sales of carbonated beverages. In recent years, the non-carbonated segments have been growing, accounting for 31% of volume in 2021, up from 20% in 2010. The company is a global enterprise, selling its products in over 200 countries around the world. The company claims that beverages bearing trademarks owned or licensed by Coca-Cola account for more than 2.1 billion of the roughly 60 billion servings of all beverages consumed around the world every day. The company's trademark Coca-Cola brands accounted for 47% of its worldwide unit case volume in 2021.

Coca-Cola manufactures syrup concentrates which are then sold to the company's network of more than 250 licensed bottlers worldwide. Concentrates are flavoring ingredients and, depending on the product, sweeteners. Coca-Cola maintains ownership of the brands and formula and is responsible for national consumer brand marketing. The bottlers manufacture, package, sell, and distribute the branded beverages to retailers and vending machine partners, who then sell the products to end consumers. Bottlers are also responsible for marketing and promotions within their territory.

Concentrate manufacturing involves relatively little capital. According to some estimates, a concentrate plant of sufficient scale to serve the entire United States probably costs on the order of $100 million to construct. In 2021, Coca-Cola had 32 concentrate plants around the world, 11 of which were in North America. In the concentrate part of its business Coca-Cola enjoys gross margins of around 60%, with most of its remaining costs being in the form of product development and marketing.

Historically Coca-Cola has relied on a network of independent bottling franchises to manufacture and distribute its products, a system that the company believes served it well. The cost of an efficient scale modern plant with multiple bottling lines and warehousing can reportedly reach $250 million.[5] As of 2010, Coca-Cola and Pepsi-ColaCo. each had about 100 company=owned and partner bottling plants in the United States. While Coca-Cola long relied upon independent bottlers to manufacture and distribute its product, in the early 1980s, Coca-Cola started to purchase bottlers. It spun them off in 1986 into a minority-owned subsidiary, Coca-Colas Enterprises, but started to acquire them again in 2010, only to reduce its exposure to the bottling business once more after 2015. In 2015, Coca-Cola had 63 company-owned bottling plants in North America. By 2021, this number had been reduced to just seven, while another four plants were leased.

In 2015, 63% of Coca-Cola's net operating revenues came from finished product operations (i.e., selling bottled drinks) and 37% from concentrate operations. In 2021, as a result of bottler spinoffs, 44% came from finished product operations and 56% from concentrate operations. The reduction in ownership of bottling had reduced the amount of physical assets on Coca-Cola's balance sheet. As of December 31, 2021, the carrying value of Coca-Cola's property, plant and equipment, net of depreciation, was $9.92 billion, or 10.5% of total assets, down from $12.6 billion, or 14% of total assets as of December 31, 2015.

Although Coca-Cola relies upon bottlers for much of its distribution, in the United States it has long reserved the right to sell its concentrate directly to owners of soda fountains, which includes restaurants, sports arenas, and convenience stores. Outside the United States, bottlers are typically authorized to sell to fountain owners and fountain wholesalers.

C8-3 The Early History of Coca-Cola[6]

Coca-Cola was invented by an Atlanta pharmacist, John Pemberton, in 1886. Pemberton, who had been wounded in the American Civil War and subsequently became addicted to morphine, was seeking a cure for his addiction. The product he concocted contained two main ingredients, coca (the basis for cocaine, which remained an ingredient of Coca-Cola until 1904) and kola, a tropical nut with a high concentration of caffeine, hence the name Coca-Cola. Pemberton produced a concentrate syrup, which he sold to drug stores with soda fountains, who added carbonated water and sold the refreshing drink as a medicinal tonic. Pemberton claimed that the drink was a valuable brain tonic and a cure for all manner of nervous affections. It was particularly valued as a hangover cure. In making these claims, Pemberton was hardly unique. All sorts of tonic drinks were being sold out of drug stores at that time. Pemberton applied for, and was granted, a trademark patent for Coca-Cola in 1887. In 1888, an ailing Pemberton sold the rights to Coca-Cola to one of his business partners, Asa Candler. Pemberton died shortly afterwards. Candler went on to transform Coca-Cola into a national drink.

Candler formally incorporated The Coca-Cola Company in 1892. Rather than sell his drink directly to consumers, Candler continued to sell the concentrate to distributors and fountain owners. Like Pemberton before him, he kept the formula of the concentrate secret to limit imitation, a tactic that the company still adheres to. The concentrate was priced low, giving distributors a healthy profit margin. In 1895, Frank Robinson, who had worked first for Pemberton and then Candler, said to Candler that by focusing on the medicinal uses of Coca-Cola the company was limiting its market. After all, he argued, not everyone got sick, but everyone got thirsty. It was Robinson who had coined the name Coca-Cola. Robinson was also responsible for writing the Coca-Cola name in its recognizable Spencerian Script that became the classic logo. After consulting with Candler, Robinson, who was now in charge of Coke's advertising, made a brilliant tactical move, he created simple ads that emphasized how refreshing Coca-Cola was. His goal was to advertise to the masses, rather than the few. It worked. Sales started to accelerate.

In 1899, two lawyers from Tennessee, Benjamin Thomas and Joseph Whitehead, came to see Candler with a proposition; they wanted to bottle Coca-Cola. Candler was skeptical; he thought the fountain business was where the money was. Moreover, bottling was an imperfect technology with a reputation for poor seals and spoiled product. However, the lawyers were persuasive. Wouldn't it be wonderful, one said, "if a fellow could put this stuff in a bottle and stop it up so the gas wouldn't get away, and he could drink it whenever he wanted?" They also pointed out that a company called Crown Cork and Seal had recently developed a crimpled crown bottle cap with a much tighter seal, solving the problem of spoiled product. Convinced by their arguments, Candler signed the 600-word contract the lawyers had prepared. It was a momentous decision.

Although the contract went through several iterations as Coca-Cola grew, the original bottling contract with the two Tennessee lawyers proved to be a template for bottler relations for the next 80 years. What in essence was a franchising contract, bound the bottlers to use only Coca-Cola syrup, banning any imitation colas. The contract excluded the soda fountain business, which would remain the preserve of The Coca-Cola Company. Bottlers were allowed to bottle non-cola carbonated beverages made by other companies, although there were few of those in evidence at the time the original contract was drafted. Each bottler was given an exclusive geographic territory. The contract specified that if the bottlers failed to supply the demand in the territory they embraced, the contract would be forfeit. The syrup concentrate was sold to the bottlers at a fixed price. There was no provision for modifying the price of the syrup should the cost of the ingredients increase. Nor was there any specified time limit to the contract. If the bottlers fulfilled their end of the deal, the contract was in effect permanent. For their part, the bottlers agreed to be responsible for advertising and promotion in their territory. The bottlers paid $1 for these rights and obligations. As Candler saw it, there was little risk in the contract. If the bottlers were successful, Coca-Cola would make a lot of money selling concentrate to them. If they were not, the company had no money at risk, the bottlers having put up the capital to build their plants.

By 1904, there were over 120 bottlers in almost every state of the Union. By 1919, there were 1,200 Coca-Cola bottling plants across America, putting almost every town within reach of a bottler. The number of franchisees peaked at 1,263 in 1928, gradually consolidating over the next 50 years to around 800. The distribution efficiency of the bottlers had been vastly increased by the development of the automobile. Coca-Cola trucks were becoming a familiar sight on America's rapidly expanding paved road network. The bottlers blanketed their territories with the Coca-Cola logo, placing advertising signs wherever they could. As one bottler noted, the bottling agreement put Coca-Cola into the hands of thousands of merchants in the suburbs and outlying districts of every city, in the stores of every country town and village, and in the homes of thousands of people where it had not been possible to put Coca-Cola. As a result, "an enormous field was opened up….and hundreds of thousands of people who had never before tasted or seen Coca-Cola were introduced to this product first in bottles." Along the way, the bottlers became the richest men in their communities.

As the bottling network expanded at a rapid clip, and Coca-Cola appeared everywhere, so did imitators. Soon there were a multitude of them, many with names that played off the Coca-Cola brand, such as Coca and Cola, Coca-Kola, Cola Coke, and Pepsi-Cola Cola. In 1905, Congress passed the Trademark Law. Coca-Cola registered under a clause giving legal status to any trademark that had been in continuous use since 1895. Encouraged by the trademark's secure status, Coca-Cola's top lawyer, Harold Hirsch, began to bring cases against the imitators. Hirsch sued any cola drink that dared to use a script logo, a diamond label like Coca-Cola, or red barrels. If the name was too similar, Hirsch objected. Hirsch opposed registration of many colas at the U.S. Patent Office, nipping them in the bud. It was Hirsch who pushed for the development of Coca-Cola's distinctive "Hobble skirt" bottle, a design that Coca-Cola patented, and he encouraged all bottlers to rapidly adopt the unique design.

By 1926, one reporter estimated that more than 7,000 copycat imitators had been buried under Hirsch's sustained legal assault. Hirsch was relentless. Adverse decisions were appealed all the way to the Supreme Court if necessary. Writing for the majority in one famous case, Supreme Court Justice Oliver Wendell Holmes noted that Coca-Cola "was a single thing coming from a single source, and well known to the community." Hirsch virtually created American trademark law, filing an average of one case per week. Despite his efforts, Hirsch couldn't shut down every rival. Among the handful of survivors was Pepsi-Cola Cola.

In 1919, Asa Candler had sold the Coca-Cola company to a group of investors. They took the company public the same year. In 1923, the son of one of those investors, Robert Woodruff, became president of Coca-Cola. Only 33 at the time, Woodruff would stay at the helm until 1954 and remained on the board of directors until 1984. It was Woodruff who articulated the vision that Coca-Cola should be "within arm's reach of desire." He identified the service station as a major new outlet and started an initiative that led to the development of Coca-Cola's distinctive red open-top coolers that were placed in service stations and stores all over the nation. Coke was also one of the early adopters of the vending machine. The first Coca-Cola vending machines started to appear in the 1930s, although they had to be attended by a clerk. Coin-operated versions started to arrive after World War II.

Woodruff was a stickler for product standardization. He wanted Coca-Cola to taste the same, and be packaged and advertised the same way, no matter where it was sold. In 1924, he formed a standardization committee to ensure that bottlers adopted the same packaging. The committee worked with bottlers and fountain outlets to make sure that the taste was consistent.

Under Woodruff's leadership, Coca-Cola's advertising evolved in the direction of lifestyle advertising. The company had long shown a flare for advertising. By 1912, the company was spending well over a million a year on advertising. Coca-Cola was already probably the single best advertised product in the United States. During 1913, Coca-Cola advertised on over 100 million items, including thermometers, carboard cutouts, metal signs, calendars, matchboxes, and baseball cards. The Coca-Cola logo started to permeate every aspect of American life. No matter where you were, you could hardly avoid seeing the logo. Celebrities started to promote it. The movies and Coca-Cola were made for each other. Buster Keaton drank it on-screen. Film stars appeared in Coca-Cola ads. And then there were the Coca-Cola girls who appeared in ads or on calendars clutching a bottle of Coke. As one critic noted, they were the "bewitching siren who lure us to Coca-Cola with their display of charms."

Under Woodruff's early years, the ad message that resonated was that Coca-Cola was always delightful and could be enjoyed at work or at play. Copy was kept to a minimum, while pictures conveyed the message that active, contented, good looking, successful young men and women enjoyed the drink. By 1929, the company had coined the phrase that Coca-Cola was "The Pause that Refreshes," a tag line that was used in one form or another for the next three decades. Increasingly, Coca-Cola ads made an appeal to American nostalgia. These images included the Coca-Cola Sant Claus and Norman Rockwell ads with freckle-faced boys at the old fishing hole, complete with dog and a bottle of Coca-Cola. Through these means, Coca-Cola became tightly woven into the fabric of American life. It became the American drink.

It was Woodruff who began to push Coca-Cola to establish foreign operations. His early efforts in the 1920s met with only limited success. However, America's entry into the Second World War after Pearl Harbor gave Woodruff a golden opportunity to extend the company's reach. As America went to war, Woodruff proclaimed "We will see that every man in uniform gets a bottle of Coca-Cola for five cents, wherever he is an whatever the costs to our company." Woodruff's commitment yielded benefits for the company; Coca-Cola was exempted from the wartime sugar rationing that bedeviled other soft drink companies (and nearly bankrupted Pepsi-ColaCo.). Coca-Cola employees followed the military overseas, establishing 64 bottling plants in the process on every continent except Antarctica, largely at government expense. Coca-Cola was apparently indispensable to the war effort. General Patton reputedly regarded Coca-Cola as a necessity, perhaps because he himself drank it constantly. He made sure Coca-Cola transported a bottling plant wherever he went. When he was in North Africa, General Eisenhower requested enough bottling equipment to fill 20,000 bottles a day. In 1944, Army Chief of Staff George Marshall issued an order specifically allowing commanders to requisition Coca-Cola plants by name, along with the company personnel to install and operate them. This expansion set the stage for a boom in Coca-Cola's international sales after the war.

C8-4 The Postwar Period: Pepsi-Cola Strikes Back[7]

Coca-Cola emerged from World War II in a dominant position domestically, and with the benefit of a fast-growing international presence. The company had 70% of the domestic market for colas, far ahead of second-place Pepsi-Cola-Cola Company, which had 20%. Unlike many other cola companies, Pepsi-Cola-Cola Company. had managed to survive despite three brushes with bankruptcy and Coca-Cola's legal assault. Following a blizzard of lawsuits and counter suits between the two companies, in 1941, Robert Woodruff had signed a deal with Walter Mack, Pepsi-Cola's president, under which Coca-Cola agreed to recognize Pepsi-Cola-Cola's trademark in the United States. Mack, an old friend of Woodruff, had been brought in to run Pepsi-Cola-Cola by outside investors in 1938. The friendship may have influenced Woodruff's decision to make a deal. The agreement was drafted without the input or knowledge of Coca-Cola's lawyers, who were furious when they found out.

Pepsi-Cola-Cola's survival through the Great Depression owed much to its strategy of promoting a 12-ounce bottled drink for the same nickel Coca-Cola got for its 6 ½ ounce bottle, which made it a hit in blue-collar neighborhoods. Under Mack's leadership, Pepsi-Cola-Cola doubled down on this strategy. In 1939, the company started to promote Pepsi-Cola-Cola using a 30-second radio jingle with a catchy tune that immediately caught on: "Pepsi-Cola-Cola hits the spot, twelve full ounces that's a lot, twice as much for a nickel too, Pepsi-Cola-Cola is the drink for you." The jingle was the first of its kind; most radio ads at the time lasted 5 minutes and were full of hard-sell verbiage. In 1941, the jingle was played nearly 300,000 times on the airwaves.

Mack also had a clever strategy for building out Pepsi-Cola-Cola's network of franchised bottlers. He found that the Coca-Cola bottler was always the wealthy bottler in each region, so he focused on well-run small bottlers who had missed the Coca-Cola train, and tried to persuade them to hitch their wagon to Pepsi-Cola. Mack awarded larger territories to Pepsi-Cola-Cola bottlers than Coca-Cola, the former company having started building out its franchisee bottler network at a time when a territory was defined by how far a horse-drawn carriage could go.

Under Mack's leadership, Pepsi-Cola-Cola started to claw market share away from Coca-Cola. Woodruff's lieutenants tried to persuade him to match Pepsi-Cola-Cola's offering with larger Coke bottles, but he refused. One of those lieutenants was the brash vice president of marketing at Coca-Cola, Alfred Steele. In 1949, Steele left Coca-Cola for Pepsi-Cola-Cola and in 1950 he became president of the company. Steele's vision for Pepsi-Cola-Cola was simple, "Beat Coke." Steele reduced the sugar content of Pepsi-Cola and promoted the drink as "the light refreshment which would refresh without filling." He pushed into the vending machine market, which Mack had seceded to Coke because a 12-ounce Pepsi-Cola bottle wouldn't fit in the standard machine. Steele created an 8-ounce bottle that fit the vending machines. He arranged for low interest loans for the machines, with payment to start 6 months after purchase. This allowed poorer bottlers to purchase the $1,000 machines of credit and pay for them out of profits. Steele also pushed bottlers to focus their attention on the take-home market, and build distribution in supermarkets, which were rapidly springing up all over America, particularly in the rapidly growing suburbs. To support the take-home market, Pepsi-Cola-Cola introduced a 26-ounce bottle.

Steele was a master at motivating Pepsi-Cola-Cola's bottlers, persuading franchisees to plow money back into their business and local advertising. You can "conserve yourself into bankruptcy," he told them, or "spend your way into prosperity." Practicing what he preached, he doubled Pepsi-Cola-Cola's marketing budget, targeting 25 metropolitan areas for heavy spending. Steele also bought out Pepsi-Cola-Cola bottlers who were failing to push the product hard enough and installed his own men.

In 1955, Steele became the fourth husband of the iconic American actress Joan Crawford (it was his third marriage). Crawford, who ironically had been a Coca-Cola girl in the 1930s, was no mere adornment. She accompanied him on his travels, logging over 100,000 miles a year and opening up new Pepsi-Cola-Cola plants in country after country. In 1957, they visited 20 foreign countries, where the actress, always holding a Pepsi-Cola bottle, was greeted by ecstatic fans. After Steele died suddenly of a heart attack in 1959, Joan Crawford took his place on the board. She continued as a brand ambassador for Pepsi-Cola-Cola and stayed on the board until 1973.

Steele's overhaul was effective. Pepsi-Cola-Cola's share of the U.S. market increased from 21% to 35% in 5 years. Pepsi-Cola-Cola also started to expand rapidly outside of the United States, reducing Coke's worldwide market share lead from five to one to three to one. Coca-Cola's response to this brash upstart was underwhelming. The company was accused of slumbering, of being self-satisfied with all of its past progress, although to be fair, Coca-Cola was financially healthy and international sales were growing at a strong clip. Still, to some critics the company was starting to look old and fat. The same could be said for some of the bottlers who were now managed by second- or third-generation owners who took profits for granted.

Pepsi-Cola continued to make headway against its rival in the 1960s and early 1970s. In 1961, Donald Kendall was appointed president of Pepsi-Cola. Kendall, who was to lead Pepsi-Cola for the next 25 years, continued on the trajectory set by Steele. In 1963, he presided over the launch of the Pepsi Generation marketing campaign, which targeted the "young and the young at heart." The 1960s was a time of social change led by the young. The campaign, which featured young energetic healthy beautiful people doing exotic things, told consumers that Pepsi drinkers were on the side of change. If you were a Pepsi drinker, you were young (or young at heart), and the future was on your side. This was a stark contrast to the nostalgia messages of the Normal Rockwell–era Coke ads and represented a sharp break from the "twice as much for half the price" theme of prior Pepsi campaigns. In 1964, Pepsi-Cola introduced Diet Pepsi, a zero-calorie variant of its core brand that catered to the changing dietary habits of the young Baby Boom generation. Coca-Cola had introduced its own diet drink, Tab, the year before, but unlike Pepsi-Cola, Coke chose to not associate Tab with its core Coke brand.

From 1962 through until 1980, Coca-Cola was led by Paul Austin, first as president and then as CEO. Austin had devoted much of his attention to growing Coca-Cola's international operations, where the company had done well. In the United States, Austin struggled to motivate Coca-Cola's bottlers to adopt a more aggressive posture towards Pepsi-Cola, and to bottle Coca-Cola's growing portfolio of non-colas, which included Tab, Fanta, Fresca, and Sprite. Both companies also had to deal with the Federal Trade Commission (FTC), which in 1972 alleged that the exclusive territories awarded to Coca-Cola and PepsiCo. bottlers, by giving bottlers a territorial monopoly, violated the Sherman Antitrust Act. Coca-Cola and PepsiCo fought back, lobbying Congress for specific legislation to exempt them from prosecution. These efforts were rewarded with the passage of the Soft Drink Interbrand Competition Act in 1980. This Act maintained that Interbrand competition between PepsiCo. and Coca-Cola was so strong that this particular market could be exempt from the Sherman Act.

C8-5 The Pepsi Challenge and Its Aftermath[8]

While Pepsi-Cola continued to grind out market share gains from Coca-Cola in the United States, the larger company remained focused on overseas expansion. This seemed to make sense. Per capita consumption of carbonated beverages was much lower outside of the United States while the American market looked saturated. However, PepsiCo was about to wake Coca-Cola out of its complacency by firing the opening shots in what would come to be known as the "Cola Wars."

Ground zero for this new round of rivalry between the two soft drink companies was Dallas, where PepsiCo.'s market share was a miserable 4%. In an attempt to fix things, the local brand manager hired the Dallas-based Stanford Advertising Agency. It turned out that the proprietor, Bob Stanford, had discovered that Pepsi beat Coke in a blind taste test while promoting a 7-Eleven generic cola. He suggested that Pepsi-Cola try out a blind taste test. What was dubbed "The Pepsi Challenge" was first in rolled out in Dallas in 1975. Backed by TV ads that showed long-time Coke drinkers astonished that they preferred Pepsi to Coke, the campaign had a dramatic impact. Pepsi-Cola's market share in Dallas doubled. The local Coca-Cola bottler responded by cutting prices and launching an advertising blitz mocking the challenge. Pepsi-Cola matched the price cuts and continued to promote the Pepsi Challenge. Within 2 years, Pepsi's share in Dallas had increased to 14%.

Encouraged by what was occurring in Dallas, other Pepsi-Cola bottlers soon adopted the challenge. Coca-Cola's response was to cut prices and to run ads that questioned the validity of The Pepsi Challenge. Pepsi-Cola matched Coca-Cola's price cuts with cuts of its own, starting a price war that depressed returns for both concentrate companies and their bottlers. Meanwhile, in Atlanta, Coke's technical people ran their own version of the Pepsi challenge. To their consternation, they found that consumers preferred Pepsi to Coke by a 58–42 split. By the end of the decade, Pepsi had edged passed Coke in supermarket sales in the United States, although thanks to its strong position in fountain and vending machine sales, Coke remained the overall market leader. In 1980, PepsiCo. raised the stakes yet again when it rolled out The Pepsi Challenge nationally. By this point, retail price discounting was the norm, and consumers were coming to expect it.

The pressure of the "Cola Wars" pushed Coca-Cola to revise its archaic bottling contract, which had fixed the price for concentrate, and did not allow for increased costs with the exception of sugar. After contentious negotiations, in 1979, Coca-Cola and its bottlers agreed that the cost of the concentrate could be raised to match increases (a) sugar prices, and (b) the cost of other ingredients as measured by the Consumer Price Index.

In 1980, Roberto Goizueta was appointed president of Coca-Cola, and in 1981 he became CEO and chairman. The replacement of Paul Austin was overdue. As early as 1975, some of his associates started to notice that Austin was developing memory problems. By 1978, it was clear to those around him that something was wrong. Initially, people put his memory lapses and increasing irritability down to Austin's penchant for alcohol, but he was in fact developing Alzheimer's. Goizueta was a Cuba American who had risen through the ranks at Coca-Cola. The chain-smoking Goizueta had a reputation for being highly intelligent, dedicated to Coca-Cola, with a good grasp of the business and an eye for detail. Although he had an affable manner, he could also be ruthless, holding people to account, but he also rewarded good results and was open to points of view other than his own.

Goizueta moved fast to wake Coca-Cola up from its slumbers. In 1980, he oversaw the replacement of cane sugar in the United States with high fructose corn syrup (HFCS), a less expensive sweetener. The price of cane sugar in the United States was higher than elsewhere in the world due to sugar quotas that limited foreign supply. In June 1980, he announced a plan to refranchise bottling operations in the United

States. In the 1970s, Coca-Cola still had around 800 bottlers in the United States. Many smaller bottlers lacked the capital resources to invest in new lines, new packaging, and aggressive sales and promotion activities. Under Goizueta, the company would actively promote consolidation among its bottlers, sometimes buying an interim equity position while looking for new owners. This cumulated in 1986 when Coca-Cola purchased a controlling interest in two large bottlers who had come on the market for $2.4 billion. Together, with bottlers Coca-Cola already owned, this gave the company control of over one-third of bottling operations in the United States.

The problem with buying bottlers is that they added a lot of physical assets to the balance sheet and took the company into the low margin capital intensive bottling business. The solution, first suggested by the CFO Douglas Ivester, was to spin off the acquired bottlers into a subsidiary in which it took a 49% stake, guaranteeing control over the operation which pushing the capital intensity off the balance sheet. The bottling subsidiary, known as Coca-Cola Enterprises (CCE), continued to acquire smaller bottlers after the spin-off, becoming the world's biggest bottler. Coca-Cola continued to purchase smaller bottlers and sell them to CCE. Coca-Cola referred to CCE as an *anchor bottler*. Ivester served as chairman of CCE's board, while continuing as CFO at Coca-Cola. CCE consolidated territories, introduced new automated bottling lines, and over time pushed new products through its distribution system. By 2009, CCE was responsible for three quarters of Coca-Cola's North American bottle and can volume. At the same time, because it retained effective control over CCE, Coca-Cola was able to sell concentrate to CCE at a relatively high price, and influence CCE's strategy. This strategy was so successful for Coca-Cola that over the next two decades the company sought to replicate it outside of the United States, encouraging bottlers in a country or region to merge in order to achieve economies of scale. The company also took a minority equity position in many of them so that it could exercise a degree of control.

Goizueta pushed to develop a better diet drink to respond to the success of Diet Pepsi and leverage off its flagship Coke brand. The result was Diet Coke. Introduced in 1982, the product surpassed all of the company's expectations, outselling Diet Pepsi and becoming the third best-selling carbonated drink in the United States by decade's end. The introduction of Diet Coke paved the way for other drinks that used the Coke name, including Caffeine Free Coke (introduced in 1983) and Cherry Coke (introduced in 1985). Pepsi-Cola also introduced new carbonated beverages, and both companies introduced a range of different packaging and sizes.

While Coca-Cola seemed to be gaining vigor under Goizueta, one problem remained, its flagship brand was still struggling in the United States against Pepsi. Goizueta had a solution for this too, New Coke, a reformulation of its classic brand. New Coke hit the market in 1985. Introducing the product at a press conference for 700 journalists in February, Goizueta explained that the new flavor had been discovered as a result of experimentation on Diet Coke. Coca-Cola President Donald Keough claimed that the new formula beat old Coke 55–44 in 190,000 blind taste tests, and that its margin increased to 61–39 when both drinks were identified. The journalists weren't buying the story. One asked, "Did you change the formula in response to the Pepsi challenge?" "Oh gosh no," replied Goizueta, "The Pepsi challenge, when did that happen?" Meanwhile, Pepsi-Cola claimed that New Coke mimicked Pepsi's taste.

Despite the negative publicity, Goizueta and his lieutenants were confident that New Coke would win out. What they didn't anticipate was the back lash from long time Coke consumers. The company was besieged by letters, 40,000 of them by June, complaining of the taste. As one letter writer put it: *Changing Coke is like breaking the American dream, like not selling hot dogs at a ballgame.* Another noted: *I do not drink alcoholic beverages, I do not smoke. I don't chase other women; my only vice has been Coke. Now you have taken that pleasure from me.*

Three months after the introduction of New Coke, Goizueta relented and stated that Coca-Cola would reintroduce its old formula, selling it side by side with New Coke as Coca-Cola Classic. Three months later, Coca-Cola announced that it would treat Coca-Cola Classic as its flagship brand, and New Coke started to disappear from store shelves. It had been a disaster, or had it? As Donald Keough stated later, the experience had taught Coke's management a useful lesson; its customers still valued the original product. Despite everything, the brand was alive and well in America. Indeed, while it cost Coca-Cola $4 million to research and develop New Coke, the original Coca-Cola formulation garnered far more than $4 million in free publicity. The classic formulation surged back to regain its position as the premier American soft drink. Coke had snatched an unlikely victory from the jaws of defeat. The "fiasco" had cemented the importance of the Coca-Cola brand in the American psyche.

Meanwhile PepsiCo. had been vertically integrating forward into the fountain business, an area where Coke had long held a lead. PepsiCo. acquired Pizza Hut, Taco Bell, and then in 1985 Kentucky Fried Chicken. Coca-Cola turned this strategy against PepsiCo., telling other fast-food chains that PepsiCo. was now their rival. Wendy's and Domino's Pizza were among those that switched to serving Coke. By 1995, Coca-Cola had over 60% of sales of high margin concentrate to restaurants, convenience stores, and food service companies, while PepsiCo.'s share was under 25%. In 1997, PepsiCo. announced that it would spin off its restaurant business, a move it hoped would revitalize its flagging fountain sales.[9]

C8-6 End of an Era and the New Millennium

By 1997, Goizueta has been CEO for 16 years. Under his leadership, Coca-Cola had transformed itself from a slumbering giant with an inefficient bottler network and poor focus that was losing market share to PepsiCo. into an efficient marketing machine. Coca-Cola increased its domestic market share of carbonated beverages from 35% to 44%. Worldwide Coca-Cola's market share had grown from 35% to 50%. By this point, 80% of Coca-Cola's business was outside of the United States. The company's market value had surged from $4.3 billion to $145 billion. If not vanquished, PepsiCo. had been beaten back down into second place. And then, at the peak of his success, Goizueta was diagnosed with lung cancer. Six weeks later he was dead.

His replacement was Douglas Ivester, the financial wiz who was the brains behind Coca-Cola's purchase and spin-off of the company's bottlers in 1986. Ironically, Ivester ascended to the CEO position just as investors and journalists were starting to question their strategy of purchasing and then spinning off bottlers. The critics pointed out that Coca-Cola had pushed off its debt from bottler acquisitions onto Coca-Cola Enterprises and moreover, extracted high profits from CCE by raising concentrate prices, leaving the anchor bottler to survive on razor thin margins. Without CCE, they argued, Coca-Cola's profits would have been much lower.

By this time Coca-Cola had other problems to worry about. The 1997 Asian economic crisis was followed by a slowdown in international business. This was compounded by a strong U.S. dollar that compressed Coca-Cola's international profits when translated back into dollars. Moreover, there were growing concerns about the health impact carbonated sodas. Caffeine, high-fructose corn syrup, sugar, and artificial sweeteners all came in for criticism. Sodas were blamed for obesity and diabetes, both of which were increasing in the United States and elsewhere. Consumption of carbonated sodas finally seemed to have peaked. Demand for bottled water, fruit drinks, specialty beverages, and sports drinks were all growing, taking share away from Coca-Cola's traditional market.

Coca-Cola's response was to accelerate its diversification into non-carbonated beverages. In 1999, the company launched its own brand of bottled water, Dasani. PepsiCo. had been in the bottled water business since 1994 with its Aquafina brand. Coca-Cola also purchased established beverage brands that could take advantage of its marketing savvy and distribution systems. Notable acquisitions included Odwalla Inc. (maker of fresh fruit and vegetable juices), Planet Java (coffee drinks), Mad River Traders (New Age teas, juices, lemonades, and sodas), and Energy Brands (makers of VitaminWater). PepsiCo., too, made several acquisitions, including Quaker Oats (makers of the best-selling sports drink Gatorade) and SoBe (teas, fruit juices, and enhanced beverages).

By 2006, Coca-Cola was dealing with another problem, the company's relationship with its bottlers was coming under strain again. One trigger was a request from Walmart that Coca-Cola deliver it Powerade sports drink directly to Walmart distribution centers.[10] Until that point, individual bottlers had always delivered to Walmart stores and stocked the shelves themselves to make sure their products were well displayed. Worried that Walmart would develop its own brand of sports drink if Coke did not agree, the company acquiesced, asking Coca-Cola Enterprises to deliver directly to Walmart distribution centers. Fifty-six smaller Coca-Cola bottlers, fearing that the practice might spread to other drinks, sued Coca-Cola and CCE, claiming the agreement violated the distribution contract with bottlers that gave them the rights to deliver directly to stores within their own exclusive territories. In response, Coca-Cola tried to buy back the distribution rights for Powerade from the bottlers, but the price was reportedly too high. Ultimately the suit was settled out of court, with the bottlers agreeing to allow for the delivery of Powerade to Walmart warehouses, but with the bottlers receiving some of the profits.

There were also disagreements between Coca-Cola and CCE, which at the time was still 36% owned by Coca-Cola. CCE was dissatisfied with sales of Coca-Cola's Golden Leaf bottled tea products and decided to carry non-Coke products instead. Coca-Cola thought that CCE's execution was very poor, and pressured CCE's board to remove the company's CEO, John Alm, which they did in 2005. But the new CEO of CCE, John Brock, continued to irritate Coca-Cola by raising prices for Coke products, which eroded Coca-Cola's market share. Coca-Cola responded by raising concentrate prices.

The tensions between Coca-Cola and its bottlers simmered for a few more years, then in early 2010 Coca-Cola announced that it would acquire the North American territories of Coca-Cola Enterprises for $12.4 billion.[11] The acquired territories accounted for about 80% of Coca-Cola's North American business. The deal came just months after PepsiCo. had announced a similar deal to purchase its two largest bottlers. In explaining the rationale, Coca-Cola executives noted that the goal was to close some bottling plants, modernize others, and create a national manufacturing footprint that would allow it to more rapidly introduce new products to satisfy consumers with rapidly changing tastes. Under the old structure, every time Coca-Cola wanted to introduce a new product, they had to negotiate with their bottlers. The new structure was also aimed at helping Coca-Cola negotiate directly with big retailers.[12]

Following the acquisition, Coca-Cola created a new company-owned bottling business, Coca-Cola Refreshments (CCR). In 2013, CCR started "refranchising" its U.S. territories, parceling out distribution rights and selling its bottling plants to trusted partners under a new franchising agreement, known as the *Comprehensive Beverage Agreement*. This agreement gives the bottlers exclusive territories, requires them to take major Coke products and commits them to production, marketing and distribution of those products. As before, Coca-Cola makes its money by selling concentrate to the bottlers. The agreement is for a stated period, typically 10 years, and is renewable for successive 10-year terms. The agreement can be terminated by Coca-Cola if the bottler does not live up to its core performance requirements under the contract. As with the old agreements, the company retains the right to manufacture and sell fountain syrups to authorized fountain wholesalers and some fountain retailers.[13]

The refranchising process was completed at the end of 2017. It involved 60 transactions transferring 350 distribution centers, 51 production facilities, 55,000-plus employees, and over 1.3 billion physical cases of volume. At the end of this process in late 2017, Coca-Cola was left with 70 independent bottlers in the United States, 10 of which were very large, had territories that covered cover multiple states, and accounted for the bulk of Coca-Cola's U.S. volume. The smaller bottlers were for the most part older bottlers who had remained independent through Coca-Cola's two forays into the bottling business. Some of them still operated under their original franchising agreement that granted rights in perpetuity for trademark Coca-Cola or other cola-flavored beverages. The company claims that the refranchising better serves the changing customer and consumer landscape in the United States and creates a more aligned, agile, and efficient network of bottlers.[14]

Outside of the United States, Coca-Cola has also pushed for bottler consolidation.[15] For example, in 2013, three Coca-Cola bottlers in Europe agreed to merge across 13 countries as part of a push by the company to cut costs and speed up new product introduction against the background of slowing sales of legacy products. Bottlers outside of the United States have long operated under contracts of a stated duration that are subject to termination if the bottler doesn't perform, or if other specified events occur.

C8-7 Looking Forward

With the bottler refranchising complete, the pressure was on CEO James Quincey to craft a strategy for profitably growing Coca-Cola's sales going forward. His initial strategy seemed to center on product innovation.[16] Most notably, he directed Coca-Cola's global subsidiaries to launch more local flavors, and to reduce time to market. In the first year of this initiative, the company launched 500 new drinks, a record, and an increase of 25% over the prior year. The company's Indian subsidiary came up with a chunky mango juice, a spicy cumin-flavored soda, and a gritty guava drink. In Japan, recent launches include a laxative Sprite (really!) and the company's first alcoholic drink, Lemon-Duo, a carbonated lemonade beverage. The Russian subsidiary launched a cumbered Sprite, there was a line of whey shakes introduced into Brazil, a sesame-and-walnut drink in China, and a salty lemon tonic in France. This surge of local innovation represents a break from established practice, which largely consisted of foreign subsidiaries rolling out drinks first developed for Americans. Quincey argued that while some of these new offerings would fall flat, others would be successfully locally, and some would become regional or global drinks.

By 2022, Quincey could look back on five successful years as CEO. The company had navigated the disruptions caused by the COVID-19 pandemic better than most, and registered strong sales rebounds in 2021 and the first half of 2022 after a pandemic-related decline in 2020. The company had also continued to expand its beverage portfolio, primarily through acquisitions. For example, in 2017, Coca-Cola acquired the Mexican sparkling water brand, Topo Chico, from one of its Mexican bottlers for $220 million. By leveraging its distribution system, Coca-Cola was able to grow Topo Chico's U.S. sales by 40% between 2018 and 2019. In 2018, Coca-Cola acquired a 15% stake in Bodyarmor, a fast-growing line of sports performance and hydration beverages. Coca-Cola already had a large stake in this business thanks to its successful Powerade business. When Coca-Cola acquired its 15% stake, Bodyarmor gained access to Coca-Cola's distribution system, which enabled it to accelerate its growth. By

2021, Bodyarmor was the number two sports drink sold in the U.S. retail sector with $1.4 billion in sales. Coca-Cola acquired the outstanding 85% stake in Bodyarmor for $5.6 billion in cash in November 2021. Similarly, in 2020, Coca-Cola acquired the 57.5% stake in fairlife L.L.C. that it did not own. Fairlife makes lactose free "ultra-filtered" milk products that are enhanced with protein and flavorings. The company started out in 2012 as a joint venture between Coca-Cola and select milk producers. Access to Coca-Cola's distribution system helped fairlife to grow to over $1 billion in sales by 2020.. Finally, in a sign that Coca-Cola is getting serious about entering the coffee space, in 2018, the company acquired the U.K. coffee retailer Costa for $4.9 billion. Costa has some 4,000 stores in 32 countries, including over 2,800 in the United Kingdom where it has a significant lead over its U.S. rival Starbucks. Although the pandemic delayed plans to open Costa stores in the United States, in mid-2022 Costa opened its first U.S. store in Atlanta.

Notes

[1]J. Maloney, "Coke's New CEO James Quincey to Staff: Make Mistakes," *Wall Street Journal*, May 9, 2017.

[2]"Americans Are Now Drinking More Bottled Water than Soda," *Reuters*, March 10, 2017.

[3]R. Grantham, "New CEO's Challenge: Make Things go Better with Coke," *Seattle Times*, May 6, 2017.

[4]Primary sources for this section are The Coca-Cola Company Annual 10K reports for 2016, 2017, and 2018.

[5]O. Pulsinelli, "Coca-Cola Bottler to Build $250 Million Production, Distribution Facility in Houston," *Houston Business Journal*, June 7, 2018.

[6]F. Allen, *Secret Formula* (Open Road, 1994). B. Elmore, *Citizen Coke* (W.W. Norton & Company, 2015). M. Pendergrast, *For God, Country and Coca-Cola* (Basic Books, 2013). J. Hamblin, "Why We Took the Cocaine out of Soda," *The Atlantic*, January 31, 2013.

[7]F. Allen, *Secret Formula* (Open Road, 1994). B. Elmore, *Citizen Coke* (W.W. Norton & Company, 2015). M. Pendergrast, *For God, Country and Coca-Cola* (Basic Books, 2013).

[8]F. Allen, *Secret Formula* (Open Road, 1994). B. Elmore, *Citizen Coke* (W.W. Norton & Company, 2015). M. Pendergrast, *For God, Country and Coca-Cola* (Basic Books, 2013).

[9]G. Colling, "Pepsi-Colaco to Spin Off its Fast Food Business," *New York Times*, January 24, 1997.

[10]M. Warner, "Coke Bottlers Challenge Walmart Deliveries," *New York Times*, March 3, 2006.

[11]W. Spain, "Bottler Acquisition Could Be a Risky Proposition for Coke," *Market Watch*, February 25, 2010. M. Esterl and P. Ziobro, "New Coke: Bottlers Are Back," *Wall Street Journal*, April 16, 2013.

[12]Timberwolf Equity Research, "The Coke System: How it Works," *Seeking Alpha*, October 1, 2015.

[13]The Coca-Cola Comapny, 2018 10K Form.

[14]J. Moye, "Coca-Cola Completes Decade Long Effort to Return Ownership of Bottling Operations to Local Partners," *The Coca-Cola Company*, November 8, 2017.

[15]M. Esterl, "The Coca-Cola Bottlers Confirm Merger," *Wall Street Journal*, August 6, 2015.

[16]E. Bellman and J. Maloney, "Coca-Cola Launched 500 Drinks Last Year. Most Taste Nothing Like Coke," *Wall Street Journal*, August 23, 2018.

Jose Cuervo: The Making of a Legendary Tequila Brand

By Melissa Schilling

In 2022, Cuervo (listed on the stock market as Becle) was the world's oldest and largest tequila producer with a global market share of 29%,[1] sales of USD $1.9 billion and net profits of USD $386 million in 2021 (see Exhibits 1 and 2).[2] Sixty-five percent of its sales were in the United States and 21% were in Mexico. Despite having been the target of several would-be takeovers, the Cuervo Group remained a (mostly) privately owned family firm. In 2017, the company raised $900 million in an IPO as "BECLE, S.A.B. de C.V."[3] but retained a majority of ownership within the family (of the 3.59 billion shares outstanding, only 1.76 billion shares are floated publicly as of 2022). The company was controlled by the Beckman family who are seventh-generation direct-line descendants of the original José Cuervo.[4]

C9-1 History

Tequila's history traces back to mezcal (wine made from agave) first produced at least as early as the 16th century and perhaps earlier (mezcal's origins are disputed).[5] Mezcal wines were an important export product for Mexico and mezcal from the town of Tequila was noted for its superior quality.[6] In 1758, King Ferdinand VI of Spain granted José Antonio de Cuervo y Valdés land near the town of Tequila in Jalisco, Mexico. José Cuervo began planting blue agave on his farm, and by 1781 was already producing 800,000 liters of "mezcal de Tequila" per year.[7] Then in 1795, his son, José Maria Guadalupe Cuervo y Montana, obtained the first commercial license to produce and distribute tequila from King Carlos IV.[8] The family's distillery, La Rojeña, remains the oldest active distillery in Latin America today.[9]

In 1852 (or 1873, depending on which account you believe), Cuervo tequila was first exported to the United States in barrels,[10] and then in 1880, Cuervo became the first company to make individual bottles of tequila (rather than barrels or large jugs), which made it easier to transport and export. This enabled much greater exportation to the United States and helped to establish "Jose Cuervo" as a brand name.

In 1938, a bartender at the Tail O' the Cock restaurant in Los Angeles invented a drink that would spark a huge increase in tequila demand–the margarita. As the story goes, a bartender named Johnny Durlesser had admired a pretty lady who had come into the bar several times. To impress her, he made her a drink with Cuervo and a "touch of sweet just like her," and the margarita was born. As noted by Oli Pergl, Cuervo's resident Tequila educator in the United Kingdom, "It wasn't, in my opinion, until the Margarita was created that the Americans really saw the true versatility of the spirit and how incredible it was. It was so different from the barrel-aged spirits they had, like Bourbon, rye, brandy or rum. The Margarita completely changed their opinion of Tequila."[11] Cuervo began launching advertisements based on the margarita in 1945 with the slogan "Margarita; It's more than a girl's name," and exports of tequila surged.

Tequila gained a reputation as a "badass" liquor that was sexier and younger than Scotch whiskey or Cognac. The Rolling Stones tour of 1972 was dubbed "the cocaine and Tequila Sunrise" tour and tequila began to be featured in songs and movies. By 1999, Cuervo's global annual sales had reached 5 million cases.

C9-2 The Market

From 2015 to 2020, tequila was the fastest-growing major spirits category in the United States and second-fastest category in the world.[12] Furthermore, by 2022, Cuervo controlled 29% of the global tequila market[13] and was selling over 43 million liters of tequila per year in the United States alone.[14] Cuervo's tequila portfolio included three of the seven largest tequila brands in the world: Jose Cuervo, 1800, and Centenario. The volume of Cuervo's tequila sales was almost three times the size of its nearest competitor, Bacardi (see Figure 1). The company had also received numerous international awards for its tequila, including the Gold Medal and Double Gold Medal in competitions such as the Bartender Spirits Awards, International Spirits Challenge, San Francisco Spirits Competition, and World Tequila Awards.[15]

C9-3 Vertical Integration at Cuervo

Cuervo was heavily vertically integrated, from the sourcing of raw materials, through the bottling and distribution of its finished products. Cuervo also grew its own Agave Azul (blue agave) and owned the largest blue agave farm in the "tequila" Appellation of Origin (AOC) region. This was a significant competitive advantage because in 1974

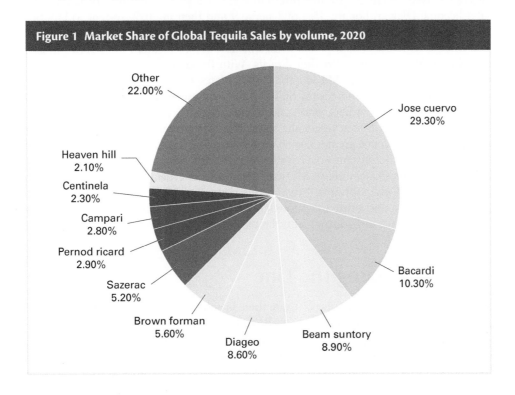

Figure 1 Market Share of Global Tequila Sales by volume, 2020

Other 22.00%
Jose cuervo 29.30%
Heaven hill 2.10%
Centinela 2.30%
Campari 2.80%
Pernod ricard 2.90%
Sazerac 5.20%
Brown forman 5.60%
Diageo 8.60%
Beam suntory 8.90%
Bacardi 10.30%

tequila was awarded "destination of origin," meaning that in order for a spirit to be called "tequila" it has to be made in certain states of Mexico. Owning the largest plantation there gave Cuervo significant control over the agave sourcing and tequila production.

C9-4 Manufacturing

Blue agave is a large spiky plant that takes 7 years to mature. After harvesting, the spiky leaves are cut off and the fleshy cores, the "piñas," are roasted, ground, and smashed to extract the agave juice known as must. This must then be placed into fermentation tanks for 50 to 60 hours. The fermented juice then goes through a process of distillation, condensation, and rectification, after which it is a drinkable product known as white tequila. However, to achieve the more complex flavors that people seek in tequila requires aging. Thus, most of the white tequila is put into oak barrels where it will be slowly aged, giving it woody and smokey flavors. Much of the flavor difference in the tequilas produced is obtained by how long the oak barrels are toasted before aging. Light, medium, and strong toasting each produce different aromatic features in the tequila that is aged in the barrel.[16] "Pure tequila" (such as Cuervo Tradicional or Cuervo Platino) is distilled 100% from the sap of the blue agave; "mixto tequila" (such as Cuervo Especial Silver or Cuervo Gold) need contain only 51.5% agave with the remainder of the alcohol coming from cheaper sugarcane spirits.[17]

Cuervo's agave farms, distilleries, and bottling plant were all in the Tequila appellation region of Jalisco Mexico. As of 2022, all Cuervo tequila is still made only in Cuervo's two distilleries, La Rojeña and Los Camichines. Cuervo also owned its own processing and bottling plant, EDISA, that included both manual and automatic bottling lines. Cuervo's other spirits were manufactured in distilleries in the United States and Ireland.

C9-4a Distribution and Marketing

In 1989, Cuervo's main distributor International Distillers and Vintners (which would later become Diageo) bought 45% of Cuervo,[18] and then in 2012, sought to buy the rest of the company. However, 18 months of intense negotiations failed to yield a deal and Cuervo remained a family-held firm. The fallout also resulted in Cuervo starting its own distribution arm —Proximo Spirits. With Proximo, the company operated a direct distribution model in Mexico, the United States, Canada, the United Kingdom, Ireland, and Australia. This meant that in most of these areas, it distributed directly to liquor stores, supermarkets, wholesalers, and convenience stores using its own sales force. In the United States where the regulation pertaining to alcohol sales varied across the states, it made greater use of wholesalers and independent distributors.

Cuervo spent heavily on advertising. In 2021, for example, the company spent USD $422 million (8,689 million Mexican pesos) on advertising, marketing, and promotion across all of its brands. Most of the company's spending was on premium national television and print ads, though it had also become famous for sponsoring beach volleyball and surf tournaments, helping to fuel its young and dynamic image.

C9-5 Expanding the Line

By 2022, Cuervo had a portfolio of more than 30 spirits and non-alcoholic beverages, including those that were acquired (e.g., Boodles Gin, Old Bushmills Distillery, Three Olives, Stranahans, Proper No. Twelve), and those that were developed internally (e.g., 1800, Maestro Dobel, Centenario, Kraken, Jose Cuervo Margaritas, and more).[19] Tequila, however, still made up the bulk of sales (see Figures 2 and 3).

Figure 2 Sales and Volume Levels of Brands

Family	9-liter cases	Sales (in thousands of Mexican pesos)	% of sales
Jose Cuervo	7,909,180	$ 13,554,501	34.39%
1800	2,288,349	$ 6,766,100	17.16%
Other Tequilas	2,242,243	$ 4,909,696	12.46%
Portfolio Tequila	**12,439,772**	**$ 25,230,297**	**64.01%**
Bushmills	934,436	$ 1,771,614	4.49%
Kraken	950,881	$ 1,696,264	4.30%
Other spirits	2,874,112	$ 5,161,242	13.09%
Non-Tequila	**4,759,429**	**$ 8,629,120**	**21.88%**
Ready-to-drink	4,877,812	$ 4,175,525	10.59%
Non-alcoholic beverages	3,479,740	$ 1,384,458	3.51%
Total	25,556,753	$ 39,419,400	100.00%

C9-6 Looking to the Future: Consumers Trading Up

In 2022, the global tequila market was $10.43 billion and was expected to grow to $15.57 billion by 2029.[20] However, that growth would not be evenly shared across the brands. From 2007 to 2022, U.S. consumers had been shifting to super-premium tequila, which in 2022 accounted for 43% of total sales. Growth in the super-premium tequila segment averaged 19% from 2017– 2022.[21] Twenty percent of tequila consumers were now opting to drink tequila "neat" (without mixers or ice).[22]

Cuervo's 1800 brand was the leader in the super premium tier, selling nearly 1.8 million cases in 2021 (see Figure 4).[23] Other premium brands, however, were coming up fast.

Figure 4 Leading Tequilas in the U.S. Retailing at $25–$40 (thousands of 9-liter cases)

Brand	Importer	2020	2021	Percent Change[1]
1800	Proximo Spirits	1,528	1,755	14.90%
Espolòn	Campari America	768	979	27.50%
Teremana	Mast-Jägermeister US	230	614	+
Cazadores	Bacardi USA	561	602	7.20%
Milagro	William Grant & Sons	349	498	42.80%
Altos	Pernod Ricard USA	359	339	−5.60%
Corralejo	Infinium Spirits	197	218	10.50%
Gran Centenario	Proximo Spirits	141	184	30.10%
Total Leading Brands[2]		4,133	5,190	25.60%

Source: Impact Databank 2022

Campari-owned Espolòn, for example, broke the 1 million case mark in 2021, and Milagro Tequila hit nearly one-half million cases. Dwayne "The Rock" Johnson's Teremana brand catapulted up to the number three spot in the super premium tier and was already among the top ten tequilas in the United States after only 2 years in the market.[24] As described by Nicole Austin, senior brand manager at Teremana, "Consumers caught on to Teremana quickly...we were out of stock a lot due to the unprecedented demand." Bacardi's super premium Tequila Cazadores was also experiencing double-digit growth.

Despite the rapid proliferation of luxury brands, Cuervo's management believed it was well positioned for the future. As noted by Lander Otegui, head of marketing at Jose Cuervo, "Jose Cuervo is synonymous with tequila and has been at the forefront of tequila premiumization worldwide...Most are unaware that we introduced tequila into the U.S. decades ago and popularized it with the margarita; the time is now to celebrate our founding father story and share it in a way that everyone can appreciate."[25]

Exhibit 1 Becle S.A.B. de C.V. (Cuervo) Income Statement, in MXN millions

	2021	2020	2019	2018	2017
Sales/Revenue	39,419	35,036	29,705	28,158	25,958
Sales Growth	12.51%	17.95%	5.49%	8.48%	–
Cost of Goods Sold (COGS) incl. D&A	18,193	16,847	14,096	11,975	10,022
COGS excluding D&A	17,579	16,132	13,410	11,444	9,587
Depreciation & Amortization Expense	614	714	685	531	435
Depreciation	–	–	–	466	416
Amortization of Intangibles	–	–	–	65	19
COGS Growth	7.99%	19.52%	17.71%	19.48%	–
Gross Income	21,226	18,189	15,609	16,183	15,936
Gross Profit Margin	53.85%	–	–	–	–
SG&A Expense	14,160	11,388	10,359	10,581	9,200
Other SG&A	–	11,388	10,359	10,581	9,200
EBIT	7,066	6,801	5,250	5,603	6,736
Unusual Expense	–	−304	–	–	–
Non Operating Income/Expense	289	151	234	−208	−397
Non-Operating Interest Income	251	144	191	193	110
Interest Expense	699	545	529	432	485
Gross Interest Expense	699	545	529	432	485
Pretax Income	6,908	6,854	5,147	5,156	5,963
Pretax Margin	17.52%	–	–	–	–
Income Tax	1,874	1,702	1,430	1,113	758
Income Tax - Current Domestic	3,532	1,152	796	782	1,670

Exhibit 1 Becle S.A.B. de C.V. (Cuervo) Income Statement, in MXN millions (continued)

	2021	2020	2019	2018	2017
Income Tax - Deferred Domestic	−1,658	550	633	331	−912
Equity in Affiliates	–	–	–	−9	−8
Consolidated Net Income	5,034	5,152	3,718	4,033	5,197
Minority Interest Expense	14	6	6	8	4
Net Income	5,020	5,146	3,712	4,025	5,193
Net Margin	12.73%	–	–	–	–
Net Income After Extraordinaries	5,020	5,146	3,712	4,025	5,193
Net Income Available to Common	5,020	5,146	3,712	4,025	5,193
EPS (Basic)	1.4	1.43	1.04	1.12	1.48
Basic Shares Outstanding	3,591	3,591	3,586	3,584	3,515
EBITDA	7,680	7,515	5,936	6,133	7,171
EBIT	7,066	6,801	5,250	5,603	6,736

Source: https://www.wsj.com/market-dataRetrieved October 14, 2022

Exhibit 2 Becle S.A.B. de C.V. (Cuervo) Balance Sheet, in MXN millions

Assets	2021	2020	2019	2018	2017
Cash & Short Term Investments	12,791	7,950	9,628	12,028	19,996
Cash Only	12,791	7,646	9,628	12,028	19,996
Total Accounts Receivable	11,264	11,187	10,818	10,234	8,504
Accounts Receivables, Net	10,284	9,214	9,295	8,536	7,260
Accounts Receivables, Gross	10,349	9,323	9,366	8,611	7,336
Bad Debt/Doubtful Accounts	−65	−109	−72	−75	−76
Other Receivables	–	1,973	1,523	1,697	1,244
Accounts Receivable Turnover	3.5	3.13	2.75	2.75	3.05
Inventories	13,027	11,486	10,353	8,162	7,419
Finished Goods	4,834	4,468	4,573	3,478	3,180
Work in Progress	6,068	–	–	–	3,232
Raw Materials	1,360	1,258	1,066	4,233	525
Progress Payments & Other	764	5,760	4,714	451	481
Other Current Assets	1,077	1,005	851	805	679
Prepaid Expenses	1,077	1,005	851	805	679
Total Current Assets	38,159	31,627	31,650	31,228	36,598

(continued)

Exhibit 2 Becle S.A.B. de C.V. (Cuervo) Balance Sheet, in MXN millions (continued)

Assets	2021	2020	2019	2018	2017
Net Property, Plant & Equipment	20,093	17,417	11,710	5,506	5,280
Property, Plant & Equipment - Gross	24,361	21,152	14,961	8,388	7,854
Buildings	1,889	1,852	1,386	1,355	1,304
Land & Improvements	1,220	1,221	647	647	556
Machinery & Equipment	6,647	6,046	5,423	4,971	3,916
Construction in Progress	4,345	3,553	1,670	488	486
Computer Software and Equipment	285	238	202	174	180
Transportation Equipment	373	361	333	280	249
Other Property, Plant & Equipment	7,230	5,528	3,253	472	1,164
Accumulated Depreciation	4,268	3,735	3,251	2,882	2,574
Total Investments and Advances	648	1,580	267	311	90
LT Investment - Affiliate Companies	648	1,568	230	311	90
Other Long-Term Investments	–	12	37	–	–
Intangible Assets	27,619	22,338	20,483	21,017	17,639
Net Goodwill	6,992	6,891	6,253	6,354	6,274
Net Other Intangibles	–	15,447	14,230	14,664	11,365
Other Assets	7,085	6,263	5,300	7,194	4,381
Deferred Charges	435	235	251	270	100
Tangible Other Assets	6,650	6,028	5,050	6,924	4,281
Total Assets	95,540	81,582	70,725	66,711	64,933

Source: https://www.wsj.com/market-dataRetrieved October 14, 2022

Notes

[1] 2022 Becle Investor Presentation, https://www.cuervo.com.mx/documents/presentations/2022/IR%20Investor%20Presentation%20March%202022.pdf.

[2] 2022 Cuervo Annual Report.

[3] "Mexico's Jose Cuervo Raises More Than $900 Million in IPO," *Reuters*, February 9, 2017.

[4] E. Bell, "15 Things You Didn't Know About Jose Cuervo," Vinepair, May 25, 2021.

[5] http://www.ianchadwick.com/tequila/16-17th%20centuries.htm, retrieved October 14, 2022.

[6] http://www.ianchadwick.com/tequila/18-19th%20centuries.htm, retrieved October 14, 2022.

[7] E. Bell, "15 Things You Didn't Know About Jose Cuervo," Vinepair, May

[8] https://cuervo.com/history/, retrieved October 14, 2022; T. Bruce-Gardyne, "Jose Cuervo: A Brand History," *The Spirits Business*, June 12, 2019.

[9] T. Bruce-Gardyne, "Jose Cuervo: A Brand History," *The Spirits Business*, June 12, 2019.

[10] https://cuervo.com/history/, retrieved October 14, 2022; http://www.ianchadwick.com/tequila/18-19th%20centuries.htm.

[11] T. Bruce-Gardyne, "Jose Cuervo: A Brand History," *The Spirits Business*, June 12, 2019.

[12]2022 Becle Investor Presentation, https://www.cuervo.com.mx/documents/presentations/2022/IR%20Investor%20Presentation%20March%202022.pdf.

[13]"Becle: World's Largest Tequila Producer at Stretched Valuations," *Seeking Alpha*, July 13, 2020.

[14]J. Conway, "Jose Cuervo Tequila's Sales Volume in the U.S. 2013-2020," *Statista*, November 5, 2021.

[15]2022 Cuervo Annual Report.

[16]https://cuervo.com/about/, retrieved October 14, 2022.

[17]J. Preston, "Drinking Tequila but Thinking Cognac, Maybe?" *New York Times*, January 4, 1996.

[18]J. Preston, "Drinking Tequila but Thinking Cognac, Maybe?" *New York Times*, January 4, 1996.

[19]2022 Cuervo Annual Report.

[20]"2022 Tequila Market Size, Share & The Global Tequila Market Is Expected to Grow from $10.43 Billion in 2022 to $15.57 Billion by 2029, at a CAGR of 5.89% in Forecast Period, 2022-2029," *Fortune Business Insights*, May.

[21]"Super-Premium Tequila: Rapid Growth in the $25-$40 Segment," *Shanken News* daily, June 22, 2022.

[22]A. Brooker, "Tequila 'Dominates Growth' in Spirits," *The Spirits Business*, September 13, 2022.

[23]A. Brooker, "Tequila 'Dominates Growth' in Spirits," *The Spirits Business*, September 13, 2022.

[24]A. Brooker, "Tequila 'Dominates Growth' in Spirits," *The Spirits Business*, September 13, 2022.

[25]"Jose Cuervo Pays Homage to its 250 Year History with New "Father of Tequila" Campaign," Jose Cuervo press release, June 17, 2019.

Boeing Commercial Aircraft

By Charles W. L. Hill School of Business University of Washington, Seattle, 98195 July 2022

C10-1 Introduction Boeing 737 MAX Crash

Boeing is one of the world's largest aerospace firms. The bulk of its revenue is generated by its commercial aircraft segment, where it is one part of a global duopoly that dominates the market (the other firm being Airbus). Boeing's commercial segment can be divided into two parts; narrow bodied aircraft that are idea for short-haul high-frequency routes, and wide-bodied aircraft that are used for transcontinental flights. In 2018, Boeing had a strong position in both segments, a full order book, and was posting record revenues and profits. It was starting to ramp up production of its latest offering, the 737 MAX, for which it had over 5,200 orders. The future looked bright. Then disaster struck.

On October 29, 2018, Lion Air Flight 610 crashed into the sea 13 minutes after taking off from Jakarta Indonesia. All 189 passengers and crew on the Boeing 737 MAX aircraft were killed. Preliminary investigations suggested flight control problems linked to a flaw on the Maneuvering Characteristics Augmentation System (MCAS) used in Boeing's 737 MAX aircraft. Following the crash, the U.S. Federal Aviation Administration (FAA) and Boeing issued warnings and training advisories to all operators of the 737 MAX. Despite these warnings, on March 19, 2019, a second Boeing 737 MAX aircraft operated by Ethiopian Airlines crashed 6 minutes after takeoff, killing all 157 people on board. The FAA immediately grounded all Boeing 737 MAX aircraft in the United States. Regulators around the world did the same.

The 737 MAX fleet would remain grounded for 20 months in the United States, and longer in some other important jurisdictions, such as China. Investigations confirmed significant flaws in the design of the MCAS, and in Boeing's training manuals and procedures for pilots, all of which had to be fixed before the 737 MAX could be recertified. Moreover, investigations by Congress and the FAA concluded that Boeing had exerted undue pressure on FAA aircraft inspectors to certify the 737 MAX back in March 2017, and that some Boeing personnel, including the chief technical pilot, had disparaged and deceived airline customers about the MCAS.[1]

For Boeing, the crashes and subsequent grounding were a huge blow to the engineering reputation, competitive position, and financial strength of the aircraft maker. CEO Dennis Muilenberg, who initially denied that there were any flaws in the design of the MCAS, was fired. The accident cost Boeing an estimated $20 billion in fines, compensation, and legal fees, with an indirect loss around $60 billion from some 1,200 cancelled orders for the 737 MAX. The MAX had been introduced as a competitor to Airbus' fuel-efficient A320neo aircraft, which had been getting large orders from airlines. Initially it looked as if the 737 MAX would allow Boeing to recapture the lead in new orders for narrow-bodied aircraft, but in the aftermath of the MAX grounding, Airbus widened its lead.

C10-1a History of the MAX Debacle

The MAX debacle came at the end of two decades of ups and downs for Boeing Commercial Airplane, the commercial aircraft division of the world's largest aerospace company. In the late 1990s and early 2000s, Boeing had struggled with several ethics scandals and production problems that had tarnished the reputation of the company and led to sub-par financial performance. Compounding matters, its global rival, Airbus, had been gaining market share. Between 2001 and 2005, the European company regularly garnered more new orders than Boeing.

Boeing started to gain an edge over its rival in 2003 when it formally launched its next generation jet, the 787. Built largely out of carbon fiber composites, the wide-bodied 787 was billed as the most fuel-efficient wide-bodied jet liner in the world. The 787 was forecasted to consume 20% less fuel than Boeing's older wide-bodied jet, the 767. By 2006, the 787 was logging significant orders. This, together with strong interest in Boeing's best-selling narrow-bodied jet, the 737, helped the company to recapture the lead in new commercial jet aircraft orders. Moreover, in 2006 Boeing's rival, Airbus, was struggling with significant production problems and weak orders for its new aircraft, the A380 super jumbo. Airbus was also late to market with a rival for the 787, the wide-bodied Airbus A350, which would also be built largely out of carbon fiber. While the 787 was scheduled to enter service in 2008, the A350 would not do that until 2012, giving Boeing a significant lead.

Over the next few years, Boeing encountered several production problems and technical design issues with the 787 that resulted in the introduction of the 787 being delayed five times. The 787 finally entered service in 2011, more than 3 years later than planned. From that point on, production ramped up rapidly. By the end of 2014, Boeing had delivered 225 787s, helping to propel the company's revenues and earnings. Boeing also had a very healthy backlog of over 843 firm orders for the 787. Meanwhile, Airbus encountered some production problems of its own with the A350 and the company did not deliver its first A350 until late 2014, more than 2 years behind schedule. Still, Airbus had grown its order book for the A350, and by 2014 had 779 firm orders.

By 2011, Boeing had to make another important decision regarding its narrow-bodied 737 aircraft family, which accounted for some 60% of Boeing's total aircraft deliveries. The main competitor for the 737 has long been Airbus' A320. In late 2010, Airbus announced that it would build a new version of the A320 designed to use advanced engines from Pratt & Whitney, which were estimated to be 10–15% more efficient than existing engines. Known as the A320neo (neo stands for "new engine option"), by August 2011 the aircraft had garnered an impressive 1,029 orders.

Airbus' success forced Boeing's hand. Boeing stated that they would offer a version of the 737 using new engines, and the 737 MAX was born. Initially the company was considering a complete redesign of the 737 to incorporate the carbon fiber technology used in the 787. However, management opted not to go down this road on the grounds that the redesign would have pushed out delivery of the new plane too far, enabling Airbus to gain a lead in the narrow-bodied market. Moreover, an all-new design would have cost significantly more in R&D costs, hurting Boeing's near-term cash flows. Instead, management decided to retrofit the venerable 737 with the new fuel-efficient engines, which were larger than the old 737 engines. The first planes entered service in May 2017. At that time Airbus had a backlog of 3,621 orders for the A320neo and Boeing had over 4,000 orders for the MAX.

C10-2 The Competitive Environment (Airline Industry History)

By the 2000s, the market for large commercial jet aircraft was dominated by just two companies: Boeing and Airbus. A third player in the industry, McDonnell Douglas, had been significant historically but had lost share during the 1980s and 1990s. In 1997, Boeing acquired McDonnell Douglas, primarily for its strong military business. Starting in the mid-1990s, Airbus had been gaining orders at Boeing's expense. However, thanks to the success of the 787, and an expanding order book for the 737 MAX, by 2018 Boeing was once again toe to toe with its global rival.

Both Boeing and Airbus have a full range of aircraft. Boeing offers three passenger aircraft "families" that range in size from 138 to 450 seats. They are the narrow-bodied 737 MAX and the wide-bodied 777 and 787 families (the Boeing 747 and 767 aircraft are still produced, but only offered as freighters). Each family comes in various forms. For example, there are currently four main variants of the 737 MAX passenger aircraft. They vary in size from 138 to 230 seats, and in range from 3,300 to 3,850 miles. List prices vary from around $100 million for the smallest member of the 737 MAX family to $300 million for the new 777X, the largest passenger plane in Boeing's portfolio.[2]

Airbus also offers four "families," the narrow-bodied A220 and A320neo families, and the wide-bodied A330 and A350 families. These aircraft vary in size from 100 to 410 seats. The range of list prices is similar to Boeing's. The A220 lists for around $81 million, while the largest A350 lists for up to $360 million.[3] Both companies also offer freighter versions of their wide-bodied aircraft.

Airbus was a relatively recent entrant into the market. Airbus began its life as a consortium between a French company and Germany company in 1970. Later, a British and Spanish company joined the consortium. Initially, few people gave Airbus much chance for success, but the consortium gained ground by innovating. It was the first aircraft maker to build planes that "flew by wire," made extensive use of composites, had only two flight crew (at the time most had three), and used a common cockpit layout across models. It also gained sales by being the first company to offer a wide-bodied twin-engine jet, the A300, that was positioned between smaller single aisle planes like the 737 and large aircraft such as the Boeing 747. In 2001, Airbus became a fully integrated company. It is now known as Airbus SE. The head office is in France, although the company is registered in the Netherlands as a "European" company, with shares traded in France, Germany, and Spain.

C10-2a Development and Production of Commercial Airplanes

The economics of development and production in the industry are characterized by several facts. First, the R&D and tooling costs associated with developing a new airliner are very high. Boeing spent some $5 billion to develop the original 777 in the early 1990s. The 787 was initially expected to cost $8 billion to develop but delays increased that to at least $15 billion. Development costs for Airbus' A380 super jumbo were initially estimated to be around $8 billion but reportedly reached $25 billion, in part due to delays getting certification. Estimates suggested that a clean sheet replacement for Boeing's original 737 would have cost $20 billion in R&D costs, which is a major reason why Boeing's management decided to retrofit the 737 with large engines to produce the 737 MAX, rather than design an all-new plane.

Second, given the high upfront costs, to break even, a company must capture a significant share of projected world demand over the next 20 years. For example, the breakeven point for the Airbus super jumbo, the A380, was originally estimated to have been between 250 and 270 aircraft, but then rose to 350 aircraft as development costs soared. While it was being developed, estimates of the total potential market for this aircraft varied widely. Boeing suggested that the total world market would be for no more than 320 aircraft over the first 20 years of its existence—Airbus believed that there would be demand for some 1,250 aircraft of this size. In the event, Airbus only sold 251 of the A380 before ending production in December 2021. The company did not recoup its $25 billion investment.[4]

Third, there are significant learning effects in aircraft production.[5] On average unit costs fall by about 20 percent each time *cumulative* output of a specific model is doubled. The phenomenon occurs because managers and factory workers learn over time how to assemble a particular model of plane more efficiently, reducing assembly time, boosting productivity, and lowering the marginal costs of producing subsequent aircraft.

Fourth, the assembly of aircraft is an enormously complex process. Modern planes have over one million component parts that have to be designed to fit with each other, and then produced and brought together at the right time to assemble the aircraft. At several times in the history of the industry, problems with the supply of critical components have held up production schedules and resulted in losses. In 1997, Boeing took a charge of $1.6 billion against earnings when it had to halt the production of its 737 and 747 models due to a lack of component parts. In 2008, Boeing had to delay production of the 787 due to a shortage of fasteners.

Historically, airline manufacturers tried to manage the supply process through vertical integration, making many of the component parts that went into an aircraft (engines were long the exception to this). Over the last three decades, however, there has been a trend to contract out production of components and even entire sub-assemblies to independent suppliers. On the 777, for example, Boeing outsourced about 65% of the aircraft production, by value, excluding the engines.[6] On the 787, the percentage outsourced reached 70%. While helping to reduce costs, contracting out has placed enormous onus on airline manufacturers to work closely with its suppliers to coordinate the entire production process.

Fifth, there is considerable regulatory risk associated with developing new passenger aircraft. Regulators in the United States, Europe, and China have exacting standards and can hold up development of aircraft for years, adding billions of dollars to the development process. Following the two 737 MAX crashes, the Chinese Civil Aviation Administration was the first regulator to ground the aircraft, and the last to approve it for a return to service (in December 2021). Historically, Boeing has had a close relationship to the FAA. This was long viewed as a source of advantage for Boeing, particularly as many other regulators followed the lead of the FAA. However, in the wake of the 737 MAX crashes, the FAA seems be taking a much more demanding line with Boeing. In the case of Boeing's new version of the 777, the 777X, the FAA has expressed multiple concerns about aspects of the aircraft, which have pushed back certification by at least 4 years (to 2023), adding billions in development costs to the project.[7]

C10-2b Customers (Legacy and Budget Airlines)

Demand for commercial jet aircraft is volatile and tends to reflect the financial health of the commercial airline industry, which is prone to boom and bust cycles (see Exhibit 1). The airline industry has long been characterized by new entry, intense price competition, and a perception among the traveling public that airline travel is a commodity. After a moderate boom during the 1990s, the airline industry went through a nasty downturn during 2001–2005. The downturn started in early 2001 due to a slowdown in business travel after the boom of the 1990s. It was compounded by a dramatic slump in airline travel after the terrorist attacks on the United States on September of 2001. Between 2001 and 2005, the entire global airline industry lost some $40 billion, more money than it had made since its inception.[8] The industry recovered in 2006 and 2007, only to rack up big losses again in 2008 and 2009 due to the recession that was ushered in by the 2008–2009 global financial crisis.

High fuel prices periodically make things worse for airlines. Due to a surge fuel prices, the bill for jet fuel represented over 25% of the industry's total operating costs in 2006, compared to less than 10% in 2001.[9] By 2014, because of high prices for jet fuel, fuel accounted for 33% of operating expenses for U.S. airlines. Wages and benefits were the second biggest operating expense, accounting for 25% of costs in 2014.[10] Due to the importance of fuel costs, airlines have a strong preference for more fuel-efficient aircraft.

During 2015–2019, the economy recovered, fuel prices fell, airline profitability went up, and orders flowed into Boeing and Airbus. Then, in March of 2020, the COVID-19 pandemic hit, lockdowns spread around the world, and airline travel collapsed, falling by more than 50% worldwide. Before pandemic-related financial assistance from the government, the U.S. airline industry lost over $20 billion in 2021. Globally, the airline industry lost $138 billion in 2020, and $52 billion in 2021. Although demand for airline travel recovered strongly in 2022 as the COVID-19 pandemic moved into the endemic phase, record high prices for jet fuel continued to strain the financial position of many airlines.[11]

In addition to volatile demand for air travel, and periodic spikes in fuel prices, one of the big factors hurting established "legacy" airlines around the world has been the rise of budget carriers, such as Southwest Airlines and Jet Blue in the United States, and Ryan Air and EasyJet in Europe. In the United States, for example, in 2000, the

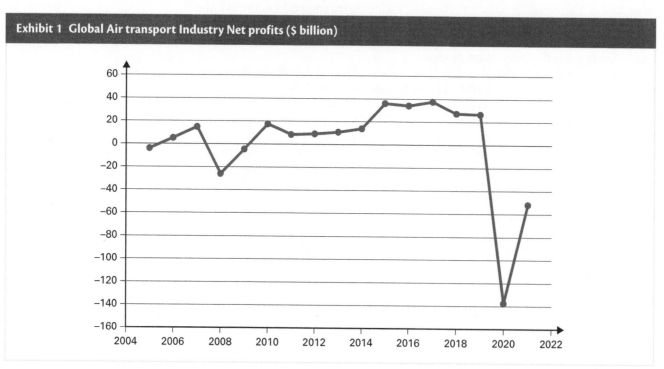

Exhibit 1 Global Air transport Industry Net profits ($ billion)

Source: International Air travel Association Annual Review, 2022.

long-established "legacy" airlines such as United, Delta, and American Airlines carried 73% of all domestic traffic. By 2021, their share had fallen to 53%.[12]

The key to the success of the budget airlines is a strategy that gives them a 30–50 percent cost advantage over legacy airlines. The budget airlines all follow the same basic script—they purchase just one type of aircraft (some standardize on Boeing 737s, others on Airbus 320s). They hire non-union labor and cross-train employees to perform multiple jobs (e.g., to help meet turnaround times, the pilots might help check tickets at the gate). As a result of flexible work rules, in 2005, Southwest needed only 80 employees to support and fly an aircraft, compared to 115 at traditional airlines. The budget airlines also favor flying "point to point," rather than through hubs, and often use cheap secondary airports, rather than major hubs. They focus on large markets with lots of traffic (e.g., up and down the East Coast of the United States). There are no frills on the flights, no in-flight food, or complementary drinks, and often only one class of seating (coach). And prices are set low to fill up the seats.

In contrast, the operations of major legacy airlines are based on the network or "hub and spoke" system. Under this system, the network airlines route their flights through major hubs. Often, a single airline will dominate a hub (thus, United dominates Chicago O'Hare airport, American Airlines dominates Dallas, and so on). This system was developed for good reason—it was a way of efficiently using airline capacity when there wasn't enough demand to fill a plane flying point to point. By using a hub-and-spoke system, the major network airlines have been able to serve some 38,000 city pairs, some of which generate fewer than 50 passengers per day. But by focusing a few hundred city pairs where there is sufficient demand to fill their planes and flying directly between them (point to point) the budget airlines seem to have found a way around this constraint. The network carriers also suffer from a higher cost structure due to their legacy of a unionized workforce. In addition, their costs are pushed higher by their superior in-flight service. In good times, the network carriers could recoup their costs by charging higher prices than the discount airlines, particularly for business travelers, who pay more to book late, and to fly business or first class. In the competitive environment of the 2000s, however, this was no longer always the case. Between 2000 and 2022, the price of an average round-trip domestic ticket in the United States increased 15%, while the consumer price index increased 168% (in other words, adjusted for inflation there had been a substantial decline in the price of airline travel).[13]

Due to the impact of increased competition from budget airlines, the real yields that airlines get from carrying passengers have fallen steadily for decades. The real yield that U.S. airlines got from passengers fell from 8.70 cents per mile in 1980 to 6.37 cents per mile in 1990, 5.12 cents per mile in 2000, and 4.00 cents per mile in 2005 (these figures are expressed in constant 1978 cents).[14] Real yields have also declined elsewhere. With real yields declining, the only way that airlines can become profitable is to reduce their operating costs—and two of the airlines' biggest costs are that of purchasing or leasing new aircraft, and fuel costs. Thus, airlines bargain hard to reduce the price they pay to Airbus and Boeing for new aircraft, often playing the two companies off against each other, and they have a strong preference for purchasing more fuel-efficient planes.

By the 2000s, legacy airlines in the United States were improving their operating efficiency to better compete with budget airlines, often by adopting many of the practices of budget airlines. This helped to grow traffic volumes, raise load factors, and reduce operating costs per passenger mile. Load factor refers to the percentage of a plane that is full on average. Prior to the COVID-19 pandemic, load factors for U.S. airlines had increased from around 65% in 2000 to consistently over 80% in 2019.

C10-2c Demand Projections

Both Boeing and Airbus issue annual projects of likely future demand for commercial jet aircraft. These projections are based upon assumptions about future global economic growth, the resulting growth in demand for air travel, and the financial health of the world's airlines.

In its 2022 report, Boeing assumed that the world economy would grow by 2.6% per annum over the next 20 years, and since airline travel is income elastic, Boeing forecasts that this will generate air traffic growth of 3.8% per annum.[15] To service this growing demand, Boeing forecasts that airlines will expand their fleets from 25,900 aircraft in service in 2019, to 47,080 in service by 2041. Factoring in the retirement of existing aircraft, this will require 41,170 new aircraft deliveries by 2041, valued at over $3.5 trillion. Narrow-bodied single-aisle planes (such as the 737 MAX and A320neo) are forecast to account for 70% of the global fleet in 2041, up from 68% today. The wide-bodied fleet (such as the 787 and A350) will comprise 18% of the fleet in 2041. Cargo aircraft (7%) and regional jets (5%) will comprise the balance. In terms of geographic demand, Asia is expected to lead with way, accounting for 42% of all new deliveries between 2022 and 2041 (with China alone accounting for 21%). North America will account for 23% of deliveries and Europe for 21%. Airbus' 20-year forecast was similar to Boeing's.

C10-3 Boeing's History[16]

William Boeing established the Boeing Company in 1916 in Seattle. In the early 1950s, Boeing took an enormous gamble when it decided to build a large jet aircraft that could be sold both to the military as a tanker, and to commercial airlines as a passenger plane. Known as the Dash 80, the plane had swept-back wings and four jet engines. Boeing invested $16 million to develop the Dash 80, two-thirds of the company's entire profits during the postwar years. The Dash 80 was the basis for two aircraft—the KC-135 Air Force (Stratotanker) and the Boeing 707. Introduced into service in 1957, the 707 was the world's first commercially successful passenger jet aircraft. Boeing went on to sell some 856 Boeing 707s along with 820 KC-135s. The final 707, a freighter, rolled off the production line in 1994 (production of passenger planes ended in 1978). The closest rival to the 707 was the Douglas DC 8, of which some 556 were ultimately sold.

The 707 was followed by several other successful jet liners, including the 727 (entered service in 1962), the 737 (entered service in 1967), and the 747 (entered service in 1970). The single-aisle 737 went on to become the workhorse of many airlines. In the 2000s, a completely redesigned version of the 737 that could seat between 110 and 180 passengers was still selling strong. Cumulative sales of the 737 totaled 6,500 by mid-2006, making it by far the most popular commercial jet aircraft ever sold.

It was the 747 "jumbo jet," however, that probably best-defined Boeing. In 1966, when Boeing's board made the decision to develop the 747, they were widely viewed as betting the company on the jet. The 747 was born out of the desire of Pan Am, then America's largest airline, for a 400-seat passenger aircraft that could fly 5,000 miles. Pan Am believed that the aircraft would be ideal for the growing volume of trans-continental traffic. However, beyond Pan Am, which committed to purchasing 25 aircraft, demand was very uncertain. Moreover, the estimated $400 million in development and tooling costs placed a heavy burden on Boeing's financial resources. To make a return on its investment, the company estimated it would have to sell close to 400 aircraft. To complicate matters further, Boeing's principal competitors, Lockheed and McDonnell Douglas, were each developing 250-seat jumbo jets.

Boeing's big bet turned out to be auspicious. Pan Am's competitors feared being left out behind, and by the end of 1970, almost 200 orders for the aircraft had been placed. Successive models of the 747 extended the range of the aircraft. The 747-400, introduced in 1989, had a range of 8,000 miles and a maximum seating capacity of 550 (although most configurations seated around 400 passengers). By this time, both Douglas and Lockheed had exited the market, giving Boeing a lucrative monopoly in the very large commercial jet category. By 2005, the company had sold some 1,430 747s, and was actively selling its latest version of the 747 family, the 747-8 which was scheduled to enter service in 2008.

By the mid-1970s Boeing was past the break-even point on all of its models (707, 727, 737, and 747). The positive cash flow helped to fund investment in two new aircraft, the narrow-bodied 757 and the wide-bodied 767. The 757 was designed as a replacement to the aging 727, while the 767 was a response to a similar aircraft from Airbus. These were the first Boeing aircraft to be designed with two-person cockpits, rather than three. Indeed, the cockpit layout was identical, allowing crew to shift from one aircraft to the other. The 767 was also the first aircraft for which Boeing subcontracted a significant amount of work to a trio of three Japanese manufacturers—Mitsubishi, Kawasaki, and Fuji—who supplied about 15% of the airframe. Introduced in 1981, both aircraft were successful. Some 1,049 757s were sold during the life of the program (which ended in 2003). Over 1,346 767s had been sold by 2022, and the program was still ongoing (although only freighter versions were now being built).

The next Boeing plane was the 777. A two-engine wide-bodied aircraft with seating capacity of up to 400 and a range of almost 8,000 miles, the 777 program was initiated in 1990. The 777 was seen as a response to Airbus' successful A330 and A340 wide-bodied aircraft. Development costs were estimated at some $5 billion. The 777 was the first wide-bodied long-haul jet to have only two engines. It was also the first to be designed entirely on computer. To develop the 777, for the first time Boeing used cross-functional teams composed of engineering and production employees. It also bought major suppliers and customers into the development process. As with the 767, a significant amount of work was outsourced to foreign manufacturers including the Japanese trio of Mitsubishi, Kawasaki, and Fuji who supplied 20% of the 777 airframe. In total, some 60% of parts for the 777 were outsourced. By mid-2006, the 777 proved to be another successful venture—850 had been ordered, far greater than the 200 or so required to break even.

In December 1996, Boeing stunned the aerospace industry by announcing it would merge with longtime rival McDonnell Douglas in a deal estimated to be worth $13.3 billion. The merger was driven by Boeing's desire to strengthen its presence in the defense and space side of the aerospace business areas where McDonnell Douglas was traditionally strong. On the commercial side of the aerospace business, McDonnell Douglas had been losing market share since the 1970s. By 1996, Douglas accounted for less than 10% of production in the large commercial jet aircraft market and only 3% of new orders placed that year. The dearth of new orders meant the long-term outlook for McDonnell Douglas's commercial business was increasingly murky. With or without the merger, many analysts felt that it was only a matter of time before McDonnell Douglas would be forced to exit from the commercial jet aircraft business. In their view, the merger with Boeing merely accelerated that process.

The merger transformed Boeing into a broad-based aerospace business within which commercial aerospace accounted for 40–60% of total revenue depending upon the stage of the commercial production cycle. In 2001, for example, the commercial aircraft group accounted for $35 billion in revenues out of a corporate total of $58 billion, or 60%. In 2005, with the delivery cycle at a low point (but the order cycle rebounding), the commercial airplane group accounted for $22.7 billion out of a total of $54.8 billion, or 41%. The balance of revenue was made up by a wide range of military aircraft, weapons and defense systems, and space systems.

In the early 2000s, in a highly symbolic act, Boeing moved its corporate headquarters from Seattle to Chicago. The move was an attempt to put some distance between top corporate officers and the commercial aerospace business, the headquarters of which remained in Seattle. The move was also intended to signal to the investment community that Boeing was far more than its commercial businesses.

To some extent, the move to Chicago may have been driven by several production missteps in the late 1990s that hit the company at a time when it should have been enjoying financial success. During the mid-1990s orders had boomed as Boeing cut prices in an aggressive move to gain share from Airbus. However, delivering these aircraft meant that Boeing had to more than double its production schedule between 1996 and 1997. As it attempted to do this, the company ran into some severe production bottlenecks.[17] The company scrambled to hire and train some 41,000 workers, recruiting many from suppliers, a move it came to regret when many of the suppliers could not meet Boeing's demands and shipments of parts were delayed. In the fall of 1997, things got so bad that Boeing shut down its 747 and 737 production lines so that workers could catch up with out-of-sequence work and wait for back-ordered parts to arrive. Ultimately, the company had to take a $1.6 billion charge against earnings to account for higher costs and penalties paid to airlines for the late delivery of jets. As a result, Boeing made very little money out of its mid-1990s order boom. The head of Boeing's commercial aerospace business was fired, and the company committed itself to a major acceleration of its attempt to overhaul its production system, elements of which dated back half a century.

C10-4 Boeing in the 2000s

In the 2000s, three things dominated the development of Boeing Commercial Aerospace. First, the company accelerated a decade long project aimed at improving the company's production methods by adopting the lean production systems initially developed by Toyota and applying them to the manufacture of large jet aircraft. Second, the company considered and then rejected the idea of building a successor to the 747. Third, Boeing decided to develop a new wide-bodied long-haul jetliner, the 787.

C10-4a Lean Production at Boeing

Boeing's attempt to revolutionize the way planes were built dates to the early 1990s. Beginning in 1990, the company started to send teams of executives to Japan to study the production systems of Japan's leading manufacturers, and particularly Toyota. Toyota had pioneered a new way of assembling automobiles, known as lean production (in contrast to conventional mass production).

Toyota's lean production system was developed by one of the company's engineers, Ohno Taiichi.[18] After working at Toyota for 5 years and visiting Ford's U.S. plants, Ohno became convinced that the mass production philosophy for making cars was flawed. He saw numerous problems, including three major drawbacks. First, long production runs created massive inventories, which had to be stored in large warehouses. This was expensive because of the cost of warehousing and because inventories tied up capital in unproductive uses. Second, if the initial machine settings were wrong, long production runs resulted in the production of a large number of defects (that is, waste). And third, the mass production system was unable to accommodate consumer preferences for product diversity.

In looking for ways to make shorter production runs economical, Ohno developed a number of techniques designed to reduce setup times for production equipment, a major source of fixed costs. By using a system of levers and pulleys, he was able to reduce the time required to change dies on stamping equipment from a full day in 1950 to 3 minutes by 1971. This advance made small production runs economical, which allowed Toyota to respond better to consumer demands for product diversity. Small production runs also eliminated the need to hold large inventories, thereby reducing warehousing costs. Furthermore, small product runs, and the lack of inventory meant that defective parts were produced only in small numbers and entered the assembly process immediately. This reduced waste and made it easier to trace defects to their source and fix the problem. In sum, Ohno's innovations enabled Toyota to produce a more diverse product range at a lower unit cost than was possible with conventional mass production.

Impressed with what Toyota had done, in the mid-1990s, Boeing started to experiment with applying Toyota like lean production methods to the production of aircraft. Production at Boeing use to be all about producing parts in high volumes, and then storing them in warehouses until they were ready to be used in the assembly process. After visiting Toyota, engineers realized that Boeing was drowning in inventory. A huge amount of space and capital was tied up in things that didn't add value. Moreover, expensive specialized machines often took up a lot of space and were frequently idle for long stretches of time.

Like Ohno at Toyota, the company engineers started to think about how they could modify equipment and processes at Boeing to reduce waste. Boeing set aside space and time for teams of creative plant employees—design engineers, maintenance technicians, electricians, machinists, and operators—to start experimenting with machinery. They called these teams "moonshiners." The term "moonshine" was coined by Japanese executives who visited the United States after World War II. They were impressed by two things in the United States: supermarkets and the stills built by people in the Appalachian hills. They noticed that people built these stills with no money. They would use salvaged parts to make small stills that produced alcohol that they sold for money. The Japanese took this philosophy back home with them and applied it to industrial machinery, which is where Boeing executives saw the concept in operation in the 1990s. With the help of Japanese consultants, they decided to apply the moonshine creative philosophy at Boeing—to produce new "right-sized" machines with very little money that could be used to make money.

The moonshine teams were trained in lean production techniques, given a small budget, and then set loose. Initially many of the moonshine teams focused on redesigning equipment to produce parts. Underlying this choice was a Boeing study that showed that more than 80% of the parts manufactured for aircraft are less than 12 inches long, and yet the metal working machinery is huge, inflexible, and could only economically produce parts in large lots.[19]

Soon, empowered moonshine teams were designing their own equipment—small-scale machines with wheels on that could be moved around the plant and took up little space. A case in point, one team replaced a large stamping machine that cost six figures and was used to produce L-shaped metal parts in batches of 1,000 with a miniature stamping machine powered by a small hydraulic motor that could be wheeled around the plant. With the small machine that cost a couple of thousand dollars, parts could be produced very quickly in small lots, eliminating the need for inventory. They also made a sanding machine and a parts cleaner of equal size. Now the entire process—from stamping the raw material to the finished part—is completed in minutes (instead of hours or days) just by configuring these machines into a small cell and having them serviced by a single person. The small scale and quick turnaround now made it possible to produce these parts just in time, eliminating the need to produce and store inventory.[20]

Another example of a moonshine innovation concerned the process for loading seats onto a plane during assembly. Historically, this was a cumbersome process. After the seats would arrive at Boeing from a supplier, wheels were attached to each seat, and then the seats were delivered to the factory floor in a large container. An overhead crane lifted the container up to the level of the aircraft door. Then the seats were unloaded and rolled into the aircraft, before being installed. The process was repeated until all the seats had been loaded. For a single aisle plane this could take twelve hours. For a wide-bodied jet it would take much longer. A moonshine team adapted a hay elevator to perform the same job. It cost a lot less, delivered seats quickly through the passenger door, and took just 2 hours, while eliminating the need for cranes.[21]

With multiple such examples, soon the company started to have a very significant impact on production costs. A drill machine was built for 5% of the cost of a full-scale machine from Ingersoll-Rand; portable routers were built for 0.2% of the cost of a large fixed router; one process that took 2,000 minutes for a 100-part order (20 minutes per part because of setup, machining, and transit) now took 100 minutes (1 minute per part). Employees building 737 floor beams reduced labor hours by 74%, increased inventory turns from 2 to 18 per year, and reduced manufacturing space by 50%. Employees building the 777 tail cut lead time by 70% and reduced space and work in progress by 50%.; production of parts for landing gear support used to take 32 moves from machine to machine, and required 10 months' production now took 3 moves and 25 days.[22]

In general, Boeing found that it was able to produce smaller lots of parts economically, often from machines that it built itself, which were smaller and cost less than the machines available from outside vendors. In turn, these innovations enabled Boeing to switch to just in time inventory systems and reduce waste. Boeing was also able to save on space. By eliminating large production machinery at its Auburn facility, replacing

Exhibit 2 The Converted Hay Loader at Work

Davdi Vardi/Shutterstock.com

much of it with smaller more flexible machines, Boeing was able to free up 1.3 million square feet of space, and sold seven buildings.[23]

In addition to moonshine teams, Boeing also adopted other process improvement methodologies, using them when deemed appropriate. Six Sigma quality improvement processes are widely used within Boeing. The most wide-reaching process change, however, was the decision to switch from a static assembly line to a moving line. In traditional aircraft manufacture, planes are docked in angled stalls. Ramps surround each plane, and workers go in and out to find parts and install them. Moving a plane to the next workstation was a complex process. The aircraft had to be down jacked from its workstation, a powered cart was bought in, the aircraft was towed to the next station, and then it was jacked up. This could take two shifts. A lot of time was wasted bringing parts to a stall and moving a plane from one stall to the next.

In 2001, Boeing introduced a moving assembly line into its Renton plant near Seattle, which manufactures the 737 (see Exhibit 3). With a moving line, each aircraft is attached to a "sled" that rides a magnetic strip embedded in the factory floor, pulling the aircraft at a rate of 2 inches per minute, moving past a series of stations where tools and parts arrive when needed, allowing workers to install the proper assemblies. The setup eliminates wandering for tools and parts, as well as expensive tug pulls or crane lifts (just having tools delivered to workstations, rather than having workers fetch them, was found to save 20–45 minutes on every shift). Preassembly tasks are performed on feeder lines. For example, inboard and outboard flaps are assembled on the wing before it arrives for joining to the fuselage.[24]

Like a Toyota assembly line, the moving line can be stopped if a problem arises. Lights are used to indicate the state of the line. A green light indicates a normal workflow, the first sign of a stoppage brings a yellow warning light, and if the problem isn't solved within 15 minutes, a purple light indicates that the line has

Exhibit 3 The Moving Line

First Class Photography/Shutterstock.com

stopped. Each work area and feeder line has their own lights, so there is no doubt where the problem is.[25]

The cumulative effects of these process innovations have been significant. By 2005, assembly time for the 737 had been cut from 22 days to just 11 days. By 2019, it was down to 9 days. In addition, work-in-process inventory had been reduced by 55% and stored inventory by 59%.[26] By 2006, all of Boeing's production lines except that for the 747 had shifted from static bays to a moving line. The 747 shifted to a moving line in the late 2000s.

C10-4b The Super-Jumbo Decisions

In the early 1990s, Boeing and Airbus started to contemplate new aircraft to replace Boeing's aging 747. The success of the 747 had given Boeing a monopoly in the market for very large jet aircraft, making the plane one of the most profitable in the jet age, but the basic design dated back to the 1960s, and some believed there might be sufficient demand for a super-jumbo aircraft with as many as 900 seats.

Initially, the two companies considered establishing a joint venture to share the costs and risks associated with a developing a super-jumbo aircraft, but Boeing withdrew in 1995, citing costs and uncertain demand prospects. Airbus subsequently concluded that Boeing was never serious about the joint venture, and the discussions were nothing more than a ploy to keep Airbus from developing its own plane.[27]

After Boeing withdrew, Airbus started to talk about offering a competitor to the 747 in 1995. The plane, then dubbed the A3XX, was to be a super jumbo with capacity for over 500 passengers. Indeed, Airbus stated that some versions of the plane might carry as many as 900 passengers. Airbus initially estimated that there would be demand for some 1,400 planes of this size over 20 years, and that development costs would total around $9 billion (estimates ultimately increased to some $15 billion). Boeing's latest 747 offering—the 747-400—could carry around 416 passengers in three classes.

Boeing responded by drafting plans to develop new versions of the 747 family: the 747-500X and the 747-600X. The 747-600X was to have a new (larger) wing, a fuselage almost 50 feet longer than the 747-400, would carry 550 passengers in three classes and have a range of 7,700 miles. The smaller 747-500X would have carried 460 passengers in three classes and had a range of 8,700 miles.

After taking a close look at the market for a super-jumbo replacement to the 747, in early 1997, Boeing announced that it would not proceed with the program. The reasons given for this decision included the limited market and high development costs, which at the time were estimated to be $7 billion. There were also fears that the wider wingspan of the new planes would mean that airports would have to redesign some of their gates to take the aircraft. Boeing, McDonnell Douglas (prior to the merger with Boeing) and the major manufacturers of jet engines all forecast demand for about 500–750 such aircraft over the next 20 years. Airbus alone forecast demand has high as 1,400 aircraft. Boeing stated that the fragmentation of the market due to the rise of "point-to-point" flights across oceans would limit demand for a super-jumbo. Instead of focusing on the super-jumbo category, Boeing stated that it would develop new versions of the 767 and 777 aircraft that could fly up to 9,000 miles and carry as many as 400 passengers.

Airbus, however, continued to push forward with plans to develop the A3XX. In December 2000, with more than 50 orders in hand, the board of EADS, Airbus' parent company, approved development of the plane, which was now dubbed the A380. Development costs at this point were pegged at $12 billion, and the plane was forecasted to enter service in 2006 with Singapore Airlines. The A380 was to have two passenger decks, more space per seat, and wider aisles. It would carry 555 passengers in great comfort, something that passengers would appreciate on long transoceanic flights. According to Airbus, the plane would carry up to 35% more passengers than the most popular 747-400 configuration yet cost per seat would be 15–20% lower due to operating efficiencies. Concerns were raised about turnaround time at airport gates for such a large plane, but Airbus stated that dual boarding bridges and wider aisles meant that turnaround times would be no more than those for the 747-400.

Airbus also stated that the A380 was also designed to operate on exiting runways and for within existing gates. However, London's Heathrow airport found that it had to spend some $450 million to accommodate the A380, widening taxiways and building a baggage reclaim area for the plane. Similarly, 18 U.S. airports had reportedly spent some $1 billion just to accommodate the A380.[28]

C10-4c The 787

While Airbus pushed forward with the A380, in March 2001, Boeing announced the development of a radically new aircraft. Dubbed the sonic cruiser, the plane would carry 250 passengers 9,000 miles and fly just below the speed of sound, cutting 1 hour off transatlantic flights and 3 hours off transpacific flights. To keep down operating costs, the sonic cruiser would be built out of low-weight carbon fiber "composites." Although the announcement created considerable interest in the aviation community, in the wake of the recession that hit the airline industry after September 11, 2001, both Boeing and the airlines became considerably less enthusiastic. In March 2002, the program was canceled. Instead, Boeing said that it would develop a more conventional aircraft using composite technology. The plane was initially known as the 7E7 with the E standing for "efficient" (the plane was renamed the 787 in early 2005).

In April 2004, the 7E7 program was launched with an order for 50 aircraft worth $6 billion from All Nippon Airlines of Japan. It was the largest launch order in Boeing's history. The 7E7 was a twin-aisle, wide-bodied, two-engine aircraft designed to carry 200–300 passengers up to 8,500 miles, making the 7E7 well suited for long-haul point-to-point flights. The range exceeded all but the longest-range plane in the 777 family, and the 7E7 could fly 750 miles more than Airbus' closest competitor, the mid-sized A330-200. With a fuselage built entirely out of composites, the aircraft was lighter and would use 20% less fuel than existing aircraft of comparable size.

The plane was also designed with passenger comfort in mind. The seats would be wider, as would the aisles, and the windows were larger than in existing aircraft. The plane would be pressurized at 6,000 feet of altitude, as opposed to 8,000 feet, which is standard industry practice. Airline cabin humidity was typically kept at 10% to avoid moisture buildup and corrosion, but composites don't corrode so humidity would be closer to 20–30%.[29]

Initial estimates suggested that the jet would cost some $7–8 billion to develop and enter service in 2008. Boeing decided to outsource more work for the 787 than on any other aircraft to date. Some 35% of the plane's fuselage and wing structure would be built by Boeing. The trio of Japanese companies that worked on the 767 and 777, Mitsubishi Heavy Industries, Kawasaki Heavy Industries, and Fuji Heavy Industries, would build another 35%, and some 26% would be built by Italian companies, particularly Alenia.[30] For the first time, Boeing asked its major suppliers to bear some of the development costs for the aircraft.

The plane was to be assembled at Boeing's wide-bodied plant in Everett, Washington State. Large sub-assemblies were to be built by major suppliers, and then shipped to Everett for final assembly. The idea was to "snap together" the parts in Everett in 3 days, cutting down on total assembly time. To speed up transportation, Boeing would adopt air freight as its major transportation method for many components.

Airbus' initial response was to dismiss Boeing's claims of cost savings as inconsequential. They pointed out that even if the 787 used less fuel than the A330, that was equivalent to just 4% of total operating costs.[31] However, even by Airbus' calculations, as fuel prices starting to accelerate, the magnitude of the savings rose. Moreover, Boeing quickly started to snag some significant orders for the 787. In 2004, Boeing booked 56 orders for the 787 and in 2005 some 232 orders. Another 85 orders were booked in the first 9 months of 2006 for a running total of 373—well beyond break-even point.

In December 2004, Airbus announced that it would develop a new model, the A350, to compete directly with the 787. The planes were to be long-haul twin-aisle jets, seating 200–300 passengers, and constructed of composites. The order flow, however, was slow, with airlines complaining that the A350 did not match the Boeing 787 on operating efficiency, range, or passenger comfort. Airbus went back to the drawing board and in mid-2006 it announced a new version of the A350, the A350 XWB for "extra Wide Body." Airbus estimated that the A350 XWB would cost $10 billion to develop and enter service in 2012, several years behind the 787. The two-engine A350 XWB will carry between 250 and 375 passengers and fly up to 8,500 miles. The largest versions of the A350 XWB will be competing directly with the Boeing 777, not the 787. Like the 787, the A350 XWB it will be built primarily of composite materials. The "extra wide body" is designed to enhance passenger comfort. To finance the A350 XWB, Airbus stated that it would seek launch aid from Germany, France, Spain, and the United Kingdom, all countries where major parts of Airbus are based.[32]

C10-5 Trade Tensions

It is impossible to discuss the global aerospace industry without touching on trade issues. Over the last three decades, both Boeing and Airbus have charged that their competitor benefited unfairly from government subsidies. Until 2001, Airbus functioned as a consortium of four European aircraft manufacturers: one British (20.0% ownership stake), one French (37.9% ownership), one German (37.9% ownership), and one Spanish (4.2% ownership). In the 1980s and early 1990s, Boeing maintained that subsidies from these nations allow Airbus to set unrealistically low prices, to offer concessions and attractive financing terms to airlines, to write off development costs, and to use state-owned airlines to obtain orders. According to a study by the U.S. Department of Commerce, Airbus received more than $13.5 billion in government subsidies between 1970 and 1990 ($25.9 billion if commercial interest rates are applied). Most of these subsidies were in the form of loans at below-market interest rates and tax breaks. The subsidies financed R&D and provided attractive financing terms for Airbus' customers. Airbus responded by pointing out that Boeing had benefited for years from hidden U.S. government subsidies, and particularly Pentagon R&D grants.

In 1992, the two sides appeared to reach an agreement that put to rest their long-standing trade dispute. The 1992 pact, which was negotiated by the European Union on behalf of the four member states, limited direct government subsidies to 33% of the total costs of developing a new aircraft and specified that and such subsidies had to be repaid with interest within 17 years. The agreement also limited indirect subsidies, such as government-supported military research that had applications to commercial aircraft, to 3% of a country's annual total commercial aerospace revenues, or 4% of commercial aircraft revenues of any single company on that country. Although Airbus officials stated that the controversy had now been resolved, Boeing officials argued that they would still be competing for years against subsidized products.

The trade dispute heated up again in 2004 when Airbus announced the first version of the A350 to compete against Boeing's 787. What raised a red flag for the U.S. government were signs from Airbus that it would apply for $1.7 billion in launch aid to help fund the development of the A350. As far as the United States was concerned, this was too much. In late 2004, U.S. Trade Representative Robert Zoellick issued a statement that formally renounced the 1992 agreement and called for an end to launch subsidies. According to Zoellick, "since its creation 35 years ago, some Europeans have justified subsidies to Airbus as necessary to support an infant industry. If that rationalization were ever valid, its time has long passed. Airbus now sells more large civil aircraft than Boeing." Zoellick went on to claim that Airbus had received some $3.7 billion in launch aid for the A380 plus another $2.8 billion in indirect subsidies, including $1.7 billion in taxpayer-funded infrastructure improvements for a total of $6.5 billion.

Airbus shot back that Boeing too continued to enjoy lavish subsidies, and that the company had received some $12 billion from NASA to develop technology, much of which has found its way into commercial jet aircraft. The Europeans also contended that Boeing would receive as much as $3.2 billion in tax breaks from Washington State, where the 787 was to be assembled, and more than $1 billion in loans from the Japanese government to three Japanese suppliers, who would build over one-third of the 787. Moreover, Airbus was quick to point out that a trade war would not benefit either side, and that Airbus purchased some $6 billion a year in supplies from companies in the United States.

In January 2005, both the United States and European Union agreed to freeze direct subsidies to the two aircraft makers while talks continued. However, in May 2005, news reports suggested, and Airbus confirmed, that the jet maker had applied to four EU governments for launch aid for the A350, and that the British government would announce some $700 million in aid at the Paris Air Show in mid-2005. Simultaneously, the European Union offered to cut launch aid for the A350 by 30%. Dissatisfied, the U.S. side decided that the talks were going nowhere, and on May 31, the United States formally filed a request with the World Trade Organization (WTO) for the establishment of a dispute resolution panel to resolve the issues. The European Union quickly responded by filing a countersuit with the WTO, claiming that U.S. aid to Boeing exceeded the terms set out in the 1992 agreement.[33]

This dispute would carry on for the next 16 years, with Boeing and Airbus filing suits and counter suits with the WTO, each accusing the other of benefiting from government subsidies of aircraft. In 2011, the WTO ruled on the complaint by Boeing, and on Airbus' counterclaim. The WTO stated that Airbus had indeed benefited from some $15 billion in improper launch aid subsidies over the prior 40 years, and that this practice must stop. Boeing, however, had little time to celebrate. In a separate ruling, the WTO stated that Boeing too had benefited from improper subsidies, including $5.3 billion from the U.S. government to develop the 787 (the WTO stated that most of these subsidies were in the form of payments from NASA to development space technology that subsequently had commercial applications).[34]

Things got even more complicated in 2013 when Boeing announced it would build a new version of its 777 aircraft, the 777X, in Washington State after the state legislature agreed to $8.7 billion in new aerospace industry tax breaks. The European Union responded by filing another complaint with the WTO, claiming that the tax breaks were a prohibited subsidy.

In 2019, the WTO had awarded the United States the right to impose tariffs of $7.5 billion on annual imports of EU goods to counter the European Union's use of subsidies to support Airbus. Then, in 2020, the WTO granted the European Union permission to impose tariffs on $4 billion of U.S. goods is response to Washington State's tax breaks for Boeing.

By 2021, it was clear that this constant back and forth was benefiting neither party. In June 2021, the two sides announced a truce in the ongoing trade war, and to suspend all retaliatory tariffs for the next 5 years. The deal included a commitment for collaboration between the United States and European Union to confront a new threat—China's growing ambitions to build an aircraft sector based on "non-market practices."[35]

C10-6 Boeing in the 2010s

By the 2010s, huge financial bets had been placed on somewhat different visions of the future of airline travel—Airbus with the A380 and Boeing with the 787. By mid-2011, Airbus had delivered 51 A380s and had a backlog of 236 orders. The rate of new orders had been slow, however. Boeing had a backlog of 827 787s on order. Airbus also hedged its bets by announcing the A350 XWB, and after a slow start, the aircraft now known as the A350, has amassed some 567 orders as compared to 827 for the 787.

C10-6a Supply Chain Issues

Both companies experienced substantial production problems and faced significant delays in producing their new aircraft. In mid-2006, Airbus announced that deliveries for the A380 would be delayed by 6 months while the company dealt with "production issues" arising from problems installing the wiring bundles in the A380. Estimates suggest that the delay would cost Airbus some $2.6 billion over the next 4 years.[36] Within months, Airbus had revised the expected delay to 18 months, and stated that the number of A380s it now needed to sell to break even had increased from 250 to 420 aircraft. The company also stated that due to production problems, it would only be able to deliver 84 A380 planes by 2010, compared to an original estimate of 420 (in fact it delivered only half of this amount).[37]

Boeing ran into several production and design problems with the 787 that resulted in five delay announcements, pushing out the first deliveries more than 3 years. For the 787, Boeing outsourced an unprecedented amount of work to suppliers. This was seen at the time as a risky move, particularly given the amount of new technology incorporated into the 787. As it turns out, several suppliers had problems meeting Being's quality specification, supplying substandard parts that had to be reworked or redesigned. The issues included a shortage of fasteners, a misalignment between the cockpit section and the fuselage, and microscopic wrinkles in the fuselage skin. In addition, Boeing found that it had to redesign parts of the section where the wing met the fuselage. Boeing executives complained that their engineers were often fixing problems "that should not have come to us in the first place."[38]

Some company sources suggested that Boeing erred by not managing its supplier relationships as well as it should have done. There may have been a lack of ongoing communication between Boeing and key suppliers. Boeing tended to throw design specifications "over the wall" to suppliers, and then was surprised when they failed to comply fully with the company's expectations. In addition, Boeing's dependency on single suppliers for key components meant that a problem in any one of those suppliers could create a bottleneck that would hold up production.

To fix some of the supply chain issues, in 2009, Boeing purchased a Vought Industries Aircraft plant for $580 million. Vought had been in a joint venture with the Italian company, Alenia Aeronautical, to make fuselage parts for the 787. Vought had not been able to keep up with the demands of the program and Boeing's acquisition had been seen as a move to exert more control over the production process and inject capital into Vought.

C10-6b New Entrants

Another issue confronting Boeing and Airbus in the 2010s was the emergence of two potential new entrants into the narrow-bodied segment of the commercial aerospace industry—Bombardier of Canada and the Commercial Aircraft Corporation of China, Ltd. (COMAC).

The Canadian regional jet manufacturer, Bombardier, was developing a 110- to 160-seat aircraft that made extensive use of composites to reduce weight and was powered by new fuel-efficient geared turbofan engines from Pratt & Whitney. These features were forecasted to reduce operating costs by about 15% compared to the older 737 and A320 models. Known as the CSeries, by early 2015, Bombardier had 243 firm orders for this aircraft plus options for another 162. The first CSeries aircraft entered service in 2016 with Swiss Global Airlines and AirBaltic. Also in 2016, Delta placed an order for 75 Cseries aircraft, with options on 50 more.

Boeing responded to the Delta order by filing a "dumping" complaint with the United States International Trade Commission (ITC), claiming that Bombardier was selling its aircraft to Delta at $19.6 million each, significantly below their $33.2 million production cost. Bombardier could do this, Boeing claimed, because it was receiving subsidies from Canadian national and provincial government. The ITC issued a preliminary ruling in which it agreed with Boeing and imposed a 292% duty on the sale of Bombardier aircraft in the United States.

Facing the possibility of being locked out of the United States, its largest potential market, by anti-dumping tariffs, in October 2017, Bombardier entered an alliance with Airbus, forming the Airbus Canada Limited Partnership, in which Airbus took a 50.1% ownership stake. Airbus renamed the CSeries aircraft the A220 and announced that it would start a second production line for the A220 in Mobile, Alabama, to supply the A220 to U.S. carriers. Because this facility was in the United States, the anti-dumping tariffs would not apply to aircraft produced there.

Interestingly, the ITC issued a final ruling in early 2018, overturning its initial decision and determining that the U.S. industry was not threatened, and no duty would be imposed. Bombardier decided to exit the partnership in February 2020, selling its share to Airbus. As of mid-2022 Airbus has accumulated 762 orders for the A220, delivered 218 aircraft, with Delta being the largest customer.

As for the second new entrant, the COMAC, this remains a threat, particularly in the Chinese market, which, according to Boeing, could account for 21% of all new aircraft orders over the next 20 years. COMAC has developed a narrow-bodied aircraft, the C919, with 150–170 seats. Although the C919 completed its maiden flight in 2017, certification has been slow, and it is yet to be approved for service by any regulator, including the Chinese. The C919 is not expected to enter service until 2023 or later. The C919 has over 1,000 commitments for orders, mostly from Chinese airlines. Most aviation analysts view the C919 as inferior in almost every way to the A320neo and the Boeing 737 MAX, and they do not expect it to gain significant market share outside of China.[39] Nevertheless, some fear that China is now on the path to developing its own commercial aerospace business.

C10-6c The A320neo and 737 MAX

By 2010, the main issue confronting both Airbus and Boeing was what to do about their aging narrow-bodied planes, the A320 and the 737, respectively. These aircraft had been the workhorses of many airlines, comprising some 70% of all units produced by the two manufacturers. Strong demand was expected for this category going forward. Ideally, both Boeing and Airbus would probably have preferred to wait for a few more years before bearing the R&D costs associated with new product development. The argument was that this would give time for new technologies to mature and make for a better aircraft at the end of the day. However, events conspired to force their hands.

First, new engine technologies developed by Pratt & Whitney increased fuel efficiency by 10–15%. CFM International, a 50/50 joint venture between GE Aviation and Safran of France, also developed its own new engine technology, known as LEAP, to compete with Pratt & Whitney. Given the importance of fuel costs in the operating costs of airlines, both Airbus and Boeing realized that they need to incorporate this new engine technology on their aircraft. The new engines were lighter but had a larger diameter than the ones they were meant to replace. This was not a problem for Airbus, given that there was plenty of room under the wings of a A320 for attaching a larger-diameter engine. However, it did create a dilemma for Boeing, since the low-slung wings of the 737 did not leave enough clearance directly under the wings to safely attach the new generation of larger-diameter engines. A particular problem was that there would not be enough clearance at takeoff and landing.

In late 2010. Airbus announced that it would introduce a redesigned version of the A320 that utilized the Pratt & Whitney or LEAP engines. Known as the A320neo (new engine option), the offering garnered strong interest from airlines, quickly racking up over 1,000 orders by August of 2011.

These developments presented Boeing with a major strategic dilemma. Should they design a high technology successor to the 737 that would incorporate many of the technologies developed for the 787, and would have room under the wings to safely attach the larger engines? Effectively, this would be an entirely new aircraft, with development costs of at least around $20 billion. Given the time it would take to design and build a new aircraft, Boeing recognized that if they pursued this option, they would have to sell the existing 737 family at a discount to airlines, given their disadvantage relative to the A320neo. A second option was to find a way to attach the new engines to the existing 737 airframe.

Boeing originally seemed to be favoring designing an entirely new aircraft, but in August 2011, it changed course, and announced that it would sell a reengineered version of the 737, known as the 737 MAX. Boeing's design engineers had come up with a solution for attaching the new engines to the existing 737 airframe. This involved placing the new engines higher and thrusting forward from the wing on the plane. This solution had three benefits for Boeing. First, it would allow for quicker development of an offering that would compete with the A320neo. Second it would reduce development costs by as much as 85%. Third, since the 737 MAX was not a new aircraft, it would not require extensive recertification by the FAA and other regulatory agencies, and nor would it require the retraining of pilots, all of which would help to get the reengineered aircraft in service quicker. Indeed, because the 737 MAX did not involve a significant redesign of the airframe or cockpit, the FAA was apparently comfortable delegating some of the certification work to Boeings own inspectors.

However, there was a catch. By moving the engines forward, Boeing changed the aerodynamics of the 737, such that the plane did not handle properly at a high angle of attack (as when taking off and ascending). This created a danger that the aircraft would stall. This in turn led to the creation of the Maneuvering Characteristics Augmentation System (MCAS), which was designed to fix the angle of attack problem by automatically pushing the nose downwards if a sensor detected that the angle of attack was too steep.[40]

Boeing quickly gained orders following the announcement of the 737 MAX. The aircraft went into service in 2017, and by 2018, some 5,200 were on order. Then disaster struck. The Lion Air crash in October 2018, and the Ethiopian Airlines crash in March 2019, indicated something was seriously wrong with the aircraft, and regulators grounded the 737 fleet. It transpired that the MCAS system relied on data from two angles of attack sensors on the nose of the aircraft, but alternated between sensors, only sampling one at a time. This implied that if a single sensor was faulty, this would result in the MCAS system erroneously and automatically pushing the nose down. There was no redundancy built into the system, which was a major design flaw.[41] In contrast, the A320neo, which does not have the same angle of attack problem, relies on three sensors, takes the average reading between them, and stops using one if it is out of line with the others, alerting the pilots of the problem.

To compound matters, pilots had not been told about the MCAS system, so that when the nose was automatically pushed down, they did not know why. Had the pilots in the two aircraft that crashed realized what was going on, they could have quickly disconnected the MCAS system and flown it themselves, but they had not been informed or trained to handle such a problem, and in the heat of the moment, as they struggled to control an aircraft whose nose was automatically being pushed down, they did not realize that there was a ready solution to the problem and 346 people lost their lives.

Boeing was subsequently faulted for relying on a single sensor to inform the MCAS, for not having a warning light in the cockpit to let the pilots know that the sensors were not in alignment, for writing software that seemed to overcorrect for too steep an angle of attack and forcing the nose downwards, and for not training pilots how to deal with such a situation. The FAA was also faulted for delegating work to Boeing's own inspectors. While the problem could be fixed by relying on two sensors, having warning lights flash when the sensors were not in agreement, rewriting the MCAS software, and properly training pilots on how to deal with the situation, the reputational, financial, and competitive loss to Boeing were enormous, to say nothing of a tragic loss of life.

One conclusion that some critics have reached, is that in its rush to respond to Airbus' A320neo, Boeing's top managers put financial considerations before engineering decisions and safety.[42] Boeing's management appeared to have become obsessed with maximizing short-run shareholder returns at the expense of engineering excellence. To keep Wall Street happy, the company had ploughed over $30 billion into stock buybacks while the 737 MAX was being developed, more than it would have cost to build an all-new aircraft. Although the CEO who oversaw the development of the 737 MAX, Dennis Muilenberg, was ultimately fired, he had made over $100 million in stock-based compensation while CEO and walked away from Boeing with a $60 million golden parachute. He arguably fared better than Boeing, which now had to rebuild its reputation and its order book.

Notes

1. D. Gates, "Boeing 737 MAX Can Return to the Skies, FAA Says," *Seattle Times*, November 18, 2020.

2. Boeing website.

3. Airbus website.

4. J. Palmer, "Big Bird," *Barron's*, December 19, 2005, pp. 25–29. http://www.yeald.com/Yeald/a/33941/both_a380_and_787_have_bright_futures.html

5. G. J. Steven, "The Learning Curve; from Aircraft to Space craft," *Management Accounting*, May 1999, pp. 64–66.

6. D. Gates, "Boeing 7E7 Watch: Familiar Suppliers Make Short List," *Seattle Times*.

7. D. Gates, "Citing a Serious Flight Test Incident and Lack of Design Maturity, FAA Slows Boeing 777X Certification," *Seattle Times*, June 27, 2021.

8. The figures are from the International Airline Travelers Association (IATA).

9. IATA, "2006 Loss Forecast Drops to US$1.7 Billion," Press Release, August 31, 2006.

10. Air Transport Association, Industry Review and Outlook, April 29, 2015.

11. International Air Travel Association Annual Review, June 2022.

12. Air Transport Association, *A4A Presentation: Industry Review and Annual Outlook*, July 13, 2022.

13. Air Transport Association, *A4A Presentation: Industry Review and Annual Outlook*, July 13, 2022.

14. Data from the Air Transport Association at www.airlines.org

15. Boeing, *Commercial Market Outlook 2022-2041*.

16. This material is drawn from an earlier version of the Boeing case written by Charles W.L. Hill. See C. W. L. Hill, "The Boeing Corporation: Commercial Aircraft Operations," in C. W. L. Hill and G. R. Jones, *Strategic Management*, third edition (Boston: Houghton Mifflin, 1995). Much of Boeing's history is described in R .J. Sterling, *Legend and Legacy* (New York: St Martin's Press, 1992).

17. S. Browder, "A Fierce Downdraft at Boeing," *BusinessWeek*, January 26, 1988, p. 34.

18. Source: M. A. Cusumano, *The Japanese Automobile Industry* (Cambridge, Mass.: Harvard University Press, 1989). Ohno Taiichi, *Toyota Production System* (Cambridge, Mass.: Productivity Press, (1990). J. P. Womack, D. T. Jones, and D. Roos, *The Machine That Changed the World* (New York: Rawson Associates, 1990).

19. J. Gillie, "Lean Manufacturing Could Save Boeing's Auburn Washington Plant," *Knight Ridder Tribune Business News*, May 6, 2002, p. 1.

20. P. V.Arnold, "Boeing Knows Lean," *MRO Today*, February 2002.

21. Boeing Press Release, "Converted Farm Machine Improves Production Process," July 1, 2003.

22. P. V.Arnold, "Boeing Knows Lean," *MRO Today*, February 2002.. Also "Build in Lean: Manufacturing for the Future," on Boeing's website http://www.boeing.com/aboutus/environment/create_build.htm. J. Gillie, "Lean Manufacturing Could Save Boeing's Auburn Washington Plant," *Knight Ridder Tribune Business News*, May 6, 2002, p. 1.

23. J. Gillie, "Lean Manufacturing Could Save Boeing's Auburn Washington Plant," *Knight Ridder Tribune Business News*, May 6, 2002, p. 1.

24. P. V.Arnold, "Boeing Knows Lean," *MRO Today*, February 2002.

25. M. Mecham, "The Lean, Green Line," *Aviation Week*, July 19, 2004, pp. 144–148.

26. Boeing Press Release, "Boeing Reduces 737 Airplane's Final Assembly Time by 50 Percent," January 27, 2005.

27. *The Economist*, "A Phony War," May 5, 2001, pp. 56–57.

28. J. D. Boyd, "Building Room for Growth," *Traffic World*, August 7, 2006, p. 1.

29. W. Sweetman, "Boeing, Boeing, Gone," *Popular Science*, June 2004 p. 97.

30. Anonymous, "Who Will Supply the Parts?," *Seattle Times*, June 15, 2003.

31. W. Sweetman, "Boeing, Boeing, Gone," *Popular Science*, June 2004 p. 97.

32. D. Michaels and J. L. Lunsford, "Airbus Chief Reveals Plans for New Family of Jetliners," *Wall Street Journal,* July 18, 2006, p. A3.

33. J. Reppert-Bismarck and W. Echikson, "EU Countersues over U.S. Aid to Boeing," *Wall Street Journal*, June 1, 2005, p. A2. United States Trade Representative Press Release, "United States Takes Next Steps in Airbus WTO Litigation," May 30, 2005.

34. N. Clark, "WTO Rules U.S. Subsidies for Boeing Unfair," *New York Times*, March 31, 2011.

35. P. Blenkinsop, "U.S., EU Agree Truce in 17-Year Airbus-Boeing Conflict," *Reuters*, June 15, 2021.

36. Anonymous, "Airbus Agonistes," *Wall Street Journal*, September 6, 2006, p. A20.

37. Anonymous, "Forecast Dimmer for Profit on Airbus' A380," *Seattle Times*, October 20, 2006, Web Edition.

38 J. Weber, "Boeing to Rein in Dreamliner Outsourcing," *Bloomberg Business Week*, January 16, 2009.

39 B. Huey, "Boeing's Lack of a Middle of the Market Aircraft Causes Us to Downgrade Its Moat Trend to Negative," *Morningstar*, May 12, 2022.

40 S. Bryen, "A Kludge Too Far," *Asia Times*, August 4, 2019.

41 M. Baker and D. Gates, "Lack of Redundancies on Boeing 737 MAX System Baffles Some Involved in Developing the Jet," *Seattle Times*, March 26, 2019.

42 P. Robison, *Flying Blind* (New York: Doubleday, 2021).

Charles Schwab in 2022

Charles Hill School of Business University of Washington Seattle, WA 98105 October 2022

C11-1 Introduction

In 1971, Charles Schwab, who was 32 at the time, set up his own stock brokerage enterprise, First Commander. Later he would change the name to Charles Schwab & Company, Inc. In 1975, when the Securities and Exchange Commission abolished mandatory fixed commissions on stock trades, Schwab moved rapidly into the discount brokerage business, offering rates that were as much as 60% below those offered by full commission brokers. Over the next 25 years, the company experienced strong growth, fueled by a customer centric focus, savvy investments in information technology, and a number of product innovations, including a bold move into online trading in 1996.

By 2000, the company was widely regarded as one of the great success stories of the era. Revenues had grown to $7.1 billion and net income to $803 million, up from $1.1 billion and $124 million, respectively, in 1993. Online trading had grown to account for 84% of all stock trades made through Schwab, up from nothing in 1995. The company's stock price had appreciated by more than that of Microsoft over the prior 10 years. In 1999, the market value of Schwab eclipsed that of Merrill Lynch, the country's largest full-service broker, despite Schwab's revenues being more than 60% lower.

The 2000s proved to be a more difficult environment for the company. Between March 2000 and mid-2003, share prices in the United States tumbled, with the technology heavy NASDAQ index losing 80% of its value from peak to trough. The volume of online trading at Schwab slumped from an average of 204,000 trades a day in 2000 to 112,000 trades a day in 2002. In 2003, Schwab's revenues and net income fell sharply and the stock price tumbled from a high of $51.70 a share in 1999 to a low of $6.30 in early 2003. During this period, Schwab expanded through acquisition into the asset management business for high-net-worth clients with the acquisition of U.S. Trust, a move that potentially put it in competition with independent investment advisors, many of who used Schwab accounts for their clients. Schwab also entered the investment banking business with the purchase of Soundview Technology Bank.

In July 2004, Founder and Chairman Charles Schwab, who had relinquished the CEO role to David Pottruck in 1998, fired Pottruck and returned as CEO. Before stepping down in 2008, he refocused the company back on its discount brokering roots, selling off Soundview and U.S. Trust. At the same time, he pushed for an expansion of Schwab's retail banking business, allowing individual investors to hold investment accounts and traditional bank accounts at Schwab. Schwab remains chairman of the company.

In 2007–2009, a serious crisis gripped the financial services industry. Some major financial institutions went bankrupt, including Lehman Brothers and Washington Mutual. The widely watched Dow Industrial Average Index plunged from over 14,000 in October of 2007 to 6,600 in March 2007. Widespread financial collapse was only averted when the government stepped in to support the sector with a $700 billion loan to troubled companies. Almost alone amongst major financial service firms, Schwab was able to navigate through the crisis with relative ease, remaining solidly profitable and having no need to place a call on government funds.

By the second decade of the 21st century. Schwab was once again on a growth path, fueled by expanded offerings including the establishment of a marketplace for Exchange Traded Funds (ETFs). Schwab's asset base expanded at around 6% per annum during this period. In late 2019, Schwab stunned the financial community when it announced that it would acquire rival discount broker TD Ameritrade for $26 billion. The combined company held $7 trillion in total assets by May 2022 and was the second-largest brokerage by self-directed assets in the world, trailing only Fidelity. The TD Ameritrade acquisition was widely seen as a response to ongoing price competition in the brokerage industry, with commissions on stock trades falling towards zero. In this environment, discount brokerages like Schwab were increasingly relying for their earnings on revenue from interest rates on assets held by the company, and on the asset management and administrative fees they charged clients. The theory behind the acquisition was that the combined company would be able to reap substantial economies of scale, enabling it to make more than its cost of capital in a world where commissions on stock trades were effectively zero.

C11-2 The Securities Brokerage Industry[1]

A security refers to financial instruments, such as a stocks, bonds, commodity contracts, stock option contracts, and foreign exchange contracts. The securities brokerage industry is concerned with the issuance and trading of financial securities, as well as a number of related activities. A broker's clients may be individuals, corporations, or government bodies. Brokers undertake one or more of the following functions; assist corporations to raise capital by offering stocks and bonds, help governments raise capital through bond issues, give advice to businesses on their foreign currency needs, assist corporations with mergers and acquisitions, help individuals plan their financial future and trade financial securities, provide detailed investment research to individuals and institutions so that they can make more informed investment decisions.

C11-2a Industry Background

In 2021, there were 3,394 broker-dealers registered in the United States, down from 9,515 in 1987. The industry is concentrated with some 200 firms that are members of the New York Stock Exchange (NYSE) accounting for 87% of the assets of all broker-dealers, and 80% of the capital. The 10 largest NYSE firms accounted for around 57% of the gross revenue in the industry in 2016, up from 48% in 1998. The consolidation of the industry has been driven in part by deregulation, which is discussed in more detail below.

Broker-dealers make their money in a number of ways. They earn **commissions** (or fees) for executing a customer's order to buy or sell a given security (stocks, bonds, option contracts, etc.). They earn **trading income**, which is the realized and unrealized gains and losses on securities held and traded by the brokerage firm. They earn money from **underwriting fees**, which are the fees charged to corporate and government clients for managing an issue of stocks or bonds on their behalf. They earn **asset management fees**, which represent income from the sale of mutual fund securities, from account supervision fees, or from investment advisory or administrative service fees. They earn **margin interest**, which is the interest that customers pay to the brokerage when they borrow against the value of their securities to finance purchases. They earn **other securities related revenue** comes from private placement fees (i.e., fees from private equity deals) subscription fees for research services, charges for advisory work on proposed mergers and acquisitions, fees for options done away from an exchange and so on. Finally, many brokerages earn **non-securities revenue** from other financial services, such as credit card operations or mortgage services.

C11-2b Industry Groups

Historically, brokerage firms have been segmented into five groups. First, there **are national full line firms**, which are the largest full-service brokers with extensive branch systems. They provide virtually every financial service and product that a brokerage can offer to both households (retail customers) and institutions (corporations, governments, and other non-profit organizations such as universities). Examples of such firms include Merrill Lynch and Morgan Stanley. Most of these firms are headquartered in New York. For retail customers, national full line firms provide access to a personal financial consultant, traditional brokerage services, securities research reports, asset management services, financial planning advice, and a range of other services such as margin loans, mortgage loans, and credit cards. For institutional clients, these firms will also arrange and underwrite the issuance of financial securities, manage their financial assets, provide advice on mergers and acquisitions, and provide more detailed research reports than those normally provided to retail customers, often for a fee.

Large investment banks are a second group. This group includes Goldman Sachs. These banks have a limited branch network and focus primarily on institutional clients, although they also may have a retail business focused on high-net-worth individuals (typically individuals with more than $1 million to invest). In 2008, Lehman Brothers went bankrupt, a casualty of bad bets on mortgage-backed securities, while the large bank, JP Morgan, acquired Bear Stearns, leaving Goldman Sachs as the sole stand-alone representative in this class.

A third group, **regional brokers**, are full-service brokerage operations with a branch network in certain regions of the country. Regional brokers typically focus on retail customers, although some have an institutional presence.

Fourth, there are a number of **New York City–based** brokers, who conduct a broad array of financial services, including brokerage, investment banking, traditional money management, and so on.

Finally, there are the **discounters**, who are primarily involved in the discount brokerage business and focus on executing orders to buy and sell stocks for retail customers. Commissions have historically been their main source of business revenue, although in recent years some have shifted their business model sometimes charging zero commission fees and making money on asset management fees instead. The discounters charge lower commissions than full-service brokers, but do not offer the same infrastructure such as personal financial consultants and detailed research reports. The discounters provide trading and execution services at deep discounts online. Many discounters, such as Ameritrade and E*Trade, do not maintain branch offices. Schwab, which was one of the first discounters, and remains the largest, has a network of brick-and-mortar offices, as well as a leading online presence.

C11-2c Earnings Trends

Industry revenues and earnings are volatile, being driven by variations in the volume of trading activity (and commissions), underwriting, and merger and acquisition activity. All of these tend to be highly correlated with changes in the value of interest rates and the stock market. In general, when interest rates fall, the cost of borrowing declines so corporations and governments tend to issue more securities, which increases underwriting income. Also, low interest rates tend to stimulate economic growth, which leads to higher corporate profits, and thus higher stock values. When interest rates decline, individuals typically move some of their money out of low interest-bearing cash accounts or low yielding bonds, and into stocks, in an attempt to earn higher returns. This drives up trading volume and hence commissions. Low interest rates, by reducing the cost of borrowing, can also increase merger and acquisition activity. Moreover, in a rising stock market, corporations often use their stock as currency with which to make acquisitions of other companies. This drives up drives up merger and acquisition activity, and the fees brokerages earn from such activity.

The 1990s was characterized by one of the strongest stock market advances in history. This boom was driven by a favorable economic environment, including falling interest rates, new information technology, productivity gains in American industry, and steady economic expansion, all of which translated into growing corporate profits and rising stock prices.

Also feeding the stock market's advance during the 1990s were favorable demographic trends. During the 1990s, American baby boomers started to save for retirement, pumping significant assets into equity funds. The percentage of household liquid assets held in equities and mutual funds increased from 33.8% in 1990 to 66.9% in 1999, while the number of households that owned equities increased from 32.5% to 50.1% over the same period.

Adding fuel to the fire, by the late 1990s, stock market mania had taken hold. Stock prices rose to speculative highs rarely seen before as "irrationally exuberant" retail investors who seemed to believe that stock prices could only go up made increasingly risky and speculative "investments" in richly valued equities.[2] The market peaked in late 2000 as the extent of overvaluation became apparent. It fell significantly over the next 2 years as the economy struggled with a recession. This was followed by a recovery in both the economy and the stock market, with the S&P 500 returning to its old highs by October of 2007. However, as the global credit crunch unfolded in 2008, the market crashed, falling precipitously in the second half of 2008 to return to levels not seen since the mid-1990s. The market has since recovered. By 2016, almost 60% of the financial assets of U.S. households was once again held in equities and mutual funds. At that point, U.S. households held equities valued at $24.5 trillion. A strong stock market increased the value of the equity holding of U.S. households to a $49.2 trillion by 2021, a figure that was more than twice the size of U.S. GDP.

The long stock market boom of the 1990s drove an expansion of industry revenues, which for brokerages that were members of the NYSE, grew from $54 billion in 1990 to $245 billion in 2000. As the bubble burst and the stock market slumped in 2001 and 2002, and brokerage revenues plummeted to $144 billion in 2003, forcing brokerages to cut expenses. By 2007, revenues had recovered again and were a record $352 billion. In 2008, the financial crisis hit, and industry revenues contracted $178 billion. In that year, the industry lost $42.6 billion. By 2021, with the stock market booming again, revenues were back up to $230 billion and the industry booked $58.4 billion in pretax net income.

The expense structure of the brokerage industry is dominated by two big items: interest expenses and compensation expenses. Together these account for about three quarters of industry expenses. Interest expenses reflect the interest rate paid on cash deposits at brokerages and rise or fall with the size of deposits and interest rates. As such, they are generally not regarded as a controllable expense (since the interest rate is ultimately set by the U.S. Federal Reserve and market forces). Compensation expenses reflect both employee headcount and bonuses. For some brokerage firms, particularly those dealing with institutional clients, bonuses can be enormous, with multi-million-dollar bonuses being awarded to productive employees. Compensation expenses and employee headcount tend to grow during bull markets, only to be rapidly curtailed once a bear market sets in.

The profitability of the industry is volatile and depends critically upon the overall level of stock market activity. Profits were high during the boom years of the 1990s. The bursting of the stock market bubble in 2000–2001 bought a period of low profitability, and although profitability improved after 2002 it did not return to the levels of the 1990s. The financial crisis and stock market crash of 2007–2009 resulted in large losses for the industry but profits in the next decade.

C11-2d Deregulation

The industry has been progressively deregulated since May 1, 1975, when a fixed commission structure on securities trades was dismantled. This development allowed for the emergence of discount brokers such as Charles Schwab. Until the mid-1980s, however, the financial services industry was highly segmented due to a 1933 Act of Congress known as the Glass-Steagall Act. This Act, which was passed in the wake of widespread bank failures following the stock market crash of 1929, erected regulatory barriers between different sectors of the financial services industry, such as commercial banking, insurance, saving and loans, and investment services (including brokerages). Most significantly, Section 20 of the Act erected a wall between commercial banking and investment services, barring commercial banks from investing in shares of stocks, limiting them to buying and selling securities as an agent, prohibiting them from underwriting and dealing in securities, and from being affiliated with any organization that did so.

In 1987, Section 20 was relaxed to allow banks to earn up to 5% of their revenue from securities underwriting. The limit was raised to 10% in 1989 and 25% in 1996. In 1999, the Gramm-Leach-Bliley (GLB) Act was passed, which finalized the repeal of the Glass-Steagall Act. By removing the walls between commercial banks, broker-dealers, and insurance companies, many predicted that the GLB Act would lead to massive industry consolidation, with commercial banks purchasing brokers and insurance companies. The rationale was that such diversified financial services firms would become one-stop financial supermarkets, cross-selling products to their expanded client base. For example, a financial supermarket might sell insurance to brokerage customers, or brokerage services to commercial bank customers. The leader in this process was Citigroup, which was formed in 1998 by a merger between Citicorp, a commercial bank, and Traveler's, and insurance company. Since Traveler's had already acquired Salmon Smith Barney, a major brokerage firm, the new Citigroup seemed to signal a new wave of consolidation in the industry. The passage of the GLB Act allowed Citigroup to start cross selling products.

However, industry reports suggest that cross selling is easier in theory than practice, in part because customers were not ready for the development.[3] In an apparent admission that this was the case, in 2002, Citigroup announced that it would spin off Traveler's Insurance as a separate company. At the same time, the fact remains that the GLB Act has made it easier for commercial banks to get into the brokerage business, and there have been several acquisitions to this effect. Most notably, in 2008, Bank of America purchased Merrill Lynch, and JP Morgan Chase purchased Bear Stearns. Both of the acquired enterprises were suffering from serious financial troubles due to their exposure to mortgage-backed securities.

C11-3 The Growth of Schwab

The son of an assistant district attorney in California, Charles Schwab started to exhibit an entrepreneurial streak from an early age. As a boy, he picked walnuts and bagged them for $5 per 100-pound sack. He raised chicken in his backyard, sold the eggs door to door, killed and plucked the fryers for market, and peddled the manure as fertilizer. Schwab called it "my first fully integrated businesses."[4]

As a child, Schwab had to struggle with a severe case of dyslexia, a disorder that makes it difficult to process written information. To keep up with his classes, he had to resort to Cliffs Notes and Classics Illustrated comic books. Schwab believes, however, that his dyslexia was ultimately a motivator, spurring him on to overcome the disability and excel. Schwab excelled enough to gain admission to Stanford, where he received a degree in economics, which was followed by an MBA from Stanford Business School.

Fresh out of Stanford in the 1960s, Schwab embarked upon his first entrepreneurial effort, an investment advisory newsletter, which grew to include a mutual fund with $20 million under management. However, after the stock market fell sharply in 1969, the State of Texas ordered Schwab to stop accepting investments through the mail from its citizens because the fund was not registered to do business in the State. Schwab went to court and lost. Ultimately, he had to close his business, leaving him with $100,000 in debt and a marriage that had collapsed under the emotional strain.

C11-3a The Early Days

Schwab soon bounced back. Capitalized by $100,000 that he borrowed from his uncle Bill, who had a successful industrial company of his own called Commander Corp, in 1971, Schwab started a new company, First Commander. Based in San Francisco, a world away from Wall Street, First Commander was a conventional brokerage that charged clients fixed commissions for securities trades. The name was changed to Charles Schwab the following year.

In 1974, at the suggestion of a friend, Schwab joined a pilot test of discount brokerage being conducted by the Securities and Exchange Commission. The discount brokerage idea instantly appealed to Schwab. He personally hated selling, particularly cold calling; the constant calling on actual or prospective customers to encourage them to make a stock trade. Moreover, Schwab was deeply disturbed by the conflict of interest that seemed everywhere in the brokerage world, with stock brokers encouraging customers to make questionable trades in order to boost commissions. Schwab also questioned the worth of the investment advice brokers gave clients, feeling that it reflected the inherent conflict of interest in the brokerage business and did not empower customers.

Schwab used the pilot test to fine-tune his model for a discount brokerage. When the SEC abolished mandatory fixed commission the following year, Schwab quickly moved into the business. His basic thrust was to empower investors by giving them the information and tools required to make their own decisions about securities investments, while keeping Schwab's costs low so that this service could be offered at a deep discount to the commissions charged by full-service brokers. Driving down costs meant that unlike full-service brokers, Schwab did not employee financial analysts and researchers who developed proprietary investment research for the firm's clients. Instead, Schwab focused on providing clients with third-party investment research. These "reports" evolved to include a company's financial history, a smatter of comments from securities analysts at other brokerage firms that had appeared in the news and a tabulation of buy and sell recommendations from full commission brokerage houses. The reports were sold to Schwab's customers at cost (in 1992 this was $9.50 for each report plus $4.75 for each additional report).[5]

A founding principle of the company was a desire to be the most useful and ethical provider of financial services. Underpinning this move was Schwab's own belief in the inherent conflict of interest between brokers at full-service firms and their clients. The desire to avoid a conflict of interest caused Schwab to rethink the traditional commission-based pay structure. As an alternative to commission-based pay, Schwab paid all of its employees, including its brokers, a salary plus a bonus that was tied to attracting and satisfying customers and achieving productivity and efficiency targets. Commissions were taken out of the compensation equation.

The chief promoter of Schwab's approach to business, and marker of the Schwab brand, was none other than Charles Schwab himself. In 1977, Schwab started to use pictures of Charles Schwab in its advertisements, a practice it still follows today.

The customer centric focus of the company led Schwab to think of ways to make the company accessible to customers. In 1975, Schwab became the first discount broker to open a branch office and to offer access 24 hours a day 7 days a week. Interestingly, however, the decision to open a branch was not something that Charles Schwab initially embraced. He wanted to keep costs low and thought it would be better if everything could be managed by way of a telephone. However, Charles Schwab was forced to ask his Uncle Bill for more capital to get his nascent discount brokerage off the ground. Uncle Bill agreed to invest $300,000 in the company, but on one condition, he insisted that Schwab open a branch office in Sacramento and employee Uncle Bill's son in law as manager![6] Reluctantly, Charles Schwab agreed to Uncle Bill's demand for a show of nepotism, hoping that the branch would not be too much of a drain on the company's business.

What happened next was a surprise; there was an immediate and dramatic increase in activity at Schwab, most of it from Sacramento. Customer inquiries, the number of trades per day, and the number of new accounts, all spiked upwards. Yet there was also a puzzle here, for the increase was not linked to an increase in foot traffic in the branch. Intrigued, Schwab opened several more branches over the next year, and each time noticed the same pattern. For example, when Schwab opened its first branch in Denver it had 300 customers. It added another 1,700 new accounts in the months following the opening of the branch, and yet there was a big spike up in foot traffic at the Denver branch.

What Schwab began to realize is that the branches served a powerful psychological purpose—they gave customers a sense of security that Schwab was a real company. Customers were reassured by seeing a branch with people in it. In practice, many clients would rarely visit a branch. They would open an account, and execute trades over the telephone (or later, via the Internet). But the branch helped them to make that first commitment. Far from being a drain, Schwab realized that the branches were a marketing tool. People wanted to be "perceptually close to their money," and the branches satisfied that deep psychological need. From 1 branch in 1975, Schwab grew to have 52 branches in 1982, 175 by 1992, and 430 in 2002. The next few years bought retrenchment however, and Schwab's branch fell to around 300 by 2008.

By the mid-1980s, customers could access Schwab in person at a branch during office hours, by phone day or night, by a telephone voice recognition quote and trading service known as TeleBroker, and by an innovative proprietary online network. To encourage customers to use TeleBroker or its online trading network, Schwab reduced commissions on transactions executed this way by 10%, but it saved much more than that because doing business via computers was cheaper. By 1995, Telebroker was handling 80 million calls and 10 million trades a year, 75% of Schwab's annual volume. To service this system, in the mid-1980s Schwab invested $20 million in four regional customer call centers, routing all calls to them rather than branches. Today, these call centers have 4,000 employees.

Schwab was the first to establish a PC-based online trading system in 1986, with the introduction of its Equalizer service. The system had 15,000 customers in 1987, and 30,000 by the end of 1988. The online system, which required a PC with a modem, allowed investors to check current stock prices, place orders, and check their portfolios. In addition, an "offline" program for PCs enabled investors to do fundamental and technical analysis on securities. To encourage customers to start using the system, there was no additional charge for using the online system after a $99 sign-up fee. In contrast, other discount brokers with PC-based online systems, such as Quick and Riley's (which had a service known as "Quick Way"), or Fidelity's (whose service was called "Fidelity Express") charged users between 10 cents and 44 cents a minute for online access depending on the time of day.[7]

Schwab's pioneering move into online trading was in many ways just an evolution of the company's early utilization of technology. In 1979, Schwab spent $2 million, an amount equivalent to the company's entire net worth at the time, to purchase a used IBM System 360 computer, plus software, that was left over from CBS's 1976 election coverage. At the time, brokerages generated and had to process massive amounts of paper to execute buy and sell orders. The computer gave Schwab a capability that no other brokerage had at the time; take a buy or sell order that came in over the phone, edit it on a computer screen, and then submit the order for processing without generating paper. Not only did the software provide for instant execution of orders, it also offered what were then sophisticated quality controls, checking a customer's account to see if funds were available before executing a transaction. As a result of this system, Schwab's costs plummet as it took paper out of the system. Moreover, the cancel and rebill rate—a measure of the accuracy of trade executions—dropped from an average of 4% to 0.1%.[8] Schwab soon found it could handle twice the transaction volume of other brokers, at less cost, and with much greater accuracy. Within 2 years, every other broker in the nation had developed similar systems, but Schwab's early investment had given it an edge and underpinned the company's belief in the value of technology to reduce costs and empower customers.

By 1982, the technology at Schwab was well ahead of that used by most full-service brokers. It was this commitment to technology that allowed Schwab to offer a product that was similar in conception to Merrill Lynch's revolutionary Cash Management Account (CMA), which was introduced in 1980. The CMA account automatically sweeps idle cash into money market funds and allows customers to draw on their money by check or credit card. Schwab's system, known as the Schwab One Account, was introduced in 1982. It went beyond Merrill's in that it allowed brokers to execute orders instantly through Schwab's computer link to the exchange floor.

In 1984, Schwab moved into the mutual fund business, not by offering its own mutual funds, but by launching a mutual fund marketplace, which allowed customers to invest in some 140 no-load mutual funds (a "no-load" fund has no sales commission). By 1990, the number of funds in the market place was 400 and the total assets involved exceeded $2 billion. For the mutual fund companies, the mutual fund marketplace offered distribution to Schwab's growing customer base. For its part, Schwab kept a small portion of the revenue stream that flowed to the fund companies from Schwab clients.

In 1986, Schwab made a gutsy move to eliminate the fees for managing Individual Retirement Accounts (IRAs). IRAs allow customers to deposit money in an account where it accumulates tax free until withdrawal at retirement. The legislation establishing IRAs had been passed by Congress in 1982. At the time, estimates suggest that IRA accounts could attract as much as $50 billion in assets within 10 years. In actual facts, the figure turned out to be $725 billion!

Initially Schwab followed industry practice and collected a small fee for each IRA. By 1986, the fees amounted to $9 million a year, not a trivial amount for Schwab in those days. After looking at the issue, Charles Schwab himself made the call to scrap the fee, commenting that "It's a nuisance, and we'll get it back."[9] He was right; Schwab's No-Annual Fee IRA immediately exceeded the company's most optimistic projections.

Despite technological and product innovations, by 1983, Schwab was scrapped for capital to fund expansion. To raise funds, he sold the company to Bank of America for $55 million in stock and a seat on the bank's board of directors. The marriage did not last long. By 1987, the bank was reeling under loan losses, and the entrepreneurially minded Schwab was frustrated by banking regulations that inhibited his desire to introduce new products. Using a mix of loans, his own money, and contributions from other managers, friends, and family, Schwab led a management buyout of the company for $324 million in cash and securities.

Six months later on September 22, 1987, Schwab went public with an IPO that raised some $440 million, enabling the company to pay down debt and leaving it with capital to fund an aggressive expansion. At the time, Schwab had 1.6 million customers, revenues of $308 million, and a pre-tax profit margin of 21%. Schwab announced plans to increase its branch network by 30% to around 120 offices over the next year. Then on Monday, October 19, 1987, the U.S. stock market crashed, dropping over 22%, the biggest one-day decline in history.

C11-3b October 1987–1995

After a strong runup over the year, on Friday, October 16, 1987, the stock market dropped 4.6%. During the weekend, nervous investors jammed the call centers and branch offices, not just at Schwab, but at many other brokerages, as they tried to place sell orders. At Schwab, 99% of the orders taken over the weekend for Monday morning were sell orders. As the market opened on Monday morning, it went into free fall. At Schwab, the computers were overwhelmed by 8 a.m. The toll-free number to the call centers was also totally overwhelmed. All the customers heard when they called were busy signals. When the dust had settled, Schwab announced that it had lost $22 million in the fourth quarter of 1987, $15 million of which came from a single customer who had been unable to meet margin calls.

The loss which amounted to 13% of the company's capital, effectively wiped out the company's profit for the year. Moreover, the inability of customers to execute trades during the crash damaged Schwab's hard-earned reputation for customer service. Schwab responded by posting a two-page ad in the Wall Street Journal on October 28, 1987. On one page, there was a message from Charles Schwab thanking customers for their patience, on the other an ad thanking employees for their dedication.

In the aftermath of the October 1987 crash, trading volume fell by 15% as customers, spooked by the volatility of the market, sat on cash balances. The slowdown prompted Schwab to cut back on its expansion plans. Ironically, however, Schwab added a significant number of new accounts in the aftermath of the crash as people looked for cheaper ways to invest.[10]

Beset by week trading volume through the next 18 months, and reluctant to lay off employees, Schwab sought ways to boost activity. One strategy started out as a compliance issue within Schwab. A compliance officer in the company noticed a disturbing pattern; a number of people had given other people limited power of attorney over their accounts. This in itself was not unusual–for example, the middle-aged children of an elderly individual might have power of attorney over their account–but what the Schwab officer noticed was that some individuals had power of attorney over dozens, if not hundreds, of accounts.

Further investigation turned up the reason–Schwab had been serving an entirely unknown set of customers, independent financial advisors who were managing the financial assets of their clients using Schwab accounts. In early 1989, there were some 500 financial advisors who managed assets totaling $1.5 billion at Schwab, about 8% of all assets at Schwab.

The advisors were attracted to Schwab for a number of reasons, including cost and the company's commitment not to give advice–which was the business of the advisors. When Charles Schwab heard about this, he immediately saw an opportunity. Financial advisors, he reasoned, represented a powerful way to acquire customers. In 1989, the company rolled out a program to aggressively court this group. Schwab hired a marketing team and told them to focus explicitly on financial planners, set apart a dedicated trading desk for them, and gave discounts of as much as 15% on commissions to financial planners with significant assets under management at Schwab accounts. Schwab also established a Financial Advisors Service, which provided its clients with a list of financial planners who were willing to work solely for a fee, and had no incentive to push the products of a particular client. At the same time, the company stated that it wasn't endorsing the planners' advice, which would run contrary to the company's commitment to offer no advice. Within a year, financial advisors had some $3 billion of client's assets under management at Schwab.

Schwab also continued to expand its branch network during this period, at a time while many brokerages, still stunned by the October 1987 debacle, were retrenching. Between 1987 and 1989, Schwab's branch network increased by just five, from 106 to 111, but in 1990 it opened up an additional 29 branches and another 28 in 1991.

By 1990s, Schwab's positioning in the industry had become clear. Although a discounter, Schwab was by no means the lowest price discount broker in the country. Its average commission structure was similar to that of Fidelity, the Boston-based mutual fund company that had moved into the discount brokerage business, and Quick & Reilly, a major national competitor (see Exhibit 1). While significantly below that of full-service brokers, the fee structure was also above that of deep discount brokers. Schwab differentiated itself from the deep discount brokers, however, by its branch network, technology, and the information (not advice) that it gave to investors.

In 1992, Schwab rolled out another strategy aimed at acquiring assets—OneSource, the first mutual fund "supermarket." OneSource was created to take advantage of America's growing appetite for mutual funds. By the early 1990s, there were more mutual funds than individual equities. On some days, Fidelity, the largest mutual fund company, accounted for 10% of the trading volume on the New York Stock Exchange. As American baby boomers aged, they seemed to have an insatiable appetite for mutual funds. But the process of buying and selling mutual funds had never been easy. As Charles Schwab explained in 1996:

> In the days before the supermarkets, to buy a mutual fund you had to write or call the fund distributor. On Day Six, you'd get a prospectus. On Day Seven or Eight you call up and they say you've got to put your money in. If you're lucky, by Day Ten you've bought it……It was even more cumbersome when you redeemed. You had to send a notarized redemption form.[11]

Exhibit 1 Becle S.A.B. de C.V. (Cuervo) Income Statement, in MXN millions	
Type of Broker	Average Commission Price on 20 trades averaging $8,975 each.
Deep Discount Brokers	$54
Average Discounters	$73
Banks	$88
Schwab, Fidelity and Quick & Reilly	$92
Full Service Brokers	$206

Source: E.C.Gottschalk, "Schwab forges ahead as other brokers hesitate", **Wall Street Journal**, May 11th, 1990, page C1.

OneSource took the hassle out of owning funds. With a single visit to a branch office, telephone call, or PC-based computer transaction, a Schwab client could buy and sell mutual funds. Schwab imposed no fee at all on investors for the service. Rather, in return for shelf space in Schwab's distribution channel and access to the more than 2 million accounts at Schwab, Schwab charged the fund companies a fee amounting to 0.35% of the assets under management. By inserting itself between the fund managers and customers, Schwab changed the balance of power in the mutual fund industry. When Schwab sold a fund through OneSource, it passed along the assets to the fund managers, but not the customers' names. Many fund managers did not like this, because it limited their ability to build a direct relationship with customers, but they had little choice if they wanted access to Schwab's customer base.

OneSource quickly propelled Schwab to the number three position in direct mutual fund distribution, behind the fund companies Fidelity and Vanguard. By 1997, Schwab customers could choose from nearly 1,400 funds offered by 200 different fund families and Schwab customers had nearly $56 billion in assets invested through OneSource.

C11-3c 1996–2000: eSchwab

In 1994, as access to the World Wide Web began to diffuse rapidly throughout America, a 2-year-old start-up run by Bill Porter, a physicist and inventor, launched its first dedicated website for online trading. The company's name was E*Trade. E*Trade announced a flat $14.95 commission on stock trades, significantly below Schwab's average commission, which at the time of $65. It was clear from the outset that E*Trade and other online brokers, such as Ameritrade, offered a direct threat to Schwab. Not only were their commission rates considerably below those of Schwab, but the ease, speed, and flexibility of trading stocks online suddenly made Schwab's proprietary online trading software, Street Smart, seem limited. (Street Smart was the Windows-based successor to Schwab's DOS-based Equalizer program.) To compound matters, talented people started to leave Schwab for E*Trade and its brethren, which they saw as the wave of the future.

At the time, deep within Schwab, William Pearson, a young software specialist who had worked on the development of Street Smart, quickly saw the transformational power of the web and believed that it would make proprietary systems like Street Smart obsolete. Pearson believed that Schwab needed to develop its own online software, and quickly. Try as he might, though, Pearson could not get the attention of his supervisor. He tried a number of other executives, but found support hard to come by. Eventually he approached Anne Hennegar, a former Schwab manager whom he knew and who now worked as a consultant to the company. Hennegar suggested that Pearson meet with Tom Seip, an executive vice president at Schwab, who was known for his ability to think outside of the box. Hennegar approached Seip on Pearson's behalf, and Seip responded positively, asking her to set up a meeting. Hennegar and Pearson turned up expecting to meet just Seip, but to their surprise in walked Charles Schwab, Chief Operating Officer David Pottruck, and the vice presidents in charge of strategic planning and the electronic brokerage arena.

As the group watched Pearson's demo of how a web-based system would look and work, they became increasingly excited. It was clear to those in the room that online system based on real-time information, personalization, customization, and interactivity all advanced Schwab's commitment to empowering customers. By the end of the meeting, Pearson had received a green light to start work on the project.

It soon transpired that several other groups within Schwab had been working on projects that were similar to Pearson's. These were all pulled together under the control of Dawn Lepore, Schwab's chief information officer, who headed up the effort to develop an online service that would ultimately become eSchwab. Meanwhile, significant strategic issues were now beginning to preoccupy Charles Schwab and David Pottruck. They realized that Schwab's established brokerage and online brokerage business were based on very different revenue and cost models. The online business would probably cannibalize business from Schwab's established brokerage operations, and that might lead people in Schwab to slow down or even derail the online initiative. As Pottruck later put it:

> The new enterprise was going to use a different model for making money than our traditional business, and we didn't want the comparisons to form the basis for a measurement of success or failure. For example, eSchwab's per trade revenue would be less than half that of the mainstream of the company, and that could be seen as a drain on resources rather than a response to what customer would be using in the future.[12]

Pottruck and Schwab understood that unless eSchwab was placed in its own organization, isolated and protected from the established business, it might never get off the ground. They also knew that if they did not cannibalize their own business with eSchwab, someone would do it for them. Thus, they decided to set up a separate organization to develop eSchwab. The unit was headed up by Beth Sawi, a highly regarded marketing manager at Schwab, who had very good relations with other managers in the company. Sawi set up the development center in a unit physically separated from other Schwab facilities.

eSchwab was launched in May 1996, but without the normal publicity that accompanied most new products at Schwab. Schwab abandoned its sliding scale commission for a flat-rate commission of $39 (which was quickly dropped to $29.95) for any stock trade up to 1,000 shares. Within 2 weeks, 25,000 people had opened eSchwab accounts. By the end of 1997, the figure would soar to 1.2 million, bringing in assets of about $81 billion, or 10 times the assets of E*Trade.

Schwab initially kept the two businesses segmented. Schwab's traditional customers were still paying an average of $65 a trade while eSchwab customers were paying $29.95. While Schwab's traditional customers could make toll-free calls to Schwab brokers, eSchwab clients could not. Moreover, Schwab's regular customers couldn't access eSchwab at all. The segmentation soon gave rise to problems. Schwab's branch employees were placed in the uncomfortable position of telling customers that they couldn't set up eSchwab accounts. Some eSchwab customers started to set up traditional Schwab accounts with small sums of money so that they could access Schwab's brokers and Schwab's information services, while continuing to trade via eSchwab. Clearly, the segmentation was not sustainable.

Schwab began to analyze the situation. The company's leaders realized that the cleanest way to deal with the problem would be to give every Schwab customer online access, adopt a commission of $29.95 on trading across all channels, and maintain existing levels of customer service at the branch level and on the phone. However, internal estimates suggested that the cut in commission rates would reduce revenues by $125 million, which would hit Schwab's stock. The problem was compounded by two factors; first, employees owned 40% of Schwab's stock, so they would be hurt by any fall in stock price, and second, employees were worried that going online would result in a decline in business at the branch level, and hence a loss of jobs there.

An internal debate raged within the company for much of 1997, a year when Schwab's revenues surged 24% to $2.3 billion. The online trading business grew by more than 90% during the year, with online trades accounting for 37% of all Schwab trades during 1997, and the trend was up throughout the year.

Looking at these figures, Pottruck, the COO, knew that Schwab had to bite the bullet and give all Schwab customers access to eSchwab (Pottruck was now running the day-to-day operations of Schwab, leaving Charles Schwab to focus on his corporate marketing and PR role). His first task was to enroll the support of the company's largest shareholder, Charles Schwab. With 52 million shares, Charles Schwab would take the biggest hit from any share price decline. According to a *Fortune* article, the conversation between Schwab and Pottruck went something like this:[13]

Pottruck: "We don't know exactly what will happen. The budget is shaky. We'll be winging it."
Schwab: "We can always adjust our costs."
Pottruck: "Yes, but we don't have to do this now. The whole year could be lousy. And the stock!"
Schwab: "This isn't that hard a decision, because we really have no choice. It's just a question of when, and it will be harder later."

Having the agreement of Schwab's founder, Pottruck formed a task force to look at how best to implement the decision. The plan that emerged was to merge all of the company's electronic services into Schwab.com, which would then coordinate Schwab's online and offline business. The base commission rate would be $29.95 whatever channel was used to make a trade—online, branch, or the telephone. The role of the branches would change, and they would start to focus more on customer support. This required a change in incentive systems. Branch employees had been paid bonuses on the basis of the assets they accrued to their branches, nut now they would be paid bonuses on assets they came in via the branch, or online. They would be rewarded for directing clients online.

Schwab implemented the change of strategy on January 15, 1998. Revenues dropped 3% in the first quarter as the average commission declined from $63 to $57. Earnings also came in short of expectations by some $6 million. The company's stock had lost 20% of its value by August 1998. However, over much of 1998, new money poured into Schwab. Total accounts surged, with Schwab gaining a million new customers in 1998, a 20% increase, while assets grew by 32%. As the year progressed, trading volume grew, doubling by year end. By the third quarter, Schwab's revenues and earnings were surging past analysts' expectations. The company ultimately achieved record revenues and earnings in 1998. Net income ended up 29% over the prior year, despite falling commission rates, aided by surging trading volume and the lower cost of executing trades online. By the end of the year, 61% of all trades at Schwab were made online. After its summer lows, the stock price recovered, ending the year up 130%, pushing Schwab's market capitalization past that of Merrill Lynch.[14]

C11-3d 2000–2004: After the Boom

In 1998, Charles Schwab appointed his long-time number two, David Pottruck, co-CEO. The appointment signaled the beginning of a leadership transition, with Schwab easing himself out of day-to-day operations. Soon Pottruck had to deal with some major issues. The end of the long stock market boom of the 1990s hit Schwab hard. The average number of trades made per day through Schwab fell from 300 million to 190 million between 2000 and 2002. Reflecting this, revenues slumped from $7.1 billion to $4.14 billion and net income from $803 million to $109 million. To cope with the decline, Schwab was forced to cut back on its employee headcount, which fell from a peak of nearly 26,000 employees in 2000 to just over 16,000 in late 2003.

Schwab's strategic reaction to the sea change in market conditions was already taking form as the market implosion began. In January 2000, Schwab acquired U.S. Trust for $2.7 billion. U.S. Trust was a 149-year-old investment advisement business that manages money for high-net-worth individuals whose invested assets exceed $2 million. When acquired, U.S. Trust had 7,000 customers and assets of $84 billion, compared to 6.4 million customers and assets of $725 billion at Schwab.[15]

According to Pottruck, widely regarded as the architect of the acquisition, Schwab made the acquisition because it discovered that high net worth individuals were starting to defect from Schwab for money managers like U.S. Trust. The main reason, as

Schwab's clients got older and richer, they started to need institutions that specialized in services that Schwab didn't offer–including personal trusts, estate planning, tax services, and private banking. With baby boomers starting to enter middle to late middle age, and their average net worth projected to rise, Schwab decided that it needed to get into this business or lose high-net-worth clients.

The decision though, started to bring Schwab into conflict with the network of 6,000 or so independent financial advisors that the company has long fostered through the Schwab Advisers Network, and who funneled customers and assets into Schwab accounts. Some advisors felt that Schwab was starting to move in on their turf, and they were not too happy about it.

In May 2002, Schwab made another move in this direction when it announced that it would launch a new service targeted at clients with more than $500,000 in assets. Known as Schwab Private Client, and developed with the help of U.S. Trust employees, for a fee of 0.6% of assets, Private Client customers can meet face to face with a financial consultant to work out an investment plan and return to the same consultant for further advice. Schwab stressed that the consultant would not tell clients what to buy and sell–that is still left to the client. Nor will clients get the legal, tax and estate planning advice offered by U.S. Trust and independent financial advisors. Rather, they get a financial plan and consultation regarding industry and market conditions.[16]

To add power to this strategy, Schwab also announced that it would start a new stock rating system. The stock rating system is not the result of the work of financial analysts. Rather, it is the product of a computer model, developed at Schwab, that analyzes more than 3,000 stocks on 24 basic measures, such as free cash flow, sales growth, insider trades, and so on, and then assigns grades. The top 10% get an A, the next 20% a B, the middle 40% a C, the next 20% a D, and the lowest 10% an F. Schwab claims that the new system is "a systematic approach with nothing but objectivity, not influenced by corporate relationships, investment banking, or any of the above."[17]

Critics of this strategy were quick to point out that many of Schwab's branch employees lacked the qualifications and expertise to give financial advice. At the time the service was announced, Schwab had some 150 qualified financial advisers in place, and planned to have 300 by early 2003. These elite employees required a higher salary than the traditional Schwab branch employees, who in many respects were little more than order takers and providers of prepackaged information.

The Schwab Private Client service also caused further grumbling among the private financial advisors affiliated with Schwab. In 2002, there were 5,900 of these. In total, their clients amounted to $222 billion of Schwab's $765 billion in client assets. Several stated that they would no longer keep clients' money at Schwab. However, Schwab stated that it would use the Private Client Service as a device for referring people who wanted more sophisticated advice than Schwab could offer to its network of registered financial advisers, and particularly an inner circle of 330 advisers who have an average of $500 million in assets under management and 17 years of experience.[18] According to one member of this group, "Schwab is not a threat to us. Most people realize the hand holding it takes to do that kind of work and Schwab wants us to do it. There's just more money behind the Schwab Advisors Network. The dead wood is gone, and firms like ours stand to benefit from even more additional leads."[19]

In 2003, Charles Schwab finally stepped down as co-CEO, leaving Pottruck in charge of the business (Charles Schwab stayed on as chairman). In late 2003, Pottruck announced that Schwab would acquire Soundview Technology Group for $321 million. Soundview was a boutique investment bank with a research arm that covered a couple of hundred companies and offered this research to institutional investors, such as mutual fund managers. Pottruck justified the acquisition by arguing that it would have taken Schwab years to build similar investment research capabilities internally. His plan was to have Soundview's research bundles for Schwab's retail investors.

C11-3e 2004–2008: The Return of Charles Schwab

The Soundview acquisition proved to be Pottruck's undoing. It soon became apparent that the acquisition has a huge mistake. There was little value to be had for Schwab's retail business from Soundview. Moreover, the move had raised Schwab's operating costs. By mid-2004, Pottruck was trying to sell Soundview. The board, which was disturbed at Pottruck's vacillating strategic leadership, expressed their concerns to Charles Schwab. On July 15, 2004, Pottruck was fired, and 66-year-old Charles Schwab returned as CEO.

Charles Schwab moved quickly to refocus the company. Soundview was sold to the investment bank UBS for $265 million. Schwab reduced the workforce by another 2,400 employees, closed underperforming branches, and removed $600 million in annual cost. This allowed him to reduce commissions on stock trades by 45%, and take market share from other discount brokers such as Ameritrade and E*Trade.

Going forward, Charles Schwab reemphasized the tradition mission of Schwab–to empower investors and provide them with ethical financial services. He also reemphasized the importance of the relationships that Schwab had with independent investment advisors. He noted: "Trading has become commoditized. The future is really about competing for client relationships."[20] One major new focus of Charles Schwab was the company's retail banking business. This had been established in 2002, but it had been a low priority for Pottruck. Now Schwab wanted to make the company a single source for banking, brokerage, and credit card services—one that would give Schwab's customers something of value: a personal relationship they could trust. The goal was to lessen Schwab's dependence on trading income, and give it a more reliable earnings stream and a deeper relationship with clients.

In mid-2007 Schwab's reorientation back to its traditional mission reached a logic conclusion when U.S. Trust was sold to Bank of America for $3.3 billion. Unlike in the past, however, Schwab was no longer earning the bulk of its money from trading commissions. As a percentage of net revenues, trading revenues (mostly commissions on stock trades) was down from 36% in 2002 to 17% in 2007. By 2007, asset management fees accounted for 47% of Schwab's net revenue, up from 41% in 2002, while net interest revenue (difference between earned interest on assets such as loans and interest paid on deposits) was 33%, up from 19% in 2002.[21] Schwab's overall performance had also improved markedly. Net income in 2007 was $1.12 billion, up from a low of $396 million in 2003.

C11-3f The Great Financial Crisis and Its Aftermath

The great financial crisis that hit the financial services industry in 2008–2009 had its roots in a bubble in housing prices in the United States. Financial service firms had been bundling thousands of home mortgages together into bonds, and selling them to investors worldwide. The purchasers of those bonds thought that they were buying a solid financial asset with a guaranteed payout–but it turned out that the quality of many of the bonds was much lower than indicated by bond rating agencies such as Standard & Poor's. Put differently, there was an unexpectedly high rate of default on home mortgages in the United States.

At the top of the housing bubble, many people were paying more than they could afford to for homes. Banks were only too happy to lend them this money because they assumed, incorrectly as it turned out, that if the borrower faced default, the home could be sold for a profit and the balance on the mortgage paid off. The flaw in this reasoning was the assumption that the underlying asset–the house–could be sold and that home pricing would continue to advance. There had been massive overbuilding in the United States. By 2007, home prices were falling as it became apparent that there was too much excess inventory in the system. The net result: many supposedly high-quality mortgage-backed bonds turned out to be nothing more than junk and prices for these bonds fell precipitously. Institutions holding these bonds had to write down their value, and their balance sheets started to deteriorate rapidly. As this occurred, other financial institutions became increasingly reluctant to lend money to those institutions seen as being overexposed to the housing market. Suddenly the banking system was facing a major credit crunch.

As the crisis unfolded, several major financial institutions went bankrupt, including Lehman Brothers (a major player in the market for mortgage-backed securities) and Washington Mutual (one of the nation's largest mortgage originators). AIG, a major insurance company that had built a big business in the 2000s selling default insurance to the holders of mortgage-backed securities, faced massive potential claims and had to be rescued from bankruptcy by the U.S. government. The government took an 80% stake in AIG in return for providing loans worth $182 billion. The U.S. government also created a $700 billion fund–the Troubled Asset Relief Program–that banks could draw upon the shore up their balance sheets and meet short-term obligations. While these actions managed to arrest what was the most serious crisis to hit the global financial system since the Great Depression of 1929, they could not stave off a severe and prolonged recession and a major decline of the market value of most financial institutions.

Almost alone among major financial institutions, Schwab sailed through the financial crisis with relative ease. The firm had steered well clear of the feeding frenzy in the U.S. housing and mortgage markets. Schwab did not originate mortgages, and nor did it hold mortgage-backed securities on its balance sheet. Schwab had no need to draw on government funds to shore up its balance sheet. The company remained profitable, and although revenues and earnings did fall from 2007 through to 2009, the balance sheet remained strong.

By 2010, Schwab was once more on a growth path, although extremely low interest rates in the United States and elsewhere limited its ability to earn money from the spread between what it paid to depositors, and the amount it could earn by investing depositors' money on the short-term money markets. Some 40% of Schwab's revenues are tied to interest rates, and so long as interest rates remain very low, Schwab's ability to earn profit here is limited. On the other hand, earnings could expand significantly if rates return to pre-crisis levels.

Charles Schwab himself stepped down as CEO on July 22, 2008, passing the reins of leadership to Walter Bettinger, although Schwab continues to be involved in major strategic decisions as an active chairman. Under Bettinger the company has charted a conservative course. The main goal has been to grow the net asset base of the firm by attracting more clients. The stellar performance of Schwab though the financial crisis, and its continuing strong brand, has certainly helped in this regard. From 2008 to 2016, Schwab has been able to generate 5–8% annual growth in its asset base. To keep doing so going forward, the company has launched a couple other initiatives.

First, in 2011, it announced a plan to start expanding its physical retail presence. Schwab's branches had declined in number from 400 in 2003 to around 300 by 2011 as more and more customers transacted online with the company. Despite this decline, Schwab has concluded that a physical retail presence remains a powerful means of gathering in new accounts and holding onto existing accounts. Rather than open more storefronts itself, however, which entails significant costs, the company has opted for a different strategy; it has decided to open additional retail branches using independents operators in what amounts to a franchise system. The goal is to ultimately triple the branch network to around 1,000. Detractors worry that Schwab risks diluting its powerful brand if the independent operators do not offer the same level of service that people have become accustomed to at traditional Schwab branches. For its part, Schwab executives have stated that it is their intention that a client walking into an independently owned Schwab branch will not know the difference and would get the same service and products as at company owned branches.[22]

Second, Schwab has made a big push into the exchange traded fund business (ETFs). ETFs are passively managed index funds, such as an S&P 500 index fund. Introduced 30 years ago, by 2021, ETFs had grown into a $7.2 trillion-dollar industry. ETFs are attractive because they trade like stocks on a regulated exchange while providing diversity within a single investment product. Since ETFs are passively managed, expense ratios are lower than those for actively managed mutual funds. Schwab started to offer ETFs in the 2000s. In 2013, it announced the launch of Schwab ETF OneSource trading platform. Modeled on Schwab's successful mutual fund market place, this provides access to more than 200 ETFs and offers $0 online trade commissions. Schwab will make money from charging administrative fees, the same way as it does with mutual funds.

C11-3g Acquiring TD Ameritrade[23]

In the 2010s, Schwab and other discount brokers were facing increased competition from a fresh wave of startups, such as Robin Hood. These new companies were offering commission free online trading. They made money from interest earned on customer's cash balances, selling order information to high-frequency traders, and margin lending (lending to customers to enable them to purchase financial instruments such as stocks, bonds, and options). By the late 2010s, these companies were growing rapidly, cutting into Schwab's business. In 2020, for example, Robin Hood had 22.8 million funded accounts.

Faced with this new competition, Schwab and others moved towards zero commissions for much of their trading. This increased their need to generate revenue from other sources, such as interest related revenue from investing customers cash balances and margin loans, and asset management and administrative fees from EFTs and other offerings. In this commodity business, economies of scale have become increasingly important. Large scale allows retail brokerages to process additional trades at low costs, which produces incrementally higher operating margins. In addition, retail brokerages such as Schwab also have banking subsidiaries that rank well against traditional banks given their low operating costs and lack of physical presence. Moreover, the generally higher net worth of their clients makes them less sensitive to interest rates than traditional bank customers.

Schwab had been reducing its reliance on commissions since the 2008–2009 great financial crises. In October 2019, Schwab took this shift to its logical conclusion when the company announced that it would no longer charge commissions on stock trades–a move that forced other discount brokers to follow suit. This was quickly followed by an announcement in November 2019 that Schwab would acquire rival discount brokerage, TD Ameritrade, for $26 billion. The acquisition would make Schwab the second-largest firm by self-directed customer assets, behind Fidelity, which held about one-third of the market. With TD Ameritrade, Schwab would account for about 27% of the market. The deal would enable Schwab to increase its customer base, while cutting expenses. The acquisition closed on October 6. 2020.

C11-4 Conclusion

As of 2022, Schwab seemed to be firing on all cylinders. The company now had over $7 trillion in assets under management. By 2022, more than 50% of earnings came from interest-related revenue, around 30% from asset management and administrative fees, and the remaining 20% coming from trading revenue. While headline commissions are now zero, the company still charges for certain types of trades and receives payments for order flow from market makers.

The top line goal is to continue to grow the business by offering low costs, excellent customer service, and a wide range of investment options. The company articulated five principles to guide its growth over the next decade: (1) Trust is everything, earned over time, lost in an instant. (2) Price matters, more than ever, and in our industry, more than most. (3) Clients deserve efficient experiences, every time. (4) Every prospective or existing client is critical to our future growth, no matter how large or small. (5) Actions matter more than words, clients, press, influencers, and employees will give credit to what we do rather than what we say. The company was clear that to achieve its growth goal and be true to its principles, it would have to continue to innovate and challenge the status quo.[24]

Notes

[1]Material for this section is drawn from *Securities Industry and Financial Markets Association 2022 Capital Markets Fact Book* (New York: SIFMA, 2022), and from SCFMA Facts Books for prior years.

[2]R. E. Shiller, *Irrational Exuberance* (Princeton, NJ: Princeton University Press, 2002).

[3]A. O'Donnell, "New Thinking on Convergence," *Wall Street & Technology*, May 2002, pp. 16–18.

[4]T. P. Pare, "How Schwab Wins Investors," *Fortune*, June 1, 1992, pp. 52–59.

[5]T. P. Pare, "How Schwab Wins Investors," *Fortune*, June 1, 1992, pp. 52–59.

[6]J. Kador, *Charles Schwab: How One Company Beat Wall Street and Reinvented the Brokerage Industry* (New York: John Wiley & Sons, 2002).

[7]E. C. Gottschalk, "Computerized Investment Systems Thrive as People Seek Control over Portfolios," *Wall Street Journal*, September 27, 1988, p. 1.

[8]J. Kador, *Charles Schwab: How One Company Beat Wall Street and Reinvented the Brokerage Industry* (New York: John Wiley & Sons, 2002).

[9]J. Kador, *Charles Schwab: How One Company Beat Wall Street and Reinvented the Brokerage Industry* (New York: John Wiley & Sons, 2002), p. 73.

[10]G. C. Hill, "Schwab to Curb Expansion, Tighten Belt Because of Post Crash trading Decline," *Wall Street Journal,* December 7, 1987, p. 1.

[11]J. Kador, *Charles Schwab: How One Company Beat Wall Street and Reinvented the Brokerage Industry* (New York: John Wiley & Sons, 2002), p. 185.

[12]J. Kador, *Charles Schwab: How One Company Beat Wall Street and Reinvented the Brokerage Industry* (New York: John Wiley & Sons, 2002), p. 217.

[13]E. Schonfeld, " Schwab Puts It All Online," *Fortune*, December 7, 1998, pp. 94–99.

[14]Anonymous, "Schwab's e-Gambit," *BusinessWeek,* January 11, 1999, p. 61.

[15]A. Kover. "Schwab Makes a Grand Play for the Rich," *Fortune*, February 7, 2000, p. 32.

[16]L. Lee and E. Thornton, "Schwab v Wall Street," *BusinessWeek*, June 3, 2002, pp. 64–70.

[17]Quoted in L. Lee and E. Thornton, "Schwab v Wall Street," *BusinessWeek*, June 3, 2002, pp. 64–70.

[18]E. E. Arvedlund, "Schwab Trades Up," *Barron's*, May 27, 2002, pp. 19–20.

[19]E. E. Arvedlund, "Schwab Trades Tp," *Barron's*, May 27, 2002, p. 20.

[20]B. Morris, "Charles Schwab's Big Challenge," *Fortune*, May 30, 2005, pp. 88–98.

[21]Charles Schwab, 2007 10K form.

[22]E. MacBride, "Why Schwab Is Embracing a Franchise Like Strategy to Fast Forward Branch Growth," *Forbes*, February 14, 2011.

[23]T. S. Bernard and M. Phillips, "Charles Schwab to Buy TD Ameritrade as Free Trading Takes Over," *New York Times*, November 25, 2019.

[24]Charles Schwab, Winter Business Update, February 6, 2018.

Case 12

Uber in 2022

Charles W. L. Hill Foster School of Business University of Washington, Seattle, WA 98195 October 2022

"Uber is software eats taxis" Marc Andreesen[1]

"I have had some terrible experiences with the taxi service; twice this past year I ordered a taxi to my house to go to the airport and they just didn't show up" Kevin Kane[2]

"Cab driver robbed, stabbed overnight in Salt Lake City" KUTV News headline.[3]

C12-1 Introduction

In June 2014, a 5-year-old company, Uber Technologies, the developer of the car hailing smart phone app, secured $1.2 billion in funding from a consortium of investors led by mutual fund giant Fidelity Investments. On the basis of the funding, Uber was valued at $18.2 billion, making it one of the world's most valuable privately held companies. This placed Uber's valuation above that of the rental car companies Hertz and Avis, as well as other well-known private technology companies such as Airbnb and Dropbox. In justifying the valuation, CEO Travis Kalanick noted that Uber was already using its app to offer ride for hire services in 130 cities in 36 countries and that revenues were "at least doubling every 6 months."[4]

At the same time, Uber was facing challenges from incumbent taxi services around the globe who argued that Uber was circumventing existing regulations and competing against them unfairly. On June 12th, 2014, European taxi drivers protested the rise of Uber, stopping in the middle of streets and shutting down major portions of several major European cities including London, Lyon, Madrid, and Milan. Uber responded by offering discounts to stranded commuters in major cities. The day after the protests, Uber reported that its ridership in London had soared by 850%.[5] In the United States, regulators in numerous cities issued cease-and-desist orders against Uber, which the company has generally ignored and in several high-profile instances, overturned.

C12-2 The "Ride for Hire" Marketplace in the United States

Historically in the United States, two different types of providers have operated in the ride for hire marketplace. There have been taxicab services and limousine services, each of which operates under a different set of rules. Both taxi cabs and limousine services are regulated by the states and/or cities in which they operate. In most cases, taxicabs are regulated at the municipal level, whereas limousine services are regulated at the city or state level. The regulations that apply to taxicab and limousine-type services are roughly similar from jurisdiction to jurisdiction, although they may differ in detail.[6]

Regulations typically address who can operate a taxicab or limousine, how service providers are contacted, the fare structure, and the labeling and appearance of vehicles. The motive for regulation is to ensure that services are safe, reliable, and affordable, and that owners and drivers are adequately compensated.

Customers can contact ride providers in two ways: by hailing on the street or by prearrangement. In general, only licensed taxicabs can be hailed on the street; limousine services must be prearranged. Moreover, unlike taxicabs, in many cities, limousine services cannot respond immediately to pick-up requests—they typically have a minimum prearrangement time, often at least an hour. This requirement works to protect taxicabs from direct competition from limousine services.

Most large urban markets are served by a significant number of local taxicab companies who operate fleets of cars. For example, there are 31 cab companies in San Francisco and 10 taxi dispatch companies that schedule rides. No one firm is dominant. There are about 1,500 licensed taxicabs within the city. Some 57% of taxi drivers in San Francisco are immigrants, a pattern that is repeated in many other cities. The average mean wage of a San Francisco driver was reported to be $22,440 in 2013.[7]

In New York, which has the largest ride-for-hire fleet in the United States, licenses have been issued for 13,437 taxicabs. There are an estimated 42,000 drivers in the city, with a licensed vehicle being used by two to three drivers a day. In 2014, only 6% of cab drivers in New York were born in the United States, and 36% came from Bangladesh and Pakistan. The New York taxi fleet picks up 600,000 passengers per day. There are also an estimated 25,000 livery cars that provide for hire service by pre-arrangement, and carry 500,000 passengers per day. There are 10,000 "black cars" that provide services mostly for corporate clients.[8]

Regulators have long required that taxicabs available to be hailed on the street be licensed. The license is to ensure that the taxi service is safe and reliable, and that fares are fair. For-hire vehicles must be insured to cover drivers and passengers, meet safety standards, and (if taxicabs) have a sealed meter. Regulations also require that licensed cabs be quickly and easily identifiable. This is normally achieved by a distinctive color (e.g., yellow cabs). Cabs must also display whether they are in service or not.

Taxicabs charge a regulated fare, set by a government agency, based on the time and distance of the trip, as measured by a meter. Some trips to and from established destinations, such as an airport, may have a fixed price and will displayed in the cab. Taxicabs are required to carry standardized meters that must be prominently displayed, are sealed and periodically checked to ensure that the proper fare is being charged. Limousine services are generally prohibited from charging fares based on time and distance, and they do not carry a meter. Typically, fees are based on time, often with a minimum billed time. The fee normally has to be agreed on in advance.

In many jurisdictions, the licensing system limits the supply of taxicabs. One common variant of licensing is the medallion system that is used in cities such as New York, Boston, Chicago, and San Francisco. Medallions are small metal plates attached to the hood of a taxi, certifying it for passenger pickup throughout a defined area (normally metropolitan boundaries). When the medallion system was first introduced in New York in 1937, the idea was to make sure that taxi driver was not a criminal luring passengers into his vehicle. To get a medallion, the taxi service has to adhere to the regulatory requirements in that jurisdiction and be approved by the appropriate regulatory agency. Medallions may be given to individual taxi drivers who own their own cars, but more typically taxi companies that own fleets of cars acquire them. The taxi companies then lease cars and medallions to drivers on a daily or weekly basis. In some locations, the driver may own the car, but lease or purchase the medallion from an agent who has acquired it. An example would be Medallion Financial, a publicly traded company that owns hundreds of medallions in New York, sells them to aspiring young cabbies, and arranges for loans to finance their purchase.

In cities that utilize a medallion system the supply of medallions has often been limited. The rationalizations for doing this include ensuring quality, guaranteeing a fair return to taxi companies, and helping to support demand for other forms of public transportation, such as buses, trains, and the subway. It has also been argued that limiting the number of cabs helps to reduce congestion and pollution.[9]

In practice, the supply of medallions has often not kept pace with growing population. In New York, Chicago, and Boston, for example, the number of medallions issued has barely budged since the 1930s. In New York, there were 11,787 medallions issued after World War II, a number that remained constant until 2004. By 2014, there were 13,437 medallions issued in New York.

Medallions can be traded. Thus, over time, a secondary market in medallions has developed. In this market, the price is not set by the agency issuing them, but by the laws of supply and demand. The effect of limited supply has been to drive up the price of medallions. In New York, taxi medallions were famously selling for over $1 million in 2012. In Boston, the price was $625,000. In San Francisco, the price was $300,000 and the city took a $100,000 commission on the sale of medallions.[10] The average annual price of medallions surged during the 2000s. In New York, prices increased 260% between 2004 and 2012. The inflation adjusted annualized return for medallions over this time period in New York was 19.5%, compared to a 3.9% annual return for the S&P 500.[11]

As noted above, drivers often do not own the medallions. There are three players in many taxi markets: the medallion holders (often taxi companies) who have acquired the right to operate a taxi from the regulatory agency, the taxi driver, and taxi dispatch companies. A taxi dispatch company is a middleman or broker, who typically matches available cabs with customers and takes a fee for its scheduling services. While an individual taxi driver may own a medallion, most often taxi companies own them. Tax companies own a fleet of cabs, which they lease out to drivers (with a medallion). A minority of drivers may own their own cab. In New York, about 18% of cabs were owner operated in 2014, putting most medallions in the hands of taxi companies.

In New York, regulations allow medallion owners to lease them out to drivers for 12-hour shifts. The critical problem facing a driver is that they must get access to a medallion in order to make a living. Due to this, companies that own medallions can extract high fees from drivers. There are also reports that some taxi dispatch companies use their position as schedulers to extract payment in the form of bribes from drivers in return for good shifts.[12]

Drivers, who legally are viewed as "independent contractors," can begin a 12-hour shift owing as much as $130 to their medallion leasing company. They may not break even until halfway through their shift. One consulting company report found that in 2006 a driver's take-home pay in New York for a 12-hour shift averaged $158. In 2011, the New York transportation authority calculated that it was $96.[13] A study of taxi drivers in Los Angeles found that drivers worked on average 72 hours a week for a median take-home wage of $8.39 an hour. The LA drivers were paying $2,000 in leasing fees per month to taxi companies. None of the drivers in the LA study had health insurance provided by their companies, and 61% were completely without health insurance.[14] Given the compensation, it is perhaps not surprising that some drivers can be rude, impatient, and prone to drive fast and take poor care of their cabs.

The LA study noted that because city officials heavily regulate the taxi business, taxi companies are active politically, paying lobbyists to advocate their interests and contributing to the campaign funds of local politicians. The same is true in New York, where the medallion owners trade association, the Metropolitan Taxi Board of Trade, lobbies hard to influence public policy. In 2011, for example, medallion owners were initially able to block plans to create a fleet of green colored "Boro" cabs to serve New York's outer boroughs. They argued that doing so would drive down the price of their medallions. In June 2013, however, the New York Supreme Court overruled lower-court rulings and allowed the licensing of Boro cabs to go ahead. The intention now is to issue 18,000 new licenses to green cabs. These cabs, however, will not be able to pick up passengers in Lower Manhattan, which remains the territory of yellow cabs.[15]

C12-3 The Ride for Hire Market in Other Countries

Many of the regulations seen in the U.S. ride-for-hire marketplace have their analog in other countries. In London, for example, there are 22,000 black cabs (taxis that can be hailed) and 49,000 vehicles licensed for private hire that cannot be hailed on the street. Although there is no regulatory limit on the number of taxis in London, before London taxi drivers can join the workforce, they must navigate byzantine licensing procedures that include memorizing the city's street maps, which is referred to as "the knowledge." Acquiring "the knowledge" constitutes the most demanding taxi driver-training program in the world. On average, it takes 12 attempts at the final test and 34 months of preparation to pass the knowledge exam. The effect of "the knowledge" requirement is to limit the supply of taxis in London. Similar, though less demanding, knowledge tests are found in Austria, Brussels, Finland, Germany, and Hungary.[16]

In Paris, the number of taxi permits was capped at 14,000 in 1937. By 2014, a much bigger and vastly richer Paris was receiving 27 million tourist visits a year, yet the number of cabs had edged up just 14% to 15,900. The result: Parisians must stand in long lines for cabs that never come. In 2007, the government of Nicolas Sarkozy proposed to license 6,500 new cabs in Paris. The proposal triggered a strike among transportation workers that shut the city down for a day and frightened Sarkozy into surrender.[17]

Italy is another country with a restrictive licensing system for taxis. This has been a problem in Milan, for example. In 2002, the ratio of taxis to inhabitants was 1 for every 1,094 inhabitants, compared to 1 for every 387 in London and 1 for every 414 in Paris. At the time, there were 4,571 taxis in Milan, a number that had been frozen for 20 years. The shortage of taxis resulted in long waiting periods at peak demand times. The price of taxi licenses on the secondary market had risen to between EUR 100,000 and EUR 130,000. In 2002, the city government moved to alleviate the cab shortage, announcing that it would issue 500 new cab licenses. Milan's taxi drivers mounted a vigorous campaign against this. The city responded by reducing the number of proposed new licenses to 300. The taxi drivers still objected and protested by forming "go-slow" convoys of taxis that paralyze the city's traffic for 2 days. The city effectively backed off.[18]

In contrast, Dublin offers a view of what can happen when regulations are relaxed. Due to the limited availability of licenses, between 1979 and 1998 the number of licenses in Dublin barely budged even though demand had soared as the population grew. Deregulation in 2000 reduced the cost of entry (car plus license) by 74%. The result was more than three times as many cabs on the road, shorter waiting times, better cab quality, and higher passenger satisfaction—all in 2 years.[19]

Interestingly, Tehran, the capital of Iran, has a highly deregulated ride-for-hire market. In addition to private taxis, a shared taxi system operates which allows any private car to pick up passengers. Since travelers can hop on and off as they please, a driver can carry passengers traveling to different destinations at the same time, which increases utilization of the vehicle. The system also means that the supply of taxis is very fluid, increasing during rush hour as commuters pick up passengers on their way home.[20]

C12-4 Uber's Service

Uber was founded in San Francisco 2009 by Garrett Camp and Travis Kalanick to develop a smartphone app that facilitates the creation of a new ride-for-hire service. The company raised $1.25 million in angel investments in 2010 to help fund the initial service rollout. From the outset, the goal was to overcome common frustrations that customers often experience when trying to find a taxi. Passengers can find taxicabs to be unpleasant, poorly maintained, dirty, and unsafely driven. Taxicabs can be difficult to find in certain areas—many avoid areas of a city where there are few passengers, or where they are unlikely to find a return fare. There can also be a shortage of cabs at peak commute times, or at special events, such as New Year's Eve, which leads to long wait times. Sometimes taxicabs just don't turn up, leaving a traveler stranded. This author once missed a plane flight because a taxicab booked the day before simply didn't appear. On another occasion, a scheduled ride turned up very late because the taxi driver got lost.

C12-4a Business Model

Uber exploited the opportunity created by customer frustrations to develop a smartphone application that effectively enabled customers to hail a limousine immediately from the comfort of a couch or a bar stool, rather than standing on a cold street and waiting for a cab to drive by. The app also shows customers the location of cars. In general, a car will arrive a few minutes after being hailed. The fare, including a tip, is charged directly to the customer's credit card. This means that no cash changes hands, which is a major plus for drivers who do not like to carry large quantities of cash (there is a long history of taxi drivers being robbed by their rides). The fee is based on time and distance, as determined by the Uber application using the GPS capability of the driver's mobile device. Under the initial model, the fee was split between the driver, who kept 80%, and Uber, which got 20%. When Uber started its service in 2010, the company was charging 40–100% more than a similar trip using a taxicab. However, over time, the price differential between Uber cars and regular taxicabs fares has declined substantially.

Uber does not own cars. Instead, it relies upon a network of established, licensed, limousine drivers and companies that wish to be part of its system. In effect, the Uber app allows limousines to be transformed into a service that can be hailed from any location, albeit by an app rather than hand signaling. Uber makes use of big data analytics to determine the best locations for drivers to wait in order to speed up response time to customer requests for rides. The more data Uber gets, the better its predictive models, the more optimal its placement of vehicles, and the higher vehicle utilization.

Uber has also used data analytics to pioneer the use of what it calls "surge pricing."[21] Instead of using fixed pricing like a conventional taxi service, Uber adjusts prices for a ride, depending upon the state of demand. For example, prices have been known to surge on New Year's Eve. Similarly, if there is an unforeseen event such as a snowstorm that makes everyone want a car at the same time, prices will go up, often dramatically. There have been reports of Uber fares increasing to as much as seven times the normal level during periods of peak demand. In turn, the higher prices attract more Uber vehicles onto the road, and prices drop back down towards normal levels. Uber argues that a benefit of this system is that it encourages more supply at periods of peak demand, and vice versa. However, there have been some reports of grumbling on the part of customers who find that they are paying unexpectedly high prices. Conversely, if Uber's network of drivers responds quickly to price signals, dramatic prices surges should be a very transitory phenomenon.

An added benefit of the Uber app is that it has a feature that allows riders to rate drivers, which translates into an implicit guarantee of driver reliability based on prior reputation. There is a corresponding feature on the driver's app, which enables them to rate customers, and to red flag and avoid troublesome clients.

Limousine and other private car owners have been attracted to the Uber model by a number of factors. First, the Uber app has enabled limo drivers to circumvent regulations that prohibit them from being hailed on the street. As such, it has increased demand for their services. Second, the app increases vehicle utilization, which drives more revenues to the vehicle owner. Third, owners of the vehicle benefit from the surge pricing methodology that enables them to charge more than regulated fares at times of peak demand. Fourth, the fact that no cash changes hands, and that payment is guaranteed when a ride is booked, increases the safety of the driver, as does the client-rating feature on the driver's app. Fifth, the Uber system means that drivers can work flexible hours, driving when they want to rather than when a taxi company tells them they must take a shift.

There have been reports of Uber drivers earning multiples of what the driver of a regulated taxicab could earn. In early 2014, Uber itself suggested that while a typical taxi cab driver could earn $30,000 a year, an Uber driver working a 40-hour week could earn nearly $91,000 a year in New York and $74,000 in San Francisco.[22] Attracted by such financial inducements, in 2014, the company claimed that 20,000 drivers a month were signing up with Uber worldwide.

Some financial journalists have questioned Uber's claims about driver income. Uber's estimates were based on a sample of drivers who drove over 40 hours a week. The earnings figure also excluded the cost of gas, insurance, parking, maintenance, repairs, and paying for tolls. One journalist concluded that in order to earn $75,000 a year driving for Uber in San Francisco, you would have to work 58 hours a week.[23]

C12-4b Expansion Strategy

Uber began offering its service in June 2010 in San Francisco under the name Uber-Cab. New York was added in May 2011. By April 2012, the company was in seven U.S. cities, Paris, and Toronto. Two years later, Uber was operating in 130 cities in 36 countries around the world. Initially, Uber limited its service to drivers with high-end limo-type cars. In San Francisco, Uber explicitly targeted members of the tech community in its early marketing efforts, sponsoring local tech and venture capital events and providing free rides to attendees. Uber's bet was that its service would immediately resonate with this demographic, who would rapidly spread the news via word of mouth and social networks. According to CEO Travis Kalanick:

> Uber spends virtually zero dollars on marketing, spreading almost exclusively via word of mouth. I'm talking old school word of mouth, you know at the water cooler in the office, at a restaurant when you're paying the bill, at a party with friends – "Who's Ubering home?" 95% of all our riders have heard about Uber from other Uber riders. Our virality is almost unprecedented. For every 7 rides we do, our users' big mouths generate a new rider.[24]

One of Uber's business development managers elaborated on this:

With Uber everything is very local-focused as transportation is a local topic. For that reason we have an operations team on the ground in all the cities where Uber exists, and that team is working with both local drivers, and local clients to grow the business there.

We've also found that our growth is driven substantially by word of mouth. When someone sees the ease of use, the fact that they press a button on their phone and in under 5 minutes a car appears, they inevitably become a brand advocate. We've also done our best to reach out to folks who are influencers in our markets, who obviously have a stronger reach and bigger audience.[25]

To drive rapid growth Uber picked cities that have what Kalanick refers to as "accelerants". These accelerants indicate a concentrated need for Uber's service. They include: (1) lots of restaurants and nightlife, (2) holidays and events, (3) weather, and (4) sports.[26] For example, in Chicago, a city with lots of nightlife, intense weather, and numerous sporting events, Uber's initial viral growth was double what they normally experienced. Special events and holidays also provided an opportunity to showcase Uber's model. Uber's ability to deliver rides on New Year's Eve in San Francisco, a city notorious for its lack of taxis, drove spikes in new ridership. Kalanick has also noted that Uber is getting better at local market entry over time:

Every city, every subsequent city that we go to we're getting better at rolling the city out and growing the city faster. And so a lot of the cities where there's constrained number of taxis, no liquid black car market, those are the cities where we launch and things explode from the start. We have other cities where there's tons of taxis, in some cases way too many and in those situations often the quality of service being delivered is really poor, so we go in there and explode as well. But there's all kinds of different cities in terms of regulatory, and in terms of what the industry looks like, an industry which we're disrupting in a substantial way.

We think that cities deserve to have another transportation alternative. It sounds crazy to have to say that but you have to do that because you have incumbent interests which are often trying to curtail innovation and curtail sort of transportation alternatives that might compete with their existing business. And, because of that, it requires us to take a very local approach to how we go after a city. We have launchers that go into [cities] … and turn nothing into something. I like to say they drop in with parachutes and machetes [and] get highly involved with the suppliers, people who own cars and run car services, and really just make sure that we can launch a service that is high quality from the start. Being local and speaking with local voice is important when you're doing transportation and means you know what's going on for the city.[27]

To achieve rapid expansion, Uber needs to be able to quickly build a network of drivers in each city in which it enters. The company certainly touts the financial and safety advantages of working for Uber, but it is also taking other actions to make sure there are plenty of drivers available. In December 2013, Uber lined up $2.5 billion in outside financing for low interest rate loans for Uber X drivers with Toyota and GM. This was designed to make it possible for up to 200,000 drivers to buy their own cars at very low interest rates, under the condition that they use those cars on the Uber network for the duration of the loan. In effect, drivers are locked in for the duration of the loan unless they want to see their interest rates balloon. Reportedly drivers have to agree to two financing rates, one that reflects the cost savings of them partnering with Uber, and one that doesn't.[28]

C12-4c Regulatory Responses

Uber had not been operating in San Francisco long before there was rumbling among taxicab companies that Uber might not be legal. A taxi driver brought objections against Uber up at City's Taxi Advisory Council Meeting. Among the concerns were the following:[29]

- Uber operates much like a cab company but does not have a taxi license.
- Its cars don't have insurance equivalent to taxi insurance.
- Uber may threaten taxi dispatcher's way of making a living.
- Limos usually have to book an hour in advance, by law, while only licensed taxis can pick someone up right away, but Uber picks people up immediately, without a license to do so.

On October 20th, the San Francisco Metro Transit Authority and the Public Utilities Commission of California issued a cease-and-desist order against the company. Uber continued its service under threat of penalties including fines of up to $5,000 per instance of Uber's operation, and potentially 90 days in jail for each day the company remained in operation past the order to desist.

Undeterred, Uber stated that it would work with the agencies involved to figure out their exact concerns, and to make sure that the service complied. On the company blog, the following statement was posted:

> Uber is a first to market, cutting edge transportation technology and it must be recognized that the regulations from both city and state regulatory bodies have not been written with these innovations in mind. As such, we are happy to help educate the regulatory bodies on this new generation of technology and work closely with both agencies to ensure our compliance and keep our service available.

However, the company did however quietly change the name of its service from UberCab to just plane Uber.

The dispute between Uber and regulatory authorities in California simmered on for 3 years. During this time, Uber continued to operate, and indeed, dramatically expanded its service. At one point, CEO Kalanick joked that he probably had 20,000 years of jail time in front of him.[30] In 2013, influenced by evidence of strong public demand for Uber's service, the California Public Utilities Commission struck a deal with Uber, lifted the (ignored) cease-and-desist order, and eliminated fines.

As Uber expanded its service, what happened in California was repeated in cities around the United States, and then the globe. In Washington, D.C., where existing taxi services were rated as poor by many residents, demand for Uber cars rapidly took off after the company started service in December 2011. The local regulatory authority, The DC Taxicab Commission, deemed the service illegal. Uber continued to operate. At one point, the Commission conducted sting operations against Uber, hailing Uber cars via the Uber app, then impounding cars and ticketing drivers. Responding to intense lobbying from D.C.'s 150 taxicab companies, in mid-2012 the City Council drafted legislation to fix the price for Uber's service so that it would be five times the minimum cost of cabs. Uber CEO Kalanick responded with a social media campaign, urging D.C. customers to sign a petition and send emails to council members to protest the legislation. The council members were swamped with thousands of emails, and quickly withdrew the legislation. In a major victory for Kalanick, in short order, a new bill was drafted and passed that exempted Uber from regulation by the Taxicab Commission.[31]

In Seattle, after initially ignoring Uber, the City Council responded to its increasing popularity by passing an ordinance that limited the number of Uber drivers to just 150. At the time, Uber already had 1,000 drivers in the city. The City Council said that it was concerned about the safety and insurance coverage of Uber cars. Council member Kshama Sawant, a self-proclaimed socialist, argued in favor of the cap as a means to protect traditional taxi drivers. However, in Seattle, city ordinances can be suspended if enough citizens sign a petition requesting this. The day after the ordinance was passed, a group that received some $400,000 in funding from Uber and similar services submitted more than 36,000 signatures to the City Clerk's office, more than double the required number to suspend an ordinance. In July 2014, the City Council voted 8–1 in favor of legislation that legalized Uber and similar services and removed any caps on driver numbers.[32]

In New York, a city with a long tradition of limo services, Uber initially operated unimpeded. When Uber tried to expand its operations to include New York's traditional yellow cabs, the City's Taxi and Limousine Commission (TLC) stepped in, telling cab owners that it had "not authorized any electronic hailing of payment applications for use in New York City taxicabs," and further that "drivers and owners are reminded that violations of Commission rules can lead to fines, and in some cases, the suspension or revocation of their license."[33] Interestingly, the TLC took this position despite strong interest among taxi drivers. Uber responded by withdrawing its yellow taxi service, but its limo service continued to operate.

In London, taxi drivers responded to the growing popularity of Uber with a day of protests, stopping in the middle of streets and causing significant congestion. The protests backfired. Uber reported a surge in app downloads and registration by London residents. In France, where similar protests by taxi drivers also took place, the Senate passed a law that requires online car service companies to return to their headquarters or a parking garage between each client, unless they have a prior reservation—a requirement that would substantially reduce Uber's ability to respond in a timely manner. In Brussels, Uber was banned after a court ruled it did not have the appropriate permits to operate in the city. In Berlin, the chairman of the Berlin Taxi Association won an injunction against Uber in April 2014, barring the company from operating there.[34]

Commenting on legal attempts to stop Uber, CEO Kalanick argues that they are classic example of regulators trying to stifle innovation. Kalanick also asserts that Uber's strategy of marching into new cities without asking permission is necessary. "If you put yourself in the position to ask for something that is already legal, you'll never be able to roll it out........the corruption of the taxi industries will make it so you will never get to market."[35]

C12-4d Competition

No good idea goes long without imitation, and Uber soon found itself facing several rivals, including most notably Lyft. Lyft is a privately held company based in San Francisco backed by venture capital. By mid-2014, it had raised over $300 million in financing. Logan Green and John Zimmer launched Lyft in the summer of 2012. It was originally conceived as a local service of Zimride, a ride-sharing service the two founded in 2007 that was focused on long-distance ride sharing, typically between cities. Lyft uses a smartphone app that facilitates peer-to-peer ride sharing and electronic hailing by enabling passengers who need a ride to request one from the available community of drivers nearby.

Lyft is different from Uber in that the drivers are regular citizens using their own cars. Drivers and passengers can rate each other on a five-star scale after each ride. The ratings establish the reputations of both drivers and passengers within the Lyft network. Ratings are displayed on the Lyft smartphone app, enabling drivers to avoid bad customers, and customers to avoid drivers with poor ratings. Lyft initially did not charge fixed prices, but instead relied upon voluntary donations to the driver. This changed in November 2013, when the company said that it would institute a fixed price schedule, with a 25% surcharge for peak periods. As with Uber, payment is automatic, made through the Lyft app, and Lyft takes 20% of the fare.[36]

By mid-2014, Lyft had established itself in 60 cities in the United States. Like Uber, Lyft has run into significant regulatory headwinds. Indeed, if anything, Lyft has faced more regulatory opposition since its drivers are using their own private cars. To counter claims regarding safety, Lyft insures each driver with a $1 million "excess" liability policy. Any driver with an average user rating of less than 4.5 out of 5 stars is also dropped from the service.

Lyft faced the same headwinds as Uber in California and stuck a similar deal with regulators in mid-2013. In New York, the TLC, who declared Lyft an unauthorized service that had not demonstrated compliance with safety and licensing requirements, initially blocked Lyft from operating in the city. The restriction was lifted in July 2014 after Lyft agreed to use licensed commercial drivers within the city. To grow its network in New York, Lyft was reportedly offering a guaranteed $10,000 a month to drivers with a license from the TLC who would agree to work 60 hours a week, and $5,000 to those who would work 40 hours a week.[37]

C12-4e Product Extensions and Price Cuts: UberX

Uber started out using traditional black limo cars. In July 2012, Uber created a new service category, known as UberX, which allowed Uber drivers to use vehicles beyond the traditional black limo, giving them a choice that included Toyota Prius Hybrids and SUVs like the Cadillac Escalade. By 2014, UberX drivers were also using basic sedans like the Toyota Camry or Honda Accord. Initially, the pricing for UberX cars was a $5 base fee, with a $3.25 per mile charge thereafter, making UberX 35% cheaper than Uber's "black car" rates. The introduction of UberX was seen as a competitive response to the emergence of Lyft as a low-cost competitor.[38]

In June 2013, Uber reduced the price of its UberX service in San Francisco by 25%. In October 2013, it announced similar fare reductions in Los Angeles, San Diego, and Washington, D.C. At the time, Uber stated that its fare was 18–37% cheaper than hailing a traditional taxicab, depending upon location. Although Uber compares its prices to traditional taxicabs, its price reductions have often come in cities where Lyft has recently launched its service. For example, Uber launched its UberX service in Indianapolis and St. Paul just a week after Lyft introduced its service to riders in those cities. Uber also offered a free month of service to riders in those cities.

Uber dropped its prices again in January 2014. To push back against resistance from drivers, it argued that the price cuts meant more rides, and thus greater revenue. Uber announced a further round of 25% price cuts in the summer of 2014 for its UberX service in select cities, including San Francisco. These cuts are meant to be for a limited time only. However, Uber also stated that drivers would still pocket 80% of the original fare *before* the cut. This implies that in some cases, Uber was now paying drivers more than they earn. For example, a 25% cut implies that a rider would now pay $11.25 for a ride that previously cost $15. But the driver would still keep 80% of the original $15 fee, which meant that Uber had to pay the driver $0.75 to make up the $12 salary for the driver. Under the new pricing scheme, UberX was now cheaper than taxicab services in many locations. For example, a fare from Union Square to the Mission District in San Francisco cost $11 via taxicab, and $6 by UberX.[39] On July 7th, 2014, Uber dropped their New York fare by 20%, making UberX cheaper than a taxi in the New York market.

C12-5 Uber Hits Some Potholes

The 2015–2018 period proved to be a challenging one for Uber's expansion strategy. On the positive side, the service continued to grow, particularly in the Americas. An interesting data point comes from Certify, which tracks business expense reimbursement in the United States. Certify found that Uber and Lyft are taking substantial share away from both traditional taxis and rental car companies. In the second quarter of 2018, Uber and Lyft combined had a 72.5% share of all ground transportation travel reimbursements in the United States, up from less than 10% in early 2014. The share of taxis fell from 38% to 5% over the same period, and rental cars fell from 55% to 22%.[40] This suggested that for business travel, an important segment, Uber and Lyft were decimating the incumbent taxi and rental car businesses.

On the other hand, Lyft has gained share from Uber. In 2017, Uber made a number of high-profile missteps (discussed below), which hurt the company's image and opened the door for Lyft to take share. By May 2018, Lyft claimed that it had 35% of the U.S. ride-share market, up from 20% at the end of 2016. Uber claims that it had 70–72% of the U.S. rid- share market in early 2018, which would leave Lyft with 28–30%.[41] No matters whose figures are correct, it is clear that Lyft gained some ground during this period.

A couple of academic studies published by the National Bureau of Economic Research suggested why Uber (and Lyft) have been doing so well in the United States. One study compared Uber's service to that of traditional taxi cabs in five U.S. cities. The study concluded that Uber drivers were significantly more productive than traditional taxi drivers.[42] For example, in Los Angeles, taxi drivers had a passenger in their car for 40.7% of the miles they drove, whereas UberX drivers had passengers in their car for 64.2% of their miles, resulting in a 58% higher capacity utilization rate for UberX drivers. In Seattle, the capacity utilization rate was 41% higher for UberX drivers.

A second study looked at the consumer surplus created by Uber.[43] The study used Uber's data on demand changes in response to surge pricing to estimate the company's demand curve. The study estimated that in 2015 the overall consumer surplus generated by UberX in the United States was around $7 billion. In other words, consumers valued the service so highly that they would have been willing to pay $7 billion more than they actually paid for their UberX rides.

The high value and productivity of Uber's service has not been enough to ensure success in a lot of international markets. Due to regulatory pressure, in 2014 and 2015, Uber was forced to suspend its service in Germany, France, Italy, Spain, and Belgium on the grounds that it relied on unlicensed non-professional drivers using their own vehicles. Uber continued to operate in some European cities, such as Berlin and Munich, but did so by working with existing licensed taxi companies and limousine services, a strategy that constrained its growth potential.

In September 2017, transportation authorities in London, one of Uber's most profitable markets, pulled the company's license. In doing so, the authorities stated that the company was not fit and proper to run a taxi service. Among the issues cited were Uber's failure to report assaults and other criminal offences to the police, a poor approach to vetting its drivers, and the use of a software tool known as "Greyball" to identify and deny service to certain riders. While Uber claimed that Greyball was used to identify riders who were suspected of violating its terms of service, authorities in London claimed that it was also used to deny rides to individuals who were flagged as regulatory or law enforcement agents. In June of 2018, Uber won a probationary license to continue operating in London for 15 months on the understanding that it would reform its practices.[44]

In China, which CEO Travis Kalanick had identified as a major growth opportunity for Uber, the company exited the market in mid-2016 after heavy initial investments.

Uber had partnered with the dominant Chinese search engine and mapping company, Baidu, something that many through was a smart move, but Uber faced intense competition from Didi Chunxing, a home-grown ride for hire operator in the Uber mold. Didi and Uber were fighting an intense price war. Didi had some very powerful backers of its own, Internet giants Alibaba and Tencent. China's influential sovereign wealth fund had also invested in Didi, a move that signaled Uber was facing an uphill battle. Seeing the writing on the wall, Uber traded its China operations for a 20% stake in Didi, which was worth about $7 billion, and a $1 billion investment from its Chinese rival. Although Uber had to pull out, the $8 billion value applied to the exit deal were about the same as its investments in the country and gave Uber a stake in the upside from growth at Didi.[45]

In 2017, Uber pulled out of Russia, combining its ridesharing business with that of the dominant local rival Yandex in a joint venture that was valued at close to $4 billion. Uber has a 36.6% share in the joint venture, but operational control was handed to Yandex. In 2018, Uber exited eight Southeast Asian nations when it sold its business there to Grab, a Singapore-based competitor. Uber will get a 27.5% stake in Grab, again giving it a share in the upside. The deal was another admission by Uber that it is finding it hard to gain traction in many nations against well-run and/or well-connected local rivals.

On the other hand, Uber registered solid growth in India and Latin America. Uber entered India in August 2013 and by July 2018 had registered 1 billion rides in the country. That being said, Uber faces intense competition in India from local rival Ola, which by at least one measure, number of cities served, is running ahead of Uber in the county.[46] In Brazil, one of the company's best markets where it had 20 million customers and 500,000 drivers in early 2018, the government passed legislation eliminating requirements that would have made it more difficult for Uber to operate. Most significantly, the bill did not require drivers to acquire licenses from the authorities.

C12-6 Management Missteps

In 2017, Uber was embroiled in several lawsuits and scandals that hurt its image. Things got off to a rocky start in 2017 when President Donald Trump issued an executive order banning immigration from seven countries. Most tech industry CEOs slammed Trump's ban, but Uber CEO Kalanick, who served on Trump's strategic forum for business leaders, issued a statement on Facebook that was only mildly critical. Then, Uber halted surge pricing during a taxi strike that was aligned with immigration policy protests at New York's JFK. Uber's move was seen as both breaking the strike and profiting off the demonstrations. Within days, a #DeleteUber campaign went viral on social media. Uber lost an estimated 200,000 accounts due to the hashtag. The main beneficiary was rival Lyft. Within days, the Lyft smartphone app had moved up from the No. 39 spot to the No. 4 spot on Apple's App store list of popular downloads.[47]

To compound matters, on January 19th, 2017, the Federal Trade Commission leveled a $20 million fine on Uber for recruiting drivers while exaggerating their earning potential. The FTC alleged that Uber claimed on its website that UberX drivers' annual median income was more than $90,000 in New York and over $74,000 in San Francisco. The FTC said, however, that drivers' annual median income was actually $61,000 in New York and $53,000 in San Francisco. In all, less than 10% of all drivers in those cities earned the yearly income Uber touted.[48]

Then on February 19, 2017, a former Uber engineer, Susan Fowler, posted a blog post that quickly went viral. The post detailed a prevailing atmosphere of sexual harassment and discrimination at the company. It opened the floodgates for more complaints and resulted in the company hiring former U.S. Attorney General Eric

Holder to lead a task force looking into the company's workplace culture, which had been characterized as "toxic." To make matters worse, on February 27, Uber senior VP of engineering Amit Singhal exited the company after it was revealed that he had left Google a year earlier due to a "credible" sexual harassment complaint. Uber claimed that they had done extensive background checks of Singhal and not uncovered any evidence of sexual harassment. The Holder report was released on June 13, 2017. It made 47 recommendations for helping Uber to improve its workplace values and environment. Some 20 staff members at Uber were fired for unethical behavior as a result of the Holder investigation.

On February 23, Waymo, a subsidiary of Alphabet (Google's parent) filed a lawsuit against Uber claiming that former Waymo employee Anthony Levandowski stole secrets related to autonomous vehicle technology. Both Uber and Waymo have been working on autonomous vehicle technology and envisage a future in which driverless cars are common on the road. On May 30, Uber fired Levandowski, stating that he did not fully comply with the court overseeing the lawsuit, or with helping Uber prove its case.

On February 28, CEO Travis Kalanick was forced to apologize after he was caught on film arguing with an Uber driver, Fawzi Kamel, about Uber's new plans to lower fares. "Some people don't like to take responsibility for their own s---. They blame everything in their life on somebody else. Good luck," Kalanick told his driver. Kalanick's troubles did not stop there. In early June of 2018, a letter surfaced that Kalanick had written in 2013 to employees going to a company conference in Miami. Filled with expletives, the letter painted a picture of a party atmosphere at the company, with references to fines for "puking," and laid out rules for sex between those attending in a manner that some believe helped to create an atmosphere of pervasive sexism and sexual harassment at the company.

This was too much for several powerful investors in the still private company. They insisted that Kalanick step down. He resigned on June 20, 2017. In August 2018, after a quick search, Kalanick was replaced by Dara Khosrowshahi, the CEO of Expedia. Khosrowashahi is an Iranian American whose family emigrated to the United States in 1978 just before the Iranian revolution. He had been CEO of Expedia for the prior 12 years, during which time revenues had quadrupled. His "fair" management style had earned him a 94% approval rating from Expedia employees on the job site Glassdoor. Uber reportedly paid him over $200 million to take the CEO position, although he did give up $180 million in future incentive compensation from Expedia to take the position.

C12-7 Khosrowshahi Takes Over

In his first year, Khosrowashahi earned accolades both within and outside the company (his Glassdoor rating has climbed to 97%). "He's an exceptional leader—a rare combination of keen financial acumen, an eye for a great product and incredible people skills," according to Expedia CEO Mark Okerstrom, who served under Khosrowashahi at Expedia.[49]

In his first 2 weeks, Khosrowashahi held a roundtable discussion with drivers to hear their complaints and shadowed Uber's customer support representatives to listen to what passengers were saying. He hired the company's first diversity officer and its first COO, Barney Harford, the former CEO of Orbitz. (Kalanick reportedly dragged his feet on hiring a COO, because he didn't want to share duties in running the company.)

It was Khosrowshahi who made nice with London lawmakers after the city revoked Uber's license to operate. He has held meetings that Kalanick never did during regulatory battles with cities around the world. In a letter to London regulators, he wrote that "While Uber has revolutionized the way people move in cities around the world, it's equally true that we've got things wrong along the way. . . .On behalf of everyone at Uber globally, I apologize for the mistakes we've made."[50] Similarly, in a technology conference in Germany in early 2018, Khosrowashahi stated that Uber had shifted from "growth at all costs to responsible growth . . .Germany as a market for Uber is a market with enormous promise that hasn't been realized. Our strategy in Germany is a total reset."[51]

Khosrowashahi was also central to settling the lawsuit between Uber and Waymo. Waymo had been seeking $1.8 billion in damages. Under an agreement reached in early 2018 that he helped broker, Waymo got 0.34% of Uber's equity, worth about $245 million given Uber's estimated valuation of $72 billion at the time. Uber also agreed not to incorporate Waymo's confidential information into hardware and software used in its self-driving cars.[52]

Under Kalanick, Uber had a list of 14 cultural values that were displayed around its headquarters, and that new hires were asked to subscribe to. They called for things such as meritocracy, toe-stepping, principled confrontation, and always be "hustling." Khosrowshahi has rewritten these values as eight "cultural norms." He crystalized these norms from 1,200 ideas sent in from Uber employees. They include credos such as "we celebrate differences, we encourage different voices and opinions to be heard," "we are customer obsessed, we work tirelessly to earn our customers' trust and business by solving their problems," and "we value ideas over hierarchy." They also include one that seems to typify Khosrowshahi's leadership approach: "We do the right thing. Period."[53]

Khosrowshahi also oversaw negotiations that led to a substantial investment by the Japanese firm Softbank in Uber that closed in early 2018. The deal was structured around a large purchase of shares by Softbank from existing Uber investors and shareholders, including ex CEO Kalanick (who sold 1/3 of his 10% stake for about $1.4 billion). Softbank also invested $1.25 billion in cash. The deal left Softbank with about 15% of Uber's outstanding stock, making the Japanese company Uber's largest shareholder. Softbank also brought two representatives to Uber's board. Softbank reportedly wanted Uber to focus on growing in the United States, Europe, Latin America, and Australia—but not Asia, where Uber has struggled against indigenous rivals. Softbank also had equity positions in India's Ola, Singapore's Grab, and China's Didi, making the company a major investor in the global ride for hire market.[54]

C12-8 IPO and Beyond

Uber went public in May of 2019 at $45 a share, raising $8.1 billion in an initial public offering (IPO) that valued the firm at around $72 billion.[55] While one of the largest IPOs ever on the NYSE, Uber's IPO was something of a disappointment given that the initial expectations in late 2018 were that Uber might be able to get as much as $75 a share, which would have valued the company at $120 billion. In the months leading up to the IPO, the offering price had been reduced several times. One reason for the decline in value were diminished growth prospects due to the continued rise of competitors around the world. For example, Chinese rival Didi was investing heavily in Latin America, once seen as a primary growth market for Uber. In 2019, Didi acquired 99, the Brazilian rival to Uber. In addition, investors were questioning the ability of ride hailing companies to make money given regulatory headwinds from state and federal government officials who wanted to classify contract drivers as employees, a move that would increase the operating expenses of Uber and Lyft.

To compound matters, in 2020, the COVID pandemic hit Uber hard, with gross bookings declining by 46%. However, the pandemic did result in more people ordering restaurant food for delivery to their home. Uber Eats, Uber's online food ordering and delivery platform (which uses the same drivers and technology as Uber's main business), saw its gross bookings surge by 109% in 2020. By 2022, it was estimated that Uber Eats had captured 20% of the U.S. food delivery market.

While the COVID pandemic proved challenging for Uber's main business, by late 2022, there were clear signs that Uber was emerging from the pandemic in a strong position.[56] For the 3 months ending June 30, 2022, Uber's gross bookings were up 33% compared to the same period a year earlier, hitting a record high. Revenue for the quarter more than doubled to $8.1 billion, again a record. While the company was still not profitable, it did generate $382 million in free cash flow for the quarter, compared to negative cash flow of $398 million a year earlier. Most analysts expect the company to be cash flow positive going forward, generating over $700 million in free cash flow for all of 2022, with operating profitability occurring in 2024. Despite increased competition and setbacks in many foreign markets, with around 30% of the global market Uber remains the largest on-demand ride-for-hire business in the world (outside of China where Didi dominates). Despite promising trends, Uber still faces stiff competition from Lyft in the United States, and other companies (such as Didi) elsewhere.

Moreover, the status of Uber contract drivers in the United States remains unresolved, with some politicians and regulators continuing to push for rules to reclassify ride-share contract drivers as employees, or at least, to give drivers the option to become employees if they wish. Another proposal under discussion is to give contractors access to some limited benefits, a model known as "contractor plus." In the worst-case scenario (for Uber), reclassifying all contract drivers as employees would raise operating costs by an estimated 30%.

Notes

[1]P. Sloan "Marc Andreesen: Predictions for 2012 and Beyond," *CNET*, December 19, 2011.

[2]J. Kartch, "Uber Battle of New Orleans Pits Old Guard vs New," *Forbes*, July 7, 2014.

[3]http://kutv.com/news/features/archive-10/stories/vid_650.shtml

[4]E. Rusli, "Uber CEO Travis Kalanick: We're Doubling Revenue Every Six Months," *Wall Street Journal,* June 6, 2014.

[5]G. Sullivan, "Uber Said Ridership up 850% after Taxis Hold London to 'Ransom,'" Morning Mix Blog, *Washington Post*, June 12, 2014.

[6]D. Hoyt and S. Callander, "Uber: 21st Century Technology Confronts 20th Century Regulation," Stanford Business School case, September 25, 2012.

[7]D. Bond-Graham, "Uber and Lyft Get a Lot of Hype—but Ridesharing in a Parasitic Business Model," AlterNet, October 22, 2013.

[8]New York City Taxi and Limousine Commission, 2014 Taxicab Factbook.

[9]M. W. Frankena and P. Pautler, "An Economic Analysis of Taxicab Regulation," Federal Trade Commission, Bureau of Economics Staff Report, May 1984.

[10]R. Dhar, "The Tyranny of the Taxi Medallions," Priceonomics blog, April 10, 2013. (http://blog.priconomics.com)

[11]New York City Taxi and Limousine Commission, 2014 Taxicab Fact book.

[12]Globe Staff Reporters, "For Boston Cabbies, a Losing Battle Against the Numbers," *Boston Globe*, March 31, 2013.

[13]J. Horwitz and C. Cumming, "Taken for a Ride," *Slate*, June 6, 2012.

[14]J. Leavitt and G. Blasi, "The Los Angeles Taxi Workers Alliance," University of California Transportation Center, UCTC Research paper No. 893, Fall 2009.

[15]D. Wiessner, "Court OKs Plan That Will Double the Number of Cabs in New York," *Reuters*, June 6, 2013.

[16]J. T. Bekken, "Experiences with Regulatory Changes of the Taxi Industry," 9th Conference on Competition and Ownership in Land Transportation (http://www.thredbo-conference-series.org/downloads/thredbo9_papers/thredbo9-workshopD-Bekken.pdf)

[17]D. Frum, "Paris Taxi Shortage: It's about Jobs," CNN Opinion, July 10, 2012.

[18]Eironline, "Milan Taxi Drivers Protest Against Increased Licenses," March 7, 2003, http://www.eurofound.europa.eu/eiro/2003/02/feature/it0302206f.htm

[19]"A Fare Fight," *The Economist*, February 11, 2011.

[20]"A Fare Fight," *The Economist*, February 11, 2011.

[21]"Pricing the Surge," *The Economist*, May 29, 2014.

[22]M. McFarland, "Ubers Remarkable Growth Could End the Era of Poorly Paid Cab Drivers," *Washington Post*, May 27, 2014.

[23]M. R. Dickey, "Here's How Much Money You Can Really Earn as an Uber Driver," *Business Insider*, June 28, 2014.

[24]Travis, "Chicago: Uber's Biggest Launch Date?" Uber Blog, September 22, 2011.

[25]S. Ellis, E. Taylor, D La Com, "Uber—What's Fueling Uber's Growth Engine?" GrowthHackers, http://growthhackers.com/companies/uber/

[26]S. Ellis, E. Taylor, D La Com, "Uber—What's Fueling Uber's Growth Engine?" GrowthHackers, http://growthhackers.com/companies/uber/

[27]N. Carter and T. Rice, "How Uber Rolls out, City by City," *Inc*, April 25, 2012.

[28]K. Rose, "Uber Might Be More Valuable Than Facebook Someday. Here's Why," *New York Magazine*, December 6, 2013.

[29]L. Kolodny, "Uber Ordered to Cease and Desist," *TechCrunch*, October 24, 2010.

[30]M. G. Siegler, "Uber CEO: I Think I've Got 20,000 Years of Jail Time in Front of Me," *TechCrunch*, May 25, 2011.

[31]B. X. Chen, "Uber, Maker of Summon a Car App, Wins in Washington," *Bits*, July 10, 2012.

[32]Z. Miners, "Seattle City Council Legalizes Uber, Lyft, Sidecar without Caps," *PC World*, July 14, 2014.

[33]C. Albanesius, "Uber Drops Taxi-Hailing App in New York," *PC Mag*, October 16, 2012.

[34]M. Scott, "European Taxi Drivers Snarl Traffic in Protest Against Car-Paging Service," *New York Times,* June 12, 2014, p. B3.

[35]B. X. Chen, "A Feisty Startup Is Met with Regulatory Snarl," *New York Times,* December 2, 2012.

[36]D. Bond-Graham, "Uber and Lyft Get a Lot of Hype—but Ridesharing in a Parasitic Business Model," AlterNet, October 22, 2013.

[37]Staff Reporter, "Lyft Offers $10K a Month to Lure Drivers in NYC," *Crain's New York Business*, August 1, 2014.

[38]R. Lawler, "SeeUber—This Is What Happens When You Cannibalize Yourself," *TechCrunch*, March 15, 2013.

[39]E. Huet, "Uber's Newest Tactic: Pay Drivers More Than They Earn," *Forbes*, July 2, 2014.

[40]W. Richter, "Numbers Are in: Uber, Lyft v. Rental Cars and taxis in the US in Q2," *Wolf Street*, July 29, 2018.

[41]D. Bosa, "Lyft Claims That It Now Has More Than One-Third of the US Ride Share Market," CNBC, May 14, 2018.

[42]J. Cramer and A. Krueger, "Disruptive Change in the Taxi Business: The Case of Uber," National Bureau of Economic Research, March 2016.

[43]P. Cohen, et al., "Using Big Data to Estimate Consumer Surplus: The Case of Uber," National Bureau of Economic Research, September 2016.

[44]G. Volpicelli, "Uber's London License Has Been Approved—but There's a Big Catch," *Wired*, June 26, 2018.

[45]A. Frangos, "Uber in China: Why Foreigners Never Win in Tech," *Wall Street Journal*, August 1, 2018.

[46]J. Russell, "Uber's Indian Rival Ola Is Aiming for an IPO in 3-4 Years," *TechCrunch*, July 23, 2018.

[47]D. Kerr, "Lyft Tops Apple App Store, Because #DeleteUber," *CNet*, January 31ˢ 2017.

[48]"Uber Agrees to Pay $20 Million to Settle FTC Charges," Federal Trade Commission, January 19, 2017.

[49]D. Kerr, "Uber's U-Turn," *CNet*, April 27, 2017.

[50]D. Kerr, "Uber's U-Turn," *CNet*, April 27, 2017.

[51]E. Auchard and D. Busvine, "Uber CEO Focused on 'Responsible Growth,' Seeks Fresh Start in Germany," *Reuters*, January 22, 2018.

[52]D. Kerr, "Four Days, $245 Million," *CNet*, February 9, 2018.

[53]S. Musil, "Uber CEO Wants Employees to Do the Right Thing. Period," *CNet*, November 7, 2018.

[54]A. Griswold, "Softbank Not Uber Is the Real King of Ride Hailing," *Quartz*, January 23, 2018.

[55]M. Isaac, "How the Promise of a $120 Billion Uber IPO Evaporated," *New York Times,* May 15, 2019.

[56]A. Mogharabi, "Risk of DOL's Proposal and Reactions of Uber, Lyft, and Door Dash Stocks, Exaggerated, in Our View," *Morningstar*, October 11, 2022.

Case 13

Failure to Launch at Uber Elevate

By Melissa Schilling

In April of 2017, Jeff Holden, the chief product officer at Uber Technologies Inc. announced a radically new product: Uber AIR, an on-demand air transportation service that would be part of its broader "flying car" project, Uber Elevate.

> On-demand aviation, has the potential to radically improve urban mobility, giving people back time lost in their daily commutes...Just as skyscrapers allowed cities to use limited land more efficiently, urban air transportation will use three-dimensional airspace to alleviate transportation congestion on the ground. A network of small, electric aircraft that take off and land vertically (called Vertical Take-off and Landing, or VTOL, and pronounced vee-tol), will enable rapid, reliable transportation between suburbs and cities and, ultimately, within cities.[1]

Uber's on-demand ride sharing service had seriously disrupted traditional taxi and livery, and induced many people to eschew car ownership altogether. However, that service was based on an innovative business model and a software application—it did not require technological advances in either automobiles or driving infrastructure. Uber Elevate, was almost the opposite: It would leverage Uber's existing business model and software programs, but would require major technological development in air transportation technology, infrastructure for air traffic control, and a network of landing pads. It was an ambitious project, to put it mildly.

C13-1 Uber's Rise

Uber was founded in 2009 as a taxi-like ride sharing service. Customers could request a ride using a smartphone application, and the software would notify Uber drivers in the area of the request. When one accepted, it would show the customer the car's approach on a map in real time. The driver would take the user to their destination, and payment would occur automatically using the customer's credit card information that was stored online.

Perhaps the most unique part of the business model was that Uber drivers did not technically work for Uber. Drivers were independent contractors; they only needed a smartphone, a driver's license, a car, insurance, and a clean driving record to quality to become an Uber driver.[2] A dynamic pricing model raised prices when demand was high and drivers were few, and the higher prices, in turn, lured more Uber drivers to start accepting ride requests.

Over time, the company added different classes of ride options (such as UberPool, UberX, UberXL, Uber Select), different services such as food delivery (UberEats), freight service (Uber Freight), and pet transport (Uber Pets). It also had development under way for its own fleet of autonomous cars.

Though the firm had endured numerous early conflicts with taxi unions and some highly public scandals involving one of the company's founders, Travis Kalanick, the service was a huge success. By 2015, it had completed its one billionth ride, making it the second-largest ride-sharing service worldwide, after Didi Chuxing in China. By 2021, it was operating in more than 900 cities in 69 countries worldwide. Its 2020, revenue was $11.14 billion, and in May 2021, its market capitalization was over $86 billion.

C13-2 Opportunities and Challenges for Uber AIR

At the time of Uber's announcement there were more than 70 companies developing electric VTOLs (eVTOLS), including Karem Aircraft, Embraer, Aurora Flight Sciences, and Bell Helicopter. However, there many obstacles that had to be overcome to make Uber's air taxi ambitions a reality. First, eVTOLs used enormous amounts of energy and would be heavily reliant on advances on battery development and charging infrastructure. Second, there would be numerous legal and safety issues to be worked out pertaining to air traffic control, pilot training and licensing, compatibility with city infrastructures, noise, dealing with adverse weather, and more.

Last-but-not-least was cost. The technology to vertically take off and land already existed in the form of helicopters, but most people have never ridden in one because it is an extremely expensive mode of transportation, estimated to be at least $8.93 per passenger per mile. How would Uber AIR be different? First, electric propulsion was expected to be much more fuel efficient and require less maintenance. Second, the much smaller eVTOLs could land at flexible "skyports" rather than the large helipads or airports that helicopters used. Uber estimated that its initial operating costs would be $5.73 per passenger per mile, and with efficient pooling it believed it could get the operating costs down to $1.84 per passenger per mile. As people began to use eVTOLs in large numbers, scale economies would also drive down the cost of producing the eVTOLs themselves. The final major cost cutting measure would be to eliminate pilots with fully autonomous eVTOLs, saving training costs, salaries, and making room for an additional passenger. Uber estimated that with fully autonomous operation at scale, the long-run operating costs of Uber AIR could be as low as 44 cents per passenger mile—less than the operating cost of many cars.[3]

Uber's CEO, Dara Khosrowshahi was initially doubtful about the project. However, after several rounds of discussion on the economics of it, he began to be persuaded. "For me the 'aha' moment came when I started understanding that Uber isn't just about cars," Khosrowshahi said. "Ultimately where we want to go is about urban mobility and urban transport, and being a solution for the cities in which we operate."[4]

In 2018, the company publicly announced that it planned to have commercial deployment of the service by 2023. However, Uber's businesses had yet to become profitable and investors were beginning to get impatient with Uber's grand ambitions. After racking up massive losses in 2019 and 2020 (of 8.5 and 6.8 billion, respectively) the company began paring back its projects. In early December 2020, it announced it would sell off its autonomous vehicles division to Aurora Innovation and its air taxi division to Joby Aviation, in efforts to get to profitability by 2021.[5] Uber had previously invested $50 million in Joby Aviation and though the terms of the deal by which it transferred its Elevate assets to Joby were not disclosed, it was revealed that Uber agreed to invest an additional $75 million in Joby. The deal also called for Joby and Uber to integrate their respective services into each other's applications to create "seamless integration between ground and air travel for future customers."[6]

C13-3 Battle for the Skies

As of mid-2022, no company had yet launched an air taxi service using eVTOLs,[7] but a few appeared to be getting close. Notably, German company Lilium announced that it would begin commercial inter-city transportation with its five-seat, all-electric Lilium Jet in 2025. Another German company, Volocopter, was betting that it could beat Lilium to the commercial market with its VoloCity, a two-person craft that looked like an egg suspended under a halo of 18 rotors designed for intra-city travel (see Figure 1 below).[8] Guangzhou-based Ehang also looked like it was making great strides, but then in early 2021 it was the subject of a scandal when an investment group accused the company of inflating its value "with a collection of lies about its products, manufacturing, revenues, partnerships and potential regulatory approval."[9] Finally, in the United States, both Palo Alto–based Archer and Santa Cruz–based Joby Aviation were promising to launch commercial operations by 2024.[10] By mid-2022, Archer had already sold $1 billion worth of pre-orders to United Airlines and planned to begin volume production in 2023.[11]

All of these companies had already repeatedly demonstrated their aircraft; the hurdles were now largely based on regulation and infrastructure. For example, in May of 2022, Joby Aviation received an important license from the FAA titled Part 135 air carrier certificate, which permits the company to operate a commercial air taxi service. However, it still needed two additional FAA badges to be fully operational: a type of certificate proving its aircraft adheres to all FAA standards, and a production certificate to allow manufacturing aircraft for commercial use.[12]

Figure 1 Volocopter (left) and Joby Aviation (right)

Source: Volocopter

Source: Joby Aviation

Case Discussion Questions

1. Will there be increasing returns to adoption for an early mover in air taxi service? If so, what will they be?
2. What are the disadvantages of entering the air taxi market early?
3. What are the important complementary goods and enabling technologies for the air taxi market? Are they available in sufficient quality and economy?
4. Was Uber well positioned to be a dominant player in this market? What resources would it have needed to be successful?
5. Overall, would you say Uber's entry into the air taxi market was too early, too late, or about right?
6. Based on the stage of development of eVTOLs and the complementary and enabling technologies and infrastructure, what companies do you think stand the best chance of success in this market?

Notes

[1] J. Holden, and N. Goel, "Fast-Forwarding to a Future of On-Demand Urban Air Transportation," San Francisco: Uber Elevate, October 27, 2016.

[2] E. Pancer, K. Gulliver, and M. MacLeod, *Uber Elevate: The Case for Flying Cars*, Ivey Publishing, case W18135, 2018.

[3] A. Goodwin, "Will You Be Able to Afford UberAir's Flying Car Service?" www.cnet.com, May 8, 2018.

[4] M. R. Dickey, "Uber's Aerial Taxi Play," *Techcrunch.com*, May 9, 2018.

[5] R. Neate, R. "Uber Sells Loss-Making Flying Taxi Division to Joby Aviation," *The Guardian*, December 9 , 2020.

[6] J. Szczesny, "Uber Selling Its Flying Taxi Business to Joby Aviation," *The Detroit Bureau*. December 10, 2020.

[7] There were, of course, some air taxi services using regular helicopters.

8 https://evtol.news/volocopter-volocity, retrieved May 17, 2021.

[9] C. Stonor, "Ehang Shares Tumble after Wolfpack Analyst Report Says "Revenues Are Largely Fabricated," *Urban Air Mobility News,* Feb 17, 2020.

[10] "Archer Announces Commitment to Launching Its Urban Air Mobility Network in Miami by 2024," Press Release, March 9, 2021, www.jobyaviation.com; L. Blain, "Archer Outlines What Its Early eVTOL Air Taxi Service Will Look Like," *New Atlas,* June 24, ,2022.

[11] S. Cao, "Hey, Air Taxi! Why You Will Soon Hail a Cab to the Sky," *Observer*, June 24, 2022.

[12] S. Cao, "Hey, Air Taxi! Why You Will Soon Hail a Cab to the Sky," *Observer*, June 24, 2022.

14

Microsoft (A): The Gates and Ballmer Years

Charles W. L. Hill Foster School of Business University of Washington, Seattle, WA 98195 August 2022

C14-1 Introduction

On February 4, 2014, Satya Nadella become CEO of Microsoft Corporation (Microsoft). Nadella, a native of Hyderabad in India, was only the third CEO in Microsoft's 39-year history. The first co-founder, Bill Gates, was CEO from Microsoft's establishment in April 1975 through January 2000, when he passed the reins over to his longtime friend and business partner, Steve Ballmer. Gates remained chairman until February 2014. The Gates years were characterized by dramatic growth as Microsoft expanded from a small start-up to become the largest and most dominant software company on the planet, and in the process making Gates' the world's richest person from 1995–2010 and again from 2013–2017. The foundations of Microsoft's success during this period were its two monopolies; the Windows operating system, which at its peak was used on 95% of the world's personal computers, and Office, which had a 90% market share in 2012.[1]

Microsoft continued to expand both revenues and profits under the leadership of Steve Ballmer. During his tenure, revenues expanded from $25 billion to $70 billion while net income grew 215% to $23 billion. One area that did particularly well during the Ballmer years was the Windows server business, a division that Satya Nadella ran prior to becoming CEO. Servers sit at the center of networks of PCs and are used to perform a variety of functions including database hosting, file services, web services, print services, and applications services. Microsoft makes a version of Windows, Windows Server, which runs on servers. The Windows Server business was a $20 billion division by 2014. Microsoft gained share from competitors such as IBM, which promoted the rival Linux operating system. By 2014, 75% of servers built around Intel microprocessors used Windows Server as their operating system, as did around 50% of all servers.[2] The Linux and Unix operating systems took the number two and three spots.

Despite impressive growth, Microsoft's stock price stagnated during the Ballmer era. This reflected a growing concern that Microsoft had lost its leadership in the computer industry to three firms—Google, Apple and Amazon—Google had grown dramatically during the 2000s on the back of its dominant Internet search business. Along the way, Google had developed an operating system for smartphones (Android) and laptops (Chrome) that were now challenging Windows on computing devices, a category that had expanded beyond traditional PCs to included smartphones and tablets. Google was also offering a "cloud-based" suite of productivity tools, Google Docs, which competed directly with Office.

Apple, a firm that was nearly bankrupt in 1997, had done more than any other company to expand the definition of computing devices to include smartphones and tablets. Apple had introduced the first version of its smartphone, the iPhone, in 2007. Differentiated by elegant design and ease of use, two Apple hallmarks, the iPhone was a sensation that redefined what a smartphone should look like and do. Apple followed the iPhone with the 2010 introduction of the iPad, a tablet device that created an entirely new computing category, and one that cannibalize sales of laptop PCs. Both devices run Apple's iOS operating system, further reducing the relevance of Windows.

As smartphones and tablets gained popularity, more and more computing was being done using these mobile devices— accessing applications and data stored on servers "in the cloud"— rather than on a traditional PC. According to Microsoft's own estimate, by mid-2014 while 90% of traditional desktop and laptop PCs still used Windows, only 14% of *all* computing devices, a definition which included PCs, smartphones, and tablets, used Windows.[3] Although under Ballmer's leadership Microsoft had tried to grow its share by introducing a Windows smartphone in 2010 and the Surface tablet in 2012, these offerings failed to gain traction. By 2014, Windows Phone had less than 3% of the global smartphone operating system market, while Apple's iOS held 15.2% and Android 81.1%.[4] In the tablet market, Android had a 65.8% share, Apple's iOS had 28.4%, and Windows tablets had 5.8%.[5] Microsoft was assumed to be losing significant amounts of money on its phone and tablet businesses. To compound matters, after three decades of sustained growth, PC sales were now declining as ever more computing was done through smartphones and tablets. PC sales fell by 4% in 2012 and 9.8% in 2013, although demand stabilized in 2014.[6]

Amazon, the world's largest Internet retailer, was challenging Microsoft from another direction. By the mid-2000s tens of thousands of servers were being grouped together into "server farms" located "in the cloud" to host high traffic Internet websites. Google had built server farms to host its Internet search business, Microsoft likewise had server farms for its Bing search business and MSNBC web offerings, and Amazon had built server farms to host its large online retail business. In 2005, Amazon leveraged the knowledge and capacity it had accumulated building server farms to start a new business, Amazon Web Services (AWS). AWS hosted data, web services, and applications for paying customers. These data, services, and applications could be accessed from anywhere by a user with a computing device and an appropriate wireless or hardwire connection. By 2014, AWS was viewed as the market share leader in the emerging cloud computing business.

Microsoft entered the cloud computing business in 2010 with an offering known as Azure (later renamed Microsoft Cloud). Azure was founded within the Windows Server division that Satya Nadella ran prior to becoming CEO. In addition to hosting data and websites, Azure allows clients to build and run applications that reside on Microsoft's "cloud." By 2014, Azure was thought to be number two in the emerging cloud business, with Google and IBM rounding out the top four. Industry-wide, the cloud computing business generated $16 billion in sales in 2014, but it was growing very rapidly and was thought by many to represent the future of computing.[7]

Commenting on Microsoft's overall competitive position in 2014, the general manger of one business unit noted that: "I think we have about 18–24 months to get it right. If we don't, Microsoft is finished."[8] This statement reflected a widespread belief within the company that the computer industry was undergoing a massive paradigm shift, away from the client server world based on PC architecture in which Microsoft had been so dominant, and towards a world of mobile devices and cloud computing, a world in which Microsoft faced significant competitive challenges. Satya Nadella was as cognizant of this as anyone. By March 2014, he had already honed his vision for the company. Microsoft, he said, was competing in a "mobile first, cloud first" world.[9] The task facing Nadella was deciding what actions to take to ensure that Microsoft survived and prospered in this brave new mobile first, cloud first world— and he knew he had to act fast.

C14-2 Bill Gates and the Early History of Microsoft

Bill Gates and Paul Allen established Microsoft in 1975. Gates was a 19-year-old Harvard dropout.[10] Allen, who was 22, had dropped out of Washington State University to go and work as a programmer at Honeywell in Boston. Gates and Allen had both attended Seattle's elite Lakeside High School, where they had bonded over their common interest in computers.

By all accounts, the young Bill Gates was extremely intelligent, hypercompetitive, ambitious, hardworking, and a gifted programmer. One of his former teachers at Lakeside described him as the most intelligent student she had ever had. He could also be dismissive of people who lacked his technical acumen, abrasive, and hypercritical. One story widely circulated in Microsoft is that if he disagreed with the technical or product presentations of Microsoft employees, he would interject with sharp comments along the lines of "that's the stupidest thing I have ever heard" or that the idea was "brain damaged." Legend has it that on more than one occasion Gates reduced a presenter to tears, although Gates would argue that it was never the person he criticized, just the idea. Gates respected people who were smart and hardworking like him, who marshaled their facts, and who stuck to their guns when challenged by him if they knew they had the facts on their side. Gates ultimately relied upon such people to lead projects and businesses within Microsoft.

In 1975, Allen persuaded Gates to drop out of Harvard and start Microsoft to write a version of the computer programming language, BASIC, to run on the world's first commercially available personal computer, the MITS Altair 8800, which used an Intel 8080 microprocessor. Gates and Allen met with the founder of MITS and demonstrated their version of BASIC for the Altair 8800. This resulted in a deal under which MITS distributed Microsoft BASIC for the Altair 8800, making Microsoft the first company to sell software to run on a personal computer. Microsoft subsequently wrote versions of Microsoft BASIC that ran on other personal computers of the time, including Apple's first successful offering, the legendary Apple II that was introduced in 1979.

In June 1980, Steve Ballmer joined Microsoft. Ballmer had been a friend of Gates at Harvard and was the only person who had outscored Gates on mathematics and microeconomics classes. Ballmer has gone to work at Procter & Gamble after Harvard, and then moved on to Stanford Business School. Gates' persuaded Ballmer to drop out of Stanford and manage business operations at Microsoft. He was employee number 30.

In July 1980, IBM approached Microsoft about using a version of Microsoft BASIC for the IBM PC, which was then in development. Gates persuaded IBM to adopt a 16-bit Intel processor (originally IBM had been considering a less powerful 8-bit processor). Gates was also instrumental is pushing IBM to adopt an open architecture, arguing that IBM would benefit from the software and peripherals that other companies could make.

Initially IBM was intent on licensing the CP/M operating system, produced by Digital Research, for the IBM PC. However, the current version of CP/M was designed to work on an 8-bit processor, and Gates had persuaded IBM that it needed a 16-bit processor. In a series of quick moves, Gates purchased a 16-bit operating system from a nearby company, Seattle Computer, for $50,000. Gates then hired the designer of the operating system, Tim Paterson, renamed the system MS-DOS, and offered to license it to IBM. In what turned out to be a masterstroke, Gates persuaded IBM to accept a non-exclusive license for MS-DOS (which IBM called PC-DOS). MS-DOS had a command-line text-based interface, and could only run one program at a time, but for 1981 it was state of the art.

To drive sales, IBM commissioned developers to build several applications for the IBM PC. In addition to Microsoft Basic, these included a version of VisiCalc, an early spreadsheet that was a popular application for the Apple II, a word processor, EasyWriter, and well-known series of business programs from Peachtree Software. Introduced in August 1981, the IBM PC was an instant success. Over the next 2 years, IBM would sell more than 500,000 PCs, seizing leadership from Apple, which had dominated the PC market with the Apple II. IBM had what Apple lacked, an ability to sell into corporate America. As sales of the IBM PC mounted, more independent software developers started to write program to run on the IBM PC. These included two applications that drove adoptions of the IBM PC: word processing (Word Star and Word Perfect) and a spreadsheet (Lotus 1-2-3).

The success of IBM gave birth to clone manufacturers who made "IBM compatible" PCs that also utilized an Intel microprocessor and Microsoft's MS-DOS operating system. The "clone" industry was born when engineers at Compaq Computer reverse engineered the BIOS chip in the original IBM PC. The BIOS chip converted the operating system into machine language and was integral to the operation of the PC. It was the only key component of the IBM PC that IBM had not bought off the shelf from other manufacturers. Compaq's BIOS chip was functionally equivalent to the chip in the IBM PC, but used different code, and thus did not violate IBMs copyright. Other PC companies soon followed Compaq's lead, including Tandy, Zenith, Leading Edge, and Dell. The birth of the clone industry was a huge boon to Microsoft. By virtue of its non-exclusive license with IBM, Microsoft had the ability to sell MS-DOS to a growing number of clone makers.

In 1983, Microsoft expanded its product offering with the introduction of Word for MS-DOS, the company's first word processor. Word was differentiated from other word processors at the time by being the first to use a mouse. In 1985, Microsoft introduced a version of Word to run on Apple's latest machine, the Macintosh. In 1985, Microsoft released the first version of Excel, the company's spreadsheet offering that competed with the best-selling Lotus 1-2-3. In 1987, Microsoft purchased a start-up company that had developed presentation software for the Macintosh. This product ultimately became PowerPoint, the first version of which was introduced in 1990.

The lead developer for Word and Excel was Charles Simonyi, a key hire at Microsoft who had formally worked at PARC, Xerox's legendary research center that had pioneered the development of the computer mouse, on screen icons, a graphical user interface (GUI), objected-oriented programming, and the laser printer. In one of the quirks of business history, senior management at Xerox had passed on the opportunity to commercialize these innovations, which opened the doors to Apple and Microsoft to pick up the ideas and run with them.

In 1982, with business booming, Paul Allen was diagnosed with Hodgkin's lymphoma. His cancer was successfully treated with radiation therapy, but he took an extended leave and never again held an operating position at Microsoft. In 2000, he resigned from the company's board of directors.

C14-3 Building the Double Monopoly

By the mid-1980s Microsoft was doing very well. It became apparent that the MS-DOS business had some compelling economics. While Microsoft bore the costs of developing successive versions of MS-DOS, the incremental or marginal costs of producing individual copies of MS-DOS were very low. In the case of new PCs, Microsoft simply gave the master code to the manufacturer, who installed MS-DOS on every machine built, and paid Microsoft a licensing fee per machine. This resulted in gross margins as high as 90%. In contrast, the gross margins of PC makers at the time were closer to 40%.

C14-3a The Development of Windows and Office

In 1986, Microsoft went public. The IPO raised $61 million and valued Microsoft at $650 million. Microsoft now had over 700 employees. The company's position, however, was not secure. Although MS-DOS was the most widely used operating system for PCs, Apple had shown what the future looked like in 1984 when it introduced the Macintosh. Borrowing many ideas from Xerox PARC, the Mac had a graphical user interface (GUI) that displayed programs as on-screen icons. It also used a computer mouse with its point-and-click methodology for selecting tasks. This intuitive interface was a big improvement in usability over the clunky command line interface of MS-DOS, which could be intimidating for people without a computing background.

Gates realized that a GUI interface was the future. Microsoft worked closely with Apple to develop the first version of Word for the Mac, which took full advantage of the Mac's GUI interface and mouse capabilities. Word for the Mac soon became one of the best-selling Mac applications. At the same time, Microsoft took what it learned from Apple and used it to start developing its own GUI interface, which was christened Windows.

Apple inadvertently helped Microsoft in two ways. First, it licensed its "visual displays" to Microsoft in 1985, enabling Microsoft to legally develop its own GUI that had a similar look and feel to the Mac, without fear of being shut down by a legal challenge. Second, the Mac was not easy to develop applications for. Apple did a poor job of providing tools to help third-party software developers write programs for the Mac. In contrast, Gates often said that the most important strategic business unit at Microsoft was its tools business. Microsoft invested heavily in the development of tools to boost developer productivity. This made it easy for third-party developers to write applications for MD-DOS, and later Windows, and drove adoption of Microsoft's operating system offerings.

The first version of Windows was introduced in November 1985. It was a GUI shell that displayed programs as on-screen icons and allowed for multitasking (using more than one program at a time). Windows sat on top of MS-DOS. It was a commercial failure. Many users lacked sufficiently powerful hardware to run Windows, and there were few programs available that took advantage of its features. Nevertheless, Microsoft continued development work on Windows.

IBM, too, saw the importance of a GUI interface. IBM was losing market share to the clone makers, so IBM decided to replace MS DOS with its own GUI operating system, OS/2. IBM contracted with Microsoft to develop OS/2. However, the arrangement was a difficult one. IBM resented the fact that Microsoft had facilitated the emergence of the clone businesses by licensing MS-DOS to IBM's competitors. IBM was also concerned that Microsoft continued to work on Windows, even while it developed OS/2. For its part, Microsoft knew that IBM was also investing in the UNIX operating systems, and had licensed a UNIX-based PC operating system, NeXTSTEP, from NeXT, a PC company that Apple founder Steve Jobs established after he left Apple in 1985. Microsoft knew it would be in trouble if IBM scrapped OS/2 in favor of a UNIX alternative. The pivotal event was when IBM announced that it would release two versions of OS/2, a more powerful version that would only be put on IBM machines, and a basic version for other PC makers. That wasn't news that Microsoft wanted to hear. Gates decided to sever the links with IBM and go for broke on Windows.

The fruit of this effort, Windows 3.0, was introduced in 1990. Windows 3.0 was a big improvement over earlier versions. Windows 3.0 was well reviewed and became a major commercial success. IBM's OS/2, meanwhile, garnered mixed reviews and limited market traction. PC manufacturers, seeing a chance to deliver a body blow to IBM, which after all was a direct competitor, adopted Windows 3.0, bundling it with most new PCs. Market momentum towards Windows 3.0 was also helped by the introductory versions of Microsoft's increasingly popular applications: Word, Excel, and PowerPoint. At the time, each of these products was number two in its market space (Word was behind WordPerfect, Excel behind Lotus 1-2-3, and PowerPoint trailed Harvard Graphics). Microsoft's rivals, however, were slow to introduce versions of their products for Windows, resulting in big market share gains for Microsoft's offerings. To further drive adoption of Windows, Microsoft also redoubled its effort to provide developers with the best tools, and to persuade them that Windows was best platform to develop applications for.

In 1992, Microsoft combined its three leading application programs—Word, Excel, and PowerPoint—into a single offering for Windows, which it called Office. Office was priced slightly below the combined price of each individual offering. Microsoft also promised interoperability between the three programs, although this took several versions to perfect. Microsoft's rivals, including most notably Word Perfect and Lotus, lacked a comparable suite of offerings and were unable to match Office. From this point on, Office became the dominant suite of information worker productivity programs.

During the late 1980s, Microsoft started another operating system development project, this one targeted primarily at servers. Servers were specialized PCs that sat at the heart of corporate networks of "client" PCs, and "served" those "clients," holding shared files and applications programs used by many machines, such as email systems. Dubbed Windows NT, this was a powerful 32-bit operating system that could run on servers. Unlike Windows 3.0, it was not DOS based (the NT stood for new technology). To develop Windows NT, Microsoft hired a team of software developers led by Dave Cutler from Digital Equipment Corporation (DEC). Cutler's team drew on their prior experience of developing 32-bit systems for DEC to develop Windows NT.

The move into the server OS business represented recognition by Microsoft of the growing importance of client-server systems within large enterprises. The development of Windows NT constituted a strategic shift by Microsoft towards the enterprise market, which was where the primary demand for client server systems resided. Windows NT was an attempt to make secure, stable software that could run "mission critical" applications within enterprises. Client server networks were taking business away from the mainframes and minicomputers sold by the likes of IBM, DEC, and Hewlett Packard. Microsoft wanted a piece of this business and with Windows NT it intended to get it. Introduced in 1993, Windows NT was a solid, stable, secure system that gained increasing acceptance within enterprises. Windows NT marked the beginning of Microsoft's server business.

To gain further enterprise business, Microsoft added an email client to its Office suite, Outlook, which could be used to connect with corporate email hosted on severs. By the time Windows NT was introduced, Microsoft was also selling a relational database offering, Microsoft SQL Server. A relational database is a product whose primary function is to store and retrieve data as requested by other software applications, be those on the same computer or those running on another computer across a network. Microsoft SQL Server was the company's entry into the enterprise-level database market, and it pitted Microsoft against Oracle and IBM, both of whom had relational data base offerings.

The 32-bit technology underlying Windows NT was subsequently incorporated into the next two releases of Windows for PCs, Windows 95, and then Windows XP (introduced in 1995 and 1998, respectively). This increasingly made Windows more than just a GUI that sat on top of MS-DOS. Windows was becoming a fully fledged operating system in its own right. By the time Windows 2000 was introduced, Windows had effectively shed it DOS heritage.

Windows 95 was a landmark release since the enhanced graphics of that offering effectively closed the gap between Windows and Apple's Macintosh. Since the introduction of the IBM PC, Apple had been a niche player in the PC business focused primarily on the education, graphic artist, and desktop publishing markets, where its graphic displays and ease of use gave it maximum advantage. With Windows 95, however, the differential appeal of the Mac all but vanished. By 1997, Apple was facing bankruptcy.

C14-3b The Internet Tidal Wave

One other event occurred during the 1990s that helped to cement the dominance of Microsoft: the explosive growth of the World Wide Web (WWW). Tim Berners Lee, a British researcher at CERN in Europe, invented the WWW during the early 1990s. The WWW sits on top of the Internet, which itself had been developed by American researchers during the 1960s and 1970s. As Berners Lee conceived it, the WWW used Hyper Text Markup Language (HTML) and Hypertext Transfer Protocol (HTTP) to enable links to be made to information anywhere on the Internet, thereby creating an enormous "web" of information. In 1993, a team at the University of Illinois led by a 22-year-old student, Marc Andreessen, developed the Mosaic web browser. Mosaic could display information on the web graphically. This was the beginning of enormous growth in the WWW. After graduation, Andreessen joined up with Jim Clark, the former CEO of Silicon Graphics, to form Netscape. Netscape further developed the Mosaic Browser, releasing its version, Netscape Navigator, in November 1994. Netscape Navigator quickly became the dominant web browser. In August 1995, Netscape did an IPO. The stock was offered at $28 a share, but closed its first day at $75, valuing Netscape at $2.9 billion.

Prior to the explosive growth of the WWW, Microsoft's Internet strategy involved the creation of a dial-up online service, Microsoft Network (MSN), which was developed to be included with Windows 95. MSN was similar in conception to early versions of AOL, with email capabilities, message boards, chat rooms, and some news and weather offerings. The first version of MSN did not have a web browser and users could not connect to the WWW. With MSN and Windows 95 in late development, Gates became aware of the rapid growth of the WWW. Microsoft legend has it that the WWW was brought to the attention of Gates by memos from two junior engineers, Steve Sinofsky and Jay Allard. Gates immediately saw the strategic significance of the WWW. In May 1995, Gates wrote a memo to his executive staff and direct reports, calling the growth of the WWW an Internet "tidal wave." Gates wrote that the Internet "is crucial to every part of our business" and "the most important single development to come along since the IBM PC was introduced in 1981." In his memo, Gates went on to say that Netscape was a "new competitor," and that Microsoft's strategy should be to make it clear that "Windows machines are the best choice for the Internet."[11]

To fulfill Gates' vision, Microsoft acted rapidly. It licensed a version of the Mosaic web browser from a company called Spyglass, improved on it, and released it as Internet Explorer (IE) version 1.0 in August 1995. IE 1.0 was bundled with Windows 95 and appeared as an icon on the start screen. Although it was too late to change MSN in time for the release on Windows 95, MSN was reworked to utilize HTML and HTTP and give users access to the WWW. In late 1996, the new version of MSN, MSN 2.0, was released. Microsoft also quickly added the ability to insert hypertext links into Office documents, allowing readers of those documents to navigate to websites.

C14-3c Antitrust Issues

All these moves were successful for Microsoft. However, the bundling of IE with Windows brought Microsoft to the attention of the U.S. Department of Justice. The DOJ argued that the bundling strategy put Netscape at a competitive disadvantage and was a deliberate attempt on Microsoft's part to "squash" their rival. Whereas Netscape charged consumers for their browser, IE was perceived as being a "free" product. Moreover, the DOJ contented that Microsoft configured the Windows code such that it was slow and difficult for users to download Netscape Navigator and install it on the Windows desktop. For its part, Microsoft claimed that IE was part of the operating system and that users expected it to be there.

In the end, the DOJ prevailed. The judge in the case ruled that Microsoft was a monopoly, and that the bundling strategy represented an abuse of Microsoft's monopoly power. In 2002, Microsoft and the DOJ reached a settlement that required Microsoft to share its application programming interfaces (APIs) with third-party companies so that they could write programs that worked well with Windows. Microsoft, however, was allowed to continue bundling IE and other products with Windows. For Netscape, this was a pyric victory. The company continued to lose market share against IE and was not helped by reports that its products were inferior in quality to IE. In 1999, Netscape was sold to AOL for $10 billion, a price tag that left many scratching their heads. AOL discontinued the Netscape browser in 2008. At the time, it had less than a 1% share of the browser market, down from over 90% in 1995.

C14-4 Managing the Company

From the outset. Gates made a point of hiring people who were like him—young, bright, driven, competitive, technically sharp, and able to argue effectively for what they believed in. A small but influential number of these hires came from Xerox PARC, including Charles Simonyi, who led the development of the first versions of Word and Excel. Ballmer hired some of the more business types. One of these was an aggressive salesman named Vern Raeburn. Gates had insisted that Microsoft should not sell directly to end users, but Raeburn marshaled his arguments and persuaded Gates to change course. Raeburn quickly pulled together a team to market and sell Microsoft's products to consumers.

This was the genesis of a split within Microsoft into two distinct functions that persist to this day: an engineering function that develops products and a sales and marketing function that sells them. For years, Gates was the de facto head of engineering with responsibility for product development, whereas Ballmer was responsible for sales and marketing. Although Microsoft went on to create different business units—Windows, Windows Server & Tools, and Office all had their own business units for example—the engineering and sales and marketing functions would cut across these units, creating a loose matrix organization. Finance, legal, and human relations functions also cut across business units.

To motivate key employees and encourage them to work long hours and stay at the company, Microsoft gave them stock options. When the company did well, and the stock price rose, these employees made substantial sums of money. As the stock price surged after the IPO in 1986, Microsoft stock options became a major draw, enabling Microsoft to hire the best and the brightest. By 2000, it is estimated that the surging stock price had created over 10,000 millionaires amongst Microsoft employees.[12] Paradoxically, by the mid-1990s, some of the early employees were so secure financially that their competitive edge had been blunted. Some were said to have retired on the job. Many other key employees simply left the company to pursue other interests.

Another notable feature of Microsoft that emerged over time was the tendency for people to move around a lot within the company. It was not unusual for people to change their jobs every 18 months and move from business to business.

C14-4a Formalizing Management Processes

As the company's growth began to accelerate in the early 1980s, Gates brought in people with business experience to help take the load off his shoulders and manage the day-to-day operations and finance side of the business, leaving him to focus on product development, technology and strategy, and Ballmer of sales. A key early hire was John Shirley. Shirley worked for Tandy Corporation, the parent company of Radio Shack. Shirley joined Microsoft as president in 1983 and stayed through until 1990. He remained on the board until 2008. People within the company would joke that Shirley was there to provide some adult supervision.

In 1994, Gates hired Bob Herbold as chief operating officer (COO). Herbold had a PhD in computer science and had worked at Procter & Gamble for 25 years, where he was responsible for P&Gs worldwide marketing and brand management. Herbold stayed at Microsoft until 2001. Another "adult" in charge of day-to-day operational issues, Herbold saw it as his job to bring discipline to the company without undermining the characteristics that had made it competitive. Herbold describes arriving at a company that was chaotic: "Incompatible systems and divergent practices companywide were causing all kinds of problems. Bills from suppliers weren't being paid on time. We never knew precisely how many people worked for the company. Business units set projections using incompatible frameworks and measures that prevented a comparison of their performance."[13]

Much of this chaos was the result of rapid revenue growth often exceeding 30% a year. Herbold notes "a balkanized system had grown up because, for years, Bill had focused on product development and Steve had focused on sales. Meanwhile, business and geographical units had relatively free rein to create local functional staffs, set business practices, and build stand-alone information systems. They weren't particularly interested in giving up their autonomy."[14]

Herbold moved fast to standardize basic businesses processes at Microsoft, including financial reporting, vendor payments, and human resources policies. He also found a company with no formal strategic planning process in place. Herbold developed a rolling 3-year planning process based on a standardized format that included historic and future projections of market share, revenues, costs, and profits. The process distinguished between established products, such as Windows and Office, and new products where there was a much greater degree of uncertainty. The plans were modified and streamlined every year based on new data.

Herbold also formalized a human resources performance appraisal process that had originally been developed by Gates. The appraisal process required managers to evaluate their direct reports and utilized a forced curve, such that some members of a team would always end up being classified as star performers, and others as poor performers. The star performers would get big pay increases, whereas the underperformers would be "encouraged to find a job outside of the company" if they couldn't bring up their rating over time. Critics of this system, known as stack ranking, noted that it pitted employees on a team against each other, encouraged backstabbing, and created a real problem for managers who had built strong teams, since they were forced to classify some of their team as underperformers, even though in an absolute sense they might be good.[15]

C14-4b The Product Development Process

Given the nature of Microsoft's business, a key aspect of the company's organization and management structure relates to the way it formalizes development of its software products. In the early years, "super programmers" such as Charles Simonyi and Gates himself drove the vision for products. Gates came to the realization that this was not a model that would scale well. Super programmers were in short supply, had little interest in updating a product once it had been created, might not understand the market well, and were prone to clash with other super programmers. In response, a formal system for developing, testing, and releasing products emerged in the mid-1980s.[16]

The process starts with a *program manager*, who is responsible for specifying the vision of the product, its key features, development schedule, development process, and implementation trade-offs. The program manager works closely with senior software developers and with product managers in marketing to achieve all of this. Their role, in other words, is to coordinate engineering and marketing, and to distill out of this what the product should do, what its key features should be, and the schedule. The program manager is then responsible for managing the overall development effort, and they must make the call on features to add or cut to hit goals, such as the schedule. On complex products, such as Windows and Office, there is a hierarchy of program managers. For example, while there may be an overall program manager for a new version of Office, there will also be program managers for each of the constituent programs, Word, Excel, PowerPoint, and so on.

It is important to understand that many of the ideas for a product's features come from developers and marketers. Program managers are leaders and facilitators of the process, rather than bosses, and they must work through persuasion and negotiation. In part, this may be due to the high status that developers have within Microsoft's culture, something that can be traced back to Gates and Simonyi. Indeed, most program managers were star developers who rose through the engineering ranks.

Once the product vision, key features, schedules, and the like have been mapped out, it is up to software *developers* to implement the vision and features. It is the developers who write the code. Typically, a small team of senior developers and program managers will take charge of the product architecture, and developer leads (first-line managers) will provide detailed guidance to their teams of programmers. While developers may be the source of ideas for new features, they are required to clarify what each feature accomplishes, and to help program managers decide what to include in a product, and what to cut to stay on schedule.

Testing the code is the responsibility of developers and *testers*. Developers are meant to test their own code frequently (typically every day). They also work with testers and are required to hand their code over to a tester for testing before adding their work to the "official build." The goal in this process is to reduce the bug count to zero. Microsoft also has a specially trained group of specially trained people who perform final tests on completed products to see if it is ready for shipment. As part of this process, beta versions of the product will be released to key customers for feedback, and the product will be tested in a usability lab. Microsoft has approximately one tester for every developer, an unusually high ratio, but one that is consistent with the goal of producing stable secure software that can run mission critical applications for enterprises.

Overtime Microsoft routinized this process, with offerings such as Windows, Office, and SQL Server going through 3- to 5-year definition, development, test, and release schedules. As these products grew in complexity and features, there was a tendency for the process to become more bureaucratic and harder to manage. This was made more challenging by the fact that many program managers, senior developers, and development leads were themselves people who excelled in a technical sense, but had little management training or experience. In the mid-2000s, this led to some serious issues when Microsoft ran over budget and over schedule while trying to develop Windows Vista (discussed later in this case).

C14-5 The Ballmer Years

When Bill Gates handed the CEO role over to Steve Ballmer in February 2000, the company was at the top of its game. Windows and Office dominated their respective markets, generating prodigious amounts of free cash flow. The stock price had hit an all-time high of $58.72 on December 23, 1999. Microsoft was the most valuable company on the planet, and Gates the world's richest man. Gates continued to work full time at Microsoft until 2008, assuming the role of chief software architect with primary oversight for product development. He also remained chairman of the company.

During the Ballmer era, revenues increased 280% to $70 billion, while net profit expanded by 215% to $23 billion. The stock price, however, dropped below $40 a share in mid-2000 and did not break through that level again until 2014, after Ballmer had resigned. The failure of the stock price to advance despite growing top and bottom lines reflected a widely held belief among investors that Microsoft had lost its leadership position in the industry. Moreover, critics believed that the company was destroying economic value by investing in businesses that did not generate a positive ROI. These included the Xbox videogame business; Internet search; and the device businesses that encompassed the Zune music player, smartphones, and tablet computers. By the end of the Ballmer era, it was widely believed that the shift to a world characterized by mobile devices and cloud computing presented an existential threat to Microsoft's core operating system business.

One of the first problems that Ballmer had to confront was the risk of a slowdown in the rate of growth of both Windows and Office. The markets for both products were now mature in most developed nations, implying that revenues would increasingly come from replacement rather than first-time demand. Although there was still plenty of room for growth in developing nations, those markets were also characterized by extremely high levels of piracy, as much as 90% in markets like China and Vietnam. Indeed, even in developed markets such as the United States, piracy rates for software products are as high as 20–25%.[17]

Two trends helped Microsoft weather the maturation of its two primary product offerings. First, a significant number of consumers in developed markets purchased multiple devices: a laptop and a desktop, for example. Second, Microsoft continued to grow its share of the enterprise markets for Windows Server and SQL Server, taking business from UNIX, LINUX, Oracle, and IBM. Microsoft's success in the enterprise space reflected the fact that to a considerable extent, the company had succeeded in building stable, secure software that could run mission-critical applications in enterprises. Given that Windows for the desktop client and Office were also widely used within enterprises, Microsoft was increasingly focused on its enterprise business. Indeed, by the early 2000s Microsoft was more of an enterprise company than a consumer company.

C14-5a Product Diversification: Xbox

Under Ballmer, Microsoft continued to diversify its product offerings, entering new markets. The first was the videogame market with its Xbox gaming console. By the late 1990s, Sony dominated this market with its PlayStation console and related game offerings. The market was worth $20 billion globally and was growing. Microsoft saw the PlayStation as a threat. The PlayStation was a specialized computer that ran a non-Microsoft operating system and could theoretically be connected to the Internet via a TV cable. Moreover, the PlayStation was often located in the living room. Bill Gates had long dreamed of having Internet-enabled computing devices in the living room that operated an interactive TV, and could also be used for web browsing, playing games, and online shopping; but Gates wanted those devices to run Windows.

Microsoft had capabilities that persuaded management that the gaming market was a viable target. Microsoft had produced one of the best-selling PC games of all times— *Microsoft Flight Simulator*—and had published another, *Age of Empires*. Through MSN it also had the world's largest online gaming site, MSN Gaming Zone, which had 12 million subscribers in the early 2000s. Moreover, Microsoft intended to use a customized version of the Windows operating system to power Xbox. This would save development costs and make it easier for developers to write games for the Xbox, since many were already familiar with Windows programming APIs and tools.

What Microsoft lacked was an ability to produce hardware, so it decided to outsource this to a contract manufacturer, Flextronics. Microsoft's strategy was to price the Xbox at or below cost to drive adoption, and then make money on the sales of games, either directly in the case of games developed in house, or from royalty fees in the case of games developed by third parties. For this strategy to work, it had to guarantee Flextronics a profit margin, which meant paying Flextronics a subsidy on every machine manufactured.

Xbox was introduced in late 2001 after $1.5 billion in development costs. The company faced tough competition from Sony's new offering, PlayStation 2 (PS2). To drive adoption, it cut prices for hardware aggressively. By 2003, Microsoft was thought to be losing $100 on every Xbox it sold. To make that back and turn a profit, Microsoft reportedly had to sell six to nine games per Xbox.[18] By late 2004, Xbox was still a distant second of PS2 in the videogame market, having sold 14 million consoles against Sony's 70 million. While Sony was making good money from the business, Microsoft was registering losses. Microsoft's home and entertainment division, of which Xbox was a part, lost $4 billion between the launch of Xbox and mid-2006.

In November 2005, Microsoft introduced its next generation console, Xbox 360. Again, contract manufacturers made the machine, and again Microsoft paid them a subsidy to ensure their profit margins. Sony followed a year later with its PS3 console, as did Nintendo with the Wii console. The Wii was a less powerful machine than either Xbox 360 or PS3, but it came with a motion sensor controller than changed the way players interacted with games. The Wii bought a new generation of casual gamers into the market and turned into a surprise hit for Nintendo. Meanwhile, Microsoft and Sony slugged it out in the hard-core gaming market. Demand for Xbox was helped by Microsoft's enormously popular *Halo* franchise. As the market expanded, all three companies were able to make a profit on an operating basis in the business. However, both Microsoft and Sony hurt themselves with quality problems and component shortages early in the product cycle (Microsoft had to take a $1.05 billion write off in 2007 for replacing poor-quality consoles).

Although Microsoft did achieve profitability on an operating basis for Xbox business by late in the Xbox 360 cycle, on a cumulative basis the return on investment was still believed to be negative. One of the bright spots for Microsoft was the growth of its online game subscription service, Xbox Live. Introduced in 2002, by mid-2013 Xbox Live had around 45 million paying subscribers who used it for everything from playing multiplayer games online to streaming movies from Netflix and browsing Facebook. At the time, Microsoft was thought to be generating annual revenues in excess of $3 billion from Xbox Live.[19] Microsoft also garnered strong reviews and sales for its Kinect motion sensor controller. Introduced in late 2010 for the Xbox 360, Kinect was developed as a response to Nintendo's Wii controller.

In late 2013, Microsoft launched its third-generation game console, Xbox One. Sony matched with the launch of its PS4 system. At launch, Microsoft positioned Xbox One as an all-purpose entertainment system for the living room, controlling the TV, music, and film streaming services through the Kinect motion and voice sensor, in addition to being a game console. Sony focused its marketing for the PS4 on the core gaming market. By mid-2014, Sony was believed to have sold 7 million PS4 consoles, versus 5 million Xbox One consoles. With Satya Nadella now in charge, Microsoft changed the marketing strategy for Xbox One, and emphasized its capabilities as a gaming machine, co-promoting it with new iterations of its popular *Halo* and *Call of Duty* franchises.

C14-5b Product Diversification: Internet Search

Another hallmark of the Ballmer era was Microsoft's expansion into Internet search. Microsoft had primitive Internet search functionality on its MSN service, but it had never seen search as a central feature. What changed this was the rise of Google, a company that didn't even exist until 1998. At the core of Google's rise was its search algorithm that cleverly ranked the relevance of a page for a search query according to the number of pages that linked into that page. Google went to great lengths to make sure that its search results were "pure." It did not mix organic and paid search results, thereby improving relevance to the user (paid search results were originally placed on the right-hand side of a search page, separate from organic search results).

What turned Google into a valuable company was the combination of highly relevant search results with a business model that made money out of search, lots of it. This was the "pay-for-click" model, where advertisers paid Google every time someone clicked on an advertiser's link. From a standing start in 2001, by 2014, Google had grown into a colossus with $68 billion in revenues, almost $21 billion in net profits, 67% of the market for Internet search in the United States, and an estimated 70% of worldwide search marketing spending.

Along the way, Google had moved aggressively into Microsoft's turf. Reasoning that with the growth of smartphones, ever more searches would come through mobile devices, Google had pushed into the smartphone business with its Android operating system, which it licensed to hardware manufacturers for free. The economic logic was that Google would be the default search engine on Android phones, so every time someone searched for something on an Android phone, and clicked on an advertising link, Google would make money. Google also developed its own web browser, Chrome, which it distributed for free. The economic reasoning was similar. Since search is conducted within a web browser environment, and Google was the default search engine on Chrome, Google would capture more search-based advertising collars if its own browser were widely used. Both products were phenomenally successful. By mid-2014, Android was found on 85% of the world's smartphones, and Chrome was the browser of choice on 46% of all desktops and tablets (relegating Microsoft's Internet Explorer, the longtime market leader, to second place with 20%).[20]

Microsoft tried to counter Google's rise in the Internet search business, but its success was limited—and very expensive. Microsoft adopted Google's pay-for-click search model, and developed a similar search algorithm, but was unable to gain much market traction and its market share remained stuck under 10%. Part of the problem was brand confusion. Microsoft's search feature was initially known as MSN Search; it sounded dull and uninspiring next to Google. In 2006, MSN search was rebranded as Windows Live Search and given some new features. A year later, the name was changed again to Live Search. Ultimately, Microsoft came to the realization that the "Live" brand was not resonating with consumers, who found it confusing. In June 2009, Microsoft's search engine was rebranded Bing. Microsoft supported the Bing launch with a $100 million ad campaign.

C14-5c Product Diversification: Smartphones and Tablets

Microsoft was one of the early leaders in the smartphone business. It first offered an operating system for smartphones, Windows Mobile, in 2002. By 2007, 42% of all smartphones used the Windows Mobile operating system. Smartphone manufactures such as Motorola and HTC paid a licensing fee to Microsoft to use Windows Mobile. As was normal at the time, Windows Mobile–powered smartphones had a physical keyboard and a small screen. The devices were primarily sold to enterprise customers, who used the phones for email, appointments, text messaging, and web browsing.

In 2007, Apple introduced the first iPhone. This revolutionized the smartphone market and significantly expanded demand (see Table 1). The combination of a touch screen, virtual keyboard, larger screen size, elegant design, and ease of use made the iPhone a huge hit in the consumer marketplace. Businesspeople, too, bought iPhones in droves, leading many companies to adopt a policy of "bring your own device" with regard to

Table 1 Global Smartphone Sales (millions) 2007-2013

Year	Android	iOS (Apple)	Microsoft	BlackBerry	Nokia
2007		3	15	12	78
2008		11	17	23	73
2009	7	25	15	34	81
2010	67	47	12	47	112
2011	200	89	9	52	93
2012	451	130	17	34	0
2013	759	151	31	19	0

Source: Gartner.com, various press releases.

smartphones. Growth of the iPhone had a further boost from the development of third-party applications, and the opening of the Apple App store in 2008, which made it easy for users to find and download apps onto their phones. The supply of apps was facilitated by efforts on Apple's part to make it easy for third-party developers to write apps for the iPhone. In 2010, Apple followed up the iPhone with the introduction of its tablet offering, the iPad. The iPad used the same iOS operating system as the iPhone and had most of the same attributes, including elegant design, a touch screen, and access to the App store through wireless connectivity. All of this helped drive rapid growth in consumer demand.

When Apple released the iPhone, Google already had its own operating systems for a touch-screen phone in development. Google had acquired the original developer, Android Inc., in 2005. The first smartphones running on Android started to appear in 2008. Google's business model was to give away Android for free, and to make money from advertising linked to mobile searches. By 2013, Android was the dominant smartphone OS, followed by Apple's iOS (see Table 1). Tablets that ran on Android stated to appear soon after the launch of the iPad in 2010 and, by 2014, Android was also dominating the tablet OS market (see Table 2).

The introduction of the iPhone, and then Android phones, decimated Microsoft's market share (see Table 1). By 2011, Microsoft's OS was found on just 9 million smartphones shipped that year. Android was on 220 million phones, and Apple sold 89 million iOS phones. The situation in the tablet market was no better, where Microsoft was caught completely flat-footed by the introduction of the iPad. Google, on the other hand, adapted very quickly and soon gained market leadership.

In response to the rapid emergence of Apple and Android, Microsoft developed a new operating system for touch-screen smartphones, *Windows Phone*. Windows Phone had an "active tile"–based "Metro" interface, rather than the on-screen icons used by Apple and Android. The first Windows Phones started to appear in late 2010. Microsoft also established its own app store, the Windows Phone Store.

Table 2 Global Tablet Sales (millions) 2010-2014

Year	Android	iOS (Apple)	Nokia
2011	17	40	0
2012	53	61	1
2013	121	70	4
2014	160	65	11

Source: Gartner.com, various press releases

In early 2011, Microsoft entered an alliance with Nokia to jointly develop Windows Phones. Like Microsoft, Nokia had been caught off guard by the emergence of the iPhone and had seen its market share slide. Nokia had used its own Symbian operating system in its smartphones. Like Windows Mobile, Symbian was a primitive first-generation smartphone OS that lacked the full features and functions of Android and iOS, including touch-screen capability, a virtual keyboard, and a supply of third-party apps that could be downloaded onto the device. Under the alliance, Nokia agreed to phase out Symbian and switch to Microsoft's Windows Phone OS. The first products of this alliance, Nokia's Lumina phones, were introduced in late 2011.

Despite some favorable reviews, the Lumina phones grew more slowly than the market, and Microsoft's market share remained in the low single digits in most nations. Reasons given to explain this included the lack of appeal of the Metro interface, and relative paucity of third-party apps for Windows Phone.

In September 2013, Microsoft announced its intention to acquire Nokia's mobile phone business for $7.2 billion. In justifying the acquisition, Steve Ballmer argued that merging together the two companies would streamline product development processes, lower costs, and result in better phones and higher gross profit margins.[21] It was also noted that Nokia was the only company left that was willing to make Windows phones. If Nokia stopped making Window's phones, Microsoft's phone business would be dead. Critics wondered whether an acquisition that made Microsoft a phone maker might not alienate other phone makers, such as HTC, who would now see Microsoft as a direct competitor.

In addition to the phone business, Microsoft entered the tablet business with its Surface offering. The Surface was positioned as a crossover between a conventional laptop and a tablet. Introduced in late 2012, it used a Windows 8.1 operating system, which by that time was also being used for Windows Phone. Like the Windows Phone, the Surface garnered some favorable reviews, but sales were slow to pick up and the product initially failed to make a dent in the dominance of Android and iOS in the tablet market. However, following the introduction of the Surface Pro 3 in mid-2014, sales appeared to be accelerating. In the last 6 months of 2014, Microsoft sold $2 billion worth of Surface tablets.

C14-5c Windows Offerings under Ballmer

Windows Vista was the first version of Windows completely developed under Ballmer's leadership (although Bill Gates oversaw the project). Vista started out as a more ambitious project with the code name of Longhorn, but when that ran into difficulties, it was recast as Vista. A primary goal for Vista was to increase security. Released in January 2007, more than 5 years after its predecessor, Windows XP, it was not well received by the marketplace. Vista took 2 years longer than expected to develop and it was several billion dollars over budget. It was a huge program—with 50 million plus lines of code—and utilized a lot of computer memory to run, resulting in unacceptably slow performance for many users. It quickly drained battery life on laptop computers. Moreover, it irritated users with constant pop-up authorization prompts for user account control. Many potential adopters simply stuck with Windows XP rather than switching to the much-maligned Vista. By October 2009, Windows Vista had 19% of the PC operating system marketplace, while Windows XP, an 8-year-old OS, still enjoyed a 63% share.

Many insiders blamed the poor performance of Vista on a development process that got out of hand. One problem was "too many VPs in reporting structures too narrow." There were 12 layers of management between Bill Gates and a developer at the base of the Windows organization. As one former Windows development lead noted: "I once sat in a scheduled review meeting with at least six VPs and ten general managers. When that many people have a say, things get confusing. Not to mention, since so many bosses are in the room, there are often negotiations between project managers prior to such meetings to make sure no one looks bad......In general, Windows suffers from a proclivity for *action control*, not *results control*. Instead of clearly stating desired outcomes, there is a penchant for telling people exactly what steps they must take."[22]

Other insiders complained about a lack of accountability, constant churning of features and specifications, with new features often being added without adequate testing, leading to system crashes and further development delays. Several people also noted that with Bill Gates heading Vista, CEO Steve Ballmer was unwilling to step in and resolve problems that were resulting in delays and cost overruns.

Once Vista shipped, many of the top engineers on the project retired. Steve Sinofsky, who had been running Office, was brought in to run Windows. At Office, Sinofsky had run a very tight ship, shipping new versions on schedule like clockwork. The Office organization was also much flatter than the Windows division, with only four levels of management.

Sinofsky flattened the Windows organization, reducing the number of levels of management from 12 to 5. He pushed developers to get Vista's successor, Windows 7, to market quickly. Originally conceived as an incremental update to Vista, Windows 7 was a more streamlined program that fixed many of the performance problems and irritations with Vista. Introduced in 2009, reviewers saw Windows 7 as a big improvement over Vista, and the operating system sold well.

Once Windows 7 shipped, Sinofsky and his team turned their attention to Windows 8. Released in 2012, Windows 8 was positioned as an operating system for the new era of digital devices. Windows 8 used the same "Metro" style tile-based interface that had first been used on Windows Phone. Despite the lukewarm reception of the Metro interface on the phone, Microsoft saw the interface as an important differentiator. Sinofsky was a major advocate of the Metro interface, going as far as to push Microsoft to kill a competing interface for tablets being developed within the company since it was inconsistent with the Metro theme that he wanted on all devices.[23] Known as the Courier, the tablet was the brainchild of a group within Microsoft's Entertainment and Devices division headed by Jay Allard. The Courier was on track to hit the market in 2010, just months behind the iPad. Widely admired within Microsoft, Allard was the force behind the creation of the Xbox business and was instrumental in pushing Microsoft to embrace the web back in 1995.

The Courier was a two-screen tablet that folded like a book and had a touch screen. Early prototypes had elicited rave reviews from outsiders who had seen it, some preferring what they saw to prototypes of the iPad that was then under development. But the Courier used a modified version of Windows as its operating system, and the interface departed substantially from the Windows norm.

When the Courier dispute surfaced, Ballmer found himself in the position of having to choose between two of his best managers. Unable to make his mind up, he brought Gates into the decision. Gates, who by now had given up all day-to-day operating responsibility, met with Allard and his team. His criticism was that Courier didn't align with Microsoft's key Windows and Office franchises. Not only did it use a customized version of Windows, and a nonstandard interface, but it also did not include an Outlook email client (Allard pointed out that users could get email through an onboard web browser). For Gates, this was a fatal flaw, and the Courier was canceled. Within months, Allard had left Microsoft, along with his boss, Robbie Bach. It would be another 2 years before Microsoft had a tablet offering, the Surface.

In addition to the Metro interface, Windows 8 also supported touch-screen technology and could be used on a tablet in addition to desktop and laptop PCs. Released in 2012, Windows 8 received decidedly mixed reviews. Although the reaction towards its performance improvements, security enhancements, and improved support for touchscreen devices was positive, the new user interface of the operating system was widely criticized for being potentially confusing and difficult to learn. Many users particularly disliked the fact that Microsoft had removed the start menu.

Market take-up of Windows 8 was slower than Microsoft had hoped. Sinofsky abruptly left Microsoft in December 2012. Recognizing that the Metro interface was not resonating with many users, Microsoft announced that it would release an update, Windows 8.1, in October 2013. Windows 8.1 tried to address some of the criticisms and gave users the ability to dispense with the Metro interface and revert to the traditional start button and menu. Despite this, adoption continued to be slow. By mid-2014, only 12.5% of PCs were using Windows 8 or 8.1. Most consumers and corporations stuck with Windows 7.

C14-6 Ballmer Steps Down

By early 2013, Steve Ballmer was coming under increasing pressure from Microsoft's board of directors. Despite robust revenue and earnings growth under his leadership, Microsoft's stock price had stagnated. Microsoft had lost its technological leadership in the industry to Apple and Google. The company's problems with Vista and Windows 8, and its failures in the smartphone, tablet, and Internet search businesses had led directors to question the direction of the company. Ballmer agreed that it was time for someone else to take the helm, and the board started to look for his successor.

Notes

[1] A. Covert, "Will Google Docs Kill Off Microsoft Office," CNN Money, November 13, 2013.

[2] International Data Corporation, "Worldwide Server Market Revenues Declines 3.7% in the Third Quarter," International Data Corporation, February 24, 2014.

[3] K. Mackie, "Microsoft Admits Windows Use at 14%," Redmondmag.com, July 14, 2014.

[4] International Data Corporation, "Smartphone OS Market Share, Q1 2014."

[5] E. Protalinski, "Strategy Analytics: Android Tablet Shipments up to 65.8% in Q1 2014," The Next Web, April 28, 2014.

[6] IDC Press Release, "IDC Expects PC Shipments to Fall by 6% and Decline through 2018," March 4, 2014.

[7] J. D'onfro, "Here's a Reminder of How Massive Amazon's Web Services Business Is," Business Insider, June 16, 2014.

[8] Comment made to the author.

[9] S. Nadella, "Mobile First, Cloud First Press Briefing," San Francisco, March 27, 2014.

[10] Much of the material in this section is drawn from (1) P.

Freiberger and M. Swaine, Fire in the Valley: The Making of the Personal Computer (McGraw Hill, 2000). (2) A. R. Harris, Microsoft: The Company and its Founders (ABDO Publishing Company, 2013). (3) J. Wallace and J. Erickson, "Hard Drive: Bill Gates and the Making of the Microsoft Empire," Harper Business, 1992. (4) Information gleaned by the author during nearly two decades of teaching in house executive education courses at Microsoft.

[11] The full Gates memo is archived at "May 26 1995: Gates, Microsoft Jump on the Internet Tidal Wave," Wired, May 26, 2010.

[12] J. Bick, "The Microsoft Millionaire Come of Age," New York Times, May 29, 2005.

[13] B. Herbold, "Inside Microsoft: Balancing Creativity and Discipline," Harvard Business Review, January 2002.

[14] B. Herbold, "Inside Microsoft: Balancing Creativity and Discipline," Harvard Business Review, January 2002

[15] J. Brustein, "Microsoft Kills Its Hated Stack Rankings. Does Anyone Do Employee Reviews

Right?," Bloomberg BusinessWeek, November 13, 2013.

[16] The best description of this process can be found in M. Cusumano and R. Selby, Microsoft Secrets (Touchstone Book, 1995).

[17] Business Software Alliance, Ninth Annual BSA Global Software Piracy Study, May 2010.

[18] K. Powers, "Showdown," Forbes, August 11, 2003, pp 86–87.

[19] A. Wilhelm, "Inside Microsoft's Earnings: Windows 8 and the Xbox Money Machine," The Next Web, April 19, 2013.

[20] P. Dekho, "Google Android Lords over 85% of Smartphone OS Market Share," Financial Express, September 1, 2014. C. Buckler, "Browser Trends September 2014," Site Point, September 2, 2014.

[21] T. B. Lee, "Here's Why Microsoft Is Buying Nokia's Phone Business," The Washington Post, September 3, 2013.

[22] Cited at http://blogs.msdn.com /b/philipsu/archive/2006/06/14/631438 .aspx

[23] J. Greene, "The Inside Story of How Microsoft Killed Its Courier Tablet," CNET, November 1, 2011.

Microsoft (B): Satya Nadella and the Push into Cloud Computing

Charles W. L. Hill Foster School of Business University of Washington, Seattle, WA 98195 August 2022

C15-1 Introduction

Satay Nadella was picked to succeed Steve Ballmer as CEO of Microsoft Corporation (Microsoft) and took charge on February 4, 2014. Nadella was a native of Hyderabad, India. In 1988, he received an engineering degree from the Manipal Institute of Technology. He then traveled to the United States and earned a master's in computer science from the University of Wisconsin. Later, while working full time at Microsoft, he earned an executive MBA from the University of Chicago. Nadella had worked at Microsoft since 1992. He was senior VP of R&D for the Online Service division from March 2007 until February 2011, when he was appointed president of the Server and Tools division. This division grew at a healthy pace under his leadership. Moreover, the strategically important Azure cloud computing initiative was based within this division. Nadella was credited for his adept leadership of the nascent cloud computing business.[1]

C15-2 Satya Takes Over

Nadella was a different kind of leader than either Ballmer or Gates. A lover of the graceful game of cricket, he embraced Buddhist beliefs, talked frequently about the need for managers to have empathy, and built a reputation over his career for being calm, even in the most contentious circumstances. He focused on positive feedback to reinforce good habits. As a manager and leader, Nadella made it clear that aggressive behavior was no longer welcome. Never raising his voice or showing anger at employees or executives, Nadella constantly worked to create a more comfortable work environment. He never wrote angry emails, or berated employees, and refused to tolerate anger or yelling in executive meetings. This was in stark contrast to Gates, who could be abrasive in his criticism, and Ballmer, who was known for his yelling. In one famous story that circulated around Microsoft, Ballmer picked up an iPhone from an executive, and threw it against the wall in anger, breaking it, to make the point (presumably) that Apple was the "enemy" and Microsoft executives should not use iOS devices. Nadella would never do this.[2]

Nadella moved quickly to put his stamp on Microsoft. Emphasizing a break with the past, Microsoft, he said, was competing in a "mobile first, cloud first" world. In this world, said Nadella, Microsoft must empower people to get things done. By June

2014, he was talking about Microsoft being the premier "productivity and platform company for the mobile first cloud first world."

In a sharp shift from the company's prior strategy, in March 2014, Nadella announced that Microsoft would offer a version of Office 365 for the iOS (the iPad and iPhone). A version had been in the works for some time, but the release had been blocked by Steve Ballmer because of fears that it would boost demand for the iPad and hurt sales of Microsoft's Surface tablet and Windows Phone. Nadella asserted that in a world where Android and iOS are widely used, Microsoft had to make its applications run on those platforms too. By the fall of 2014, Office for the iPad had over 30 million downloads. Also in March 2014, Nadella announced that Windows would be free for devices smaller than 9 inches, meaning smartphones and tablets. This was seen as an attempt to jump-start adoption of Windows on digital devices, and to match Google's strategy of giving away Android for free. As it turns out, the gambit did not work, but it did reinforce the impression that Nadella was willing to try bold strategies.

In June 2014, Nadella sent a long letter to employees stating that the company would be taking "important steps to visibly change our culture." He talked about the need to obsess over customers, to streamline engineering processes and reduce the time and energy it takes to get things done, to limit the number of people involved in making decisions, to drive greater accountability, and to flatten the organization. In making these statements, Nadella was implicitly acknowledging that Microsoft's culture had been too bureaucratic, too political, and that there had not been sufficient accountability.

Nadella also announced that as part of its efforts to streamline the organization, Microsoft would layoff 18,000 employees, 12,500 of them in the newly acquired Nokia unit. These were the most significant layoffs in Microsoft's history. Coming at a time when the company was still making very healthy profits, they sent a clear signal that Nadella believed that company needed to become more efficient to compete effectively going forward.

The headcount reductions at Microsoft's Nokia unit were followed in June 2015 by the announcement that Microsoft would cut another 7,800 positions globally, primarily in the Nokia unit. The company also stated that it would write off $7.6 billion in assets related to its 2013 acquisition of Nokia, more than the $7.2 billion Microsoft paid for Nokia in September 2013. It was a stunning reversal, and yet another break from the prior strategy. In making this announcement, Nadella stated that "we are moving from a strategy to grow a standalone phone business to a strategy to grow and create a vibrant Windows ecosystem including first party device family."[3] The underlying message was clear, Microsoft was admitting defeat in the phone business, and would move on from trying to establish its offering as a standard in the phone business. Instead, Microsoft would support other offerings, including iOS, Android, and Linux.

In January of 2015, Microsoft unveiled its next version of Windows, Windows 10, which was introduced in late 2015 (Microsoft decided to skip the Windows 9 designation). Windows 10 represented a move away from the tile-based Metro interface. The traditional start menu that was in Windows 7 was put back in. Microsoft stated that Windows 10 would run on all devices, from desktops and laptops to tablets and smart phones. Applications written to run on Windows 10 would run on any device, which promised to remove a major headache for app developers. Moreover, the ability to tap into the wider Windows ecosystem was seen as creating an incentive for developers to write more apps for Windows devices. In a departure from its prior strategy, Microsoft announced that Windows 10 would be free to any Windows 7 or 8 users that downloaded it in the first year after its release. Estimates suggests that this would result in $500 million in lost revenue for the first year Windows 10 was on the market.

C15-3 The Cloud Computing Initiative

As CEO Nadella repeatedly emphasized, Microsoft's cloud computing business was central to the future of the company. This was not surprising. As the executive in charge of the Server and Tools division, he had had responsibility for nurturing that business since 2011. Conversations about "cloud computing" had been taking place at Microsoft since 2004 when Amazon had launched its Amazon Web Services (AWS) cloud computing offering. The "cloud" referred to the idea that data, operating systems, and applications could be hosted on public "server farms" or "data centers" comprising of thousands of machines that were run by third parties (such as AWS), rather than on company-owned servers and PCs located within an enterprise. The interest in cloud computing was based on a realization that in a world where computing device users were always connected to the Internet through wired or wireless links, there were compelling economic reasons for moving computing power and programs off servers located within enterprises (on premises), and onto public server farms. Specifically, the cloud could deliver more value to users at a lower cost than traditional client server networks.

On the value side, there was clearly great utility associated with storing files on the cloud and being able to access those files anywhere anytime through any connected device. The files could be in the form of documents, music, video, or databases. Moreover, by reaching out and accessing programs and data stored on the cloud, users with simple devices such as smartphones and tablets could theoretically access vast amounts of computing power when they needed it.

On the cost side, it was apparent that moving computing resources onto a public cloud could save businesses a lot of money. Corporate IT departments traditionally shouldered the costs of buying and maintaining computer hardware and software, activities that accounted for almost 90% of all IT costs. Servers, however, often only ran at 5–10% capacity, while much of the software installed on corporate servers and PCs was only rarely used. By moving data and applications onto a server farm owned by someone else, demand for computing resources could be aggregated and servers could be run at closer to 90% capacity. This implied significant economies of scale in the costs of computation. Microsoft's own estimates suggested that under optimal conditions, shifting to a cloud-based model could reduce IT costs by as much as 80%.[4] Moreover, instead of paying for software that was rarely used, corporations might be able to pay for software only when they used it (this is the utility model of pricing).

Microsoft proposed to build a public cloud computing business that would host data and applications for corporations, taking the burden of infrastructure and maintenance costs off their hands. In return, corporations would pay a fee for storing data, and either a subscription or runtime fee for executing applications. As early as 2006, Steve Ballmer had stated that Microsoft had no choice but to go "all in" on the cloud.[5] By 2010, this commitment had developed into Microsoft's Azure cloud computing initiative, which had been located within the company's Server and Tools division.

Cloud computing was initially seen as comprising of three segments: infrastructure as a service (IaaS), platform as a service (PaaS), and software as a service (SaaS). IaaS refers to basic hosting of data, websites, and the like. Amazon's AWS started out as an IaaS offering. PaaS refers to the idea of building a software platform upon which software applications can be built and run. Microsoft's Azure platform is a PaaS offering that uses Windows Server technology. Think of Azure as Windows for a server farm (data center) of 100,000 machines. Azure balances workflow and loads across servers to achieve efficient capacity utilization, economies of scale, and fast response time to computing queries. There are significant security protocols built into Azure to protect the data of customers. Azure also comes with tools that help clients analyze data and manage their own workload, and protocols that enable third-party developers to write applications that run on top of Azure. Unlike the old Windows model, however, Microsoft Azure explicitly supports clients that wish to use other platforms, such as Linux, to manage their data and run applications on top of Azure. Azure does this by enabling customers to run "virtual machines" that use another operating system if they so wish (thus, for example, a company could run Linux servers on top of Azure). Over time, the distinction between IaaS and PaaS has become somewhat blurred, as the three big players in this area—Amazon, Microsoft, and Google—will often bundle IaaS and PaaS together for clients.

SaaS is the idea that software applications can be hosted and run on the cloud and accessed through a desktop or mobile device anywhere anytime. Salesforce.com was an early leader in the SaaS space with its customer relationship management (CRM) software. Introduced in 2000, this was the first notable software product that was entirely cloud based. Office 365, launched in 2011, was Microsoft's first SaaS product.

By 2011, when Nadella was running the server and tool's division, Microsoft was committed to competing in all three segments. The company would host data for enterprises and consumers (IaaS). It would continue to develop Azure so that enterprises could write applications, such as data analytics, that would run well on the cloud (PaaS). And Microsoft would reposition many of its products, such as Office, SQL Server, and Dynamics, as software SaaS offerings. In June 2011, Microsoft introduced Office 365 to enterprise users. Office 365 was a cloud version of its best-selling Office Suite. In 2013, Office 365 was offered to consumers. Enterprises paid a licensing fee and consumers an annual subscription fee for Office 365. Users could download the program onto multiple devices (for consumers the limit was five). They could also store Office documents on Microsoft's Cloud using its One Drive storage offering. Microsoft shifted to a rolling release model for developing Office 365, updating the program on an as-needed basis (initially quarterly), a marked departure from the historic 3- to 5-year development schedule at Microsoft.

One of the problems Microsoft had to grapple with in shifting towards a cloud-computing model was that it represented a change in the underlying economics of its business. In the traditional model, most of Microsoft's costs were associated with the fixed costs of developing programs such as Windows and Office. The marginal costs of producing more versions of a program were very low, a fact that at high volumes enabled Microsoft to earn gross margins in the 90% range on Windows and Office. In the cloud computing model, however, Microsoft had to build and maintain server farms, which could cost anywhere from $200 million to $1 billion each in fixed costs, and which consumed large amounts of electricity. There was a general belief that even at high volumes, the gross margins associated with a cloud computing business would be lower than what Microsoft was accustomed to. As people within the company were fond of saying, "in the cloud business we actually have costs of goods sold."

By 2021, Microsoft had 200 data centers (server farms) based in 34 countries around the world. These data centers contained more than 4 million individual servers and were linked together with 165,000 miles of fiber-optic cable that wrapped around the world. According to a Microsoft spokesperson, the company was planning to open between 50 and 100 new data centers each year for the foreseeable future.[6] Estimates suggest that building a 700,00 square foot, 60-megawatt load data center in the United States in 2022 would cost between $420 million and $770 million, with a yearly operating cost in the order of $25 million (much of which is in the form of electricity to power the servers and the associated cooling systems).[7] The largest data centers require more than 100 megawatts of power capacity.

C15-4 Microsoft in 2022

While cloud computing was still a small business in 2013, generating perhaps less than $10 billion in revenues industry-wide, rapid growth was predicted going forward. Industry revenues were projected to balloon to $150 billion by 2020. Clearly, Microsoft had to embrace this business and Nadella made doing so the centerpiece of his strategy for the company. By 2022, Nadella's efforts to transform Microsoft were bearing significant fruit. Between 2014 and 2022, Microsoft's revenues had expanded from $87 billion to $198 billion, and net income from $22 billion to $73 billion. The company's market cap now exceeded $2 trillion. Driving this impressive growth had been the expansion of Microsoft's cloud computing businesses.

The global cloud computing business had grown significantly between 2014 and 2022. This was due to the compelling economics of moving data onto the cloud, the widespread adoption of mobile computing devices, the spread of high bandwidth fixed line and wireless connections, and the emergence of businesses that could take advantage of these developments to deliver new services to consumers, or enhance their existing services, and do so productively. Helping to drive the growth of cloud computing services were the development of big data analytics, artificial intelligence, and machine learning—all software technologies that benefited from analyzing big data stored on the cloud, often in real time, to deliver superior value at a lower cost to businesses and their customers. A related factor has been the growth of the Internet of Things (IoT), which refers the large number of digital devices connected to the Internet that are now found in a wide range of products, including automobiles, phones, watches, home security systems, medical equipment, logistics tracking equipment, payment devices, and a myriad of other products.

A company like Uber, for example, could not have existed in 2005—the technology simply wasn't there. But by 2015, by harnessing the power of the cloud and ubiquitous wireless connections to perform real-time location mapping and data analytics, Uber could deliver a value-added ride for hire service that would not have been possible a decade earlier, and which transformed the established taxi business globally. Similarly, the transformation of Netflix from a company that delivered CD-ROMs of movies via the mail, into a streaming video behemoth that delivers customized content to users, was made possible by the marriage of data storage on the cloud with high bandwidth wired and wireless connections. The cloud allows for the establishment of such novel services, and at the same time drives demand for more services.

From a standing start in 2006, the global cloud services market, including IaaS, PaaS, and SaaS offerings, reached $387 billion in 2021. The market was forecast to surpass $1.63 trillion by 2030, representing a compound annual growth rate of 17.32% from 2022 to 2030. North America dominated the cloud services market in 2021, accounting for 40% of global revenue. The SaaS segment was the largest, accounting for 54% of global revenue in 2021.[8]

Although Amazon's AWS had a large early lead in IaaS/PaaS offerings, by 2022 Microsoft had an estimated 22% share of the global IaaS/PaaS market, second only to Amazon, which had a 33% share. Moreover, Microsoft has been steadily gaining on AWS. Google, with 10%, rounded out the top three companies. The overall IaaS/PaaS market was expected to be around $250 billion in 2022, up 30% from 2021.[9]

Microsoft's success in IaaS/PaaS has been helped by the fact that the company had an established customer base among corporations who have long used Microsoft desktop and server operating systems, and Microsoft applications such as Office. Azure offers corporate clients a painless way to experiment with moving select data and workloads onto the cloud, since the customers remain within the same Microsoft environment. In other words, Microsoft offers long-standing corporate customers a very easy "on-ramp" onto the cloud. Amazon lacked this advantage, and indeed, in its early days, Amazon focused on marketing AWS to start-ups and smaller enterprises, since they were likely to be less invested in Microsoft products.

Microsoft gained a significant advantage by pursuing a "hybrid cloud strategy," helping customers to move some of their data and workloads onto Microsoft's "public" cloud, while keeping other data and workloads "on premises" in private data centers that run on Azure. The great advantage of this is that all operate within the same Microsoft environment. This has been a particularly successful strategy in sectors such as finance and health services, where government regulations mandate that some workloads and data be kept on premises. In addition, Microsoft has established a strong reputation for maintaining the security of data on the cloud, and for being able to deliver a high degree of uptime (Microsoft aims for 99.999% uptime). This contrasts with AWS, which in the last month of 2021, for example, suffered three outages, briefly shutting down a vast number of online services now critical to everyday life.[10]

In addition to its success with IaaS/PaaS, Microsoft has transformed its traditional on-premises products to become SaaS cloud applications, simultaneously changing its perpetual licensing business model into a subscription model. The most obvious example of this is the Office bundle. Long the dominant information worker productivity suite with a global monopoly, the on-premises version of Office is now rapidly being replaced by the cloud-based version, Office 365, which as of 2022 had more than 345 million active subscribers, up from 70,000 in early 2016.[11]

Microsoft is trying to work the same magic with Dynamics 365. Introduced in July 2016, Dynamics 365 is a comprehensive suite of business tools, built to handle a wide variety of work processes. Aimed at small and medium-sized businesses, it operates on the Microsoft Azure cloud computing platform. Dynamics contains 11 core modules, or applications, including 5 of the customer relationship management (CRM) type; sales, customer service, field service, project service automation, and marketing. Other modules fall under the category of enterprise resource planning (ERP), talent management (HRM), finance, and operations. The company is competing against Salesforce.com, Oracle, Workday, and SAP, among others in this area. Although far more competitive than the Office market, Microsoft has been gaining market share in this area, and while its share remains in the single digits, the future potential is significant.

To support Microsoft's push into the cloud, in 2018, Nadella implemented a major reorganization of Microsoft. He split the long-dominant Windows engineering team into two separate teams. One team was to focus on "experiences and devices," with a mission to "install a unifying product ethos across our end user experiences and devices." The other team was to focus on Microsoft's "cloud and artificial intelligence platform," with a mission to "drive platform coherence and compelling value across all levels of the tech stack starting with the distributed computing fabric (cloud computing and the Azure platform) to AI (higher level services that sit on top of Microsoft's cloud platform)."[12] These changes were widely interpreted as signaling that the Windows era at Microsoft was over. The reorganization is "really doubling down on the cloud as the fundamental platform for Microsoft," noted an analyst at Gartner.[13]

Microsoft had also continued to make some significant investments in developer tools to support the push into mobile and cloud computing. The company offers Visual Studios to developers, which is an integrated development environment used to develop computer applications, mobile apps, websites, and web apps. Visual Studios supports 35 different programming languages with code editing, automated code compiling, and debugging. In 2016, Microsoft acquired Xamarin, a leading platform for mobile app development on iOS and Android. Xamarin has since been integrated into Visual Studios and allows for cross-platform application development. Thus, a set of code written for one operating system can be quickly used for the same app on another. Like so many other moves made in the Nadella era, this represents a break from Microsoft's past and embraces a platform agnostic view of the world.

Another notable acquisition was that of GitHub in October 2018 for $7.5 billion. GitHub is a repository for open-source (non-proprietary) software code, and an online collaboration community for software developers. It's sometimes described as the "Facebook for programmers." As CEO, Nadella has embraced the open-source movement, and he clearly sees GitHub as a critical source for software code that will help to unleash the power of the cloud, not just for Microsoft, but for everybody. By 2018, over 27 million software developers had contributed some 80 million lines of code to GitHub. Programmers working at Microsoft, Amazon, Apple, and Google all had a significant presence at GitHub, and actively used it as a repository for documentation and code, and as a medium for collaboration.[14]

Some questioned whether Microsoft's rivals would continue to allow their developers to use GitHub following the acquisition. However, in the 12 months up to June 2021 the number of monthly active organizations using GitHub increased 70%. One analyst noted that GitHub is flourishing not because Microsoft is marketing the heck out of it, but because Microsoft has insisted that GitHub retain its open-source ethos and developer-first culture.

Nadella himself observed in 2021 that "As every organization looks to build its own digital capability, they will need to modernize existing apps, build new apps, and have a standard way of doing both…..We offer the most popular tools to help developers rapidly grow from idea to code and code to cloud. Visual Studio has more than 25 million monthly active users and GitHub is home to nearly 65 million developers…. Some of the most groundbreaking technological achievements of the past year, including critical COVID-19 vaccine trials as well as the first powered flight on Mars were only possible because of the contributions of the open-source communities on GitHub."[15]

In another acquisition aimed at boosting its cloud presence, in April 2021, Microsoft announced that it would purchase Nuance Communications for $16 billion. Nuance is a provider of artificial intelligence (AI) and speech recognition software. Nuance was a pioneer in speech recognition, and provided part of the technology for Siri, the talking digital assistant that made its debut on the Apple iPhone in 2011. Nuance has several successful product offerings in the healthcare sector, including Dragon, the market-leading speech-to-text software. It also offers cloud-based AI products that help physicians make diagnostic and treatment decisions for patients. While Microsoft is undoubtedly interested in expanding its footprint in the large field for medical software, observers also expect the company to leverage Nuance's technology and apply it to other fields.[16]

Although Microsoft's success in moving enterprise customers onto the cloud received the most press, the company had not forgotten the retail consumer. In the retail space, its Surface laptop was still selling well and getting good reviews, versions of Office 365 for individuals and students had strong sales (although the challenges presented by Google Docs is very real), and the company had moved its successful gaming business onto Azure. Although Microsoft still produced a physical Xbox console, many thought that the future lay in streaming games to any device over the cloud. Microsoft's Xbox Live offering positioned the company to make this move. Signaling its continuing commitment to gaming, in January of 2022, Microsoft announced that it would acquire Activision Blizzard for $68.7 billion. Activision Blizzard has a stable of major games, including *World of Warcraft, Call of Duty*, and *Diablo*, while Microsoft has major hits including *Minecraft, Gears of War,* and the *Halo* franchise. If the merger goes through (it's still under regulatory review at the time of writing), it will transform Microsoft into one of the world's largest game companies.

Why does Microsoft want to be so big in gaming? In an email to employees, Nadella explained that gaming "is the largest and fastest growing form of entertainment, and as the digital and physical worlds come together, it will pay a critical role in the development of the metaverse platform." In other words, Microsoft has plans to use its growing competence in virtual reality to enhance the gaming experience, allowing players to fully immerse themselves in a multiplayer digital world that exists on the cloud. And perhaps it will also encourage developments to flow the other way, taking lessons learned from gaming in virtual reality, and applying them to business settings.[17]

C15-5 Looking Forward

As Microsoft reported its financial results for 2022, Satya Nadella could look back on a successful 8 years as CEO of the world's largest software company. When he took over in 2014, the company, while still very profitable, was no longer considered a leader in the information technology sector. Apple had seized the initiative in the consumer space with innovative products including the iPhone, iPad, and newer versions of the Mac such as the Air Book. Google, too, had leveraged its successful search business to develop Android, now the world's most widely used mobile operating system, while Apple held the number two spot on mobile devices with iOS. Microsoft's Windows Phone, on the other hand, had been a dismal failure. In the corporate arena, Amazon had pioneered the IaaS/PaaS sector of the nascent cloud computing business with AWS, while Salesforce had been the first to introduce a successful enterprise SaaS product. Microsoft was trying to respond to these developments, but its Windows-centric strategy, backward-looking leadership, somewhat dysfunctional culture, and lack of innovation was holding the company back.

Satya Nadella had been a breath of fresh air, changing the strategy, organization, and culture of Microsoft in meaningful ways. The company had walked away from its Windows-centric strategy; embraced open source; regularly ran non-Microsoft operating systems on top of Azure; wrote versions of Microsoft programs to run on other operating systems; leveraged its long relationship with enterprise customers to move them onto the cloud; invested heavily in AI and data analytics so that it could better serve its enterprise customers; and moved its legacy product offerings such as Office onto the cloud, building a strong SaaS business in the process. The company was now growing remarkably fast for such a large enterprise. Revenues had increased 230% since 2014 and net income 330%. The company was yet again enormously profitable with an ROIC for fiscal 2022 of 33.23%. The task for Nadella and his team was to build on this foundation to drive more profitable growth going forward.

Notes

[1] S. Nadella, *Hit Refresh: The Quest to Rediscover Microsoft's Soul and Imagine a Better Future for Everyone* (Harper Business, 2017).

[2] V. Wadhwa, I. Amla, and A. Salkever, "How Microsoft Made the Stunning Transformation from Evil Empire to Kool Kid," *Fortune*, December 21, 2021.

[3] T. Warren, "Microsoft Writes Off $7.6 Billion from Nokia Deal," *The Verge*, July 8, 2015.

[4] "The Economics of the Cloud," *Microsoft White Paper*, November 2010.

[5] The author was an observer at a Microsoft strategy conference when Ballmer made this comment in response to a presentation suggesting that Microsoft take a cautious approach to the cloud. "No," said Ballmer, "this is wrong, we have to go all in on this one."

[6] J. Roach, "Microsoft's Virtual Data Center Grounds "the Cloud" in Reality," *Microsoft Innovation Stories*, April 20, 2021.

[7] M. Zhang, "How Much Does It Cost to Build a Data Center?," *Dgtl Infra*, May 30, 2022.

[8] "Cloud Services Market Size to Surpass US$1,630 Billion by 2030," *Precedence Research*, June 10, 2022.

[9] S. Sharwood, "Cloud a Three-Player Market Dominated by AWS, Google, Microsoft," *The Register*, May 2, 2022.

[10] A. Gregg and D. Harwell, "Amazon Web Services Third Outage in a Month Exposes Weak Point in the Internet's Backbone," *Washington Po,* December 22, 2021.

[11] T. Redmond, "Office 365 Reaches 345 Million Paid Seats," April 28, 2022, https://office365it-pros.com/2022/04/28/office-365-number-of-users/

[12] "Satya Nadella Email to Employees: Embracing Our Future: Intelligent Cloud and Intelligent Edge," *Microsoft News Center*, March 29, 2018.

[13] S. Lohr, "Microsoft Reorganizes to Fuel Cloud and AI Businesses," *New York Times*, March 29, 2018.

[14] S. Rogers, "Microsoft Reportedly Agreed to Buy Coding Resources GitHub," *Interesting Engineering*, June 3, 2018.

[15] B. Evans, "Microsoft's Killer Acquisition: GitHub Soars 70%," *Acceleration Economy*, May 6, 2021.

[16] M. de la Merced, C. Metz, and K. Weise, "Microsoft to Buy Nuance for $16 Billion," *New York Times*, April 12, 2021.

[17] B. Woods, "In Microsoft's Activision Deal, It's Not Just Stock Price but a Future World at Stake," *CNBC*, May 7, 2022.

Console Wars: Half a Century of Conflict in the Home Videogame Market

This case was prepared by Charles W. L. Hill, Foster School of Business, University of Washington.
Copyright © Charles W.L. Hill, 2022

C16-1 An Industry Is Born

In 1968, Nolan Bushell, the 24-year-old son of a Utah cement contractor graduated from the University of Utah with a degree in engineering.[1] Bushell then moved to California, where he worked briefly in the computer graphics division of Ampex. At home, Bushell turned his daughter's bedroom into a laboratory. There, he created a simpler version of *Space War*, a computer game that had been invented in 1962 by an MIT graduate student, Steve Russell. Bushell's version of Russell's game, which he called *Computer Space*, was made of integrated circuits connected to a 19-inch black-and-white television screen. Unlike a computer, Bushell's invention could do nothing but play the game, which meant that, unlike a computer, it could be produced cheaply.

Bushell envisioned video games like his standing next to pinball machines in arcades. With hopes of having his invention put into production, Bushell left Ampex to work for a small pinball company that manufactured 1,500 copies of his video game. The game never sold, primarily because the player had to read a full page of directions before he or she could play the game—way too complex for an arcade game. Bushell left the pinball company and with a friend, Ted Dabney, put up $500 to start a company that would develop a simpler video game and in the summer of 1972, Atari Incorporated was established.

One of the new company's employees, Al Alcorn, came up with a very simple game. People knew the rules immediately, and it could be played with one hand. The game was modeled on table tennis, and players batted a ball back and forth with paddles that could be moved up and down sides of a court by twisting knobs. Bushell named the game *Pong* after the sonar-like sound that was emitted every time the ball connected with a paddle. In the fall of 1972, Bushell installed his prototype for *Pong* in Andy Capp's tavern in Sunnyvale, California. The only instructions were "avoid missing the ball for a high score." In the first week, 1,200 quarters were deposited in the casserole dish that served for a coin box in Bushell's prototype. Bushell was ecstatic; his simple game had brought in $300 in a week. The pinball machine that stood next to it averaged $35 a week.

Lacking the capital to mass-produce the game, Bushnell approached established amusement game companies, only to be repeatedly shown the door. Down but hardly out, Bushnell cut his hair, put on a suit, and talked his way into a $50,000 line of credit from a local bank. He set up a production line in an abandoned roller-skating rink and he hired people to assemble machines while Led Zeppelin and the Rolling Stones were played at full volume over the speaker system of the rink. Among his first batch of employees was a skinny 17-year-old named Steve Jobs, who would later establish Apple Computer. Jobs had been attracted by a classified ad that read "Have Fun and Make Money."

In no time at all, Bushnell was selling all the machines that his small staff could make—about 10 per day—but to grow, he needed additional capital. While the ambience at the rink, with its mix of rock music and marijuana fumes, put off most potential investors, Don Valentine, one of the country's most astute and credible venture capitalists, was impressed with the growth story. Armed with Valentine's money, Atari began to increase production and expand their range of games. New games included *Tank* and *Breakout*; the latter was designed by Jobs and a friend of his (and later Apple co-founder), Steve Wozniak. By 1974, 100,000 *Pong*-like games were sold worldwide. Although Atari manufactured only 10% of the games, the company still made $3.2 million that year.

With the *Pong* clones coming on strong, Bushnell decided to make a *Pong* system for the home. Bushnell's team managed to compress Atari's coin-operated *Pong* game down to a few inexpensive circuits that were contained in a game console. Bushnell then went on a road show, demonstrating *Pong* to toy buyers, but he received an indifferent response and no sales. A dejected Bushnell returned to Atari with no idea of what to do next. Then the buyer for the sporting goods department at Sears came to see Bushnell, reviewed the machine, and offered to buy every home *Pong* game Atari could make. With Sears' backing, Bushnell boosted production. Sears ran a major television ad campaign to sell home *Pong*, and Atari's sales soared, hitting $450 million in 1975. The console-based home videogame market had arrived.

C16-2 Atari Era Boom and Bust

By 1976, about 20 different companies were crowding into the home videogame market, including National Semiconductor, RCA, Coleco, and Fairchild Semiconductors. Recognizing the limitations of existing console designs, in 1976, Fairchild came out with a game system capable of playing multiple games. The Fairchild system, Channel F, consisted of three components—a console, controllers, and cartridges. The console was a small computer optimized for graphics processing capabilities. It was designed to receive information from the controllers, process it, and send signals to a television monitor. The controllers were handheld devices used to direct on-screen action. The cartridges contained chips encoding the instructions for a game. The cartridges were designed to be inserted into the console.

In 1976, Bushnell sold Atari to Warner Communications for $28 million. Bushnell stayed on to run Atari. Backed by Warner's capital, in 1977, Atari developed and bought out its own cartridge-based system, the Atari 2600. The 2600 system was sold for $200, and associated cartridges retailed for $25–$30. Sales surged during the 1977 Christmas season. Atari claimed to have sold about 400,000 units of the 2600 VCA in 1977, about 50% of all cartridge-based systems in American homes. Atari had also earned more than $100 million in sales of game cartridges. By this point, second-place Fairchild sold around 250,00 units of its system. Cartridge sales for the year totaled about 1.2 million units, with an average selling price of around $20. Fresh from this success and fortified by market forecasts predicting sales of 33 million cartridges and an installed base of 16 million machines in American households by 1980, Bushnell committed Atari to manufacturing 1 million units of the 2600 for the 1978 Christmas season. Atari estimated that total demand would reach 2 million units. Bushnell was also encouraged by signals from Fairchild that it would again be limiting production to around 200,000 units. At this point, Atari had a library of nine games. Fairchild had 17. Importantly, games written for the Fairchild console could not run on an Atari machine, and vice versa.[2]

In 1978, about a dozen other electronics companies entered the console market with incompatible cartridge-based home systems (they included Coleco, National Semiconductor, and Magnavox). However, the 1978 Christmas season brought unexpectedly low sales. Consumers were put off by the lack of standardization. Only Atari, and Coleco with its Telstar console, survived an industry shakeout. Atari lost Bushnell, who was ousted by Warner executives. Bushnell later stated that part of the problem was a disagreement over strategy. Bushnell wanted Atari to price the 2600 at cost and make money on sales of software; Warner wanted to continue making profits on hardware sales.[3]

Several important developments occurred in 1979. First, several game producers and programmers defected from Atari to set up their own firm, Activision, and to make games compatible with the Atari 2600. Their success encouraged others to follow suit. Second, Coleco developed an expansion module that allowed its machine to play Atari games. Atari and Mattel (which entered the market in 1979) did likewise. The expansion module created a degree of standardization in the market. Third, the year 1979 saw the introduction of three new games to the home market—*Space Invaders, Asteroids*, and *Pac-Man*. All three were adapted from popular arcade games and all three helped drive demand for players.

Demand recovered strongly in late 1979 and kept growing for the next 3 years. In 1981, U.S. sales of home video games and cartridges hit $1 billion. In 1982, they surged to $3 billion, with Atari accounting for half of this amount. It seemed as if Atari could do no wrong; the 2600 was everywhere. About 20 million units were sold, and by late 1982, a large number of independent companies, including Activision, Imagic, and Epyx, were now producing hundreds of games for the 2600. Second-place Coleco, with its new ColecoVision console, was also doing well, partly because of a popular arcade game, *Donkey Kong*, which it had licensed from a Japanese company called Nintendo.

Atari was also in contact with Nintendo. In 1982, the company very nearly licensed the rights to Nintendo's Famicom, a cartridge-based videogame system machine that was a big hit in Japan. Atari's successor to the 2600, the 5200, was not selling well and the Famicom seemed like a good substitute. The negotiations broke down, however, when Atari discovered that Nintendo had extended its *Donkey Kong* license to Coleco. This allowed Coleco to port a version of the game to its home computer, which was a direct competitor to Atari's home computer. [4]

After a strong 1982 season, the industry hoped for continued growth in 1983. Then the bottom dropped out of the market. Sales of home video games plunged to $100 million. Atari lost $500 million in the first 9 months of the year. Part of the blame for the collapse was laid at the feet of an enormous inventory overhang of unsold games. About 15 to 20 million surplus game cartridges were left over from the 1982 Christmas season (in 1981, there were none). On top of this, around 500 new games hit the market in 1993. The average price of a cartridge plunged from $30 in 1979 to $16 in 1982, and then to $4 in 1983. As sales slowed, retailers cut back on the shelf space allocated to video games. It proved difficult for new games to make a splash in a crowded market. Atari had to dispose of 6 million units of *ET: The Extraterrestrial*. Meanwhile, big hits from previous years, such as *Pac-Man*, were bundled with game players and given away free to try to encourage system sales. [5]

Surveying the rubble, commentators claimed that the console market was dead. The era of dedicated game machines was over. Personal computers were taking their place.[6] It seemed to be true. Mattel sold off its game business, Fairchild moved on to other things, Coleco folded, and Warner decided to break up Atari and sell its constituent pieces—at least those pieces for which it could find a buyer. No one in America seemed to want to have anything to do with the console business; no one, that is, except for Minoru Arakawa, the head of Nintendo's U.S. subsidiary, Nintendo of America (NOA). Picking through the rubble of the industry, Arakawa noticed that there were people who still packed video arcades, bringing in $7 billion a year, more money than the entire movie industry. Perhaps it was not a lack of interest in home video games that had killed the industry. Perhaps it was bad business practice.

C16-3 The Nintendo Monopoly

Nintendo was a century-old Japanese company that had built up a profitable business making playing cards before diversifying into the videogame business. Based in Kyoto and still run by the founding Yamauchi family, the company started to diversify into the videogame business in the late 1970s. The first step was to license videogame technology from Magnavox. In 1977, Nintendo introduced a home videogame system in Japan based on this technology that played a variation of *Pong*. In 1978, the company began to sell coin-operated video games.

C16-3a The Famicom

In the early 1980s, the company's boss, Hiroshi Yamauchi, decided that Nintendo had to develop its own videogame console for the home. He pushed the company's engineers to develop a machine that combined superior graphics-processing capabilities and low cost. Yamauchi wanted a machine that could sell for $75, less than half the price of competing machines at the time. He dubbed the machine the Family Computer, or Famicom. The machine that his engineers designed was based on the controller, console, and plug in the cartridge format. It contained two custom chips—an 8-bit central processing unit and a graphics-processing unit. Both chips had been scaled down to perform only essential functions. A 16-bit processor was available at the time, but to keep costs down, Yamauchi refused to use it.

Nintendo approached Ricoh, the electronics giant, which had spare semiconductor capacity. Nintendo told Ricoh that the chips had to cost no more that 2,000 yen. Ricoh replied that the 2,000-yen price point was absurdly low. Yamauchi's response was to guarantee Ricoh a 3-million-chip order within 2 years. Since the leading companies in Japan were selling, at most, 30,000 video games per year at the time, it seemed like an outrageous commitment, but Ricoh agreed to the price given the size of the order.[7]

Another feature of the machine was its memory—2,000 bytes of random access memory (RAM), compared to the 256 bytes of RAM in the Atari machine. The result was a machine with superior graphics-processing capabilities and faster action that could handle more complex games than other consoles. Nintendo's engineers also built a new set of chips into the game cartridges. In addition to chips that held the game program, Nintendo developed memory map controller (MMC) chips that took over some of the graphics-processing work from the chips in the console and enabled the system to handle more complex games. Over time, Nintendo's engineers developed more powerful MMC chips, enabling the basic 8-bit system to do things that originally seemed out of reach. The engineers also figured out a way to include a battery backup system in cartridges that allowed games to store information independently, saving the state of the game so that a player could pick up where they had left off. In turn, this enabled game designers to create longer, more complex and engaging multilevel games that lasted not for minutes, but for hours or even days.

C16-3b The Games

Yamauchi recognized that great hardware would not sell itself. The key to the market, he reasoned, was great games. Yamauchi had instructed the engineers, when they were developing the hardware, to make sure that "it was appreciated by software engineers." Nintendo decided that it would become a haven for game designers. "An ordinary man," Yamauchi said, "cannot develop good games no matter how hard he tries. A handful of people in this world can develop games that everyone wants. Those are the people we want at Nintendo."[8]

Yamauchi had an advantage in Sigeru Miyamoto. Miyamoto had joined Nintendo at the age of 24. Yamauchi had hired Miyamoto, a graduate of Kanazawa Munici College of Industrial Arts, as a favor to his father and an old friend, although he had little idea what he would do with an artist. For 3 years, Miyamoto worked as Nintendo's staff artist. Then, in 1980, Yamauchi called Miyamoto into his office. Nintendo had started selling coin-operated video games, but one of the new games, *Radarscope*, was a disaster. Could Miyamoto come up with a new game? Miyamoto was delighted. He had always spent a lot of time drawing cartoons, and as a student, he had played video games constantly. Miyamoto believed that video games could be used to bring cartoons to life.[9]

The game Miyamoto developed was nothing short of a revelation. At a time when most coin-operated video games lacked characters or depth, Miyamoto created a game around a story that had both. Most games involved battles with space invaders or heroes shooting lasers at aliens; Miyamoto's game did neither. Based loosely on *Beauty and the Beast* and *King Kong,* Miyamoto's game involved a pet ape who runs off with his master's beautiful girlfriend. His master is an ordinary carpenter called Mario, who has a bulbous nose, a bushy mustache, a pair of large pathetic eyes, and a red cap (which Miyamoto added because he was not good at hairstyles). He does not carry a laser gun. The ape runs off with the girlfriend to get back at his master, who was not especially nice to the beast. The man, of course, has to get his girlfriend back by running up ramps, climbing ladders, jumping off elevators, and the like, while the ape throws objects at the hapless carpenter. Since the main character is an ape, Miyamoto called him Kong; because the main character is as stubborn as a donkey, he called the game *Donkey Kong.*

Released in 1981, *Donkey Kong* was a sensation in the world of coin-operated video arcades and a smash hit for Nintendo. In 1984, Yamauchi again summoned Miyamoto to his office. He needed more games, this time for Famicom. Miyamoto was made the head of a new research and development (R&D) group and told to come up with the most imaginative video games ever.

Miyamoto began with Mario from *Donkey Kong.* A colleague had told him that Mario looked more like a plumber than a carpenter, so a plumber he became. Miyamoto gave Mario a brother, Luigi, who was as tall and thin as Mario was short and fat. They became the Super Mario Brothers. Since plumbers spend their time working on pipes, large green sewer pipes became obstacles and doorways into secret worlds. Mario and Luigi's task was to search for the captive Princess Toadstool. Mario and Luigi are endearing bumblers, unequal to their tasks yet surviving. They shoot, squash, or evade their enemies—a potpourri of inventions that includes flying turtles and stinging fish, man-eating flowers, and fire-breathing dragons—while they collect gold coins, blow air bubbles, and climb vines into smiling clouds.[10]

Super Mario Brothers was introduced in 1985. For Miyamoto, this was just the beginning. Between 1985 and 1991, Miyamoto produced eight *Mario* games. About

60 to 70 million were sold worldwide, making Miyamoto the most successful game designer in the world. After adapting *Donkey Kong* for Famicom, he also went on to create other top-selling games, including multiple variations of *Super Mario Brothers* (e.g., *Mario Kart*) and another classic, *The Legend of Zelda*. While Miyamoto drew freely from folklore, literature, and pop culture, the main source for his ideas was his own experience. The memory of being lost among a maze of sliding doors in his family's home was re-created in the labyrinths of the *Zelda* games. The dog that attacked him when he was a child attacks Mario in *Super Mario*. As a child, Miyamoto had once climbed a tree to catch a view of far-off mountains and had become stuck. Mario gets himself in a similar fix. Once Miyamoto went hiking without a map and was surprised to stumble across a lake. In the *Legend of Zelda*, part of the adventure is in walking into new places without a map and being confronted by surprises.

C16-3c Nintendo in Japan

Nintendo introduced Famicom into the Japanese market in May 1983. Famicom was priced at $100, more than Yamauchi wanted, but significantly less than the products of competitors. When he introduced the machine, Yamauchi urged retailers to forgo profits on the hardware because it was just a tool to sell software, and that is where they would make their money. Backed by an extensive advertising campaign, 500,000 units of Famicom were sold in the first 2 months. Within a year, the figure stood at 1 million, and sales were still expanding rapidly. With the hardware quickly finding its way into Japanese homes, Nintendo was besieged with calls from retailers frantically demanding more games.

At this point, Yamauchi told Miyamoto to come up with the most imaginative games ever. However, Yamauchi also realized that Nintendo alone could not satisfy the growing thirst for new games, so he initiated a licensing program. To become a Nintendo licensee, companies had to agree to an unprecedented series of restrictions. Licensees could publish only five Nintendo games per year, and they could not write those titles for other platforms. The licensing fee was set at 20% of the wholesale price of each cartridge sold (game cartridges wholesaled for around $30). It typically cost $500,000 to develop a game and took around 6 months. Nintendo insisted that games not contain any excessively violent or sexually suggestive material and that they review every game before allowing it to be produced.[11]

Despite these restrictions, six companies (Bandai, Capcom, Konami, Namco, Taito, and Hudson) agreed to become Nintendo licensees, not least because millions of customers were now clamoring for games. Bandai was Japan's largest toy company. The others already made either coin-operated video games or computer software games. Because of these licensing agreements, they saw their sales and earnings surge. For example, Konami's earnings went from $10 million in 1987 to $300 million in 1991.

After the six licensees began selling games, reports of defective games began to reach Yamauchi. The original six licensees were allowed to manufacture their own game cartridges. Realizing that he had given away the ability to control the quality of the cartridges, Yamauchi decided to change the contract for future licensees. Future licensees were required to submit all manufacturing orders for cartridges to Nintendo. Nintendo charged licensees $14 per cartridge, required that they place a minimum order for 10,000 units (later the minimum order was raised to 30,000), and insisted on cash payment in full when the order was placed. Nintendo outsourced cartridge manufacturing to other companies, using the volume of its orders to get rock-bottom prices. The cartridges were estimated to cost Nintendo between $6 and $8 each. The licensees then picked up the cartridges from Nintendo's loading dock and were responsible for distribution. In 1985, there were 17 licensees. By 1987, there were 50. By this point, 90% of the home videogame systems sold in Japan were Nintendo systems.

C16-3d Nintendo in America

In 1980, Nintendo established a subsidiary in America to sell its coin-operated video games. Yamauchi's American-educated son-in-law, Minoru Arakawa, headed the subsidiary. All of the other essential employees were Americans, including Ron Judy and Al Stone. For its first 2 years, Nintendo of America (NOA), based originally in Seattle, struggled to sell second-rate games such as *Radarscope*. The subsidiary seemed on the brink of closing. NOA could not even make the rent payment on the warehouse. Then they received a large shipment from Japan: 2,000 units of a new coin-operated video game. Opening the box, they discovered *Donkey Kong*. After playing the game briefly, Judy proclaimed it a disaster. Stone walked out of the building, declaring that "it's over."[12] The managers were appalled. They could not imagine a game less likely to sell in video arcades. The only promising sign was that a 20-year employee rapidly became enthralled with the game.

Arakawa, however, knew he had little choice but to try to sell the machine. Judy persuaded the owner of the Spot Tavern near Nintendo's office to take one of the machines on a trial basis. After one night, Judy discovered $30 in the coin box, a phenomenal amount. The next night there was $35 and $36 the night after that. NOA had a hit on its hands.

By the end of 1982, NOA had sold over 60,000 copies of *Donkey Kong* and had booked sales in excess of $100 million. The subsidiary had outgrown its Seattle location. They moved to a new site in Redmond, a Seattle suburb, where they located next to a small but fast-growing software company called Microsoft.

By 1984, NOA was riding a wave of success in the coin-operated videogame market. Arakawa, however, was interested in the possibilities of selling Nintendo's new Famicom system in the United States. Throughout 1984, Arakawa, Judy, and Stone met with numerous toy and department store representatives to discuss the possibilities, only to be repeatedly rebuffed. Still smarting from the 1983 debacle, the representatives wanted nothing to do with the home videogame business. They also met with former managers from Atari and Caleco to gain their insights. The most common response they received was that the market collapsed because the last generation of games was awful.

Arakawa and his team decided that if they were going to sell Famicom in the United States, they would have to find a new distribution channel. The obvious choice was consumer electronics stores. Arakawa asked the R&D team in Kyoto to redesign Famicom for the U.S. market so that it looked less like a toy (Famicom was encased in red and white plastic), and more like a consumer electronics device. The redesigned machine was renamed the Nintendo Entertainment System (NES).

Arakawa's big fear was that illegal, low-quality Taiwanese games would flood the U.S. market if NES was successful. To stop counterfeit games being played on NES, Arakawa asked Nintendo's Japanese engineers to design a security system into the U.S. version of Famicom so that only Nintendo-approved games could be played on NES. The Japanese engineers responded by designing a security chip to be embedded in the game cartridges. NES would not work unless the security chips in the cartridges unlocked, or shook hands with, a chip in NES. Since the code embedded in the security chip was proprietary, the implication of this system was that no one could manufacture games for NES without Nintendo's specific approval.

To overcome the skepticism and reluctance of retailers to stock a home videogame system, Arakawa decided in late 1985 to make an extraordinary commitment. Nintendo would stock stores and set up displays and windows. Retailers would not have to pay for anything they stocked for 90 days. After that, retailers could pay Nintendo for what they sold and return the rest. NES was bundled with Nintendo's best-selling game in Japan, *Super Mario Brothers*. It was a low-risk proposition for retailers, but even with this, most were skeptical. Ultimately, 30 Nintendo personnel descended on the New York area. Referred to as the Nintendo SWAT team, they persuaded some stores to stock NES after an extraordinary blitz that involved 18-hour days. To support the New York product launch, Nintendo also committed itself to a $5 million advertising campaign aimed at the 7- to 14-year-olds who seemed to be Nintendo's likely core audience.

By December 1985, between 500 and 600 stores in the New York area were stocking Nintendo systems. Sales were moderate, about half of the 100,000 NES machines shipped from Japan were sold, but it was enough to justify going forward. The SWAT team then moved first to Los Angeles, then to Chicago, and then to Dallas. As in New York, sales started at a moderate pace, but by late 1986 they started to accelerate rapidly, and Nintendo went national with NES.

In 1986, around 1 million NES units were sold in the United States. In 1987, the figure increased to 3 million. In 1988, it jumped to over 7 million. In the same year, 33 million game cartridges were sold. Nintendo mania had arrived in the United States. To expand the supply of games, Nintendo licensed the rights to produce up to five games per year to 31 American software companies. Nintendo continued to use a restrictive licensing agreement that gave it exclusive rights to any games, required licensees to place their orders through Nintendo, and insisted on a 30,000-unit minimum order. [13]

By 1990, the home videogame market was worth $5 billion worldwide. Nintendo dominated the industry, with a 90% share of the market for game equipment. The parent company was, by some measures, now the most profitable company in Japan. By 1992, it was netting over $1 billion in gross profit annually, or more than $1.5 million for each employee in Japan. The company's stock market value exceeded that of Sony, Japan's premier consumer electronics firm. Indeed, the company's net profit exceeded that of all the American movie studios combined. Nintendo games, it seemed, were bigger than the movies.

As of 1991, there were over 100 licensees for Nintendo, and over 450 titles were available for NES. In the United States, Nintendo products were distributed through toy stores (30 percent of volume), mass merchandisers (40% of volume), and department stores (10% of volume). Nintendo tightly controlled the number of game titles and games that could be sold, quickly withdrawing titles as soon as interest appeared to decline. In 1988, retailers requested 110 million cartridges from Nintendo. Market surveys suggested that perhaps 45 million could have been sold, but Nintendo allowed only 33 million to be shipped.[14] Nintendo claimed that the shortage of games was in part due to a worldwide shortage of semiconductor chips.

Several companies had tried to reverse-engineer the code embedded in Nintendo's security chip, which competitors characterized as a lockout chip. Nintendo successfully sued them. The most notable was Atari Games, one of the successors of the original Atari, which in 1987 sued Nintendo of America for anticompetitive behavior. Atari claimed that the purpose of the security chip was to monopolize the market. At the same time, Atari announced that it had found a way around Nintendo's security chip and would begin to sell unlicensed games.[15] NOA responded with a countersuit. In a March 1991 ruling, Atari was found to have obtained Nintendo's security code illegally and was ordered to stop selling NES-compatible games. However, Nintendo did not always have it all its own way. In 1990, under pressure from Congress, the Department of Justice, and several lawsuits, Nintendo rescinded its exclusivity requirements, freeing up developers to write games for other platforms. However, developers faced a real problem: what platform could they write for?

C16-4 Sega's *Sonic* Boom

Sega was founded in 1954 by David Rosen, a 20-year-old American who settled in Japan after a tour of duty with the U.S. Air Force.[16] The company began as an operator of photo booths. In the 1960s, it diversified into the Japanese arcade business. As part of that business, Sega started to develop its own arcade games, some of which were successful not only in Japan, but also in the United States and Europe. When arcade games started to become electronic in the 1970s following the introduction of *Pong*, Sega invested in the development of electronic games.

Nintendo's success with the Famicom persuaded Sega to develop its own console for the home market. Launched in Japan in 1986, Sega's first offering, an 8-bit machine, never commanded more than 5 percent of the Japanese market. Sega, however, was not about to give up. From years in the arcade business, the company understood that great games drove sales. Sega also realized that more powerful technology gave game developers the tools to develop more appealing games. This philosophy underlay Sega's decision to develop a 16-bit game system, the Sega Genesis.

Sega took the design of its 16-bit arcade machine and adapted it for Genesis. Compared to Nintendo's 8-bit machine, the 16-bit console featured an array of superior technological features, including high-definition graphics and animation, a full spectrum of colors, two independent scrolling backgrounds that created an impressive depth of field, and near CD quality sound. The design strategy also made it easy to port Sega's catalog of successful arcade games to the Genesis.

The Genesis was launched in Japan in 1989 and in the United States in 1990. In the United States, the machine was priced at $199. The company hoped that sales would be boosted by the popularity of its arcade games, such as the graphically violent *Altered Beast*. Sega also licensed other companies to develop games for the Genesis console. In an effort to recruit licensees, Sega asked for lower royalty rates than Nintendo, and it gave licensees the right to manufacture their own cartridges. Independent game developers were slow to climb on board, however, and the $200 price tag for the console held back sales.

One of the first independent game developers to sign up with Sega was Electronic Arts. Established by three former Apple employees, Trip Hawkins, Electronic Arts had focused on designing games for personal computers and consequently had missed the Nintendo 8-bit era. Now Hawkins was determined to get a presence in the home video game market and aligning his company with Sega seemed to be the best option. The Nintendo playing field was already crowded, and Sega offered a far less restrictive licensing deal than Nintendo. Electronic Arts subsequently wrote several popular games for Genesis, including *John Madden* football and several gory combat games.[17]

Nintendo had not been ignoring the potential of the 16-bit system. Nintendo's own 16-bit system, Super NES, was ready for market introduction in 1989—at the same time as Sega's Genesis. Nintendo introduced Super NES in Japan in 1990, where it quickly established a strong market presence and outsold Sega's Genesis. In the United States, however, the company decided to hold back longer to reap the full benefits of the dominance it enjoyed with the 8-bit NES system. Yamauchi was also worried about the lack of backward compatibility between Nintendo's 8-bit and 16-bit systems. (The company had tried to make the 16-bit system so that it could play 8-bit games but concluded that the cost of doing so was prohibitive.) These concerns may have led the company to delay market introduction until the 8-bit market was saturated.

Meanwhile, in the United States, the Sega bandwagon was beginning to gain momentum. One development that gave the Genesis a push was the introduction of a new Sega game, *Sonic the Hedgehog*. Developed by an independent team that was contracted to Sega, the game featured a cute hedgehog that impatiently tapped his paw when the player took too long to act. Impatience was Sonic's central feature—he had places to go, and quickly. He zipped along, collecting brass rings when he could find them, before rolling into a ball and flying down slides with loops and underground tunnels. Sonic was Sega's Mario.

In mid-1991, in an attempt to jump-start slow sales, Tom Kalinske, head of Sega's American subsidiary, decided to bundle *Sonic the Hedgehog* with the game player.

He also reduced the price for the bundled unit to $150, and he relaunched the system with an aggressive advertising campaign aimed at teenagers. The campaign was built around the slogan "Genesis does what Nintendon't." The shift in strategy worked, and sales accelerated sharply.

Sega's success prompted Nintendo to launch its own 16-bit system. Nintendo's Super NES was introduced at $200. However, Sega now had a 2-year head start in games. By the end of 1991, about 125 game titles were available for the Genesis, compared to 25 for Super NES. In May 1992, Nintendo reduced the price of Super NES to $150. At this time, Sega was claiming a 63% share of the 16-bit market in the United States, and Nintendo claimed a 60% share. By now, Sega was cool. It began to take more chances with mass media–defined morality. When Acclaim Entertainment released its bloody *Mortal Kombat* game in September 1992, the Sega version let players rip off heads and tear out hearts. Reflecting Nintendo's image of their core market, its version was sanitized. The Sega version outsold Nintendo's two to one. [18] By January 1993, there were 320 titles available for Sega Genesis, and 130 for Super NES. In early 1994, independent estimates suggested that Sega had 60% of the U.S. market and Nintendo had 40%, figures Nintendo disputed.

C16-5 3DO

Trip Hawkins, whose first big success was Electronic Arts, founded 3DO in 1991.[19] Hawkins's vision for 3DO was to shift the home videogame business away from the existing cartridge-based format and toward a CD-ROM–based platform. The original partners in 3DO were Electronic Arts, Matsushita, Time Warner, AT&T, and the venture capital firm Kleiner Perkins. Collectively, they invested over $17 million in 3DO, making it the richest start-up in the history of the home videogame industry. 3DO went public in May 1993 at $15 per share. By October of that year, the stock had risen to $48 per share, making 3DO worth $1 billion—not bad for a company that had yet to generate a single dollar in revenues.

The basis for 3DO's $1 billion market cap was patented computer system architecture and a copyrighted operating system that allowed for much richer graphics and audio capabilities. The system was built around a 32-bit RISC microprocessor and proprietary graphics processor chips. Instead of a cartridge, the 3DO system stored games on a CD-ROM that was capable of holding up to 600 megabytes of content, sharply up from the 10 megabytes of content found in the typical game cartridge of the time. The slower access time of a CD-ROM compared to a cartridge was alleviated somewhat by the use of a double-speed CD-ROM drive. [20]

The belief at 3DO—a belief apparently shared by many investors—was that the superior storage and graphics-processing capabilities of the 3DO system would prove very attractive to game developers, allowing them to be far more creative. In turn, better games would attract customers away from Nintendo and Sega. Developing games that used the capabilities of a CD-ROM system altered the economics of game development. Estimates suggested that it would cost approximately $2 million to produce a game for the 3DO system and could take as long as 24 months to develop. However, at $2 per disc, a CD-ROM cost substantially less to produce than a cartridge.

The centerpiece of 3DO's strategy was to license its hardware technology for free. Game developers paid a royalty of $3 per disc for access to the 3DO operating code. Discs typically wholesaled for $30 each.

Matsushita introduced the first 3DO machine into the U.S. market in October 1993. Priced at $700, the machine was sold through electronic retailers that carried Panasonic high-end electronics products. Sega's Tom Kalinsky noted, "It's a noble effort. Some people will buy 3DO, and they'll have a wonderful experience. It's impressive, but it's a niche. We've done the research. It does not become a large market until you go below $500. At $300, it starts to get interesting. We make no money on hardware. It's a cutthroat business. I hope Matsushita understands that." [21] CD-ROM discs for the 3DO machine retailed for around $75. The machine came bundled with *Crash n Burn*, a high-speed combat racing game. However, only 18 3DO titles were available by the crucial Christmas period, although reports suggested that 150 titles were under development. [22]

Sales of the hardware were slow, reaching only 30,000 by January 1994. [23] In the same month, AT&T and Sanyo both announced that they would begin to manufacture the 3DO machine. In March, faced with continuing sluggish sales, 3DO announced that it would give hardware manufacturers two shares of 3DO stock for every unit sold at or below a certain retail price. Matsushita dropped the price of its machine to $500. About the same time, Toshiba, LG, and Samsung all announced that they would start to produce 3DO machines.

By June 1994, cumulative sales of 3DO machines in the United States stood at 40,000 units. Matsushita announced plans to expand distribution beyond the current 3,500 outlets to include the toy and mass merchandise channels. Hawkins and his partners announced that they would invest another $37 million in 3DO. By July, there were 750 3DO software licensees, but only 40 titles were available for the format. Despite these moves, sales continued at a very sluggish pace and the supply of new software titles started to dry up. [24]

By 1996, it was clear that 3DO's console was not gaining sufficient traction in the marketplace. Trip Hawkins' gambit had failed. In September 1996, 3DO announced that it would sell its hardware system business. [25] The company announced that about 150 people, one-third of the workforce, would probably lose their jobs in the restructuring. According to Trip Hawkins, 3DO would now focus on developing software for online gaming. Hawkins stated that the Internet and Internet entertainment constituted a huge opportunity for 3DO. The stock dropped $1.375 to $6.75.

C16-6 Sony's PlayStation

In the fall of 1995, Sony entered the fray with the introduction of the Sony PlayStation. [26] PlayStation used a 32-bit RISC microprocessor running at 33 MHz and using a double-speed CD-ROM drive. PlayStation cost an estimated $500 million to develop. The machine had actually been under development since 1991, when Sony decided that the home videogame industry was getting too big to ignore. Initially, Sony was in an alliance with Nintendo to develop the machine. Nintendo walked away from the alliance in 1992, however, after a disagreement over who owned the rights to any future CD-ROM games. Sony went alone. [27]

From the start, Sony felt that it could leverage its presence in the film and music business to build a strong position in the home video game industry. A consumer electronics giant with a position in the Hollywood movie business and the music industry (Sony owned Columbia Pictures and the Columbia record label), Sony believed that it had access to significant intellectual property that could form the basis of many popular games.

In 1991, Sony established a division in New York: Sony Electronic Publishing. The division was to serve as an umbrella organization for Sony's multimedia offerings. Headed by Iceland native Olaf Olafsson, then just 28 years old, this organization ultimately took the lead role in both the market launch of PlayStation and in developing game titles. [28] In 1993, as part of this effort, Sony purchased a well-respected British game developer, Psygnosis. By the fall of 1995, this unit had 20 games ready to complement PlayStation: *The Haldeman Diaries, Mickey Mania* (developed in collaboration with Disney), and *Johnny Mnemonic*, based on the William Gibson short story. To entice independent game developers such as Electronic Arts, Namco, and Acclaim Entertainment, Olafsson used the promise of low royalty rates. The standard royalty rate was set at $9 per disc, although developers that signed on early enough were given a lower royalty rate. Sony also provided approximately 4,000 game development tools to licensees in an effort to help them speed games to market. [29]

To distribute PlayStation, Sony set up a retail channel separate from Sony's consumer electronics sales force. It marketed the PlayStation as a hip and powerful alternative to the outdated Nintendo and Sega cartridge-based systems. Sony worked closely with retailers before the launch to find out how it could help them sell the PlayStation. To jump-start demand, Sony set up in-store displays to allow potential consumers to try the equipment. Just before the launch, Sony had lined up an impressive 12,000 retail outlets in the United States.[30]

Sony targeted its advertising for PlayStation at males in the 18- to 35-year age range. The targeting was evident in the content of many of the games. One of the big hits for PlayStation was *Tomb Raider*, whose central character, Lara Croft, combined sex appeal with savviness and helped to recruit an older generation to PlayStation.[31] PlayStation was initially priced at $299, and games retailed for as much as $60. Sony's Tokyo-based executives had reportedly been insisting on a $350–$400 price for PlayStation, but Olafsson pushed hard for the lower price. Because of the fallout from this internal battle, in January 1996, Olafsson resigned from Sony. By then, however, Sony was following Olafsson's script. [32]

Sony's prelaunch work was rewarded with strong early sales. By January 1996, more than 800,000 PlayStations had been sold in the United States, plus another 4 million games. In May 1996, with 1.2 million PlayStations shipped, Sony reduced the price of PlayStation to $199. Sega responded with a similar price cut for its Saturn. The prices on some of Sony's initial games were also reduced to $29.99. The weekend after the price cuts, retailers reported that PlayStation sales were up by between 350% and 1,000% over the prior week.[33] The sales surge continued through 1996. By the end of the year, sales of PlayStation and associated software amounted to $1.3 billion, out of a total for U.S. sales at $2.2 billion for all videogame hardware and software. In March 1997, Sony cut the price of PlayStation again, this time to $149. It also reduced its suggested retail price for games by $10 to $49.99. By this point, Sony had sold 3.4 million units of PlayStation in the United States, compared to Saturn's 1.6 million units.[34] Worldwide, PlayStation had outsold Saturn by 13 million to 7.8 million units, and Saturn sales were slowing. [35] The momentum was clearly running in Sony's favor, but the company now had a new challenge to deal with: Nintendo's latest generation game machine, the N64.

C16-7 Nintendo Strikes Back

In July 1996, Nintendo launched Nintendo 64 (N64) in the Japanese market. This release was followed by a late fall introduction in the United States. N64 is a 64-bit machine developed in conjunction with Silicon Graphics. Originally targeted for introduction a year earlier, N64 had been under development since 1993. The machine used a plug-in cartridge format rather than a CD-ROM drive. According to Nintendo, cartridges allow for faster access time and are far more durable than CD-ROMs (an important consideration with children).[36]

N64 was targeted at children and young teenagers. It was priced at $200 and launched with just four games. Despite the lack of games, initial sales were very strong. Indeed, 1997 turned out to be a banner year for both Sony and Nintendo. The overall U.S. market was strong, with sales of hardware and software combined reaching a record $5.5 billion. Estimates suggest that PlayStation accounted for 49% of machines and games by value. N64 captured a 41% share, leaving Sega trailing badly with less than 10% of the market. During the year, the average price for game machines had fallen to $150. By year-end, there were 300 titles available for PlayStation, compared to 40 for N64. Games for PlayStation retailed for $40, on average, compared to over $60 for N64.[37]

By late 1998, PlayStation was widening its lead over N64. In the crucial North American market, PlayStation was reported to be outselling N64 by a two-to-one margin, although Nintendo retained a lead in the under-12 category. At this point, there were 115 games available for N64 versus 431 for PlayStation.[38] Worldwide, Sony had now sold close to 55 million PlayStations. The success of PlayStation had a major impact on Sony's bottom line. In fiscal 1998, PlayStation business generated revenues of $5.5 billion for Sony, 10% of its worldwide revenues, but accounted for $886 million, or 22.5%, of the company's operating income.[39]

C16-8 Microsoft enters the fray

Microsoft was first rumored to be developing a videogame console in late 1999. In March 2000, Bill Gates made it official when he announced that Microsoft would enter the home videogame market in fall 2001 with a console code named Xbox. In terms of sheer computing power, the 128-bit Xbox had the edge over competitors. Xbox had a 733-megahertz Pentium III processor, a high-powered graphics chip from Nvidia Corp, a built-in broadband cable modem to allow for online game playing and high-speed Internet browsing, 64 megabytes of memory, CD and DVD drives, and an internal hard disk drive. The operating system was a stripped-down version of its popular Windows system optimized for graphics-processing capabilities. Microsoft claimed that because the Xbox was based on familiar Windows PC technology, it would be much easier for software developers to write games for, and it would be relatively easy to convert games from the PC to run on the Xbox.[40]

Although Microsoft was a new entrant to the videogame industry, it was no stranger to games. Microsoft had long participated in the PC gaming industry and was one of the largest publishers of PC games, with hits such as *Microsoft Flight Simulator* and *Age of Empires I and II* to its credit. Sales of Microsoft's PC games had increased 50% annually between 1998 and 2001, and the company accounted for about 10% of the PC game market by 2001. Microsoft had also offered online gaming for some time, including its popular MSN Gaming Zone site. Started in 1996, by 2001, the website had become the largest online PC gaming hub on the Internet with nearly 12 million subscribers paying $9.95 a month to play premium games such as *Asheron's Call* or *Fighter Ace*. Nor was Microsoft new to hardware; its joysticks and game pads outsold all other brands, and it had an important mouse business.

To build the Xbox, Microsoft chose Flextronics, a contract manufacturer that already made computer mice for Microsoft. Realizing that it would probably have to cut Xbox prices over time, Microsoft guaranteed Flextronics a profit margin, effectively agreeing to subsidize Flextronics if selling prices fell below a specified amount. By 2003, Microsoft was thought to be losing $100 on every Xbox sold. To make that back and turn a profit, Microsoft reportedly had to sell between six and nine video games per Xbox.[41]

Analysts speculated that Microsoft's entry into the home videogame market was a response to a potential threat from Sony. Microsoft was worried that Internet-ready consoles might take over many web-browsing functions from the personal computer. Some in the company described Internet-enabled videogame terminals as Trojan horses in the living room. In Microsoft's calculation, it made sense to get in the market to try and keep Sony and others in check. With annual revenues of more than $20 billion worldwide, by 2003, the home videogame market was an important source of potential growth for Microsoft. Still, by moving away from its core market, Microsoft was taking a big risk, particularly given the scale of investments required to develop the Xbox, reported to run as high as $1.5 billion.

C16-8a Mortal Combat: Microsoft versus Sony

Entering the market in late 2001, Microsoft found itself engaged in head-to-head competition with Sony's latest offering, the 128-bit PlayStation 2 (PS2), which had been launched in Japan in early 2000 and the United States in October 2000. Initially priced at $299, PlayStation 2 was a powerful machine. At its core was a 300-megahertz graphics processing chip that was jointly developed with Toshiba and consumed about $1.3 billion in R&D. Referred to as the Emotion Engine processor, the chip allowed the machine to display graphic images previously found only on supercomputers.

The machine was set up to play different CD and DVD formats, as well as proprietary game titles. As was true with the original PlayStation, PS2 could play audio CDs. The system was also compatible with the original PlayStation: any PlayStation title could be played on the PS2. To help justify the initial price tag, the unit doubled as a DVD player with picture quality as good as current players. The PlayStation 2 did not come equipped with a modem, but it did have networking capabilities and a modem could be attached using one of two USB ports.[42]

Nintendo also upped its game, introducing its own 128-bit console, the GameCube, in late 2001. Nintendo tried to make the GameCube easy for developers to work with rather than focusing on raw peak performance. While developers no doubt appreciated this, by the time GameCube hits store shelves in late 2001, the PS2 had been on the market for 18 months and boasted a solid library of games. Despite its strong brand and instantly recognized intellectual property that included *Donkey Kong, Super Mario Brothers*, and the Pokémon characters, Nintendo was playing catchup to Sony.

Although both Xbox and Nintendo initially racked up strong sales, the momentum started to slow significantly in 2002. By September 2002, Sony had sold 11.2 million units of PS2 in the United States, versus 2.2 million units of Xbox and 2.7 million units of Nintendo's Game Cube. Unable to hold onto market share in the wake of the new competition, in late 2002, Sega withdrew from the console market, announcing that henceforth, it would focus just on developing games for other platforms.

In June 2002, Sony responded to the new entry by cutting the price for PS2 from $299 to $199. Microsoft quickly followed, cutting the price for Xbox from $299 to $199, while Nintendo cut its price from $299 to $149.[43] A year later, Sony cut prices again, this time to $179 a console. Again, Microsoft followed with a similar price cut, and in March 2004 it took the lead, cutting Xbox prices to $149. Sony followed suit 2 months later.[44]

Microsoft's strategy, however, involved far more than just cutting prices. In November 2002, Microsoft announced that it would introduce a new service for gamers, Xbox Live. For $50 a year, Xbox Live subscribers with broadband connections would be able to play online enabled versions of Xbox games with other online subscribers. To support Xbox Live, Microsoft invested some $500 million in its own data centers to host online game playing.

Online game playing was clearly a strategic priority for Microsoft from the outset. Unlike the PS2 and Game Cube, Xbox came with a built-in broadband capability. The decision to make the Xbox broadband capable was made back in 1999 when less than 5% of U.S. homes were linked to the Internet with a broadband connection. Explaining the decision to build broadband capabilities into the Xbox at a time when rivals lacked them, the head of Xbox, Jay Allard, noted that "my attitude has always been to bet on the future, not against it."[45] While Sony's PS2 could be hooked up to the Internet via a broadband connection, doing so required purchase of a special network adapter for $40.

By mid-2003, Xbox Live had some 500,000 subscribers, versus 80,000 who had registered to play PlayStation 2 games online. By this point in time, there were 28 online games for Xbox and 18 for PS2. By January 2004, the comparative figures stood at 50 for Microsoft and 32 for Sony. By mid-2004, Xbox Live reportedly had over 1 million subscribers, with Sony claiming a similar number of online players.[46] In May 2004, Microsoft struck a deal with Electronic Arts, the world's largest videogame publisher, to bring EA games, including its best-selling *Madden Football*, to the Xbox Live platform. Until this point, EA had only produced live games for Sony's platform.

Despite all these strategic moves, by late 2004, Xbox was still a distant second of PS2 in the videogame market having sold 14 million consoles against Sony's 70 million (Nintendo had sold 13 million GameCube consoles by this point). While Sony was making good money from the business, Microsoft was registering significant losses. In fiscal 2004, Microsoft's home and entertainment division, of which Xbox is the major component, registered $2.45 billion in revenues but lost $1.135 billion. By way of contrast, Sony's game division had $7.5 billion of sales in fiscal 2004 and generated operating profits of $640 million.

Microsoft, however, indicated that it was in the business for the long term. In late 2004, the company got a boost from the release of *Halo 2*, the sequel to *Halo*, one of its best-selling games. As first day sales for *Halo 2* were totaled up, executives at Sony had to be worried. Microsoft announced that *Halo 2* had sales of $125 million in its first 24 hours on the market in the United States and Canada, an industry record. These figures put *Halo 2* firmly on track to be one of the biggest video games ever with a shot at surpassing Nintendo's *Super Mario 64*, which had sold $308 million in the Unites States since its September 1996 debut. Moreover, the company was rumored to be ahead of Sony by as much as a year to bring the next-generation videogame console to market. In late 2004, reports suggest that Xbox 2 would be on the market in time for the 2005 Christmas season, probably a full year ahead of Sony's PlayStation 3. Sony was rumored to be running into technical problems as it tries to develop PlayStation 3.[47]

C16-9 The Next Generation

Over the next 15 years, Microsoft, Sony, and Nintendo continued to battle it out in the console market. Each company developed and released newer, more powerful, versions of their respective consoles with higher graphics resolution, higher framerates, high-speed internal storage, and backward compatibility with earlier systems. In 2020, Sony launched its fifth-generation console, the PS5, while Microsoft offered its fourth-generation consoles, the Xbox Series X and Series S. Meanwhile, Nintendo was on its eighth-generation console, the Nintendo Switch, which was first introduced in March 2017. Sony and Microsoft competed in the hard-core gaming segment of the market, while Nintendo continued to focus on a younger demographic, and on casual gamers.

By 2021, the console segment of the broader videogame market generated revenues of around $65 billion, up from $35 billion in 2018.[48] Breaking these revenues down, 34% were attributed to sales of hardware, 25% to sales of packaged games, and 41% to online revenue, which included digital downloads of complete games and subscription fees for services that streamed games to consoles.[49] Sony was estimated to have a 46% share of the global market for console hardware and games in 2021, Nintendo had a 29% share, while Microsoft had a 25% share.[50] Forecasts suggested that the console gaming market would continue to expand, reaching over $100 billion worldwide by 2026. Console games accounted for about 28% of total videogame market revenues in 2021, with smartphone games (45%), PC games (19%), and tablet games (7%) accounting for the remainder.[51] In total, over 3 billion people worldwide now played video games.

The technological advancements contained in successive generations of consoles enabled game developers to write increasingly realistic and complex games. The downside of this is that even with development tools that reduce programming costs, the costs of developing leading-edge video games for consoles continued to rise with each successive generation. The costs of developing complex console games are estimated to be between $15 million and $30 million, with development times stretching out to between 24 and 36 months.[52] Top-of-the-line "AAA" games can cost significantly more than this. For example, Activision's *Call of Duty: Modern Warfare 2*, which was released in 2009, reportedly cost some $50 million to develop. In addition, Activision spent another $200 million promoting the game. *Grand Theft Auto IV*, released in 2008, reportedly had a development budget of $100 million. More recently, unconfirmed estimates suggest that Microsoft may have spent as much as $500 million to develop and market *Halo Infinite*, the sixth addition to Microsoft's long running *Halo* franchise, which was released in late 2021.[53]

As the cost of game development have surged, so have the risks. If an expensive game fails in the marketplace, it can take down the developer. For example, Majesco, a mid-sized game developer, saw its stock price crash after two highly anticipated console games–*Psychonauts* and *Advent Rising*–failed to gain a following among gamers. The high risks associated with developing console games favor large game publishers, who can spread development risks over a wide portfolio of offerings. In addition, the risks have created a tendency for publishers to focus on developing new editions (or expansions) to successful franchises–such as *Halo, Call of Duty, Gears of War*, or *Grand Theft Auto*–since these games already have an established user base.[54]

The important role of successful franchises has increased the bargaining power of game developers, relative to console companies. Microsoft and Sony often vie with each other to be the first to offer a new expansion of a successful franchise on their platform. While the implications of this for royalty rates are not public, it seems likely that the consoled companies must accept lower royalty rates on popular game franchises to lock in exclusivity, or to gain an earlier release to a new edition of a best-selling game. This may have increased the bargaining power of successful game developers such as Activision Blizzard and Electronic Arts.

Given the changing economics of the industry, all three console companies have increased their investment in their own game studios, developing their own in-house games and reducing their reliance on third-party developers. For example, as of late 2021, Sony reportedly had 25 different exclusive games in development for the PS5.[55] Microsoft too has several exclusive games developed in-house, including *Halo* and *Gears of War*. Significantly, the original versions of these games were created by third-party developers, who were then acquired and bought into Xbox Game Studios, the company's own in-house development arm. The original version of *Halo*, for example, was developed by Bungie Studios, which was acquired by Microsoft in 2000.

Microsoft now has 23 game development studios within Xbox Game Studios. Several of these studios have been added through acquisitions. In 2014, Microsoft acquired Mojang AB, the developer of the best-selling game *Minecraft*, for $2.5 billion. *Minecraft*, however, is not exclusive to Xbox and Microsoft continues to develop it for multiple platforms, including Sony's PlayStation. The Mojang acquisition was followed in 2020 by the acquisition of ZeniMax Media for $7.5 billion. ZeniMax had developed several successful games including *Doom, The Elder Scrolls,* and *Fallout*. In early 2022, Microsoft rocked the industry when it made a $68.7 billion bid for Activision Blizzard, one of the top three videogame companies in the world, and publisher of several major game franchises including *World of Warcraft, Call of Duty, Diablo*, and *Overwatch*. To gain the approval of regulators, Microsoft has indicated that it will continue to make versions of Activision's games for other platforms, including Sony's PlayStation.

Another significant development in the industry has been the ongoing shift towards streaming games over the Internet, either to just consoles, or increasingly to a variety of platforms including PCs, tablets, and smartphones. This "any screen strategy" has been facilitated by the development of cloud computing infrastructure, high-bandwidth wired and wireless links, and the increasing power of digital devices including PCs, tablets, and smartphones. Microsoft's heavy investments in its Azure cloud computing infrastructure is seen by many as giving it a distinct advantage in the streaming business. Taken to its logical conclusion, some in the industry believe that the growth of cloud-based game streaming services may mean that there will come a time when dedicated consoles are obsolete.

Microsoft pioneered the online gaming business model among console companies with its Xbox Live service, introduced in 2002. Xbox Live now allows for multiplayer games online, for the digital distribution of games to consoles, and for streaming games to consoles and other devices. By 2021, Xbox Live had more than 100 million active users. The premium Xbox Live Game Pass service, which allows subscribers to stream games from a curated library for a monthly fee, had over 18 million subscribers in 2021, up from 10 million in early 2020. Estimates suggest that by mid-2022 there were some 25–30 million Game Pass subscribers, with some industry observers speculating that the Activision Blizzard acquisition could add tens of millions more to Game Pass.[56]

Sony too, has a growing presence in the online arena via its PlayStation Plus offering. Like Xbox live, PlayStation Plus supports multiplayer games, digital downloads, and game streaming. As of March 2022, Sony had some 47.4 million active subscribers to its premium PS Plus offering, and 106 million users in total, putting it ahead of Microsoft. However, Microsoft's streaming service appears to be growing faster, with the pending Activision Blizzard acquisition potentially vaulting Microsoft into the lead.

This case is intended to be used as a basis for class discussion rather than as an illustration of either effective or ineffective handling of the situation. Reprinted by permission of Charles W. L. Hill.

Notes

[1]A good account of the early history of Bushnell and Atari can be found in S. Cohen, *Zap! The Rise and Fall of Atari* (New York: McGraw-Hill, 1984).

[2]R. Isaacs, "Video Games Race to Catch a Changing Market," *BusinessWeek*, December 26, 1977, p. 44B.

[3]P. Pagnano, "Atari's Game Plan to Overwhelm Its Competitors," *BusinessWeek*, May 8, 1978, p. 50F; and D. Sheff, *Game Over* (New York: Random House, 1993).

[4]S. Cohen, *Zap! The Rise and Fall of Atari* (New York: McGraw-Hill, 1984).

[5]L. Kehoe, "Atari Seeks Way out of Video Game Woes," *Financial Times*, December 14, 1983, p. 23.

[6]M. Schrage, "The High Tech Dinosaurs: Video Games, Once Ascendant, Are Making Way," *Washington Post*, July 31, 1983, p. F1.

[7]D. Sheff, *Game Over* (New York: Random House, 1993).

[8]Quoted in D. Sheff, *Game Over* (New York: Random House, 1993), p. 38.

[9]D. Sheff, *Game Over* (New York: Random House, 1993).

[10]D. Golden, "In Search of Princess Toadstool," *Boston Globe,* November 20, 1988, p. 18.

[11]N. Gross and G. Lewis, "Here Come the Super Mario Bros.," *BusinessWeek*, November 9, 1987, p. 138.

[12]D. Sheff, *Game Over* (New York: Random House, 1993).

[13]D. Golden, "In Search of Princess Toadstool," *Boston Globe,* November 20, 1988, p. 18.

[14]Staff Reporter, "Marketer of the Year," *Adweek*, November 27, 1989, p. 15.

[15]C. Lazzareschi, "No Mere Child's Play," *Los Angeles Times*, December 16, 1988, p. 1.

[16]For a good summary of the early history of Sega, see J. Battle and B. Johnstone, "The Next Level: Sega's

Plans for World Domination," *Wired*, release 1.06, December 1993.

[17]D. Sheff, *Game Over* (New York: Random House, 1993).

[18]J. Battle and B. Johnstone, "The Next Level: Sega's Plans for World Domination," *Wired*, release 1.06, December 1993.'

[19]For background details, see J. Flower, "3DO: Hip or Hype?" *Wired*, release 1.02, May/June 1993.

[20]R. Brandt, "3DO's New Game Player: Awesome or Another Betamax?" *BusinessWeek*, January 11, 1993, p. 38.

[21]J. Flower, "3DO: Hip or Hype?" *Wired*, release 1.02, May/June 1993.

[22]S. Jacobs, "Third Time's a Charm (They Hope)," *Wired*, release 2.01, January 1994.

[23]A. Dunkin, "Video Games: The Next Generation," *BusinessWeek*, January 31, 1994, p. 80.

[24]J. Greenstein, "No Clear Winners, Though Some Losers; the Video Game Industry in 1995," *BusinessWeek*, December 22, 1995, p. 42.

[25]Staff Reporter, "3DO Says 'I Do' on Major Shift of Its Game Strategy," *Los Angeles Times*, September 17, 1996, p. 2.

[26]S. Taves, "Meet Your New Playmate," *Wired*, release 3.09, September 1995.

[27]I. Kunni, "The Games Sony Plays," *BusinessWeek*, June 15, 1998, p. 128.

[28]C. Platt, "WordNerd," *Wired*, release 3.10, October 1995.

[29]I. Kunni, "The Games Sony Plays," *BusinessWeek*, June 15, 1998, p. 128.

[30]J. A. Trachtenberg, "Race Quits Sony Just Before U.S. Rollout of Its PlayStation Video-Game System,"

Wall Street Journal, August 8, 1995, p. B3.

[31]S. Beenstock, "Market Raider: How Sony Won the Console Game," *Marketing*, September 10, 1998, p. 26.

[32]J. A. Trachtenberg, "Olafsson Calls It Quits as Chairman of Sony's Technology Strategy Group," *Wall Street Journal*, January 23, 1996, p. B6.

[33]J. Greenstein, "Price Cuts Boost Saturn, PlayStation Hardware Sales," *Video Business*, May 31, 1996, p. 1.

[34]J. Greenstein, "Sony Cuts Prices of PlayStation Hardware," *Video Business*, March 10, 1997, p. 1.

[35]D. Hamilton, "Sega Suddenly Finds Itself Embattled," *Wall Street Journal,* March 31, 1997, p. A10.

[36]Staff Reporter, "Nintendo Wakes Up," *The Economist*, August 3, 1996, pp. 55–56.

[37]D. Takahashi, "Game Plan: Video Game Makers See Soaring Sales Now—And Lots of Trouble Ahead," *Wall Street Journal*, June 15, 1998, p. R10.

[38]D. Takahashi, "Sony and Nintendo Battle for Kids Under 13," *Wall Street Journal*, September 24, 1998, p. B4.

[39]I. Kunni, "The Games Sony Plays," *BusinessWeek*, June 15, 1998, p. 128.

[40]D. Takahashi, "Microsoft's X-Box Impresses Game Developers," *Wall Street Journal,* March 13, 2000, p. B12.

[41]K. Powers, "Showdown," *Forbes*, August 11, 2003, pp. 86–87.

[42]T. Oxford and S. Steinberg, "Ultimate Game Machine Sony's PlayStation 2 Is Due on Shelves Oct. 26. It Brims with Potential—But at This Point Sega's Dreamcast

Appears a Tough Competitor," *Atlanta Journal/Atlanta Constitution*, October 1, 2000, p. P1.

[43]*The Economist*, "Console Wars," June 22, 2002, p. 71.

[44]R. A. Guth, "Game Gambit: Microsoft to cut Xbox price*," Wall Street Journal*, March 19, 2004, p. B1.

[45]K. Powers, "Showdown," *Forbes*, August 11, 2003, pp. 86–87.

[46]E. Taub, "No Longer a Solitary Pursuit: Video Games Move Online," *New York* Times, July 5, 2004, p. C4.

[47]J. Greene and C. Edwards, "Microsoft Plays Video Leapfrog," *BusinessWeek*, May 10, 2004, pp. 44–45.

[48]"$65.4 Billion Worldwide Console Games Industry to 2031," *Business Wire*, April 4, 2022.

[49]A. Palumbo, "Xbox Expected to Gain Console Software Market Share," *wccftech*, March 25, 2022.

[50]"Console Market Reaches New Heights with Growth to $60 Billion," *Ampere Analysis*, March 1, 2022.

[51]"Console Gaming Statistics, 2022," *wepc.com*, accessed September 8, 2022.

[52]C. Morris, "As Video Game Development Costs Rise, So Do Risks," *CNBC*, September 13, 2013.

[53]D. Trock, "How Much Did Halo Infinite Cost to Make?," *Gamer Journal*, December 27, 2021.

[54]C. Morris, "As Video Game Development Costs Rise, So Do Risks," *CNBC*, September 13, 2013.

[55]J. Moore, "As PS5 Turns a Year Old, More Than 25 Exclusives Are Currently in Development," *IGN*, November 12, 2021.

[56]J. Corden, "Could Xbox Game Pass Really Hit 100 Million Subscribers?," *windowscentral.com*, accessed September 8, 2022.

SpaceX: Disrupting the Space Industry

By Melissa Schilling

In October of 2022, SpaceX was valued at $127 billion, making it one of the most valuable privately held companies in the world.[1] In just 20 years since its founding, the company had developed revolutionary space vehicle technology including the world's first reusable orbital class rocket (the Falcon 9) and the world's most powerful rocket (the Starship). Perhaps even more remarkable, the company offered commercial space launches at a price dramatically lower than that offered by its leading competitors. It was estimated that by 2022, SpaceX had already seized over 65% of the global market share for commercial space launches.[2] The meteoric rise of SpaceX, a start-up from an industry outsider, was completely rewriting the rules of competition in the space industry.

C17-1 Musk's Moonshot Idea: Colonizing Mars

In 2002, Elon Musk was 31 years old, had $180 million, and was trying to decide what to do with the rest of his life.[3] He had already created and sold one of the first successful internet portals, Zip2, a platform that enabled newspapers to create and host their own online "city guides." The timing of the venture had been perfect; in the mid-1990s, the penetration of the Internet had grown exponentially, but most businesses did not yet fully understand how to harness it. As Musk noted, "When we tried to get funding in November 1995, more than half the venture capitalists we met with didn't know what the internet was and had not used it."[4] Soon, Musk's company was hosting the websites of nearly 200 media companies, including the *New York Times'* local directory site called "New York Today" and newspapers owned by Hearst, Times Mirror, and Pulitzer Publishing.[5] In February of 1999, Compaq bought Zip2 for $307 million in hopes that it could use the platform to help one of its other products, AltaVista, become a top portal for search, media, and shopping.[6]

Musk then founded an online financial services and email payment company called X.com. This company later merged with a company called Confinity that had developed a person-to-person email system called PayPal, and the merged companies worked together to make PayPal the most successful online payment system in the world. When eBbay bought PayPal for $1.5 billion in stock in 2002, Musk personally got $165 million from the sale.

Musk now had a pretty serious nest egg and wondered what he should do next. Money no longer motivated him; instead, he wondered what he could do that would be most important to the world. Worried about the human population's overreliance on finite energy sources, he helped to build Tesla Motors and Solar City during this time, but another unusual possibility had also begun to take shape in his mind. Musk had been very disturbed to discover that NASA had no intentions of going to Mars, and he began to ponder what it would take. The major problem was not one of technological feasibility, he concluded, but rather expense. Rockets could get into orbit, but they were expensive, and typically not reusable. This, he reasoned, was like throwing away your Boeing 747 after every flight across the Atlantic and it made space travel ludicrously impractical. Musk made the astonishing decision to pick up where NASA had left off.

Musk began to study rocket science texts such as *Rocket Propulsion Elements, Fundamentals of Astrodynamics*, and *Aerothermodynamics of Gas Turbine and Rocket Propulsion*. He traveled to Russia with Jim Cantrell, Adeo Ressi, and Mike Griffin to see if he could buy an affordable intercontinental ballistic missile to use as a launch vehicle. Though the team met with the Russians three times over a period of 4 months, in the end, when Musk suggested he wanted two missiles for $8 million, the Russians sent him away, telling him his plan was impossible. As Cantrell recounted, "They looked at us like we were not credible people...One of their chief designers spit on me and Elon because he thought we were full of shit."[7] On the plane ride home, as Griffin, Ressi, and Cantrell somberly toasted the end of the Russian expedition, Musk sat in the row in front of them, frenetically typing on his computer. Suddenly he wheeled around showing them a spreadsheet, and said, "Hey, guys, I think we can build this rocket ourselves."[8]

The other men were skeptical, to say the least. However, Musk passed his computer over to Griffin and Cantrell, showing them a document that detailed the cost of materials needed to build, assemble, and launch a rocket. Musk's calculations suggested that they could build a modest-sized rocket that would specialize in carrying smaller satellites and research payloads to space, and they could do so much cheaper than what the Russians were offering. The spreadsheet also laid out the performance characteristics of the rocket in impressive detail. Cantrell recalls, "I looked at it and said, I'll be damned—*that's* why he's been borrowing all my books. He'd been borrowing all my college textbooks on rocketry and propulsion. You know, whenever anybody asks Elon how he learned to build rockets, he says, 'I read books.' Well, it's true. He *devoured* those books. He knew everything. He's the smartest guy I've ever met, and he'd been planning to build a rocket all along."[9]

Investing $100 million of his own funds, Musk founded a company in June 2002 in Hawthorne California called Space Exploration—or SpaceX—and began developing a method that would streamline the production of rockets that could be used more than once. If NASA was not going to bring humanity to Mars, Musk would do it himself.

Creating a rocket company is an expensive and risky venture and most of the space industry found it highly improbable that an outsider with a small team and budget could be successful. As Tom Mueller, one of SpaceX's first engineers notes, "At TRW I had an army of people and government funding. Now we were going to make a low-cost rocket with a small team. People just didn't think it could be done."[10]

Musk, however, felt that the space industry was overdue for modernization. Aerospace companies had little competition and made extremely expensive high-performance rockets for every launch. Musk, on the other hand, intended to apply Silicon Valley's techniques of running lean and capitalizing on massive advancements in computing and materials technology. Musk's conversations with aerospace contractors convinced him that they all charged too much money and worked too slowly. He decided that SpaceX should try to make as much of the componentry as possible inhouse, including engines, guidance systems, and more. SpaceX would ultimately become an extremely vertically integrated rocket company. These decisions also made it easy to recruit the brightest of engineers—young aeronautics experts were keen to design rockets from the ground up and work for an exciting company without the bureaucracy of a government contractor.

On March 24, 2006, the first Falcon 1, a two-stage rocket,[1] was launched from the Kwajalein Islands as a nervous Musk and others watched. Twenty-five seconds into the flight a fire broke out on the rocket and it began to spin and fall back to Earth. It took a year to build a new Falcon 1. On March 21, 2007, the second Falcon 1 was launched, and this one made it to the 5-minute mark, successfully separating the first stage of the rocket from the second stage, with the second stage continuing into orbit. The team was elated and began to breathe easier. However, just after the 5-minute mark passed the second stage of the rocket started to wobble and then break apart. It was a devastating blow to SpaceX employees; many had spent almost 2 years shuttling between California and Kwajalein working to prepare for this launch.

Musk assured everyone that he would persist until they were successful, but everyone knew there was a risk that the company would simply run out of money. Unlike traditional aerospace companies that had huge multi-year government contracts, most of SpaceX's funding had come from Musk's personal savings, and SpaceX and Musk's other major venture, Tesla Motors, had already burned through more than half of Musk's cash. Kevin Brogan, one of SpaceX's first employees remembered, "We were burning through a hundred thousand dollars per day...Sometimes he wouldn't let you buy a part for two thousand dollars because he expected you to find it cheaper or invent something cheaper. Other times, he wouldn't flinch at renting a plane for ninety thousand dollars to get something to Kwaj because it saved an entire workday, so it was worth it."[11]

The third Falcon 1 was launched on August 2, 2008. The launch initially appeared to go perfectly, but at the moment the stages were supposed to separate, unexpected thrust from the first stage caused it to bump the second stage and damage it. Both parts then fell to Earth. As recounted by Dolly Singh, a recruiter at SpaceX, "It was like the worst [expletive] day ever. You don't usually see grown-ups weeping but there they were. We were tired and broken emotionally."[12] An exhausted and discouraged Musk tried to keep a positive front, telling the team: "Look. We are going to do this. It's going to be okay. Don't freak out."[13] Musk knew, however, that a fourth flight would be the last—he had spent $100 million on SpaceX and had no more money to inject into the company because the rest had all gone into Tesla Motors. There simply wouldn't be enough money for a fifth launch.

On September 28, 2008, the team prepared for the fourth Falcon 1 launch. The employees had worked non-stop shifts under intense pressure to reach this point, many of them separated from their families for long periods, living on the tiny island near the launch site under difficult conditions. Now many were queasy with anxiety about what would happen on this launch. This fourth launch, at last, went perfectly. Nine minutes into its journey, the Falcon 1 reached orbit, making it the first privately built space vehicle ever to do so. The employees of SpaceX roared their cheers, and many (including Musk) fought back tears.

Antonio Gracias, chief executive officer of Valor Equity Partners, investor in both Tesla and SpaceX, and Musk's friend, noted how deeply impressed he was by Musk's strength and resolve during this time: "He has this ability to work harder and endure more stress than anyone I've ever met. What he went through in 2008 would have broken anyone else. He didn't just survive. He kept working and stayed focused." He adds, "Most people who are under that sort of pressure fray. Their decisions go bad. Elon gets hyperrational. He's still able to make very clear, long-term decisions. The

---

[1]Multi-stage rockets are designed so that different parts of the rocket have their own engine and propellant. This enables stages to be separated from the rocket after they have used up their fuel, thereby reducing the mass of the rest of the craft.

harder it gets, the better he gets. Anyone who saw what he went through firsthand came away with more respect for the guy. I've just never seen anything like his ability to take pain."[14]

The successful launch was a watershed moment that reinvigorated everyone's faith in the company, but SpaceX was still in a financially precarious position. It already had two other projects under way, the Falcon 9 (a much bigger rocket), and the Dragon capsule (a reusable cargo spacecraft that would be launched by the Falcon 9 and used to deliver supplies to the International Space Station), and Musk had to borrow money from his friends just to make the company's payroll. To make matters worse, Tesla Motors was also in dire financial straits—both companies were on the verge of bankruptcy. However, on December 23, SpaceX was notified that NASA would be awarding the company a $1.6 billion contract to service the Space Station, effectively saving the company. Then on December 24, just hours before Tesla would have entered bankruptcy, Musk negotiated an investment from Draper Fisher Jurvetson that saved the auto company. As the deals went through, Musk broke down in tears.

C17-2 Next Steps

Having demonstrated the company's ability to successfully launch the Falcon 1, SpaceX turned its attention to its other, even bigger projects. First, it developed the Falcon 9, a rocket with nine Merlin engines and the ability to able to carry just over 50,000 pounds into orbit. The Falcon 9 was designed to be human-rated, requiring extreme reliability. Its avionics and controls were made triple-redundant, and according to Musk its flight computers will "issue the right commands even if there's severe damage to the system." The Falcon 9 can also keep flying if it suffers an engine shutdown; after about 90 seconds, it can even survive a second engine shutdown.[15]

By 2010, SpaceX proved that the Falcon 9 could carry the Dragon capsule into space and then the capsule could be recovered safely after an ocean landing. In 2012, the SpaceX Dragon capsule became the first private company to dock with the International Space Station. In 2015, SpaceX demonstrated its Falcon 9 could be vertically landed, the first time this had been achieved for an orbital class rocket, and then in 2017 it successfully reused a Falcon 9 in a second flight, achieving what most stalwarts of the space industry had said was impossible.

The Falcon 9 competed directly against the Delta IV and Atlas V launch systems made by United Launch Alliance (ULA), a joint venture of Boeing and Lockheed Martin. The Delta and Atlas launch families had been the standard space launch systems used by the U.S. government for more than 50 years, carrying payloads including weather, telecommunications, and national security satellites, as well as deep space and interplanetary exploration missions in support of scientific research. ULA had a virtual monopoly before SpaceX's jarring arrival,[16] but after the introduction of the Falcon 9, it was clear that the space industry had changed. Traditionally in the United States, rockets were designed by government agencies (e.g., NASA) and then companies like Lockheed Martin were commissioned to build them as external contractors. Now for the first time, the government could choose from rockets designed and built by a private U.S. company that were not only as powerful as those designed by NASA, but were also remarkably less expensive. Launch contracts awarded to SpaceX and ULA by the U.S. Air Force in 2018, for example, indicated that ULA's launch prices for the Atlas V were almost double those for the Falcon 9. The government decided to give both companies contracts because having two launch companies better assured the U.S. government's access to space; however, it was clear that pressure would now be on ULA to bring their costs down as well. This was implicitly stated by Air Force Secretary Heather Wilson in her testimony to the U.S. House Defense Appropriations subcommittee, "The cost of launch is plummeting" and commercial space ventures now "have multiple choices" ... "We're coming to a point," she said, that low-cost launchers are "enabling business plans to close in space that never were possible before."[17]

In 2011, SpaceX had also began developing the Falcon Heavy, which at the time was by far the world's most powerful rocket (see Figure 1) with 27 Merlin engines and the ability to carry 140,660 pounds into orbit. Falcon Heavy's maiden

Figure 1 Rocket Size and Payload Comparison, 2022

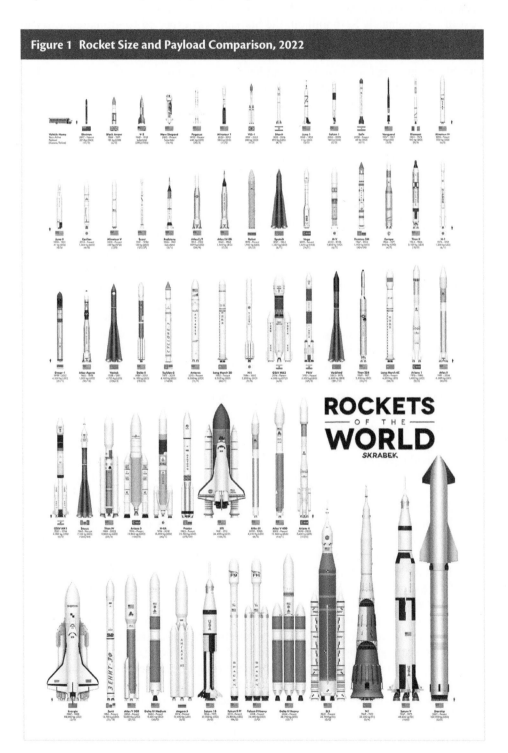

launch was on February 6, 2018, and carried a Tesla Roadster on board. Soon it was certified for the National Security Space Launch program.[18] The Falcon Heavy can carry equipment and supplies to Mars and both its stages can be recovered and used repeatedly.

In 2021 and 2022, SpaceX conducted several test flights of its Starship (which collectively refers to SpaceX's Starship spacecraft and Super Heavy Rocket), the tallest and most powerful launch vehicle ever built.[19] Starship was designed to carry both crew and cargo to Earth orbit, the Moon, Mars, and more. Developed at an estimated cost of approximately $216 million, the Starship was expected to ultimately carry up to 100 passengers and at a price per launch of approximately $2 million (by comparison, NASA's Space Launch System, Starship's closest competitor in functionality, was capable of carrying four astronauts and has a price per launch of *$4.1 billion*, making it over 2,000 times the price of the Starship launch!).[20] Starship was the key vehicle for achieving Musk's ultimate goal: colonizing Mars.

C17-3 Doing Things Differently at SpaceX

There were numerous ways in which SpaceX's strategies diverged from space industry norms, and almost all of them had direct implications for the cost of its launch systems. First, whereas most aerospace companies give their designs to myriad third-party contractors who create the hardware for them, SpaceX produced roughly 80% of its launch hardware inhouse.[21] SpaceX builds its own motherboards and circuits, vibration sensors, radios, and more. In most industries, vertical integration *increases* the costs of firms by not enabling them to benefit from competitive bidding between efficient suppliers. In the aerospace industry, however, the entrenchment of norms around using parts specialized for the space industry ("space grade"), and the bureaucratic rules defined by government contractors, had kept supply costs high–*very* high. SpaceX decided instead to build many of its own parts, or to buy parts not considered "space grade" and modify them to achieve "space grade." For example, rather than paying $50,000 to $100,000 for an industrial-grade radio, SpaceX was able to build its own for $5,000, and shaved 20% of the weight off at the same time.

SpaceX's willingness to produce their own parts came as a shock to suppliers. For example, Tom Mueller recounts a time when he asked a vendor for an estimate on a particular engine valve: "They came back [requesting] like a year and a half in development and hundreds of thousands of dollars. Just way out of whack. And we're like, 'No, we need it by this summer, for much, much less money.' They go, 'Good luck with that,' and kind of smirked and left." Mueller's team created the valve themselves, and by summer they had qualified it for use with cryogenic propellants. "That vendor, they iced us for a couple of months," Mueller said, "and then they called us back: 'Hey, we're willing to do that valve. You guys want to talk about it?' And we're like, 'No, we're done.' He goes, 'What do you mean you're done?' 'We qualified it. We're done.' And there was just silence at the end of the line. They were in shock."[22]

As noted, a big factor driving savings at SpaceX is that it often builds its components out of readily available consumer electronics rather than equipment already deemed "space grade" by the rest of the industry. Twenty years ago, "space grade" equipment would have had far superior performance characteristics compared to consumer electronics, but today that is no longer the case—standard electronics can now compete with more expensive, specialized gear. For example, at one point SpaceX needed an actuator that would steer the second stage of the Falcon 1. The job fell to engineer Steve Davis to find the important part and, since he had never built a part like that before, he sought out suppliers who could make it for them. Their quoted price for the device was $120,000. As Davis recalls, "Elon laughed. He said, 'That part is no more complicated than a garage door opener. Your budget is five thousand dollars. Go make it work.'"[23] Davis ended up designing an actuator that cost $3,900. Another example is provided by the computers that provide avionics for a rocket. Traditionally NASA's Jet Propulsion Laboratory bought expensive, specially toughened computers that cost over $10 million each to operate its rockets. Musk told engineer Kevin Watson that he wanted the bulk of the computer systems for Falcon 1 and Dragon to cost no more than $10,000. Watson was floored, noting, "In traditional aerospace, it would cost you more than ten thousand dollars just for the food at a meeting to discuss the cost of the avionics."[24] Watson was inspired by the challenge, however, and ended up creating a fully redundant avionics platform that used a mix of off-the-shelf computer parts and in-house components for just over $10,000. That same system was then also adapted for use in the Falcon 9.

SpaceX's willingness to experiment with new designs and technologies was a huge competitive advantage. For example, by using "friction stir welding," SpaceX was able to fuse large, thin sheets of metal together without rivets or other fasteners, reducing the weight of the rocket body by hundreds of pounds. This technology had previously not been considered feasible for such a large structure but SpaceX proved it could work. The technology was then also transferred to Tesla, where it could help make lighter and stronger cars.

Vertical integration also gave SpaceX more control over when and how things are done, making it significantly more nimble than traditional aerospace companies, and having almost all of SpaceX's engineers under one roof greatly streamlines the process of designing, testing, and improving the launch systems. For example, if a fault was found in a launch sensor, NASA would have traditionally responded with paperwork, meetings with suppliers, and a 3-month delay to wait for a new launch window. SpaceX, on the other hand, is known for fixing faults fast and on the fly—often enabling the launch to continue as planned. As Tom Mueller describes, "We make our main combustion chambers, turbo pump, gas generators, injectors, and main valves…We have complete control. We have our own test site, while most of the other guys use government test sites. The labor hours are cut in half and so is the work around the materials. Four years ago, we could make two rockets a year and now we can make twenty a year."[25]

SpaceX's rockets are also designed with commonality of parts and modularity in mind, which also reduces costs and development time. Consider, for example, the contrast between the Falcon 9 and ULA's Atlas V. Atlas V was the workhorse of the space industry, used for everything from probing distant planets to launching spy satellites. The Atlas V uses up to three kinds of rockets, each tailored for a specific phase of flight. In the first stage, RD-180 engines (built in Russia) burn a highly refined form of kerosene called RP1. Optional solid-fuel strap-on boosters provided additional thrust at liftoff, and a liquid hydrogen engine in the upper stage takes over in the final phase of flight. Using three kinds of rockets helped to optimize the performance of the Atlas V, but at a steep price. As Musk noted, "To a first-order approximation, you've just tripled your factory costs and all your operational costs." All of the engines on SpaceX's Falcon 9 and Falcon Heavy rockets, by contrast, are its own SpaceX-designed Merlin engines powered by RP1 and liquid oxygen. Having all of the engines be the same reduced the amount of tooling and the number of processes required, resulting in what Musk calls "huge cost savings."[26]

SpaceX's vertical integration has also led to it creating advances in state-of-the-art space technology. For the Dragon's heat shield, for example, the company intended to use a material called PICA (phenolic impregnated carbon ablator), first developed for NASA's Stardust comet-sample-return spacecraft. The prices they were offered by the manufacturer, however, were too high so they decided instead to work with NASA's

Ames Research Center to make the material themselves. What they came up with, PICA-X, turned out to be better than the original material and 10 times less expensive. In fact, Musk states that a single PICA-X heat shield can withstand hundreds of returns from low Earth orbit, and can even handle the much higher energy reentries from the moon or Mars.[2]

The largest cost advantage SpaceX has, far and away, is the fact that its rockets use reverse thrusters to lower themselves safely back to the ground so that they can be reused. Reusing the rockets means that much of the cost of producing the rocket will be amortized over multiple flights, dramatically lowering the cost of space travel relative to systems in which the rockets are considered expendable. In fact, SpaceX estimates indicated that with a larger volume of launches and improvements in launch technology, it could get the cost of a Falcon 9 launch down to about $20 million. This cost difference between SpaceX and traditional space vehicle manufacturing was a game changer. SpaceX was not just undercutting the U.S. manufacturers in price, it was also well under the price of its rivals in Europe, Japan, Russia, and China. As gleefully noted by venture capitalist and SpaceX board member Steve Jurvetson, "SpaceX lowered the cost of going into space by 10x. The ministers of China say, 'We can't compete on price with that. In how many industries have you heard ministries of China say ever say that?"[28]

C17-4 New Competition

Now that SpaceX had proven that reusable rockets were feasible, other rocket companies were beginning to take up the challenge. For example, in December 2021, the government of France announced that it would fund the development of a new reusable rocket called Maia by a French rocket firm ArianeGroup. As stated by French Finance Minister Bruno Le Maire, "We will have our SpaceX, we will have our Falcon 9. We will make up for a bad strategic choice made ten years ago."[29] The Maia would actually be tiny compared to Falcon 9, but it signaled France's intent to not be left behind in the space race. Rocket Lab, a U.S.- and New Zealand–based company, aimed to also make reusable rockets but would focus on smaller rockets that could service the small satellite launch industry.[30] The company was also developing a larger reusable launch vehicle intended for human spaceflight called Neutron.[31] Blue Origin, the rocket company founded by Amazon's Jeff Bezos, was also working on making its own heavy-lift orbital launch vehicle, New Glenn, fully reusable. The first stage of the New Glenn rocket was designed to be reusable in 2016; in 2021, the company began working on approaches to making the second stage reusable also.[32]

C17-5 Staying Private and Focused on Mars

Despite pressure from employees and would-be investors, Musk has resisted the urge to take SpaceX public. Shareholders tend to put intense focus on quarterly earnings, which can create pressures that are at odds with a firm's long-term goals and investments. The board of directors of a publicly held firm would thus undoubtedly force SpaceX to make changes that would improve its profitability at the expense of its chances for reaching Mars. As Musk wrote in a letter to his SpaceX employees, "Creating the technology needed to establish life on Mars is and always has been the fundamental goal of SpaceX. If being a public company diminishes that likelihood, then we should not do so until Mars is secure." [33]

Notes

[1] A. Konrad and M. Durot, "South Korean Investors Pour More Cash into SpaceX at $125 Billion Price Tag," *Forbes*, August 11, 2022.

[2] T. Hughes, Testimony to the House Subcommittee on Space, Science and Technology, July 13, 2017.

[3] M. A. Schilling, *Quirky: The Remarkable Story of the Traits, Foibles, and Genius of Breakthrough Innovators Who Changed the World* (New York: Public Affairs, 2018).

[4] Computer History Museum. An evening with Elon Musk (interview), January 24, 2013.

[5] S. Outing, "Zip2's Evolving City Site and Portal Strategy," *The Editor and Publisher*. August 31, 1998.

[6] Anonymous, "Compaq Buys Software Firm Zip2," *Los Angeles Times*, February 2, 1999.

[7] A. Vance, *Elon Musk: Tesla, SpaceX, and the Quest for a Fantastic Future* (New York: Harper Collins, 2015), p. 106.

[8] A. Vance, *Elon Musk: Tesla, SpaceX, and the Quest for a Fantastic Future* (New York: Harper Collins, 2015), p. 107.

[9] T. Junod, "Elon Musk: Triumph of His Will," *Esquire*, November 14, 2012.

[10] A. Vance, *Elon Musk: Tesla, SpaceX, and the Quest for a Fantastic Future* (New York: Harper Collins, 2015), p. 116.

[11] A. Vance, *Elon Musk: Tesla, SpaceX, and the Quest for a Fantastic Future* (New York: Harper Collins, 2015), p. 188.

[12] A. Vance, *Elon Musk: Tesla, SpaceX, and the Quest for a Fantastic Future* (New York: Harper Collins, 2015), p. 199.

[13] A. Vance, *Elon Musk: Tesla, SpaceX, and the Quest for a Fantastic Future* (New York: Harper Collins, 2015), p. 199.

[14] A. Vance, *Elon Musk: Tesla, SpaceX, and the Quest for a Fantastic Future* (New York: Harper Collins, 2015), p. 211.

[15] A. Chaikin, "Is SpaceX Changing the Rocket Equation?," Air & Space Smithsonian, January 2012.

[16] A. Pasztor, "SpaceX and United Launch Alliance Split $640 Million in Pentagon Rocket Contracts," *Wall Street Journal*, March 15, 2018.

[17] A. Pasztor, "SpaceX and United Launch Alliance Split $640 Million in Pentagon Rocket Contracts," *Wall Street Journal*, March 15, 2018.

[18] W. Harwood, "SpaceX Falcon Heavy Launch Puts on a Spectacular Show in Maiden fFight," CBS News, February 6, 2018; S. Erwin, "Air Force Certified Falcon Heavy for National Security Launch but More Work Needed to Meet Required Orbits," *SpaceNews*, April 27, 2019.

[19] J. Amos, "Biggest Ever Rocket Is Assembled Briefly in Texas," *BBC News*, August 11, 2021.

[20] S. Tonkin, "How Does Elon Musk's Starship Stackup Against NASA's Space Launch System? MailOnline Compares the World's Two Most Powerful Rockets Ahead of Their Maiden Launches Next Month," *DailyMail*, October 10, 2022.

[21] A. Chaikin, "Is SpaceX Changing the Rocket Equation?," Air & Space Smithsonian, January 2012.

[22] A. Chaikin, "Is SpaceX Changing the Rocket Equation?," Air & Space Smithsonian, January 2012.

[23] A. Vance, *Elon Musk: Tesla, SpaceX, and the Quest for a Fantastic Future* (New York: Harper Collins, 2015), p. 236.

[24] A. Vance, *Elon Musk: Tesla, SpaceX, and the Quest for a Fantastic Future* (New York: Harper Collins, 2015), p. 237.

[25] A. Vance, *Elon Musk: Tesla, SpaceX, and the Quest for a Fantastic Future* (New York: Harper Collins, 2015), p. 258.

[26] A. Chaikin, "Is SpaceX Changing the Rocket Equation?," Air & Space Smithsonian, January 2012.

[27] A. Chaikin, "Is SpaceX Changing the Rocket Equation?," Air & Space Smithsonian, January 2012.

[28] J. Bort, "Here's Why Investor Steve Jurvetson Saved Elon Musk's Space Dreams," *Business Inside*, September 14, 2012.

[29] E. Berger, "Concerned About SpaceX, France to Accelerate Reusable Rocket Plans," ARSTechnica, December 7, 2021.

[30] https://www.rocketlabusa.com/launch/electron/, retrieved October 11, 2022.

[31] Rocket Lab press release, "Rocket Lab Reveals Neutron Launch Vehicle's Advanced Architecture," December 2, 2021.

[32] E. Berger, "First Images of Blue Origin's "Project Jarvi" Test Tank," *ARS Technica*, August 24, 2021.

[33] Elon Musk, in A. Vance, *Elon Musk: Tesla, SpaceX, and the Quest for a Fantastic Future* (New York: Harper Collins, 2015), p. 260.

Alibaba Group: The Rise of a Platform Giant

Melissa A. Schilling

Alibaba, a company founded in 1999 to facilitate export transactions for small Chinese businesses, grew to become a platform ecosystem with astonishing reach. Many described Alibaba as being Amazon, Yelp, YouTube, and PayPal wrapped into one company. When the company went public in 2014 (its stock symbol is BABA), it raised US$25 billion, making it the largest IPO in history. For the fiscal year ending in 2021, Alibaba posted revenues of over CNY 717 billion, or $US 109 billion, making it the third-largest retailer in the world (behind Amazon and Walmart).[1] In terms of gross merchandise volume moved, Alibaba was larger than Amazon, Walmart, and eBay *combined*.[2]

C18-1 The History of Alibaba

Alibaba was founded in 1999 by 18 friends, led by a man named Jack Ma. Jack Ma's story is an inspiring rags-to-riches tale. He was born in Hangzhao, China, in 1964 to a poor family. He was slight in build, and often got into fights with classmates.[3] Ma struggled both to get into university and to find a job. As he told Charlie Rose in an interview in 2015, "There's an examination for young people to go to university. I failed it three times. I failed a lot. So I applied to 30 different jobs and got rejected. I went for a job with the police; they said, "You're no good." I even went to KFC when it came to my city. Twenty-four people went for the job. Twenty-three were accepted. I was the only guy [who wasn't]." Ma was also rejected by Harvard 10 times. He ultimately accepted a job as an English teacher that paid $12 month.

In 1995, Ma traveled to the United States for the first time, serving as an interpreter for a Chinese government trade delegation. There, on a lark, he did an online search for "beer" and "China," but was surprised to find that no Chinese beers came up. He decided at that moment to form a company called China Pages, which would help Chinese companies build websites. China Pages would eventually merge into an unsuccessful joint venture with China Telecom. Ma next headed up an Internet company backed by the Chinese Ministry of Foreign Trade and Economic Cooperation in Beijing. Ma worried, however, that being connected to the government would keep him from capitalizing on the rapid change and opportunities created by the Internet. Ma thus persuaded his team at the ministry to go back to Hangzhao with him where they founded Alibaba.

The company began as a business-to-business wholesale platform that enabled companies around the world to easily buy products from China. The platform was particularly useful for small to medium-sized Chinese businesses that would normally not be able to easily tap the export market. Ma had the objective of democratizing business in China by helping small businesses overcome the advantages large businesses wielded. As Ma noted, "What we do is give small companies e-commerce ability by helping them source partners and information around the world."

Unlike Amazon, Alibaba would not take ownership over inventory; instead Alibaba would provide access to all of the resources that an online business would need to succeed. It would serve as a platform hub at the center of an ecosystem of interacting partners of all types: suppliers, buyers, advertisers, financiers, logistics providers, information technology providers, and more. As put by Ming Zeng, chairman of the Academic Council of Alibaba Group, "Alibaba does what Amazon, eBay, PayPal, Google, FedEx, wholesalers, and a good portion of manufacturers do in the United States, with a healthy helping of financial services for garnish."[4] Alibaba did not charge transaction fees or fees to list goods; instead, its business model relied on selling advertising. The free listing service attracted sellers in droves, and by 2001 it already had 450,000 users and had achieved profitability.

C18-2 Expanding Alibaba's Market Reach

In 2002, eBay entered the Chinese market by purchasing a large stake in EachNet, a Chinese consumer-to-consumer sales platform, and Ma sensed the threat eBay and EachNet posed. Much of Alibaba's business came from small firms that could just as easily use a consumer-oriented platform like EachNet, and if EachNet grew quickly, it might lure Alibaba users away. Furthermore, individual consumers were already placing orders on Alibaba when they wanted to buy goods in bulk, revealing the potential for a consumer market for Alibaba. Thus in 2003, Alibaba created a subsidiary platform called Taobao ("treasure hunt"), focused on consumer-to-consumer sales. Unlike eBay, Taobao did not charge fees, and because Chinese users were more comfortable with face-to-face transactions, it created Taobao WangWang, an instant messaging service that simulated face-to-face negotiations between buyers and sellers.[5] The strategy was successful—by 2004, Alibaba controlled the majority of the consumer-to-consumer e-commerce market in China, and eBay announced its exit from the country.

In 2004, Alibaba partnered with four of China's largest banks to create an e-payment system called Alipay. Though initially Alipay was designed just to work with Taobao and Tmall, soon the payment system had evolved to be a complete mobile payment service. Using a smartphone, Alipay users can make payments online and at brick-and-mortar stores. They can also use it to make person-to-person money transfers, purchase bus and train tickets, hail taxis, and as digital identification for many public services.

The company grew rapidly, and by 2008, Alibaba's annual revenues were 3.9 billion yuan (or $US 562 million).[6] Unfortunately, the free and open nature of Taobao was both a strength and a weakness. While sellers of any size could join easily, Taobao also began to have a reputation for having counterfeit products. To counter this, Alibaba launched a business-to-consumer retail platform called Taobao Mall, later referred to simply as Tmall. Unlike Taobao, TMall screened sellers, and set standards for quality and reliability. It also collected annual fees and transaction fees from sellers. The combination of standards and fees effectively limited sellers to larger and more established players. This, in turn, gave consumers more confidence in the products and transaction process.

C18-3 Deepening the Platform Strategy

Transaction volume grew quickly and the firm turned its focus away from growing its user base and instead invested in improving the efficiency of its logistics, finance, and data infrastructure and providing additional services to members of its ecosystem (see Figure 1).

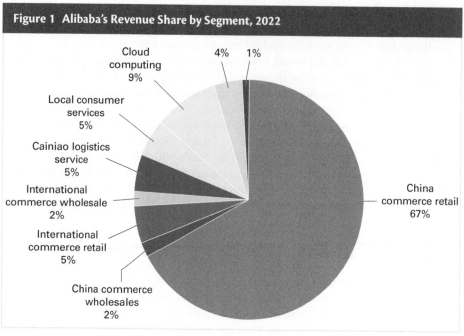

Figure 1 Alibaba's Revenue Share by Segment, 2022

- Cloud computing 9%
- Local consumer services 5%
- Cainiao logistics service 5%
- International commerce wholesale 2%
- International commerce retail 5%
- China commerce wholesales 2%
- 4%
- 1%
- China commerce retail 67%

Source: Data from Statista, 2022

Cainiao. In 2011, the company spent over US $4 billion on logistics and an integrated network of warehouses across China, and in 2013, Alibaba and a consortium of logistics companies formed Cainiao, a logistics network that links warehouses, distribution centers, and delivery companies. Mirroring Alibaba's strategy for e-commerce, Cainiao owns no warehouses and does not employ delivery personnel itself; instead, it just coordinates them efficiently, enabling participants to confidentially exchange information, provide real-time status on deliveries, and more. By late 2017, Cainiao was coordinating over 57 million deliveries a day.

The AliMe Chatbot. In 2016, Alibaba introduced an AI-powered chatbot called Ali Xiaomi (later changed to AliMe) that can handle both spoken and written customer queries on Taobao and Tmall. AliMe can handle a wide range of customer requests, including product returns, making product suggestions, and answering questions about delivery status.[7] The chatbot uses machine learning to continuously improve its ability to diagnose and fix customer issues, enabling it to handle increasingly complex problems over time. Automating customer service improves the efficiency of both Alibaba and its merchants. As noted by Ming Zeng, "Previously, most large sellers on our platform would hire temp workers to handle consumer inquiries during big events. Not anymore." AliMe helped Alibaba handle a record number of sales on its Single's Day shopping festival in 2019, responding to 300 million queries, i.e., 97% of the customer services on Alibaba e-commerce platforms, an amount that would have normally required a human staff of 85,000.[8]

Ant Financial Services. Alibaba also started two microfinance subsidiaries that would provide microloans to small sellers on Taobao and Alibaba.com. At banks in China, the minimum loan amount was typically about 6 million RMB (about $1 million), which was well above the needs of a typical small business. Furthermore, most small businesses lacked the credit history and documentation of their business performance needed to apply for such loans. This meant that tens of millions of small businesses in China were struggling to gain access to the capital they needed to grow their businesses.[9] Alibaba realized it already had real-time accurate data on the performance of millions of small businesses on its platform, and it could use that data to create a credit assessment program. Alibaba was able to not only provide microloans to businesses, but also performed all steps of its loan process online, making it fast

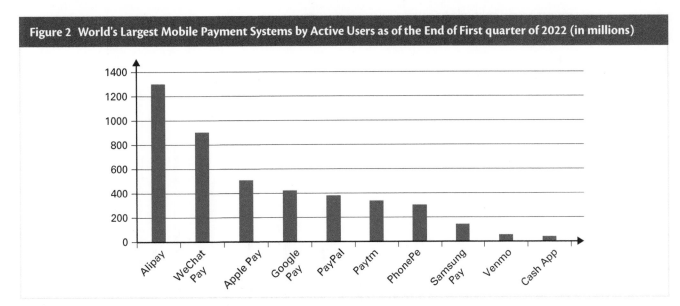

Figure 2 World's Largest Mobile Payment Systems by Active Users as of the End of First quarter of 2022 (in millions)

Source: https://www.fintechnews.org/alipay-is-the-most-popular-digital-wallet-in-the-world-in-2022/

and convenient. These two programs were later merged into Ant Financial Services. As noted by Ming Zeng, "Ant can easily process loans as small as several hundred RMB (around $50) in a few minutes. How is this possible? When faced with potential borrowers, lending institutions need answer only three basic questions: Should we lend to them, how much should we lend, and at what interest rate? Once sellers on our platforms gave us authorization to analyze their data, we were well positioned to answer those questions. Our algorithms can look at transaction data to assess how well a business is doing, how competitive its offerings are in the market, whether its partners have high credit ratings, and so on."[10]

Alipay was also brought under the umbrella of the Ant Financial Services group, and by 2022, Alipay had grown to become the largest mobile payment system in the world, with roughly 1.3 billion active users, followed by Chinese rival Tencent's WeChat Pay (see Figure 2). The size and success of Ant Financial Services had the unfortunate side effect of attracting the scrutiny of the Chinese government, which would begin to place increasingly difficult restrictions on the company.

Artificial Intelligence and Cloud Services. The cornerstone of Alibaba's advantage was data. All of the transactions handled by Alibaba, Taobao, Tmall, Alipay, Cainiao, and Aliyun generate data, and that data, in turn, is fed into algorithmic engines that yield increasingly precise predictions about things like consumer preferences, inventory needs, and investment returns.[11] In the same way that each Google search makes the Google search engine more accurate at gauging what a user is looking for, each transaction in Alibaba's rapidly growing ecosystem makes its platform smarter. In systems based on data and networks, size matters; the volume of data input into the system can create a self-reinforcing advantage. Alibaba also created a spinoff company, Aliyun, that offered cloud-based services to Chinese e-commerce vendors, banks, game developers, and more.

C18-4 Revenue Growth and Profitability

Analysts noted that though Alibaba's sales were only about one-third of Amazon's in 2021, for most of its history Alibaba had been far more profitable than Amazon, earning more net income in every year between 2012 and 2020 (see Figures 3 and 4, and

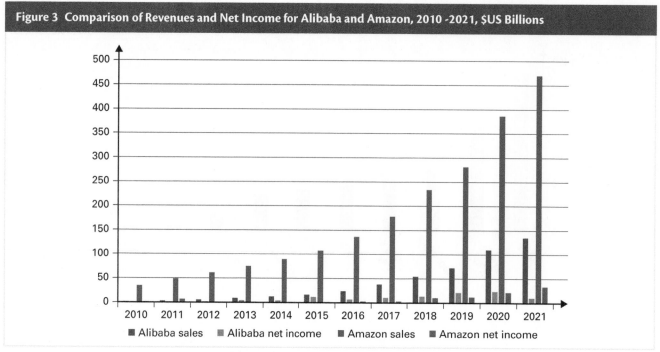

Source: U.S. Securities and Exchange Commission

Exhibits 1 and 2). The financial ratios told a powerful story about Alibaba's strategy of owning the platform but not the products: in most years, Alibaba was significantly more profitable, enjoying a much higher return on sales and return on assets.

C18-5 Plans to Expand Its International Presence

Alibaba's early growth had been primarily driven by the enormous and underserved population of Chinese consumers and small businesses, but in 2017, Jack Ma made it clear that it was time for Alibaba to have a bigger presence in the United States and Europe. While many pressed Ma to use Taobao and Tmall to sell to U.S. consumers, Ma demonstrated his political savvy by turning the equation around and focusing on helping U.S. businesses reach the Chinese market. In a meeting with U.S. President Donald Trump in 2017, Ma promised to sign up 1 million U.S. small businesses to Taobao and Tmall to sell to Chinese consumers over the next 5 years and predicted that each small business would likely hire at least one new employee as a result of increased sales, hence providing 1 million new jobs in the United States. Trump was delighted by the promise, and declared to a roomful of press, "Jack and I are going to do some great things."[12]

However, on September 10, 2018, Jack Ma's 54th birthday, he stunned the world by announcing that he would be retiring as Alibaba's chairman in exactly 1 year. Ma was now China's richest man with a net worth of $40 billion, and was determined to now focus his efforts on education and philanthropy. As he wrote in his letter to customers, employees, and shareholders:

> I still have lots of dreams to pursue. Those who know me know that I do not like to sit idle. I plan on continuing my role as the founding partner in the Alibaba Partnership and contribute to the work of the partnership. I also want to return to education, which excites me with so much blessing because this is

Figure 4 Comparison of ROA and ROS for Alibaba and Amazon

	2010	2011	2012	2013	2014	2015	2016	2017	2018	2019	2020	2021
Alibaba												
ROA	12%	9%	15%	26%	13%	23%	10%	11%	10%	12%	10%	3%
ROS	27%	21%	24%	44%	32%	71%	28%	26%	24%	29%	21%	7%
Amazon												
ROA	7%	3%	0%	1%	−1%	1%	3%	3%	7%	6%	8%	9%
ROS	4%	13%	0%	0%	0%	1%	2%	2%	4%	4%	6%	7%

Source: US Securities and Exchange Commission

*Alibaba's fiscal year ends in March so dates are adjusted to show the previous year to facilitate comparison to Amazon (e.g., Alibaba FY ending 03/22 shown as 2021)

what I love to do. The world is big, and I am still young, so I want to try new things—because what if new dreams can be realized?!

The one thing I can promise everyone is this: Alibaba was never about Jack Ma, but Jack Ma will forever belong to Alibaba.

Exhibit 1 Alibaba Group's Consolidated Income Statement, $US Thousands

Period Ending:	3/31/2022	3/31/2021	3/31/2020	3/31/2019
Total Revenue	$134,487,000	$109,426,000	$71,860,000	$56,076,000
Cost of Revenue	$85,045,000	$64,257,000	$39,809,000	$30,792,000
Gross Profit	$49,441,000	$45,169,000	$32,051,000	$25,284,000
Operating Expenses				
Research and Development	$8,744,000	$8,732,000	$6,074,000	$5,571,000
Sales, General and Admin.	$23,919,000	$20,861,000	$11,119,000	$9,623,000
Non-Recurring Items	$3,964,000	–	$81,000	–
Other Operating Items	$1,836,000	$1,896,000	$1,887,000	$1,596,000
Operating Income	$10,979,000	$13,681,000	$12,890,000	$8,494,000
Add'l income/expense items	−$816,000	$12,262,000	$11,334,000	$6,596,000
Earnings Before Interest and Tax	$10,162,000	$25,943,000	$24,224,000	$15,090,000
Interest Expense	$774,000	$683,000	$730,000	$772,000
Earnings Before Tax	$9,388,000	$25,260,000	$23,494,000	$14,318,000
Income Tax	$4,227,000	$4,467,000	$2,899,000	$2,463,000
Minority Interest	$2,261,000	$1,065,000	−$808,000	$84,000
Equity Earnings/Loss				
Unconsolidated Subsidiary	$2,392,000	$1,113,000	$1,281,000	$1,139,000
Net Income-Cont. Operations	$9,814,000	$22,971,000	$21,067,000	$13,078,000
Net Income	$9,814,000	$22,971,000	$21,067,000	$13,078,000
Net Income Applicable to	$9,768,000	$22,930,000	$21,043,000	$13,035,000
Common Shareholders				

Data from Nasdaq.com

Exhibit 2 Alibaba Group's Balance Sheet, $US Thousands

Period Ending:	3/31/2022	3/31/2021	3/31/2020	3/31/2019
Current Assets				
Cash and Cash Equivalents	$35,843,000	$54,381,000	$48,777,000	$29,537,000
Short-Term Investments	$41,807,000	$24,742,000	$4,612,000	$1,963,000
Net Receivables	–	–	–	–
Inventory	–	–	–	–
Other Current Assets	$23,016,000	$19,025,000	$11,875,000	$8,718,000
Total Current Assets	$100,666,000	$98,148,000	$65,264,000	$40,218,000
Long-Term Assets				
Long-Term Investments	$69,880,000	$66,729,000	$49,479,000	$35,943,000
Fixed Assets	$27,085,000	$22,488,000	$14,576,000	$13,695,000
Goodwill	$42,500,000	$44,664,000	$39,021,000	$39,424,000
Intangible Assets	$9,338,000	$10,806,000	$8,593,000	$10,159,000
Other Assets	$17,838,000	$15,016,000	$8,175,000	$4,169,000
Deferred Asset Charges	–	–	–	–
Total Assets	$267,307,000	$257,852,000	$185,107,000	$143,608,000
Current Liabilities				
Accounts Payable	$46,225,000	$43,694,000	$25,620,000	$20,148,000
Short-Term Debt / Current				
Portion of Long-Term Debt	$1,394,000	$2,050,000	$1,152,000	$4,571,000
Other Current Liabilities	$12,885,000	$11,824,000	$7,328,000	$6,183,000
Total Current Liabilities	$60,504,000	$57,568,000	$34,100,000	$30,902,000
Long-Term Debt	$20,889,000	$20,704,000	$16,957,000	$16,641,000
Other Liabilities	$5,025,000	$4,692,000	$3,561,000	$921,000
Deferred Liability Charges	$10,278,000	$9,574,000	$6,474,000	$3,569,000
Misc. Stocks	$19,558,000	$20,975,000	$16,234,000	$17,310,000
Minority Interest	$1,522,000	$1,323,000	$1,283,000	$1,015,000
Total Liabilities	$116,255,000	$113,513,000	$77,326,000	$69,343,000
Stock Holders Equity				
Common Stocks	–	–	–	–
Capital Surplus	$88,846,000	$84,657,000	$57,279,000	$38,375,000
Retained Earnings	−$350,000	–	–	–
Treasury Stock	$64,717,000	$60,154,000	$48,457,000	$34,490,000
Other Equity	−$3,683,000	−$1,794,000	$762,000	$385,000
Total Equity	$149,529,000	$143,016,000	$106,498,000	$73,250,000
Total Liabilities & Equity	$267,307,000	$257,852,000	$185,107,000	$143,608,000

Data from Nasdaq.com

C18-6 Facing Economic and Regulatory Headwinds

In late 2020, China launched a regulatory crackdown on Chinese tech firms, accusing Alibaba, Tencent, and Meituan of monopolistic behavior, false advertising, and mistreating users. Alibaba and Meituan were fined $2.75 billion and $527 billion, respectively, and the Chinese government began to impose strict oversight over the algorithms used by the companies to target customers, ordered the platforms to open up to each other, and set tight limits on online lending (of which Ant was a big player). Even more devastatingly, the state-owned People's Bank of China halted Ant Group's IPO, sending the stock price into a downward spiral.[13] On top of that, a sharply slowing economy in China had caused Alibaba's growth to slow. Revenue from its Taobao and Tmall e-commerce platforms fell 1.3% in 2021, compared to a year earlier. The company admitted that it believed it had substantially captured all customers in China with purchasing power, and now would need to focus on retaining them and inducing them to spend more.[14] This, understandably, did not promise the double-digit growth Alibaba had enjoyed up to now.

Alibaba's other businesses, such as international e-commerce, cloud, and logistics posted more growth, but were still unprofitable and would continue to require significant investment for at least several years.

These challenges had delivered an outsized hit to Alibaba's market capitalization; by September 2022, Alibaba's market capitalization had fallen to $US 208.6 billion, down about one-third from its peak market cap of $US 310 billion in late 2020 (before the crackdown was imposed). Alibaba's business model had proven remarkably successful and it held dominant positions in several industries. However, the Chinese government appeared intent on clipping its wings and the stock market had become suddenly wary about Alibaba's prospects. What would the future hold for the company that had been China's shooting star?

Notes

[1]https://www.forbes.com/sites/laurendebter/2022/05/12/worlds-largest-retailers-2022-amazon-walmart-alibaba/?sh=3bca441959e3

[2]A Cheng, "Alibaba vs. the World," *Institutional Investor,* July 25, 2017.

[3]"The Rags-to-Riches Story of Alibaba Founder Jack Ma," *Business Insider*, March 2, 2017.

[4]M Zeng, "Alibaba and the Future of Business," *Harvard Business Review*, September-October 2018.

[5]S. H. Park and Z. Zhao, "Alibaba Group: Fostering an E-Commerce Ecosystem." (Ivey Publishing, case W16858.

[6]Data retrieved from Morningstar.com on September 27, 2018.

[7]J. Erickson and S. Wang, "At Alibaba, Artificial Intelligence Is Changing How People Shop Online," *Alizila*, June 5, 2017.

[8]A. Dong, "AI Chatbot Behind Alibaba's $38 Million Single's Day Miracle," *HBS Digital Initiative*, April 20, 2020.

[9]M. Zeng, "Alibaba and the Future of Business," *Harvard Business Review*, September-October, 2018.

[10]M. Zeng, "Alibaba and the Future of Business," *Harvard Business Review*, September-October, 2018.

[11]M. Zeng, "Alibaba and the Future of Business," *Harvard Business Review*, September-October, 2018.

[12]A Lashinsky, "Jack Ma's Strategy to Take Alibaba Global," *Intheblack*, October 1, 2017.

[13]"Factbox: How China's Regulatory Crackdown Has Reshaped Its Tech, Property Sectors," *Reuters*, April 29, 2022.

[14]J. Wong, "Alibaba Shares Are Cheap, but Not a Bargain," *Wall Street Journal*, February 25, 2022.

19

3M: The Innovation Engine

Charles W. L. Hill School of Business University of Washington Seattle, WA 98105 August 2022

C19-1 Introduction

Established in 1902, 3M is one of the largest technology-driven enterprises in the United States. Its 2021 revenues were $35.4 billion, 60% of which generated were outside the United States. The company was solidly profitable, earning $5.93 billion in net income and generating a return on invested capital of 19.1%. Throughout its history, 3M's researchers had driven much of the company's growth. The company commits 6% of its revenues to R&D. In 2017, around 8,100 of the company's 91,000 employees were scientists and researchers. The company has over 118,000 patents, 9,000 of which had been accumulated since 2001.[1]

This innovation engine had helped 3M to develop many of the 60,000 products that it sold in 2021. These products included Post-it Notes, Flex Circuits, various kinds of Scotch tape, abrasives, specialty chemicals, Thinsulate insulation products, Nexcare bandage, optical films, fiber-optic connectors, drug delivery systems, and much more. According to a Boston Consulting Group study, in 2018, 3M's return on its investment in R&D outpaced each name on a list of the 10 most innovative companies in America. For every dollar of R&D spent in 2017, 3M yielded $8.60 in gross profit, versus an average of $5.50 for the top 10. Over a 3-year period, 3M outpaced every firm on the list except the number one ranked Apple.[2] How had 3M built this innovation machine, and could it continue to keep innovating and growing profitably going forward?

C19-2 The History of 3M: Building Innovative Capabilities

The story of 3M goes back to 1902 when five Minnesota businessmen established the Minnesota Mining and Manufacturing company to mine a mineral that they thought was corundum, which is ideal for making sandpaper. The mineral, however, turned out to be low-grade anorthosite, nowhere near as suitable for making sandpaper, and the company nearly failed. To try and salvage the business, 3M turned to making the sandpaper itself using materials purchased from another source.

In 1907, 3M hired a 20-year-old business student, William McKnight, as assistant bookkeeper. This turned out to be a pivotal move in the history of the company. The hardworking McKnight soon made his mark. By 1929, he was CEO of the company and in 1949 he became chairman of 3M's board of directors, a position that he held through until 1966.

C19-2a From Sandpaper to Post-it Notes

It was McKnight, then 3M's vice-president, who hired the company's first scientist, Richard Carlton, in 1921. Around the same time, McKnight's interest had been peaked by an odd request from a Philadelphian printer by the name of Francis Okie for samples of every sandpaper grit size that 3M made. McKnight dispatched 3M's East Coast sales manager to find out what Okie was up to. The sales manager discovered that Okie had invented a new kind of sandpaper that he had patented. It was waterproof sandpaper that could be used with water or oil to reduce dust and decrease the friction that marred auto finishes. In addition, the lack of dust reduced the poisoning associated with inhaling the dust of paint that had a high lead content. Okie had a problem though; he had no financial backers to commercialize the sandpaper. 3M quickly stepped into the breach, purchasing the rights to Okie's Wetordry waterproof sandpaper, and hiring the young printer to come and join Richard Carlton in 3M's lab. Wetordry sandpaper went on to revolutionize the sandpaper industry, and was the driver of significant growth at 3M.

Another key player in the company's history, Richard Drew, also joined 3M in 1921. Hired straight out of the University of Minnesota, Drew would round out the trio of scientists, Carlton, Okie, and Drew, who, under McKnight's leadership, would do much to shape 3M's innovative organization.

McKnight charged the newly hired Drew with developing a stronger adhesive to better bind the grit for sandpaper to paper backing. While experimenting with adhesives, Drew accidentally developed a weak adhesive that had an interest quality–if placed on the back of a strip of paper and stuck to a surface, the strip of paper could be pealed off the surface it was adhered to without leaving any adhesive residue on that surface. This discovery gave Drew an epiphany. He had been visiting auto-body paint shops to see how 3M's Wetordry sandpaper was used, and he noticed that there was a problem with paint running. His epiphany was to cover the back of a strip of paper with his weak adhesive, and use it as "masking tape" to cover parts of the auto body that were not to be painted. An excited Drew took his idea to McKnight, and explained how masking tape might create an entirely new business for 3M. McKnight reminded Drew that he had been hired to fix a specific problem, and pointedly suggested that he concentrate on doing just that.

Chastised, Dew went back to his lab, but he could not get the idea out of his mind, so he continued to work on it at night, long after everyone else had gone home. Drew succeeded in perfecting the masking tape product, and then went to visit several auto-body shops to show them his innovation. He quickly received several commitments for orders. Drew then went to see McKnight again. He told him that he had continued to work on the masking tape idea on his own time, had perfected the product, and got several customers interested in purchasing it. This time it was McKnight's turn to be chastised. Realizing that he had almost killed a good business idea, McKnight reversed his original position and gave Drew the go ahead to pursue the idea.[3]

Introduced into the market in 1925, Drew's invention of masking tape represented the first significant product diversification at 3M. Company legend has it that this incident was also the genesis for 3M's famous 15% rule. Reflecting on Drew's work, both McKnight and Carlton both agreed that technical people could disagree with management, and should be allowed to go and do some experimentation on their own. The company then established a norm that technical people could spend up to 15% of their own workweek on projects that might benefit the consumer, without having to justify the project to their manager.

Drew himself was not finished. In the late 1920s, he was working with cellophane, a product that had been invented by DuPont, when lightning struck for a second time. Why, Drew wondered, couldn't cellophane be coated with an adhesive and used as a sealing tape? The result was Scotch Cellophane Tape. The first batch was delivered to a customer in September 1930, and Scotch Tape went on to become one of 3M's best-selling products. Years later, Drew noted that, "Would there have been any masking or cellophane tape if it hadn't been for earlier 3M research on adhesive binders for 3M™ Wetordry™ Abrasive Paper? Probably not!"[4]

Over the years, other scientists followed Drew's footsteps at 3M, creating a wide range of innovative products by leveraging existing technology and applying it to new areas. Two famous examples illustrate how many of these innovations occurred–the invention of Scotch Guard and the development of the ubiquitous "Post-it Notes."

The genesis of Scotch Guard was in 1953 when a 3M scientist named Patsy Sherman was working on a new kind of rubber for jet aircraft fuel lines. Some of the latex mixture splashed onto a pair of canvas tennis shoes. Over time, the spot stayed clean while the rest of the canvas soiled. Sherman enlisted the help of fellow chemist Sam Smith. Together they began to investigate polymers, and it didn't take long for them to realize that they were on to something. They discovered an oil- and water-repellant substance, based on the fluorocarbon fluid used in air conditioners, with enormous potential for protecting fabrics from stains. It took several years before the team perfected a means to apply the treatment using water as the carrier, thereby making it economically feasible for use as a finish in textile plants.

Three years after the accidental spill, the first rain and stain repellent for use on wool was announced. Experience and time revealed that one product could not, however, effectively protect all fabrics, so 3M continued working, producing a wide range of Scotch Guard products that could be used to protect all kinds of fabrics.[5]

The story of Post-it Notes began with Spencer Silver, a senior scientist studying adhesives.[6] In 1968, Silver had developed an adhesive with properties like no other; it was a pressure-sensitive adhesive that would adhere to a surface but was weak enough to easily peel off the surface and leave no residue. Silver spent several years shopping his adhesive around 3M, to no avail. It was a classic case of a technology in search of a product. Then, one day in 1973, Art Fry, a new product development research who had attended one of Silver's seminars, was singing in his church choir. He was frustrated that his bookmarks kept falling out of his hymn book, when he had a "Eureka" moment. Fry realized that Silver's adhesive could be used to make a wonderfully reliable bookmark.

Fry went to work next day, and using 15% time, started to develop the bookmark. When he started using a sample to write notes to his boss, Fry suddenly realized that he had stumbled on a much bigger potential use for the product. Before the product could be commercialized, however, Fry had to solve a host of technical and manufacturing problems. With the support of his boss, Fry persisted and after 18 months, the product development effort moved from 15% time to a formal development effort funded 3M's own seed capital.

The first Post-it Notes were test marketed in 1977 in four major cities, but customers were lukewarm at best. This did not gel with the experience within 3M, where people in Fry's division were using samples all the time to write messages to each other. Further research revealed that the test marketing effort, which focused on ads and brochures, didn't resonate well with consumers, who didn't seem to value Post-it Notes until they had the actual product in their hands. In 1978, 3M tried again, this time descending on Boise, Idaho, and handing out samples. Follow-up research revealed that 90% of consumers who tried the product said they would buy it. Armed with this knowledge, 3M rolled out the national launch of Post-it Notes in 1980. The product subsequently went on to become a best seller.

C19-2b Institutionalizing Innovation

Early on, McKnight set an ambitious target for 3M–a 10% annual increase in sales and 25% profit target. He also indicated how he thought that should be achieved with a commitment to plow 5% of sales back into R&D every year. The question though, was how to ensure that 3M would continue to produce new products?

The answer was not apparent all at once, but rather evolved over the years from experience. A prime example was the 15% rule, which came out of McKnight's experience with Drew. In addition to the 15% rule and the continued commitment to push money back into R&D, a number of other mechanisms evolved at 3M to spur innovation.

Initially research took place in the business units that made and sold products, but by the 1930s 3M had already diversified into several different fields, thanks in large part to the efforts of Drew and others. McKnight and Carlton realized that there was a need for a central research function. In 1937, they established a central research laboratory that was charged with supplementing the work of product divisions and undertaking long-run basic research. From the outset, the researchers at the lab were multidisciplinary, with people from different scientific disciplines often working next to each other on research benches.

As the company continued to grow, it became clear that there was a need for some mechanism to knit together the company's increasingly diverse business operations. This led to the establishment of the 3M Technical Forum in 1951. The goal of the Technical Forum was to foster idea sharing, discussion, and problem solving between technical employees located in different divisions and the central research laboratory. The Technical Forum sponsored "problem-solving sessions" at which businesses would present their most recent technical nightmares in the hope that somebody might be able to suggest a solution–and that often was the case. The forum also established an annual event in which each division put up a booth to show off its latest technologies. Chapters were also created to focus on specific disciplines, such as polymer chemistry or coating processes.

During the 1970s, the Technical Forum cloned itself, establishing forums in Australia and England. By 2001, the forum had grown to 9,500 members in 8 U.S. locations and 19 other countries, becoming an international network of researchers who could share ideas, solve problems, and leverage technology.

According to Marlyee Paulson, who coordinated the Technical Forum from 1979 to 1992, the great virtue of the Technical Forum is to cross pollinate ideas. To quote:

> 3M has lots of polymer chemists. They may be in tape; they may be medical or several other divisions. The forum pulls them across 3M to share what they know. It's a simple but amazingly effective way to bring like mind together.[7]

In 1999, 3M created another unit within the company, 3M Innovative Properties (3M, IPC) to leverage technical know-how. 3M IPC is explicitly charged with protecting and leveraging 3M's intellectual property around the world. At 3M, there has been a long tradition that while divisions "own" their products; the company as a whole "owns" the underlying technology, or intellectual property. One task of 3M IPC is to find ways in which 3M technology can be applied across business units to produce unique marketable products. Historically, the company has been remarkably successful at leveraging company technology to produce new product ideas.

Another key to institutionalizing innovation at 3M has been the principle of "patient money." The basic idea is that producing revolutionary new products requires substantial long-term investments, and often repeated failure, before a major payoff occurs. The principle can be traced back to 3M's early days. It took the company 12 years before its initial sandpaper business started to show a profit, a fact that drove home the importance of taking the long view. Throughout the company's history, similar examples can be found. Scotchlite Reflective Sheeting, now widely used on road signs, didn't show much profit for 10 years. The same was true of flurochemicals and duplicating products. Patient money doesn't mean substantial funding for long periods of time, however. Rather, it might imply that a small group of five researchers is supported for 10 years while they work on a technology.

More generally, if a researcher creates a new technology or idea, they can begin working on it using 15% time. If the idea shows promise, they may request seed capital from their business unit managers to develop it further. If that funding is denied, which can occur, they are free to take the idea to any other 3M business unit. Unlike the case in many other companies, requests for seed capital do not require that researchers draft detailed business plans that are reviewed by top management. That comes later in the process. As one former senior technology manager has noted:

In the early stages of a new product or technology, it shouldn't be overly managed. If we start asking for business plans too early and insist on tight financial evaluations, we'll kill an idea or surely slow it down.[8]

Explaining the patient money philosophy, Ron Baukol, a former executive vice president of 3M's international operations, and a manager who started as a researcher, has noted that:

> You just know that some things are going to be worth working on, and that requires technological patience.....you don't put too much money into the investigation, but you keep one to five people working on it for twenty years if you have to. You do that because you know that, once you have cracked the code, it's going to be big.[9]

An internal review of 3M's innovation process in the early 1980s concluded that despite the liberal process for funding new product ideas, some promising ideas did not receive funding from business units, or the central research budget. This led to the establishment in 1985 of Genesis Grants, which provide up to $100,000 in seed capital to fund projects that do not get funded through 3M's regular channels. About a dozen of these grants are given every year. One of the recipients of these grants, a project that focused on creating a multilayered reflective film, has subsequently produced a breakthrough reflective technology that may have applications in a wide range of businesses, from better reflective strips on road signs to computer displays and the reflective linings in light fixtures. Company estimates in 2002 suggest that the commercialization of this technology might ultimately generate $1 billion in sales for 3M.

Underlying the patient money philosophy is recognition that innovation is a very risky business. 3M has long acknowledged that failure is an accepted and essential part of the new product development process. As former 3M CEO Lew Lehr once noted:

> We estimate that 60% of our formal new product development programs never make it. When this happens, the important thing is to not punish the people involved.[10]

In an effort to reduce the probability of failure, in the 1960s, 3M started to establish a process for auditing the product development efforts ongoing in the company's business units. The idea has been to provide a peer review, or technical audit, of major development projects taking place in the company. A typical technical audit team is composed of 10 to 15 business and technical people, including technical directors and senior scientists from other divisions. The audit team looks at the strengths and weaknesses of a development program, and its probability of success, both from a technical standpoint and a business standpoint. The team then makes non-binding recommendations, but they are normally taken very seriously by the managers of a project. For example, if an audit team concludes that a project has enormous potential, but is terribly underfunded, managers of the unit would often increase the funding level. Of course, the converse can also happen, and in many instances, the audit team can provide useful feedback and technical ideas that can help a development team to improve their project's chance of success.

By the 1990s, the continuing growth of 3M had produced a company that was simultaneously pursuing a vast array of new product ideas. This was a natural outcome of 3M's decentralized and bottom-up approach to innovation, but it was problematic in one crucial respect, the company's R&D resources were being spread too thinly over a wide range of opportunities, resulting in potentially major projects being underfunded.

To try and channel R&D resources into projects that had blockbuster potential, in 1994, 3M introduced what was known as the Pacing Plus Program.

The program asked business to select a small number of programs that would receive priority funding, but 3M's senior executives made the final decision on which programs were to be selected for the Pacing Plus Program. An earlier attempt to do this in 1990 had met with limited success because each sector in 3M submitted as many as 200 programs. The Pacing Plus Program narrowed the list down to 25 key programs that by 1996 were receiving some 20% of 3M's entire R&D funds (by the early 2000s, the number of projects funded under the Pacing Plus Program had grown to 60). The focus was on "leapfrog technologies," revolutionary ideas that might change the basis of competition and led to entirely new technology platforms that might, in typical 3M fashion, spawn an entire range of new products.

To further foster a culture of entrepreneurial innovation and risk taking, over the years, 3M established a number of reward and recognition programs to honor employees who make significant contributions to the company. These include the Carton Society award, which honors employees for outstanding career scientific achievements and the Circle of Technical Excellence and Innovation Award, which recognizes people who have made exceptional contributions to 3M's technical capabilities.

Another key component of 3M's innovative culture has been an emphasis on dual-career tracks. Right for its early days, many of the key players in 3M's history, people like Richard Drew, chose to stay in research, turning down opportunities to go into the management side of the business. Over the years, this became formalized in a dual-career path. Today, technical employees can choose to follow a technical career path or a management career path, with equal advancement opportunities. The idea is to let researchers develop their technical professional interests, without being penalized financially for not going into management.

Although 3M's innovative culture emphasizes the role of technical employees in producing innovations, the company also has a strong tradition of emphasizing that new product ideas often come from watching customers at work. Richard Drew's original idea for masking tape, for example, came from watching workers uses 3M Wetordry sandpaper in autobody shops. As with much else at 3M, the tone was set by McKnight, who insisted that salespeople needed to "get behind the smokestacks" of 3M customers, going onto the factory floor, talking to workers, and finding out what their problems were. Over the years, this theme has become ingrained in 3M's culture, with salespeople often requesting time to watch customer work, and then bringing their insights about customer problems back into their organization.

By the mid-1990s, McKnight's notion of getting behind the smokestacks had evolved into the idea that 3M could learn a tremendous amount from what were termed "lead users," who were customers working in very demanding conditions. Over the years, 3M had observed that in many cases, customers themselves can be innovators, developing new products to solve problems that they face in their work setting. This was most likely to occur for customers working in very demanding conditions. To take advantage of this process, 3M has instituted a lead user process in the company in which cross-functional teams from a business unit go and observe how customers work in demanding situations.

For example, 3M has a $100 million business selling surgical drapes, which are drapes backed with adhesives that are used to cover parts of a body during surgery and help prevent infection. As an aid to new product development, 3M's surgical drapes business formed a cross-functional team that went to observe surgeons at work in very demanding situations – including on the battlefield, hospitals in developing nations, and in vets' offices. The result was a new set of product ideas, including low-cost surgical drapes that were affordable in developing nations, and devices for coating a patient's skin and surgical instruments with antimicrobial substances that would reduce the chance of infection during surgery.[11]

The company has also formalized the process for identifying promising avenues for research, developing potential products, and then taking those products to market. This process involves three-part teams known as "scouts," "entrepreneurs," and "implementers." The role of *scouts* is to identify problems that 3M might solve through innovation. Once an interesting problem has been identified, the project is handed over to the *entrepreneurs,* who attempt to come up with a solution. Once a solution has been found, the *implementers* step in to commercialize that solution and bring it to market. The *scouts* are predominantly research scientists, whereas the *entrepreneurs* and *implementations* are typically cross-functional teams.[12]

A case in point; in 2007, two *scouts* were talking to customers, visiting hospitals and clinics, and reviewing the medical research when they learned that concern was rising about surgical site infections (SSIs) caused by methicillin-resistant *Staphylococcus aureus* (MRSA), and other potentially deadly forms of that bacterial strain. Roughly 20% of people are persistent carriers of it, and 60% are intermittent carriers. Since *S. aureus* is typically found in the nose, that put a lot of people at risk for infection during surgical procedures.

The *scouts* had found a problem. They then sat down with a team of 3M *entrepreneurs*, whose job it is to figure out how to capitalize on opportunities then scouts have identified. They ultimately came up with the idea of using iodine as a nasal treatment before each operation.

The *scouts* then stepped aside and the *entrepreneurs* took over. They fleshed out an initial prototype and developed a number of chemical formulations for the product. Each was rigorously modeled, tested, analyzed, tweaked, and tested. The scouting phase took only 3 months, whereas the entrepreneurial development phase took about 9 months. Once the *entrepreneurs* had gone through enough trials and due diligence to reach a viable solution, they passed it along to a team of around a dozen *implementers* to get it ready for commercialization. This was a longer process, stretching across roughly 18 months of rigorous market testing, seeking and adapting to regulatory guidelines, nailing down supply chain quality and performance metrics, and building out the go-to-market road map. In 2010, the 3M™ Skin and Nasal Antiseptic Patient Preoperative Skin Preparation hit the market. Since then, it's been used in healthcare facilities and has helped reduce the likelihood of SSIs.

Driving the entire innovation machine at 3M has been a series of stretch goals set by top managers. The goals date back to 3M's early days and McKnight's ambitious growth targets. In 1977, the company established "Challenge 81," which called for 25% of sales to come from products that had been on the market for less than 5 years by 1981. By the 1990s, the goal had been raised to the requirement that 30% of sales should come from products that had been on the market less than 4 years.

The flip side of these goals were that over the years, many products and businesses that had been 3M staples were phased out. More than 20 of the businesses that were 3M mainstays in 1980, for example, had been phased out by 2000. Analysts estimate that sales from mature products at 3M generally fall by 3–4% per annum. The company has a long history of inventing businesses, leading the market for long periods of time, and then shutting those businesses down, or selling them off, when they can no longer meet 3M's own demanding growth targets. Notable examples include the duplicating business, a business 3M invented with Thermo Fax copiers (which were ultimately made obsolete my Xerox's patented technology) and the video and audio magnetic tape business. The former division was sold off in 1985, and then later in 1995. In both cases, the company exited these areas because they had become low-growth commodity businesses that could not generate the kind of top-line growth that 3M was looking for.

Still, 3M was by no means invulnerable in the realm of innovation and on occasion squandered huge opportunities. A case in point was the document copying business. 3M invented this business in 1951 when it introduced the world's first commercially successful Thermo Fax copier (which used specially coated 3M paper to copy original typed documents). 3M dominated the world copier business until 1970, when Xerox overtook the company with its revolutionary xerographic technology that used plain paper to make copies. 3M saw Xerox coming, but rather than try and develop their own plain paper copier, the company invested funds in trying to improve its (increasingly obsolete) copying technology. It wasn't until 1975 that 3M introduced its own plain paper copier, and by then it was too late. Ironically, 3M turned down the chance to acquire Xerox's technology 20 years earlier, when the company's founders had approached 3M.

C19-2c Building the Organization

McKnight, a strong believer in decentralization, organized the company into product divisions in 1948, making 3M one of the early adopters of this organizational form. Each division was set up as an individual profit center that had the power, autonomy, and resources to run independently. At the same time, certain functions remained centralized, including significant R&D, human resources, and finance.

McKnight wanted to keep the divisions small enough that people had a chance to be entrepreneurial and focused on the customer. A key philosophy of McKnight's was "divide and grow." Put simply, when a division became too big, some of its embryonic businesses were spun of into a new division. Not only did this new division then typically attain higher growth rates, but the original division had to find new drivers of growth to make up for the contribution of the businesses that had gained independence. This drove the search for further innovations.

At 3M, the process of organic diversification by splitting divisions became known as "renewal." The examples of renewal within 3M are legendary. A copying machine project for Thermo-Fax copiers grew to become the Office Products Division. When Magnetic Recording Materials was spun off from the Electrical Products division, it grew to become its own division, and then in turn spawned a spate of divisions.

However, this organic process was not without its downside. By the early 1990s, some of 3M's key customers were frustrated that they had to do businesses with a large number of different 3M divisions. In some cases, there could be representatives from 10 to 20 3M divisions calling on the same customer. To cope with this problem, in 1992, 3M started to assign key account representatives to sell 3M products directly to major customers. These representatives typically worked across divisional lines. Implementing the strategy required many of 3M's general managers to give up some of their autonomy and power, but the solution seemed to work well, particularly for 3M's consumer and office divisions.

Underpinning the organization that McKnight put in place was his own management philosophy. As explained in a 1948 document, his basic management philosophy consisted of the following values:[13]

> As our business grows, it becomes increasingly necessary to delegate responsibility and to encourage men and women to exercise their initiative. This requires considerable tolerance. Those men and women to whom we delegate authority and responsibility, if they are good people, are going to want to do their jobs in their own way.
>
> Mistakes will be made. But if a person is essentially right, the mistakes he or she makes are not as serious in the long run as the mistakes management will make if it undertakes to tell those in authority exactly how they must do their jobs.
>
> Management that is destructively critical when mistakes are made kills initiative. And it's essential that we have many people with initiative if we are to continue to grow.

At just 3% per annum, employee turnover rate at 3M has long been among the lowest in corporate America, a fact that is often attributed to the tolerant, empowering, and family-like corporate culture that McKnight helped to establish. Reinforcing this culture has been a progressive approach towards employee compensation and retention. In the depths of the Great Depression, 3M was able to avoid laying off employees while many others did because the company's innovation engine was able to keep building new businesses even through the worst of times.

In many ways, 3M was ahead of its time in management philosophy and human resource practices. The company introduced its first profit sharing plan in 1916, and McKnight instituted a pension plan in 1930 and an employee stock purchase plan in 1950. McKnight himself was convinced that people would be much more likely to be loyal in a company if they had a stake in it. 3M also developed a policy of promoting from within, and of giving its employees a plethora of career opportunities within the company.

C19-2d Going International

The first steps abroad occurred in the 1920s. There were some limited sales of Wetor-dry sandpaper in Europe during the early 1920s. These increased after 1929 when 3M joined the Durex Corporation, a joint venture for international abrasive product sales in which 3M was involved along with eight other United States companies. In 1950, however, the Department of Justice alleged that the Durex Corporation was a mechanism for achieving collusion among U.S. abrasive manufactured, and a judge ordered that the corporation be broken up. After the Durex Corporation was dissolved in 1951, 3M was left with a sandpaper factory in Britain, a small plant in France, a sales office in Germany, and a tape factory in Brazil. International sales at this point amounted to no more than 5% of 3M's total revenues.

Although 3M opposed the dissolution of the Durex Corporation, in retrospect it turned out to be one of the most important events in the company's history, for it forced the corporation to build its own international operations. By 2010, international sales amounted to 63% of total revenues.

In 1952, Clarence Sampair was put in charge of 3M's international operations and charged with getting them off the ground. He was given considerable strategic and operational independence. Sampair and his successor, Maynard Patterson, worked hard to protect the international operations from getting caught up in the red tape of a major corporation. For example, Patterson recounts how....

> I asked Em Monteiro to start a small company in Columbia. I told him to pick a key person he wanted to take with him. "Go start a company," I said, "and no one from St Paul is going to visit you unless you ask for them. We'll stay out of your way, and if someone sticks his nose in your business you call me."[14]

The international businesses were grouped into an International Division that Sampair headed. From the get-go, the company insisted that foreign ventures pay their own way. In addition, 3M's international companies were expected to pay a 5% to 10% royalty to the corporate head office. Starved of working capital, 3M's International Division relied heavily on local borrowing to fund local operations, a fact that forced those operations to quickly pay their own way.

The international growth at 3M typically occurred in stages. The company would start by exporting to a country and working through sales subsidiaries. In that way, it began to understand the country, the local marketplace, and the local business environment. Next, 3M established warehouses in each nation and stocked those with goods paid for in local currency. The next phase involved converting products to the sizes and packaging forms that the local market conditions, customs, and culture dictated. 3M would ship jumbo rolls of products from the United States, which were then broken up and repackaged for each country. The next stage was designing and building plants, buying machinery and getting them up and running. Over the years, R&D functions were often added, and by the 1980s, considerable R&D was being done outside of the United States.

Both Sampair and Patterson set an innovative, entrepreneurial framework that according to the company, still guides 3M's International Operations today. The philosophy can be reduced to several key and simple commitments: (1) Get in early (within the company, the strategy is known as FIDO–"First in Defeats Others"). (2) Hire talented and motivated local people. (3) Become a good corporate citizen of the country. (4) Grow with the local economy. (5) American products are not one size fit all around the world; tailor products to fit local needs. (6) Enforce patents in local countries.

As 3M stepped into the international market vacuum, foreign sales surged from less than 5% in 1951 to 42% by 1979. By the end of the 1970s, 3M was beginning to understand how important it was to integrate the international operations more closely with the U.S. operations, and to build innovative capabilities overseas. It expanded the company's international R&D presence (there are now more than 3,000 technical employees outside the United States), built closer ties between the U.S. and foreign research organizations, and started to transfer more managerial and technical employees between businesses in different countries.

In 1978, the company started the Pathfinder Program to encourage new product and new business initiatives born outside the United States. By 1983, products developed under the initiative were generating sales of over $150 million a year. 3M Brazil invented a low-cost, hot melt adhesive from local raw materials, 3M Germany teamed up with Sumitomo 3M of Japan (a joint venture with Sumitomo) to develop electronic connectors with new features for the worldwide electronics industry, 3M Philippines developed a Scotch-Brite cleaning pad shaped like a foot after learning that Filipinos polished floors with their feet, and so on. On the back of such developments, in 1992, international operations exceeded 50% for the first time in the company's history.

By the 1990s, 3M started to shift away from a country-by-country management structure to more regional management. Drivers behind this development included the fall of trade barriers, the rise of trading blocks such as the European Union and NAFTA, and the need to drive down costs in the face of intense global competition. The first European Business Center (EBC) was created in 1991 to manage 3M's chemical business across Europe. The EBC was charged with product development, manufacturing, sales and marketing for Europe, but also with paying attention to local country requirements. Other EBCs soon followed, such as EBCs for disposable products and pharmaceuticals.

As the millennium ended, 3M was transforming the company into a transnational organization characterized by an integrated network of businesses that spanned the globe. The goal was to get the right mix of global scale to deal with competitive pressures, while at the same time maintaining 3M's traditional focus on local market differences and decentralized R&D capabilities.

C19-3 The New Era

C19-3a The DeSimone Years

In 1991, Desi DeSimone became CEO of 3M. A long-time 3M employee, the Canadian born DeSimone, was the epitome of a 21st-century manager—he had made his name by building 3M's Brazilian business and spoke five languages fluently. Unlike most prior 3M CEOs, DeSimone came from the manufacturing side of the business, rather than the technical aide. He soon received praise for managing 3M through the recession of the early 1990s. By the late 1990s, however, his leadership had come under fire from both inside and outside the company.

In 1998 and 1999, the company missed its earnings targets, and the stock price fell as disappointed investors sold. Sales were flat, profit margins fell and earnings slumped by 50%. The stock had underperformed the widely tracked S&P 500 stock index for most of the 1980s and 1990s.

One cause of the earnings slump in the late 1990s was 3M's sluggish response to the 1997 Asian crisis. During the Asian crisis, the value of several Asian currencies fell by as much as 80% against the U.S. dollar in a matter of months. 3M generated a quarter of its sales from Asia, but it was slow to cut costs there in the face of slumping demand following the collapse of currency values. At the same time, a flood of cheap Asian products cut into 3M's market share in the United States and Europe as lower currency values made Asian products much cheaper.

Another problem was that for all of its vaunted innovative capabilities, 3M had not produced a new blockbuster product since Post-it Notes. Most of the new products produced during the 1990s were just improvements over existing products, not truly new products.

DeSimone was also blamed for not pushing 3M hard enough earlier in the decade to reduce costs. An example was the company's supply chain excellence program. Back in 1995, 3M's inventory was turning over just 3.5 times a year, subpar for manufacturing. An internal study suggested that every half point increase in inventory turnover could reduce 3M's working capital needs by $700 million and boost its return on invested capital. But by 1998, 3M had made no progress on this front.[15]

By 1998, there was also evidence of internal concerns. Anonymous letters from 3M employees were sent to the board of directors, claiming that DeSimone was not committed to research as he should have been. Some letters complained that DeSimone was not funding important projects for future growth, others that he had not moved boldly enough to cut costs, and still others that the company's dual-career track was not being implemented well, and that technical people were underpaid. Critics argued that he was a slow and cautious decision maker in a time that required decisive strategic decisions. For example, in August 1998, DeSimone announced a restructuring plan that included a commitment to cut 4,500 jobs, but reports suggest that other senior managers wanted 10,000 job cuts, and DeSimone had watered down the proposals.[16]

Despite the criticism, 3M's board, which included four previous 3M CEOs among its members, stood behind DeSimone until he retired in 2001. However, the board began a search for a new top executive in February 2000 and signaled that it was looking for an outsider. In December 2000, the company announced that it had found the person they wanted, Jim McNerney, a 51-year-old General Electric veteran who ran GE's medical equipment businesses, and before that GE's Asian operations. McNerney was one of the front runners in the race to succeed Jack Welsh as CEO of GE but lost out to Jeffrey Immelt. One week after that announcement, 3M hired him.

C19-3b McNerney's Plan for 3M

In his first public statement days after being appointed, McNerney said that his focus would be on getting to know 3M's people and culture and its diverse lines of business:

> I think getting to know some of those businesses and bringing some of GE here to overlay on top of 3M's strong culture of innovation will be particularly important.[17]

It soon became apparent that McNerney's game plan was exactly that: to bring the GE play book to 3M and use it to try and boost 3M's results, while simultaneously not destroying the innovative culture that had produced the company's portfolio of 50,000 products.

The first move came in April 2001, when 3M announced that the company would cut 5,000 jobs, or about 7% of the workforce, in a restructuring effort that would zero in on struggling businesses. To cover severance and other costs of restructuring, 3M announced that it would take a $600 million charge against earnings. The job cuts were expected to save $500 million a year. In another effort to save costs, the company streamlined its purchasing processes, for example, by reducing the number of packaging suppliers on a global basis from 50 to 5, saving another $100 million a year in the process.

Next, McNerney introduced the Six Sigma process, a rigorous statistically based quality control process that was one of the drivers of process improvement and cost savings at GE. At heart, Six Sigma is a management philosophy, accompanied by a set of tools, that is rooted in identifying and prioritizing customers and their needs, reducing variation in all business processes, and selecting and grading all projects based on their impact on financial results. Six Sigma breaks every task (process) in an organization down into increments to be measured against a perfect model.

McNerney called for Six Sigma to be rolled out across 3M's global operations. He also introduced a 3M-like performance evaluation system at 3M under which managers were asked to rank every single employee who reported to them.

In addition to boosting performance from existing business, McNerney quickly signaled that he wanted to play a more active role in allocating resources between new business opportunities. At any given time, 3M has around 1,500 products in the development pipeline. McNerney stated that was too many, and he indicated that wanted to funnel more cash to the most promising ideas, those with a potential market of $100 million a year or more, while cutting funding to weaker-looking development projects.

He also scrapped the requirement that each division get 30% of its sales from products introduced in the past 4 years, noting that:

> To make that number, some managers were resorting to some rather dubious innovations, such as pink Post it Notes. It became a game, what could you do to get a new SKU?[18]

Some long-time 3M watchers, however, worried that by changing resource allocation practices McNerney might harm 3M's innovative culture. If the company's history proves anything, they say, it's that it is hard to tell which of today's tiny products will become tomorrow's home runs. No one predicted that Scotch Guard or Post-it Notes would earn millions. They began as little experiments that evolved without planning into big hits. McNerney's innovations all sound fine in theory, they say, but there is a risk that he will transform 3M into "3E" and lose what is valuable in 3M in the process.

In general, though, securities analysts greeted McNerney's moves favorably. One noted that "McNerney is all about speed," and that there will be "no more Tower of Babel-everyone speaks-one language." This "one company" vision was meant to replace the program under which 3M systematically spun off successful new products into new business centers. The problem with this approach, according to the analyst, was that there was no leveraging of best practices across businesses.[19]

McNerney also signaled that he would reform 3M's regional management structure, replacing it with a global business unit structure that will be defined by either products or markets.

At a meeting for investment analysts, held on September 30, 2003, McNerney summarized a number of achievements.[20] At the time, the indications seemed to suggest that McNerney was helping to revitalize 3M. Profitability, measured by return on invested capital, had risen from 19.4% in 2001 and was projected to hit 25.5% in 2003. 3M's stock price had risen from $42 just before McNerney was hired to $73 in October 2003 (see Exhibit 5 for details).

Like his former boss, Jack Welsh at GE, McNerney seemed to place significant value on internal executive education programs as a way of shifting to a performance-oriented culture. McNerney noted that some 20,000 employees had been through Six Sigma training by the third quarter of 2003. Almost 400 higher level managers had been through an Advanced Leadership Development Program set up by McNerney and offered by 3M's own internal executive education institute. Some 40% of participants had been promoted on graduating. All of the company's top managers had graduated from an Executive Leadership Program offered by 3M.

McNerney also emphasized the value of five initiatives that he put in place at 3M; indirect cost control, global sourcing, e-productivity, Six Sigma, and the 3M Acceleration program. With regard to indirect cost control, some $800 million had been taken out of 3M's cost structure since 2001, primarily by reducing employee numbers, introducing more efficient processes that boost productivity, benchmarking operations internally and leveraging best practices. According to McNerney, internal benchmarking highlighted another $200–$400 million in potential cost savings over the next few years.

On global sourcing, McNerney noted that more than $500 million had been saved since 2000 by consolidating purchasing, reducing the number of suppliers, switching to lower-cost suppliers in developing nations, and introducing dual sourcing policies to keep price increases under control.

The e-productivity program at 3M embraced the entire organization, and all functions. It involves the digitalization of a wide range of processes, from customer ordering and payment, through supply chain management and inventory control, to managing employee process. The central goal is to boost productivity by using information technology to more effectively manage information within the company, and between the company and its customers and suppliers. McNerney cited some $100 million in annual cost savings from this process.

The Six Sigma program overlays the entire organization, and focuses on improving processes to boost cash flow, lower costs (through productivity enhancements), and boost growth rates. By late 2003, there were some 7,000 Six Sigma projects in process at 3M. By using working capital more efficiently, Six Sigma programs had helped to generate some $800 million in cash, with the total expected to rise to $1.5 billion in by the end of 2004. 3M has applied the Six Sigma process to the company's R&D process, enabling researcher to engage customer information in the initial stages of a design discussion, which according to Jay Inlenfeld, the VP of R&D, Six Sigma tools:

> Allow us to be more closely connected to the market and give us a much higher probability of success in our new product designs.[21]

Finally, the 3M Acceleration program is aimed at boosting the growth rate from new products through better resource allocation, particularly by shifting resources from slower growing to faster growing markets. As McNerney noted:

> 3M has always had extremely strong competitive positions, but not in markets that are growing fast enough. The issue has been to shift emphasize into markets that are growing faster.[22]

Part of this program is a tool termed 2X/3X, 2X is an objective for two times the number of new products that were introduced in the past, and 3X is a business objective for three times as many winning products as there were in the past. 2X focuses on generating more "major" product initiatives, and 3X on improving the commercialization of those initiatives. The process illustrated in Exhibit 3 is 3M's "stage gate" process, where each gate represents a major decision point in the development of a new product, from idea generation to post launch.

Other initiates aimed at boosting 3M's organization growth rate through innovation include Six Sigma process, leadership development programs, and technology leadership. The purpose of these initiatives was to help implement the 2X/3X strategy.

As a further step in the Acceleration Program, 3M decided to centralize its corporate R&D effort. Prior to the arrival of McNerney, there were 12 technology centers staffed by 900 scientists that focused on core technology development. The company is replacing these with one central research lab, staffed by 500 scientists, some 120 of whom will be located outside the United States. The remaining 400 scientists will be relocated to R&D centers in the business units. The goal of this new corporate research lab is to focus on developing new technology that might fill high-growth "white spaces," which are areas where the company currently has no presence, but where the long-term market potential is great. An example is research on fuel cells, which is currently a big research project within 3M.

Responding to critics' charges that changes such as these might impact on 3M's innovative culture, VP of R&D Inlenfeld noted that:

> We are not going to change the basic culture of innovation at 3M. There is a lot of culture in 3M, but we are going to introduce more systematic, more productive tools that allow our researchers to be more successful.[23]

For example, Inlenfeld repeatedly emphasized that the company remains committed to basic 3M principles, such as the 15% rule and leveraging technology across businesses.

By late 2003, McNerney noted that some 600 new product ideas were underdevelopment and that collectively, they were expected to reach the market and generate some $5 billion in new revenues between 2003 and 2006, up from $3.5 billion 18 months earlier. Some $1 billion of these gains were expected to come in 2003.

C19-3c George Buckley Takes Over

In mid-2005 McNerney announced that he would leave 3M to become CEO and chairman of Boeing, a company on whose board he had served for some time. He was replaced in late 2005 by another outsider, George Buckley, the highly regarded CEO of Brunswick Industries. Buckley, a Brit with a PhD in electrical engineering, describes himself as a scientist at heart. Over the next year, in several presentations, Buckley outlined his strategy for 3M, and it soon became apparent that he was sticking to the general course laid out by McNerney, albeit with some important corrections.[24]

Buckley did not see 3M as an enterprise that needed radical change. He saw 3M as a company with impressive internal strengths, but one that had been too cautious about pursuing growth opportunities.[25] Buckley's overall strategic vision for 3M was that the company must solve customer needs through the provision of innovative and differentiated products that increase the efficiency and competitiveness of customers. Consistent with long-term 3M strategy, he saw this as being achieved by taking 3M's multiple technology platforms and applying them to different market opportunities.

Controlling costs and boosting productivity through Six Sigma continued to be a major thrust under Buckley. This was hardly a surprise, since Buckley had pushed Six Sigma at Brunswick. By late 2006, some 55,000 3M employees had been trained in Six Sigma methodology, 20,000 projects had been completed, and some 15,000 were under way. 3M was also adding techniques gleaned from Toyota's lean production methodology to its Six Sigma tool kit. As a result of Six Sigma and other cost control methods, between 2001 and 2005 productivity measured by sales per employee increased from $234 to $311, and some $750 million were taken out of overhead costs.

However, Buckley departed from McNerney's playbook in one significant way, he removed Six Sigma from the labs. The feeling of many at 3M was that Six Sigma rules choked those working on innovation. As one 3M researcher noted, "It's really tough to schedule innovation."[26] When McNerney left 3M in 2005, the percentage of sales from new products introduced in the last 5 years had fallen to 21%, down from the company's long-term goal of 30%. By 2010, after 5 years of Buckley's leadership, the percentage was back up to 30%. According to many in the company, Buckley has been a champion of researchers at 3M, devoting much of his personal time to empowering researchers and urging them to restore the luster of 3M.

Buckley stressed the need for 3M to more aggressively pursue growth opportunities. He wanted the company to use its differentiated brands and technology to continue to develop core businesses and extend those core businesses into adjacent areas. In addition, like McNerney, Buckley wanted the company to focus R&D resources on emerging business opportunities, and he too seemed to be prepared to play a more proactive role in this process. Areas of focus included filtration systems, track and trace information technology, energy and mineral extraction, and food safety. 3M made a number of acquisitions since 2005 to achieve scale and acquire technology and other assets in these areas. In addition, it increased its own investment in technologies related to these growth opportunities, particularly nanotechnology.

Buckley made selective divestures of businesses not seen as core. Most notably, in November 2006, 3M reached an agreement to sell its pharmaceutical business for $2.1 billion. 3M took this step after deciding that a combination of slow growth, and high regulatory and technological risk, made the sector an unattractive one that would dampen the company's growth rate.

Finally, Buckley was committed to continuing internationalization at 3M. 3M doubled its capital investment in the fast-growing markets of China, India, Brazil, Russia, and Poland between 2005 and 2010. All of these markets are seen as expanding two to three times as fast as the United States.

Judged by the company's financial results, the McNerney and Buckley eras did seem to be improving 3M's financial performance. The first decade of the twenty-first century was a difficult one, marked by sluggish growth in the United States, and in 2008–2009, a steep recession triggered by a global financial crisis. 3M weathered this storm better than most, bouncing out of the recession in 2010 with strong revenue and income growth, helped in large part by its new products and exposure to fast growing international markets. For the decade, revenues expanded from $16 billion in 2001 to $26.66 billion in 2010, earnings per share expanded from $1.79 to $5.63, while ROIC increased from the mid-teens in the 1990s to the mid-20s form most of the decade.

C19-3d Back to the Future

In early 2012, Georg Buckley retired after a successful tenure during which he had skillfully navigated 3M through the great financial crisis of 2008–2009. The company's COO, Inge Thulin replaced him. Thulin was originally from Sweden and first joined 3M in 1979. Fluent in five languages, Thulin had worked for 3M in Europe, the Middle East, Canada, and Hong Kong. Within the company he was seen as one of the chief architects of 3M's successful international business, which he oversaw as executive vice president for international operations. He was also seen as an insider who knew 3M's culture intimately, and who placed a high value on innovation. In his first shareholder meeting, he reaffirmed this, stating that "innovation is the center of our plan," and committing the company to increasing R&D spending to 6% of company sales, up from 5.4% of sales in 2012. More generally, Thulin stated that he would be continuing to follow the road map laid out by George Buckley, with whom he worked closely.

Thulin retired in 2018 after a successful tenure and was replaced by another company insider, Michael Roman. Roman joined 3M as a design engineer in 1988. Like Thulin, Roman has significant international experience, including a stint leading 3M Korea. He was chief strategy officer at 3M for 10 years before becoming COO in 2017, and then CEO in 2018. Upon becoming CEO, Roman indicated that he would not deviate from 3M's prior playbook, as developed under Buckley and Thulin, and for the most part he has done that. In July 2022, however, 3M announced that it would spin off its large healthcare division into a separate company. This division generated $8.6 billion in sales in 2021, about a quarter of 3M's total. Explaining the rational for the spin-off, Roman emphasized that a stand-alone healthcare business would be better positioned to deliver industry leading innovations in its sector.[27]

References

1. J. C. Collins and J. I. Porras, *Built to Last* (New York: Harper Business, 1994).
2. M. Conlin. "Too Much Doodle?," *Forbes*, October 19, 1998, pp. 54–56.
3. M. Dickson, "Back to the Future," *Financial Times*, May 30 1994, p. 7.
4. J. Hallinan, "3M's Next Chief Plans to Fortify Results with Discipline He Learned at GE Unit," *Wall Street Journal*, December 6, 2000, p. B17.
5. E. Von Hippel, et al, "Creating Breakthroughs at 3M," *Harvard Business Review*, September-October 1999.
6. R. Mullin, "Analysts Rate 3M's New Culture," Chemical Week September 26, 2001, pp. 39–40.

7. 3M. A Century of Innovation, the 3M Story. 3M, 2002. Available at http://www.3m.com/about3m/century/index.jhtml

8. 3M Investor Meeting, September 30, 2003, archived at http://www.corporate-ir.net/ireye/ir_site.zhtml?ticker=MMM&script=2100

9. T. Studt, "3M—Where Innovation Rules," *R&D Magazine*, April 2003, vol 45, pp. 20–24.

10. D. Weimer, "3M: The Heat Is on the Boss," *BusinessWeek,* March 15, 1999, pp. 82–83.

11. J. Useem, "(Tape) + (Light Bulb) = ?," *Fortune*, August 12, 2002, pp. 127–131.

12. M. Gunther, M. Adamo, and B. Feldman, "3M's Innovation Revival," *Fortune*, September 27. 2010, pp. 73–76.

Notes

[1]3M Annual report, 2021. Archived at http://investors.3m.com/financials/annual-reports-and-proxy-statements/default.aspx

[2]J. Aguilar, "Is Decisively Taking the Right Action, but Additional Concerns Still Loom Large," *Morningstar*, July 27, 2021.

[3]Sources: M. Dickson. "Back to the Future," *Financial Times*, May 30, 1994, p. 7. http://www.3m.com/profile/looking/mcknight.jhtml.

[4]http://www.3m.com/about3M/pioneers/drew2.jhtml

[5]Source: http://www.3m.com/about3M/innovation/scotchgard50/index.jhtml

[6]3M. A Century of Innovation, the 3M Story. 3M, 2002. Available at http://www.3m.com/about3m/century/index.jhtml

[7]3M. A Century of Innovation, the 3M Story. 3M, 2002, p. 33. Available at http://www.3m.com/about3m/century/index.jhtml

[8]3M. A Century of Innovation, the 3M Story. 3M, 2002, p. 78. Available at http://www.3m.com/about3m/century/index.jhtml

[9]3M. A Century of Innovation, the 3M Story. 3M, 2002, p. 78. Available at http://www.3m.com/about3m/century/index.jhtml

[10]3M. A Century of Innovation, the 3M Story. 3M, 2002, p. 42.

Available at http://www.3m.com/about3m/century/index.jhtml

[11]E. Von Hippel, et al, "Creating Breakthroughs at 3M," *Harvard Business Review*, September-October 1999.

[12]M. Scholz, "The Three Step Process That's Kept 3M Innovative for Decades," *Fast Company,* July 10, 2017.

[13]From 3M website at http://www.3m.com/about3M/history/mcknight.jhtml

[14]3M. A Century of Innovation, the 3M Story. 3M, 2002, pp. 143–144. Available at http://www.3m.com/about3m/century/index.jhtml

[15]M. Conlin, "Too Much Doodle?," *Forbes*, October 19, 1998, pp. 54–56.

[16]De'Ann Weimer, "3M: The Heat Is on the Boss," *BusinessWeek*, March 15, 1999, pp. 82–83.

[17]J. Hallinan, "3M's Next Chief Plans to Fortify Results with Discipline He Learned at GE Unit," *Wall Street Journal*, December 6, 2000, p. B17.

[18]J. Useem, "(Tape) + (Light Bulb) = ?," *Fortune*, August 12, 2002, pp. 127–131.

[19]R. Mullin, "Analysts Rate 3M's New Culture," *Chemical Week*, September 26, 2001, pp. 39–40.

[20]3M Investor Meeting, September 30, 2003, archived at http://www.corporate-ir.net/ireye/ir_site.zhtml?ticker=MMM&script=2100

[21]T. Studt, "3M—Where Innovation Rules," *R&D Magazine*, April 2003, p. 22.

[22]3M Investor Meeting, September 30, 2003, archived at http://www.corporate-ir.net/ireye/ir_site.zhtml?ticker=MMM&script=2100

[23]T. Studt, "3M—Where Innovation Rules," *R&D Magazine*, April 2003, p. 21.

[24]Material here drawn from George Buckley's presentation to Prudential's investor conference on "Inside our Best ideas," September 28, 2006. This and other relevant presentations are archived at http://investor.3m.com/ireye/ir_site.zhtml?ticker=MMM&script=1200

[25]J. Sprague, "MMM: Searching for Growth with New CEO Leading," *Citigroup Global Markets*, May 2, 2006.

[26]M. Gunther, M. Adamo, and B. Feldman, "3M's Innovation Revival," *Fortune*, September 27, 2010, p. 74.

[27]S. Balasubramanian, "Manufacturing Titan 3M Is Spinning Off Its Healthcare Business into a Separate Company," *Forbes,* July 26, 2022.

20

Upside Foods: Changing the World Through Cultivated Meat[1]

By Melissa Schillin

In late 2017, Microsoft founder Bill Gates and a group of other high-powered investors- who comprise Breakthrough Energy Ventures-like Amazon's Jeff Bezos, Alibaba's Jack Ma, and Virgin's Richard Branson-announced their intention to fund a San Francisco-based startup called Memphis Meats with an unusual business plan: it grew "clean" meat using stem cells, eliminating the need to breed or slaughter animals. The company had already produced beef, chicken and duck, all grown from cells.[2]

There were many potential advantages of growing meat without animals. First, growth in the demand for meat was skyrocketing due to both population growth and development. When developing countries become wealthier, they increase their meat consumption. While humanity's population had doubled since 1960, consumption of animal products had risen fivefold and was still increasing. Many scientists and economists had begun to warn of an impending "meat crisis". Even though plant protein substitutes like soy and pea protein had gained enthusiastic followings, the rate of animal protein consumption had continued to rise. This suggested that meat shortages were inevitable unless radically more efficient methods of production were developed.

Large-scale production of animals also had a massively negative effect on the environment. The worldwide production of cattle, for example, resulted in a larger emissions of greenhouse gasses than the collective effect of the world's automobiles. Animal production is also extremely water intensive: To produce each chicken sold in a supermarket, for example, requires more than one-thousand gallons of water, and each egg requires fifty gallons. Each gallon of cow's milk required nine hundred gallons of water. A study by Oxford University indicated that meat grown from cells would produce up to 96% lower greenhouse gas emissions, use 45% less energy, 99% less land, and 96% less water.[3]

Scientists also agreed that producing animals for consumption was simply inefficient. Estimates suggested, for example, that it required roughly 23 calories worth of inputs to produce one calorie of beef. "Clean" meat promised to bring that ratio down to three calories of inputs to produce a calorie of beef–more than seven times greater efficiency. "Clean" meat also would not contain antibiotics, steroids, or bacteria such as *E-coli* – it was literally "cleaner", and that translated into both greater human health and lower perishability.

C20-1 The Development of Cultivated Meat

In 2004, Jason Matheny, a twenty-nine-year-old recent graduate from the John Hopkins Public Health program decided to try to tackle the problems with production of animals for food. Though Matheny was a vegetarian himself, he realized that convincing enough people to adopt a plant-based diet to slow down the meat crisis was unlikely. As he noted, "You can spend your time trying to get people to turn their lights out more often, or you can invent a more efficient light bulb that uses far less energy even if you leave it on. What we need is an enormously more efficient way to get meat."[4]

Matheny founded a non-profit organization called New Harvest that would be dedicated to promoting research into growing real meat without animals. He soon discovered that a Dutch scientist, Willem van Eelen was exploring how to culture meat from animal cells. Van Eelen had been awarded the first patent on a cultured meat production method in 1999. However, the eccentric scientist had not had much luck in attracting funding to his project, nor in scaling up his production. Matheny decided that with a little prodding, the Dutch government might be persuaded to make a serious investment in the development of meat culturing methods. He managed to get a meeting with the Netherland's minister of agriculture where he made his case. Matheny's efforts paid off: The Dutch government agreed to invest two million euros in exploring methods of creating cultured meat at three different universities.

By 2005, cultivated meat was starting to gather attention. The journal *Tissue Engineering* published an article entitled "*In Vitro-Cultured Meat Production*", and in the same year, the *New York Times* profiled cultivated meat in its annual "Ideas of the Year." However, while governments and universities were willing to invest in the basic science of creating methods of producing clean meat, they did not have the capabilities and assets needed to bring it to commercial scale. Matheny knew that to make cultivated meat a mainstream reality, he would need to attract the interest of large agribusiness firms.

Matheny's initial talks with agribusiness firms did not go well. Though meat producers were open to the idea conceptually, they worried that consumers would balk at cultivated meat and perceive it as unnatural. Matheny found this criticism frustrating; after all, flying in airplanes, using air conditioning, or eating meat pumped full of steroids to accelerate its growth were also unnatural.

Progress was slow. Matheny took a job at the Intelligence Advanced Research Projects Activity (IARPA) of the U.S. Federal government while continuing to run New Harvest on the side. Fortunately, others were also starting to realize the urgency of developing alternative meat production methods.

C20-2 Enter Sergey Brin of Google

In 2009, the Brin Wojcicki Foundation, co-founder of Google, contacted Matheny to learn more about cultured meat technologies. Matheny referred Brin's foundation to Dr. Mark Post at Maastricht University, one of the leading scientists funded by the Dutch government's cultivated meat investment. Post had succeeded in growing mouse muscles in vitro and was certain his process could be replicated with the muscles of cows, poultry, and more. As he stated, "It was so clear to me that we could do this. The science was there. All we needed was funding to actually prove it, and now here was a chance to get what was needed."[5] It took more than a year to work out the details, but in 2011, Brin offered Post roughly three quarters of a million dollars to prove his process by making two cultured beef burgers, and Post's team set about meeting the challenge.

In early 2013, the moment of truth arrived: Post and his team had enough cultured beef to do a taste test. They fried up a small burger and split it into thirds to taste. It tasted like meat. Their burger was 100% skeletal muscle and they knew that for commercial production they would need to add fat and connective tissue to more closely replicate the texture of beef, but those would be easy problems to solve after passing this milestone. The press responded enthusiastically, and the *Washington Post* ran an article headlined, "Could a test-tube burger save the planet?"[6]

C20-3 Going Commercial

In 2015, Uma Valeti, a cardiologist at the Mayo Clinic founded his own cultured-meat research lab at the University of Minnesota. "I'd read about the inefficiency of meat-eating compared to a vegetarian diet, but what bothered me more than the wastefulness was the sheer scale of suffering of the animals".[7] As a heart doctor, Valeti also believed that getting people to eat less meat could improve human health: "I knew that poor diets and the unhealthy fats and refined carbs that my patients were eating were killing them, but so many seemed totally unwilling to eat less or no meat. Some actually told me they'd rather live a shorter life than stop eating the meats they loved." Valeti began fantasizing about a best-of-both-worlds alternative–a healthier and kinder meat. As he noted, "The main difference I thought I'd want for this meat I was envisioning was that it'd have to be leaner and more protein-packed than a cut of supermarket meat, since there's a large amount of saturated fat in that meat…Why not have fats that are proven to be better for health and longevity, like omega-3s? We want to be not just like conventional meat but healthier than conventional meat."[8]

Valeti was nervous about leaving his successful position as a cardiologist–after all, he had a wife and two children to help support. However, when he sat down to discuss it with his wife (a pediatric eye surgeon), she said, "Look, Uma. We've been wanting to do this forever. I don't ever want us to look back on why we didn't have the courage to work on an idea that could make this world kinder and better for our children and their generation."[9] And thus Valeti's company –which would later be named Memphis Meats-was born.

Building on Dr. Post's achievement, Valeti's team began experimenting with ways to get just the right texture and taste. The company developed a process that began with selecting specific types of animal cells that could be grown into meat. Next those cells are put into a "cultivator" (similar to a fermentation tank) where they grew and formed muscle and connective tissue. The process was similar to how breweries grew yeast cells to make beer.[10]

After much trial and error to refine the texture and taste of the end product, and a growing number of patents, they hosted their first tasting event in December 2015. On the menu: a meatball. This time the giant agribusiness firms took notice. At the end of 2016, Tyson Foods, the world's largest meat producer, announced that it would invest $150 million in a venture capital fund that would develop alternative proteins, including meat grown from self-reproducing cells.

In 2017 Memphis meats raised $17 million in an A round that included investments from agribusiness giants Cargill and Tyson, as well as celebrity investors such as Bill Gates, Kimball Musk and Richard Branson. In January of 2020 Memphis Meats closed a B round of investment for $186 million that included new and returning investors that included Tyson, Cargill, Gates, Musk, Branson, Threshold Ventures, Finistere, Future Ventures, Fifty Years, CPT Capital, KBW Ventures and Vulcan Capital.[11] Now called "Upside Foods" (Memphis Meats had changed its name to Upside in 2017).[12]

The company used those funds to build a pilot production facility that would enable it to begin bringing its products to market. By November 2021 it had opened a 53,000 square-foot engineering, production and innovation center called "EPIC" in Emeryville, California. This facility was designed to produce any species of meat, poultry or seafood, and would initially make more than 50,000 pounds of finished product with intention to scale to a future capacity of more than 400,000 pounds per year.[13]

The world was becoming more and more convinced that the initially science-fiction-like idea of cultured meat would soon become a commercially viable reality. As evidence of this, in April of 2022 Upside Foods raised a $400 million C round that brought in investors such as Temasek, the Abu Dhabi Growth Fund, and more.[14] This funding was intended to be used to build a commercial-scale facility, educate consumers and built out a robust and effective supply chain for cell feed and other inputs. Valeti believed it would take roughly 18 to 24 months to transition to the new site to scale to "tens of millions of pounds of product." In the meantime, Upside would produce small batches of products, including a chicken product that would be launched to consumers in late 2022. Valeti also had faith that the company would be able to make cultured meat not only competitive with traditional meat, but more affordable. "Our costs have continued to come down significantly over the last three years…We have a clear path to bringing a cost competitive product to market as we scale our production," Valeti noted.[15]

C20-4 Looking to the Future

By early 2022, it was estimated that there were over one hundred startups making cultivated meat, including Eat Just, BlueNalu, Finless Foods, Wild Earth, Aleph Farms, Meatable, Higher Steaks, and many more. Over $2 billion had been invested in the space.[16]

That first meatball had cost $1200; to make cultured meat a commercial reality required bringing costs down substantially. But analysts were quick to point out that the first iPhone had cost $2.6 billion in R&D – much more than the first cultured meats. Scale and learning curve efficiencies would drive the cost down of cultured meat down. Growing meat rather than whole animals had, after all, inherent efficiency advantages.

Some skeptics believed the bigger problem was not production economies, but consumer acceptance: would people be willing to eat meat grown without animals? Sergey Brin, Bill Gates, Jeff Bezos, Jack Ma and Richard Branson were willing to be that they would. Branson was a firm believer that they would, stating in 2017: "I believe that in 30 years or so we will no longer need to kill any animals and that all meat will either be clean or plant-based, taste the same and also be much healthier for everyone."[17] Valeti noted that a considerable part of Upside's budget would go to consumer education, stating, "Our goal is to introduce consumers to cultivated meat to dispel any confusion with meat alternatives…This is going to open up the entire cultivated meat space, and as the pioneer, we are writing the playbook and sharing it with people. In the next two decades, so many products will be brought to market, so our goal is to engage with consumers and B2B businesses. The consumer has to fall in love with this."[18]

Discussion questions:

1. What were the potential advantages of developing cultivated meat? What were the challenges of developing it and bringing it to market?
2. What kinds of organizations were involved in developing cultivated meat? What were the different resources that each kind of organization brought to the innovation?
3. Should organizations with a social mission such as those dedicated to improving the environment or reducing human or animal suffering be evaluated in a different way than other organizations? Why do you think so many individuals and firms were willing to make such major investments in cultivated meat?
4. Do you think people will be willing to eat cultivated meat? Do you think cultivated meat will be profitable? Can you think of other products or services that faced similar adoption challenges?

Notes

[1] Adapted from a NYU teaching case by Paul Shapiro and Melissa Schilling.

[2] Friedman, Z. 2017. Why Bill Gates and Richard Branson invested in "Clean" meat. *Forbes*, August 25th.

[3] Tuomisto, HL & de Mattos, MJ. 2011. Environmental impacts of cultured meat production. Environmental Science & Technology, 14:6117-2123.

[4] Shapiro, P. *Clean Meat: How growing meat without animals will revolutionize dinner and the world.* New York: Gallery Books, pg. 35.

[5] Shapiro, P. 2018. *Clean Meat: How growing meat without animals will revolutionize dinner and the world.* New York: Gallery Books, pg. 60.

[6] 2013. "Could a test-tube burger save the planet?" *Washington Post,* August 5th.

[7] Shapiro, P. 2018. *Clean Meat: How growing meat without animals will revolutionize dinner and the world.* New York: Gallery Books, pg. 113.

[8] Shapiro, P. 2018. *Clean Meat: How growing meat without animals will revolutionize dinner and the world.* New York: Gallery Books, pg. 115.

[9] Shapiro, P. 2018. *Clean Meat: How growing meat without animals will revolutionize dinner and the world.* New York: Gallery Books, pg. 118.

[10] Aubrey, A. 2020. Ready for meat grown from animal cells? A startup plans a pilot facility. NPR, January 22nd.

[11] Byrne B & Crosser N. 2020. Upside Foods' $161 million Series B is a turning point for the meat industry. Good Food Institute, January 22nd.

[12] 2021. Memphis Meats changes name, plans to roll out lab-grown chicken this year. *Food Processing,* May 12th.

[13] Hall C 2022. Upside Foods bites into $400M round to serve cultivated meat later this year. Techcrunch, April 21st.

[14] Hall C 2022. Upside Foods bites into $400M round to serve cultivated meat later this year. Techcrunch, April 21st.

[15] Aubrey, A. 2020. Ready for meat grown from animal cells? A startup plans a pilot facility. NPR, January 22nd.

[16] Rogers K 2022. Lab-grown meat could make strides in 2022 as start-ups push for U.S. approval. CNBC January 23rd.

[17] Friedman, Z. 2017. Why Bill Gates and Richard Branson invested in "Clean" meat. *Forbes*, August 25th.

[18] Hall C 2022. Upside Foods bites into $400M round to serve cultivated meat later this year. Techcrunch, April 21st.

General Electric: Jack Welch, Jeffery Immelt, and the Rise and Fall of GE

By Charles W. L. Hill Foster School of Business University of Washington Seattle, WA 98105 August 2022

C21-1 Introduction

On November 9, 2021, The General Electric Company (GE) announced that it was going to split itself into three independent companies—a healthcare business, an energy business, and an aerospace company. The split marked the end of the road for a 130-year-old industrial company that in the 1990s was considered one of the best managed diversified enterprises in the world, and for a time held the title as the world's most valuable industrial corporation. The 2000s, however, were not kind to GE. When the legendary CEO of GE, Jack Welch, retired in 2001, he was succeeded by Jeffery Immelt. Welch's two-decade tenure had seen dramatic improvements in GE's performance, but Immelt's 16-year reign as CEO was characterized by crisis and decline. When Immelt stepped aside in June of 2017, the company was loaded with debt, cash flow was under pressure, and operating performance in several of GE's business units was weak. The stock price was below the level where it was 16 years earlier when Immelt had become CEO, even though the S&P 500 had risen by 240%. Immelt's successors tried to turn the behemoth around, but in the end admitted defeat and decided to break the company up instead. Many wondered how this could have happened to such a storied corporation that for years was held up as an example of managerial excellence.

C21-2 The Evolution of GE

The history of GE dates to 1890 when Thomas Edison established the Edison General Electric Company. Thomas Edison was a prolific entrepreneur and inventor with over a thousand patents to his name. His inventions included the phonograph, the motion picture camera, and a long-lasting incandescent lightbulb. In 1892, Edison merged the Edison General Electric Company with Thomson-Huston Electric Company to form General Electric. Edison remained associated with GE for the rest of his life through his patents and consulting duties. GE was one of the original components of the Dow Jones Industrial Index when it was established in 1896. It was the sole survivor of the founding companies when it was finally removed from the Index on June 25, 2018.

C21-2a General Electric in the 1960s and 1970s

By the early 1970s, GE was an extensively diversified corporation with activities ranging from plastics, home appliances and lighting, to power generation equipment and jet engines. Reg Jones, who became CEO in 1973, worried about the lack of industrial logic tying together the company's disparate businesses. He felt that the company had become too decentralized. His predecessor as CEO, Ralph Cordiner, had broken the company down into departments that were "the size that a man could get his arms around." His philosophy was to give an executive a $50 million business and say, "here grow this into a $125 million business." If he achieved that, the department would then be split into two departments. As a result of this policy, by the time Jones took over, GE had 190 departments that were grouped into 46 divisions and 10 groups.

While the company had been growing its revenues, profit growth under Cordiner had been disappointing. In part this was because the company was undertaking simultaneous large investments with long payback periods into nuclear power, jet engines, and computers. More generally, Jones attributed the profitless growth to an engineering culture where "we *can* do it" all too often became "we *should* do it." The company was the champion of make not buy, of volume and diversification, but it was not focused on the bottom line.

Following a detailed study by management consultants McKenzie & Co, Jones' solution was to reorganize the company into 43 strategic business units (SBU), each of which served a clearly defined end market. Jones tried to improve GE's profit performance by developing a sophisticated strategic planning system that required each SBU to develop a strategy in close consultation with strategic planners at the head office. The idea was that the head office would add value by helping business until managers develop and improve their strategy. However, it wasn't clear that planners at the head office had the skill set to help develop strategies in businesses as diverse as plastics, power generation systems, jet engines, and appliances. Moreover, there were complaints that the formal planning system was overly bureaucratic, centralized, involved a lot of game playing and upward merchandizing of plans, and devalued the contributions of SBU managers, who often thought that the planners at the head office lack the expertise to understand their businesses. The planning system also made it difficult to assign accountability.

By the end of his tenure, Jones acknowledged that the corporate office didn't have the bandwidth to adequately review 43 different business unit plans. As another CEO who knew Jones at the time commented, he was "drowning in paper, his office was full of stacks of planning books." Nevertheless, Jones believed that the strategic planning systems had injected necessary discipline into the performance review process and improved capital allocation at GE. For the first time, GE had exited businesses that were underperforming, including computers. However, it still wasn't clear to Jones, or many outside observers, how GE was more than the sum of its parts.

C21-2b The Welch Years; 1981–2001

When Jones retired in 1981, he chose as his successor a brash, hard driving, and abrasive young executive who had made his reputation running GE's plastics business. His name was Jack Welch. Welsh was just 45 when he became CEO in April 1981. He would run the company for the next two decades. In 1999, 2 years before his retirement, *Fortune Magazine* ran an article that called Welch not just the best executive of the year, but quite possibly the best manager of the 20th century.

One of Welch's first actions was to dramatically reduce the strategic planning function of the head office. Welch thought that business-level strategy should be done by the people who ran the businesses. Most of the planners at the head office were laid off or sent down to the businesses. Welch replaced the extensive planning process with a "real-time" discussion of each business's strategy that was built around a five-page strategy "playbook," which Welch and his business leader discussed without the benefit of staff.

To remain part of GE, Welch told each business that it had to be number one or two in its market, and that it had to have a strategy for growing its profitability at 15% per annum. If the business was not number one or two, the dictum was "fix, sell or close." Of the 43 SBUs that Welch inherited from Jones, 14 passed the test of either being number one or two or having a plan for getting there. The remainder were either sold or closed. By 1990, Welch had sold off 200 product lines, raising $11 billion in the process. During the same time period, Welch made over 370 acquisitions, investing more than $21 billion. These acquisitions both strengthened the company's core businesses and took GE into new areas such as financial services and network broadcasting with the acquisitions of Kidder Peabody (an investment bank), Polaris (an aircraft leasing company), and NBC (a network broadcasting company that came with the acquisition of RCA). As part of the restructuring process, GE eliminated over 120,000 employee positions between 1981 and 1988, with about the same number leaving the company due to divestments. The layoffs earned Welch the nickname "Neutron Jack." In 1980, GE had 404,000 employees. By 1990, even with extensive acquisitions, GE's headcount was down to around 290,000.

In 1986, Welch shocked the company when he came in one Monday morning and replaced 12 of his 14 business unit heads. In Welch's view these executives were wedded to the old way of doing things and were the wrong people to lead the cultural change that he envisaged. He thought the company was moving too slow and behaving too cautiously, partly due to push-back from his own top management team. He replaced them with people that were more in his own mold.

Welch was explicit about the kind of managers he wanted at GE. They had to be able to make a decision and take *ownership* for their actions. They had to be good *stewards* of the assets under their control. They had to be *entrepreneurial*, willing to take risks. He also valued *excellence, reality and candor*, and *open communication*, all attributes he felt had not been valued under prior leadership. As part of the performance review process, Welch rated senior managers not only on their ability to hit financial objectives, but also on whether they lived up to the values he espoused.

By the late 1980s, Welch had the mix of growth businesses that he wanted. He now started to develop strategies for continually improving performance. His view was that while productivity could be increased by restructuring, that only got you so far. To continue to improve productivity over the long run, processes needed to be put in place that created the right incentives for employees to look for ways of reducing costs and adding value. The first such process was known as *work out*. Under *work-out* groups, 40 to 100 employees were invited to share their views about how their business could be improved with their boss. Employees worked with facilitators on ideas over 3 days, at the end of which they were presented to their supervisor. The rules of the process required managers to make instant decisions about proposals on the spot in front of everyone. A manager's supervisor normally sat behind them as they made decisions. About 80% of proposals got an immediate yes. By 1992, around two-thirds of GE's employees had participated in *work out*. The result; productivity increases at GE which had been running at an annual rate of 2% from 1981 to 1987 doubled to 4% between 1988 and 1992.

Work out was followed by a series of additional productivity initiatives during the 1990s. These included *best practices* (an initiative aimed at learning of the best practices of market leading organizations and implementing them within GE), *boundaryless behavior* (which required managers to share best practices across businesses), and perhaps most famously, the *Six Sigma quality improvement process*. Introduced in 1996, by 1999, GE had invested $500 million to train 85,000 employees in Six Sigma. As a result of Six Sigma programs, the company was reporting productivity improvements from more efficient product design, fewer production errors, less wasted materials and time, and better capacity utilization. To make sure that all of these initiatives were adopted,

Welch insisted that a manager's success at implementing an initiative would be a major component of their annual performance review, and that bonuses would be tied to this.

Welch devoted an enormous amount of time to human resource initiatives. He made stock options a major component of employee performance, expanding the number of option recipients from 300 to 30,000. He introduced a stack ranking system for performance evaluation. This required every manager to rank their subordinates into one of five categories. The bottom 10% were scored five and encouraged to leave the company (a practice that led to the system being known as "rank and yank"). He championed the introduction of 360-degree performance reviews, in which an employee's performance was evaluated not just by their supervisor , but also by peers and subordinates. Perhaps most notably, he monitored, mentored, and evaluated the performance of the top 500 managers at GE. Welch saw his role as developing great managers who could lead any business. To him, allocating human capital was every bit as important as allocating financial capital. Welch estimated that he spent up to 70% of his time on HR issues.

On the strategy side, the biggest trend during the Welch years was the expansion of GE's financial services business. GE had been involved in financial services through GE Capital since the 1930s. First established to help consumers buy home appliances such as refrigerators, under Welch, GE Capital expanded into a mammoth profit machine. Much of this growth was driven by a series of major acquisitions in the 1980s that included insurance, investment banking, leasing, credit card, and mortgage companies. By the mid-1990s, over 40% of GE's profits were coming from GE Capital. GE Capital had become a financial conglomerate in its own right, making car loans, issuing credit cards, owning and leasing commercial aircraft, investing in commercial real estate, issuing mortgages, offering insurance, and a host of other activities. GE Capital helped GE's industrial businesses by offering financing for the customers that purchased its expensive heavy equipment, from jet engines and power turbines to locomotives and MRI machines. In return, GE's industrial businesses helped GE Capital by furnishing reliable earnings and tangible assets that helped the whole company to maintain a triple A credit rating. That rating allowed GE to borrow funds in world capital markets at a lower rate than any purely financial corporation could achieve. The result was a lower cost of capital that for years was a major source of advantage for the financial services business.

GE Capital also performed another critical function for its parent company—it helped GE to manage its earnings. Since financial assets are under normal conditions far more liquid than tangible assets, GE Capital was able to buy or sell assets in the final days of a quarter to make sure that GE's reported earnings rose smoothly and in line with Wall Street expectations. Investors seem willing to pay more for a company that can produce a steady and predictable stream of growing earnings. GE Capital helped GE to achieve this. This helped the stock to trade at a premium to purely industrial companies.

GE also grew its product services under Welsh. GE realized that since it sold expensive capital equipment that often remained in service for years, if not decades, it could make good money by offering life-of-equipment service contracts that provided ongoing diagnostics and preventative maintenance. In 1994, Welch noted that there was an installed base of 9,000 GE commercial jet engines, 10,000 turbines, 13,000 locomotives, and 84,000 pieces of diagnostic medical imaging equipment. The strategy was to monetize this installed base. For example, by putting diagnostic sensors in an MRI machine and remotely monitoring that data, GE could detect when a critical component was failing and replaced it before the part failed. Customers placed a high value on such services. They limited downtime and kept expensive capital equipment functioning efficiently. For GE, in addition to creating a new income stream, service contracts provided a steady and predictable earnings flow, which again helped the company to deliver the predictable earnings growth that pleased Wall Street.

On the face of it, the achievements of the Welch years were impressive. Over his 20 years as CEO, the stock was up 2,790%. When Welch became CEO, GE's earnings were $1.65 billion; when he left, they were $12.74 billion. According to the company's own data, productivity at GE increased by 5% per annum compounded during Welch's tenure. On retirement, Welch collected a $417 million severance package, the largest in corporate history. Was that large payout justified? GE's board clearly thought so. However, Welch had his critics. Some argued that the reliance of GE Capital was risky. Unlike a traditional bank, GE Capital had no large stable source of deposits to fall back on in a financial crisis and carried a heavy debt load. Others believed that the increasing complexity and diversity of GE made it difficult to analyze the company's financial statements. They worried that the practice of drawing on GE Capital to smooth out earnings was an accounting trick that might be used to obscure serious operating problems in certain businesses. They were perplexed as to how to value a company that now included not just traditional industrial businesses, but also financial services and network broadcasting. Another concern was that GE in its current form was very much the creation of one man. It was unclear whether anyone could truly replace Welch.

C21-3 The Immelt Era, 2001–2017

When Jack Welsh retired in 2001, GE was at the top it its game. In a sense though, he had been lucky. He took over in 1981 when the U.S. economy was in recession. He was helped in his early years by the robust economic recovery that followed. Apart from a brief recession in 1990–1991, the 1990s were also a period of economic vitality in the United States. The stock market boomed, carrying many companies to record highs (GE's stock hit an all-time high of $33.69 a share in August 2000 when it sported a price earnings ratio of close to 60). His successor, Jeffery Immelt, would have no such tailwinds.

Immelt joined GE in 1982 after graduating from Harvard with an MBA. He rose through the ranks to lead GE's medical equipment business. He was also on the board of GE Capital. He was selected to succeed Welch in October 2000 and assume the CEO position on September 7, 2001. Four days later, two hijacked passenger aircraft slammed into the World Trade Center towers in the largest terrorist attack on U.S. soil in history. The stock market—already in retreat from its all-time highs in 2000—tumbled and the economy slipped into a recession. GE's insurance business took a direct hit from the attack and had to pay out $600 million in claims. GE's aircraft engine and aircraft leasing businesses were also hurt by the attacks. By the end of Immelt's first week as CEO, the stock had lost 20% of its value.

Despite these adverse events, Immelt seemed committed to sticking with GE's diversification strategy. In the company's 2001 annual report, he noted that:

> Our businesses are closely integrated. They share four leading-edge business initiatives: excellent financial disciplines and Controllership; a tradition of sharing talent and best practices; and a culture whose cornerstone is absolute, unyielding integrity. Without these powerful ties, we actually could merit the label "conglomerate" that people often inaccurately apply to us. That word just does not apply to GE.........Instead, what we have is a Company of diverse businesses whose sum truly is greater than the parts; a Company executing with excellence despite a brutal global economy to deliver over $17 billions of cash flow in 2001. Try "managing" your way to cash flow of that magnitude – year after year......Some companies are different. We believe GE is different, and one of the things that makes us different is that—in good times and bad - we deliver. That is who we are.

C21-3a Reshaping the Portfolio: Acquisitions and Divestments

If there were any doubts that Immelt would continue Welch's strategy of diversification via acquisitions into industries seen as having growth prospects, they were quickly dispelled by his early moves. Immelt made a series of acquisitions to strengthen several businesses, enter new ones, and reposition the company to capitalize from what he saw as major growth opportunities. Over his tenure he did hundreds of deals, claiming with some pride that he was the only CEO who has ever bought and sold over $100 billions of businesses. By the company's own calculations, during Immelt's tenure GE made 380 acquisitions that came at a cost of over $175 billion. It also sold off 370 business and product lines worth around $400 billion. Put differently, during Immelt's tenure GE made an average of 46 acquisitions and divestitures annually at an average value of $35 billion per year, churning roughly 9% of its total current enterprise value every year.

Before 2001 was over, Immelt had already made some significant acquisitions. He expanded GE's NBC business with the acquisitions of Telemundo (which served the rapidly growing Hispanic market) and with the purchase of the Bravo network. He took GE deeper into the media business in 2003 when the company acquired 80% of the Universal entertainment business from the French firm, Vivendi, for $5.5 billion. The acquisition included Universal's film library, film studio, cable services, and theme park. The venture was rebranded as NBCUniversal Media L.L.C. While critics wondered what GE was doing in the entertainment business, Immelt countered that "This is about stuff we know how to do....we understand the nuances of this industry and where it is going."

Between 2001 and 2007, GE made $75 billion worth of acquisitions in areas like energy, aviation, water treatment, health care, and financial services. Some of these acquisitions were great successes. For example, GE purchased Enron's wind turbine business for $358 million in a bankruptcy auction, creating the foundation for a business that by 2016 bought in over $10 billion in revenue. To help fund the acquisitions, the company also sold off businesses seen as having low growth potential. Among the divestments was GE's plastics business, which was sold to a Saudi company for $11.6 billion, just before the 2008–2009 financial crisis. The price was more than analysts had expected and the deal was generally regarded as excellent for GE.

Not all of Immelt's bets paid off. Following the events of September 11, 2001, GE dived into the security business, buying two explosive detection companies for well over $1 billion. In 2009, these businesses were packaged as GE Homeland Security and sold off for just $760 million. Immelt's security bet turned out to be a bust. In another example, in 2004, with home prices surging GE paid $500 million for America's six largest subprime mortgage company, WMC. In 2007, the market for subprime loans collapsed and WMC lost $1 billion. GE shut the company down and laid off most of its employees. As of 2018, however, WMC was still causing headaches for GE. Several investors that purchased mortgage-backed securities from WMC were suing the company, claiming that it misrepresented the quality of its mortgages. The Justice Department had also launched an investigation of WMC. In 2018, GE set aside $1.5 billion to cover potential losses from the investigation.

Perhaps Immelt's worst acquisition was his biggest, the purchase of the French power company Alstom for $10.6 billion in 2015. Alstom, a competitor of GE Power, made and serviced the turbines that utilities use to generate power. Alstom's profit margins were low, but GE thought it could improve them. GE's strategy relied heavily upon selling services, but to comply with antitrust laws regulators made GE divest Alstom's service business. The acquisition added more than 30,000 high-cost employees, many in Europe. GE thought that they would pay for themselves, but the acquisition was mistimed. GE invested in Alstom's fossil fuel–fired turbine business just as renewables were become cost competitive. The result was that global demand for GE Power's products collapsed and the unit's profit plunged by 45%.

GE also made nine acquisitions valued at more than $14 billion in the oil and gas industry between 2010 and 2014. These were made at a time when oil prices were hovering around $100 a barrel. In 2016, with oil prices slumping to under $40 a barrel, GE agreed to combine its oil and gas unit with Baker Hughes, a publicly traded oilfield services provider. The deal created the second-largest oilfield service provider in the world with revenues of $23 billion and operations in 120 countries.

Immelt also made a series of acquisitions to bulk up GE Capital before the 2008–2009 global financial crisis (these included WMC). By 2007, GE Capital was accounting for 55% of the company's profit, more than at any time under Welch. However, this growth came at a price. Between 2001 and 2007, GE Capital took on over $250 billions of additional debt to finance its lending and investment activities (unlike a traditional bank, GE Capital did not have a large deposit base, so it financed its lending and investments by issuing debt). Immelt allowed GE Capital to take greater risks, most notably by making direct investments in commercial real estate. It all worked well until the global financial crisis hit, when most of GE Capital's profits evaporated. Immelt had to cut GE's dividend for the first time since the Great Depression and was forced to ask Warren Buffet for a $3 billion loan to meet GE Capital's short-term commitments.

GE Capital never fully recovered from the financial crisis. Investors who had favorably viewed GE Capital prior to the crisis now saw it as a volatile and risky business and attached a discount to GE's shares. In June of 2015, GE announced its intention to exit from most of GE Capital, refocusing the portfolio on its industrial businesses. At the time, GE Capital controlled assets worth approximately $500 billion, making it the seventh-largest financial institution in the United States. GE's plan was to sell off the majority of GE Capital's assets. What would remain were assets directly related to GE's industrial business. By March 2017, this divestiture was largely complete. After shedding itself of most of GE Capital, GE said that it expected operating earnings from its industrial businesses to comprise over 90% of its earnings in 2018, up from 58% in 2014.

The global financial crisis also prompted Immelt to rethink GE's media strategy. GE decided to exit this business in order to raise capital and refocus on its industrial engineering core. In 2009, GE sold a 51% stake in NBCUniversal to Comcast for $13.75 billion. Comcast paid GE $6.5 billion in cash, and another $7.25 billion in cable TV assets that Comcast owned, which became part of NBCUniversal. However, as part of the deal, GE had to pay Vivendi $5.8 billion for the 20% of NBCUniversal that it still owned, leaving GE with less than a billion in cash. In 2013, Comcast purchased the remaining 49% of NBCUniversal for $12 billion. The deal was widely regarded as something of a coup for Comcast, which by several calculations acquired NBCUniversal assets at a discount to their underlying value.

Another major divestment occurred in 2016 when GE sold its home appliances business to Haier, a Chinese company, for $5.4 billion. Immelt had decided that home appliances didn't fit with the industrial core of the new GE he was building. Plus, the unit's profitability was subpar.

C21-3b Infrastructure, Globalization, and Ecomagination

Three interrelated strategic themes that came to represent the Immelt era were *infrastructure*, *globalization*, and *ecomagination*. Immelt stressed the need for GE to position itself to benefit from the enormous spending on infrastructure that was taking place in fast-growing developing countries. He often noted that when he was getting started at GE, some 80% of revenues came from developed countries. He was positioning GE for a time when 80% of revenues would come from developing nations like China, India, Brazil, and the like. To better drive growth in infrastructure sales to developing nations, he reorganized GE into six large groups, one of which was infrastructure. This sector included aircraft engines, rail products, power generation equipment, water treatment systems, and oil and gas equipment. The idea was to provide customers with one-stop shopping for all infrastructure projects. Immelt's belief was that by focusing on the needs of an underserved customer group—the governments of developing nations—GE could benefit from the anticipated surge in developing country infrastructure projects.

Surprisingly for such a big company, when Immelt took charge, GE was still doing 60% of its business in the United States. By the time he left in 2017, GE was operating in 180 countries and generated 61% of its revenues outside of the United States. Moreover, annual revenues from emerging markets had grown from $10 billion to $45 billion over his tenure. On the other hand, some analysts complained that this growth was bought at too high a price. Immelt himself acknowledged that doing businesses in China and India was more difficult than he had anticipated.

Related to the infrastructure play was Immelt's ecomagination strategy. The idea behind ecomagination came out of a top management strategic planning review in 2004. The management team came to the realization that several of the company's core businesses were deeply involved in environment and energy-related projects. The appliance business was exploring energy conservation. The energy business was looking into alternatives to fossil fuels, including wind, solar, and nuclear. Other businesses were looking at ways to reduce emissions and use energy more efficiently. What was particularly striking was that GE had initiated almost all of these projects in response to requests from its customers.

When these common issues surfaced across different lines of business, the group realized that something deeper was going on that they needed to understand. They initiated a data-gathering effort. They made an effort to educate themselves on the science behind energy and environmental issues, including greenhouse gas emissions. As CEO Jeff Immelt later explained, "We went through a process of really understanding and coming to our own points of view on the science." Immelt himself became convinced that climate change was a technical fact. GE executives engaged in "dreaming sessions" with customers in energy and heavy industry companies to try and understand their concerns and desires. What emerged was a wish list from customers that included cleaner ways to burn coal, more efficient wastewater treatment plants, better hydrogen fuel cells, and so on. At the same time, GE talked to government officials and regulators to try and get a sense for where public policy might be going.

This external review came to the conclusion that energy prices would likely increase going forward, driven by rising energy consumption in developing nations, and creating demand for energy efficient products. The team also saw tighter environmental controls, including caps on greenhouse gas emissions, as all but inevitable. At the same time, they looked inside GE. While the company had already been working on numerous energy efficiency and environmental projects, the team realized there were some gaps in technological capabilities, and there was a lack of overarching strategy. What emerged from these efforts was a belief that GE could build strong businesses by helping its customers to improve their energy efficiency and environmental performance. As Immelt soon became fond of saying, "green is green."

First rolled out in 2005, the ecomagination strategy cut across business. Immelt tapped one of the company's promising young leaders to head the program. GE established targets for doubling investments in clean technology to $1.5 billion per year by 2010 and growing annual revenues from eco-products to $20 billion from $10 billion in 2004. In its own operations, GE set out to cut greenhouse gas emissions per unit of output by 30 percent by 2008, and to cut absolute emissions by 1% by 2010 (as opposed to a forecasted increase of 40% due to the growth of the business). These corporate goals were broken into sub goals and handed down to the relevant businesses. Performance against goal was reviewed on a regular basis and the compensation of executives was tied to their ability to meet these goals.

The effort started to bear fruit. These included a new generation of energy-efficient appliances, a new jet engine that burned 10% less fuel, a hybrid locomotive that burned 3% less fuel and put out 40% lower emissions than its immediate predecessor, lightweight plastics to replace the steel in cars, and technologies for turning coal into gas in order to drive electric turbines, while stripping most of the CO_2 from the turbine exhaust.

By the end of its first 5-year plan, GE had met or exceeded most of its original goals, despite the global financial crisis that hit in 2008. Not only did GE sell more than $20 billion worth of eco-products in 2010, according to management, these products were also among the most profitable in GE's portfolio. In total, GE reported that its ecomagination portfolio included over 140 products and solutions that had generated $105 billion in revenues by 2011. One of the great growth stories in the company has been its wind turbine business, which it bought from Enron in 2002. In that year it sold $200 million worth of wind turbines. By 2008, this was a $6 billion business that had installed 10,000 turbines. By 2012, GE had installed over 20,000 turbines worldwide and was predicting a surge in orders from developing nations. Sales from Brazil alone were forecasted to be in the range of $1 billion a year for the next decade.

C21-3c Downfall

Despite all of Immelt's acquisitions, divestments, and grand strategic initiatives, GE's performance failed to live up to that of the Welch era. The profit growth simply wasn't there. By early 2017, the stock was trading in the high 20s, still below the peak reached in the Welch years. To be sure, the PE multiple had compressed from a high of 50 in 2000 to 20, but even at that level it seemed expensive. GE's stock had tracked the rebound in the S&P 500 from the market's 2009 lows that followed the global financial crisis until 2015, but then it started to lag. The first problem to become evident was GE's ill-timed expansion into the oil and gas business. This was made at a time when oil prices were around $100 a barrel. New supply from American producers using fracking technology, combined with an attempt by Saudi Arabia to drive marginal American producers out of business by expanding its own output, led to a sharp fall in the price of oil, which ended 2015 trading below $40 a barrel. This resulted in a decline in new exploration activity, and a fall in demand for GE's oil and gas services. In addition, restructuring charges related to divestments from GE Capital and strategic changes at Alstom resulted in GE booking $6.1 billion loss for the year, or –$0.62 a share. Despite the loss, Immelt confidently predicted that GE would earn $2 a share in 2018. The promise was enough to induce the Train Fund, run by activist investor Nelson Peltz's, to buy a $2.5 billion stake in GE. It was a big bet that Immelt was now on the hook to deliver.

By 2016, astute investors noticed was that GE was spending far more cash than it was generating. The company could pay its bills, but its cash reserves were being run down. Despite this, Immelt continued to use cash flow to buyback stock and maintain the dividend. From 2015 through until 2017, GE generated about $30 billion in free cash flow and asset sales, but it spent about $75 billion on stock buybacks, dividends, and acquisitions. Some $29 billion was spent on share repurchases at an average price of $30 a share. Immelt had been encouraged to buyback stock by Peltz. Peltz had actually urged GE to borrow $20 billion for additional repurchases (something the company didn't do), based on his belief that the stock would surge when the earnings promised by Immelt arrived.

What bought things to a head were problems at GE Power, a unit which after the 2015 Alston acquisition accounted for a third of GE's revenues. As recently as May 2017, Immelt was telling Wall Street that the operating profit outlook for GE Power was very positive. Just 2 months later, GE reported that the unit's quarterly profit was down, orders were down, and the outlook wasn't good. To compound matters, to gain market share in a weak market, GE Power had been sharply discounting prices which pressured margins.

The problems at GE Power were the end for Immelt. He lost the support of the board and stepped down. At Immelt's retirement in August 2017, the stock was below the level when he took over 16 years earlier. Including dividends, GE gained just 8% with Immelt at the helm. The S&P 500 had risen 214% over the same period. It wasn't until Immelt had departed that the board leaned the full scope of problems at GE Power. Orders dropped 25% in the fourth quarter of 2017 from a year earlier and the unit's profit fell in half. In December 2017, GE said that it would lay off 12,000 people in its power business, nearly 18% of the workforce. Management at Siemens, GE's main competitor in the power business, said they had seen this decline coming for several years, and had been proactively reducing capacity, while GE had been buying more.

After Immelt's ouster, some insiders at GE voiced the opinion to reporters at the *Wall Street Journal* that the company's problems were exacerbated by what they called Immelt's "success theater." Immelt and his deputies projected optimism about GE's business and its future that didn't always match the reality of its operations and markets. According to several of the executives interviewed by the *Wall Street Journal*, Immelt didn't like to hear bad news and he didn't like delivering bad news either. He stressed the positive and downplayed the negative. One insider linked this to GE's culture: "GE itself has never been a culture where people say "I can't,'" she said. An outside stock analyst noted that "the history of GE is to only provide positive information….there is a credibility gap between what they say and the reality of what is to come."

C21-4 Flannery and Culp

Immelt was replaced by John Flannery, another GE veteran who had risen to prominence running GE's medical equipment business. Flannery lost no time in telling the market that Immelt's projections had been overly optimistic, and that the company would have to go through some wrenching changes. In October 2017, GE reported poor third-quarter results that were barely half of what Wall Street expected. After stripping out restructuring charges, GE earned 29 cents per share in the third quarter of 2017 compared to Wall Street expectations of 49 cents a share. Profits fell 50% at the company's power business. GE also posted a loss in its oil and gas business. The company lowered its profit forecast for 2017 to $1.05–$1.10 a share from $1.60–$1.70 a share. Flannery told analysts: "The results I am about to share with you are completely unacceptable." "Things will not stay the same at GE," he said. "Everything is on the table and there are no sacred cows."

Flannery took some steps immediately. He decided to cut GE's dividend in half, a move that would save $4 billion annually. He vowed to transform GE's culture, particularly with regard to capital allocation decisions. He promised to be more disciplined and data driven in his decisions. He stated that he would realign pay for top executives so that they were rewarded when the firm generated more free cash flow. He reformed the board of directors, shrinking it from 18 to 12, and replacing several long-standing directors. He also put a representative from outside investor Train Partners on the board.

Still the hits kept on coming. In December 2017, GE announced that 12,000 employees at GE Power would be laid off. In January 2018, GE wrote off $6.2 billion in connection with a long-term care insurance business that was part of GE Capital. Flannery stated that the insurance business would require another $15 billion in write-offs over the next 7 years. The charge was so big and unexpected that the SEC opened an investigation. In February, GE revealed that the Justice Department was investigating WMC Mortgage, a business that GE had shut down a decade earlier. In April 2018, GE announced that it would put $1.5 billion in reserve for potential liabilities associated with the WMC investigation. The stock market did not respond well to this stream of bad news. There was speculation that another dividend cut was in the offing. By June 2018, the stock was trading at around $13 a share, less than half of its value a year earlier.

Shortly after taking over, Flannery launched a top to bottom strategic review of all of GE's activities. On June 26, 2018, Flannery announced the results of this review. They were dramatic (see Figure 1). The company would sell two big businesses, the profitable healthcare business, best known for making diagnostic equipment such as MRI scanners, and its oil and gas business, Baker Hughes. The company had announced earlier that it was selling its locomotive business for $11 billion, and Flannery indicated that the lighting business would also be sold off. These sales would cut GE's revenues by over a third. GE would hold onto its troubled power business, its profitable jet engine business, and its renewable energy business, along with the parts of GE Capital that were tied to sales of its industrial equipment.

In addition to asset disposals, Flannery stated that his plans called for a change in how GE was being managed, shifting from a centralized top-down approach to a culture where the business units are the center of gravity. The company's headquarters staff would be cut, saving $500 million in annual cost. Flannery also indicated that GE would reduce its dividend after the sale of its healthcare business, and that it will still need to pump cash into its GE Capital in 2019. The initial reaction from the stock market was favorable, with the stock rising $1 to close at $13.76 on the news.

In defending his choices about what to keep and what to sell, in an interview with the *Wall Street Journal*, Flannery started that "Unlike health care and Baker Hughes, there is significant shared technology (between power, aviation and renewables) …. We get technology for GE fan blades for aircraft engines that we put into the renewable business, so there's a lot of technology sharing back and forth, and we feel they can innovate and share investment in ways other parts of the company couldn't… The business model is very similar. Big high-technology differentiation, installed base, long-term service." As for GE Capital, Flannery noted that the broad strategy was to leverage the expertise in GE Capital employees to help support the industrial businesses, but from a balance sheet and investment perspective, the strategy was to "shrink materially the balance sheet of GE Capital."

Flannery's moves were not enough to quickly turn GE around. Frustrated by Flannery's slow progress, the board lost patience with him. By the fall of 2018, Flannery was out. He was replaced by Larry Culp, the former CEO of Danaher, an engineering conglomerate that makes scientific, medical, and automotive equipment. The first outside CEO in GE's history, Culp moved quickly to turn around GE. He slashed GE's 119-year-old dividend from 12 cents a share to a nominal 1 cent a share. Over the next 2 years, he oversaw several major divestments. He sold GE's BioPharma unit for $21.4 billion; GE's controlling stake in oil service firm Baker Hughes for $2.7 billion; and GE's jet leasing business Gecas to a rival, AirCap, for an estimated $24 billion. Gecas was the largest asset in GE Capital. Proceeds from these asset sales were used to pay down debt. Culp also pushed GE's managers to improve operating performance by implementing lean production methods. As a result of asset sales and improvements

Figure1 GE Sales and Spinoffs Announced June 26, 2018

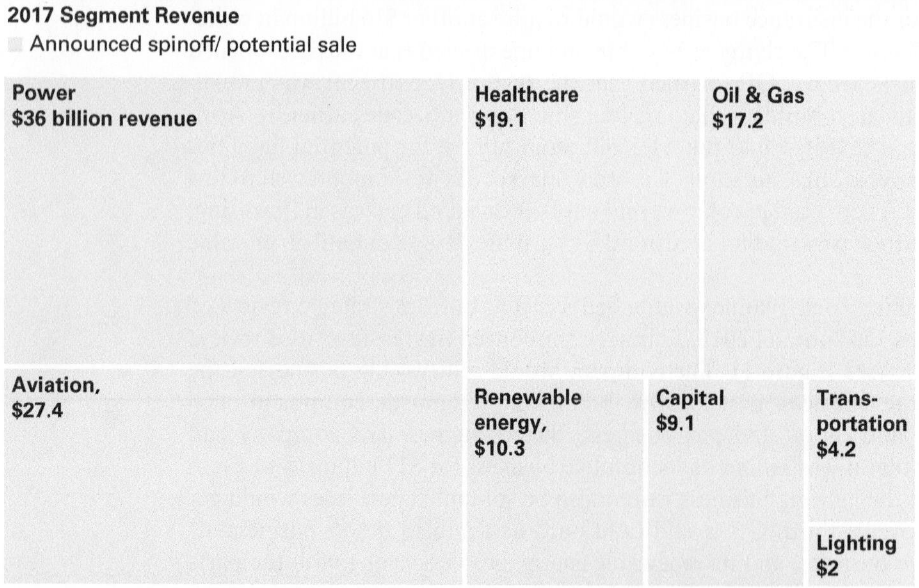

2017 Segment Revenue
☐ Announced spinoff/ potential sale

Power $36 billion revenue	Healthcare $19.1	Oil & Gas $17.2
Aviation, $27.4	Renewable energy, $10.3 / Capital $9.1	Trans-portation $4.2 / Lighting $2

in operating cash flow, between 2018 and 2021, GE was able to reduce its debt load by $75 billion.

Culp's initial game plan was to transform GE into a more tightly focused industrial conglomerate with a strong position in jet engines, medical equipment, and power generation equipment (he reversed Flannery's plan to sell off the medical business). However, the stock price remained stubbornly low, despite a booming stock market. In November 2021, he shifted course, announcing that GE would split into three independent companies. The healthcare division would be called GE HealthCare. The amalgamation of GE's remaining gas power, renewable energy, and digital assets would be called GE Vernova. The remaining aerospace operations would be called GE Aerospace. GE Aerospace would retain the rights to the GE trademark, which it would license long term to the other companies. GE said its brand was worth almost $20 billion and provides a competitive advantage with customers.

Sources

Anonymous, "How Comcast "Stole" NBC Universal from General Electric," *The Street*, February 13, 2013.

Anonymous, "General Electric Is Making a Big Investment in Oil and Gas," *Reuters*, July 3, 2017.

Anonymous, "Understanding GE Capital's Exit Plan," *Forbes*, June 2, 2015.

Anonymous, "GE Completes Last Major Sale of GE Capital Exit Plan," *Zack.com*, March 29, 2017.

Anonymous, "Flannery Unveils his Strategy to Revive GE," *The Economist*, November 16, 2017.

C. Bartlett, "GE's Two-Decade Transformation: Jack Welch's Leadership," *Harvard Business School Case,* January 6, 2000.

J. Byrne, "Jack," *BusinessWeek,* June 8, 1998.

J. Cornell, "General Electric Announces Plan to Separate into Three Independent Publicly Traded Companies," *Forbes*, December 14, 2021.

General Electric Annual Reports, various years.

G. Colvin, "GE Under Siege," *Fortune*, October 9, 2008.

G. Colvin, "What the Hell Happened at GE?," *Fortune*, May 24, 2018.

A. Gara, "For GE's Jeff Immelt, Hundreds of Deals and $575 Billion Didn't Yield a Higher Stock Price," *Forbes*, June 15, 2017.

T. Gryta, J. Lublin, and D. Benoit, "How Jeffrey Immelt's "Success Theater" Masked the Rot at GE," *Wall Street Journal*, February 21, 2018.

T. Gryta, "Q&Q: GE CEO Explains Strategy, Smaller HQ," *Wall Street Journal*, June 26, 2018.

T. Gryta, "GE Narrows Focus to Power, Aviation in Latest Revamp," *Wall Street Journal*, June 26, 2018.

J. Immelt, "Growth as a Process," *Harvard Business Review*, June 2006.

S. Lohr, "GE Goes With What It Knows: Making Stuff," *New York Times*, December 5, 2010.

K. Kranhold, "GE's Environment Push Hits Business Realities," *Wall Street Journal*, September 14, 2007.

J. Makower, "Ecomagination at 10: A Status report," *GreenBiz,* May 11, 2015.

J. Welch and J. Byrne, *Jack: Straight from the Gut* (Warner Books, 2001).

A. Winston, "GE Is Avoiding Hard Choices About Ecomagination," *Harvard Business Review*, August 1, 2014.

N. Schwartz, "Is GE Too Big for Its Own Good?," *New York Times*, July 22, 2007.

M. Sheetz, "General Electric CEO Says Third Quarter Results are Completely Unacceptable," *CNBC*, October 20, 2017.

R. Slater, *Jack Welch and the GE Way* (McGraw-Hill, 1998).

B. Sutherland and B. Schott, "It's Time for GE to Let Go of GE," *Washington Post*, July 20, 2022.

Case 22

Competition in the U.S. Market for Wireless Telecommunications

Over the last two decades, the wireless telecommunications industry in the United States has been characterized by strong growth as demand for mobile phones—and, since 2007, smartphones—drove industry revenues forward. In 2000, there were 109 million wireless subscribers in the United States. By 2020, the number had risen to almost 470 million, representing a penetration rate of over 100% (some people had multiple phones). Moreover, smartphone penetration had risen from 37% of the population in 2010 to 85% by 2021. The growth in demand has been driven by the value of mobile communications devices, and since the arrival of smartphones, by the increasing ubiquity of high-bandwidth (4G and now 5G) wireless connections, and the commensurate demand for the streaming of digital content to smartphones.

As this market has grown, the competitive structure of the industry has become increasingly consolidated. By 2022, three companies dominated the industry: AT&T with 44% of subscriptions, Verizon with 31%, and T-Mobile with 24%. Much of the consolidation has been achieved through mergers and acquisitions. In 2004, AT&T bought Cingular for $41 billion; in 2005, Sprint and Nextel closed a $36-billion merger; and in 2009, Verizon bought Alltel for $28.1 billion. In 2011, AT&T tried to purchase T-Mobile, but was blocked by regulators. Merger talks between T-Mobile and Sprint broke down in 2014. However, in 2018, the two companies came back to the table, and in 2020 T-Mobile and Sprint merged, a move that put T-Mobile on an equal footing with Verizon and AT&T.

The merger wave was driven by a realization among wireless companies that only the largest firms can reap the scale economies necessary to be profitable in this capital-intensive industry. Building out network infrastructure, such as cell towers, and constantly upgrading that infrastructure to deliver fast, reliable voice and data service, has consumed over $600 billion in capital spending since 1985; $300 billion of that has been spent since 2010. By the early 2020s, capital expenditures in the industry were running at around $50 billion a year. Wireless companies have also spent over $160 billion so far to acquire from the government the right to use the wireless spectrum. The government periodically auctions off the spectrum, and competition among wireless providers typically drives up the price. The big three wireless companies had spent an estimated $100 billion between 2020 and 2022 to acquire the rights to 5G spectrum from the U.S. government. Companies in the industry have also had to spend heavily on marketing to establish their brands, and on building out a nationwide network of retail stores to provide point-of-sale service to their customers.

Until recently, competition in the industry primarily focused on non-price factors such as service coverage and reliability, handset equipment, service packages, and brand. Verizon, for example, emphasized its superior coverage and the high speed of its network; AT&T gained share when it signed a deal in 2007 to be the exclusive supplier of Apple's iPhone for 1 year; and T-Mobile branded itself as the hip network for young people looking for value. To reduce customer churn and limit price competition, service providers required customers to enter 2-year contracts with early termination fees in exchange for new equipment (the cost of which was heavily subsidized), or to purchase updated service plans.

However, with the market now saturated, and regulators likely to block any further merger attempts, competition is increasingly based on price. The shift began in early 2013, when T-Mobile broke ranks with the industry and began discarding 2-year contracts and early-termination fees and eliminating subsidies of several hundred dollars for new phones, instead offering customers the option to pay for new devices in monthly installments. When merger talks broke down between Sprint and T-Mobile in mid-2014, Sprint quickly shifted its strategy and went after market share by offering customers who switch from rivals' lower prices and more data. T-Mobile responded with a similar offering of its own, and the price war started to accelerate in the industry. In December 2014, T-Mobile upped the stakes with further price cuts that would save a family of four 50% in their monthly payments compared to a similar plan from Verizon (Verizon continues to subsidize the cost of handsets; T-Mobile does not). Both AT&T and Sprint rolled out their own offers to keep pace with T-Mobile. In a sign that the price war was starting to hurt the industry, in December 2014, both AT&T and Verizon warned investors that their profits might take a hit going forward due to declining average revenues per customer and high capital expenditures.

The price war has persisted since 2014, although it has waxed and waned in intensity depending on the underlying rate of demand growth. By 2022, however, with demand growth slowing once more in a saturated market, the big three providers reaching parity in terms of the scope and quality of geographic coverage, and with each provider facing a need to capture more demand to cover the fixed costs of spectrum acquisition and infrastructure buildout, price competition heated up again.

Sources: C. Lobello, "Wireless Merger Madness," *The Week*, April 25, 2013; M. De la Merced and B. Chen, "No Merger of Sprint and T-Mobile," *New York Times*, August 6, 2014; "Number of Wireless Subscribers in the United States," *Statista*, www.statista.com; *CTIA* Wireless Industry Association Survey Results, 1985–2017, CTIA, archived at www.ctia.org; P. Dave, "Wireless Price Wars Drive Down Costs for Consumers, Sales for Carriers," *Los Angeles Times*, December 9, 2014; S. Price, "Big 4 Wireless Carriers Spent $100B on 5G spectrum," *S&P Global Market Intelligence*, January 26, 2022; "Wireless Telecommunications Carriers in the US—Market Research Report," *IBIS World*, September 2, 2022.

Case Discussion Questions

1. What have been the main growth drivers of demand for wireless telecommunications services in the United States?
2. What are the barriers to entry into the market for wireless telecommunications?
3. What are the implications of these entry barriers for new entry?
4. What stage of development is the industry now at? What are the implications of this for the incumbent wireless carriers?
5. Why has the intensity of price competition increased in the industry? What, if anything, can the main players do to limit price competition?

Case 23

The Rise of lululemon

In 1998, self-described snowboarder and surfer dude Chip Wilson took his first yoga class. The Vancouver native loved the exercises but hated doing them in the cotton clothing that was standard yoga wear at the time. For Wilson, who had worked in the sportswear business and had a passion for technical athletic fabrics, wearing cotton clothes to do sweaty, stretchy, power yoga exercises seemed inappropriate. Thus, the idea for lululemon was born.

Wilson's vision was to create high-quality, stylishly designed clothing for yoga and related sports activities using the very best technical fabrics. He built a design team, but outsourced manufacturing to low-cost producers in Southeast Asia. Rather than selling clothing through existing retailers, Wilson elected to open his own stores. The idea was to staff the stores with employees who were passionate about exercise, and who could act as ambassadors for healthy living through yoga and related sports such as running and cycling.

The first store, opened in Vancouver, Canada, in 2000, quickly became a runaway success, and other stores followed. In 2007, the company went public, using the capital raised to accelerate its expansion plans. By 2022, lululemon had over 600 stores, mostly in North America, and sales in excess of $6.4 billion. Sales per square foot in 2021 were estimated to be around $1,443—the highest for any large apparel retailer in North America. Between 2018 and 2022, average return on invested capital—an important measure of profitability—was around 25%, outpacing that of other well-known specialty retailers.

How did lululemon achieve this? It started with a focus on an unmet consumer need: the latent desire among yoga enthusiasts for high-quality, stylish, durable, technical athletic wear. Getting the product offering right was a central part of the company's strategy. lululemon was so successful in bringing a design ethos to athletic clothing that it is often credited with creating the athleisure apparel trend. Also of note is that its products are well made, moisture wicking, and include its own "anti-stink" technology. As the product line developed, lululemon added men's workout clothes and athleisure ware, broadening its scope, and bringing another demographic into its stores.

An equally important part of the product strategy was to stock a limited supply of an item. New colors and seasonal items, for example, get a 3- to 12-week life cycle, which keeps the product offerings feeling fresh. The goal is to sell gear at full price, and to condition customers to buy it when they see it rather than wait, because if they do, it may soon be "out of stock." The company only allows product returns if the clothes have not been worn and still have the price tags attached. The scarcity strategy worked. Until recently, lululemon never held sales, and its clothing sells for a premium price. Even today, only a small selection of items is placed "on sale." Most items sell for full price.

To create the right in-store service, lululemon hires employees who are passionate about fitness. Part of the hiring process involves taking prospective employees to a yoga or spin class. Some 70% of store managers are internal hires; most started on the sales floor and grew up in the culture. Store managers are given funds to repaint their stores, any color, twice a year. The interior design of each store is largely up to its manager. Each store is also given $2,700 a year for employees to contribute to a charity or local event of their own choosing. One store manager in Washington, D.C., used the funds to create, with regional community leaders, a global yoga event in 2010. The result, Salutation Nation, is now an annual event in which over 70 lululemon stores simultaneously host a free, all-level yoga practice.

Employees are trained to eavesdrop on customers, who are called "guests." Clothes-folding tables are placed on the sales floor near the fitting rooms rather than in a back room so that employees can overhear complaints. Nearby, a large chalkboard lets customers write suggestions or complaints, which are sent back to headquarters. This feedback is then incorporated into the product design process.

Despite the company's focus on providing a quality product, it has not all been clear sailing. In 2010, Wilson caused a stir when he emblazoned the company's tote bags with the phrase "Who is John Galt?" the opening line from Ayn Rand's 1957 novel, *Atlas Shrugged*. *Atlas Shrugged* has become a libertarian bible, and the underlying message that lululemon supported Rand's brand of unregulated capitalism did not sit well with many of the stores' customers. After negative feedback, the bags were quickly pulled from stores. Wilson himself stepped down from day-to-day involvement in the company in January 2012 and resigned from his chairman position in 2014.

In early 2013, lululemon found itself dealing with another controversy when it decided to recall black yoga pants that were too sheer, and effectively "see through," when stretched due to the lack of "rear-end coverage." In addition to the negative fallout from the product itself, some customers report being mistreated by employees who demanded that customers put the pants on and bend over to determine whether the clothing was see-through enough to warrant a refund. One consequence of this PR disaster was the resignation of then CEO Christine Day. The company is also facing increasing competition from rivals such as Gap's Athleta Urban Outfitters' Without Walls, and Nike Stores. Most observers in the media and financial community believe that the company can handle these challenges and continue its growth trajectory.

Sources: D. Mattoili, "Lululemon's Secret Sauce," *Wall Street Journal*, March 22, 2012; C. Leahey, "Lululemon CEO: How to Build Trust Inside Your Company," *CNN Money*, March 16, 2012; T. Hsu, "'Pantsgate' to Hurt Lululemon Profit: Customer Told to Bend Over," *latimes.com*, March 21, 2013; C. O'Commor, "Billionaire Founder Chip Wilson Out at Yoga Giant Lululemon," *Forbes*, January 9, 2012; B. Weishaar, "No-Moat Lululemon Faces Increasing Competition but Is Regaining Its Customer Base," *Morningstar*, December 17, 2014; D. Swartz, "Narrow Most Lululemon Continues to Ride a Wave of Popularity," *Morningstar*, September 6, 2022.

Case Discussion Questions

1. What opportunity did Chip Wilson see that led to the establishment of lululemon?
2. Why are lululemon's sales per square foot so high?
3. How would you characterize lululemon's business-level strategy?
4. What are the main threats to lululemon's business?
5. What are lululemon's main strengths? What are its weaknesses?
6. What must the company do to maintain its competitive advantage?

Southwest Airlines

Southwest Airlines has long been the standout performer in the U.S. airline industry. It is famous for its fares, which are often some 30% lower than those of its major rivals. These low fares are balanced by an even lower cost structure, which has enabled Southwest to record superior profitability even in its down years. Indeed, Southwest has been profitable since its inception with the sole exception of 2020, when the COVID-19 pandemic dramatically depressed demand across the entire industry by over 60%. This record has made it the envy of an airline industry that has seen more than 180 bankruptcies since 1978. Even during 2001 to 2005—quite possibly the worst four years in the history of the airline industry—when every other major airline lost money, Southwest made money each year and earned a return on invested capital of 5.8%. Today, Southwest is the third-largest airline in the United States with 17% of the market, only fractionally less than that of American Airlines and Delta.

Southwest operates differently than many of its competitors. While operators like American Airlines and Delta route passengers through hubs, Southwest Airlines flies point-to-point, often through smaller airports. By operating this way, Southwest has found that it can reduce total travel time for its passengers. They are not routed through hubs and spend less time on the ground—something that most passengers value. This boosts demand and keeps planes full. Moreover, because it avoids many hubs, Southwest has experienced fewer long delays, which again helps to reduce total travel time. In 2017, a delayed flight at Southwest was on average 49.11 minutes late leaving the gate, compared to 69.99 minutes at Delta and 60.28 minutes at American Airlines. Southwest's high reliability translates into a solid brand reputation and strong demand, which further helps to fill its planes and, consequently, reduce costs.

Furthermore, because Southwest flies point to point rather than through congested airport hubs, there is no need for dozens of gates and thousands of employees to handle banks of flights that come arrive and depart within a 2-hour window, leaving the hub empty until the next flight arrives a few hours later. The result: Southwest operates with far fewer employees than do airlines that fly through hubs.

To further reduce costs and boost reliability, Southwest flies only one type of plane, the Boeing 737. This reduces training costs, maintenance costs, and inventory costs while increasing efficiency in crew and flight scheduling. The operation is nearly ticketless and there is no seat assignment, which reduces costs associated with back-office functions. There are no in-flight meals or movies, and the airline will not transfer baggage to other airlines, reducing the need for baggage handlers. Southwest also has high employee productivity, which means fewer employees per passenger. All of this helps to keep costs low. In 2017, for example, Southwest's cost per available seat miles flown was 11.35 cents, compared to 15.30 cents at Delta and 15.63 cents at American Airlines.

To help maintain high employee productivity, Southwest devotes enormous attention to its staff. On average, the company hires only 3% of candidates interviewed in a year. When hiring, it emphasizes teamwork and a positive attitude. Southwest reasons that skills can be taught, but a positive attitude and a willingness to pitch in cannot. Southwest also creates incentives for its employees to work hard. All employees are covered by a profit-sharing plan, and at least 25% of each employee's share in the plan must be invested in Southwest Airlines stock. This gives rise to a simple formula: The harder employees work, the more profitable Southwest becomes and the more well off the employees become. The results are clear. At other airlines, one would never see a pilot helping to check passengers onto the plane. At Southwest, pilots and flight attendants have been known to help clean the aircraft and check in passengers at the gate to get a plane back into the air as quickly as possible, because no plane makes money when it is sitting on the ground. This flexible, motivated workforce leads to higher productivity and reduces the need for more employees.

Sources: M. Brelis, "Simple Strategy Makes Southwest a Model for Success," *Boston Globe*, November 5, 2000, p. F1; M. Trottman, "At Southwest, New CEO Sits in the Hot Seat," *Wall Street Journal*, July 19, 2004, p. B1; J. Helyar, "Southwest Finds Trouble in the Air," *Fortune*, August 9, 2004, p. 38; Southwest Airlines 10-K 2013; C. Higgins, "Southwest Airlines," *Morningstar*, January 25, 2018; Bureau of Transportation Statistics at www.transtats.bts.gov/.

Case Discussion Questions

1. What resources underlie Southwest's strong position in the U.S. airline industry?
2. How do these resources enable Southwest to improve one or more of the following: efficiency, quality, customer responsiveness, and innovation?
3. Apply the VIRO framework and describe to what extent these resources can be considered valuable, rare, inimitable, and well organized.
4. What must Southwest do to maintain its competitive advantage going forward in the U.S. airline industry?

Case

25

Virgin America

Prior to its 2016 acquisition by Alaska Airlines, Virgin America was consistently rated as one of the top U.S. airlines. Founded in 2004, the airline served 20 destinations out of its main hub in San Francisco. Virgin America was known for its leather seats, cocktail-lounge-style lighting, onboard Wi-Fi, in-seat power outlets for electronic devices, full-service meals, and that most scarce of all assets in coach class, legroom. The airline has earned a host of awards since its launch in 2007, including being named the "Best U.S. Airline" in the *Condé Nast* Traveler Readers' Choice Awards every year from 2008–2014; and "Best Domestic Airline" in the *Travel and Leisure* World's Best Awards for 7 years in a row. Furthermore, *Consumer Reports* named Virgin America the "Best U.S. Airline" in 2013 and 2014. Industry statistics supported these accolades. In 2014, Virgin was #1 in on-time arrivals in the United States, with 83.5% of aircraft arriving on time. Virgin America also had the lowest level of denied boardings (0.07 per 1,000 passengers), and mishandled baggage (0.87 per 1,000 passengers), and the fewest customer complaints (1.50 per 1,000 passengers).

Virgin America was an offshoot of the Virgin Group, the enterprise started by British billionaire Richard Branson. Branson got his start in the music business with Virgin Records stores (established in 1971) and the Virgin Record record label (established in 1973). In 1984, he leveraged the Virgin brand to enter an entirely new industry, airlines, with Virgin Atlantic. Virgin Atlantic became a major competitor to British Airways on a number of long-haul routes out of London, winning market share through superior customer service, innovative perks for premium travelers, and competitive pricing. Branson has also licensed the right to use the Virgin brand name across a wide array of businesses, including Virgin Media (a major U.K. cable operator), Virgin Money (a U.K. financial services company), and Virgin Mobile (a wireless brand that exists in many countries). This strategy has made Virgin one of the most recognizable brands in the world. Interestingly, Branson makes money from royalty payments irrespective of whether companies licensing the Virgin brand are profitable or not. Branson himself describes the Virgin brand as representing, "innovation, quality, and a sense of fun."

For all its accolades and the power of the Virgin brand, Virgin America has had a hard time making money. One problem is that, as a small airline, Virgin only has a few flights a day on many routes and is unable to offer consumers the choice of multiple departure times, something that many travelers value. For example, on the popular route for tech workers between San Francisco and Austin, Texas, United offers six flights a day and Jet Blue offers two, compared with just one for Virgin America.

Another serious problem is that providing all the extra frills necessary to deliver a high-quality experience costs money. In its first 5 years of operation, Virgin America accumulated $440 million in losses before registering a small profit of $67 million on revenues of $1.4 billion in 2013. In 2014, Virgin America went public and managed to post a respectable $150 million in net profits on revenues of close to $1.5 billion. The company was helped by an improving economy, strong demand, and lower jet fuel costs.

The key competitive issue the company faced was that it was a niche player in a much larger industry where low-cost carriers such as Southwest Airlines and Jet Blue put constant pressure on prices and crowded out routes with multiple flights daily. Virgin America charged prices that were 10% to 20% above those of its no-frills rivals, but it could not raise prices too far without losing customers and flying with empty seats, which is a recipe for failure in an industry where margins are slim. On the route between New York's Kennedy Airport and Los Angeles during late 2012, for example, Virgin passengers were paying an average of $305 a ticket compared to an industry average of $263. Virgin's passenger-load factor on that route was 96% of the industry average during the same period. Virgin CEO David Cush, however, was adamant that the airline "… won't get into a fare war. Our product is good; we've got good loyalty. People will be willing to pay $20 or $30 more." Was he correct? We will never know. In 2016, Virgin was acquired by West Coast rival Alaska Airlines, reportedly because Alaska wanted Virgin's landing slots at the San Francisco hub. Although Virgin continued to operate as a division of Alaska for a while, in April 2018 it was fully merged into Alaska's operating structure, and the brand disappeared.

Sources: M. Richtel, "At Virgin America, a Fine Line Between Pizazz and Profit," *New York Times*, September 7, 2013; B. Tuttle, "Why an Airline That Travelers Love Is Failing," *Time*, October 25, 2012; T. Huddleston, "Virgin America Goes Public," *Fortune*, November 13, 2014; A. Levine-Weinberg, "How Richard Branson Built a $5-Billion Fortune from Scratch," *Motley Fool*, October 19, 2014, www.fool.com.

Case Discussion Questions

1. What was Virgin America's segmentation strategy? Who did it serve?
2. With regard to its core segment, what did Virgin America offer its customers?
3. Using the Porter model, which generic business-level strategy was Virgin America pursuing?
4. What actions taken at the functional level enabled Virgin America to implement its strategy?
5. Do you think Virgin America would have been able to survive had it remained independent? (The company was acquired by Alaska Airlines in 2016.)

Case

26

McDonald's

For most of its history, McDonald's has been an extraordinarily successful enterprise. It began in 1955, when the legendary Ray Kroc decided to franchise the McDonald brothers' fast-food concept. Since its inception, McDonald's has grown into the largest restaurant chain in the world, with almost 38,000 stores in 120 countries and annual revenues of $22 billion in 2021.

For decades, McDonald's success was grounded in a simple formula: Give consumers value for money, good quick service, and consistent quality in a clean environment, and they will return time and time again. To deliver value for money and consistent quality, McDonald's standardized the process of order taking, making food, and providing service. Standardized processes raised employee productivity while ensuring that customers had the same experience in all branches of the restaurant. McDonald's also developed close ties with wholesalers and food producers, managing its supply chain to reduce costs. As it became larger, buying power enabled McDonald's to realize economies of scale in purchasing of inputs from food ingredients to paper, and pass on cost savings to customers in the form of low-priced meals, which drove increased demand. There was also the ubiquity of McDonald's; their restaurants could be found everywhere. This accessibility, coupled with the consistent experience and low prices, built brand loyalty.

The formula worked well until the early 2000s. By then, McDonald's was under attack for contributing to obesity. Its low-priced, high-fat foods were dangerous, claimed critics. By 2002, sales were stagnating, and profits were falling. It seemed that McDonald's had lost its edge. The company responded with several steps. It scrapped its supersize menu and added healthier options such as salads and apple slices. Executives mined data to discover that people were eating more chicken and less beef. So, McDonald's added grilled chicken sandwiches, chicken wraps, Southern-style chicken sandwiches, and more recently, chicken for breakfast to their menu. Chicken sales doubled at McDonald's between 2002 and 2008. Today, the company buys more chicken than beef.

McDonald's also shifted its emphasis on beverages. For decades, drinks were an afterthought, but executives couldn't help but note the rapid growth of Starbucks. In 2006, McDonald's decided to offer better coffee, including lattes. McDonald's improved the quality of its coffee by purchasing high-quality beans, using better equipment, and filtering its water. The company did not lose sight of the need to keep costs low and service quick, however, and continues to add coffee-making machines that produce lattes and cappuccinos in 45 seconds, at the push of a button. Starbucks it is not, but for many people a latte from the McDonald's drive-through window is comparable. Today, the latte machines have been installed in almost half of the stores in the United States.

All of these strategies seemed to work. Revenues, net profits, and profitability all improved between 2002 and 2013. By 2014, however, McDonald's was once more running into headwinds. Same-store sales declined in 2014, impacting profitability. Among the problems that analysts identified at McDonald's was an inability to attract customers in the 19- to 30-year-old age group. Rivals offering healthier alternatives, such as Chipotle Mexican Grill, and "better burger" chains that appeal to this demographic, such as Smashburger, were gaining ground at the expense of McDonald's. A *Consumer Reports* survey ranked McDonald's burgers the worst among its peers. Another problem was that the quality of customer service at McDonald's seemed to have slipped. Many customers say that employees at McDonalds are rude and unprofessional. One reason why McDonald's employees might be feeling stressed out is that the menu has grown quite large in recent years, and many restaurants were not adequately staffed given the diversity of the menu.

In 2015, management at McDonald's took steps to fix these problems. The company emphasized a number of "velocity growth accelerators" including (1) an "Experience of the Future" layout, which features a combination of ordering flexibility (including counter, kiosk, online, and mobile ordering), customer experience (including a blend of front counter, table service, and curbside delivery), and a more streamlined "core" menu (but one that still allows for personalization); (2) mobile ordering and payments; and (3) delivery alternatives. The results of these initiatives have been promising, as McDonald's saw its growth rate accelerate once more. In 2020, McDonald's built upon its successful velocity growth plan, introducing a new strategic framework for growth known as "Accelerating the Arches." This framework has three primary pillars: A renewed commitment to core menu products like burgers, chicken, and coffee to tap into consumer demand for familiarity; doubling down on what it calls the "3 Ds,"—digital ordering, delivery, and drive-thru; and maximizing marketing by "investing in new, culturally relevant approaches to effectively communicate the story of brand, food, and purpose." In essence, what McDonald's wants is its best customers using its mobile app to order classics for takeout and delivery, while making them feel good about being so loyal to the company. The early results suggest that the program is working, with both revenues and profit accelerating in 2021 and early 2022 as the program was rolled out. Revenues increased from $19.2 billion to $23.33 billion from 2020 to 2021, while net income grew from $4.73 billion to $7.55 billion.

Sources: Jonathan Beer, "5 Reasons McDonald's Has Indigestion," *CBS Money Watch*, August 12, 2014; A. Martin, "McDonald's, the Happiest Meal is Hot Profits," *New York Times*, January 11, 2009; M. Vella, "A New Look for McDonald's," *Business Week Online*, December 4, 2008; M. Warner, "Salads or No, Cheap Burgers Revive McDonald's," *New York Times*, April 19, 2006. Virginia Chamlee, "The McDonald's of the Future Has Table Service and Touch Screen Ordering," *Eater*, September 27, 2017; J. Beer, "Inside McDonald's Bold—But Maybe Not Bold Enough—Strategy to Turn Customers into Super Fans," *Fast Company*, November 9, 2020; S. Dunlop, "Recession Resistant McDonald's Offers Attractive Restaurant Exposure Amidst Tough Times," *Morningstar*, July 29, 2022.

Case Discussion Questions

1. How would you characterize McDonald's business-level strategy?
2. What functional-level strategies has McDonald's pursued to boost its efficiency?
3. What functional-level strategies has McDonald's pursued to boost its customer responsiveness?
4. What does product quality mean for McDonald's? What functional-level strategies has it pursued to boost its product quality?
5. How has innovation helped McDonald's improve its efficiency, customer responsiveness, and product quality?
6. Do you think that McDonald's has any rare and valuable resources? In what value creation activities are these resources located?
7. How sustainable is McDonald's competitive position in the fast-food restaurant business?

Starbucks—
Expanding Globally

Forty years ago, Starbucks was a single store in Seattle's Pike Place Market selling premium-roasted coffee. Today, it is a global roaster and retailer of coffee, with more than 28,000 stores in 76 countries. Starbucks set out on its current course in the 1980s when the company's director of marketing, Howard Schultz, came back from a trip to Italy, enchanted with the Italian coffeehouse experience. Schultz, who later became CEO, persuaded the company's owners to experiment with the coffeehouse format—and the Starbucks experience was born. The strategy was to sell the company's own premium roasted coffee and freshly brewed espresso-style coffee beverages, along with a variety of pastries, coffee accessories, teas, and other products, in a tastefully designed coffeehouse setting. From the outset, the company focused on selling "a third-place experience," rather than just the coffee. The formula led to spectacular success in the United States, where Starbucks went from obscurity to one of the best-known brands in the country in a decade. Thanks to Starbucks, coffee stores became places for relaxation, chatting with friends, reading the newspaper, holding business meetings, or (more recently) browsing online.

In 1995, with 700 stores across the United States, Starbucks began exploring foreign opportunities. The first target market was Japan. The company established a joint venture with a local retailer, Sazaby Inc. Each company held a 50% stake in the venture: Starbucks Coffee of Japan. Starbucks initially invested $10 million in this venture, its first foreign direct investment. The Starbucks format was then licensed to the venture, which was charged with taking over responsibility for growing Starbucks's presence in Japan.

To make sure the Japanese operations replicated the "Starbucks experience" in North America, Starbucks transferred some employees to the Japanese operation. The joint venture agreement required all Japanese store managers and employees to attend training classes similar to those given to U.S. employees. The agreement also required that stores adhere to the design parameters established in the United States. In 2001, the company introduced a stock option plan for all Japanese employees, making it the first company in Japan to do so. Skeptics doubted that Starbucks would be able to replicate its North American success overseas, but by the end of 2018 Starbucks' had some 1,286 stores and a profitable business in Japan. Along the way, in 2015, Starbucks acquired Starbucks Coffee of Japan, making the stores wholly owned as opposed to licensed.

After Japan, the company embarked on an aggressive foreign investment program. In 1998, it purchased Seattle Coffee, a British coffee chain with 60 retail stores, for $84 million. An American couple, originally from Seattle, had started Seattle Coffee with the intention of establishing a Starbucks-like chain in Britain. By 2018, Starbucks had almost 1,000 stores in the United Kingdom.

In the late 1990s, Starbucks also opened stores in Taiwan, China, Singapore, Thailand, New Zealand, South Korea, and Malaysia. In Asia, Starbucks's most common strategy was to license its format to a local operator or joint venture partner in return for initial licensing fees and royalties on store revenues. As in Japan, Starbucks insisted on an intensive employee-training program and strict specifications regarding the format and layout of the store.

China has developed into Starbucks's fastest-growing market and is now second only to the United States in terms of store count and revenues. Although China has historically been a nation of tea drinkers, the third-place coffee culture pioneered by Starbucks has gained significant traction in the nation's large cities where wealthy and middle-class customers will pay $5 for a cup of coffee. As with many other nations, Starbucks originally entered China by setting up a joint venture with a local company and licensing its format to that entity. That changed in 2018 when Starbucks bought out its East China venture partner in order to attain greater control over its growth strategy. According to Belinda Wong, CEO of Starbucks's China operations, "Full ownership will give us the opportunity to fully leverage the company's robust business infrastructure to deliver an elevated coffee, in-store third place experience and digital innovation to our customers, and further strengthen the career development opportunities for our people." The company now aims to have 6,000 wholly owned stores in China by the end of 2022, up from 3,500 at the end of fiscal 2018.

Sources: Starbucks 2018 10K; J. Ordonez, "Starbucks to Start Major Expansion in Overseas Market," *Wall Street Journal*, October 27, 2000, p. B10; S. Homes and D. Bennett, "Planet Starbucks," *BusinessWeek,* September 9, 2002, pp. 99–110; "Starbucks Outlines International Growth Strategy," *Business Wire*, October 14, 2004; A. Yeh, "Starbucks Aims for New Tier in China," *Financial Times*, February 14, 2006, p. 17; Laurie Burkitt, "Starbucks to Add Thousands of Stores in China," *Wall Street Journal*, January 12, 2016; "Starbucks to Acquire Remaining Shares of East China JV," Starbucks press release, July 27, 2017; Jon Bird, "Roasted: How China Is Showing the Way for Starbucks in the US," *Forbes*, January 15, 2019; Eric Sylvers, "After 25,000 Stores in 78 Countries, Starbucks Turns to Italy," *Wall Street Journal*, September 6, 2018.

Case Discussion Questions

1. Where did the original idea for Starbucks's format come from? What lessons can be learned from this?
2. What drove Starbucks to start expanding internationally? Is this strategy in the best interests of its company's shareholders?
3. Why do you think Starbucks decided to enter the Japanese market via a joint venture with a Japanese company? What lessons can be drawn from this?
4. What drove Starbucks to shift from a joint venture strategy in China to run the operation through a wholly owned subsidiary? What are the benefits here? What are the potential risks and costs? Do you think this was the correct decision?

Starbucks: Taking a Stand on Social Issues

By Melissa Schilling

When Howard Schultz founded Starbucks in 1987, he wanted to create a company that would genuinely care for the well-being of its employees. He had been very influenced by his memories of his father, noting that his father "struggled a great deal and never made more than $20,000 a year, and his work was never valued, emotionally or physically, by his employer ... This was an injustice ... I want our employees to know we value them." He also believed that happy employees are the key to competitiveness and growth. As he stated: "We can't achieve our strategic objectives without a work force of people who are immersed in the same commitment as management. Our only sustainable advantage is the quality of our work force. We're building a national retail company by creating pride in–and stake in–the outcome of our labor."

Schultz set out to accomplish his goals by creating an empowering corporate culture, exceptional employee benefits, and employee stock ownership programs. While Starbucks enforces almost fanatical standards of coffee quality and customer service, the culture at Starbucks towards employees is laid back and supportive. Employees are empowered to make decisions without constant referral to management, and are encouraged to think of themselves as partners in the business. Starbucks wants employees to use their best judgment in making decisions and will stand behind them. This is reinforced through generous compensation and benefits packages.

In 2000, Schultz announced that he was resigning as CEO and left the firm to pursue other ventures (though he remained chairman of the board of directors). However, after Starbucks began to suffer from slumping net income and decreasing share price, Schultz returned to the helm in 2008. Rather than cutting costs and reducing the workforce, Schultz announced his "Transformation Agenda"—a controversial plan to invest in Starbucks's employees, environment, and community. The plan included equity-based compensation even for non-executive employees, industry-leading health and retirement benefits, tuition reimbursement, ethical sourcing requirements, and more. Today, Starbucks remains an industry leader in the investment it makes in having a positive impact on employees, its suppliers, the community, and the planet.

Employees

As of 2022, all U.S.-based employees who work at least 20 hours a week were eligible for:

- Comprehensive health insurance
- 100% college tuition coverage for a first-time bachelor's degree through Arizona State University's online program

- Equity in the form of stock ("Bean Stock")
- 401(k) retirement plan
- Partner and family sick time benefit
- Vacation time
- Paid parental leave and reimbursement for certain uncovered fertility services, adoption and surrogacy expenses.
- Child and adult back-up care
- 10 no-cost mental health sessions a year and free Headspace subscriptions
- Coverage for transgender procedures
- A free pound of coffee a week

As of June 2022, Starbuck's U.S. hourly employees averaged $17/hour with all U.S. employees earning at least $15/hour. Its U.S.-based employees were 71.3% female and 48.2% Black, Indigenous, and People of Color (BIPOC). It had also achieved 100% pay equity for women in its company operated stores in the United States, Canada, China, and Great Britain. Its licensed stores had achieved 100% pay equity for women in Singapore, the Philippines, and India. Starbucks was also recognized as a top employer for LGBTQ+ workplace equity and received a 100% rating from the Human Rights Campaign's Corporate Equality Index. The company scored a perfect 100 on the Disability Equality Index. The company also was committed to hiring veterans and refugees and, by the end of 2020, had hired almost 32,000 veterans and military spouses and 2,600 refugees.

Suppliers

Starbucks had long committed to an ethical sourcing approach it had created in 2004 (in partnership with Conservation International) called Coffee and Farmer Equity (C.A.F.E.). The C.A.F.E. Practices program created supplier transparency by requiring Starbucks suppliers to submit evidence of payments made throughout the supply chain, including how much was paid directly to farmers for their coffee. It also set strict criteria around wages and benefits, hiring practices, hours of work and use of protective equipment, as well as criteria for sustainable agricultural practices. Starbucks also sourced 99.7% of its tea from Rainforest Certified Farms and 100% of its cocoa beans from COCOA Practices-verified or UTZ certified farms.

To meet the unmet financing needs of farmers and help improve supply chain resiliency, Starbucks operated a $100 million Global Farmer Fund that offered loans at modest interest rates. Last but not least, Starbucks operated 10 Farmer Support Centers globally to share tools and information with coffee farmers (whether they sold to Starbucks or not) that would enhance their productivity, quality, and profitability.

Community

In 2021, Starbucks partnered with Community Development Financial Institutions to invest $10 million in small-business development loans to focus on underserved communities in Chicago. It also committed $100 million to a program to advance racial equity and environmental resilience in BIPOC communities in 12 U.S. metro areas and their surrounding regions. It participated in hunger relief efforts, including food donation programs in the United States, Canada, United Kingdom, Japan, and Mexico, and in 2021 had committed to reinvesting $100 million in hunger relief over the next 10 years. Its employees donated more than 34,000 volunteer hours to local non-profit organizations and Starbucks matched employee donations up to $1,000 per employee per year. In the same year, it also donated $4 million to support nonprofits that serve BIPOC youth, and another $4 million for disaster relief.

Planet

In 2021, Starbucks set out a set of 2030 goals that included:

- A 50% reduction in greenhouse emissions
- A 50% conservation or replenishment of water withdrawal across direct operations, stores, packaging, and the agricultural supply chain
- A 50% reduction in waste sent to landfills

To achieve this, Starbucks planned to expand its plant-based menu options, shift to reusable packaging, invest in regenerative agriculture and reforestation, experiment with incentives to induce consumers to choose reusable cups over single-use cups, and use 100% renewable energy in company operated stores in the United States, Canada, and Europe and 72% of company-operated stores globally.

The company sometimes drew ire in taking on issues that bore little relationship to its core activities. Critics admonished that such initiatives risked alienating some consumers and investors, and risked elevating expectations that the company might not always be able to meet. As Schultz noted, "I can tell you the organization is not thrilled when I walk into a room and say we're now going to take on veterans (issues)." But, he adds, "The size and the scale of the company and the platform that we have allows us, I think, to project a voice into the debate, and hopefully that's for good ... We are leading [Starbucks] to try to redefine the role and responsibility of a public company."

Sources: C. Birkner, "Taking Care of Their Own," *Marketing News*, February, pp. 44–49; M. Rothman, "Into the Black," *Inc.*, January 1993, p. 58; D. Ritter, "3 Reasons It's Hard to Hate Starbucks," *Wall Street Cheat Sheet*, July 6, 2014; www.usatoday.com, A. Gonzalez, "Starbucks as Citizen: Schultz Acts Boldly on Social, Political Issues," *Seattle Times*, March 15, 2015; www.seattletimes.com, www.starbucks.com (accessed April 28, 2015); Yahoo Finance; Hoovers; Data from www.glassdoor.com retrieved October 13, 2018; Starbucks 2021 Global Environmental & Social Impact Report; Starbucks 2022 Notice of Annual Meeting of Shareholders and Proxy Statement; Starbuck C.A.F.E. Practices (https://www.starbucksathome.com/ca/en-ca/story/cafe-practices).

Case Discussion Questions

1. What are the pros and cons of Starbucks taking a stance on ethical issues such as minimum wage requirements, sustainable growing practices, and more? What do you think motivated Schultz to implement these standards?
2. Do you think it makes sense for companies to hold themselves to a higher standard than the law? Do you think it makes sense for companies to utilize ethical standards that might not increase profitability?
3. How much influence do you think a company with the size and reach of Starbucks could have on the legal and ethical environment of the countries in which it operates?

JCB in India

In 1979, JCB, the large British manufacturer of construction equipment, entered into a joint venture with Escorts, an Indian engineering conglomerate, to manufacture backhoe loaders for sale in India. Escorts held a majority 60% stake in the venture, and JCB 40%. The joint venture was a first for JCB, which historically had exported as much as two-thirds of its production from Britain to a wide range of nations. However, high tariff barriers made direct exports to India difficult.

JCB would probably have preferred to go it alone in India, but government regulations at the time required foreign investors to create joint ventures with local companies. JCB believed the Indian construction market was ripe for growth and could become very large. The company's managers believed that it was better to get a foothold in the nation, thereby gaining an advantage over global competitors, rather than wait until the growth potential was realized.

Twenty years later, the joint venture was selling some 2,000 backhoes in India and had an 80% share of the Indian market for that product. After years of deregulation, the Indian economy was booming. However, JCB felt that the joint venture limited its ability to expand. For one thing, much of JCB's global success was based upon the utilization of leading-edge manufacturing technologies and relentless product innovation, but the company was very hesitant about transferring this know-how to a venture where it did not have a majority stake and therefore lacked control. The last thing JCB wanted was for these valuable technologies to leak out of the joint venture into Escorts, which was one of the largest manufacturers of tractors in India and might conceivably become a direct competitor in the future. Moreover, JCB was unwilling to make the investment in India required to take the joint venture to the next level unless it could capture more of the long-run returns.

In 1999, JCB took advantages of changes in government regulations to renegotiate the terms of the venture with Escorts, purchasing 20% of its partner's equity to give JCB majority control. In 2002, JCB took this to its logical end when it responded to further relaxation of government regulations on foreign investment to purchase all of Escorts's remaining equity, transforming the joint venture into a wholly owned subsidiary. Around the same time, JCB also invested in wholly owned factories in the United States and Brazil.

Having gained full control, in early 2005, JCB increased its investment in India, announcing it would build a second factory that it would use to serve the fast-growing Indian market. At the same time, JCB also announced it would set up another wholly owned factory in China to serve that market. India and China, the two most populous nations in the world, were growing rapidly, construction was booming, and JCB, then the world's fifth-largest manufacturer of construction equipment, was eager to expand its presence to match its global rivals, particularly Caterpillar, Komatsu, and Volvo, which were also expanding aggressively in these markets.

By 2008 JCB's foreign investment was bearing fruit. The product line had been expanded from 120 machines in 2001 to over 250. JCB had 47 dealers and some 275 outlets around India, and it claimed a market share in India of 53%. Over the next few years, JCB continued to gain business in India. By 2016 it was the market leader for construction equipment in India with a 66% share and a network of 60 dealers and 600 outlets. Boosted by strong demand growth due to heavy infrastructure investment in India, in 2016, JCB opened two new factories in the country, increasing its local workforce to 5,000. By 2018, JCB was generating £2.62 billion in annual sales, over £1.4 billion of which came from India. In addition to strong demand in India, JCB's Indian factories were also now exporting to 93 other countries. India had become the jewel in the crown for JCB.

Sources: P. Marsh, "Partnerships Feel the Indian Heat," *Financial Times*, June 22, 2006, p. 11; P. Marsh, "JCB Targets Asia to Spread Production," *Financial Times,* March 16, 2005, p. 26; D. Jones, "Profits Jump at JCB," *Daily Post,* June 20, 2006, p. 21; R. Bentley, "Still Optimistic about Asia," *Asian Business Review,* October 1, 1999, p. 1; and "JCB Launches India-Specific Heavy Duty Crane," *The Hindu,* October 18, 2008. Michael Pooler, JCB Piles up Big Profits Despite Dwindling Global Markets," *Financial Times*, July 12, 2016. Malyaban Ghosh, "JCB India Revenues Rise," *Livemint.com*, April 16, 2018.

Case Discussion Questions

1. What was the strategic rational underlying JCB's entry into India in 1979 and China in 2005? Given that capital to fund expansion is limited, does it make more sense for JCB to expand its presence in these markets, as opposed to more developed markets, such as those of Western Europe?
2. Why do you think JCB chose to enter India via a joint venture, as opposed to some other entry mode?
3. Why did JCB not simply license its technology to Escorts?
4. What were the potential disadvantages of JCB's joint venture with Escorts?
5. What were the benefits of gaining full control of the Indian joint venture in 2002? Can you think of any drawbacks?
6. Why do you think JCB has been so successful in India?

Case 30

Organization Change at Google (Alphabet)

In April 2011, Larry Page, one of Google's two founders, became CEO of the company. Page had been CEO of Google from its establishment in 1998 through 2001, when Eric Schmidt took over. After 10 years, Schmidt decided to step down and handed the reins back to Page. One of Page's first actions was to reorganize the company into business units.

Under Schmidt, Google operated with a functional structure that was split into two main entities—an engineering function and a product management function. The engineering group was responsible for creating, building, and maintaining Google's products. The product management group focused on selling Google's offerings, particularly its advertising services. There were, however, two main exceptions to this structure: YouTube and the Android group. These were both acquisitions, and both were left to run their own operations in a largely autonomous manner. Notably, both had been more successful than many of Google's own internally generated new-product ideas.

The alleged great virtue of Google's functional structure was that it was flat, with very few layers in the hierarchy and wide spans of control. Innovation was encouraged. Indeed, numerous articles were written about Google's "bottom-up" new product development process. Engineers were encouraged to spend 20% of their time on projects of their own choosing. They were empowered to form teams to flesh out product ideas, and could get funding to take those products to market by going through a formal process that ended with a presentation in front of Page and Google cofounder Sergey Brin. The products that emerged from this process included Google News, Google Earth, Google Maps, Gmail, and Google Apps.

By 2011, it was becoming increasingly clear that there were limitations to this structure. There was a lack of accountability for products once they had been developed. The core engineers might move on to other projects. Projects could stay in the beta stage for years, essentially unfinished offerings. No one was really responsible for taking products and making them into stand-alone businesses. Many engineers complained that the process for approving new products had become mired in red tape. It was too slow. A structure that had worked well when Google was still a small start-up was no longer scaling. Furthermore, the structure did not reflect the fact that Google had become a multibusiness enterprise, albeit one in which search-based advertising income was still the main driver of the company's revenues. Indeed, that in itself was viewed as an issue, for despite creating many new-product offerings, Google was still dependent upon search-based advertising for the bulk of its income.

Page's solution to this problem was to reorganize Google into seven core business units: Search, Advertising, YouTube, Mobile (Android), Chrome, Social (Google + and Blogger), and Commerce (Google Apps). Senior vice presidents, who report directly to Page, head each unit. Each VP has full responsibility (and accountability) for the fate of his or her unit. Getting a new product started no longer requires convincing executives from across the company to get on board. And once a product ships, engineers and managers can't jump to the next thing and leave important products like Gmail in unfinished beta for years. "Now you are accountable not only for delivering something, but for revising and fixing it," said one Google spokesperson.

In 2015, Google reorganized again. A new corporate entity was created, Alphabet, which functions as a holding company for Google's core businesses and several "moonshot bets" that the company is pursuing. Under the holding company structure, the Google subsidiary continues to be organized on a divisional basis (which now includes divisions for Internet Search, Google Cloud, YouTube, Android, and Chrome). In addition, as of 2018, there are 11 other subsidiaries that Larry Page refers to as "bets in area that might seem speculative or even strange."

These businesses have included its self-driving car unit, a robotics unit, an artificial intelligence business, a unit focusing on longevity research, smart home technology maker Nest, and Google ventures (the company's own venture capital unit). Page argued that the reorganization helped to separate out the core revenue generating businesses from the moonshots, which allowed for greater transparency, particularly for investors. He also stated that the reorganization created a leaner more efficient Alphabet. Currently, the Google subsidiary generates 99% of Alphabet's revenues and all of its profits.

Sources: Miguel Helft, "The Future According to Google's Larry Page," *CNNMoney,* January 3, 2013; Liz Gannes, "GoogQuake: The Larry Page Reorg Promotes Top Lieutenants to SVP," *All Things Digital,* April 7, 2011; Jessica Guynn, "Google CEO Larry Page Completes Major Reorganization of Internet Search Giant," *Los Angeles Times,* April 7, 2011. A. Palmer, "Alphabet at Two: How Google's Radical Reorganization Has Paid Off," *The Street*, August 19, 2017.

Case Discussion Questions

1. Describe the benefits of Google's functional structure as it emerged during the early 2000s.
2. What were the limitations of Google's functional structure? Why did these limitations start to become obvious by 2011?
3. What objective was Larry Page trying to achieve when he reorganized Google in 2011? Do you think he chose the correct organizational form?
4. Why do you think Page created the Alphabet holding company structure in 2015? What are the benefits of this structure? Can you see any drawbacks?

Case 31

A Battle for Dominance in Mobile Payments

By Melissa Schilling

By 2021, there were roughly 6.5 billion mobile broadband subscribers in the world and the number was growing fast (see Figure 1).

[1]As smartphones spread worldwide, so do mobile payment systems. The fastest growth is in developing economies in Asia, Africa, and Latin America, where many people did not have credit cards or bank cards and are transitioning directly from cash payments to mobile payments.

The Competing Mobile Payment Systems

The largest mobile payment system in the world, Alipay (owned by AliBaba group in China), uses a system based on QR codes. With Alipay, a merchant generates a barcode at the point of sale, and the consumer scans with their phone. An application

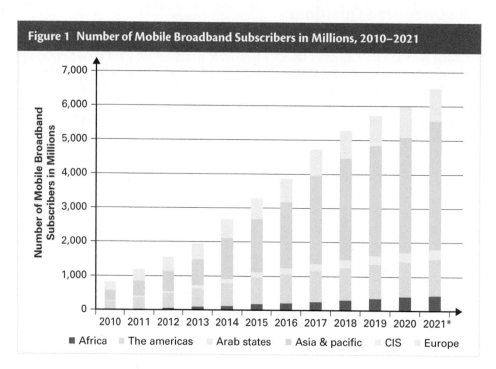

Figure 1 Number of Mobile Broadband Subscribers in Millions, 2010–2021

Number of Mobile Broadband Subscribers in Millions

Legend: Africa, The americas, Arab states, Asia & pacific, CIS, Europe

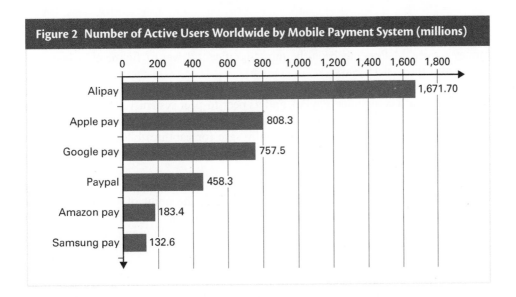

Figure 2 Number of Active Users Worldwide by Mobile Payment System (millions)

Mobile Payment System	Active Users (millions)
Alipay	1,671.70
Apple pay	808.3
Google pay	757.5
Paypal	458.3
Amazon pay	183.4
Samsung pay	132.6

then shows the details of the transaction and the consumer enters a pin to confirm payment. Alipay reports that by the end of 2021 it had 1.67 billion active users, more than double the largest U.S. mobile payment system (Apple Pay) (see Figure 2).

Many of the other large mobile payment systems, such as Apple Pay, Samsung Pay, or Google Pay, use Near Field Communication (NFC) chips in smartphones. NFC chips enable communication between a mobile device and a point-of-sale system just by having the devices in close proximity.[2] These systems transfer the customer's information wirelessly, and then merchant banks and credit card systems such as Visa or MasterCard complete the transaction. These systems were thus very much like existing ways of using credit cards, but enabled completion of the purchase without contact. In emerging markets such as Asia-Pacific and Latin America, where NFC-enabled smartphones are less common, mobile payment systems are more likely to use QR codes (machine readable bar codes), contactless stickers, and magnetic secure transmission (MST). MST sends a magnetic signal from a mobile device to a payment terminal.

Still other competitors, such as PayPal, use a downloadable application and the Web to transmit a customer's information. By the end of 2021, PayPal had over 458 million active registered accounts. With PayPal, customers could complete purchases simply by entering their phone numbers and a pin number or use a PayPal-issued magnetic stripe cards linked to their PayPal accounts. Users could opt to link their PayPal accounts to their credit cards, or directly to their bank accounts. PayPal also owns a service called Venmo that enables peer-to-peer exchanges with a Facebook-like interface that is growing in popularity as a way to exchange money without carrying cash. Venmo charges a 3% fee if the transaction uses a major credit card, but it is free if the consumer uses it with a major bank card and debit card.

In India and Africa, the proportion of people with mobile phones vastly exceeds the proportion of people with credit cards. Not surprisingly, then, in these regions, mobile payment systems were growing fast. In parts of Africa, a system called M-Pesa ("M" for mobile and "pesa," which is Kiswahili for money) enables any individual with a passport or national ID card to deposit money into their phone account, and transfer money to other users using Short Message Service (SMS).[3] By 2022, there were roughly 51 million M-Pesa users in seven countries.[4] The system had grown to offer a range of services including international transfers, loans, and health provision. The platform processes more than 61 million transactions a day. A 2022 World Economic Forum report stated that 84% of Internet users in Kenya and 60% in Nigeria regularly made payments with mobile phones in 2021, a much higher adoption rate than in Europe.[5] As noted by Nick Read, CEO of Vodafone Group, "As the original mobile money service, M-Pesa has been the most significant driver of financial inclusion in Africa over the past 15 years."[6]

As noted above, some of the mobile systems did not require involvement of the major credit card companies. PayPal, and its peer-to-peer system Venmo, for instance, did not require credit cards, nor does Alipay. A mobile payment system that cuts out the credit card companies could potentially save (or capture) billions of dollars in transaction fees. Credit card companies and merchants thus both had high incentives to influence the outcome of this battle.

For consumers, the key dimensions that influenced adoption were convenience (e.g., would the customer have to type in a code at the point of purchase? Was it easily accessible on a device the individual already owned?), risk of fraud (e.g., was the individual's identity and financial information at risk?), and ubiquity (e.g., could the system be used everywhere? Did it enable peer-to-peer transactions?). For merchants, the primary concerns were fraud and cost (e.g., what were the fixed costs and transaction fees of using the system?) Apple Pay had a significant convenience advantage in that a customer could pay with their fingerprint.[7] QR code–based systems, by contrast, required the customer to open the application on their phone and get a QR code that would need to be scanned at checkout or to type in a pin.

Banking the Unbanked

According to the 2021 Global Financial Index (Findex) survey, by 2020, 76% of the world's adult population had a bank account—50% increase from the 51% that was recorded in 2011. However, 1.4 billion adults were still unbanked.[8] This is a serious obstacle to overcoming poverty—access to banking is a very important resource for people to save money and utilize credit. Fortunately, the rise of mobile payment systems is having enormously beneficial social and economic consequences by helping the unbanked become banked.

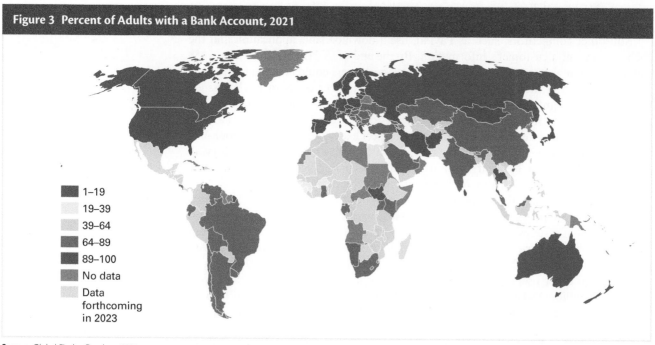

Figure 3 Percent of Adults with a Bank Account, 2021

1–19
19–39
39–64
64–89
89–100
No data
Data forthcoming in 2023

Source: Global Findex Database 2021.

By 2022, it was clear that mobile payments represented a game-changing opportunity that could accelerate e-commerce, smartphone adoption, and the global reach of financial services. However, lack of compatibility between many of the mobile payment systems raised a lingering question: Which payment systems would survive, and which would be ultimately locked out?

Case Discussion Questions

1. What are some of the advantages and disadvantages of mobile payment systems in a) developed countries and b) developing countries?
2. What are the key factors that differentiate the different mobile payment systems? Which factors do consumers care most about? Which factors do merchants care most about?
3. Are there forces that are likely to encourage one of the mobile payment systems to emerge as dominant? If so, what do you think will determine which becomes dominant?
4. Is there anything the mobile payment systems could do to increase the likelihood of them becoming dominant?
5. How do these different mobile systems increase or decrease the power of a) banks, b) credit cards?

Notes

[1] International Telecommunications Union ICT Facts and Figures 2017.

[2] J. Kent, "Dominant Mobile Payment Approaches and Leading Mobile Payment Solution Providers: A Review," *Journal of Payments Strategy & Systems* 6:4 (2012): 315–324.

[3] V. Govindarajan and M. Balakrishnan, "Developing Countries Are Revolutionizing Mobile Banking," *Harvard Business Review* Blog Network, April 30, 2012.

[4] A. Rolfe, "M-Pesa –51 Million Users in 7 Countries –Turns 15." www.paymentscardsandmobile. com, March 7, 2022.

[5] M. Armstrong, "Mobile Payment in Africa Is More Popular Than You May Think-Here's Why," *World Economic Forum*, March 18, 2022.

[6] A. Rolfe, "M-Pesa–51 Million Users in 7 Countries–Turns 15."

www.paymentscardsandmobile. com, March 7, 2022.

[7] D. Pogue, "How Mobile Payments Are Failing and Credit Cards Are Getting Better," *Scientific American*, January 20, 2015.

[8] T. Zimwara, "Latest Global Findex Survey: Share of Adult Population with a Bank Account Now 76%–1.4 Billion Adults Still Unbanked," *Bitcoin.com*, July 16, 2022.

Case

32

The Proposed Merger of Comcast and Time Warner Cable

By Melissa Schilling

In February 2014, Comcast and Time Warner Cable announced their intention to merge—a deal worth about $45 billion. The merger would form the largest cable TV and Internet provider in the United States and enable the company to control 27 of the top 30 markets in the United States, and three-fourths of the overall cable market. The merger first had to be approved, however, by the Department of Justice (to assess antitrust concerns) and the Federal Communications Commission (the FCC, which evaluates media deals to assess their influence on the public interest).

Comcast and Time Warner Cable argued that the deal would not significantly influence competition in the cable industry because the companies operated in nonoverlapping geographic markets, so customers would not be losing an option for getting cable service. They also argued that the merger would enable the companies to make investments that would provide customers with faster broadband, greater network reliability and security, better in-home Wi-Fi, and greater video on-demand choices. As argued by David Cohen, Comcast's executive vice president, in front of a Senate panel: "I can make you and the members of this committee one absolute commitment, which is that there is nothing in this transaction that will cause anybody's cable bills to go up."

Opponents of the merger, however, argued that the size and scale of the merged company would make the company dangerously powerful (particularly given that Comcast had recently acquired NBC Universal). Whereas the merger might not change the cable options available for end consumers, it definitely would change the options available for content providers such as Disney and Viacom, or on-demand programming providers such as Netflix, Cinema Now, Hulu, and others. The merged company's overwhelming bargaining power over suppliers could also create cost advantages other TV or Internet providers might be unable to match, thereby enabling it to squeeze competitors out of the market. For example, satellite operator Dish Network argued that the combined company would be able to use its size to force providers of content to lower their prices, and that companies such as Dish Network would be at a competitive disadvantage. Dish also argued that the merged company might undermine video services such as Netflix or Cinema Now by altering streaming speeds either at the "last mile" of the Internet (where it is delivered into people's homes) or at interconnection points between Internet providers. Netflix noted that Comcast had already required the Netflix to pay "terminating access fees" to ensure that customers did not get a downgraded signal. If the cable companies downgraded the signal for on-demand providers, customers would abandon services like Netflix and turn to on-demand options the cable operators themselves were providing. Senator Al Franken pointed out that when Comcast had acquired NBC Universal in 2010, it had defended that vertical integration move by referring to Time Warner Cable as a fierce competitor. "Comcast can't have it both ways," Franken argued. "It can't say that the existence of competition among distributors, including Time Warner Cable, was a reason to approve the NBC deal in 2010 and then turn around a few years later and say the absence of competition with Time Warner Cable is reason to approve this deal."

For Brian Roberts, CEO and chairman of Comcast, the merger would be yet another milestone in the megadeal acquisition spree he has used to grow the company into a $68-billion media behemoth. The deal was a more nuanced proposition for Robert Marcus, who had been CEO at Time Warner Cable for less than 2 months when the deal was announced: He would get a $79.9-million severance payoff to walk away. The investment bankers advising the deal also stood to rake in $140 million in fees. After a year of reviewing the proposed merger, the Department of Justice announced that it planned to file an antitrust lawsuit against the merger, citing the reduction of competition in the broadband and cable industries that would result, and making Comcast "an unavoidable gatekeeper for internet-based services." Thus, on April 24, 2015, Comcast announced that it would no longer seek to acquire Time Warner Cable. As stated by Brian Roberts, Comcast CEO, "We structured this deal so that if the government didn't agree, we could walk away."

Sources: J. Brodkin, "Comcast/TWC Merger May Be Blocked by Justice Department," *ARS Technica*, April 17, 2005; V. Luckerson, "Dish Network Slams Potential Comcast-Time Warner Merger," www.Time.com, July 10, 2014; A. Fitzpatrick, "Time Warner Cable Outage Raises Questions about Comcast Merger," www.Time.com, August 28, 2014; A. Rogers, "Comcast Urges Congress to Back Time Warner Cable Merger," www.Time.com, April 11, 2014; D. Pomerant, "Netflix Calls on the FCC to Deny the Time Warner Comcast Merger," www.Forbes.com, August 26, 2014, p. 1; A. Timms, "Deals of the Year 2014: Comcast Faces Screen Test," *Institutional Investor*, December 2014; H. Fuchtgott-Roth, "Comcast and Time Warner Cable: Autopsy of a Failed Merger," *Forbes*, April 24, 2015; A. Holmes, "Analysis: Failure of Comcast-Time Warner Deal May Spark New Wave of Mergers," *The Center for Public Integrity*, April 24, 2015.

Case Discussion Questions

1. What do you think are the advantages and disadvantages of vertical integration between content producers and distributors?
2. Do you think both of these companies were above minimum efficient scale? If so, what does that suggest about whether and where they would reap savings from the merger?
3. Do you think this merger would have been good for consumers? Why or why not?

Case 33

HP's Disastrous Acquisition of Autonomy

By Melissa Schilling

In 2011, Hewlett-Packard (HP) was churning on many fronts simultaneously. It had decided to abandon its tablet computer and was struggling with a decision about whether to exit its $40 billion-a-year personal computer (PC) business altogether. It also had a new CEO, Leo Apotheker (formerly the head of German software company SAP AG), who was intent on making a high-impact acquisition that would transform the firm from being primarily a hardware manufacturer into a fast-growing software firm. The firm also had a new chairman of the board, Ray Lane, who was also a software specialist as well as former president of Oracle.

Leo Apotheker had proposed buying two mid-sized software companies, but both deals fell through. The first was nixed by the board's finance committee, and the second fell apart during negotiations over price. In frustration, Apotheker told Lane, "I'm running out of software companies."

Then, in the summer of 2011, Apotheker proposed looking at Autonomy, a British company that makes software firms use to search for information in text files, video files, and other corporate documents. Lane was enthusiastic about the idea. When Apotheker brought the proposal to the board members in July 2011, half of them were already busy analyzing the decision to jettison the PC business, so only half of the board evaluated the acquisition proposal. The board approved a price for Autonomy that was about a 50% premium over its market value, which was already high at about 15 times its operating profit. HP announced the acquisition on August 18, 2011—the same day that it announced it would abandon its tablet computer and was considering exiting the PC industry. The price of the acquisition was $11.1 billion—12.6 times Autonomy's 2010 revenue. Notably, Oracle had already considered acquiring Autonomy and decided that, even if the numbers Autonomy was presenting were taken at face value, it was not worth buying even at a $6-billion price tag. HP's stock fell by 20% the next day.

In the days following the announcement, HP's stock continued to tumble, and backlash from shareholders and others in the investment community was scathing. Ray Lane asked HP's advisers if the company could back out of the deal and was told that, according to U.K. takeover rules, backing out was only possible if HP could show that Autonomy engaged in financial impropriety. HP began frantically examining the financials of Autonomy, hoping for a way to get out of the deal. In the midst of harsh disapproval from HP's largest stockholders and other senior executives within the firm, HP fired Leo Apotheker on September 22, 2012, less than a month after the acquisition's announcement, and only 11 months into his tenure as CEO.

By May 2012, it was clear that Autonomy was not going to hit its revenue targets, and Michael Lynch, Autonomy's founder (who had been asked to stay on and run the company) was fired. In late November 2012, HP wrote down $8.8 billion of the acquisition, essentially admitting that the company was worth 79% less than it had paid for it. Then the finger pointing began in earnest. HP attributed more than $5 billion of the write-down to a "willful effort on behalf of certain former Autonomy employees to inflate the underlying financial metrics of the company in order to mislead investors and potential buyers. . . . These misrepresentations and lack of disclosure severely impacted management's ability to fairly value Autonomy at the time of the deal."

Michael Lynch denied the charges, insisting he knew of no wrongdoing at Autonomy, arguing that auditors from Deloitte had approved its financial statements, and pointing out that the firm followed British accounting guidelines, which differ in some ways from American rules. Lynch also accused HP of mismanaging the acquisition, saying "Can HP really state that no part of the $5-billion write-down was, or should be, attributed to HP's operational and financial mismanagement of Autonomy since acquisition? ... Why did HP senior management apparently wait six months to inform its shareholders of the possibility of a material event related to Autonomy?"

Many shareholders and analysts also pointed their fingers at HP, saying that the deal was shockingly overpriced. Sanford C. Bernstein & Company analyst Toni Sacconaghi wrote, "We see the decision to purchase Autonomy as value-destroying," and Richard Kugele, an analyst at Needham & Company, wrote, "HP may have eroded what remained of Wall Street's confidence in the company" with the "seemingly overly expensive acquisition of Autonomy for over $10B." Apotheker responded by saying, "We have a pretty rigorous process inside HP that we follow for all our acquisitions, which is a D.C.F.-based model.... Just take it from us. We did that analysis at great length, in great detail, and we feel that we paid a very fair price for Autonomy." However, when Ray Lane was questioned, he seemed unfamiliar with any cash flow analysis done for the acquisition. He noted instead that he believed the price was fair because Autonomy was unique and critical to HP's strategic vision.

According to an article in *Fortune*, Catherine A. Lesjak, the chief financial officer at HP, had spoken out against the deal before it transpired, arguing that it was not in the best interests of the shareholders and that HP could not afford it. Furthermore, outside auditors for Autonomy apparently informed HP (during a call in the days leading up to the announcement) that an executive at Autonomy had raised allegations of improper accounting at the firm, but a review had deemed the allegations baseless and they were never passed on to HP's board or CEO.

In the third quarter of 2012, HP lost $6.9 billion, largely because of the Autonomy mess. Its stock was trading at $13—almost 60% less than it had been worth when the Autonomy deal was announced. By April 4, 2013, Ray Lane stepped down as chairman of the board (although he continued on as a board member).

Did Autonomy intentionally inflate its financial metrics? Did Apotheker and Lane's eagerness for a "transformative acquisition" cause them to be sloppy in their valuation of Autonomy? Or was the value of Autonomy lost due to the more mundane cause of integration failure? Financial forensic investigators are trying to answer these questions, but irrespective of the underlying causes, Sacconaghi notes that Autonomy "will arguably go down as the worst, most value-destroying deal in the history of corporate America."

Sources: J. Bandler, "HP Should Have Listened to Its CFO," *Fortune*, November 20, 2012, www.fortune.com; J. B. Stewart, "From HP, a Blunder That Seems to Beat All," *New York Times*, November 30, 2012, www.nytimes.com; M. G. De La Merced, "Autonomy's Ex-Chief Calls on HP to Defend Its Claims," *New York Times*, Dealbook, November 27, 2012, www.nytimes.com/pages/business/dealbook; B. Worthen and J. Scheck, "Inside H-P's Missed Chance to Avoid a Disastrous Deal," *Wall Street Journal*, January 21, 2013, pp. A1–A16.

Case Discussion Questions

1. Why do you think Apotheker was so eager to make an acquisition?
2. Why do most acquisitions result in paying a premium over the market price? Was the 50% premium for Autonomy reasonable?
3. Was it unethical for Apotheker to propose the acquisition at the 50% premium? Was it unethical for Autonomy to go along with the price at a 50% premium? Who suffers the consequences of an overpriced acquisition?
4. Is there anything HP and Autonomy could have done differently to avoid the public backlash and share price drop the company suffered?

LVMH: Getting Big While Staying Beautiful

By Melissa Schilling

In 1854, Louis Vuitton founded a trunk-making company in Paris. He had observed that most trunks could not be easily stacked because they had rounded tops; he thus began producing trunks with flat bottoms and tops out of trianon canvas, which was lightweight and airtight. The style became extremely popular, and soon competitors were imitating his design. To deter imitation, he began creating trunks with special patterns and a logo—creating the iconic look that distinguishes Louis Vuitton products today. After his death, his son, Georges Vuitton, took over the company and began to expand worldwide. He exhibited the trunks at the Chicago World's Fair in 1893, and toured cities such as New York, Chicago, and Philadelphia, selling the trunks to retailers. Over the next 80 years, Louis Vuitton stores opened around the world, including Bombay (now Mumbai); London; Washington, D.C.; Buenos Aires; Taipei; Tokyo; and Seoul. In 1987, Moët Hennessy and Louis Vuitton merged to create the LVMH group, one of the world's largest and best-known luxury goods companies.

Many brands that came to be owned by the LVMH group were even older than Louis Vuitton: Moët & Chandon, the champagne company, had been founded in 1743; Veuve Clicquot Ponsardin dated back to 1772; Hennessy (maker of fine cognac) was originally formed in 1765, and perfumery Guerlain dated back to 1829. The oldest company in the group, Château d'Yquem, began making wine in 1593. Each company brought a legacy of craftsmanship and a loyal following of customers. However, LVMH's biggest brand by far has continued to be Louis Vuitton, which accounts for about one-third of its sales and almost half of its profit.

Much of LVMH's growth into the diversified, luxury goods group that it has become can be attributed to Bernard Arnault. Arnault's career in luxury goods began in 1984, when he bought Dior in the bankruptcy sale of an industrial group. A few years later, he bought Luis Vuitton, which at the time had 125 stores. He subsequently transformed the group into a luxury conglomerate with over 60 brands. One of his first moves was to take production and distribution back from license-holders to begin restoring the exclusivity of the brands. In the years that followed, he bought Celine, Givenchy, Fendi, Kenzo, Bulgari, Sephora, Tag Heuer, and more. In 2014, LVMH also opened a stunning new arts center in Paris, the Foundation Louis Vuitton. The center, designed by world-renowned architect Frank Gehry, generated a flurry of publicity for the group.

Perhaps ironically, luxury goods benefit from economies of scale: A large luxury group can help a new brand grow faster through its distribution reach and expertise in brand management. Prestigious, high-traffic locations such as London's Bond Street can cost millions in rent. On top of that, a vendor must pay to outfit the shop. A large luxury group can make such investments and wait for them to pay off; small brands usually cannot. Furthermore, large luxury groups have more bargaining power with

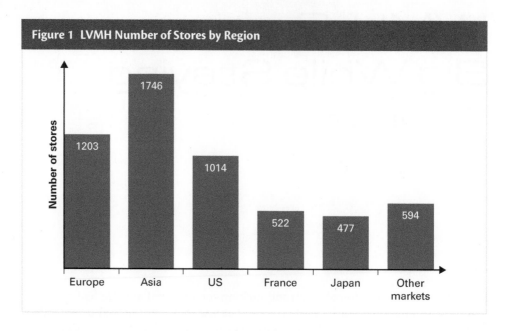

Figure 1 LVMH Number of Stores by Region

Number of stores

- Europe: 1203
- Asia: 1746
- US: 1014
- France: 522
- Japan: 477
- Other markets: 594

fashion magazines, more access to important fashion shows, and more influence with "key opinion leaders." They can also better attract and retain managers because they offer a deep, broad career path. At LVMH, for example, managers can move from fashion to wine to jewelry, and can live in a range of the world's biggest cities, vastly increasing their experience and marketability. As a result of these effects, the top luxury brands were expected to account for one-third of sales in 2022.

According to Bain & Company, over the past 20 years, the number of luxury goods consumers has more than tripled to 330 million, and their spending on luxury goods has risen at double the rate of global GDP. After a sharp 2020 contraction due to the COVID-19 pandemic, the luxury industry roared back, achieving sales of just over $1 trillion in 2021. Asia was the leading region for luxury goods sales, followed by the Americas, and then Europe.

By 2021, LVMH was earning almost $71 billion in revenues, had a net profit margin of 19.8%, and operated 5,556 stores worldwide. LVMH had proven that a company could be big and global, yet have prestigious and exclusive brands. As noted by Arnault, "People said in 1989 that Louis Vuitton was already too big. Now it's ten times the size." The company bought Tiffany for $16 billion in 2021, and though Arnault had indicated he was in no hurry to pursue another major deal, analysts suspected more acquisitions might be expected. With a sizeable war chest of cash, "Just about any deal is open to them, if the potential targets are willing to sell," noted Bernstein analyst Luca Solca.

Sources: www.lvmh.com; Anonymous, "Beauty and the Beasts: The Business Case," *The Economist*, December 13, 2014, pp. 6–8; Anonymous, "Exclusively for Anybody," *The Economist*, December 13, 2014, pp. 3–5; Yahoo Finance; C. D'Arpizio, F. Levato, C. Gault, J. Montgolfier, and L. Jaroudi, "From Surging Recovery to Elegant Advance: The Evolving Future of Luxury," *Bain & Company Report*, December 2021; "How LVMH Bounced Back with Record Profits in 2021: Buying Tiffany & Co., Raising Chanel Prices, and Tempting Luxury Shoppers Back to Louis Vuitton, Celine and Loewe Boutiques," *South China Morning Post*, February 7; 2021; "LVMH Completes the Acquisition of Tiffany & Co.," LVMH Press Release, January 7.

Case Discussion Questions

1. Do LVMH's acquisitions pass the "better-off test"? If so, how?
2. What kinds of companies make ideal acquisition targets for LVMH?
3. Do you think there are any limits to how big and diversified LVMH could (successfully) become?

Glossary

A

absolute cost advantage A cost advantage that is enjoyed by incumbents in an industry and that new entrants cannot expect to match.

acquisition When a company uses its capital resources to purchase another company.

advanced factors of production Resources such as process knowledge, organizational architecture, and intellectual property that contribute to a company's competitive advantage.

anticompetitive behavior A range of actions aimed at harming actual or potential competitors, most often by using monopoly power, and thereby enhancing the long-run prospects of the firm.

autonomous subunit A subunit that has all the resources and decision-making power required to run the operation on a day-to-day basis.

availability error A bias that arises from our predisposition to estimate the probability of an outcome based on how easy the outcome is to imagine.

B

barriers to entry Factors that make it costly for companies to enter an industry.

barriers to imitation Factors or characteristics that make it difficult for another individual or company to replicate something.

basic factors of production Resources such as land, labor, management, plant, and equipment.

benchmarking Measuring how well a company is doing by comparing it to another company, or to itself, over time.

better-off test Is additional value created by having these businesses under one roof and does it achieve more value than these businesses could achieve under any non-ownership configuration?

brand loyalty Preference of consumers for the products of established companies.

broad differentiation strategy When a company differentiates its product in some way, such as by recognizing different segments or offering different products to each segment.

broad low-cost strategy When a company lowers costs so that it can lower prices and still make a profit.

bureaucratic control Control through a formal system of written rules and procedures.

bureaucratic costs The costs associated with solving the transaction difficulties between business units and corporate headquarters as a company obtains the benefits from transferring, sharing, and leveraging competencies.

business ethics Accepted principles of right or wrong governing the conduct of businesspeople.

business-level strategy A business's overall competitive theme: the way it positions itself in the marketplace to gain a competitive advantage, and the different positioning strategies that it can use in different industry settings.

business model The conception of how strategies should work together as a whole to enable the company to achieve competitive advantage.

business unit A self-contained division that provides a product or service for a particular market.

C

capabilities Another term for "process knowledge."

capital productivity The sales produced by a dollar of capital invested in the business.

carve-out A carve-out is a partial divestiture of a business where a parent company sells some portion of a business unit to outside investors, such as to a strategic buyer or to the public in an initial public offering.

causal ambiguity When the way that one thing, A, leads to an outcome (or "causes"), B, is not clearly understood.

centralization Structure in which decision-making authority is concentrated at a high level in the management hierarchy.

chaining A strategy designed to obtain the advantages of cost leadership by establishing a network of linked merchandising outlets interconnected by information technology that functions as one large company.

code of ethics Formal statement of the ethical priorities to which a business adheres.

cognitive biases Systematic errors in decision making that arise from the way people process information.

commonality A skill or competency that, when shared by two or more business units, allows them to operate more effectively and create more value for customers.

competitive advantage The achieved advantage over rivals when a company's profitability is greater than the average profitability of firms in its industry.

confirmation bias Refers to the fact that decision makers who have strong prior beliefs tend to make decisions on the basis of these beliefs, even when presented with evidence that their beliefs are wrong.

control The process through which managers regulate the activities of individuals and units so that they are consistent with the goals and standards of the organization.

controls The metrics used to measure the performance of subunits and make judgments about how well managers are running them.

corruption Can arise in a business context when managers pay bribes to gain access to lucrative business contracts.

cost-of-entry test Can the better-off test be met even after accounting for the cost of entering these businesses?

credible commitment A believable promise or pledge to support the development of a long-term relationship between companies.

cross-selling When a company takes advantage of or leverages its established relationship with customers by way of acquiring additional product lines or categories that it can sell to them. In this way, a company increases differentiation because it can provide a "total solution" and satisfy all of a customer's specific needs.

customer defection The percentage of a company's customers who defect every year to competitors.

customer response time Time that it takes for a good to be delivered or a service to be performed.

D

decentralization Structure in which decision-making authority is distributed to lower-level managers or other employees.

delayering The process of reducing the number of levels in a management hierarchy.

devil's advocacy A technique in which one member of a decision-making team identifies all the considerations that might make a proposal unacceptable.

dialectic inquiry The generation of a plan (a thesis) and a counterplan (an antithesis) that reflect plausible but conflicting courses of action.

diseconomies of scale Unit cost increases associated with a large scale of output.

distinctive competencies Firm-specific strengths that allow a company to differentiate its products and/or achieve substantially lower costs to achieve a competitive advantage.

diversified company A company that makes and sells products in two or more different or distinct industries.

diversification The process of entering new industries, distinct from a company's core or original industry, to make new kinds of products for customers in new markets.

divestment strategy When a company exits an industry by selling its business assets to another company.

dominant design Common set of features or design characteristics.

E

economies of scale Reductions in unit costs attributed to larger output.

economies of scope The synergies that arise when one or more of a diversified company's business units are able to lower costs or increase differentiation because they can more effectively pool, share, and utilize expensive resources or capabilities.

employee productivity The output produced per employee.

environmental degradation Occurs when a company's actions directly or indirectly result in pollution or other forms of environmental harm.

escalating commitment A cognitive bias that occurs when decision makers, having already committed significant resources to a project, commit even more resources after receiving feedback that the project is failing.

ethical dilemmas Situations where there is no agreement over exactly what the accepted principles of right and wrong are, or where none of the available alternatives seems ethically acceptable.

ethics Accepted principles of right or wrong that govern the conduct of a person, the members of a profession, or the actions of an organization.

experience curve The systematic lowering of the cost structure and consequent unit cost reductions that have been observed to occur over the life of a product.

exit barriers Economic, strategic, and emotional factors that prevent companies from leaving an industry.

external stakeholders All other individuals and groups that have some claim on the company.

F

first mover A firm that pioneers a particular product category or feature by being first to offer it to market.

first-mover disadvantages Competitive disadvantages associated with being first to market.

fixed costs Costs that must be incurred to produce a product regardless of level of output.

flat hierarchies Organizational structures with very few layers of management.

flexible production technology A range of technologies designed to reduce setup times for complex equipment, increase the use of machinery through better scheduling, and improve quality control at all stages of the manufacturing process.

focus differentiation strategy When a company targets a certain segment or niche and customizes its offering to the needs of that particular segment through the addition of features and functions.

focus low-cost strategy When a company targets a certain segment or niche and tries to be the low-cost player in that niche.

focus strategy When a company decides to serve a limited number of segments, or just one segment.

format wars Battles to control the source of differentiation, and thus the value that such differentiation can create for the customer.

fragmented industry An industry composed of a large number of small- and medium-sized companies.

franchising A strategy in which the franchisor grants to its franchisees the right to use the franchisor's name, reputation, and business model in return for a franchise fee and, often, a percentage of the profits.

functional-level strategies Actions that managers take to improve the efficiency and effectiveness of one or more of value creation activities.

functional managers Managers responsible for supervising a particular function; that is, a task, activity, or operation, such as accounting, marketing, research and development (R&D), information technology, or logistics.

functional structure An organizational structure built upon the division of labor within the firm, with different functions focusing on different tasks.

G

general managers Managers who bear responsibility for the overall performance of the company or for one of its major self-contained subunits or divisions.

general organizational competencies Competencies that result from the skills of a company's top managers and that help every business unit within a company perform at a higher level than it could if it operated as a separate or independent company.

generic business-level strategy A strategy that gives a company a specific form of competitive position and advantage vis-à-vis its rivals, resulting in above-average profitability.

goal A desired future state that an organization attempts to realize.

global standardization strategy A business model based on pursuing a low-cost strategy on a global scale.

global strategic alliances Cooperative agreements between companies from different countries that are actual or potential competitors.

greenmail A source of gaining wealth whereby corporate raiders either push companies to change their corporate strategy to one that will benefit stockholders, or charge a premium for stock when the company wants to buy it back.

H

harvest strategy When a company reduces to a minimum the assets it employs in a business to reduce its cost structure and extract ("milk") maximum profits from its investment.

holdup When a company is taken advantage of by another company it does business with after it has made an investment in expensive specialized assets to better meet the needs of the other company.

horizontal differentiation The formal division of the organization into subunits.

horizontal integration The process of acquiring or merging with industry competitors to achieve the competitive advantages that arise from a large size and scope of operations.

hostage taking A means of exchanging valuable resources to guarantee that each partner to an agreement will keep its side of the bargain.

I

illusion of control A cognitive bias rooted in the tendency to overestimate one's ability to control events.

incentives The devices used to encourage desired employee behavior.

industry A group of companies offering products or services that are close substitutes for each other.

influence costs The loss of efficiency that arises from deliberate information distortions for personal gain within an organization.

information asymmetry A situation where an agent has more information about the resources he or she is managing than the principal has.

information manipulation When managers use their control over corporate data to distort or hide information in order to enhance their own financial situation or the competitive position of the firm.

inside directors Senior employees of the company, such as the CEO.

integrating mechanisms Processes and procedures used for coordination subunits.

intellectual property Knowledge, research, and information that is owned by an individual or organization.

internal capital market A corporate-level strategy whereby the firm's headquarters assesses the performance of business units and allocates money across them. Cash generated by units that are profitable but have poor investment opportunities within their business is used to cross-subsidize businesses that need cash and have strong promise for long-run profitability.

internal new venturing The process of transferring resources to, and creating a new business unit or division in, a new industry to innovate new kinds of products.

internal stakeholders Stockholders and employees, including executive officers, other managers, and board members.

J

just-in-time (JIT) inventory system System of economizing on inventory-holding costs by scheduling components to arrive just in time to enter the production process or only as stock is depleted.

K

killer applications Applications or uses of a new technology or product that are so compelling that customers adopt them in droves, killing competing formats.

knowledge network A network for transmitting information within an organization that is based not on formal organization structure but on informal contacts between managers within an enterprise and on distributed-information systems.

L

leadership strategy When a company develops strategies to become the dominant player in a declining industry.

learning effects Cost savings that come from learning by doing.

leveraging competencies The process of taking a distinctive competency developed by a business unit in one industry and using it to create a new business unit in a different industry.

limit price strategy Charging a price that is lower than that required to maximize profits in the short run to signal to new entrants that the incumbent has a low-cost structure that the entrant likely cannot match.

localization strategy A strategy focused on increasing profitability by customizing a company's goods or services so that they provide a favorable match to tastes and preferences in different national markets.

location economies The economic benefits that arise from performing a value creation activity in an optimal location.

M

market controls The regulation of the behavior of individuals and units within an enterprise by setting up an internal market for valuable resources such as capital.

market development When a company searches for new market segments for its existing products in order to increase sales.

market segmentation The way a company decides to group customers, based on important differences in their needs, in order to gain a competitive advantage.

marketing strategy The position that a company takes with regard to pricing, promotion, advertising, product design, and distribution.

mass customization The use of flexible manufacturing technology to reconcile two goals that were once thought to be incompatible: low cost and differentiation through product customization.

mass market A market into which large numbers of customers enter.

matrix structure An organizational structure in which managers try to achieve tight coordination between functions, particularly R&D, production, and marketing.

merger An agreement between two companies to pool their resources and operations and join together to better compete in a business or industry.

mission The purpose of the company, or a statement of what the company strives to do.

modularity The degree to which a system's components can be separated and recombined.

multidivisional company A company that competes in several different businesses and has created a separate, self-contained division to manage each.

multidivisional structure An organizational structure in which a firm is divided into divisions, each of which is responsible for a distinct business area.

multinational companies Companies that do business in two or more national markets.

N

network effects The network of complementary products as a primary determinant of the demand for an industry's product.

niche strategy When a company focuses on pockets of demand that are declining more slowly than the industry as a whole in order to maintain profitability.

non-price competition The use of product differentiation strategies to deter potential entrants and manage rivalry within an industry.

norms Social rules and guidelines that prescribe the appropriate behavior in particular situations.

O

on-the-job consumption A term used by economists to describe the behavior of senior management's use of company funds to acquire perks (lavish offices, jets, and the like) that will enhance their status, instead of investing the funds to increase stockholder returns.

opportunism Seeking one's own self-interest, often through the use of guile.

opportunistic exploitations Unethical behavior sometimes used by managers to unilaterally rewrite the terms of a contract with suppliers, buyers, or complement providers in a way that favors to the firm.

opportunities Elements and conditions in a company's environment that allow it to formulate and implement strategies that enable it to become more profitable.

output controls Setting goals for units or individuals and monitoring performance against those goals.

outside view Identification of past successful or failed strategic initiatives to determine whether those initiatives will work for the project at hand.

organizational architecture The combination of the organizational structure of a company, its control systems, its incentive systems, its organizational culture, and its human-capital strategy.

organizational culture The norms and value systems that are shared among the employees of an organization.

organizational design skills The ability of a company's managers to create a structure, culture, and control systems that motivate and coordinate employees to perform at a high level.

organizational processes The manner in which decisions are made and work is performed within the organization.

organizational structure The combination of the location of decision-making responsibilities, the formal division of the organization into subunits, and the establishment of integrating mechanisms to coordinate the activities of the subunits.

outside directors Directors who are not full-time employees of the company, needed to provide objectivity to the monitoring and evaluation of processes.

P

parallel sourcing policy A policy in which a company enters into long-term contracts with at least two suppliers for the same component to prevent any incidents of opportunism.

peer control The pressure that employees exert on others within their team or work group to perform up to or in excess of the expectations of the organization.

people The employees of an organization, as well as the strategy used to recruit, compensate, motivate, and retain those individuals; also refers to employees' skills, values, and orientation.

performance ambiguity The difficulty of identifying with precision the reason for the high (or low) performance of a subunit such as a function or team.

personal control Control by personal contact with and direct supervision of subordinates.

personal ethics Generally accepted principles of right and wrong governing the conduct of individuals.

platform ecosystem "Ecosystem," a contraction of "ecological" and "system," refers to a system where elements share some form of mutual dependence. A platform in this context is a stable core that mediates the relationship between a range of components, complements, and end users. Thus "platform ecosystem" refers to a system of mutually dependent entities mediated by a stable core.

positioning strategy The specific set of options a company adopts for a product based upon four main dimensions of marketing: price, distribution, promotion and advertising, and product features.

potential competitors Companies that are currently not competing in the industry but have the potential to do so if they choose.

price leadership When one company assumes responsibility for determining the pricing strategy that maximizes industry profitability.

price signaling The process whereby companies increase or decrease product prices to convey their intentions to other companies and influence the price of an industry's products.

process innovation

primary activities Activities related to the design, creation, and delivery of the product, its marketing, and its support and after-sales service.

process innovation Development of a new process for producing and delivering products to customers.

process knowledge Knowledge of the internal rules, routines, and procedures of an organization that managers can leverage to achieve organizational objectives.

product bundling Offering customers the opportunity to purchase a range of products at a single, combined price; this increases the value of a company's product line because customers often obtain a price discount when purchasing a set of products at one time, and customers become used to dealing with only one company and its representatives.

product development The creation of new or improved products to replace existing products.

product innovation Development of products that are new to the world or have superior attributes to existing products.

product proliferation strategy The strategy of "filling the niches" or catering to the needs of customers in all market segments to deter entry by competitors.

profit growth The increase in net profit over time.

profitability The return a company makes on the capital invested in the enterprise.

public domain Government- or association-set standards of knowledge or technology that any company can freely incorporate into its product.

Q

quasi integration The use of long-term relationships, or investment in some activities normally performed by suppliers or buyers, in place of full ownership of operations that are backward or forward in the supply chain.

R

razor and blade strategy Pricing the product low in order to stimulate demand, and pricing complements high.

reasoning by analogy Use of simple analogies to make sense out of complex problems.

related diversification A corporate-level strategy based on the goal of establishing a business unit in a new industry that is related to a company's existing business units by some form of commonality or linkage between their value-chain functions.

representativeness A bias rooted in the tendency to generalize from a small sample or even a single, vivid anecdote.

resources Assets of a company.

restructuring The process of reorganizing and divesting business units and exiting industries to refocus upon a company's core business and rebuild its distinctive competencies.

return on invested capital (ROIC) Return on invested capital is equal to net profit divided by capital invested in the company.

risk capital Equity capital invested with no guarantee that stockholders will recoup their cash or earn a decent return.

S

scenario planning Formulating plans that are based upon "what-if" scenarios about the future.

segmentation strategy When a company decides to serve many segments, or even the entire market, producing different offerings for different segments.

self-dealing Managers using company funds for their own personal consumption.

self-managing teams Teams where members coordinate their own activities and make their own hiring, training, work, and reward decisions.

shareholder value Returns that shareholders earn from purchasing shares in a company.

socially complex Something that is characterized by, or is the outcome of, the interaction of multiple individuals.

span of control The number of a manager's direct reports.

split-off A split-off can occur after a carve-out and is when shareholders in the parent company are offered the opportunity to hold shares in the subsidiary instead of some or all of their shares in the parent company (i.e., they can trade some or all of their shares in the parent for shares in the subsidiary according to an exchange ratio based on the value of the two stocks).

spinoff A spinoff is when a corporation makes a division or subsidiary a separate legal entity.

spinout A spinout is when employees decide to leave the firm and form their own venture.

stakeholders Individuals or groups with an interest, claim, or stake in the company—in what it does and in how well it performs.

standard A performance requirement that the organization is meant to attain on an ongoing basis.

standardization strategy When a company decides to ignore different segments and produces a standardized product for the average consumer.

standardized interface A point of interconnection between two systems or parts of a system that adheres to a standard to ensure those systems or parts can connect or exchange information, energy, or other resources (e.g., a USB slot on a computer enables it to communicate and power a range of peripherals); USB is a type of standardized interface.

stock options The right to purchase company stock at a predetermined price at some point in the future, usually within 10 years of the grant date.

strategic alliances Long-term agreements between two or more companies to jointly develop new products or processes that benefit all companies that are a part of the agreement.

strategic commitments Investments that signal an incumbent's long-term commitment to a market or market segment.

strategic leadership Creating competitive advantage through effective management of the strategy-making process.

strategic outsourcing The decision to allow one or more of a company's value-chain activities to be performed by independent, specialist companies that focus all their skills and knowledge on just one kind of activity to increase performance.

strategy A set of related actions that managers take to increase their company's performance.

strategy formulation Selecting strategies based on analysis of an organization's external and internal environment.

strategy implementation Putting strategies into action.

subgoal An objective, the achievement of which helps the organization attain or exceed its major goals.

substandard working conditions Arise when managers underinvest in working conditions, or pay employees below-market rates, to reduce their production costs.

supply chain management The task of managing the flow of inputs and components from suppliers into the company's production processes to minimize inventory holding and maximize inventory turnover.

support activities Activities that provide inputs that allow the primary activities to take place.

sustained competitive advantage A company's strategies enable it to maintain above-average profitability for a number of years.

switching costs Costs that consumers must bear to switch from the products offered by one established company to the products offered by a new entrant.

SWOT analysis The comparison of strengths, weaknesses, opportunities, and threats.

T

tacit A characteristic of knowledge or skills such that they cannot be documented or codified but may be understood through experience or intuition.

takeover constraint The risk of being acquired by another company.

tall hierarchies Organizational structures with many layers of management.

tapered integration When a firm uses a mix of vertical integration and market transactions for a given input. For example, a firm might operate limited semiconductor manufacturing while also buying semiconductor chips on the market. Doing so helps to prevent supplier holdup (because the firm can credibly commit to not buying from external suppliers) and increases its ability to judge the quality and cost of purchased supplies.

technical standards A set of technical specifications that producers adhere to when making a product or component.

technology upgrading Incumbent companies deterring entry by investing in costly technology upgrades that potential entrants have trouble matching.

technological paradigm shifts Shifts in new technologies that revolutionize the structure of the industry, dramatically alter the nature of competition, and require companies to adopt new strategies in order to survive.

threats Elements in the external environment that could endanger the integrity and profitability of the company's business.

total quality management (TQM) Increasing product reliability so that it consistently performs as it was designed to and rarely breaks down.

transfer prices The prices that one division of a company charges another division for its products, which are the inputs the other division requires to manufacture its own products.

transferring competencies The process of taking a distinctive competency developed by a business unit in one industry and implanting it in a business unit operating in another industry.

transnational strategy A business model that simultaneously achieves low costs, differentiates the product offering across geographic markets, and fosters a flow of skills between different subsidiaries in the company's global network of operations.

turnaround strategy When managers of a diversified company identify inefficient, poorly managed companies in other industries and then acquire and restructure them to improve their performance—and thus the profitability of the total corporation.

U

unrelated diversification A corporate-level strategy based on a multibusiness model that uses general organizational competencies to increase the performance of all the company's business units.

V

value chain The concept that a company consists of a chain of activities that transforms inputs into outputs.

value innovation When innovations push out the efficiency frontier in an industry, allowing for greater value to be offered through superior differentiation at a lower cost than was previously thought possible.

values The ideas or shared assumptions about what a group believes to be good, right, and desirable.

vertical differentiation The location of decision-making responsibilities within a structure, referring to centralization or decentralization, and also the number of layers in a hierarchy, referring to whether the organizational structure is tall or flat.

vertical disintegration When a company decides to exit industries, either forward or backward in the industry value chain, to its core industry to increase profitability.

vertical integration When a company expands its operations either backward into an industry that produces inputs for the company's products (backward vertical integration) or forward into an industry that uses, distributes, or sells the company's products (forward vertical integration).

virtual corporation When companies pursued extensive strategic outsourcing to the extent that they only perform the central value creation functions that lead to competitive advantage.

vision The articulation of a company's desired achievements or future state.

VRIO framework A framework managers use to determine the quality of a company's resources, where V is value, R is rarity, I is inimitability, and O is for organization.

Index